CASSESE'S INTERNATIONAL LAW

CASSESE'S INTERNATIONAL LAW

Third Edition

PAOLA GAETA
Professor of International Law
The Graduate Institute, Geneva

JORGE E. VIÑUALES
Harold Samuel Professor of Law
University of Cambridge

SALVATORE ZAPPALÀ
Professor of International Law
University of Catania

OXFORD
UNIVERSITY PRESS

Great Clarendon Street, Oxford, OX2 6DP,
United Kingdom

Oxford University Press is a department of the University of Oxford.
It furthers the University's objective of excellence in research, scholarship,
and education by publishing worldwide. Oxford is a registered trade mark of
Oxford University Press in the UK and in certain other countries

© Cassese Estate, Paola Gaeta, Jorge Viñuales,
and Salvatore Zappalà 2020

The moral rights of the authors have been asserted

First Edition 2001
Second Edition 2005
Impression: 1

All rights reserved. No part of this publication may be reproduced, stored in
a retrieval system, or transmitted, in any form or by any means, without the
prior permission in writing of Oxford University Press, or as expressly permitted
by law, by licence or under terms agreed with the appropriate reprographics
rights organization. Enquiries concerning reproduction outside the scope of the
above should be sent to the Rights Department, Oxford University Press, at the
address above

You must not circulate this work in any other form
and you must impose this same condition on any acquirer

Public sector information reproduced under Open Government Licence v3.0
(http://www.nationalarchives.gov.uk/doc/open-government-licence/open-government-licence.htm)

Published in the United States of America by Oxford University Press
198 Madison Avenue, New York, NY 10016, United States of America

British Library Cataloguing in Publication Data
Data available

Library of Congress Control Number: 2020939613

ISBN 978–0–19–923128–7

Printed in Great Britain by
Bell & Bain Ltd., Glasgow

Links to third party websites are provided by Oxford in good faith and
for information only. Oxford disclaims any responsibility for the materials
contained in any third party website referenced in this work.

PREFACE

We undertook the work on this third edition of Antonio Cassese's leading textbook on *International Law* both to pay tribute to his memory and profound influence on the field and, no less importantly, to contribute to the dissemination of his thought. Nino's moral and yet realistic vision of international law is greatly needed in the present international context. We are deeply grateful to Sylvia Fano Cassese, for her confidence in our project. Her trust and support have been very important to us.

We have done our utmost to preserve Nino's voice and normative stances throughout the book while, at the same time, integrating the many developments of the last 15 years and some additional material on areas which have become central to the study of international law, such as territorial disputes, maritime delimitation, extraterritorial application of human rights, international and domestic criminal prosecution, trade, foreign investment, and environmental protection, among others. The format also follows earlier editions, including in the referencing of cases, which are referred to only by name because the full reference is provided in the table of cases.

To the best of our ability, we have preserved Nino's rare combination of a historically informed, conceptually strong, and practice-infused analysis of international law, which have provided the basis for the training of many generations of international lawyers in the four corners of the world.

The authors of these lines are amongst those who greatly benefited from Nino's teaching and work. It is our hope that, with this new edition, his classic textbook will contribute to form the 'judicious reformers' in whom, at the end of his life, he placed his trust for the improvement of the international legal order.

Paola Gaeta, Geneva
Jorge E. Viñuales, Cambridge,
Salvatore Zappalà, Catania
7 April 2020

CONTENTS

Preface v
Principal abbreviations xix
Table of cases xxiii
Table of statutes xli
Table of treaties and instruments xliii

PART I: ORIGINS AND FOUNDATIONS OF THE INTERNATIONAL COMMUNITY

1. THE MAIN LEGAL FEATURES OF THE INTERNATIONAL COMMUNITY — 3
2. THE HISTORICAL EVOLUTION OF THE INTERNATIONAL COMMUNITY — 20
3. THE FUNDAMENTAL PRINCIPLES GOVERNING INTERNATIONAL RELATIONS — 45

PART II: SUBJECTS OF THE INTERNATIONAL COMMUNITY

4. STATES AS THE PRIMARY SUBJECTS OF INTERNATIONAL LAW — 79
5. THE SPATIAL DIMENSIONS OF STATE ACTIVITIES — 92
6. IMMUNITIES OF STATES AND STATE OFFICIALS — 122
7. INTERNATIONAL ORGANIZATIONS — 140
8. INDIVIDUALS AND OTHER LEGAL SUBJECTS — 156

PART III: INTERNATIONAL LAW-MAKING AND NORMATIVE INTERACTIONS

9. LAW-MAKING PROCESSES — 181
10. THE LAW OF TREATIES — 204
11. NORMATIVE INTERACTIONS: IMPLEMENTATION AND HIERARCHY OF NORMS — 218

PART IV: IMPLEMENTATION OF INTERNATIONAL LAW

12. INTERNATIONAL STATE RESPONSIBILITY FOR WRONGFUL ACTS   245
13. PEACEFUL SETTLEMENT OF INTERNATIONAL DISPUTES   276
14. ENFORCEMENT   294

PART V: CONTEMPORARY ISSUES IN INTERNATIONAL LAW

15. THE ROLE OF THE UNITED NATIONS   313
16. COLLECTIVE SECURITY AND THE USE OF ARMED FORCE   335
17. LEGAL RESTRAINTS ON VIOLENCE IN ARMED CONFLICT   366
18. THE PROTECTION OF HUMAN RIGHTS   404
19. THE REPRESSION OF INTERNATIONAL CRIMES   427
20. THE PROTECTION OF THE ENVIRONMENT   454
21. INTERNATIONAL LAW AND THE GLOBAL ECONOMY   490

Index   527

DETAILED TABLE OF CONTENTS

Preface v
Principal abbreviations xix
Table of cases xxiii
Table of statutes xli
Table of treaties and instruments xliii

PART I: ORIGINS AND FOUNDATIONS OF THE INTERNATIONAL COMMUNITY

1. **THE MAIN LEGAL FEATURES OF THE INTERNATIONAL COMMUNITY** 3

    1.1. Introduction 3
    1.2. The nature of international legal subjects 3
    1.3. The lack of a central authority, and decentralization of legal 'functions' 4
    1.4. Collective responsibility 6
    1.5. The need for most international rules to be translated into national legislation 8
    1.6. The range of States' freedom of action 9
    1.7. The overriding role of effectiveness 12
    1.8. Traditional and new trends 12
        1.8.1. Reciprocity as the basis of international rights and obligations 12
        1.8.2. Community obligations and community rights 14
        1.8.3. Article 1 common to the four 1949 Geneva Conventions as indicative of current merits and flaws of community rights and obligations 16
    1.9. Coexistence of the old and new patterns 19

2. **THE HISTORICAL EVOLUTION OF THE INTERNATIONAL COMMUNITY** 20

    2.1. Introduction 20
    2.2. The emergence of the present international community before the Peace of Westphalia 20
    2.3. From the Peace of Westphalia to the end of the First World War 23
        2.3.1. The composition of the international community 23
        2.3.2. The balance of power 26
        2.3.3. The main features of the law 28
        2.3.4. Efforts to restrain the Great Powers' dominance: the Calvo and Drago doctrines 30

2.4.	From the First to the Second World War	32
	2.4.1. The turning point: the First World War and its consequences	32
	2.4.2. The Soviet Union's presence splits the international community	32
	2.4.3. An experiment in collective co-ordination of force: the League of Nations	34
	2.4.4. Legal output	36
2.5.	From the UN Charter to the end of the Cold War	37
	2.5.1. The main consequences of the Second World War	37
	2.5.2. The establishment of the United Nations	38
	2.5.3. Changes in the composition of the international community	39
	2.5.4. Legal change	40
2.6.	From the end of the Cold War to the present	41
	2.6.1. 'Unipolarity'	42
	2.6.2. Emerging 'multipolarity'	43

3. THE FUNDAMENTAL PRINCIPLES GOVERNING INTERNATIONAL RELATIONS — 45

3.1.	Characterization of fundamental principles	45
3.2.	The sovereign equality of States	49
	3.2.1. General observations	49
	3.2.2. Sovereignty	50
	3.2.3. Legal equality	52
3.3.	The principle of non-intervention	52
	3.3.1. General observations	52
	3.3.2. Development of non-intervention by the UN General Assembly	54
	3.3.3. Specific forms of intervention	55
3.4.	Prohibition of the threat or use of force	57
	3.4.1. General observations	57
	3.4.2. Legal scope of the principle	58
3.5.	Peaceful settlement of international disputes	60
	3.5.1. General observations	60
	3.5.2. Legal scope of the principle	61
3.6.	The duty to co-operate	62
	3.6.1. General observations	62
	3.6.2. Dimensions of co-operation	62
3.7.	The principle of good faith	64
	3.7.1. General observations	64
	3.7.2. Specific expressions of good faith	65
3.8.	Self-determination of peoples	66
	3.8.1. How the principle evolved in the world community	66
	3.8.2. Legal scope of the principle	67
	3.8.3. Rights and obligations	69
	3.8.4. Limits of the principle	71
3.9.	Respect for human rights	71
	3.9.1. General observations	71
	3.9.2. Legal scope of the principle	72
3.10.	Prevention of significant environmental harm	73
	3.10.1. General observations	73
	3.10.2. Legal scope of the principle	74
3.11.	Interactions among fundamental principles	75

PART II: SUBJECTS OF THE INTERNATIONAL COMMUNITY

4. STATES AS THE PRIMARY SUBJECTS OF INTERNATIONAL LAW 79

4.1. The continuing pre-eminence of States 79
4.2. The creation of States in international law 80
4.3. The role of recognition 82
    4.3.1. Concept and effects of the recognition of States 82
    4.3.2. Contested statehood 84
4.4. Continuity, succession, and extinction of States 86
    4.4.1. Changes in government and in territory 86
    4.4.2. State succession 87
4.5. The evolving concept of sovereignty 90

5. THE SPATIAL DIMENSIONS OF STATE ACTIVITIES 92

5.1. Introduction 92
5.2. Sovereignty, competence, and jurisdiction 94
    5.2.1. Conceptual distinctions 94
    5.2.2. Exercise of jurisdiction 95
5.3. Land territory 97
    5.3.1. Acquisition of territory 98
    5.3.2. Titles, *effectivités*, and their interactions 99
    5.3.3. Delimitation of boundaries: the *uti possidetis* doctrine 102
5.4. The law of the sea 103
    5.4.1. The codification of the law of the sea 103
    5.4.2. Territorial sea 104
    5.4.3. Internal waters 106
    5.4.4. Bays 107
    5.4.5. The contiguous zone 108
    5.4.6. The exclusive economic zone 108
    5.4.7. The continental shelf 110
    5.4.8. Delimitation of maritime areas 112
    5.4.9. The high seas 114
5.5. The international seabed and the concept of the common heritage of mankind 116
5.6. The law of airspace 118
5.7. The law of outer space 120
5.8. Concluding observations 121

6. IMMUNITIES OF STATES AND STATE OFFICIALS 122

6.1. Sovereignty and immunities 122
6.2. State immunities from jurisdiction and execution 122
    6.2.1. Jurisdictional immunity 122
    6.2.2. Employment disputes 124
    6.2.3. Jurisdictional immunity and *jus cogens* 126
    6.2.4. Immunity from execution 129
6.3. Immunities of foreign State officials 130
    6.3.1. Types of immunities 130
    6.3.2. Functional immunities 131

6.3.3.	Immunities of diplomatic and consular agents	133
6.3.4.	Immunities of high-rank State officials	135

7. INTERNATIONAL ORGANIZATIONS 140

7.1. The development of international organizations — 140
7.2. Types of international organizations — 142
7.3. Recognition of their legal personality — 143
7.4. Scope and limits: implied powers and the principle of speciality — 145
7.5. Immunities of international organizations and their agents — 147
    7.5.1. The right to immunity from jurisdiction of State courts for acts and activities performed by the organization — 148
    7.5.2. The immunity of agents of the organization in their official capacity as international civil servants — 150
7.6. Other rights of international organizations — 153
7.7. The responsibility of international organizations — 154

8. INDIVIDUALS AND OTHER LEGAL SUBJECTS 156

8.1. The expansion of international legal personality — 156
8.2. Individuals: rights and duties — 158
    8.2.1. General remarks — 158
    8.2.2. Customary rules imposing obligations on individuals — 159
    8.2.3. The holders of the corresponding rights — 160
    8.2.4. Treaty provisions conferring rights on individuals — 161
8.3. Peoples and national liberation movements — 165
8.4. Insurgents — 167
8.5. *Sui generis* entities and other subjects (corporations and NGOs) — 173
    8.5.1. General — 173
    8.5.2. The Holy See — 173
    8.5.3. The Sovereign Order of Malta — 174
    8.5.4. The International Committee of the Red Cross (ICRC) — 174
    8.5.5. Transnational corporations — 175
    8.5.6. Non-governmental organizations (NGOs) — 176
8.6. Concluding remarks — 177

PART III: INTERNATIONAL LAW-MAKING AND NORMATIVE INTERACTIONS

9. LAW-MAKING PROCESSES 181

9.1. Introduction — 181
9.2. Treaties as law-making processes — 182
9.3. Custom: formation and identification — 184
    9.3.1. General — 184
    9.3.2. Elements of custom — 184
    9.3.3. The existence of customary rules — 187
    9.3.4. The 'persistent objector' — 188
    9.3.5. Local customary rules — 190
    9.3.6. The present role of custom — 191

9.4.	General principles of law recognized in domestic systems	192
	9.4.1. General	192
	9.4.2. The attempt to codify resort to principles in 1921	193
	9.4.3. The past and present role of principles	194
9.5.	Other international law-making processes	195
	9.5.1. Unilateral acts of States	195
	9.5.2. Binding decisions of international organizations	197
	9.5.3. Is equity a formal source?	197
9.6.	Identification and development of international law	199
	9.6.1. Jurisprudence and doctrine	199
	9.6.2. Codification	200
	9.6.3. Soft law	201
9.7.	Interactions among sources	202

10. THE LAW OF TREATIES 204

10.1.	Introduction	204
10.2.	Notion and types of treaties	205
10.3.	Conclusion of treaties	207
	10.3.1 Standard procedure	207
	10.3.2 Expression of consent and entry into force	208
10.4.	Effects and scope of application	209
10.5.	Reservations	210
10.6.	Interpretation	212
10.7.	Amendment and modification	214
10.8.	Grounds of invalidity	214
	10.8.1 Innovation in the Vienna Convention	214
	10.8.2 Absolute and relative grounds of invalidity	215
10.9.	Termination and suspension	216

11. NORMATIVE INTERACTIONS: IMPLEMENTATION AND HIERARCHY OF NORMS 218

11.1.	Three inquiries: transposal, effects, and norm hierarchy	218
11.2.	The need for transposal: dualism, monism, and reality	218
11.3.	Effects: implementing international law within domestic systems	221
	11.3.1. General	221
	11.3.2. Modalities of implementation: trends in domestic systems	223
	11.3.3. The rank of international rules within domestic systems	224
	11.3.4. Domestic implementation of customary international law	225
	11.3.5. Domestic implementation of treaty law	226
	11.3.6. Hierarchical relations between international and domestic law	231
11.4.	Hierarchical relations among international legal norms: emergence and development of *jus cogens*	232
	11.4.1. General	232
	11.4.2. The emergence of *jus cogens*: establishment and scope	233
	11.4.3. Examples of peremptory norms	236
	11.4.4. Legal effects of *jus cogens*	237
	11.4.5. The limited reliance of *jus cogens* in international dealings	240

PART IV: IMPLEMENTATION OF INTERNATIONAL LAW

12. INTERNATIONAL STATE RESPONSIBILITY FOR WRONGFUL ACTS   245

- 12.1. Introduction   245
- 12.2. The codification of the law of State responsibility   246
- 12.3. Preliminary notions   248
- 12.4. The internationally wrongful act   249
  - 12.4.1. Attribution of conduct to a State   249
  - 12.4.2. Inconsistency of State conduct with an international obligation   255
  - 12.4.3. The relevance of fault   256
- 12.5. The question of damage   256
- 12.6. Circumstances precluding wrongfulness   258
  - 12.6.1. The codification of the ILC Articles   258
  - 12.6.2. The relevance of *jus cogens*   262
  - 12.6.3. The relationship with the obligation to pay compensation   262
- 12.7. Consequences of the internationally wrongful act   263
  - 12.7.1. Obligations of the responsible State and forms of reparation   263
  - 12.7.2. The notion of injured State   265
- 12.8. Aggravated State responsibility   267
  - 12.8.1. The regulation in the ILC Articles   268
  - 12.8.2. Aggravated State responsibility in light of international practice   271
  - 12.8.3. The current role of aggravated responsibility   275

13. PEACEFUL SETTLEMENT OF INTERNATIONAL DISPUTES   276

- 13.1. Introduction   276
- 13.2. Obligation and means of dispute settlement   277
- 13.3. Diplomatic means of dispute settlement   279
- 13.4. Judicial means of dispute settlement   283
- 13.5. Interplay between diplomatic and judicial means   289
- 13.6. Non-compliance and supervisory procedures   291

14. ENFORCEMENT   294

- 14.1. Decentralized enforcement in historical perspective   294
  - 14.1.1. General   294
  - 14.1.2. Forcible intervention   295
  - 14.1.3. Reprisals   296
  - 14.1.4. War   297
- 14.2. Enforcement of international rules in contemporary international law   297
  - 14.2.1. General   297
  - 14.2.2. Retortion   298
  - 14.2.3. Countermeasures in general   299
  - 14.2.4. Limitations on countermeasures   300
  - 14.2.5. Countermeasures and aggravated State responsibility   303
- 14.3. Can national courts enforce international rules?   303
- 14.4. Collective enforcement measures (sanctions proper)   306
  - 14.4.1. General   306
  - 14.4.2. Sanctions and respect for human rights   308

PART V: CONTEMPORARY ISSUES IN INTERNATIONAL LAW

15. THE ROLE OF THE UNITED NATIONS — 313

15.1. The grand design of the post-Second World War period — 313
15.2. Goals and structure of the organization — 315
15.3. Principal achievements and failures of the UN — 318
    15.3.1. General — 318
    15.3.2. Maintenance of peace and security — 318
    15.3.3. Promotion of the peaceful settlement of disputes likely to endanger peace — 321
    15.3.4. Self-determination of peoples — 323
    15.3.5. Economic and social co-operation — 324
    15.3.6. Human rights — 326
    15.3.7. Disarmament — 327
    15.3.8. Codification and progressive development of international law — 329
15.4. The current role of the UN — 331

16. COLLECTIVE SECURITY AND THE USE OF ARMED FORCE — 335

16.1. Introduction — 335
16.2. Measures short of armed force and the UN system — 337
    16.2.1. General — 337
    16.2.2. Economic and other 'sanctions' — 339
    16.2.3. Non-recognition of illegal situations — 340
    16.2.4. The establishment of international criminal tribunals — 341
    16.2.5. Action by the General Assembly in case of gross violations of international law — 341
16.3. Peace operations—from peacekeeping to peace enforcement and peace building — 343
16.4. Enforcement action upon authorization of the Security Council — 346
16.5. Self-defence and its many faces — 349
    16.5.1. Individual and collective self-defence — 349
    16.5.2. Is anticipatory self-defence admissible? — 353
    16.5.3. Self-defence against armed infiltration and indirect aggression — 357
    16.5.4. Forcible protection of nationals abroad — 358
    16.5.5. Armed intervention with the consent of the territorial State — 360
    16.5.6. Armed reprisals against unlawful small-scale use of force — 362
    16.5.7. Humanitarian intervention — 364

17. LEGAL RESTRAINTS ON VIOLENCE IN ARMED CONFLICT — 366

17.1. Introduction — 366
17.2. The core international legal framework — 368
    17.2.1. The origin of international humanitarian law and early key instruments — 368
    17.2.2. The Hague Conventions (1899–1907) and the Martens Clause — 369
    17.2.3. The 1949 Geneva Conventions and common Article 3 — 370
    17.2.4. The 1977 Additional Protocols — 372
    17.2.5. Other legal instruments and customary international law — 374
    17.2.6. International humanitarian law and international human rights law — 375

17.3. Combatant status	380
17.3.1. Requirements for combatant status	381
17.3.2. Recognition of belligerency	384
17.4. Members of non-State armed groups	384
17.5. Direct participation in hostilities	386
17.5.1. Unlawful combatants?	387
17.5.2. Targeted killings and the 'war on terror'	388
17.6. Restriction on the use of military force and the choice of weapons	390
17.6.1. The principle of distinction	390
17.6.2. The principle of proportionality	391
17.6.3. Restrictions on the choice of weapons	393
17.7. Protection of war victims	395
17.8. Preventive and repressive measures to ensure compliance	397
17.8.1. Specific institutions	398
17.8.2. Reactions to violations	400
17.8.3. Compensation for damage	401
17.9. An overall assessment	402
18. THE PROTECTION OF HUMAN RIGHTS	**404**
18.1. Introduction	404
18.2. Classical international law	404
18.3. The turning point: the UN Charter	406
18.4. Trends in the evolution of international action on human rights	408
18.4.1. General	408
18.4.2. The Universal Declaration (1948)	408
18.4.3. Human rights treaties	409
18.4.4. The tendency to overrule the objection of domestic jurisdiction	410
18.4.5. Expansion of the territorial scope of human rights obligations	412
18.4.6. Universal supervisory mechanisms	414
18.4.7. Regional supervisory mechanisms	416
18.4.8. Human rights, humanitarian law, and litigation before domestic courts	419
18.5. Human rights and customary international law	420
18.6. The impact of human rights on classical international law	422
18.7. The present role of human rights	423
19. THE REPRESSION OF INTERNATIONAL CRIMES	**427**
19.1. International crimes	427
19.2. Categories of international crimes	428
19.2.1. War crimes	428
19.2.2. Crimes against humanity	431
19.2.3. Genocide	434
19.2.4. The crime of aggression	437
19.2.5. Torture	440
19.2.6. Terrorism	442
19.3. Prosecution and punishment of international crimes	444
19.3.1. Prosecution and punishment by State courts	444
19.3.2. The demand for international criminal justice	446
19.3.3. The establishment of international criminal courts and tribunals	448
19.3.4. Merits and disadvantages of international criminal trials	452

20. THE PROTECTION OF THE ENVIRONMENT — 454

20.1. Introduction — 454
20.2. Precedents — 455
20.3. The principles of international environmental law: 1972–2020 — 458
20.4. Contemporary regulation of environmental challenges — 471
    20.4.1. Overview — 471
    20.4.2. The role of 'soft law' instruments — 471
    20.4.3. Multilateral environmental agreements (MEAs) — 473
    20.4.4. Mechanisms to promote and manage compliance — 478
    20.4.5. International institutions in charge of environmental protection — 482
20.5. Responsibility and liability for environmental harm — 483
    20.5.1. Overview — 483
    20.5.2. Compensation *ex gratia* or strict liability of States — 484
    20.5.3. State responsibility for environmental harm or risk — 485
    20.5.4. Civil liability of economic operators — 487

21. INTERNATIONAL LAW AND THE GLOBAL ECONOMY — 490

21.1. Introduction — 490
21.2. The post-1945 global economic architecture — 491
    21.2.1. Two foundational conferences: Bretton Woods and Havana — 491
    21.2.2. The International Monetary Fund (IMF) — 494
    21.2.3. The International Bank for Reconstruction and Development (World Bank) — 495
    21.2.4. The General Agreement on Tariffs and Trade (GATT) — 496
21.3. Decolonization, development, and the struggle for a NIEO — 499
    21.3.1. The North–South divide — 499
    21.3.2. The economic structure of under-development — 499
    21.3.3. The struggle for a New International Economic Order (NIEO) — 501
    21.3.4. Multilateral co-operation for development — 504
21.4. International law and the global economy today — 509
    21.4.1. The post-1990 global economic architecture — 509
    21.4.2. The World Trade Organization (WTO) — 510
    21.4.3. The rise of international investment law and arbitration — 518

Index — 527

PRINCIPAL ABBREVIATIONS

ACHR	American Convention on Human Rights
AFDI	*Annuaire Français de Droit International*
AJIL	*American Journal of International Law*
AILC	B. D. Reams, Jr., ed., *American International Law Cases* (1783–1968) (New York: Oceana Publications, 1971)
Ann. Dig.	J. Fischer Williams and H. Lauterpacht, eds., *Annual Digest of Public International Law Cases* (London, New York, Toronto: Longmans, Green and Co., 1932–53)
Anzilotti, *Corso*	D. Anzilotti, *Corso di diritto internazionale* (1912, 1928), i, 4th edn (Padua: Cedam, 1955)
Anzilotti, *Cours*	D. Anzilotti, *Cours de droit international*, I (trans. G. Gidel) (Paris, 1929)
ASDI	*Annuaire Suisse de Droit International*
ASIL	American Society of International Law
AU	African Union
BIICL	British Institute of International and Comparative Law
BILC	*British International Law Cases* (London, 1965)
1912 British Manual	*Land Warfare, an Exposition of the Laws and Usages of War on Land, for the Guidance of Officers of His Majesty's Army*, by Colonel J. E. Edmonds and L. Oppenheim (London: His Majesty's Stationery Office, 1912)
1958 British Manual	*The Law of War on Land, being Part III of the Manual of Military Law*, The War Office (edited by Sir Hersch Lauterpacht and Colonel G. I. D. Draper) (London: Her Majesty's Stationery Office, 1958)
2004 British Manual	*The Manual of the Law of Armed Conflict*, UK Ministry of Defence, under the general editorship of Major General (retired) Anthony Rogers (Oxford: Oxford University Press, 2004)
Bulletin crim.	*Bulletin des arrêts de la Cour de Cassation, Chambre criminelle*
BYIL	*British Yearbook of International Law*
CICR	Comité International de la Croix Rouge
CJTL	*Columbia Journal of Transnational Law*
CYIL	*Canadian Yearbook of International Law*
DSB	Dispute Settlement Body (of the WTO)
DSU	Understanding on Rules and Procedures Governing the Settlement of Disputes (annexed to the WTO Agreement)
ECB	*European Communities Bulletin*
ECHR	European Court of Human Rights
ECJ	European Court of Justice

ECOSOC	Economic and Social Council (of the UN)
EJIL	*European Journal of International Law*
El Derecho, Jurisprudencia	Consejo general del poder judicial (Madrid), Centro de Documentación Judicial, *El Derecho, Jurisprudencia penal, constitucional*, http://www.elderecho.com, also on CDRom
Encyclopedia	R. Bernhardt, ed., *Encyclopedia of Public International Law*, 4 vols (North Holland: 1992, 1995, 1997, 2000)
FAO	Food and Agriculture Organization of the United Nations
FCO	Foreign and Commonwealth Office
Friedman	L. Friedman, ed., *The Law of War—A Documentary History*, 2 vols (New York: Random House, 1972)
FRUS	*Foreign Relations of the United States* (Washington, DC: Government Printing Office) many volumes; some of them are entitled: *Diplomatic Papers on the Foreign Relations of the United States*
FSIA	Foreign Sovereign Immunity Act 1976 (USA)
GA	General Assembly (of the UN)
GAOR	UN General Assembly Official Records
GATT	General Agreement on Tariffs and Trade
GDR	German Democratic Republic (former)
GYIL	*German Yearbook of International Law*
Hackworth	G. H. Hackworth, *Digest of International Law* (Washington, DC: Government Printing Office, 1942)
HRLJ	*Human Rights Law Journal*
IACHR	Inter-American Court of Human Rights
ICAO	International Civil Aviation Organization
ICC	International Criminal Court
ICCPR	International Covenant on Civil and Political Rights
ICJ	International Court of Justice
ICJ Reports	Reports of the International Court of Justice
ICLQ	*International & Comparative Law Quarterly*
ICRC	International Committee of the Red Cross
ICTR	International Criminal Tribunal for Rwanda
ICTY	International Criminal Tribunal for the Former Yugoslavia
IFOR	Implementation Force (NATO)
IHR	*The International History Review*
IJIL	*Indian Journal of International Law*
ILC	UN International Law Commission
ILM	International Legal Materials
ILO	International Labour Organization
ILR	International Law Reports (since 1950; edited first by Sir H. Lauterpacht and at present by Sir E. Lauterpacht, C. J. Greenwood, and A. G. Oppenheimer)
IMT	International Military Tribunal
IOLR	*International Organizations Law Review*
IRRC	*International Review of the Red Cross*
IYIL	*Italian Yearbook of International Law*
JAIL	*Japanese Annual of International Law*

JDI	*Journal du droit international*
JICJ	*Journal of International Criminal Justice*
JIDS	*Journal of International Dispute Settlement*
JPL	*Journal of Public Law*
JWTL	*Journal of World Trade Law*
JYIL	*Japanese Yearbook of International Law*
Kelsen, *Principles*	H. Kelsen, *Principles of International Law*, 2nd edn, revised and edited by R. W. Tucker (New York: Holt, Rinehart & Winston, Inc., 1966)
La Fontaine, *Pasicrisie*	H. La Fontaine, *Pasicrisie internationale—Histoire documentaire des arbitrages internationaux* (Berne: Impr. Stämpfli and Co., 1902)
Lapradelle and Politis	A. de Lapradelle and N. Politis, *Recueil des Arbitrages internationaux*, 3 vols (Paris: Pedone, 1905, 1923, 1954)
LJIL	*Leiden Journal of International Law*
Moore, *Digest*	J. B. Moore, *A Digest of International Law*, 8 vols (Washington, DC: Government Printing Office, 1906)
Moore, *History and Digest*	J. B. Moore, *History and Digest of the International Arbitrations to which the United States has been a Party*, 6 vols (Washington, DC: Government Printing Office, 1898)
Moore, *International Adjudications*	J. B. Moore, *International Adjudications, Ancient and Modern, History and Documents*, 6 vols (New York: Oxford University Press, 1929–31)
MPEPIL	*Max Planck Encyclopedia of Public International Law*
NAFO	Northwest Atlantic Fisheries Organization
NGO	Non-governmental organization
NIEO	New International Economic Order
NYIL	*Netherlands Yearbook of International Law*
OAS	Organization of American States
OAU	Organization of African Unity
ONUC	United Nations Operation in Congo
ONUMOZ	United Nations Operation in Mozambique
ONUSAL	United Nations Observer Mission in El Salvador
OSCE	Organization for Security and Co-operation in Europe
Parry	*The Consolidated Treaty Series*, edited and annotated by C. Parry, 155 vols plus Indexes (Dobbs Ferry, NY: Oceana Publications, 1969–86)
PCA	Permanent Court of Arbitration
PCIJ	Permanent Court of International Justice
PLO	Palestine Liberation Organization
POW	Prisoner of war
QIL	*Questions of International Law*
RBDI	*Revue Belge de Droit International*
RCADI	*Recueil des Cours de l'Académie de Droit International de La Haye*
RDI	*Rivista di Diritto Internazionale*
RECIEL	*Review of European, Comparative and International Environmental Law*
RGDIP	*Revue Générale de Droit International Public*
RIAA	Reports of International Arbitral Awards

RDIPP	*Rivista di diritto internazionale privato e processuale*
RUF	Revolutionary United Front of Sierra Leone
SC	Security Council (of the UN)
SCOR	UN Security Council Official Records
SFDI	Société française pour le droit international
SFOR	Stabilisation Force (NATO)
SG	Secretary-General (of the UN)
SOM	Sovereign Order of Malta
Trial Nuremberg	Trial of the Major War Criminals before the International Military Tribunal, Nuremberg, 14 November 1945–1 October 1946 (Nuremberg 1946)
UN	United Nations
UNAMI	United Nations Assistance Mission for Iraq
UNAMIR	United Nations Assistance Mission for Rwanda
UNAVEM	United Nations Angola Verification Mission
UNCIO	Documents of the United Nations Conference on International Organization, San Francisco, 1945, 16 vols (London and New York: United Nations Information Organizations, 1945–46)
UNEF	United Nations Emergency Force
UNEP	United Nations Environment Programme
UNFICYP	United Nations Peace-keeping Force in Cyprus
UNIFIL	United Nations Mission in Lebanon
UNITA	National Union for the Total Independence of Angola
UNMIK	United Nations Mission in Kosovo
UNMOGIP	United Nations Observer Group in India and Pakistan
UNOSOM	United Nations Operation in Somalia
UNPROFOR	United Nations Protection Force
UNTAC	United Nations Transitional Authority in Cambodia
UNTAET	United Nations Transitional Administration in East Timor
UNTEA	United Nations Temporary Executive Authority
UNY	*United Nations Yearbook*
USSR	Union of Soviet Socialist Republics
WEU	Western European Union
Whiteman	M. M. Whiteman, *Digest of International Law*, 15 vols (Washington, DC: Government Printing Office, 1963–70)
WHO	World Health Organization
WTO	World Trade Organization
YIEL	*Yearbook of International Environmental Law*
YILC	*Yearbook of the International Law Commission*
ZaöRV	*Zeitschrift für ausländisches öffentliches Recht und Völkerrecht*

TABLE OF CASES

A

Abaclat and Others v Argentine Republic ICSID Case No. ARB/07/5, Decision on Jurisdiction and Admissibility, 4 August 2011, 52 ILM (2013) 671 . . . 523

Abbasi v Secretary of State for Foreign and Commonwealth Affairs and others, UK, Court of Appeal (Civil Division), 6 November 2002, [2002] EWCA Civ 1598 (UK Court of Appeal) . . . 520

Abdel Basset Ali Al-Megrahi and Lamen Khalifa Fhimah, Lockerbie Special Court (High Court of Justiciary at Camp Zeist), 31 January 2001 case no. 1475/99, online at: https://www.scotcourts.gov.uk/search-judgments/lockerbie-trial . . . 420

Accordance with International Law of the Unilateral Declaration of Independence in Respect of Kosovo ICJ, Advisory Opinion, 22 July 2010, ICJ Reports 2010, 403 . . . 69, 76

Advisory Opinion OC-16/99, (Mexico Request), The Right to Information on Consular Assistance in the Framework of the Guarantees of the Due Process of Law', IACHR, 1 October 1999, online at: www.corteidh.or.cr/docs/opiniones/seriea_16_ing

Advisory Opinion OC-21/14, (Argentina, Brazil, Paraguay and Uruguay Request), Rights and Guarantees of Children in the Context of Migration and/or in Need of International Protection, IACHR 19 August 2014, online at: http://www.corteidh.or.cr/docs/opiniones/seriea_21_eng.pdf. . . . 418

Advisory Opinion OC-23/17 (Colombia Request): Environment and Human Rights, IACHR, 15 November 2017, online at: www.corteidh.or.cr/docs/opiniones/seriea_23_ing . . . 96, 418, 460, 469, 470

Advisory Opinion requested by the French Court of Cassation (Request no. P16-2018–001): see Request for an Advisory Opinion Submitted by the French Court of Cassation (Request no. P16-2018–001)

Aegean Sea Continental Shelf (Greece v Turkey), ICJ, Judgement, 19 December 1978, ICJ Reports 1978, 4 . . . 194, 201, 205–6

Ahmadou Sadio Diallo (Republic of Guinea v Democratic Republic of the Congo) (ICJ), Judgment, ICJ Reports 2010, 639 . . . 159, 521

Air Transport Association of America and others v Secretary of State for Energy and Climate Change (Case C-366/10), ECJ, Judgment, 21 December 2011, EU:C:2011:864 . . . 119

Akayesu, ICTR, Trial Chamber, Judgement, 2 September 1998 (Case no. ICTR–96–4–T), online at: unictr.irmct.org/cases/ictr-96-4 . . . 435

Aksoy v Turkey, ECHR, Application no. 21987/93, Judgment, 18 December 1996, online at: http://hudoc.echr.coe.int/fre?i=001-58003 . . . 441

Al-Adsani v Government of Kuwait, UK, Court of Appeal, 12 March 1996, 107 ILR 536 . . . 128

Al-Adsani v United Kingdom, ECHR, Application no. 35763/97, 21 November 2001, online at: http://hudoc.echr.coe.int/eng?i=001-59885 . . . 126

Alabama, The (United States/Great Britain) Arbitration See Alabama claims of the United States of America against Great Britain

Alabama claims of the United States of America against Great Britain, Alabama Claims Tribunal,14 September 1872, , in Lapradelle and Politis, II, 889 . . . 199, 221, 257, 287, 486

Alcom Ltd v Republic of Colombia, UK, House of Lords, 12 April 1984, 74 ILR 179 . . . 130

Alfred Dunhill of London, Inc. v Republic of Cuba et al., US, Supreme Court, 24 May 1976, 425 U.S. 682; 96 S.Ct.1954; 48 L.Ed.2d 301 . . . 123

Ambasciata di Norvegia v Quattri, Italy, Court of Cassation (plenary), 28 November 1991, no 12771, 74 RDI (1991) 993 . . . 125

Amoco Cadiz, US, District Court for the Northern District of Illinois, 15 June 1992, 794 F. Supp. 261 (1992) . . . 487

Anglo-Iranian Oil Company Ltd. v Idemitsu Kosan Kabushiki Kaisha (Nissho Maru case), Japan, Tokyo Higher Court, 1953, 20 ILR 305 . . . 304

Anglo-Iranian Oil Company Ltd v Jaffrate and others, Aden Supreme Court, 9 January 1953, 20 ILR (1953) 316 . . . 304

The Antelope, US, Supreme Court, 1825, 23 U.S. 66 (1825) 23 . . . 188

Appeal Relating to the Jurisdiction of the ICAO Council (India v Pakistan), ICJ, Judgment, 18 August 1972, ICJ Reports 1972, 46 . . . 201

Applicability of Article VI, Section 22, of the Convention on the Privileges and Immunities of the United Nations, ICJ, Advisory Opinion, 15 December 1989, ICJ Reports 1989, 177 . . . 152

Application of the Convention on the Prevention and Punishment of the Crime of Genocide (Bosnia-Herzegovina v Yugoslavia) (Serbia-Montenegro), ICJ, Judgment, 26 February

2007, ICJ Reports 2007, 43 . . . 15, 238, 251, 254, 435

Application of the Convention on the Prevention and Punishment of the Crime of Genocide (Bosnia-Herzegovina v Yugoslavia) (Serbia-Montenegro), Further Requests for the Indication of Provisional Measures, ICJ, Order, 13 September 1993, ICJ Reports 1993, 325 . . . 15

Application of the International Convention on the Elimination of All Forms of Racial Discrimination (Georgia v Russian Federation) (Preliminary Objections), ICJ, Judgment, 1 April 2011, ICJ Reports 2011, 70 . . . 277

Application of the International Convention on the Elimination of All Forms of Racial Discrimination (Qatar v United Arab Emirates) (Provisional Measures) ICJ, Order, 23 July 2018, ICJ Reports 2018, 406 . . . 8

Apurement des Comptes (Netherlands v France), 12 March 2004, RIAA XXV, 312 . . . 213

ARA Libertad (Argentina v Ghana) (Provisional Measures), ITLOS, Order, 15 December 2012 (Case no. 20), ITLOS Reports 2012, 332 . . . 130

Arafat and Salah, Italy, Court of Cassation, 28 June 1985, 109 Foro italiano (1986-II), 277; English translation in 7 IYIL (1986–7) 295 . . . 48, 166

Arbitration Agreement between Croatia and Slovenia *See* In the matter of an arbitration under the Arbitration Agreement between the Government of the Republic of Croatia and the Government of the Republic of Slovenia

Arbitration between Barbados and the Republic of Trinidad and Tobago, Relating to the delimitation of the exclusive economic zone and the continental shelf between them, 11 April 2006, RIAA XXVII, 147 . . . 280

Arbitration regarding the Iron Rhine ('Ijzeren Rijn') Railway between The Kingdom of Belgium and The Kingdom of the Netherlands, 24 May 2005, RIAA XXVII, 35 . . . 469, 470

Arbitration for the Brčko Area (The Federation of Bosnia and Herzegovina v. the Republika Srpska), Arbitral Tribunal for the Dispute over Inter-Entity Boundary in Brcko Area, Award, 14 February 1997, 36 ILM (1997) 396; Supplemental Award, UN Doc. S/1998/248, 15 March 1998, online at: http://www.ohr.int/ohr_archive/arbitral-tribunal-for-dispute-over-inter-entity-boundary-in-brcko-area-supplemental-award/; Final Award, 5 March 1999, 38 ILM (1999) 536 . . . 198

Arctic Sunrise Arbitration, (The Netherlands v Russia), Award on the Merits, 24 August 2015, online at: https://pca-cpa.org/en/cases/ 21/ . . . 110

Argentina—Measures Affecting the Export of Bovine Hides and Import of Finished Leather, WTO, Panel Report, 19 December 2000, WT/ DS155/R, online at: https://www.wto.org/ english/tratop_e/dispu_e/cases_e/ds155_e. htm . . . 514

Armed Activities on the Territory of the Congo (Democratic Republic of the Congo v Uganda), ICJ, Judgment, 19 December 2005, ICJ Reports 2005, 168 . . . 53, 55, 58, 59, 251, 259, 377

Arrest Warrant of 11 April 2000 (Democratic Republic of Congo v Belgium), ICJ, Judgement, 14 February 2002, ICJ Reports 2002, 3 . . . 94, 136, 137, 138, 446

Article 3, Paragraph 2 of the Treaty of Lausanne (Frontier between Turkey and Iraq), PCIJ, Advisory Opinion, 21 November 1925, Series B, no.12, 6 . . . 194

Asian Agricultural Products Ltd v Republic of Sri Lanka, ICSID Case No. ARB/87/3, Final Award, 27 June 1990, 30 ILM (1991) 577 . . . 525

Asylum (Colombia v Peru), ICJ, Judgment, 20 November 1950, ICJ Reports 1950, 266 . . . 189, 190

Avena and other Mexican Nationals (Mexico v United States of America), ICJ, Judgment, 31 March 2004, ICJ Reports 2004, 12 . . . 159, 264, 521

Award between the United States of America and the United Kingdom relating to the rights of jurisdiction of United States of America in the Bering's sea and the preservation of fur seals, 15 August 1893, Moore, History and Digest, I, 935 (also RIAA XXVIII, 263) . . . 105, 188, 455

B

Banco Nacional de Cuba v Sabbatino, US, Supreme Court, 23 March 1964, 376 U.S. 398 . . . 123, 304

Barcelona Traction (Belgium v Spain), ICJ, Judgment, 5 February 1970, ICJ Reports 1970, 3 . . . 199, 420, 524

Beit Sourik Village Council v Government of Israel, Supreme Court Sitting as the High Court of Justice, 30 June 2004, HCJ 2056/ 04, online at: http://62.90.71.124/eng/system/ index.htm (Israeli Supreme Court) . . . 303, 392

Belilos v Switzerland, ECHR, Admissibility, Merits and Just satisfaction, Application no. 10328/83, 29 April 1988, online at: http:// hudoc.echr.coe.int/fre?i=001-57434 (ECtHR) . . . 211

Bemba Gombo, ICC, Trial Chamber, Judgment, 21 March 2016 (Case no. ICC-01/05–01/08), online at: www.icc-cpi.int/CourtRecords/ CR2016_02238 . . . 254

Bering Fur Seal Arbitration (United States v United Kingdom) *See* Award between the United States of America and the United

Kingdom relating to the rights of jurisdiction of United States of America in the Bering's sea and the preservation of fur seals

Bernstein v N.V.Nederlandsche-Amerikaanische Stoomvaart-Maatschappij, US, US Court of Appeals, Second Circuit, 5 February 1954, 210 F.2d 375 (2nd Cir. 1954) ... 304–5

Bey di Tunisi rappresentato da Guttieres v Elmilik, Italy, Florence Court of Cassation, 25 July 1886, La giurisprudenza di diritto internazionale, II (1876–90), 1543 ... 123

Bigi, Italy, Rome Tribunal, Order, 18 February 1987, 24 RDIPP (1988) 359 (partial English translation in IYIL (1988–92) 44) ... 136, 137

Blake v Guatemala, (Preliminary Objections), IACHR, Judgment, online at: http://hrlibrary.umn.edu/iachr/C/27-ing.html ... 255

Blaise and others, CJEU, Grand Chamber, Case C-616/17, Judgment, 1 October 2019, EU:C:2019:800 ... 464

Blaškić (1996), ICTY, decision of the President, 3 April 1996, ICTY, Judicial Reports, 1996 I, 773 ... 222

Blaškić, ICTY, Trial Chamber, Judgment, 3 March 2000 (Case no. IT-95-14-T), online at: www.icty.org/cases/blaskic/tjug ... 195

Blaškić (Judgment on the request of Croatia), ICTY, Appeals Chamber, 29 October 1997 (Case no. IT-95-14-AR108 bis), online at: www.icty.org/cases/blaskic/acdec ... 124, 131, 132

Blaškić (subpoena) *See above* Blaškić (Judgment on the request of Croatia)

Border and Transborder Armed Actions (Nicaragua v Honduras) (Jurisdiction and Admissibility), ICJ, Judgment, 20 December 1988, ICJ Reports 1988, 69 ... 65

Borgers v Belgium, ECHR, Application no. 12005/86, Judgement, 30 October 1991, online at: http://hudoc.echr.coe.int/fre?i=001-57720 ... 423

Bouterse, The Netherlands, Amsterdam Court of Appeal, 20 November 2000, online at: www.icj.org/objectives/decision.htm (in English); www.rechtspraak.nl (in Dutch) ... 137

Brazil-Measures Affecting Imports of Retreaded Tyres, WTO, AB Report, 3 December 2007, WT/DS332/AB/R; Panel Report, 12 June 2007, WT/DS332/R, online at: https://www.wto.org/english/tratop_e/dispu_e/cases_e/ds332_e.htm ... 517

Brazilian Loans *See* Paiement, en or, des emprunts fédéraux brésiliens émis en France

Bufano et al., Switzerland, Tribunal Fédéral, 21 May 1986, in Arrêts du Tribunal Fédéral Suisse, Recueil Officiel, vol. 112, I, 222 ... 239

Buttes Gas and Oil Company v Hammer and others, UK, House of Lords, 29 October 1981, per Lord Wilberforce, 21 ILM (1982) 92 ... 123

C

Caire (France–Mexico Claims Commission) *See* Estate of Jean-Baptiste Caire (France) v United Mexican States

Calley, US, Instructions from the Military Judge to the Court Martial Members, March 1971, Friedman, II, 1703–27; United States, US Army Court of Military Appeals, 21 December 1973, 22 USCMA 534 ... 444

Canada—Certain Measures Affecting the Renewable Energy Generation Sector, WTO, AB Report, 6 May 2013, WT/DS412/AB/R, WT/DS426/AB/R, online at: www.wto.org/tratop_e/dispu_e/412_426abr_e ... 516

Canada/Japan—Tariff on Imports of Spruce, Pine, Fire (SPF) Dimension Lumber, GATT, Panel Report, 19 July 1989, L/6470-36S/167, online: www.wto.org/tratop_e/dispu_e/gatt_e/88lumber ... 513

Cape Horn Pigeon (United States of America v Russia), 29 November 1902, RIAA IX, 63 ... 193

The Carthage (France v Italy), 6 May 1913, RIIA XI, 457 (in French) ... 265

Case concerning filleting within the Gulf of St. Lawrence between Canada and France, 17 July 1986, RIAA XIX, 225 ... 109

Case Concerning Military and Paramilitary Activities in and Against Nicaragua (Nicaragua v United States of America), ICJ, Judgment, 27 June 1986, ICJ Reports, 1986, 14 ... 17, 53, 55, 56, 58, 59, 60, 93, 118, 171, 185, 196, 199, 240, 251, 253, 254, 268, 272, 350, 351, 354, 357, 358, 364, 375, 438

Case Concerning Military and Paramilitary Activities in and Against Nicaragua (Nicaragua v United States of America) (Jurisdiction and admissibility), ICJ, Judgment, 26 November 1984, ICJ Reports 1984, 39 ... 287, 300

Case concerning the Air Service Agreement of 27 March 1946, 9 December 1978, RIAA XVIII, 415 ... 267, 298, 299, 302

Case concerning the differences between New Zealand and France arising from the Rainbow Warrior affair, Ruling of the UN Secretary-General, 6 July 1986, RIAA XIX, 197 ... 132, 260, 261, 265, 322

Case Concerning the Gabčikovo-Nagymaros Project (Hungary/Slovakia), ICJ, Judgement, 25 September 1997, ICJ Reports 1997, 7 ... 63, 65, 66, 201, 261, 287, 302, 462, 469, 470

Case Concerning the Payment of Various Serbian Loans Issued in France (France v Kingdom of the Serbs, Croats, and Slovenes), PCIJ, Judgment, 12 July 1929, Series A, no 20, 1 ... 260

Case of Agreement on German External Debt, 16 May 1980, 84 RGDIP (1980), 1157 ... 213

Case of Sawhoyamaxa Indigenous Community v Paraguay, IACHR, Judgment, 29 March 2006,

online at: www.corteidh.or.cr/casos/articulos/seriec_146_ing . . . 525
Case of the 'Maria Luz', 17 May 1875, Moore, vol. 5, 5034–6 . . . 23
The Case of the S.S. Lotus (France v Turkey), PCIJ, Judgment, 7 September 1927, Series A, no.10, 2 . . . 94, 96, 184
Case Relating to the Territorial Jurisdiction of the International Commission of the River Oder *See* Territorial Jurisdiction of the International Commission of the River Oder (United Kingdom v Poland)
Certain activities carried out by Nicaragua in the Border Area (Costa Rica v Nicaragua), Construction of a road in Costa Rica along the river San Juan (Nicaragua v Costa Rica), ICJ, Judgment, 16 December 2015, ICJ Reports 2015, 665 . . . 62, 63, 74, 287, 461, 462, 463
Certain activities carried out by Nicaragua in the Border Area (Costa Rica v Nicaragua), Compensation owed by the Republic of Nicaragua to the Republic of Costa Rica, ICJ, Judgment, 2 February 2018, ICJ Reports 2018, 15 . . . 487
Certain Expenses of the United Nations, ICJ, Advisory Opinion, 20 July 1962, ICJ Reports 1962, 151 . . . 213, 343
Certain German Interests in Polish Upper Silesia (Germany v Poland), PCIJ, Judgment, 25 May 1926, Series A, no. 7, 4 . . . 209
Certain Questions of Mutual Assistance in Criminal Matters (Djibouti v France), ICJ, Judgment, 4 June 2008, ICJ Reports 2008, 231 . . . 64
Ceskoslovenska Obchodni Banka, A.S. v The Slovak Republic, ICSID Case No. ARB/97/4, Award, 24 May 1999, online at: www.italaw.com/files/case-documents/ita0145 . . . 523
Chagos Marine Protected Area Arbitration (Mauritius v United Kingdom), Award, 18 March 2015, online at: https://pca-cpa.org/en/cases/11/ . . . 110
Chemin de fer Liégeois-Luxembourg v Etat néerlandais, Belgium, Court of Cassation, 11 June 1903, Pasicrisie belge, 1903, I, 294 . . . 123
Chile—Price Band System and Safeguard Measures Relating to Certain Agricultural Products, WTO, Panel Report, 3 May 2002, WT/DS207/R, online at: https://www.wto.org/english/tratop_e/dispu_e/cases_e/ds207_e.htm . . . 517
Chile—Taxes on Alcoholic Beverages, WTO, Panel Report, 15 June 1999, WT/DS87/R, WT/DS110/R, online at: https://www.wto.org/english/tratop_e/dispu_e/cases_e/ds87_e.htm . . . 514
Chilean Nationalization of El Teniente Mine, Germany, Hamburg Superior Court, 13 March 1974, 13 ILM (1974) 1115 . . . 304
China—Measures Affecting Imports of Automobile Parts, WTO, AB Report, 15 December 2008), WT/DS339/AB/R, WT/DS340/AB/R, WT/DS342/AB/R, online at: www.wto.org/tratop_e/dispu_e/cases_e/ds342_e . . . 514
China—Measures Related to the Exportation of Rare Earths, Tungsten, and Molybdenum, WTO, Panel Report, 26 March 2014, WT/DS431/R ; WT/DS432/R ; WT/DS433/R, online at: https://www.wto.org/english/tratop_e/dispu_e/cases_e/ds431_e.htm . . . 469, 470
China—Measures Related to the Exportation of Various Raw Materials, WTO, AB Report, 13 January 2012, WT/ DS 394/AB/R, online at: www.wto.org/tratop_e/dispu_e/cases_e/ds394_e . . . 469, 470
Chinese Women, Japan, Tokyo District Court, 24 April 2003, in 1127 Hanrei Taimuzu 281 (in Japanese), cited in Shin Hae Bong, 'Compensation for Victims of Wartime Atrocities: Recent Developments in Japan's Court Case law', in 3 JICJ (2005) 187 . . . 402
Cicippio v. Islamic Republic of Iran, US, US Court of Appeals for the District of Columbia Circuit, 29 July 1994, 308 U.S. App. D.C. 102 . . . 128
CME Czech Republic B.V v The Czech Republic, UNCITRAL Arbitration Proceedings, Partial Award, 13 September 2001, online at: https://www.italaw.com/cases/281 . . . 519
Coard and others v US, Inter-American Commission of Human Rights, Report no. 109/99, 29 September 1999 (Case no. 10.951), online at: http://heiwwwe.unige.ch/ humanrts/cases/1999/us109–99.html . . . 412
Commonwealth v WMC Resources Ltd, Australia, High Court, 2 February 1998) [1998] 194 CLR 1 . . . 111
Compagnie générale des asphaltes de France Case, British-Venezuelan Mixed Claims Commission, RIIA IX, 389 . . . 264
Competence of the ILO Concerning Personal Work of the Employer, PCIJ, Advisory Opinion of 23 July 1926, Series B, no. 13, 18 . . . 146, 213
Condor e Filvem v Ministero di Grazia e Giustizia, Italy, Constitutional Court, 15 July 1992, 75 RDI (1992) 395 (English translation in 8 IYIL (1988–92) 31) . . . 129
Consolato generale britannico in Napoli v Toglia, Italy, Court of Cassation (plenary), 15 May 1989, no. 2329, 72 RDI (1989) 687 . . . 125
Continental Shelf (Libyan Arab Jamahiriya/Malta), ICJ, Judgment, 3 June 1985, ICJ Reports 1985, 13 . . . 104, 109, 111, 113
Continental Shelf (Tunisia/Libyan Arab Jamahiriya), ICJ, Judgment, 24 February 1982, ICJ Reports 1982, 59 . . . 112, 113, 198
Controller and Auditor General v Sir Ronald Davidson, New Zealand, Court of Appeal, 16 February 1996, 2 New Zealand Law Reports (1996) 278 . . . 128

TABLE OF CASES

Corfu Channel (United Kingdom v Albania), ICJ, Judgement, 9 April 1949, ICJ Reports 1949, 4 . . . 50, 53, 59, 62, 63, 72, 106, 265, 287, 322, 364, 375, 463, 486

The Creole, US-Great Britain Mixed Commission, 15 January 1855, La Pradelle and Politis vol. I, 704 . . . 260

Cristiani v Istituto italo–latino–americano, Italy, Corte of Cassation, 23 November 1985, 69 RDI (1986) 146 . . . 144

D

Danzig Railway Officials: *See* Jurisdiction of the Courts of Danzig

Davy, Great Britain-Venezuela Mixed Claims Commission, 1903, RIAA IX, 467 . . . 250

De Guieros Magalhaes Abrantes v Republic of Portugal, Belgium, Labour Court of Brussels, 22 September 1992, Pasicrisie belge, I, 1992, 104 . . . 125

De Meeüs v Forzano, Italy, Corte of Cassation, 16 November 1939, 19 RDI (1940), 93 . . . 187

Decision on Confirmation of Charges against Omar Hassan Ahmad Al Bashir, ICC, PTC, 4 March 2009 (Case no. ICC-02/05-01/09-3), online at: https://www.icccpi.int/pages/record.aspx?uri=639096 . . . 138, 436

Decision on the Authorization of an Investigation into the Situation in the Republic of Kenya, ICC, 31 March 2010 (Case no. ICC-01/09), online at: www.icc-cpi.int/CourtRecords/CR2010_02409 . . . 434

Decision on the Prosecution's Request for a Ruling on Jurisdiction under Article 19(3) of the Statute, ICC, PTC, 6 September 2018, (Case no. ICC-RoC46(3)-01/18), online at: https://www.icc-cpi.int/Pages/record.aspx?docNo=ICC-RoC46(3)-01/18-37 . . . 450

Delcourt v Belgium, ECHR, Application no. 2689/65, Judgment, 17 January 1970, online at: hudoc.echr.coe.int/webservices/content/pdf . . . 423

Delia Saldías de Lopez (on behalf of a husband, Sergio Euben Lopez Burgo) v Uruguay, HRC, 29 July 1981, communication no. R. 12/52, Human Rights Committee, Selected Decisions (Second to Sixteenth Sessions) (1985), 91 . . . 412

Delimitation of the Maritime Boundary between Guinea-Bissau and Senegal, 31 July 1989, RIAA XX, 119 . . . 167

Delimitation of the Maritime Boundary in the Gulf of Maine Area (Canada/United States of America), ICJ, Judgment, 12 October 1984, ICJ Reports 1984, 246 . . . 112–13, 198

Delimitation of the Maritime Frontier between Guinea and Guinea-Bissau, 14 February 1985, RIAA XIX, 147 . . . 213

Demizpence, France, Council of State, 10 March 1995, no. 141083, 99 RGDIP (1995) 1013 . . . 227

Denmark ACCC/C/2006/18, Aarhus Compliance Committee, 29 April 2008, ECE/MP.PP/2008/5/Add.4 . . . 468

Diallo (Republic of Guinea v Democratic Republic of the Congo): *see* Ahmadou Sadio Diallo (Republic of Guinea v Democratic Republic of the Congo)

Dickinson v Del Solar, United Kingdom, King's Bench Division, 31 July 1929, [1930] 1 K.B. 376, 6 BILC 142 . . . 131

Difference Relating to Immunity from Legal Process of a Special Rapporteur of the Commission on Human Rights, ICJ, Advisory Opinion, 29 April 1999, ICJ Reports 1999, 62 . . . 152, 250

Dispute Concerning Delimitation of the Maritime Boundary between Ghana and Côte d'Ivoire in the Atlantic Ocean (Ghana/Côte d'Ivoire) (Provisional Measures), ITLOS, Order, 25 April 2015 (Case no. 23), ITLOS Reports 2015, 146 . . . 62, 460, 462

Dispute regarding Navigational and Related Rights (Costa Rica v. Nicaragua), ICJ, Judgment, 13 July 2009, ICJ Reports 2009, 213 . . . 191

District of Columbia v Vinard L. Paris, US, Police Court of the District of Columbia, 1937, 33 AJIL (1939) 787 . . . 135

Doe v Lumintang, US, District Court for the District of Columbia, 10 September 2001, online at: www.cja.org / etimorjudgement.htm . . . 420

Dogger Bank (Great Britain/Russia), Commission of Inquiry, Report, 26 February 1905, 2 AJIL (1908) 931 . . . 280

Dominguez v State, US, Court of Appeals, 2 October 1921, 90 Tex.Crim. 609, 234 S.W. 79 (1921), 17 AILC (1783–1968), 8 . . . 51

E

Eagle Star and British Dominions Insurance Company (Limited) and Excess Insurance Company (Limited) (Great Britain v United Mexican States), Great Britain––Mexico Claims Commission, 23 April 1931, RIAA V, 139 . . . 257

East Timor (Portugal v Australia), ICJ, Judgment, 30 June 1995, ICJ Reports 1995, 90 . . . 48, 69, 278

Eastern Extension, Australasia and China Telegraph Co., 9 November 1923, RIAA VI, 112 . . . 192

Ecole française de Rome v Guadagnino, Italy, Court of Cassation (plenary), 9 September 1997 no. 8768, 34 RDIPP 1(998) 816 . . . 125

Effect of Awards of Compensation made by the United Nations Administrative Tribunal, ICJ, Advisory Opinion, 13 July 1954, ICJ Reports 1962, 151 . . . 213

E.H.P. v Canada, HRC, Communication No. 67/1980, 27 October 1982, UN Doc. CCPR/C/OP/1 (1984) 20 . . . 466

Eichmann, Israel, District Court of Jerusalem, 12 December 1961, 36 ILR 5(English translation); Supreme Court, 29 May 1962, 36 ILR 277 (English translation) . . . 51, 419, 444, 446, 453

Empire, The v Chang and others, Japan, Supreme Court, Annual Digest, 1919–22, 288 . . . 137

Erdemović (Appeal), ICTY, Appeals Chamber, 7 October 1997 (Case no. IT-96-22-A), online at: www.icty.org/cases/erdemovic/acjug . . . 195

Erdemović (Sentencing), ICTY, Trial Chamber, Judgment, 29 November 1996 (Case no. IT-96-22-T), online at: www.icty.org/cases/erdemovic/tjug . . . 195

Estate of Jean-Baptiste Caire (France) v United Mexican States, French-Mexican Claims Commission, 7 June 1929, RIAA V, 516 . . . 250

European Community ACCC/C/2007/21, Aarhus Compliance Committee, 3 April 2009, ECE/MP.PP/C.1/2009/2/Add.1 . . . 468

European Communities—Conditions for the Granting of Tariff Preferences to Developing Countries, WTO, AB Report, 7 April 2004, WT/DS246/AB/R, online at: www.wto.org/tratop_e/dispu_e/cases_e/ds246_e . . . 515

European Communities—Measures Affecting Asbestos and Products Containing Asbestos, WTO, AB Report, 12 March 2001, WT/DS135/AB/R, online at: www.wto.org/tratop_e/dispu_e/cases_e/ds135_e . . . 513, 514

European Communities—Measures Affecting the Approval and Marketing of Biotech Products (EC—Biotech), Panel Report, 29 September 2006, WT/DS291/R, WT/DS292/R, WT/DS293/R, online at: www.wto.org/tratop_e/dispu_e/cases_e/ds291_e . . . 463

European Communities—Measures Affecting Trade in Commercial Vessels, WTO, Panel Report, 20 June 2005, WT/DS301/R, online at: www.wto.org/tratop_e/dispu_e/cases_e/ds301_e . . . 513

European Communities—Measures Concerning Meat and Meat Products (Hormones), Arbitration under Article 21.3(c) of the Dispute Settlement Understanding, AB Report, 29 May 1998, WT/DS26/15 and WT/DS26/15,1833, online at: www.wto.org/tratop_e/dispu_e/cases_e/ds26_e . . . 463

European Communities—Measures Prohibiting the Importation and Marketing of Seal Products ((EC—Seal Products), WTO, AB Report, 22 May 2014, WT/DS400/AB/R, WT/DS401/AB/R, online at: www.wto.org/tratop_e/dispu_e/cases_e/ds400_e . . . 514, 517

European Communities and Certain Member States—Measures Affecting Trade in Large Civil Aircraft, WTO, AB Report, 18 May 2011, WT/DS316/AB/R, online at: www.wto.org/tratop_e/dispu_e/cases_e/ds316_e . . . 515

European Union ACCC/C/2008/32 (Part I), Aarhus Compliance Committee, 24 August 2011, ECE/MP.PP/C.1/2011/4/Add.1 . . . 468

Ex parte Quirin, US, Supreme Court, 31 July 1942, 17 AILC 457 . . . 387

Exchange of Greek and Turkish Populations, PCIJ, Advisory Opinion, 21 February 1925, Series B, no.10, 21 . . . 222

F

Fabiani, French-Venezuelan Claims Commission, 31 July 1905, RIAA X, 85 . . . 193

Factory at Chorzow (Germany v. Poland) (Jurisdiction), PCIJ, Judgment, 26 July 1927, PCIJ, Series A, no. 9, 7.....66; Judgment, 13 September 1928, Series A, no. 17, 4 . . . 194

Ferrini v Federal Republic of Germany, Italy, Court of Cassation (plenary-civil matters), 11 March 2004, no. 5044, 87 RDI (2004) 540 . . . 133, 240, 304, 305, 402

Fidel Castro, Spain, Audiencia Nacional, Order, 4 March 1999 (no.1999/2723), CD Rom, EL DERECHO, 2002, Criminal Case Law . . . 136, 137

Filartiga v Peña-Irala, US, Court of Appeals, Second Circuit, 30 June 1980, 630 F 2d 876 (2nd Circ. 1980) . . . 420, 441

Filipino 'comfort' women v Japan, Tokyo District Court, 9 October 1998, in 45 Sosho Geppo no.9, 1597; 1683 Hanrei Jiho 57; 1029 Hanrei Taimuzu 96, cited in Shin Hae Bong, 'Compensation for Victims of Wartime Atrocities: Recent Developments in Japan's Court Case law', in 3 JICJ (2005) 187 . . . 402

Fishbach and Friedericy, German-Venezuelan Mixed Claims Commission, 1903, RIAA X, 388 . . . 188

Fishel v BASF Group and others, US, District Court for the Southern District of Iowa, Central Division, 11 March 1998, 175 F.R.D. 525 (S.D. Iowa 1997) . . . 402

Fisheries (United Kingdom v Norway), ICJ, Judgment, 18 December 1951, ICJ Reports 1951, 116 . . . 105, 107, 108, 189

Fisheries Jurisdiction (Spain v Canada) (Jurisdiction), ICJ, Judgment, 4 December 1998, ICJ Reports 1998, 432 . . . 115

Fisheries Jurisdiction (United Kingdom v Iceland) and (Federal Republic of Germany v Iceland), ICJ, Judgements, 25 July 1974, ICJ Reports 1974, 3 and 175 . . . 105, 107, 201

Fogarty v United Kingdom, ECHR, Application no. 37112/97, Judgment, 21 November 2001, online at: hudoc.echr.coe.int/app/conversion/pdf/library= . . . 124

Forced transportation and labour of Chinese, Japan, Tokyo District Court, 11 March 2003, unreported, cited in Shin Hae Bong, 'Compensation for Victims of Wartime Atrocities: Recent Developments in Japan's Court Case law', 3 JICJ (2005) 187 . . . 304

Forced transportation and labour of Chinese workers, Japan, Niigata District Court, 26 March 2004, unreported, cited in Shin Hae Bong, 'Compensation for Victims of Wartime Atrocities: Recent Developments in Japan's Court Case law', 3 JICJ (2005) 187 . . . 304

Ford et al. v García et al., US, Court of Appeals for the Eleventh Circuit, 30 April 2002, online at: www.law.emory.edu/ 11circuit/apr2002/01–10357.opn.html . . . 420

Forti v Suarez-Mason, US, District Court for the Northern District of California, 6 October 1987, 672 F. Supp. 1531, 1548–50 (N.D. Cal., 1987) . . . 123, 305, 420

Foster and Elam v Neilson, United States, US, Supreme Court, 1829, 27 U.S. (2 Pet) 253 (1829), AILC (1783–1968) vol. 2, 412 . . . 227

Francisco Mallén (United Mexican States) v United States of America, Mexico-US General Claims Commission, 27 April 1927, RIAA IV, 173 . . . 250

Franco-Canadian Fisheries Arbitration See Case concerning filleting within the Gulf of St. Lawrence between Canada and France

François v State of Canada, Belgium, Labour Court of Brussel, 1st Chamber, 23 May 1989, 115 ILR 418 . . . 125

Free Zones of Upper Savoy and the District of Gex (France v Switzerland), PCIJ, 7 June 1932, Series A/B no. 46, 96 . . . 221

Frontier Dispute (Benin/Niger), ICJ, Judgment, 12 July 2005, ICJ Reports 2005, 90 . . . 99

Frontier Dispute (Burkina Faso/Republic of Mali), ICJ, Judgment, 22 December 1986, ICJ Reports 1986, 554 . . . 71, 99, 101, 102, 194, 196

Fujii v State of California, US, Supreme Court of California, 1952, 242 Pac (2nd) 617, 46 AJIL (1952), 559 . . . 227

Furundžija, ICTY, Trial Chamber, Judgment, 10 December 1998 (Case no. IT-95–17/1-T), online at: www.icty.org/cases/furundzija/tjug . . . 195, 222, 236, 238, 239, 240, 441

G

Galić, ICTY, Appeals Chamber, Judgment, 30 November 2006 (Case no. IT-98-29-A), online at: www.icty.org/cases/galic/acjug/galacjud061130 . . . 430

Galvan (Salome Lerma Vda. De Galvan), Mexico-United States General Claims Commission, 21 July 1927, RIAA IV, 273 . . . 250

Garcia José Guillermo and Vides Casanova Carlos Eugenio, United States, US District Court, Southern District of Florida, verdict of 23 July 2002 and order of 31 July 2002, online at: www.cja.org/RomagozaFinalJudgment.htm Instructions of the judge to the jury, online at: www.cja.org/RomagozaFinalJudgment.htm . . . 139

Genocide (Bosnia and Herzegovina v Yugoslavia (Serbia and Montenegro) case See Application of the Convention on the Prevention and Punishment of the Crime of Genocide (Bosnia-Herzegovina v Yugoslavia) (Serbia-Montenegro)

Georges Pinson (France) v United Mexican States, French-Mexican Claims Commission, 19 October 1928, RIAA V, 327 . . . 222

Ghaddafi, France, Cour de Cassation, 13 March 2001, no.1414, Bulletin des arrêts de la Cour de Cassation, Chambre criminelle, March 2001, no. 64, 218; Paris Court of appeal, Chambre d'accusation, 20 October 2000, no. 1999/05921, RGDIP (2001) 475 . . . 136, 137

Giamahiria Araba Libica v Soc. Rossbeton, Italy, Court of Cassation (plenary), 25 May 1989, 72 RDI (1989) 692 . . . 130

Giamahira Araba Libica v Trobbiani, Italy, Court of Cassation (plenary), 25 May 1989, no. 145, 73 RDI (1990) 403 . . . 125

Gill: see John Gill (Great Britain) v United Mexican States

Gladys M. Lafontant v Jean-Bertrand Aristide, US, District Court for the Eastern District of New York, 27 January 1994, 844 F.Supp.128 . . . 136

Godínez Cruz v Honduras, IACHR, 20 January 1989, online at: http://www1.umn.edu/humanrts/ iachr/b_11_14d. html . . . 389

Göring and others, IMT Nuremberg, Trial of the Major War Criminals before the International Military Tribunal, vol. I, Nuremberg 1947, 171 . . . 158

Gowan Comércio Internacional e Serviços Lda v Ministero della Salute, CJEU, Case C-77/09, Judgment, 22 December 2010, EU:C:2010:803 . . . 464

Gramajo: See Xuncax Teresa v Gramajo Hector

Grand Jury Proceedings, US, US Court of Appeals 4th Circuit, 5 May 1987, 817 F.2d, 1108 . . . 137

Greifelt and others, United States Military Tribunal sitting at Nuremberg, 10 March 1948, in Trials of War Criminals before the Nüremberg Military Tribunals under Control Council Law no.10 (Washington, D.C., US Govt Printing Office, 1950), vol. 5, 88 . . . 434

Guatemala Genocide Case, Decision No. 327/2003, Spain, Supreme Court, 25 February 2003, online at: ihl-databases.icrc.org/CASE_TEXT . . . 139

Guyana v Suriname, PCA Case 2004/04, Award, 17 September 2007, online at: https://pca-cpa.org/en/cases/9/ . . . 113

H

Hamdi v Rumsfeld, US Supreme Court, 542 US 507 (2004) ... 380, 388

Harry Roberts (United States) v United Mexican States, Mexico-USA General Claims Commission, 2 November 1926, RIAA IV, 77 ... 519

Hartford Fire Insurance Co. v California et al., US, US Supreme Court, 28 June 1993, 509 U.S. 764 ... 95

Hassan v UK, ECHR, Grand Chamber, Application no. 29750/09, Judgment, 16 September 2014, online at: hudoc.echr.coe.int/app/conversion/pdf ... 379

Hatton v UK, ECHR, Grand Chamber, Application no. 36022/97, Judgment, 8 July 2003, online at: hudoc.echr.coe.int/app/conversion/pdf/library= ... 469, 470

Haya de la Torre (Colombia v Peru), ICJ, Judgment, 13 June 1951, ICJ Reports 1951, 71 ... 288

Hirute Abebe-Jira and others v Kelbessa Negewo, US, US Court of Appeals for the Northern District of Georgia, 10 January 1996, 72 F.3d 844 (11th Circ. 1996) ... 420

Hissène Habré, Extradition Request, Judgment, Court of Appeal of Dakar, 25 November 2005 at http://www.internationalcrimesdatabase.org/Case/762 ... 137

H.J.M.M. v Public Prosecutor, The Netherlands, Supreme Court, 23 September 1980, 13 NYIL 1982, 366 ... 227

Hoess, Rudolf Franz Ferdinand, Poland, Supreme National Tribunal, March 1947, LRTWC, VII, 11 ... 434

Home Frontier and Foreign Missionary Society of the United Brethren in Christ (United States of America) v Great Britain, 18 December 1920, RIAA VI, 42 ... 254

I

I Congreso del Partido, UK, Hight Court, 28 January 1977, in 64 ILR, 154; Court of Appeal, 1 October 1979, ibid., 277; House of Lords, 16 July 1981, ibid., 307 ... 123

ICAO Council: see Appeal Relating to the Jurisdiction of the ICAO Council (India v Pakistan)

In the matter of an arbitration under the Arbitration Agreement between the Government of the Republic of Croatia and the Government of the Republic of Slovenia, signed on 4 November 2009, PCA Case No. 2012-04, Final Award, 29 June 2017, online at: https://pca-cpa.org/en/cases/3/ ... 101, 102, 103

In the matter of the Indus Waters Kishenganga Arbitration before the Court of Arbitration constituted in accordance with the Indus Waters Treaty 1960 between the Government of India and the Government of Pakistan signed on 19 September 1960 (Islamic Republic of Pakistan v Republic of India), PCA, Partial Award, 18 February 2013, online at: https://pca-cpa.org/en/cases/20/... ... 469, 470

In the matter of the South China Sea Arbitration before and Arbitral Tribunal constituted under Annex VII of the United Nations Convention on the Law of the Sea (Republic of the Philippines v People's Republic of China), PCA Case No. 2013-19, Award, 12 July 2016, online at: http://www.pcacases.com/web/view/7 ... 62, 97, 460, 462

In the matter of Oil Spill by the Amoco Cadiz off the Coast of France on March 16, 1978, US, Court of Appeals Seventh Circuit, 24 January 1992, 954 F. 2d 1279 (7th Cir. 1992) 1299 ... 487

Incident in the North Sea: See Dogger Bank (Great Britain/Russia)

India—Certain Measures Relating to Solar Cells and Solar Modules, WTO, AB Report, 16 September 2016, WT-DS456/AB/R, online at: www.wto.org/english/tratop_e/dispu_e/456abr_e ... 517

India—Quantitative Restrictions on Imports of Agricultural, Textile and Industrial Products, WTO, AB Report, 23 August 1999, WT/SD90/AB/R, online at: www.wto.org/tratop_e/dispu_e/cases_e/ds90_e ... 516, 517

Indus Water Kishenganga Arbitration (Islamic Republic of Pakistan v Republic of India): see In the matter of the Indus Waters Kishenganga Arbitration before the Court of Arbitration constituted in accordance with the Indus Waters Treaty 1960 between the Government of India and the Government of Pakistan signed on 19 September 1960 (Islamic Republic of Pakistan v Republic of India)

Interhandel (Switzerland v United States) (Preliminary Objections), ICJ, Judgement, 21 March 1959, ICJ Reports 1959, 6 ... 521

Interlocutory Decision on the Applicable Law: Terrorism, Conspiracy, Homicide, Perpetration, Cumulative Charging, STL, Appeals Chamber, STL-11-01/I, 16 February 2011, online at: www.legal-tools.org/doc/ceebc3/pdf ... 443

Interpretation of Peace Treaties with Bulgaria, Hungary and Romania (first phase), ICJ, Advisory Opinion, 30 March 1950, ICJ Reports 1950, 65 ... 277

Interpretation of the Agreement of 25 March 1951 between the WHO and Egypt, ICJ, Advisory Opinion, 20 December 1980, ICJ Reports 1980, 73 ... 154, 203

Interpretation of the Statute of the Memel Territory (Britain, France, Italy, Japan v Lithuania), PCIJ, Judgment, 11 August 1932, Series A/B No. 49, 250 ... 100

Island of Palmas (Netherlands/United States of America), 4 April 1928, RIAA II, 831) ... 81, 94, 97, 99, 100, 199

Istituto internazionale di Agricoltura v Profili. Italy, Court of Cassation, 13 May 1931, Giurisprudenza italiana, 1931, I, 738 . . . 143

J

Jadhav (India v Pakistan), ICJ, Judgement, 17 July 2019, (unreported), online at: https://www.icj-cij.org/en/case/168/judgments . . . 287

Jam et al v International Finance Corp., US, Supreme Court, 27 February 2019, 586 U.S. ___ 2019 . . . 148

Japan—Taxes on Alcoholic Beverages, WTO, AB Report, 4 October 1996, WT/DS8/AB/R,WT/DS10/AB/R, WT/DS11/AB/R, online at: www.wto.org/tratop_e/dispu_e/cases_e/ds8_e . . . 513, 514

Jelisić, ICTY, Trial Chamber, Judgment, 14 December 1999 (Case no. IT-95-10-T), online at: www.icty.org/cases/jelisic/tjug . . . 435

John Gill (Great Britain v United Mexican States), Claims Commission, Decision No. 44, 19 May 1931, RIIA, V, 157 . . . 260

Jones and others v United Kingdom, ECHR, Applications nos. 34356/06 and 40528/06, Judgment, 14 January 2014, online at: http://hudoc.echr.coe.int/fre?i=001-140005 . . . 126

Judgment no. 963 of the ILO Administrative Tribunal (Niesing, Peeters and Roussot), ILO Administrative Tribunal, 27 June 1989, online: http://www.ilo.org/public/english/tribunal/fulltext/0963.htm . . . 194

Jurisdiction of the Courts of Danzig, PCIJ, Advisory Opinion, 3 March 1928, Series B no. 15, 6 . . . 158

Jurisdiction of the European Commission of the Danube, PCIJ, Advisory Opinion, 8 December 1927, Series B, no. 14, 6 . . . 213

Jurisdiction Immunities (Germany v Italy): . . . see Jurisdictional Immunities of the State (Germany v Italy: Greece intervening)

Jurisdictional Immunities of the State (Germany v Italy: Greece intervening), ICJ, Judgment, 3 February 2012, ICJ Reports 2012, 99 . . . 126, 128–9, 240, 287

K

Kadi *See* Yassin Abdullah Kadi and Al Barakaat International Foundation v Council of the European Union and Commission of the European Communities (C-402/05 and C-415/05)

Kadić S. v Karadic Radovan, United States, Court of Appeals Second Circuit, 13 October 1995, 70 F.3d 232 . . . 420

Kalogeropoulou and others v Greece and Germany, ECHR, Application no. 59021/00, Judgement, 12 December 2002, 129 ILR (2002) 537 . . . 402

Kasikili/Sedudu Island (Botswana/Namibia), ICJ, Judgment, 13 December 1999, ICJ Reports 1999, 1045 . . . 98, 213

Kassab, France, Court of Cassation, 23 April 1969, Bulletin des arrêts de la Cour de Cassation (Cassation civile), 1969, 109 . . . 304

Kassem, Israel, Israeli Military Court sitting in Ramallah, 13 April 1969, 42 ILR, 470 . . . 381, 389

Katanga, ICC, Trial Chamber, Judgment, 7 March 2014 (case no. ICC-01/04–01/07), online at: www.icc-cpi.int/Pages/record/07-3436-tENG . . . 254

Kayishema and Ruzindana, ICTR, Trial Chamber, Judgment, 21 May 1999 (Case no. ICTR-95-1-T), online at: unictr.irmct.org/cases/ictr-95-1 . . . 435

Kenya Decision: *See* Decision on the Authorization of an Investigation into the Situation in the Republic of Kenya

Kilroy v Windsor, US, District Court, Northern District of Ohio, Eastern Division, 7 December 1978, 81 ILR 605 . . . 136

Kingdom of Morocco v DR, Belgium, Labour Court of Brussels, 6th Chamber, 6 November 1989, 115 ILR, 421 . . . 125

Korea—Measures Affecting Imports of Fresh, Chilled and Frozen Beef, WTO, AB Report 11 December 2000, WT/DS161/AB/R, WT/DS169/AB/R, online at: www.wto.org/tratop_e/dispu_e/161-169abr_e . . . 514, 517

Korean 'comfort' women v Japan, Japan, Shimonoseki Branch, Yamaguchi District Court, 27 April 1998, 1642 Hanrei Jiho, 24, or 1081 Hanrei Taimuzu 137 (in Japanese), cited in Shin Hae Bong, 'Compensation for Victims of Wartime Atrocities: Recent Developments in Japan's Court Case law', in 3 JICJ (2005) 187 . . . 304, 402

Krstić, ICTY, Trial Chamber, Judgment, 2 August 2001 (Case no. IT-98–33-T), online at: www.icty.org/cases/krstic/tjug; Appeals Chamber, Judgment, 19 April 2004 (Case no. IT-98–33-A), online at: www.icty.org/cases/krstic/acjug . . . 435, 436

Kunarac, ICTY, Appeals Chamber, Judgement 12 June 2002 (Cases nos. IT-96-23 and IT-96-23/1-A), online at: www.icty.org/cases/kunarac/acjug . . . 431, 434

Kupreškić et al., ICTY, Trial Chamber, Judgment, 14 January 2000 (Case no. IT-95-16-T), online at: www.icty.org/cases/kupreskic/tjug . . . 194, 195, 236, 400

L

La Belle-Anschlag, Germany, Berlin District Court (*Landgericht*), 13 November 2001, 366 pp. (unpublished); German Supreme Court (*Bundesgerichtshof*), 24 June 2004, 57 Neue Juristische Wochenschrift (2004), 3051 . . . 7, 352

Labita v Italy, ECHR, Application no. 26772/95, Judgment, 6 April 2000, online at: http://hudoc.echr.coe.int/rus?i=001-58559 . . . 423

Lac Lanoux (Spain/France), Arbitral Tribunal, 16 November 1957, RIAA XII, 281 . . . 63, 457, 463

LaGrand (Germany v United States of America), ICJ, Judgment, 27 June 2001, ICJ Reports 2001, 466 . . . 66, 159, 213, 265, 521

Land and Maritime Boundary between Cameroon and Nigeria (Cameroon v Nigeria: Equatorial Guinea intervening), ICJ, Judgment, 1 0 October 2002, ICJ Reports 2002, 303 . . . 63, 100

Land and Maritime Boundary between Cameroon and Nigeria (Cameroon v Nigeria: Equatorial Guinea intervening) (Preliminary Objections), ICJ, Judgment, ICJ Reports 1998, 275 . . . 64, 65, 66, 462

Land, Island and Maritime Frontier Dispute (El Salvador/Honduras) (Application to Intervene), ICJ, Judgment, 13 September 1990, ICJ Reports 1990, 92 . . . 66

Land, Island and the Maritime Frontier Dispute (El Salvador/Honduras, Nicaragua intervening), ICJ, Judgement, 11 September 1992, ICJ Reports 1992, 351 . . . 101, 102, 107, 108

Land Reclamation in and around the Straits of Johor (Malaysia v Singapore) (Provisional Measures), ITLOS, Case No. 12, Order, 10 September 2003, ITLOS Report 2003, 4 . . . 62

Laperdrix and Penquer v Kouzouboff and Belin, France, Paris Court of Appeal, 9 April 1925, 53 JDI (1926) 64 . . . 137

Law on 'Procedures Concerning Certain Crimes Committed During the 1956 Revolution', Hungary, Constitutional Court, 12 October 1993, no. 53, in Az Alkotmánybíróság Határozatai, 1994, 2832 (in Hungarian) . . . 236

Le Louis, Forest, UK, High Court of Admiralty, 15 December 1817, 3 BILC, 691 . . . 14

Legal Consequences for States of the Continued Presence of South Africa in Namibia (South West Africa) notwithstanding Security Council Resolution 276 (1970), ICJ, Advisory Opinion, 21 June 1971, ICJ Reports 1971, 16 . . . 68, 70, 200–1, 213

Legal Consequences of the Construction of a Wall in the Occupied Palestinian Territory, ICJ, Advisory Opinion, 9 July 2004, ICJ Reports 2004, 136 . . . 17, 58, 59, 68, 213, 262, 269, 350, 377, 413

Legal Consequences of the Separation of the Chagos Archipelago from Mauritius in 1965, ICJ, Advisory Opinion, 25 February 2019, (unreported) online at: https://www.icj-cij.org/en/case/169/advisory-opinions . . . 68, 69, 70, 99, 167, 240–1, 287

Legal Status of Eastern Greenland (Denmark v Norway), PCIJ, Judgment, 5 April 1933, Series A/B No. 53, 22 . . . 100, 195

Legality of the Threat or Use of Nuclear Weapons, ICJ, Advisory Opinion, 8 July 1996, ICJ Reports 1996, 226 . . . 62, 63, 72, 73, 94, 147, 201, 236, 240, 280, 300, 350, 374, 376, 394, 396, 462, 466, 475

Legality of the Use by a State of Nuclear Weapons in Armed Conflict, ICJ, Advisory Opinion, 8 July 1996, ICJ Reports 1996, 66 . . . 141, 146, 213, 355

Letelier v Republic of Chile, US, US District Court, 11 March 1980, 488 F. Supp. 665 (DDC 1980); US District Court for the District of Columbia, 5 November 1980, 502 F.Supp 259; Court of Appeals Second Circuit, 20 November 1984, 748 F 2d 790, 53 USLW 2286 . . . 305

Leitelier and Moffit, Dispute concerning responsibility for the deaths of Letelier and Moffitt (United States/Chile), Commission of Inquiry, 11 January 1992, RIIA XXV, 1 . . . 280

L.F.H. Neer and Pauline Neer (United States.) v United Mexican States (1926) RIAA IV, 60 . . . 519, 520

Lilian Celiberti de Casariego v Uruguay, HRC, 29 July 1981, communication No. R. 13/56, in UN Doc. Supp. No. 40 (A/36/40) . . . 412

Lockheed: See Olivi and Lefebvre d'Ovidio

Loizidou v Turkey (Preliminary Objections), ECHR, Application no. 15318/89, Judgment, 23 March 1995, online at: http://hudoc.echr.coe.int/fre?i=001-57920 . . . 211, 412

Lubanga Dyilo, ICC, Trial Chamber, Judgment, 14 March 2012 (Case no. ICC-01/04–01/06), online at: www.icc-cpi.int/CourtRecords/CR2012_03942 . . . 254

Luna v Repubblica socialista di Romania, Italy, Court of Cassation, 23 November 1974, 58 RDI 1975, 597 . . . 125

M

M. Kallon and B. Bazzy Kamara, SCSL, Decision on Challenge to Jurisdiction: Lomé Accord Amnesty, Appeals Chamber, 13 March 2004, online at: ww.rscsl.org/AFRC/Appeal/SCSL-04-16-PT-033 . . . 170

Maffezini v Kingdom of Spain (Jurisdiction), ICSID Case No. ARB/97/7, Decision on Jurisdiction, 25 January 2000, online at: https://www.italaw.com/cases/641 . . . 525

Malaysian Historical Salvors v Malaysia, ICSID Case No. ARB/05/10, Decision on the application for annulment, 16 April 2009, online at: https://www.italaw.com/cases/646 . . . 523

Mallén: See Francisco Mallén (United Mexican States) v United States of America

The Manouba (France v Italy), 6 May 1913, RIIA XI, 471 (in French) . . . 265

Marcello Viola v Italy (No. 2), ECHR, Application no. 77633/16, Judgement, 13 June 2019, online at: http://hudoc.echr.coe.int/fre?i=002-12494 . . . 423

Marcinkus and others, Italy, Court of Cassation (plenary), 23 July 1987, 24 RIDPP (1988) 327 (partial English translation in 8 IYIL (1988–92) 51) . . . 173

Marcos: *See* Trajano v Marcos

Margellos v Germany, Greece, Supreme Special Court (Anotato Eidiko Dikasterio responsible under Article 100.1 (f) for pronouncing on cases involving the interpretation of international rules), 17 September 2002, cited in A. Gattini, 'To What Extent are State Immunity and Non-Justiciability Major Hurdles to Individuals' Claims for War Damages?', 1 JICJ (2003) 36 . . . 304

Maritime Boundary Between Timor-Leste And Australia (The "Timor Sea Conciliation"), Pca Case Nº 2016-10, Report And Recommendations of The Compulsory Conciliation Commission Between Timor-Leste And Australia On The Timor Sea, 9 May 2018, online at: https://pca-cpa.org/en/cases/132/ . . . 278, 283

Maritime Boundary (Ghana/Côte d'Ivoire) *See* Dispute Concerning Delimitation of the Maritime Boundary between Ghana and Côte d'Ivoire in the Atlantic Ocean

Maritime Delimitation and Territorial Questions between Qatar and Bahrain (Qatar v Bahrain), ICJ, Judgment, 16 March 2001, ICJ Reports 2001, 40 . . . 105, 106

Maritime Delimitation and Territorial Questions between Qatar and Bahrain (Qatar v Bahrain) (Jurisdiction and Admissibility), ICJ, Judgment, 1 July 1994, ICJ Reports 1994, 112.....201, 206; Judgment, 15 February 1995, ICJ Reports 1995, 6 . . . 213

Maritime Delimitation and Territorial Questions between Qatar and Bahrain (Qatar v. Bahrain), ICJ, Judgment, 16 March 2001, ICJ Reports 2001, . . . 40

Maritime Delimitation in the Black Sea (Romania v Ukraine), ICJ, Judgment, 3 February 2009, ICJ Reports 2009, 61 . . . 111, 112, 113

Maritime Dispute (Peru v Chile), ICJ, Judgment, 27 January 2014, ICJ Reports 2014, 3 . . . 113

Marshall Islands (Marshall Islands v United Kingdom; Marshall Islands v Pakistan; Marshall Islands v India) cases: *See* Obligations concerning Negotiations relating to Cessation of the Nuclear Arms Race continued to Nuclear Disarmament (Marshall Islands v United Kingdom), (Marshall Islands v Pakistan) and (Marshall Islands v India)

Martini, Italy-Venezuela Arbitration, 3 May 1939, RIAA II, 978 . . . 264

Mavrommatis Palestine Concessions (Greece v United Kingdom) (Objections to the Jurisdiction), PCIJ, 30 August 1924, Series A, no. 2, 6 . . . 277, 288, 520

M.C. v Bulgaria, ECHR, Application no. 39272/98, Judgement, 4 December 2003, online at: http://hudoc.echr.coe.int/ ENG?i=001-104387 . . . 423

McCann and others, ECHR, Application no. 18984/91, Judgment, 27 September 1995, online at: http://hudoc.echr.coe.int/ fre?i=001-57943 . . . 389

McCulloch v The State of Maryland, US, Supreme Court, 1819, 17 U.S. 316 (1819); 4 Wheat. 316 . . . 213

McLeod: *See* People v McLeod

Ministère Public v Hissein Habré, Senegal, Extraordinary African Chambers, Appeals Chamber, Judgment, 27 April 2017, online at: www.chambresafricaines.org . . . 137

Ministère Public v P., Belgium, Court of Brussels, 5 June 1965, Journal des Tribunaux (Brussels), 1966, 30 . . . 137

Ministero delle Finanze v Associazione dei Cavalieri italiani dello Sovrano Militare Ordine di Malta, Italy, Court of Cassation, 3 May 1978, no. 2051, 61 RDI 1978, 558 . . . 174

Minors Oposa v Secretary of the Department of Environment and Natural Resources (DENR), Philippines, Supreme Court, 30 July 1993, 33 ILM (1994) 173 . . . 466

The Miriella (Anglo-Iranian Oil Company Ltd v Supor Company), Italy, Venice Court, 11 March 1953, 22 ILR (1955) 19 . . . 304

Missionary Society: *See* Home Frontier and Foreign Missionary Society of the United Brethren in Christ (United States of America) v Great Britain

Missouri v Holland, US, Supreme Court, 1920, AILC (1783–1968), Vol. 10, 373 . . . 213

Mohamed Ali and another v Public Prosecutor, UK, Privy Council (Judicial Committee), 29 July 1968, [1969] A.C. 430, online at: www.icrc.org/ ihl-nat. nsf/0/ 383128666c8ab799c1256a1e- 00366ad3?OpenDocument . . . 389

Moldova ACCC/C/2008/30, Aarhus Compliance Committee, 8 February 2011, ECE/ MP.PP/C.1/2009/6/Add.3 . . . 468

Monetary Gold Removed from Rome in 1943 (Italy v France, United Kingdom of Great Britain and Northern Ireland and United States of America) (Preliminary Question), ICJ, Judgment, 15 June 1954, ICJ Reports 1954, 19 . . . 284

Montero v Uruguay, HRC, 31 March 1983, communication No. 106/1081, UN Doc. CCPR/C/OP/2 . . . 412

Moraly et société "Maison Moraly", France, Council of State, 31 January 1969, 73 RGDIP (1969) 1151 (in French)

Mosul Boundary: *See* Article 3, Paragraph 2 of the Treaty of Lausanne (Frontier between Turkey and Iraq)

Mothers of Srebrenica Association and others v State of the Netherlands, The Netherlands,

Supreme Court, 13 April 2012, Case no. 10/04437, 51 ILM 2012, 1322 . . . 150

MOX Plant Case, The (Ireland v United Kingdom) (Provisional Measures), ITLOS, Order, 3 December 2001 (Case no. 10), ITLOS Report 2001, 95 . . . 62

Musema, ICTR, Trial Chamber, Judgment, 27 January 2000 (Case no. ICTR-96-13-T), online at: unictr.irmct.org/cases/ictr-96-13 . . . 435

M/V Norstar, The (Panama v Italy), ITLOS, Judgment, 10 April 2019 (Case no. 25) (unreported), online at: https://www.itlos.org/en/cases/list-of-cases/case-no-25/ . . . 115–16

The M/V 'Saiga' (No.2) Case (Saint Vincent and the Grenadines v Guinea), ITLOS, Judgment, 1 July 1999 (Case no. 2), ITLOS Reports 1999, 10 . . . 109, 114

N

Nachova and others v Bulgaria, ECHR, Applications nos. 43577/98 and 43579/98, Grand Chamber, Judgment, 6 July 2005, online at: http://hudoc.echr.coe.int/eng?i=001-69630 . . . 377

Nanni and others v Sovrano Militare Ordine di Malta, Italy, Court of Cassation, 13 March 1935, 8 ILR 2 . . . 174

Naulilaa (Portugal v Germany): See Responsabilité de l'Allemagne à raison des dommages causés dans les colonies portugaises du Sud de l'Afrique (affaire de Naulilaa) (Portugal v Germany)

Neira Alegría et al., IACHR, Judgment, 19 January 1995, online at: http://www1.umn.edu/humanrts/iachr/C/20-ing/html . . . 389

Neptune (United States v Great Britain), United States-Great Britain Mixed Commission, 25 June 1797, Lapradelle and Politis, 1, 137 . . . 193, 261

New Jersey v Delaware, US, Supreme Court, 5 February 1934, 291 U.S. 361 (1934) . . . 188

Nicaragua (Nicaragua v United States of America): see Case Concerning Military and Paramilitary Activities in and against Nicaragua (Nicaragua v United States of America)

Nicaragua (Nicaragua v United States of America) (Jurisdiction and admissibility): see Case Concerning Military and Paramilitary Activities in and against Nicaragua (Nicaragua v United States of America) (Jurisdiction and admissibility)

Nobili v Emperor Charles I of Austria, Italy, Court of Cassation, 11 March 1921, Giurisprudenza italiana, 1921, I, 371; English summary in Annual Digest (1919–1922) 136 . . . 136

North Atlantic Coast Fisheries Case (Great Britain/United States of America), 7 September 1910, RIAA XI, 167 . . . 92

North Sea Continental Shelf (Federal Republic of Germany/Denmark; Federal Republic of Germany/Netherlands), ICJ, Judgment, 20 February 1969, ICJ Reports 1969, 4 . . . 60, 61, 62, 63, 66, 111, 112, 113, 184, 185, 186, 196, 198, 199, 201, 239, 280, 462

Norwegian Fisheries case (United Kingdom v Norway) See Fisheries (United Kingdom v Norway)

Nottebohm (Liechtenstein v Guatemala), ICJ, Judgment, 6 April 1955, ICJ Reports 1955, 4 . . . 199

Nuclear Tests (Australia v France), ICJ, Judgement, 20 December 1974, ICJ Reports 1974, 253 . . . 64, 65, 194, 195, 196, 199

NV. Assurantje Machtshappij de Nederlanden van 1845 v. Pt. Escomptobank, the Netherlands, Hague District Court, 20 February 1962, 33 ILR (1962) 30 . . . 304

O

Obligations concerning Negotiations relating to Cessation of the Nuclear Arms Race and to Nuclear Disarmament (Marshall Islands v United Kingdom) (Preliminary Objections), ICJ, Judgment, 5 October 2016, ICJ Reports 2016, 833; (Marshall Islands v Pakistan) (Jurisdiction and Admissibility), ICJ, Judgment, 5 October 2016, ICJ Reports 2016, 552; (Marshall Islands v India) (Jurisdiction and Admissibility), ICJ, Judgment, 5 October 2016, ICJ Reports 2016, 255 . . . 62, 277

Obligation to Negotiate Access to the Pacific Ocean (Bolivia v Chile), ICJ, Judgment, 1 October 2018, (unreported), online at: https://www.icj-cij.org/en/case/153/judgments . . . 61, 62, 280, 462, 524

Ogoni case: see Social and Economic Rights Action Center (SERAC) and others v Nigeria

Oil Platforms (Islamic Republic of Iran v United States of America) (Preliminary Objections), ICJ, Judgment, 12 December 1996, ICJ Reports 1986, 803 . . . 213

Oil Platforms (Islamic Republic of Iran v United States of America), ICJ, Judgment, 6 November 2003, ICJ Reports 2003, 161 . . . 350, 351

Olivi and Lefebvre d'Ovidio, Italy, Constitutional Court, 6 February 1979, 63 RDI (1980), 512; English translation: 4 IYIL (1978–79) 186 . . . 227

Opinion no. 1 Yugoslavia (Dissolution of Yugoslavia), Arbitration Commission of the Peace Conference on Yugoslavia, 29 November 1991, 3 EJIL (1992) 182 . . . 48

Opinion no. 2 (Serbian Minorities in Bosnia-Herzegovina and Croatia), Arbitration Commission of the Peace Conference on Yugoslavia, 11 January 1992, 3 EJIL (1992) 183 . . . 48, 102

Opinion no. 5 (Recognition of Croatia), Arbitration Commission of the Peace Conference on Yugoslavia, 11 January 1992, 4 EJIL (1993) 76 . . . 84

Opinion no. 10 (Federal Republic of Yugoslavia and Serbia Montenegro), Arbitration Commission of the Peace Conference on Yugoslavia, 4 July 1992, 4 EJIL (1993) 90 . . . 238

Opinion no. 14 (State succession), Arbitration Commission of the Peace Conference on Yugoslavia, 13 August 1993, 96 ILR, 729–32 . . . 89

P

Paiement, en or, des emprunts fédéraux brésiliens émis en France (*France/Brazil*), PCIJ, Jugement, 12 July 1929, série A, no. 21, 243 . . . 194

Palmarejo (The) and Mexican Gold Fields Ltd, UK–Mexican Claims Commission, 6 August 1931, RIAA V, 298 . . . 264

Pamuk and others, Italy, Crotone Court (Tribunale di Crotone), 27 September 2001, 84 RDI (2001) 1155 . . . 114

Parlement Belge, Great Britain, Divorce and Admiralty Division, 15 March 1879, 3 BILC, 305; Court of Appeal, 27 February 1880, 3 BILC, 322 . . . 123

Paul v Avril, US, District Court, S.D. Florida, 14 January 1993, 812 F. Suppl. 207 (SD Florida 1993) . . . 137, 420

Pauline Fraisse, France, Court of Cassation, 2 June 2000, no. 450, RGDIP (2000) 985 . . . 228

Pellat, France-Mexico Claims Commission, 7 June 1929, RIAA V, 534 . . . 250

People v McLeod US, New York Supreme Court, 1841, 25 Wend. 483, 37 A. Dec. 328 . . . 131, 132

Perrini v Académie de France à Rome, Italy, Court of Cassation (plenary), 26 May 1994, no. 5126, 78 RDI (1995) 229 . . . 125

Pfizer Animal Health SA v Council, EU, Court of First Instance, n° T-13/99, 11 September 2002, EU:T:2002:209 . . . 463, 464

Philippine Embassy, Germany, German Federal Constitutional Court (Bundesverfassungsgericht), 13 December 1977, 65 ILR 146 . . . 130

Phillip Morris Asia Limited v Commonwealth of Australia, PCA Case No 2012-12, Award on Jurisdiction and Admissibility, 17 December 2015, online at: https://pca-cpa.org/en/cases/5/ . . . 66

Pinochet, Belgium, Brussels Investigating Judge (*juge d'investigation*), Order, 6 November 1998, 79 Revue de droit pénal et de criminologie (1999) 278 . . . 237

Pinochet, Spain, Audiencia Nacional, order (*auto*), 5 November 1998, online at: www.derechoshumanos.net/jurisprudencia/1998-11-05-A-N-(Pinochet)-Auto-Competencia-Spain-Genocidio-Chile.htm . . . 240

Pinochet, UK *See* R v Bow Street Stipendiary Magistrate and others, ex parte Pinochet Ugarte

Pious Funds of the Californias (United States of America v The United Mexican States), 14 October 1902, RIAA IX, 11 . . . 193

P.M. v Zappi Mentore, Italy, Court of Appeal of Venice, 8 May 1971, Rivista penale, 1971, II, 1255 . . . 137

Polish Nationals in Danzig: *See* Treatment of Polish Nationals and Other Persons of Polish Origin or Speech in the Danzig Territory

Polo Castro, Italy, Court of Cassation, 8 May 1989, 73 RDI (1990), 1038 . . . 228

Poštová banka, a.s. and Istrokapital s.e. v Hellenic Republic, ICSID Case No. ARB/13/8, Award, 9 April 2015, online at: https://www.italaw.com/cases/2073 . . . 523

Prefecture of Voiotia v Germany, Greece, Court of Cassation, case no. 11/2000, 4 May 2000, in 49 Nomiko Vima (2001) 212 (in Greek), summarized in 3 YIHL (2000) 511 and 95 AJIL (2001) 198 . . . 304, 402

Presidenza Consiglio dei Ministri v Markovic et al., Italy, Court of Cassation, 2 June 2002, no. 8157, 85 RDI (2002) 800 . . . 402

Princz v Federal Republic of Germany, United States, Court of Appeal of the District of Columbia Circuit, 1 July 1994, 26 F.3d 1166 (1994) . . . 128, 239, 240, 402

Prise d'eau à la Meuse (Netherlands v Belgium), PCIJ, Judgment, 28 June 1937, Series A/B, no. 70, 4 . . . 194, 198

Prisoners of War––Ethiopia's Claim 4, Eritrea-Ethiopia Claims Commission, partial award, 1 July 2003, online at: www.cpa-pca.org . . . 396

Prisoners of War––Ethiopia's Claim 17, Eritrea-Ethiopia Claims Commission, partial award, 1 July 2003, online at: www.cpa-pca.org . . . 396

Public Prosecutor v Koi et al., UK, Privy Council, 4 December 1967, BILC 9, 235 . . . 380

Pulp Mills on the River Uruguay (Argentina v Uruguay), ICJ, Judgment, 20 April 2010, ICJ Reports 2010, 14 . . . 61, 62, 63, 64, 74, 75, 280, 460, 461, 462, 463, 464, 469

Q

Queisser v Germany, CJEU, Case C-282/15, Judgment, 19 January 2017, EU:C:2017:26 . . . 464

Questions relating to the Obligation to Prosecute or Extradite (Belgium v Senegal), ICJ, Judgment, 20 July 2012, ICJ Reports 2012, 554 . . . 16, 72, 96

R

R v Bow Street Stipendiary Magistrate and others, ex parte Pinochet Ugarte, United Kingdom, House of Lords, 24 March 1999, in [1999] 2 All ER 97 . . . 128, 137, 236, 237, 240, 441, 445, 446

R v Gul (Mohemed), UK, Court of Appeal (Criminal Division), 22 February 2012, [2012] EWCA Crim 280 . . . 443

R v Gul (Mohemed), UK, Supreme Court, 25 October 2013, [2013] UKSC 64 . . . 443

R v Horseferry Road Magistrates' Court, UK, House of Lords, 24 June 1993, [1992] 3 WLR 90; 95 ILR 380 . . . 97

R v Keyn (The Franconia), Great Britain, Court for Crown Cases Reserved, 6 May–13 November 1876, (1876) L.R. 2 Exch.Div.63, BILC, vol. 2, 701 . . . 184

R v Palacios, Canada, Court of Appeal for Ontario, 10 February 1984, 23 CYIL (1985) 412 . . . 135

R v Plymouth Justices and another (ex parte Driver), UK, High Court (Decisional Court), [1986] 1 QB 95 . . . 97

R v Reeves Taylor, UK, Supreme Court, 13 November 2019([2019] UKSC 51 . . . 441

Radio Corporation of America v The National Government of the Republic of China, Arbitration, Award, 13 April 1935, online at: https://pca-cpa.org/en/cases/16/ . . . 285

Rahimtoola v Nizam of Hyderabad, UK, House of Lords, 7 November 1957, [1958] AC 379 . . . 123

Rainbow Warrior case See Case concerning the differences between New Zealand and France arising from the Rainbow Warrior affair

Rainbow Warrior (New Zealand v. France), Arbitral Tribunal, Award, 30 April 1990, 82 ILR, . . . 499

Rasul v Bush, US, Supreme Court, 28 June 2004, 542 US 466 (2004) . . . 388

Rau, Vanden Abel v Duruty, Belgium, Cour d'appel de Gand, 14 March 1879, in Pasicrisie belge, I, 1879, 75 . . . 123

Rawle Kennedy v Trinidad and Tobago, HRC, 31 December 1999, communication no. 845, CCPR/C67/D/845/ 1999, online at: https://juris.ohchr.org/Search/Details/957 . . . 211

Reference re Secession of Quebec, Supreme Court of Canada, 20 August 1998, [1998] 2 S.C.R, 217, online at: https://scc-csc.lexum.com/scc-csc/scc-csc/en/item/1643/index.do . . . 68, 76

Rein v Libya, US, Court of Appeals Second District, 15 December 1998, 38 ILM (1999) 450 . . . 128

Reparation for Injuries Suffered in the Service of the United Nations, ICJ, Advisory Opinion, 11 April 1949, ICJ Reports 1949, 174 . . . 144, 146–7, 153, 199, 213

Request for an Advisory Opinion Submitted by the French Court of Cassation (Request no. P16-2018–001), ECHR, Grand Chamber, 10 April 2019, online at: http://hudoc.echr.coe.int/spa?i=003-6380464-8364383 . . . 417

Request for an Advisory Opinion Submitted by the Sub-Regional Fisheries Commission (SRFC), ITLOS, Advisory Opinion, 2 April 2015 (Case no. 21), ITLOS Reports 2015, 4 . . . 62, 75, 460, 462

Reservations to the Convention on the Prevention and Punishment of Genocide, ICJ, Advisory Opinion, 28 May 1951, ICJ Reports 1951, 15 . . . 199, 210, 435

Responsabilité de l'Allemagne à raison des dommages causés dans les colonies portugaises du Sud de l'Afrique (affaire de Naulilaa) (Portugal v Germany), 31 July 1928, RIAA II, 1019 . . . 257, 296–7, 298, 302

Responsibilities and obligations of States sponsoring persons and entities with respect to activities in the Area, ITLOS, Advisory Opinion, 1 February 2011 (Case no. 17), ITLOS Reports 2011, 10 . . . 74, 117–18, 460, 461, 463

Right of Passage over Indian Territory (Portugal v India), ICJ, Judgment, 12 April 1960, ICJ Reports, 1960, 6 . . . 191

Rio Tinto Zinc Corp. v Westinghouse Electric Corp., UK, Court of Appeal, 26 May 1977, 73 ILR 296; House of Lords, 11 December 1977, ibid., 311 . . . 96

Rohingya Decision: see Decision on the Prosecution's Request for a Ruling on Jurisdiction under Article 19(3) of the Statute

Ronald S. Lauder v The Czech Republic, UNCITRAL Arbitration Proceedings, Final Award 3 September 2001, online at: https://www.italaw.com/cases/documents/611 . . . 519

Rose Mary: See Anglo-Iranian Oil Company Ltd v Jaffrate and others

Rousseau v Republic of Upper Volta, Belgium, Labour Court of Brussels (Third Chamber), 25 April 1983, 82 ILR 118 . . . 125

Royaume de Grèce v Banque Julius Bär et Cie., Switzerland, Tribunal Fédéral, 6 June 1956, Recueil des arrêts du Tribunal Fédéral suisse, vol. 82, I, 75 . . . 130

Russel v S.r.l. Immobiliare Soblim, Italy, Constitutional Court, 24 Giurisprudenza costituzionale (1979) I, 373–7; English translation in 4 IYIL (1978–9) 146 . . . 133

Russia—Measures Concerning Traffic in Transit, WTO, Panel Report, 5 April 2019), WT/DS512/R, online at: www.wto.org/english/tratop_e/dispu_e . . . 516

Russian Claim for Interest on Indemnities (Russia/Turkey), 11 November 1912, online at: https://pca-cpa.org/en/cases/89/ . . . 193

Rutaganda, ICTR, Trial Chamber, Judgment, 6 December 1999 (Case no. ICTR-96-3-T), online at: unictr.irmct.org/cases/ictr-96-3 . . . 435

TABLE OF CASES

S

S.A. Fromagerie Franco-Suisse 'Le Sky' v État Belge, Belgium, Court of Cassation, 25 May 1971, Journal des Tribunaux, 1971, 460; English translation: Common Market Law Reports (1972) 330 . . . 230

The S.S. Wimbledon (United Kingdom, France, Italy, Japan v Germany), PCIJ, Judgment, 28 June 1923, Series A, No. 1, 16 . . . 257

Saltany v Reagan, US, District Court for the District of Columbia, 23 December 1988, 702 F. Supp. 319 (D.D.C 1988) . . . 136

Sarran, Levacher et al., France, Council of State, 30 October 1998, 14 Revue française de droit administratif, 1998, 1081 . . . 228

Savarkar (France v Great Britain), 24 February 1911, RIAA XI, 247 . . . 259

Sayce v Ameer Ruler Sadiq Mohsammad Abbasi Bahawalpur State, UK, King's Bench Division, 21 January 1952, 7 BILC 657; Court of Appeals, 20 May 1952, 7 BILC 662 . . . 136

The Schooner Exchange v McFaddon, US, Supreme Court, 1812, 11 U.S. (7 Cranch) 116, 3 L.Ed.287 (1812) . . . 136

Scilingo, Spain, Sentencia por crímenes contra la humanidad en el caso Adolfo Scilingo, N° 16/2005, Spain, Audiencia Nacional, 19 April 2005, online at: http://www.derechos.org/nizkor/espana/juicioral/doc/sentencia.html . . . 139

Scilingo, Spain, Central Criminal Court (Audiencia nacional), Order (auto) of the Investigating Judge, 25 March 1998, in EL DERECHO, 21; Order (auto) of 4 November 1998, no. 1998/22605, rec.173/1998, in EL DERECHO, 8; . . . 240

Selmouni v France, ECHR, Application no. 25803/94, Judgment, 28 July 1999, online at: http://hudoc.echr.coe.int/rus?i=001-58287 . . . 423, 441

Sentenza no. 238/2014, Italy, Constitutional Court, 22 October 2014, online at: https://www.cortecostituzionale.it/actionJudgment.do . . . 127

Sentenza no. 238/2014, Italy, Constitutional Court, 22 October 2014, online at: https://www.cortecostituzionale.it/actionJudgment.do . . . 127

SERAP v Federal Republic of Nigeria, ECOWAS Court of Justice, Judgment No ECW/CCJ/JUD/18/12, 14 December 2012, online at: www.worldcourts.com/ecowasccj/eng/decisions . . . 460

Serbian Loans *See* Case Concerning the Payment of Various Serbian Loans Issued in France (France v Kingdom of the Serbs, Croats, and Slovenes)

Serdar Mohammed v Ministry of Defence, UK, Court of Appeal, 30 July 2015, [2015] EWCA Crim 843; Supreme Court, 17 January 2017, [2017] UKSC 2 . . . 380

SGS Société Générale Islamic Republic of Pakistan, ICSID Case No. ARB/01/13, Decision Jurisdiction, 27 August 2003, online at : https://www.italaw.com/cases/1009 . . . 523

SGS Société Générale de Surveillance S.A. v Republic of the Philippines (Objections to Jurisdiction), ICSID Case No. ARB/02/6, Decision of the Tribunal on Objections to Jurisdiction, 29 January 2004, online at: https://www.italaw.com/cases/documents/1019 . . . 523

SGS Société Générale de Surveillance S.A. v Islamic Republic of Pakistan (Jurisdiction), ICSID Case No. ARB/01/13, Decision on Jurisdiction, 27 August 2003, online at : https://www.italaw.com/cases/1009 . . . 523

Shahin Shaine Ebrahimi and others v The Government of the Islamic Republic of Iran, Iran-US Claims Tribunal, Nos 44, 46, and 47, Final Award, 12 October 1994, online at: https://jusmundi.com/en/document/decision/en-shahin-shaine-ebrahimi-and-others-v-the-government-of-the-islamic-republic-of-iran-final-award-award-no-560-44-46-47-3-thursday-9th-february-1984 . . . 522

Sharon and Yaron, HSA v SA (Ariel Sharon) and YA (Amos Yaron), Final appeal/Cassation (concerning questions of law), Belgium, Court of Cassation, 12 February 2003, P.02.1139.F/2 . . . 136, 137, 138, 139

Shaw v Shaw, UK, High Court, 9 February 1979, 78 ILR 483 . . . 135

Shimoda and others, Japan, Tokyo District Court, 7 December 1963, L. Friedmann, II, 1688–1702, online at: www.icrc.org/ihl-nat.nsf (in English) . . . 304, 394, 402, 419

Siderman de Blake v Republic of Argentina, US, Court of Appeals Ninth Circuit, 22 May 1992, 965 F.2n 699 . . . 420

Simon Julio, Del Cerro Juan Antonio, Argentina, Federal Judge Gabriel R. Cavallo, judgment, 6 March 2001, case no. 8686/2000, online at: http://www.mpf.gov.ar/Institucional/UnidadesFE/Simon-Juzgado-4.pdf (in Spanish); http://hrlibrary.umn.edu/research/argentina/jfcc4-cavallo.html (in English) . . . 240

Sjoerd Albert Lapre and others v Japan, Japan, Tokyo District Court, 30 November 1998, online at: https://secureservercdn.net/198.71.188.149/891.924.myftpupload.com/wp-content/uploads/2015/02/Dutch-11.30.98.pdf (in Japanese) . . . 402

Social and Economic Rights Action Center (SERAC) and others v Nigeria, African Commission on Human and Peoples' Rights, Application no. 155/96, 27 May 2002, online at : ww.achpr.org/file/English/achpr30_155_96_eng . . . 460, 469

xxxviii ...Machain and others, US, Supreme Court, 29 June 2004, online at: www.findlaw. com ... 420
South China Sea Arbitration (Republic of the Philippines v People's Republic of China) See In the matter of the South China Sea Arbitration before and Arbitral Tribunal constituted under Annex VII of the United Nations Convention on the Law of the Sea (Republic of the Philippines v People's Republic of China)
South West Africa Cases (Ethiopia v South Africa; Liberia v South Africa), ICJ, Judgment, 18 July 1966, ICJ Reports 1966, 4 ... 48, 191, 199
South West Africa Cases (Ethiopia v South Africa; Liberia v South Africa), (Preliminary Objections), Judgment, 21 December 1962, ICJ Report 1962, 319 ... 277
Sovereignty over Certain Frontier Land (Belgium/Netherlands), ICJ, Judgment, 20 June 1959, ICJ Reports 1959, 209 ... 102
Sovereignty over Pedra Branca/Pulau Batu Puteh, Middle Rocks and South Ledge (Malaysia/Singapore), ICJ, Judgment, 23 May 2008, ICJ Reports 2008, 12 ... 66, 99, 100
Sovereignty over Pulau Ligitan and Pulau Sipadan (Indonesia/Malaysia), ICJ, Judgment, 17 December 2002, ICJ Reports 2002, 625 ... 100, 213
Sovrano Militare Ordine di Malta v Amministrazione delle finanze dello Stato, Italy, Court of Cassation, 5 November 1991, 75 RDI (1992) 176 ... 174
Sovrano Militare Ordine di Malta v Brunelli, Tacchi and others, Italy, Court of Cassation, 17 November 1931, ILR 1931–2, 88 ... 174
Sovrano Militare Ordine di Malta v Grisi, Italy, Court of Cassation (plenary), 3 February 1988, 71 RDI (1988) 905 ... 174
Sovrano Militare Ordine di Malta v Guidetti, Italy, Court of Cassation (plenary), 18 March 1999, Foro italiano, II, 1999, 1822 ... 174
Sovrano Militare Ordine di Malta v Salimei, Italy, Court of Cassation (plenary), 18 February 1989, 72 RDI (1989) 411 ... 174
Spanish Zone of Morocco Claims (Great Britain v Spain), 1 May 1925, RIAA II, 627 ... 264
Stakić, ICTY, Trial Chamber, Judgment, 31 July 2003 (Case no. IT-97-24-T), online at: www.icty.org/cases/stakic/tjug ... 435
State of Himachal Pradesh and others v Ganesh Wood Products and others, India, Supreme Court, 11 September 1995, 1995 (6) SCC 363, online at: https://indiankanoon.org/doc/1149168/ ... 466
Status of Eastern Carelia, PCIJ, Advisory Opinion, 23 July 1923, Series B, No 5, 8 ... 61, 278
Stichting Mothers of Srebrenica and others against the Netherlands, ECHR, Application no. 65542/12, Judgment, 11 June 2013, online at: http://hudoc.echr.coe.int/eng?i=001-122255 ... 150

T

Tadić (Interlocutory Appeal), ICTY, Appeals Chamber, Decision on the Defence Motion for Interlocutory Appeal on Jurisdiction, 2 October 1995 (Case no. IT-94-1-AR72), online at: www.icty.org/cases/tadic/acdec ... 172, 199, 238, 253, 254, 330, 367, 374, 375, 422, 429, 434
Tadić, ICTY, Trial Chamber, Opinion and Judgment, 7 May 1997 (Case no. IT-94-1-T), online at: www.icty.org/cases/tadic/tjug; Appeals Chamber, Judgment, 15 July 1999 (Case no. IT-94-1-A), online at: www.icty.org/cases/tadic/acjug ... 434
Taskın and others v Turkey, ECHR, Application no. 46117/99, Judgment, 10 November 2004, online at: http://hudoc.echr.coe.int/eng?i=001-67401 ... 468
Tatar v Romania, ECHR Application No. 67021/01, Judgment, 27 January 2009, Final 6 July 2009, online at: http://hudoc.echr.coe.int/eng?i=001-90909 (in French) ... 463
Temple of Preah Vihear (Cambodia v Thailand), ICJ, Judgment, 15 June 1962, ICJ Reports 1962, 6 ... 100
Territo, In Re, US, Court of Appeals 9th Circuit, 8 June 1946, 156 F.2d 142 (9th Circ. 1946)
Territorial Dispute (Lybian Arab Jamahiriya/Chad), ICJ, Judgment, 3 February 1994, ICJ Reports 1994, 8 ... 100, 213
Territorial and Maritime Dispute (Nicaragua v Colombia) (Preliminary Objections), ICJ, Judgement, 13 December 2007, ICJ Reports 2007, 832 ... 100
Territorial and Maritime Dispute (Nicaragua v Colombia), ICJ, Judgment, 19 November 2012, ICJ Reports 2012, 624 ... 113
Territorial and Maritime Dispute between Nicaragua and Honduras in the Caribbean Sea (Nicaragua v Honduras), ICJ, Judgment, 8 October 2007, ICJ Reports 2007, 659 ... 100, 113
Territorial Dispute (Libyan Arab Jamahiriya/Chad), ICJ, Judgment, 3 February 1994, ICJ Reports 1994, 8 ... 101
Territorial Jurisdiction of the International Commission of the River Oder (United Kingdom v Poland), PCIJ, Judgment, 10 September 1929, Series A, no 23, 5 ... 14, 63
Texaco Overseas Petroleum Company and California Asiatic Oil Company v The Government of the Libyan Arab Republic, Arbitral Award, 19 January 1977, 17 ILM 1978, 1 ... 40, 502
Timor Sea Conciliation (Timor-Leste v Australia): see Maritime Boundary Between Timor-Leste and Australia (The "Timor Sea Conciliation")
Tinoco Case (Great Britain v Costa Rica), 18 October 1923, RIAA I, 369 ... 87
Todd v Panjaitan, US, District Court, District of Massachussets, 26 October 1994 (default judgment), 1994 WL 827111 ... 420

Tomasi v France, ECHR, Application no. 12850/87, Judgement, 27 August 1992, online at: http://hudoc.echr.coe.int/fre?i=001-57796 . . . 423

Trail Smelter (United States of America/Canada), 16 April 1938 and 11 March 1941, RIAA III, 1905-1982 . . . 287, 457, 460, 486

Trajano v Marcos, US, Court of Appeals, 21 October 1992, 978 F. 2d 493, 501–3 (9th Cir. 1992), cert. denied, 508 US 972, 113 S. Ct 2960, 125 L. Ed. 2d 661 (1993) . . . 420

Treatment of Polish Nationals and Other Persons of Polish Origin or Speech in the Danzig Territory, PCIJ, Advisory Opinion, 4 February 1932, Series A/B, no.44, 4 . . . 221

Turkey—Restrictions on Imports of Textile and Clothing Products, WTO, AB Report, 22 October 1999), WT/DS34/AB/R, online at: www.wto.org/tratop_e/dispu_e/cases_e/ds34_e . . . 512, 516

Typaldos v Manicomio di Aversa, Italy, Naples Court of Cassation (Corte di cassazione di Napoli), 25 February 1886, La giurisprudenza di diritto internazionale, II (1876–90), 1491 . . . 123

U

Underhill v Hernandez, US, Supreme Court, 1897, 168 U.S.250, 18 S.Ct. 83 . . . 123, 171

United Kingdom ACCC/C/2008/27, Aarhus Compliance Committee ECE/MP.PP/C.1/2010/6/Add.2, 24 September 2010 . . . 468

United Kingdom ACCC/C/2010/53, Aarhus Compliance Committee, 11 January 2013, ECE/MP.PP/C.1/2013/3 . . . 468

U.S.—Import Prohibition of Certain Shrimp and Shrimp Products, WTO, AB Report, 12 October 1998, WT/DS58/AB/R, online at: www.wto.org/tratop_e/dispu_e/cases_e/ds58_e . . . 469, 517

United States v Aluminium Co. of America et al., US, Circuit Court of Appeals, Second Circuit, 12 March 1945, 148 F.2nd 416 (1945) (2nd Cir.1945), online at: https://law.justia.com/cases/federal/appellate-courts/F2/148/416/1503668/ . . . 96

United States v Alvarez-Machain, US, Supreme Court, 15 June 1992, 504 U.S. 655 (1992), online at: https://supreme.justia.com/cases/federal/us/504/655/ . . . 96, 97

United States—Definitive Safeguard Measures on Imports of Circular Welded Carbon Quality Line Pipe from Korea, WTO, AB Report,15 February 2002, WT/DS202/AB/R, online at: www.wto.org/tratop_e/dispu_e/cases_e/ds202_e . . . 517

United States Diplomatic and Consular Staff in Teheran (United States of America v Iran) (Provisional Measures), ICJ, Order, 15 December 1979, ICJ Reports 1979, 7 . . . 240

United States Diplomatic and Consular Staff in Teheran (United States of America v Iran), ICJ, Judgment of 24 May 1980, ICJ Reports 1980, 3 . . . 252–3, 287, 301

United States—Final Anti-Dumping Measures on Stainless Steel from Mexico, WTO, AB Report, 30 April 2008, WT/DS344/AB/R, online at: www.wto.org/tratop_e/dispu_e/cases_e/ds344_e . . . 515

United States—Measures Concerning the Importation, Marketing and Sale of Tuna and Tuna Products, WTO, AB Report, 16 May 2012, WT/DS381/AB/R, online at: www.wto.org/tratop_e/dispu_e/cases_e/ds381_e . . . 513

United States v Palestine Liberation Organization, US, Southern District Court of New York, 29 June 1988, 12 AILC (second series) 386 . . . 229

United States—Standards for Reformulated and Conventional Gasoline, WTO, AB Report, 29 April 1996, WT/DS2/AB/R, online at: www.wto.org/english/tratop_e/envir_e/gas1_e . . . 517, 518

United States—Tax Treatment of 'Foreign Sales Corporations'—Recourse to Article 21(5) of the DSU by the European Communities, WTO, AB Report, 14 January 2002, WT/DS108/AB/RW, online at: www.wto.org/tratop_e/dispu_e/cases_e/ds108_e . . . 514

V

Velásquez Rodríquez, IACHR, Judgment, 29 July 1988, online at: http://www1.umn.edu/humanrts/iachr/b_11_12d. html . . . 389

The Venezuelan Preferential Case (Germany, Great Britain, Italy, Venezuela et al.), 22 February 1904, RIAA IX, 99 . . . 10

Vienna Convention on Consular Relations (Paraguay v United States of America) (Provisional Measures), ICJ, Order, 9 April 1998, ICJ Reports 1998, 248 . . . 521

W

Weber v Switzerland, ECHR, App No 11034/84, Judgment, 22 May 1990, online at: http://hudoc.echr.coe.int/tur?i=001-57629 . . . 211

West Rand Central Gold Mining Co. Ltd. v The King, Great Britain, King's Bench Division, 1 June 1905, [1905] 2.K.B. 391, BILC, vol. 2, 283 . . . 814

Western Sahara, ICJ, Advisory Opinion, 16 October 1975, ICJ Reports 1975, 12 . . . 48, 68, 70, 98, 100

Whaling in the Antarctic (Australia v Japan: New Zealand intervening), Judgment, 31 March 2014, ICJ Reports 2014, 226 . . . 16

Whittingham (I) & Sons Ltd. v Fratelli D'Amico, Italy, Court of Cassation, 16 July 1954, no. 2539, Diritto Marittimo (1955) 195 . . . 229

X

Xuncax Teresa and others v Gramajo Hector, US, District Court, 12 April 1995, 886 F. Suppl. 162 (D.Mass. 1995) . . . 420

Y

Yassin Abdullah Kadi and Al Barakaat International Foundation v Council of the European Union and Commission of the European Communities (C-402/05 and C-415/05), ECJ, Grand Chamber, 3 September 2008, EU:C:2008:461 . . . 339

Youmans, USA-Mexico General Claims Commission, 23 November 1926, RIAA IV, 110 . . . 250

Yuille, Shortridge and Co. (United Kingdom/Portugal), Hamburg, Hamburg Senate, 21 October 1861, in Lapradelle and Politis, II, 101 . . . 257

Yunis, US, District Court for the District of Columbia, 23 February 1988, 681 F. Supp. 896 . . . 419

Z

Zoerrsch v Waldock and another, UK, London Court of Appeal, 24 March 1964, 8 BILC 837 . . . 137

TABLE OF STATUTES

ARMENIA

Constitution
    Art 6 . . . 228

AUSTRALIA

Foreign Sovereign Immunities Act 1985
    s 11 . . . 124

AZERBAIIJAN

Constitution
    Art 151 . . . 228

BELGIUM

Law of 1993 . . . 445
Law of 1999 . . . 445

BULGARIA

Constitution
    Art 5(4) . . . 228

CANADA

State Immunity Act 1985
    s 5 . . . 124

CROATIA

Constitution . . . 84

CUBA

Democracy Act 1992 . . . 95

ESTONIA

Constitution
    Art 123 . . . 228

FRANCE

Constitution 1958
    Art 53 . . . 228
    Art 55 . . . 228
Criminal Code
    Art 211-1 . . . 436

GEORGIA

Constitution
    Art 6 . . . 228

GREECE

Constitution
    Art 100.1(b) . . . 402
    Art 100.1(f) . . . 304

IRAQ

Law Number 7 of 1958
    Art 1 . . . 438

ITALY

Constitution
    Art 10 . . . 127
    Art 96 . . . 227
Maritime Code 1932 . . . 229

KAZAKHSTAN

Constitution
    Art 4 . . . 228

MOLDOVA

Constitution
    Art 8 . . . 228

NETHERLANDS

Constitution . . . 228

RUSSIA

Constitution of the Russian Federation 1993
    Art 15(4) . . . 228
Federal Law on International Treaties of the Russian Federation
    Art 5 . . . 227

SOUTH AFRICA

Constitution 1996 . . . 226
    s 233 . . . 229

SPAIN

Constitution 1978 . . . 228
    Art 94 . . . 231
Law on Judicial Powers 1985
    Art 23 . . . 445

SWITZERLAND

Federal Civil Code . . . 175
    Art 60 *et seq.* . . . 175
Penal Code
    Art 271 . . . 51
    Art 273 . . . 51

TADZHIKISTAN

Constitution
    Art 11 . . . 228

UNITED KINGDOM

Abnormal Importation (Customs Duties) Act 1931 . . . 492
Anti-Terrorism Act 1988 . . . 229
Anti-terrorism, Crime and Security Act 2001 . . . 95
    s 51 . . . 95
Criminal Justice 1988
    s 134 . . . 441
Import Duties Act 1932 . . . 492
State Immunity Act . . . 124
    s 1 . . . 124
    s 2 . . . 124
    s 13(2) . . . 130

UNITED STATES

Abnormal Importation Act . . . 492
Alien Torts Claim Act 1789 . . . 419
Constitution . . . 213, 219
    Art VI(2) . . . 227
D'Amato Act 1996 . . . 95, 302
Foreign Sovereign Immunities Act 1976, as amended in 1988, and part of the US Code . . . 305
    Art 1604 . . . 124
    Art 1605 . . . 124
    Art 1605(a)(2) . . . 124
    Art 1609 . . . 130
Helms–Burton Act 1996 . . . 95, 302
International Organizations Immunities Act 1945 . . . 148
Justice Against Sponsors of Terrorism Act (JASTA) . . . 128
National Environmental Policy Act, 42 USC, Chap 55 . . . 461
Omnibus Diplomatic Security and Antiterrorism 1986 . . . 95
Restatement of the Law Third (1986) . . . 189
Smoot-Hawley Tariff Act 1930 . . . 491
Torture Victim Protection Act (28 USC § 1350 note). . . . 139
US Navy Regulations
    Art 0614 . . . 359

TABLE OF TREATIES AND INSTRUMENTS

Aarhus Convention on Access to Information, Public Participation in Decision-making and Access to Justice in Environmental Matters 1998 . . . 468
    Art 9(3) . . . 468
African Charter on Human and Peoples' Rights 1981 . . . 410, 418
    Art 4 . . . 377
    Art 6 . . . 378
    Art 24 . . . 460
    Protocol 1998 . . . 418
    Protocol, Art 34(6) . . . 418
Agenda for Sustainable Development 2030 . . . 73, 468, 469, 472–3
Agreement entered into by the government of Nicaragua with Nicaraguan rebels 1988 . . . 170
Agreement Establishing the World Trade Organization (WTO Agreement) *See* Marrakesh Agreement establishing the World Trade Organization 1994 (WTO Agreement)
Agreement for the Implementation of Part XI of the United Nations Convention on the Law of the Sea, 28 July 1994, 1836 UNTS 3 . . . 104
Agreement for the Implementation of the Provisions of the United Nations Convention on the Law of the Sea of 10 December 1982 relating to the Conservation and Management of Straddling Fish Stocks and Highly Migratory Fish Stocks 1995 . . . 115, 469
    Art 24(1) . . . 469
Agreement Establishing the Common Fund for Commodities 1980 (CFC) . . . 503
Agreement of ICRC with Bosnia and Herzegovina 1998 . . . 175
Agreement of ICRC with Cameroon 1999 . . . 175
Agreement of ICRC with Hungary 1997 . . . 175
Agreement of ICRC with ICTY by exchange of letters 28 April 1995 and 5 May 1995 . . . 175
Agreement of ICRC with Sierra Leone 2000 . . . 175
Agreement of ICRC with Switzerland on the legal status of the Committee in Switzerland 1993 . . . 175
    Art 1 . . . 175
    Art 3 . . . 175
Agreement of ICRC with the Republic of Macedonia 1999 . . . 175
Agreement on the International Military Tribunal (IMT) for the Punishment of War Criminals 1945 . . . 37
Agreement on Trade Related Aspects of Intellectual Property Rights (TRIPs Agreement) . . . 510, 515
    Art 66(1) . . . 515
Agreements entered into by the government of Angola with the 'National Union for the Total Independence of Angola' (UNITA) 1991 . . . 170
Algiers Accord . . . 285
Algiers Agreement 2000
    Art 5 . . . 397–8
Amended Protocol on Prohibitions or Restrictions on the Use of Mines, Booby-Traps and Other Devices 1996 . . . 172
American Convention on Human Rights 1969 . . . 255, 299, 410, 418, 525
    Art 4 . . . 377
    Art 7 . . . 378
    Art 26 . . . 460
    Art 44 . . . 163
American Declaration on the Rights and Duties of Man 1948 . . . 412–13, 418
American Treaty on Pacific Settlement (Pact of Bogotá) 1948
    Art XXXI . . . 287
Arab Charter of Human Rights 1994 (not yet in force) . . . 410
    Art 14 . . . 378
Arms Trade Treaty 2013 . . . 177, 328
    Art 22(1) . . . 328
Articles of Agreement of the International Monetary Fund: adopted at the United Nations Monetary and Financial Conference, Bretton Woods, New Hampshire 1944 . . . 494, 495
    Art IV(1)(iii) . . . 495
    Art IV(2)(b) (new) . . . 495
    Art VI, section 3 . . . 494
Atlantic Charter 1941 . . . 314, 406, 492
Basel Convention on the Control of Transboundary Movements of Hazardous Wastes and their Disposal 1989 (Basel Convention) . . . 475
Basel Protocol on Liability and compensation for damage resulting from transboundary movements of hazardous wastes and their disposal 1999 . . . 489
Briand-Kellogg Pact 1928 (Paris Pact of 27 August 1928 on the Prohibition of War) . . . 11, 35, 57, 335
Brussels Convention 1924 . . . 229
Cartagena Protocol on Biosafety to the Convention on Biological Diversity 2000 (Biosafety Protocol) . . . 474, 475
Charter of Paris . . . 84
Charter of the International Military Tribunal (IMT; Nuremberg Tribunal) . . . 160, 432, 433, 437, 447

Art 6(a) ... 437
Charter of the OAS ... 361
Charter of the United Nations See UN Charter 1945
Charter on Economic Rights and Duties of States 1974 ... 324, 522
　Art 2(2)(c) ... 522
Chicago Convention on International Civil Aviation 1944 ... 118–19
　Art 1 ... 93, 118
　Art 3 ... 118
　Art 84 ... 119
　Annex 9, Chap 2 ... 119
Cobden-Chevalier Treaty 1860 (Treaty of Commerce between the United Kingdom and France 1860) ... 497
Constitutive Act of the African Union 2000
　Art 4(h) ... 365
　Art 7(1) ... 365
Convention between the United States and Other Powers Respecting the Limitation of the Employment of Force for the Recovery of Contract Debts 1907 ... 32
Convention Concerning the Protection of the World Cultural and Natural Heritage 1972 (World Heritage Convention (WHC)). ... 474, 475, 477, 479
Convention for the Establishment of a Central American Court of Justice ... 286
Convention for the Prevention and Punishment of Terrorism 1937 ... 442
Convention for the Prevention and Repression of the Crime of Genocide 1948 ... 410, 434, 435, 436
　Art I, §§113–115 ... 15
　Art II ... 435
　Art IV ... 435
　Art VIII ... 435
　Art IX ... 435
Convention on Biological Diversity 1992 (CBD) ... 474, 475
　Art 20(4) ... 467
　Art 26 ... 479
　Annex I (Nagoya Protocol) See Nagoya Protocol
Convention on Certain Conventional Weapons 1980 ... 393, 395
　Protocol 1 ... 393
　Protocol 2 ... 393
　Protocol 3 ... 393
　Protocol 4 ... 393
Convention on Chemical Weapons 1993 ... 329
Convention on Civil Liability for Damage Resulting from Activities Dangerous to the Environment 1993 (Lugano Convention) ... 489
Convention on Civil Liability for Nuclear Damage 1963 (Vienna Convention) ... 488
　Art I(a) ... 488
　Art I(c) ... 488
　Art II(3)(a) ... 488
　Art IV(1) ... 488
　Art IV(2)–(3) ... 488
　Art VII ... 488
　Art XIII ... 489
　Amending Protocol 1997 ... 488
Convention on Enforced Disappearances 2006 ... 410, 414
Convention on Fishing and Conservation of the Living Resources of the High Seas 1958 (CFCLR) ... 103, 200
Convention on International Liability for Damage Caused by Space Objects 1972 ... 483
　Art II ... 483
　Art III ... 484
　Art VI ... 484
　Art VI.1 ... 484
　Art VI.2 ... 484
Convention on State Succession 1978 ... 200
Convention on State Succession 1983 ... 200
Convention on Stateless Persons 1954 ... 173
Convention on Supplementary Compensation for Nuclear Damage 1997 ... 488
Convention on Wetlands of International Importance especially as Waterfowl Habitat 1971 (Ramsar Convention) ... 474, 475
Convention on the Conservation of Migratory Species of Wild Animals 1979 (CMS) ... 474, 475
Convention on the Continental Shelf 1958 (CCS) ... 103, 200
　Art 1 ... 201
　Art 3 ... 201
Convention on the Elimination of Discrimination Against Women 1979 ... 414
　Art 4 ... 410
　Optional Protocol 1999 ... 414
Convention on the Elimination of Racial Discrimination 1965 ... 410, 414
　Art 1(4) ... 410
　Art 14 ... 163
Convention on the High Seas 1958 (CHS) ... 103, 200
Convention on the International Trade of Endangered Species 1973(CITES) ... 474, 475, 477, 480
　Art VIII ... 479
　Art 13 ... 479
Convention on the Law of Treaties with International Organizations 1986 ... 200
Convention on the Prevention and Punishment of Crimes against Humanity ... 433
Convention on the Prevention of Marine Pollution by Dumping of Wastes and Other Matter 1972 (London Convention) ... 474, 475, 480
Convention on the Prohibition of the Development, Production and Stockpiling of Bacteriological (Biological) and Toxin Weapons and on Their Destruction 1972 ... 266
Convention on the Prohibition of the Development, Production, Stockpiling and Use of Chemical Weapons and on Their Destruction 1993 ... 266

Convention on the Protection and Use of Transboundary Watercourses and International Lakes 1992 (Helsinki Convention) . . . 475
Convention on the Rights of Migrant Workers and Their Families 1990 . . . 410, 414
Convention on the Rights of Persons with Disabilities 2007 . . . 410, 414
  Optional Protocol 2007 . . . 414
Convention on the Rights of the Child 1989 . . . 326, 410, 414
Convention on the Settlement of Investment Disputes between States and Nationals of Other States 1965 (ICSID Convention) . . . 496, 525
  Preamble, para 1 . . . 522
  Art 27(1) . . . 519
Convention on the Territorial Sea and the Contiguous Zone 1958 (CTS) . . . 103, 200
Convention on the Privileges and Immunities of the United Nations . . . 151
  Art II, section 2 . . . 148
  Art V, section 18(a) . . . 151
  Art V, section 19 . . . 151
  Art V, section 20 . . . 151
  Art V, section 22 . . . 152
Convention on Third Party Liability in the Field of Nuclear Energy 1960 (Paris Convention) . . . 488
  Art 1(a)(vi) . . . 488
  Art 3 . . . 488
  Art 5(b) . . . 488
  Art 9 . . . 488
  Art 10 . . . 488
  Art 14(a) . . . 489
Convention Relating to Third Party Liability in the Field of Maritime Carriage of Nuclear Material 1971 . . . 489
Convention Supplementary to the Paris Convention 1960 on Third Party Liability in the Field of Nuclear Energy 1963 . . . 488
Covenant of the League of Nations 1919 . . . 22, 34, 35, 68, 276, 297, 327
  Art 5 . . . 411
  Art 12 . . . 34, 57
  Art 13 . . . 34, 57
  Art 14 . . . 57, 286
  Art 15 . . . 34
  Art 22 . . . 99
Dayton-Paris Accord 1995 . . . 282
  Annex II, Art V(3) . . . 198
Declaration of Brussels 1874 . . . 369
Declaration of St Petersburg 1868 . . . 369
  Preamble . . . 369
Declaration on a New International Economic Order 1974 . . . 330
Declaration on International Economic Co-operation and the Revitalization of Economic Growth and Development of Developing Countries 1990 . . . 325
Declaration on permanent sovereignty over natural resources 1962 . . . 330

Declaration on principles governing activities in outer space 1963 . . . 330
Declaration on principles governing the seabed and ocean bed beyond national jurisdiction 1970 . . . 330
Declaration on the Definition of Aggression 1974 . . . 330
Declaration on the Granting of Independence to Colonial Countries and Peoples 1960 . . . 68
  Art 73e . . . 68
Declaration on the 'Guidelines on the Recognition of New States in Eastern Europe and in the Soviet Union' . . . 84
Declaration on the Inadmissibility of Intervention in the Domestic Affairs of States and the Protection of Their Independence and Sovereignty 1965 . . . 54
Declaration on the Right to Development 1986 . . . 324–5, 503
  Art 1 . . . 503
  Art 2(1) . . . 503
  Art 2(3) . . . 503
  Art 4(1) . . . 503
Understanding on Rules and Procedures Governing the Settlement of Disputes (Dispute Settlement Body (DSU)) annexed to WTO Agreement . . . 290
  Art 21(3) . . . 518
  Art 21(3)(c) . . . 518
  Art 22(2) . . . 518
  Art 22(6) . . . 518
Draft Articles on the Law of Treaties 1963 . . . 48
Draft Articles on the Prevention of Transboundary Harm from Hazardous Activities 2001 . . . 460
Draft Code of Crimes against Peace and Security of Mankind . . . 437
  Art 16 . . . 437
Draft Comprehensive Convention on International Terrorism 2000 . . . 442
Escazú Agreement (Regional Agreement on Access to Information, Public Participation and Justice in Environmental Matters in Latin America and the Caribbean) 2018 . . . 468
EU Treaty
  Art 42(7) . . . 353
European Community Treaty . . . 299
European Convention for the Peaceful Settlement of Disputes 1957
  Art 1 . . . 287
European Convention for the Prevention of Torture 1987 . . . 398
European Convention for the Protection of Human Rights and Fundamental Freedoms 1950 1950 (ECHR) . . . 126, 163, 299, 377, 380, 408, 410, 416, 417, 423
  Art 1 . . . 412
  Art 2 . . . 377
  Art 3 . . . 423
  Art 5 . . . 378, 379

Art 5(1)(f) ... 228
Art 8 ... 227
Protocol 11, 1994 ... 416
Protocol 14, 2004 ... 416
Protocol 14, Art 2 ... 416
Protocol 14, Art 6 ... 416
Protocol 14, Art 7 ... 416
Protocol 14, Art 8 ... 416
Protocol 14, Art 12 ... 416
Protocol 14, Art 16 ... 416
Protocol 14, Art 17 ... 416
Protocol 14, Art 19 ... 416
Protocol 15 ... 416
Protocol 16, 2013 ... 416, 417
Protocols ... 417
European Convention on State Immunity 1972 ... 125
  Art 5(1) ... 125
  Art 5(2) ... 125
Final Act of the Uruguay Round 1994 ... 510
  WTO Agreement *See* WTO Agreement
First Additional Protocol (I) 1977 of the Geneva Conventions: Protection of Victims of International Armed Conflict (AP I) ... 166, 368, 370, 372, 373, 374, 381, 382, 383, 387, 390, 391, 394, 396, 397, 399, 400, 401, 429, 430, 445
  Art 1(1) ... 16
  Art 1(2) ... 370
  Art 1(4) ... 372
  Art 5 ... 399
  Art 8(2)(a) ... 429
  Art 8(2)(b) ... 430
  Art 8(2)(c) ... 430
  Art 8(2)(e) ... 430
  Arts 43–44 ... 374
  Art 43(1) ... 381, 382
  Art 43(2) ... 381, 382
  Art 44 ... 382, 383
  Art 44(3) ... 382, 383
  Art 44(4) ... 383
  Art 47 ... 383
  Art 47(1) ... 384
  Art 47(2) ... 384
  Art 51 ... 390
  Art 51(2) ... 430
  Art 51(3) ... 386
  Art 51(5)(b) ... 392
  Art 51(6) ... 400
  Art 52 ... 390
  Art 52(2) ... 390
  Art 53(c) ... 400
  Art 54 ... 392
  Art 54(4) ... 400
  Art 55(2) ... 400
  Art 56 ... 392
  Art 56(4) ... 400
  Art 57(2)(a)(ii) ... 392
  Art 57(2)(a)(iii) ... 392
  Art 57(2)(b) ... 392
  Art 85(3)(b) ... 392
Art 90 ... 281, 372, 400
Art 91 ... 401
Art 96(3) ... 166
Friendly Relations Declaration 1970 *See* UN Declaration on Friendly Relations 1970
GA Declaration on the Inadmissibility of Intervention and Interference in the Internal Affairs of States 1981 ... 363
GA Declaration on the New International Economic Order and the Programme of Action relating thereto 1974 ... 324
General Act of the Berlin Congo Conference 1885 ... 26
General Agreement on Tariffs and Trade 1947 (GATT 1947) ... 490, 491, 493, 494, 496–9, 507, 510, 511, 513, 517
  Pt IV: Trade and Development ... 507
  Art I ... 497, 513
  Art I(1) ... 513, 514
  Art III ... 497, 513, 514
  Art III(2) ... 513, 514
  Art III(2), 1st sentence ... 514
  Art III(2), 2nd sentence ... 514
  Art III(4) ... 513, 514
  Art III(8) ... 513
  Art VI ... 498
  Art XI ... 498, 511
  Art XI (1) ... 512
  Arts XII–XIV ... 498
  Art XVI ... 498
  Art XVIII ... 507
  Art XIX ... 498
  Art XX ... 498
  Art XXI ... 498
  Art XXIV ... 498
  Art XXV ... 498
  Art XXVIII*bis* ... 498, 512
  Amending Protocol ... 507
General Agreement on Tariffs and Trade 1994 (GATT 1994) ... 497, 510, 516
  Art I ... 517
  Art III ... 517
  Art III(8)(a) ... 516
  Art VI ... 510, 515
  Art VII ... 512
  Art XI ... 517
  Art XI(2)(a) ... 516
  Art XII ... 516
  Art XVII ... 515
  Art XVIII:A ... 515
  Art XVIII:B ... 516
  Art XIX ... 516
  Art XX ... 517
  Art XXI ... 516
  Art XXI(b)(iii) ... 516
  Art XXIV ... 516
  Art XXIV(4) ... 516
  Art XXIV(8) ... 516
  Art XXIV(5) ... 516
  Art XXIV(8) ... 516

Art XXIV(12) ... 516
Marrakesh Protocol ... 510
General Agreement on Trade in Services
  (GATS) ... 510
  Art II ... 513
  Art XVII ... 513
Geneva Convention (I) for the Amelioration of the Condition of the Wounded and Sick in Armed Forces in the Field. Geneva 1949 ... 371
  Art 63 ... 370
Geneva Convention (II) for the Amelioration of the Condition of the Wounded and Sick and Shipwrecked Members of the Armed Forces at Sea 1949 ... 368, 371
  Art 12(1) ... 16
  Art 62 ... 370
Geneva Convention (III) relative to the Treatment of Prisoners of War 1949 ... 371, 381, 383, 387, 388, 396
  Art 4 ... 387
  Art 4(A) ... 381
  Art 4(A)(2) ... 381, 382
  Art 5 ... 387
  Art 21 ... 379
  Art 130 ... 430
  Art 142 ... 370
Geneva Convention (IV) relative to the Protection of Civilian Persons in Time of War 1949 ... 371, 387, 388, 389, 396
  Art 42 ... 379
  Art 78(1) ... 379
  Art 147 ... 430
  Art 158 ... 370
Geneva Convention for the Amelioration of the Condition of the Wounded and Sick in Armies in the Field 1906 ... 396
Geneva Convention for the Amelioration of the Condition of the Wounded in Armies in the Field 1929 ... 370, 396
Geneva Convention on Maritime Warfare 1864 ... 369, 396
Geneva Convention on the Continental Shelf 1958 ... 110, 187
  Art 6 ... 112, 186
Geneva Convention on the Territorial Sea 1958 ... 93
Geneva Convention relative to the Treatment of Prisoners of War 1929 ... 370, 1971, 395
Geneva Conventions (I), (II), (III) and (IV)1949 ... 17, 18, 175, 222, 236, 268, 368, 370–1, 372, 373–4, 378, 379, 381, 382, 390, 394, 396, 397, 399, 400, 429, 445, 448
  Common Art 1 ... 16, 17, 18, 268
  Common Art 2 ... 372
  Common Art 2(1) ... 367
  Common Art 2(3) ... 371
  Common Art 3 ... 171, 370–1, 372, 373, 375, 379, 384, 386, 396, 397, 430, 448
  Common Art 3(3) ... 170
  Common Art 10(3) ... 175, 399
  Common Art 10(5) ... 399
  Common Art 10(6) ... 399
  Common Art 11(3) ... 399
  Common Art 11(5) ... 399
  Common Art 11(6) ... 399
  Common Art 11 ... 175
First Additional Protocol 1977 See First Additional Protocol (I) 1977 of the Geneva Conventions: Protection of Victims of International Armed Conflict (AP I)
Second Additional Prototocol 1977 See Second Additional Protocol (II) 1977 of the Geneva Conventions: Protection of Victims of Non-International Armed Conflicts (AP II)
Geneva Protocol 1925 ... 393
Genocide Convention 1948 See Convention for the Prevention and Repression of the Crime of Genocide
German-Polish Treaty 1922 ... 411
Gothenburg Protocol on the Reduction of Acidification, Eutrophication and Ground-Level Ozone 1999 ... 476
Hague Agreement 1928 between the President of the PCIJ and the Netherlands ... 187
Hague Convention II containing Regulations on the Laws and Customs of War on Land 1899 ... 369, 370, 381, 396
  Martens Clause See Martens Clause
  Preamble ... 369
Hague Convention IV respecting the Laws and Customs of War on Land and its annex: Regulations concerning the Laws and Customs of War on Land 1907 ... 369, 370, 371, 393, 396, 401
  Art 3 ... 401
  Martens Clause See Martens Clause
  Annex (Hague Regulations 1907) ... 371, 381, 382, 390, 393, 396, 401
  Annex, Art 1 ... 381
  Annex, Art 23(b) ... 390
  Annex, Art 23(c) ... 390
  Annex, Art 23(d) ... 390
  Annex, Art 23(f) ... 390
  Annex, Art 28 ... 390
  Annex, Art 29 ... 132
  Annex, Art 42 ... 396
  Annex, Art 46(1) ... 429
Hague Convention V respecting the Rights and Duties of Neutral Powers and Persons in Case of War on Land 1907 ... 394
Hague Convention XIII concerning the Rights and Duties of Neutral Powers in Naval War 1907 ... 394
Hague Convention for the Peaceful Settlement of Disputes 1899 (revised/improved 1907) ... 280, 284, 297
  Art 9 (1907 Convention) ... 280
  Art 41 (1907 Convention) ... 284

Hague Convention for the Protection of Cultural
  Property in the Event of Armed Conflict
  1954 . . . 172, 374
  Protocol . . . 374
Hague Conventions 1899–1907 . . . 368, 369–70,
  372, 393
Hague Protocol II for the Protection of Cultural
  Property in the Event of Armed Conflict
  1999 . . . 430
  Art 15 . . . 430
Hague Regulations *See* Annex of Hague Convention IV respecting the Laws and Customs
  of War on Land and its annex: Regulations
  concerning the Laws and Customs of War on
  Land 1907
Havana Convention of 28 February 1928
  Art 19 . . . 187
Helsinki Convention *See* Convention on the
  Protection and Use of Transboundary Watercourses and International Lakes 1992 (Helsinki
  Convention),
Helsinki Final Act 1975 . . . 84, 201, 421
ICC Elements of Crime . . . 429, 436, 440, 441
  Art 7(1)(f) . . . 440
  Art 8(2)(a)(ii) . . . 440
  Art 8(2)(c)(i) . . . 440
ICSID Convention *See* Convention on the Settlement of Investment Disputes between States
  and Nationals of Other States
ILC Articles on Prevention of Transboundary
  Harm from Hazardous Activities . . . 472, 485
  Art 2 . . . 485
  Art 2(a) . . . 460
  Art 3 . . . 460, 485
ILC Articles on State Responsibility . . . 247, 248,
  249, 255, 256, 258, 259, 262, 263, 265, 267, 268,
  269, 270, 271, 272, 273
  Art 1 . . . 249
  Art 2 . . . 249
  Art 4–11 . . . 249
  Art 4 . . . 251
  Art 4(2) . . . 251
  Art 4 . . . 250
  Art 5 . . . 252
  Art 6 . . . 252
  Art 7 . . . 250, 252
  Art 8 . . . 253, 254
  Art 9 . . . 252
  Art 10 . . . 254
  Art 11 . . . 253
  Art 12 . . . 255
  Art 13 . . . 255
  Art 14(1) . . . 255
  Art 14(2) . . . 255
  Art 16 . . . 256
  Art 17 . . . 256
  Art 18 . . . 256
  Art 20 . . . 258
  Art 21 . . . 258
  Art 22 . . . 258
  Art 23 . . . 258
  Art 23(1) . . . 259
  Art 24 . . . 258, 260
  Art 24(1) . . . 260
  Art 25 . . . 258, 262
  Art 25(1) . . . 261
  Art 26 . . . 262
  Art 27(b) . . . 262
  Art 30 . . . 263
  Art 31 . . . 263
  Art 35 . . . 264
  Art 36 . . . 264
  Art 37 . . . 264
  Art 39 . . . 256
  Art 40 . . . 268, 269
  Art 40(2) . . . 268
  Art 41 . . . 268, 269
  Art 42 . . . 265, 266, 273
  Art 42(a) . . . 265
  Art 42(b) . . . 265, 271
  Art 43 . . . 266
  Art 48 . . . 258, 268
  Art 48(1)(b) . . . 271
  Art 48(2)(a) . . . 270
  Art 48(2)(b) . . . 270
  Art 50(1)(a) . . . 300
  Art 50(1)(b) . . . 300
  Art 50(1)(d) . . . 301
  Art 50(2)(b) . . . 301
  Art 52(1) . . . 267
  Art 52(1)(b) . . . 266
  Art 54 . . . 268, 270, 273
  Art 55 . . . 247
ILC Draft Articles on State Responsibility . . . 170
  Art 19 . . . 236, 268
  Art 54(3) (Draft 2000) . . . 274
ILC Draft Articles on Prevention of Transboundary Harm from Hazardous Activities . . . 248
ILC Draft Articles on the Protection of Persons
  in the Event of Disasters 2014 . . . 56
ILC Draft Articles on the Responsibility of International Organizations . . . 154, 155
ILC Draft Declaration on the Rights and Duties
  of States 1949 . . . 90
  Art 1 . . . 90
  Art 3 . . . 90
  Art 14 . . . 90
ILC Principles on the Allocation of Loss in the
  Case of Transboundary Harm Arising out of
  Hazardous Activities 2006 . . . 248, 487, 488
  Art 4 . . . 488
ILO Constitution
  Art 22 . . . 291
  Art 22(3) . . . 292
  Art 24 . . . 36, 163
  Art 24(5) . . . 292
  Art 26 . . . 281
  Art 26(9) . . . 292
  Art 34 . . . 281
ILO Conventions . . . 405

TABLE OF TREATIES AND INSTRUMENTS

Indian Bilateral Investment Treaty 2015
   Art 1(2)1 . . . 523
   Art 1(6) . . . 523
International Convention for the Prevention of Pollution from Ships, 2 November 1973, amended by the Protocol 1978 (MARPOL 73/78) . . . 474, 475, 479
International Convention for the Regulation of Whaling 1946 (Whaling Convention) . . . 475
   Schedule (adopted 1971) . . . 479
International Convention for the Suppression of Acts of Nuclear Terrorism 2005 . . . 442
International Convention for the Suppression of the Financing of Terrorism 1999 . . . 442, 443
   Art 2(1)(b) . . . 443
International Convention on Civil Liability for Oil Pollution Damage 1992 (CLC 92) . . . 487
   Art I(3) . . . 488
   Art III(1) . . . 488
   Art III(2)–(3) . . . 488
   Art III(4) . . . 488
   Art IV . . . 488
   Art V(2) . . . 488
   Art VII(1) . . . 488
   Art VII(8) . . . 488
   Art X(2) . . . 489
   Amending Protocol . . . 487
International Convention on Liability and Compensation for Damage in Connection with the Carriage of Hazardous and Noxious Substances 1996
Amending Protocol 2010 . . . 489
International Convention on the Establishment of an International Fund for Compensation for Oil Pollution Damage 1992 (FUND/92) . . . 487
   Art 4 . . . 489
   Art 4(2) . . . 489
   Amending Protocol 2003 . . . 487
International Trade Organization (ITO) Charter (Havana Charter) . . . 493, 497
International Wheat Agreement 1959 . . . 173
Jay Treaty between Great Britain and the US 1794 . . . 284
Joint Protocol Relating to the Application of the Vienna Convention and the Paris Convention 1988 . . . 488
Kyoto Protocol to the United Nations Framework Convention on Climate Change 1997 (Kyoto Protocol) . . . 474, 475, 476, 477
   Art 2(1) . . . 469
   Art 3 . . . 467
   Art 4(3) . . . 477
   Art 4(9) . . . 477
   Art 10 . . . 467, 469
   Art 12(2) . . . 469
   Annex A . . . 469
   Annex B . . . 476
Lieber Code . . . 368
Lomé Agreement 7 July 1999 . . . 170
London Agreement 1945 . . . 432, 433, 437
London Convention on Dumping 1972 *See* Convention on the Prevention of Marine Pollution by Dumping of Wastes and Other Matter 1972 (London Convention)
London Protocol 1996 *See* Protocol of 7 November 1996 to the Convention of 1972 on the Prevention of Marine Pollution by Dumping of Wastes and Other Matter, 7 November 1996 (London Protocol)
Lugano Convention *See* Convention on Civil Liability for Damage Resulting from Activities Dangerous to the Environment 1993
Lusaka Protocol 1994 . . . 170
Madrid Protocol *See* Protocol to the Antarctic Treaty on Environmental Protection 1991 (Madrid Protocol)
Manila Declaration on the Peaceful Settlement of Disputes 1982 . . . 60, 61, 278
   §3 . . . 61
   §5 . . . 61
   §7 . . . 61
   §8 . . . 61
   §10 . . . 61
   §12 . . . 61
Maritime Boundary Treaty Annex 28: Conciliation Between the Democratic Republic of Timor-Leste and the Commonwealth of Australia, Report and Recommendations of the Compulsory Conciliation Commission Between Timor-Leste and Australia on the Timor Sea 2018 . . . 283
MARPOL 73/78 Convention *See* International Convention for the Prevention of Pollution from Ships
Marrakesh Agreement establishing the World Trade Organization 1994 (WTO Agreement) . . . 290, 497, 510, 511
   Annex I, A (Goods) . . . 510
   Annex I, B (Services) . . . 510
   Annex I, C (Intellectual Property Rights) . . . 510
   Annex IA . . . 510
   Annex 1B . . . 510
   Annex 1C . . . 510
   Annex II . . . 510, 517
   Annex III . . . 510
   Annex IV . . . 510
   Annexes I–IV . . . 510
Martens Clause (Hague Conventions II and IV) . . . 185, 186, 193, 369–71
Minamata Convention on Mercury 2013 . . . 475
Montego Bay Convention on the Law of the Sea *See* UN Convention on the Law of the Sea 1982 (UNCLOS)
Montevideo Convention on the Rights and Duties of States 1933
   Art 1 . . . 81
Montreal Protocol on Substances that Deplete the Ozone Layer 1987 (Montreal Protocol) . . . 474,

475, 476, 477, 479, 480, 481
 Art 5 . . . 477, 478
 Art 5(1) . . . 467
 Art 10 . . . 477
 Art 10A . . . 477
 Annex V . . . 480
 Kigali Amendment 2016 . . . 476
Moscow Treaty on nuclear testing in outer space 1963 . . . 329
Munich Treaty 1938 . . . 431
Nagoya–Kuala Lumpur Supplementary Protocol on Liability and Redress to the Cartagena Protocol on Biosafety 2010 . . . 489
Protocol of 7 November 1996 to the Convention of 1972 on the Prevention of Marine Pollution by Dumping of Wastes and Other Matter, 7 November 1996 (London Protocol) . . . 474, 475
Nagoya Protocol to the Convention on Biological Diversity on Access to Genetic Resources and the Fair and Equitable Sharing of the Benefits arising from their Utilization 2010 (Nagoya Protocol) . . . 469, 472, 475
 Preamble . . . 469
New York Convention on the Recognition and Enforcement of Foreign Arbitral Awards 1958 . . . 306, 525
New York Convention 1997 See UN Convention on the Law of the Non-Navigational Uses of International Watercourses 1997
New York Convention on the Recognition and Enforcement of Foreign Arbitral Awards 1958 . . . 525
Niue Treaty on Co-operation in Fisheries Surveillance and Law Enforcement in the South Pacific Region 1992 . . . 479
North-American Free Trade Agreement (NAFTA) . . . 516
 Art 1128 . . . 518
Northwest Atlantic Fisheries Organization (NAFO) Convention . . . 115
Optional Protocol on the Involvement of Children in Armed Conflict 2000 . . . 410
Optional Protocol on the Sale of Children, Child Prostitution and Child Pornography 2000 . . . 410
Ottawa Convention on the prohibition of the use, stockpiling, production, and transfer of antipersonnel mines and on their destruction . . . 393
Panama Canal Treaty
 Art V . . . 361
Panamanian Declaration
 §3 . . . 362
Paris Agreement on Climate Change 2015 . . . 326, 470, 474, 475, 476, 477, 478, 481
 Preamble . . . 469
 Art 2(1) . . . 469
 Art 2(2) . . . 467
 Art 4(1) . . . 469

Art 4(2) . . . 477
 Art 6(1) . . . 469
 Art 6(2) . . . 469
 Art 6(4) . . . 469
 Art 6(8) . . . 469
 Art 6(9) . . . 469
 Art 7(1) . . . 469
 Art 8 . . . 484
 Art 8(1) . . . 469
 Art 9 . . . 484
 Art 10(5) . . . 469
Paris Pact 1928 . . . 276
Peace of Westphalia 1648 . . . 20, 22, 23, 335
Peace Treaty of Paris 1898 . . . 26
Principles of International Law concerning Friendly Relations and Co-operation among States (UN General Assembly resolution 2625 (XXV)) . . . 278
Protocol on Civil Liability and Compensation for Damage Caused by the Transboundary Effects of Industrial Accidents on Transboundary Waters 2003 . . . 489
Protocol on the Compulsory Settlement of Disputes . . . 103
Protocol on Water and Health to the Convention on the Protection and Use of Transboundary Watercourses and International Lakes 1992, 1999 (Protocol on Water and Health)
 Preamble . . . 469
 Art 1 . . . 469
 Art 4(4)(c) . . . 469
Protocol to the Antarctic Treaty on Environmental Protection 1991(Madrid Protocol) . . . 475, 479
Ramsar Convention on Wetlands 1971 See Convention on Wetlands of International Importance especially as Waterfowl Habitat 1971 (Ramsar Convention)
Rio Declaration on Environment and Development 1992 . . . 63, 74, 330, 459, 462, 464, 471
 Preamble . . . 459
 Principle 1 . . . 460
 Principle 2 . . . 73, 459, 460, 484
 Principle 3 . . . 460, 466
 Principle 4 . . . 460, 470
 Principle 6 . . . 467
 Principle 7 . . . 63, 460, 462, 467
 Principle 10 . . . 460, 467
 Principle 15 . . . 459, 463, 464
 Principle 16 . . . 460, 465
 Principle 17 . . . 459, 461
 Principle 18 . . . 63, 459, 462
 Principle 19 . . . 63, 459, 462
 Principle 27 . . . 63, 462
Rotterdam Convention on the Prior Informed Consent Procedure for Certain Hazardous Chemicals and Pesticides in International Trade 1998 (Rotterdam Convention) . . . 469, 472, 475, 477
 Preamble . . . 469

San Salvador Protocol
  Art 11 . . . 460
Second Additional Protocol (II) 1977 of the Geneva Conventions: Protection of Victims of Non-International Armed Conflicts (AP II) . . . 172, 368, 370, 372, 373, 374, 448
  Preamble . . . 370
  Art 1(1) . . . 373
  Art 1(2) . . . 373
  Art 4 . . . 373
  Art 5(1) . . . 379
  Art 5(2) . . . 379
  Art 6 . . . 379
  Art 6(5) . . . 379
  Art 13 . . . 373, 384, 390
  Art 13(2) . . . 430
  Art 13(3) . . . 386
  Art 14 . . . 373
Settlement of Westphalia 1648 . . . 34
Slavery Convention 1926 . . . 36
  Art 2(b) . . . 36
Slavery Convention 1956
  Art 8 . . . 292
Soviet-German Treaty 1921
  Art 8 . . . 34
  Art 9 . . . 34
Start I/Start II Agreements of 31 July 1991/3 January 1993 respectively . . . 329
Statute of the International Atomic Energy Agency 1956, as amended 1989
  Art III.A.6 . . . 472
Statute of the International Court of Justice (ICJ) . . . 200, 286, 434, 435
  Art 4 . . . 284
  Art 8 . . . 316
  Art 10 . . . 317
  Art 36(2) . . . 287
  Art 38 . . . 181, 195, 197
  Art 38(1) . . . 181, 192
  Art 38(1)(a)–(c) . . . 181, 199
  Art 38(1)(b) . . . 184
  Art 38(1)(d) . . . 182, 199
  Art 38(2) . . . 181, 197
  Art 50 . . . 280
  Art 59 . . . 181, 199
  Art 65 . . . 286
Statute of the International Criminal Court 1998 (ICC) (Rome Statute) . . . 138, 161, 222, 228, 392, 431, 433, 434, 436, 437, 438, 439, 449, 450
  Preamble . . . 449, 450
  Art 1 . . . 450
  Art 4(1) . . . 144
  Art 5(1) . . . 449
  Art 5bis . . . 437
  Art 7(1) . . . 428
  Art 7(1)(h) . . . 433
  Art 7(2) . . . 434
  Art 7(3) . . . 433
  Art 8 . . . 429
  Art 8(1) . . . 430
  Art 8(2) . . . 375
  Art 8(2)(b)(iv) . . . 392
  Art 8bis . . . 438, 439, 440
  Art 8bis(1) . . . 439
  Art 8bis(2) . . . 439
  Art 12 . . . 450
  Art 12(2)(a) . . . 450
  Art 12(3) . . . 450
  Art 13 . . . 449
  Art 15bis. . . . 438
  Art 15ter . . . 438
  Art 17 . . . 451
  Art 21 . . . 195
  Art 25bis . . . 438
  Art 30 . . . 431
Statute of the International Criminal Tribunal for Rwanda (ICTR) . . . 138, 222, 230, 434, 435
  Art 2–4 . . . 449
  Art 4 . . . 375
Statute of the International Criminal Tribunal for the former Yugoslavia (ICTY) . . . 138, 222, 230, 433, 434, 435
  Arts 2–5 . . . 449
Statute of the Permanent Court of International Justice (PCIJ) . . . 192, 286
  Art 38 . . . 181
  Art 38(1)(c) . . . 193, 194
Stockholm Convention on Persistent Organic Pollutants 2001 (Stockholm Convention) . . . 475, 477
  Art 7(3) . . . 469
  Annex A (Elimination) . . . 477
  Annex B (Restriction) . . . 477
  Annex C (Unintentional Production) . . . 477
Stockholm Declaration on the Human Environment 1972 . . . 74, 330, 459, 470, 471
  Principle 1 . . . 460
  Principle 21 . . . 73, 459, 460, 485
Straddling Fish Stocks Agreement, See Agreement for the Implementation of the Provisions of the United Nations Convention on the Law of the Sea 1982 relating to the Conservation and Management of Straddling Fish Stocks and Highly Migratory Fish Stocks 1995
Tlatelolco Treaty Banning Nuclear Weapons in Latin America 1967 . . . 266, 329
Treaty banning the placing of nuclear weapons on the ocean floor 1971 . . . 329
Treaty between Italy and the Holy See 1929
  Art 11 . . . 173
Treaty between the USSR and the US on antiballistic missiles 1972 (modified Salt I (1974) followed by Salt II (1979)) . . . 329
Treaty for the Complete Ban on Nuclear Tests 1996 . . . 329
Treaty of Bangkok for the denuclearization of South East Asia 1995 . . . 329
Treaty of Guarantee between Cyprus, Greece, Turkey, and the UK, 1960
  Article IV . . . 361

Treaty of Münster ... 22
　Art 3 ... 23
　Art 65 ... 22
　Art 123 ... 22
　Art 124 ... 23
Treaty of Paris, 30 May 1814 ... 174
Treaty of Paris, 26 September 1815 ... 27
Treaty of Paris, 27 August 1928 ... 340
Treaty of Peace and Friendship between Chile and Argentina 1984 ... 282
Treaty of Pelindaba (South Africa) for the denuclearization of Africa 1996 ... 329
Treaty of Rarotonga (Cook Islands) denuclearizing the South Pacific 1985 ... 329
Treaty of Versailles 1919 ... 292
Treaty on Nuclear Tests 1996 ... 329
Treaty on Principles Governing the Activities of States in the Exploration and Use of Outer Space 1967 ... 120, 202
　Art 1 ... 120
　Art 2 ... 120
　Art 4 ... 328
　Art XII ... 292
Treaty on the Antarctic 1959 ... 479
　Art I ... 328
　Art IV ... 97
　Art V ... 328
　Art VII ... 292
Treaty on the European Union
　Art 5 ... 146
Treaty on the Functioning of the European Union 2007 (TFEU)
　Art 2 ... 94
　Art 288 ... 230
Treaty on the International Agency for Atomic Energy
　Art 12(6) ... 292
Treaty on the Moon and Other Celestial Bodies 1979 ... 120, 121, 484
　Art 3 ... 328
　Art 4 ... 120
　Art 4(1) ... 121
　Art 11(1) ... 121
Treaty on the Non-Proliferation of Nuclear Weapons 1968 (NPT) ... 328
　Art VI ... 63, 277, 280
　Art X(1) ... 266
Treaty on the Prohibition of Nuclear Weapons 2017 ... 328, 394
　Art 15 ... 394
Treaty on the Warsaw Pact ... 351
Troppau Protocol 1818 ... 27
　Arts 2-4 ... 27
UN Charter 1945 ... 11, 37, 38, 39, 42, 45, 46, 49, 54, 57, 58, 60, 62, 64, 65, 72, 73, 74, 84, 148, 236, 267, 269, 274, 276, 277, 278, 286, 298, 303, 314, 315, 317, 318, 319, 320, 321, 323, 324, 326, 327, 329, 331, 336, 337, 338, 343, 346, 349, 350, 352, 354, 355, 357, 358, 359, 360, 361, 364, 365, 366, 406, 408, 411, 425, 432, 439, 454, 459, 484

Preamble ... 316, 329
Chap VI ... 54, 60, 277, 289, 321, 322, 425
Chap VII ... 38, 54, 57, 197, 203, 230, 319, 322, 330, 336, 338, 341, 344, 345, 346, 349, 355, 425, 448, 449
Chap VIII ... 54, 425
Chap XI ... 323
Chap XII ... 99
Art 1 ... 45, 68, 407, 456
Art 1(1) ... 315, 323, 329
Art 1(2) ... 316
Art 1(3) ... 62, 316, 462
Art 2 ... 45, 197, 456
Art 2(1) ... 49, 93
Art 2(2) ... 64
Art 2(3) ... 60, 61, 263, 277, 278, 318, 321
Art 2(4) ... 38, 48, 57, 58, 272, 298, 300, 315, 318, 320, 349, 361, 362, 363, 437
Art 2(5) ... 62
Art 2(6) ... 197
Art 2(7) ... 47, 54, 314, 315, 326, 407, 408
Art 3 ... 456
Art 4 ... 437, 456
Art 5(2) ... 437
Art 6 ... 456
Art 10 ... 314
Art 11(1) ... 316, 327
Art 12 ... 314, 316
Art 13(1) ... 326
Art 13(1)(a) ... 329
Art 13(1)(b) ... 316, 324
Art 14 ... 322
Art 15 ... 449
Art 16 ... 449
Art 17(2) ... 316, 343, 505
Art 18(2) ... 316
Art 18(3) ... 316
Art 21 ... 316
Art 22 ... 316
Art 25 ... 197, 317
Art 27(3) ... 39, 317, 319, 357
Art 30 ... 439
Art 33 ... 60, 61, 267, 277
Art 33(1) ... 277, 321
Art 33(2) ... 321
Art 34 ... 322
Art 35(2) ... 321
Art 36(1) ... 322
Art 37(2) ... 322
Art 39 ... 274, 319, 338, 346
Art 41 ... 197, 274, 319, 330, 337–8, 339, 341, 348
Art 42 ... 319, 338
Arts 43–45 ... 317
Art 43 ... 319, 337, 346
Art 51 ... 57, 58, 59, 199, 314, 319, 320, 349, 350, 351, 352, 353, 354, 355, 357, 358, 359, 360, 361, 362, 363, 364
Arts 52–54 ... 333
Art 53 ... 57

Art 55 ... 68, 227, 316, 323, 324, 327, 407
Art 55(c) ... 326
Art 56 ... 227, 327, 407
Art 62 ... 324, 326
Art 68 ... 317
Art 71 ... 333
Art 73 ... 314, 323
Art 73(e) ... 323
Art 76(b) ... 323
Art 83 ... 317
Art 86 ... 317
Art 92 ... 286
Art 96 ... 286
Art 97 ... 316, 317
Art 99 ... 281, 322
Art 103 ... 203, 314
Art 104 ... 144
Art 105(1) ... 148
Art 105(2) ... 151
Art 106 ... 57, 319
Art 107 ... 57
Art 108 ... 331, 357
UN Convention against Torture and Other Cruel, Inhuman or Degrading Treatment or Punishment 1984 (CAT) ... 96, 410, 414, 440, 441, 442
   Art 1(1) ... 440, 441
   Art 6(2) ... 96
   Art 7 ... 445
   Art 7(1) ... 96
   Art 19 ... 292
   Optional Protocol 2002 ... 410
UN Convention on Jurisdictional Immunities of States and Their Property 2004 ... 124, 125
   Art 2.1(c) ... 124
   Art 3 ... 126
   Art 7 ... 129
   Art 10 ... 124
   Art 11 ... 125
   Art 18 ... 129
   Art 19 ... 129
   Art 20 ... 129
   Art 21(1) ... 130
UN Convention on Racial Discrimination ... 40, 291–2
   Art 9 ... 292
UN Convention on the Law of the Non-Navigational Uses of International Watercourses 1997 (New York Convention) ... 469, 475
   Art 24(2)(a) ... 469
UN Convention on the Law of the Sea 1958 ... 200
UN Convention on the Law of the Sea 1982 (UNCLOS) ... 93, 104–16, 117, 118, 200, 220, 279, 283, 474, 475
   Pt II ... 105
   Pt V ... 109
   Pt VI ... 110
   Pt VII ... 114
   Pt XI ... 104, 117, 121

Pt XII ... 104, 474
Pt XIII ... 104
Pt XIV ... 104
Pt XV ... 104
Art 3 ... 105
Art 5 ... 105
Art 7 ... 106, 107
Art 7(1) ... 105
Art 8(2) ... 106
Art 9 ... 107
Art 10 ... 107
Art 10(1) ... 107
Art 10(2) ... 107
Art 10(4) ... 107
Art 10(5) ... 107
Art 10(6) ... 107
Art 11 ... 107
Art 13 ... 97
Art 15 ... 112
Art 19(1) ... 106
Art 27(1) ... 106
Art 33 ... 108
Art 46 ... 105
Art 47 ... 105
Art 49 ... 106
Art 50 ... 107
Art 52 ... 106
Art 53 ... 106
Art 56(1) ... 110
Art 58(1) ... 110, 116
Art 60(2) ... 109
Art 62(4) ... 109
Art 73(1) ... 109
Art 74(1) ... 112
Art 76 ... 111
Art 76(1) ... 110
Art 76(8) ... 111
Art 76(10) ... 111
Art 78 ... 111
Art 80 ... 111
Art 83(1) ... 111
Art 87 ... 110, 116
Art 87(1) ... 115, 116
Art 92 ... 115
Art 101 ... 427
Art 110 ... 114
Art 110(3) ... 114
Art 111 ... 114
Art 121(1) ... 97
Art 121(2) ... 97
Art 121(3) ... 97
Art 136 ... 117, 502
Art 137 ... 117
Arts 141–145 ... 117
Art 160 ... 117
Art 194 ... 266
Art 283(1) ... 279, 280
Art 284 ... 283
Art 293 ... 109
Annex II ... 111

Annex II, art 4 . . . 111
Annex VI . . . 288
Annex VII . . . 288
Annex VIII . . . 288
UN Convention to Combat Desertification in those Countries Experiencing Serious Drought and/or Desertification, Particularly in Africa 1994 (UNCCD) . . . 469, 474
Preamble . . . 469
Art 1(b) . . . 469
Art 5(b) . . . 469
Art 9(1) . . . 469
Art 18(1) . . . 469
Annex I, Art 6 . . . 469
Annex II, Art 3(1) . . . 469
Annex III, Art 2(c) . . . 469
Annex V, Art 2(i) . . . 469
UN Covenant on Civil and Political Rights 1966 (ICCPR) . . . 68, 72, 161, 217, 239, 291, 301, 327, 330, 376, 408, 410, 412, 414
Common Art 1 . . . 40, 68, 69
Art 2 . . . 412
Art 2(1) . . . 412
Art 2(3) . . . 410
Art 6 . . . 376, 377, 378
Art 9(1) . . . 378
Art 14(5) . . . 227
Art 16 . . . 292
Optional Protocol . . . 163, 410, 414
Optional Protocol, Art 1 . . . 412
UN Covenant on Economic, Social and Cultural Rights 1966 (ICESCR) . . . 68, 72, 301, 308, 327, 330, 408, 410, 413, 414
Common Art 1 . . . 40, 68, 69
Art 40 . . . 292
Optional Protocol 2008 . . . 414
UN Declaration on Friendly Relations 1970 . . . 41, 46, 47, 49, 54, 55, 58, 60, 61, 62, 63, 65, 74, 98, 165, 200, 267, 330, 363, 421, 462
§§161–165 . . . 55
§162 . . . 55
§§202–203 . . . 55
§205 . . . 55
§206 . . . 55
§§207–209 . . . 55
Principle 1, §6 . . . 300
Principle 1, §10 . . . 59
Principle 2, §3 . . . 61
Principle 2, §4 . . . 61
Principle 2, §5 . . . 61
Principle 3, §2 . . . 56
Principle 5, §1 . . . 69
Principle 5, §2 . . . 69
Principle 5, §4 . . . 68, 69
Principle 5, §5 . . . 69
UN Framework Convention on Climate Change 1992 (UNFCCC) . . . 474, 475, 476, 481
Art 3(1) . . . 467
Art 3(4) . . . 469
Art 12 . . . 479

Art 14 . . . 478
Annex I . . . 476, 478
UNCITRAL Arbitration Rules . . . 525
UNECE Convention on Long-Range Transboundary Air Pollution 1979 (LRTAP) . . . 474, 475, 476, 480
Gothenburg Protocol . . . 476
Protocols 1–8 . . . 475
Universal Declaration of Human Rights 1948 (UDHR) . . . 72, 217, 327, 330, 408–9
Art 3 . . . 377
Art 9 . . . 378
Art 28 . . . 409
US Model BIT (2012)
Art 1 . . . 523
Vienna Convention on Consular Relations 1963 . . . 66, 135, 200, 240
Art 41(1) . . . 135
Art 41(2) . . . 135
Art 49 . . . 135
Art 50 . . . 135
Optional Protocol, Art 1 . . . 287
Vienna Convention on Diplomatic Relations 1961 . . . 133, 200, 240
Art 9 . . . 134
Art 29 . . . 9
Art 31 . . . 134
Art 31(1) . . . 13
Art 34 . . . 9
Art 34(a)–(f) . . . 134
Art 38(1) . . . 134
Art 39(2) . . . 135
Art 40(1) . . . 135
Optional Protocol, Art 1 . . . 287
Vienna Convention on Succession of States in respect of State property, Archives and Debts 1983 . . . 89
Art 40 . . . 89
Vienna Convention on Succession of States in respect of Treaties 1978 . . . 88, 201, 205
Art 2(1) . . . 88
Art 12 . . . 88, 201
Art 34 . . . 88
Art 35 . . . 88
Vienna Convention on the Law of Treaties 1969 (VCLT) . . . 200, 204, 205, 206, 210, 211, 212, 213, 214, 215, 216, 217, 222, 234, 235, 237, 238, 259, 282, 300
Art 1 . . . 205
Art 2(1)(a) . . . 206
Art 2(1)(c) . . . 206
Art 4 . . . 205
Art 7(1)(a) . . . 207
Art 7(1)(b) . . . 207
Art 7(2) . . . 207
Art 7(2)(b) . . . 207
Art 7(2)(c) . . . 207
Art 8 . . . 207
Art 9(1) . . . 207
Art 9(2) . . . 207

Art 10 . . . 207
Art 12 . . . 208
Art 13 . . . 208
Art 14 . . . 208
Art 15 . . . 208
Art 16 . . . 209
Art 18(a) . . . 208
Arts 19–23 . . . 210
Art 21(3) . . . 210
Art 24(1) . . . 208
Art 25 . . . 209
Art 26 . . . 65, 209
Art 26(4) . . . 208
Art 27 . . . 222
Art 28 . . . 209, 255
Art 29 . . . 209
Art 30 . . . 210
Arts 31–33 . . . 212
Art 31 . . . 213, 354
Art 31(1) . . . 66, 212
Art 32 . . . 213
Art 33 . . . 213
Art 33(4) . . . 213
Arts 34–36 . . . 172
Arts 35–36 . . . 209
Art 40 . . . 214
Art 41 . . . 214
Art 44(5) . . . 215, 238
Art 45 . . . 215
Art 47 . . . 207, 215
Art 48 . . . 215
Art 49 . . . 215
Art 50 . . . 215, 235
Art 51 . . . 215
Art 52 . . . 201, 215
Art 53 . . . 48, 205, 215, 234, 235
Art 54 . . . 215
Art 56 . . . 217
Art 60 . . . 201, 216, 266
Art 60(5) . . . 216, 300
Art 61 . . . 217
Art 62 . . . 201, 217
Art 62(1)(a) . . . 217
Art 62(1)(b) . . . 217
Art 62(2)(a) . . . 217
Art 62(2)(b) . . . 217
Art 64 . . . 205, 217, 235
Art 65 . . . 215
Art 66(a) . . . 235, 287
Art 66(b) . . . 282
Annex, Art 5 . . . 282
Annex, Art 6 . . . 282

Vienna Convention on the Law of Treaties between States and International Organizations or between International Organizations 1986 (not yet in force) . . . 65, 205, 234
Preamble . . . 65
Art 26 . . . 65
Art 66.2 . . . 235
Vienna Convention on the Protection of the Ozone Layer 1985 . . . 474, 476
Art 2(2) . . . 467
Art 11 . . . 478
Washington Treaty on short-range missiles 1987 . . . 329
Warsaw Pact 1955 . . . 320
WHO International Health Regulations 2005 . . . 119, 120
Art 43 . . . 119
World Heritage Convention 1972 (WHC) *See* Convention Concerning the Protection of the World Cultural and Natural Heritage, 16 November 1972 (World Heritage Convention (WHC))
WTO Agreement *See* Marrakesh Agreement establishing the World Trade Organization 1994 (WTO Agreement)
WTO Agreement on Implementation of Article VII of the General Agreement on Tariffs and Trade 1994 (Anti-Dumping Agreement) . . . 510, 512, 515
Art 15 . . . 515
WTO Agreement on Import Licensing Procedures . . . 510, 512
WTO Agreement on Preshipment Inspection . . . 510
WTO Agreement on Rules of Origin . . . 510, 512
WTO Agreement on Safeguards . . . 510
WTO Agreement on Subsidies and Countervailing Measures (SCM Agreement) . . . 510
Arts 3–9 . . . 515
Arts 10–23 . . . 515
Art 27 . . . 515
WTO Agreement on Technical Barriers to Trade (TBT Agreement) . . . 510, 511, 512, 513
WTO Agreement on Textiles and Clothing . . . 510
WTO Agreement on Trade-Related Investment Measures (TRIMs) . . . 510
WTO Agreement on the Application of Sanitary and Phytosanitary Measures (SPS Agreement) . . . 510, 511, 512
WTO Agreement Trade Facilitation Agreement (TFA) . . . 512

PART I
ORIGINS AND FOUNDATIONS OF THE INTERNATIONAL COMMUNITY

PART I

1
THE MAIN LEGAL FEATURES OF THE INTERNATIONAL COMMUNITY

1.1 INTRODUCTION

We all live within the framework of national legal orders. We therefore tend to assume that each legal system should be modelled on State law, or at least strongly resemble it. Accordingly, and almost unwittingly, we take the view that all legal systems should address themselves to individuals or groups of individuals, and in addition that they should include certain centralized institutions responsible for making law, adjudicating disputes, and enforcing legal norms.

However, the picture offered by the international community is significantly different. This enquiry should therefore begin with a note of warning. The features of the world community are quite unique. Failure to grasp this crucial fact would inevitably entail a serious misinterpretation of the operation of law on this community.

1.2 THE NATURE OF INTERNATIONAL LEGAL SUBJECTS

The first salient feature of international law is that most of its rules aim at regulating the behaviour of States, not that of individuals. States are the principal actors on the international scene. They are legal entities, aggregates of human beings dominated by an apparatus that wields authority over them. Their general goals are distinct from the goals of each individual or group. Each State owns and controls a separate territory; and each is held together by political, economic, cultural (and frequently also ethnic or religious) links.

Within States, individuals are the principal legal subjects, and such legal entities as public corporations, private associations, etc. are merely secondary subjects whose possible suppression would not result in the demise of the whole legal system. In the international community the reverse holds true: States are the primary subjects and, despite major developments in the second half of the twentieth century and the beginning of the twenty-first, individuals play a limited role (see **8.2** and **Chapters 18** and **19**). The latter are as puny Davids confronted by overpowering Goliaths holding all the instruments of power.

Although the protagonists of international life are States as legal entities or corporate structures, of course they can only operate through individuals, who do not act on their own account but as State officials, as the vehicles of the structures to which they belong. Thus, for instance, if a treaty of extradition is concluded by France with China, this deal should not blind us to what actually happens, namely that the international instrument is brought into being by individuals and is subsequently implemented by individuals. The agreement is negotiated by diplomats belonging to the two States; their Ministers of Foreign Affairs sign the treaty; the instrument of ratification is formally approved and signed by the Heads of State, if necessary after authorization by parliamentary assemblies. Once the treaty has entered into force, it is implemented by the courts of each country (indeed, it is generally for the courts to grant or refuse extradition in each particular case) and, if required, also by officials of the respective Ministries of Justice.

Similarly, a State may consider that another country has committed an internationally wrongful act, and therefore decides to react by resorting to peaceful reprisals (today called countermeasures; see **14.2**) such as the expulsion of all the nationals of the State in question. This response is decided upon and carried out by individuals acting as State agents: the decision is normally taken, at the suggestion of the Foreign Minister, by the Minister for Home Affairs, after possible deliberation by the Cabinet; the actual expulsion is carried out by police officers or officials of other enforcement agencies.

Indeed, in international law more than in any other field, the phenomenon of the 'fictitious person' manifests itself in a conspicuous form: individuals engage in transactions or perform acts not in their personal capacity, that is to protect or further their own interests, but on behalf of collectivities or a multitude of individuals.

Why is it that the world community consists of sovereign and independent States, while human beings as such play a lesser role? We shall see in **Chapter 2** how the international community evolved and how, after the first modern States (England, France, and Spain) came into being in the fifteenth century, the various communities in Europe and elsewhere gradually consolidated and 'hardened' into States. It may suffice now to stress that this powerful drive has been a constant and salient feature of the world community, so much so that most individuals now belong to one State or another: the world population of about 7.7 billion human beings is currently divided up amongst nearly two hundred States. In the Middle Ages it was usual to say that outside the Church no salvation could be found (*extra Ecclesiam nulla salus*)—at least, this was what the Church encouraged people to believe. Today it could be maintained with greater truthfulness that without the protection of a State human beings are likely to endure more suffering and hardship than what is likely to be their lot in the normal course of events—witness the plight of stateless persons, which has only lately been taken up by international institutions. In the decades to come, this may come to be said of cities, where most of the world population is expected to live. That would have profound implications for international law that are only now starting to be perceived.[1]

1.3 THE LACK OF A CENTRAL AUTHORITY, AND DECENTRALIZATION OF LEGAL 'FUNCTIONS'

National legal systems are highly developed. In addition to substantive rules, which enjoin citizens to behave in a certain way, sophisticated organizational rules have evolved. Special machinery exists in relation to the 'life' of the legal order. These developments resulted from the emergence within the State community of a group of individuals who succeeded in wielding effective power: they considered it convenient to create a special structure

---

[1] Reflecting this prospective development, a new study group was established in 2017 by the International Law Association (ILA) focusing on 'The Role of Cities in International Law'. On this issue see J. Nijman, 'The Renaissance of the City as a Global Actor: The Role of Foreign Policy and International Law in the Construction of Cities as Global Actors' in G. Hellman, A. Fahrmeir, and M. Vec (eds), *The Transformation of Foreign Policy* (Oxford: Oxford University Press, 2016), 209.

aimed at institutionalizing that power and crystallizing the relationships between the ruling group and their fellow members. In devising the institutional apparatus, a common pattern evolved in all modern States. First, the use of force by members of the community was forbidden, except for emergency situations such as self-defence (the right to use force to impede unlawful violence which would otherwise be unavoidable); States monopolized lawful coercion. Secondly, the central organs acting on behalf of the whole community were responsible for the three main functions typical of any legal system (law-making, law determination, and law enforcement). Accordingly, first the monarch and subsequently an assembly (generally called a parliament) held the power to create and modify law, courts ascertained breaches of law, and special bodies of professionals (police officers) were the law enforcers. It should be added that these were functions proper and not simple powers. For all these bodies had to exercise their powers in the interest of the whole community and not in their own interest; they were vested with a power but also a legal duty to make the law, to establish whether legal rules had been breached, and to enforce them, if necessary.

By contrast, in the international community no State or group of States has managed to hold the lasting power required to impose its will on the whole world community. Power is fragmented and dispersed. True, political and military alliances, and even empires, have occasionally emerged, or a strong convergence of interests between two or more members of the community has evolved. However, these have not hardened into a permanent power structure that has lasted until the present day. The relations between the States comprising the international community remain largely *horizontal*. Despite important developments, particularly in international adjudication,[2] no *vertical* structure has as yet crystallized, as is, in contrast, the rule within the domestic systems of States.

This situation is all the more striking and unsatisfactory today. At present, most components of national structures and of the international community (individuals, groups, associations, State-like entities, multinational corporations, transnational organizations, multinational financial structures, telecommunication networks, and social media and other internet-based networks, etc.) are so closely intertwined across national borders that they constitute the phenomenon usually called 'globalization'. However, the global governance structures initially developed to address the challenges of global problems do not, or no longer, match this factual situation. Relative anarchy still prevails at the level of central management.

The major consequence of the *horizontal* structure of the international community is that organizational rules are at a very embryonic stage. There are no rules setting up special machinery for discharging the three aforementioned functions of States at the global level, nor for entrusting them to any particular body or member of the international community. All three 'functions' are decentralized. Clearly, in relation to the international community, one cannot speak of functions proper: when making law, settling disputes, or enforcing the law, States do not act in the interest and on behalf of the international community; they do not fulfil an obligation, but primarily pursue their own interests. It is for each State, acting together with other States under the impulse of overriding economic, political, or other factors, to set new legal standards or to change them, either deliberately (as in the case of *treaties*, that is, contractual stipulations entered into by two or more States, and only binding upon the contracting parties; see **9.2** and **Chapter 10**) or almost unwittingly (as in the case of *customary law*, that is, general rules evolved through a spontaneous process and binding upon all international legal subjects; see **9.3**). It is for each of them to decide how to

---

[2] For a general assessment see P.-M. Dupuy and J. E. Viñuales, 'The Challenge of Proliferation: An Anatomy of the Debate' in C. Romano, K. Alter, and Y. Shany (eds), *The Oxford Handbook of International Adjudication* (Oxford: Oxford University Press, 2014), 135.

settle disputes or to impel compliance with law, that is, whether to iron out disagreements peacefully or enforce the law unilaterally or collectively. Of particular significance is the fact that each State has the power of 'auto-interpretation' of legal rules, a power that necessarily follows from the absence, as a matter of principle, of courts endowed with general and compulsory jurisdiction. Indeed, on the international plane, despite the major development of adjudication systems in the last 70 years, jurisdiction remains entirely based on consent.

In addition, in classical international law, that is, the law which came into being and governed international relations between—as two symbolic benchmarks—the Peace of Westphalia of 1648 and the First World War (see **2.3** and **2.4**), resort to force was lawful both to enforce a right and to protect economic, political, or other interests. This state of affairs greatly favoured powerful States. As we shall see, some improvements, including the ban on the use of force by individual States, are defining features of the present international legal system (**3.4** and **Chapter 16**).

1.4 COLLECTIVE RESPONSIBILITY

As in all embryonic legal systems where groups play a much greater role than individuals, responsibility for violations of the rules governing the behaviour of States does not fall upon the transgressor (the individual State agent) but on the group to which he or she belongs (the State community). Here again we are confronted with a striking deviation from domestic legal systems.

Within the national legal orders which frame our daily lives, we are accustomed to the notion of individual responsibility: the person who commits a tort or any other breach of law shall suffer the consequences that law attaches to such reprehensible conduct. The responsible person either must make good the damage or, in the case of crime, is liable to a criminal penalty. Such is the rule. There are, however, exceptions. One is 'vicarious responsibility', which comes into play when the law provides that someone bears responsibility for actions performed by another person with whom the former has special ties (e.g. parents are legally responsible for damage caused by their children); sometimes a whole group is held responsible for the acts performed by one of its representatives on behalf of the group (as in the civil liability of corporations for torts).

In the international legal system, the exception becomes the rule. A State official may break international law: for instance, a military commander orders his pilots to intrude upon the airspace of a neighbouring State, or a court disregards an international treaty granting certain rights to foreigners, or a police officer infringes diplomatic immunities by arresting a diplomat or maltreating her. In these and similar cases the wronged State is allowed to take measures against the whole community to which that State official belongs, even though the community has neither carried out nor ordered the infraction. For instance, the State which has become the victim of the international transgression can claim the payment of a sum of money (to be drawn from the State treasury), or it may resort to countermeasures (traditionally called reprisals) damaging individuals other than the actual authors of the offence (e.g. the expulsion of foreigners, the suspension of a commercial treaty, and so on).

Hence, collective responsibility means both that the whole State community is liable for any breach of international law committed by any State official and that the whole State community may suffer from the consequences of the wrongful act (on this matter see **12.7**). A classic illustration is the Corfu incident of 1923. On 27 August 1923, the Italian members of the International Commission charged by the Conference of Ambassadors (a body consisting of diplomats from France, the UK, Italy, and Japan and responsible for the implementation of the peace treaties) to delimit the Graeco-Albanian frontier were killed at Zepi, near the town of Janina, on Greek territory, at the hands of unknown terrorists. Two days later, Italy requested Greece to formally apologize, hold a solemn religious ceremony, pay honour to the Italian flag and military honours to the dead, conduct a most serious inquiry within five days, inflict the death penalty on all culprits, and pay an indemnity of 50 million Italian lire within five days. The next day the Greek government responded that it regarded as unjust the Italian charges that Greece was responsible for the assassination of the Italians; it also dismissed the requests concerning a criminal inquiry, the imposition of the death penalty, and the payment of compensation. At the same time, Greece submitted the matter to the Council of the League of Nations, with a view to an amicable settlement of the matter. Nevertheless, the next day upon the orders of the Italian dictator, Mussolini, Italian ships bombarded Corfu, causing numerous casualties among civilians (16 people were killed and more than three times that number wounded); Italian troops occupied the island, to force Greece to comply with the Italian requests. In the event, following the initial report by an international commission of inquiry it had set up, the Conference of Ambassadors found that Greece had been negligent in pursuing the perpetrators of the crime; on 27 September Italian troops evacuated Corfu, and Italy was awarded in compensation 50 million lire (which Greece had previously deposited as security in the Swiss National Bank, on the understanding that the Permanent Court of International Justice (PCIJ) would determine the amount of the indemnity due; a determination which, however, never took place). Thus, even assuming that Greece was responsible, a matter that was never fully clarified, Greek civilians and the Greek Treasury bore the brunt of the consequences of the assassination perpetrated by some bandits at Zepi.[3]

Among similarly instructive instances of collective responsibility, one may mention the reaction, in 1982, to the unlawful invasion by Argentina of the Falklands (Malvinas). The (then ten) members of the (then) European Economic Communities adopted economic countermeasures (essentially the suspension of imports of textiles and meat from Argentina) and the US followed suit, by among other things suspending new export-import credits and guarantees; the parties adversely affected by such sanctions were individuals and corporations, that is, persons and entities other than the Argentine dictatorship that had decided the invasion. Another illustration of collective responsibility can be seen in the US air strikes on Tripoli and Benghazi on 14 April 1986 as a response to the bombing in Berlin, organized by Libyan agents on 5 April, of the *La Belle* disco, where two US soldiers and a Turkish woman were killed and more than 200 people were wounded. According to Libya, 41 people died and 226 were wounded as a result of those air strikes. In 2001, the Berlin District Court ruled that the Libyan secret service was behind the bombing of the Berlin disco, and the ruling was confirmed in 2004 by the German Supreme Court in *La Belle—Anschlag*.[4] Yet another instance can be found in the economic sanctions adopted in 1992 by States against Libya, at the request of the UN Security Council (SC resolution 748–1992) and as a reaction to the terrorist act at Lockerbie; these measures included the blocking of air communications with Libya; they clearly affected all Libyans as well as

---

[3] For a contemporaneous report of this incident see [Anonymous], 'L'incidente italo-greco e l'occupazione di Corfu' (1924) 16 *Rivista di diritto internazionale* 337.

[4] BBC reported that on 10 August 2004 Libya concluded an agreement to pay a total of $35 million compensation into a US compensation fund for relatives of victims of the terror attacks blamed on Tripoli, including the attack against the Berlin disco: BBC News, 31 October 2008, online at: http://news.bbc.co.uk/2/hi/americas/7703110.stm.

interests of Libyan corporations, in addition to Libyan State officials. A number of more recent cases have been identified and discussed in the reports of the Special Rapporteur of the Human Rights Council on the negative impact of unilateral coercive measures on the enjoyment of human rights.[5] They include a discussion of the 50-year-old US embargo on Cuba, which, after being lifted by the Obama administration, was re-introduced by the subsequent administration, and of the severe restrictions (including restriction of maritime, air, and land movement to and from Qatar; blacklisting of individuals; and restrictions on financial transactions) imposed in June 2017 by Bahrain, Egypt, Saudi Arabia, the United Arab Emirates, and Yemen against Qatar, allegedly for its support of terrorist organizations in the region.[6]

Leaving aside the lawfulness of each of the measures reviewed, which requires a case-by-case analysis, the cases mentioned are illustrative of a form of responsibility analogous to that found in rudimentary legal systems.[7] Indeed, the law governing the international community is typical of embryonic societies, with the aggravating circumstance—rightly emphasized by Hoffmann[8]—that, unlike such communities (which are highly integrated, with all the ensuing benefits), the world community is largely based on the non-integration of its subjects, from the viewpoint of their social interrelations.

Later on we shall see that two new trends have significantly altered the picture of classical international law. First, next to traditional State accountability for 'ordinary' breaches of international rules, a new class of State responsibility has emerged for gross violations of fundamental rules enshrining essential values (so-called 'aggravated' responsibility: see **12.8**). Secondly, while in earlier times the only category of individuals criminally liable under international law was that of pirates, since the end of the nineteenth century *individual responsibility* has gradually evolved. It was considered that serious offences committed by State officials in exceptional circumstances, for example war crimes, should entail the personal liability of their authors in addition to the possible international responsibility of the State to which they belonged. The category of war crimes gradually expanded after the Second World War and further categories were added: those of crimes against peace (chiefly aggression) and of crimes against humanity and genocide (see **Chapter 19**). However, despite these momentous advances, collective responsibility still remains the rule.

1.5 THE NEED FOR MOST INTERNATIONAL RULES TO BE TRANSLATED INTO NATIONAL LEGISLATION

As we shall see in **Chapter 11**, international rules to be applied by States within their own legal systems generally need to be incorporated into national law. This is because the international community is composed of sovereign States, each eager to control the individuals

---

[5] Report of the Special Rapporteur of the Human Rights Council on the negative impact of unilateral coercive measures on the enjoyment of human rights, 29 August 2017, UN Doc. A/72/370.

[6] At the request of Qatar, the International Court of Justice has indicated provisional measures. See *Application of the International Convention on the Elimination of All Forms of Racial Discrimination (Qatar v United Arab Emirates) (Provisional Measures)*.

[7] Kelsen was one of the first authors to draw attention to this phenomenon. He pointed out that: 'collective responsibility exists in case of blood revenge which is directed not only against the murderer but also against all the members of his family. Collective responsibility is established in the Ten Commandments where Yahweh threatens to punish the children and the children's children for the sins of their fathers' (*Principles*, 9).

[8] S. Hoffmann, 'International Law and the Control of Force' in K. Deutsch and S. Hoffmann (eds), *The Relevance of International Law* (Garden City, NY: Anchor Books, 1971), 36.

subject to its jurisdiction and consequently to decide on the extent to which they may hold rights and obligations. Hence, when international rules need to be applied within a State, or by a State official, in most cases they must be turned into municipal law.

Thus, for instance, for an international rule forbidding the use of certain categories of weapon (such as chemical or biological weapons) to take effect, the Minister of Defence and the military commanders of a given State must be under a national obligation to comply with the rule, become cognizant of the scope of the rule, and take all the necessary measures to implement it. A provision such as Article 29 of the Vienna Convention of 1961 on diplomatic relations[9] obliges the enforcement agencies of a State to refrain from arresting or detaining foreign diplomats, and to take all necessary measures to prevent undue attacks on them. Similarly, Article 34 of the same Convention[10] requires the tax authorities of the 'receiving State' (that is the State where they perform their diplomatic activity) to take the requisite regulatory or administrative steps to exempt foreign diplomats from all the dues and taxes to which they may not be subjected.

It is therefore apparent that most international rules cannot work without the constant help, co-operation, and support of national legal systems. Exaggerating somewhat (on account of his strictly dualistic approach), the German publicist H. Triepel observed in 1923 that international law is like a field marshal who can only give orders to generals. It is solely through the generals that his orders can reach the troops. If the generals do not transmit them to the soldiers in the field, he will lose the battle.[11]

1.6 THE RANGE OF STATES' FREEDOM OF ACTION

To illustrate yet another typical feature of the international community it is useful to refer once again, by way of comparison, to domestic legal systems.

In most national orders, individuals—the primary legal subjects—enjoy great freedom in their private transactions. They can variously enter into agreements with other persons, or refrain from so doing, or they can set up companies, create associations, and so on. Their broad contractual freedom is not unfettered, however, in that central authorities usually place legal restraints upon them. Thus, for instance, one cannot make private transactions which are contrary to public order and morals (such as a contract whereby one party undertakes to hand over to another a next of kin, for the purposes of prostitution); if such a transaction is made, it is null and void. It should be noted that national public orders include norms prohibiting physical persons from disposing of their body or their freedom. Thus, a contract whereby one party undertakes to mutilate his body or to deliver to another party one of his limbs is normally contrary to public order and consequently null and void. The same consideration applies to a contract whereby one party undertakes to commit suicide or to submit permanently to a position akin to slavery in relation to another party. Every domestic system contains a core of values that members of the community cannot disregard, not even when they engage in private transactions *inter se*. In the case of any such

---

[9] Vienna Convention on Diplomatic Relations, 14 April 1964, 500 UNTS 95, Article 29: 'The person of a diplomatic agent shall be inviolable. He shall not be liable to any form of arrest or detention. The receiving State shall treat him with due respect and shall take all appropriate steps to prevent any attack on his person, freedom or dignity.'

[10] Ibid., at Article 34: 'A diplomatic agent shall be exempt from all dues, taxes, personal or real, national, regional or municipal, except for certain categories of taxes enumerated in the same provision.'

[11] H. Triepel, 'Les rapports entre le droit interne et le droit international' (1923) 1 *RCADI* 73, at 106.

disregard, the response of the central authorities is to make the private undertaking devoid of legal effect. *A fortiori*, individuals are not allowed to depart from certain basic values, which are held in such high esteem as to be embodied in rules governing criminal behaviour. If two or more persons enter into an agreement for the setting up of a criminal association, not only will their agreement be null and void, they will also incur penal responsibility and are punishable accordingly. A third set of restrictions on individual freedom derives from all the norms of public law concerning the functioning of State institutions: thus, for instance, in a State where political elections take place by law once every four years, citizens are not free to vote whenever they would like to do so. Limitations also derive from constitutional rules restraining the exercise of certain rights and liberties (as in the case of freedom of thought or association), and from labour laws (which often restrict freedom of contract in labour relations with regard to working time and working conditions, normally with a view to protecting the weaker party).

By contrast, subjects of the international community enjoy wide-ranging freedom of action. In classical international law, their freedom was in fact untrammelled. The international legal system was not interested in requesting States to give their internal legal order a specific content. With a few exceptions (for instance, international customary rules on the treatment of foreigners or on immunities to be granted to foreign diplomats), States were completely free to decide upon the tenor and scope of their national legislation. States also enjoyed complete freedom as regards the conduct of their foreign policy. It was up to them to decide whether or not to enter into international agreements; they also were free to choose their partners and the contents of agreements. They could shape their international relations as they pleased; they could recognize a new State or withhold recognition; they were free to enter into alliance with one or more States or refrain from doing so. The legal order even authorized States to use as much force as they wished and on any grounds they chose. States could engage in a war or resort to forcible measures short of war, either on the grounds that one of their legal rights had been violated, or because they considered it politically and economically expedient forcibly to attack another State (e.g. in order to occupy and annex part, or the whole, of its territory, or to set up a government subservient to their commands, etc.). Law was so 'generous' as also to allow States to intervene in the domestic and international affairs of other members of the world community, either by political pressure or by threatening the use of force, for the purpose of inducing the 'victim' of the intervention to change its policy. A prominent illustration was the blockade of Venezuelan ports by the UK, Germany, and Italy in December 1902, which was subsequently condoned by an arbitral tribunal which decided that these three countries had a right to preferential treatment in the payment of money claims against Venezuela precisely because they had incurred higher costs—the blockade—when enforcing their claims.[12] Furthermore, even when they undertook to submit their legal disputes to arbitration, States usually excluded from the obligation to submit to arbitration all the disputes affecting their 'vital interests', and each State retained the right to decide whether a specific case fell within that category. Freedom in the economic field was even greater. Lack of legal restraints even allowed States to agree with other States that one of them must extinguish itself: they could

---

[12] *The Venezuelan Preferential Case (Germany, Great Britain, Italy, Venezuela et al.)* It has been argued that the arbitral award was an important impetus for the so-called Roosevelt corollary to the Monroe doctrine, namely the claim that the US was entitled to exercise an 'international police power' (military intervention) in the Americas: see M. Maass, 'Catalyst for the Roosevelt Corollary: Arbitrating the 1902–1903 Venezuela Crisis and Its Impact on the Development of the Roosevelt Corollary to the Monroe Doctrine' (2009) 20 *Diplomacy & Statecraft* 383.

conclude an agreement whereby one of them was incorporated into the other; or they could merge; or else one of them could agree to cede a portion of its territory to another State. No imperative rule prohibited self-mutilation or self-destruction.

We have, of course, been speaking of legal freedom. Power politics, the constant need for a balance of power, economic and social considerations, the geographical situation of States, prestige and traditions, as well as other factors—all these conspired to reduce that freedom. Nevertheless, the legal order adopted a laissez-faire attitude, thereby leaving an enormous field of action to individual States.

It is not difficult to understand why international law developed in this way. No State or group of States proved capable of wielding permanent control over the world community so as to impose a set of basic standards of behaviour calculated to govern the action of members. Hence, it was necessary to fall back on a negative regulation, leaving all members free to act as they liked, provided they did not grossly and consistently trespass on the freedom of other members. Clearly, this approach heavily favoured the Great Powers. In practice, international law was modelled in such a way as to legitimize, 'codify', and protect their interests.

The unrestricted freedom of States has been subjected to increasing qualification since the First World War. Three factors account for new developments in this area. First of all, there is the ever-expanding scope of the network of international treaties. Most States are now party to a very large number of treaties impinging upon their domestic legal systems. Consequently, at present most members of the world community are bound to obey a number of obligations that greatly restrict their latitude, as regards both their own internal system and their freedom in the international sphere. Many States have assumed obligations in the field of commercial, political, and judicial co-operation, in the realm of human rights, and so on. Similarly, as far as international action is concerned, many are parties to international organizations, to treaties of alliance, etc. True, all these undertakings derive from treaties; in theory, States can therefore get rid of them if they wish to do so. However, in practice, it is difficult for them to release themselves from all their various commitments: political, economic, diplomatic, military, and psychological factors stand in the way.

A second important reason is the increasing number of legal restrictions on the right to use force. The Covenant of the League of Nations, adopted in June 1919, placed considerable restraints on a number of States. These restraints curtailed the power of these States to wage war. The 1928 Briand-Kellogg Pact, promoted by the US and France, reinforced and extended them to a larger (and, in some respects, different) group of States by 'outlawing war' in their relations. They became radical and sweeping in 1945, when the UN Charter required members to refrain from using or threatening the use of any sort of military force, with or without the label of 'war'. The ban on the use of force has now turned into a principle encompassing the whole international community, although the resulting limitation on State freedom is unfortunately beset with loopholes, which chiefly affect the enforcement mechanisms (see **3.4** and **Chapter 16**).

Thirdly, in the 1960s a customary rule evolved in the international community to the effect that certain general norms have greater legal force than other rules, in that States cannot derogate from them through international agreements. This set of peremptory norms was called *jus cogens* (see **11.4**). It follows that States are now duty-bound to refrain from entering into agreements providing for one of the activities prohibited by peremptory norms; if they nevertheless do so, their agreements will be null and void.

However, as we shall see throughout this book, despite these major advances, in reality and at least in some respects, the condition of the present international community is not far removed from that of classical international law.

1.7 THE OVERRIDING ROLE OF EFFECTIVENESS

International law is a realistic legal system. It takes account of existing power relationships and endeavours to translate them into legal rules. It is largely based on the principle of effectiveness, that is to say, it provides that only those claims and situations which are effective can produce legal consequences. A situation is effective if it is solidly implanted in real life. Thus, for instance, if a new State emerges from secession, it will be able to claim international status only after it is apparent that it undisputedly controls a specific territory and the human community living there. Control over the State community must be real and durable. The same consideration holds true for insurgents. If civil strife breaks out within a State, the rebels cannot claim international rights and duties unless they exercise effective authority over a part of the territory concerned. Similarly, in the case of the military occupation of a foreign territory, the occupying Power cannot claim all the rights and privileges deriving from the international law of warfare, until the territory is actually placed under that Power's authority and it is in a position to assert itself.

The principle of effectiveness permeates the whole body of rules making up international law. Under classical international law, one of its corollaries has long been that legal fictions had no place on the international scene. New situations were not recognized as legally valid unless they could be seen to rest on a firm display of authority. No new regime could claim international legitimacy if it failed to demonstrate that it had firmly supplanted the former authority. Force was the principal source of legitimation.

One may well wonder why force has played such an overriding role in the world community, giving the international legal system a 'conservative' slant. The answer probably lies in the fact that power has always been diffused and a superior authority capable of legitimizing new situations has not emerged, nor have States evolved a core of legally binding principles serving this purpose (because they are too divided to be able to do so). In consequence, legal rules must of necessity rely upon force as the sole standard by which new facts and events are to be legally appraised.

The foregoing observations essentially apply to the *traditional* setting of the international community. Since the First World War a number of States have attempted to make 'legality' prevail over sheer force or authority. The main impetus came from the so-called 'Stimson doctrine', named after the (then) US Secretary of State Henry Stimson who, in a letter to Japan and China of 7 January 1932, stated that no de facto situation obtained by force would be recognized by the United States. The letter concerned the Japanese forceful seizure of Chinese territory in Manchuria.[13] This doctrine suggested withholding legitimation from certain situations which, although effective, offended values that were increasingly regarded as fundamental.

1.8 TRADITIONAL AND NEW TRENDS

1.8.1 RECIPROCITY AS THE BASIS OF INTERNATIONAL RIGHTS AND OBLIGATIONS

The international community has long been characterized by a horizontal structure and the lack of strong political, ideological, and economic links between its members. These features have thus resulted in the tendency for every State to be self-seeking. Self-interest has held sway.

---

[13] For two contemporaneous accounts of the legal basis of the Stimson doctrine see A. McNair, 'The Stimson Doctrine of Non-Recognition' (1933) 14 *BYIL* 65; Q. Wright, 'The Legal Foundation of the Stimson Doctrine' (1935) 4 *Pacific Affairs* 439.

This phenomenon is also apparent in the way substantive rules govern the behaviour of States. International rules, even though they address themselves to all States (in the case of customs) or groups of States (in the case of multilateral treaties), confer rights or impose obligations on *pairs of States*. As a result, each State has a right or an obligation in relation to one other State at a time. That is so even in the case of customary rules imposing obligations *erga omnes*, that is, towards all other States. This is because, in their concrete application, they boil down to standards applying to pairs of States. One major illustration from classical international law is the principle requiring respect of sovereignty. Each State could claim from all other States full respect for its territorial integrity and political independence. Yet, as soon as this norm was violated, the ensuing legal relationship linked only the aggrieved State and the offending party. Indeed, once a State had infringed the sovereignty of another State, it was for the victim to claim reparation. Other States could intervene in support of the victim. But the underlying conception of classical international law was that, even for obligations that today we call *erga omnes*, the basis of obligation was reciprocity.[14] By way of illustration, the US response—through the Stimson doctrine—to the Japanese aggression against China in 1931 emphasized the non-opposability to the US of any situation de facto or *de jure* arising from such aggression.

The same holds true, in modern international law, for most areas of international regulation. For example, although the rules on diplomatic immunities are general in character and directed to all States, in their specific operation, they split into a number of binary rules based on considerations of reciprocity, each regulating a pair of States. Thus, for instance, the rule that '[a] diplomatic agent shall enjoy immunity from the criminal jurisdiction of the receiving State' (codified in the 1961 Vienna Convention on Diplomatic Relations, Article 31(1)) entails that in the relations between, say, the UK and Indonesia, either State has the right to claim from the other that its diplomatic agents be immune from the criminal jurisdiction of the other State.

The same reasoning applies to most international treaties. For instance, a treaty on international trade providing for the establishment of a certain customs duty on a particular good confers on each contracting party the right to demand of all the other contracting parties fulfilment of that obligation; as soon as a contracting party breaches that obligation with regard to goods imported from another contracting party, the latter is entitled to claim reparation for that breach. In practice, this multilateral treaty can be broken down into a set of substantially similar bilateral treaties, each regulating the relationships between a particular pair of States. It is as if each contracting party were bound by as many bilateral treaties as there are other contracting parties.

Plainly, we are far from the situation of all national legal systems. There, in cases of serious breach (e.g. most criminal offences), a representative of the entire community (the Public Prosecutor or a similar institution) can initiate legal proceedings irrespective of the attitude or action of the injured party. The system prevailing in international law has a number of serious drawbacks, among them the fact that the reaction to a wrong ultimately depends on whether the victim is stronger than or at least as strong as the culpable State. In the final analysis, respect for law is made dependent on power.

One of the few exceptions to this network of legal rights and obligations in classical international law was constituted by the general rule on piracy. This rule authorized every State to seize and capture pirates on the high seas, whatever their nationality and whether or not they had attacked one of its ships or threatened to do so. Thus, this rule (which imposed on

---

[14] See M. Virally, 'Le principe de réciprocité dans le droit international contemporain' (1967) 122 *RCADI* 1. Two decades later, the same intuition was formulated in the language of international relations by R. Keohane, 'Reciprocity in international relations' (1986) 40 *International Organization* 1.

all individuals in the world the obligation to refrain from piracy) granted a right to all States unconnected to actual damage. However, when exercising this right, States did not act on behalf of the world community, for the protection of a community value; rather they acted merely to safeguard a *joint interest*. As a British court put it in 1817 in *Le Louis, Forest*, pirates are 'enemies of the human race, renouncing every country, and ravaging every country in its coasts and vessels indiscriminately, and thereby creating universal terror and alarm'. Hence, the right to capture piratical vessels 'has existed upon the ground of repelling injury, and as a measure of self-defence' (*Le Louis, Forest*, at 704–5). This proposition clearly spells out that the right to capture pirates rested on both the joint interest of all States and that of each one of them to fight a common danger (and consequent damage), be it real or potential.

An analogous situation concerned the rights of riparian States with regard to navigable international rivers in classical international law. Under the customary law developed since 1815, every riparian State had a right to free navigation and to equality of treatment. Consequently, if one of those States performed an act preventing another State's free navigation, it simultaneously infringed upon the right of any and all other riparian State(s), whether or not it actually caused damage to them (with the consequence that, at least in principle, any other riparian State could demand cessation of the wrongful act). This is because, as the PCIJ put it in 1929 in *Territorial Jurisdiction of the International Commission of the River Oder*, the 'community of interest in a navigable river becomes the basis of a common legal right, the essential features of which are the perfect equality of all riparian States in the use of the whole course of the river and the exclusion of any preferential privilege of any one riparian State in relation to the others' (at 27).

1.8.2 COMMUNITY OBLIGATIONS AND COMMUNITY RIGHTS

In the *present* international community, traditional rules based on reciprocity still constitute the bulk of international law. Nevertheless, one can also find new rules with a different content and import. A number of treaties, many of which came into being after the First World War and more particularly in the aftermath of the Second World War, provide for obligations that are incumbent upon each State towards all other contracting parties and which are in no way reciprocal.

This category of rules has evolved from the emergence of *new values* that the international community has come to regard as being worthy of special protection. Thus, after the First World War, as a result of the ideological and political pressure of socialist doctrines, and also because, following the catastrophe of war, the condition of workers was growing worse, the lot of workers was regarded as deserving greater international action. Consequently, the International Labour Organization (ILO) was set up and international conventions for the protection of workers were drafted and adopted, their implementation being under the scrutiny of the ILO.[15] Similarly, after the Second World War, as a reaction to the mass murder by the Nazis of ethnic and religious groups (chiefly Jews, as well as the Roma people) and the total disregard for the basic human rights of thousands of individuals both in Germany and elsewhere, the Allies decided to create better safeguards against genocide and other egregious violations of human rights. By the same token, the Nazi aggression against a number of European States and the attack by Japan on the US

---

[15] For a review of the literature on the ILO see J. van Daele, 'The International Labour Organization (ILO) in Past and Present Research' (2008) 53 *International Review of Social History* 485. Van Daele refers to E. J. Solano (ed.), *Labour as an International Problem* (London: Macmillan, 1920), which includes essays from the ILO intellectual architects, George Barnes, Emile Vandervelde, Harold Butler, Sophy Sanger, Arthur Fontaine, Minoru Oka, and James Shotwell.

prompted the UN to enact a sweeping ban on all forms of aggression. As stated earlier, all these new values resulted in numerous international treaties as well as a few international customary rules (see **Chapters 3, 18,** and **19**).

Community obligations possess the following unique features: (i) they are obligations protecting fundamental values (such as peace, human rights, self-determination of peoples, protection of health and the environment); (ii) they are obligations *erga omnes*, that is towards all the member States of the international community (or, in the case of multilateral treaties, all the other contracting States); (iii) they are attended by a correlative *right* that belongs to every State (or to every other *contracting* State, in the case of obligations provided for in multilateral treaties); (iv) this right may be exercised by every other (contracting) State, whether or not it has been materially or morally injured by the violation (i.e. all States are deemed to be affected by an impairment of the norm protecting community values); (v) the right is exercised *on behalf of the whole international community* (or the community of the contracting States) to *safeguard fundamental values* of this community. For example, when a State makes a remonstrance to, or forcefully protests against, another State on account of atrocities committed by the latter against its own nationals, and demands the immediate cessation of those atrocities, it is not motivated by the desire to safeguard its own interests or to prevent any possible future damage; its sole (or primary) purpose is to vindicate humanitarian values on behalf of the whole international community. These rights can therefore be termed 'community rights'. However, the existence of community rights arising from community obligations does not depend on the preponderance of the community interest over the individual interest. For example, the due diligence duty to take measures to prevent the spread of a pandemic, such as Ebola or COVID-19, is *erga omnes* in nature, and the corresponding community right to require its performance is based on both community and individual interests.

In a way, this body of values makes up what the Spanish international lawyer Francisco de Vitoria (1483–1546), a follower of modern natural law theory, termed *bonum commune totius orbis*, that is, the common good of the whole world—in other words, the assets and values that are shared by the whole of mankind and to which the particular interests and demands of individual States should yield. As we shall see, this is yet another confirmation that the emergence in modern times of the notions of community obligations and rights (and of the cognate concept of *jus cogens*, see **11.4**) translates into positive law ideas and constructs propounded by the advocates of natural law between the sixteenth and the eighteenth centuries.

How can the 'community rights' we are discussing be exercised? Customary rules do not provide for any particular mechanism. It follows that it is possible to resort to traditional means of redress (diplomatic steps, diplomatic pressure, peaceful countermeasures; see **14.2**). As for treaties, some simply proclaim a right, without specifying the means by which it can be put into effect. The means of redress just mentioned can also be used in such cases. By contrast, a number of other treaties set up special procedures or special machinery to facilitate the task of the claimant State. We shall return to this point later on (see **13.4, 13.5, 13.6,** and **14.4**).[16]

---

[16] In a resolution adopted in 1989, the *Institut de Droit International* (in 63-II *Annuaire* (1990), 338), authoritatively restating and spelling out existing customary law, pointed out that the obligation to ensure observance of fundamental human rights as 'a direct expression of the dignity of the human person' is *erga omnes*; in case of breaches of human rights any other State is empowered to react by means of 'diplomatic representations as well as purely verbal expressions of concern or disapproval', whereas if the breaches are large scale or systematic, other States are entitled to take diplomatic, economic, and other peaceful measures towards the responsible State. Furthermore, as Judge ad hoc Lauterpacht implicitly held in his Separate Opinion in *Genocide (Bosnia and Herzegovina v Yugoslavia (Serbia and Montenegro))*, Further Requests for the Indication of Provisional Measures, §§113–115, under Article I of the 1948 Genocide Convention each contracting party is authorized to react to any acts of genocide by any other contracting State. Customary law restates and broadens these obligations and rights in the area of genocide.

Nevertheless, the significance of the recent emergence of 'community obligations', though considerable, should not be overemphasized.[17] For one thing, the treaties or customary rules laying down these obligations are still relatively rare. For another, even those rules are seldom put into effect.[18] An important feature of the international community, namely the major gap between norms and their actual implementation, is more conspicuous in this area than anywhere else. Although States have the opportunity of acting in the interest of the whole international community, or of all the other contracting parties, they usually prefer to avoid meddling in other States' internal affairs. They end up exercising their 'community rights' only when their own economic, military, health, or political interests are at stake. In the final analysis, most procedures based on State-to-State complaints have ended in failure, or, at least, have not been exploited fully.

1.8.3 ARTICLE 1 COMMON TO THE FOUR 1949 GENEVA CONVENTIONS AS INDICATIVE OF CURRENT MERITS AND FLAWS OF COMMUNITY RIGHTS AND OBLIGATIONS

A telling illustration of the current flaws of community rights and obligations can be seen in Article 1 common to the four Geneva Conventions of 1949 (protecting such 'war victims' as civilians, the wounded and the sick, prisoners of war, etc.: see **17.2.3**), as well as Article 1(1) of the 1977 First Additional Protocol updating the 1949 Convention with respect to international armed conflicts (see **17.2.4**), on which it is therefore worth dwelling at some length.

These provisions stipulate that each contracting State undertakes to respect the four Conventions (and Protocol) 'in all circumstances', and by the same token assumes the obligation 'to ensure respect' for these instruments 'in all circumstances'. Common Article 1 is not a substantive legal provision, that is, a provision that lays down a specific obligation (such as, for instance, Article 12(1) of the First Geneva Convention, whereby '[m]embers of the armed forces and other persons mentioned in the following Article, who are wounded and sick, shall be respected and protected in all circumstances'). In other words, common Article 1 does not provide for a specific conduct with regard to a specific matter. It is not a *primary* rule,[19] that is, a rule that requires legal subjects to perform or abstain from certain actions. Instead, that Article lays down a general obligation relating to *how* all the specific obligations laid down in the Geneva Conventions must be fulfilled by each specific contracting State both as regards its own compliance with those obligations and compliance by other contracting States. Article 1 is thus an 'adjective' provision; it describes the 'modalities' in which the 'verbs' in the primary rules of the Conventions are to be performed. Article 1 thus clarifies the requirements

---

[17] On the various instances of current international protection of 'community interests' see the important considerations by B. Simma, 'From Bilateralism to Community Interest in International Law' (1994) 250 *RCADI* 217, at 256ff.

[18] For two examples where community interests were put into effect see the ICJ in *Questions relating to the Obligation to Prosecute or Extradite (Belgium v Senegal)* and *Whaling in the Antarctic (Australia v Japan: New Zealand intervening)*.

[19] H. L. A. Hart, *The Concept of Law* (Oxford: Clarendon Press, 1961), 78.

of all other provisions, in that the prescribed conduct must not only be performed by each State but, in addition, each State has an obligation to ensure that each other State performs such obligations in all circumstances.[20]

How does Article 1 operate with regard to the other, primary rules? It provides, first, that each contracting State is bound to abide by all the provisions of the Conventions regardless of any misbehaviour of another State party. In other words, it provides that those other (primary) provisions are not subject to the principle of reciprocity; hence, a contracting party may not disregard a provision if another State party breaches that provision to the detriment of the former State. Disregard of a Convention provision by way of countermeasure is not allowed. Secondly, Article 1 provides that each State party is bound to ensure respect for the Conventions by any other contracting State. It follows that (a) the obligation incumbent upon each contracting State to comply with the Conventions' provisions operates towards all the other contracting States. It is an obligation *erga omnes partes* (towards all the other States parties). It also follows that (b) any State party has a *legal claim* to compliance with the Conventions by any other State party. Any contracting State, faced with violations of the Conventions by a belligerent (or, more generally, a party to an armed conflict) may take action and demand cessation of the breach. Thus, we are faced here with community obligations and community rights proper.

Let us now concentrate on this second feature of the legal mechanism instituted by Article 1. It should be clear from the above that, back in 1949, the Geneva Conventions set up an innovative legal system that departed from the traditional principles governing international relations essentially geared to self-interest (reciprocity, bilateralism) and enshrined the principle of community protection of universal values. Each State party to the Conventions, even if it was not involved in or directly affected by an armed conflict, was granted a *legal entitlement* to demand observance of Convention provisions, in that they enshrine respect for fundamental humanitarian values. The *common interest* in compliance with humanitarian treaty rules was thus recognized and translated into a legal mechanism.

However, in 1949 States stopped *halfway*. They did not specify how States parties could exercise that legal entitlement *at the interstate level*; they did not spell out through which international means or according to what interstate modalities that legal entitlement could operate. They only mentioned the system of Protecting Powers (see **17.8.1**), which, however: (i) has not as its primary duty that of ensuring compliance with the law; (ii) is confined to those third States that each of the belligerents accepts (or proposes and the other belligerent accepts); and, in addition, (iii) has been scantily applied, on a number of grounds. Furthermore, (iv) the Conventions envisage only general tasks for the International Committee of the Red Cross (ICRC).

---

[20] This is the interpretation that the authors of International Committee of the Red Cross (ICRC) Commentary, under the general editorship of J. S. Pictet, first propounded; it was taken up both by the UN Tehran Conference on Human Rights in 1968 res. XXIII, §9 of the Preamble ('States Parties to the Red Cross Geneva Conventions sometimes fail to appreciate their responsibility to take steps to ensure the respect of these humanitarian rules in all circumstances by other States, even if they are not themselves directly involved in an armed conflict') and then by the UN General Assembly in res. 2444 (XXIII) of 19 December 1968 (the UN Secretary-General was asked to take steps in consultation with the ICRC, to study 'steps which could be taken to secure the better application' of humanitarian law). The ICJ has confirmed this interpretation in *Nicaragua (Nicaragua v United States of America)*, §220, and *Legal Consequences of the Construction of a Wall in the Occupied Palestinian Territory*, §§158–159.

Thus, by and large, common Article 1 left in the hands of *each contracting State* faced with serious infringements of the Conventions by other States, the decision whether or not to undertake action and, in the affirmative, what form such action should take. However, the Conventions pointed to the possible reaction to serious violations of the Conventions, at the *national* level. The Conventions specified that the courts of each contracting party were endowed with universal jurisdiction over 'grave breaches' of the Conventions (i.e. very serious violations specified in those Conventions), wherever and by whomever perpetrated, on condition that the suspect or accused be present on the territory of the prosecuting contracting State (see **19.3.1**).

It is thus clear that the Conventions set up a universally oriented, or community-oriented mechanism, but did not coherently take the further step of envisaging the establishment of centralized machinery capable of activating and vindicating the community interest. Absent any such machinery, enforcement was left to each individual contracting State, both at the interstate level (relating to action to be taken as between States) and at the national (judicial) level. From community interest one was taken back to bilateralism, to individual action based on national self-interest.

State practice since 1950, when the Conventions entered into force, shows that self-interest and unilateralism have indeed tended to prevail. At the *interstate level*, few States took action, and always at the bilateral level: they sent diplomatic notes, or undertook diplomatic demarches, vis-à-vis belligerents grossly violating the Conventions.[21] As these actions were rarely made public, one cannot gauge their importance and establish whether they had any follow-up. At the *national judicial level*, courts did not act at least until 1994, when, prodded by the establishment of the International Criminal Tribunal for the Former Yugoslavia (ICTY), they started instituting proceedings against alleged authors of crimes in the former Yugoslavia. The ICRC occasionally took steps. When it did so, it normally published appeals to the belligerents concerned as well as to all States parties,[22] or issued press releases.[23] Again, it is difficult to appraise whether such action was consequential. It is thus clear that in most cases the action of States and the ICRC was not co-ordinated. In particular, it would seem that the ICRC tends not to act as the representative and spokesman of the community of States parties to the Geneva Conventions.

---

[21] See H. P. Gasser, 'Ensuring Respect for the Geneva Conventions and Protocols: the Role of Third States and the United Nations' in H. Fox and M. M. Meyer (eds), *Armed Conflict and the New Law*, vol. II (London: British Institute of International and Comparative Law, 1993), 31 ('Although no clear evidence is available, we have reason to believe that governments actually do act in support of better respect for humanitarian law by States parties to an armed conflict, confidentially and on a bilateral level'). It should be noted that when he wrote these words Mr Gasser was the Legal Adviser of the ICRC.

[22] For example, it issued appeals to all States in 1979 concerning the war in Rhodesia (ICRC *Annual Report* 1979, at 13); the war between Iran and Iraq (ICRC *Annual Report* 1983, at 56; 1984, at 60; 1989, at 85); the armed conflict in the former Yugoslavia (see the statements and press releases issued in 1991–95 and collected in CICR, *Ex-Yougoslavie, Déclarations du Comité International de la Croix-Rouge, 1994* (doc. DP (1994) 49); CICR, *Ex-Yougoslavie, Communiqués de presse et communications à la presse du CICR, 1995* (doc. DP (1994) 51); the NATO attack against the Federal Republic of Yugoslavia (Serbia and Montenegro) in 1999 (in ICRC, 2000, no. 837, at 258–62); the war in Iraq in 2003–04 (ICRC press release no. 04/26 of 8 April 2004)).

[23] See e.g. the press releases no. 1479 of 15 December 1983 (on the Iran–Iraq war), no. 1481 of 7 March 1984 (on the same war), no. 1489 of 7 June 1984 (on the same war), no. 1574 of 1 June 1988 (on the use of antipersonnel mines and other prohibited weapons), no. 06 of 2003 (update) of 9 April 2003 (on ICRC activities in Iraq), and no. 03/28 of 11 April 2003 (on the protection of civilians in the war in Iraq).

This assessment ought, however, to be qualified to some extent. *A few international procedures exist which can be set in motion not by States but either at the request of the aggrieved individuals or ex officio*, that is by the international body responsible for supervising compliance with the treaty concerned (see **18.4.6, 18.4.7, 20.4.4**, and **21.4.3**). Thus, in such cases fulfilment of community obligations is sought by entities other than the various contracting States. Although these procedures are few in number, their significant operation eventually compensates for the lack of consideration still shown in the international community to ideals of a common good.

1.9 COEXISTENCE OF THE OLD AND NEW PATTERNS

Every legal system undergoes constant change, for law must steadily adjust itself to new realities. This sometimes results in old and new institutions living together: even in the case of revolutions, it is difficult to cast aside all the existing legal structures overnight. However, as a rule, fresh pieces of the legal fabric supplant outmoded ones so as to eliminate the most glaring inconsistencies.

In the international community two different patterns in law, one traditional, the other modern, live side by side. Taking up the distinction drawn by a distinguished British political scientist, M. Wight,[24] and developed by another British scholar, H. Bull,[25] we could call the traditional model 'Grotian' and the new one 'Kantian'. Under the former model the international community is based on a 'statist' vision of international relations; it is characterized by co-operation and regulated intercourse among sovereign States, each pursuing its own interests. In contrast, the Kantian paradigm is based on a universalist or cosmopolitan outlook, 'which sees at work in international politics a potential community of mankind' and lays stress on the element of 'trans-national solidarity' (*jus cosmopoliticum*).

The new 'Kantian' legal institutions, which have developed within the setting of the international community approximately since the First World War (and with greater intensity since 1945), have not uprooted or supplanted the old framework, the 'Grotian' strand. Rather, they appear to have been superimposed on it, even though their main purpose is to mitigate the most striking defects of the old system. This creates, in turn, a complex interplay of old and new, horizontal and vertical, sovereignty and humanity. Such interplay must be kept in mind when studying the legal concepts and institutions discussed in this book, for they provide a key to understanding the many inconsistencies presented by contemporary international law.

---

[24] See M. Wight, 'Western Values in International Relations' in H. Butterfield and M. Wight (eds), *Diplomatic Investigations* (London: Allen and Unwin, 1967); M. Wight, G. Wight, and B. Porter (eds), *International Theory— The Three Traditions* (Leicester and London: Leicester University Press, 1991), in particular at 137ff. Wight distinguishes between the Machiavellian, Grotian, and Kantian traditions.

[25] H. Bull, *The Anarchical Society: A Study of Order in World Politics* (London and Basingstoke: Macmillan, 1977), 24; H. Bull, 'The Importance of Grotius in the Study of International Relations' in H. Bull, B. Kingsbury, and A. Roberts (eds), *Hugo Grotius and International Relations* (Oxford: Oxford University Press, 1990), esp. at 71–93. Bull distinguishes between the Hobbesian or realist tradition, the Kantian or universalist tradition, and the Grotian or internationalist tradition. R. Falk has taken up these notions and discussed them in many articles (see, in particular, 'A New Paradigm for International Legal Studies: Prospects and Proposals' in R. Falk, F. Kratochwil, and S. H. Mendlovitz (eds), *International Law: A Comparative Perspective* (Boulder, CO, and London: Westview, 1985), 651). See also R. Jackson, *The Global Covenant: Human Conduct in a World of States* (Oxford: Oxford University Press, 2000), 378.

2

THE HISTORICAL EVOLUTION OF THE INTERNATIONAL COMMUNITY

2.1 INTRODUCTION

We should now ask how the law of the international community acquired the unique features it currently shows. As a result of what historical events did it evolve in such a way as to appear so markedly different from all domestic legal systems?

In tracing this historical process, it is useful to divide it into various stages. Periodization is, of course, always a construct, and therefore arbitrary to some extent;[1] nevertheless, it may prove helpful for a better understanding of some major turning points. The evolution of the international community can be broadly divided into four major stages: from its gradual emergence (sixteenth–early seventeenth century) to the First World War; from the establishment of the League of Nations to the end of the Second World War (1919–45); from the establishment of the United Nations to the end of the Cold War (1945–89); and the present period.

2.2 THE EMERGENCE OF THE PRESENT INTERNATIONAL COMMUNITY BEFORE THE PEACE OF WESTPHALIA

The origin of the international community in its present structure and configuration is usually traced back to the sixteenth century. The symbolic starting-point where it is deemed to have crystallized is the Peace of Westphalia (1648), which concluded the ferocious and sanguinary Thirty Years War.[2] Of course, international intercourse between groups and

---

[1] The periodization on which the following presentation relies is based on the widely influential W. G. Grewe, *Epochen der Völkerrechtsgeschichte* (Baden-Baden: Nomos, 1984), translated into English by M. Byers in 2000 under the title *The Epochs of International Law* (Berlin: De Gruyter, 2000). Grewe's 'epochs' were defined by reference to the preponderance of one or more Powers. It has been simplified for present purposes. For a recent analysis of the periodization question see I. de la Rasilla, 'The Problem of Periodization in the History of International Law' (2019) 37 *Law and History Review* 275.

[2] This is the start of what Grewe calls the French age of the 'droit public de l'Europe', *Epochen*, part III. A century earlier, E. Nys had selected the Peace of Westphalia as the moment at which international law crystallized, see E. Nys, *Les origines du droit international* (Bruxelles: Castaigne, 1894). For a study placing the European origins of international law in the wider perspective of different legal orders prevailing in different regions see Y. Onuma, 'When Was the Law of the International Society Born? An Inquiry on the History of International Law from an Intercivilizational Perspective' (2000) 2 *Journal of the History of International Law* 1. Even within Eurocentric accounts, the 1648 symbolic starting-point has been questioned. See e.g. A. Osiander, 'Sovereignty, International Relations, and the Westphalian Myth' (2001) 55 *International Organization* 251; M. Koskenniemi, 'Histories of International Law: Dealing with Eurocentrism' (2011) 19 *Rechtsgeschichte* 152.

nations had existed previously. From time immemorial there had been consular and diplomatic relations between different communities, as well as treaties of alliance or of peace.[3] Reprisals had been regulated for many years and during the Middle Ages a body of law on the conduct of belligerent hostilities had gradually evolved. And yet all these relations were radically different from current international dealings, for the fabric of the international community itself was different. Even in the late Middle Ages, when international relations of a kind resulted from the splitting of communities into various groups headed by feudal lords, the international community differed from the present one, and this for two main reasons.

First, fully fledged States—in the modern sense—did not yet exist. Centralized structures, which had gradually come into being in Europe between 1100 and 1300, did not assume the typical features of a modern State until after 1450. Of the various historical enquiries into the origin of the modern State, one may quote here those of J. R. Strayer.[4] In his view, what characterizes the modern State and differentiates it from both 'the great, imperfectly integrated empires' of the past and the small, but highly cohesive units, such as the Greek 'city State', are the following characteristics: 'the appearance of political units persisting in time and fixed in space, the development of permanent, impersonal institutions, agreement on the need for an authority which can give final judgments, and acceptance of the idea that this authority should receive the basic loyalty of its subjects'. Underlying them are 'a shift in loyalty from family, local community, or religious organization to the State, and the acquisition by the State of a moral authority to back up its institutional structure and its theoretical legal supremacy'. In addition to these features, the modern State shows a very important distinguishing trait: the emergence of centralized bureaucracies, which gradually turn into ministerial departments.[5] It was no doubt a slow evolution; nevertheless, in the seventeenth century the permanent core of the State was the bureaucracy although, as Jellinek pointed out, one had to wait until the adoption on 25 May 1791 of the French décret establishing the various ministries for the 'principle of division of labour to be completely carried through in public administration, and for ministers in the sense of administrative law to side by the monarch'.[6]

The period following the Peace of Westphalia inaugurated a new era also in a second respect. Previously there had been the overpowering presence of two poles of authority: the Pope at the head of the Catholic Church, and the Emperor at the head of the Holy Roman Empire (which had been set up as early as AD 800 by Charlemagne and had encompassed most of Europe, but dwindled in the seventeenth century to the German territory in central Europe). The necessary premise for the development of the present international community was the demise of the previous structure and the rise of modern national States between the fifteenth and seventeenth centuries. This momentous phenomenon, indisputably favoured by the conquest of America (1492) and the dissemination of Protestantism after the Reformation, led to the formation of a number of strong States, all of which sought to be independent of any superior authority. Western countries such as England, Spain, and France, followed by the Netherlands and Sweden, as well as the Ottoman Empire, China, and

---

[3] For a remarkable study of the legal aspects of such interactions see D. J. Bederman, *International Law in Antiquity* (Cambridge: Cambridge University Press, 2001), chapters 4 and 5.

[4] J. R. Strayer, *On the Medieval Origins of the Modern State* (Princeton, NJ: Princeton University Press, 1979), 9.

[5] In an important book, H. J. Berman has argued that the first such legally organized bureaucracy was the Western church after Pope Gregory VII. See H. J. Berman, *Law and Revolution: The Formation of the Western Legal Tradition* (Cambridge, MA: Harvard University Press, 1983).

[6] G. Jellinek, 'Die Entwicklung des Ministeriums in der Konstitutionellen Monarchie' (1883), in *Ausgewählte Schriften und Reden* (Berlin: O. Häring, 1911), ii, 98.

Japan in the East, increasingly regarded one another as separate and autonomous entities, and each struggled to overpower the other. New standards of behaviour became necessary. Consequently, either the old rules were given a new shape or new norms were developed.

In this respect an important contribution was made by a number of imaginative and forward-looking jurists, such as the Spaniards Francisco de Vitoria (1483–1546)[7] and Francisco Suárez (1548–1617),[8] the Italian Alberico Gentili (1552–1608),[9] a Protestant who fled to England, where he taught at Oxford, and above all the Dutchman Hugo Grotius (1583–1645).[10] They set out to lend a lucid legal justification to the interests of the emerging States in general, and of their own countries in particular.

The Peace of Westphalia concluded a most appalling war, which had caused 'great effusion of Christian blood and the desolation of several provinces' (preamble to the Treaty of Münster). The major countries of Europe had been involved; the conflict had started in 1618 for religious reasons, namely the struggle between Catholics and Protestants, but it soon turned into an all-out struggle for military and political hegemony in Europe. The treaties of peace were signed in the Westphalian towns of Münster and Osnabrück. Questions of prestige accounted for the choice of two places for negotiating peace: France and Sweden, the former Catholic, the latter Protestant, quarrelled over the question of precedence; consequently France was given priority in Catholic Münster and Sweden in Protestant Osnabrück. However, from the legal point of view, the treaties made up an integrated whole.

The treaties constitute a watershed in the evolution of the modern international community. First, they recognized Protestantism at an international level and consequently legitimized the existence of States based on Calvinist or Lutheran faith. Henceforth, even from the point of view of religion, it was recognized that the State was independent from the Church. Secondly, the treaties granted members of the Holy Roman Empire (some three hundred small States) the *jus foederationis*, that is, the right to enter into alliances with foreign Powers and to wage war, provided that those alliances or wars were neither against the Empire 'nor against the public peace' and the 'treaty' (Treaty of Münster, Article 65). Thus, a number of small countries were upgraded to the status of members of the international community with quasi-sovereign rights. Thirdly, the treaties crystallized a political distribution of power in Europe that lasted for more than a century. France, Sweden, and the Netherlands were recognized as the new emerging big Powers; Switzerland (and the Netherlands) were given the status of neutral countries; Germany was split up into a number of relatively small States. In short, the Peace of Westphalia testified to the rapid decline of the Church (an institution which had already suffered many blows) and to the de facto disintegration of the Empire. By the same token, it recorded the birth of an international system based on a plurality of independent and rival States, recognizing no superior authority over them.

The treaties signed in 1648 also set up a scheme for collective security, which remained, however, dead letter. It is nevertheless worth recalling it, as it provides background for the discussion, later in this chapter, of the Covenant of the League of Nations. Under this scheme, peace was to be enforced. Pursuant to Article 123 of the Treaty of Münster, the

---

[7] See J. Brown Scott, *The Spanish Origin of International Law: Francisco de Vitoria and His Law of Nations* (Oxford: Clarendon Press, 1932). A critical appraisal of Vitoria is provided by A. Anghie, 'Francisco de Vitoria and the Colonial Origins of International Law' (1996) 5 *Social & Legal Studies* 321.
[8] See J. Soder, *Francisco Suárez und das Völkerrecht* (Frankfurt am Main: Metzner, 1973).
[9] See G. van Molen, *Alberico Gentili and the Development of International Law* (Leiden: Sijthoff, 1968).
[10] See the monumental P. Haggenmacher, *Grotius et la doctrine de la guerre juste* (Paris: PUF, 1983).

victim of a threat to peace or any serious violation was not to resort to war, but should 'exhort the offender not to come to any hostility, submitting the cause to a friendly composition or to the ordinary proceedings of justice'. Article 124 envisaged a cooling-off period, lasting as long as three years; if at its expiry no settlement had been reached, the injured State was entitled to wage war, and all the other contracting parties were to assist it by using force. In addition, States were duty-bound to refrain from giving military assistance to the offender, nor could they allow the latter's troops to pass through or stay in their territories (Article 3). Thus, the collective security system envisaged in 1648 hinged on the following notions: (i) a sweeping ban on the use of force; (ii) a prohibition on individual self-defence, except after the expiry of a long period; (iii) the duty of all States other than the victim of a wrong to act in collective self-defence. This scheme was never put into effect. Though weak and rudimentary by modern standards, it was too far ahead of its time and in harsh conflict with the interests and predispositions of States. Members of the international community followed a different pattern of behaviour, based on both the untrammelled right of individual States to resort to war whenever they considered it appropriate and the lack of any obligation to give military assistance to the victims of attacks by other States.

2.3 FROM THE PEACE OF WESTPHALIA TO THE END OF THE FIRST WORLD WAR

2.3.1 THE COMPOSITION OF THE INTERNATIONAL COMMUNITY

Since its inception, the world community has encompassed States belonging to different geographic, cultural, and religious areas. While a significant body of practice concerns relations between European States, treaties were also concluded with other States with which Europe had come into contact, chiefly the Mogul Empire in India, the Ottoman Empire, Persia, China, Japan (since 1854), Burma, and Siam (which has been called Thailand since 1939), as well as with the States of Ethiopia and Liberia (the latter independent since 1847), and Haiti (independent since 1804). Only one year after the Peace of Westphalia, on 1 July 1649, the Holy Roman Empire concluded a treaty with the Ottoman Empire for the continuation of the peace which had been agreed in 1642.

The practice of European States, joined by the US in 1783 and by the Latin American countries between 1811 and 1821, is of particular relevance for the understanding of how international law emerged. Grewe's characterization of the period following 1648 as that of a European public law captures a particular moment in the process of development of international law, even if this process is situated in the wider context of different legal orders prevailing in different regions of the world.[11] All the States just mentioned had a common religious matrix: they were Christian. This common background made for a certain sense of belonging. Despite political, economic, and military conflicts, culture and religion acted as cement uniting them. As late as the 1870s, this common trait was a mark of 'civilization', such that, to signal modernism and seek acceptance by the community, Japan displayed its adherence to values of human dignity through the rejection of the coolie (contractual slave) trade.[12] Another strong unifying factor was the pattern of internal economic and

---

[11] See Onuma, 'When Was the Law of the International Society Born?' (n 2).
[12] This can be illustrated by reference to the *Case of the 'Maria Luz'*. On the historical circumstances of this case see S. Jones Crawford, 'The Maria Luz Affair' (1984) 46 *The Historian* 546.

political development. All Western States were the outgrowth of capitalism and its equivalent phenomenon in the political field: absolutism (followed in subsequent years by parliamentary democracy).

In a number of respects, non-Christian States, even powerful ones such as the Ottoman Empire, lived for many years on the margin of this international community defined by European Powers: they did not take a very active part, nor did they play any major role, in it. For several centuries, from the beginning of the sixteenth to the eighteenth century, some Asian Powers (namely all State entities in the East Indies, as well as Persia, Burma, and Siam) entertained international relations with European countries on a footing of complete equality. However, the industrial revolution that took place in Europe in the late eighteenth century introduced power inequalities and created a gap between Europe and non-European States. This gap steered the bellicose appetites of European Powers which, in the nineteenth century, set out to conquer vast swathes of territory from the latter or open their markets in a process closely intertwined with the emergence and consolidation of classical international law.[13]

The debate on the relations between international law and imperialism is vivid, and it has many strands.[14] Be that as it may, three points are difficult to question. First, since its inception the world community consisted not only of European States, but embraced other countries and nations as well, and there was some degree of intercourse between all sections of the community; however, many factors including geographical distance and the slowness of communication and transport rendered transactions between European and other countries particularly difficult. Secondly, for various reasons, the European Powers set the tone, at least in the last three centuries, and they played a dominant role throughout. Thirdly, Western jurists played a major role in supporting the domination penchants of European Powers. Indeed, they consistently theorized about and buttressed the idea of 'European' superiority.

As pointed out above, non-European States bowed to Western 'superiority' and eventually submitted to the rules elaborated by European countries. Western States tended to develop two distinct classes of relations with the 'outside' world, depending on whether this 'world' consisted of States proper (the Ottoman Empire, China, Japan, etc.) or was instead made up of communities lacking any organized central authority (tribal communities or communities dominated by local rulers, in Africa and Asia). With the former, Europe and the United States to a large extent based their relations on the 'capitulation' system. They considered the latter largely as objects of conquest and appropriation, and consequently turned them into colonial territories.[15]

Let us consider first the capitulation system. Capitulations were unilateral concessions, later construed by European writers as agreements, concluded by Western States with Moslem rulers (later on with the Ottoman Empire); with some Arab countries (Egypt, Iraq, Syria, Morocco, Palestine); with Persia, Siam, China, and Japan ever since the sixteenth

---

[13] On the relations between imperialism and the development of classical international law see A. Anghie, *Imperialism, Sovereignty and the Making of International Law* (New York: Cambridge University Press, 2007).

[14] See M. Koskenniemi, W. Rech, and M. Jimenez Fonseca (eds), *International Law and Empire: Historical Explorations* (Oxford: Oxford University Press, 2016); B. Fassbender and A. Peters (eds), *The Oxford Handbook of the History of International Law* (Oxford: Oxford University Press, 2012), part V (devoted to 'encounters' between, on the one hand, European Powers and, on the other hand, China, Japan, India, Russia, and North American indigenous peoples).

[15] However, an extensive study by M. Hébié has shed new light upon these relations, emphasizing the use by colonial Powers of standard treaty techniques with local rulers to gain sovereignty. See M. Hébié, *Souveraineté par traité: Une études des accords entre puissances coloniales et entités politiques locales* (Paris: PUF, 2015).

century. The capitulations regime was consolidated in the seventeenth and eighteenth centuries: the treaty of 1740 between France and the Ottoman Empire is usually mentioned as being of great significance for the delineation of the main traits of this regime.[16] Capitulations served to define conditions for the residence of Europeans (later also US nationals) in the territory of non-European countries. They tended to include the following basic provisions: (i) Europeans who were nationals of a party to the agreement could not be expelled from the country without the consent of their consul; (ii) they had the right to practise public worship of their Christian faith; to this end they could erect churches and have their own graveyards; (iii) they enjoyed freedom of trade and commerce and were exempted from certain import and export duties; (iv) reprisals against them were prohibited, especially in case of insolvency; (v) jurisdiction over disputes between Europeans belonged to the consul of the defendant or, in criminal cases, of the victim (hence not to the territorial court), while in the case of disputes between a European and a national of the territorial State the jurisdiction devolved upon the judges of the latter State.

Three features of this legal regime are striking. First, Europeans came to make up a legal community completely separate from the local one and actually subject to their own national authorities, which thereby extended their control extraterritorially. Secondly, this regime was not based on reciprocity: it consisted of a number of privileges granted to Europeans on non-European territory, with no counterpart in favour of non-European nationals.[17] The overwhelming inequality on which capitulations rested was clearly indicative of the existing relations. Thirdly, at least in the eighteenth and early nineteenth centuries, certain non-Western States did not see capitulations as detrimental to their sovereignty. Thus, for instance, a Japanese author stated that '[t]he Japanese authorities in those days, which had little knowledge of the concept of extraterritoriality, regarded national laws of Japan as something sacred, for the benefit of which foreigners were not worthy of enjoyment'.[18] And Alexandrowicz has pointed out that capitulations rested on an ancient Asian tradition akin to a *lex mercatoria*.[19] Nonetheless, Western rights of extraterritoriality constituted serious restraints on the sovereignty of the territorial State. Later on, towards the end of the nineteenth century, they were deeply felt as an undue encroachment even by the Japanese authorities, and they were gradually terminated (see **2.4.4**).

Let us now turn to the relations of European States with another class of 'other' countries, namely those lacking comparably developed State-like structures, or governed by a great number of local authorities frequently feuding with one another. These countries and territories were gradually subjected to the colonial domination of Western Powers. Europeans first colonized the Americas in the fifteenth century. As soon as the first signs of rebellion were apparent in America, Asia became a desirable area. In the eighteenth century, first France and then Britain appropriated large portions of India, until in 1772 most of India actually became a British colony. In the nineteenth century, after many Latin American countries became independent, Europeans turned to Africa, while at

---

[16] Initially, capitulations consisted of unilateral concessions granted by the Ottoman Empire at its discretion and revocable, although by the late nineteenth century they came to be seen as agreements binding on the parties. On this point see U. Özsu, 'Ottoman Empire' in Fassbender and Peters, *The Oxford Handbook* (n 14), at 431.

[17] The few instances adduced by Alexandrowicz of privileges granted in Europe to non-European partners are exceptional and cannot be considered representative. See C. H. Alexandrowicz, 'The Afro-Asian World and the Law of Nations: Historical Aspects' (1968) 123 *RCADI* 117, at 125.

[18] H. Otsuka, 'Japan's Early Encounter with the Concept of the Law of Nations' (1969) 13 *JYIL* 56.

[19] Alexandrowicz, 'The Afro-Asian World' (n 17), at 151 ('ancient custom in Asia allowed foreign merchants to govern themselves by their own personal law instead of submitting to the jurisdiction and the law of the host country and possibly to a different way of life').

the same time intensifying their interest in Asia. One major stepping stone in the strategy of appropriation was the Berlin Conference of 1884–85, attended by such European countries as Austria-Hungary, Belgium, Denmark, France, Germany, Britain, Italy, the Netherlands, Portugal, Russia, Spain, Sweden-Norway, plus the Ottoman Empire and the US, and resulting in the General Act of the Berlin Congo Conference of 26 February 1885.[20] The interior of the African continent was split up among Britain, France, Portugal, Belgium, Germany, and Italy. Meanwhile, Britain, France, and the Netherlands either appropriated or consolidated their control over Asia. Even a State formerly under colonial domination, the US, took part in the colonialist trend. It seized power over the Philippines in 1898 as a result of the war with Spain, concluded by the Peace Treaty of Paris in 1898.

An important question which should be raised here is that of the role of international law in the process of colonial conquest. It has been argued that this body of law greatly facilitated the task of European Powers,[21] offering them, as it did, a large number of legal instruments designed to render conquest smooth and easy. International law authorized States to acquire sovereignty over those territories, both by downgrading the latter to *terrae nullius*, namely, territories belonging to no one, and by depriving the local communities or rulers of international standing. Although the latter point has been called into question on the basis of an important body of documentary evidence,[22] the fact remains that effective occupation and de facto control over the territory (coupled with the intent of appropriation) were sufficient, or have been considered to be sufficient in retrospect, for the acquisition of sovereign rights. Furthermore, if local rulers opposed the colonial conquest, international law offered two instruments: either war (without all the legal restraints applicable to wars between 'civilized' States), or the conclusion of treaties (indeed a great number of agreements with 'local rulers' or chieftains were entered into by European States, and they normally lacked any reciprocity). The same legal instruments were available in case of conflict between colonial Powers and other Western countries wishing to appropriate the same territories: either the waging of a war or the conclusion of an agreement settled the matter.

2.3.2 THE BALANCE OF POWER

Throughout the whole period under consideration power was spread out: no single State became so strong as to subject all the other countries to its will. Legally, all members of the international community were on an equal footing. In practice, a group of Great Powers (France, Britain, Spain, Portugal, the US, Russia, Austria, Prussia, Sweden, and the Netherlands) dominated the international scene. However, this group never presented a united front because there were constant rivalries. A balance of power proved necessary and was in fact established.

It is against this general background that an early experiment in collective systems for restraining power and enforcing the law should be considered. It was made in 1815 after

---

[20] See J. Fisch, 'Africa as terra nullius: The Berlin Conference and International Law' in S. Förster, W. Momsen, and R. Robinson (eds), *Bismarck, Europe and Africa: The Berlin Africa Conference 1884–85 and the Onset of Partition* (Oxford: Oxford University Press, 1988), 347.

[21] See e.g. Anghie, *Imperialism* (n 13).

[22] See Hébié, *Souveraineté par traité* (n 15).

the defeat of Napoleon.[23] The French Revolution and the genius of Napoleon had shattered deep-rooted principles and upset the existing order. The victors felt they had to protect the interests of European monarchies against the seeds of revolution. To this end, they met to devise a system capable of putting a straitjacket on these new forces, which were urging the abolition of inequitable practices and the dismantling of aristocratic privileges. The new system, called the Concert of Europe, was set up in a number of treaties worked out in 1815 and supplemented by subsequent agreements. It rested on three principal elements:

(1) A *declaration of principles*, binding all States except for Britain, the Papal States, and the Ottoman Empire. It proclaimed that the contracting parties would adopt as standards of behaviour, both in their internal orders and in international relations, the precepts of the Christian religion.

(2) A *military alliance*. The 'Holy Alliance' was instituted by the Treaty of Paris of 26 September 1815, concluded by Austria, Prussia, and Russia, to which France acceded in 1818.[24] It envisaged a system for collective security based on the agreement of the big Powers, designed to forestall or stifle any recurrence of Bonapartism, either in France or elsewhere. Under Articles 2 to 4 of the treaty, the contracting States undertook to agree upon the measures to be taken against those infringing upon the 'tranquillity' and the 'established order' in Europe; they also pledged themselves to agree upon the number of troops which each of them was bound to provide 'for the pursuit of the common cause'. While, at the outset, the main object was that of averting any threat to the stability of post-Napoleonic France, the system was subsequently extended—through the treaty of 1818 and the Troppau Protocol of 1818—so as to function against any revolutionary movement likely to overthrow European monarchies. The Troppau Protocol, ratified by Austria, Russia, and Prussia, provided for three measures in cases of revolution: (i) the State in which a revolution broke out would cease to be a member of the Concert of Europe; (ii) the new government resulting from a revolution would not be recognized; and (iii) the States directly concerned, or otherwise the Holy Alliance, would intervene to put an end to the revolution.

This system proved quite effective in practice. It was actually resorted to on two occasions: in 1821, when Austrian troops were sent to Naples and Turin to suppress liberal insurgents on behalf of the Holy Alliance; and in 1823, when French troops were dispatched to Spain, again to thwart a liberal attempt at independence. On both occasions, one State only—the one directly concerned—made a military intervention. But the right to take action was considered as delegated by all the partners of the Holy Alliance, and it was authorized by a general meeting (the Conference of Troppau and Laybach in the former case, the Conference of Verona in the latter).

(3) A *new procedure for the settlement of political questions*, consisting of meetings of all the sovereigns concerned where they might discuss 'great interests in common', consider measures conducive to the 'tranquillity and prosperity of peoples', and attempt to maintain peace in Europe. In short, a new diplomatic method was propounded: multilateral diplomacy, based on *periodical summit meetings*. It proved most useful and was indeed resorted to on a number of occasions in later years.

---

[23] See generally C. K. Webster, *The Congress of Vienna* (London: Humphrey Milford, 1934); K. Griewank, *Die Wiener Kongress und die europäische Restauration, 1814–1815* (Leipzig: Koehler & Amelang, 1954); A. Sked (ed.), *Europe's Balance of Power 1815–1848* (London: Macmillan, 1979); M. Schulz, *Normen und Praxis: Das Europäische Konzert des Grossmächte als Sicherheitsrat 1815–60* (Oldenbourg: De Gruyter, 2009).

[24] See M. Bourquin, *Histoire de la Sainte-Alliance* (Geneva: Georg, 1954).

As soon as European monarchies came under strong attack from nationalist movements and were gradually overthrown or forced to turn into parliamentary democracies, the system set up in 1815 was replaced by the traditional policy of the *balance of power*: only the diplomatic method of summit meetings survived. Protected—at least in some respects—by this policy, the European Powers revived their tendency to exercise hegemony, endeavouring not to trespass upon the respective spheres of influence.

Within this general framework, the emergence of the US set a limit to European influence and power in the Americas. The new trend was formally proclaimed by the American president, Monroe, in the doctrine propounded in the famous message to Congress of 2 December 1823.[25] This message stated, first, that 'the American continents ... are henceforth not to be considered as subjects for future *colonization* by any European powers'. Secondly, while the US would not intervene in European matters including European Powers' 'colonies and dependencies', by the same token it could not allow European Powers to *intervene* in America: the US 'would not view any interposition for the purpose of oppressing them [i.e. independent Governments of the "American continents"] or controlling in any other manner their destiny, by any European power in any other light than as the manifestation of an unfriendly disposition toward the United States'.[26] Thus, a check was placed on European expansionism and, at the same time, the basic principle was enunciated that the American continent was under the control of the most powerful State of the area.

2.3.3 THE MAIN FEATURES OF THE LAW

The very expression 'international law' dates back to this period.[27] The legal regulation created in this period possesses two salient features:

(1) International rules and principles were the product of Western civilization and bore the imprint of Eurocentrism, Christian ideology, and of a 'free market' outlook (they rested on a laissez-faire philosophy, that is, on the idea that all States should be legally equal and free to pursue their own interests, irrespective of any economic or social imbalance).

(2) International norms and principles were mainly framed by the Great Powers or middle-sized States, particularly by those States which had built up extensive colonial empires by dint of conquest and expansion. They elaborated the rules to serve their own interests. Among the norms of this category, particular emphasis should be laid on those concerning force: they placed no restraint on the threat or use of belligerent violence. Other important

---

[25] On this crucial development and its implications see A. Alvarez, *The Monroe Doctrine: Its Importance in the International Life of the States of the New World* (New York: Oxford University Press, 1924). For a more recent study of the doctrine's many faces see J. Sexton, *The Monroe Doctrine: Empire and Nation in Nineteenth-Century America* (New York: Hill and Wang, 2011).

[26] J. B. Moore, *History and Digest of International Arbitrations* (Washington, DC: Government Printing Office, 1898), vol. 6, 368.

[27] It was first used in 1780 by J. Bentham in his *Introduction to the Principles of Morals and Legislation*. Since then it has increasingly replaced the previous terms 'law of nations' and 'droit des gens'. As the Italian philologist P. Peruzzi showed ('A European Word-Formation Pattern' (1976) 41 *Archivio filologico italiano* 76), other factors besides the strictly linguistic one motivated this change, or were instrumental in making it widespread: the emotional appeal and the growing importance of the concept of 'nation', the spread of 'international industrial exhibitions', and the setting up in 1864, in London, of the 'International Working Men's Association', commonly known as the 'First International' or simply, 'The International'. Some authors have gone beyond locating the emergence of the expression at this time and considered that the very field of international law, as it is known today, emerged in the second half of the nineteenth century as a professional practice. See M. Koskenniemi, *The Gentle Civilizer of Nations. The Rise and Fall of International Law 1870–1960* (Cambridge: Cambridge University Press, 2001).

rules were those on the diplomatic and judicial protection of nationals abroad: whenever the citizen of a certain State claimed that a foreign government had behaved unlawfully towards him, he could request his national government to step in and claim reparation for the alleged international wrongful act. Clearly, these rules constituted important legal tools in the hands of those Great Powers whose nationals went abroad to set up commercial enterprises.

A notable contribution to the elucidation and development of international customary rules, that often led to the elaboration of international treaties, was made by a group of eminent European and American scholars, who were instrumental in the establishment, in 1873, in Ghent (Belgium) of an association of distinguished academics, some of them involved in international affairs in different capacities: the *Institut de Droit International*. Among them some stood out: the Dutch T. M. C. Asser, the Swiss (teaching in Germany) J. C. Bluntschli, the Argentinian C. Calvo, the British J. Lorimer, the Italian P. S. Mancini, the Swiss G. Moynier, and the Belgian G. Rolin-Jaequemyns.[28] The aims of the *Institut* were: promotion of the 'progress of international law' by stating its principles 'according to the judicial conscience of the civilized world'; promotion of 'progressive codification'; and the 'official acknowledgement' of the principles of international law. Over the years, the *Institut* has discussed important topics and passed resolutions that have been influential in the development of international law: in particular those on the liberty of navigation and neutrality within the Congo Basin, on rules concerning arbitration proceedings, on land and sea warfare, on international prize courts, on codification, on the recognition of States, etc.

Two qualifications should be made to the above remarks on the principal features of law in this period. First, in some cases Great Powers were impelled to make concessions to smaller States (see, for example, the rules on lawful combatants, **17.3**). The second qualification is that a number of treaties were dictated by humanitarian demands, while others met the exigencies of all members of the international community, whether powerful or weak. The former category includes not only treaties on the slave trade,[29] but also some international agreements placing restraints on the use of weapons causing inhuman suffering (see **17.6.3**). At least one of the treaties banning weapons should be mentioned at this juncture, namely the Declaration prohibiting the use of expanding bullets, adopted by the Hague Conference in 1899. Soft-nosed bullets which expanded on contact, thus causing gaping wounds and appalling suffering, had been developed by the British at the Dum-Dum arsenal in Calcutta in the nineteenth century. As E. M. Spiers recalled, the British authorities justified their production by saying that

> the demands of small colonial warfare warranted this deviation from the standards of European armaments. The enemies whom Britain encountered were not armies from the European countries who had signed the St Petersburg Declaration [of 1868, prohibiting the use in time of war of explosive projectiles under 400 grammes weight], but 'fanatical natives', 'savages', and 'barbarians'. The difference was deemed substantial: 'civilised man is much more susceptible to injury than savages ... the savage, like the tiger, is not so impressionable, and will go on fighting even when desperately wounded.'[30]

---

[28] On the origins, project and ideology of the *Institut de Droit International*, see Koskenniemi, *The Gentle Civilizer* (n 27), at 11.

[29] See S. Drescher, *Abolition: A History of Slavery and Antislavery* (New York: Cambridge University Press, 2009); S. Drescher and P. Finkelman, 'Slavery' in Fassbender and Peters, *The Oxford Handbook* (n 14), at 890.

[30] E. M. Spiers, 'The Use of Dum Dum Bullets in Colonial Warfare' (1976) 4 *Journal of Imperial and Commonwealth History* 6. It should be noted that the distinction between civilized peoples and barbarians, as far as the use of weapons was concerned, was certainly not new. Back in 1625, Grotius had written that poisoning weapons and waters was 'contrary to the law of nations, not indeed of all nations but of European nations and of such others as attain to the higher standards of Europe', H. Grotius, *On the Law of War and Peace*, trans. F. W. Kelsey (Oxford: Clarendon Press, 1925), 653 (Book III, Ch. IV).

Although Britain assured other Western Powers that it would not use those bullets in European wars, they managed to have the Hague Peace Conference pass the Declaration referred to above. Britain grudgingly adhered to it in 1907, and the prohibition gradually expanded so as to cover any international armed conflict. The other category of rules intended to meet the demands of all States irrespective of their strength included treaties such as those on diplomatic and consular immunities, as well as the norms on neutrality and the neutralization of States. Although some of these norms were also motivated by particular interests, their intrinsic significance for the whole international community transformed them into lasting principles which continue to display their effects today.

2.3.4 EFFORTS TO RESTRAIN THE GREAT POWERS' DOMINANCE: THE CALVO AND DRAGO DOCTRINES

Timid attempts were made to restrain the domination of the Great Powers by international or national legislation. The first and probably the most important instance was the clause that, from the middle of the nineteenth century, many Latin American States began to insert into concession contracts with nationals of foreign countries, chiefly for the exploitation of national resources. It was the Argentine jurist C. Calvo (1824–1906) who had developed the doctrine (named after him) of sovereign equality and national treatment underlying this clause.[31] It stipulated that in cases of dispute arising out of contracts, foreigners relinquished the right to request the diplomatic and judicial protection of their national State and agreed to have the dispute settled by local tribunals.

Plainly, the Calvo clause sought to limit the legal and political interventions of Western capital-exporting countries, which often constituted the pretext or the occasion for armed expeditions, strong political pressure, or other forms of interference. The attempt was ill-fated: numerous international courts and claims commissions ruled that the clause was legally ineffective, in that it could not deprive States of their rights of protection, since the latter derived from international law only. Consequently, the clause was either set aside or downgraded to a proviso requiring the exhaustion of local remedies before international diplomatic or judicial action could be initiated. No doubt the refusal to apply the clause was legally correct in the light of the international rules applicable at the time. The failure of the Calvo stipulation only proved that it was vain to seek to undermine existing conditions by means which fell short of a radical change in the legal regulation of the treatment of nationals abroad.

Another important attempt to place restraints on the Great Powers' hegemony was made, in the early twentieth century, by the Foreign Minister of Argentina, Luis María

---

[31] See C. Calvo, *Derecho Internacional Teórico y Práctico de Europa y América* (Paris: D'Amyot/Durand et Pedone-Lauriel, 1868), subsequently translated into French and expanded through four other editions, the last one published as C. Calvo, *Le droit international théorique et pratique* (Paris: Arthur Rousseau, 1896). On the specific context in which the Calvo doctrine arose see J. E. Viñuales and M. J. Langer, 'Foreign Investment in Latin-America: Between Love and Hatred' in C. Auroi and A. Helg (eds), *Latin America: Dreams and Legacy 1810–2010* (London: Imperial College Press, 2011), 319.

Drago (1859–1921).[32] He argued that the Great Powers must not use military force to seek payment of debts from poor countries. The unfettered right of States to resort to force included their right forcibly to recover payments due by foreign States to the nationals of the former. Three European countries, Britain, Germany, and Italy, used this right against Venezuela in 1902. They had requested Venezuela (i) to pay compensation for damage caused to their nationals during the civil strife which raged between 1898 and 1900, and for the seizure of fishing boats and other commercial ships by the Venezuelan authorities, and (ii) to repay loans made to Venezuela for the building of its railway. Venezuela demanded that the European claims be settled by a Venezuelan commission. This commission, however, partly rejected and partly reduced the European demands. The European Powers found the settlement unacceptable. After imparting an ultimatum, their forces sank three Venezuelan ships, bombarded the locality of Puerto Cabello, and, on 20 December 1902, instituted a naval blockade off the Venezuelan coast. Venezuela gave in. A few days later, on 29 December, Drago sent a diplomatic note to the US State Department, in which he claimed, first, that the European armed intervention was contrary to the Monroe doctrine (which he declared he was willing to uphold), and, secondly, that financial troubles and the consequent need to postpone payment of debts was no justification for foreign military intervention, since 'the collection of loans by military means requires territorial occupation to make them effective, and territorial occupation signifies the suppression or subordination of the governments of the countries on which it is imposed'.[33]

This note, which enunciated what was subsequently termed the 'Drago doctrine', elicited a lukewarm response from the US. In his note of 17 February 1903, the US Secretary of State, J. M. Hay, substantially dismissed Drago's claims and pointed out that, so long as Latin American countries fulfilled their international duties towards foreign States, they need not fear any foreign intervention. Hay quoted a message sent to Congress by President Theodore Roosevelt on 2 December 1902, which stated: 'It behoves each one to maintain order within its own borders and to discharge its just obligations to foreigners. When this is done, they [the independent nations of America] can rest assured that, strong or weak, they have nothing to dread from outside interference' (USFR (1903), at 5). In sum, the US considered protection of foreign property to override the need to keep Europeans from intervening militarily on the American continent.[34] It is hardly surprising that the so-called Drago doctrine was assailed by leading European jurists as being at variance with international law—a proposition which was indeed correct, in the light of the rules obtaining at the time.

No substantial headway was made in 1907, when Latin American countries endeavoured to pass, at the second Hague Peace Conference, a convention forbidding the use of force for the recovery of contract debts. The US delegate, General Horace Porter, took up, but also watered down, the ideas put forward by Drago in 1902. General Porter proposed to make resort to force conditional on the non-acceptance by the debtor State of international

---

[32] See L. M. Drago, 'State Loans in their Relations to International Policy' (1907) 1 *AJIL* 692. For a retrospective assessment see L. M. Drago and H. E. Nettles, 'The Drago Doctrine in International Law and Politics' (1928) 8 *The Hispanic American Historical Review* 204.

[33] (1907) *AJIL*, Supp I, 1.

[34] It should be noted that, in planning their intervention, the intervening European Powers were careful not to upset the US as a regional Power. They even sought to have the dispute arbitrated by US President Roosevelt, albeit the latter declined. See J. E. Viñuales, 'Experiments in International Adjudication: Past and Present' in I. de la Rasilla and J. E. Viñuales (eds), *Experiments in International Adjudication: Historical Accounts* (Cambridge: Cambridge University Press, 2019), 11, at 19–20.

arbitration or its failure to carry out an arbitral award. The Conference largely accepted General Porter's proposals and set up a Convention on the matter.[35] Significantly, it was not ratified by any European country, thus showing again that even in an emasculated form, the efforts of Latin American countries to restrain international legitimation of force were to no avail.

2.4 FROM THE FIRST TO THE SECOND WORLD WAR

Two major events mark the beginning of a new era: (i) the First World War which, although fought solely in Europe, involved the greater part of the international community and caused the members of that community to strive to rebuild it on better foundations; (ii) the Soviet Revolution and the consequent rise of the first State openly to oppose the economic and ideological roots of other States and of international relations.

2.4.1 THE TURNING POINT: THE FIRST WORLD WAR AND ITS CONSEQUENCES

The Great War had many important repercussions. It marked the passing of the 'European Age'.[36] When the war was over, it became apparent that Europe no longer played a crucial part in the world community: the gradual erosion of its importance, initiated long before, culminated in Europe's demotion to the rank of merely one of the areas of power. Among the chief factors affecting its position were: (i) the rise of the US; (ii) the emergence in 1917 of the Soviet Union (as it was called from 30 December 1922 onwards) and the falling to pieces of the substantial ideological and political unity of the 'old' community; and (iii) the end of colonial expansion—a striking phenomenon which marked the beginning of that long process that culminated in the collapse of colonial empires in the 1960s. The decline of Europe made itself felt in the field of economic, military, and political power, but also in that of culture and ideology. Europe's pivotal role in the previous centuries as the world's storeroom of values, institutions, political concepts, and standards of behaviour came to an end.

The war united the whole world—albeit in a forced and somewhat sinister way. For the first time a conflict assumed such magnitude as to involve all major members of the international community. The war proved that some major events were crucial to the world community at large. It became difficult for States to keep aloof from what was happening in other areas of the world.

2.4.2 THE SOVIET UNION'S PRESENCE SPLITS THE INTERNATIONAL COMMUNITY

It has already been pointed out that although some members of the international community (the Ottoman Empire, China, Japan, Persia, and Siam) had a different economic and ideological outlook to that of European States, they had actually yielded to the Christian majority geared to liberalism, which indeed set the tone throughout the development of the international community. In 1917, one government came into being with an ideology and

---

[35] Convention between the United States and Other Powers Respecting the Limitation of the Employment of Force for the Recovery of Contract Debts, 18 October 1907, 36 *Statutes at Large* 2241.

[36] R. Albrecht-Carrié, *The Meaning of the First World War* (Englewood Cliffs, NJ: Prentice Hall, 1965), vi.

a political philosophy radically at odds with those upheld by all other States. In the international field, the USSR advocated the following principles:[37]

(1) *Self-determination of peoples*, to be applied both to national groups in Europe (for example, the nationalities in Austria-Hungary) and to peoples under colonial domination (see **3.8**).

(2) The *substantive equality of States* (by contrast with their legal equality). Point 6 of the proposals forming the basis for negotiations submitted by Adolph Joffe, the head of the Russian delegation to the Brest-Litovsk Peace Conference (which opened on 22 December 1917), proposed that the contracting parties should condemn the attempt by strong nations to restrict the freedom of the weaker nations by such indirect methods as economic boycotts, economic subjection by means of compulsory commercial agreements, separate customs agreements, restricting the freedom of trade with third countries, naval blockade without direct military purpose, etc. Thus, for the first time, there was outright condemnation of economic coercion, as a means of subduing weaker States, and unequal treaties.

(3) *Socialist internationalism*, whereby the USSR pledged itself to assist the working class and the political parties struggling for socialism in any State. Thus, again for the first time, a member State of the international community proclaimed a policy aimed at disrupting the fabric of other States and their colonial possessions (and the USSR officially pursued such a policy until at least 1927).

The potential implications of this new state of affairs were soon fully appreciated by the American Secretary of State, Robert Lansing. In a memorandum of 2 December 1917, speaking of Lenin and Trotsky, Lansing, among other things, wrote the following:

> How can anyone deal with such people? They are wanting in international virtue. International obligations and comity mean nothing to them. The one thing they are striving to bring about is the 'Social Revolution', which will sweep away national boundaries, racial distinctions and modern political, religious and social institutions, and make the ignorant and incapable mass of humanity dominant in the earth. They indeed plan to destroy civilization by mob violence . . . the Bolshevik program is to make way with the military and political authority in Russia and to incite similar destruction in other countries.[38]

(4) The *partial rejection of international law*. The USSR proclaimed that since all the existing legal norms and institutions of the international community were the upshot of 'bourgeois' and 'capitalist' tendencies, they were by definition contrary to socialist interests, and would be endorsed by the new regime only to the extent that they proved useful to it. Consequently, many existing treaties were denounced.

In fact, the Soviet government did not reject international law wholesale. Indeed, it could not have done so without becoming an outcast in the world community. One cannot be a member of a social group and at the same time dismiss all its rules. One must comply with at least some of them since otherwise international relations become impossible, with the group as a whole ostracizing the recalcitrant member by condemning it to complete isolation. The USSR rejected a number of bilateral and even multilateral treaties, but it tacitly or

---

[37] For a concise statement of the Soviet doctrine see S. Krylov, 'Les notions principales du droit des gens: la doctrine soviétique du droit international' (1947) 70 *RCADI* 407. Professor Krylov was the first Soviet judge of the ICJ, in addition to being a distinguished academic and a legal adviser to the Soviet government. His views were stated in many works, including S. Krylov, E. Korovin, and F. Kojevnikov, *Mejdunarodnoe pravo* [International Law] (Moscow: Gosjurizdat, 1957). For an external appraisal of Soviet doctrines and their operation see B. Meissner (ed.), *Sowjetunion und Völkerrecht 1917 bis 1962* (Köln: Verlag Wissenschaft und Politik, 1963); B. Meissner, 'The Soviet Concept of Nation and the Right of National Self-Determination' (1976) 32 *International Journal* 56.

[38] R. Lansing, *War Memoirs* (Indianapolis: The Bobbs-Merrill Co., 1935, repr. Westport, CT: Greenwood Press, 1970), 341.

expressly bowed to a great many international standards. Thus, for example, in addition to emphasizing the importance of the customary rules protecting State sovereignty, it invoked a general norm (the rule *rebus sic stantibus*, see **10.9**) to justify its repudiation of unacceptable treaties. Similarly, the USSR upheld many customary rules on treaty making (witness its entering into a great number of bilateral and multilateral treaties), and on diplomatic and consular immunities and privileges. In addition, it tacitly accepted the bulk of customary rules on the treatment of foreigners, as is proved by Articles 8 and 9 of the Soviet-German Treaty of 6 May 1921, which stated that Germany guaranteed to Soviet citizens 'the prescriptions of international law and of the German common law'.

Nevertheless, the basic Soviet attitude towards the legal instruments of the international community inevitably undermined some of the community's basic doctrines. The USSR eroded—to a greater or lesser extent—many sacred principles, such as that on protection of investments abroad, while it resolutely opposed others, such as those concerning the rights of colonial Powers.

2.4.3 AN EXPERIMENT IN COLLECTIVE CO-ORDINATION OF FORCE: THE LEAGUE OF NATIONS

Following the First World War, the victors decided to set up an international institution designed to prevent the recurrence of worldwide armed conflict. The League of Nations was created, with a relatively small membership (42 States including five British dominions: India, New Zealand, Canada, Australia, and South Africa).[39] For domestic reasons the US held aloof. Its absence undisputedly weakened the institution from the outset.

The system set up in 1919 resembles the one devised in 1648 in the form of the Settlement of Westphalia (see **2.2**). Recourse to force was not generally prohibited, except for a limited number of cases. Articles 12, 13, and 15 of the Covenant subjected resort to war to a cooling-off period of three months. If a dispute was submitted to the League Council or to the Permanent Court of International Justice (PCIJ) or an arbitral tribunal, war could only be resorted to three months after the arbitral or judicial decision or the Council report. Consequently, there was a general prohibition on wars initiated before that delay or waged against a State which was complying with an arbitral award or a judgment of the PCIJ, or with a report adopted unanimously by the League Council.

The League system had major flaws. There was no ban on resort to force short of war. This qualification manifestly induced States to engage in war operations while claiming that they were merely using coercion short of war and were therefore not breaking any provision of the Covenant. An instance is the case of Manchuria, when Japan attacked China (1932), which triggered the assertion of the Stimson doctrine (see **1.7**). In addition, war was not banned altogether; it was only subjected to a cooling-off period, in the hope that States' bellicose moods would lose momentum after a certain delay, and that the procedures for the settlement of disputes provided for in the Covenant would meanwhile induce them to refrain from using force. This proved illusory, as is shown by the case of the Italian aggression against Abyssinia, in 1935–36.[40] Furthermore, no collective system

---

[39] On this important institution see F. P. Walters, *A History of the League of Nations* (Oxford: Oxford University Press, 1952). For a legal analysis of the Covenant of the League of Nations see R. Kolb (ed.), *Commentaire sur le Pacte de la Société des Nations* (Bruxelles: Bruylant, 2014). For a survey of work on the League of Nations see S. Pedersen, 'Back to the League of Nations' (2007) 112 *American Historical Review* 1091.

[40] For a contemporaneous account see Q. Wright, 'The Test of Aggression in the Italo-Ethiopian War' (1936) 30 *AJIL* 45. For two retrospective analyses see E. Santarelli, 'La guerra d'Etiopia, imperialismo e terzo mondo' (1969) 97 *Il Movimento di Liberazione in Italia* 35; G. W. Baer, *The Coming of the Italo-Ethiopian War* (Cambridge, MA: Harvard University Press, 1967).

was set up for enforcing law against a State that broke the procedural prohibitions of the Covenant. If a member State waged war contravening the Covenant's stipulations, all the other member States were duty-bound to assist the victim against the aggressor—as long as they considered the use of force in the case at issue to be a breach of the Covenant. The League of Nations Assembly or Council had no power to send in troops against the aggressors; they could only recommend the use of force to member States. In short, the Covenant merely envisaged *joint voluntary action* on the part of States. There was no provision for an institutionalized enforcement procedure, there was no monopoly of force granted to the League organs, much less was an international army for the maintenance of peace and order set up. Plainly, the League system was a far cry from the enforcement machinery that existed within each State system. Indeed, in the only case when there was resort to sanctions (namely against Italy, 1935–36) they proved a failure, for political reasons. A further deficiency was that the Covenant's prescriptions remained treaty law; consequently, they did not bind States outside the League (the US, as well as a number of European and Asian countries, including at a certain stage Germany, the USSR, and Japan). As a result, the customary international rules authorizing war remained unaffected as far as third States were concerned.

Differences between member States, the lack of co-operation, the fact that the League gradually became a political instrument of Britain and France only, along with its inherent institutional deficiencies—all these account for its failure. A number of States resorted to force without being the subject of military sanctions or at any rate without the League bringing about a satisfactory settlement.

The US and France endeavoured to obviate the most conspicuous deficiencies of the League by promoting the Paris Pact of 27 August 1928 on the Prohibition of War, also known as the Briand-Kellogg Pact (or Kellogg-Briand Pact), after the names of the French Minister of Foreign Affairs, Aristide Briand, and the US Secretary of State, Frank B. Kellogg.[41] The Pact, however, did not make much headway, for once again it was only war that was prohibited (although the ban was now more sweeping), and in addition there was no provision for an enforcement mechanism. Furthermore, the correspondence between the parties before the signing of the Pact made it clear that the right of self-defence was unaffected, and that a very liberal construction was placed on that right. Thus, Britain stated that it included its right to defend 'certain regions of the world, the welfare and integrity of which constitute a special and vital interest for our peace and security'. And the US contended that self-defence embraced any action decided on by the US government to prevent an infringement of the Monroe doctrine. The conspicuous merits of the Pact were that it laid down a more general prohibition of war, and that it was binding on States not parties to the Covenant, such as the US. In fact, Briand had seen the Pact as a tactic to bring the US closer to the Covenant. However, the Pact itself was unable to supplant the customary rule authorizing war, in that it did not turn into a customary rule abrogating the latter.

In short, even in the period between the two world wars, States gradually endeavoured to retrieve their traditionally unfettered right to use military force in international relations. The League served to slow down the process and reduce the instances of recourse to force. It was, however, unable to introduce a fundamental change in one particular structural element of the old international community.

---

[41] On this highly symbolic instrument see R. H. Ferrell, *Peace in Their Time: The Origins of the Kellogg-Briand Pact* (New Haven, CT: Yale University Press, 1952). For the views of Kellogg and Briand themselves see F. B. Kellogg, 'The War Prevention Policy of the United States' (1928) 22 *AJIL* 253; A. Briand, *Discours et écrits de politique étrangère: la paix, l'Union européenne, la Société des nations*, ed. A. Elisha (Paris: Plon, 1965).

2.4.4 LEGAL OUTPUT

During this period there was no conspicuous success in elaborating new rules. In its isolation, the Soviet Union remained to a great extent on the defensive; on a number of occasions it challenged existing international institutions, but it was unable to affect the new rules.

The principal area in which marked progress was made was that of the arbitral and judicial settlement of disputes. In the inter-war period international adjudication was in full bloom. The PCIJ, set up in 1921, delivered 32 judgments, and 27 Advisory Opinions. The parties to the contentious proceedings were mostly European. Similarly, the members of the Court were mostly from European countries or from the US (from 1922 to 1930, four of 16 judges were non-Western, while from 1931 to 1942 the proportion changed to 7 out of 21). Numerous ad hoc arbitral tribunals were also set up. Indeed, most European States strongly believed that arbitration was the best means of settling disputes and preventing the outbreak of wars. This, however, was an overoptimistic view, both because on a number of occasions arbitral awards were not heeded, and because arbitration was inherently unable to restrain power politics. However, frequent recourse to international adjudication made it possible for international courts, particularly the PCIJ, to pronounce on many international legal issues. The case law which evolved was instrumental in filling many gaps in international law. Principles and rules were specified, elucidated, and elaborated upon. This, by itself, was a remarkable contribution to the improvement of the technical aspects of international law.

In addition, a new wind began to blow through the international community, bringing with it a drive towards limiting inequalities between States, and greater concern for the demands of individuals. The tendency to do away with the most glaring forms of inequality can be seen in the gradual abolition of capitulations. The only country where this regime had already been dismantled before the First World War was Japan (in 1899). Capitulations with other countries were gradually abrogated.

The emergence of a fresh concern with the situation of individuals manifested itself in two forms. First, while the slave trade had been prohibited long before, and slavery itself had been banned in many States, the Slavery Convention adopted on 26 September 1926 under the aegis of the League of Nations introduced a general obligation to 'bring about progressively and as soon as possible, the complete abolition of slavery in all its forms' (Article 2(b)).[42] Secondly, a body of instruments to protect minorities was developed under the aegis of the League.[43] Of note, groups of individuals were granted the right to lodge complaints with international bodies. Religious, ethnic, and linguistic minorities protected by post-war treaties were authorized to submit to the Council of the League of Nations 'petitions' designed to inform it of alleged violations of minority rights. Under Article 24 of the ILO Constitution, trade union associations were entitled to file

---

[42] For a retrospective account see A. Ribi Forclaz, *Humanitarian Imperialism: The Politics of Anti-Slavery Activism, 1880–1940* (Oxford: Oxford University Press, 2015), 46. See also B. Metzger, 'Towards an International Human Rights Regime during the Inter-War Years: The League of Nations' Combat of Traffic in Women and Children' in K. Grant, P. Levine, and F. Trentmann (eds), *Beyond Sovereignty: Britain, Empire and Transnationalism, c.1880–1950* (Basingstoke: Palgrave Macmillan, 2007), 54. For the discussions leading to the Slavery Convention see J. Allain, *The Slavery Conventions: The Travaux Préparatoires of the 1926 League of Nations Convention and the 1956 United Nations Convention* (Leiden: Brill, 2008); J. Allain, *Slavery in International Law* (Leiden: Brill, 2012), 379 (on the 1926 Slavery Convention) and 384 (on the Forced Labour Convention).

[43] For two retrospective accounts see J. Jackson Preece, *National Minorities and the European Nation-States System* (Oxford: Oxford University Press, 1998), 67; C. Gütermann, *Das Minderheitenschutzverfahren Völkerbundes* (Berlin: Duncker & Humblot, 1979). For a contemporaneous account see J. Stone, *International Guarantee of Minority Rights* (Oxford: Oxford University Press, 1932).

complaints with the ILO Governing Body. These normative innovations were indicative of the new tendency to pay greater attention to the interests of human beings, who until then had had no say whatsoever in the international community. As the Greek international lawyer Politis stated in 1927:

> Beforehand, the sovereign State was for its subjects an iron cage whence they could communicate legally with the outside world only through narrow bars. Under the pressure of the necessities of life, those bars have progressively loosened. The cage is starting to wobble. It will eventually fall to bits. Men will then be able to communicate beyond the frontiers of their respective countries freely and without any hindrance.[44]

2.5 FROM THE UN CHARTER TO THE END OF THE COLD WAR

2.5.1 THE MAIN CONSEQUENCES OF THE SECOND WORLD WAR

In 1945, over a period of less than two months, three momentous events occurred: on 26 June the Charter of the United Nations was signed in San Francisco (it came into force on 24 October 1945); on 6 August the atomic bomb was dropped on Hiroshima (two days later Albert Camus commented in France that 'the mechanical civilization has just reached its last degree of savagery';[45] on 9 August a second bomb was dropped on Nagasaki; and on 8 August the Agreement on the International Military Tribunal (IMT) for the Punishment of War Criminals was signed in London (the first session of the Tribunal was held in Berlin on 18 October). These three events were not formally linked to one another. Arguably they did, however, result from a unitary design: to put an end to the war, punish those responsible for it, and set the ground for a new international community.

In a way, these seemingly disparate events were destined to have a radical effect on the future of the international community. They increased the existing tension between the opposite poles of law and force. This tension was now dramatically enhanced: on the one hand, States came to possess potentially unrestricted physical power; on the other, new rules and principles were proclaimed and acted upon, and a new international organization was established with a view to placing an ever-increasing number of legal restraints on State sovereignty.

Peace became the principal goal of the international community at large. In the past, wars had never been of worldwide magnitude; in addition, States had never possessed the means of destruction capable of annihilating mankind. The new appalling advances in humans' ability to wreak havoc made it necessary to regard peace as the fundamental purpose of all States, a purpose to which all others—including respect for international law and promotion of justice—ought to be subordinated. However, when the framers of the UN Charter upgraded peace to such high rank, they did not naïvely pursue the goal of permanent and universal peace. They were aware that international friction and interstate armed conflict would not disappear by legislative fiat. They more realistically set about building up a system designed to make armed clashes exceptional events, to be controlled and terminated by means of international institutionalized co-operation. In short, States aimed at achieving a state of affairs where the absence of war was to be a fairly normal condition.

---

[44] N. Politis, *Les nouvelles tendances du droit international* (Paris: Librairie Hachette, 1927), 91.
[45] 'La civilisation mécanique vient de parvenir à son dernier degré de sauvagerie', *Combat*, 8 August 1945, reprinted in A. Camus, *Essais* (Paris: Gallimard, 1984), 291.

One means of pursuing this new purpose was to render the unleashing of wars more onerous than before. Waging war in breach of international law (that is, a war of aggression) was made an 'international crime' entailing the personal responsibility of its authors (in addition, of course, to that of the State for which they acted).

The Second World War had yet another remarkable consequence: it precipitated the downfall of colonial empires. It accelerated a process which had started earlier, and whose principal components were the gradual economic and political decline of European Powers; the disruptive presence of the Soviet Union on the world scene; and the growing political and economic power of the US, which (despite its colonial domination of the Philippines, and the de facto direct or indirect exploitation of some Latin American countries) propounded an anti-colonialist ideology. These were the international factors that contributed to the demise of colonialism. There were, however, also domestic reasons, which various authors have rightly stressed. After the First World War, at least some Western European countries had witnessed both a gradual opening to democracy and also a drive towards the 'welfare State', largely motivated by greater sensitivity to and concern for the underprivileged. Thus, when the cost of maintaining colonial rule over distant territories increased (among other things because of rising unrest there), the metropolitan masses were able to transmit a clear message to their rulers: since the principal profits from colonial exploitation went to limited groups of people, whereas the military costs and also some welfare costs were becoming an increasingly heavy burden on the budget of the colonial country, it was no longer in the interest of the population to persist with colonial domination.

2.5.2 THE ESTABLISHMENT OF THE UNITED NATIONS

One of the major reactions to the devastations of the Second World War and the unfettered recourse to violence marking those dark years was the keen desire to set up a world organization that would be capable of preventing 'the scourge of war' and peacefully settling all major disputes between States. Thus, the UN was created. As this organization is analysed in **Chapter 15**, it suffices here to outline briefly its main features.

The political premise to this major turning point was the rapprochement between two former political opponents, the US and the USSR, which had gradually come about during the war and had led to some form of political co-operation. The major victorious Powers conceived of the UN as a sort of prolongation of their wartime alliance.

The UN Charter banned the use or threat of force (Article 2(4)) and at the same time granted to the Security Council the power to take sanctions and measures involving the use of force against any State breaking that ban (Chapter VII of the Charter). It also regulated the gradual demise of the colonial empires, by providing for the trusteeship system with a view to ensuring a slow passage of colonial countries to self-government or independence. In addition, the Charter endeavoured to strengthen international co-operation in various fields.

No doubt the UN was a far better and more advanced experiment in world security than the previous ones (that of 1648, which to a large extent remained on paper; the Concert of Europe of 1815; and the League of Nations of 1919). Suffice it to mention just one element: for the first time, the Charter prohibited not just war, but any threat of or resort to the use of military force. This, by itself, marked an enormous advance in international institutions. More specifically, the system for collective security created in 1945 bears a strong resemblance to the Concert of Europe of 1815 (see **2.3.2**). As in the post-Napoleonic era, in 1945 the main Powers considered it necessary to assume control of international affairs and to decide themselves on joint action to be taken in case of serious threats or breaches of peace. They therefore set up a 'directorate', consisting of the two superpowers (the US and the

USSR) plus a few other States which, although already on the wane, could still be regarded as indispensable to any effective direction of international affairs (the UK, France, and China, the latter being at that time formally represented by the 'nationalist' government of Chiang Kai-shek). The superiority of a few powerful countries was formally acknowledged in law: Article 27(3) of the UN Charter lays down that the Security Council cannot adopt any deliberation on matters of substance unless all five *permanent* members agree (either by voting in favour or, according to the practice evolved later, by abstaining). This is the so-called *veto* by any of the Big Five. By the same token, the Charter envisaged a system of collective security: if the Security Council, with the concurring vote of the permanent members, agreed that there was a threat to peace, a breach of the peace, or an act of aggression, it could either take sanctions or dispatch UN armed forces against the offending State.

However, two events undermined from the outset the whole edifice built at San Francisco. First, less than two months after the adoption of the Charter, the US dropped atomic bombs on Hiroshima and Nagasaki: this immediately posed new and dramatic problems. Secondly, nearly a year after June 1945, the Cold War set in, breaking up the political and military alliance born during the war and practically dividing the world into two conflicting camps. The disagreement between the Western Powers and the Soviet Union, which surfaced in 1946, with the Cold War spreading everywhere, in most cases prevented the collective security system from working. As a consequence, the international community had to fall back on the traditional devices for preventing war or enforcing international law. Once again, an attempt at centralizing the use of force ended in failure, and the old institution of self-help acquired new importance, albeit with a number of qualifications.

2.5.3 CHANGES IN THE COMPOSITION OF THE INTERNATIONAL COMMUNITY

Following the Second World War, the make-up of the world community changed radically. First, a handful of Eastern European countries, already under the influence of the Soviet Union (which had freed them from the Nazis), became socialist 'democracies' (the German Democratic Republic, Poland, Bulgaria, Hungary, Romania, and Czechoslovakia, to which Yugoslavia should be added). As a consequence, the Soviet Union no longer felt isolated in its ideological and political fight against capitalist States. Secondly, a number of countries subjected to colonial domination gained political independence as a result of the erosion of the colonial empires of France, the UK, Belgium, the Netherlands, Portugal, Spain, and Italy.

Syria and Lebanon were granted independence in 1945 and 1946 respectively; India and Pakistan became formally independent in 1947; in 1948 the State of Israel was founded, and Burma became independent; independent status was granted to Libya in 1951, to Tunisia, Morocco, Sudan, and Ghana in 1956, to the Federation of Malaya in 1957, and to Guinea in 1958. Many other colonial countries gained independence in the 1960s.

After 1960 the bulk of the international community consisted of so-called 'Third World' countries, after the expression used by French intellectual Alfred Sauvy, by analogy with Sieyès' 'tiers Etat'.[46] Together with the socialist States they could easily muster a two-thirds majority in any international gathering. The new make-up of the world community differs radically from that represented in its first phase. While in the seventeenth and eighteenth

---

[46] A. Sauvy, 'Trois mondes, une planète', *L'Observateur*, no. 118, 14 August 1952, 14.

centuries a number of European countries dominated the world scene, and non-Western States were far less numerous and of marginal importance, now non-Western States constituted the overwhelming majority. However, one should refrain from jumping to the conclusion that the new position was the exact reverse of the former. In fact, the Western minority still wielded enormous economic and military power, while the majority was chiefly endowed with political and rhetorical authority. Hence, the situation was now more complex and contradictory than before.

Along with newly independent States, a new category of international subjects became active in the international arena: intergovernmental organizations (see **Chapter 7**). They mushroomed in a short period of time, covering several fields (political, economic, social, technical, etc.) with a broad variety of activities, which had considerable impact on international affairs. Their existence had many consequences. It may suffice to emphasize one, which relates to the political field. Previously, some States, particularly middle-sized and small Powers, were to some extent able to refrain from becoming involved in international affairs which were not directly relevant to them. Once they started participating in the activities of international organizations where all major world events were discussed, often forming the subject of resolutions or leading to the taking of some sort of joint action, it became almost impossible for them to remain aloof. They were required to express their views on the matter, to take sides, to join in praising, condemning, or exhorting. In short, the creation of a wide network of intergovernmental organizations aroused or strengthened, if not a sense of solidarity, at least the sense of belonging to the same community and therefore of being concerned by any crucial event occurring in it. If the First World War made each State feel that it could no longer live in relative isolation, the emergence of organizations buttressed this trend and definitively established the notion that certain occurrences (aggression in one area of the world, one particular country's pursuit of a policy of destabilization of other States, widespread injustice in economic relations between two or more groups of States, etc.) were of concern to the whole international community.

2.5.4 LEGAL CHANGE

Once developing countries had, with the active support of socialist States, firmly established their command over the UN General Assembly, they started devising and propounding a complex strategy. First, the powers of the UN were enhanced (at least at the rhetorical level), except in the area of collective security, and they were increasingly expanded to new areas, particularly international development. Secondly, developing and socialist States kept insisting on self-determination, permanent sovereignty over natural resources, and racial equality, and demanded that these be turned into legal principles. They achieved these demands starting in 1960, with the adoption by the General Assembly of the 'Declaration on the Granting of Independence to Colonial Countries and Peoples' (Resolution 1514 (XV)),[47] followed, in 1962, by Resolution 1803 (XVII) on 'Permanent Sovereignty over Natural Resources',[48] then, in 1965, when the UN Convention on Racial Discrimination was adopted, and again in 1966 when the two UN International Covenants on Human Rights were adopted. The Covenants included a common article (Article 1) laying down the principle of self-determination. These instruments were followed and amplified by a number of resolutions laying down ancillary rules (see **3.8**). Thirdly, the two groups of States proposed

---

[47] This resolution was, years later, recognized as having crystallized customary international law at the time of its adoption. See *Legal Consequences of the Separation of the Chagos Archipelago from Mauritius in 1965*, §150.

[48] This resolution was soon recognized as codifying customary international law, see *Texaco Overseas Petroleum Company and California Asiatic Oil Company v The Government of the Libyan Arab Republic*, §87.

that all the basic principles governing international relations should be recast in such a way as to take account of their views. This was achieved in 1970, after many years of labour, when the UN General Assembly adopted the Declaration on Friendly Relations[49] (see **Chapter 3**). Fourthly, codification, that is, the transformation of customary rules into written form (treaty provisions or other written expressions), was expanded to cover a wide range of subjects.[50] Finally, developing countries tried to bring about radical changes in the economic set-up of the international community. After long and untiring efforts, the so-called Group of 77 (in 1964, when they first united their efforts on an institutional basis, the African, Asian, and Latin American States numbered 77) succeeded in having the General Assembly adopt a Declaration and a plan of action on the 'New International Economic Order' (NIEO).[51] The outcome took the form of a series of resolutions, for it would have been both unrealistic and premature to impose new economic principles with legally binding force on industrialized countries. The adoption of recommendations was seen as the stage preceding the gradual transformation of political guidelines into international legal rules.

During this period, the contribution of the *Institut de Droit International* and, more generally, of individual writers, to the elaboration or codification of international law increasingly dwindled. This was mainly due to the UN's establishment of the International Law Commission (ILC), which is charged with the task of contributing to the codification and progressive development of international law, as well as the increasing adoption, by the General Assembly, of normative resolutions or Declarations concerning important issues of international law.

2.6 FROM THE END OF THE COLD WAR TO THE PRESENT

The fall, in 1989, of the Berlin Wall and the subsequent break-up of the group of socialist States led to the demise of the whole of this group. The Russian Federation, despite being technically the continuator of the USSR (see **4.4**), did not inherit the Soviet Union's position as a superpower.[52]

---

[49] On this important instrument see M. K. Nawaz et al. (eds), *The Legal Principles Governing Friendly Relations and Co-Operation among States* (Leiden: Sijthoff, 1966); G. Arangio Ruiz, 'The Normative Role of the General Assembly of the United Nations and the Declaration of Principles of Friendly Relations' (1972) 137 *RCADI* 419; M. Sahovic, 'Codification des principes du droit international des relations amicales et de la coopération entre les Etats' (1972) 137 *RCADI* 243; G. Abi-Saab, 'La reformulation des principes de la charte et la transformation des structures juridiques de la communauté internationale' in *Le droit international au service de la paix, de la justice et du développement: mélanges Michel Virally* (Paris: Pedone, 1991), 1; I. Sinclair, 'The Significance of the Friendly Relations Declaration' in C. Warbrick and V. Lowe (eds), *The United Nations and the Principles of International Law, Essays in Memory of Michael Akehurst* (London: Routledge, 1994), 1; J. E. Viñuales (ed.), *The UN Friendly Relations Declaration at 50: An Assessment of the Fundamental Principles of International Law* (Cambridge: Cambridge University Press, 2020).

[50] See SFDI, *La codification du droit international: Colloque d'Aix-en-Provence* (Paris: Pedone, 1999).

[51] On the economic dimensions of the NIEO see J. Bhagwati (ed.), *The New International Economic Order: The North–South Debate* (Cambridge, MA: MIT Press, 1977). For different views on the legal dimensions see G. A. C. White, 'A New International Economic Order' (1975) 24 *ICLQ* 542; D. Carreau, 'Le nouvel ordre économique international' (1977) 104 *JDI* 595; S. Marchisio, *La cooperazione per lo sviluppo nel diritto delle Nazioni Unite* (Naples: Jovene, 1977); M. Bedjaoui, *Towards a New International Economic Order* (Paris: UNESCO, 1979); R.-J. Dupuy (ed.), *The New International Economic Order* (Leiden: Martinus Nijhoff, 1981); G. Abi-Saab, 'Le droit au développement' (1988) 44 *Annuaire suisse de droit international* 9.

[52] On the implications of the transition from the USSR to the Russian Federation from the perspective of international law see T. Långström, *Transformation in Russia and International Law* (Leiden: Martinus Nijhoff, 2003).

At present, there no longer exist in the world community three distinct groupings. The global system characterized, in the two decades following the collapse of the USSR, by 'unipolarity', with the US as the only superpower, is giving way to a new variant of the old 'multipolar' system, where newly emerging countries, sometimes referred to as the BRIICS (Brazil, Russia, India, Indonesia, China, and South Africa), as well as the EU, occupy an increasingly important place in global affairs. This diversification of the poles of power has called into question the short-lived 'end of history' that some saw in the political and ideological influence of the US. China, which has grown increasingly assertive in international relations, has challenged the pre-eminent position of the US, which, faced with domestic division and inward policies, has lost much of its prestige and influence in the global arena.

The beginning of this multipolarity can be tentatively found in the 2008 world economic crisis. Two distinct periods can thus be identified: one which goes from the end of the Cold War to the 2008 crisis, and the other that began with the latter crisis and is unfolding before our very eyes.

2.6.1 'UNIPOLARITY'

During the first period, the US, dubbed the 'lonely superpower',[53] tended to act as a world policeman, that is, it endeavoured to settle political disputes or to promote settlements, as well as to contribute to the maintenance of peace and the enforcement of international law. This role, however, was played selectively, that is, only to the extent that it proved consonant with, and favoured, the strategic and geopolitical interests of the US. Thus, in many cases where these interests were at stake, the US acted forcibly through the UN (Iraq, 1990–91, Somalia, 1992, Bosnia-Herzegovina, 1992–95); in other instances, where UN support was not forthcoming, it acted through NATO, in clear disregard of the UN Charter (Kosovo, 1999). In yet other instances, it either refrained from taking military action, because its interests were not involved (e.g. Rwanda, 1994, Sierra Leone, 2000, etc.) or engaged in military operations without any UN authorization (Iraq, 2003–04). The US also exercised its political role as a global mediator in many trouble-spots (e.g. in the Middle East, Northern Ireland, etc.).

The former socialist countries, no longer united, tended to lean on Western countries. Developing States are no longer divided into one group siding with socialist States and another siding with the West. They seem to be no longer ideologically oriented. They are instead united by their demands for more international economic and financial assistance and greater access to world markets. In the UN, these countries have sometimes negotiated as the 'Group of 77' (see **2.5.4**), when discussing economic and, to some extent, environmental matters, but they have also acted in other formations, in relation to political matters.

What also characterized the first post-Cold War period were: (i) the relative decline of the UN as an international institution for the maintenance of peace and stability; (ii) the tendency of States to strengthen and broaden the role of military alliances such as NATO; (iii) the growing trend towards regionalization (a trend that appeared more conspicuously in Europe, with the European Union); and (iv) the devastating importance of terrorism. The impact of terrorism on the life of the international community since the 11 September 2001 attacks on the US signalled, in fact, a dramatic turning point in the evolution of the world community: as a result of those attacks, the increasing spread of terrorism, and the consequent forcible reaction of many States, a number of international legal categories and instrumentalities have been called into question or, at the very least, suffered an overstretch

---

[53] See S. Huntington, 'The Lonely Superpower' (1999) 78 *Foreign Affairs* 2.

(e.g. in the area of self-defence, see **16.5**), which in the long run could potentially lead to a significant change in international legal standards and institutions.

2.6.2 EMERGING 'MULTIPOLARITY'

Turning to the second period of the post-Cold War world, it would seem that the main divide today is that resulting from socio-economic development, with broad categories of countries labelled as part of the 'Global North' or the 'Global South'. These labels are, to be sure, very approximative, and they mask wide variation within them. But they can be borrowed, for present purposes, to briefly characterize the agendas of different groups of countries.

At present, the industrialized countries of the 'Global North' see as the main international problems the fight against terrorism; free trade; nuclear disarmament; protection of the environment (particularly climate change); prevention of viral outbreaks and disease spread; and the need to prevent ethnic, racial, and religious conflicts—increasingly rife in so many parts of the world—from spreading across the borders of the countries where they break out. No fully fledged common legal strategy may be discerned in this group of countries.

As for the wide range of developing States, in the so-called 'Global South', they consider that the major problems are their poverty and development challenges, the lack of fair access of their products to world markets, and the dangerously widening gap with industrialized States. Their legal strategy in the world community reflects these concerns. As for the legal means of action they pursue, it would seem that they have drawn an important lesson from (a) the failure of both the NIEO and their doctrine of the so-called right to development, and (b) the fact that they now lack the ideological and political support they previously attracted from socialist States. They therefore no longer insist on passing General Assembly resolutions proclaiming new rights or outlining new economic strategies. They have realized that it is more constructive to come to some sort of agreement or compromise with the industrialized countries.

A characteristic feature of modern developments in international law deserves to be emphasized. Over several decades, a certain degree of specialization in the rules governing some matters led to the consolidation of recognizable bodies of norms, sometimes called 'branches' or—confusingly—'special regimes' of international law. This process of specialization concerns, for instance, human rights law, the humanitarian law of armed conflict, environmental law, international health law, international trade law, international investment law, international criminal law, or the law of the sea. For some time, they tended to appear as separate and tight legal compartments, which gave international lawyers the false impression that international law was legally fragmented. Whereas that may have been true from a sociological perspective, with groups of lawyers, scholarship, academic degrees, and even professional groups identifying themselves by reference to a 'branch', the law itself never supported such a conclusion.[54]

At present, these groups and therefore the labels are becoming less homogeneous and water-tight, and the profound connections between different bodies of norms are becoming gradually understood and fleshed out in legal scholarship and practice. Thus, for instance, two bodies of law, namely international rules and guidelines on the protection of the environment and international trade law, are increasingly linked to—and, to some extent, made

---

[54] See P.-M. Dupuy, 'L'unité de l'ordre juridique international: cours général de droit international public (2000)' (2002) 297 *RCADI* 9.

contingent on the application of—the law of development as well as human rights law; international criminal law is more and more influenced by human rights law and linked to humanitarian law; the operation of human rights and investment law is influenced by that of international health law; the law of State responsibility is increasingly overlapping, or being influenced by, the law on individual criminal liability; in many respects the law of the sea has been connected to the law of development and is seen as a possible means of promoting the take-off of the economies of poor countries.

This gradual interpenetration and cross-fertilization of previously somewhat compartmentalized areas of international law is a significant development: it shows that, at least at the normative level, the international community is becoming more integrated and—what is even more important—that such values as human rights, environmental protection, and the need to promote development are increasingly permeating various sectors of international law that previously seemed impervious to them.

3

THE FUNDAMENTAL PRINCIPLES GOVERNING INTERNATIONAL RELATIONS

3.1 CHARACTERIZATION OF FUNDAMENTAL PRINCIPLES

Most States have written constitutions that lay down the fundamental principles regulating social relations. Principles are the pinnacle of the legal system and are intended to serve as basic guidelines for the life of the whole community. Besides imposing general obligations, they also set out the policy lines and the basic goals of State agencies. Furthermore, they can be relied upon for the interpretation of legal provisions, whenever the ordinary rules on interpretation prove insufficient.

The position is different in the world community. When this community came into existence, no State or other authority set forth any fundamental principles for regulating international dealings: no State had enough power to impose standards of behaviour on all other members. A body of law gradually evolved under the impulse of convergent interests and exigencies of States, but no general overarching principle was agreed upon. However, the increase in the corpus of rules by the gradual accretion of new norms made it clear that States spontaneously and almost unwittingly based their relations on a few fundamental tenets from which they drew inspiration. Close scrutiny of the legal standards emerging in the first stages of development of the international community shows that States substantially acted upon at least three *postulates*: freedom, equality, and effectiveness. These postulates differ from the general principles of national legal systems, which are legally binding. The three postulates are merely legal constructs reached through an inductive process based on generalization of some of the distinguishing traits of international rules. Through such a process, the conclusion can be reached that, in the early days, most international rules granted a wide sphere of action to States; they proclaimed or relied on the legal equality of States; and tended to legitimize situations which had acquired de facto force.

The three postulates are clearly the synthesis of what could be concisely defined as the 'laissez-faire approach' of classical international law. Under this approach, all States were equally free to do what they liked provided they followed certain 'rules of the game'. Moreover, if, in the exercise of this almost unfettered freedom, they could bring about new situations by force, the law would give its blessing to these situations.

The adoption of the UN Charter in 1945 heralded a very significant change: the drafters laid down in Articles 1 and 2 a set of fundamental purposes and principles by which all the members of the UN were to abide. They ranged from the recognition of the self-determination of peoples or of individual human rights, to the sovereign equality of States, the prohibition of the use of force, the obligation to settle disputes peacefully, or the need to behave in good faith. Thus, an international treaty of overriding importance set forth the fundamental standards governing State action and established the main goals of international institutions. This new state of affairs was the direct consequence of the shake-up in the world community brought about by the Second World War, in particular of the keen desire of all States to lay the foundations of an international system more conducive to peace and justice. However, in spite of the great impact of the Charter principles on the evolution of the international community, it gradually emerged in the 1960s that they were too loose and did not meet the demands of new States. Indeed, far-reaching changes had taken place in the international community in the aftermath of the Second World War as a result of the demise of colonialism and the spread of the socialist State model. More particularly, the world community had been joined by numerous new members whose political outlook differed substantially from that of older States.

Socialist and developing countries thus initiated a process of revision that involved the expansion and updating of the Charter principles, with a view to turning them into standards of universal value. These groups of countries were motivated by two basic factors. On the one hand, they were keen to inject their own basic demands into international law so as to make it more consonant with current international realities. On the other hand, they felt that, in order to satisfy the need for predictability and security underlying social relations, they had to discuss, negotiate, agree upon, and set down in black letter the basic standards of conduct with the traditional members of the world community. The principles agreed upon in the 1960s and proclaimed in the 1970 UN Friendly Relations Declaration (resolution 2625, adopted by consensus, but not legally binding per se[1]), while to a large extent restating those already set forth in the UN Charter, gave them greater emphasis or fleshed them out, and in addition extended their application to all States (whereas those laid down in the Charter only applied to members of the Organization). They were seven: the ban on the threat or use of force, the peaceful settlement of disputes, the prohibition of intervention in other States' affairs, the duty to co-operate, self-determination of peoples, the sovereign equality of States, and good faith.

It should not be thought, however, that the mere fact of being included in the list proclaimed in the Declaration upgrades a standard of behaviour to the rank of a universal and fundamental principle. It is also necessary for the standard to be laid down in a set of norms of general import. Standards such as those on co-operation, or on good faith, as long as they are not enshrined in instruments elevating them to the rank of legal principles governing the conduct of international subjects, may remain expressions of policy guidelines. By the same token, it is not true that only those principles laid down in the Declaration make up the body of fundamental principles of international law. What is determinative of the matter is careful consideration of international practice: a wide range of factors (treaties; GA resolutions; declarations of States; statements by government representatives in the UN; diplomatic practice; case law, if any) must be taken into account when trying to determine whether certain international pronouncements have engendered a principle of universal scope and legally binding force. This is particularly true of the need to protect human rights and the environment, neither of which is listed as an independent principle in the Friendly Relations Declaration.

In the present world community, even after the collapse of the Soviet Union and most other socialist countries, States are divided economically, politically, and culturally and often their relations are beset with tensions. The principles therefore represent the

---

[1] Resolution 2625 (XXV), Declaration on Principles of International Law concerning Friendly Relations and Cooperation among States in accordance with the Charter of the United Nations, 24 October 1970. On this important instrument see J. E. Viñuales (ed.), *The UN Friendly Relations Declaration at 50: An Assessment of the Fundamental Principles of International Law* (Cambridge: Cambridge University Press, 2020).

fundamental set of standards on which they are not divided, and which allow a degree of relatively smooth international dealings. They make up the apex of the whole body of international law. They constitute *overriding legal standards* that may be regarded as the *constitutional principles* of the international community. As such, they share certain common features.

Firstly, the principles reflecting the traditional structure of the world community, grounded in equality of States and marked by individual State interest, were not only standards that underpinned most rules of the international community and expressed the thrust of that body of law; they were also enshrined in general rules that attracted unanimous support and accurately described the way States intended to conduct their international dealings. By contrast, the new principles are the expression and the result of conflicting views of States on matters of crucial importance, which they try to conciliate. At present, when States cannot agree upon definite and specific standards of behaviour because of their principled, opposing attitudes, but need nevertheless some sort of basic guidelines for their conduct, they tend to fall back on principles. Principles, being general, loose, and multifaceted, may be tainted with some ambiguity. They therefore lend themselves to various and even contradictory applications, and they are also susceptible to being manipulated and used for conflicting purposes. In this respect *modern* principles are a typical expression of the present world community, whereas in the old community—narrower and relatively homogeneous—fairly well-defined and unanimously supported principles tended to prevail, in addition of course to treaty and customary rules.

Secondly, with some exceptions (e.g. sovereign equality), these principles seek to govern not only the conduct of States but also that of other international legal subjects (in particular, insurgents, peoples represented by liberation movements, and international organizations). All the legal entities operating in the international community must abide by them to certain degrees. By way of illustration, the principle of non-intervention as initially formulated in Article 2(7) of the UN Charter sought to prevent unlawful intervention of the UN in the internal affairs of member States. The customary principle, as it emerged from the inter-American practice, had a wider scope and concerned the relations among States, and it is this understanding that was later codified in the Friendly Relations Declaration. But the reference in Article 2(7) of the UN Charter highlights the scope of application of fundamental principles, which in most cases exceeds the sole interstate relations.

Thirdly, the rights and claims deriving from the principles accrue, in many cases, to all members of the international community, who are thereby entitled to claim their observance. In other words, some principles legally entitle any relevant international subject to claim compliance by any other international subject, whether or not non-compliance has damaged the former subject. Thus, for instance, any State can demand respect for the ban on the use of force by any other State; in case of violation, it is entitled to insist on its cessation or, more generally, demand reparation. Similarly, the principle requiring the protection of human rights or the principle of prevention of environmental harm entitles all members of the community to demand compliance and, in the case of gross and large-scale infringements, to request their cessation (as well as punishment of the responsible authorities, if allowed by the circumstances).

Fourthly, certain principles have been vested with higher authority, in that they are accepted by the international community as standards from which no derogation is permitted. Such principles are referred to as peremptory norms or *jus cogens*. As will be specified later on (see **11.4**), the special force of such peremptory principles lies in rendering null and void any international treaty contrary to them. Importantly, the fundamental character of a principle must not be equated with its peremptory character. For example, the principle of sovereign equality does not produce the effects of peremptory norms. Indeed, this principle can be derogated from by treaty, as demonstrated by a plethora of treaties and conventions, as long as the limitations thus placed are freely accepted by the State. If two or more States enter into an agreement providing for impairment or restriction of the sovereignty of a third State, short of the use of force, such an agreement is not null and void. But its conclusion and implementation trigger the international responsibility of the States concerned for breach of a fundamental rule of international law. This also holds true for the principle of non-intervention, as emphasized by the UN General Assembly in resolution 36/103.[2] By contrast, a treaty in breach of the principle prohibiting the threat or the use of force is null and void *ab initio*.[3] This would also be the case for a treaty in breach of the principle commanding respect for fundamental human rights, which belongs to the category of *jus cogens*. For one thing, this character derives from the fact that certain general rules protecting specific human rights (those on racial discrimination, apartheid, slavery, genocide, and the self-determination of peoples) have had the nature of peremptory norms ascribed to them in official statements by government representatives.[4] Logically, if a treaty that allows or makes provision for genocide, slavery, or racial discrimination is null and void on account of its inconsistency with *jus cogens*, there is no reason for denying the same character to a treaty authorizing large-scale infringements of similar gravity of human rights (e.g. massive denial of civil and political freedoms; of trade union rights; or of basic economic, social, and cultural rights). Yet another example of a principle enjoying *jus cogens* character is the *self-determination of peoples*. Many countries made statements to this effect in the UN General Assembly on the occasion of the discussion on the Draft Articles on the Law of Treaties in 1963, at the Vienna Conference on the Law of Treaties in 1968–69, as well as in the UN General Assembly in 1970, on the occasion of the discussion on the Friendly Relations Declaration.[5] A treaty that deprives a people of its right to self-determination is therefore null and void *ab initio*.

---

[2] Operative paragraph II(*h*) of resolution 36/103, 9 December 1981, provides that one of the consequences of the principle is the duty of States 'to refrain from entering into agreements with other States with a view to intervening or interfering in internal or external affairs of other States'.

[3] In a memorandum of 29 December 1979 to the Acting Secretary of State Warren Christopher, the Legal Adviser of the US Department of State stressed that if the Treaty of Friendship, Good Neighborliness and Co-operation between the USSR and Afghanistan, of 1978, lent itself 'to support of Soviet intervention of the type in question in Afghanistan, it would be void under contemporary principles of international law, since it would conflict with what the Vienna Convention on the Law of Treaties describes as a "peremptory norm of general international law" (Article 53), namely, that contained in Article 2(4) of the Charter' (in (1980) 74 *AJIL* 418, in particular at 419).

[4] Countries belonging to various groups made a number of statements to this effect at the Diplomatic Conference on the Law of Treaties in Vienna. See, in particular, the statements by the representative of Finland (United Nations Conference on the Law of Treaties, First Session (Vienna, 26 March–24 May 1968), *Official Records*, at 295, §13), Kenya (ibid., 296, §31), Sierra Leone (ibid., 300, §9), Uruguay (ibid., 303, §48), Cyprus (ibid., 306, §69), France (ibid., 309, §32), Canada (ibid., 323, §22), and the Federal Republic of Germany (United Nations Conference on the Law of Treaties, Second Session (Vienna, 9 April–22 May 1969), *Official Records*, at 96, §26). See also the strong Dissenting Opinion of Judge Tanaka in the *South West Africa Cases* (1966) (where he expressed the view that 'surely the law concerning the protection of human rights may be considered to belong to the *jus cogens*' (at 298)) and, in the case law of the Arbitration Commission of the Peace Conference on Yugoslavia, the Opinions No. 1 (Dissolution of Yugoslavia) and No. 2 (Serbian Minorities in Bosnia-Herzegovina and Croatia).

[5] Spain, Algeria, and (to some extent) Morocco adopted the same attitude in their submissions in 1975 before the ICJ in the *Western Sahara* case (§§48–53). It would seem that Italy also supported the view at issue in 1975, in the UN Human Rights Commission (see UN Doc. E/CN. 4/SR.1300, at 91), as did the US in the aforementioned 1979 Memorandum on the Soviet invasion of Afghanistan. The Italian Court of Cassation in 1985, in the *Arafat and Salah* case, also stated that self-determination is part of *jus cogens* (at 886), as did the Arbitration Commission of the International Conference on Yugoslavia, in its Opinions No. 1 and No. 2, at 182. In its decision in the *East Timor (Portugal v Australia)* case, the ICJ seemed to support this view in asserting that Portugal's view that the right to self-determination has *erga omnes* character was 'irreproachable', §29.

Finally, another common feature of the principles ought to be stressed. Although valid for and applicable to every State, they rely heavily for their implementation and enforcement on the UN. Plainly, the momentous advance represented by the emergence of a network of normative standards has not gone hand in hand with commensurate progress in the setting up of international law enforcement machinery. In other words, no *specific* mechanism has as yet been established in the international community to flesh out and give teeth to the basic tenets destined to act as the backbone of the community. In this vacuum, the UN has been called upon to play the role of an implementation mechanism, by monitoring and enforcing the observance of the principles. In doing so, the UN acts in the interest and on behalf of the entire world community.

The foregoing discussion of the main common features of fundamental principles must be kept in mind when studying the specific contents and operation of each principle, to which we now turn.

3.2 THE SOVEREIGN EQUALITY OF STATES

3.2.1 GENERAL OBSERVATIONS

Traditional international law was based on a set of rules protecting the sovereignty of States and establishing their formal equality in law.[6] In 1945, while drafting the UN Charter, the drafters proclaimed the 'sovereign equality of all its Members' (Article 2(1)) as one of the Organization's principles. This formula was not adopted without opposition. The Belgian delegate to one of the Committees in the San Francisco Conference that drafted the Charter pointed out that 'the smaller States would regard it as somewhat ironical, in view of the striking inequalities evident in the Organization, to find at the head of the statement of principles a bold reference to the "sovereign equality" of all Members'.[7] By contrast, and for obvious reasons, neither the labours of the Special Committee on Friendly Relations (1962–70) nor the debates in the General Assembly reveal any radical differences on this principle, so much so that 'the principle of sovereign equality of States' was reaffirmed in the Friendly Relations Declaration along the lines of Article 2(1) of the Charter. However, in this resolution, it was extended to *all* States, irrespective of their membership in the UN.

Of the various principles, this is unquestionably one on which there is nowadays unqualified agreement and which has the support of all groups of States, regardless of ideologies, political leanings, and circumstances. It is safe to conclude that sovereign equality constitutes the lynchpin of the whole body of international legal standards, the fundamental premise on which all international relations rest.

This being so, its present import is not entirely clear. Admittedly, the principle is an umbrella concept, covering various general rules, of which it provides a synthesis. Consequently, it can only be fully appreciated if these general rules are spelled out. As the principle embraces two logically distinct notions (sovereignty and legal equality), it is useful to consider them separately.

---

[6] See generally M. Koskenniemi and V. Kari, 'Sovereign Equality' in Viñuales, *The UN Friendly Relations Declaration* (n 1), chapter 8.
[7] UNCIO, vi, at 332.

3.2.2 SOVEREIGNTY

Sovereignty includes sweeping powers and rights, including most prominently:

(1) The power to wield authority over all the individuals living in the territory. This power might even be regarded as the quintessence of sovereignty. As a political leader and publicist stated in 1923, the famous Cartesian dictum, if applied to States, should be set out as follows: '*iubeo, ergo sum*' (I command, hence I exist).[8] The power of the authorities of a State to exercise public functions over individuals located in a territory is called 'jurisdiction'. Normally jurisdiction may manifest itself in various forms: *prescriptive jurisdiction* (i.e. the power to enact legal commands or authorizations binding upon the individuals and State instrumentalities in the territory belonging to the State, and also, under certain circumstances, upon individuals abroad); *adjudicative jurisdiction* (this is a form of prescriptive jurisdiction defining the scope of the power to settle legal disputes through binding decisions, or to interpret the law with binding force for all the persons and entities concerned); and *enforcement jurisdiction* (i.e. the power to ensure through coercive means that legal commands and entitlements are complied with). The doctrine of jurisdiction is further discussed in section **5.2**.

(2) The power to freely use and dispose of the territory under the State's jurisdiction and perform all activities deemed necessary or beneficial to the population living there. In 1921 the US Secretary of State Robert Lansing aptly synthesized, in *political* terms, the primary goal pursued by States in the exercise of this power, as follows: '[T]he chief object in the determination of the sovereignty to be exercised within a certain territory is national safety. National safety is as dominant in the life of a nation as self-preservation is in the life of an individual. It is even more so, as nations do not respond to the impulse of self-sacrifice.'[9] This power is not without limitations, which evolve over time following the conclusion by States of new treaties and the development of general international law. Some important limitations arise from the principle of prevention of significant environmental harm (see **3.10**) and, more generally, from several duties requiring the exercise of due diligence or aimed at upholding elementary considerations of humanity or, still, at allowing navigation through international straits (see *Corfu Channel (United Kingdom v Albania)* case, at 22), among many others.[10]

(3) The right that no other State intrude in the State's territory (the so-called *jus excludendi alios*, or the right to exclude others). States have always vigorously protested and claimed compensation when foreign States have exercised on their territory public activities that had not been previously authorized. They have also reacted in this way when the public action on their territory had been performed secretly or by State agents allegedly acting as private individuals.

In some cases, the doctrine has been invoked with regard to actions performed publicly by foreign authorities. Thus, in 1921 a company of US soldiers, authorized by the US War Department to go into the territory of Mexico in pursuit of bandits, arrested a Mexican who had perpetrated a crime in Texas. The Mexican national was brought to trial before a

---

[8] V. E. Orlando, 'Francesco Crispi' (1923), in *Scritti varii di diritto pubblico e scienza politica* (Milano: Giuffrè, 1940), 400.

[9] R. Lansing, *The Peace Negotiations: A Personal Account* (Boston and New York: Houghton Mifflin Co., 1921), 102.

[10] See generally N. Schrijver, *Sovereignty over Natural Resources: Balancing Rights and Duties* (New York: Cambridge University Press, 1997).

Texas court. On appeal, a US court held in *Dominguez* v *State* that the US soldiers' 'entry of Mexico for the purpose of apprehending offenders would have been a violation of the law of nations in the absence of consent of the Mexican Government'. Since, however, that government had given its consent, the arrest of Dominguez had not been illegal and he could be tried in the US (at 8–9). Another illustration concerns activities by Italian officials in Switzerland. On 8 May 2003, a delegation (consisting of two parliamentarians, a judge acting as a consultant, and two unarmed police officers) of the Italian Parliamentary Enquiry Committee charged with investigating the 'Telekom Serbia' affair visited, unauthorized, the bankruptcy office (*Ufficio fallimenti*) of Lugano (Switzerland) to collect evidence on alleged embezzlement, corruption, and other offences in the purchase of 'Telekom Serbia' by the Italian public telephone company Telecom. The Italian officials were briefly detained by the Swiss police at the request of the Swiss Federal prosecutor, questioned, and charged with breach of Articles 271 and 273 of the Swiss Penal Code (punishing respectively unauthorized acts performed in Switzerland on behalf of a foreign State, and economic espionage). The Federal Prosecutor rightly contended that the Italian authorities were under an obligation to request the evidence through official channels, by means of a rogatory letter. Subsequently, by reasons of comity, the Swiss authorities dropped the criminal charges brought against the Italian officials.[11]

In other cases, States have protested against actions carried out on their territory by a foreign country acting through private individuals or by foreign agents disguised as private individuals. One example is the *Salomon Jacob* case. In 1935 a German national was kidnapped in Switzerland by other Germans acting on behalf of Germany and taken to Germany; Switzerland protested; in the end Mr Jacob was returned to Switzerland and a German civil servant was punished by the German authorities.[12] Another illustration is the *Eichmann* case. In 1960 Eichmann was kidnapped in Argentina by Israeli agents posing as private individuals, and taken to Israel; Argentina, not content with the apology offered by Israel, took the case to the UN Security Council, which called upon Israel to pay adequate compensation.[13] A third illustration is provided by the *Argoud* case. In 1963 the French colonel Argoud was kidnapped in Germany by French agents and taken to France to stand trial. Germany protested and demanded the return of Argoud, adding that it stood ready to subsequently extradite him to France. The French authorities claimed however that they were not responsible for the alleged kidnapping of Argoud, adding that, in any case, it was not even certain that he had been kidnapped, for perhaps he had in fact returned to France voluntarily. Eventually, Germany renounced its claim to the restitution of the French colonel.[14]

(4) The right to immunity from the jurisdiction of foreign courts for acts or actions performed by the State in its sovereign capacity, and for execution measures taken against the use or planned use of public property or assets for the discharge of public functions. The question, however, of defining these classes of acts or actions, or the public nature of assets, is not entirely settled (see **6.2**).

(5) The right to immunity for State representatives for acts, past or present, in their official capacity (the so-called *functional immunity*) and for other acts, while they hold an official position (the so-called *personal immunity*) (see **6.3**).

---

[11] See *Corriere della sera*, 9 May 2003, at 5; 10 May 2003, at 6; 17 May 2003, at 6.
[12] See (1935) 29 *AJIL* 502; (1936) 30 *AJIL* 123.
[13] See Whiteman, v, 208; (1960) *UNYB* 196.
[14] For references concerning the *Argoud* case, see N. Ronzitti, in (1965) 48 *RDI* 74.

(6) The right to respect for life and property of the State's nationals and State officials abroad (see **21.4.3**).

3.2.3 LEGAL EQUALITY

Legal equality implies that, formally speaking, every State is fully and equally sovereign or, in other words, that the rights and duties arising from sovereignty are the same for all States and, as a result, no State enjoys a hierarchical position with respect to other States. As Emeric de Vattel stated as early as 1758, 'a dwarf is as much a man as a giant; a small republic is no less a sovereign State than the most powerful kingdom'.[15]

Consequently, possible legal hindrances or limitations may be the result simply of factual circumstances, such as those concerning landlocked States or States without any natural or mineral resources and therefore heavily dependent on foreign aid. Alternatively, legal constraints, if any, are only valid if freely accepted by the State concerned. An example is the status of a neutralized State, which entails a series of limitations on freedom of action in international relations; or the legal condition of member States of the UN, which, unlike permanent members, enjoy neither a permanent seat nor a right of veto in the Security Council.

3.3 THE PRINCIPLE OF NON-INTERVENTION

3.3.1 GENERAL OBSERVATIONS

The principle of non-intervention in the affairs of other States also belongs to the old pattern of the world community.[16] Indeed, it constitutes one of the most significant tenets of the 'Grotian' model. Together with the principle of sovereign equality, and as a corollary of it, the principle of non-intervention is designed to ensure that each State respects the fundamental prerogatives of the other members of the community. The community at the time was limited to European States and, over time, some other States such as the United States of America and some Latin American States. In fact, historically, the 'accession' of the latter to the circle of political units considered to be States helped to consolidate the principle of non-intervention, firstly as non-(European) intervention in the Americas, under the banner of the Monroe doctrine, and later as non-intervention in general. In fact, the principle of non-intervention was affirmed with increasing strength and clarity in the inter-American context. Over time, the principle has crystallized in a few more specific applications:

(1) The first is the rule prohibiting a State from interfering in the internal organization of a foreign State. For instance, one State may not decide which organ of a foreign State is competent to perform a certain act, nor may it enjoin a foreign State agent to discharge certain activities or accomplish a certain act. Another rule prohibits States from encroaching upon the internal affairs of other States. Thus, for instance, a State is not allowed to bring pressure to bear on specific national bodies of other countries (the legislature, enforcement

---

[15] E. de Vattel, *Le droit des gens, ou principes de la loi naturelle* (Paris: J.-P. Aillaud, 1830), i, at 47 ('Préliminaires', §18).

[16] See generally D. Tladi, 'The Duty not to Intervene in Matters within Domestic Jurisdiction' in Viñuales, *The UN Friendly Relations Declaration* (n 1), chapter 5.

agencies, or the judiciary), nor may it interfere in the relations between foreign government authorities and their own nationals. As an illustration of the invocation of this principle it may be recalled that in 1999, when asked what action the British authorities were undertaking in respect of British nationals on trial overseas, the Minister of State for the Foreign and Commonwealth Office (FCO) replied that

> [i]nternational law does not allow the FCO to interfere in the judicial procedures of other sovereign States, just as we would not tolerate other countries interfering in our own judicial procedures. The FCO therefore cannot intervene in the trials of British nationals overseas. However, the FCO will do everything it can to ensure that such nationals have access to legal representation, and insist that they are treated as well as nationals of the countries concerned.[17]

(2) Another expression of the non-intervention principle requires States to refrain from instigating, organizing, or officially supporting the organization on their territory of activities prejudicial to foreign countries. Measures to enforce compliance with the obligation imposed by this rule include the expulsion of foreigners who take advantage of the asylum granted to them to conspire against foreign countries; imposition of restrictions on the traffic of arms and ammunitions; prohibition against the creation of armed bands and the supply of the means of disturbing the domestic order of foreign countries.

(3) A third expression of the non-intervention principle has a more specific scope in that it deals only with civil strife: it stipulates that whenever a civil war breaks out in a foreign country, States are duty-bound to refrain from assisting insurgents, unless they qualify for the status of national liberation movements (see **8.3** and **8.4**).

(4) A fourth expression concerns conduct that is also banned by other principles such as the prohibition of the threat or the use of force, the principle of territorial integrity, and, more generally, the principle of sovereign equality. These are discussed in other sections of this chapter (see **3.2** and **3.4**). For present purposes, it will suffice to mention two aspects. Firstly, in the *Nicaragua (Nicaragua v United States of America)* case the ICJ recognized that whenever the prohibition on the use of force is breached, there is also a breach of the non-intervention principle.[18] The two principles entertain a relationship of implication. Any breach, however mild, of the prohibition of the use of force will necessarily amount to a breach of non-intervention. But the reverse is not true, as there may be conduct which constitutes a prohibited intervention and falls nevertheless short of breaching the prohibition of the use of force. Secondly, unauthorized intervention in the territory of another State violates the non-intervention principle, unless the wrongdoer can rely on a circumstance precluding wrongfulness (e.g. consent, for an intervention by invitation[19]). This can be illustrated by reference to the *Corfu Channel (United Kingdom v Albania)* case, where the UK unlawfully intervened in Albanian territorial waters to remove mines (at 35), or to the *Armed Activities on the Territory of the Congo (Democratic Republic of the Congo v Uganda)* case, where Uganda's personnel conducted unauthorized activities in the Congolese section of the border (at §163). In both cases, the ICJ affirmed the unlawfulness of the intervention.

---

[17] See (1999) 70 *BYIL* 422.
[18] *Nicaragua (Nicaragua v United States of America)*, §209.
[19] Ibid., at §246; *Armed Activities on the Territory of the Congo (Democratic Republic of the Congo v Uganda)*, §§42–53. See G. Nolte, 'Intervention by Invitation', *Max Planck Encyclopedia of Public International Law* (2015) (emphasizing the need for valid consent from a legitimate government).

3.3.2 DEVELOPMENT OF NON-INTERVENTION BY THE UN GENERAL ASSEMBLY

The rules discussed in the previous section are still in force. However, in the period before 1945, States were allowed not to comply with these rules if they considered that their interests overrode the rules. If a State did consider its interests to be paramount, it was legally authorized to intervene by force, or by the threat of force, in the domestic or external affairs of another State, and impose a certain course of action. Consequently, the protection afforded by the aforementioned rules was precarious.

In the period after the First World War, and particularly in the years following the Second World War, instead of losing its significance and impact, the principle acquired new vigour. At present, a number of States, notably such States as Cuba and China, insist strongly on upholding it. Three major developments brought new life and authority to the principle. First, the introduction of far-reaching legal restraints on the use or threat of force, which conferred on the principle of non-intervention a less precarious existence and a more clear-cut delimitation. Secondly, the drive towards international co-operation, which entailed the expansion of intergovernmental organizations and increasing opportunities for both these organizations and States to meddle with the interests of other States. This brought about the correlative need for States to define more clearly the areas where they were entitled to remain immune from outside interference. The third development was the spread of human rights and environmental doctrines, with the ensuing possibility for States and individuals to pressure other States to comply with international standards. The principle of non-intervention thus acquired the fundamental value of a solid and indispensable 'bridge' between the traditional, sovereignty-oriented structure of the international community and the 'new' attitude of States, based on more intense social intercourse and closer co-operation.

Article 2(7) of the UN Charter included the non-intervention principle as one of the fundamental principles governing the new order established after the Second World War. These principles govern the conduct of 'the Organization and its Members' but Article 2(7) was specifically formulated as a limitation of the scope of intervention of the UN itself: '[n]othing contained in the present Charter shall authorize the United Nations to intervene in matters which are essentially within the domestic jurisdiction of any state'. A more general statement of the non-intervention principle, applicable to all States (not only members), was formulated in two subsequent resolutions from the UN General Assembly. Resolution 2131 (XX), adopted in 1965,[20] can be seen as a first effort to integrate the classical law of non-intervention, discussed earlier, with the new imperatives of decolonization, (non-)alignment (through an emphasis on non-intervention on neither the 'internal' nor the 'external' affairs of States), and the prohibition of the use of force. Of note is that, unlike Article 2(7), which focused on limiting intervention by the UN and only reserved chapter VII of the UN Charter, resolution 2131 (XX) is addressed to States and, at the same time, it reserves a wider set of chapters (VI, VII, and VIII) of the UN Charter. Five years later, this synthesis between the old and the new laws of non-intervention was restated in the Friendly Relations Declaration and the reservation was made more general, encompassing all the 'relevant provisions of the Charter relating to the maintenance of international peace and security'. It is this restatement that has been considered to accurately reflect customary international law and has been applied as such in a number of international disputes.

---

[20] Resolution 2131 (XX), Declaration on the Inadmissibility of Intervention in the Domestic Affairs of States and the Protection of Their Independence and Sovereignty, 21 December 1965. See also resolution 36/103, Declaration on the Inadmissibility of Intervention and Interference in the Internal Affairs of States, 9 December 1981.

A brief reference to such disputes appears useful also to show how a rather abstract formulation can be brought to bear upon very specific factual circumstances.

In the *Nicaragua* case, the ICJ discussed the practice and *opinio juris* relating to the principle of non-intervention, referring to the Friendly Relations Declaration as the authoritative expression of customary law on the matter (at §§202–203). It specifically clarified the two core components of non-intervention, namely that a 'prohibited intervention must ... be one bearing on matters in which each State is permitted, by the principle of State sovereignty, to decide freely' and that it must involve the use of 'methods of coercion in regard to such choices, which must remain free ones' (at §205). Significantly, the Court rejected the existence of a right of intervention for ideological reasons (at §§207–209). It also stated that the existence of coercion was particularly discernible when force had been used, either directly or indirectly, by granting support to subversive armed activities in other States, thus making clear that there may be other forms of coercion short of armed force (at §206). *In casu*, the Court found that certain acts of the United States (supporting the *contra* forces, a paramilitary group acting against the Nicaraguan government, short of using force) were in breach of the non-intervention principle only, whereas others (e.g. laying mines in the internal and territorial waters of Nicaragua) were violations of both non-intervention and the prohibition of the use of force. In a subsequent case brought by the Democratic Republic of the Congo against Uganda in connection with armed activities in the border region between the two countries, the ICJ referred to the *Nicaragua* case to clarify the operation of the non-intervention principle in the specific circumstances of the case. After stating that the Friendly Relations Declaration was 'declaratory of customary international law' on the matter (*Armed Activities on the Territory of the Congo (Democratic Republic of the Congo v Uganda)*, at §162), it relied on the *Nicaragua* case to conclude that, although the action of the Congo Liberation Movement (MLC) was not attributable to Uganda, Ugandan support for the MLC's military wing constituted an unlawful intervention in the civil strife taking place in the DRC, as well as a breach of the prohibition of the use of force (at §§161–165).

3.3.3 SPECIFIC FORMS OF INTERVENTION

The question arises of whether the ban on intervention in the internal and external affairs of other States also encompasses a number of situations where intervention takes certain specific forms (e.g. economic pressure or cyber-intervention) or relies on special circumstances (e.g. humanitarian intervention in its old and more recent forms).

With respect to international economic relations, not every form of economic pressure, be it direct or effected through international economic institutions, can be regarded as forbidden. Thus, for instance, the decision simply to withhold economic assistance to developing countries, or to stop the financing of international institutions promoting development, does not amount to an infringement of the principle, if such a decision is warranted by serious difficulties on the part of the granting State or by a change in its policy that is not motivated by matters falling under the domaine reservé of the recipient. Another situation that became very controversial in the 1990s (in the debate regarding the so-called 'Washington consensus') and, again, with the Euro zone debt crisis starting in late 2009 and the ensuing austerity policies in countries such as Greece or Portugal, concerns conditional financing by a State, a group of States, or an international financial institution. In some cases, such financing is made available only on the condition that the recipient State makes structural reforms, with potentially far-reaching consequences. If the State concerned agrees to such reforms, conditionality could not amount to a breach of the non-intervention principle but it could, however, contravene other international norms, including human rights.

The dividing line between what constitutes forbidden intervention and what does not in the area of economic relations hinges upon the existence of coercion. Only those economic measures designed 'to coerce another State in order to obtain from it the subordination of the exercise of its sovereign rights and to secure from it advantages of any kind'[21] may be regarded as inconsistent with the principle of non-intervention.

Another peculiar form of potential intervention is interference through cyberspace with the activities of other countries, whether in the form of surveillance programmes (e.g. the US National Security Agency's secret surveillance programme unveiled by the documents disclosed by former US official Edward Snowden in 2013), hacking of another State's public or private networks (e.g. reports of Russian hacking of Georgia's network during the 2008 conflict or of the 2016 US presidential election), or the unleashing of viruses capable of interfering with the activities of another State (e.g. the Stuxnet virus introduced into Iranian nuclear facilities that led to the destruction of the centrifuges used to enrich uranium).[22] Whether such forms of interference meet the requirements of an unlawful intervention will depend on the specific circumstances of the case. The *Tallinn Manual on the International Law Applicable to Cyber Warfare*, a private initiative from a group of experts, sees some forms of interference—for example with elections in the targeted State—as unlawful intervention, whereas others—for example the NSA's surveillance programme—would lack the coercive element.[23] It should be noted that even in those cases where the non-intervention principle is not breached, such actions might be inconsistent with other fundamental principles, such as the sovereign equality of States.

One important debate in both the classical and the modern law of non-intervention concerns the extent to which certain purposes (e.g. humanitarian motives broadly understood or pro-democratic intervention) may make intervention lawful. The debate has been more vivid in connection with armed intervention to protect human rights, including in the context of the 'Responsibility to Protect' doctrine,[24] but it also extends to non-armed intervention, for example, for the protection of persons in the event of disaster[25] or other forms of assistance to populations in another State. Cases where humanitarian reasons were alleged to provide some justification for forcible intervention, among many others, include NATO-led interventions against Yugoslavia (1999) and Libya (2011), the US-led invasion of Iraq (2003), and the military interventions of several States against the Islamic State of Iraq and the Levant (ISIL, also known as Islamic State or ISIS/Daesh), starting in 2014. These issues will be discussed in more detail later (see **16.5.4** and **16.5.7**). For present purposes, it must be noted that humanitarian intervention is not recognized as an exception to the prohibition of the use of force. In those cases where force is not used, absent an element of coercion, the intervention would remain lawful. The humanitarian purpose may be important in determining whether or not the intervention concerns, in the wording of the *Nicaragua* case, 'matters in which each State is permitted, by the principle of

---

[21] Friendly Relations Declaration, Principle 3, §2.

[22] See C. S. Yoo, 'Cyber Espionage or Cyberwar?: International Law, Domestic Law, and Self-Protective Measures' (2015) *Faculty Scholarship Paper* 1540.

[23] M. N. Schmitt (ed.), *The Tallinn Manual on the International Law Applicable to Cyber Warfare* (Cambridge: Cambridge University Press, 2013), 44.

[24] Resolution 60/1, 2005 World Summit Outcome, 24 October 2005, §§138–139, subsequently elaborated in a Report from the UN Secretary-General, Implementing the Responsibility to Protect, 12 January 2009, UN Doc. A/63/677. This policy doctrine has been referred to by the UN Security Council several times, including in connection with Darfur (2006), Libya (2011), Côte d'Ivoire (2011), South Sudan (2011), Yemen (2011), Syria (2012), and the Central African Republic (2013). See N. Michel, 'La responsabilité de protéger—Une vue d'ensemble assortie d'une perspective suisse' (2012) 131 *Revue de droit suisse* 5.

[25] ILC, Draft Articles on the Protection of Persons in the Event of Disasters, UN Doc. A/CN.4/L.831, 15 May 2014.

State sovereignty, to decide freely'. All States are indeed required under international law to protect the human rights of the populations under their jurisdiction.

3.4 PROHIBITION OF THE THREAT OR USE OF FORCE

3.4.1 GENERAL OBSERVATIONS

The prohibition of the threat or use of force is perhaps the most fundamental principle laid down in the UN Charter (Article 2(4)).[26] Previous attempts at restricting or banning the use of force in the Covenant of the League of Nations (Articles 12, 13, and 14) or the 1928 Briand-Kellogg Pact had either been narrower in scope (e.g. introducing a moratorium to be respected before using force, or banning force against States complying with a decision of the PCIJ or the League's Council) or devoid of any implementation mechanism (as for the 1928 Pact). That the prohibition of the use of force was proclaimed and strongly emphasized in 1945 is hardly surprising. As already pointed out, after 1945 peace became the supreme goal of the world community and States decided to agree upon sweeping self-limitations of their sovereign prerogatives in the form of a mutual obligation to refrain from using or threatening force. The need to avert armed conflict likely to endanger the very survival of mankind prompted the international community to take a step that genuinely broke new ground in the conduct of international relations.

Given the importance of this principle and its legal manifestations in international law, **Chapter 16** is fully devoted to it. However, understanding the role of this principle in the context of the other fundamental principles of international law calls for some further observations. Some comments concern specifically the way in which the principle was enshrined in the UN Charter. Firstly, the ban on force is an 'absolute all-inclusive prohibition', as was stated by the US delegate at the San Francisco Conference that led to the adoption of the UN Charter.[27] The threat or use of force was banned in all circumstances except for those provided for in: Chapter VII (collective enforcement measures); Article 51 (preserving the customary right of self-defence); Article 53 (enforcement action by regional agencies authorized by the Security Council); and in other provisions (Articles 106 and 107, on former 'enemy States', which have since fallen into desuetude). Secondly, only military force was proscribed. A Brazilian amendment calculated to prohibit also 'the threat or use of economic measures in any manner inconsistent with the purposes of the UN' was indeed rejected,[28] for reasons which unfortunately were not reported. Thirdly, only the threat or use of force in interstate relations was banned. Consequently, member States were by implication allowed to resort to forcible measures to suppress insurgents on their own territory, or to fight against liberation movements struggling for independence in territories subject to colonial domination—territories considered by colonial Powers as an integral part of their own territory inasmuch as they were under their exclusive authority. This implication was to come under great strain due to the emergence of the principle of self-determination of peoples.

---

[26] See generally O. Corten, 'The Prohibition of the Use of Force' in Viñuales, *The UN Friendly Relations Declaration*, chapter 3; C. Gray, *International Law and the Use of Force*, 4th edn (Oxford: Oxford University Press, 2018); O. Corten, *Le droit contre la guerre: L'interdiction du recours à la force en droit international contemporain*, 2nd edn (Paris: Pedone, 2014); I. Brownlie, *International Law and the Use of Force by States* (Oxford: Oxford University Press, 1963).

[27] UNCIO, vi, at 355.

[28] Ibid., at 559; see also 720–1.

After 1945 the ban in Article 2(4) was gradually transformed into a general rule of international law, binding on non-member States as well, and its implications for a wider set of circumstances of international relations became the object of great doctrinal scrutiny and often debate. One major question arose from the spread of wars of national liberation in colonial territories as well as in territories under foreign occupation (e.g. the Arab territories occupied by Israel following the war of 1967), or under racist regimes (e.g. in Namibia and South Africa as well as in Rhodesia during the period 1965–80). Under existing international law the Powers against which liberation wars were being waged were authorized to use force to quell liberation movements, and this seemed to socialist and developing countries a negative feature of the Charter. Another question was the increasing use by powerful States of economic coercion to subjugate developing countries, which easily fell prey to economic pressure and dependency. Moreover, in some instances States resorted to war and managed to conquer foreign territory without there being any effective sanction on the part of the international community capable of bringing about the evacuation of the occupied territory (e.g. the Arab territories occupied by Israel in 1967).

3.4.2 LEGAL SCOPE OF THE PRINCIPLE

The clash between the demands of the West, sometimes backed up by some of the Latin American States, and those of socialist and developing countries, resulted in lengthy and tiresome discussions within the UN. The ensuing compromise was set forth in two major UN General Assembly resolutions that can be considered to reflect the international customary law on this matter, namely the Friendly Relations Declaration[29] and resolution 3314 (XXIX) of 1974 on the 'Definition of Aggression'.[30] None of the competing groups had the upper hand. The resulting situation can be summarized as follows:

(1) The threat or use of armed force must not be resorted to against (a) *States* or (b) *peoples* having a representative organization (i.e. national liberation movements) and falling within one of the categories entitled to self-determination (colonial peoples, peoples under foreign occupation, or under racist regimes).

(2) As the ICJ held in *Nicaragua (Nicaragua v United States of America)* (at §195), it is necessary to distinguish 'the most grave forms of the use of force (those constituting an armed attack) from other less grave forms'. For instance, according to the Court, 'assistance to rebels in the form of the provision of weapons or logistical or other support' may be regarded as a threat or use of force (or amount to prohibited intervention in the internal or external affairs of other States). However, it does not amount to 'armed attack'. In the opinion of the Court, it follows that a State that is the victim of the threat or use of force not amounting to an 'armed attack' is not entitled to the right of individual or collective self-defence (see **16.5**).

(3) Force must not be used for the purpose of forestalling an imminent attack by another State (that is, an attack which is presumed to be imminent). This is the concept of *anticipatory or pre-emptive self-defence*. The question has led to vivid debates among legal commentators. On the one hand, the proponents of this anticipatory self-defence argue that it would be unrealistic not to admit such a possibility and that Article 51 of the UN Charter

---

[29] *Nicaragua (Nicaragua v United States)*, §§187–190; *Legal Consequences of the Construction of a Wall in the Occupied Palestinian Territory*, §87; *Armed Activities on the Territory of the Congo (Democratic Republic of the Congo v Uganda)*, §162.
[30] Resolution 3314 (XXIX), Definition of Aggression, 14 December 1974.

left intact the customary rule on self-defence, which authorized such action.[31] On the other hand, an equally distinguished strand of commentators consider that there was no customary basis for such an anticipatory self-defence in the first place and, at all events, such a possibility has been entirely excluded by Article 51 of the UN Charter.[32] The ICJ has refrained on two occasions from taking a position on this question.[33] However, analysis of State and UN practice shows that the overwhelming majority of States consider that there are no legal grounds to admit anticipatory or pre-emptive self-defence (see **16.5.2**). Moreover, at a policy level, the doctrine certainly weakens the prohibition of the use of force, and it may operate as a double-edged sword, turning against those States that have invoked it.[34]

(4) Force in self-defence may not be used to repel an indirect armed aggression (i.e. 'self-defence' that does not respond immediately to armed attack but only occurs later, or delayed armed retaliation), although it might be admitted as an immediate ('on-the-spot') armed reaction to a minor use of force (e.g. a border patrol or a warship passing through an international strait that comes under fire would be entitled to return fire, even if the initial use of force is not an armed attack or an aggression).[35]

(5) Territory belonging to a State (or to which a 'people' entitled to self-determination may legitimately make a claim) may not be 'the object of *acquisition* by another State resulting from the threat or the use of force'.[36] This consequence of the principle was emphasized by the ICJ in its Advisory Opinion on the *Legal Consequences of the Construction of a Wall in the Occupied Palestinian Territory* as an expression of international customary law (at §§87 and 117). This means that conquest does not transfer a legal title of sovereignty, even if it is followed by de facto occupation, and assertion of authority, over the territory. Furthermore, all other States are enjoined to withhold recognition of the territorial situation resulting from the threat or use of force. The difference between the territory of a State and that of a people is a very delicate matter that may lend itself to controversy. The Russian annexation of Crimea between February and March 2014 must be characterized as a clear violation of the prohibition of the use of force with a view to acquiring territory belonging to another State (Ukraine). However, careful steps were taken to present the situation as a declaration of independence by Crimea followed by a request to join the Russian Federation.[37] From

---

[31] This doctrine has been expounded by authors such as McDougall ('The Soviet-Cuban Quarantine and Self-Defence' (1963) 57 *AJIL* 601); Waldock ('The Regulation of the Use of Force by Individual States in International Law' (1952) 82 *RCADI* 498); Schwebel ('Aggression, Intervention and Self-Defence in Modern International Law' (1972-II) 136 *RCADI* 479ff); Schachter (*International Law in Theory and Practice* (Nijhoff, 1991), 151); and Higgins (*Problems and Process: International Law and How to Use It* (Clarendon Press, 1994), 242).

[32] Opponents include Kelsen (*The Law of the United Nations* (Stevens, 1950), 797); Wehberg ('L'interdiction du recours à la force. Le principe et les problèmes qui se posent' (1951-I) 78 *RCADI* 81); Jessup (*A Modern Law of Nations: An Introduction* (Macmillan, 1952), 165); Brownlie (*International Law and the Use of Force by States* (Oxford University Press, 1963), 264ff); Lamberti Zanardi (*La leggitima difesa nel diritto internazionale* (Giuffre, 1972), 191ff).

[33] *Nicaragua* (*Nicaragua* v *United States*), §194; *Armed Activities on the Territory of the Congo (Democratic Republic of the Congo* v *Uganda)*, §143.

[34] The doctrine has been resorted to by Israel on various occasions, including in 1967 against Egypt, in 1975 against Palestinian camps in Lebanon, and in 1981 against Iraq. Iraq also resorted to it, in 1980, to attempt to justify its use of force against Iran. In 2003, the US and the UK invoked this doctrine to justify the invasion of Iraq.

[35] On the difference between 'delayed' response to an armed attack and 'immediate' armed reaction to a minor use of force see Brownlie, *International Law and the Use of Force*, at 305. The expression 'on-the-spot' is used by Y. Dinstein, *War, Aggression and Self-Defence*, 2nd edn (Cambridge: Cambridge University Press, 1994), 214. The border patrol example is derived from Dinstein, whereas the warship example is derived from *Corfu Channel (United Kingdom* v *Albania)*, 31.

[36] Friendly Relations Declaration, Principle 1, §10.

[37] On the Crimea situation see the proceedings of the symposium on 'The Incorporation of Crimea by the Russian Federation in the Light of International Law' edited by C. Marxsen, A. Peters, and M. Hartwig and published in *ZaöRV* 75 (2015) (particularly the contributions by Marxen, Bílková, and Christakis).

a legal perspective, this remains a prohibited territorial acquisition effected through the unlawful use of force, and third States are under a duty not to recognize the territorial situation arising from it.

(6) Extreme forms of *economic coercion* could potentially amount to a threat to the peace and therefore be unlawful under the prohibition of the threat or the use of force. Such cases would in addition constitute a breach of the non-intervention principle.

The prohibition of the threat or the use of force must, of course, be considered in the light of the general rules which allow the use of force under specific circumstances (see **Chapter 16**). It is precisely the need for this principle to be qualified by these rules that constitutes its 'Achilles' heel'. Indeed, it is by dint of a broad interpretation of, or even by bypassing, those rules that various States—particularly the Great Powers or the countries certain of their support—have endeavoured to dodge the principle, thereby also abusing the exceptions laid down in the rules.

3.5 PEACEFUL SETTLEMENT OF INTERNATIONAL DISPUTES

3.5.1 GENERAL OBSERVATIONS

The UN Charter requires member States to settle their international disputes peacefully (Articles 2(3) and 33) so as generally to prevent peace and security, as well as justice, from being endangered.[38] Chapter VI of the UN Charter strengthens this obligation with regard to disputes likely to endanger the maintenance of peace and security. The Security Council may call upon parties to such disputes to settle them by peaceful means (or may 'investigate' the dispute or even make recommendations to the parties with regard to both the choice of the procedure and the settlement of the dispute).

This obligation has gradually been extended to all States as a logical corollary of the formation of a customary ban on the use of force. A customary rule has evolved on the matter, which is reflected in the Friendly Relations Declaration and in the Manila Declaration on the Peaceful Settlement of Disputes of 1982.[39] The ICJ authoritatively confirmed aspects of this principle in its jurisprudence. In the *North Sea Continental Shelf (Federal Republic of Germany/Denmark; Federal Republic of Germany/Netherlands)* cases, the Court relied on the jurisprudence of its predecessor, the Permanent Court of International Justice (PCIJ), to conclude that the States parties to the dispute were 'under an obligation to enter into negotiations with a view to arriving at an agreement' as well as 'so to conduct themselves that the negotiations are meaningful, which will not be the case when either of them insists upon its own position without contemplating any modification of it'(at §§85ff). It further stated that this obligation was but a special application of a 'principle that underlies all international relations'.[40] In the *Nicaragua* case, the Court insisted that this principle is 'complementary' to the principles of a prohibitive nature such as that banning the use of force, and that 'respect for [the principle] is essential in the world today'. The Court went on to specify that the principle 'has also the status of customary law' (*Nicaragua (Nicaragua v United States)*, at §290).

---

[38] See generally S. Hamamoto, 'Peaceful Settlement of International Disputes' in Viñuales, *The UN Friendly Relations Declaration*, chapter 4; Y. Tanaka, *The Peaceful Settlement of International Disputes* (Cambridge: Cambridge University Press, 2018); J. G. Merrills, *International Dispute Settlement*, 6th edn (Cambridge: Cambridge University Press, 2017).

[39] Resolution 37/10, Manila Declaration on the Peaceful Settlement of Disputes, 15 November 1982.

[40] Ibid., at 86.

3.5.2 LEGAL SCOPE OF THE PRINCIPLE

Regarding the scope and the purport of the principle, it has been fleshed out in more detail in a number of international instruments (e.g. the Friendly Relations Declaration and the Manila Declaration[41]) as well as in some decisions from international courts. For present purposes it can be summarized as follows:

(1) States are mandated *bona fide* to endeavour to resolve their disputes peacefully.[42] The reference to good faith is important and it has a number of practical implications, including the need to consider potential modifications of a State's position[43] or to interpret dispute settlement clauses in good faith[44] or, more generally, to avoid engaging in delaying tactics that turn the dispute settlement process into a mere *pro forma* exercise.

(2) To this end, they must try the various means and procedures available (negotiation, mediation, conciliation, resort to arbitral or judicial mechanisms, etc.; see **Chapter 13**). However, they are not bound to choose a particular means of settlement (principle of 'free choice of means').[45] As the PCIJ held in its Advisory Opinion in *Status of Eastern Carelia*, States are not obliged to submit a dispute to a particular mechanism without their consent. But if they do so (e.g. through a compromissory clause or dispute settlement agreement), they are bound by their choice, as the ability to consent to a given means of dispute settlement, including for disputes that may arise in the future, is fully consistent with sovereign equality.

(3) In the event of failure to reach a solution by one of the means of dispute settlement just mentioned, States are legally bound 'to continue to seek a settlement of the dispute by other peaceful means agreed upon by them'.[46]

(4) While trying to settle the dispute peacefully, States must 'refrain from any action which may aggravate the situation so as to endanger the maintenance of international peace and security'.[47] This requirement, read in the light of the principle of good faith, also governs action that may render more difficult or preclude a negotiated solution, even if peace and security are not endangered. By way of illustration, the ICJ held in *Pulp Mills on the River Uruguay (Argentina v Uruguay)* that good faith requires a State not to unilaterally authorize an activity while negotiations with another State concerning such activity are still ongoing (at §144).

Thus, the principle is breached whenever a State wilfully and *mala fide* refuses to resort to negotiations or other peaceful means or procedures proposed by the counterparty; or, after the failure of a particular means or procedure agreed upon by the disputing parties (for example, mediation), refuses to continue to seek a settlement; or takes action that is likely to aggravate the dispute or jeopardize peace. More generally, the principle is breached when a party manifestly engages in delaying tactics or in any other way shows that in actual fact it is not prepared to settle the matter peacefully.

If a party to the dispute considers that the counterparty has contravened the principle and that the dispute has important political overtones or implications, it may resort to

---

[41] Together with Articles 2(3) and 33 of the UN Charter, the Friendly Relations Declaration and the Manila Declaration are the two instruments to which the ICJ has referred to ascertain the operation of this duty. See *Obligation to Negotiate Access to the Pacific Ocean (Bolivia v Chile)*, §166.

[42] Manila Declaration, § 5; *Obligation to Negotiate Access to the Pacific Ocean (Bolivia v Chile)*, §165.

[43] *North Sea Continental Shelf (Federal Republic of Germany/Denmark; Federal Republic of Germany/Netherlands)* cases, §85.

[44] Manila Declaration, §12.

[45] Friendly Relations Declaration, Principle 2, §5; Manila Declaration, §3; *Obligation to Negotiate Access to the Pacific Ocean (Bolivia v Chile)*, §§165–166.

[46] Friendly Relations Declaration, Principle 2, §3; Manila Declaration, §7.

[47] Friendly Relations Declaration, Principle 2, §4; Manila Declaration, §§8 and 10.

an appropriate international body (at either the regional or universal level). Should such resort prove of no avail or unsatisfactory, the State can take countermeasures, subject to the stringent conditions provided for on the matter (see **14.2.4**). One should bear in mind that one of the purposes of peaceful countermeasures may be to impel the counterparty to reach an amicable settlement of the dispute.

3.6 THE DUTY TO CO-OPERATE

3.6.1 GENERAL OBSERVATIONS

The duty to co-operate is closely related to the principle requiring the peaceful settlement of international disputes, but it goes beyond it because it is also intended to guide non-conflicting relations, aptly referred to as 'co-operative' relations.[48] The duty was enshrined in the UN Charter as both a purpose of the United Nations (Article 1(3)) and, in a narrower form, a principle governing the relations between States parties and the United Nations (Article 2(5)). As with other principles, its most elaborate formulation appears in the Friendly Relations Declaration, which characterized it by reference to three main components, namely its nature (as a 'duty' of States), its domain ('the various spheres of international relations'), and its purposes (e.g. 'elimination of all forms of racial discrimination').

Before analysing more specifically the legal scope of this duty in the light of international instruments and cases, it is important to note that the duty to co-operate is part of international customary law, as implied by the ICJ as early as in the *Corfu Channel (United Kingdom v Albania)* case (at 22–3) and subsequently confirmed in several other decisions from the ICJ or other international tribunals.[49] Moreover, in recent years, this duty has provided the basis for a number of claims relating to questions as diverse as environmental protection,[50] nuclear disarmament,[51] or access to the sea by a landlocked State.[52]

3.6.2 DIMENSIONS OF CO-OPERATION

The main dimensions of the duty to co-operate can be identified by reference to the three components mentioned in the previous section, namely its nature, domain, and purposes:

(1) Co-operation is formulated as a 'duty' of States. Performance of this duty takes place across a spectrum defined by two extremes, namely refusal of any interaction (which is inconsistent with the duty to co-operate) and a specific result (the duty to co-operate

---

[48] See generally L. Boisson de Chazournes and J. Rudall, 'Co-operation' in Viñuales, *The UN Friendly Relations Declaration* (n 1), chapter 6.

[49] See e.g., for the ICJ: *North Sea Continental Shelf (Federal Republic of Germany/Denmark; Federal Republic of Germany/Netherlands)*, §§83–87; *Legality of the Threat or Use of Nuclear Weapons*, §§98–103; *Pulp Mills on the River Uruguay (Argentina v Uruguay)*, §§90–122, 132–150; *Certain Activities Carried Out by Nicaragua in the Border Area (Costa Rica v Nicaragua), Construction of a Road in Costa Rica along the river San Juan (Nicaragua v Costa Rica)*, §104. For the ITLOS: *The MOX Plant Case (Ireland v United Kingdom) (Provisional Measures)*, §82; *Land Reclamation in and around the Straits of Johor (Malaysia v Singapore) (Provisional Measures)*, §92; *Dispute Concerning Delimitation of the Maritime Boundary between Ghana and Côte d'Ivoire in the Atlantic Ocean (Ghana/Côte d'Ivoire) (Provisional Measures)*, §73; *Request for an Advisory Opinion Submitted by the Sub-Regional Fisheries Commission (SRFC)*, §140. See also the *South China Sea Arbitration (Republic of the Philippines v People's Republic of China)* under the Convention on the Law of the Sea, §§946, 984–985.

[50] See e.g. *South China Sea Arbitration (Republic of the Philippines v People's Republic of China)*, §§946, 984–985.

[51] See the *Marshall Islands (Marshall Islands v United Kingdom; Marshall Islands v Pakistan; Marshall Islands v India)* cases before the ICJ.

[52] See *Obligation to Negotiate Access to the Pacific Ocean (Bolivia v Chile)*.

is an obligation of means and does not require reaching a specific result[53]). Between these two extremes, the duty to co-operate carries a variety of implications, some of which have already been mentioned in section **3.4.2** in connection with conflicting relations. Other implications include: the duty to notify and consult when an activity or an accident may have significant consequences on other States,[54] although this does not amount to subjecting the pursuance of the activity to the consent of the other State[55] unless a treaty provision so requires; and the duty not to preclude the outcome of a co-operative process by unilateral action taken while the process is ongoing.[56] The implications will be a function of the objective pursued by co-operation (e.g. which may determine the appropriate time and content of a notification).

(2) The domain of the duty to co-operate is broad, as co-operation is expected in virtually all spheres of international relations. The Friendly Relations Declaration specifically refers to the maintenance of international peace and security; the promotion of human rights; international relations in the economic, social, cultural, technical, and trade fields, and others. Traditionally, co-operation has been of particular importance in connection with shared resources, such as watercourses, which the PCIJ deemed to represent a 'community of interests' among riparian States, thereby highlighting the equal position of each riparian State with respect to the resource.[57] In the decades following the adoption of the Friendly Relations Declaration perhaps the main new area requiring international co-operation has been the protection of the environment. The 1992 Rio Declaration on Environment and Development specifically states the duty to co-operate in both a transboundary (Principles 18 and 19) and a global context (Principles 7 and 27). More recently, the outbreak of viral disease, such as SARS (2002–04), H1N1 (2009), MERS (which emerged in 2012), Ebola (2014–16), or COVID-19 (2019–present), has required States to co-operate to contain the spread of the disease through a range of channels, most notably the World Health Organization. It has also tested the limits of co-operation when certain materials (e.g. medical protective gear or testing substances) are in short supply, and States compete for them. The domain of co-operation is not devoid of practical interest, to the extent that it may have implications for the manner in which the duty to co-operate operates. By way of illustration, in the specific context of nuclear disarmament, in the Advisory Opinion on *Legality of the Threat or Use of Nuclear Weapons*, the ICJ has held that Article VI of the Non-Proliferation Treaty entails a 'twofold obligation to pursue and to conclude negotiations' or, in other terms, not 'a mere obligation of conduct; [. . . but . . .] an obligation to achieve a precise result—nuclear disarmament in all its aspects' (at §§99–100). In its Declaration appended to this Advisory Opinion, the ICJ President, M. Bedjaoui, went further and noted that 'it is not unreasonable to think that, considering the at least formal unanimity in this field, this twofold obligation to negotiate in good faith and achieve the desired result has now, 50 years on, acquired *a customary character*'.

---

[53] *North Sea Continental Shelf (Federal Republic of Germany/Denmark; Federal Republic of Germany/Netherlands)* cases, §85; *Land and Maritime Boundary between Cameroon and Nigeria (Cameroon v Nigeria: Equatorial Guinea intervening)*, §244; *Case Concerning the Gabčíkovo-Nagymaros Project (Hungary/Slovakia)*, §141.

[54] *Corfu Channel (United Kingdom v Albania)*, 22; Rio Declaration on Environment and Development, 13 June 1992, UN Doc. A/CONF.151/26, Principles 18 and 19; *Certain Activities Carried Out by Nicaragua in the Border Area (Costa Rica v Nicaragua)*, §§104, 108, and 168.

[55] *Lac Lanoux Case (Spain v France)*, §§13, 22.

[56] *Pulp Mills on the River Uruguay (Argentina v Uruguay)*, §144.

[57] *Territorial Jurisdiction of the International Commission of the River Oder (United Kingdom v Poland)*, at 27 (for navigational uses); *Case Concerning the Gabčíkovo-Nagymaros Project (Hungary/Slovakia)*, §85 (for non-navigational uses).

(3) The purposes pursued by the duty to co-operate are related but distinct from the domains where co-operation takes place. For example, co-operation in the domain of international peace and security may pursue different goals, such as defusing one specific escalation, or addressing the root causes of conflict, or achieving complete nuclear disarmament. Purposes are important for the interpretation of specific provisions, as required by the rules on treaty interpretation (see **10.6**). By way of illustration, one of the expressions of co-operation—the obligation to notify—aims to sufficiently and officially inform affected States of the situation in order to enable or continue a process of co-operation. As a result, it is not enough for notification purposes that the information could have been retrieved by the affected State in the public domain[58] or that a private company or an entity other than the State of origin has made that State aware of the situation.[59]

3.7 THE PRINCIPLE OF GOOD FAITH

3.7.1 GENERAL OBSERVATIONS

The principle of good faith is as ubiquitous in international law as it is difficult to circumscribe.[60] It is essentially an ethical postulate that, against all odds, pervades the law governing the relations that at times have been little more than a Hobbesian state of nature.[61] Its roots are so deep, that it would be all but impossible to understand it without inquiring into the very foundations of international law. For the very rules that make treaties binding (*pacta sunt servanda*) and that attach an obligatory character to some unilateral acts rest upon considerations of good faith.[62] The purpose of this short section, however, is not to open such a deep and vast inquiry but only to survey how this ethical postulate has found expression as a principle of international law, as well as to refer to some specific applications.

Because of its nature, the principle of good faith is inseparable from the very existence of international law. Even in those cases where States utterly disregard their international obligations or commitments, they seek to present their action as being in good faith. Abidance by good faith is virtually always claimed, even if only as lip service paid to it. In the aftermath of the Second World War, the community of States that negotiated the UN Charter deemed it important to include good faith as one of the principles governing the action of the Organization and its members. Article 2(2) states indeed that '[a]ll members, in order to ensure to all of them the rights and benefits resulting from membership, shall fulfil in good faith the obligations assumed by them in accordance with the present Charter'.[63] Thus, good faith is formulated as an enabling principle, without which the very

---

[58] *Certain Questions of Mutual Assistance in Criminal Matters (Djibouti v France)*, §150.
[59] *Pulp Mills on the River Uruguay (Argentina v Uruguay)*, §§110, 113, and 115.
[60] See generally G. Futhazar and A. Peters, 'Good Faith' in Viñuales, *The UN Friendly Relations Declaration* (n 1), chapter 9; R. Kolb, *La bonne foi en droit international public: Contribution à l'étude des principes généraux de droit* (Paris: PUF, 2000); E. Zoller, *La bonne foi en droit international public* (Paris: Pedone, 1977).
[61] See A. Cassese, *International Law in a Divided World* (Oxford: Clarendon Press, 1986), 153.
[62] *Nuclear Tests (Australia v France)*, §46.
[63] See *Land and Maritime Boundary between Cameroon and Nigeria (Cameroon v Nigeria: Equatorial Guinea intervening) (Preliminary Objections)*, §38, referring to the body of authority supporting the recognition of the principle of good faith.

regime of the Charter would be devoid of content. As for other principles, the Friendly Relations Declaration provided a statement that is not limited to the obligations of the UN Charter but encompasses 'obligations under the generally recognized principles and rules of international law' and 'under agreements valid' under such principles and rules.

Thus stated, the principle encompasses the entire field of international law. But to understand how it may operate in practice, it is necessary to identify some of its major expressions. Indeed, the ICJ has stated on different occasions that although the principle governs 'the creation and performance of legal obligations ... it is not in itself a source of obligation where none would otherwise exist'.[64]

3.7.2 SPECIFIC EXPRESSIONS OF GOOD FAITH

The expressions of good faith reviewed in this section are only a selection from the many specific and general forms in which good faith may have a bearing on the creation, interpretation, and application of international law. But they provide a good indication of how good faith operates legally at the international level:

(1) *Pacta sunt servanda* is a foundational norm that confers its binding character on international agreements of all sorts. In the specific context of agreements qualifying as treaties under the 1969 Vienna Convention on the Law of Treaties (VCLT), this principle is stated in Article 26: '[e]very treaty in force is binding upon the parties to it and must be performed by them in good faith'. The scope of the principle, which is part of international customary law,[65] goes beyond the VCLT and governs all types of agreements, including those between States and international organizations or between international organizations.[66]

(2) Good faith is also the basis for the recognition of the binding character of unilateral acts of States as well as of a number of other utterances that do not technically qualify as unilateral acts. In the *Nuclear Tests* case, before determining the legal import of certain declarations made by French authorities regarding the discontinuance of atmospheric nuclear tests, the ICJ identified a number of features that must be present for such declarations to create a legal obligation and concluded that such a binding character rested upon considerations of good faith: '[j]ust as the very rule of *pacta sunt servanda* in the law of treaties is based on good faith, so also is the binding character of an international obligation assumed by unilateral declaration' (§46). Although these occurrences may be exceptional, the implications of good faith for certain utterances or indications from State officials have gained renewed importance in the context of foreign investment disputes. Investors often claim that they have received specific assurances from the host State or its officials in order to either buttress the existence of a legitimate expectation or to defeat a State's argument based on the police powers doctrine[67] (see further **21.4.3**).

---

[64] *Border and Transborder Armed Actions (Nicaragua v Honduras) (Jurisdiction and Admissibility)*, §94; *Land and Maritime Boundary between Cameroon and Nigeria (Cameroon v Nigeria: Equatorial Guinea intervening) (Preliminary Objections)*, §39.

[65] *Case Concerning the Gabčíkovo-Nagymaros Project (Hungary/Slovakia)*, §142.

[66] See Vienna Convention on the Law of Treaties between States and International Organizations or between International Organizations, 21 March 1986, not yet in force, noting in the preamble that 'the principles of free consent and of good faith and the *pacta sunt servanda* rule are universally recognised' and then restating the rule in Article 26.

[67] See the discussion in J. E. Viñuales, 'Sovereignty in Foreign Investment Law' in Z. Douglas, J. Pauwelyn, and J. E. Viñuales (eds), *The Foundations of International Investment Law* (Oxford: Oxford University Press, 2014), 339.

(3) Negotiations and the duty to co-operate must be conducted in good faith, which carries a number of legal implications, as discussed in sections **3.5.2** and **3.6.2**.

(4) An expression of the good faith principle of particular practical importance concerns the rules on the interpretation of treaties. As further discussed in section **10.6**, the overarching rule codified in Article 31(1) of the VCLT states that treaties 'shall be interpreted in good faith in accordance with the ordinary meaning to be given to the terms of the treaty in their context and in the light of its object and purpose'.

(5) The principle of good faith is also spelled out through a number of more specific concepts that preclude a party from exercising a right in an abusive manner (prohibition of *abus de droit*) or benefiting from its own wrongdoing (clean hands doctrine) or its inconsistency if another party has relied upon it (estoppel). Some practical illustrations will help elucidate this point. In some foreign investment disputes, the restructuring of an investment transaction for the purpose of gaining protection under an investment agreement after a dispute arose has been considered by investment tribunals as an abuse of right leading to the dismissal of the claim.[68] The clean hands doctrine has been applied in a variety of contexts, although these specific terms—which stem from the common law language—have not been used. For example, in the *LaGrand* case, the ICJ reasoned that the United States could not rely on the fact that the LaGrand brothers had not pleaded the violation of their rights under the Vienna Convention on Consular Relations because such an omission resulted from the United States' own omission to inform the LaGrand brothers of their rights, as required by the Convention (§60). Similarly, in the *Case Concerning the Gabčíkovo-Nagymaros Project* case, the ICJ concluded that the right of Hungary to terminate a 1977 treaty for the development of a hydroelectric project as a result of Slovakia's development of an alternative project was precluded because such alternative was itself the result of Hungary's prior wrongdoing.[69] As for estoppel, the doctrine has been recognized in international law as a form of unilateral act giving rise to a binding commitment when certain elements are present: 'a statement or representation made by one party to another and reliance upon it by that other party to his detriment or the advantage of the party making it'.[70] Thus, estoppel rests on good faith without requiring wrongdoing or illegality.

3.8 SELF-DETERMINATION OF PEOPLES

3.8.1 HOW THE PRINCIPLE EVOLVED IN THE WORLD COMMUNITY

It may be useful to begin by tracing the gradual emergence of self-determination as a general principle. Propounded by the French Revolution and then strongly supported, albeit in differing versions, by such statesmen as Lenin and Wilson, self-determination was intended—at the international level—to brush aside the old, State-oriented approach

---

[68] *Phillip Morris Asia Limited* v *Commonwealth of Australia*, §§538–554, 569 (reviewing the investment jurisprudence on this point).

[69] *Case Concerning the Gabčíkovo-Nagymaros Project (Hungary/Slovakia)*, §110, referring to a prior statement of the principle by the PCIJ in *Factory at Chorzow (Jurisdiction)*, 31.

[70] *Land, Island and Maritime Frontier Dispute (El Salvador/Honduras)(Application to Intervene)*, 118. See also *North Sea Continental Shelf (Federal Republic of Germany/Denmark; Federal Republic of Germany/Netherlands)*, §30; *Land and Maritime Boundary between Cameroon and Nigeria (Cameroon v Nigeria: Equatorial Guinea intervening) (Preliminary Objections)*, §57; *Sovereignty over Pedra Branca/Pulau Batu Puteh, Middle Rocks and South Ledge (Malaysia/Singapore)*, §228.

prevailing in international dealings. Under this old approach, the world community consisted of potentates, the sovereign States, each of them primarily concerned with the interests of its own political elite. Relations between international subjects in actual fact were relations between ruling groups that took into account the interests of their own nationals only when these were threatened by foreign Powers, and only so long as those interests were of some relevance to the ruling elite concerned. By contrast, self-determination meant that peoples and nations were to have a say in international dealings: sovereign Powers could no longer freely dispose of them, for example by ceding or annexing territories without paying any regard to the wishes of the populations concerned, through plebiscites or referendums. Peoples were also to have a say in the conduct of domestic and foreign business; self-determination was thus advocated as a democratic principle calling for the consent of the governed in any sovereign State. Furthermore, peoples and nations were entitled to be free from any external oppression, chiefly in the form of colonial rule.

Clearly, this set of principles was directed toward undermining the very core of the traditional principles on which international society had rested since its inception: dynastic legitimation of power, despotism (albeit in increasingly attenuated forms), and agreements between rulers only. Self-determination suddenly introduced a new standard for judging the legitimacy of power in the international setting: respect for the wishes and aspirations of peoples and nations. This struck at the very heart of traditional arrangements. Self-determination also eroded one of the basic postulates of the old international community: territorial sovereignty. Territorial sovereignty meant that every international subject was to pay full respect to any other Power wielding authority over a territory and the population living there, regardless both of how it had acquired its territorial title (whether by conquest, hereditary succession, or barter with another sovereign ruler) and in particular of the aspirations of the populations concerned.

By promoting the formation of international entities based on the free will of the populations concerned, self-determination delivered a lethal blow to multinational empires. By the same token, it sounded the death knell for colonial rule. In short, the redistribution of power in the international community, advocated by self-determination, introduced a highly dynamic factor of change that deeply undermined the status quo. The US Secretary of State, R. Lansing, was therefore right when in 1919 he wrote that the 'phrase so deeply cherished and so warmly advocated by President Wilson was simply loaded with dynamite' and went on to point out that the 'fixity of national boundaries and of national allegiance, and political stability would disappear if this principle was uniformly applied'.[71] Further, he raised some interrogations that were soon to become prophetic: '[w]hat effect will it have on the Irish, the Indians, the Egyptians, and the nationalists among the Boers—Will it not breed discontent, disorder and rebellion—Will not the Mohammedans of Syria and Palestine and possibly of Morocco and Tripoli rely on it—How can it be harmonized with Zionism, to which the President is practically committed?'[72]

3.8.2 LEGAL SCOPE OF THE PRINCIPLE

Like sovereign equality, this principle relates to international subjects. In particular, it touches upon both the inner structure and the legal legitimation of subjects on the international plane. However, unlike sovereign equality, the principle of self-determination

---

[71] R. Lansing (n 9), 93, in particular at 96–7.
[72] Ibid., at 97 (quoting from a note he wrote on 20 December 1918, in Paris).

strikingly reflects the new trends emerging in the world community.[73] In addition, it has a markedly ideological matrix. This explains why its transformation into a legal standard of behaviour has been a gradual process, and it has elicited strong opposition from many Western countries with colonial possessions.[74]

Self-determination appears firmly embedded in the corpus of international law in only three areas: as an *anti-colonialist standard*, as a *ban on foreign military occupation*, and as a requirement that all *racial groups be given full access to government*. Peoples under colonial domination have the right to *external* self-determination, that is, to opt for the establishment of a sovereign State, or the free association or integration with an independent State, or 'the emergence into any other political status freely determined by the people'.[75] The same right accrues to peoples subjected to foreign military occupation, both before and after they reach (or recover) independence. Any racial group denied full access to government in a sovereign State is entitled to either *external* self-determination (e.g. to achieve independence, integration into an existing State, etc.) or *internal* self-determination (as stated by the Supreme Court of Canada in the—different—context of Quebec, that means the 'pursuit of its political, economic, social and cultural development within the framework of an existing State'[76]).

More specifically, there now exists in the body of international law both a *general principle*, serving as an overarching guideline, and a set of specific *customary rules* dealing with individual issues (particularly the *right* to self-determination of colonial peoples, peoples under foreign occupation, and racially oppressed peoples; and the right to self-determination as a fundamental human right, even outside the context of decolonization[77]). These rules specify, with regard to certain areas, the general principle. The role of the principle is to cast light on borderline situations and to serve as a general standard for the interpretation of both customary and treaty law. The principle therefore transcends, and gives unity to, the customary rules. It sets out the *essence* of self-determination. As the ICJ put it in the Advisory Opinion on *Western Sahara*, self-determination 'requires a free and genuine expression of the will of the peoples concerned'.[78] In other words, the principle lays down the *method* by which States must reach decisions concerning peoples: heeding their freely expressed will. By contrast, the principle points neither to the various specific areas in which self-determination should apply, nor to the final goal of self-determination (internal self-government, independent statehood, association with or integration into another State, or the free choice of any other political status).

---

[73] See generally A. Cassese, *Self-Determination of Peoples: A Legal Reappraisal* (Cambridge: Cambridge University Press, 1995); M. Kohen, 'Self-determination' in Viñuales, *The UN Friendly Relations Declaration* (n 1), chapter 7.

[74] An important milestone of this transformation is an Advisory Opinion of the ICJ relating to the situation in Namibia, where the 'sacred trust of civilization' envisioned in the Covenant of the League of Nations is read in the light of the principle of self-determination: *Legal Consequences for States of the Continued Presence of South Africa in Namibia (South West Africa) notwithstanding Security Council Resolution 276 (1970)*, §53.

[75] Friendly Relations Declaration (XXV), Principle 5, §4. See also Articles 1 and 55 of the UN Charter and Article 1 common to the International Covenant on Civil and Political Rights, 16 December 1966, 999 UNTS 171 (ICCPR) and the International Covenant on Economic, Social and Cultural Rights, 16 December 1966, 993 UNTS 3 (ICESCR).

[76] *Reference re Secession of Quebec*, §126.

[77] *Legal Consequences of the Separation of the Chagos Archipelago from Mauritius in 1965*, §§144, 148, and 150–153.

[78] *Western Sahara*, §§58–59; resolution 1514 (XV), Declaration on the Granting of Independence to Colonial Countries and Peoples, 14 December 1960; resolution 1541 (XV), Principles which should guide members in determining whether or not an obligation exists to transmit the information called for under Article 73e of the Charter, 15 December 1960. The importance of this principle has been subsequently reaffirmed on several occasions: *East Timor*, §29 ('one of the essential principles of contemporary international law'); *Legal Consequences of the Construction of a Wall in the Occupied Palestinian Territory*, §§88 and 156.

This ambiguity has been particularly acute in cases outside the context of decolonization where the possibility of external self-determination is not clearly recognized. One illustration is the declaration of independence of Kosovo. Asked whether this declaration was lawful under international law, the ICJ issued a hesitant Advisory Opinion, avoiding the key issue at stake, that is, the legality of secession, and merely concluding that by reason of the specific characteristics of the declaration's authors, the declaration was not unlawful (*Accordance with International Law of the Unilateral Declaration of Independence in Respect of Kosovo*). The situation has arisen again in connection with the Russian annexation of Crimea, which was legally organized so as to appear as secession followed by integration with another State (Russia). International law neither confers a right to secession nor bans it, except when the secession results from a violation of a fundamental principle such as the prohibition of the use of force, in which case secession is unlawful and there is an obligation not to recognize the new territorial situation (see **3.4.2**). From a systemic standpoint, putting both the *Kosovo* and *Crimea* cases in perspective is important to emphasize that the weakening of the territorial integrity rule in Serbia (in the *Kosovo* case), favoured by Western countries, may have paved the way for the encroachment on the territorial integrity of Ukraine (in relation to Crimea). Self-determination is inherently fact-sensitive. Yet, the ambiguity in its understanding has profound systemic implications.

3.8.3 RIGHTS AND OBLIGATIONS

The elaboration of the law of self-determination has taken place in the context of decolonization and, more specifically, of colonial peoples, peoples subjected to foreign occupation, as well as groups subjected to racial oppression. These are not the only contexts where the right to self-determination may operate, as noted by the ICJ in its Advisory Opinion on *Legal Consequences of the Separation of the Chagos Archipelago from Mauritius in 1965*,[79] but they provide the historical and legal context in which the principle and the right to self-determination developed. In this context, self-determination carries both specific rights and obligations (1–3) and systemic implications (4–7):

(1) First and foremost, the peoples entitled to self-determination have a legal right, in relation to the oppressor or territorial State, to external or internal self-determination[80] (see **3.8.2**), as well as a host of rights and claims in regard to other States,[81] chiefly the claim that third States refrain from sending troops to assist the State denying self-determination (see **8.3**).

(2) States which oppress peoples falling within one of the three categories are duty-bound to allow the free exercise of the right to self-determination. In particular they are enjoined not to deny this right forcibly.[82] This is in addition to the obligations arising for such States from the right to self-determination as a human right beyond the context of decolonization.[83]

---

[79] *Legal Consequences of the Separation of the Chagos Archipelago from Mauritius in 1965*, §144 ('The Court is conscious that the right to self-determination, as a fundamental human right, has a broad scope of application. However, to answer the question put to it by the General Assembly, the Court will confine itself, in this Advisory Opinion, to analysing the right to self-determination in the context of decolonization').

[80] Resolution 1514 (XV) (n 78), §2; Friendly Relations Declaration (n 1), Principle 5, §§1 and 4; Article 1 common to ICCPR and ICESCR (n 75); *Legal Consequences of the Separation of the Chagos Archipelago from Mauritius in 1965*, §§177–179.

[81] *East Timor (Portugal v Australia)*, §29; *Legal Consequences of the Separation of the Chagos Archipelago from Mauritius in 1965*, §180.

[82] Resolution 1514 (XV) (n 78), §1; Friendly Relations Declaration (n 1), Principle 5, §§2 and 5.

[83] *Legal Consequences of the Separation of the Chagos Archipelago from Mauritius in 1965*, §144.

(3) Third States are legally authorized to support peoples entitled to self-determination, by granting them any assistance short of armed force. Conversely, they must refrain from aiding and abetting oppressor States. Furthermore, they are entitled to claim respect for the right by States denying self-determination. If self-determination is forcibly denied they can bring the question before the competent UN bodies and even resort to peaceful countermeasures, particularly if there has been a previous finding by the UN to the effect that the right at issue is illegally infringed.[84] States also have a 'legal interest' to invoke, before an international tribunal, the international responsibility of the State denying the right to self-determination of a people entitled to it.[85]

In addition, self-determination has had a profound impact on the very foundations of the international legal order. At least three major systemic implications can be discerned:

(4) In the area of the use of force, self-determination has had a twofold impact. On the one hand, it has *extended* the general ban on force (previously existing for States in their relations with other States). It has imposed on States the prohibition against using force to deny self-determination, against colonial peoples, peoples subjected to foreign occupation, and racial groups denied equal access to government. On the other hand, self-determination has resulted in granting to liberation movements a legal licence to use force—akin to the right of States to self-defence—for the purpose of reacting to the forcible denial of self-determination by a colonial State, an occupying Power, or a State refusing a racially oppressed group equal access to government.

(5) Self-determination has also left a mark in international humanitarian law, particularly as regards the law applicable to wars of national liberation, which became a frequent occurrence throughout the decolonization process (see **17.2.4** and **17.3.1**).

(6) Self-determination has also had a significant impact on the most traditional segment of international law, namely the acquisition, transfer, and loss of title over territory. It has cast doubt on traditional legal titles such as colonial conquest and acquisition by cession of sovereignty over overseas territories. Furthermore, it is no longer possible for valid legal title to be acquired where territories are annexed in breach of self-determination or where part of the territory of a non-self-governing territory is detached by the administering Power at the time of independence.[86] Self-determination also prevents States from regarding as *terra nullius* territories inhabited by organized aggregates lacking the hallmarks of State authority, in cases where, for example, the sovereign State previously wielding authority over a territory has abandoned that territory.[87]

(7) Finally, self-determination renders null and void treaties providing for the transfer of territories whenever such treaties do not include provision for any prior and genuine consultation of the population involved (see **10.8**).

---

[84] These consequences were addressed in some detail by the ICJ in *Legal Consequences for States of the Continued Presence of South Africa in Namibia (South West Africa) notwithstanding Security Council Resolution 276 (1970)*, §§117–127.

[85] *Legal Consequences of the Separation of the Chagos Archipelago from Mauritius in 1965*, §180 ('Since respect for the right to self-determination is an obligation *erga omnes*, all States have a legal interest in protecting that right').

[86] *Legal Consequences of the Separation of the Chagos Archipelago from Mauritius in 1965*, §160 ('any detachment by the administering Power of part of a non-self-governing territory, unless based on the freely expressed and genuine will of the people of the territory concerned, is contrary to the right to self-determination').

[87] See *Western Sahara*, §§80–83.

3.8.4 LIMITS OF THE PRINCIPLE

The acceptance of the principle into the realm of law has been *selective* and *limited* in many respects. In particular, the international law on self-determination developed in the context of decolonization is not applicable to the demands of *ethnic groups and national, religious, cultural, or linguistic minorities* (not otherwise falling under the law of decolonization). International law refrains from granting any right of external self-determination to these groups, but it does grant them certain rights based either on self-determination as a fundamental human right or on other collective rights. The increasing recognition of collective rights for indigenous and tribal peoples and other minorities,[88] particularly in the Inter-American[89] and African[90] contexts, goes some way towards providing legal protection to the claims of such groups and minorities, but it falls short of the more comprehensive scope of powers entailed by self-determination.

Clearly, political stability and the territorial integrity of States are important values that States hold dear. In their view, indiscriminately granting the right to self-determination to all ethnic groups and minorities would pose a serious threat to peace and bring about the fragmentation of States into a myriad of entities unable to survive. It should not come as a surprise that it is precisely those States that benefited from self-determination when they liberated themselves from colonial rule, which are now among the staunchest supporters of a strict interpretation of the principle.[91] It would thus seem that most States have heeded the warning issued as early as 1952 by a leading champion of human rights, Eleanor Roosevelt, who, speaking as a US delegate, stated that, '[j]ust as the concept of individual human liberty carried to its logical extreme would mean anarchy, so the principle of self-determination given unrestricted application could result in chaos'.[92]

3.9 RESPECT FOR HUMAN RIGHTS

3.9.1 GENERAL OBSERVATIONS

Unlike the principles of sovereign equality and non-intervention—a typical expression of the Grotian model, to which dissensions in the world today have given a new lease of life— the principle imposing respect for human rights, like the ban on the threat or use of force, is typical of a new stage of development in the international community following the Second

---

[88] See Office of the High Commissioner for Human Rights, *Minority Rights: International Standards and Guidance for Implementation* (New York and Geneva: OHCHR, 2010).

[89] See Inter-American Commission on Human Rights, *Indigenous and Tribal Peoples' Rights over their Ancestral Lands and Natural Resources: Norms and Jurisprudence of the Inter-American Human Rights System*, doc. OEA/Ser.L/V/II, doc. 56/09, 30 December 2009.

[90] See G. Pentassuglia, 'Indigenous Groups and the Developing Jurisprudence of the African Commission on Human and Peoples' Rights' (2010) 3 *UCL Human Rights Review* 150.

[91] The ICJ took note of such a preference in affirming the general scope of the *uti possidetis* principle. See *Frontier Dispute (Burkina Faso/Republic of Mali)*, §§20–26 (particularly at paragraph 25 where it is stated: '[a]t first sight this principle [*uti possidetis*] conflicts outright with another one, the right of peoples to self-determination. In fact, however, the maintenance of the territorial status quo in Africa is often seen as the wisest course, to preserve what has been achieved by peoples who have struggled for their independence, and to avoid a disruption which would deprive the continent of the gains achieved by much sacrifice').

[92] E. Roosevelt, 'The Universal Validity of Man's Right to Self-Determination' in 27 *US Dept of State Bulletin*, 8 December 1952, at 919.

World War.[93] It is, in fact, competing—if not at loggerheads—with the traditional principles of sovereign equality of States and of non-intervention. It is for this very reason that the principle is difficult to co-ordinate with the other two.

The foundations of this obligation must be sought in two strands of sources. On the one hand, the adoption of the UN Charter and the subsequent enactment of such fundamental international instruments as the Universal Declaration of 1948, the two Covenants on Human Rights of 1966, and a host of specific conventions and international resolutions (see **Chapter 18**), had such an impact on the international community that almost no State currently challenges the concept that human rights must be respected everywhere in the world. But this principle is not simply an aggregation derived from instruments formulated in terms of specific human rights. There is also authority for the existence of a State duty formulated as such, in the form of a general obligation. The ICJ has acknowledged the duty of States to protect 'elementary considerations of humanity'[94] and the Friendly Relations Declaration includes a statement to the effect that '[e]very State has the duty to promote through joint and separate action universal respect for and observance of human rights and fundamental freedoms in accordance with the Charter'. Moreover, the ICJ characterized the obligations arising from a human rights treaty (*in casu* the Convention against torture) as having an *erga omnes* character, hence every State party to that Convention—and indeed every State—has an interest in their observance, even in the absence of any specific injury.[95] The two strands converge and result in a general prohibition of gross and large-scale violations of basic human rights and fundamental freedoms.

3.9.2 LEGAL SCOPE OF THE PRINCIPLE

States have gradually come to accept the idea that massive infringements of basic human rights are reprehensible; they make the delinquent State accountable to the whole international community. In contrast, isolated and sporadic instances of violation are not necessarily of *general* international concern. Thus, the principle at issue does not impose on States the obligation to abide by specific regulations on human rights, although such obligation may arise from human rights treaties. Rather it requires States to refrain from seriously and repeatedly infringing a basic right (e.g. the right not to be subjected to torture; or the right to a fair trial; or freedom from arbitrary arrest), and from trampling upon a whole series of rights (e.g. the fundamental civil and political rights, or social, economic, and cultural rights).

As in the case of other general principles, respect for human rights derives its most solid guarantee from the UN system. Legally, any State whatsoever is entitled to insist that the offending party discontinue its violations (and make reparations, as the case may require). However, for a number of historical, political, and diplomatic reasons States eschew bilateral action and prefer to bring the issue of gross disregard for human rights before international organizations, chiefly the UN. This practice is, to some extent, a healthy phenomenon, for

---

[93] See generally E. Riedel, 'Human Rights Protection as a Principle' in Viñuales, *The UN Friendly Relations Declaration* (n 1), chapter 10; A. A. Cançado Trindade, *International Law for Humankind: Towards a New 'Jus Gentium'* (Leiden: Martinus Nijhoff, 2010); T. Meron, *The Humanization of International Law* (Leiden: Martinus Nijhoff, 2006); G. Le Moli, *Human Dignity in International Law* (Cambridge: Cambridge University Press, 2020).

[94] See *Corfu Channel (United Kingdom v Albania)*, 22; *Legality of the Threat or Use of Nuclear Weapons*, §79.

[95] *Questions relating to the Obligation to Prosecute or Extradite (Belgium v Senegal)*, §§64–70.

in the UN a less partial examination of allegations can be made, and 'collective sanctions' (see **14.4**) may be resorted to, which tend to be more effective than individual (peaceful) countermeasures.

3.10 PREVENTION OF SIGNIFICANT ENVIRONMENTAL HARM

3.10.1 GENERAL OBSERVATIONS

Much like respect for human rights, the protection of the environment is a new development that became a subject of international law mainly in the late 1960s, although some conservation, natural resource, and oil pollution instruments existed prior to that date.[96] Importantly, the prevention principle, which remains the cardinal principle of international environmental law, may not be easily harmonized with principles such as sovereign equality or self-determination. In fact, its initial and still main challenge was the quest for development by both developing and newly independent States as well as for growth in developed States. Principles relating to environmental protection were perceived as a hindrance for much-needed development, and an inequitable one given that developed countries had not paid attention to environmental protection during their development process in the nineteenth century. This development–environment equation has haunted most environmental negotiations since the late 1960s, and it is still with us today.[97] The 17 Sustainable Development Goals (SDGs) adopted by the UN General Assembly in 2015 as part of the 2030 Agenda for Sustainable Development are an attempt, much like the introduction of the concept of 'sustainable development' and Agenda 21 before them, at downplaying the tensions between economic prosperity, social development, and environmental protection, and at (perhaps over-)emphasizing their synergies.

At the same time, the scale of the environmental challenges faced today is such that almost no State dares to totally ignore them. As a result, a vast body of treaties and instruments relating to environmental protection has developed over the past five decades (see **Chapter 20**), as well as a limited number of principles with unquestionable customary grounding. Among the latter, the prevention principle takes pride of place. Initially formulated in Principle 21 of the 1972 Stockholm Declaration on the Human Environment,[98] it was slightly adjusted in 1992 to incorporate a developmental dimension in Principle 2 of the Rio Declaration on Environment and Development: 'States have, in accordance with the Charter of the United Nations and the principles of international law, the sovereign right to exploit their own resources pursuant to their own environmental and developmental policies, and the responsibility to ensure that activities within their jurisdiction or control do not cause damage to the environment of other States or of areas beyond the limits of national jurisdiction.' Subsequently, it came to be widely recognized by international courts and tribunals, including the ICJ,[99] as a principle of international customary law.

---

[96] See generally L.-A. Duvic-Paoli and J. E. Viñuales, 'Prevention of Environment Harm' in Viñuales, *The UN Friendly Relations Declaration* (n 1), chapter 12; L.-A. Duvic-Paoli, *The Prevention Principle in International Environmental Law* (Cambridge: Cambridge University Press, 2018); Xue Hanqin, *Transboundary Harm in International Law* (Cambridge: Cambridge University Press, 2003).

[97] For an overview of five decades of global environmental governance see J. E. Viñuales, 'The Rise and Fall of Sustainable Development' (2013) 22 *RECIEL* 3.

[98] Declaration of the United Nations Conference on the Human Environment, Stockholm, 16 June 1972, UN Doc. A/CONF 48/14/Rev.1, pp. 2ff.

[99] The first recognition as such came in 1996, see *Legality of the Threat or Use of Nuclear Weapons*, §29.

In its present understanding, the prevention principle is the expression in environmental matters of the broader due diligence obligation under international law, and it is further fleshed out, procedurally, by two other customary duties, namely the duty to co-operate in good faith and the requirement to conduct an environmental impact assessment (see **20.3**). Importantly, it is this customary matrix, as well as a number of other environmental principles (e.g. precaution, polluter-pays, intergenerational equity, common but differentiated responsibilities, participation, etc.), that gives legal expression to the 'sustainable' dimension of the concept of sustainable development. From an international legal standpoint, development is 'sustainable' if it respects environmental principles, chiefly the prevention principle.[100] Largely due to its novelty, as compared to the immediate concerns in the aftermath of the Second World War, environmental protection was not mentioned in the UN Charter. Nor was it referred to in the Friendly Relations Declaration of 1970. It was only after the 1972 Stockholm Declaration, as well as the creation of the United Nations Environment Programme (UNEP, today called UN Environment) following the Stockholm Conference, that environmental considerations started to feature among the principles of international law. An illustration of this trend is provided by the work of the International Law Commission, starting in 1978, which would lead to the adoption of two sets of draft articles, one on prevention (2001) and another on allocation of loss (2006). In the meantime, the end of the Cold War and the 1992 Rio Conference on Environment and Development gave renewed impetus to environmental matters, and throughout the 1990s the ICJ and other international courts integrated them into their jurisprudence. In what follows, as with other principles, we provide a concise characterization of the customary law of environmental protection as it stands today.

3.10.2 LEGAL SCOPE OF THE PRINCIPLE

As noted earlier, the customary matrix of environmental protection consists of four principles that were identified by the ICJ in 2015:[101] the general obligation of due diligence, the prevention principle, the duty to co-operate, and the requirement to conduct an environmental impact assessment (EIA). Overall, they can be summarized by reference to the prevention principle, which is the expression of due diligence as regards prevention of environmental harm, and it is further extended through co-operation and the EIA requirement:

(1) The starting-point of the prevention principle is a restatement of States' sovereign right to make use of their natural resources. Before achieving independence, such sovereignty is protected by the principle of permanent sovereignty over natural resources, initially stated in the 1962 resolution 1803 (XVII).[102] This principle remains applicable after achieving independence to the extent that the powers granted by States to foreigners over their natural resources are essentially transient and do not amount to a definitive alienation.

(2) The exercise of such power is however limited by the need not to cause significant harm to the environment of other States or of areas beyond national jurisdiction. This limitation must be understood from three different perspectives. Firstly, the obligation imposed on States is one of conduct, rather than one of result.[103] States must display '*due diligence*' in taking action to prevent significant environmental harm. That entails not only adopting appropriate legal frameworks

---

[100] See J. E. Viñuales, 'Sustainable Development' in L. Rajamani and J. Peel (eds), *The Oxford Handbook of International Environmental Law*, 2nd edn (Oxford: Oxford University Press, 2020), chapter 17.

[101] *Certain Activities Carried Out by Nicaragua in the Border Area (Costa Rica v Nicaragua)*, §104.

[102] Resolution 1803 (XVII), Permanent Sovereignty over Natural Resources, 14 December 1962.

[103] *Pulp Mills on the River Uruguay (Argentina v Uruguay)*, §197; *Responsibilities and Obligations of States Sponsoring Persons and Entities with respect to Activities in the Area*, §§111–116.

consistent with international standards and the current scientific understanding of the problem but also taking proactive steps to ensure that such frameworks are effectively applied.[104] The level of diligence is thus a demanding one, although it is not to be equated with strict—or no-fault—liability (*responsabilité objective*). Secondly, such action must aim to prevent '*significant*' harm. The threshold to consider harm as 'significant' depends on each specific situation but it is understood that the harm must be more than merely detectable without the need for it to reach a serious or irreversible character. Less than significant harm must be tolerated by affected States as part of the State of origin's sovereign right to use its resources. The State of origin must nevertheless regulate such harm under the polluter-pays principle, which aims to internalize—that is, allocate to the polluter—the cost of negative externalities (undesirable effects on third parties) of activities that are otherwise beneficial (e.g. electricity production, transportation, etc.). Thirdly, the duty seeks to prevent significant harm to the *environment as such*, whether of other States or of areas beyond any State jurisdiction (the global commons). It may be asked whether States have a duty to prevent significant harm to their own environment. This point has not been settled in the jurisprudence but there are important policy and legal reasons to conclude that the prevention principle also limits harm to a State's own environment.[105] This is an additional indication of the difficulties involved in conciliating sovereign equality and prevention.

(3) The prevention principle is, in turn, further implemented by two other customary principles, namely the *duty to co-operate* in good faith and the requirement to conduct an *environmental impact assessment*. Importantly, these duties are not the only expression of the prevention principle. Indeed, the prevention principle requires a high level of due diligence to prevent significant environmental harm. Within the broad spectrum of measures necessary to discharge this due diligence obligation, some procedures can be specifically demanded by potentially affected States or other States (for harm to the global commons). Hence, these other States can only require the State of origin to exercise due diligence in *general terms* (without indication of specific procedures) but they are entitled, under international law, to *specifically* demand from it certain forms of co-operation (notification and consultation) and the conduct of an environmental impact assessment. More detail on these procedural duties is provided in section **20.3**.

3.11 INTERACTIONS AMONG FUNDAMENTAL PRINCIPLES

The principles discussed in this chapter are closely intertwined.[106] They supplement and support one another and also condition each other's application. Subjects of international law must comply with all of them. Also, in the application of any one of the principles, all the others must simultaneously be borne in mind.

By way of illustration one may mention that the principles on respect for human rights and on non-intervention in the internal affairs of States are tightly connected. For example, the question of whether States can intervene to prompt a third State to discontinue alleged violations of human rights can only be settled in the light, and on the combined strength, of

---

[104] *Pulp Mills on the River Uruguay (Argentina v Uruguay)*, §197; *Request for an Advisory Opinion Submitted by the Sub-Regional Fisheries Commission (SRFC)*, §§131–140.

[105] See Duvic-Paoli and Viñuales (n 96), at 119.

[106] See P.-M. Dupuy, 'The Friendly Relations Declaration at 50' in Viñuales, *The UN Friendly Relations Declaration* (n 1), chapter 15.

the two principles, which—taken together—can provide a correct solution to the question in specific cases.[107] It follows that any peaceful initiative aimed at requiring a State to discontinue large-scale and gross violations of human rights is consistent with the principle of non-intervention. Such an initiative can also take the form of a proposal, within an international organization, that non-forcible sanctions be taken against a State systematically engaging in violations of basic human rights. The situation is different in the case of sporadic infringements or single occurrences of serious disregard for human rights. In this case a balance between the two principles may consist in allowing foreign countries to take steps solely via diplomatic channels. Consequently, the State where the alleged violations have occurred must not regard as an unfriendly act a *démarche* by another State aimed at expressing concern and calling upon the former State to do its utmost to end the violations. By contrast, the State on whose territory the violations took place can reject as undue interference any attempt by other States to exercise direct pressure on its State officials or on individuals or groups and associations acting on its territory.

Serious difficulties also arise as regards the question of how to co-ordinate the right of peoples to self-determination with that of the sovereign equality and territorial integrity of States. While many complexities arise in specific cases, given the highly fact-sensitive nature of the interaction between these two principles, the following propositions seem warranted. International law tends strongly to protect the territorial integrity of sovereign States. As a consequence, the international community does not expressly authorize secession (i.e. external self-determination outside the context of decolonization, foreign occupation, or racial oppression). As for peoples entitled to internal self-determination, it does not follow from this legal entitlement that they have a right to secession. In 1998, the Supreme Court of Canada in *Reference re Secession of Quebec* rightly held that '[a] State whose government represents the whole of the people or the peoples resident within its territory, on a basis of equality and without discrimination, and respects the principles [sic] of self-determination in its own internal arrangements, is entitled to the protection under international law of its territorial integrity' (at §130). In the Advisory Opinion on the Declaration of independence of Kosovo, the ICJ considered the argument advanced by some States according to which Kosovo would have a right to secession, despite the fact that the situation took place outside of the three contexts above or, alternatively, that it would have a right of 'remedial secession' as a result of its oppression by Serbia. The Court did not take a position on either of these issues, but it did emphasize that there existed widely divergent views on them.[108]

However, the absence of a right must not be equated with the existence of a prohibition. An important caveat is that secession is clearly prohibited in a number of situations: (i) in the absence of a people enjoying the right to self-determination; (ii) when the new territorial situation results from a violation of the prohibition on the use of force, as in the Crimea case; or (iii) when it results from a prohibited intervention in the internal affairs of another State to support a group outside the context of decolonization, foreign occupation, or racial oppression.

---

[107] S. Hoffmann, *Duties Beyond Borders: On the Limits and Possibilities of Ethical International Politics* (Syracuse, NY: Syracuse University Press, 1981), 124, suggested a useful criterion: 'We must make a distinction between what one can normally call interference or meddling, which is practiced by every sovereign State, and which essentially consists of trying to change a sovereign regime so as to make it more favourable to one's own political or economic interests, and the kinds of measures I am advocating here [that is, peaceful steps to be taken on the bilateral and multilateral level, and within international organizations] and which are essentially aimed at getting governments to observe rules of behavior to which they have committed themselves.'

[108] *Accordance with International Law of the Unilateral Declaration of Independence in Respect of Kosovo* §§82–83.

PART II
SUBJECTS OF THE INTERNATIONAL COMMUNITY

4

STATES AS THE PRIMARY SUBJECTS OF INTERNATIONAL LAW

4.1 THE CONTINUING PRE-EMINENCE OF STATES

National systems encompass many legal subjects of different natures: ranging from citizens to foreigners residing in the territory of the State, including corporate bodies, NGOs, as well as public institutions at national and local level. In national legal systems *individuals* are the primary subjects. By contrast, the legal subjects of the international community are relatively fewer. In addition, the fundamental subjects are not individuals, but *States*. They are entities which, besides controlling territory in a stable and permanent manner, exercise the principal law-making and executive 'functions' proper to any legal order. All other subjects either exercise effective authority over territory for a limited period of time only or have no territorial basis whatsoever.

States are the backbone of the international community. States created the international legal order as we know it, and international law has been modelled on the evolving needs and interests of States. They possess full *legal capacity* and the full spectrum of entitlements under international law, that is, the ability to be vested with rights, powers, and obligations. Were they to disappear, the present international community would either fall apart, or radically change in its fundamental structure. For historical reasons, there are at present about two hundred States, including a few mini-States. As a matter of legal principle, all States are equal. However, one particular class—a handful of States with strong economic and military systems—enjoys a pre-eminent position in the shaping and implementation of international law.

Traditionally, there has been another category of international subjects, namely *insurgents* (a category which tends to be blurred today within the broader label of non-State actors), who come into being through their struggle against the State to which they belong. They are born from a wound in the body of a particular State, and they are therefore not easily accepted by the international community unless they can prove their ability to exercise some of the sovereign rights typical of States. They assert themselves by force, and acquire international status proportionate to their power and authority. However, their existence is by definition provisional: they either win and turn into fully fledged States or are defeated and disappear.

States and insurgents are 'traditional' subjects of the international community, in the sense that they have been the *dramatis personae* (the characters of the play) on the international scene since its inception. Throughout the twentieth century, and particularly since the end of the Second World War, other poles of interest and activity have gained international status. They include *international organizations*, *national liberation movements* (i.e. some categories of *peoples* possessed of a representative organization), and *individuals*. In addition, in the late twentieth and early twenty-first centuries, new categories have developed under the general label of *non-state actors*. These can include NGOs, corporations, and armed groups not necessarily meeting the requirements of insurgency. The emergence of these subjects is a distinct feature of contemporary international law and will be further examined in **Chapter 8**.

Unlike States, which are the primordial subjects of international law, all the other subjects just mentioned, on account of their inherent characteristics (e.g. lack of permanent, or at least stable, authority over a territory, etc.) possess a *limited legal capacity* in the area of international rights and obligations. They also have a *limited capacity to act*, that is, to put into effect their rights and powers in judicial and other proceedings, or to enforce their rights.

4.2 THE CREATION OF STATES IN INTERNATIONAL LAW

As already stated, States are the primary subjects of the international community, just like individuals in national legal systems. However, while individuals are normally very numerous, there are only some two hundred States, and they are profoundly different. This does not simplify matters but rather complicates them in the world community. As the distinguished British political scientist, M. Wight, pointed out:

> The smaller the numerical membership of a society, and the more various its members, the more difficult it is to make rules not unjust to extreme cases: this is one reason for the weakness of international law. As a *reductio ad absurdum*, imagine a society of four members: an ogre twenty feet high, flesh-eating, preferably human; an Englishman six feet high, speaking no Japanese; a Japanese samurai, a military noble, speaking no English; and a Central African pygmy, early palaeolithic; and all on an island the size of Malta. This is a parable of what is called international society.[1]

A further factor complicates matters. Generally municipal law lays down rules establishing when an individual or a body acquires legal status or legal capacity—that is, when they become holders of rights and duties. To this effect, most national legal systems provide that individuals become legal subjects at birth (or even on conception), although they may only exercise their rights and obligations when they come of age. As for entities (corporations, foundations, public agencies, etc.), domestic law usually specifies the requirements they must satisfy in order to be granted rights and duties. In short, municipal law normally includes special provisions on the 'birth' of juridical subjects. In a way, the application of such rules constitutes a kind of precondition to the operation of all other substantive and procedural norms.

By contrast, there is no international legislation laying down detailed rules concerning the creation of States. Yet, on careful analysis, it is possible to infer from the body of general international law that it presupposes certain general characteristics in the entities whose conduct they regulate. Reliance upon general international law, that is, customary law, is necessary for this purpose because the international legal personality must operate towards all the other members of the international community.[2]

The rules under discussion usually require the following elements: a *central structure* capable of exercising *effective control*, in an *independent* manner, over a *human community*

---

[1] M. Wight, ed. B. Porter and G. Wight, *International Theory: The Three Traditions* (London: Leicester University Press, 1991), 139.

[2] See generally J. Crawford, *The Creation of States in International Law*, 2nd edn (Oxford: Oxford University Press, 2007).

living in a given *territory*.³ Hence three structural elements: government (an apparatus, a structure), population, and territory, interconnected, and connected to the rest of the international community, through two fundamental principles: effectiveness and independence. The bodies endowed with supreme authority must be distinct from, and independent of, any other State, that is to say, endowed with an original (not derivative) legal order—they must possess autonomous 'sovereignty'. According to the well-known expression used by the sole arbitrator Max Huber in the *Palmas Island* case, 'sovereignty in the relations between States signifies independence. Independence in regard to a portion of the globe is the right to exercise therein, to the exclusion of any other State, the functions of a State.'⁴ However, some forms of international interference by other subjects have in the past been considered compatible with statehood. An example is provided by protectorates, where the protecting State—for example France in relation to Morocco and Tunisia—was legally authorized to control the defence and foreign policy of the protected State.

Other required elements are that the *territory* must not belong, or no longer belong, to any other sovereign State, and the members of the community living therein (the people) do not owe allegiance to other outside authorities. Territory is an essential element of statehood; it may be large or small, but it is indispensable if an organized structure is to qualify as a State as international subject. International law requires *effective* possession of, and control over, a territory. Only in exceptional circumstances does it allow governmental entities that have lost effective control over territory to survive as international entities for some time. Such was the case of the so-called 'Governments-in-exile' created during the Second World War: they were hosted in Britain and represented countries occupied by Germany, namely Poland, Norway, the Netherlands, Belgium, Luxemburg, Yugoslavia, and Greece.⁵ In those cases, the 'survival' of the international subject rests on a legal fiction—politically motivated—and is warranted by the hope of recovering control over territory. Once this prospect vanishes, the other States discard this legal fiction. The same may apply to States that lose their territory as a result of sea-level rise induced by climate change, although the specificity of this situation may receive a *sui generis* solution, for example territory transferred, leased, or otherwise made available to the affected entities, recognition of artificial structures as territory, or possibly the redefinition of statehood in such cases.⁶

Furthermore, there are cases in which claims to statehood cannot be entertained because the entity *lacks independence* (and hence is not considered the bearer of original and autonomous sovereignty) under international law. This is the case with the so-called 'puppet states', for example those created in occupation areas by the Axis Powers (the Manchukuo to cover the Japanese occupation of Manchuria from 1932 to 1945, Vichy France, the Italian Social Republic by Germany, respectively in France after the occupation and in northern

---

³ Broadly speaking these requirements are set out in the 1933 Montevideo Convention on the Rights and Duties of States (entered into force on 23 December 1934), which under Article 1 provides that '[t]he state as a person of international law should possess the following qualifications: a. a permanent population; b. a defined territory; c. government; and d. capacity to enter into relations with the other states'. Generally, the latter requirement is seen as a consequence of Statehood. For a critical assessment of reliance of this instrument see T. Grant, 'Defining Statehood: The Montevideo Convention and its Discontents' (1998) 37 *Colum J Transn'l L* 403.
⁴ *Island of Palmas Case (Netherlands/United States of America)*, 838.
⁵ See generally A. Koberg, *Die Exilregierung im Völkerrecht: Eine Untersuchung ihrer rechtlichen Klassifikation* (Frankfurt am Main: Lang, 2004) and S. Talmon, *Recognition of Governments in International Law: with particular reference to Governments in Exile* (Oxford: Clarendon Press, 1998).
⁶· See A. Torres Camprubí, *Statehood under Water: Challenges of Sea-Level Rise to the Continuity of Pacific Island States* (Leiden: Martinus Nijhoff, 2016).

Italy after 1943); or those established in the 1970s in South Africa with the creation of the Bantustan or Black Homeland States (e.g. Transkei in 1976 or Venda in 1979 and Ciskei in 1981). In these cases, there normally is a lack of any independence and autonomy, and fictional entities are created by other States to circumvent international law and cover their own activities in that territory.[7]

Another complex matter concerns the so-called *failed or collapsed* States,[8] which are entities that do not, or no longer, possess effective control over the territory or population; in such cases, the prevailing tendency has been to preserve statehood and provide assistance to the government to help re-establish authority (e.g. this has been the case in Somalia, Liberia, or Sierra Leone, where the UN has supported governmental authorities in regaining control and starting the processes of state-rebuilding). In these cases, one might say that there is a principle of stability that prevails, which suggests preserving formal authority for as long as might be necessary to seek to re-establish control, with the assistance and involvement of the international community, normally through the United Nations.

Finally, there are also cases in which, despite the fact that formal elements are present (territory, population, and government), the UN Security Council has pronounced against recognizing certain situations as meeting the requirements of statehood on account of some form of illegality affecting their genesis, for example the pronouncements contained in resolution 541 (1983) on the Turkish Republic in Northern Cyprus, or resolutions 216 and 217 (1965) concerning Southern Rhodesia (for more detail see **4.3.2**). These cases are an illustration of the tension that exists in contemporary international law between effectiveness and legality.[9] Once it was only the factual dimension of force that would determine the establishment of sovereignty over given territory and the emergence of a new State. Today, there are a number of rules that play a role and affect such a process. On the one hand, there is the requirement that control over territory and population be effective for statehood to emerge. On the other, a more relaxed approach to such a requirement is possible where there is a pre-existing legal basis (failed or collapsed States), or where the legal claim for statehood is anchored to other fundamental legal principles (self-determination, protection, and promotion of human rights). Conversely, if the entity is created with the purpose of somehow circumventing international law, despite its factual existence, there can be resistance in the international community for it to be considered as fully established under international law. Often, and particularly in the more controversial cases, the approach taken by the international community of States towards specific situations might also assume relevance.

4.3 THE ROLE OF RECOGNITION

4.3.1 CONCEPT AND EFFECTS OF THE RECOGNITION OF STATES

It is clear that the norms already referred to do not lay down very specific criteria. They merely provide a general yardstick. It is, therefore, difficult to ascertain in practice whether a State fulfils the requisite conditions. The existence of a State is to a large extent characterized by a rather powerful factual dimension, and the attitude of existing States, as reflected

---

[7] See R. Wun, 'Beyond Traditional Statehood Criteria: The Law and Contemporary Politics of State Creation' (2013) 26 *Hague Yrbk Intl L* 316.

[8] On this rather vague political science category see R. Rotberg (ed.), *State Failure and State Weakness in a Time of Terror* (Washington: Brookings Institution, 2003), chapter 1.

[9] See S. Zappalà, 'Can Legality Trump Effectiveness in Today's International Law' in A. Cassese (ed.), *Realizing Utopia. The Future of International Law* (Oxford: Oxford University Press, 2012), 105.

in their recognition, or non-recognition, of the new entity, may be a factor that helps in addressing the issue.¹⁰

The act of recognition has no legal effect on the international personality of the entity: it does not confer rights, nor does it impose obligations on it. Many jurists, chiefly in the past, have advocated the view that recognition entails 'constitutive' effects, namely that it creates the legal personality of States. This view is, however, fallacious because it is in strident contradiction with the principle of effectiveness (*effectivités*) whereby certain 'effective' situations are for that sole reason given legal effects. If one were to follow the theory of constitutive recognition, a State would not possess legal personality if not recognized, even where it possessed effectiveness. Furthermore, the theory is inconsistent with the principle of the sovereign equality of States, for existing States would be authorized to decide when a new entity exhibiting all the hallmarks of a State might or might not be admitted to membership in the world community. The theory is also logically unsound, for it implies that a certain entity is an international subject in relation to those States which have recognized it, while it lacks legal personality as far as other States are concerned; thus, the international personality would be split quite artificially, in defiance of reality. In fact, this theory is an outmoded survival from the nineteenth century, when, as pointed out earlier, European States claimed the right to admit other States to, or exclude them from, the 'family of nations'. As mentioned, even at that time such a right was questionable, and the policy was devoid of formal legitimization. Thus, a different account of the act of recognition is needed.

At present, recognition of States has a threefold significance. First, it is politically important in that it testifies to the will of the recognizing States to initiate international interaction with the new State. Secondly, it is legally relevant for it proves that the recognizing States consider that, in their view, the new entity fulfils all the factual conditions considered necessary for becoming an international subject. Of course, this assessment is not binding on other States. It is, however, indicative of the attitude of States and can therefore prove useful in deciding whether the new entity may be regarded as an international legal subject. In a community lacking any central authority responsible for formally passing judgment on legally relevant situations, the attitude of single States acquires considerable weight as evidence for, or against, the existence of new legal subjects. Thirdly, recognition is legally relevant in that, once granted, it bars the recognizing State from altering its position and claiming that the new entity lacks statehood. In other words, the granting of recognition creates an *estoppel* precluding the recognizing State from contesting the legal personality of the new State.¹¹

In addition, recognition may have legal consequences when precipitately granted, particularly when the new entity results from secession from an existing State or from a civil war. *Premature* recognition, that is, recognition accorded before the basic factual conditions for statehood are met, may amount to unlawful interference in the internal affairs of the State concerned. For example, according to some commentators,¹² the recognition of Croatia by

---

¹⁰ On recognition of States see H. Lauterpacht, 'Recognition of States in International Law' (1944) 53 *Yale LJ* 385; I. Brownlie, 'Recognition in Theory and Practice' (1982) 53 *BYIL* 197; S. Talmon, 'The Constitutive Versus the Declaratory Doctrine of Recognition: Tertium Non Datur?' (2004) 75 *BYIL* 101; E. Wyler, *Théorie et pratique de la reconnaissance d'État* (Bruxelles: Bruylant, 2013).

¹¹ It is widely recognized that international law upholds the common law concept of estoppel, whereby a party is barred from alleging or denying a fact or claiming a right, to the detriment of another party entitled to rely upon such conduct in consequence of previous allegation, denial, or conduct, or admission by the former party.

¹² See e.g. R. Müllerson, *International Law, Rights and Politics* (London: Routledge, 1994), 130; R. Rich, 'Recognition of States: the Collapse of Yugoslavia and the Soviet Union' (1993) 4 *EJIL* 36.

the members of the European Communities, Austria, and Switzerland on 15 January 1992 was premature, because Croatia only controlled one-third of its territory. The Arbitration Commission on Yugoslavia, in its Opinion No. 5 of 11 January 1992, held that, subject to a reservation (the Croatian Constitution did not incorporate some treaty provisions specified by the Arbitration Commission), Croatia met 'the necessary conditions for its recognition by the Member States of the European Community' (in 4 EJIL (1993), at 76–7).

State practice shows that over the years the *factual conditions many States require for recognition* have changed. In the past, it was sufficient for the new State to wield *effective control* over a human community and the territory where such community lived. In the 1930s some States began also to require that *the new State must not contravene some fundamental standards* of the international community (such as the ban on wars that were either in breach of international treaties or initiated to aggress a foreign country). If these values had been disregarded, States withheld recognition, even if the new State was firmly in control of population and territory. More recently, some States, chiefly of Western Europe, have begun also to require *respect for human rights and the rights of minorities* as well as *respect for existing international frontiers*, as further conditions for granting recognition.[13]

4.3.2 CONTESTED STATEHOOD

New States are rarely successful in achieving recognition by all members of the international community within a short period of time, unless they obtained independence peacefully, as part of a 'consensual' or negotiated process. A case in point, in this regard, could be considered the recent 'birth' of South Sudan as a new State.[14] The Republic of South Sudan declared independence from Sudan on 9 July 2011, on the basis of the 2005 Peace Agreement that ended a long-lasting civil war, and the result of a referendum held in January 2011. On 14 July 2011, only a few days after its declaration of independence, South Sudan was admitted to the UN by consensus, as the 193rd member State.[15]

More frequently, however, the emergence of new States attracts much more controversy. Only a few States grant recognition and accordingly initiate dealings with the new entity, exchanging diplomatic envoys, entering into agreements, and so on. A segment of the international community may decide to remain aloof for some time: this attitude is usually motivated by political considerations (a lack of ideological or political affinity, or even open opposition, or else the existence of strong economic or geographic obstacles to the subsistence of the new entity). If this is the case, the new State will not be able to enter into active relations with those States: no treaties are concluded, diplomats are not exchanged, the nationals of the new State are not allowed to enter the non-recognizing countries and

---

[13] Following the break-up of the Soviet Union and the radical changes that occurred in eastern European countries, on 16 December 1991 the Foreign Ministers of the Member States of the European Community adopted a Declaration on the 'Guidelines on the Recognition of New States in Eastern Europe and in the Soviet Union' (in (1993) 4 *EJIL* 74). In this Declaration they among other things required for the formal recognition of new States in eastern Europe: (i) respect for the UN Charter, the Helsinki Final Act, and the Charter of Paris, 'especially with regard to the rule of law, democracy and human rights'; (ii) guarantees for the rights of ethnic and national groups and minorities; (iii) respect for the inviolability of all frontiers 'which can only be changed by peaceful means and by common agreement'; (iv) acceptance of all relevant commitments with regard to disarmament and nuclear non-proliferation as well as security and regional stability; (v) commitment to settle by agreement, including where appropriate by recourse to arbitration, all questions concerning State succession and regional disputes. In addition, the Declaration stipulated that 'the Community and its member States will not recognize entities which are the result of aggression'.

[14] See generally M. Öhm, *War and Statehood in South Sudan* (Baden-Baden: Nomos, 2014).

[15] See A/Res/65/308; see also press release GA/11114, 14 July 2011 and press release SC/10323, 13 July 2011.

vice versa. Yet, this does not necessarily mean that the new entity is devoid of legal personality in relation to non-recognizing nations. General international rules such as those concerning the high seas, or respect for territorial and political sovereignty, etc. do apply in the relationships between the new State and all other members of the community. It follows that non-recognizing States are duty-bound to refrain from invading or occupying the new State or from jeopardizing its political independence. Also, they are not allowed to subvert its domestic political system. Furthermore, they must respect its right to sail the high seas. In particular, no interference in the navigation of its warships is allowed.

It should be added that extreme situations may exist where a State, although it exhibits at least the traditional requirements based on effectiveness, is still not recognized by the overwhelming majority of the members of the world community. This anomalous situation results from the clash of two conflicting principles: the old principle of effectiveness and the new principle of withholding legitimacy to facts and situations inconsistent with the general values of the present world community. The coexistence of these two principles (because the latter has not been capable of displacing the former) may give rise to the disconcerting situation of a State meeting all the conditions and showing all the trappings of statehood but deprived of international intercourse. Such was the case of Southern Rhodesia,[16] from its Unilateral Declaration of Independence (UDI, 1965) until the point when its internal political system accepted majority rule (1980). By resolutions 216 and 217 of 12 and 20 November 1965 the UN Security Council had called upon all States 'not to recognize this illegal act'. Until 1980 all States (except for South Africa) withheld recognition on account of Southern Rhodesia's racist policy. This general stand only meant that no other State (except for South Africa) was ready to enter into relations with Southern Rhodesia as long as it refused to change its domestic policies. Socially, Southern Rhodesia was regarded as an outcast, a pariah State. Legally speaking, other States looked upon Southern Rhodesia as a territory under British colonial administration. It did, nonetheless, possess autonomous rights and duties, although it was unable to make use of most of them. Another illustration of this hypothesis is Taiwan (Formosa). Although it might be regarded as an entity possessing all the hallmarks of a State, China's claim that it is part of its territory and subject to its sovereignty prevents Taiwan from entertaining State-to-State relationships with all other States.[17]

There have also been cases in which it was doubtful that a new State had actually been created, or else a new entity had been set up but in gross breach of international rules, and, in addition, other States did not consider it to be really independent of the State that had been instrumental in its establishment (with the consequence that they withheld recognition). This last instance occurred with regard to the 'Turkish Republic of Northern Cyprus', proclaimed on 15 November 1983 and recognized by Turkey only.[18] The UN Security Council, the Commonwealth Heads of Government, and the Committee of Ministers of the Council of Europe considered the declaration of independence 'legally invalid', required its 'withdrawal', and called upon all States 'not to recognize any Cypriot State other than the Republic of Cyprus' (see in particular SC resolution 541 of 18 November 1983).

A more recent relevant case is the situation of Kosovo.[19] Today recognized by over 110 States, the Republic of Kosovo declared independence from Serbia on 17 February 2008. The statehood of Kosovo is still contested by a segment of the international community.

---

[16] See generally V. Gowlland Debbas, *Collective Responses to Illegal Acts in International Law: United Nations Action in the Question of Southern Rhodesia* (Leiden: Martinus Nijhoff, 1990).

[17] See H.-C. Chiang and J.-Y. Hwang, 'On the Statehood of Taiwan: A Legal Reappraisal' in P. C. Y. Chow (ed.), *The 'One China' Dilemma* (New York: Palgrave, 2008), 57.

[18] See F. Hoffmeister, *Legal Aspects of the Cyprus Problem: Annan Plan and EU Accession* (Leiden: Martinus Nijhoff, 2006).

[19] See P. Hilpold (ed.), *Kosovo and International Law* (Leiden: Martinus Nijhoff, 2012).

In 2010, the ICJ rendered an Advisory Opinion (requested by the UN General Assembly) in which, although it did not shed so much light on the establishment of a new State, it determined that the declaration of independence per se was not illegal under international law, possibly opening the path for recognition not to be seen as an undue interference in Serbia's internal affairs. Today, Kosovo is active in international relations, has been recognized by a majority of States in the world community, and is engaged, together with Serbia, in a negotiating process overseen by the European Union. Nonetheless, clearly it will continue to face hurdles in fully establishing itself, with the difficulties in acceding to several 'universal' treaties, including those establishing international organizations, such as the United Nations, as long as a significant group of States (including some UN Security Council permanent members) continues to oppose its statehood.

Last but not least, when discussing the issue of statehood and recognition one must mention the developments which have occurred in the last 10 years regarding the status of Palestine.[20] Despite frequent reiteration by several members of the international community of the need for a negotiated settlement with Israel and recurring reference to the 'two-State solution' as a prospect for the future, Palestine has taken steps since 2010 to advance its statehood through legal process. To a certain extent it might be considered to have obtained a form of collective recognition through the combined effect of its admission to UNESCO in 2011 and its status 'upgrade' as non-member observer State by the UN General Assembly in 2012 through resolution 67/19.[21] This resolution was subsequently reaffirmed by resolution 73/5 adopted on 16 October 2018, whereby the General Assembly allowed for some limited specific rights to be exercised by the Observer State of Palestine on account of its being the Chair of the G77 for 2019.[22]

4.4 CONTINUITY, SUCCESSION, AND EXTINCTION OF STATES

4.4.1 CHANGES IN GOVERNMENT AND IN TERRITORY

We now move to the examination of a distinct aspect of the life of States: how do changes in the life or existence of States affect their legal personality? Normally international law has an inclination for stability and continuity. A revolutionary change in government does not have any major impact on personality. The principal problem that may arise in the case of revolutionary change following a civil war is whether acts performed by a government

---

[20] See BIICL, *The Palestine Question in International Law* (London: BIICL, 2008); P. Eden, 'Palestinian Statehood: Trapped Between Rhetoric and Realpolitik' (2013) 62 *ICLQ* 225.

[21] See UN Doc. A/RES/67/19.

[22] On 23 September 2011 Palestine submitted its application for full membership in the UN. This did not go forward as it remained blocked at the stage of examination by the Security Council (it is up to the General Assembly to take a decision on admission, on the basis of a recommendation of the Council—since the Council never took action on Palestine's request, the procedure did not move forward); see UN Doc. A/66/371-S/2011/592, annex I. In October 2011 Palestine obtained admission to UNESCO, a specialized agency of the UN; thereafter—on account of the clause contained in several multilateral treaties according to which these are open to the accession of members of specialized agencies—Palestine started to deposit a number of instruments of ratification/accession/adhesion to a number of international agreements, strengthening its stance as a 'State' in international relations. In 2012, Palestine obtained an upgrade of its status at the UN by being recognized in the position of non-member observer State (operative paragraph 2 of UNGA resolution 67/19). In such a scenario, one might opine that a form of collective recognition took place. In any case, even if there is disagreement on this point, it would seem that the effects of GA resolution 67/19 would at least be that UN organs are bound to consider the observer State of Palestine as a non-member State for the purpose of their activities.

are binding upon a State if that government is succeeded by another one. In *Tinoco Case* (*Great Britain* v *Costa Rica*), in 1923, the arbitrator Taft satisfactorily clarified the matter. In 1917, Tinoco, a political leader, overthrew the government of Costa Rica and proclaimed a new constitution. In 1919, the Tinoco government was toppled and the old authorities reinstated. In 1922, the government passed legislation quashing all the rights Tinoco had granted by contract to a number of British companies. The arbitrator held that, as Tinoco 'was in actual and peaceable administration without resistance or conflict or contest by anyone until a few months before the time when he retired and resigned' (at 379), those contracts were binding on Costa Rica. This case illustrates a generally accepted principle in international law: revolutionary or extra-constitutional changes in the government do not have any bearing on the identity of a State and consequently States are bound by international acts performed by previous governments.

In contrast, changes in the territory of a State may affect its legal personality. This happens when a State becomes extinct as a result of its break-up (*dismemberment*), or of its *merger* with one or more States (in which case all the merging States become extinct and at the same time give birth to a new legal subject), or when a State *incorporates* another one which, as a consequence, becomes extinct. In contrast, in case of *secession* of a part of the State's population and territory, the State continues to exist as a legal subject, but the seceding part may acquire international statehood.

4.4.2 STATE SUCCESSION

Whenever on a territory a State replaces another one, the problem arises of whether there is a State succession, namely whether the rights and obligations of the former State are transferred to the other international subject (or subjects, in case of dismemberment) that has (or have) de facto replaced the old State, or part of it, in its control over the territory and the population living there.[23] The question is far from academic, as is shown by the merger of Egypt and Syria into the United Arab Republic in 1958 (which lasted until 1961), the merger of Tanganyika and Zanzibar to form Tanzania in 1964, the secession of Bangladesh from Pakistan in 1970, the merger of North and South Yemen in 1990, the incorporation of the German Democratic Republic into the Federal Republic of Germany in 1990, the acquisition (or, rather, the re-acquisition) of independence from the Soviet Union of the three Baltic States (Estonia and Latvia in 1990 and Lithuania in 1991), the break-up of the Soviet Union in 1991, of Yugoslavia in 1991, Czechoslovakia in 1992–93, and the separations of Eritrea from Ethiopia in 1993, of Montenegro from the Union of Serbia and Montenegro in 2006, as well as, more recently, of South Sudan from Sudan in 2011.

This matter is regulated by a number of customary rules addressing the succession of States in relation to treaties and concerning matters such as assets/debts, State archives, and membership of international organizations. In 2017, the UN International Law Commission began a study of the rules relating to State succession with respect to State responsibility, which have already been analysed in some detail by the *Institut de Droit International*.[24] Given that the latter area is still under consideration, we focus on the other two areas here, for which there are well-developed sets of rules.

---

[23] See generally D. P. O'Connell, *State Succession in Municipal Law and International Law*, 2 vols (Cambridge: Cambridge University Press, 1967); B. Stern, 'La succession d'états' (1996) 262 *RCADI* 9; P. M. Eisemann and M. Koskenniemi (eds), *State Succession: Codification Tested against the Facts* (The Hague: Martinus Nijhoff, 2000).

[24] IDI Resolution, Succession of States in Matters of International Responsibility, Tallinn Session, 14th Commission (28 August 2015). See generally M. Kohen and P. Dumberry, *The Institute of International Law's Resolution on State Succession and State Responsibility: Introduction, Text and Commentaries* (Cambridge: Cambridge University Press, 2019); P. Dumberry, *State Succession to International Responsibility* (Leiden: Martinus Nijhoff, 2007).

Let us first consider the question of *succession to treaties*. This is governed by the customary rules partly codified by the 1978 Vienna Convention on Succession of States in respect of Treaties.[25] This regime is based on a distinction between various categories of treaties:

(1) The first are the so-called *localized treaties*, which impose obligations and confer rights with regard to specific territories (for instance, they regulate frontier matters, lay down a right of transit over certain specific areas, demilitarize a territory, establish fishing rights in certain waters or rights of navigation in specific rivers, etc.). Since these treaties attach to a specific territory, for the sake of international stability they are not affected by the mere fact of State succession; in other words, those treaties bind the new entity (see the 1978 Vienna Convention, Article 12).

(2) With regard to *non-localized treaties* customary law, as codified in the 1978 Vienna Convention, provides for a differentiated legal regime. For 'newly independent States' (namely successor States 'the territory of which immediately before the date of the succession of States was a dependent territory for the international relations of which the predecessor State was responsible', 1978 Vienna Convention, Article 2(1)), the 'clean slate' principle applies, namely the principle whereby the new States are not bound by the treaties in force for the territory at the date of succession. This 'anti-colonialist' approach has been clearly dictated by the necessity to take into account the legal condition and the specific needs of States resulting from the decolonization process.

(3) By contrast, with regard to other States, the need to ensure international stability has encouraged upholding the principle of continuity, whereby normally treaties binding on the predecessor State also apply to the successor State (see the 1978 Vienna Convention, Articles 34 and 35). However, these provisions of the Vienna Convention do not correspond to customary law, which is instead based on the 'clean slate' rule, subject to the exception of localized treaties.

(4) For a particular category of treaties, namely those on *human rights*, it would seem that a general rule has gradually evolved whereby the successor State (whether or not it belongs to the category of 'newly independent States') must respect them. The rationale for this rule is that human rights treaties are intended to protect and benefit individuals vis-à-vis the central authorities; hence, whatever the nature, character, and political allegiance of these authorities, what matters is that individuals should continue to be protected even after a change in sovereignty over a particular territory. In addition, human rights are now considered so essential that it would be inconsistent with the whole thrust of the present world community to discontinue protecting them only because one State has replaced another in operating as the governing entity responsible for the international relations of a particular territory.[26]

---

[25] Vienna Convention on Succession of States in respect of Treaties, 22 August 1978, 1946 UNTS 3.

[26] In 1997, the UN Human Rights Committee stated in its General Comment No. 26 that 'once the people are accorded the protection of the rights under the Covenant, such protection devolves with territory and continues to belong to them, notwithstanding change in government of the State party, including dismemberment in more than one State or State succession or any subsequent action of the State party designed to divest them of the rights guaranteed by the Covenant'. Human Rights Committee, General Comment No. 26 (61), UN Doc. A/53/40, Annex VII, 8 December 1997, §4. See also http://www1.umn.edu/humanrts/gencomm/hrcom26.htm. On this matter see M. T. Kamminga, 'State Succession in Respect of Human Rights Treaties' (1996) 7 *EJIL* 469ff; B. Simma, 'From Bilateralism to Community Interest in International Law' (1994) 250 *RCADI* 354.

As noted earlier, the question of succession also arises with regard to *State assets and debts, State archives, and membership of international organizations.* The matter has been addressed in the Vienna Convention on Succession of States in respect of State Property, Archives and Debts.[27] But this instrument is not in force and the extent to which it codifies customary international law remains uncertain.

(1) As for *State property*, the definition of what belongs to a State must be drawn from the relevant national law applicable at the moment of succession, as is laid down in Article 8 of the Vienna Convention of 1983 and was restated by the Arbitration Commission on Yugoslavia in its Opinion no. 14 on *State Succession* (at 732). Once it has been established whether the assets are public, it may normally be held that the State that wields control over the territory where the assets are located succeeds the previous territorial State with regard to ownership. The same holds true for *State archives.*

(2) The question of succession with regard to *public debts* (that is, debts owed by the State) is more difficult, also because State practice is rather confusing. Under Article 40 of the 1983 Vienna Convention, when a State breaks up and new entities come into being, unless they otherwise agree, the State debt of the predecessor State passes to the successor States 'in an equitable proportion'.

(3) With regard to membership of *international organizations*, it is reasonable to believe that, if two member States merge thereby creating a new State, this State should apply for admission to the organization. However, in UN practice, no admission has been required (this happened in 1958, when Egypt and Syria merged to form the United Arab Republic, and in 1990, when North Yemen and South Yemen merged). If a member State breaks up into two or more States, all of them must apply for membership (this happened in 1992–93, after the dissolution of Yugoslavia and the birth of six Yugoslav Republics; five were admitted immediately thereafter while the Federal Republic of Yugoslavia (Serbia and Montenegro) applied for, and gained, membership in 2000). Subsequently, in 2003, the Federal Republic was renamed Union of Serbia and Montenegro and it dissolved in 2006, when Montenegro left the Union. In 2006, Montenegro applied for UN membership and was admitted to the UN as the 192nd member State. On the other hand, however, the Republic of Serbia did not have to apply again for membership and continued to hold the seat of the Federal Republic, as admitted on 1 November 2000. This can be seen as confirmation that an exception can be admitted for the one component that may successfully claim to be a continuation of the old State, as far as membership is concerned (this happened in 1990, when the Soviet Union broke up, and all newly born republics had to apply for admission, except for the Russian Federation which was considered a continuation of the Soviet Union, and Byelorussia and Ukraine which were already members of the UN in their own right). If a new State-like entity comes into being as a result of secession from a member State, it too must apply for membership.

---

[27] Vienna Convention on Succession of States in respect of State Property, Archives and Debts, 7 April 1983 (not in force).

4.5 THE EVOLVING CONCEPT OF SOVEREIGNTY

As mentioned earlier, 'sovereignty' is the key trait of statehood, and sovereign equality is recognized as one of the fundamental principles of international law (see **3.2**). However, in modern international law, sovereignty is not unfettered. Interdependence became the rule and, between the end of the nineteenth and the beginning of the twentieth centuries, the development of international law increasingly placed restraints on sovereignty and addressed the clashes between States, offering legal solutions. This was done through the conclusion of a growing number of international agreements, in the form of bilateral and multilateral treaties, and the establishment of international organizations. The process prospered after the Second World War for two main reasons: the wounds of two tragic world wars in 30 years, with millions of victims; and the confidence placed by the major Powers in an international rule-based order. And yet, there is a tension between State sovereignty and the supremacy of international law. This tension is well reflected in the 1949 ILC *Draft Declaration on the Rights and Duties of States* which, on the one hand, indicated that '[e]very State has the right to independence and hence to exercise freely, without dictation by any other State, all its legal powers, including the choice of its own form of government' (Article 1) and that '[e]very State has the duty to refrain from intervention in the internal or external affairs of any other State' (Article 3), while at the same time, it stipulated, in Article 14, that '[e]very State has the duty to conduct its relations with other States in accordance with international law and with the principle that the *sovereignty* of each State *is subject to the supremacy of international law*' (emphasis added).[28]

Between the end of the twentieth century and the first decade of the twenty-first, the panoply of multilateral treaties and broad variety of international institutions 'governing' world affairs might have created the perception that States and State sovereignty were in retreat.[29] Since the 2008 financial crisis, even more than in the past, globalization and interdependence have been seen as affecting the very heart of statehood by setting aside the power of States to take decisions and replacing it with an opaque network of faceless actors that would dictate the direction the world should take. The reaction to this understanding, which seems to be very much unfolding before our eyes as we write these lines, has taken the form of new doctrines labelled 'sovereignism' or 'patriotism', whether for economic, health, security, or other reasons. This is in many ways a return to a more traditional and confrontational version of the international legal order. It may reflect a defensive reflex, akin to the one observed during the inter-war years, or perhaps yet another populist lapse, having this time reached the States that, in the past, had stood against such tendencies.

It is difficult to say at this stage whether we are witnessing a systemic change that will reshape the international community (and hence will inevitably impact international law) or a significant, but transient, moment without systemic implications. What is beyond doubt is that this phenomenon merits the attention of international lawyers,[30] since the State—that some considered to be 'in crisis'—would appear to be resurrecting and coming back to the centre of the international legal system, a position it likely never left in the first place, despite appearances. Does this situation mean that international law will go back to

---

[28] Available on the ILC Analytical Guide: https://legal.un.org/ilc/texts/instruments/english/commentaries/2_1_1949.pdf.

[29] L. Condorelli and A. Cassese, 'Is Leviathan Still Holding Sway over International Dealings?' in A. Cassese (ed.), *Realizing Utopia* (Oxford: Oxford University Press, 2012), 14, as well as J. Alvarez, 'State Sovereignty is not Withering Away: A Few Lessons for the Future' in the same volume, 26. See also the Report of the Secretary-General A/59/312, *Globalization and Interdependence*, 31 August 2004.

[30] See e.g. J. Brunnée, 'Multilateralism in Crisis' (2018) 112 *ASIL Proceedings* 335.

the law of mere coexistence? Or, even more challenging, does this mean that international law will largely be set aside to make room for 'confrontation' and 'might is right'? Will multilateral institutions be undermined to the point of becoming irrelevant, or disappear?

A radical change seems difficult to imagine at this stage. Many of the problems that the international community is facing today, such as the existence of weapons of mass destruction, serious environmental challenges, large-scale movements of people, global terrorism, the emergence and spread of viruses and disease, among others, do require, more than ever, State co-operation and efforts for a co-ordinated approach. Moreover, the interconnection among economies and societies is a fact which can hardly be denied, although current political realities in some countries may give expression to a renewed faith in sovereignty as the instrument to better ensure governance of these challenges. The main (and yet largely utopian) objective of any constructive attempt to strengthen the international system, while respecting State sovereignty, would be to establish true and effective accountability for sovereign States and international actors both when they act, and when they 'fail to act'.

At this stage, however, and despite current trends, there seems to be little doubt that international rules will have to continue to aim at guiding State sovereignty towards shared goals and channelling the display of State authority through a set of norms and procedures, in order to maintain the predictability of a rule-based legal order. Traditionally, in addition to treaty rules, which vary from State to State, limitations have been imposed upon State sovereignty by customary international law. Some of these rules are the *natural legal consequence of the obligation to respect the sovereignty of other States*. At the same time, there are rules that restrict sovereignty on account of shared values, some of which ought to be protected in the interest of the international community as a whole (*jus cogens*).

There are two main categories of limitations of the power of sovereign States in their own territory. One arises from the need to respect the sovereignty of other States, in its many manifestations. A State may not exercise its sovereign powers over, or otherwise interfere with actions legally performed by, foreign States. This legal inability stems from the general principle imposing respect for the independence and dignity of foreign States (*par in parem non habet imperium*, that is, equals have no jurisdiction over one another). The other broad category of limitations results from the requirement, under both treaties and customary international law, to protect certain common, or even better, community values (human dignity underpinning humanitarian law, human rights, and international criminal law, or the need to preserve the environment) or specific activities (e.g. investments by foreign entities). **Chapter 6** will focus on two important areas belonging to the first category, namely State immunities and the immunities of State officials. The second category will be discussed in its various aspects in several other chapters of this book (see **Chapters 17, 18, 19,** and **20**).

5
THE SPATIAL DIMENSIONS OF STATE ACTIVITIES

5.1 INTRODUCTION

Most activities performed by the primary subjects of the world community, States, take place within a geographic area. Territory is crucial not only to the very existence of States (a State without a territorial basis, however tiny it may be, is inconceivable).[1] Territory also constitutes the dimension within which States deploy their main activities.

In traditional international law the physical dimension of State activity was regulated in fairly uncomplicated terms. The earth, portions of the sea, and the air were divided up into areas subject to the sovereign authority of States. Also, the general principles regulating the carving up of areas among sovereign States were relatively simple. Subject to the discussion, later in this chapter, of the complex relations between title and *effectivités*, these principles can be broadly characterized as follows. First, whoever possessed a territory and exercised actual control over it acquired a legal title. Secondly, for areas subject to no one (*terrae nullius*), mere discovery following the logic of 'first come, first served' rapidly became insufficient. Actual display of sovereignty, coupled with the intent to wield authority, has been needed since, at least, the Berlin Conference of 1884–85. On the strength of these elementary principles, land on the whole planet gradually became subject to the rule of one or other sovereign State. In addition to land, a small portion of sea around land, the so-called territorial waters, was also subject to State sovereignty. The air above each territory up to the stars (*usque ad sidera*) was considered subject to the sovereignty of the territorial State; of course, this stipulation was only theoretical in nature, for States did not possess any means of exercising de facto control over the airspace above their land.

Clearly, this distribution of space among members of the world community was inspired by aggressive individualism and a laissez-faire attitude: whoever had the physical means of acquiring and effectively controlling a portion of territory on land was legitimized to claim sovereign rights over it. As a consequence, the more powerful—militarily and economically—a State, the greater its chance of acquiring a larger territory.

The only exception to this partition was the high seas, which—since the seventeenth century—were considered to belong to everybody (*res communis omnium*): every State could sail its ships or use the high seas' resources as it pleased, as long as it did not hamper their free use by other States. However, the fact that the high seas were considered a 'common good' should not lead us to believe that this legal regime was motivated by solidarity. Had a State, or group of States, proved strong enough to claim and enforce the exclusive right to use that area or large portions thereof, it would have had no hesitation in depriving other

---

[1] See *North Atlantic Coast Fisheries Case (Great Britain/United States of America)*, 180 ('one of the essential elements of sovereignty is that it has to be exercised within territorial limits [. . .] failing proof to the contrary, the territory is coterminous with Sovereignty').

members of the international community of access thereto. Furthermore, the *res communis* concept means that every State is authorized to use a certain good for its own purposes and its own interest. It is not a community-oriented concept; it is geared to self-interest.

After the Second World War, new technological means brought to the attention and the grasp of States the potential resources of the seabed and subsoil off the coast of States, an area called the continental shelf. In addition, advances in shipping rendered it possible to exploit fishing resources in areas far removed from the coast and up to the high seas. It was also expected that mineral resources would be found on the ocean floor. The world community faced a choice: (i) to allow each and every State freely to appropriate or at least exclusively exploit the resources within its reach, on the individualistic principle of free competition; or (ii) to act on a community-oriented principle, whereby resources beyond the territorial waters of each State should be commonly exploited and shared, or at least should be used by the more industrialized and powerful States in such a manner as to take into account also the needs of other States.

States immediately opted for the first alternative. The whole development of the law of the sea was thus dictated by State sovereignty, nationalism, and a laissez-faire attitude. In the scramble for economic, scientific, and/or military control over the new resources, almost all new notions were inspired by self-interest and geared to competition. The only area where developing countries managed to achieve the adoption of new concepts was the ocean floor and the subsoil thereof, beyond the limits of national jurisdiction. With respect to this 'Area', they launched the notion of the 'common heritage of mankind'; they propounded the view that the mineral resources of the Area should be exploited in such a way as to take into consideration the needs of poor countries. However, as discussed in section **5.5**, the concept proved unworkable and, to a large extent, was watered down in both treaty and actual practice.

Thus, in the whole area of the international law of the sea, a nationalist self-centred approach has displaced community interests and any idea of solidarity or joint utilization of resources. As we shall see in section **5.7**, some headway was instead made in the legal regulation of outer space, a layer of the atmosphere that is above the airspace normally used by aircraft, although it has never been delimited (it is conventionally and approximately considered to be beyond 90–100 miles from the earth's surface). The very limits of technology, which did not yet allow the application of sovereignty-oriented notions to this area, largely account for this relative progress in law-making and equitable distribution.

All in all, the spatial dimension of State activities unfolds in land, sea, and air spaces. Some of them are subject to the sovereignty of the State. They constitute the 'territory' of the State in technical terms. The International Court of Justice (ICJ) summarized the contemporary understanding of what is covered by a State's territory under general international law in the following terms:

> The basic legal concept of State sovereignty in customary international law, expressed in, *inter alia*, Article 2, paragraph 1, of the United Nations Charter, extends to the internal waters and territorial sea of every State and to the air space above its territory. As to superjacent air space, the 1944 Chicago Convention on International Civil Aviation (Art. 1) reproduces the established principle of the complete and exclusive sovereignty of a State over the air space above its territory. That convention, in conjunction with the 1958 Geneva Convention on the Territorial Sea, further specifies that the sovereignty of the coastal State extends to the territorial sea and to the air space above it, as does the United Nations Convention on the Law of the Sea adopted on 10 December 1982. The Court has no doubt that these prescriptions of treaty-law merely respond to firmly established and longstanding tenets of customary international law.[2]

---

[2] *Nicaragua (Nicaragua v United States of America)*, §212.

Some other spaces are subject to the jurisdiction of the State, where it may exercise 'sovereign rights' (to be distinguished from sovereignty) over certain matters. These are the exclusive economic zone and the continental shelf. Yet, some other spaces are beyond State jurisdiction and constitute the global commons (e.g. the high seas, the seabed and subsoil underneath it, outer space). For presentation purposes, this chapter distinguishes the three main domains of State activity—land, sea, and air—and discusses the legal concepts on which the assertion of State powers over them relies. Before undertaking this discussion, the chapter introduces some distinctions regarding the concepts of sovereignty, competence, and jurisdiction, and the exercise of jurisdiction.

5.2 SOVEREIGNTY, COMPETENCE, AND JURISDICTION

5.2.1 CONCEPTUAL DISTINCTIONS

We characterized the concept of sovereignty in sections **3.2** and **4.5**, and some of its manifestations (e.g. immunities) in **Chapter 6**. As noted in the previous section, sovereignty is intrinsically related to the spatial dimension where it is exercised, namely the territory of the State. The sole arbitrator, Max Huber, in the *Island of Palmas* case emphasized this connection in the following terms: '[s]overeignty in the relations between States signifies independence. Independence in regard to a portion of the globe is the right to exercise therein, to the exclusion of any other State, the functions of a State.'[3]

The 'full' range of competences (functions of a State) exclusively pertain to a State by virtue of its sovereignty over its territory. Thus, competences must be understood as the range of functions (powers and duties) that flow from sovereignty. Aside from some significant terminological complexity, competences can thus be easily distinguished from sovereignty. A subject of international law which is not sovereign, for example an international organization (see **Chapter 7**), may have competences dictated or implicitly covered by its mandate, but such competences are not full, nor are they exclusive within a spatially delimited area. Such is the case even for an organization like the European Union, which exercises its functions within a defined area. Indeed, the competences exercised by the EU have been transferred by agreement among EU Member States, and many of them are shared with States.[4]

The competences of a State are exercised through the assertion of jurisdiction. Jurisdiction can be asserted over the State territory (territorial jurisdiction) or beyond (extraterritorial jurisdiction). The exercise of extraterritorial jurisdiction has been a matter of great controversy in international law since the classic statement by the Permanent Court of International Justice (PCIJ) that: '[f]ar from laying down a general prohibition to the effect that States may not extend the application of their laws and the jurisdiction of their courts to persons, property and acts outside their territory, it [international law] leaves them in this respect a wide measure of discretion which is only limited in certain cases by prohibitive rules'.[5] The continued accuracy of this observation has been often called into question, including by several judges of the ICJ.[6] Suffice it to say that the ICJ as well as other international and domestic courts and tribunals have recognized the extension of jurisdiction

---

[3] *Island of Palmas (Netherlands/United States of America)*, 838.
[4] See Treaty on the Functioning of the European Union (TFEU), 13 December 2007, 2008/C 115/01, Article 2.
[5] *The Case of the S.S. Lotus (France v Turkey)*, 18–19.
[6] *Legality of the Threat or Use of Nuclear Weapons*, Declaration of President Bedjaoui, §13, and Dissenting Opinion of Judge Weeramantry, 495–6; *Arrest Warrant of 11 April 2000 (Democratic Republic of the Congo v Belgium)*, Joint Separate Opinion of Judges Higgins, Kooijmans, and Buergenthal, §§50–51.

for the purpose of prosecuting international crimes (see **19.3.1**) or to bring remote situations under the scope of a State's human rights obligations (see **18.4.5**). More prosaically, coastal States do not exercise territorial jurisdiction over certain maritime spaces, such as the exclusive economic zone and the continental shelf. They only exercise functional jurisdiction arising not from sovereignty but from the more limited basis of 'sovereign rights'. As discussed next, the exercise of jurisdiction can take different forms, which are relevant from an international law perspective.

5.2.2 EXERCISE OF JURISDICTION

A distinction is usually made between prescriptive, adjudicative, and enforcement jurisdiction. The limits placed by international law on the spatial scope of these three forms of jurisdiction differ.

(1) *Prescriptive jurisdiction* normally extends to the territory over which a State is sovereign. In other words, States may normally pass binding legislation applicable to persons and entities in the territory of the State. However, States may also enact legislation binding upon their nationals abroad, as well as applicable to other facts or conduct engaged in abroad and considered prejudicial to the State (e.g. the counterfeiting of the national currency by foreigners or nationals abroad; the smuggling of drugs and other prohibited goods from abroad into the territory). Or States can go so far as to pass legislation applicable to acts performed abroad by foreigners against other foreigners.

This extraterritorial extension of jurisdiction takes three main forms in contemporary international law. Firstly, it has found expression in what could be called 'market power laws', namely laws adopted by a State requiring certain actors based abroad to behave in certain ways to avoid being penalized (and commercially affected) in the State adopting the law. By way of illustration, the US has enacted various laws that provided for sanctions against foreign companies making commercial transactions with States inimical to the US.[7] Once put into effect, however, these laws infringed fundamental principles of international law, and in particular the principle of respect for the sovereignty of foreign States. As a result of protests by European and Latin American countries, the measures envisaged in those laws were suspended.[8] Secondly, the scope of certain laws has been extended extraterritorially for the purpose of exercising universal jurisdiction over terrorism[9] or other serious international crimes, such as genocide or torture.[10] In these two hypotheses, the State deliberately seeks to address

---

[7] See e.g. the Cuban Democracy Act of 1992, prohibiting the granting of licences for transactions between European subsidiaries of US companies or US-controlled firms and Cuba; the Helms–Burton Act of 1996, under which sanctions were envisaged for foreign companies that purchased property in Cuba confiscated in the 1960s from US owners; and the 1996 D'Amato Act, which provided for sanctions against foreign companies conducting business with Libya and Iran. On the resurgence of this wielding of market power see P. Terry, 'Unilateral Economic Sanctions and their Extraterritorial Impact: One Foreign Policy for All?' (2019) 18 *Chinese JIL*, 425.

[8] See further *Hartford Fire Insurance Co. v California*, where the US Supreme Court held that the relevant US legislation was intended to apply to 'foreign conduct that was meant to produce and did in fact produce some substantial effect in the United States', (at 2909).

[9] See e.g. the 1986 US Omnibus Diplomatic Security and Antiterrorism Act, which asserted US jurisdiction over attacks on US citizens in foreign countries; or the UK Anti-terrorism, Crime and Security Act 2001, which in section 51 asserted jurisdiction over such offences as causing a nuclear explosion without authorization, developing or transferring nuclear weapons, and assisting or inducing certain weapons-related acts overseas.

[10] As the British Home Secretary stated in 2000 in the House of Commons, 'the principle of universal jurisdiction in respect of very serious crimes such as torture is now established', in (2000) 71 *BYIL* 588 (see, however, (2000) 71 *BYIL* 620). See generally A. Cassese and P. Gaeta, *Cassese's International Criminal Law*, 3rd edn (Oxford: Oxford University Press, 2013), chapter 15.

situations beyond its territory. The third hypothesis is somewhat different. Here, a situation is deemed to be under the jurisdiction of the State, often against the will of the State, for purposes of allocating responsibility. Such is the case of the growing body of jurisprudence on the extraterritorial scope of human rights obligations[11] and of environmental harm caused abroad.[12]

(2) *Adjudicative jurisdiction* is the power to pronounce upon legal disputes. Normally this judicial jurisdiction is based on the principles of territoriality: the active (or, less frequently, passive) nationality principle, that is, respectively, jurisdiction based on the nationality of the offender or that of the victim; or the protective principle, according to which courts assert jurisdiction over offences that, although committed abroad, infringe upon or seriously affect national interests[13]. As noted earlier, however, in the last two decades, the principle of universality (jurisdiction over offences committed abroad by foreigners against foreigners) has been taking shape with regard to international crimes.

The ICJ analysed the question of universal jurisdiction under the UN Convention against Torture (CAT) in the case concerning *Questions relating to the Obligation to Prosecute or Extradite (Belgium v Senegal)*. In this case, Belgium had requested the Court to judge that Senegal was in breach of its obligations under the CAT as a result, *inter alia*, of its failure to conduct a 'preliminary inquiry' (Article 6(2) of the CAT) and to prosecute (Article 7(1) of the CAT) the former dictator of Chad, Hissène Habré, who had been granted political asylum in Senegal in 1990. The Court found Senegal in breach of both provisions, but it refrained from addressing the question of whether there is an obligation under customary international law for a State to prosecute alleged perpetrators of international crimes committed by a foreign national abroad (at §§53–55). Yet, it fleshed out the scope and operation of this same obligation as provided for in Article 7(1) of the CAT, clarifying that a State might be relieved from its obligation to prosecute if it acceded to a request for extradition from a foreign State. Thus, whereas the duty to prosecute was an obligation, the possibility to extradite was an option (at §§94–95). The principle of universality is further discussed in section **19.3.1**.

(3) *Enforcement jurisdiction* is normally confined to acts committed on the territory. As the PCIJ stated, this type of jurisdiction 'cannot be exercised by a State outside its territory except by virtue of a permissive rule derived from international custom or from a convention'.[14] On this point, the reasoning of the PCIJ remains valid.

The US government has occasionally claimed that it had the authority to take enforcement measures abroad, for example for the purpose of punishing criminal offences perpetrated in Mexico against US nationals. The US Supreme Court in *United States v Alvarez-Machain* in 1992 admitted that these measures (which were clearly contrary to international law, for they breached the sovereign rights of the foreign country) may be inconsistent with general international law, but confirmed that the abducted individuals could be prosecuted

---

[11] See generally M. Milanovic, *Extraterritorial Application of Human Rights Treaties* (Oxford: Oxford University Press, 2011).

[12] See generally J. E. Viñuales, 'A Human Rights Approach to Extraterritorial Environmental Protection? An Assessment', in N. Bhuta (ed.), *The Frontiers of Human Rights* (Oxford: Oxford University Press, 2016), 177 (expounding a theory of extension resulting from the effective control of the source of harm (at 218–19), subsequently endorsed by the Inter-American Court of Human Rights in its *Advisory Opinion OC-23/17 (Colombia Request): Environment and Human Rights*, §§102, 103, and 104(h)).

[13] US courts have asserted jurisdiction over foreign companies that are members of a cartel, whose activities have brought about effects in the US by affecting imports and exports from the US. See *United States v Aluminium Co. of America et al*. See also *Rio Tinto Zinc Corp. v Westinghouse Electric Corp.*, brought before British courts. The US decisions met with protests by other States.

[14] *The Case of the S.S. Lotus (France v Turkey)*, 19.

in the US.[15] Also, English courts have asserted jurisdiction over persons in custody in the UK, but kidnapped abroad.[16] However, in *R. v Horseferry Magistrates' Courts*, the House of Lords held that British courts must decline jurisdiction in such cases. *In casu*, the defendant had been brought to the UK after being abducted by South African police in collusion with English police. For other cases where States have unlawfully accomplished public acts abroad see section **3.2.2**.

The foregoing distinctions between sovereignty, competence and jurisdiction, including the different forms in which it is exercised, must be kept in mind for the understanding of the following discussion of the spatial dimensions of State activity.

5.3 LAND TERRITORY

Land territory is the portion of emerged land, including islands,[17] subject to the sovereign authority of a State. At present no territory exists that is not subject to a sovereign Power. The only exception is the Antarctic continent, where claims to territorial sovereignty by some adjacent and other States—Argentina, Australia, Chile, France, New Zealand, Norway, and the UK—based on discovery or symbolic annexation or the doctrine of contiguity called the 'sector principle', are suspended by treaty.[18] Today there consequently exists an absolute nexus between territory and sovereignty. In 1928, in his celebrated judgment in *Island of Palmas*, Max Huber held that 'sovereignty in relation to a portion of the surface of the globe is the legal condition necessary for the inclusion of such portion in the territory of any particular State'.[19]

---

[15] In 1990 a Mexican national, Alvarez-Machain, had been kidnapped on Mexican territory and taken to the US. A US District Court—before which Alvarez-Machain had been brought to trial for the alleged torture and murder of a US national in Mexico—found that US officials were responsible for the abduction, although they were not personally involved in it. The court dismissed the indictment on the ground that it lacked jurisdiction since the abduction contravened the 1978 Extradition Treaty between the US and Mexico, and it ordered Alvarez-Machain's repatriation. The Court of Appeals affirmed, holding that US jurisdiction was improper. The US Supreme Court held instead that US jurisdiction could be exercised, as the abduction was not contrary to the Extradition Treaty. It admitted that Alvarez-Machain's abduction might be 'in violation of general international law principles' and that Mexico had 'protested the abduction through diplomatic notes'. It added however that 'the decision of whether the respondent should be returned to Mexico, as a matter outside of the Treaty, is a matter for the Executive Branch' (at 5–7). Hence a US court could lawfully try Alvarez-Machain.

[16] See e.g. *R. v Plymouth Justices*, at 351.

[17] Islands *lato sensu* include all 'naturally formed' and permanently (during low or high tide) emerged land entirely surrounded by water. See Article 121(1) of the United Nations Convention on the Law of the Sea, 10 December 1982, 1833 UNTS 397 (UNCLOS). If an island can 'sustain human habitation or economic life of [its] own' (Article 121(3), UNCLOS), it is an 'island' within the meaning of Article 121(1) of the UNCLOS, and it projects a territorial sea as well as an exclusive economic zone and a continental shelf (Article 121(2) of the UNCLOS). Otherwise, it is merely a 'rock' (Article 121(3) of the UNCLOS), which only projects a territorial sea. Rocks are therefore also emerged land and part of the territory. By contrast, 'low tide elevations' (Article 13 of the UNCLOS) are not permanently emerged and, therefore, are only part of the territory of a State if they are located within the territorial sea, but they do not constitute in and of themselves territory. On these distinctions and their important implications see *South China Sea Arbitration*, §§303–311 and 473–511.

[18] Antarctic Treaty, 1 December 1959, 402 UNTS 71, Article IV. On the Antarctic Treaty System see R.-J. Dupuy, 'Le statut de l'Antarctique' (1958) 4 *AFDI* 196; R.-J. Dupuy, 'Le Traité sur l'Antarctique' (1960) 6 *AFDI* 111; G. Battaglini, *La condizione dell'Antartide nel diritto internazionale* (Padova: Cedam, 1961); R. E. Guyer, 'The Antarctic System' (1973) 139 *RCADI* 147; W. Bush, *Antarctica and International Law*, 3 vols (Dobbs Ferry, NY: Oceana Publications, 1982–88); H. K. Cohen (ed.), *Handbook of the Antarctic Treaty System*, 9th edn (Washington, DC: US Department of State, 2002); A. D. Hemmings, D. R. Rothwell, and K. N. Scott (eds), *Antarctic Security in the Twenty-First Century: Legal and Policy Perspectives* (Abingdon: Routledge, 2012).

[19] *Island of Palmas (Netherlands/United States of America)*, 838.

States are entitled to exercise over their territories all those powers inherent in their sovereignty (see **3.2.2**). Such powers are subject to the limitations arising from an ever-expanding body of international law concerning matters such as human rights and environmental protection but also economic relations in the areas of foreign investment and international trade, among others.

5.3.1 ACQUISITION OF TERRITORY

Traditionally, the legal bases underlying the powers exercised over territory were framed as 'modes of acquisition' of territory.[20] The principal modes of acquiring territory were extrapolated from Roman law: (i) occupation of a *terra nullius*, that is, land belonging to no one (as stated above, occupation must be effective and accompanied by *animus domini*, that is, the intent to appropriate the territory); (ii) cession by treaty, followed by the effective peaceful transfer of territory; (iii) conquest (occupation following resort to armed violence); (iv) accretion (a physical process whereby new land is formed close to existing land, for example a new island in a river mouth or the formation of dry land as a result of the change of flow of a river; normally the new land is held to be under the sovereignty of the State within whose territory it has come into being); and, depending on the author, (v) acquisitive prescription (uncontested effective possession of a territory with animus for a long period of time).[21]

At present, conquest is no longer admissible, as 'no territorial acquisition resulting from the threat or use of force shall be recognized as legal' (Declaration on Friendly Relations, of 1970) (see **3.4.2**). Moreover, the occupation of a *terra nullius* is no longer possible, because there are no longer any known *terrae nullius*. Thus, with the exception of accretion, which is exceptional, all current modes of acquisition of territory are 'derivative' in nature, that is, they presuppose a prior acquisition of 'title' over the territory that is passed on or, in other words, an 'original' title.[22] However, knowledge of the law relating to the historical and present modes of acquisition of territory is not irrelevant. This is because contemporary territorial conflicts often have deep historical roots and, as a result, the validity of a current 'title' to territory is often dependent on either historical events or a previous title secured in a more or less remote past.[23] For that reason, understanding the contemporary law of territory requires knowledge of (i) both present and past law, (ii) including of fundamental principles of international (e.g. the post-1945 prohibition of the use of force or the emergence of the right to self-determination (see **3.4** and **3.8**)), and (iii) the so-called 'technical'

---

[20] See R. Y. Jennings, *The Acquisition of Territory in International Law*, 2nd edn, with an introduction by M. G. Kohen (Manchester: Manchester University Press, 2017).

[21] Acquisitive prescription remains controversial. In *Kasikili/Sedudu Island (Botswana/Namibia)*, the ICJ refrained from pronouncing on acquisitive prescription despite the fact that both parties to the dispute, Namibia and Botswana, had recognized this mode of acquisition (§97).

[22] For contemporary statements see M. Kohen and M. Hébié (eds), *Research Handbook on Territorial Disputes in International Law* (Cheltenham: Edward Elgar, 2018), chapters 2 and 3 (by Mamadou Hébié); M. Shaw, *International Law*, 8th edn (Cambridge: Cambridge University Press, 2017), chapter 9; G. Giraudeau, *Les différends territoriaux devant le juge international* (Leiden: Martinus Nijhoff, 2013); M. Shaw (ed.), *Title to Territory* (Aldershot: Ashgate, 2005); J. A. Barberis, *El territorio del Estado y la soberanía territorial* (ábaco Buenos Aires: Abaco, 2003); G. Distefano, *L'ordre international entre légalité et effectivité: Le titre dans le contentieux territorial* (Paris: Pedone, 2002); S. P. Sharma, *Territorial Acquisition, Disputes and International Law* (The Hague: Kluwer, 1997).

[23] The ICJ has expressly recognized the need to form an opinion on the legal relevance of events in the past to address present questions relating to territorial powers. See *Western Sahara*, §52.

rules determining their interactions (i.e. the 'critical date'[24] and the inter-temporal law[25] rules).[26] The terminology used in this area has tended to shift from that of 'modes of acquisition' to that of 'titles' to territory, past and present.[27] That is because the traditional modes of acquisition could properly account for situations such as the title to territory of States coming into existence (whether in the decolonization, succession, or secession context) or for title conferred by a third party in a process of political or equitable attribution or allocation. Moreover, it is less the acquisition and more the actual title to territory that must be ascertained. A complex question is the role of effective displays of sovereign power over a certain territory, the so-called '*effectivités*', and their interaction with titles to territory. These interactions are often key for the determination of territorial conflicts.

In the following paragraphs, we briefly review the contemporary international law of territory and then discuss the determination of boundaries with respect to former colonial or other non-self-governing territories in accordance with the *uti possidetis* principle.

5.3.2 TITLES, *EFFECTIVITÉS*, AND THEIR INTERACTIONS

In a landmark decision rendered by a Chamber of the ICJ in 1986, in the *Case Concerning the Frontier Dispute (Burkina Faso v Republic of Mali)*, the Chamber made several statements of great relevance for the contemporary law of territory. It characterized the concept of 'title' as the 'source' of a right and, also, as the evidence of the existence of such a source (at §18). Leaving aside the latter, by 'title' it is therefore understood the 'root' or the 'source' that gives a State certain powers over territory. Such powers may vary in scope because a State may hold title to territorial sovereignty or only to administration[28] or to ownership or property.[29] Thus, different titles confer different powers over spaces.

---

[24] The 'critical date' is generally understood as the dividing temporal line between 'those acts which should be taken into consideration for the purposes of establishing or ascertaining sovereignty and those acts occurring after such date', *Sovereignty over Pedra Branca/Pulau Batu Puteh, Middle Rocks and South Ledge (Malaysia/Singapore)*, §32. It is normally set at the time the dispute crystallized, although there may be significant deviations depending on the circumstances of the case. See J. Crawford, *Brownlie's Principles of Public International Law*, 8th edn (Oxford: Oxford University Press, 2012), 219.

[25] This rule serves to identify the law applicable to the assessment of title or loss thereof. Since the *Island of Palmas* case, it is generally understood as requiring the determination of the law applicable to the creation of rights (which may be the law in force in a distant past) and that of the law applicable to determine the continued existence of rights. As noted by arbitrator Huber, '[t]he same principle which subjects the act creative of a right to the law in force at the time the right arises, demands that the existence of the right, in other words its continued manifestation, shall follow the conditions required by the evolution of law', *Island of Palmas (Netherlands/United States of America)*, 845. This distinction is key to give effect to principles that have emerged after a right was created, e.g. the right to self-determination.

[26] See Kohen and Hébié, *Research Handbook* (n 22), chapter 1.

[27] See ibid., chapter 4 (by M. Kohen); Crawford, *Brownlie's Principles*, 220.

[28] E.g. the territories administered by colonial Powers under the Trusteeship system established under Chapter XII of the UN Charter and, previously, the mandate system established by Article 22 of the Covenant of the League of Nations. One important difference between title to sovereignty and title of administration is that, in the latter case, the administrating Power cannot dispose of or dismember the territory of the non-self-governing territory under administration, as this contravenes the principles of territorial integrity and the right to self-determination. See *Legal Consequences of the Separation of the Chagos Archipelago from Mauritius in 1965*, §160.

[29] The question of ownership is distinct and independent from that of sovereignty. See *Frontier Dispute (Benin/Niger)*, §124. States often own property located in other States for a variety of purposes, such as diplomatic, consular, or even merely investment purposes. In some cases, ownership may be an indication, among others, that a State holds a title such as effective occupation.

Titles that confer territorial sovereignty are of different natures. Title may arise from the *coming into existence of a State*. That may happen in different ways, such as the exercise of the right to self-determination by the people of a non-self-governing territory (see **5.3.3**), the succession (by contrast to mere continuation) of a State to one or more other States (see **4.4.2**), or the secession of an entity which becomes a new State in respect to a portion of a territory of the State from which it seceded.[30] Title may also arise from a *treaty lawfully concluded* (without coercion) and ratified by all relevant States, even in the absence of actual transfer of the territory. Treaties transferring territory (cession), or delimiting a boundary, or formally recognizing the sovereignty of another State over a certain area, or general peace settlements allocating different portions of territory among the contracting parties, or agreements entered into by colonial Powers with local rulers[31] all are deemed to confer title. Importantly, by virtue of the principle of stability of boundaries, a boundary set by treaty is maintained even if the treaty is terminated.[32] Title to territory may also be conferred by *political adjudication or attribution*, that is, by the decision of a third party empowered to allocate territory to one or more States on its authority. Historically, title was thus attributed by Papal adjudication.[33] There are also examples of such attribution during the twentieth century, such as the attribution of the Memel territory to Lithuania[34] or that of Eritrea to Ethiopia by a resolution of the UN General Assembly.[35] Importantly, the decisions of international courts and tribunals on land and/or maritime boundary disputes based on international law (by contrast with decisions on the basis of pure equity) cannot be seen as the basis for attribution, because they are declaratory, that is, they simply draw the conclusions resulting from the application of rules of international law. Certain unilateral acts, such as the renunciation of a territory (the recognition that another State has sovereignty over it)[36] or the *acquiescence* by a State to the continued display of sovereign prerogatives by another State,[37] may also confer title. In addition, *effective occupation* of a territory by a State with the requisite *animus domini* (possession *à titre de souverain*)[38] can also confer title, not only when exercised over a *terra nullius* but also when exercised on a territory over which no other State holds a firmer title.[39]

---

[30] E.g. Eritrea. See R. Goy, 'L'indépendance de l'Erythrée' (1993) 39 *AFDI* 337.

[31] On this point, the holding of the sole arbitrator in *Island of Palmas* to the effect that such agreements are merely a domestic organization of colonial territory no longer reflects the accepted understanding under international law. Following the *Western Sahara* Advisory Opinion, agreements with local rulers have been deemed to constitute title to territory. See *Western Sahara*, §80; *Land and Maritime Boundary between Cameroon and Nigeria (Cameroon v Nigeria: Equatorial Guinea intervening)*, §§203–205. For a comprehensive study of the relevant practice see M. Hébié, *Souveraineté par traité: Une étude des accords entre puissances coloniales et entités politiques locales* (Paris: PUF, 2015).

[32] See *Territorial Dispute (Libyan Arab Jamahiriya/Chad)*, §§72–73; *Territorial and Maritime Dispute (Nicaragua v Colombia), (Preliminary Objections)*, §§88–90.

[33] A well-known illustration is Pope Alexander VI's Bull *Inter Caetera*, issued on 4 May 1493, granting Spain the exclusive right over lands discovered west of a line set one hundred leagues west of the Azores and Cape Verde.

[34] See *Interpretation of the Statute of the Memel Territory (Britain, France, Italy, Japan v Lithuania)*, at 250–1 (recalling that after the First World War, the Allied Powers had received the territory of Memel from Germany and, acting through a Conference of Ambassadors, decided to transfer it to Lithuania through the adoption of a Statute for the Memel territory).

[35] See e.g. the UN General Assembly resolution 390 (V), of 2 December 1950, recommending that 'Eritrea shall constitute an autonomous unit federated with Ethiopia under the Sovereignty of the Ethiopian Crown' (§1).

[36] See e.g. *Legal Status of Eastern Greenland (Denmark v Norway)*, 71–2.

[37] See e.g. *Temple of Preah Vihear (Cambodia v Thailand)*, 30–1; *Sovereignty over Pedra Branca/Pulau Batu Puteh, Middle Rocks and South Ledge (Malaysia/Singapore)*, §§120–122.

[38] See e.g. *Legal Status of Eastern Greenland (Denmark v Norway)*, 63, at 65–6; *Sovereignty over Pulau Ligitan and Pulau Sipadan (Indonesia/Malaysia)*, §§127–149 (reviewing the role of *effectivités* as title, in the absence of a treaty); *Territorial and Maritime Dispute between Nicaragua and Honduras in the Caribbean Sea (Nicaragua v Honduras)*, §176; *Territorial and Maritime Dispute (Nicaragua v Colombia)*, §§82–83.

[39] *Sovereignty over Pulau Ligitan and Pulau Sipadan (Indonesia/Malaysia)*, §127.

The latter point raises the complex question of the interactions between title and *effectivités*. Effective administration *à titre de souverain* can by itself confer title but only in the absence of a stronger title. In cases where another title exists, the role of *effectivités* will vary from that of mere confirmation of that title, to a challenge to such title (which may yield if additional factors are met, e.g. acquiescence), to a title in its own right (when the other State also claims *effectivités* but these are weaker or less well established), to evidence of the geographical extent of a title. In the *Burkina Faso/Mali* case, the ICJ Chamber clarified the different possible interactions in a limpid manner:

> [The Chamber] must however state forthwith, in general terms, what legal relationship exists between such acts and the titles on which the implementation of the principle of uti possidetis is grounded. For this purpose, a distinction must be drawn among several eventualities. Where the act corresponds exactly to law, where effective administration is additional to the uti possidetis juris, the only role of effectivité is to confirm the exercise of the right derived from a legal title. Where the act does not correspond to the law, where the territory which is the subject of the dispute is effectively administered by a State other than the one possessing the legal title, preference should be given to the holder of the title. In the event that the effectivité does not co-exist with any legal title, it must invariably be taken into consideration. Finally, there are cases where the legal title is not capable of showing exactly the territorial expanse to which it relates. The effectivité can then play an essential role in showing how the title is interpreted in practice.[40]

As it arises from this excerpt, legal title prevails over *effectivités*.[41] This is further reflected by the increasingly discernible approach followed by the ICJ when addressing a territorial dispute.[42] The Court and its Chambers usually begin by considering whether a treaty confers title on one of the parties. If such is the case, the treaty is the *lex specialis* and there is no need to examine other titles;[43] if there is no treaty, the Court will examine whether other legal titles recognized in general international law are controlling in the circumstances of the case. The second step concerns the analysis of *effectivités* and their relations with the title previously ascertained. The second step aims at assessing whether the subsequent behaviour of the parties to the dispute confirms or modifies the situation arising from the legal title. The assessment of the first and second steps will often rely on the application of the technical rules on the critical date and inter-temporal law. The third step concerns reliance on equity *infra legem*, characterized in *Burkina Faso/Mali* as 'a form of equity which constitutes a method of interpretation of the law in force, and one of its attributes'.[44] This involves an equitable interpretation of the applicable rules, particularly the relevant title. For example, in *Frontier Dispute (El Salvador/Honduras)*, the ICJ Chamber noted that, as it could not ascertain the boundary line inherited from the colonial period on a specific segment, equity *infra legem* allowed it to rely on the line set by an unratified agreement.[45]

---

[40] *Frontier Dispute (Burkina Faso/Republic of Mali)*, §63.

[41] For a recent restatement see *Arbitration Agreement between Croatia and Slovenia*, §340.

[42] See *Territorial Dispute (Libyan Arab Jamahiriya/Chad)*; M. Kohen, 'Le règlement des différends territoriaux à la lumière de l'arrêt de la C.I.J. dans l'affaire Libye/Tchad' (1995) 100 *RGDIP* 301, at 310–11.

[43] *Territorial Dispute (Libyan Arab Jamahiriya/Chad)*, §§75–76.

[44] *Case Concerning the Frontier Dispute (Burkina Faso/Republic of Mali)*, §28 (on the principle) and §§148–149 (on the application).

[45] See e.g. *Land, Island and Maritime Frontier Dispute (El Salvador/Honduras; Nicaragua intervening)*, §§262–263.

The rules and the approach followed for the settlement of disputes relating to land territory differ from the approach followed for the delimitation of maritime boundaries (see **5.4.8**). There are, however, some commonalities between the two,[46] such as the application of the fundamental principles of international law (e.g. prohibition of the use of force, the principle of territorial integrity, the right to self-determination), that of the *uti possidetis* principle, the principle of the stability of boundaries, the exclusion of the *rebus sic stantibus* clause (see **10.9**), and the role played by equity *infra legem*, which is also required by the legal rules governing the delimitation of maritime spaces. But the two sets of rules and approaches remain distinct.

5.3.3 DELIMITATION OF BOUNDARIES: THE *UTI POSSIDETIS* DOCTRINE

Towards the beginning of the nineteenth century, a practice developed in Spanish America whereby, on the accession of the various former colonies of Spain to independence, their boundaries followed the former colonial frontiers ('you will have sovereignty over those territories you possess as of law': *uti possidetis juris*). This sound practice, aimed at averting endless territorial claims and clashes, took shape in a host of bilateral treaties, as well as the national constitutions of some newly independent Latin American countries. It is not clear whether the practice turned into a customary rule of international law endowed with a regional scope, or remained a simple practice devoid of any binding force, or rather crystallized into a general principle of law, as two Latin American judges of the ICJ held in 1959 in a case involving Belgium and the Netherlands.[47]

The wave of decolonization in Africa, which started in the 1950s and continued until 1963, posed the crucial problem of the borders of the new independent countries. Except for a few cases where the boundaries were agreed upon within the framework of the UN, the general trend was to accept the colonial boundaries that existed at the time of independence. This practice was sanctioned in various UN resolutions as well as an important resolution of the Organization of African Unity (OAU) (resolution 16 of the 1964 Meeting of Heads of State and Government of the OAU). Importantly, in the aforementioned *Burkina Faso/Mali* case, the ICJ Chamber held that *uti possidetis* 'is a general principle, which is logically connected with the phenomenon of obtaining independence, wherever it occurs. Its obvious purpose is to prevent the independence and stability of new States being endangered by fratricidal struggles provoked by the challenging of frontiers following the withdrawal of the administering power.'[48]

The Arbitration Commission established by the Conference on Yugoslavia, in its Opinion No. 2, applied the principle as having a universal and not only a regional purport. The Arbitration Commission, called upon to pronounce on whether 'the Serbian population in Croatia and Bosnia-Herzegovina, as one of the constituent peoples of Yugoslavia, have the right to self-determination', stated that 'whatever the circumstances, the right to self-determination must not involve changes to existing frontier[s] at the time of independence (*uti possidetis juris*) except where the States concerned agree otherwise'.[49] In the 2017 award rendered in *Croatia/Slovenia*, the arbitration tribunal constituted to settle

---

[46] Kohen and Hébié, *Research Handbook* (n 22), chapter 1, at 17.

[47] *Sovereignty over Certain Frontier Land (Belgium/Netherlands)*, Dissenting Opinion of Judge Armand-Ugon, at 240 (calling this principle 'an obvious and convenient procedure'); Dissenting Opinion of Judge Moreno Quintana, at 255 (recalling the 'well-known principle' of *uti possidetis*).

[48] *Case Concerning the Frontier Dispute (Burkina Faso/Republic of Mali)*, §20; *Land, Island and the Maritime Frontier Dispute (El Salvador/Honduras, Nicaragua intervening)*, §§40–43.

[49] Opinion no. 2 (Serbian Minorities in Bosnia-Herzegovina and Croatia), Arbitration Commission of the Peace Conference on Yugoslavia.

the territorial dispute noted that the parties had agreed that the principle of *uti possidetis* was applicable to their relations,[50] thus confirming the relevance of the principle beyond the context of decolonization. Importantly, following the agreement of the parties, the tribunal gave priority to the former administrative boundaries (under the law of the Socialist Federal Republic of Yugoslavia) over the so-called 'practical' boundary defined by *effectivités*.[51] Such *effectivités* were deemed useful only as confirmation of the title arising from the *uti possidetis* principle.[52]

5.4 THE LAW OF THE SEA

5.4.1 THE CODIFICATION OF THE LAW OF THE SEA

The historical development of the law of the sea is largely consubstantial with that of international law as a whole.[53] From the early writings of authors such as Grotius on the law of prize (*De jure praedae*), the exercise of State powers in areas beyond State control, such as the seas sufficiently removed from the shore, called for common rules of interaction among sovereigns, no less so than the restraints on the conduct of hostilities. For most of its existence, the law of the sea was of customary nature. Only after the First World War were serious attempts made at codifying such law, most notably under the aegis of the League of Nations. The Conference held in 1930 at The Hague, organized by the League, was intended to focus on four key questions, namely territorial waters, the status of government vessels, piracy, and the exploitation of natural resources. Despite important preparatory work on these topics, only territorial waters were eventually discussed,[54] and the codification of this specific topic remained elusive for another half a century.

After the Second World War, the UN International Law Commission undertook the codification of several aspects of the law of the sea. The final report of the ILC, submitted in 1956, provided the basis for the convening of the First United Nations Conference on the Law of the Sea (UNCLOS I), held in Geneva in 1958. Although the Conference did not result in a comprehensive codification instrument, it adopted four major instruments, namely the Convention on the Territorial Sea and the Contiguous Zone (CTS), the Convention on the High Seas (CHS), the Convention on Fishing and Conservation of the Living Resources of the High Seas (CFCLR), and the Convention on the Continental Shelf (CCS) as well as an Optional Protocol on the Compulsory Settlement of Disputes. As no agreement could be reached on the width of the territorial sea, in 1960 a Second United Nations Conference on the Law of the Sea (UNCLOS II) was convened to address this point; alas, unsuccessfully. The third attempt resulted from the forces underpinning the decolonization and development movements, which during the 1960s sought to redefine the rules of international law that had been prescribed without their participation in the international community. The Third United Nations Conference on the Law of the Sea (UNCLOS III) grew out of a Committee established

---

[50] *Arbitration Agreement between Croatia and Slovenia*, §§251–263.
[51] Ibid., at §§337–338.
[52] Ibid., at §262.
[53] For a concise account see T. Treves, 'Historical Development of the Law of the Sea' in D. R. Rothwell et al. (eds), *The Oxford Handbook of the Law of the Sea* (Oxford: Oxford University Press, 2015), 1. See also T. Scovazzi, 'The Evolution of the International Law of the Sea: New Issues, New Challenges' (2000) 286 *RCADI* 39.
[54] See S. Rosenne, *League of Nations Conference on the Codification of International Law (1930)* (Dobbs Ferry, NY: Oceana Publications, 1975).

within the UN General Assembly to examine the exploration and exploitation of the natural resources of the seabed beyond national jurisdiction. This Committee was turned into the Preparatory Committee for UNCLOS III, which after little less than a decade (1973 to 1982) was able to adopt a landmark instrument, the 1982 UN Convention on the Law of the Sea (UNCLOS).[55]

The very impetus that had prompted this third attempt went beyond what many industrialized countries were ready to accept with respect to the exploitation of the global commons. The system established in Part XI of the UNCLOS over the so-called 'Area', that is, the seabed and subsoil beyond national jurisdiction, came under much criticism from developed countries and prevented the ratification of the UNCLOS for more than a decade. Eventually, an agreement reached in 1994 regarding the implementation of Part XI[56] paved the way for the entry into force of the UNCLOS that year. But the provisions of the UNCLOS had in the meantime been relied upon, throughout the 1980s, as reflections of customary international law, including for novel concepts such as the recognition of an exclusive economic zone.[57]

The UNCLOS has been rightly called 'a constitution of the oceans' as it covers, in a single overall instrument, a wide range of topics previously scattered in separate treaties or simply not formulated in treaty form. The instrument follows a 'zonal approach', essentially defining the rights and duties of coastal and flag States (and in some cases also port States) in a range of areas characterized mostly by reference to their distance from the shore.[58] As a result, the sea has been *divided up* into sections or areas subject to State jurisdiction to varying degrees. There are, however, exceptions to the zonal approach for which the UNCLOS provides 'transversal' regulation, whether for specific topics (e.g. Part XII: Protection of the marine environment (see **Chapter 20**); Part XIII: Marine scientific research; Part XIV: Development and transfer of marine technology) or for dispute settlement (Part XV), which, quite remarkably, is compulsory for all States parties.

5.4.2 TERRITORIAL SEA

The territorial sea of States consists of the waters surrounding a State's territory and including its bays, gulfs, and straits up to 12 nautical miles from the 'baselines', which are normally the low-tide water line as it appears in large-scale official charts from the State.

As noted earlier, the width of the territorial waters has long been the subject of extensive dispute. In the past, the principle was often advocated that the breadth of that belt was the same as the effective range of shore artillery, namely three nautical miles. However, probably on account of the development of more powerful guns and, perhaps more importantly, due to the increasing interest in the fisheries in areas more and more removed from the shore, many States claimed a broader area. The question remained intractable during the 1930 Conference and, years later, throughout UNCLOS I and II. In the meantime, States tended to assert what has been called 'creeping jurisdiction' over increasingly wide areas of

---

[55] United Nations Convention on the Law of the Sea, 10 December 1982, 1833 UNTS 3.
[56] Agreement for the Implementation of Part XI of the United Nations Convention on the Law of the Sea, 28 July 1994, 1836 UNTS 3.
[57] *Continental Shelf (Libyan Arab Jamahiriya/Malta)*, §§27 and 34.
[58] See T. Treves, 'Law of the Sea', *MPEPIL* (April 2011), §§23–25.

their coastal waters.[59] At present the question is settled by Part II of the UNCLOS, Article 3 of which provides that States have the right to establish the breadth of their territorial sea up to a limit not exceeding 12 nautical miles from the baselines.

The question of *from where to measure the width of the territorial sea*, that is, of how to define baselines, has been somewhat controversial in the past. It is now regulated by Article 5 of the UNCLOS, which reflects a customary rule. Under this provision 'the normal baseline for measuring the breadth of the territorial sea is the low-water line along the coast as marked on large-scale charts officially recognized by the coastal State'. This general principle of the 'low-water line' is however derogated from in the case of States whose coast is deeply indented, or if there is a fringe of islands along the coast in its immediate vicinity.

In the first case, Article 7(1) of the UNCLOS provides, partly in keeping with, partly developing, customary international law, that 'the method of straight baselines joining appropriate points may be employed in drawing the baseline from which the breadth of the territorial sea is measured'. Some general criteria for the drawing of straight baselines are laid down in the same provision: (i) one 'must not depart to any appreciable extent from the general direction of the coast'; (ii) 'the sea areas lying within the lines must be sufficiently closely linked to the land domain to be subject to the regime of internal waters'; (iii) 'account must be taken . . . of economic interests peculiar to the region concerned'; (iv) the system in question 'may not be applied by a State in such a manner as to cut off the territorial sea of another State from the high seas or an exclusive economic zone'. This provision partly reflects earlier findings by the ICJ in the *Norwegian Fisheries Case*. The UK challenged the validity of a decree issued by Norway in 1935 whereby the baselines from which Norway's territorial waters were measured were drawn as 'straight baselines', due to the heavily indented coast. That had the result that fishing rights in a more extensive area fell within Norway's territorial waters, thus excluding UK's fishing vessels. The Court found that due to the form of the Norwegian coast, the drawing of straight baselines was consistent with international law.

In the second case, Article 47 of the UNCLOS envisions the possibility for archipelagic States to draw archipelagic baselines characterized as straight baselines 'joining the outermost points of the outermost islands and drying reefs of the archipelago', subject to a series of limitations regarding *inter alia* the length of such lines and the areas that are enclosed by them. Importantly, only archipelagic States (as defined in Article 46 of the UNCLOS) are entitled to draw such baselines. A State whose territory consists of both land and an archipelago is not entitled to do so in its islands. The situation created some controversy at the time of the negotiation of the UNCLOS. The Greek ambassador, Constantine Stavropoulos, claimed that the very word 'archipelago' came from the Greek language and originally designated the Aegean Sea. Greece should therefore be entitled, despite having a territory with both continental land and islands, to claim the status of an archipelagic State for its islands. However, the definition of archipelagic State retained in Article 46 of the UNCLOS excludes cases such as Greece. The ICJ has confirmed that the use of straight baselines, including as archipelagic baselines, is subject to specific conditions and must be applied restrictively.[60]

---

[59] For an early example see *Bering Fur Seals Arbitration (United States of America/United Kingdom)*. A more emblematic case concerns the unilateral extension by Iceland of its exclusive fisheries jurisdiction from a limit of 12 to one of 50 nautical miles. This extension was challenged by the UK and Germany before the ICJ, which decided that the unilateral extension was not opposable either to the UK or Germany: see *Fisheries Jurisdiction (United Kingdom v Iceland; Federal Republic of Germany v Iceland)*. Another example is provided by the *Norwegian Fisheries (United Kingdom v Norway)* case discussed later in this section.

[60] *Maritime Delimitation and Territorial Questions between Qatar and Bahrain (Qatar v Bahrain)*, §§212–215.

Within the territorial sea (plus its airspace, seabed, and subsoil) the coastal State enjoys *full sovereignty*, subject to the *right of innocent passage* of foreign merchant ships and warships[61] (however, for submarines it is required that they must navigate on the surface and show their flag). This right entails that foreign ships may pass through the territorial waters if their passage 'is not prejudicial to the peace, good order or security of the coastal State' (Article 19(1) of the UNCLOS). Of course, major Powers have always insisted on this right and tend to favour a broadening of the notion; they contend, in particular, that no prior notification or authorization is required. In contrast, lesser States have for long maintained that prior notification and authorization are needed for warships (currently some 40 States insist on this requirement). The UNCLOS strikes a satisfactory balance between these conflicting demands. The passage is *'innocent'* if, for example, foreign ships do not engage in threat or use of force, spying, propaganda, breach of customs, fiscal, immigration, or sanitary regulations, interference with coastal communications, serious and wilful pollution, etc., and as long as they comply with the laws and regulations enacted by the coastal State, notably in the area of transport, fishing, and navigation. Thus, if a foreign fishing vessel breaches the legislation of the coastal State on fishing in the territorial waters, passage may not be held to be 'innocent'.

It is not absolutely clear whether the determination of the 'innocent' nature of the passage exclusively falls to the coastal State. In 1949, in *Corfu Channel* (at 30–1), the ICJ held that the assessment may be objective and the opinion of the coastal State is not decisive (e.g. the violation of local laws by the foreign ship is not in itself sufficient to prove that the coastal State has suffered a prejudice). In *Qatar v Bahrain*, the ICJ similarly noted that Bahrain was not entitled to unilaterally set straight baselines and, for that reason, there were areas that constituted Bahrain's territorial sea rather than its internal waters, and therefore Qatari vessels like those of all other States 'enjoy[ed] in these waters the right of innocent passage accorded by customary international law'.[62] The coastal State may not exercise criminal jurisdiction over offences committed on board ships within territorial waters, except for the situations enumerated in Article 27(1) of the UNCLOS.

5.4.3 INTERNAL WATERS

Unlike the territorial sea, internal waters (comprising not only rivers and lakes but also sea waters within the baselines) are subject to the full and exclusive sovereignty of the State. Hence, in internal waters along the coast of a State, no right of innocent passage accrues to other States. Foreign vessels may enter these waters only if the coastal State consents to such ingress and subject to the restrictions that it may impose. Exceptions to the unfettered right of the coastal State are: (i) cases of distress, and (ii) cases where 'the establishment of a straight baseline in accordance with the method set forth in Article 7 [referred to above] has the effect of enclosing as internal waters areas which had not previously been considered as such' (Article 8(2) of the UNCLOS); in the latter case the foreign ship enjoys the right of innocent passage. When the waters enclosed within straight baselines are archipelagic waters (Article 49 of the UNCLOS) a right of innocent passage (Article 52) and a regime of archipelagic sea lanes (Article 53) apply, although, within the archipelagic waters, the archipelagic State may 'draw closing lines for the delimitation of internal waters,

---

[61] On the historical origins and opposing doctrinal views regarding this passage see D. P. O'Connell, *The International Law of the Sea*, vol. I (Oxford: Oxford University Press, 1982), chapter 7.

[62] *Maritime Delimitation and Territorial Questions between Qatar and Bahrain (Qatar v Bahrain)*, at §223.

in accordance with articles 9, 10 and 11' (Article 50). The provisions referred to introduce specifications for mouths of rivers, bays, and ports.

Foreign ships allowed to enter internal waters are subject to the legislation of the coastal State. Offences committed on board foreign ships in a port of the coastal State are normally subject to the criminal jurisdiction of the flag State, unless such offences infringe customs legislation or disrupt the peace of the port, or the captain of the foreign vessel requests intervention of the coastal State's enforcement authorities. Incidents occurring in the foreign port or offences perpetrated there are subject to the jurisdiction of the coastal State.

5.4.4 BAYS

A particular problem may be posed by States having bays, defined in Article 10(2) of the UNCLOS as: 'a well-marked indentation whose penetration is in such proportion to the width of its mouth as to contain land-locked waters and constitute more than a mere curvature of the coast. An indentation shall not however be regarded as a bay unless its area is as large as, or larger than, that of the semi-circle whose diameter is a line drawn across the mouth of that indentation.'

For these bays, under Article 10(4) and 10(5), if the distance between the low-water marks of the natural entrance points of the bay does not exceed 24 nautical miles, 'a closing line may be drawn between these two low-water marks, and the waters enclosed thereby shall be considered as internal waters'. If the bay's entrance exceeds 24 nautical miles, 'a straight baseline of 24 nautical miles shall be drawn within the bay in such a manner as to enclose the maximum area of water that is possible with a line of that length'.

Particular problems arise when the coasts of bays belong to more than one State. According to the ICJ in the *Land, Island and Maritime Frontier Dispute* there may exist 'pluri-State bays' where the coast may belong to more States and yet it is possible to draw a closing line.[63] The case of the Gulf of Fonseca was particularly interesting because, in addition to a pluri-State bay, it was also considered a historic bay. 'Historic bays' are indentations claimed by the coastal State as part of its internal waters, hence submitted to its sovereignty, by virtue of a customary title based on consistent claims by that State, and the absence of protest by other States. The ICJ upheld the notion in 1951 in *Norwegian Fisheries*[64] and in 1992 in the *Land, Island and Maritime Frontier Dispute*.[65] The limitations for the drawing of straight baselines enclosing the waters of bays (Articles 7 and 10 of the UNCLOS) are not applicable to pluri-State bays and historic bays (Article 10(1) and (6) of the UNCLOS). Thus, in such cases, a straight baseline of more than 24 nautical miles can be drawn to enclose the relevant waters and the semi-circle test is not applicable.

Nevertheless, although the notion is clear, so far claims by some coastal States to such bays have not been settled. One may mention, for instance, the Canadian claims to the Hudson bay,[66] or by Libya to the Gulf of Sirte (Sidra), which is about 300 miles broad.[67] Other bays over which States have put forward claims include: the Granville Bay (in France,

---

[63] *Land, Island and Maritime Frontier Dispute (El Salvador/Honduras; Nicaragua intervening)*, §§395ff. The ICJ Chamber concluded that the term 'condominium' used in a 1917 decision from the Central American Court of Justice meant co-sovereignty resulting from succession by the three States, at the time of their independence, to a colonial territory that was undelimited in this area (at §401).

[64] *Fisheries (United Kingdom v Norway)*, §§130–131.

[65] *Land, Island and Maritime Frontier Dispute (El Salvador/Honduras; Nicaragua intervening)*, §§404–405.

[66] See a Canadian statement of 1957 (in Canada, *House of Commons Debates*, 1957–58, 14 November 1957, 1163). See also (1966) 4 *CYIL* 282 and (1974) 12 *CYIL* 278.

[67] See the Libyan statement of 1973 in UN Legislative Series, *National Legislation and Treaties Relating to the Law of the Sea*, ST/LEG/SER.B/18, 26–7.

between Normandy and Brittany),[68] Shark Bay (in Australia),[69] and Bangkok bay (in Thailand).[70] The complexity of these claims lies in the factual nature of the test for the recognition of historic bays, that is, the consistent exercise of governmental powers (although the ICJ Chamber in *Land, Island and Maritime Frontier Dispute (El Salvador/Honduras)* spoke of 'claims') and absence of protest or acquiescence by other States.[71]

5.4.5 THE CONTIGUOUS ZONE

The contiguous zone goes beyond the territorial sea and can extend to up to 24 nautical miles from the baselines.[72] This zone was originally agreed upon by States to enable the coastal State to prevent persons who commit offences in the territorial waters from evading apprehension by the coastal authorities by simply moving into the high seas. At a time when the recognized width of the territorial waters was barely 3 nautical miles from the shore, smuggling and the related evasion of custom duties would have been very difficult to control.[73]

Over time, the same rationale was extended to entitle the coastal State to exercise 'control' over matters relating to customs, taxation, immigration, and sanitary regulation so as to prevent and punish infringements (Article 33 of the UNCLOS). In the contiguous zone, States do not have sovereignty. They only exercise functional jurisdiction for the specific purposes recognized by the rule. This right of the coastal State implies that it can both prevent ships from entering its territorial waters if they are suspected of engaging in prohibited activities, and arrest vessels that have already perpetrated offences in its territorial waters.

5.4.6 THE EXCLUSIVE ECONOMIC ZONE

The exclusive economic zone has been gradually established in recent years following the discovery of important natural resources off the coast of many States. It is an area beyond and adjacent to the territorial sea, that may extend up to 200 miles (from the baselines from which the breadth of the territorial sea is measured). In this area, the coastal State enjoys 'sovereign rights' *in some specific matters*, namely only for the purpose of exploring, exploiting, conserving, and managing *living and non-living natural resources*. In addition, it has 'jurisdiction' over artificial islands, installations and infrastructures, marine scientific research, and the protection and preservation of the marine environment. Importantly, States must proclaim an exclusive economic zone in order to enjoy the attendant powers and, although they frequently do so, there are cases such as in the Mediterranean Sea where several States have refrained from making such proclamations.

---

[68] See the French note of 1928 in *League of Nations* doc. C.74. M.39.1929.V, 159–60.

[69] See the statement of the Australian Government of 1967, in UN Legislative Series, *National Legislation and Treaties Relating to the Law of the Sea*, ST/LEG/SER.B/15, 46.

[70] See the statement made in 1959 by the Government of Thailand, in UN Legislative Series, *National Legislation and Treaties Relating to the Law of the Sea*, ST/LEG/SER.B/16, 34.

[71] See *Fisheries (United Kingdom v Norway)*, §§130–131 (with the ICJ implicitly endorsing the admission made by the UK in regard to Norway's historic waters); *Juridical Regime of Historic Waters Including Historic Bays—Study prepared by the Secretariat*, UN Doc. A/CN.4/143, reproduced in the Yearbook of the ILC, 1962, vol. II, §§80–133.

[72] On the historical development of this concept since 1850 see A. V. Lowe, 'The Development of the Concept of the Contiguous Zone' (1981) 52 *BYIL* 109.

[73] See e.g. the case of the *Petit Jules*, discussed in ibid., at 111–14.

As a consequence of its rights over the zone, the coastal State has broad prescriptive jurisdiction (legislative and regulatory powers) relating to such a zone. The current regime is formulated in Part V of the UNCLOS, which in many respects reflects customary international law.[74] Under Article 62(4), the coastal State may issue laws and regulations, which must however be consistent with the provisions on the zone contained in the UNCLOS, on a wide range of matters, such as: (i) licensing of fishermen, fishing vessels, and equipment, including payment of fees; (ii) determining the species which may be caught, and fixing quotas of catch; (iii) regulating seasons and areas of fishing as well as the types, sizes, and amount of gear; (iv) fixing the age and size of fish and other species that may be caught; (v) requiring, under the authorization and control of the coastal State, the conduct of specified fisheries research programmes and regulating their conduct; (vi) enforcement procedures, and so on. It is notable that, in 1986, a French-Canadian arbitral tribunal held in *Franco-Canadian Fisheries Arbitration*[75] that a ship engaged in fish processing in the exclusive economic zone was not subject to the jurisdiction of the coastal State, for fish processing did not come within the purview of the matters over which that State had jurisdiction. This is an example of the 'functional' nature of the jurisdiction exercised by the coastal State in the exclusive economic zone, which can therefore not be fully equated with the full jurisdiction arising from sovereignty.[76]

The coastal State also has extensive powers of enforcement. Under Article 73(1) of the UNCLOS it may 'take such measures, including boarding, inspection, arrest and judicial proceedings, as may be necessary to ensure compliance with the laws and regulations adopted by it in conformity with [the] Convention'. By way of illustration, in 1997 Guinea arrested in its exclusive economic zone the *Saiga*, a vessel belonging to St Vincent and the Grenadines, claiming that it had the right to do so because the ship had been supplying gas-oil to other fishing vessels, thus avoiding paying customs duties. The International Tribunal for the Law of the Sea (ITLOS), in *The M/V 'Saiga' (No. 2) Case (Saint Vincent and the Grenadines v Guinea)* held that, in the area under consideration, 'the coastal State has jurisdiction to apply customs law and regulations in respect of artificial islands, installations and structures (Article 60 paragraph 2)' (at §127). However, in the view of the Tribunal, the UNCLOS 'does not empower a coastal State to apply its customs laws in respect of any other parts of the exclusive economic zone' (at §127 *in fine*). It therefore held Guinea to be in breach of the Convention. The Tribunal also held that Guinea's use of force in stopping and arresting the *Saiga* was excessive. In the Tribunal's view:

> Although the Convention does not contain express provisions on the use of force in the arrest of ships, international law, which is applicable by virtue of Article 293 of the Convention, requires that the use of force must be avoided as far as possible and, where force is unavoidable, it must not go beyond what is reasonable and necessary in the circumstances. Considerations of humanity must apply in the law of the sea, as they do in other areas of international law. (at §155)

---

[74] *Continental Shelf (Libyan Arab Jamahiriya/Malta)*, §§27 and 34.
[75] *Case concerning filleting within the Gulf of St. Lawrence between Canada and France*, §§49–54.
[76] See also the discussion of taxation of catering and entertainment services provided to oil rigs in the UK's exclusive economic zone in R. Higgins, 'International Law and the Avoidance, Containment and Resolution of Disputes: General course on public international law' (1991) 230 *RCADI* 9, at 185.

The Tribunal then noted that:

> The normal practice used to stop a ship at sea is first to give an auditory or visual signal to stop, using internationally recognized signals. Where this does not succeed, a variety of actions may be taken, including the firing of shots across the bows of the ship. It is only after the appropriate actions fail that the pursuing vessel may, as a last resort, use force. Even then, appropriate warning must be issued to the ship and all efforts should be made to ensure that life is not endangered. (at §156)

More generally, the exercise of the rights of the coastal State is subject to the duty to have 'due regard' for the rights of flag States (Article 56(1) of the UNCLOS). This duty reflects the larger freedoms enjoyed by flag States in the exclusive economic zone. In this zone, the coastal State may not prevent other States from exercising their right of navigation and overflight, as well as the right to lay cables and pipelines. Article 58(1) of the UNCLOS defines these freedoms by reference to those in the high seas (Article 87). Having 'due regard' may entail, for example, certain procedural steps (e.g. consultations) before an environmental measure is adopted.[77] The coastal State may also be required to tolerate certain freedoms not explicitly stated in the UNCLOS, such as the right to stage an environmental protest, as in the case of Greenpeace's vessel *Arctic Sunrise*, which led to a dispute between the Netherlands (the flag State) and Russia (who seized the vessel and detained its crew).[78]

5.4.7 THE CONTINENTAL SHELF

The discovery in the 1930s of oil and gas in the seabed and subsoil off the coast of some States beyond the territorial sea led many States, spearheaded by the United States (through the so-called Truman proclamation made in 1945)[79] to claim exclusive rights of exploitation over an area that previously had been part of the high seas, hence free for anybody. In a matter of a few years a customary rule evolved that was then codified first in the Geneva Convention of 1958 on the Continental Shelf and then reaffirmed in Part VI of the UNCLOS.

While the areas discussed so far embrace sea waters and their resources, the continental shelf is part of underwater land. The shelf is the natural prolongation of a coastal State's land territory into the sea, before it falls away into the ocean depths. Normally the shelf is covered with relatively shallow water (between 150 and 200 metres). Its length varies depending on the geology of the coast. For instance, off the US western coast it is no broader than five miles, while off the coast of other States it is very wide. Under Article 76(1) of the UNCLOS the outer limit of the continental shelf is set out as follows:

> The continental shelf of a coastal State comprises the seabed and subsoil of the submarine areas that extend beyond its territorial sea throughout the natural prolongation of its land territory to the outer edge of the continental margin, or to a distance of 200 nautical miles from the baselines from which the breadth of the territorial sea is measured where the outer edge of [the] continental margin does not extend up to that distance.

---

[77] See *Chagos Marine Protected Area Arbitration (Mauritius v United Kingdom)*, §§518–519 and 534–536.
[78] See *Arctic Sunrise Arbitration (The Netherlands v Russia)*, §§227–228.
[79] The text of the Presidential Proclamation no. 2667, of 28 September 1945, can be consulted online: https://www.presidency.ucsb.edu/documents/proclamation-2667-policy-the-united-states-with-respect-the-natural-resources-the-subsoil.

The coastal State has, again, 'sovereign rights'[80] *limited* to certain specific activities: exploration and exploitation of the natural resources of the shelf (essentially: petroleum and fisheries). Coastal States have a continental shelf *ipso facto*, without any need for a specific proclamation, although one is indeed made in most cases, in order to organize the regime for the exploitation of the natural resources of this area. As the ICJ put it in *North Sea Continental Shelf*:

> the rights of the coastal State [in respect of the continental shelf] ... exist *ipso facto* and *ab initio*, by virtue of its sovereignty over the land, and as an extension of it in an exercise of sovereign rights for the purpose of exploring the seabed and exploiting its natural resources. In short, there is here an inherent right. (at §19)

In addition, under Article 80 of the UNCLOS, the coastal State may construct and maintain installations for exploration of the shelf and establish safety zones around such installations up to a limit of 500 metres. These rights only relate to the shelf and its resources. Under Article 78 of the UNCLOS the status of the superjacent waters, if they are beyond the contiguous zone and part of the high seas, remain unaffected, just as does the airspace above those waters. From a legal standpoint, that is so even when the continental shelf underneath has been delimitated.[81] But, as the ICJ has recognized, the two areas are closely linked and that relation may be important for delimitation purposes.[82]

An important process which is still ongoing concerns the determination of the outer limits of the continental shelf. Under Article 76 of the UNCLOS, these may go beyond 200 nautical miles. In such cases, the coastal State has the right to establish unilaterally the outer edge of the continental margin, but such unilateralism is subject to a process whereby information is submitted to a Commission on the Limits of the Continental Shelf, which makes recommendations (Annex II to the UNCLOS). Outer limits set in accordance with such recommendations are 'final and binding' (Article 76(8)) but this system is without prejudice to the need for delimitation of the continental shelves of different States, whether adjacent or opposite (Article 76(10)). In 2008, the Meeting of the Parties to UNCLOS set the time limit for submissions to this Commission from parties at 13 May 2009.[83] Many full submissions have been filed, as well as a number of submissions with preliminary information (to meet the deadline).[84] Unless a State accedes to the UNCLOS later, no further submissions are admissible. But the process is structured in such a way that, if a State does not agree with a recommendation, it has to present a revised submission, which will be evaluated by the Commission, and so forth until agreement is reached. This approach, together with the slow pace of response of the Commission, will keep the issue of the extended continental shelf on the international agenda for many years to come.

---

[80] As in the case of the exclusive economic zone, these 'sovereign rights' are more limited than the 'sovereignty' enjoyed by the coastal State over the territorial sea. For example, in *Commonwealth v WMC Resources Ltd*, the High Court of Australia made a distinction between the powers of Australia over resources within its sovereignty and those of the continental shelf, where 'it has no property in the continental shelf at common law'.

[81] *Maritime Delimitation in the Black Sea (Romania v Ukraine)*, §69.

[82] *Continental Shelf (Libyan Arab Jamahiriya/Malta)*, §33.

[83] Report of the Meeting of the Parties, SPLOS/184, 21 July 2008, §§85–99; Issues related to the workload of the Commission on the Limits of the Continental Shelf—tentative dates of submissions, SPLOS/INF/20.

[84] Report of the Meeting of the Parties, SPLOS/184, 21 July 2008, §§85–99; Decision regarding the workload of the Commission on the Limits of the Continental Shelf and the ability of States, particularly developing States, to fulfil the requirements of article 4 of Annex II to the Convention, as well as the decision contained in SPLOS/72, paragraph (a), SPLOS/183, §1(a).

5.4.8 DELIMITATION OF MARITIME AREAS

The question of maritime delimitation became particularly important with the recognition of new maritime areas, such as the continental shelf and, later, the exclusive economic zone. On this question, when an agreement cannot be reached, the role of judicial dispute settlement has been of major importance, and it has led to the recognition of a standard approach to delimitation which takes as a starting-point the drawing of an equidistance (median) line between the adjacent (or opposite) spaces (territorial seas, exclusive economic zones, and continental shelves) and then adjusts the line to take into account special circumstances and to ensure proportionality between the maritime spaces thus delimited and the length of the coast.[85]

However, this standard approach was not the result of clear guidelines arising from codification efforts, either in 1958 or in 1982. The UNCLOS provides different guidance for the delimitation of the territorial sea, where the drawing of a median/equidistance line is expressly mentioned (Article 15), and for that of the exclusive economic zone and the continental shelf, for which Articles 74(1) and 83(1) merely refer to an 'equitable solution'. Instead, the current approach was distilled from a substantial body of cases, with the decisions of the ICJ playing a particularly important role. It is also noteworthy that throughout this process of distillation, the ICJ itself changed course, first refraining from recognizing the customary nature of the rule of equidistance for the delimitation of the continental shelf and then progressively recognizing its role as a starting-point. The following discussion summarizes a long and complex body of cases,[86] highlighting the main junctures of the overall process that led to the current approach.

An early case concerned the delimitation of the continental shelves of the UK, the Federal Republic of Germany, and Denmark in the North Sea. Under Article 6 of the 1958 Convention on the Continental Shelf, in the absence of agreement between the States concerned, the boundary had to be determined 'by application of the principle of equidistance from the nearest points of the baselines from which the breadth of the territorial sea of each State is measured'. However, applied in those specific geographical circumstances, the principle of equidistance could lead to inequitable solutions. In the *North Sea Continental Shelf* cases, the ICJ held that the principle at issue was not enshrined in customary law; in its view the relevant general rule prescribed that the delimitation was to be effected 'by agreement in accordance with equitable principles'(at 53). 'Equitable principles' remained key in judicial delimitation, but they were soon seen as not specific enough to achieve an equitable outcome.[87] Moreover, such a wide approach could lead to differences, sometimes very significant ones, between the limits of the continental shelf and those of the exclusive economic zone. Such divergence is entirely admissible, but it may be unpractical to define the rights and duties of States on this basis.

One significant development came in *Delimitation of the Maritime Boundary in the Gulf of Maine Area*, decided by an ICJ Chamber in 1984 at the request of Canada and the US.

---

[85] See *Maritime Delimitation in the Black Sea (Romania v Ukraine)*.
[86] On maritime delimitation see P. Weil, *Perspectives du droit de la delimitation maritime* (Paris: Pedone, 1988); A. de Almeida do Nascimento, *El derecho internacional de la delimitación de los espacios marinos de soberanía económica* (Madrid: Tecnos, 1999); P. Tomka, 'The Contribution of the International Court of Justice to the Law of the Sea' in D. Attard et al. (eds), *The IMLI Manual on International Maritime Law*, vol. I (Oxford: Oxford University Press, 2014), 618; M. Evans, 'Maritime Boundary Delimitation' in D. Rothwell et al. (eds), *The Oxford Handbook of the Law of the Sea* (Oxford: Oxford University Press, 2015), 254; S. Fietta and R. Cleverly, *A Practitioner's Guide to Maritime Boundary Delimitation* (Oxford: Oxford University Press, 2016); Y. Tanaka, *Predictability and Flexibility in the Law of Maritime Delimitation*, 3rd edn (Oxford: Hart, 2019).
[87] *Continental Shelf (Tunisia/Libyan Arab Jamahiriya)*, §70.

The 1981 agreement submitting the dispute requested the Chamber to draw a single line for the delimitation of both the continental shelf and the fisheries zone of the two parties in the Gulf of Maine. The Chamber relied on the considerations made by the ICJ in the *North Sea Continental Shelf* case to draw a single line delimitating the two areas. The case is significant not only because it was the first time a dispute was submitted to an ICJ Chamber but also because of the request for the Chamber to actually draw a delimitation line (rather than merely identifying the principles through which delimitation was to be effected) and, indeed, a single line for both maritime areas (at §§24–27), an approach that would become the rule thereafter.

Another significant development was the recognition of the use of the equidistance method, adjusted to take into account special circumstances, as a preliminary and provisional step. The ICJ did so in *Continental Shelf (Libyan Arab Jamahiriya/Malta)*, although it did not embrace the method as such but only its use as an embodiment of the 'equitable principles' in the light of the circumstances of the case, namely the need to delimitate two opposite continental shelves.[88] In this case, the Court also discussed an important consideration that had been given significant weight in a previous case, *Continental Shelf (Tunisia/Libyan Arab Jamahiriya)* (at §§103ff) and, even earlier, in the *North Sea Continental Shelf* cases (at §101(D)(3)), namely the criterion of proportionality between the length of the coast of a State and the area apportioned to it through the delimitation exercise.

The case law of the early 1980s, together with the *North Sea Continental Shelf* precedent and the codification process now ripe in the form of the UNCLOS, set the course for the process of distillation that was eventually consolidated in the 2009 decision of the ICJ in the case concerning the *Delimitation of the Black Sea (Romania v Ukraine)*. This case endorsed, for the delimitation of adjacent or opposite exclusive economic zones and continental shelves through a single line, a three-step method (i) starting with the drawing of a preliminary equidistance (or median) line constructed from the 'most appropriate' basepoints selected from the baselines used for the territorial sea; (ii) to be adjusted on the basis of 'special' or 'relevant' circumstances to achieve an 'equitable result';[89] and (iii) finally corrected, if necessary, to avoid an inequitable result that may arise from 'any marked disproportion between the ratio of the respective coastal lengths and the ratio between the relevant maritime area of each State' (at §§115–122).

Importantly, the Court now considers that the equidistance method must be used 'unless there are compelling reasons that make this unfeasible in the particular case'.[90] Such was the case in the ICJ's 2007 decision in *Nicaragua v Colombia*, where the Court used instead a bisector line (rather than an equidistance one) to delimitate the relevant area of the Caribbean sea.[91] But the Court expressly stated that the rule remained the resort to equidistance,[92] and it has subsequently relied on the methodology fleshed out in the *Black Sea* case for both entirely[93] and partially[94] undelimitated areas.

---

[88] *Continental Shelf (Libyan Arab Jamahiriya/Malta)*, §§43 and 60–63.

[89] For a discussion of such circumstances see *Guyana v Suriname*, §§297–305.

[90] *Maritime Delimitation in the Black Sea (Romania v Ukraine)*, §116.

[91] *Territorial and Maritime Dispute between Nicaragua and Honduras in the Caribbean Sea (Nicaragua v Honduras)*, §§272 and 287.

[92] Ibid., at §§272, 277–280.

[93] *Territorial and Maritime Dispute (Nicaragua v Colombia)*, §§190–199.

[94] *Maritime Dispute (Peru v Chile)*, §§183–195 (in this case, part of the boundary had been delimited by treaty, so the Court used the standard methodology only for the undelimited part, which started seaward at a point where the delimited part ended).

5.4.9 THE HIGH SEAS

Beyond the contiguous zone, and subject to what has already been said with regard to the exclusive economic zone, the waters belong to the high seas. They are free for every State to access, being a good available to all of them (*res communis omnium*). The applicable regime is now codified in Part VII of the UNCLOS. Each State enjoys freedom of navigation and overflight, of laying submarine cables and pipelines, fishing, scientific research, construction of artificial islands and other installations (provided they are permitted by international rules).

Each State has exclusive jurisdiction over its own ships. Under customary international law, as codified in Article 110 of the UNCLOS, exceptionally, a State, through its warships or public vessels vested with enforcement functions (e.g. coastal guard vessels), may exercise jurisdiction over *foreign* ships in the following cases:

(1) It may *approach, board, and visit* foreign merchant ships to ascertain their nationality, or to establish whether they engage in (a) piracy, or (b) slave trading, or (c) unauthorized broadcasting, or whether (d) the ship is without nationality,[95] or whether (e) though flying a foreign flag or refusing to show its flag, the ship is in reality of the same nationality as the warship. However, if the suspicions about the nature of the activity in which the ship is engaging or its nationality prove to be unfounded, and provided that 'the ship boarded has not committed any act justifying' those suspicions, the State that has proceeded to board and visit the ship shall compensate the foreign ship 'for any loss or damage that may have been sustained' (Article 110(3)).

(2) It may *arrest and seize* any ship (a merchant vessel or a warship no longer under the control of the flag State) engaging in piracy or slave trading, and bring to trial the persons engaged in such activities.

(3) It may *pursue and seize* a ship suspected of infringing its laws in its internal waters, territorial sea, or contiguous zone, or its laws relating to the exclusive economic zone or continental shelf. This right of 'hot pursuit' (regulated by Article 111 of the UNCLOS) must be initiated in one of these areas and may be exercised on the high seas; it must be uninterrupted, but shall cease as soon as the pursued ship is in the territorial waters of its own State or of a third State (in *The M/V 'Saiga' (No. 2)* case, the ITLOS held that the various conditions for the exercise of the right of hot pursuit set forth in Article 111 'are cumulative; each of them must be satisfied for the pursuit to be legitimate under the Convention') (at §146).

Except for the above cases, a State may not arrest in international waters ships flying the flag of other States. Furthermore, in undertaking law enforcement operations at sea, States may only use the degree of force that is 'reasonable and necessary in the circumstances' (at §155), and subject to the practical procedures convincingly set out by the ITLOS in that case (see **5.4.6**).

A case illustrating the importance of the legal regime of the high seas is the Spanish–Canadian dispute over the interception of a Spanish vessel by Canadian authorities (ICJ,

---

[95] In this respect, one should mention a decision rendered in 2001 by an Italian court in *Pamuk and others*. Italian customs officers had arrested on the high seas a flagless vessel transporting illegal immigrants who had been transferred, on the high seas, to another vessel directed to the Italian coast and had subsequently entered Italian territorial waters. The court held that the arrest and visit of the ship on the high seas was lawful, for it was in keeping with Article 110 of the 1982 Convention: not only was the ship flagless, but its transfer of illegal immigrants to another ship had been monitored by Italian planes and a helicopter; the Italian customs authorities were therefore right in suspecting illegal conduct, consisting of the unlawful immigration of foreigners into Italy (at 1156–7).

Fisheries Jurisdiction (Spain v Canada) (Jurisdiction)). On 5 March 1995 Canadian government vessels intercepted and boarded in international waters (some 245 miles from the Canadian coast) a Spanish fishing vessel, the *Estai*. The vessel was seized and its master arrested on charges of violations of the Canadian Coastal Fisheries Protection Act and its implementing legislation. In particular the Spaniards were charged with illegal fishing for Greenland halibut. Part of the ship's catch was confiscated; the members of the crew were released immediately; the master was released following the payment of bail; the vessel was released following the posting of a bond. The same day that the *Estai* was boarded, Spain sent two Notes Verbales to Canada protesting at the 'flagrant violation of international law' (at §20). On 10 March, it sent another Note Verbale asserting that Canada had breached 'the universally accepted norm of customary international law codified in Article 92 and articles to the same effect of the 1982 Convention on the law of the Sea' (ibid.). Also on 10 March, the European Community and its Member States sent a Note Verbale to Canada, which stated among other things that:

> [t]he arrest of a vessel in international waters by a State other than the State of which the vessel is flying the flag and under whose jurisdiction it falls, is an illegal act under both the NAFO [Northwest Atlantic Fisheries Organization] Convention and customary international law, and cannot be justified by any means. With this action Canada is not only flagrantly violating international law, but is failing to observe normal behaviour of responsible States . . . This serious breach of international law goes far beyond the question of fisheries conservation. The arrest is a lawless act against the sovereignty of a member State of the European Community. Furthermore, the behaviour of the Canadian vessels has clearly endangered the lives of the crew and the safety of the Spanish vessel concerned. The European Community and its member States demand that Canada immediately release the vessel, repair any damages caused, cease and desist from its harassment of vessels flying the flag of Community Member States and immediately repeal the legislation under which it claims to take such unilateral action. (at §21)

Canada replied that 'the arrest of the *Estai* was necessary in order to put a stop to the overfishing of Greenland halibut by Spanish fishermen' (at §20). In April the proceedings against the *Estai* and its master were discontinued by order of the Canadian Attorney-General, the bond was discharged, and the bail was repaid with interest; subsequently the confiscated portion of the catch was returned. Nevertheless, Spain brought the dispute to the ICJ, asking the Court to hold that the Canadian legislation on the matter at issue was not opposable to Spain, and that Canada had breached international law and had to pay reparation as well as refrain from future violations of international law. The Court, however, held in 1998 that it lacked jurisdiction to adjudicate upon the dispute, for the dispute came within the terms of a reservation to the Court's jurisdiction contained in a Canadian Declaration of 1994 accepting the Court's jurisdiction (at §89). The incident prompted the conclusion of the 1995 Straddling Fish Stocks Agreement[96] governing the special situations of fisheries that straddle the high seas and the areas under State jurisdiction.

Another apposite case concerns the regulation of 'bunkering', namely the refuelling of ships offshore, beyond the internal waters and territorial sea of the coastal State. In a 2019 decision in the case *The M/V 'Norstar' (Panama v Italy)*, the ITLOS concluded that Italy had interfered with the freedom of the high seas and flag State jurisdiction in breach of Article 87(1) of the UNCLOS. The measure challenged was a decree of seizure issued by an Italian public prosecutor in the course of criminal proceedings against several individuals accused of smuggling and tax fraud for the seizure of the vessel *Norstar*. The vessel had

---

[96] Agreement for the Implementation of the Provisions of the United Nations Convention on the Law of the Sea of 10 December 1982 relating to the Conservation and Management of Straddling Fish Stocks and Highly Migratory Fish Stocks, 4 August 1995, 2167 UNTS 88. See P.-M. Dupuy and J. E. Viñuales, *International Environmental Law*, 2nd edn (Cambridge: Cambridge University Press, 2018), 210.

been arrested by Spanish authorities in internal waters on the request of the Italian authorities. The ITLOS considered that the decree was in breach of the freedoms of the high seas, which are also applicable in the exclusive economic zone by virtue of Article 58(1) (which refers to Article 87), because it interfered with a lawful activity of a foreign vessel in that area. The fact that the decree was an exercise by Italy of 'prescriptive' rather than of 'enforcement' jurisdiction (the latter having taken place only in internal waters of Spain) did not change the conclusion because, according to the ITLOS 'article 87 may still be applicable and be breached if a State extends its criminal and customs laws extraterritorially to activities of foreign ships on the high seas and criminalizes them' (at §226). It must be noted that several judges expressed reservations regarding the position of the majority on Article 87(1). In a joint Dissenting Opinion, no less than seven judges considered that Article 87(1) was relevant but not applicable to the circumstances of the case, because it 'protects the free movement of vessels primarily from the exercise of enforcement jurisdiction by non-flag States on the high seas'.[97] The case remains noteworthy because it was the first time that the scope of Article 87 was litigated before the ITLOS.

5.5 THE INTERNATIONAL SEABED AND THE CONCEPT OF THE COMMON HERITAGE OF MANKIND

The international seabed is the soil and subsoil under the high seas. In the past it has been estimated to be rich in mineral nodules, notably manganese, nickel, copper, and cobalt. After a rather long period of disenchantment during which these riches were believed to have been overestimated, interest in deep seabed mining is growing again as a result of the search for rare earths and minerals used in a variety of electronic products. Yet, when the question first arose, developing countries considered that a new, community-oriented concept should govern the exploitation of undersea wealth.

Thus, as early as 1967 the Maltese Ambassador Arvid Pardo launched the notion of the *common heritage of mankind* in the UN General Assembly.[98] He noted that new technology as well as fresh developments in oceanography were making it possible for mankind to benefit from the 'immense wealth' existing on the seabed and the ocean floor beyond national jurisdictions. In his view there were two alternative courses of action. The first was to allow a 'competitive scramble for sovereign rights over the land underlying the world's seas and oceans, surpassing in magnitude and in its implications last century's colonial scramble for territory in Asia and Africa'; one of the consequences would be both a 'dramatic increase of the arms race and increasing world tension'; in addition, the 'strong would get stronger, the rich richer, and among the rich themselves there would arise an increasing and insuperable differentiation between two or three and the remainder'. The other alternative was to establish an international legal regime to ensure that the seabed and the ocean floor were exploited solely for peaceful purposes, and for the benefit of mankind as a whole. Thus the concept of the 'common heritage of mankind', as a general standard for the exploitation of new natural resources, was delineated. It incorporates five main elements: (i) the absence of a right of appropriation; (ii) the duty to exploit the resources in the interest of mankind in such a way as to benefit all, including developing countries; (iii) the obligation to explore

---

[97] *The M/V Nostar (Panama v Italy)*, Joint Dissenting Opinion of Judges Cot, Pawlack, Yanai, Hoffmann, Kolodkin and Lijnzaad and Judge Ad Hoc Treves, §15.

[98] It is reported in A. Pardo, *The Common Heritage: Selected Papers on Oceans and World Order 1967–74* (Malta: Malta University Press, 1975), 31, 64, and 85.

and exploit for peaceful purposes only; (iv) the duty to pay due regard to scientific research; (v) the duty duly to protect the environment.

Pardo's ideas were to a large extent taken up in Part XI of the UNCLOS. Article 136 provided that '[t]he Area [i.e. the seabed and ocean floor and subsoil thereof, beyond the limits of national jurisdictions] and its resources are the common heritage of mankind'. Other provisions specified that no portion of the Area and its resources could be appropriated or made subject to State sovereignty, that the Area should be used peacefully, marine scientific research must be promoted, and the marine environment must be protected (see Articles 137 and 141–145). The crucial point was of course how the resources of the Area would be exploited. In short, an organization, the International Seabed Authority, was established, consisting of an Assembly, made up of all contracting parties, and a Council, consisting of 36 States selected in accordance with special criteria. The activities of exploration or exploitation were to be carried out either by the Enterprise (an organ of the Authority also charged with transporting, processing, and marketing the minerals recovered from the Area), or by States parties, State enterprises, or natural or juridical persons having the nationality of, or being controlled by, a State party. When entities other than the Enterprise carried out the various activities, they could do so only after receiving an authorization for production from the Authority. Each area for which an entity might apply was to be divided into two parts: one to be exploited by the applicant, the other by the Enterprise. As for the modalities for sharing the financial or other economic benefits, under Article 160 the question was left to the Assembly for future decision. It was only provided that the sharing should be 'equitable' and that one ought to take into account 'the interests and needs of developing States and peoples who have not attained full independence or other self-governing status'.

Industrialized countries firmly opposed the new concepts. Led by the US, the UK, and Japan, they criticized this legal regime, on many grounds: (i) it did not ensure access to seabed minerals; (ii) majority voting did not enable industrialized States, which would have to bear the brunt of costly research and exploitation, to have a proportionate role in decision making; (iii) the legal regime of transfer of technology by industrialized countries to the Enterprise and developing States would be contrary to the free play of market forces and penalize the former category of States. This opposition prevented the UNCLOS from entering into force.

A breakthrough occurred in 1994, when States reached agreement on a text designed to revise Part XI of the UNCLOS. Thanks to this revision, an increasing number of States ratified the Convention, which entered into force in 1994. The agreement adopted in 1994 hinges on the following points: (i) the Authority shall be set up gradually, and its costs for member States will be kept at a minimum; (ii) there is no longer an obligation for States to finance the Enterprise (previously it had been provided that States parties were to grant the Enterprise long-term, interest-free loans designed to cover 50 per cent of the cost of exploring and exploiting a site in the Area, of treating and marketing the minerals retrieved, besides covering the initial administration expenses); (iii) the Enterprise is now subject to market forces; both its funding and its operations are subject to cost-effectiveness criteria; (iv) in conformity with a new voting system, the Authority's Council can no longer impose its decisions on matters that States (in particular, industrialized States) deem contrary to their interests; (v) there is no longer an obligation to transfer technology to the Enterprise or to those developing countries which apply for a contract.

In practice, the exploration of the Area has been conducted by private companies 'sponsored' by a limited number of States. In 2010, the Council of the International Seabed Authority requested an Advisory Opinion to the ITLOS Seabed Chamber on the responsibilities of States sponsoring activities in the Area. The Opinion, rendered in

February 2011, made clear that such States do not have strict liability for the potential damage caused by the sponsored entities but only a duty of due diligence, which the Chamber defined in demanding terms (requiring both the adoption of appropriate measures and their proactive enforcement) but which remains an obligation of conduct and not of result.[99]

Thus, although the notion of the common heritage of mankind has not been abandoned, in practice all its major implications for developing countries, with regard to seabed resources, have been watered down to such an extent that one may well wonder when and how this bold concept will be translated into reality. At present, a similar script is being replayed, this time in connection with marine genetic resources and, more broadly, biodiversity beyond national jurisdiction (BBNJ). A revised version of the old tension identified by Pardo between a scramble for appropriation, formulated as the maintenance of the freedom of exploitation of such resources in the high seas, and the characterization of BBNJ, including marine genetic resources, as the common heritage of mankind, has emerged in the last decade, and it is now at the heart of ongoing negotiations on a new agreement.[100]

5.6 THE LAW OF AIRSPACE

Traditionally, States have claimed sovereignty over the whole of their airspace. This of course was theoretical until balloons and then aircraft began to be used. At present each State enjoys exclusive sovereignty over the airspace above its territory and territorial sea as a matter of customary international law.[101] There is no agreed-upon determination of the height of airspace. As a British Minister of State put it in 1999, 'The UK does not have a working definition of the upper limit of UK airspace, but for practical purposes the limit is considered to be at least as high as any aircraft can fly.'[102] No foreign State may fly through its airspace without prior permission or authorization. Overflight by foreign aircraft is allowed under bilateral or multilateral agreements.

The international legal regime arising from this network of agreements makes a broad distinction between State (governmental) and civil aircraft and, within the latter, between aircraft engaged in scheduled international air services (the main bone of contention) and the rest. The 1944 Chicago Convention on International Civil Aviation[103] recognized, in its Article 1, the sovereignty of States over their airspace, and it clearly states that it applies to civil aircraft only (Article 3). For civil aircraft of one of the contracting parties, it provides for two (out of five) of the so-called 'freedoms of the air', namely 'the right, subject to the observance of the terms of this Convention, *to make flights into or in transit non-stop across its territory* and *to make stops for non-traffic purposes without the necessity of obtaining prior permission*, and subject to the right of the State flown over to require landing'. Importantly, these rights are not recognized to 'aircraft engaged in scheduled international air services'. For the latter, a regime of bilateral and sometimes multilateral agreements (known as air services agreements) has been negotiated by States to extend these two freedoms to scheduled international air services as well as to grant, depending on the case, three additional commercial freedoms, namely the rights to put down, in the territory of

---

[99] *Responsibilities and Obligations of States Sponsoring Persons and Entities with Respect to Activities in the Area*, §§107–120.
[100] See Dupuy and Viñuales, *International Environmental Law*, 244–7.
[101] *Nicaragua (Nicaragua v United States)*, §212.
[102] See (1999) 70 *BYIL* 520.
[103] Chicago Convention on International Civil Aviation, 7 December 1944, 15 UNTS 295.

the granting State, traffic coming from the home State of the carrier (third freedom); to take on, in the territory of the granting State, traffic destined for the home State of the carrier (fourth freedom); and to put down and take on, in the territory of the granting State, traffic coming from or destined to a third State (fifth freedom).[104] An important precedent for the design of air services agreements was the so-called Bermuda Agreement, signed between the US and the UK in 1946, which mutually granted, subject to some specifications, the five freedoms of the air to the respective carriers. The agreement was replaced in 1977 with a more restrictive one (so-called Bermuda II), but it is noteworthy for its influence over the approach followed by hundreds of other air services agreements concluded by other States.

The system of the 1944 Chicago Convention is managed by an international organization established by it, the International Civil Aviation Organization (ICAO), which can perform a dispute settlement function. By way of illustration, following the severe restrictions on air movement to and from Qatar imposed in June 2017 by Bahrain, Egypt, Saudi Arabia, and the United Arab Emirates, Qatar brought the dispute (concerning both the Chicago Convention and a multilateral air services agreement) before the ICAO Council under Article 84 of the Chicago Convention. In a decision rendered on 29 June 2018, the Council sided with Qatar, prompting Bahrain, Egypt, Saudi Arabia, and the UAE to file an application with the ICJ 'appealing' against that decision, as per the terms of Article 84 of the Chicago Convention, on the grounds that the Council lacked jurisdiction to render the decision. The dispute was pending at the time of writing.

The powers of States over their airspace have also been discussed in other fora. In 2011, the Court of Justice of the European Union (CJEU), upon a referral from a UK court, took position on the legality of the extension of a European Union Directive creating an emissions trading scheme (the ETS Directive) to aircraft arriving at/departing from the EU (Case C-366/10 *Air Transport Association of America and others v Secretary of State for Energy and Climate Change*). In assessing the legality of the extension, the Court (Grand Chamber) reviewed *inter alia* the principles of international customary law relating to the sovereignty of each State over its airspace and the freedom to fly over the high seas. It noted the customary grounding of these principles (at §104) and even recognized that they could be directly relied upon by individuals to challenge the validity of an EU act (at §109). It concluded in this regard that the EU had jurisdiction over the carriers of third States to the extent that the latter had chosen to operate a commercial route arriving at or departing from the EU. It further observed that the fact that EU law (the extension of the ETS Directive) applied partly to events taking place beyond the EU airspace did not call into question the validity of the act (at §§121–130).

More recently, the measures taken by States around the world to contain the spread of COVID-19, which include drastic restrictions on air traffic, illustrate the interactions between the international law of air traffic and international health law. Chapter 2 of Annex 9 to the Chicago Convention, on the 'Entry and Departure of Aircraft', states that 'Contracting States shall not prevent an aircraft from calling at any international airport for public health reasons unless such action is taken in accordance with the International Health Regulations (2005) of the World Health Organization' (at §2.4). In turn, Article 43 of the International Health Regulations (2005) sets certain standards of scientific evidence for the justification of restrictive measures on international traffic. Given that, on 30 January 2020, the WHO declared COVID-19 to be 'a public health emergency of international concern' and subsequently, on 11 March 2020, declared it a global 'pandemic', there is a sufficient basis for the adoption of short-term measures to contain the outbreak.

---

[104] See ICAO, *Manual on the Regulation of International Air Transport* (Doc. 9626, Part 4).

However, ICAO has issued guidelines on 'Aviation and COVID-19', recalling that 'longer-term restrictions are normally not effective once appropriate containment measures are in place' and that, under the International Health Regulations, States adopting such measures are required to inform the WHO about them. Thus, the powers of States to regulate air traffic are not unconstrained, even in the case of health emergencies.

5.7 THE LAW OF OUTER SPACE

As stated earlier, outer space is the space around the earth beyond an altitude still undefined. According to some commentators, it starts between 90 and 100 miles above the earth; according to others, it comprises the space beyond the height to which aircraft can ascend in the atmosphere while 'deriving support from the reactions of the air'. In 1999 the British Minister of Science stated that '[t]here is no established definition of the height at which airspace ends and outer space begins'.[105]

Theoretically, until the first rockets and satellites were launched into outer space in 1957, under the *usque ad sidera* principle (see **5.1**) each State had sovereign rights over its own portion of outer space. However, as soon as the USSR and the US began launching rockets and orbiting satellites, a consensus instantly emerged to the effect that they were not required to ask for the authorization of the States above whose territory the satellites were orbiting. All States bowed to the technological superiority of the two Powers and gave up their theoretical rights of jurisdiction over their respective outer space. As a consequence, outer space was immediately considered open to everybody for exploration and use (*res communis omnium*). In the following years the UN General Assembly approved a number of resolutions, in particular resolution 1721 (XVI) of 20 December 1961, the Declaration adopted by resolution 1962 (XVIII) of 13 December 1963, and the 1967 Treaty on Principles Governing the Activities of States in the Exploration and Use of Outer Space. Together with the 1979 Agreement Governing the Activities of States on the Moon and Other Celestial Bodies, they laid down a set of rules which, being unopposed and indeed universally accepted, may be deemed to have become part of customary law. The basic principles of the legal regime of outer space are as follows: (i) it is not subject to national appropriation by claim of sovereignty, by means of use or occupation, or by any other means; (ii) its exploration and use must be carried out 'for the benefit and in the interests of all countries, irrespective of their degree of economic or scientific development', and shall be 'the province of all mankind' (Article 1 of the 1967 Treaty and Article 4 of the 1979 Treaty); (iii) it must not be used to put into orbit round the earth, or station in any other manner, objects carrying nuclear weapons or other weapons of mass destruction.

Clearly, States did not go beyond the concept of *res communis omnium*.[106] Except for the ban on orbiting weapons of mass destruction and damaging the environment, outer space was placed under a legal regime akin to that of the high seas. The notion that the exploration and use of outer space is 'the province of all mankind' is an emphatic proposition which should not lead one to believe that outer space is subject to the legal regime of

---

[105] See (1999) 70 *BYIL* 521.

[106] As the British Under-Secretary of State for the Foreign Office stated in 1999, when asked about the legal status of outer space, 'Article 2 of the 1967 Outer Space Treaty precludes national appropriation of outer space by claim of sovereignty. Therefore, outer space cannot be *res nullius*, which would connote territory capable of appropriation. In the light of the other provisions of the Outer Space Treaty, particularly Article 2, the generally accepted view is that outer space is *res communis* like the high seas' (in (1999) 70 *BYIL* 521).

the 'common heritage of mankind'. Indeed, States exploring and using the area in question are under no specific obligation to carry out these activities in the interest of all mankind. And it is well known that major Powers are using outer space primarily, if not exclusively, in their own interests (except, of course, for certain obligations of co-operation undertaken by treaty with a few other countries).

The 1979 Treaty on the Moon and Other Celestial Bodies, the provisions of which have to a large extent become customary law, provides that all substances originating in the moon and other celestial bodies are to be regarded as natural resources belonging to the common heritage of mankind (see Articles 4(1) and 11(1)). In the event, the treaty only commanded unanimous support, after initial strong opposition from some major Powers, because the crucial point concerning the concept of common heritage, namely the question of how to share the benefits deriving from the exploitation of resources in outer space, was left unresolved.

5.8 CONCLUDING OBSERVATIONS

In the international legal regulation of territory and other spaces, more than in any other area, the tension and conflict between a traditional, State sovereignty-oriented approach and a modern, community-oriented outlook have come to the fore. However, here more than in any other area self-interest and individualism have eventually gained the upper hand even at the *legal* level. As we shall see in **Chapters 18**, **19**, and **20**, in other fields notable advances have been made at least on the legal plane; although they have not yet been fully matched by progress in practice, still legal tools are available to States enabling them to take a new path, if they so wish. The legal regulation of space has instead remained under the aegis of the 'each for himself' principle. The launching of the common heritage of mankind paradigm should not lead one to believe that, at least there, some community interest was propounded. In fact, the real lynchpin of the concept, the idea of equitable sharing of profits, was advanced in the exclusive, or primary, interest of developing countries and contrary to the interests of industrialized States. It is striking that at the very time developing countries appropriated the exclusive economic zone, they also declared that the ocean floor beyond that zone was part of the common heritage of mankind. One cannot but infer that, with regard to the exclusive economic zone, even poor coastal States preferred to appropriate those resources, on the assumption that they would be able to exploit them directly or through agreements with developed States. In the area beyond that zone, being deprived of the technological means required for exploration and exploitation, developing countries urged instead that States able to do so should act in the interests of everyone. The conclusion is warranted that they acted out of national self-interest, more than on behalf of humankind.

Nevertheless, as the concept is still embodied in Part XI of the UNCLOS as revised in 1994, as well as in the 1979 Treaty on the Moon, it remains possible that gradually, through patient and realistic compromise, it may be turned into a set of legal provisions and institutions designed to meet the needs of all countries, in particular those that are less advanced.

6
IMMUNITIES OF STATES AND STATE OFFICIALS

6.1 SOVEREIGNTY AND IMMUNITIES

State sovereignty under international law is expressed and guaranteed in several ways. One of the most distinctive traits of international law in this regard is that a sovereign State cannot rule, or otherwise exercise sovereign powers, over another equally sovereign State (see **3.2**). This notion is formulated emphatically in the Latin expressions according to which States are those entities '*quia superiorem non recognoscens*' and that '*par in parem non habet imperium*'. As discussed in **Chapter 4**, States are by definition entities that do not recognize any authority above them and operate among themselves on a formally equal footing under international law.

On the basis of the original character of statehood and of State sovereignty, as the pinnacle of authority on a given portion of the globe, no State can be subjected to the jurisdiction of another State. This implies—as a matter of legal principle (which today recognizes several exceptions as we shall see later in the chapter)—that foreign States are generally not subjected to the municipal laws of other States, that they cannot be brought to justice before the domestic courts of other States, and that they must not be subjected to enforcement measures under the national laws of other States. Moreover, as a further distinct corollary of State sovereignty, as we shall see later (see **6.3**), the agents of the State (State organs and State officials above all) are entitled to (a certain measure of) immunity, in particular for their official acts, but in certain specific instances (and for particular categories of officials) also for private acts.

The general rule under international law is thus that foreign States and foreign State officials are not subject to the legislative, executive, and judicial powers of other States. That said, it is undeniable that, since the beginning of the twentieth century, a number of exceptions to this general rule have progressively developed and, in parallel with the elaboration of a more tempered and more accountable notion of State sovereignty (see **4.5**), State immunity—albeit still fundamental under international law—is no longer seen as a monolithic sacred totem.

6.2 STATE IMMUNITIES FROM JURISDICTION AND EXECUTION

6.2.1 JURISDICTIONAL IMMUNITY

The doctrine of immunity of foreign States from the jurisdiction of the forum State is grounded on a twofold rationale. First, States must not interfere with public acts of other sovereign States out of respect for their independence, and on account of the principle of sovereign equality of States. Secondly, generally speaking and with regard to both domestic decisions and decisions made by foreign countries, the judiciary should not interfere with the conduct of foreign policy by either national or foreign governmental authorities, on the principle of the separation of powers. It follows that it is not for courts, but for the organs responsible for foreign affairs, to take matters relating to foreign acts into their own hands and use diplomatic channels to discuss, or argue over, them with the foreign State concerned.

These doctrines have been set out in many cases. For instance, in the celebrated *Underhill v Hernandez* case, in 1897, the US Supreme Court stated that '[e]very sovereign State is bound to respect the independence of every other sovereign State, and the courts of one country cannot sit in judgment on the acts of the government of another done within its own territory' (at 195).[1] In 1880, in *The Parlement belge*, the British Court of Appeal had taken the same stance. There had been a collision in British territorial waters between a Belgian postal vessel and a British steam-tug. The owners of the British vessel instituted an action of damage. The Admiralty Division, *per* Sir Robert Phillimore, held that the Belgian ship, although it performed a public function, did not belong to 'that category of public vessels, which are exempt from process of law and all private claims' (at 318). The Court of Appeal reversed the decision. It held that:

> as a consequence of the absolute independence of every sovereign authority, and of the international comity which induces every sovereign state to respect the independence and dignity of every other sovereign state, each and every one declines to exercise by means of its courts any of its territorial jurisdiction over the person of any sovereign or ambassador of any other state, or over the public property of any state which is destined to public use, or over the property of any ambassador, though such sovereign, ambassador, or property be within its territory, and therefore, but for the common agreement, subject to its jurisdiction. (at 331)

A century later, in *Buttes Gas and Oil Co. v Hammer and others*, the British House of Lords, *per* Lord Wilberforce, held that the transactions of foreign sovereign States 'are not issues upon which a municipal court can pass' (at 107).

In the past the immunity of foreign States was absolute (like sovereignty in a way). Then, gradually, towards the end of the nineteenth century a more restrictive view took shape. An exception was envisaged for acts performed *jure gestionis* or *jure privatorum*, that is, performed by a foreign State in a private capacity as a legal person subject to private law. This new trend took hold in the case law of Belgium and Italy.[2] This phenomenon has been variously accounted for. In 1958, in *Rahimtoola v Nizam of Hyderabad* Lord Denning noted that 'in all civilized countries there has been a progressive tendency towards making the sovereign liable to be sued in his own courts . . . Foreign sovereigns should not be in any different position' (at 418). In a more elaborate manner, in 1981, Lord Wilberforce held in *I Congreso del Partido* that the restrictive theory:

> arises from the willingness of States to enter into commercial, or other private law, transactions with individuals. It appears to have two main foundations: (a) it is necessary in the interests of justice to individuals having transactions with States to allow them to bring such transactions before the courts; (b) to require a State to answer a claim based on such transactions does not involve a challenge or inquiry into any act of sovereignty or governmental act of that State. It is, in accepted phrases, neither a threat to the dignity of that State nor any interference with its sovereign functions. (at 307)

---

[1] The *Underhill v Hernandez* case is at the origin of the 'Act of State' doctrine, which developed in the US and some other countries. The leading case on the matter is the US Supreme Court's decision in *Banco Nacional de Cuba v Sabbatino*, whilst other cases envisage exceptions (e.g. *Alfred Dunhill of London, Inc. v Republic of Cuba*) for commercial acts, and *Forti v Suarez-Mason* (for human rights violations).

[2] As for Belgian case law, see *Rau, Vanden Abel v Duruty*, 175, and *Chemin de fer Liégeois-Luxembourg v État néerlandais*, 301–3. For Italian case law, see *Typaldos v Manicomio di Aversa*, 1492–3, and *Bey di Tunisi rappresentato da Guttieres v Elmilik*, 1544–5.

Be that as it may, it is a fact that the tendency acquired increasing importance after the First World War, particularly after the growing participation of Soviet authorities in commercial transactions, a practice that has also spread to all modern States. At present, almost all States embrace the doctrine of restrictive immunity.[3] It would seem that only China and some Latin American States still cling to the old doctrine of absolute immunity. The doctrine currently prevailing holds that acts performed *jure gestionis*, that is, private or commercial transactions of States, are subject to foreign jurisdiction. In contrast, acts performed *jure imperii*, that is by the foreign State in its capacity as a sovereign, are immune.

However, leaving aside so-called 'sovereign acts', how can one define acts performed by a foreign State in a private capacity? Two different criteria have been suggested. One is based on the *nature* of the foreign act, the other on the *function* that the act is intended to fulfil. Yet, resort to these standards may lead to conflicting results. For example, if a foreign State purchases goods for use by its armed forces, this act, if assessed by the first standard, may be considered as being private in nature, and hence lead to denial of immunity. In contrast, if one looks at the purpose for which the goods have been acquired, one ought to emphasize the public nature of the act, and consequently to uphold immunity. The difficulty of drawing a clear-cut distinction has prompted States to spell out the doctrine of immunity and to enumerate the possible exceptions. This has been done in both national legislation (see e.g. Articles 1604 and 1605 of the US Act and sections 1 and 2 of the UK Act) and in international instruments such as the United Nations Convention on Jurisdictional Immunities of States and Their Property.[4]

6.2.2 EMPLOYMENT DISPUTES

A particular sector where issues concerning immunities have developed is the area of employment disputes. Respect for the independence and sovereignty of foreign States requires among other things that a State must not interfere with or meddle in their internal organization. In 1997, in *Blaškić (subpoena)*, the ICTY Appeals Chamber stated that 'it is well known that customary international law protects the internal organization of each sovereign State; it leaves [it] to each sovereign to determine its internal structure and in particular to designate the individuals acting as State organs or agents' (at §41). It follows that a State may not sit in judgment over employment relationships between individuals (whether or not nationals of the local State) and foreign States. Hence, for many years national courts have held that, whenever employment contracts with organs and institutions of foreign States (e.g. embassies, consulates, cultural centres) relate to the public functions of those States, they may not be subject to the jurisdiction of the forum territory. These courts have relied upon the old distinction between acts performed *jure gestionis* and those performed *jure imperii* (e.g. the European Court of Human Rights in *Fogarty v United Kingdom*). However, the vagaries of case law have caused great uncertainties.

---

[3] See e.g. the US Foreign Sovereign Immunities Act 1976, as amended in 1988, and part of the US Code, Article 1605(a)(2); the UK State Immunity Act 1978, section 2; Canada's State Immunity Act 1985, section 5; Australia's Foreign Sovereign Immunities Act 1985, section 11.

[4] Pursuant to Article 10 of the Convention, States do not enjoy immunity from jurisdiction when they engage in a 'commercial transaction' with a foreign natural or legal person. Under Article 2(1)(c) 'commercial transaction' means: (a) any commercial contract or transaction for the sale of goods or supply of services; (b) any contract for a loan or other transaction of a financial nature, including any obligation of guarantee or of indemnity in respect of any such loan or transaction; (c) any other contract or transaction, of a commercial, industrial, trading, or professional nature, but not including a contract of employment of persons.

What is even more important, whenever State courts uphold immunity the individuals who had instituted proceedings may end up having no judicial remedy at all to vindicate their rights. Thus, a serious infringement of fundamental human rights may ensue: indeed, the prevailing doctrine of human rights upholds the right of every individual to have judicial remedies available for safeguarding his substantive rights.

As a result of these new concerns, the traditional distinction gradually loosened. First, courts placed greater emphasis on the private nature of employment contracts. For instance, Brussels labour courts held that both in making and in terminating a contract of employment a foreign embassy acts as a private individual; it does not exercise a public function but performs an ordinary commercial act. In *Rousseau v Republic of Upper Volta* the Brussels Labour Court held that the employment of a Belgian driver at a foreign embassy involved manual labour and therefore 'was an act of ordinary affairs rather than an act of public power'.[5] It is notable that the nationality of the employee is not necessarily relevant, with the consequence that State immunity from the foreign jurisdiction may not be relied upon whether or not the employee has the same nationality as the State against which the claim is brought. Thus, in 1992, in *De Guieros Magalhaes Abrantes v Republic of Portugal* the Brussels Labour Court held that a Portuguese employed as a language teacher at the Portuguese embassy in Belgium was entitled to sue Portugal for unfair dismissal.

Secondly, courts have drawn a distinction between activities of persons employed by foreign agencies that are ancillary to the public functions of the foreign entities (this applied e.g. to cleaners, plumbers, and other workers), and those that are instead directly related to the discharge of those functions (think e.g. of persons fulfilling security duties).[6] Or else courts have drawn a distinction between labour disputes that revolve around compensation or patrimonial matters, and those relating to the power of the foreign agency to terminate a labour contract.[7]

Thirdly, international instruments tend to provide safer and more objective criteria for establishing whether or not a foreign State enjoys immunity from jurisdiction. For instance, Article 5(1) of the 1972 European Convention on State Immunity[8] provides that '[a] Contracting State cannot claim immunity from the jurisdiction of a court of another Contracting State if the proceedings relate to a contract of employment between the State and an individual where the work has to be performed on the territory of the State of the forum'. But, in some cases, this waiver of immunity is not applicable. Article 5(2) thus maintains the immunity of jurisdiction in some cases when a waiver is not justified as a result of the nationality of employee or of the lack of previous connection with the State of the forum or, still, in case the employment contract states otherwise, although the latter possibility remains specifically circumscribed. Article 11 of the UN Convention on Jurisdictional Immunities of States,[9] on the other hand, takes a broadly similar approach. It first provides that no immunity may be claimed for contracts of employment if the work must be performed 'in whole or in part' in the territory of the forum State. It then enumerates some exceptions to this waiver: (i) when 'the employee has been recruited to perform

---

[5] *Rousseau v Republic of Upper Volta*, 118. See also *Kingdom of Morocco v DR*, 421 (relating to a Portuguese national employed as a chauffeur by the Moroccan Embassy in Brussels); *François v State of Canada*, 418 (relating to a Belgian technician employed by the Embassy of Canada).

[6] See in this vein the decision of the Italian Court of Cassation in *Luna v Repubblica socialista di Romania*, 597–9.

[7] See e.g. the decision of the Italian Court of Cassation in *Consolato generale britannnico in Napoli v Toglia*, 690–1; *Giamahira Araba Libica v Trobbiani*, 405; *Ambasciata di Norvegia v Quattri*, 997; *Ecole française de Rome v Guadagnino*, 817–18; and *Perrini v Académie de France à Rome*, 230–1.

[8] European Convention on State Immunity, 16 May 1972, ETS No. 74.

[9] UN Convention on Jurisdictional Immunities of States and Their Property, 2 December 2004, UN Doc. A/RES/59/38.

functions closely related to the exercise of governmental authority'; (ii) when 'the subject of the proceedings is the recruitment, renewal or reinstatement of an individual'; (iii) when the employee 'was neither a national nor a habitual resident of the State of the forum at the time when the contract of employment was concluded'; (iv) when 'the employee is a national of the employer State at the time when the proceeding is instituted'; and (v) when 'the employer State and the employee have otherwise agreed in writing, subject to any considerations of public policy conferring on the courts of the State of the forum exclusive jurisdiction by reason of the subject matter of the proceeding'.

All in all, one can discern in the case law and in international instruments a tendency to restrict foreign immunity. This tendency is closely related to the growing concern with the need to grant individuals the right to a judicial remedy against any alleged breach of law.

6.2.3 JURISDICTIONAL IMMUNITY AND *JUS COGENS*

One important question that needs to be tackled is whether peremptory norms of international law (*jus cogens*) may authorize national courts to set aside State immunity. We will see (see **11.4**) that there exist in international law customary rules endowed with a special legal force. They cannot be derogated from by treaty or customary rules. Rules that are inconsistent with a peremptory norm are therefore invalid. For present purposes, the question is whether the existence of peremptory norms can preclude the application of the general rule on State immunity from jurisdiction, and consequently allow a State court to pronounce on acts performed by a foreign State in its public and official capacity. The problem may arise when courts are requested to pronounce on claims for compensation for foreign acts allegedly breaching peremptory norms.

At the dawn of the twenty-first century, domestic and international case law in this respect oscillates between, on the one hand, the aspiration to allow for justice for victims to be achieved by setting aside immunity in specific cases of serious violations of peremptory norms of international law and, on the other hand, the need to respect traditional law by recognizing that State immunity is not to be taken lightly and that justice is not necessarily best achieved through adjudication by foreign national courts.

The European Court of Human Rights already in 2001 in the *Al-Adsani v United Kingdom* case,[10] and more recently in *Jones and others v United Kingdom* (at §§186–189, 215), considered that granting State immunity even in cases of serious human rights violations did not necessarily amount to a violation of the ECHR and the right of victims to have access to justice.

However, the main blow to the efforts to defeat State immunity in case of violations of *jus cogens* came from the International Court of Justice (ICJ). Overall the debate seems to have been closed by the view taken by the ICJ in its judgment of 3 February 2012 in *Jurisdictional Immunities (Germany v Italy)*, which appears to have swung the pendulum towards the protection of sovereign immunities. The case was introduced by Germany, which filed an application with the Court on 23 December 2008, following a string of decisions by Italian courts which had set aside immunity for war crimes and crimes against humanity

---

[10] The issue in *Al-Adsani v United Kingdom* revolved around torture. According to the claimant, the general rule prohibiting torture, as well as the corresponding provision of the Convention (Article 3), belong to *jus cogens*. Hence, a foreign State, if sued before a national court for the alleged violation of those rules, is barred from invoking immunity from jurisdiction. However, in 2001, the European Court held, with many judges dissenting, that in spite of the peremptory nature of the prohibition of torture, State immunity from jurisdiction may not be set aside (at §66).

committed by the German Reich in 1944–45. In deciding the case, the ICJ eventually took the view that Italian courts had violated Germany's immunity from jurisdiction. The Court affirmed that even assuming the *jus cogens* nature of the norms violated, this would not authorize the exercise of jurisdiction over a foreign State. In support, the Court cited several domestic court cases of other States which recognized priority to immunity even in cases of alleged violations of *jus cogens* and stated that '... none of the legislation on State immunity considered [by the Court] in §§70–71 [of its judgment], has limited immunity in cases where violations of *jus cogens* are alleged' (at §96). For the Court, immunity operates in the procedural world while the nature of a rule as belonging to a core of imperative norms is a different matter, operating at the substantive level (at §92). This decision—even if it left several questions unanswered—seems to have found broad approval, at least among States. In essence the Court rejected any form of deductive reasoning (i.e. drawing consequences from the fact that there is a core of principles expressing fundamental values) and, by highlighting the lack of State practice (other than in Italy and Greece), the Court concluded that no derogation to State immunity is permitted on these grounds. The Court finally expressed regret that not all victims were properly compensated but concluded that it was not possible for domestic courts to deal with such an issue and invited the two States to negotiate appropriately (at §99).

At the international level this judgment has undermined the prospects that State immunity may be set aside for massive violations of human rights, or humanitarian law, and brought the debate back to the late 1990s. The Italian government took immediate measures to implement the judgment and the parliament approved a law to this effect. Yet, cases were still pending before Italian courts relating to the underlying crimes and, in 2014, the Italian Constitutional Court, which had been seized by some of the judges hearing those cases, declared the domestic provisions implementing the ICJ judgment null and void because they were in conflict with fundamental values protected by the Italian Constitution (Sentenza no. 238/2014). In so doing, the Italian Court 'rejected' the view propounded by the ICJ and supported a different interpretation of the relationship between fundamental principles of international law and of course, above all, fundamental principles of Italian constitutional law. In brief, the Italian Court concluded that Italy incorporates in its legal order (through Article 10 of its Constitution) the important customary principle of State immunity. This rule largely prevails over all domestic rules, including many constitutional provisions. However, it cannot prevail automatically over equally fundamental principles contained in the Constitution, such as those referring to the proscription of international crimes (e.g. genocide, crimes against humanity, and war crimes) and the protection of fundamental rights, including access to justice for victims of these crimes. As a result of these limitations, the 'absolute' understanding of State immunity expressed by the ICJ cannot 'enter' the Italian legal order and hence those domestic provisions implementing the judgment were considered (to that limited extent) to be contrary to the Constitution and nullified.

It is difficult to anticipate whether the pendulum will oscillate back to a more balanced and nuanced position on the relationship between State immunity and egregious violations of fundamental rights. There can be little doubt that, in the future, there will be further developments. The need to provide relief to victims of atrocities is an issue that can hardly be satisfied through the mere recognition of 'immunity', without any path for accountability, and the expectation that agreed solutions can be reached through negotiations (without any further specification). It is not clear at this stage that State immunity must yield to norms of *jus cogens*. Nevertheless, the debate is far from being closed. In the past, there have been precedents which can be taken into account as the reasoning underlying those decisions may still bear some relevance,[11] and further evolution of the practice and the norms might still take place, in particular in the light of work undertaken by the ILC on the topics of *jus cogens* as well as immunity of State officials from criminal jurisdiction.[12] In addition, recent developments attest that State practice in this area is continuing to evolve under the pressure of the need to provide victims with some avenues to obtain justice. For example, in 2016 in the US, legislation was passed allowing courts to set aside immunity for cases brought against States sponsoring terrorist acts.[13] Moreover, it is not always necessary to have a wealth of authorities and State practice available before asserting that *jus cogens* norms override contrary customary rules. This in particular holds true when peremptory norms are intended to protect fundamental values of the international community that are currently regarded as important enough to override traditional State concerns protected by rules on State immunities. Furthermore, and quite remarkably, in the case of torture and other international crimes (all prohibited by rules of *jus cogens*) the customary rule on the immunity of State agents (so-called functional immunity; see **6.3.2**) is disallowed and the State agent is held personally accountable for a breach of the international rule. If the violation of a general rule of *jus cogens* entails that the individual author is no longer protected by the customary rule on functional immunity (a corollary of the general rule on State immunity from any foreign interference in the internal organization of the State), it is difficult to see why the rule on State immunity from jurisdiction should not yield to *jus cogens* in similar situations.

The potential effects of the Italian immunity cases and other similarly progressive stances on sovereign immunity from jurisdiction in cases of serious violations of international law have certainly been limited by the ICJ judgment in the *Jurisdictional immunities (Germany v Italy)* case. However, a key aspect in those cases was the role of deductive reasoning, which highlights the need for judges to balance fundamental principles in specific and concrete cases. According to that line of reasoning, it would be possible to draw some consequences from principles that enshrine fundamental values in the name of the international community as a whole. It would seem that in deliberating over the *Jurisdictional immunities* case, the ICJ might have had broader 'law-making' concerns (concerns for the stability of the international legal order) rather than simply an eye to solving the specific case. In fact, the Court could not examine the dispute in its entirety, since it (rather abruptly) declined to hear Italy's counterclaim (ICJ Order 6 July 2010). The Court ended up being more preoccupied with the broader effects that could ensue from the recognition of a general rule that would allow domestic judges to set aside State immunity when confronted with international crimes (without any possibility of international control), and hence it preferred to adopt a conservative stance. The reference to the need for 'further negotiation involving the two States concerned' rests on the same due deference to State sovereignty that inspires the rest of the judgment, with its emphasis on the

---

[11] See e.g. the case law cited in the Appendix to the Annex Report, dated 6 July 1999, of the ILC Working Group, which noted the existence of such a practice indicating that States are not entitled to plead immunity where there has been a violation of human rights norms with the character of *jus cogens*: *Al-Adsani v Government of Kuwait*, 471; *Controller and Auditor General v Sir Ronald Davidson*, particularly at 290 (*per* Cooke P.); Dissenting Opinion of Justice Wald in *Princz v Federal Republic of Germany*, 1176–85; *Rein v Libya*; *Cicippio v Islamic Republic of Iran*; and the *Pinochet* case before the UK House of Lords.

[12] For a summary of the work of the ILC on the topic of *jus cogens* see https://legal.un.org/ilc/summaries/1_14.shtml and for *Immunity of State officials from foreign criminal jurisdiction*, see https://legal.un.org/ilc/summaries/4_2.shtml.

[13] See the Justice Against Sponsors of Terrorism Act (JASTA), which allows for immunity to be set aside in civil claims brought by American victims of acts of terrorism against States associated with such acts (designated as sponsors of terrorism by the State Department). The US Administration (which has been critical of the Act) tried to block this Act; however the veto by President Obama was eventually overturned by Congress and Senate with large majorities on 28 September 2016.

intergovernmental nature of international law. The same can be said of the Court's view that '[i]mmunity cannot be made dependent upon the outcome of a balancing exercise of the specific circumstances of each case to be conducted by the national court before which immunity is claimed' (but one may wonder whether the vindication of rights can be made dependent upon the discretion of governments). What appears to be at stake is the proper role of domestic courts, particularly when they carry out a balancing of interests on the basis of deductive reasoning, which leaves the final decision outside the hands of governments.

Thus, a traditional vision of State sovereignty emerges from the ICJ judgment, which paves the way for an enhanced protection for States and sacrifices access to justice for victims of serious human rights violations. Some caveats could have been placed; and some (even forceful ones) appear in the Dissenting and Separate Opinions (see for example the Opinions of Judges Bennouna, Cançado Trindade, and Yusuf). Arguably, it could be said that sovereignty can be fully respected, by recognizing immunity, only on the condition that some mechanisms are put in place to ensure compliance with the obligation to provide remedial measures to victims of international crimes.[14] Ultimately what seems unreasonable in the solution proposed, and in the long run will inevitably continue to cause tensions between immunity and accountability, is a situation whereby States are shielded by immunity, hence preventing judicial scrutiny by courts (organs which have the general role of providing access to justice for the enforcement of rights). Governments are invited, or even placed under an obligation, to negotiate appropriate forms of reparation for victims; however, nothing is done in practice, and there is no consequence nor any remedy if they do not comply. Ultimately, such a situation creates a risk of lack of accountability, which is far from being satisfactory and in itself generates the seeds of further (judicial) unilateralism, which is what might have happened with the decision of Italy's Constitutional Court in 2014.

6.2.4 IMMUNITY FROM EXECUTION

Some final remarks need to be made on the issue of immunity of States from execution. Generally speaking, immunity from execution has been seen as running in parallel to immunity from jurisdiction. Thus, the distinction between private or commercial acts of States (*jure gestionis*) and acts performed in a sovereign capacity (*jure imperii*) is mirrored in the context of execution by a distinction between assets used or intended for use for a commercial (non-governmental) or public purpose.[15] For the former category immunity has been denied while it has been upheld for the latter.

That said, the parallelism between immunity from jurisdiction and immunity from execution, as far as the rationale for such immunities is concerned, is not rigid and watertight. Article 20 of the UN Convention on Jurisdictional Immunities of States specifically provides that 'where consent to measures of constraint is required under articles 18 [pre-judgment measures] and 19 [post-judgment measures], consent to the exercise of jurisdiction under article 7 shall not imply consent to the taking of measures of constraint'. As the measures involved in execution are more intrusive into foreign sovereignty than the exercise of jurisdiction, a tendency can be discerned in the case law to be more protective of State sovereignty in granting immunity from execution, both at the domestic and at the international level. The Italian Constitutional Court rightly emphasized this trend in its judgment of 1992 in *Condor e Filvem* v *Ministero di Grazia e Giustizia*, when it stated that 'for long in the legal conviction of States the *relative* character of immunity from

---

[14] This is also in line with the position reflected in Article 5 of the resolution on universal jurisdiction adopted by the *Institut de Droit International* at its 2015 session in Tallinn.

[15] See generally H. Fox and P. Webb, *The Law of State Immunity*, 3rd edn (Oxford: Oxford University Press, 2013), 479ff.

jurisdiction has emerged in contrast to the tendency of States to view execution as being *absolute* in nature' (at 398). At the international level, the International Tribunal for the Law of the Sea (ITLOS) considered, in the Order on Provisional Measures in *ARA Libertad (Argentina* v *Ghana)*, that the retention of an Argentine warship in a Ghanaian port following an attachment order issued by a Ghanaian court was inconsistent with the immunity enjoyed by this warship under general international law (at §§95 and 98).[16]

The fact that measures of constraint may be taken against property or assets of foreign States destined for a private function, that is, intended for use for commercial or other non-governmental purposes, has been considered by courts as the logical and inescapable consequence of the fact that otherwise courts could pronounce on the substantive rights in dispute but would lack the power to order measures to put those rights into effect.[17] In contrast, the property and assets of a foreign State cannot be seized, attached, or subject to any other measure of execution (whether before—by way of interim relief—or after judgment—enforcement proper) if such property or assets are intended for the discharge of public functions.[18]

Normally courts have held that execution measures may be taken against bank accounts belonging to foreign States. However, in the case of accounts opened by foreign diplomatic missions, domestic courts have generally considered that they are destined to accomplish public functions of the foreign State and therefore immune.[19] Some other categories of property or assets are generally considered to be destined for public functions and are therefore immune from execution.[20] These include property of a military character or intended for military use; property of the monetary authorities of a country (e.g. its Central Bank); cultural heritage or historical archives (unless intended to be placed on sale); or property part of an exhibition of scientific, cultural, or historical interest (again, unless intended for sale).

6.3 IMMUNITIES OF FOREIGN STATE OFFICIALS

6.3.1 TYPES OF IMMUNITIES

Another aspect of immunity which is worth considering is the protection recognized by international law to foreign officials. In practice, various categories of immunities often apply, sometimes cumulatively, to the same official, with the risk that some confusion might arise.

The first distinction that ought to be made is that between functional (or *ratione materiae*) and personal (*ratione personae*) immunities. The functional immunity essentially derives from the fact that States act through their agents, as human beings act through their organs;

---

[16] See S. El-Sawah and J. E. Viñuales, 'L'immunité d'exécution dans l'affaire de l'Ara Libertad devant le TIDM' (2013) 140 *Journal du droit international (Clunet)* 13.

[17] Thus e.g. the decision of the Swiss Federal Tribunal in *Royaume de Grèce* v *Banque Julius Bär et Cie*. Or the Italian Court of Cassation (judging in plenary) in *Giamahiria Araba Libica* v *Soc. Rossbeton*, at 693–6.

[18] Thus, §1609 of the US Foreign Sovereign Immunities Act of 1976 (as amended in 1988), and section 13(2) of the UK State Immunities Act of 1978.

[19] The German Constitutional Court took this stand in 1977 in *Philippine Embassy* (at 164), as did the House of Lords in 1984 in *Alcom Ltd* v *Republic of Colombia and others* (at 180ff) and the Swiss Foreign Department (in a note of 28 February 1991, where mention is made of a 'presumption' that foreign embassies' bank accounts are used for public purposes and consequently enjoy immunity from execution; see text in 2 *Schweizerische Zeitschrift für internationales und europäisches Recht* (1992), 570–2).

[20] UN Convention on Jurisdictional Immunities, Article 21(1).

hence the acts that these agents/organs of the State perform are to be attributed to the State not to the officials as such. Personal immunity is a special form of protection granted to certain agents/officials/organs on account of the specificities of their role (e.g. Heads of State and Government, Ministers of Foreign Affairs, diplomats, etc.).

The two categories of immunities differ in various respects: (i) unlike functional immunities, personal immunities cover private acts and transactions; (ii) personal immunities do not consist of exemptions from the substantive law of the receiving State, but only of exemption from the jurisdiction of its courts and enforcement of its enforcement agencies;[21] (iii) personal immunities only apply as between the sending and the receiving States (as well as in relation to the State through which a diplomatic agent is passing on his or her way to or from the receiving State), whereas functional immunities, besides being absolute (with the exception relating to international crimes), may be invoked towards *any other State*, that is, *erga omnes*; (iv) personal immunities cease with the cessation of the function, whereas functional immunities remain applicable even beyond the cessation of functions for any covered acts carried out during the performance of the function.

For all categories of personnel protected by some form of immunity, it is worth noting that immunity can be waived by their State, as immunities do not accrue to the individual as such (they are not intended as a benefit for the individual but derive from State sovereignty and are protected as part of the guarantees for respect of such sovereignty). It is also important to note that particular rules have emerged with respect to prosecutions for international crimes, and hence immunities in this area require a closer look.

6.3.2 FUNCTIONAL IMMUNITIES

All State officials enjoy functional immunity for acts performed in the exercise of their functions (except in the case of international crimes). The rule was first enunciated in the famous *McLeod* incident between the US and the UK. As the British law officers put it in 1854:

> The principle of international law that an individual doing a hostile act authorized and ratified by the government of which he is a Member [*scilicet*, a subject] cannot be held individually answerable as a private trespasser or malefactor, but that the Act becomes one for which the State to which he belongs is in such a case alone responsible, is a principle too well established to be now controversial.[22]

The ICTY Appeals Chamber restated the principle and set out its rationale in *Blaškić* (*subpoena*) as follows:

> [C]ustomary international law protects the internal organization of each sovereign State: it leaves it to each sovereign State to determine its internal structure and in particular to designate the individuals acting as State agents or organs. Each sovereign State has the right to issue instructions to its organs, both those operating at the internal level and those operating in the field of international relations, and also to provide for sanctions or other remedies in case of non-compliance with those instructions. The corollary of this exclusive power is that each State is entitled to claim that acts or transactions performed by one of its organs in its official capacity be attributed to the State, so that the individual organ may not be held accountable for those acts or transactions. The general rule under discussion is well established in international law and is based on the sovereign equality of States (*par in parem non habet imperium*) (at §§41–42).

---

[21] This proposition was enunciated, among others, by British courts. See e.g. *Dickinson v Del Solar*, at 142–4. In its decision of 31 July 1929, the King's Bench Division held that '[d]iplomatic privilege does not impart immunity from legal liability, but only exemption from local jurisdiction. The privilege is the privilege of the Sovereign by whom the diplomatic agent is accredited' (at 144).

[22] See Lord McNair, *Law Officers Opinions* (Cambridge: Cambridge University Press, 1956), ii, 230.

The right to immunity for acts performed by State officials in international relations is a logical consequence of the right of States to claim immunity from the jurisdiction of foreign States and has the same rationale, that is, the need to respect the sovereign rights and internal organization of foreign States. It follows that State officials performing official acts and transactions are exempt from the foreign substantive law. Their acts and transactions may not be attributed to them, but must be imputed to the State on whose behalf they have acted. Consequently, if the acts they carry out are in breach of international law, it is their State that incurs international responsibility. As the ICTY Appeals Chamber put it in *Blaškić (subpoena)*, State officials 'cannot suffer the consequence of wrongful acts which are not attributable to them personally but to the State on whose behalf they act' (at §38). If that act is also in breach of their national law, they may only be prosecuted and punished by their own national courts. Thus, for instance, if the pilot of a military aircraft deliberately and unlawfully enters foreign territory, he may not be held internationally responsible for this international breach; it will be his State that will be held accountable. Similarly, if a State official orders the taking of measures in violation of an international treaty (e.g. a bilateral investment treaty), he may not subsequently be personally sued for damage before the courts of the victim State whenever nationals of that State have suffered economic loss as a result of that breach of treaty. International responsibility lies with the State which acted through its official.

However, if the official act (i) is in breach of international law, (ii) is performed on the territory of the foreign State, and (iii) involves the commission of a serious criminal offence under the local legislation (e.g. murder), in addition to international responsibility for the State of which the individual is agent, there may arise a personal liability for that individual, or at any rate punitive measures may be inflicted upon the State agent. This rule was clearly applied in at least two cases: *McLeod*, in 1830,[23] and *Rainbow Warrior*, in 1985.[24] A more recent example could be the unlawful killing by a Saudi squad of the journalist Jamal Khashoggi in October 2018 in Turkish territory, within the premises of a Saudi consulate.

Another exception to immunity, broader than the previous one, relates to international crimes. As held by the ICTY Appeals Chamber in *Blaškić (subpoena)* (at §41),[25] State

---

[23] See the judgment delivered by the New York Supreme Court in *People v McLeod* in 1841. McLeod, in a writ of habeas corpus, had pleaded that (i) US courts lacked jurisdiction because he had acted in an official capacity, as a member of the British armed forces in Canada, and (ii) in any event he had an alibi, in that 'he was absent, and did not at all participate in the alleged offence' (at 263). The Court rejected the first objection (and considered it improper for it to consider the other ground), by noting that since there was no war between the US and Great Britain, the latter could not legally justify the murder committed by McLeod: 'She [England] cannot turn that into lawful war which was murder in time of peace. She may, in that way, justify the offender as between him and his own government. She cannot bind foreign courts of justice by insisting that what in the eye of the whole world was a deliberate and prepared attack, must be protected by the law of self-defence ... I deny that she can, in time of peace, send her men into our territory, and render them impervious to our laws, by embodying them and putting arms in their hands. She may declare war; but if she claim the benefit of peace, as both nations have done in this instance, the moment any of her citizens enter our territory, they are as completely obnoxious to punishment by our law, as if they had been born and always resided in this country' (at 285). The Court therefore disallowed the petition and the case was remitted to another US Court, which found in October 1841 that McLeod had an alibi and acquitted him (at 299).

[24] See the UN Secretary-General's ruling of 1986, at 214–12.

[25] The Appeals Chamber held that among the exceptions to the rule of State officials' immunity are those that 'arise from the norms of international criminal law prohibiting war crimes, crimes against humanity and genocide. Under these norms, those responsible for such crimes cannot invoke immunity from national or international jurisdiction even if they perpetrated such crimes while acting in their official capacity. Similarly, other classes of persons (e.g. spies, as defined in Article 29 of the Regulations Respecting the Laws and Customs of War on Land, annexed to the Hague Convention IV of 1907), although acting as State organs, may be held personally accountable for their wrongdoing' (at §41).

officials may not claim immunity from jurisdiction or functional immunity for international crimes.[26] They are criminally liable for them. In addition, the State of which they are organs may also incur international liability for such breaches although, in practice, criminal liability of individuals tends to overshadow and set aside State responsibility. Nonetheless, as we shall see later in this chapter, diplomats and senior State officials (Heads of State or Government, Foreign Ministers), who are entitled to *personal* immunities, may not be prosecuted for international crimes as long as they hold office. The rationale for this temporary immunity resides in the need to prevent possible abuses by national courts jeopardizing smooth international dealings amongst States.

As discussed next, special categories of State officials enjoy broader immunities on account of the specific roles they discharge. These are, at least, the Heads of State and Government, and Ministers of Foreign Affairs, as well as diplomatic and consular agents. For these categories, customary law grants a host of privileges and immunities which are broader than the mere functional immunities described earlier. In addition, arguments have been advanced that other high-level officials (e.g. other members of government) may benefit from similar treatment. To the extent these officials are sent abroad to represent their own State some of these arguments could be valid as long as such immunities are limited to what is strictly needed for the time of the visit and are 'agreed' with the receiving State.

6.3.3 IMMUNITIES OF DIPLOMATIC AND CONSULAR AGENTS

For diplomatic agents, these rules are codified in the Vienna Convention on Diplomatic Relations, of 1961.[27] All these rules envisage two classes of privileges and immunities, which overlap the *functional* immunities diplomats enjoy as State officials for acts and transactions performed in their official capacity. One class encompasses immunities that attach to the premises and assets used by the foreign State official for accomplishing his or her mission (immunities *relating to property*); the other class encompasses immunities covering the personal activities of that official (*personal* immunities).

These immunities are intended to shelter foreign officials from any interference with their private life that might jeopardize the accomplishment of their official function. Traditionally, this rationale was expressed with the dictum *ne impediatur legatio*, that is, they are granted in order to save the official mission from being hampered in its work. By way of illustration, in *Russel v S.r.l. Immobiliare Soblim* the Italian Constitutional Court was asked to decide whether the immunity from civil jurisdiction enjoyed by foreign diplomats was contrary to the constitutional principle of equality. The dispute arose from a claim against the Canadian military attaché in Rome for not paying the rent on his private dwelling in Rome. The Court upheld the immunity and noted that the customary rule granting immunity to foreign diplomats for their private transactions 'sprang up not in order to bestow a personal privilege but for the purpose of assuring in all cases that the diplomat may fulfil his duties. Indeed, immunity from civil jurisdiction, although with some exceptions, became necessary precisely to guarantee complete independence in accomplishing the mission: *ne impediatur legatio*' (at 147).

Among the diplomatic *immunities relating to property* the following stand out. First, the premises of the foreign diplomatic mission are inviolable; consequently, State officials of the local country may not enter them without the consent of the head of the mission. The area where the foreign mission is located is not subject to foreign sovereignty,

---

[26] See also *Ferrini v Federal Republic of Germany*, §11.
[27] Vienna Convention on Diplomatic Relations, 18 April 1961, 500 UNTS 95.

that is, it is not foreign territory. This area is part of the territory of the host State, but the enforcement agencies of this State are not allowed to exercise their powers in that area, unless expressly authorized by the head of the foreign mission. This is why Grotius rightly stated that foreign diplomatic missions are *quasi extra territorium*: the so-called extraterritoriality of those missions does not mean that they are located on a territory not subject to the sovereignty of the host State. Secondly, the property of the foreign diplomatic mission is immune from search, requisition, attachment, or execution. Thirdly, the diplomatic bag as well as the use of a diplomatic courier and messages in code and cipher may not be violated.

Personal immunities of diplomatic agents also have several aspects. First, diplomatic agents enjoy immunity from arrest and detention. If the diplomatic agent engages in criminal activity, the host State may notify the sending State that he or she is *persona non grata* (that is, a person unacceptable to the receiving State). In any such case, according to Article 9 of the Vienna Convention, 'the sending State shall as appropriate, either recall the person concerned or terminate his functions with the mission'. If the sending State refuses to do so or fails so to act 'within a reasonable period', the host State 'may refuse to recognize the person concerned as a member of the [diplomatic] mission'. Secondly, diplomatic agents enjoy immunity from criminal, civil, and administrative jurisdiction in the receiving State. However, customary law as codified in Article 31 of the Vienna Convention provides that there is no exemption from jurisdiction with regard to action relating to: (a) private immoveable property located in the receiving State, 'unless [the agent] holds it on behalf of the sending State for the purposes of the mission'; (b) succession, 'in which the diplomatic agent is involved as an executor, administrator, heir or legatee as private person and not on behalf of the sending State'; (c) 'any professional or commercial activity exercised by the diplomatic agent in the receiving State outside his official functions'. Clearly, with regard to these three categories of action, the rationale *ne impediatur legatio* cannot ground a personal immunity from the local jurisdiction, given that they all involve a deliberate decision to engage in private activities or transactions not linked to their diplomatic functions. In addition, diplomatic agents are not exempt from administrative or civil proceedings whenever they voluntarily submit to jurisdiction; for instance, after initiating proceedings before a local court, thus waiving their right to immunity from jurisdiction, they may not invoke immunity in respect of a counterclaim directly connected with the principal claim, or in respect of an appeal. A third aspect of the personal immunity enjoyed by diplomatic agents is the inviolability of his or her private residence, papers, correspondence, and property. Fourthly, diplomatic agents are exempted from all duties and taxes, personal or real, national, regional, or municipal (except for indirect taxes and other duties or taxes enumerated in Article 34(a)–(f) of the Vienna Convention).

Of note is the fact that, in accordance with Article 38(1) of the Vienna Convention, the above immunities do not cover a diplomatic agent who has the *nationality* of the receiving State or '*permanent residence*' there (Article 38(1) of the Vienna Convention). In the absence of additional privileges and immunities specially granted by the receiving States, such an agent only enjoys 'immunity from jurisdiction, and inviolability, in respect of official acts performed in the exercise of his functions'. The rationale underlying this exception is that otherwise the diplomatic agent would be exempt from any jurisdiction and thus enjoy total unaccountability. This applies among other things to the payment of taxes and dues. It also and *a fortiori* holds true for immunity from criminal jurisdiction.

The personal immunities and privileges normally applicable to diplomatic agents are also due to members of his or her family forming part of his or her household, if they are not nationals of the receiving State. The rationale is again provided by the dictum *ne impediatur legatio*, although in this case the interference would be indirect, through the exposure of the diplomatic agent's household members to the jurisdiction and enforcement powers of the receiving State.

Customary rules on the legal status of *consular agents* were codified in the Vienna Convention of 1963.[28] Consular agents are not diplomatic envoys: they are not in charge of transactions between two States. Rather, they perform activities designed to protect the commercial and other interests of the appointing State and in particular render assistance to nationals of that State (e.g. by giving such nationals help and advice should they be arrested or detained in the host State, by communicating with nationals imprisoned by the local authorities, etc.). They also perform important notarial functions (e.g. by attesting and legalizing signatures, by administering oaths for the purpose of evidence in trial proceedings, by concluding or registering marriages, by taking charge of wills of their own nationals, legalizing adoptions, registering births and deaths, etc.).

On account of the characteristics of their functions, consular agents do not enjoy *personal* immunities. They are only immune from criminal and civil jurisdiction for acts done in the official exercise of their consular functions (*functional* immunities). In addition, under Article 41(1) of the 1963 Vienna Convention, they are not 'liable to arrest or detention pending trial, except in the case of a grave crime and pursuant to a decision by the competent judicial authority'. Except in such a case, they may not be imprisoned, and they are not 'liable to any other form of restriction on their personal freedom save in execution of a judicial decision of final effect' (Article 41(2)). Similarly, consular premises (the buildings where their activity is performed), as well as consular archives and documents, are inviolable from search and seizure. Consular agents are further exempt from taxation (Article 49 of the Vienna Convention) and from customs duties and inspection (Article 50).

Termination of a diplomat's functions in the host State does not entail *ipso facto* the cessation of immunities. As the acting US Secretary of State Adee stated in 1908, in a note to the Brazilian Ambassador in the US, 'the diplomatic immunity inherent in the persons of diplomatic agents extends for a reasonable time after the cessation of diplomatic functions in order that they may complete their arrangements to leave the country'.[29] This proposition has been borne out by case law,[30] and is codified in Article 39(2) of the Vienna Convention on Diplomatic Relations, whereby personal privileges and immunities 'cease at the moment when he [the diplomat] leaves the country, or on expiry of a reasonable period in which to do so, but shall subsist until that time, even in case of armed conflict'. Furthermore, the diplomatic agent enjoys immunity in the territory of third States while returning to his or her own country (see Article 40(1) of the 1961 Vienna Convention).

6.3.4 IMMUNITIES OF HIGH-RANKING STATE OFFICIALS

Another special class of State officials are those who serve at the highest level of the State. When on official mission abroad, Heads of State and Government, and Foreign Ministers enjoy, in addition to immunity for official acts (functional immunity), privileges and

---

[28] Vienna Convention on Consular Relations, 24 April 1963, 596 UNTS 261.
[29] See Hackworth, iv, at 458.
[30] See e.g. the decision of the Police Court of the District of Columbia in *District of Columbia* v *Vinard L. Paris*; the decision of the Court of Appeal of Ontario in *R.* v *Palacios*, 412–13; and the decision by the English High Court in *Shaw* v *Shaw*. For other cases as well as State practice see J. Salmon, *Manuel de droit diplomatique* (Bruxelles: Bruylant, 1994), 404.

immunities with regard both to the premises where they perform their official transactions or live, and also to their private acts. There are differences in the legal literature about whether the aforementioned privileges and immunities conferred on diplomatic agents may be extended in their totality to this class of persons. The better view is that this extension is admitted by international law; case law bears out this proposition.[31] National courts have grounded this conclusion in a principle parallel to that applying to diplomats, namely *ne impediatur officium* (the need to protect the foreign senior official from possible interference in his or her official functions).[32]

It should be stressed again that, unlike acts performed by these State officials in their official capacity, which are covered by functional immunity, the privileges and immunities under discussion either relate to property or are personal, and they are intended to shelter the foreign State official from any undue interference by the host State in his or her private life, thereby jeopardizing his or her action as a foreign dignitary. However, these immunities are only granted to senior State officials on an *official* visit. It would seem that when they are on a private visit and are not travelling *incognito*, the host State is bound to afford them special protection; it may also grant them privileges and immunities out of comity, that is, politeness and good will. But there is no expressly recognized obligation to do so.

Domestic courts as well as the ICJ in the *Arrest Warrant* case have set forth the view that chief among these immunities is the immunity from prosecution by a foreign court for either ordinary offences or international crimes. This view, which goes back to such famous cases as *The Schooner Exchange* v *McFaddon*, of 1812 (at 137), has been repeatedly affirmed in the case law.[33] The rationale behind the exemption from the criminal jurisdiction of foreign courts is twofold: first, as noted by a US court in *Gladys M. Lafontant* v *Jean-Bertrand Aristide*, 'Head-of-state immunity, like foreign sovereign immunity, is premised on the concept that a state and its rulers are one for the purposes of immunity' (at 10–11); secondly, the notion that all States are equal, with the consequence that no State may 'exercise judicial authority over another' (ibid.). Perhaps, for Heads of State and Government, there is the further reason that to bring them to trial in a foreign court or otherwise subject them to measures of constraint would involve disrupting the political life of their State and undermine its international prestige. A possible illustration of the latter point, which may well go under the rubric of an infringement to the 'inviolability' of foreign high officials, is provided by the alleged exercise of coercion by Saudi Arabia on Lebanon's Prime Minister Saad Hariri, during his visit to Riyadh in early November 2017, which initially led to Hariri's resignation. The crisis did not reach the courts. It was solved through political means. In mid-November, French President Emmanuel Macron made an unscheduled visit to Riyadh and invited Hariri and his family to visit him in France. Hariri was thus allowed to leave Saudi Arabia, but the incident marked an important point both in Lebanese politics and in the power relations in the Middle East.

---

[31] See e.g. *Kilroy* v *Windsor*, 605–7 (where there is also stated the position of the US State Department); the decisions of the King's Bench Division of 21 January 1952 and the Court of Appeal of 20 May 1952 in *Sayce* v *Ameer Ruler Sadiq Mohsammad Abbasi Bahawalpur State*, 657 and 662 respectively. See also the decision of the Italian Court of Cassation of 11 March 1921 in *Nobili* v *Emperor Charles I of Austria*.

[32] See the order issued on 18 February 1987 by the Rome Tribunal in *Bigi*, at 360.

[33] See e.g. *Saltany* v *Reagan*, 320, and *Gladys M. Lafontant* v *Jean-Bertrand Aristide*, 10–11, as well as *Fidel Castro* (Legal Grounds nos 1–4) (Spain); *Gaddafi* (France) and *Sharon and Yaron, HSA* v *SA (Ariel Sharon) and YA (Amos Yaron Sharon)*, 2.

Regarding Ministers of Foreign Affairs, their immunity has been asserted in national cases: see, for instance, *Bigi* (at 359), stating that the Foreign Minister of San Marino could no longer enjoy immunity from jurisdiction for acts performed in his private capacity after leaving office, and the authoritative ICJ judgment in *Arrest Warrant* (at §§53–61).

As for other State officials, the State in whose capacity the senior official acts may waive the immunity. In the absence of such waiver, *functional* immunity stands and it does not come to an end with the cessation of the functions vested in the State official, as is confirmed by case law and State pronouncements, primarily concerning diplomatic agents.[34] Conversely, *personal* privileges and immunities terminate with the cessation of the mission. A Paris court in 1925 spelled out the rationale behind this international regulation in *Laperdrix and Penquer* v *Kouzouboff and Belin*, as follows: 'the principle of diplomatic immunity is set up in the interests of governments, not in that of diplomats; it cannot apply beyond the [diplomatic] mission ... a contrary view would lead to creating to the benefit of diplomatic agents a sort of statute of limitations and an indefinite unaccountability' (at 65). Thus, for instance, if an ambassador commits an ordinary crime such as the murder of his wife in the receiving State, he is immune there from criminal jurisdiction. However, if he goes back to that country after relinquishing his diplomatic position, he may be arrested and brought to trial.[35]

Personal immunities shield all those State officials to whom they accrue from *prosecution for international crimes in foreign courts*, while such State agents remain in office. Spanish, French, and Belgian courts have clearly enunciated this notion, respectively in *Fidel Castro* (Legal grounds 1–4), *Ghaddafi* (at 218–19), and *Sharon and Yaron* (at 3). However, when they leave office the aforementioned State agents forfeit personal immunities. Accordingly, they may be prosecuted for any international crimes they may have perpetrated while in office, or before. This proposition is supported in the case law (see e.g. the decisions of the Audiencia Nacional in Spain and of the UK House of Lords in *Pinochet*, the Amsterdam Court of Appeals in *Bouterse*,[36] and the Court of Appeal of Dakar on the Extradition Request for *Hissène Habré*[37]), as well as by State declarations.[38] However, some cases seem to contradict this jurisprudential trend. In at least two decisions concerning former Heads of State, US courts held that they had jurisdiction over them because the State to which they belonged had waived immunity: see *Grand Jury Proceedings* (concerning former Philippine President Marcos, found civilly liable for failing to comply with deferral grand jury subpoenas) and *Paul* v *Avril* (concerning the former military ruler of Haiti, sued for alleged violations of human rights). If a waiver of immunity was considered necessary, this would

---

[34] See e.g. the opinion issued on 12 May 1961 by the Swiss Foreign Department, in 21 *ASDI* (1964), 171; the decision by the London Court of Appeal in *Zoerrsch* v *Waldock and another*.

[35] This proposition is clearly confirmed by State practice and case law, concerning instances where diplomats had committed a range of criminal and administrative offences, including: infringements of customs regulations (see *Ministère Public* v *P*, 30–1) or of the laws on explosives (see *The Empire* v *Chang and others*, 288); rape (see *Imp. A.B.*, 212); illegal parking; refusal to state their identity, and injury of police officers (see *P.M.* v *Zappi Mentore*, 1255–60); criminal misconduct by a former Foreign Minister (see e.g. *Bigi*, 360).

[36] The Dutch Supreme Court eventually dismissed the case against Bouterse, as it was established that there was no link with the Netherlands; however, the points concerning immunity in case of international crimes were not discussed.

[37] Subsequently, however, the former Chadian ruler was tried and convicted by the Extraordinary African Chambers in Senegal: see *Ministère Public* v *Hissein Habré*, Extraordinary African Chambers, Appeals Chambers.

[38] E.g. in 2000, the UK Foreign Secretary stated in Parliament that 'former heads of State are not immune from a process for such alleged crimes [that is, "very serious crimes such as torture"]', at (2000) 71 *BYIL* 588.

mean that otherwise the former Heads of State would have enjoyed immunity from foreign courts' jurisdiction.

This restrictive position was also taken by the ICJ in the *Arrest Warrant* case, where the Court stated that a Minister of Foreign Affairs may be prosecuted (i) in his or her own country, or (ii) in foreign courts if their home State waives the immunity, or (iii) in foreign courts after they have ceased their function for offences committed before or after their term of office or during such term, if the offence was committed 'in a private capacity', or, again, (iv) in an international criminal court or tribunal (at §61). What this conclusion leaves out is perhaps the very core of the problem. It is not conceivable that a senior State agent may perpetrate such offences as war crimes, torture, crimes against humanity, terrorism, or genocide, in 'a private capacity'. Rather, in performing, or ordering or willingly condoning the perpetration of, those acts, a senior State agent acts in the exercise of his public functions. Thus, the narrow definition of category (iii) retained by the Court would only permit the prosecution in foreign courts of high-ranking officials for international crimes committed during their term of office if such crimes could be artificially said to have been committed 'in a private capacity'.

Another issue which is worth examining is the interplay between the immunity of Heads of State (or Government or Ministers of Foreign Affairs) and requests for their arrest and surrender originating from international criminal courts or tribunals. In keeping with the ICJ *Arrest Warrant* judgment already mentioned (at §61), one may consider derogations to immunity permissible for trials before international criminal courts and tribunals. Nonetheless, what happens to immunity when a State is requested to arrest and surrender the high-ranking official to an international criminal court or tribunal is more controversial. Under the Statutes of the International Criminal Tribunals for the former Yugoslavia and Rwanda (established by SC resolutions: see **19.3.3**) it was clear that the Heads of State or Government of the relevant countries could not enjoy any immunity vis-à-vis such tribunals; the situation, however, appears to be more debatable with respect to the International Criminal Court (ICC) (see **19.3.3**) and has given rise to controversies, notably with regard to the arrest warrant against the then Sudanese President Omar Al Bashir and subsequent requests by the ICC to States parties to execute it. While there is no doubt under the ICC Statute that all high-ranking officials (including Heads of State or Government) of States parties to the Statute do not enjoy immunity before the ICC, there is more uncertainty as to whether States parties are under an obligation to set aside the immunity of Heads of State (and other high-ranking officials) of States, which are not parties to the Statute, when requested by the Court to enforce an arrest warrant. The complexity of the issue has led to several proceedings and decisions by the ICC regarding the non-execution of its requests to States parties to execute the arrest warrant against Al Bashir when he was still President of Sudan, as well as in the domestic courts of some States parties (notably South Africa), and more recently to the perspective of a request for an ICJ Advisory Opinion by the UN General Assembly at the initiative of the African Group. In line with the more recent trend towards restricting the scope of derogations to immunity so as to offer increased protection to State sovereignty, a wide array of opinions has been expressed in favour of preserving the immunity of officials of States not parties to the Statute. Broadly speaking, however, one should be mindful that to address the issue properly, attention should be paid not only to the provisions of the ICC Statute, but also to other norms including the text of relevant SC resolutions (in the case of Sudan resolution 1593 of 2005) and the rules of customary law.

Another important question concerns whether or not, and to what extent, other high-ranking officials enjoy similar immunities under customary international law. High-ranking and other State officials who do not enjoy such personal immunities (e.g. Defence

Ministers; police officers, whether or not senior; military personnel, etc.) may be prosecuted at any time, even if they are still holding office. This proposition is supported by case law. For example, in *Sharon and Yaron*, the Court of Cassation of Belgium held that one of the two defendants, Amos Yaron, former Head of Security and at the moment of proceedings senior State official in the Israeli Defence Ministry, could be prosecuted.[39] US courts have also taken a similar position, although with respect to civil cases. In *Garcia José Guillermo and Vides Casanova Carlos Eugenio*, US courts did not delve at any length into immunity issues, but recalled that under the Torture Victim Protection Act, immunity of foreign State officials is not a bar to civil claims against defendants sued for torture, war crimes, and other crimes against humanity ('[the] TVPA provides, in relevant part: (a) Liability. – An individual who, under actual or apparent authority, or color of law of any foreign nation – (1) subjects an individual to torture *shall, in a civil action, be liable* for damages to that individual' (28 USC §1350 note)).[40]

---

[39] See the decision by which the Court of Cassation of Belgium ended the proceedings against then Prime Minister Sharon (who enjoyed immunity), but excluded any obstacles to proceeding against Yaron, then director general of the Israeli Defence Ministry, and others (*Sharon and Yaron, HSA v SA (Ariel Sharon) and YA (Amos Yaron)*). See also the *Scilingo* case (Audiencia Nacional, N° 16/2005) as well as the Decision of the Supreme Court concerning the *Guatemala Genocide Case* Decision No. 327/2003.

[40] The two generals, who were both former Ministers of Defence who had taken their retirement in Florida, were ordered to pay reparation of hundreds of thousands of dollars to their victims; subsequently they were eventually deported to El Salvador (in 2014 and 2015).

7
INTERNATIONAL ORGANIZATIONS

7.1 THE DEVELOPMENT OF INTERNATIONAL ORGANIZATIONS

The emergence of international (also known as intergovernmental)[1] organizations is a phenomenon that marked the twentieth century. It is the result of the increased interaction and co-operation among States, and convenience in creating instrumentalities that would jointly act on their behalf.[2]

Historically, before international organizations as such were created, initial attempts were linked to the need to co-ordinate specific efforts on a rather occasional basis. For example, when wars broke out, States established coalitions in the form of military alliances—or when conflicts ended, the victors co-ordinated their efforts to 'organize' peace (the 1815 'Congress of Vienna' is seen by many as the first embryonic form of political organization). At that time, however, there was no, or a very minor, institutional dimension.

Subsequently, towards the end of the nineteenth century, the demand for more structured transnational handling of certain problems increasingly required the establishment of more institutionalized forms of co-operation which would be characterized as international organizations (e.g. for postal services and other international communications, the International Telegraph Union in 1865 and the Universal Postal Union in 1874; or for agreed standards on measurements, e.g. the International Bureau of Weights and Measures in 1875; or for patents and trademarks, e.g. the Union for the Protection of Industrial Property, established in 1883; or the International Institute for Agriculture, created in 1905; or for the handling of important transnational watercourses, e.g. the various 'River Commissions', for the Rhine, the Danube, etc.).

Progressively, even more matters have acquired an international or transnational dimension and can only (or better) be handled through increased interstate co-operation. It is thus natural that States decided to set up joint bodies charged with carrying out international action, in matters of common interest, on behalf of all the participating States. In setting up these institutions States have been motivated primarily by reasons of *expediency* and *practicality*, but also by some measure of *idealism*.

What is remarkable is that, particularly after the Second World War, further steps were taken, and intergovernmental agencies have been increasingly endowed with autonomous powers, with rights and duties distinct from those belonging to each member State.

---

[1] The main trait of intergovernmental organizations is that their members are States, and they are represented in the organization (and more broadly in international dealings) by the governments.

[2] There are several historical accounts of this phenomenon, most often focusing on one specific organization, such as the League of Nations, the UN, or the ILO. For a general survey see B. Reinalda, *Routledge History of International Organizations: From 1815 to the Present Day* (London: Routledge, 2009).

An ideological factor helped in strengthening the role of intergovernmental organizations and allotting international standing to them. This was the idea that, to ward off the scourge of a third world war, a strong network of international instrumentalities should be created so as to impose heavier and more far-reaching restraints on States. However illusory and naïve this 'internationalist' outlook may have been, there is no denying that it led to the proliferation of organizations and contributed to their increasing importance.

States found it convenient to establish international machinery for the purpose of carrying out tasks of mutual interest. They therefore instituted distinct centres of action that furthered the common goals (autonomy), whilst at the same time they designed them to perform only those activities that States delegate to them (principle of speciality or of conferral).

As the ICJ put it in its 1996 Advisory Opinion on *Legality of the Use by a State of Nuclear Weapons in Armed Conflict*, the object of the constituent instruments of international organizations 'is to create new subjects of law endowed with a certain autonomy, to which the parties entrust the task of realizing common goals' (at §19). On this score, organizations, when they are endowed with international legal personality, can be styled *ancillary* subjects of international law. This means that they are mere instruments in the hands of States. They cease to exist internationally the very day the groups of States that created them decide to jettison them. In other words, the very existence of the new entity, as well as the range of functions and powers conferred on it, is still very much dependent on the will of its member States. Nonetheless, as we will see, international organizations have developed, at least to some extent, in ways which were not always 'scripted' as such in the constitutive instruments and in some cases acquired great autonomy from the member States.[3]

Today, international organizations are undergoing a crisis phase which may have affected support for international organizations and the very heart of multilateralism, including that measure of idealism mentioned earlier. There are several reasons for this development, which are linked to both realities and perceptions.

First, international organizations are increasingly seen, particularly in some countries, as costly and ineffective bureaucracies. Secondly, public opinion in several countries is, or might in future be, under the impression that international organizations are 'external' entities imposing unpopular and unwanted measures at the domestic level, devoid of any legitimacy. Thirdly, international organizations are viewed, at least in some instances, as being totally unaccountable. In some extreme cases, international institutions have been considered as acting in serious violation of international law, operating in a legal vacuum and providing for no appropriate mechanism to offer redress to victims.

Inevitably this situation has created a wave of criticism and some tensions in the international system, which are yet to be addressed properly. Meanwhile, the entire idea of an international system based on co-operation and international organizations has been put in doubt.

In Western countries, existing international organizations have appeared (or have been made to appear) as both ineffective and unaccountable (as well as unable to handle the negative effects of globalization), with arguably decreasing support in committing to them. At the same time, in other sectors of the international community, there has been an increase in the creation of international 'instrumentalities'. However, the establishment of international organizations in the post-Second World War era was primarily promoted by the US and other Western countries, together with some other Latin American States, and was essentially based on liberal values and ideals, such as the free market, civil rights, and fundamental liberties. Today, the creation of new organizations is no longer viewed positively

---

[3] One major example is the development of the UN peacekeeping practice, which was largely due to the creativity of UN Secretary-General, Dag Hammarksjöld. See **15.3**.

by the US and its traditional allies; in contrast, other sectors of the international community, often inspired by different sets of values, are becoming more active in this area. For example, China, as the new emerging superpower, together with other regional States, has created new international financial institutions such as the Asian Infrastructure Investment Bank, or, together with Brazil, India, South Africa, and Russia (forming together the so-called BRICS nations), has established the New Development Bank. In parallel, groups of countries in Africa and in Asia are moving at regional or sub-regional level towards more structured interactions and, albeit with slightly different approaches, have been engaged in establishing international organizations and organizing forms of co-operation.

7.2 TYPES OF INTERNATIONAL ORGANIZATIONS

As mentioned previously, the first international organizations (created in the late nineteenth and the early twentieth centuries) were rather rudimentary, and primarily concerned with limited technical matters. Broadly speaking they could be seen merely as collective instrumentalities for the joint performance of actions that each member State would otherwise have had to undertake by itself.[4]

After the First World War, with the establishment of the League of Nations and the International Labour Organization (ILO)—institutions with more political breadth—for the first time international organizations assumed greater importance, were assigned broader objectives, and considered by scholars as endowed with legal personality. Yet even those institutions, and certainly all the more technical ones, were to a large extent conceived by member States as 'collective organs'; that is, as structures that remained under the firm control of the member States, possessing very little real independence or existence of their own. Unanimity was often required for deliberations, spontaneous adherence of member States to the recommendations of the entity was the rule, and enforcement activities were still very much in the hands of the member States, which were the lynchpin of any concrete development. At that stage (early twentieth century) States were still considering international organizations to be instrumentalities, devoid of real autonomy.

It was only after the Second World War, when many organizations were created and granted sweeping powers, that the problem of the proper role and weight of intergovernmental organizations in international affairs became more apparent. International organizations are established for specific purposes and among different groups of States. Hence, there is an enormous variety in size, membership, objectives, functioning mechanisms, resources, and so on.

After the Second World War several international institutions were set up in various fields and regions. These included: (a) *political* relations—for example, the United Nations, which has universal scope; the Organization of American States, the Council of Europe, the Organization of African Unity (now African Union), and the League of Arab States, all of which are regional in character; (b) *military* relations—for example, the North Atlantic Treaty Organization (NATO) and the former Warsaw Pact; (c) *economic* co-operation—for example, the International Monetary Fund, the World Bank, and the World Trade Organization (at the universal level); the European Union (EU) (which also has a political dimension), or the

---

[4] For a careful description of traditional international organizations active in economic fields, see W. Kaufmann, 'Les unions internationales de nature économique' (1924) 2 *RCADI* 181. For a contemporary conceptualization of international organizations see J. Klabbers, 'Formal Intergovernmental Organizations' in J. Katz Cogan, I. Hurd, and I. Johnstone (eds), *The Oxford Handbook of International Organizations* (Oxford: Oxford University Press, 2016), 134.

Southern Common Market (MERCOSUR) at the regional level; (d) *cultural* relations—for example, the United Nations Educational, Scientific and Cultural Organization (UNESCO); (e) *social* co-operation—for example, the Food and Agriculture Organization (FAO); (f) *scientific* research—for example, CERN (the European Organization for Nuclear Research, originally the European Council for Nuclear Research).

Most of these were established in the first couple of decades after the War, however, even in more recent times, although Western countries seem less supportive of the establishment of new international organizations (perhaps for financial reasons) and despite the challenges and criticism facing existing international organizations, the establishment of organizations as an instrument of collective governance still finds support.

At present there are hundreds of intergovernmental organizations at universal and regional level, of both a political and technical nature, most of them actively engaged in mutual co-operation and co-operation with the United Nations, for example, in implementing the Sustainable Development Goals by 2030. As an indication of this phenomenon one may point to the fact that, in the past decade alone (2008–18) the UN General Assembly has granted 'observer status' in the GA to about 30 international organizations, at a pace of about five new requests every year (not all of them eventually accepted).

As far as their structure is concerned, most organizations usually consist of (i) a permanent 'secretariat', headed by a secretary-general or director-general, with the required staff (here as well there are huge differences among organizations: some have only a few staff members, while others such as the UN or the EU may employ tens of thousands of people); (ii) they normally also have an 'assembly' in which all member States take part, which meets periodically and/or when needed; and (iii) a governing body, often called 'council' or 'board', made up of a more limited number of member States (generally elected by the plenary assembly), entrusted with more specific tasks and usually reporting to the assembly (this body may also have the task of steering and/or supervising the work of the secretariat and preparing the periodic meetings of the assembly).

7.3 RECOGNITION OF THEIR LEGAL PERSONALITY

As the phenomenon of international organizations developed, the question of their being endowed with international legal personality continued to crop up. Initially, some scholars rejected the idea;[5] nonetheless, courts started to answer that question in the affirmative. For example, in 1931 the Italian Court of Cassation delivered a seminal decision in *Istituto internazionale di Agricoltura* v *Profili*. Mr Profili, an employee of the International Institute for Agriculture (IIA), the international organization that was the predecessor of FAO and similarly headquartered in Rome, had been dismissed by the Organization. He sued the IIA before a court in Rome, asking among other things for severance pay. The IIA having challenged the jurisdiction of Italian courts, the case was brought before the Court of Cassation. The Court held that the Organization had international legal personality, as the States establishing the Organization had intended it to be 'absolutely autonomous *vis-à-vis* each and every member State'; consequently, it was empowered to organize its own structure and legal order autonomously and without any interference from sovereign States. It followed that Italian courts lacked jurisdiction over employment relations with the Organization.

Progressively, it became clear that international organizations were indeed often acting with a sufficient degree of autonomy and took part in several international undertakings

---

[5] See e.g. D. Anzilotti, 'Gli organi comuni nelle società di Stati' (1914) 8 *RDI* 156, repr. in his *Scritti di diritto internazionale pubblico* (Padova: Cedam, 1956), i, 605.

which required recognition of their autonomous personality. One of the first issues that was posed to the ICJ in the exercise of its advisory function concerned the subjectivity of the UN.

In this regard it should be said that not all entities referred to as international organizations necessarily possess international legal personality. Hence, it might be useful to clarify what the test is for determining whether or not they are international subjects and should be recognized as the bearer of the corresponding rights and duties under international law.

In its famous Advisory Opinion of 1949 on *Reparation for Injuries Suffered in the Service of the United Nations* the ICJ outlined two criteria. First, it must be shown that the member States, in setting up the organization and entrusting certain functions to it, with the attendant duties and responsibilities, intended to clothe it 'with the competence required to enable these functions to be effectively discharged' (at 179). In other words, it must be proved that the founding fathers intended to put into being an autonomous body, capable of occupying 'a position in certain respects in detachment from its Members' (ibid.). Secondly, it is necessary for the organization *in actual fact to enjoy the autonomy* from member States and the effective capacity necessary for it to act as an international subject. In the ICJ's words, it is necessary to show that the organization 'is in fact exercising and enjoying functions and rights which can only be explained on the basis of the possession of a large measure of international personality and the capacity to operate upon an international plane' (ibid.).

The intention to provide the organization with legal personality may also be spelled out by the draftsmen in the text of the charter or statute establishing it. The UN Charter, in Article 104, states that '[the] Organization shall enjoy in the territory of each of its Members such legal capacity as may be necessary for the exercise of its functions and the fulfilment of its purposes'. Analogous provisions are also contained in the constitutive instruments of other organizations. In this respect, mention can also be made, for example, of Article 4(1) of the 1998 Statute of the International Criminal Court (ICC), which states: 'The Court shall have international legal personality. It shall also have such legal capacity as may be necessary for the exercise of its functions and the fulfilment of its purposes.' It would not seem that such a provision per se could determine the international subjectivity of international organizations. It has often been interpreted as a rule providing the Organization with sufficient legal personality to entertain dealings with its member States, which are under an obligation to recognize the personality of international organizations, in their domestic legal systems. However, such treaty provisions together with other facts showing that the organization acts as a subject in international dealings might constitute relevant indicia of its legal personality under international law.

The *intention* of member States can be inferred from other elements. For instance, it may be deduced from, among other things, the existence of a sufficiently articulated structure, capable of acting with a degree of independence, and/or the fact that decisions must not necessarily (or must not always) be taken unanimously but can be adopted by a majority vote.

Nonetheless, ultimately what matters, besides the intentions of its founders, is that the international organization has a proper structure and effectively acts in the international system as a fully fledged participant, with autonomy vis-à-vis its creators. In 1985 the Italian Court of Cassation insisted upon this requirement in *Cristiani v Istituto italo-latino-americano*. The Court held that international legal personality is based on the effective position of an entity in the international community: the organization needs to constitute a 'collective unity detached from the member States'; it must consist of 'social organs' that are distinct from the organs of each member State and that in addition do not act as joint organs of those States; rather, they must act as organs proper to the organization.

In essence, international organizations' subjectivity or personhood under international law is both a matter of fact and of law. On the one hand, it refers to the legal dimension reflected in their constitutive instruments which assign to them specific tasks, provide for methods of deliberation which enable identification of the personality of organizations separate from that of their member States; on the other hand it requires that the organization can effectively act autonomously and that this be accepted by its member States. Once the above-mentioned twofold test is met and the organization is regarded as a distinct legal person under international law, it may be considered that it not only enjoys all the powers and competences indicated in the institutive instrument, but also possesses international rights and obligations deriving from international customary rules. On the basis of these rules the organization can interact with other subjects of international law and enter into agreements, invoke its rights, and assume its responsibilities.

As for organizations that do not satisfy the above tests, it may be said that they act on behalf of all their member States. These organizations can be considered organs common to all those States, with the consequence that acts they perform may be legally attributed to all such States. By the same token, any wrongful act perpetrated by one of the organs or officials of the organization is the responsibility of all the member States (on the responsibility of international organizations see **7.7**).

There are influential forms of co-operation among States that are not intended to become 'organizations', such as the G-7/G-8 or G-20, or the BRICS summits. These forms of political/economic co-operation do not of course present the traits of international organizations as they possess neither permanent structures nor any autonomy from the participant States.

To sum up, today there is little doubt that international organizations may possess legal personality under international law; however, the determination of the precise scope of such personality and the consequences that may be attached to it in terms of rights, duties, and responsibilities are open to more debate and are linked to a number of factors. International organizations are subjects that possess unique characteristics and the extent of their personality is very much dependent on these traits. Moreover, the way in which they act is very much dependent on their constitutive instrument, and the first issue that needs to be examined is the attribution to international organizations of specific tasks and appropriate powers to perform them.

7.4 SCOPE AND LIMITS: IMPLIED POWERS AND THE PRINCIPLE OF SPECIALITY

The determination of the competence of an international organization is very much dependent on the details contained in its constitutive instrument. Moreover, the recognition of international legal personality for international organizations entails some rights and duties derived by customary international law; against this background, it is possible to examine in more detail the scope and limits of the powers of international organizations.

It is impossible to give a definite answer valid for all international organizations, for it is to a large extent left to the instituting States to decide in each case how to structure the international entity, what powers are granted, and which obligations are imposed. Only practice will tell how these powers are effectively exercised and discharged.

The general principle inspiring the functioning of international organizations is that they can perform only those functions that are assigned to them and can exercise only those powers conferred on them by their member States through the constitutive instrument.

While international case law on the matter has been supportive of rather expansive approaches to the competences of international organizations, allowing for a certain broadening of their powers, it must also be noted that courts have consistently reaffirmed the principle that international organizations act on the basis of conferred powers and that rigorous scrutiny is required so as to determine that these are exercised in line with the organization's objectives (see e.g. the ICJ in the 1996 Advisory Opinion on *Legality of the Use by a State of Nuclear Weapons in Armed Conflict*). Hence, international organizations doubtless do not possess general competences and rights. As the ICJ had already expressed it in its Advisory Opinion on *Reparation for Injuries Suffered in the Service of the United Nations*, 'the subjects of law in any legal system are not necessarily identical in their nature or in the extent of their rights' (at 178). And, in the same Opinion, the Court also stressed that unlike States, international organizations have a limited competence and field of action. As the Court put it:

> [I]nternational organizations are subjects of international law which do not, unlike States, possess a general competence. *International organizations are governed by the 'principle of speciality'*, that is to say, they are invested by the States which create them with powers, the limits of which are a function of the common interests whose promotion those States entrust to them. (at §25, emphasis added)

This is a principle which in substance (albeit with different terminology) was already well established in the 1929 Permanent Court of International Justice (PCIJ) Opinion on *Jurisdiction of the European Commission of the Danube* and has always governed the functioning of international organizations. It is also labelled in other ways, such as, for example, the principle of conferral in the context of the European Union, where it has been explicitly reaffirmed in Article 5 of the Treaty on the European Union. In essence it indicates the same phenomenon: the powers and competences of international organizations cannot be presumed and must be anchored to the provisions of their respective constitutive instruments.

While it is true that this overarching principle applies to all international organizations and may function as a limitation to their powers, it is equally true that the precise determination of the scope of their functions and powers largely differs, depending on the interpretation of their 'constitutive' instruments. International practice, at least after the Second World War, has consistently shown that in appropriate circumstances interpretation may entail an expansion of their powers.

The PCIJ had already held that international organizations could have powers that, albeit not explicitly mentioned in the statutory instruments creating the organization, were required for the discharge of the tasks assigned, in 1926 in its Advisory Opinion on *Competence of the ILO Concerning Personal Work of the Employer*.

Hence, the notion, also known as the theory of implied powers—that international organizations need all those powers that are necessary for the performance of the functions entrusted to them to be recognized—has been applied rather frequently to international organizations. Naturally there are limits to the application of such a notion: at one extreme, some have advocated that implied powers must flow from express powers, and can be recognized only if absolutely necessary to the exercise of those powers (see the Dissenting Opinion of Judge Hackworth in the Advisory Opinion of the ICJ on *Reparation for Injuries Suffered in the Service of the United Nations*). On the other hand, the prevailing view has been to adopt a broader approach, recognizing that implied powers can derive not only from express powers, but can also ensue from the need to ensure the ability of the organization to pursue the fulfilment of the tasks and functions assigned by member States in the constitutive instrument. The ICJ expressed itself in the following terms in this respect:

> Under international law, the Organization must be deemed to have those powers which, though not expressly provided in the Charter, are conferred upon it by necessary implication as being *essential to the performance of its duties*. (*Reparation for Injuries Suffered in the Service of the United Nations*, at 182–3)

The Court also stated that:

> [...] the necessities of international life may point to the need for organizations, in order to *achieve their objectives*, to possess subsidiary powers which are not expressly provided for in the basic instruments which govern their activities. It is generally accepted that international organizations can exercise such powers, known as 'implied' powers. (*Legality of the Threat or Use of Nuclear Weapons*, at §25)

Broadly speaking, the general trend, so far, has been in favour of an expansive interpretation of international organizations' competences and promotion of their increased role in international affairs, including through recognition of their personality and the rights deriving from it.

7.5 IMMUNITIES OF INTERNATIONAL ORGANIZATIONS AND THEIR AGENTS

One of the key aspects in fully establishing the role of international organizations in international dealings has been the recognition of relevant immunities from jurisdiction for international organizations and for their agents.

These immunities are instrumental for the purpose of discharging their functions unobstructed. They both flow from international organizations' international personality and are also normally specifically provided for in the agreements establishing the organization and/or further agreements, implementing the constitutive instrument so as to better define the boundaries of such immunities (such as e.g. a headquarters agreement between the organization and the host State, or special conventions concerning the privileges and immunities of the organization).

A number of cases have confirmed the importance of the immunities of international organizations and their essential function in preserving the autonomy and independence of the organization.[6] There is little doubt that without appropriate guarantees, international organizations and their officials would be unable to perform their duties effectively and discharge their tasks unhindered. However, at the same time, recognition of the immunity of international organizations creates a potential for denial of justice, which is particularly problematic in cases where serious violations have emerged. The latter creates discontent and paves the way for challenges, which may result in weakening the credibility of organizations, eventually jeopardizing their missions.

---

[6] See C. Ryngaert, 'The Immunities of International Organizations before Domestic Courts: Recent Trends' (2010) 7 *IOLR* 121. See generally N. Blokker and N. Schrijver (eds), *The Immunity of International Organizations* (Leiden: Brill/Nijhoff, 2015).

7.5.1 THE RIGHT TO IMMUNITY FROM JURISDICTION OF STATE COURTS FOR ACTS AND ACTIVITIES PERFORMED BY THE ORGANIZATION

Article 105(1) of the UN Charter provides that '[t]he Organization shall enjoy in the territory of each of its Members such privileges and immunities as are necessary for the fulfilment of its purposes'. Immediately after the entry into force of the Charter, these provisions were further implemented through the adoption of the Convention on the Privileges and Immunities of the United Nations.[7] Article II, section 2, of the Convention indicates that '[t]he United Nations, its property and assets wherever located and by whomsoever held, shall enjoy immunity from every form of legal process except insofar as in any particular case it has expressly waived its immunity. It is, however, understood that no waiver of immunity shall extend to any measure of execution.'

More generally, international organizations have the right to claim immunity from the jurisdiction as well as the execution of national courts, with regard to activities performed to attain the goals laid down in the organization's statutes or constitution. The rationale for this immunity is that otherwise States could interfere with or affect the functioning of the organization; for instance, the State where the organization is headquartered could seize or impound its assets. Moreover, the domestic courts of many States have held that disputes relating to employment with international organizations cannot be submitted to States' jurisdiction, for they concern activities falling within the purview of the organization concerned. Normally, international organizations establish internal jurisdictional systems to deal with employment disputes.

At the same time, however, national courts did not refrain from setting aside immunity for activities akin to commercial activities (in parallel with what has been done with States), as well as for purely economic aspects of working relations. In other words, with regard to international organizations too, the principle of absolute immunity seems to have been set aside, along the lines of what happened with State immunity.

In a recent judgment (*Jam et al.* v *International Finance Corp*), the US Supreme Court (Judge Breyer dissenting), while discussing the immunity of international financial institutions, established two principles: (a) the treatment of international organizations, as far as immunity is concerned, *mirrors that of States* (and in the specific context of the case this was found to be in line with the text of US provisions governing such immunities); (b) the *immunity* of international organizations *cannot be absolute*, but needs to evolve along the lines of what happened with State immunity (which—as we have seen in **Chapter 6**—can indeed no longer be considered as absolute).

As the US Supreme Court put it:

> [The] International Organizations Immunities Act of 1945 grants international organizations such as the World Bank and the World Health Organization the 'same immunity from suit [. . .] as is enjoyed by foreign governments.' . . . At the time the IOIA was enacted, foreign governments enjoyed virtually absolute immunity from suit. Today that immunity is more limited. Most significantly, foreign governments are not immune from actions based upon certain kinds of commercial activity in which they engage. This case requires us to determine whether the IOIA grants international organizations the virtually absolute immunity foreign governments enjoyed when the IOIA was enacted, or the more limited immunity they enjoy today.

---

[7] Adopted by GA resolution 22A(I) 'Privileges and Immunities of the United Nations', 13 February 1946. See generally A. Reinisch (ed.), *The Conventions on the Privileges and Immunities of the United Nations and Specialized Agencies: A Commentary* (New York: Oxford University Press, 2016).

There can be little doubt that the approach concretely taken by the US Supreme Court reflects a general trend towards restricting immunities, which is a salient feature of contemporary international law. Such development is to be seen in a positive light as it avoids legal black holes and creates accountability spaces allowing for victims of alleged violations avenues to seek redress. However, at the same time, there are several aspects that ought to be fully considered and there is a fundamental problem that requires better clarification.

First of all, it would appear that the 'foundations' of the immunity of international organizations are different from those of State immunity. Their immunity is essentially functional and not based on the principle of sovereign equality (of States—i.e. *par in parem non habet judicium*) and hence the transposal to international organizations of the principles that were developed for State immunity would seem to require further refinement.

Secondly, the criterion adopted to determine the scope of actual immunity seems to revolve around an examination of the type of actions (e.g. whether or not they can be characterized as commercial activities); however, it may well be the case that violations occur when international organizations perform other kinds of activities which are in no way 'commercial' or private in character (rather, on the other hand, they could be part and parcel of international organizations' display of what could be described as *lato sensu* 'public powers'). Where international organizations' official acts are called into question, the issue of immunity still pops up. In these cases, arguably what should really matter is whether or not appropriate mechanisms of settlement are offered to the victims, more than the nature of the activity (i.e. 'commercial' or 'private').

Thirdly, and more generally, it would seem that the objective to be pursued should be to ensure accountability while also ensuring that international organizations remain fully independent, and that their autonomy is not put in jeopardy by invasive judiciaries.

This leads to a fundamental problem, already mentioned, which lies in the temptations of (judicial) 'unilateralism'. Every time the jurisdiction of one State elevates itself above the international legal order, every time a domestic judge considers that they can determine according to their own lights the scope of immunities under international law, then the risk is that international law is set aside altogether, without a fair balancing of competing values. That is not to say that domestic courts should refrain from engaging with international law. On the contrary, admittedly the role of national judges is essential for a more effective enactment of international rules. However, it is suggested that in interpreting and implementing international law domestic courts should fully take into account the panoply of international rules that come into play and should look to the overall array of competing interests that are at issue in each specific case.

More broadly, as far as international organizations are concerned, an alternative solution to the exercise of jurisdiction by domestic courts could be the establishment of appropriate mechanisms within the organization allowing victims of alleged violations a right of access, which would in turn increase the perception of accountability.

In this regard it might be interesting to note that in the 'Haiti cholera cases' for example, this would have allowed the complainants to be heard within the Organization and could have spared some of the controversies that tarnished the reputation of the UN. In that case, as is well known, the UN mission in Haiti was deemed responsible for bringing cholera to the island: lack of due diligence and culpable omissions were identified by the claimants and were recognized as flagrant by many observers. The UN, however, consistently maintained its position about immunity, barring any effective judicial remedy. US courts upheld the immunity claim and the cases were ultimately dismissed. Eventually an extrajudicial settlement was found, but in essence this was obtained only after a great deal of 'political' pressure on the Organization. That case was macroscopic, involving thousands of victims. However, in many instances the absence of remedies is the rule, and the Organization has only the option of bouncing back claimants, resorting to the immunity shield. Concerning the Haiti cases, some have argued that 'lawyers' in the Organization should have taken a different approach.[8] Nonetheless, arguably the issue should not be seen as confined to a single case and it appears more as a structural weakness that needs to be remedied. The Organization and, hence, its leadership, but also—and to a large extent and above all—its member States, should finally take the decision to establish appropriate settlement mechanisms to be activated in all appropriate cases.

Another relevant situation in this regard is the matter that led the association of victims of the Srebrenica massacre to bring lawsuits against the Netherlands and the United Nations. A number of decisions have been issued in this matter both at domestic level by Dutch courts as well as by the European Court of Human Rights. In essence the complainants (relatives of the victims of the Srebrenica genocide) maintained that the Dutch soldiers deployed as UN peacekeepers (Srebrenica was a UN-proclaimed safe haven, where thousands of Bosnian men were killed by the troops under the orders of Ratko Mladic, under the eyes of the Dutch soldiers of UNPROFOR, a UN peacekeeping force deployed, among other things, to protect the city) had not fulfilled their duties and had allowed the massacres to take place, and in so doing not only were there responsibilities of the State, but also of the UN. Eventually the Netherlands were deemed to be partially responsible for the deaths, but as far as the UN is concerned both the Dutch Supreme Court and the European Court of Human Rights confirmed and upheld the principle of the immunity of the Organization.[9]

While it is almost self-evident that the exercise of jurisdiction by the domestic courts of one or more member States cannot be seen as an appropriate way to deal with claims concerning the actions of international organizations, it is also clear that the lack of any jurisdictional control over the activities of international organizations is hardly consistent with the basic rule of law principles and elementary rules of good governance and responsible management, which are often invoked by the very same international organizations vis-à-vis member States.

As with State immunities, for international organizations too one needs to look at how claimants can find avenues to obtain access to justice. However, contrary to what happens in the case of State immunity, where—at least in theory—the jurisdiction of the State claiming immunity can normally be activated, in the case of international organizations often there is no available mechanism at all, or only limited alternatives which are usually impractical (such as e.g. resort to arbitration). In essence, when denied access to domestic courts on account of the immunity of international organizations, the claimants do not have any—even potential—remedy.

7.5.2 THE IMMUNITY OF AGENTS OF THE ORGANIZATION IN THEIR OFFICIAL CAPACITY AS INTERNATIONAL CIVIL SERVANTS

The immunity of international organizations normally extends to their personnel, who cannot be brought to justice for acts performed in their official capacity. Even though it is uncertain whether any customary rule in this respect has developed, it is usually through the organizations' constitutive instruments and through specific agreements between the organizations and their member States that such immunities, necessary for the unhindered performance of those organizations' tasks, are accorded.

---

[8] See J. Alvarez, 'The United Nations in the Time of Cholera' (2014) 108 *AJIL unbound* 22.
[9] For the European Court of Human Rights, see *Stichting Mothers of Srebrenica et al.* v *State of the Netherlands and the United Nations*; for the Dutch Supreme Court, see *Mothers of Srebrenica Association and others* v *the Netherlands*.

In this vein, Article 105(2) of the UN Charter indicates that 'officials of the Organization shall similarly enjoy such privileges and immunities as are necessary for the independent exercise of their functions in connection with the Organization'. The Convention on privileges and immunities of the UN mentioned earlier specifies that UN officials enjoy immunity 'from legal process in respect of words spoken or written and all acts performed by them in their official capacity'. This form of immunity, which is defined in Article V, section 18(a) of the Convention, is granted exclusively in the interests of the United Nations. Of course, immunity can and should be waived by the Secretary-General every time this is necessary in the interests of justice. This category of immunity is 'functional' in that it only refers to and covers the actions or omissions undertaken by international organizations' officials in their capacity as agents of those organizations. Moreover, on top of these functional immunities some categories of international civil servants (very high-level international organizations' officials normally) may also benefit from personal (or diplomatic) immunities; that is, immunities that are linked to their rank and that are based on the idea of letting them exercise their functions unhindered, covering even matters unrelated to their jobs. This is the case, for example, under Article V, section 19 of the Convention for the Secretary-General of the UN and a few other top-ranking UN officials (Under and Assistant Secretary-Generals), who are entitled to the same treatment as diplomatic envoys. Also, these immunities, naturally, are recognized for the benefit of the Organization and not as a personal privilege (as reflected under Article V, section 20 of the Convention)[10] and they can (and should) be waived whenever appropriate, so as to allow domestic courts to exercise jurisdiction.

The complexity and sensitivity of the issues involved with UN officials' immunities are well illustrated by a recent case regarding the immunities of a judge of the International Residual Mechanism for Criminal Tribunals (the IRMCT or just MICT or Mechanism as it is often called), the successor institution to ICTY and ICTR (see 19.3.3). In brief, in September 2016, Judge Akay, a Turkish national (and former member of the Turkish judiciary) who was serving on the MICT, was arrested and detained by Turkish authorities in the context of criminal proceedings against him on charges of membership of a terrorist organization. Almost immediately after his incarceration the United Nations Secretariat asserted immunity and requested release of Judge Akay, so as to allow him to continue to perform his tasks as judge of the MICT. In parallel, the President of the MICT raised the issue with both the General Assembly and the Security Council. After conviction at first instance, Judge Akay's appointment as MICT judge was not renewed (as the UN were informed by the Turkish government that Judge Akay no longer possessed the requirements to be a candidate for such a position, on account of his conviction). Eventually a new judge was appointed to the MICT.

In this case, while the UN Secretary-General promptly asserted immunity, and does not appear to have ever explicitly waived the claim, he may have abstained from taking a strong position and carrying through the claim to immunity 'vocally'. Of course, the decision rests with the Secretary-General as to what course of action is preferable to undertake, and through which channels; however, this case objectively creates some uncertainties. It would seem that the immunities claimed in this case appear to be akin to diplomatic or personal immunities accruing to high-ranking UN officials. Turkey indicated that the criminal

---

[10] According to section 20 of the Convention: 'Privileges and immunities are granted to officials in the interests of the United Nations and not for the personal benefit of the individuals themselves. The Secretary-General shall have the right and the duty to waive the immunity of any official in any case where, in his opinion, the immunity would impede the course of justice and can be waived without prejudice to the interests of the United Nations. In the case of the Secretary-General, the Security Council shall have the right to waive immunity.'

proceedings had nothing to do with the official functions of Judge Akay, and hence his functional immunity was not at issue (and this seems also to be the position of the UN);[11] on the other hand, the argument appears to be that Turkey maintains that the diplomatic/personal immunities could not be invoked towards the national authorities of the official (along the lines of what would occur with diplomats). Ultimately Turkish authorities did exercise jurisdiction. Judge Meron, as President of the MICT, issued a statement whereby he expressed strong disappointment, stating that 'the acquiescence to the position advanced by the Government of Turkey represents a *de facto* acceptance of a State's actions undertaken in contravention of the diplomatic immunity asserted by the United Nations, a dangerous precedent to set'.[12]

In the UN system, immunities are also accorded to special classes of people acting for the Organization, the so-called 'experts on mission'; these are figures who perform specific duties within the Organization without being 'staff members' and are protected by functional immunity on the basis of Article V, section 22 of the Convention. The ICJ was called to pronounce on the immunities of experts on mission (in two Advisory Opinions).[13] These are, for example, the 'special rapporteurs' under the Human Rights Council (and in the past the Human Rights Commission) monitoring mechanisms. The Court reaffirmed the functional nature of these immunities and the fact that these arise from the Organization's immunity; moreover, it clarified that this category of personnel enjoys immunities and that only the Secretary-General can waive them and needs to do so explicitly (in other words, restraint should be exercised by domestic authorities).[14]

Finally, special treatment—not necessarily labelled immunity—is also accorded to broader categories of personnel deployed in UN missions all over the world; the status of this class of personnel (who are often not even UN staff) is normally implemented through status of forces or mission agreements or other special regulations between the UN and the host State; these agreements deal specifically with situations where such personnel may be involved in proceedings before domestic courts for actions which are unrelated to their official functions. The agreements often provide for the exclusive jurisdiction of the State of nationality as the more convenient forum, as opposed to the territorial State (or *loci commissi delicti*), which normally agrees not to exercise its jurisdiction. These mechanisms, which are of course designed to avoid the risks of undue interference by local authorities with the work of international organizations, lend themselves to abuses and have on several occasions led the General Assembly to tackle the issue by strengthening mechanisms to establish accountability for the conduct of all categories of personnel through more robust co-operation (e.g. the zero tolerance policy concerning sexual exploitation and abuses, as well as the annual debate and resolution on the 'criminal accountability of UN officials and experts on mission'). The main objective of any measure is to ensure increased monitoring and accountability, without however jeopardizing the ability of the Organization and its personnel to perform their tasks unhindered.

---

[11] In this regard see https://www.asil.org/insights/volume/22/issue/14/immunity-judge-akay-turkey-test-case-international-judges-immunity-and#_ednref3.

[12] See http://www.irmct.org/en/news/statement-president-non-reappointment-judge-akay.

[13] See *Applicability of Article VI, Section 22, of the Convention on the Privileges and Immunities of the United Nations* (concerning the case of case of Mr Dumitru Mazilu, as Rapporteur of the Sub-Commission on the Prevention of Discrimination and Protection of Minorities of the Commission on Human Rights), and *Difference Relating to Immunity from Legal Process of a Special Rapporteur of the Commission on Human Rights* (concerning the case of Mr Cumaraswamy).

[14] *Difference Relating to Immunity from Legal Process of a Special Rapporteur of the Commission on Human Rights*, 84–5, §§52–56.

7.6 OTHER RIGHTS OF INTERNATIONAL ORGANIZATIONS

Among other rights generally recognized to be held by international organizations a few others are worth mentioning:

(1) *The right to enter into international agreements, including with non-member States, on matters within the organization's province.* Treaties concluded by the organization have all the legally binding effects of international treaties proper—provided, of course, that this was the intention of the parties to the agreement. In fact, international organizations have concluded numerous treaties covering a host of matters: ranging from headquarters agreements and conventions on privileges and immunities to treaties relating to activities performed by the organization concerned (e.g. those on technical assistance entered into by the UN), or agreements with other organizations for the co-ordination of their action, etc.

(2) *The right to protection for its agents and the right to bring an international claim.* As subjects of international law, international organizations are entitled to *invoke protection for their agents* acting as international civil servants, as well as the right to *bring international claims*.

The ICJ in its Advisory Opinion on *Reparation for Injuries* authoritatively upheld this right as early as 1949. On 17 September 1948, the UN Mediator, a Swede, Count Folke Bernadotte, and the UN Observer, a Frenchman, Colonel André Sérot, were assassinated by a Jewish terrorist organization while on an official mission for the UN. The murder took place in the eastern part of Jerusalem (then under Israeli control) after Israel had proclaimed its independence, and before it was admitted to UN membership. The Israeli authorities tried to discover and bring to justice the perpetrators and instigators of the crime but, as the Israeli representative stated to the UN General Assembly on 5 May 1948, 'the results of the investigations had been disappointingly negative' (*UNY*, 1948, at 400). The government of Israel admitted that 'failure had been reported in the functioning of its security system in the past' but it 'could not admit that any conclusions could be drawn from that event with respect to its present capacity to fulfil its international obligations'. Whatever the reasons behind its stance (it has been contended that it made a point of honouring its international obligations because it was keen to enter the UN), the fact remains that Israel declared itself to be ready to make reparation for its failure to protect the two UN agents and to punish their killers.

International organizations also possess the *right to bring a claim* with a view to obtaining reparation for any damage caused by member States or by third States to the assets of the organization or to its officials acting on behalf of the organization. The ICJ upheld this right too in the same case. The Court held unanimously that the organization could bring an international claim for damage caused to its assets, and held by a large majority (11 to 4) that the organization could also bring a claim for reparation due in respect of the damage caused to an agent of the organization (so-called *functional* protection). Accordingly, the organization may bring claims on behalf of its agents, even where the offending State is the national State of the victim. The Court correctly implied that this right was *procedural* in character and presupposed the violation of a *substantive* right of the Organization, that is, the right to respect for and protection of its agents by any State in whose territory the agents performed their official functions.

A majority of the Court adopted a very progressive stand on another issue. Instead of endorsing the traditional view whereby States alone can put forward claims on behalf of their nationals injured abroad (the so-called *diplomatic* protection), the Court held that when an individual acts on behalf of an organization, the organization may also exercise protection of its agents qua individuals. This view, needless to say, greatly privileged the *functional* bond as opposed to *national* allegiance. Some felt that this view actually undermined the authority of States over their citizens and constituted a dangerous precedent. At that time socialist countries, in particular, strongly resented and criticized the Court.

Despite the existence of these various rights, organizations do not always have the capacity to *enforce* them when member or non-member States breach them. True, organizations have the right to seek remedies before international bodies (provided of course that the defendant State has accepted the competence of such organs). However, in cases of non-compliance by States either with their own obligations or with international decisions concerning their wrongful acts, international organizations are often unable to enforce the law. They only have the power to suspend the delinquent member State from participation or voting, or to expel it from the organization. With regard to non-member States, organizations may invoke the general rules on State responsibility (see **Chapter 12**).

7.7 THE RESPONSIBILITY OF INTERNATIONAL ORGANIZATIONS

Another facet of the recognition of legal personality of international organizations is the fact that, as legal subjects, they are responsible for violations of international law. Clearly the issues of personality and responsibility are two sides of the same coin. In his very first report on the topic of Responsibility of International Organizations, the Special Rapporteur, Giorgio Gaja, stated that 'responsibility under international law may arise only for a subject of international law' (at §15). As illustrated by the ICJ in its Advisory Opinion *Interpretation of the Agreement of 25 March 1951 between the WHO and Egypt*, 'international organizations are subjects of international law and, as such, are bound by any obligations incumbent upon them under general rules of international law, under their constitutions or under international agreements to which they are parties' (at 89–90).

The violations of obligations flowing from any of these sources of law should normally entail the responsibility of international organizations for internationally wrongful acts. However, there is a distinction to be made between the consequences of violations, and hence responsibility, under general international law, and any special mechanisms which may exist in the constitutive instrument or in other internal laws of the relevant organization to redress any infringement of the applicable law.

The work carried out by the ILC had as its primary objective the codification of the general rules. The Articles on the Responsibility of International Organizations of the International Law Commission (ILC) have been modelled on the parallel Articles on State Responsibility (see **12.1**) with few adaptations. Essentially the idea is that the rules governing the responsibility of international organizations are the same as, or at least inspired by similar logic to, those relating to State responsibility, linked to the subjectivity of international organizations under international law. The approach taken by the Commission, however, has been criticized by both certain scholars and some member States, arguing that the ILC did not sufficiently take into account the specificities of international organizations.

Admittedly, setting out general rules applicable, at least in theory, to all international organizations has the merit of trying to devise a minimum group of default rules that could apply, absent specific regulation. This choice does not exclude that international organizations may operate under special rules and procedures, and the fact that these general rules would be applicable only in very limited cases does not per se mean that they are not useful. In brief: the idea of transposing the rules on State responsibility to international organizations has been criticized on account of the differences between international organizations and States as legal subjects (the scope and nature of their personality, of their powers, the breadth of their competences, and so on), as well as the huge differences among international organizations themselves, entities so varied in nature that they can hardly be regulated in the same way. Although the Articles on the Responsibility of International Organizations will probably remain at this stage a non-binding document (and case law will be further collected and analysed to see how and to what extent these provisions are resorted to), they certainly evidence the need for dealing with this issue.

As indicated earlier, one of the main problems with regard to the responsibility of international organizations is the difficulty in establishing appropriate mechanisms of redress for violations of international law (be it general international law or treaty law, including constitutive instruments) attributable to the organization, without jeopardizing their autonomy and independence (and hence their ability to fulfil their tasks unhindered). Broadly speaking, while it is clear that international organizations, at least in theory, are accountable to their member States (and member States could explore avenues to establish greater accountability through exercise of internal monitoring), it remains to be seen how responsibility of international organizations may be enforced when such avenues do not exist or are not practicable.

8

INDIVIDUALS AND OTHER LEGAL SUBJECTS

8.1 THE EXPANSION OF INTERNATIONAL LEGAL PERSONALITY

One of the main developments of the twentieth century has been the expansion of international personality. As already mentioned, while States remain the backbone of the international community, various other entities have emerged. International legal subjects also include insurgents, national liberation movements, international organizations, and individuals, as well as a few *sui generis* entities. While insurgents, like States and some of the *sui generis* entities, constitute traditional subjects of international law, the other categories are new classes of subjects. Among these new categories, individuals present distinctive traits that are worth closer scrutiny.

The rationale behind attributing international status to individuals and national liberation movements also has an *ideological aspect*. Different ideologies accounted for the emergence of each of the two classes of international subject. Western, liberal-democratic theory lay at the root of the granting of legal entitlements to individuals on the international scene: the human rights doctrine, championed by Western countries such as the US and a few Latin American countries as early as 1944–45 and subsequently taken up by a number of other Western or Western-oriented States. This doctrine did not result only in the drafting of a number of international treaties protecting human rights. Its logical corollary was that individuals were granted the opportunity to call States to account before international bodies whenever they felt that their rights had been disregarded. In addition, new doctrines emerged (or took on new vigour) in the world community. They advocated full respect for some basic values (in addition to human rights, peace, the need to spare civilians as much as possible in armed conflict and, more generally, to uphold principles of humanity). Furthermore, States increasingly envisaged the direct imposition of international obligations upon individuals, regardless of what the national legal order within which they lived might enjoin them to do. These obligations are designed to induce individuals to heed those values, with the consequence that, should they disregard them, they may be prosecuted and punished.

On the other hand, the doctrine and, subsequently, the principle of and the right to self-determination of peoples (see **3.8**) is behind the emergence of colonial peoples and peoples under racist regimes or foreign domination on the international scene. What gave impetus to the appearance of this category of subjects was the anti-colonialist version propounded by Lenin as early as 1917, rather than the moderate one put forward by Woodrow Wilson in 1918.[1]

---

[1] See M. Kohen, 'Self-determination' in J. E. Viñuales (ed.), *The Friendly Relations Declaration at 50: An Assessment of the Fundamental Principles of International Law* (Cambridge: Cambridge University Press, 2020), chapter 7.

In essence, as is often the case in international law, two main fundamental structural principles have been at play in bringing about these developments: legality, on the one hand, and effectiveness (or *effectivité*), on the other. These two elements combined, in different measures in each case, both play a role and contributed to the expansion of claims to international legal subjectivity in the second half of the twentieth century.

Some entities have emerged as legal subjects under international law primarily on account of the idea that their subjectivity was linked to adherence with new legal principles and fundamental values protected by the international legal system: for example, peoples were recognized to have legal personality under international law on the basis of the affirmation of the principle of self-determination; similarly, individuals were proposed as new subjects of international law on account of the appearance on the international scene of human rights norms as well as rules imposing individual criminal responsibility under international law—that is, the rules on war crimes, crimes against humanity, and genocide.

Other entities, on the other hand, have been treated, at least in some respects, as subjects more on the basis of their concrete ability to interact at the international level with subjects of law: for their factual relevance they have been considered as possessing some traits of subjectivity under international law. However, a measure of legality/legitimacy is still required (in the sense that any entity claiming subjectivity under international law cannot be radically in conflict with fundamental principles—for example, ISIS/Daesh despite the label 'State' did not seem to be perceived as potentially claiming subjectivity under international law for it denied the fundamental principles of the international legal system[2]).

In this respect, the dichotomy between traditional and current international law becomes even more relevant. Under traditional international law, the prevailing tendency was to consider States to be the main (or exclusive) subjects of international law. This leads to the discourse by which entities other than States are defined 'negatively' as 'non-state actors'.[3]

The truth is that the broader participation in international relations hardly made it possible to continue to limit legal personality only to the traditional actors: States, insurgents, and a few other *sui generis* entities. Some have argued in favour of different categorization (labelling these new entities as participants or actors), some have maintained that only rather limited recognition can be given to these other entities, while the traditional approach is still prevailing.

The reality is that today a large variety of entities has acquired some status under international law and actively participates in international dealings. As we have seen already, the phenomenon of international organizations has been one of the main developments of the twentieth century; another powerful driver for change has been the increasing recognition of rights and duties for actors other than States, in particular the emergence of human rights and international criminal law. Moreover, three radically different phenomena have marked the past two or three decades: the increased activism of international civil society, the advent of the internet era and an interlinked cyberworld which hardly recognizes any borders, and the renewed emergency surrounding international terrorism. These phenomena—in different ways—have further enlarged the spectrum of entities that take part in or, at the very least, greatly influence international dealings. All these developments have rendered any limited approach to the 'subjects of international law' more difficult to maintain.

---

[2] See e.g. M. Frulli (ed.), *A. Cassese, Diritto internazionale* (Bologna: Il Mulino, 2017), 161, although limiting the remark to the issue of recognition as insurgents; arguably, however, the comment can be broadened to the very existence of any such entity under international law.

[3] See P. Alston, 'The "Not-a-Cat" Syndrome: Can the International Human Rights Regime Accommodate Non-State Actors?' in P. Alston (ed.), *Non-State Actors and Human Rights, (Collected Courses of the Academy of European Union)* (Oxford: Oxford University Press, 2005), 3; A. Clapham, *Human Rights Obligations of Non-State Actors* (Oxford: Oxford University Press, 2006), chapter 1.

Certainly, a broader perspective on international subjectivity (which had already been advanced between the two world wars) has been reinvigorated since the Second World War, through the recognition that individuals assume more prominence. In particular, with the Nuremberg and Tokyo trials, international law affirms that there are duties which individuals must respect irrespective of what their domestic legal system indicates (there are offences against international law—i.e. war crimes, crimes against humanity, genocide, crimes against peace). The judgment of the International Military Tribunal sitting at Nuremberg (the IMT or the Nuremberg Tribunal) stated that 'international law imposes duties and liabilities upon individuals as well as upon States' and it added that '[c]rimes against international law are committed by men, not by abstract entities, and only by punishing individuals who commit such crimes can the provision of international law be enforced' (*Göring and others*, at 223). On the other hand, the advent of human rights law on the international scene indicates that individuals are the bearers of legal rights and may possess—to a certain extent—the ability to invoke such rights before international authorities even against their own State (the regional systems of human rights protection are the clearest example of this trend).

8.2 INDIVIDUALS: RIGHTS AND DUTIES

8.2.1 GENERAL REMARKS

Many commentators contend that individuals may not be regarded as having the legal status of international subjects. In their view, individuals are still under the exclusive control of States. If treaties provide for rights and duties of individuals, this would only mean that each State undertakes by agreement vis-à-vis the other contracting States to confer such rights and impose duties on individuals solely within its own legal system. Those commentators regard the right of individuals to petition international judicial or quasi-judicial bodies as exceptional, viewing it as no more than a procedural entitlement which lacks any attendant substantive right or the power to enforce a possible decision of the international body favourable to the individual. We will see later that the international condition of individuals is much more complex and multifaceted. In any case, here too international law has undergone dramatic changes in recent times. After briefly sketching out the condition of individuals under traditional international law, we will examine the relevant modern rules, to establish whether it may be said that they grant rights to, or impose obligations on, individuals, and whether it is therefore warranted to regard human beings as international legal subjects.

Over a long period of time—in fact during the whole of the first stage of development of the international community, from the seventeenth to the early twentieth century—human beings were under the exclusive control of States. If, in time, individuals acquired some relevance in international affairs, it was largely as 'beneficiaries' of treaties of commerce and navigation, or of conventions on the treatment to be accorded to foreigners, etc. Or else they constituted the 'reference point' of States' powers (e.g. think of the customary rule granting States the right to exercise diplomatic and, if legally possible, judicial protection of their nationals wronged by a foreign country). The general position of international law with regard to individuals was aptly set out in 1928 by the PCIJ in its Advisory Opinion on *Jurisdiction of the Courts of Danzig*, as follows:

> It may be readily admitted that, according to a well-established principle of international law, the *Beamtenabkommen* [a treaty between Poland and Germany] being an international agreement, cannot, as such, create direct rights and obligations for private individuals. But it cannot be disputed that the very object of an international agreement, according to the intention of the Contracting Parties, may be the adoption by the Parties of some definite rules creating individual rights and obligations enforceable by the national courts. (at 17–18)

Traditional international law did not include general rules conferring rights on individuals regardless of their nationality. The question of a possible international legal status for individuals mainly arose with regard to *piracy* (any attack on a ship committed for private ends, on the high seas, by the crew or the passengers of a private ship), a phenomenon that, while it was widespread in the seventeenth and eighteenth centuries, gradually disappeared, although more recently it has been to some extent revived in certain areas of the world. It thus remained a matter of controversy whether international rules reached individuals directly or through the intermediary of national legal systems.

Some leading scholars (such as Westlake and Kelsen)[4] argued that international rules imposed direct obligations concerning piracy on individuals while at the same time exceptionally authorizing any State to seize pirates on the high seas and to punish them irrespective of their nationality. Others (e.g. Anzilotti)[5] contended that, instead, international rules merely obliged States to pass legislation prohibiting piracy and at the same time authorized all States to allow their national authorities to arrest, prosecute, and punish pirates.

The question remained controversial, on two main grounds. First, when piracy was in its heyday individuals were under the full control of States. As stated earlier, they were beneficiaries of diplomatic or judicial protection only when their national State decided to exercise such protection vis-à-vis another State. Secondly, it seemed rather odd to speak of individuals as subjects of international law, when allegedly they had obligations deriving from international rules but were not at the same time granted rights and powers.

The situation appears to be different today. At present, as a result of historical events and the spread of new ideologies, States have lost their exclusive monopoly over individuals, in addition to gradually yielding some of their powers to other entities such as international organizations. Individuals have gradually come to be regarded as holders of internationally material interests but also as capable of infringing fundamental values of the world community. Their demands and concerns as well as their possibly reprehensible conduct have been taken into account. Thus, individuals have been granted legal rights that are operational at the international level. By the same token, States have deemed it fit to extend obligations to them, by enjoining them to comply with some new fundamental values and calling them to account for any breach of such values.

Moreover, the general trend has progressively recognized more room for the subjectivity of individuals and strengthened recognition for their rights: for example, the ICJ judgment in *LaGrand (Germany v United States of America)* (at §77) and the subsequent *Avena and Other Mexican Nationals (Mexico v United States of America)* seem to support a reading of diplomatic protection that strengthens the position of individuals, creating a reinforced basis for their subjectivity under international law. Also, in *Ahmadou Sadio Diallo (Republic of Guinea v Democratic Republic of the Congo)*, the Court reiterated a similar approach.

8.2.2 CUSTOMARY RULES IMPOSING OBLIGATIONS ON INDIVIDUALS

It seems unquestionable that, in recent times, a number of international rules have come into being that directly impose *obligations* upon individuals. These general rules first crystallized in the area of armed conflict. They provided that, should individuals engaging in

---

[4] J. Westlake, *Chapters on the Principles of International Law* (Cambridge: Cambridge University Press, 1894), 2; H. Kelsen, *Principles of International Law* (New York: Rinehart & Co., 1952), 203.

[5] D. Anzilotti, 'L'azione individuale contraria al diritto internazionale' (1902) 5 *Rivista di diritto internazionale e legislazione comparata* 8, repr. in his *Scritti di diritto internazionnale pubblico* (Padova: Cedam, 1956), i, 211.

an international war break the rules of warfare, they would be criminally liable for such breaches, regardless of their official position as State agents. Subsequently general rules on the punishment of other international crimes evolved (on crimes against humanity, in particular genocide, on aggression and terrorism, as well as torture). In addition, the scope of the rules on war crimes has expanded (see **19.2.1**).

Thus, individuals are at present under many international obligations, some solely relating to armed conflict, others (those on crimes against humanity, genocide, aggression, terrorism, and torture) also concerning peacetime. These obligations are incumbent upon *all individuals of the world*: they are all obliged to refrain from breaching the aforementioned rules; if they do not do so, they are accountable for their transgression. This is so regardless of whether the national legal system within which individuals live contains a similar or the same obligation (translated into national legislation). In other words, this is an area where the international legal system enters into direct contact, as it were, with individuals, without the medium of national legal systems. As the IMT at Nuremberg stated:

> [T]he very essence of the Charter [of the IMT] is that individuals have international duties which transcend the national obligations of obedience imposed by the individual State. He who violates the laws of war cannot obtain immunity while acting in pursuance of the authority of the State if the State in authorizing action moves outside its competence under international law. (*Göring and others*, at 233)

Furthermore, those obligations are incumbent on individuals both when they act as State officials (this is by far the most normal occurrence) as well as, under certain conditions, when they engage in the prohibited conduct qua individuals, that is, in a private capacity. Individuals breaching one of the obligations under discussion are criminally liable and can be prosecuted before domestic courts (see **19.3.1**) or before an international criminal court or tribunal, if such a court or tribunal has been established and has jurisdiction over the crimes (see **19.3.3**).

8.2.3 THE HOLDERS OF THE CORRESPONDING RIGHTS

Who is legally entitled to enforce the above-mentioned obligations? Two views are admissible. First, it could be maintained that, at the present stage in the development of the world community, individuals may not yet be held entitled to seek enforcement of those obligations at the *international* level. Only States would be in a position to advance such a claim, with the concomitant power to pursue enforcement by bringing to trial, before international criminal courts or tribunals (such as the International Criminal Court: ICC; see **19.3.3**), those allegedly responsible for breaches of the obligations. A different view could also be entertained. It could be contended that the 'foray' of international values, hence of international rights and obligations, into areas previously subjected to national legal systems has been so extensive as to give individuals a role that was previously unthinkable. As has just been pointed out, all individuals in the world, whatever their nationality and whether or not they are so enjoined by the national legal system of the country in which they live, are now under the strict international obligation fully to respect some important values (maintenance of peace, protection of human dignity, etc.). It would be not only consistent from the viewpoint of legal logic but also in keeping with new trends emerging in the world community to argue that the international right in respect of those obligations accrues to all individuals: they are entitled to respect for their life and limbs, and for their dignity; hence they have a right not to become a victim of war crimes, crimes against humanity, aggression, torture, or terrorism. At least for the time being, this international right, deriving from general international rules, is not, however, attended by a *specific* means, or power, of enforcement that belongs to individuals. At present, individuals can only institute criminal proceedings against the alleged culprits of such crimes before national courts possessing territorial, personal, or universal criminal jurisdiction (see **19.3.1**). Alternatively, they can bring the alleged breaches to the attention of the Prosecutor of the ICC. They can also petition international human rights bodies, calling to account the State of which the alleged author of a crime is an agent. That a substantive right is not attended by a specific legal entitlement to enforce that right is by no means novel or surprising, in legal terms.

It may be noted that the power, granted by the Statute establishing the ICC (the Rome Statute) to victims of international crimes, to put forward their legal views and concerns in proceedings set in motion before the Court by the Prosecutor, by States, or by the Security Council, may bear out, at least to some extent, the legal construction just delineated. It should be added that, strictly speaking, there is nothing to prevent States from providing in international rules for obligations incumbent upon individuals and corresponding rights accruing to them, in the international field. What matters is the intention of the law-makers. In terms of the view under discussion, it could be contended that the States that deliberately or unwittingly contributed to the formation of customary rules on international crimes intended to grant corresponding rights to individuals.

To grasp what this view implies, it may prove useful to emphasize the difference between the general rules under discussion and treaty provisions on human rights (e.g. those of the International Covenant on Civil and Political Rights). The latter provisions seem to confer *substantive* (as opposed to *procedural* or *adjective*) rights and obligations on individuals; in fact, all they do is to oblige States to grant rights and impose obligations on individuals *in their respective national systems*. As a consequence, should a contracting party fail to implement one of those provisions by legislative action in its domestic legal system, individuals would not possess the substantive rights and obligations laid down in that provision. By contrast, the rights and obligations we are discussing are *directly* conferred on individuals by international rules. They therefore accrue to, or are incumbent upon, persons even if a national legal system *has not implemented* those international rules domestically or has passed legislation contrary to them. Clearly, in this case the international legal order reaches out to individuals and international norms apply even without relying upon, or going through, national legal systems. This unique legal regulation is significant evidence of the *growing direct impact* of the international legal system on the action of individuals living in sovereign States.

Whichever of these two views is considered sounder, there is no gainsaying that the emergence of the international obligations under discussion marks a significant advance in the international community.

8.2.4 TREATY PROVISIONS CONFERRING RIGHTS ON INDIVIDUALS

In modern times, States have increasingly concluded agreements granting human rights to individuals subject to their jurisdiction. In some instances, they have also provided for the right of individuals to petition international bodies alleging that a contracting State has breached one of their human rights. The question arises of whether the *substantive* rights at issue have only a national dimension, that is, whether they may only be exercised within the municipal sphere of each contracting party, or have instead an international scope, in which case they may be exercised at the international level. The same problem also arises with regard to the *procedural* right to petition international bodies.

As pointed out previously, it is apparent from international treaties on human rights that the substantive rights they lay down may only be exercised by individuals within the *domestic* legal system of each contracting party. The position is different as regards the right to lodge a complaint with an international body established by treaty.

This trend began in Latin America. The treaty concluded by five Central American republics (Costa Rica, El Salvador, Guatemala, Honduras, and Nicaragua) for the establishment of the Central American Court of Justice (1908–18) granted to individuals, as well as to States and domestic institutions, the right to appear as parties before the Court (see **13.4**). Individuals could bring complaints against one of those States (other than their own), for violations of international law. Indeed, individuals brought five of the 10 cases heard by the Court; however, none of these cases was successful.

After the First World War, the framers of the International Labour Organization (ILO) decided to confer on industrial associations of workers and employers the right to demand compliance with ILO Conventions by member States. At the time this was a very great improvement. It went hand in hand with another similar development in the field of the international protection of minorities (racial, religious, or linguistic): representatives of such minorities gained the right to lodge 'petitions' with the League of Nations, if in their view the States concerned failed to honour their international undertakings. In both cases, the rationale behind this significant change can easily be accounted for: as ILO Conventions and international treaties on minorities were calculated to protect workers (or employers) and minorities respectively, it was quite logical to grant their beneficiaries the right to protest in the case of alleged violations. This appeared all the more sensible since the treaties in question did not lay down any synallagmatic (reciprocal) rules (see **10.2**), but imposed obligations *erga omnes* (*contractantes*) relating to acts to be performed by each contracting State within its own municipal territory, regardless of any direct interest or benefit that might accrue to other contracting States. Consequently, had the groups of individuals directly concerned not been authorized to denounce possible violations, no State would have been likely to protest.

However, the potential practical benefits of this important new right were never fully realized. Associations of workers and employers lodged very few complaints with the ILO, and minorities made scant use of their right of petition. Historical conditions were manifestly not yet propitious for a legal development that was in many respects far in advance of its time.

After the Second World War, the ILO principles were reaffirmed and the machinery for implementing them was gradually strengthened. Treaties on minorities, which had collapsed long before the outbreak of the war, were replaced by a number of Conventions on human rights, which no longer protected groups of individuals as such, but rather single human beings. Some of them granted their beneficiaries the right to make States accountable for possible contraventions. Individuals consequently came to possess a certain measure of international status.

On closer scrutiny, it appears that, as stressed earlier in the chapter, the right to petition international bodies is conferred on individuals regardless of whether or not they are accordingly *authorized* by the national legislation implementing those treaties. In other words, this right is granted to individuals *directly by international rules*, and exists whatever the content of national legislation. The right therefore is an *international right* proper. However, this right is subject to the following limitations:

(1) Individuals are given only a *procedural right*, namely, the right to initiate international proceedings before an international body, for the purpose of ascertaining whether the State complained of has violated the treaty to the detriment of those individuals. In addition, this right is usually limited to forwarding a complaint, for the complainant is not allowed to participate in international proceedings.

A notable exception is the system of the European Convention on Human Rights (ECHR): in addition to instituting proceedings, individuals may submit memorials, take part in, and make representations at the hearings; after delivery of the judgment by a Chamber, they may request that the case be referred to the Grand Chamber if they consider that it raises a serious question of interpretation or application or a serious issue of general importance.

Normally the individual has no right to enforce or promote the enforcement of any international decision favourable to him (again, a limited deviation from this rule can be found in the practice relating to the ECHR). Once the international body has pronounced upon the alleged violation, the applicant is left in the hands of the accused State: cessation of, or reparation for, the wrongful act will substantially depend on its goodwill (however, under the ECHR the State is under the obligation to comply and, in addition, the Council of Europe Committee of Ministers has the power to monitor compliance with the Court's judgment).

(2) The right in question is *only granted by treaties* (or, in a few instances, by *international resolutions*). Consequently, it exists only with respect to certain well-defined matters (e.g. labour relations, human rights).

As to the ILO, Article 24 of its Constitution grants associations of workers or employers the right to submit complaints with respect to any ILO Convention ratified by the State complained of; in addition, a few resolutions adopted in 1950 provide for the right of associations of workers to petition an ILO body (the Committee on Trade Union Freedom of Association) for alleged violations of the ILO Conventions on the matter, regardless of whether the accused State has ratified them.

In the field of human rights, mention should be made of the Optional Protocol to the International Covenant on Civil and Political Rights of 1966, the Convention on the Elimination of Racial Discrimination of 1965 (Article 14), as well as of two procedures set up by the Economic and Social Council (ECOSOC) in 1967 and 1970 respectively, whereby individuals or groups of individuals can submit 'communications' to certain human rights bodies (see **18.4.6**). On the regional level, the most noteworthy treaty is the ECHR, referred to above. An American Convention on Human Rights was adopted in 1969, one of its provisions (Article 44) granting 'any person or group of persons or any non-governmental entity legally recognized in one or more member States' of the Organization of American States (OAS) the right to lodge with the Inter-American Commission on Human Rights petitions containing denunciations or complaints of violation of the Convention by a State party to it (see **18.4.7**).

(3) Another limitation lies in the fact that *not all States that are parties to the above treaties accept being made accountable to individuals* (the ECHR being a notable exception). To enable States opposed to the presence of individuals in the international community to ratify the treaties concerned without submitting to supervisory procedures set in motion by individuals, a special device has been resorted to: the authority of international bodies to consider individuals' petitions has been laid down in particular clauses of the treaties. Consequently, only those contracting States which *also* accept the clauses explicitly, submit to the control mechanisms.

(4) A further weakness is that the *procedures individuals are authorized to initiate are quite different from those existing in domestic law*. Three things in particular stand out. First, international bodies responsible for considering petitions are generally not judicial in character, although they often tend to behave in conformity with judicial rules. Secondly, often international proceedings are themselves quite rudimentary; in particular, there are notable limitations concerning the taking of evidence. Thirdly, and even more importantly, the outcome of the procedure is not a judgment proper, but a relatively mild act, such as a report setting out the views of the international body, a recommendation, or the like: no

legally binding decision is envisaged (again, the European and the American Conventions on human rights are important exceptions).

It is thus apparent that the role of individuals' international procedural rights is limited on many scores. In addition, it is precarious, for it rests on the will of States. As soon as they decide to terminate the treaty or to repeal the international resolution granting procedural rights to individuals, these rights cease to exist in the international arena. Similarly, as soon as a State that has ratified one of the treaties in question withdraws its acceptance of the international bodies' authority to deal with complaints by individuals, the latter can no longer sue that State on the international plane.

Despite these deficiencies, the importance of individuals in relation to the right to petition international bodies directly should not be underestimated. It is not easy for States to deprive themselves of some of their sovereign prerogatives, such as their traditional claim to exercise full control over individuals subject to their jurisdiction. Given the present structure of the world community and the fact that States are still the overlords, the limited status of individuals can be regarded as remarkable progress. In addition, individuals are granted the right to petition international organs irrespective of their nationality, whether they be citizens of the State complained of, or nationals of other States (be they parties to the treaty or not), or even stateless persons. The right is therefore granted to physical persons qua human beings. No bond of nationality or any other form of allegiance is taken into account. This in itself represents a momentous advance.

Furthermore, in a great many cases where States have accepted the authority of international bodies to consider complaints of individuals, they have eventually come to respect the decisions by which those bodies have determined violations. In other words, international techniques of supervision set in motion by physical persons (or non-governmental groups) have indeed proved effective. This is hardly surprising. Once a State has taken the serious and momentous step of accepting the jurisdiction of international bodies acting at the request of individuals, it does not find it too difficult to attend to the decisions of those bodies and, if found responsible for violations, to take all the necessary measures for terminating a breach, or paying compensation to the victims.

All things considered, the existing international systems for protecting human rights that depend on the initiative of the very beneficiaries of the rights in question are no less effective than other international devices for ensuring compliance with international law. One should therefore not be discouraged by the paucity of international mechanisms based on individuals' petitions. Like all international instruments denoting a bold advance, treaties granting procedural rights to human beings are destined to be fruitful in the long run.

In sum, in contemporary international law individuals possess international legal status. They have a few *obligations*, deriving from customary international law. In addition, *procedural rights* enure to the benefit of individuals, not however vis-à-vis all States, but only towards the group of States that have concluded treaties, or the international organizations that have adopted resolutions, envisaging such rights. Clearly, the international legal status of individuals is unique: they have a *lopsided position* in the international community. As far as their obligations are concerned, they are associated with all the other members of the international community; in contrast, they do not possess rights in relation to all members of that community. Plainly, all States are willing to demand of individuals respect for some fundamental values, while they are less prepared to associate them to their international dealings, let alone to grant them the power to sue States before international bodies. To differentiate the position of individuals from that of States, it can be maintained that while States have international legal personality proper, individuals possess a *limited locus standi in international law*. Furthermore, unlike States, individuals possess a limited array of rights and obligations, that is, a *limited legal capacity* (to some extent they can therefore be equated with other non-State international subjects: insurgents, international organizations, and national liberation movements).

8.3 PEOPLES AND NATIONAL LIBERATION MOVEMENTS

The emergence of organized groups fighting on behalf of a whole 'people' against colonial Powers is a characteristic feature of the aftermath of the Second World War. Although it is not possible to discern a linear or sequential trajectory, generally speaking, liberation movements arose first in Africa, then in Asia; they then mushroomed in Latin America and—to a lesser extent—in Europe. Africa, however, has been the principal home of liberation movements. Along with the gradual expansion of the liberation phenomenon from Africa to other continents, the movements also broadened their objectives, invoking new goals in addition to anti-colonialism, namely struggles against racist regimes and alien domination. Struggles of this type were prevalent from the 1960s until the 1980s. At present they seem to be on the wane. Consequently, this class of international subjects is dwindling.[6]

A characteristic of a few of these movements has been the acquisition of control over some part of the territory they claimed (e.g. the FLN in Algeria, the two movements in Zimbabwe, the two liberation movements in Eritrea, POLISARIO in Western Sahara). However, most of them were hosted in a friendly country, from where they conducted military operations against their adversaries (e.g. the PLO, SWAPO, and the ANC). *Control of territory*, therefore, is not their distinguishing trait, in contrast to insurgents. Their chief characteristic is their *international legitimation based on the principle of self-determination*. They are given international status on account of their political goals: their struggle to free themselves from colonial domination, a racist regime, or alien occupation. It is as a consequence of this legitimation, recognized in the 1970 Friendly Relations Declaration (see **3.8**), that no ban is imposed on States to refrain from providing national liberation movements with humanitarian, economic, and military assistance short of sending armed troops; conversely, States are duty-bound to refrain from assisting a State denying self-determination to a people or a group entitled to it. Yet, this does not mean that the territorial factor is ruled out altogether:

---

[6] Algeria was the first country to witness the emergence of a liberation movement (the FLN, in 1954). Other African movements were: PAIGC (African Party for the Independence of Guinea and Cape Verde); FRELIMO (Liberation Front of Mozambique); the three movements in Angola (MPLA, UNITA, and FLNA); the two movements which fought in Zimbabwe (ZAPU and ZANU); those fighting against South Africa (ANC: African National Congress, and PAC: Pan African Congress); SWAPO (South West Africa People's Organization), in Namibia; POLISARIO, struggling against Morocco in Western Sahara (annexed by Morocco in 1975), amongst others. In the Middle East the PLO was founded in 1969. In Asia the FNLV actively participated in the struggle against South Vietnam from 1960 to 1974; FRETILIN sprang up in Timor in 1975 to fight against Indonesian rule. In Latin America similar movements emerged. Many of these movements eventually acquired statehood (e.g. in Algeria, Zimbabwe, the Comores, the Seychelles, Angola, Mozambique, Vietnam, Eritrea, South Africa, and East Timor). The ANC became an integral part of the new government in South Africa. In East Timor a new State is in the process of emerging. The PLO has been gradually given control over the Gaza Strip and parts of the West Bank, as the 'Palestinian Authority'. On the other hand, POLISARIO is still seeking independence in Western Sahara; a ceasefire signed in 1991 under UN auspices put an end to the guerrilla war that had started in 1976; however, UN-sponsored diplomatic efforts to hold a referendum on self-determination have led nowhere, for there are still many bones of contention involved in the question of how to hold the referendum.

it is present, albeit in a very singular way. Liberation movements are elevated to the rank of international subjects because they tend (or at least strive) to acquire control over territory. In this context, territory amounts to a 'prospective' factor. Liberation movements could not be recognized as members of the world community if they did not aspire to possess (once their struggle is over) the basic feature proper to primary subjects of the community, that is, effective control over a population living in a given territory.

In order to be holders of rights and subjects of obligations, it is necessary for them to have an apparatus, a representative organization that can come into contact, as necessary, with other international legal persons. Once there is a 'people', in the meaning of one of the three aforementioned categories, endowed with a representative organization or apparatus, it can claim to possess international status. This was recognized in Article 96(3) of the 1977 First Additional Protocol of the Geneva Conventions (see **17.2.4**). In indicating the categories of peoples entitled to make a Declaration for the purpose of being bound by the Protocol, it specified that such a Declaration could be made by '*the authority representing a people* engaged against a High Contracting Party in an armed conflict of the type referred to in Art. 1.4', that is, a conflict against a colonial, racist, or alien Power. In its judgment of 28 June 1985 in *Arafat and Salah*, the Italian Court of Cassation held that national liberation movements, such as the PLO,

> enjoy a limited international personality. They are granted *locus standi* in the international community for the limited purpose of discussing, on a perfectly equal footing with territorial States, the means and terms for the self-determination of the peoples they politically control, pursuant to the principle of self-determination of peoples, to be considered a customary rule of a peremptory character ... Reference to the recognition, whether *de jure* or *de facto*, of the PLO granted by some Governments is irrelevant. Indeed, recognition does not constitute the international legal personality, for it belongs to the political domain and consequently is devoid of effects from the legal viewpoint. (at 884–9)

Regarding the rights and duties of such organized peoples, they can be summarized as follows:

(1) The *right* to self-determination. This right is general in character and is opposable to all member States of the international community: it is a community right (see **3.8**).

(2) The rights and obligations deriving from general principles regulating the conduct of hostilities (*jus in bello*) (see **Chapter 17**).

(3) The rights and obligations deriving from rules on treaty making (see **10.3**). The existence of the power is evidenced by the numerous agreements various liberation movements have entered into on such matters as: the stationing of armed forces belonging to the movements on the territory of States, cessation of hostilities, and the granting of independence, as well as questions relating to borders.

(4) The right to claim respect for, and protection of, the persons acting in their official capacity as organs of the people's representative structure, as well as their immunity from the jurisdiction of States' courts for acts performed in that capacity. Arguably this right is inherent in the fact that the liberation movement acts as a distinct international entity with latent sovereign attributes. However, some national courts have denied this right, for instance the Italian Court of Cassation in its aforementioned judgment of 1985 in *Arafat and Salah*, on the questionable grounds that customary rules only confer that right on entities endowed with 'complete international personality', such as States (at 887).

Regarding the possibility for the organized peoples to dispose of the claimed territory or its natural resources, some rules can be derived from the practice in the context of the decolonization process. As long as conflict between the organized people and the colonial or dominant State is under way, the colonial or dominant Power is barred from entering into international treaties concerning the territory of the people concerned or from dismembering the territory of the people. An arbitral tribunal in *Delimitation of the Maritime Boundary between Guinea-Bissau and Senegal* laid down this principle (at §§49–52). It should be noted that in their submissions to the tribunal both Senegal and Guinea-Bissau agreed on the principle. Another relevant example concerns the situation of Timor-Leste, although the assertion of the rights of the East-Timorese people against the treaties concluded between Indonesia, the occupying Power, and Australia followed a negotiated route eventually enshrined in new treaties. More recently, in its Advisory Opinion on *Legal Consequences of the Separation of the Chagos Archipelago from Mauritius in 1965*, the ICJ expressly recognized the entitlement of peoples to their full territory as part of their right to self-determination (at §§160, 173–174).

8.4 INSURGENTS

Often political and military dissidence within a sovereign State results in large-scale armed conflict, with insurgents (and, more generally, violent non-State armed groups) succeeding in controlling a modicum of territory and setting up an operational structure capable of effectively wielding authority over the individuals living there. When this happens, the insurrectional party (or the non-State armed group) normally claims some measure of recognition as an international subject.[7] What is the reaction of international law to civil strife and other non-international armed conflicts (NIACs)? The international rules governing the conduct of hostilities, including in the context of NIACs, will be discussed in **Chapter 17**. Here we focus on the extent to which insurgents acquire some standing in the world community.

States have traditionally been hostile to insurgents in their territory for the obvious reason that they oppose any disruption to the status quo by an entity which seeks to topple the 'lawful government' and possibly change the whole fabric of the State. Consequently, they prefer to treat insurgency as a domestic occurrence and the rebels as common criminals. In their eyes, any 'interference' from the international community is bound to bolster

---

[7] Insurgency has occurred frequently since the inception of the international community. Civil strife raged in North America between 1774 and 1783: the fight between American settlers and the British colonial Power (which today would be styled a 'war of national liberation', although the rebels were white, like the colonial Power) lasted a long time and wrought havoc; it ended with the victory of the rebels. Between 1810 and 1824, other rebellions broke out on the same continent, against Spanish and Portuguese rule in Latin America. Once again, the insurgents got the upper hand. In the nineteenth century, a number of internal armed conflicts also erupted in Europe, yet the most important civil war of all took place in the US between 1861 and 1865, and was attended by such appalling devastation and cruelty that the contending parties regarded it as no different from a war proper, and consequently applied to it the bulk of the rules governing armed conflict between States. In the twentieth century, internal conflicts were particularly serious, protracted, and destructive. The Spanish Civil War 1936–39 stands out for its magnitude and far-reaching repercussions. After the Second World War, conflicts broke out in some Western and socialist countries: in Greece (1946–49), in Hungary (1956), in Czechoslovakia (1968), in Turkey (1983 to the present), in the former Yugoslavia (1991–95 and 1998–99), and in Chechnya (1991–96 and 1999 onwards). However, most major insurrections in modern times have tended to take place in developing countries (e.g. in Rwanda, the Democratic Republic of the Congo, Sudan, Nicaragua, Colombia, and so on).

insurgents and make them even more dangerous. Traditional reluctance to grant civil upheaval the status of international armed conflict has become even more marked since the second half of the twentieth century, for two reasons. The first is the rapid spread of ethnic feuds or other forms of conflict in many developing States, particularly in Africa, where the arbitrary borders decided upon by the colonial Powers may fuel calls for secession. The second is the growing centrifugal influence of nationalist or religious groups, particularly in States resulting from the break-up of bigger entities (this holds true, among others, for the new States born out of the collapse of the Soviet Union and Yugoslavia). Consequently, feeling more and more insecure, the overwhelming majority of States show a growing tendency to withhold the granting of international legal standing to rebels and to treat them under the criminal law of the country concerned.

The inimical attitude of States towards insurgents has found expression in three principal forms. First of all, the current regulation of the conditions for insurgents to acquire international legal personality remains contested and blurred. International law only establishes certain loose minimum requirements for eligibility to become an international subject. In short, (i) rebels must prove that they have effective control over some part of the territory, and (ii) civil strife must reach a certain degree of intensity and duration (it may not simply consist of riots, or sporadic and short-lived acts of violence). It is for States (both the State against which civil strife breaks out and other parties) to appraise—by granting or withholding, if only implicitly, *recognition of insurgency*—whether these requirements have been fulfilled.

If the insurrection is widespread and protracted in time, and insurgents come to acquire stable control over part of the territory, the central authorities or third States may grant the *recognition of belligerency* (see **17.3.2**). In 1870 and 1875 US President Grant cogently set out the *conditions* for such recognition when he put forth the grounds on which the United States refused to grant such recognition to Cuban rebels fighting against the central Spanish authorities (Cuba was then a Spanish colony). In his 'special message' of 13 June 1870, President Grant wrote as follows:

> The question of belligerency is one of fact not to be decided by sympathies for or prejudices against either party. The relations between the parent state and the insurgents must amount, in fact, to war in the sense of international law. Fighting, though fierce and protracted, does not alone constitute war; there must be military forces acting in accordance with the rules and customs of war—flags of truce, cartels, exchange of prisoners, etc.—and to justify a recognition of belligerency there must be, above all, a *de facto* political organization of the insurgents sufficient in character and resources to constitute it, if left to itself, a state among nations capable of discharging the duties of a state, and of meeting the just responsibilities it may incur as such toward other powers in the discharge of its national duties.

He then went on to note, with regard to the Cuban rebels, the following:

> The insurgents hold no town or city: have no established seat of government; they have no prize courts; no organization for the receiving and collecting of revenues; no seaport to which a prize may be carried or through which access can be had by a foreign power to the limited interior territory and mountain fastnesses which they occupy. The existence of a legislature representing any popular constituency is more than doubtful. In the uncertainty that hangs around the entire insurrection there is no palpable evidence of an election, of any delegated authority, or of any government outside the limits of the camps occupied from day to day by the roving companies of insurgent troops. There is no commerce; no trade, either internal or foreign; no manufactures. The late commander in chief of the insurgents, having recently come to the United States, publicly declared that 'all commercial intercourse or trade with the exterior world has been utterly cut off,' and he further added, 'To-day we have not ten thousand arms in Cuba.'[8]

---

[8] Moore, *Digest*, i, at 194.

Subsequently, in his 'annual message' of 1875, President Grant further explained why the US could not grant the recognition of belligerency. He repeated that in his view the insurgents had no

> substantial political organization, real palpable and manifest to the world, having the forms and capable of the ordinary functions of government toward its own people and other States, with courts for the administration of justice, with a local habitation, possessing such organizational force, such material, such occupation of territory, as to take the contest out of the category of a mere rebellious insurrection, or occasional skirmishes, and place it on the terrible footing of war, to which a recognition of belligerency would aim to elevate it.

If the State against which the insurgents are fighting or third States grant them the recognition of belligerency, thereby admitting that the conflict under way is *international*, insurgents are automatically upgraded to entities entitled to *all* the rights, and subject to *all* the obligations, deriving from *jus in bello* (see **17.3.2**). States are however loath to grant such recognition, as is shown by the fact that it has very seldom been given. Examples are indeed rare. During the American Civil War, on 19 April 1861, President Lincoln issued a proclamation declaring the coasts of the seceded Confederate States to be under naval blockade; 'for this purpose a competent force' was posted 'so as to prevent entrance and exit of vessels' from the ports on those coasts. This proclamation amounted to a recognition of belligerency. On 14 May 1861 Britain issued a proclamation of neutrality, thus recognizing in its turn the insurgents as belligerents.[9] Instead, in 1870 and 1875, as already mentioned, the US refused to recognize the Cuban insurgents as belligerents opposing Spain. In August–September 1918, Britain, France, Italy, and the US recognized the state of belligerency between the Czecho-Slovaks (who had taken up arms against the central authorities and were led by a National Council), on the one side, and the German and Austro-Hungarian Empires, on the other.[10]

Thus, the existence of insurgents as international legal persons largely depends on the attitude of other subjects. Theoretically, if all members of the international community were to decide that a certain insurrectional party lacked the requisite conditions, that party would hardly be in a position to exercise the rights and fulfil the obligations inherent in its international status, however strong, effective, and protracted its authority over a portion of the territory belonging to a sovereign State. In practice, things are different, for two main reasons. First, in the international community there are different political and ideological alignments; any insurrectional party is likely to enlist the support of one or more States with which it has political, religious, or ideological affinities, or because of military or strategic considerations. Consequently, there will always be one or more States inclined to grant recognition to certain insurgents. Secondly, even other States may at a particular point find it useful to concede that a group of insurgents has become a legally independent subject. This may occur when the rebellious party exercises effective authority over a territory where foreigners live and/or operate. Since it would be unrealistic for third States to claim respect for their nationals from the incumbent government, they are forced to address their claim for protection of their citizens and their property to the rebels. They thus implicitly admit that rebels have a duty under international law to protect the lives and assets of foreigners.

Be that as it may, there is no gainsaying that recognition by existing States can play a more significant role in the case of insurgents than in the 'birth' and legal personality of new States. The conspicuous reluctance of States to admit insurgents to the 'charmed circle'

---

[9] See E. W. Hall, *A Treatise on International Law*, 8th edn (Oxford: Clarendon Press, 1924), 44.
[10] Ibid., at 41–2.

of the family of nations, the inherently provisional character of insurgency, the embryonic nature of most international rules concerning NIACs, are all factors determining the practical and legal importance of recognition of insurgents.

A *second manifestation* of the reluctance to recognize the situation of insurgents concerns the duties of third States. While third States are authorized to provide assistance of any kind (including the dispatch of armed forces for wiping out the rebels) to the 'lawful' government, they are duty-bound to refrain from supplying assistance (other than humanitarian) to insurgents (whereas, they are authorized to assist national liberation movements: see **8.3**).

A *third consequence* of this reluctance is the paucity of general international rules addressed equally to rebels and to States. These rules include those, of a customary nature, on treaty making: insurgents are to some extent empowered to enter into agreements with States willing to entertain relations with them. The power of insurrectional movements (and generally violent non-State armed groups) to make international agreements is explicitly restated, with regard to a specific matter, in Article 3(3) common to the four 1949 Geneva Conventions ('The Parties to the conflict should further endeavour to bring into force, by means of special agreements, all or part of the other provisions of the present Convention'). The clause in paragraph 4 of the same Article, whereby '[t]he application of the preceding provisions shall not affect the legal status of the Parties to the conflict' was primarily intended to be a diplomatic device or gimmick for assuaging the fear of States that insurgents might be thereby politically legitimized.[11] It cannot have any bearing on the *restatement* of insurgents' customary law power to make agreements, if the rebels have a modicum of organization and control over part of a territory and as long as other international subjects are willing to entertain legal dealings with them. Indeed, insurgents have often concluded agreements with the State against which they were fighting.[12] The view the Special Court for Sierra Leone set out in its decision in *M. Kallon and B. Bazzy Kamara* (at §§36–50), that the Lomé agreement of 7 July 1999 between the government of Sierra Leone and the Revolutionary United Front (RUF) was not an international agreement proper, may be held to be wrong.

Other customary rules binding or conferring rights on insurgents are those on the treatment of foreigners: rebels must grant foreigners the treatment provided for under international law. In 1972, in his Report on the ILC Draft Articles on State Responsibility, R. Ago drew attention to three 'examples' of State practice where third States requested insurgents to make compensation for damage caused by the insurrectional authorities to the nationals of the States concerned.[13] These cases relate to (i) the American Civil War (1861–65), (ii) an insurrection which broke out in Mexico in 1914, and (iii) the Spanish Civil War

---

[11] Among others, see the ICRC Commentary to the Geneva Conventions under the general editorship of J. S. Pictet: *Commentary to the IVth Geneva Convention* (Geneva: ICRC, 1958), 44 (also online at https://ihl-databases.icrc.org/applic/ihl/ihl.nsf/vwTreaties1949.xsp).

[12] Suffice it to mention the agreement entered into by the government of Nicaragua with Nicaraguan rebels on 23 March 1988 (text in 27 ILM (1988), at 955–6); the agreements entered into by the government of Angola with the 'National Union for the Total Independence of Angola' (UNITA) of 1 May 1991 (text in UN Doc. S/22609, 17 May 1991; the detailed agreement was initialled by the heads of the two delegations, then approved by the government of Angola and UNITA, and entered into force upon the signature by the two parties); the similarly detailed Lusaka Protocol of 15 November 1994 (text in UN Doc. S/1994/1441, 22 December 1994); both agreements were mentioned with approval by the Security Council in its resolution 1118 (1997) of 30 June 1997; the agreements entered into by some of the parties to the armed conflict in the former Yugoslavia in 1991–93 (in ICRC, *Former Yugoslavia, Declarations of the ICRC*, 1994, DP (1994) 49, and CICR, *Ex-Yougoslavia, Communiqués de press du CICR*, 1995, DP (1994) 51); the agreement concluded on 7 July 1999 by the government of Sierra Leone with the 'Revolutionary United Front of Sierra Leone' (RUF) (online at http://www.sierra-leone.org/lomeaccord.html).

[13] (1972) 2 YILC §181.

(1936–39). In relation to the latter, on three occasions in 1937 the British government addressed a formal request for reparation to the Nationalist authorities, as a consequence of the destruction of a British destroyer, a merchant vessel, and two seaplanes at the hands of the insurgents. These and other precedents remain very relevant today for the protection of foreign investors in territories controlled by insurgents, typically in the extractive industries, and the infrastructure and construction sectors.

However, rebels do not have a full correlative right to claim respect for their lives and property from all third States where their 'nationals' (that is, persons owing them allegiance) may find themselves. Such respect can be exacted only by way of reciprocity. If a 'national' from an insurgent territory lives in a State unwilling to recognize rebels, that State's duty to protect that 'national' only exists in relation to the 'lawful' government, of which the individual has citizenship.

With regard to the rules on foreign representatives, practice suggests that insurgents must treat as State organs all officials of third States in the territory under their control; that is, they owe them a special duty of protection, and must grant them immunity from jurisdiction for official acts, etc. as well as respecting diplomatic immunities of foreigners entitled to such immunities. It can be contended that, in contrast, persons acting for the rebellious party can claim international protection only from those States that have granted them recognition. Other States are entitled to regard them simply as nationals of the country where civil strife is under way. It must, however, be mentioned that in 1897 the US Supreme Court held, in *Underhill* v *Hernandez*, that officials or agents of the insurgent party are entitled to immunity from the jurisdiction of foreign courts for their official acts carried out on their territory. In 1892, during the civil war in Venezuela, General Hernandez, a leader of the insurgents, allegedly ill-treated an American citizen, G. F. Underhill, who had constructed a waterworks system in the city of Bolivar. Underhill complained that, among other things, he had been refused 'a passport to leave the city of Bolivar', had been confined in his house, and had been the object of assaults and affronts by the soldiers of Hernandez' army. After the success of the insurgents (and after their government was recognized by the US as 'the legitimate government of Venezuela') Underhill brought a claim for damages against Hernandez in a US court. The US Supreme Court, to which the case was eventually taken, held that the US Court of Appeal that had dismissed the claim was right, for the Venezuelan general enjoyed immunity from foreign jurisdiction for his official acts. It stated that:

> [i]f the party seeking to dislodge the existing government succeeds, and the independence of the government it has set up is recognized, then the acts of such government from the commencement of its existence are regarded as those of an independent nation. If the political revolt fails of success, still if actual war has been waged, acts of legitimate warfare cannot be made the basis of individual liability. (at 196)

A few rules on the enforcement of international law also apply (see **Chapter 14**). Insurgents can resort to lawful countermeasures to enforce international agreements entered into with States or other subjects of international law, or the general international rules on foreigners and respect for officials, when applicable. The principles and rules on the international responsibility of States could also be transposed, *mutatis mutandis*, to insurgents (see **12.1**).

Finally, there are rules applicable in non-international armed conflicts concerning the conduct of hostilities and the protection of the victims of warfare (see **Chapter 17**). Some of them are customary in nature: for instance, those on the protection of civilians and other persons not taking part in armed hostilities as well as the norms laid down in Article 3 common to the four Geneva Conventions of 1949, which, as the ICJ authoritatively held in *Nicaragua (Nicaragua v United States of America)* (at §218), have turned into customary international rules. Furthermore, some international rules on means and methods of combat as well as those on criminal responsibility for serious violations of humanitarian law apply to rebels (see the decision the ICTY Appeals Chamber handed down in *Tadić (Interlocutory Appeal)*, at §§96–137); it follows that, among other things, such violations may amount to war crimes, for which their authors may be held criminally liable (see thereon *Tadić (Interlocutory Appeal)*, at §§94–95).

In addition to such customary rules, rebels may be bound by some *treaty rules* on non-international armed conflict, such as the 1954 Hague Convention for the Protection of Cultural Property in the Event of Armed Conflict; the Second Geneva Protocol of 1977; or the 1996 Amended Protocol on Prohibitions or Restrictions on the Use of Mines, Booby-Traps and Other Devices. The legal ground on which rebels, formally not parties to these treaties, may derive obligations and rights from them has raised much controversy in the legal literature. The problem arises because, as we shall see (see **10.4**), treaties as a rule only apply between the contracting parties. The better view is that rebels may derive rights and obligations from those treaties pursuant to Articles 34–36 of the Vienna Convention on the Law of Treaties (and the corresponding rules of customary law), which provide for the conditions on which third parties may acquire rights or draw obligations from a treaty to which they are not parties. It follows from these provisions that it is required, first, that the contracting parties intended the treaty to grant rights or impose obligations on third parties, and, secondly, that a third party should accept such rights or obligations (the assumption of obligations must however be in written form). As for the first condition, it is clear from the text of the specific treaties under discussion, the intention of their draftsmen, and the very logic of these treaties that their authors also intended legally to involve rebels. As for the condition that rebels must be ready and willing to accept the relevant treaty, it is met any time insurgents make a declaration to the effect that they expressly undertake to comply with international humanitarian law as laid down in the relevant treaty, or implicitly accept as binding the provisions of the treaty by some sort of written statement or undertaking (e.g. by requesting the ICRC to intervene and guarantee respect for the treaty). This express or implied written engagement results in rebels deriving rights and obligations from the treaty, although strictly speaking they do not become parties to it. The distinction between these two categories (*participants* in and *parties* to the treaty) can be easily explained. States tend to be stable and permanent. Rebels, in contrast, are by definition transient creatures. Their temporary character fully justifies their participation in the treaties at issue only so long as the internal armed conflict is in progress. As the treaties are designed to regulate the armed strife, it is quite right for rebels to be bound by (and draw legal entitlements from) them solely for the duration of the conflict.[14]

The provisional character of insurrectional movements has the wider consequence that they cannot claim rights contingent upon the permanent character of international subjects. Thus, *inter alia*, insurgents do not possess any right of sovereignty proper over the territory under their effective control. That is, they may not lawfully cede the territory or part of it to another international subject; they merely exercise de facto authority.

To conclude, insurgents are State-like subjects, for they exhibit all the major features of States. However, they are *transient* and, in addition, they have a *limited international capacity* in two respects. First, they have only a few international rights and duties. Secondly, they are only 'associated' with a limited number of existing States, that is, those which take the view that rebels fulfil all the conditions for international personality, and consequently engage in dealings with them.

---

[14] For an exposition of further legal implications see A. Cassese, 'The Status of Rebels under the 1977 Geneva Protocol on Non-International Armed Conflicts' (1981) 30 *ICLQ* 416–39.

8.5 *SUI GENERIS* ENTITIES AND OTHER SUBJECTS (CORPORATIONS AND NGOS)

8.5.1 GENERAL

There exist in the international community some international subjects that exhibit three characteristics: they (i) have come to acquire a legal status there on account of specific *historic circumstances*; (ii) do not possess any distinct territory or, if they do use a territory, this belongs to another entity; (iii) have a very limited international personality, not different, in practice, from that of such diminutive States as Andorra, Monaco, San Marino, Fiji, St Vincent and the Grenadines, and the like (which, however, in theory are vested with all the rights and powers belonging to sovereign States).

8.5.2 THE HOLY SEE

The Holy See consists of the central organization of the Catholic Church. Previously the Church wielded authority and control over a State, called in the past the 'Pontifical State' or the Papal States, with a fairly big territory in central Italy. After the completion of Italian unity and the birth of Italy as a sovereign State in 1865, the Pontifical State was incorporated in the Italian Kingdom in 1870. In 1929, as a result of agreements with Italy, a few buildings in Rome (covering not more than one hundred acres) were turned over to the Holy See so as to constitute what is now called the 'Vatican State' (a distinct, diminutive subject of international law, endowed with a tiny territory, but deprived of sovereignty, for it is subjected to the supremacy of the Holy See).

The Holy See can enter into international agreements, which are called 'concordats' when they regulate the treatment of Catholics and Catholic institutions by the other contracting party. One such agreement was made on 11 February 1929 with Italy (it consisted of a concordat and a treaty proper.[15] It also enters into multilateral treaties of a humanitarian character, such as the Convention on Stateless Persons of 1954 or the International Wheat Agreement of 1959. In addition, the Holy See is a member of some international organizations (e.g. the Universal Postal Union and the International Telecommunications Union) and has observer status at the UN. The Holy See also takes part in diplomatic relations, sending and receiving diplomats.

The main reason why States, even if they have no Catholic affiliation, entertain international relations with the Holy See lies in tradition and in the moral authority of the Pope, the highest official of the Holy See.

It is interesting to note that, being an international subject, the Holy See enjoys immunity from foreign jurisdiction; such immunity also accrues to its organs. Thus, in *Marcinkus and others*, the Italian Court of Cassation held that Marcinkus and two other managers of the Vatican Bank ('Institute for Religious Works' (IOR)) accused by the Italian authorities of the fraudulent bankruptcy of Banco Ambrosiano could not be brought to justice, for the Italian courts lacked jurisdiction: the three accused had not acted as private individuals but as organs or representatives of the Vatican Bank. The Court held (at 329) that it must act upon Article 11 of the 1929 treaty between Italy and the Holy See, whereby '[t]he Central bodies of the Catholic Church shall be exempt from any interference by the Italian State' (a treaty provision that among other things restated the customary rule on functional immunities of State officials (see **6.3**) and extended it to officials of the Holy See).

---

[15] See text in (1929) 23 *AJIL Suppl.* 187.

8.5.3 THE SOVEREIGN ORDER OF MALTA

The Sovereign Order of Malta, established at the beginning of the twelfth century, at the time of the Crusades, had a territory: after Jerusalem, St John in Acres, Cyprus, and Rhodes (1308–1522), the Order's territory was the island of Malta, which it possessed between 1530 and 1798 (when Napoleon dispossessed the Order of the island, which was then handed over to Great Britain by virtue of the Paris Treaty of 30 May 1814). Since 1834 it has had a building in Rome. It runs hospitals, casualty units, charitable institutions, and relief organizations in various countries.

The Order's presence in the international community, albeit slight, is primarily due to historical reasons linked to its traditional humanitarian role. It has an extremely limited, almost evanescent international personality, which, in addition, is increasingly controversial on account of the growing dependency of the Order on the Holy See. Essentially, it entertains diplomatic relations with a number of States all characterized by their Catholic tradition (Italy, Spain, Portugal, Argentina, Brazil, etc.). In some respects, though, these relations belong more to comity than to the legal sphere proper. Italian courts, in a long string of judgments, have nonetheless propounded the Order's international personality.[16] In 1935, the Italian Court of Cassation held in *Nanni et al. v Sovrano Militare Ordine di Malta* that the Order has a 'limited legal capacity to act in international relations for the purpose of achieving the goals proper to the Order' (at 1485). In 1991 the same Court held in *Sovrano Militare Ordine di Malta v Amministrazione delle finanze dello Stato* that the Order's legal personality is a 'unique form' of international personality: it is 'functional in character, in that it operates exclusively so that the Order may attain its institutional goals of health and hospital assistance' (at 177). The Court derived from this personality the Order's right to immunity from State jurisdiction as well as to fiscal exemption.

As has rightly been noted,[17] although the Order is recognized by and has relations with a limited number of States, its impact on the whole international community finds expression, mainly, in the fact that other States acknowledge that their relations with the Order are international in nature.

8.5.4 THE INTERNATIONAL COMMITTEE OF THE RED CROSS (ICRC)

Unlike the two previous entities, which are deeply rooted in the old history of Europe, the ICRC is a relatively modern institution that reflects the new trends in the international community towards the ever-expanding role of humanitarian concerns. Nonetheless the ICRC too, born as a private entity, has gradually come to possess international personality essentially for historical reasons.

The Committee was established in 1863 in Switzerland as a private association for the purpose of fulfilling a humanitarian mission with regard to armed conflicts. Initially it was called '*Comité international et permanent de secours aux militaires blessés*' (*Permanent International Committee for the Relief of Wounded Soldiers*: see **17.2.1**); it was given the

---

[16] See for instance the following decisions: *Sovrano Militare Ordine di Malta v Brunelli, Tacchi and others*; *Nanni et al. v Sovrano Militare Ordine di Malta*; *Ministero delle Finanze v Associazione dei Cavalieri italiani del Sovrano Militare Ordine di Malta*; *Sovrano Militare Ordine di Malta v Grisi* (concerning a contract of employment with the Order); *Sovrano Militare Ordine di Malta v Salimei* (concerning relations between the Order and the Italian national health service); *Sovrano Militare Ordine di Malta v Guidetti*.

[17] G. Sperduti, 'Sulla personalità internazionale dell'Ordine di Malta' (1955) 38 *RDI* 48. See also *Lezioni di diritto internazionale* (Milano: Giuffrè, 1958), 28.

present name in 1875. It was granted domestic legal personality under the Swiss federal Civil Code (adopted in 1907 and entered into force in 1912: Articles 60 *et seq.*). The increasing importance and dynamism of the Committee have resulted in its playing a significant role in international dealings and acquiring an (albeit limited) international status.

The ICRC has no territory of its own. It has its headquarters in a building in Geneva, on Swiss territory. The ICRC premises are, however, inviolable, that is, 'no agent of the Swiss public authority may enter them without the express consent of the Committee' (Article 3 of the 1993 Agreement; see later).

The ICRC promotes the drafting of multilateral humanitarian treaties on armed conflicts, and contacts States to prompt them to comply, or promotes compliance with international conventions on armed conflict. Under the 1949 Geneva Conventions it may fulfil the role of protecting entity if agreement between belligerents is not reached on the appointment of Protecting Powers (see *infra* **17.2.3** and **17.8.1**). In fulfilling this role, the ICRC not only safeguards the interests of the belligerents, but also ensures that the rights of the victims of war are duly respected. It should be noted that under some common provisions of the four Geneva Conventions of 1949 (e.g. Articles 10(3) or 11), the ICRC has the right to offer its humanitarian services to fulfil the role normally performed by Protecting Powers, and the relevant belligerent is legally bound to accept such an offer.

In addition, the ICRC may enter into international treaties with States and international organizations. It often does make such treaties or conventions with States[18] or with the UN.[19] So far the ICRC has concluded some 65 headquarters agreements with States, all considered by the contracting parties as international agreements proper (some of them explicitly say so).[20]

Moreover, the ICRC was granted observer status in the General Assembly in 1990; such status is normally granted either to States, which are not (yet) members of the UN, or to intergovernmental organizations.

8.5.5 TRANSNATIONAL CORPORATIONS

Among the entities that are often referred to as powerful actors in international relations, multinationals or transnational corporations certainly have a unique position. Not only are these economic giants the bearers—like other private persons, including individuals to a large extent—of rights and obligations under international law, but, in several instances, they are indeed able to influence the behaviour of States in many significant ways.

---

[18] See e.g. the Agreement of 19 March 1993 with Switzerland on the legal status of the Committee in Switzerland, in 293 *IRRC* (1993) 152; online at https://casebook.icrc.org/case-study/agreement-between-icrc-and-switzerland. Article 1 of the Agreement stipulates among other things that the Swiss government 'recognizes the international juridical personality' of the Committee.

[19] See e.g. the agreement with the ICTY, a subsidiary body of the UN Security Council, relating to the inspection of the UN detention unit in The Hague, where the ICTY detains persons indicted of international crimes. The Agreement was made by exchange of letters between the President of the ICTY and the President of the ICRC: see the letters of, respectively, 28 April 1995 and 5 May 1995 in ICTY, *Basic Documents* 1998, at 380–5; online at http://www.un.org/icty/legaldoc/index.htm.

[20] See A. Lorite Escorihuela, 'Le Comité international de la Croix-Rouge comme organisation *sui generis*: Remarques sur la personnalité juridique internationale du CICR' (2001) 105 *RGDIP* 607. Among relevant agreements in this regard see e.g. the Agreement of 24 March 1997 with Hungary, the Agreement of 24 February 1999 with the Republic of Macedonia, that of 26 May 1998 with Bosnia and Herzegovina, and that of 31 March 1999 with Cameroon, as well as the Agreement of 7 October 2000 with Sierra Leone. All these Agreements provide that the status of the ICRC is 'the same as that of intergovernmental organizations' (or 'comparable to the status' of those organizations) and in addition provide for all the immunities and exemptions normally granted by States to intergovernmental organizations or States.

The main approach to the issue of recognition of legal subjectivity for corporations has had to do with the need to impose on them fundamental obligations, particularly in the area of human rights, and establish their responsibility for serious violations of international law. Some see the strengthening of mechanisms that would allow the imposition of increased responsibilities on corporations as a useful and appropriate tool for enforcing international norms (as far as human rights violations are concerned, imposing responsibility on corporations could ensure that victims are provided with effective remedies which could entail reparations).

Clearly, major corporations are key players in shaping and implementing several international rules regarding trade, investments, transports, telecommunications, and so on (see **Chapter 21**). They are entitled to play some role in organizations such as WTO and ILO, and often are instrumental in the implementation of Security Council decisions; think, for example, of the banking sector and the UN Security Council sanction regimes.[21] Most of all, they have played an increasing role in the context of disputes relating to foreign investment transactions. These disputes have recognized the existence of norms that are directly addressed to such corporations in their capacity as 'investors', mostly the right to bring a claim before an international arbitral tribunal. Other substantive standards included in the investment agreements are best seen as 'disciplines' self-imposed by States as a matter of reciprocal concessions and grounded on the sole basis of nationality (see **21.4.3**).

8.5.6 NON-GOVERNMENTAL ORGANIZATIONS (NGOS)

Non-governmental organizations (NGOs) are entities which are an (organized) expression of civil society; they are defined as non-governmental to distinguish them from international organizations, also called intergovernmental organizations (IOs or IGOs, see **Chapter 7**).

Traditionally, NGOs are established as legal subjects endowed with personality under the domestic laws of one or more States; they are often created to support specific agendas, or causes, and although there are some which have a broad-ranging scope of activity, they normally focus on a limited range of issues. Generally, they promote change and stimulate States to make progress in certain areas of international law. There is little doubt that, through their influence, NGOs have been an actor in international relations.

Moreover, despite scepticism in some quarters as to their nature and the involvement of civil society in international dealings, starting at least in the 1990s, NGOs have been increasingly allowed to participate in international settings where important issues are addressed. They are enabled to observe negotiations and participate in the discussions, they also exert influence on several States by providing expert assistance, and can indeed contribute to the drafting of international legal instruments during multilateral negotiations. On a different level, NGOs are active in bringing cases before domestic and regional courts stigmatizing violations of international law by States, individuals, or corporations. Naturally, they are also vocal about violations through traditional instruments of advocacy.

NGOs do not have a general, clear standing; however in several systems there are codified mechanisms for enabling their participation or for special status within each given system (e.g. in the UN system, the Economic and Social Council has established a procedure to grant NGOs special consultative status). In the realm of environmental negotiations, NGOs have been granted ample room to be heard, and the same holds true for negotiations in

---

[21] See José Alvarez, 'Are Corporations Subjects of International Law?' (2011) 9 *Santa Clara Journal of International Law* 1.

other sectors (e.g. negotiations for the establishment of the ICC or the Arms Trade Treaty). Broadly speaking, civil society has been increasingly active.

On the other hand, given that NGOs have been increasingly active on the international scene, discussions have started as to their responsibility under international law. In this regard, international rules are not particularly developed. Clearly, NGOs may be made accountable under domestic law; at the same time, they can be excluded from meetings and negotiations if they do not respect certain standards, or in any case their entitlement to participate is often based on a decision by Member States. In other words, NGOs are fundamentally subject to the authority of States, and hence although they certainly are participants in international dealings and can of course wield great influence on many aspects of these dealings, it is not necessarily accurate to describe them as subjects of international law.

8.6 CONCLUDING REMARKS

A few final observations on subjectivity under international law are in order. Some have argued that it would be useful to avoid the debate on subjectivity altogether, and that it would be preferable to focus on rights and obligations, without determining whether or not a given entity is a subject of international law.

It is certainly important to note that the characterization of certain entities as subjects of international law must not be understood as indicating a normative role, but only as a descriptive conceptualization of reality, essential for 'scientific' purposes. In other words, it is a descriptive tool, which might assist in understanding realities, rather than an instrument of regulation. Naturally, on the basis of such an understanding regulation might ensue, for example, by adding or removing rights and duties, or by providing avenues for entering claims at international or regional level. It also helps in understanding the potential impact of various actors on the development of norms and processes in international law, which certainly goes beyond the traditional subjects.

As mentioned earlier in the chapter, the two main structural principles of international law, legality and effectiveness, come into play and determine, to a large extent, whether or not a given entity is capable of acting in the international system as a main participant and can properly interact with other subjects, with a sufficient degree of autonomy and recognition of its role; moreover, the role these actors are able to play indicates which rules are applicable to them, what rights they enjoy, and what duties are incumbent on them. In other words, it is important to understand whether these actors are merely bound to respect domestic rules, and hence only subject to national laws, or whether there are indeed international norms that are applicable to them. The combination of all these factors provides a broad indication of their potential status under international law. Clearly, as we have shown, actors other than States display limited personality under international law; in other words, these actors possess a subjectivity that varies both in breadth and in depth, depending on their structure, the area in which they operate, and the specific international rules applicable to them.

PART III
INTERNATIONAL LAW-MAKING AND NORMATIVE INTERACTIONS

PART II

9

LAW-MAKING PROCESSES

9.1 INTRODUCTION

The lack of a centralized body entrusted with law-making functions in the international legal system means that the creation of rules of international law is the outcome of unconventional processes with respect to municipal law. Traditionally, these processes were predominantly 'the exclusive preserve of States', meaning that only States were participating in the creation of international rules. The situation has changed in modern times, given that other actors such as international organizations, NGOs, multinational corporations, and more generally the so-called international or global civil society, play an active role in shaping the content of rules of international law. In addition, international law is currently created in a variety of fora, for instance through multilateral processes, by and within international organizations, through codification and progressive development of international law. International judges also play a role in the making of international rules, given the often unclear or ambiguous or loose content of the rules that they shall apply to decide the case. By opting for a specific solution, they inevitably fill gaps in the pre-existing normative framework, although this appears abhorrent under a traditional and strictly positivistic understanding of international law-making.

States continue nonetheless to be the main makers of international rules. In addition, despite the changes which have occurred in the processes of international law-making, the sources through which international rules are created have remained almost unchanged since the Statute of the Permanent Court of Justice (PCIJ) listed them for the first time. Article 38 of the Statute of the PCIJ has been reproduced in Article 38 of the Statute of the International Court of Justice (ICJ), the principal judicial organ of the United Nations (see **15.2**). The latter constitutes the unavoidable starting-point for any analysis of the making of international rules. Article 38 of the ICJ Statute reads as follows:

(1) The Court, whose function is to decide in accordance with international law such disputes as are submitted to it, shall apply:
   a. international conventions, whether general or particular, establishing rules expressly recognized by the contesting states;
   b. international custom, as evidence of a general practice accepted as law;
   c. the general principles of law recognized by civilized nations;
   d. subject to the provisions of Article 59 [binding character of judgments for the parties], judicial decisions and the teachings of the most highly qualified publicists of the various nations, as subsidiary means for the determination of rules of law.
(2) This provision shall not prejudice the power of the Court to decide a case ex aequo et bono, if the parties agree thereto.

It is generally accepted that letters a. to c. of the first paragraph of this provision list the main *formal* sources of international law, namely the processes and procedures through which legally binding rules of international law are created.[1] These are mentioned in the order that the ICJ will usually follow: international conventions (namely, treaties under all their different denominations: see **10.2**), that establish rules expressly accepted by the parties to the dispute; international custom, giving rise to the so-called customary rules; and general principles as recognized in domestic systems (although the anachronistic term 'civilized nations' is used). Treaties and custom constitute the two most important sources of international law. They are envisaged by two basic 'constitutional' rules of the international community, which lie at the very apex of the legal order (they are often designated by the Latin expressions: *consuetudo est servanda*, that is, all international subjects must comply with customary rules, and *pacta sunt servanda*, that is, the parties to international agreements must abide by them).

On the other hand, Article 38(1)(d) raises questions on whether it refers to formal sources of international law, although *subsidiary* with respect to the preceding ones. Notably, however, formal sources may also create rules that are non-binding, but nonetheless have a normative character and may produce legal effects other than obliging the addresses to comply: this is so-called *soft law*. Decisions taken by the Court *ex aequo et bono*, namely based on considerations external to the law, are not a formal source of international law although the decisions themselves are binding on the parties to the dispute.

Importantly, one should distinguish between the formal sources of international law (discussed so far and examined in the present chapter) and its *material* sources, namely the means by which the content of a rule is derived. These material sources include the relevant documents where the terms of a rule are set out, independently from its normative force (a resolution, a treaty, a judgment, a scholarly article). Material sources are also the various factors (economic, moral, humanitarian, and so on) that have an impact in shaping the content of a rule. Based on this distinction between formal and material sources, one may understand why a treaty is at the same time the formal source of certain rules for States parties and the material source where one can find the content of the rules themselves. However, if subsequently the rules contained in the treaty are generally followed by States which are not parties and thus give an impetus to the creation of corresponding rules of customary law, the formal source of these rules for non-State parties will be customary law, but the treaty will still remain one of the material sources to ascertain their content.

9.2 TREATIES AS LAW-MAKING PROCESSES

The most frequent means of creating international rules is the conclusion of agreements. These are also called treaties, conventions, protocols, covenants, acts' and so on. The terminology varies but the substance is the same: they all denote a merger of the wills of two or more international subjects for the purpose of regulating their interests by international rules (see **10.2**).

Treaties are applicable to the contracting parties only and the regulation contained therein is binding, based on the principle *pacta sunt servanda* (meaning that legally binding agreements must be performed, see **10.4**). Treaties therefore perfectly reflect the

---

[1] See generally H. Thirlway, *The Sources of International Law*, 2nd edn (Oxford: Oxford University Press, 2019); J. d'Aspremont, S. Besson, and S. Knuchel (eds), *The Oxford Handbook of the Sources of International Law* (Oxford: Oxford University Press, 2018); G. Abi-Saab, 'Les sources du droit international: essai de déconstruction' in M. Rama Montaldo (ed.), *Liber Amicorum en hommage au Professeur Eduardo Jiménez de Aréchaga* (Montevideo: FCU, 1994), I, 29; J. Barberis, *Fuentes del Derecho Internacional* (La Plata: Editora Platense, 1973).

individualism prevailing in the international community, since they respond to the basic need of not imposing obligations on States that do not wish to be bound by them. In other words, treaties set forth international rules that are created by the very States that are to comply with them, thus establishing a complete coincidence of rule-makers and those to whom rules are addressed.

One may wonder whether treaties can be considered as true law-creating processes. According to one view, treaties should be seen as sources of obligations for the contracting parties rather than sources of law.[2] However, there are treaties that go beyond the establishment of reciprocal obligations between the parties and regulate matters to establish patterns of behaviour in order to achieve the same or a common objective. The latter category of treaties, in other words, establishes rules of general purport, that may have an impact on the formation of customary rules or that codify customary international law, although formally speaking they are binding on States parties only (one may think, for instance, of treaties regulating matters such as the law of the sea, the protection of the victims of warfare, or the international protection of human rights). This is the reason why the latter treaties are usually referred to as 'normative treaties' (law-making treaties, *traités-lois*), following a terminology proposed, among others, by Hans Triepel which opposed *Vereinbarung* (treaty resembling a law or treaty-legislation, *traités-lois*) to the so-called *Vertrag* (contractual or reciprocal treaties, *traités-contracts*).

Treaties are subject to the same rules governing their formation, life, and death, comprising the so-called 'law of treaties' (see **Chapter 10**), irrespective of their content. In the past, the international rules on the law of treaties were to some extent ambiguous and did not define in detail key issues such as, for instance, the grounds for terminating a treaty or denouncing its invalidity. The emergence in the twentieth century of a great number of States, many of them with different ideological, political, and cultural backgrounds (first the socialist countries and later developing States), meant that the international regulation of treaties had to become more certain, detailed, and consonant with the demands of these new States. As a result of the consequent need to codify, reshape, and develop traditional rules, States agreed to devote a whole treaty to the 'birth', 'life', and 'death' of international agreements. This was the 1969 Vienna Convention on the Law of Treaties, which regulated all the main features of international treaties (it was followed in 1986 by the Vienna Convention on the Law of Treaties between States and International Organizations) (see **Chapter 10**).

Traditionally States were free to regulate any subject matter, and in any manner decided upon by the parties concerned, through the conclusion of treaties. This freedom is no longer unfettered, since a new category of general international rules has now come into being, designed to protect fundamental values of the international community as a whole: peremptory rules or *jus cogens* (see **11.4**). The regulation contained in a treaty cannot therefore be contrary to *jus cogens*, subject to the invalidity of the treaty.

Treaties have always been the primary source of legal relations between States, and their importance has significantly increased in the context of modern international law. The adoption of key multilateral treaties on different areas of law (e.g. human rights, environment, humanitarian law, terrorism, disarmament) has brought about the most important changes in the international legal order since the end of the Second World War.

---

[2] See e.g. G. Fitzmaurice, 'Some Problems regarding the Formal Sources of International Law' in F. M. van Asbeck et al. (eds), *Symbolae Verzijl* (The Hague: Martinus Nijhoff, 1958), 153.

9.3 CUSTOM: FORMATION AND IDENTIFICATION

9.3.1 GENERAL

Custom is the process whereby rules binding on all States are created. Unlike treaties, custom is not a deliberate law-making process. In concluding treaties, States come together willingly to agree upon legal standards of behaviour acceptable to all those participating in the law-making process. Their main and conscious intent is to bring about those standards. By contrast, in the case of custom, States, when participating in the norm-setting process, do not act for the primary purpose of laying down international rules. Their primary concern is to safeguard some economic, social, or political interests. The gradual birth of a new international rule is the side effect of States' conduct in international relations. That is why Kelsen defined custom as 'unconscious and unintentional lawmaking' and some Italian international lawyers (Giuliano, Ago, Barile) defined it as a 'spontaneous process'.[3]

In the past, some leading authors contended that custom boiled down to 'tacit agreement' (*tacitum pactum*), that is, customary rules which resulted from the convergence of will of all States.[4] This approach, assuming that it was formerly sound, is no longer tenable today. At present, when they gradually crystallize in the world community, customary rules do not need to be supported or consented to by all States. As explained in what follows, for a rule to take root in international dealings it is sufficient for a majority of States to engage in a consistent practice corresponding with the rule and to be aware of its imperative need. States will be bound by the rule even if some of them have been indifferent, or relatively indifferent, to it (one may consider the position of landlocked States with respect to the birth of customary rules on the law of the sea), or at any rate have refrained from expressing either assent or opposition. That universal (express or implicit) participation in the formation of a customary rule is not required is evidenced by the fact that no national or international court dealing with the question of whether a customary rule had taken shape on a certain matter has ever examined the views of all States of the world.

9.3.2 ELEMENTS OF CUSTOM

Article 38(1)(b) of the Statute of the ICJ contains the most authoritative definition of custom (although a number of scholars have questioned it), by referring to 'international custom, as evidence of a general practice accepted as law'. This definition reflects the widely held view that custom is made up of two elements: general practice, or *usus* or *diuturnitas*, and the conviction that such practice reflects, or amounts to, law (*opinio juris*) or is required by social, economic, or political exigencies (*opinio necessitatis*).

As for the first element, namely general practice, its scope is epitomized in a celebrated series of decisions of the ICJ in the *North Sea Continental Shelf (Federal Republic of Germany/Denmark; Federal Republic of Germany/Netherlands)* cases. There the Court

---

[3] H. Kelsen, *Principles of International Law* (New York: Rinehart & Co., 1952), 307–8; M. Giuliano, *La comunità internazionale e il diritto* (Padova: Cedam, 1950), 161ff; R. Ago, *Scienza giuridica e diritto internazionale* (Milano: Giuffrè, 1950), 78; G. Barile, 'La rilevazione e l'integrazione del diritto internazionale non scritto e la libertà d'apprezzamento del giudice' (1953) 5 *Comunicazioni e studi* 150ff. It should be noted that as early as 1928, D. Anzilotti had written that customary rules are 'spontaneous, almost unconscious manifestations of certain needs of social life' (*Corso*, at 73; *Cours*, at 74).

[4] See Anzilotti, *Corso*, i, 71–6. Various national courts took substantially the same stand, e.g. British courts (see *R. v Keyn (The Franconia)* and the *West Rand Central Gold Mining Co. Ltd v The King* cases) and in 1927 the PCIJ, in *The SS Lotus*, where the Court stated as follows: 'The rules of law binding upon States . . . emanate from their own free will as expressed in conventions or by usages generally accepted as expressing principles of law and established in order to regulate the relations between these co-existing independent communities or with a view to the achievement of common aims' (at 18).

stated that 'State practice, including that of States whose interests are specially affected, should ... [be] both extensive and virtually uniform' (at §74). As the same Court stated in *Nicaragua (Nicaragua v United States of America)* (at §186), possible instances of non-compliance with a rule do not necessarily mean that the rule has not come into being. State practice need not be absolutely uniform. Individual deviations may not lead to the conclusion that no rule has crystallized but can on the contrary confirm the existence of a rule, in that either they are regarded as breaches of international law or the State concerned claims that its conduct was justified by exceptional circumstances.[5]

Should this practice always 'show a general recognition that a rule of law or legal obligation is involved', as the ICJ put it in the *North Sea Continental Shelf* cases (at §74)? It would seem that the two elements need not both be present from the outset. Usually, a practice evolves among certain States under the impetus of economic, political, or military demands. At this stage, the practice may thus be regarded as being imposed by social or economic or political needs (*opinio necessitatis*).[6] If it does not encounter strong and consistent opposition from other States but is increasingly accepted, or acquiesced in, a customary rule gradually crystallizes. At this later stage it may be held that the practice is dictated by international law (*opinio juris*). In other words, now States begin to believe that they must conform to the practice not so much, or not only, out of economic, political, or military considerations, but because an international rule enjoins them to do so. At that moment—difficult to pinpoint exactly, since it is the result of a continuous process—a customary rule may be said to have evolved. It would seem that it is only with regard to this stage in the gradual formation of a customary rule that one may require 'a belief that ... [a given] practice is rendered obligatory by the existence of a rule of law requiring it', with the consequence that the 'States concerned must ... feel that they are conforming to what amounts to a legal obligation', as the ICJ clarified the *North Sea Continental Shelf* cases (at §77).

Arguably, in some instances, *opinio juris* acquires a prominent role in the formation of custom, among other things because it is based on evident and inherently rational grounds; this, for example, holds true for the customary rules prohibiting genocide, slavery, torture, or racial discrimination, but more prominently in the field of international humanitarian law of armed conflict (see **Chapter 17**). This is because of the celebrated Martens Clause (see **17.2.2**), adopted in 1899 at the Hague Peace Conference and couched as follows:

> Until a more complete code of the laws of war has been issued, the High Contracting parties deem it expedient to declare that, in cases not included in the Regulations adopted by them, the inhabitants and the belligerents remain under the protection and the rule (*sous la sauvegarde et sous l'empire*) of the principles of the law of nations, as they result from the usages established among civilised peoples, from the laws of humanity, and the dictates of the public conscience.

---

[5] In *Nicaragua (Nicaragua v United States of America)*, in establishing the content of customary rules on the 'non-use of force and non-intervention', the Court stated the following: 'It is not to be expected that in the practice of States the application of the rules in question should have been perfect, in the sense that States should have refrained, with complete consistency, from the use of force or from intervention in each other's internal affairs. The Court does not consider that, for a rule to be established as customary, the corresponding practice must be in absolutely rigorous conformity with the rule. In order to deduce the existence of customary rules, the Court deems it sufficient that the conduct of States should, in general, be consistent with such rules, and that instances of State conduct inconsistent with a given rule should generally have been treated as breaches of that rule, not as indications of the recognition of a new rule. If a State acts in a way prima facie inconsistent with a recognized rule, but defends its conduct by appealing to exceptions or justifications contained within the rule itself, then whether or not the State's conduct is in fact justifiable on that basis, the significance of that attitude is to confirm rather than to weaken the rule' (at §186).

[6] Telling examples of customary rules based at the outset on *opinio necessitatis*, subsequently turned into *opinio juris*, are the rules on the continental shelf (whereby each coastal State has exclusive jurisdiction over the natural resources of the subsoil and the seabed of the continental shelf contiguous to its coast, within certain limits (see **5.4.7**)). Another example is provided by the rules on outer space (see **5.7**).

The clause puts the 'laws of humanity' and the 'dictates of public conscience' on the same footing as the 'usages of States' (that is, State practice) as historical sources of 'principles of international law'. In consequence it is logically admissible to infer (and is borne out by practice) that the requirement of State practice may not need to apply to the formation of a principle or a rule based on the laws of humanity or the dictates of public conscience. Or, at least, this requirement may not be as high as in the case of principles and rules having a different underpinning or rationale. In other words, when it comes to proof of the emergence of a principle or general rule reflecting the laws of humanity (or the dictates of public conscience), as a result of the impact of the Martens Clause on international law the requirement of *usus* may be less stringent than in other cases where the principle or rule may have emerged as a result of economic, political, or military demands. By the same token, the requirement of *opinio juris* or *opinio necessitatis* may take on special prominence. As a result, the expression of legal views by a number of States and other international subjects about the binding value of a principle or a rule, or the social and moral need for its observance by States, may be held to be conducive to the formation of a principle or a customary rule, even when there is no widespread and consistent State practice, or even no practice at all, to back up those legal views. Thus, arguably the Martens Clause (in its present legal dimension) loosens, in the limited area of humanitarian law, the requirements prescribed for *usus*, while at the same time elevating *opinio* (*juris* or *necessitatis*) to a rank higher than that normally admitted.[7]

By contrast, whenever there exist at the outset conflicting (economic or political) interests, the *usus* element may acquire greater importance for the formation of a customary rule. This, for instance, applies to the creation of the rule on the continental shelf (see **5.4.7**). In other instances *usus* is less important: for example, in the case of outer space (see **5.7**), it is a fact that only two Great Powers (the Soviet Union and the US) had the technological resources for using that portion of air; hence, once their substantial convergence had come about, it was easy for a customary rule to evolve very quickly (so much so that a distinguished commentator spoke of 'instant custom').[8]

Plainly, the *time element* in the formation of customary rules may vary, depending on the circumstances of the case and the States' interests at stake. Nevertheless, what ultimately matters is that the two aforementioned elements be present, namely the subjective element (the conviction that a new standard of behaviour is necessary, or is already binding) and the objective element (that is, a well-settled State practice). In *North Sea Continental Shelf* the ICJ had to establish whether the principle of equidistance, embodied in Article 6 of the 1958 Geneva Convention on the Continental Shelf, as a method for delimiting the continental shelf as between adjacent States had turned into a rule of customary law, and was consequently binding on the Federal Republic of Germany, a State not party to the

---

[7] This conclusion is justified by the need—in the area of the law of warfare—for humanitarian demands to keep a balance between military activities and their devastating impact on human beings, even before such humanitarian demands have been translated into practice. What would be the purpose of requiring prior State practice for the formation of a general legal ban, when what is at stake is, say, the use of deadly means or methods of warfare that seriously imperil civilians? To wait for the development of practice would mean, in effect, legally to step in only after thousands of civilians have been killed. The original 'restructuring' of the norm-creating process in the area of humanitarian law, as suggested here, would thus serve as a sort of antidote to the destructiveness of war: combatants must comply with restraints on the most pernicious forms of belligerence whenever they are authoritatively required to do so by States and other international subjects, even if such restraints have not been previously put into practice. State and judicial practice concerning the Martens Clause does not run counter to the above interpretation; recent judicial pronouncements would seem to uphold it, at least in part. See further A. Cassese, 'The Martens Clause: Half a Loaf or Simply Pie in the Sky?' (2000) 11 *EJIL* 187.

[8] See B. Cheng, 'United Nations Resolutions on Outer Space: "Instant" International Customary Law?' (1965) 5 *IJIL* 23.

Convention. The Court answered the question in the negative. After noting that little time had elapsed since the Convention had entered into force, in 1964, it stated:

> Although the passage of only a short period of time is not necessarily, or of itself, a bar to the formation of a new rule of customary international law on the basis of what was originally a purely conventional rule, an indispensable requirement would be that within the period in question, short though it might be, State practice, including that of States whose interests are specially affected, should have been both extensive and virtually uniform in the sense of the provision invoked;—and should moreover have occurred in such a way as to show a general recognition that a rule of law or legal obligation is involved. (at §74)

The Court then emphasized that no 'settled practice' had emerged, and in addition the States' 'feeling' that they were conforming to what amounted to a legal obligation was lacking. It therefore concluded that no customary rule had evolved.

9.3.3 THE EXISTENCE OF CUSTOMARY RULES

Normally it is not easy to establish whether a customary rule has evolved. The matter has recently been addressed by the International Law Commission (ILC), which in 2018 provided its Draft Conclusions on Identification of Customary International Law with Commentaries, prepared under the guidance of Sir Michael Wood as Special Rapporteur.[9]

However, there are various examples of how international or national courts have established the existence of a customary rule. One of them, little known, is a case brought in 1939 before the Italian Court of Cassation (*De Meeüs* v *Forzano*, at 93–5). In 1922, the same Court had held that diplomatic agents were not immune from civil jurisdiction for acts and transactions performed in their private capacity in the receiving State. That decision had triggered a firm note of protest lodged by the dean of the diplomatic corps in Rome with the Italian Foreign Ministry.[10] When a similar case arose a few years later concerning a Belgian diplomat, and the matter was brought before the Supreme Court, the Court found that a customary rule had evolved in the international community granting foreign diplomats immunity from civil jurisdiction for private acts (on some limited exceptions, see **6.3.3**).

As evidence of the existence of such a rule the Court mentioned the *protest*, just referred to. The Court noted that it emanated not from the diplomat concerned but from the whole diplomatic corps; it therefore had 'the value of an indication of the awareness, in the international circles concerned, of the legally binding nature of the customary rule and of its recognition by civilised States' (at 94). The Court then referred to various *treaties*, some of them ratified by Italy, others to which Italy was not a party. It pointed out that, although Italian legislation did not regulate the matter by specific provisions, nevertheless it was of significance that in 1929 Italy had ratified and implemented a treaty with the Holy See that, in mentioning in Article 12 the immunity in question, did not provide for any restriction. The Court added that Italy had taken the same stand in the Hague Agreement of 22 May 1928 between the President of the PCIJ and the Netherlands concerning the immunities and privileges of members and staff of the Court; this Agreement laid down 'the rules that at the time were held applicable to diplomatic immunities and privileges'; Italy 'had not been extraneous to it' (at 94). The Court then cited the Havana Convention of 28 February 1928 on diplomatic officers, which provided in Article 19 along the same lines.[11] It concluded

---

[9] ILC, 'Draft conclusions on identification of customary international law and commentaries thereto', Report of the International Law Commission, Seventieth Session (30 April–1 June and 2 July–10 August 2018), UN Doc. A/73/10 (2018) 119.

[10] Text, in French, in (1924) 32 *Zeitschrift für internationales Recht* 474, in footnote.

[11] The Convention had been adopted by the Sixth Pan-American Conference. See text in M. O. Hudson, *International Legislation* (Washington, DC: Carnegie Endowment, 1931–50), iv, at 2401ff, and (1928) 22 *AJIL* Suppl. 138ff.

that 'the combination of all these specific elements ... proves the existence of the [customary] rule relied upon by the appellant. Hence, as there are no contrary legislative provisions in the national legal system [of Italy] and conversely there are elements showing that Italy has adhered' to the customary rule in question, this was applicable in Italy (at 95).

According to Anzilotti (*Corso*, at 74–5), it is difficult for such a rule to emerge if one or more States is not faced with the opposition or protest of other States concerned, the rule gradually evolving out of this clash of interests. And in any case it is from the existence of arbitral awards on the specific issue—so the distinguished international lawyer went on to write in 1928—that one may surely infer that a customary rule has crystallized. This position was in a sense echoed in 1934 by the US Supreme Court Judge Benjamin Cardozo in *New Jersey* v *Delaware* (for whom international customary law 'has at times, like the common law within states, a twilight existence during which it is hardly distinguishable from morality or justice, till at length the imprimatur of a court attests its jural quality', at 383).

9.3.4 THE 'PERSISTENT OBJECTOR'

According to the doctrine of the persistent objector, a State that dissociates itself from a nascent customary rule and continues to do so consistently thereafter, is not bound by it and thus remains free from the obligations it imposes. In other words, this theory postulates that any State could object to the applicability of a customary rule, at least at the moment of its formation, thereby avoiding being restrained by rules that were not to its liking. For instance, in 1893 the British counsel so (implicitly) suggested before the British-American Arbitral Tribunal in the *Bering Fur Seal (United States of America/United Kingdom)* arbitration,[12] as did (expressly) in 1825 the US Supreme Court[13] and in 1903 the German–Venezuelan Mixed Claims Commission.[14]

This doctrine can be seen as a corollary of the view according to which custom is a 'tacit agreement' or a way to defend the voluntarist conception of the sources of international law: any time a State could prove that it had tacitly or expressly opposed a customary rule

---

[12] The US counsel had invoked principles of justice and morality. The British counsel dismissed this claim, noting that '[i]nternational law, properly so called, is only so much of the principles of morality and justice as the nations have agreed shall be part of those rules of conduct which shall govern their relations one with another. In other words, international law, as there exists no external superior power to impose it, rests upon the principle of consent. In the words of Grotius, *Placuitne gentibus?* Is there the consent of nations?' (Moore, *History and Digest*, i, at 871). When the President of the Tribunal asked the counsel for Great Britain whether it only referred to written agreement, he replied: 'When I say "to which they have agreed" of course I mean not merely or necessarily by a formal or express or written agreement, but by any mode in which agreement may be manifested, by which the Tribunal may arrive at the conclusion that they have so agreed' (ibid., at 872). It should be noted that the US did not challenge the British views on this matter. The Tribunal did not pronounce on the issue, although generally speaking it upheld the British claims.

[13] In *The Antelope*, the US Supreme Court had to deal in 1825 with the question of whether the arrest by American authorities of a Spanish vessel engaged in the slave trade was lawful. It held the arrest unlawful, for, although the slave trade was at the time normally prohibited, previously it had been legal and States favourable to that trade were entitled not to abide by the new rule. The Court held that '[n]o principle of general law is more universally acknowledged, than the perfect equality of nations. Russia and Geneva have equal rights. It results from this equality, that no one can rightfully impose a rule on another. Each legislates for itself, but its legislation can operate on itself alone. A right, then, which is vested in all by the consent of all, can be devested only by consent; and this trade [of slaves] in which all have participated, must remain lawful to those who cannot be induced to relinquish it. As no nation can prescribe a rule for others, none can make a law of nations; and this traffic remains lawful to those whose governments have not forbidden it' (at 35–56, in particular at 45).

[14] In 1903, in *Fishbach and Friedricy* the umpire of the German–Venezuelan Mixed Claims Commission held that '[a]ny nation has the power and the right to dissent from a rule or principle of international law, even though it is accepted by all the other nations' (at 397).

at the moment of its birth, such rule could not be regarded as binding on it since it did not consent to it. The US *Restatement of the Law Third* (1986) clearly took this same stand: it held that this view is 'an accepted application of the traditional principle that international law essentially depends on the consent of States'.[15]

This view did not go unchallenged. Possibly, it reflected the real state of affairs existing before the Second World War, when there were few States (mostly European) and their consent was necessary for a general rule to emerge. Whether or not that view rightly reflected the reality of the time, it is submitted that it can no longer be regarded as tenable today since custom at present does not exhibit 'consensual' features. This proposition can be advanced on two grounds. First, no one could deny the current community-oriented configuration of international relations (which are much less individualistic, and more social values-oriented). At present it is extremely difficult for an individual State to eschew the strong pressure of the vast majority of members of the community. Secondly, there is no firm support in State practice and international case law for a rule on the 'persistent objector'. The only explicit judicial contention in favour of this doctrine is set out in two *obiter dicta* of the ICJ (in *Asylum (Colombia v Peru)*, at 131, and *Fisheries (United Kingdom v Norway)*, at 277–8), but neither case appears to provide a watertight pronouncement about the existence of a customary rule or principle on the matter.[16]

Nonetheless, at present the doctrine of the persistent objector seems to be taken for granted. Support for this doctrine has mushroomed, particularly since the 1960s,[17] as a Western bulwark against the attempt of the newly independent States to reshape the content of the old rules of customary international law thanks to their majority within international organizations.[18] In other words, the doctrine has developed as 'an exhaust valve so that traditional states would not be bound by the norms put forward by the Third World'.[19] The ILC has recognized the existence of the doctrine in the aforementioned 2018 Draft Conclusions on Identification of Customary International Law, 'without prejudice to any question concerning peremptory norms of general international law' (Draft Conclusion 15). However, the practical value of the doctrine has been limited: up to now, it seems that the persistent and continued opposition by a State to the formation of a customary rule since its inception has never been recognized as apt to prevent the application of that rule to the persisting objecting State. The doctrine has therefore been correctly described as a myth.[20]

---

[15] See The American Law Institute, *Restatement of the Law Third: The Foreign Relations Law of the United States* (St Paul, MN: American Law Institute Publishers, 1987), I, at 18, 26 (§102d) and 32 (note 2). The passage quoted is at 32.

[16] According to A. A. Cançado Trindade, the persistent objector doctrine is as a 'nebulous figure ... which has never found the support that it sought in vain in the international case-law' (see IACHR, *Advisory Opinion OC-16/99 (Mexico Request), The Right to Information on Consular Assistance in the Framework of the Guarantees of the Due Process of Law*, Concurring Opinion of Judge Cançado Trindade).

[17] A. B. Curtis and G. Mitu, 'Withdrawing from International Custom' (2010) 120 *Yale LJ* 233.

[18] See P. Dumberry, 'Incoherent and Ineffective: The Concept of Persistent Objector Revisited' (2010) 59 *ICLQ* 783.

[19] G. R. Bandeira Galindo and C. Yip, 'Customary International Law and the Third World: Do Not Step on the Grass' (2017) 16 *Chinese JIL* 251, at 267.

[20] P.-M. Dupuy, 'A propos de l'opposabilité de la coutume générale: enquête brève sur l'objecteur persistant' in *Le droit international au service de la paix, de la justice et du développement: Mélanges Michel Virally* (Paris: A. Pedone, 1991), 257, 270.

9.3.5 LOCAL CUSTOMARY RULES

As pointed out earlier, a second feature differentiating custom from treaties is that customary rules are normally binding upon all States (and eventually other relevant international subjects, for instance non-State armed groups, international organizations, and so on), whereas treaties only bind those States (and other relevant international subjects with treaty-making power) that ratify or adhere to them. In addition to 'general' customary rules, there may exist customary rules that are only binding upon States of a certain geographical area or region, or even two States only. The ICJ has admitted in *Asylum (Colombia v Peru)* (at 276) that such rules may exist. Colombia relied against Peru on a 'regional or local custom peculiar to Latin American States' granting diplomatic asylum and in particular conferring on the State granting asylum the right to characterize the offence committed by the asylum seeker by a unilateral and final decision, binding on the territorial State. The Court held, however, that Colombia had failed to prove the existence of such a rule.

In 1948 a military rebellion had broken out in Peru, but had been suppressed on the same day. One of the leaders of the rebels, Víctor Raúl Haya de la Torre, sought asylum in the Colombian Embassy in Lima. As the Peruvian authorities refused to give him a safe-conduct for leaving the country, Colombia invoked before the ICJ various treaties as well as a regional customary rule granting asylum to political offenders. According to Colombia, this rule conferred on the State granting asylum the right unilaterally to characterize the offence as falling under those for which asylum was authorized. The Court noted that:

> [i]n the case of diplomatic asylum, the refugee is within the territory of the State where the offence was committed. A decision to grant asylum involves a derogation from the sovereignty of that State. It withdraws the offender from the jurisdiction of the territorial State and constitutes an intervention in matters which are exclusively within the competence of that State. Such a derogation from territorial sovereignty cannot be recognized unless its legal basis is established in each particular case. (at 274–5)

With specific regard to an alleged regional customary rule, the Court held that:

> [t]he Party which relies on a custom of this kind must prove that this custom is established in such a manner that it has become binding on the other Party. The Colombian Government must prove that the rule invoked by it is in accordance with a constant and uniform usage practised by the States in question, and that this usage is the expression of a right appertaining to the State granting asylum and a duty incumbent on the territorial State. (at 276)

The Court then stated that the practice was too uncertain, fluctuating, and even contradictory, and in addition had so often been influenced by considerations of political expediency, to be able to give rise to a customary rule. It concluded that Colombia had failed to prove the existence of such a rule. The Court added that:

> even if it could be supposed that such a custom existed between certain Latin-American States only, it could not be invoked against Peru which, far from having by its attitude adhered to it, [had], on the contrary, repudiated it by refraining from ratifying the Montevideo Conventions of 1933 and 1939 [on political asylum], which were the first to include a rule concerning the qualification of the offence in matters of diplomatic asylum. (at 277–8)

It would appear from the ruling of the ICJ in this case that, according to the Court, a regional customary rule must be based on the two elements (practice and *opinio juris*) required for all customary rules. However, it also must meet two special requirements: (i) it has to be tacitly accepted by all the parties concerned (thereby boiling down to a sort of tacit agreement, as has been rightly noted by some commentators); (ii) its existence must be proved by the State that invokes it, with the consequence that if this State fails to discharge its burden of proof, the claim based on the alleged customary rule is rejected. In contrast, in the case of customary rules having general purport, it is for the international court itself to satisfy itself that a rule has or has not evolved, pursuant to the principle applicable to international courts (not however to international criminal tribunals), *jura novit curia* (that is, while the facts must be proved by the party relying upon them to advance a certain claim, it is for the court to find the applicable law).

The ICJ also held in *Right of Passage over Indian Territory (Portugal v India)* that a local custom may exist that is binding upon *two States only* (at 39). In that case Portugal relied on a local custom as regulating its right of passage over Indian territory as between the Portuguese enclaves (the Court found that Portugal did indeed have such a right, but it was limited to the passage of private individuals, civil servants, and goods (at 40)). Similarly, in *Dispute regarding Navigational and Related Rights (Costa Rica v Nicaragua)*, the ICJ recognized the existence of a local customary rule on fishing by the inhabitants of the Costa Rican bank of the San Juan River for subsistence purposes from that bank. The Court established the existence of this local customary rule by noting the failure of Nicaragua to deny 'a right arising from the practice which had continued undisturbed and unquestioned over a very long period' (at §141). It may however be contended that in such cases of 'bilateral customs' it would be more appropriate to speak of a tacit agreement.

9.3.6 THE PRESENT ROLE OF CUSTOM

The existence today of so many international organizations to a great extent facilitates and speeds up the custom-creating process, at least in those areas where States are prepared to bring general rules into being. In particular, the UN makes a major contribution as it offers a forum where States are able to exchange and, where possible, harmonize their views to arrive at some form of compromise with other groups. Within UN representative bodies, chiefly the General Assembly, as well as in other international fora, general consent on the lowest common denominator often evolves: the majority of States eventually succeed in overcoming opposition by individual States, and in achieving general standards of behaviour. The latter come to constitute the normative core of subsequent practice and the basis for the drafting of treaties (or the evolution of customary rules). In other words, those general standards of behaviour represent a sort of bridge between the previous normative vacuum and the future detailed regulation afforded by treaty making or customary law. They provide basic guidelines; the treaty provisions (or customary rules) which usually follow in time provide the nuts and bolts, as it were—the technicalities calculated to bind international standards together and make them more detailed—besides, in the case of treaties, setting up the necessary techniques of supervision.[21]

After the Second World War, however, custom increasingly lost ground in two respects: existing customary rules were eroded more and more by fresh practice, and resort to custom to regulate new matters became relatively rare. These developments were largely due to the growing assertiveness of socialist countries and the massive presence of Third World States in the international arena. Both groups insisted on the need radically to revise old customary rules, which appeared to them to be the distillation of traditional Western values, the quintessence of the outlook they opposed. They demanded legal change. Custom is not the most suitable instrument for achieving such change. The insecurity inherent in its unwritten character and its protracted process of development rendered it disadvantageous to the Third World. The majority of States accordingly turned to the codification and progressive development of international law through resolutions of the UN General Assembly and, when possible, multilateral treaties.

Another general reason for the demotion of custom is that the membership of the world community is far larger than in the heyday of international customary law (in the space of

---

[21] See Judge Tanaka's Dissenting Opinion in *South West Africa (Ethiopia v South Africa; Liberia v South Africa)* (at 291).

one hundred years the number of States has risen from about 40 to nearly 200). Even more important, members of the world community are deeply divided economically and politically. It has, therefore, become extremely difficult for general rules to receive the support of the bulk of such a large number of very diverse States. By the same token, it is nowadays exceedingly difficult to ascertain whether a new rule has emerged, for it is not always possible to get hold of the huge body of evidence required.

9.4 GENERAL PRINCIPLES OF LAW RECOGNIZED IN DOMESTIC SYSTEMS

9.4.1 GENERAL

In addition to treaties and customs, Article 38(1) of the ICJ Statute, reproducing the Statute of the PCIJ, refers to 'the general principles of law recognized by civilized nations' (or, to rid the text of its early twentieth-century formulation, recognized in domestic systems).

These principles must not be confused with the general principles of international law (see **Chapter 3**), which are sweeping, loose, but fundamental standards of conduct that can be deduced from treaty and customary rules by extracting and generalizing some of their most significant common points. They do not make up a source proper. Most of them primarily serve the purpose of filling possible gaps or of making a particular construction prevail at any time when two or more interpretations are possible. Moreover, some principles (that is those on sovereignty, on non-interference in the affairs of other States, on the prohibition of the threat or use of force, on the peaceful settlement of disputes, on respect for human rights, and on self-determination of peoples), as we have seen earlier (**Chapter 3**), play the major role of forming the 'constitutional principles' of the world community (together with other norms of *jus cogens* (see **Chapter 11**)). The need to resort to general principles of international law, which a US–British Claims Tribunal aptly emphasized in 1923 in *Eastern Extension, Australasia and China Telegraph Co.*, is all the more conspicuous in the international community, where there is no central law-making body, treaty law tends to regulate only the specific matters of concern to the relevant contracting parties, and customary rules normally come into being slowly and by definition cannot address all the interests and concerns of States. In this community, general principles constitute both the backbone of the body of law governing international dealings and the potent cement that binds together the various and often disparate cogs and wheels of the normative framework of the community. States tend to be rather wary of general principles for fear that they might unduly restrain their freedom of action; in consequence, they seldom invoke such principles, except when they consider it advantageous to use them against another State, and they claim that a certain principle exists limiting the sovereignty of that State. Normally principles are spelled out by courts, when adjudicating cases that are not entirely regulated by treaty or customary rules. In this respect courts have played and are increasingly playing an essential role: they identify and set out principles 'hidden' in the interstices of the normative network, thus considerably contributing to the enrichment and development of the whole body of international law. It cannot be denied that, by so acting, courts fulfil a meritorious function very close to, and almost verging on, the creation of law.

By contrast, general principles of law recognized in domestic systems are norm-setting processes that bring about international rules to which recourse may only be had if and when no rule produced by any other formal source of international law regulates a certain matter. In other words, general principles of law are *subsidiary* sources, made necessary only by the lack of an applicable rule based on treaty or custom or other sources (see **9.5**). Resort to such principles started in the nineteenth century and at the beginning of the twentieth century. At the time courts adjudicating disputes between States, faced with cases where no treaty or customary rule regulated the matter submitted to arbitration, felt it necessary to have recourse to some general principles common to the domestic legal systems of most countries (in that period this of course meant European countries plus some advanced States of other continents such as the US). This was an adroit manner of filling legal gaps, thereby developing the then rather rudimentary and incomplete body of international law. It should be noted that the courts set out these principles without engaging in a comparative survey of national law. They simply enunciated principles that had very general purport and which indisputably were common to all major Western legal systems. No State protested, which is not surprising since the courts applied general principles familiar to the States concerned.

The principles at issue embraced necessity (*Neptune* (*United States v Great Britain*), (Opinion of Commissioner Pinkney) at 177–8); force majeure (*Russian Claim for Interest on Indemnities (Russia/Turkey)*, at §6); res judicata (*Pious Funds of the Californias (United States of America v The United Mexican States)*, at 12); denial of justice (*Fabiani*, at 356); and, turning to more specific areas, the principle whereby in the case of wrongful acts, the delinquent State must pay compensation including both *damnum emergens* and *lucrum cessans* (*Cape Horn Pigeon (United States of America v Russia).*, at 65). Some of these principles have, since then, been recognized as norms of customary international law.

9.4.2 THE ATTEMPT TO CODIFY RESORT TO PRINCIPLES IN 1921

After the First World War, reference to these principles was codified in Article 38(1)(c) of the Statute of the PCIJ, drafted in 1921 by an Advisory Committee of Jurists appointed by the Council of the League of Nations and made up of 10 members (eight from the West, a Brazilian, and a Japanese). The Chairman, the Belgian E. E. F. Descamps, proposed that, in addition to treaties and custom, the Court should also apply 'the rules of international law as recognized by the legal conscience of civilized nations'. Interestingly, in moving to adopt such an approach, he cited in support the Martens Clause (see **9.3.2**) and explicitly insisted that the new Court should 'conform to the dictates of the legal conscience of civilised nations'.

In commenting upon and reacting to the proposal, the Committee split into two groups. The majority proved to be in favour. They had two aims in mind. First, they wished to expand the sources of international law, by making applicable 'the fundamental law of justice and injustice, deeply engraved on the heart of every human being and which is given its highest and most authoritative expression in the legal conscience of civilized nations' (Descamps). Plainly, the advocates of this doctrine endeavoured to introduce 'principles of objective justice', that is, natural law principles in international relations. Secondly, where a dispute was not governed either by a treaty or by custom, they wished to avoid the possibility that the Court might declare itself incompetent through lack of applicable rules. Three members (the American Root, the Englishman Lord Phillimore, and the Italian Ricci-Busatti) strongly opposed this approach, adopting one that was markedly positivist. In an earlier meeting the leader of this group, Root, had emphatically stated that '[n]ations will submit to positive law, but will not submit to such principles as have not been developed into positive rules supported by an accord between all States'. And he asked, 'Was it possible to compel nations to submit their disputes to a Court which would administer not merely law, but also what it deems to be the conscience of civilised peoples?' In short, the minority clung to the traditional concept that the Court should solely apply rules and principles derived from the will of States and embodied in treaties or custom.

Given this radical difference of views, Root and Lord Phillimore eventually suggested a compromise: the Court should be empowered to apply 'the general principles of law recognised by civilised nations'. The proposal was accepted and, in the end, became Article 38(1)(c) of the Court's Statute. Clearly, the formula agreed upon followed a middle course between the two opposing views. The Court was empowered to apply something more than treaties and custom, and was thus able to go beyond the law resting on the will of States. However, it could not apply general and vague 'principles of objective justice' (in which case it would ultimately have been endowed with the power to create law), but only those principles which were clearly laid down in the municipal law systems of (dominant) States.

In spite of the looseness of the formula adopted in 1921, the fact that international courts previously had already drawn upon general principles of law proclaimed in national legal systems, and had not been challenged by the States concerned, justifies the view that Article 38(1)(c) eventually codified what had become over the years an unwritten rule on general principles.

9.4.3 THE PAST AND PRESENT ROLE OF PRINCIPLES

What use did the PCIJ make of the new source of law? Even a cursory glance at the Court's case law makes it clear that the Court very seldom resorted to the principles and, what is more important, it actually relied on principles of legal logic or general jurisprudence.

Concerning the principles referred to by the Court, mention may be made of the principle *nemo judex in re sua* (*Mosul Boundary*, at 32); the duty of reparation for international wrongs (*Factory at Chorzow (Germany v Poland)*, at 29); the principle whereby one cannot take advantage of one's own misconduct (ibid., at 31); and the *inadimplenti non est adimplendum* principle (Dissenting Opinion of Judge Anzilotti, *Prise d'eau à la Meuse (Netherlands v Belgium)*, at 50). In addition, there are some principles relating to the interpretation of treaties, such as *contra proferentem* (*Brazilian Loans (France/Brazil)*, at 114). As for the method applied by the Court to identify such principles, the Court did not carry out a detailed investigation of the legal systems of the various members of the international community. This, in itself, corroborates the view that they were actually not applied qua general principles obtaining in domestic systems, but as general tenets capable of being induced from the rules of international law or deduced from legal logic. Finally, the principles resorted to were not indispensable for the final decision in the case. They were only mentioned *ad adjuvandum*, that is, to bolster a proposition that the Court could already formulate on the basis of other rules or principles.

When the ICJ replaced the PCIJ, the new Court resorted even less frequently to these principles and always *ad adjuvandum*, as other courts have also done.[22] It would seem that the main reason for the decline of these principles is that, in the meantime, in the international community a whole network of treaty rules had been established and in addition numerous customary rules had emerged, translating general principles of international law into treaty or customary rules. As a consequence, it was felt that there was no need in traditional areas of international law to have recourse to these general principles.

Could it be held that, since it was so rarely invoked, the general rule on general principles recognized in domestic systems gradually withered away? In fact it has not fallen into desuetude. It has remained dormant, as it were, for a long time. However,

---

[22] In this regard, mention may be made of the principle of good faith (ICJ, *Nuclear Tests*, at §46), the rule of law (ICJ, *Frontier Dispute (Burkina Faso/Republic of Mali)*, at §23, and judgment no. 963 of the ILO Administrative Tribunal), the principle whereby a rule must be construed 'within the framework of the entire legal system prevailing at the time of the interpretation' (ICJ, *Aegean Sea Continental Shelf*, at 33), and the principle *expressio unius est exclusion alterius* (one thing having been mentioned the other is excluded: ICTY, *Kupreškić et al.*, at §623).

as soon as it has appeared that new areas of international law contained conspicuous gaps, the rule in question and the source it envisages have been revitalized. This applies to various areas, for instance international administrative law (governing the relations between international organizations and their staff); the case law of the European Court of Human Rights and the Court of Justice of the European Union also deserve special mention, since the two courts have frequently resorted to the general principles common to member States. General principles have also been applied in the field of international criminal law (see **Chapter 19**), a body of law that is still rudimentary and replete with lacunae. In this area, international criminal tribunals (see **19.3.3**) have frequently resorted to general principles of criminal law recognized in the principal legal systems of the world—common law systems and civil law systems.[23] Also Article 21 of the Statute of the International Criminal Court (ICC) envisages the possibility that the Court might resort to such a subsidiary source.

It should be added that, as international courts have repeatedly emphasized, the general principles under discussion can only be applied at the international level if they are compatible with the essential features and legal institutions of the world community. It would be inappropriate mechanically to import into the international legal system legal constructs that are not consonant with the specificities of international relations and which consequently cannot fit into the body of international law.[24]

9.5 OTHER INTERNATIONAL LAW-MAKING PROCESSES

9.5.1 UNILATERAL ACTS OF STATES

Unilateral acts of States can give rise to binding rules and therefore shall be recognized as a source of international law, although they are not provided for in Article 38 of the Statute of the ICJ. The PCIJ adopted this view in the *Legal Status of Eastern Greenland* case, where the Court found that an oral declaration formulated by the Minister for Foreign Affairs of Norway 'in regard to a question falling within his province' [was] binding upon the country to which the Minister belongs' (at 71). The ICJ has followed the same approach in a string of cases, the first being *Nuclear Tests*, where the Court held that:

> it is well recognized that declarations made by way of unilateral acts, concerning legal or factual situations, may have the effect of creating legal obligations... An undertaking of this kind, if given publicly, and with an intent to be bound, even though not made within the context of international negotiation, is binding. (at §43)

Not all unilateral acts give rise to new binding rules. Indeed, most unilateral acts produce other legal effects, which are always predetermined by customary law, which

---

[23] In *Erdemović* (Sentencing) an ICTY Trial Chamber held that 'there is a general principle of law common to all nations... whereby the most severe penalties may be imposed for crimes against humanity'(at §31); in *Furundžija* another Trial Chamber of the same Tribunal held that the definition of rape as a crime against humanity resulted from the convergence of the principles of the major legal systems of the world (at §§174–181); in *Kupreškić et al.* the same Trial Chamber found in principles common to the various legal systems the 'criteria for deciding whether there has been a violation of one or more provisions' when the same conduct can be regarded as breaching more than one provision of criminal law (question of cumulation of offences) (at §637ff; §680ff); in *Blaškić* another ICTY Trial Chamber held that the proportionality of the penalty to the gravity of the crime is a general principle of criminal law common to the major legal systems of the world (at §796).

[24] See Judge Cassese's Dissenting Opinion in *Erdemović* (Appeal), §§1–6.

therefore means that they are not a source of international law. For instance, protest is a unilateral declaration designed to object to an act or action performed by another State; its purpose and legal effect is to show that the protesting State does not recognize, accept, or acquiesce in the act or action, or preserves the right to challenge that act or action. Similarly, recognition by a State of a situation or conduct aims to consider as legitimate that situation or conduct and thus prevents the recognizing State from subsequently challenging what had been previously recognized (in other words, it creates an estoppel: on recognition of States, see **4.3.1**). Renunciation is the willing unilateral abandonment of a right; this abandonment, although it may be explicit or tacit, must however be deliberate and clear; as Anzilotti rightly pointed out, it may not be inferred from simple inertia, or non-exercise of a right, or mere passage of time (*Corso*, at 297). Notification is the act by which a State makes other States cognizant of a certain action it has performed (e.g. in the case of naval blockade in time of war, customary law requires that the blockading State should notify neutral States of the blockade). Its legal effect is to preclude the other States from subsequently claiming that, not knowing of the action notified, they were entitled to behave differently.

Promise seems to be the only unilateral transaction giving rise to international obligations proper, that is, establishing a new rule binding the promising State towards one or more other States. Promise is a unilateral declaration by which a State undertakes to behave in a certain manner. This obligation is assumed independently of any reciprocal undertaking by other States (otherwise the declaration would amount to one element of a contractual legal transaction).

In the *North Sea Continental Shelf* cases the ICJ stressed that the unilateral assumption 'by conduct, by public statements and proclamations, and in other ways', by a State not party to a Convention, of the obligations laid down in the Convention was 'not lightly to be presumed', because 'a very definite, very consistent course of conduct' was required (at §§27–28). In *Nuclear Tests*, the same Court held that France's declaration, that it would cease conducting atmospheric nuclear tests, entailed that it had assumed an obligation to do so. The Court required, for a unilateral declaration to produce this effect, that the State making the declaration should have the clear intention to be legally bound by it, and that the undertaking be given publicly (at 267–71). Promise was also considered as a legal transaction giving rise to obligations in *Nicaragua (Nicaragua v United States of America)* (at §261), and in *Frontier Dispute (Burkina Faso/Republic of Mali)* (at §§39–40).

In 2006, the ILC adopted ten 'Guiding Principles applicable to unilateral declarations of States capable of creating legal obligations'.[25] As the ILC has explained, the Guiding Principles are limited to unilateral acts *stricto sensu*, that is, formal declarations 'publicly made and manifesting the will to be bound'. Other behaviours that can be designated as unilateral acts, but where there is no intent to produce legal effects through 'creating, recognizing, safeguarding or modifying rights, obligations or legal situations', are not taken into account by the Guiding Principles. The Guiding Principles constitute an authoritative guidance on unilateral acts of States as a formal source of international law, also considering that they have largely been overlooked by international legal scholars.

---

[25] ILC, 'Guiding Principles Applicable to Unilateral Declarations of States Capable of Creating Legal Obligations' in Report of the International Law Commission Fifty-eighth session (1 May–9 June and 3 July–11 August 2006), UN Doc. A/61/10 (2006) 366.

9.5.2 BINDING DECISIONS OF INTERNATIONAL ORGANIZATIONS

Article 38 of the Statute of the ICJ fails to refer to norm-setting processes within the framework of an intergovernmental organization. Under these norm-setting processes, usually a body of the organization is empowered to adopt binding legal standards, in most cases by majority vote. The rules enacted by the body entrusted with this function by the treaty bind only the member States of the organization.

That these sources of international law are hedged around with these limitations is quite understandable. States only accept being bound by written rules other than those based on consent if they have previously accepted the norm-creating process through a treaty, that is, have previously manifested in writing their willingness to be bound in future by rules set by an international body. Furthermore, just as the treaty rules that make up the statute of an organization bind only the member States of that organization, similarly the rules enacted by a constituent body of the organization cannot bind third States.

It is apparent that the existence of this category of sources of law is a characteristic feature of modern international law. The needs it was intended to meet are clear: in some specific and well-defined areas it would be difficult and time-consuming for States to get together and unanimously agree upon a set of rules as soon as the necessity for such rules arises. It is easier and more expeditious for an international body to enact such rules.

Among the international organizations that can issue binding decisions, the United Nations deserves special mention. The power to pass binding resolutions is provided for the Security Council when acting under Chapter VII of the UN Charter (concerning action with respect to threats to peace, breaches of the peace, and acts of aggression). Article 41 of the UN Charter provides that '[t]he Security Council may decide what measures not involving the use of armed force are to be employed to give effect to its decisions'. When the Security Council decides not to resort to recommendations but to issue decisions, these are binding on the strength of Article 25 of the UN Charter ('The Members of the United Nations agree to accept and carry out the decisions of the Security Council in accordance with the present Charter'). The UN may impel compliance with these decisions by third States, namely those very few States that are still not members of the UN, through sanctions or other measures taken on the strength of Article 2(6) of the UN Charter ('The Organization shall ensure that States which are not members of the United Nations act in accordance with these Principles [laid down in Article 2] so far as may be necessary for the maintenance of international peace and security') (see **14.4** and, more generally, **Chapter 15**). Particularly since the end of the Cold War, the UN Security Council has passed many decisions on sanctions, such as bans on exports and imports and other economic relations with particular States (e.g. Iraq, the Federal Republic of Yugoslavia (Serbia-Montenegro), Somalia, Liberia, Libya, Haiti, etc.). It also adopted the Statutes of ad hoc international criminal tribunals (see **19.3.3**).

9.5.3 IS EQUITY A FORMAL SOURCE?

In the Anglo-American tradition, equity refers to rules and jurisprudence that developed parallel to common law, giving rise to courts of equity (Chancery courts) dealing only with equitable relief.

In international law, courts and tribunals may be granted the power to make decisions based not on existing law, but rather on principles of equity. Article 38(2) of the ICJ Statute envisages this possibility, although States have never granted the Court specific jurisdiction to make decisions *ex aequo et bono*. Whenever an international court or tribunal applies equity to solve a dispute, it issues a binding decision for the parties by departing from or adjusting existing rules. Clearly, therefore, in this scenario equity is not a source of law, but a means to correct it.[26]

Equity can also be a material component of the category of general principles of law applied in domestic systems (see **9.4**). For instance, in a Dissenting Opinion, Judge Anzilotti stated that the principle of *inadimplenti non est inadimplentum* is 'so just, so equitable, so universally recognised that it must be applied in international relations... [and is] one of the general principles of law recognised by civilised nations' (*Prise d'eau à la Meuse*, Dissenting Opinion Judge Anzilotti, at 50). In his dissent in the same case, Judge Manley Hudson asserted that certain maxims of equity are 'general principles of law recognized by civilized nations' (*Prise d'eau à la Meuse*, Dissenting Opinion Judge Hudson, at 76) and concluded that, based on maxims such as 'equality is equity' and 'he who seeks equity must do equity' (at 76), a judge shall ensure that 'where two parties have assumed an identical or reciprocal obligation, one party which is engaged in a continuing non-performance of that obligation should not be permitted to take advantage of a similar non-performance of that obligation by the other party' (at 77). Here again, however, equity will not be a formal source of international law, but a material source to establish general principles of law applied in domestic systems.

Finally, equity may play a role in the interpretation of the relevant applicable rules, whenever the latter allow the judge a sufficient margin of discretion to adapt them to the circumstances of the case (equity *infra legem*: see **5.3.2**). In this scenario, however, the line between interpretation of existing law and creation of new law by resorting to equity may be blurred. One prominent example is the *North Sea Continental Shelf* cases, where the ICJ was confronted with the application of the so-called principle of equidistance to delimit the lateral continental shelf boundaries between Germany and two other countries (Denmark and the Netherlands). The application of the principle of equidistance would have produced a manifestly unjust result on Germany, in light of the concavity of its coastlines. The Court resorted to equity, arguing that it was 'applying a rule of law which itself require[d] the application of equitable principles' (at §85). However, as Judge Morelli put forward, the Court actually resorted to equity to derive principles and criteria not prescribed by the relevant rules. In other words, equity was applied to fill in the gaps of existing applicable law (*praeter legem*), absent an express consent of the parties to resort to equitable principles.[27]

---

[26] E.g. under Article V(3) of Annex II to the Dayton-Paris Accord of 1995 the Arbitral Tribunal, charged with pronouncing on the establishment of an Inter-Entity Boundary Line between the Federation of Bosnia and Herzegovina and the Republika Srpška in the Brčko area, was authorized to apply 'the relevant legal and equitable principles'. In its award of 14 February 1997, the Arbitral Tribunal drew upon 'the demands of impartiality, justice and reason' (*Arbitration for the Brčko Area*, at 399ff). In its second, 'supplemental award', of 15 March 1998, the Arbitral Tribunal put off a final decision on the matter, deciding that the interim international supervisory system set up by the first award should continue. It justified this decision as being equitable and not based on 'purely political considerations'. In its third and final award, of 5 March 1999, the Arbitral Tribunal went so far as to legislate on the matter: it established a permanent self-governing Brčko District, independent of the two Entities, to be held in condominium by them, and subject to the sovereignty of Bosnia and Herzegovina (at 536ff).

[27] In two cases (*Continental Shelf (Tunisia/Libyan Arab Jamahiriya)* and *Delimitation of the Maritime Boundary in the Gulf of Maine Area (Canada/United States of America)*), the ICJ has further developed the approach followed in the *North Continental Shelf* cases and has recognized that equity may be applied as a self-standing applicable principle of law *praeter legem*. This approach was however harshly criticized in the Dissenting Opinions of some judges of the Court as well as in legal scholarship.

9.6 IDENTIFICATION AND DEVELOPMENT OF INTERNATIONAL LAW

9.6.1 JURISPRUDENCE AND DOCTRINE

Article 38(1)(d) of the ICJ refers to 'judicial decisions and teaching of the most qualified publicists' as 'subsidiary means for the determination of rules of law'. According to the prevalent view, this provision does not list additional formal sources of international law but two material sources, namely two means of determining the content of the rules created through the formal sources under previous letters (a) to (c)[28] (according to Article 59 of the ICJ Statute, however, the Court's decisions have binding force between the parties of the dispute and in respect of that particular case).

Given the rudimentary character of international law, and the lack of both a central law-making body and a central judicial institution endowed with compulsory jurisdiction, in practice many decisions of the most authoritative courts (in particular the ICJ) are bound to have crucial importance in establishing the existence of customary rules, or in defining their scope and content, or in promoting the evolution of new concepts.[29] In addition, in a few instances the ICJ has in fact even gone so far as to set new international rules, in spite of its aforementioned lack of formal power to do so. As one distinguished commentator noted, this happened when the ICJ set out the implied powers doctrine whereby international organizations may be deemed to possess all the powers necessary for the fulfilment of their functions or goals (*Reparations for Injuries Suffered in the Service of the United Nations*, at 182); developed a new regime of reservations to treaties (*Reservations to the Convention on the Prevention and Punishment of Genocide*, at 24); held that in the exercise of diplomatic protection, even in the case of a single nationality what matters is the effective link between an individual and a State (*Nottebohm (Liechtenstein v Guatemala)*, at 22–54); and set forth the doctrine of 'equitable principles' in matters of delimitation of the continental shelf (*North Sea Continental Shelf* cases, at 46–8). It is notable that no State has ever objected to, or complained about, these pronouncements. Thus, States have implicitly accepted or at least acquiesced in the normative role sometimes played by the ICJ.

As to the teaching of publicists, by the late twentieth century they had certainly become far less influential than in the past, arguably because of the 'maturation of international

---

[28] Among others, see G. Schwarzenberger, *International Law as Applied by International Courts and Tribunals*, vol. I, 3rd edn (London: Stevens and Sons Ltd, 1957), 26.

[29] It may suffice here to mention a few landmark decisions: the award rendered in 1872 in *Alabama (United States/Great Britain)*, which laid down the basic principles on neutrality (at 543–682); the award made in 1928 by the Swiss arbitrator Max Huber in *Island of Palmas (Netherlands/United States of America)*, where the notion of territorial sovereignty was set out (at 838–40); the arbitral award in *Naulilaa (Portugal v Germany)* (Portugal v Germany), spelling out the requirements of reprisals (at 1025–8). One should also mention various judgments handed down by the ICJ: that in *Barcelona Traction (Belgium v Spain)*, which propounded, in a celebrated *obiter dictum*, the notion of obligations *erga omnes* (at §33) and in effect reversed the judgment of 1966 in the *South West Africa* cases (where the Court, by the President's casting vote, had held that a member of the League of Nations did not have legal standing to vindicate a right belonging to any member of the League, because *actio popularis*, that is, the right to institute proceedings on behalf of the community, did not exist in international law; the Court had consequently denied legal standing to Ethiopia and Liberia in their action against South Africa; at 38–47); the judgment in the *North Sea Continental Shelf* cases, where the relations between treaties and custom were delineated in a masterly manner (at 32–43); the judgment in *Nuclear Tests*, where the Court enunciated the doctrine of legal effects of unilateral acts of States (at 267–71); that in *Nicaragua*, where the Court set out in compelling terms (i) the principal aspects of the body of customary law on the imputability to a State of acts of individuals not having the status of, or not acting as, State officials or agents; (ii) the principles on the use of force, in particular under Article 51 of the UN Charter; (iii) the principle of non-intervention; and (iv) the fundamental principles of humanitarian law (at 38–66, 94–106, 106–12, and 113–15). One may also mention the judgment of the ICTY in *Tadić (Interlocutory Appeal)*, delineating the category of war crimes in internal armed conflicts (at §§94–137).

law since the era of the founding fathers'.[30] In addition, the ICJ Statute refers 'to the most qualified' publicists, which suggests that the category of publicist can be broken down into different categories and that factors may exist to assess the weight of 'teachings'.[31]

9.6.2 CODIFICATION

As pointed out earlier, most States tend to prefer treaties to custom, for the former are more certain and result from the willing participation of contracting parties in the negotiating process. Between the 1960s and the 1980s, this natural preference for treaties became more pronounced, because new States began actively to participate in international relations and insisted that the old law be changed so as to take account of their needs and concerns. The 'old' States considered it advisable to update the law by a treaty-making process, so as to be in a position actively to discuss and negotiate the adaptation of the law to new realities. This process is called 'codification'.

Two major channels have been used to this end. In the more traditional and classical areas of codification (in particular, the law of the sea, diplomatic and consular immunities, the law of treaties, State succession, and State responsibility) draft treaties were elaborated by the UN ILC (made up of 34 experts, many with diplomatic experience and, therefore, sensitive to States' demands) and subsequently discussed by the Sixth Committee of the General Assembly. They were then the subject of negotiation in diplomatic conferences. Thus, important codification treaties were adopted, such as four Conventions on the Law of the Sea of 1958 (superseded by the 1982 Convention on the Law of the Sea); the 1961 Vienna Convention on Diplomatic Relations, and that on Consular Relations of 1963; the Vienna Convention on the Law of Treaties of 1969, followed by the Convention on the Law of Treaties with International Organizations, of 1986; and two Conventions on State Succession, of 1978 and 1983, etc.

In other areas, or in the same areas when existing law was in need of radical change or major differences persisted, the technical co-operation of the ILC was shunned: States preferred to keep the discussion and negotiation under their direct control. Accordingly, a Special Committee consisting of their representatives was set up to report to the General Assembly. In some instances where the matter was too controversial for a detailed agreement to be reached, the upshot was the adoption of a Declaration (such as the 1970 Declaration on Friendly Relations). In other cases the General Assembly, after taking account of the discussions in the Special Committee, referred the matter to a diplomatic Conference. An important illustration of this process is the laborious work carried out from 1973 to 1982 on the new law of the sea, which led to the adoption of the 1982 Convention. In 1958, when four Conventions on the matter were adopted, the main purpose was to restate, codify, and update existing law, and consequently the co-operation of the ILC proved indispensable. By contrast, in the 1970s the main object was to change the law radically; to this end, direct negotiation among States was regarded as a more suitable method.

The ICJ has lucidly stressed the relations between codification treaties and customary international law in a string of important judgments, and the legal literature has produced forceful theoretical treatment of the subject.[32] Codification treaties may have the following effects.

---

[30] S. Sivakumaran, 'The Influence of Teachings of Publicists on the Development of International Law' (2017) 66 *ICLQ* 1, at 2.

[31] For a recent study on the matter, see S. T. Helmersen, 'Finding "the Most Highly Qualified Publicists": Lessons from the International Court of Justice' (2019) 30 *EJIL* 509.

[32] See in particular the comments by E. Jimenez de Aréchaga, 'International Law in the Past Third of a Century' (1978-I) 159 *RCADI* 14–26.

(1) A *declaratory effect*, that is they simply codify or restate an existing customary rule (as the ICJ noted in *Legal Consequences for States of the Continued Presence of South Africa in Namibia* (at 47), and *ICAO Council* (at 67), where the Court noted that Article 60 of the Vienna Convention on the Law of Treaties concerning termination of a treaty relationship on account of breach was merely declaratory of existing law; the Court stated the same with regard to Article 62 of the same Convention, on termination of treaties on the ground of change of circumstances, in *Fisheries Jurisdiction* (at 18); see also the *Case Concerning the Gabčíkovo-Nagymaros Project* (§§46–47; see also §§101–104); in this same case the Court held that Article 12 of the 1978 Vienna Convention on Succession of States in Respect of Treaties reflected a rule of customary law (at §123)).

(2) A *crystallizing effect*, in that they bring to maturity an emerging customary rule, that is, a rule that was still in the formative stage (as the ICJ stressed in the *North Sea Continental Shelf* cases (at 39), with regard to Articles 1 and 3 of the Convention on the Continental Shelf defining the continental shelf and the rights of States relating thereto, and in *Fisheries Jurisdiction (United Kingdom v Iceland)* (at 14), with regard to Article 52 of the Vienna Convention on the Law of Treaties, on coercion as a ground for the invalidity of treaties).

(3) A *generating effect*, which materializes whenever a treaty provision creating new law sets in motion a process whereby it gradually brings about, or contributes to, the formation of a corresponding customary rule (in the *North Sea Continental Shelf* case the ICJ considered as legally admissible a process whereby a treaty provision, while only conventional or contractual in its origin, subsequently passes into the general *corpus* of international law and is 'accepted as such by the *opinio juris*' so as to have binding effects even for countries other than the parties to the treaty (at 41); subsequently in the *Fisheries Jurisdiction Case (United Kingdom v Iceland)* it returned to the matter, although it did not find that the effect at issue had come about *in casu* (at 23–6)).

9.6.3 SOFT LAW

The term soft law is used as opposed to 'hard law', (which makes up binding international law), to describe a body of standards, commitments, joint statements, or declarations of policy or intention (e.g. think of the Helsinki Final Act of 1975), or resolutions adopted by the UN General Assembly or other multilateral bodies, that do not have per se binding character but nonetheless possess high normative value. For instance, the ICJ has clarified that the resolutions of the UN General Assembly may (i) 'provide evidence important for establishing the existence of a rule or the emergence of an *opinio juris*', or they may (ii) 'show the gradual evolution of the *opinio juris* required for the establishment of a new rule'. The Court went on to examine various resolutions on nuclear weapons and found that they did not evince the existence of a customary rule prohibiting the use of nuclear weapons in any circumstances; this was proved, among other things, by the fact that those resolutions had been adopted 'with substantial numbers of negative votes and abstentions' (*Legality of the Threat or Use of Nuclear Weapons*, at §§70–73).

How can one distinguish 'soft law' from a legally binding undertaking? It all depends on the intention of the authors of the specific document, as it may be inferred from the relevant elements: the drafters of the text may have intended to attach to it the legal value of a binding agreement, or they may have envisaged the document as a piece of 'soft law' (in this respect one could usefully make reference to two cases: *Aegean Sea Continental Shelf (Greece v Turkey)*, decided by the ICJ in 1978, and *Maritime Delimitation and Territorial Questions between Qatar and Bahrain (Qatar v Bahrain) (Jurisdiction and Admissibility)*, decided by the same Court in 1994 (see **10.2**)).

The instruments or documents belonging to soft law have three major features in common. First, they are indicative of the modern trends emerging in the world community, where international organizations or other collective bodies have the task of promoting action on matters of general concern. Secondly, they deal with matters that reflect new concerns of the international community, to which previously this community was not sensitive or not sufficiently alert. Thirdly, for political, economic, or other reasons, it is, however, hard for States to reach full convergence of views and standards on these matters so as to agree upon legally binding commitments. As a consequence, the standards, statements, and other instruments at issue do not impose legally binding obligations. Nevertheless, these matters, although they remain legally unregulated, become the object of agreed guidelines, or statements of common positions or policies. These may thus lay the ground, or constitute the building blocks, for the gradual formation of treaty provisions (or, as clarified in what follows, new customary rules). In other words, gradually 'soft law' may turn into 'hard law'.

Soft law instruments and documents, as in the case of codification convention, may in some cases codify existing customary international rules, or crystallize their formation or contribute to the development of new rules of customary international law. The conditions on which a piece of 'soft law' may be regarded as declaratory, or indicative, of a customary rule, or instead as helping to crystallize such a rule, are the general conditions to be fulfilled for establishing whether a customary rule exists or is in the process of formation: ascertaining whether *usus* and *opinio juris* have evolved on a certain subject. Thus, for instance, the consent that evolved among States in the late 1950s on the use of outer space as soon as the first rockets and satellites were launched, was reflected and crystallized in a Declaration (1962-XVIII) adopted in 1963 by the UN General Assembly (Article 2). It was subsequently restated and spelled out in the 1967 Treaty on Principles Governing the Activities of States in the Exploration and Use of Outer Space. This treaty clearly elaborated upon a set of principles that were already part of general law. By the same token, arguably some provisions of the treaty led to the formation of corresponding rules of customary international law.

9.7 INTERACTIONS AMONG SOURCES

The sources of international law may create rules on the same subject matter. These rules may not be in conflict, as also explained earlier: for instance, because the treaty rule reflects the content of a corresponding rule of customary international law, or vice versa, the treaty rule crystallizes the content of the emerging customary rule.

Rules of international law on the same subject matter may however have a different content. This does not necessarily imply that a conflict between them arises. As the ILC has aptly pointed out in its study on the Fragmentation of International Law, 'when several norms bear on a single issue they should, to the extent possible, be interpreted so as to give rise to a single set of compatible obligations'.[33] If this is not the case, the question of establishing their hierarchy arises.

In this respect, the traditional principle is that there is no hierarchy between treaties and customs as sources of law, and arguably between them and unilateral acts of States as formal sources that can be considered as 'primary sources'. In other words, rules created

---

[33] This is what the ILC called the 'principle of harmonization': ILC, 'Conclusions of the Study Group on the Fragmentation of International Law: Difficulties Arising from the Diversification and Expansion of International Law', in Report of the International Law Commission, Fifty-eighth session (1 May–9 June and 3 July–11 August 2006) UN Doc. A/61/10 (2006) 403, at 408.

by any of these primary sources are at the same level, and possess equal rank and status. It follows that the relations between rules generated by the aforementioned three sources are governed by the general principles which in all legal orders regulate the relations between norms deriving from the same source: a later law repeals an earlier one (*lex posterior derogat priori*); a later law, general in character, does not derogate from an earlier one, which is special in character (*lex posterior generalis non derogat priori speciali*); a special law prevails over a general law, or *lex specialis derogat generali*. However, as it will be further explained later (see **11.4**), a set of rules comprising the so-called *jus cogens* has now emerged: these rules set forth obligations that cannot be contracted out of by way of treaties and that can only be derogated from by rules having the same peremptory character. These rules are hierarchically superior to any other rule of international law not belonging to *jus cogens*.

As for binding decisions of international organizations, they must be enacted in conformity with the procedures envisaged in the constituent treaty. This is the reason why the norm-setting processes by which binding decisions are issued are often termed 'secondary' sources, because they are provided for by rules produced by a primary source (treaties). Arguably, decisions of international organizations must be in conformity with customary international law. In this regard, the ICJ has stated: '[i]nternational organizations are subjects of international law, and, as such, are bound by any obligations incumbent upon them under general rules of international law' (*Interpretation of the Agreement of 25 March 1951 Between the WHO and Egypt*, at 89). There are however scholars who find the matter far from settled and describe it as a hard question.[34] Notably, the decisions of the Security Council adopted under Chapter VII of the UN Charter prevail over any other conflicting treaty obligations of UN member States. This is by virtue of Article 103 of the UN Charter, which provides that:

> [i]n the event of a conflict between the obligations of the Members of the United Nations under the present Charter and their obligations under any other international agreement, their obligations under the present Charter shall prevail.[35]

Concerning general principles of law recognized in domestic systems, they are a subsidiary source of international law to which courts can resort only where there are gaps or an unclear regulation in the rules created by the other sources of international law. The reason for so proceeding is that, logically, one should first of all apply rules and principles that are peculiar to international law, hence more specifically suited to regulate a matter arising within the international community. Only subsequently may one turn to more sweeping principles that underpin domestic systems of law.

---

[34] J. Alvarez, 'Review of Dan Sarooshi, International Organizations and Their Exercise of Sovereign Powers' (2007) 101 *AJIL* 674.
[35] The exact scope of this provision is however a matter of debate. See among others: R. Lijova, 'The Scope of the Supremacy Clause of the United Nations Charter' (2008) 57 *ICLQ* 583.

10
THE LAW OF TREATIES

10.1 INTRODUCTION

International rules regulating the birth, life, and death of an international treaty form the so-called 'law of treaties'. Despite the indispensable role that international agreements have played since the inception of the modern international society (and even before),[1] in the past there was much uncertainty as regards the existence, content, and scope of the rules of customary international law on the law of treaties. In particular, to an even greater extent than the 'birth' and life of treaties, their 'death' was regulated by a handful of rules containing numerous loopholes. Major Powers made treaties to their advantage and released themselves from treaty obligations when they deemed fit. If the other contracting party was also a Great Power, resort to war could prove necessary. This explains the scepticism expressed as early as the eighteenth century by Frederick II of Prussia on the relative weights of treaties and State interests (in his view the latter must always prevail in the final analysis).[2] It also explains some acerbic comments made by Bismarck, in 1879[3]—which in recent times, it is reported, were (not surprisingly) taken up to some extent by de Gaulle.[4]

Codification efforts to clarify the content of the customary rules on the law of treaties were made by the League of Nations and other institutions (such as the International Commission of American Jurists) but to no avail. In 1948, a study prepared by the UN Secretariat in relation to the work of codification of the International Law Commission (ILC) emphasized that 'there is hardly a branch of the law of treaties which is free from doubt and, in some cases, from confusion'.[5] Against this background, the adoption in 1969 of the Vienna Convention on the Law of Treaties (VCLT) is therefore amongst the prominent achievements of ILC, thanks to the work of eminent British jurists as Special Rapporteurs on the topic (James L. Brierly, Sir Hersch Lauterpacht, Sir Gerald Fitzmaurice, and Sir Humphrey Waldock).

The VCLT entered into force on 27 January 1980 and, as of today, it counts 116 States parties. It is the 'treaty on treaties'[6] since it codifies, and to some extent progressively

---

[1] On the use of international treaties in ancient times, see S. A. Korff, 'An Introduction to the History of International Law' (1924) 18 *AJIL* 246, at 249.

[2] Frédéric II, 'Histoire de mon temps, Avant-propos' in *Oeuvres posthumes de Frédéric II, roi de Prusse* (Berlin: Voss et Fils, 1789), i, at 11, 14.

[3] Bismarck wrote the following: 'Observance of treaties between Big States is relative indeed, as soon as it is put to test "in the struggle for existence". No big nation will be prompted to sacrifice its existence on the altar of fidelity to a treaty, if obliged to choose between the two. The [maxim] *ultra posse nemo tenetur* [no one is bound beyond what he can do] cannot be invalidated by any treaty clause' (Otto Fürst von Bismarck-Schönhauser, *Gedanken und Erinnerungen* (Stuttgart and Berlin: Cotta, 1922), ii, at 287).

[4] Reportedly President de Gaulle, upon signing an important treaty with Germany, stated that international agreements 'are like roses and young girls; they last while they last' (see *The Economist*, 18 March 1972, 6).

[5] Survey of International Law in Relation to the Work of Codification of the International Law Commission: Preparatory work within the purview of article 18, paragraph 1, of the International Law Commission—Memorandum submitted by the Secretary-General, A/CN.4/1/Rev.1, p. 51, §91.

[6] See R. D. Karney and R. E. Dalton, 'The Treaty on Treaties' (1970) 64 *AJIL* 495.

develops, the customary rules of the law of treaties. There are however some limitations. First, the Convention applies only to treaties concluded after its entry into force (Article 4). Treaties made before that date are still governed by the pre-existing rules, to the extent that they differ from those codified in the Convention as 'new' customary rules or as a progressive development of international law. Secondly, the Convention applies only to treaties concluded between States (Article 1). However, the rules of the Convention may reflect the content of rules of customary international law that apply also to treaties concluded by States with other subjects of international law. Thirdly, the Convention applies only to treaties concluded in a written form (see later in this chapter). Oral treaties (which are however rare) are not per se regulated by the Vienna Convention, although nothing precludes their being regulated by rules of customary international law having the same content as those contained in the Convention. Finally, the Convention deals exclusively with the 'birth, life, and death' of treaties, which means that it does not deal at all with their specific substance, which is for States to agree upon. However, the Vienna Convention contains an important limitation to the pre-existing unfettered freedom of States in deciding the substance of treaties: *jus cogens*. The Convention indeed provides that treaties whose content is contrary to peremptory rules of international law are null and void (Article 53) or become null and void (Article 64) (see **11.4**).

Two other Vienna Conventions are also relevant in the field of the law of treaties. The first is the 1986 Vienna Convention on the Law of Treaties between States and International Organizations or between International Organizations. This Convention mainly extends the provisions contained in the 1969 Vienna Convention to the treaties mentioned in its title, with the relevant adjustments. As of today, it is not in force. The second Convention worth mentioning is the 1978 Vienna Convention on Succession of States in respect to Treaties, which entered into force in 1996 and whose provisions do not fully reflect the content of corresponding rules of customary international law (see **4.4.2**).

10.2 NOTION AND TYPES OF TREATIES

Under international law, States enjoy full freedom as regards the modalities and form of treaties, for there are no rules *prescribing* any definite procedure or formality. In other words, States can conclude a treaty by reaching an agreement by joint declarations, exchange of notes or letters, agreed minutes, and so on. It is for States to decide how to bring into being legally binding undertakings. It all depends on their will.

In addition, a treaty may be termed in a variety of ways, such as convention, protocol, pact, or covenant, to mention just a few. What matters in determining whether a treaty exists is whether the relevant parties have reached an agreement regulated by international law. The latter is a key requirement, since there may be agreements concluded by States with other subjects of international law which, however, intend to create legal situations regulated by national law and cannot therefore be considered international treaties (think of the purchase of property of one State by another State).

There may be cases where it is not clear whether a State has entered into an international binding agreement proper, or has instead undertaken only a political commitment. The problem arose before the International Court of Justice (ICJ) in *Aegean Sea Continental Shelf*, in 1978. The Court had to satisfy itself that its jurisdiction was based on a communiqué jointly issued in Brussels by the Prime Ministers of Greece and Turkey. The document was not signed or even initialled; it had been directly issued to the press during a press conference held at the conclusion of the Prime Ministers' meeting. The Court first pointed out that it knew 'of no rule of international law which might preclude a joint communiqué from constituting an international agreement to submit a dispute to arbitration or judicial settlement' (at §96). It then noted that whether or not the communiqué constituted an agreement:

> essentially depends on the nature of the act or transaction to which the Communiqué gives expression; and it does not settle the matter simply to refer to the form—a communiqué—in which that act or transaction is embodied. On the contrary, in determining what was indeed the nature of the act or transaction embodied in the Brussels Communiqué, the Court must have regard above all to its actual terms and to the particular circumstances in which it was drawn up. (at §96)

The Court then carefully considered the positions taken by the two States prior to the issuing of the communiqué (at §§100–106). It concluded as follows:

> Having regard to the terms [of the communiqué] and to the context in which it was agreed and issued, the Court can only conclude that it was not intended to, and did not, constitute an immediate commitment by the Greek and Turkish Prime Ministers, on behalf of their respective Governments, to accept unconditionally the unilateral submission of the present dispute to the Court. (at §107)

By contrast, in *Maritime Delimitation and Territorial Questions between Qatar and Bahrain (Qatar v Bahrain) (Jurisdiction and Admissibility)* the ICJ held that the minutes of a meeting of 25 December 1990 of the Foreign Ministers of Bahrain and Qatar, in the presence of the Foreign Minister of Saudi Arabia, constituted an international agreement serving as the basis for the Court's jurisdiction. After examining the contents of the minutes, the Court noted that the minutes:

> include a reaffirmation of obligations previously entered into; they entrust King Fahd [of Saudi Arabia] with the task of attempting to find a solution to the dispute during a period of six months; and lastly, they address the circumstances under which the Court could be seised after May 1991. Accordingly, and contrary to the contentions of Bahrain, the Minutes are not a simple record of a meeting . . . ; they do not merely give account of discussions and summarize points of agreement and disagreement. They enumerate the commitments to which the Parties have consented. They thus create rights and obligations in international law for the Parties. They constitute an international agreement. (at §25)

Under Article 2(1)(a) of the VCLT: '"treaty" means an international agreement concluded between States in written form and governed by international law, whether embodied in a single instrument or in two or more related instruments and whatever its particular designation'. The written form is not required for a treaty to exist under customary international law (since States can also enter oral agreements), but in the 1969 Vienna Convention it serves to delimit the scope of application of the Convention itself.

Treaties may be concluded by two or by more than two States (bilateral or multilateral treaties). Some multilateral treaties aim at universal participation, and are therefore called 'universal treaties': this is for instance the case of treaties for the protection of fundamental values of the international community, such as the protection of the environment or human rights. To achieve universality, these treaties are 'open' to States that have not taken part in their formation. By contrast, treaties are 'closed' when they limit the number of States parties to it, or when they establish that participation by new States is subject to the unanimous acceptance of the pre-existing parties.

Finally, the distinction can also be made between so-called 'normative treaties' (*traités-lois*) and 'contractual treaties' (*traités-contrats*), depending on whether the treaty establishes a common international regulation of a specific subject matter or regulates the individual interests of the parties through reciprocal or synallagmatic obligations (see **9.2**). It may often be the case, however, that normative treaties contain also synallagmatic obligations; the term normative treaties is, in any case, proposed if the normative provisions of the treaty are predominant.

10.3 CONCLUSION OF TREATIES

As mentioned previously, States can choose the procedures and means to conclude international agreements. Nonetheless, the standard procedure for the making of treaties starts with negotiations, aiming at the adoption and authentication of the text of the treaty. The negotiating States will then have to express their consent to be bound by the treaty, which will enter into force once the relevant requirements have been met. Let us examine each of these phases in turn.

10.3.1 STANDARD PROCEDURE

(1) *Negotiations* are conducted by persons possessing the so-called 'full powers' (Article 7(1)(a) VCLT). Full powers are defined as follows:

> [A] document emanating from the competent authority of a State designating a person or persons to represent the State for negotiating, adopting or authenticating the text of a treaty, for expressing the consent of the State to be bound by a treaty, or for accomplishing any other act with respect to a treaty ... (Article 2(1)(c) of the Vienna Convention)

State representatives may be dispensed from presenting the full powers when it appears from the practice of the States concerned, or from other circumstances, that their intention was to consider those persons as representing the State for any relevant treaty-making activity (Article 7(1)(b) VCLT). In addition, Heads of States, Heads of Government, Ministers for Foreign Affairs, and, to a limited extent, heads of diplomatic missions and representatives accredited by States to an international conference or an international organization or one of its organs[7] do not have to present full powers in virtue of their functions as State representatives (Article 7(2) VCLT). Any act relating to the conclusion of a treaty carried out by an unauthorized person is without legal effect, unless the relevant State subsequently confirms the act (Article 8 VCLT). By contrast, if there is a specific restriction to the authority of a representative of a State to express the consent of that State to be bound by a particular treaty, and the restriction was not notified to the other negotiating States prior to the expression of such consent, the omission to observe that restriction does not invalidate the consent of the State to be bound by the treaty (Article 47 VCLT).

Negotiations for the adoption of the text of a treaty are not subject to any specific requirements, unless they are carried out within international organizations or in the framework of international conferences specifically convened for that purpose.

(2) *Adoption and authentication of the text.* Successful negotiations end with the adoption of the text of the treaty. Article 9(1) VCLT clarifies that this requires the consent of all negotiating States. At the same time, however, it provides that treaties negotiated in the context of an international conference are adopted by the vote of two-thirds of the States present and voting, unless by the same majority they shall decide to apply a different rule (Article 9(2)). The next step is the *authentication* of the text of the treaty, which makes it definitive. The treaty itself may provide the procedure for its authentication, otherwise the text of the treaty is established as authentic and definitive by the signature, signature ad referendum, or initialling by the representatives of those States of the text of the treaty or of the Final Act of a conference incorporating the text (Article 10).

---

[7] Heads of diplomatic missions and representatives accredited by States to an international conference or an international organization or one of its organs do not have to present full powers with respect only to treaties negotiated, respectively, between the accrediting State and the State to which they are accredited and for the purpose of adopting the text of a treaty in that conference, organization, or organ (Article 7(2)(b) and (c) VCLT).

10.3.2 EXPRESSION OF CONSENT AND ENTRY INTO FORCE

(1) *Means to express consent.* The main means by which States express their consent to be bound by the regulation contained in the text of the treaty are (i) ratification (and its equivalents, namely acceptance or approval), (ii) accession, (iii) signature, and (iv) exchange of instruments forming the treaty.

Ratification does not mean *ex post* endorsement or confirmation of the manifestation of the State's will to be bound by the treaty. In fact, it is by enacting a formal document constituting the instrument of ratification that a State expresses its intent to be legally bound by a treaty. The treaty is thus concluded in *solemn form*. Usually modern constitutions require the intervention of the legislature before the Head of State—or some other prominent State agency—signs and enacts the aforementioned instrument of ratification. States that have signed a treaty are not obligated to ratify it. Until ratification (and until the treaty enters into force), the State that has signed the treaty must refrain from acting in such a way as to stultify the object and purpose of the treaty (see Article 18(a) of the Vienna Convention). Article 14 of the VCLT establishes that ratification (or acceptance or approval, equivalent to ratification) is required (i) when the treaty so provides, (ii) when it is otherwise established that the negotiating States so agreed, (iii) when the relevant representative of the State signed the treaty subject to ratification, and (iv) when it so appears from the full powers of the representative of the State or it was so expressed during the negotiations.

Accession allows States that have not negotiated the treaty to become parties to it. Article 15 VCLT clarifies that accession constitutes a means to express consent to be bound by a treaty (i) when the treaty so provides, (ii) when it is otherwise established that the negotiating States so agreed, (iii) when all the parties to the treaty have subsequently agreed that consent may be expressed by accession.

Signature of the treaty (and in some cases initialling) by the relevant State representatives and/or the exchange of notes between them are *simplified forms* to express the consent to be bound by the treaty. These agreements (also called 'executive agreements') do not call for ratification (or equivalent instrument) by the Head of State, and consequently do not involve parliaments in their elaboration. The reasons behind their appearance are self-evident. There is a need to regulate urgent matters by procedures that have the merit of being expeditious and 'economically functional' (e.g. think of agreements between postal administrations of two States). And there is the advantage of bypassing national legislatures in areas where the Executive deems it advisable to preserve a certain flexibility and latitude of power. Articles 12 and 13 regulate the expression of consent in simplified forms, namely by signature (and in some cases by initialling) and by exchange of the instruments constituting the treaty. Consent to be bound is expressed by signature in three situations, namely when (i) the treaty so establishes, (ii) when it is otherwise established that the negotiating States agreed that signature should have that effect, and (iii) when the intention of the State to give that effect to signature appears from the full powers of its representative or was expressed during the negotiations (Article 12). Similarly, the exchange of instruments constituting the treaty expresses the consent to be bound (i) when the relevant instruments so provide or (ii) it is otherwise established that States intended to give the exchange of instruments that effect (Article 13).

(2) *Entry into force.* A treaty becomes binding on the States which have expressed their consent to that effect based on the relevant provisions contained in the treaty itself or as otherwise established by the parties (Article 24(1) VCLT). This naturally implies that some provisions of the treaty apply before the treaty has entered into force (Article 26(4) VCLT). Failing any such provision or agreement, a treaty enters into force as soon as the consent to be bound by the treaty has been established for all the negotiating States.

For treaties concluded in the solemn form, the default rule provides that the consent is established when the instruments of ratification, acceptance, approval, or accession are exchanged between the contracting States, or they are deposited with the depositary, or they are notified to the contracting States or to the depositary, if so agreed (Article 16 VCLT). States can also agree that a treaty or part of it is provisionally applied pending its entry into force (Article 25 VCLT).

10.4 EFFECTS AND SCOPE OF APPLICATION

Once a treaty enters into force, the regulation contained therein is binding for the parties, which must therefore comply with it. Article 26 VCLT enunciates this fundamental rule (expressed by the Latin maxim *pacta sunt servanda*), adding that the parties to the treaty must perform it in good faith. The treaty is binding on each party in respect of its entire territory, unless a different intention appears from the treaty or is otherwise established (Article 29 VCLT). The term 'entire territory' of a State describes all the land, the territorial waters, and the airspace that constitute the territory of the State. The obligation of performance, however, does not apply in relation to any act or fact which took place or any situation which ceased to exist before the date of the entry into force of the treaty with respect to each party to the treaty. In other words, the regulation contained in a treaty does not have retroactive effects, unless a different intention appears from the treaty or is otherwise established (Article 28 VCLT). Importantly, a State cannot invoke its internal law to justify its failure to perform a treaty (unless there has been the manifest violation of an internal rule on the competence to conclude a treaty, which may constitute a ground of invalidity of the treaty, as further clarified later in the chapter).

Another major feature of treaties is that they only bind the parties to them, that is the States that have agreed to be bound by their provisions. As the Permanent Court of International Justice (PCIJ) in 1926 put it in *Certain German Interests in Polish Upper Silesia (Germany v Poland)*, 'a treaty only creates law as between the States which are parties to it' (at 29). Hence, for third States treaties are devoid of any legal consequence: they are a thing made by others (*res inter alios acta*). To put it differently, treaties may neither impose obligations on, nor create legal entitlements for, third States (*pacta tertiis nec nocent nec prosunt*). Both in the old law and in the law that has gradually emerged in modern times and was codified in Articles 35–36 of the VCLT, it is provided that third States may derive rights and obligations from a treaty only if they consent to assuming the obligations or exercising the rights laid down in the treaty. (In the case of rights, the third State's assent may be presumed 'as long as the contrary is not indicated, unless the treaty otherwise provides'; in contrast, in the case of obligations, their acceptance by a third State must be in writing.) That means that only after entering with the contracting parties into a tacit (or, in the case of obligations, written) agreement designed to extend the rights or obligations of the treaty, may a third State derive a legal entitlement or an obligation from the treaty. In short, nothing can be done without or against the will of a sovereign State.

If States conclude a subsequent treaty regulating the same subject matter as a treaty already in force, the provisions of the latter prevail if the former so establishes. If the earlier treaty is not terminated or suspended, and all the parties to the earlier treaty are also parties to the later treaty, the provisions of the earlier treaty apply only to the extent that they are compatible with the later treaty. If, however, not every State party to the earlier treaty is also a party to the later one, the earlier treaty continues to apply between the parties to both treaties and those which are parties only to the earlier treaty (which means that the parties to both treaties may face situations of conflicting treaty obligations). The provisions of the earlier treaty apply only to the extent that they are compatible with the later treaty among the States which are parties to both treaties (Article 30 VCLT, on the application of successive treaties relating to the same subject matter).

10.5 RESERVATIONS

Traditionally, when a State participating in the negotiations for a *multilateral* treaty found that some of its clauses were too onerous but nonetheless wished to enter into the treaty, it made reservations, that is, unilateral statements intended to either (i) exclude the application of one or more provisions, or (ii) place a certain interpretation on them. However, reservations (attached to the signature or to ratification of the treaty) had to be accepted by *all* other contracting parties for the reserving State to become bound by the treaty. The principle of unanimity favoured the 'integrity of treaties'. However, in practice it gave a sort of right of veto to all other parties. (The situation is, however, different for bilateral treaties; 'reservations' to such a treaty in fact amount to a proposal for a new text and consequently they may only produce legal effects if accepted by the other party.)

This old regulation of reservations proved totally inadequate when membership in the international community increased (and there was a greater need for so-called universal treaties), the more so because the newcomers belonged to political, economic, and cultural areas different from those of Western Christian countries. The very liberal doctrine of 'universality of treaties' came therefore to be upheld. Thus, a regime was envisaged, first in the important Advisory Opinion delivered in 1951 by the ICJ on *Reservations to the Convention on the Prevention and Punishment of Genocide* (at 15–30) and then in the VCLT.

Under the regime established in the Vienna Convention (Articles 19–23), States can append reservations at the time of ratification or accession, unless such reservations (i) are expressly prohibited by the treaty (because the treaty either prohibits any reservation or only allows reservations to provisions other than the one that is the object of a reservation), or (ii) prove incompatible with the object and purpose of the treaty. The treaty comes into force between the reserving State and the other parties (as modified, between the State and the other parties, by the reservation). One of the latter States may object to the reservation within 12 months of its notification (among other things, because it considers the reservation to be contrary to the object and purpose of the treaty). The objection may have a considerable legal effect if the objecting State so wishes: this State may oppose the entry into force of the treaty between itself and the reserving State. However, the objection may be not intended to have such effect. In this regard, Article 21(3) of the VCLT provides that, '[w]hen a State objecting to a reservation has not opposed the entry into force of the treaty between itself and the reserving State, the provisions to which the reservation relates do not apply as between the two States to the extent of the reservation'.

By following this rule, therefore, when the reservation is aimed at excluding the applicability of a particular provision, there is no difference between acceptance of a reservation and objection to it: in both cases the treaty applies, except for the excluded provision, as between the reserving and the objecting State (or all non-objecting States). However, when the reservation places a certain interpretation on a treaty provision, what are the legal consequences of the objection under Article 21(3)? Arguably, in light of the principle of universality of treaties, the treaty should apply as between the reserving and the objecting State with the exception of the provision (or part thereof) covered by the interpretative reservation. Instead, as between the reserving State and the States which have not objected to the reservation, the treaty applies in full, but the provision covered by the reservation will have the scope suggested in the reservation.

This legal regime has the great merit of allowing as many States as possible to take part in treaties that include provisions unacceptable to some of them. However, it may impair the integrity of multilateral treaties (since they may end up being split into a series of bilateral agreements). Furthermore, in practice it leaves the question of whether or not a reservation is contrary to the object and purpose of a treaty to be decided by each contracting party. To be workable, this regime should always rely on the possibility that there is an international body to monitor and assess the admissibility of reservations, and rule on the matter. However, most multilateral treaties to date lack such a body. Hence, the extreme subjectivity of any appraisal of reservations.

Important innovations have been recently introduced in the area of treaties on human rights by two monitoring bodies. First the European Court of Human Rights (notably in a number of cases: *Belilos v Switzerland* (at §60), *Weber v Switzerland* (at §§38–40), and *Loizidou v Turkey (Preliminary Objections)*, (at §§90–98)), and then the UN Human Rights Committee (in a General Comment of 1994[8] and in a decision of 1999 on the *Rawle Kennedy v Trinidad and Tobago* case (at §§6.4–6.7)), have propounded the following view: if a State enters a reservation to a human rights treaty that is inadmissible either because it is not allowed by the treaty itself or because it is contrary to its object and purpose, it does not follow that the provision reserved does not operate with regard to the reserving State, or that this State may not join the treaty. It only follows that the reservation must be regarded as null and void, at least in those parts that prove to be incompatible with the object and purpose of the treaty. Clearly, under this view standards on human rights must prevail over the concerns of sovereign States. If there is conflict between the two requirements (the international community's need for contracting parties to remain bound as far as possible by international standards on human rights, and the intent of one of these parties to eschew the legal impact of such a standard), the former must prevail.

This view, although some major Powers have attacked it, is in keeping with the object and purpose of human rights law. It therefore commends itself as appropriate, as long as there exists an international independent body empowered to pronounce on the matter. It could also be extended to other treaties, whenever they set up supervisory bodies charged with monitoring compliance. These bodies, if endowed with judicial or quasi-judicial powers, could be in a position to appraise impartially whether a reservation is consonant with the purpose and object of the treaty, or even forbidden by the treaty, and decide accordingly.

---

[8] Human Rights Committee, General Comment 24/52 on Issues relating to Reservations to the UN Covenant on Civil and Political Rights, adopted on 2 November 1994, §17, in 34 ILM (1995), 845. The Committee has offered the following rationale for the conclusion just referred to: '[Human rights] treaties, and the [UN] Covenant [on Civil and Political Rights] specifically, are not a web of inter-State exchanges of mutual obligations. They concern the endowment of individuals with rights. The principle of inter-State reciprocity has no place ... And because the operation of the classic rules on reservations is so inadequate for the Covenant, States have often not seen any legal interest in or need to object to reservations. The absence of protest by States cannot imply that a reservation is either compatible or incompatible with the object and purpose of the Covenant. Objections have been occasional, made by some but not by others, and on grounds not always specified ... In short, the pattern is so unclear that it is not safe to assume that a non-objecting State thinks that a particular reservation is acceptable. In the view of the Committee, because of the special characteristics of the Covenant as a human rights treaty, it is open to question what effect objections have between States *inter se* ... It necessarily falls to the Committee to determine whether a specific reservation is compatible with the object and purpose of the Covenant' (ibid., at §§17 and 20). It should be noted that the US, the UK, and France strongly objected to the Committee's views on the severability of reservations contrary to the object and purpose of human rights treaties: see (1995) 16 *HRLJ* 422ff. See also Special Rapporteur A. Pellet's Second Report to the ILC (A/C.N.4/447/Add.I) and *YILC* (1997-II) Part Two, at 48–9, 53–6, §§75–87 and 124–156.

In light of some unresolved issues in the relevant provisions on reservations in the VCLT, and on account of the subsequent developments, in 1993 the ILC decided to include the topic of 'the law and practice relating to reservations to treaties' in its agenda and appointed the French jurist, Alain Pellet, as Special Rapporteur. The ILC concluded its works on the topic in 2011, by adopting the 'Guide to Practice on Reservations to Treaties'.[9] This is a non-binding document, which from the start was not intended to be transformed into a binding instrument. It addresses issues such as the distinction between interpretative reservations and interpretative declarations, the permissibility of reservations, and the question of the unity or diversity of the legal regime applicable to reservations.

10.6 INTERPRETATION

As Anzilotti emphasized in 1912,[10] in the past there were no binding rules on interpretation. The criteria for construing treaty law were merely 'rules of logic', borrowed from national law or developed by arbitral courts, or 'those very general criteria which could be inferred from the nature and character of the [international] legal order'. States and courts tended to agree that the main purpose of treaty interpretation was to identify and spell out the intention of the draftsmen. However, views differed when it came to specifying how this intention could be found. Some States, under the influence of their own legal systems, favoured resort to the negotiating history (so-called preparatory work or *travaux préparatoires*). This held true for such countries as France, Italy, and the US. Some commentators termed this approach 'subjective interpretation'. Other countries, such as Britain, preferred instead a construction based on the text of the treaty and the wording of its provisions (termed by some commentators 'objective interpretation'). Courts tended to take different views depending on the cultural background of the judges.

The adverse consequences of the lack of legally binding rules in such a delicate area are self-evident. Furthermore, the absence proved ultimately to be to the advantage of bigger States. It is hardly surprising that one of the few maxims on interpretation that evolved in this period stemmed directly from the structure of the world community and the overriding principle of States' freedom: the criterion whereby international obligations should be so construed as to place fewer curtailments on States, and no treaty could be taken to restrict by implication the exercise of sovereignty or self-preservation (*in dubio mitius*: if in doubt, the interpretation least unfavourable to the subject of an obligation must be chosen; in other words, limitations of sovereignty must be strictly construed).

This tricky area received a balanced and satisfactory regulation in Articles 31–33 of the VCLT. Although some important questions, such as inter-temporal interpretation, were left out, the rules on construction upheld the most advanced views. Basically the Convention gave pride of place to literal, systematic, and teleological interpretation (Article 31(1): 'A treaty shall be interpreted in good faith in accordance with the ordinary meaning to be given to the terms of the treaty in their context and in the light of its object and purpose'). Thus, great weight was attributed to the purpose pursued by contracting parties, as laid down in the text of the treaty. Also, the authors of the VCLT set great store by the principle of 'effectiveness' (*ut res magis valeat quam pereat*), whereby a treaty must be given

---

[9] Report of the International Law Commission Sixty-third session (26 April–3 June and 4 July–12 August 2011), UN Doc. A/66/10/Add.1 (2011) 1. See also A. Pellet, 'The ILC Guide to Practice on Reservations to Treaties: A General Presentation by the Special Rapporteur' (2003) 24 *EJIL* 1061.

[10] D. Anzilotti, *Corso*, at 102, 104, 107. Anzilotti had already made this statement in the first edition of his *Corso*, i (*Parte generale*) (Roma: Athenaeum, 1912), 203.

an interpretation that enables its provisions to be 'effective and useful', that is, to have the appropriate effect. This principle is plainly intended to expand the normative scope of treaties, to the detriment of the old principle whereby in case of doubt limitations of sovereignty were to be strictly interpreted.

Under the VCLT recourse to preparatory work may only be regarded as 'a supplementary means of interpretation'. Pursuant to Article 32 the records of the negotiating history of a treaty may only be relied upon 'in order to confirm the meaning' resulting from literal, systematic, and teleological interpretation, or to determine the meaning when the interpretation based on those criteria either leaves the text 'ambiguous or obscure' or 'leads to a result which is manifestly absurd or unreasonable'. It is interesting to note that the ICJ,[11] as well as some arbitral courts,[12] has held that both Article 31 and Article 32 reflect customary law.

Under Article 33, when a treaty has been authenticated in two or more languages, the text is equally authoritative in each language, and the terms of the treaty are presumed to have the same meaning in each authentic text. When, however, there appears to be a difference of meaning, the meaning must prevail which best reconciles the texts, having regard to the object and purpose of the treaty (paragraph 4 of Article 33, which the ICJ in *LaGrand (Germany v United States of America)* (at §101) held to reflect customary international law).

In modern times, international courts have increasingly applied the 'implied powers doctrine' when interpreting a particular category of treaties, that is, the constitutive instruments of international organizations. This doctrine was first suggested by the US Supreme Court when interpreting the US Constitution with a view to broadening the powers of the federal authorities with respect to those of member States: it was propounded in 1819 by Chief Justice Marshall in *McCulloch v The State of Maryland* (at 407–37), and reaffirmed, *inter alia*, in 1920 in *Missouri v Holland* (at 376–7). It was taken up at the international level by the PCIJ[13] and then the ICJ[14] to broaden the powers of the ILO and UN respectively vis-à-vis member States. Under this doctrine, organs of international organizations may be deemed to possess all the powers necessary for the discharge of their express powers or the fulfilment of the organization's goals. This doctrine, based on the so-called federal analogy (namely, the equation of relations between member States of a federal State and the federal authorities, to the relations between member States of international organizations and organs of these organizations) is controversial. In particular, opponents argue that this doctrine ends up granting excessively broad powers to organs of international organizations, especially when it is relied upon to derive implied powers from general and loosely worded goals of the organizations (as in the case of the UN).

---

[11] See *Territorial Dispute (Lybian Arab Jamahiriya/Chad)*, §41; *Maritime Delimitation and Territorial Questions between Qatar and Bahrain (Qatar v Bahrain) (Jurisdiction and Admissibility)* 1995, §33; 1996, §23; *Oil Platforms (Islamic Republic of Iran v United States of America) (Preliminary Objections)*, §23; *Kasikili/Sedudu Island (Botswana/Namibia)*, §18; *LaGrand (Germany v United States of America)*, §99; *Sovereignty over Pulau Litigan and Pulau Sipadan (Indonesia/Malaysia)*, §37; *Legal Consequences of the Construction of a Wall*, §94.

[12] See e.g. *Case of the Agreement on German External Debt*, §16; *Delimitation of the Maritime Frontier between Guinea and Guinea-Bissau*, §41; the case concerning *Apurement des Comptes (Netherlands v France)*, §§57–67.

[13] PCIJ, Advisory Opinions on *Competence of the ILO Concerning Personal Work of the Employer*, 18, and on *Jurisdiction of the European Commission of the Danube*, 64.

[14] See the Advisory Opinions in *Reparation for Injuries Suffered in the Service of the United Nations*, 182, in *Effects of Awards of Compensation made by the U.N. Administrative Tribunal*, 56–7, in the *Certain Expenses of the United Nations* case, 167–8, and in *Legal Consequences for States of the Continued Presence of South Africa in Namibia (South West Africa) notwithstanding Security Council Resolution 276 (1970)*, 47–9, 52. See also the Court's Advisory Opinion in *Legality of the Use by a State of Nuclear Weapons in Armed Conflict*, 78–81, §§25–26.

10.7 AMENDMENT AND MODIFICATION

All parties to a multilateral treaty can subsequently change its regulation by way of an amendment. Article 40 of the VCLT provides that, unless the treaty provides otherwise, proposals to amend the treaty shall be notified to all the States parties which will have the right to take part in the decision as to the action to be taken in regard to such a proposal and in the negotiation and conclusion of any agreement for the amendment of the treaty. However, a State which is already a party to the treaty is not bound by the amending agreement if that State does not become a party to it: in such a scenario, the relationship between this State and the States which are parties to the amending agreement are regulated by the rule on successive treaties relating to the same subject matter (see **10.4**). A State that becomes a party to the treaty after the entry into force of the amending agreement shall be considered as a party to the treaty as amended, failing an expression of a different intention by that State; however, it shall be considered as a party to the unamended treaty in relation to any party to the treaty not bound by the amending agreement. It shall be noted that the term 'revision' of a treaty is often used in international practice, although it is unclear whether this term refers to amendment or to a process that envisages more substantial changes to the treaty rather than changes to some of its provisions.

Amendment shall be distinguished from modification, since the latter aims at an agreement concluded between two or more States parties to a treaty, but not all of them. Article 41 of the VCLT stipulates that modification shall be provided in the treaty, or—when the modification is not prohibited—it shall not affect the enjoyment by the other parties of their rights under the treaty or the performance of their obligations; and shall not relate to a provision, derogation from which is incompatible with the effective execution of the object and purpose of the treaty as a whole.

10.8 GROUNDS OF INVALIDITY

10.8.1 INNOVATION IN THE VIENNA CONVENTION

In the past, the law also turned a blind eye to possible coercion of weaker States by stronger ones. Thus duress—economic, political, or military coercion exerted by one State over another to compel it to enter into a given agreement—was not considered to invalidate a treaty. Similarly, corruption of the State officials negotiating or, more generally, concluding a treaty did not render it null and void. Furthermore, there were no rules placing restrictions on the freedom of States as to the object of treaties. States were therefore allowed to regulate their own interests as they thought best, and even to agree on offences or attacks on other States or on the partition of their territory. The only grounds of invalidity were minor ones: (i) using force or intimidation against the State official making the treaty; (ii) inducing the other party through misrepresentation to enter into an agreement (e.g. the conclusion of a boundary treaty based on a map fraudulently altered by one of the parties); (iii) the circumstance that consent was based on errors as to facts (e.g. an incorrect map, in the case of a boundary treaty). In addition, all of these grounds of invalidity were on the same legal footing. Consequently, they could all make a treaty voidable if the party against which the grounds of invalidity had been invoked was willing to consider the treaty null and void, or a dispute resolution mechanism made it possible for the parties to reach agreement. Furthermore, only the party to a treaty allegedly damaged by the treaty's invalidity was legally entitled to claim that the treaty was not valid; the other parties (in the case of a multilateral treaty) had no say in the matter.

The fact that it is not possible to glean many instances of grounds of invalidity from the international practice of the past is ample proof of their relative irrelevance. The paucity of international rules on this matter clearly played into the hands of the Great Powers.

Under the VCLT, a major cause of injustice in the making of treaties—*coercion* exercised by a powerful State against another *State*—has been regarded as rendering the treaty null and void. Article 52 of the Convention covers coercion by the threat or use of military force contrary to the UN Charter, while a Declaration adopted by the Vienna Diplomatic Conference calls upon States to refrain from economic and political coercion as well. Thus, the foundations have been laid for the gradual emergence of a customary rule on the matter. Article 53 of the VCLT constitutes another novelty, for it provides that treaties are null and void if contrary to *jus cogens* (see **11.4**). In addition, Article 50 of the VCLT stipulates that *corruption* of a State official of one of the negotiating parties is a cause of invalidity. Furthermore, the Convention provides significant clarification as regards *error* (Article 48), *fraud* (Article 49), and use of coercion against the *State representatives* negotiating the treaty (Article 51). Besides, Article 47 regulates a matter that was previously the subject of dispute: whether a State could claim that a treaty it had concluded was invalid because its consent had been expressed in violation of a provision of its internal law (it is now necessary for that violation to be 'manifest' and to concern a national rule 'of fundamental importance').

10.8.2 ABSOLUTE AND RELATIVE GROUNDS OF INVALIDITY

What is very novel, and marks a momentous advance in the field of the law of treaties, is the distinction drawn in the Convention between '*absolute*' and '*relative*' grounds of invalidity. The former (coercion against a State representative; coercion against the State as a whole; incompatibility with *jus cogens*) implies that: (i) any State party to the treaty (that is, not merely the State which has suffered from possible coercion or which might be prejudiced by actions contrary to a peremptory rule) can invoke the invalidity of the treaty; (ii) a treaty cannot be divided into valid and invalid clauses, but stands or falls as a whole (Article 44(5) VCLT); and (iii) possible acquiescence does not render the treaty valid (Article 45 VCLT). If one of these grounds is established, the treaty is null and void *ex tunc*, that is from the moment it was concluded.

In contrast, grounds of relative invalidity are: error, fraud, corruption, manifest violation of internal law, or of the restrictions of the powers of the State representative who has concluded the treaty. These grounds may only be invoked by the State that has been the *victim* of error, fraud, corruption, or whose representative has acted in manifest breach of internal law or of the restrictions on his powers. Furthermore, these grounds of invalidity may be *cured* by acquiescence or subsequent express consent by the aggrieved party. Finally, these grounds of nullity may vitiate only *some provisions* of the treaty. Also these grounds of invalidity operate *ex tunc*, that is, they render the treaty or some of its provisions null and void as from the conclusion of the treaty. However, acts performed bona fide by the aggrieved party before the treaty is declared null and void may be regarded as valid and legally effective, depending upon the specific circumstances of each case.

The important question arises of whether, when a treaty is tainted with absolute nullity, this nullity may be invoked by a *State not party to the treaty*. Under Article 65 of the VCLT, only a party to the defective treaty may invoke its inconsistency with *jus cogens*, and the same seems to apply to other grounds of absolute invalidity (see Articles 52 and 54). However, customary rules corresponding to the Vienna Convention's provisions on invalidity of treaties might have developed to allow *any State concerned*, whether or not party to the treaty, to invoke *jus cogens* or coercion of a State representative or of a State.

The development of such customary rules would be in keeping with the spirit, object, and purpose of the distinction between the two classes of invalidity or nullity. The distinction is of great importance, for it points to an area of values which the international community has upgraded by establishing a specific regulation: use of force or other behaviour inconsistent with a peremptory rule has been stigmatized to such an extent as to render treaties concluded by resorting to either of them particularly vulnerable. If this is so, one fails to see why one should deny the right to invoke the nullity of the treaty to a third State that may be *directly affected* by a treaty. Think, for example, of a treaty concluded by two or more States and providing for unlawful forcible action in a territory subject to the sovereignty of a third State, or genocide of ethnic groups, or the forcible suppression of the right of self-determination of peoples having ramifications in a third State. By the same token, a third State is arguably entitled to invoke the nullity of a treaty between two other States resulting from the threat or use of force by one of them against the other, if the conclusion of such a treaty may have serious repercussions for the State in question (e.g. the treaty stipulates that force may be used to invade the third State).

Before which international institutions is the third State authorized to invoke the absolute invalidity? Arguably, before an international court or tribunal having jurisdiction under the relevant jurisdictional clauses; if such jurisdiction is lacking, the third State is entitled to call upon the relevant contracting States or State to either undertake negotiations with a view to legally settling the matter, or bring the issue before an arbitral or judicial body.

10.9 TERMINATION AND SUSPENSION

Treaties may contain provisions regulating the termination, suspension, or withdrawal by one party with respect to all the other parties. Termination, suspension, or withdrawal may also be effected by consent of all parties to the treaty. The VCLT also codifies some grounds that may be invoked to terminate or suspend a treaty, or to withdraw from it.

Article 60 VCLT regulates the termination or suspension of the operation of a treaty as a consequence of its breach by another party, according to the principle *inadimplenti non est adimplendum*. It stipulates that the breach shall be a 'material breach', which consists in '(a) a repudiation of the treaty not sanctioned by the present Convention; or (b) the violation of a provision essential to the accomplishment of the object or purpose of the treaty'. In the case of bilateral treaties, the material breach by one party allows the other party to decide whether to terminate or to suspend the operation of the treaty. Similarly, in the case of multilateral treaties, all the parties can by unanimous decision decide whether to terminate the treaty or suspend its operation in whole or in part, in the relations between themselves and the defaulting State, or as between all the parties. In addition, a party specially affected by the material breach can invoke it as a ground for suspending the operation of the treaty in whole or in part in the relations between itself and the defaulting State. Finally, any party other than the defaulting State can invoke the breach as a ground for suspending the operation of the treaty in whole or in part with respect to itself if the treaty is of such a character that a material breach of its provisions by one party radically changes the position of every party with respect to the further performance of its obligations under the treaty. Importantly, however, Article 60(5) establishes that the material breach of the treaty cannot be invoked as a ground for termination or suspension of 'provisions relating to the protection of the human person contained in treaties of a humanitarian character, in particular to provisions prohibiting any form of reprisals against persons protected by such treaties'. The distinction between the termination/suspension of a treaty based on the material breach of one party and recourse to countermeasures by the victim State in the framework of State responsibility is not entirely settled (on countermeasures, see **14.2**).

Another ground for termination/suspension of the operation of a treaty or withdrawal from it is based on the principle of the fundamental changes of circumstances (*rebus sic stantibus*). According to Article 62 of the VCLT, the change of circumstances cannot constitute a ground for termination or suspension unless the following two requirements are met: 'the existence of those circumstances constituted an essential basis of the consent of the parties to be bound by the treaty'; and 'the effect of the change is radically to transform the extent of obligations still to be performed under the treaty' (Article 62(1)(a) and (b)). This ground of termination/suspension or withdrawal, however, cannot be invoked 'if the treaty establishes a boundary'; and 'if the fundamental change is the result of a breach, by the party invoking it, either of an obligation under the treaty or of any other international obligation owed to any other party to the treaty' (Article 62(2)(a) and (b)).

A third ground for termination/suspension or withdrawal is the supervening impossibility of performance, codified in Article 61 of the VCLT. The impossibility of performance shall not be the result of a breach by that party either of an obligation under the treaty or of any other international obligation owed to any other party to the treaty. It shall concern the permanent disappearance or destruction of an object indispensable for the execution of the treaty. If the impossibility is temporary, it may be invoked only as a ground for suspending the operation of the treaty.

Fourthly, *jus cogens* (see **11.4**) is called into play for the termination of treaties as well. Under Article 64 of the VCLT, 'if a new peremptory norm of general international law emerges, any existing treaty which is in conflict with that norm becomes void and terminates'.

Finally, Article 56 of VCLT establishes that denunciation of or withdrawal from a treaty, when the treaty does not contain any clause to that effect, is not allowed unless it is established that the parties had the intention of allowing for this possibility, or a right of denunciation or withdrawal may be implied by the nature of the treaty. In light of these provisions the UN Human Rights Committee, in its General Comment 26(61) of 1997, held that the UN Covenant on Civil and Political Rights is not subject to denunciation or withdrawal because 'the drafters of the Covenant deliberately intended to exclude the possibility of denunciation', and 'the Covenant is not the type of treaty which, by its nature, implied a right of denunciation ... [it] codifies in treaty form the universal human rights enshrined in the Universal Declaration of Human Rights ... As such, the Covenant does not have a temporary character typical of treaties where a right of denunciation is deemed to be admitted, notwithstanding the absence of a specific provision to that effect.'[15]

The Vienna Convention spells out a cardinal principle, namely that, except for what is stipulated by Article 64, the various causes of termination do not make treaties come to an end automatically but can only be invoked by one of the parties as a ground for discontinuing the treaty. It is also provided that, in addition to authorizing a party to claim that a treaty should cease, the above clauses could also have a more limited effect: that is to say, they could authorize a party to claim the mere suspension of the treaty.

There are a few grounds of termination (or suspension) of treaties that are not regulated by the VCLT, namely the effect of war on treaties, the so-called 'desuetude' (namely, when it is clear from the conduct of the parties that they no longer consider the treaty as binding), and the termination of bilateral treaties because of the extinction of one of the parties.

---

[15] Human Rights Committee, General Comment 26(61), adopted by the Committee at its 1631st meeting, CCPR/C/21/Rev.1/Add.8/Rev.1, 8 December 1997, §§2–3.

11
NORMATIVE INTERACTIONS: IMPLEMENTATION AND HIERARCHY OF NORMS

11.1 THREE INQUIRIES: TRANSPOSAL, EFFECTS, AND NORM HIERARCHY

This chapter deals with three separate and yet intertwined aspects of normative interactions concerning international legal norms. It relates to the mechanisms for the implementation of international law at domestic level, the effects international norms display within municipal legal orders, and the hierarchy of norms both within international law, as well as in the relationships between international law and domestic legal systems.

First, the chapter deals with some fundamental realities of international law as a body of legal rules which requires implementation at domestic level through transposal (see **11.2**). Secondly, it tackles the issue of the effects that international law may display in concrete situations, including within national systems (see **11.3**). Thirdly, the chapter discusses the verticalization of the international legal order with the affirmation in the second half of the twentieth century of the notion of *jus cogens* (or peremptory norms) and the effects it has (or might have) within international law and in its relationships with municipal laws (see **11.4**). As we shall see, these issues not only have an intriguing theoretical dimension, but also bear consequences in real life, as the law as concretely applied often depends on the interpretations of international law accepted at domestic level by national authorities (governments, legislators, but above all judicial bodies).

11.2 THE NEED FOR TRANSPOSAL: DUALISM, MONISM, AND REALITY

The question whether international rules make up a body of law not only different, but also radically autonomous and distinct, from municipal (or national) legal orders has been the subject of much controversy. Historically, some theoretical constructs have been advanced: first, the so-called national or internal monistic view advocating the supremacy of municipal law; then the dualistic doctrine, suggesting the existence of two distinct sets of legal orders (international law, on the one hand, and municipal legal systems on the other); and, finally, the internationalist monistic theory maintaining the unity of the various legal systems under the primacy of international law.

The first group of theories began to be propounded in the eighteenth century, subsequently refined in the nineteenth and early twentieth centuries.[1] It was based on the idea

---

[1] German scholar, J. J. Moser (1701–85). It was later elaborated, on the basis of Hegel's views (set forth in *Encyclopaedia*, 1817, and *Philosophy of Right*, 1821), into a fully fledged doctrine by some German international lawyers (C. Bergbohm, A. Zorn, and M. Wenzel) in the late nineteenth century and the early twentieth century.

that the State was the largest societal unit, and that States acted towards each other in a merely contractualistic way free from superior norms (after all States had been created to oppose 'universal' entities like the Empire and the Roman Pope as sources of legitimacy). Under this doctrine, national law subsumed, and prevailed over, any international legal rules, which were seen as 'external State law' (the law to be used in international dealings). It followed that international law proper did not exist, for it was made up of the 'external law' of the various members of the international community. International law was not a body of binding standards of behaviour. It was only a set of guidelines whose provisional value was removed as soon as a powerful State thought that they were contrary to its interests. Thus, this doctrine actually asserted the existence of a single set of legal systems, the domestic legal orders, and denied the existence of international law as a distinct and autonomous body of law. It clearly reflected the extreme nationalism and authoritarianism of a few great Powers, anxious to protect their respective interests.

Instead, towards the second half of the nineteenth century, a dualistic approach emerged. Dualistic theories were developed upon observation of the attitude towards international law taken in such countries as Britain and the United States.[2] English case law and the US Constitution recognized the authority of international customary rules and duly ratified treaties approved by the competent constitutional authorities. Although international rules were only considered internally binding to the extent that they had been approved or accepted by the foreign policy-makers (as well as, in the case of treaties, by the national legislators), the fact remains that these States in principle recognized the effect of international law in their domestic legal orders. The doctrine started from the assumption that international law and municipal legal systems constitute two distinct and formally separate categories of legal orders (hence dualism). They differ as to (i) their subjects (individuals and groups of individuals in the case of domestic legal systems, States in the case of international law); (ii) their sources (parliamentary statutes or judge-made law being the main sources of internal law, while treaties and custom are the two principal law-creating processes in international law); and (iii) the contents of the rules (national law regulating the internal functioning of the State and the relations between the State and individuals, whereas international law chiefly governs relations between sovereign States). It followed, among other things, that international law cannot directly address itself to individuals. To become binding on domestic authorities and individuals, it must be 'transformed' into national law through the various mechanisms for the national implementation of international rules freely decided upon by each sovereign State. As Anzilotti stated in 1928, 'international rules are only possible to the extent that they can rely on national rules'. In addition, international rules cannot alter or repeal national legislation and, by the same token, national laws cannot create, modify, or repeal international rules. Clearly, this conception was inspired by a far more moderate nationalism: it advocated the need for national legal systems to comply with international rules by turning them into national norms binding at the domestic level. However, it envisaged at the same time a sort of 'emergency exit' for States in the case of serious conflict between international and national values: since international law is effective to the extent that it is actually applied within domestic legal systems, when national interests are regarded as prevalent, States may go as far as to thwart the legal import of international prescriptions by refraining from implementing them at the domestic level (although of course by so doing they may incur international responsibility).

---

[2] This attitude was in some respects developed into a theoretical construct in 1899 by the German publicist H. Triepel (1868–1946) and significantly elaborated upon by the Italian D. Anzilotti (1869–1950) between 1902 and 1928.

A third group of theories, which can be labelled an internationalist monistic conception, advocated the primacy of international law.[3] This view is based on a number of postulates. First, there exists a unitary legal system, embracing all the various legal orders operating at various levels. Secondly, international law is at the top of the pyramid and validates or invalidates all the legal acts of any other legal system. Consequently, municipal law must always conform to international law. In cases of conflict, the latter declares all domestic rules or acts contrary to it to be illegal. A further corollary is that the 'transformation' of international norms into domestic law 'is not necessary from the point of view of international law'. This is because international and national law are 'parts of one normative system'. Thirdly, the subjects of international law are not radically different from those of national law: both in municipal law and in international law individuals are the principal subjects of law, although in international law individuals are often taken into account in their position as State officials. In addition, the sources of international law belong to a legal system that is hierarchically superior to municipal systems, not radically different from them. As a result, international rules can be applied as such by domestic courts, without any need for transformation. However, allowance is made for certain qualifications. National constitutions (be they written or unwritten) may require domestic courts to apply only statutes enacted by national legislatures. In this case courts will only apply international treaty rules after they have been transformed into national statutes. Nevertheless, this necessity of transformation is a question of national, not of international law. Furthermore, national courts may be required to apply statutes that are contrary to international rules. For Kelsen, although this occurrence shows the weakness of international law, nevertheless the fact remains that the State incurs international responsibility for this non-compliance with international rules. According to this conception, the international legal system controls, however imperfectly, all national systems, which are subordinate to it. It follows that international values override national ones and State officials must always strive to achieve the objectives set by international rules.

It is clear that this theory rests on two basic ideological principles: internationalism and pacifism. Kelsen spelled out this underpinning with great clarity. He concluded, however, that the choice in favour of the primacy of international law cannot be based on scientific considerations but is dictated by ethical or political preferences. This somewhat agnostic attitude was probably motivated by Kelsen's adhesion to the philosophy of relativity. It is plausible that there was also another reason; Kelsen was aware that the international community was still far from the condition postulated by his theory: it still lacked the machinery for repealing those municipal provisions which are inconsistent with international rules.

In real life, none of the above-mentioned abstract constructs are able on their own to capture the complexity of the interaction between international and domestic laws and, at the same time, all of them contain some measure of truth. How then should we explain the relation between the sphere of international law and that of municipal law? The first monistic theory is indisputably devoid of scientific value and was essentially intended to underpin ideological and political positions. It also reflected a time when the nation State was emerging. In contrast, the dualistic approach did reflect the legal reality, particularly in the nineteenth and the first half of the twentieth century, although it was unable convincingly to explain some exceptional phenomena, such as the fact that a few international rules directly imposed obligations on individuals (e.g. the rules prohibiting piracy as an

---

[3] It was first outlined in 1899 by the German W. Kaufmann (1858–1926), was propounded as a fully fledged doctrine after the First World War, between 1920 and 1934, by the Austrian H. Kelsen (1881–1973), and was subsequently embraced by a number of distinguished scholars including A. Verdross (from Austria) and G. Scelle (from France).

international crime). Indeed, in that period international society consisted of sovereign States, and their dealings belonged to a sphere of law substantially separate and distinct from that of each national legal order. The Kelsenian monistic theory, an admirable theoretical construction, was in advance of its time; in many respects it was utopian and did not reflect the reality of international relations. However, for all its inconsistencies and practical pitfalls, it had significant ideological impact. It brought new emphasis to the role of international law as a controlling factor of State conduct. It was instrumental in consolidating the notion that State officials should abide by international legal standards and ought therefore to put international imperatives before national demands.

At present, as we shall see in the next section, the dualistic conception is no longer valid in its entirety, whereas some of the postulates of the conception put forward by Kelsen are gradually taking a foothold in the international community. In short, international law no longer constitutes a sphere of law tightly separate and distinct (subject to one or two exceptions) from that of national legal systems. In many areas international law has made significant inroads into national legal systems, piercing their 'armour'. It no longer constitutes a different legal realm from the various municipal systems; quite to the contrary, it has a huge direct daily impact on these systems. It conditions their life in many areas and even contributes to shaping their internal functioning and operation. In addition, many international rules address themselves directly to individuals, without the intermediary of national legal systems: they impose obligations on them (this chiefly applies to rules on international crimes) or grant them rights (e.g. the right to petition international bodies). Those obligations must be fulfilled, and the rights may be exercised, regardless of what national legal orders may provide. In short, in many respects, individuals have become international legal subjects. Thus, international law is no longer *jus inter potestates* (a law governing only relations among sovereign entities). It also embraces individuals, by directly legitimizing, or issuing commands to, them. Subject to the limitations set out at the start of the book (see **Chapter 1**), it may be gradually heading, at least in some respects, towards a *civitas maxima* (a human commonwealth encompassing individuals, States, and other aggregates cutting across the boundaries of States). By the same token, it is increasingly becoming, more than a *jus inter partes* (a body of law governing relations among subjects 'in a horizontal manner'), a *jus super partes* (a corpus of legal standards regulating international dealings 'from above' (see **11.4** and **Chapters 13** and **16**).

11.3 EFFECTS: IMPLEMENTING INTERNATIONAL LAW WITHIN DOMESTIC SYSTEMS

11.3.1 GENERAL

Whichever of the three visions just outlined is preferred, it is a fact that most international rules, to become operative, need to be applied by State officials or individuals within domestic legal systems. National implementation of international rules is thus of crucial importance. One would therefore expect there to be some form of international regulation of the matter, or at least a certain uniformity in the ways in which domestic legal systems put international law into effect. The reality is quite different, however.

International law provides that States cannot invoke the legal procedures of their municipal system as a justification for not complying with international rules. This principle, famously asserted in the so-called *Alabama* (*United States of America/Great Britain*) arbitration, has been firmly rooted in the case law of the Permanent Court of International Justice (PCIJ) (in *Polish Nationals in Danzig*, at 24, and in *Free Zones of Upper Savoy and* the District of Gex (France v Switzerland), at 167) and other courts (e.g. in *Georges Pinson (France)* v *United Mexican States*, at 393–4, and in *Blaškić 1996*, at §7), and is now laid down, with regard to treaties, in the 1969 Vienna Convention on the Law of Treaties, Article 27 of which provides that '[a] party [to a treaty] may not invoke the provisions of its internal law as justification for its failure to perform a treaty' (see **10.8.1**).

The PCIJ held in the Advisory Opinion on *Exchange of Greek and Turkish Populations* (at 20), and some commentators have contended, that there exists a general duty for States to bring national law into conformity with obligations under international law. If such a duty existed, each time a State fails to comply with an international rule as a result of the failure of its domestic law-making body to pass the necessary implementing legislation, it would breach both that rule and the general principle imposing the duty in question. However, a perusal of State practice shows that no such general duty exists. When a State breaches an international obligation because the national legislation necessary for implementing the rule is lacking or inadequate, other States claim cessation of the wrongdoing or reparation only for that breach, without enquiring about the reasons for non-compliance or protesting at the lack or inadequacy of legislation. In other words, States are only interested in the final result: fulfilment or non-fulfilment of an obligation. They show no interest in the factors that brought about that result. Again, this state of affairs reflects the individualistic structure of the international community and the paramount importance of respect for other States' internal affairs.

What has just been pointed out primarily applies to traditional international law. The current regulation of the international community shows two important developments. First, a number of treaties, in addition to laying down a set of obligations, also explicitly impose upon contracting States the duty to enact legislation for implementing the various provisions (or at least some provisions) of the treaties. One may mention some rules of the four 1949 Geneva Conventions on the victims of war, as well as a number of treaties on human rights, or other international instruments such as the Statutes of the International Criminal Tribunal for the former Yugoslavia (ICTY), the International Criminal Tribunal for Rwanda (ICTR), and the International Criminal Court (ICC). Secondly, some general rules that have acquired the rank and status of peremptory norms or *jus cogens* (see **11.4**) require that States adopt the necessary implementing legislation. Thus, for instance, the ICTY Trial Chamber held in *Furundžija* that one of the consequences of the peremptory nature of international rules prohibiting and criminalizing torture is that States are bound to enact legislation prohibiting that heinous practice at the national level (at §§145, 148–149). The motivation behind these two developments is clear: States regard certain treaties or general rules as so crucial that they take care to require that members of the international community change their national systems so as to ensure the international rules are implemented. The common goal is to cover even potential breaches of those international rules. International legislators seek to forestall breaches by ensuring that States take all the national measures necessary to prevent or punish at the national level deviations from those international rules. In this way such deviations may not reach the level of international delinquencies, for they may be remedied within the national sphere. It follows that a State may be called to account even if it simply fails to pass the necessary implementing legislation; it need not actually have engaged in any specific conduct inconsistent with the relevant international rule. In addition, if a State breaches one of those rules through lack of implementing legislation, it is answerable for a twofold delinquency.

Admittedly, even in the instances just mentioned, State practice does not contain many cases of complaints or requests by members of the international community that other States pass implementing legislation. The simple fact is that, in their day-to-day dealings, States still tend to cling to the old dogma of respect for the internal affairs of other international subjects. Fortunately, in some cases international monitoring mechanisms have been established, which among other things scrutinize whether parties to a specific international treaty have taken all the necessary legislative measures.

Apart from the general rule barring States from adducing domestic legal problems for not complying with international law, and the treaty or customary rules just mentioned that impose the obligation to enact implementing legislation, international law does not contain any regulation of implementation. It thus leaves each country complete freedom with regard to how it fulfils, nationally, its international obligations.

A survey of national systems shows a conspicuous lack of uniformity. This anarchic state of affairs can be easily accounted for: States consider that the translation of international commands into domestic legal standards is part and parcel of their sovereignty, and are unwilling to surrender it to international control. National self-interest stands in the way of a sensible regulation of this crucial area. As a consequence, each State decides, on its own, how to make international law binding on State agencies and individuals and what status and rank to assign to it in the hierarchy of municipal sources of law.

As there is no international legal regulation of this matter, it falls to the commentator to undertake an analysis of comparative national law. The following paragraphs discuss the major tendencies that have taken shape among States. This examination serves to pinpoint both the legal technicalities involved in each of the prevailing systems and the political and ideological motivations underlying each such system.

11.3.2 MODALITIES OF IMPLEMENTATION: TRENDS IN DOMESTIC SYSTEMS

Generally speaking, in the second half of the twentieth century domestic systems gradually opened the door to international values and States became increasingly willing to bow to international law. Although each State is free to choose its own mechanisms for implementing international rules, even a cursory survey of national legal systems shows that two basic modalities prevail. The first is automatic standing incorporation of international rules. Such incorporation occurs whenever the national constitution, or a law (or, in the case of judge-made law, judicial decisions) enjoins all State officials as well as all nationals and other individuals living on the territory of the State to apply certain present or future rules of international law. In other words, an internal norm provides in a permanent way for the automatic incorporation into national law of any relevant rule of international (customary or treaty) law, without there being any need for the passing of an ad hoc national statute (subject to the exception of non-self-executing international rules; see **12.4.2(b)**). It follows that any time a treaty is duly approved and published in the State's Official Gazette or a customary rule of international law evolves in the world community, State officials and individuals must *ipso facto* and without further ado comply with it. This mechanism, among other things, enables the national legal system to adjust itself continuously and automatically to international legal standards. As soon as an international rule comes into existence, a corresponding legal provision evolves in the national legal system (subject to publication of the treaty, in the case of this category of international norms). By the same token, as soon as an international rule is terminated or changes in content, corresponding modifications in the national legal system take place (again, in the case of amendment of treaties, subject to publication of the amending provisions).

The second approach is legislative ad hoc incorporation of international rules. Under this approach international rules become applicable within the State legal system only if and when the relevant parliamentary authorities pass specific implementing legislation. This legislation may take one of two principal forms. First, it may consist of an Act of Parliament translating the various treaty provisions into national legislation, setting out in detail the various obligations, powers, and rights stemming from those international provisions (statutory ad hoc incorporation of international rules). Secondly, the Act of

Parliament may confine itself to enjoining the automatic applicability of the international rule within the national legal system, without reformulating that rule ad hoc (automatic ad hoc incorporation of international law). Under this second modality, in substance the mechanism works in a similar way to the one that we have termed above 'automatic standing incorporation' (the only difference being that now the incorporation is effected on a case-by-case basis). Now, as well, State officials, and all the individuals concerned, become duty-bound to abide by the international provisions to which the Act of Parliament makes reference. The enabling legislation simply consists of one or two provisions stating that the treaty at issue must be complied with; the text of the treaty is annexed as a schedule. Courts, State officials, and individuals must infer the various provisions to be applied at the national level by way of interpretation. That is, these bodies or individuals must deduce from the text of the treaty, to which the piece of legislation refers, all the various rules to be applied at the national level.

For the purpose of ensuring a more complete and effective implementation of international law, preference should always be given to the legislative ad hoc incorporation of international rules whenever they turn out to be non-self-executing (see **11.3.5**). Conversely, whenever international rules are self-executing, it would be preferable to resort to the automatic (whether permanent or ad hoc) incorporation of international rules. Indeed, this mechanism better safeguards the correct application of international rules because it does not ossify them: instead, it enables the national legal system to adjust itself fully to international rules as they are construed and applied in the international sphere.

11.3.3 THE RANK OF INTERNATIONAL RULES WITHIN DOMESTIC SYSTEMS

Once we have established that, often, for international rules to become operative, these need to be translated into domestic legal systems, we can also tackle the distinct issue of what kind of rank rules of international origin assume within domestic legal systems. A survey of national legislation and case law shows that some States tend to put the international rules incorporated into the national legal system (whether automatically or through ad hoc legislative enactment) on the same footing as national legislation of domestic origin. As a consequence, the general principles governing relationships between rules having the same rank apply: a subsequent law repeals or modifies or at any rate supersedes a previous law; a special law prevails over a general law; a subsequent general law does not derogate from a prior special law. It follows that the national legislature may at any time pass a law amending or repealing a rule of international origin. True, in this case the State, if it applies the national law in lieu of the international rule, incurs international responsibility for a breach of international law. The fact remains, however, that the international rule is set aside by a simple Act of Parliament.

In contrast, other States tend to accord international rules a status and rank higher than that of national legislation. Such an approach is normally linked to the nature of their national constitution. Where the constitution is 'flexible' (that is, it can be amended by simple Act of Parliament), or in any case the principle of legislative supremacy obtains, the only way of giving international rules overriding importance would be to entrench them, so that it is not possible for legislation passed by simple majority to modify them. Such a course of action, however, does not seem to have been followed so far in those States which have a 'flexible' constitution.

Things are different where the constitution is 'rigid', in particular where it is 'functionally rigid' (that is, the constitution lays down special requirements for constitutional amendments and in addition sets up a court authorized to undertake judicial review of legislation so as to establish whether the legislature exceeds its powers and infringes the constitution). In these constitutional systems, if the constitution provides for the incorporation of international rules, normally those rules enjoy constitutional or quasi-constitutional status and therefore rank higher than normal law. It follows that the legislature is precluded from passing a law contrary to an international rule, unless of course this law is enacted through the special procedure required for constitutional legislation. The logic behind this approach is that international legal standards should always be regarded as having overriding importance. Therefore, in addition to binding the executive branch and all citizens, they cannot be set aside by simple parliamentary majority. Only under special circumstances, when compelling national interests prevail and a special majority (say, a two-thirds majority) is mustered in parliament, may those rules be overridden.

States tend to regulate national incorporation of international rules on the basis of two different requirements. First, they may have to choose between a statist (or nationalist) and an internationalist approach. Secondly, they may have to take into account the question of the relationship between the executive and legislative branches of government, and shape the mechanism for implementing international law accordingly.

States choosing a statist or nationalist approach incline (i) to adopt legislative ad hoc incorporation, and (ii) to put international rules on the same footing as national legislation of domestic origin. In contrast, States taking an international outlook tend (i) to opt for the automatic incorporation (whether standing or ad hoc) of international rules, and (ii) to accord international rules a status and rank higher than that of national legislation.

States often take into account a second requirement, which concerns the general question of reserving to the legislative branch a competence that belongs to it alone and not to the executive branch. In those States where the government (chiefly the foreign ministry) makes international treaties without any parliamentary participation, a special problem may arise in two sets of circumstances: (i) whenever the treaty covers areas that come within the purview of the legislature; (ii) whenever parliaments do not play any role, or play a limited role, in the decision to be bound by a treaty. In the first case, it is necessary to prevent the government from bypassing parliament by making a treaty and having it incorporated into national legislation without going through parliament. Hence, in these countries the intervention of parliament is always required for the treaty to be transformed into national legislation. Consequently, these countries do not opt for the automatic standing incorporation of treaties, but rather for their ad hoc incorporation (whether legislative or automatic). In other words, parliament may be required to enact a special law either setting out in detail the various rules contained in the treaty or simply enjoining all the relevant State agencies and the individuals concerned to abide by the treaty.

In the second case, where parliaments are excluded from the decision on whether or not to be bound by a treaty, to enable parliaments to exercise some control over foreign policy-making they may be required to formally give their consent to the incorporation of the treaty, for the treaty to take effect at the municipal level. In this case as well, the automatic standing incorporation mechanism proves to be inadequate and States resort to the legislative ad hoc incorporation system.

11.3.4 DOMESTIC IMPLEMENTATION OF CUSTOMARY INTERNATIONAL LAW

Although there is very great diversity in the ways of implementing customary rules, nevertheless a common feature stands out. All national systems adopt the same basic modality of implementation: automatic standing incorporation. National constitutions or statutes or judicial decisions of most States stipulate that customary international rules become domestically binding *ipso facto*, that is, by the mere fact of their evolving in the international community. As soon as they come into being in the world community international customary rules become binding within national legal systems; in addition, they have, at the national level, the same content as that of the corresponding international rules.

The reason for the choice of this implementation system is self-evident: it is the only suitable one for rules that emerge gradually in the world community and whose content is not immediately definable. Were States to decide that a customary rule only becomes binding upon State officials and individuals after the enactment of a statute setting out the contents of such a rule, the parliamentary assembly would have to play a very difficult role, namely, to decide whether the customary rule has taken shape, and with what contents. Given the characteristics of customary law, it is far more fitting and practical to leave it to judges and other State officials to establish whether and to what extent a customary rule is binding within the legal system of a State.

Clearly, there may be customary rules that need to be supplemented by national legislation, in order for them to become operative at the domestic level. As an example of such non-self-executing customary rules, one may mention the rule providing that the maximum outer limit of the territorial sea should be 12 nautical miles. Plainly, it is for each State to decide on the width of its territorial sea, by enacting national legislation or regulation on the matter.

Having made this general point, let us now consider the rank of customary international law within major national systems.

In some States with 'rigid' constitutions, constitutional provisions and judicial practice proclaim that international customary law overrides any inconsistent 'ordinary' national legislation. This holds true for Italy, Germany, Japan, and Greece; the same also applies to Uzbekistan, Turkmenistan, and Belarus. In some of these States (e.g. Italy, Germany, and Japan) there is a constitutional court entrusted with judicial review of legislative acts and consequently responsible for ensuring that no law is passed which conflicts with the constitution. Hence, the enactment of any ordinary law contrary to international customary rules is safeguarded through judicial review.

Other States (e.g. the US, China, France, and the UK) do not lay down provisions according customary international law a rank higher than that of ordinary legislation. In the UK this is also due to the lack of a written constitution and the upholding of legislative supremacy. Consequently, should Parliament pass a law clearly conflicting with a customary rule of international law, the national law, being later in time, would prevail. However, in some countries such as Russia, there appears to be a judicial tendency to extend to customary rules the applicability of the constitutional provision granting treaties a rank higher than that of subsequent laws, and consequently to hold that customary rules take precedence over subsequent contrary legislation (although this tendency might be fading away in the light of more recent trends eroding the supremacy of international law over domestic norms). This approach, also upheld in such countries as Belgium, has been laid down in terms in the 1996 South African Constitution (in spite of the fact that this is a 'rigid' constitution and the country has a constitutional court endowed with the power to undertake judicial review of legislation).

11.3.5 DOMESTIC IMPLEMENTATION OF TREATY LAW

While, as shown in the previous section, customary international law is normally incorporated by means of the automatic standing mechanism, with regard to treaties States tend to resort to all three aforementioned mechanisms of incorporation: automatic standing; statutory ad hoc incorporation; automatic ad hoc incorporation.

Some national systems provide that domestic authorities are to comply with treaties upon their publication in the Official Bulletin (see e.g. France and many African countries);

in the case of the US, treaties duly ratified by the President after the Senate's approval are 'the supreme Law of the Land and the Judges in every State shall be bound thereby, anything in the Constitution or laws of any State to the contrary not with standing' (Article VI(2) of the Constitution). By contrast, other domestic systems (such as the UK and Israel) provide that treaties do not bind national authorities unless they are translated into national legislation (in the UK, however, this principle does not apply to treaties concerning the conduct of war or to treaties of cession). At least with regard to these two countries, it would seem that the main reason for this incorporation scheme is that treaties are only made by the executive and consequently the parliament necessarily must be involved, by virtue of the separation of powers doctrine, for the treaty to become part of national law. In other countries, such as Italy and Germany, practice shows frequent resort to automatic ad hoc incorporation.

A particular problem may arise with regard to treaties containing non-self-executing provisions, that is, provisions that cannot be directly applied within the national legal system because they need to be supplemented by additional national legislation for them to be implemented. Whenever treaties contain such provisions, even in those national legal systems where the mere publication of international treaties is sufficient for them to produce effects domestically, the passing of implementing legislation proves necessary.

The notion was formulated as early as 1829 by Chief Justice Marshall (of the US Supreme Court) in *Foster and Elam v Neilson*. He wrote (at 427):

> Our Constitution declares a treaty to be the law of the land. It is, consequently, to be regarded in courts of justice as equivalent to an act of the legislature, whenever it operates of itself without the aid of any legislative provision. But when the terms of the stipulation import a contract, when either of the parties engages to perform a particular act, the treaty addresses itself to the political, not the judicial department; and the legislature must execute the contract, before it can become a rule for the court.

In *Fujii v State of California* the Supreme Court of California held, in 1952, that Articles 55 and 56 of the UN Charter, on human rights, were non-self-executing and could not be applied unless the requisite state legislation was enacted (at 312). Similarly, in 1979 the Italian Constitutional Court held in *Lockheed* that Article 14(5) of the UN Covenant on Civil and Political Rights (whereby '[e]veryone convicted of a crime shall have the right to his conviction and sentence being reviewed by a higher tribunal according to law') was not applicable to the judicial proceedings that could be instituted against the Prime Minister and other members of cabinet under Article 96 of the Constitution, unless and until the legislature passed a law governing appellate proceedings in this matter (at 94–5). In 1980 the Dutch Supreme Court delivered a similar decision in *H.J.M.M. v Public Prosecutor* (at 367). The distinction between self-executing and non-self-executing treaty provisions was taken up, in practice, in the Russian Federal Law on International Treaties of the Russian Federation, adopted by the Duma on 16 June 1995 and entered into force on 21 July 1995. Article 5 of the Law provides, *inter alia*, that:

> [t]he provisions of the officially published international treaties of the Russian Federation which do not require the adoption of internal acts for their application are directly applicable. Corresponding legal acts shall be adopted for the application of other provisions of the international treaties of the Russian Federation.

It should be emphasized that national courts often tend to broaden the notion of non-self-executing treaty provisions, with a view to wittingly or unwittingly shielding national legal systems from legal change. Thus, for instance, not until 1991 did the French Council of State (Conseil d'État), after many contrary decisions, come to the right conclusion, in *Demizpence* (at 1013), that Article 8 of the European Convention on Human Rights (the right to private and family life) is self-executing. Similarly, it was only in 1989 that the Italian Court of Cassation held, in *Polo Castro* (at 1042–4), that Article 5(1)(f) of the same Convention (on the condition of a person who has been arrested or detained with a view to preventing his unauthorized entry into the country, or pending his deportation or extradition) is self-executing.

The legal standing of treaties within domestic legal orders and the possibility of conflict between international treaties and subsequent national legislation vary greatly, depending upon the rank and status of the national rule providing for the incorporation of international treaties within the legal system. In countries where a constitutional provision (of a 'rigid' constitution) provides for the incorporation of treaties, duly ratified treaties override national legislation.

Thus, in France treaties acquire a status higher than national 'ordinary' legislation, with the obvious consequence that, in the case of conflict, the former prevails. Article 55 of the 1958 Constitution provides that '[t]reaties and agreements duly ratified and approved shall, upon their publication, have an authority superior to that of laws, subject, for each agreement or treaty, to its application by the other party'. However, as the Conseil d'État stated in *Sarran, Levacher et al.* (at 1081–90), and as did the plenary Court of Cassation in *Pauline Fraisse*, international treaties may not override constitutional provisions. It is for this reason that, following a decision of the Constitutional Council (*Conseil constitutionnel*), the French Parliament decided that, to implement the Statute of the ICC and those provisions of the Statute that were contrary to the French Constitution, it needed to pass a constitutional law. Such a law was indeed enacted: it added to Article 53 of the Constitution a new paragraph providing that the French legal order shall conform to the Rome Statute. This Statute has thus been given constitutional rank in the French legal system, or at least constitutional safeguard.

Similar provisions on the incorporation of treaties are contained in the constitutions of such countries as Greece and a number of French-speaking African countries, such as the Ivory Coast. The Spanish Constitution of 1978 also contains such a provision, but without the reciprocity clause. Furthermore, Article 15(4) of the 1993 Constitution of the Russian Federation provides that 'the generally recognized principles and norms of international law and the international treaties of the Russian Federation shall constitute an integral part of its legal system' and goes on to state that 'if an international treaty of the Russian Federation establishes other rules than those stipulated by the law, the rules of the international treaty shall be applied'.

The supremacy of international treaties is also laid down in the constitutions of such States as Bulgaria (Article 5(4)), Moldova (Article 8), Estonia (Article 123), Armenia (Article 6), Azerbaijan (Article 151), Kazakhstan (Article 4), Georgia (Article 6), and Tadzhikistan (Article 11). In the Netherlands, treaties are granted a status that is even higher than the Constitution, at least in some cases. It should be added that in many countries that have constitutional courts, these courts have acted upon the principle of primacy of international treaties over 'ordinary legislation'.

In contrast, in other countries, constitutions or national laws provide, either explicitly or implicitly, that treaties possess the same rank as laws enacted by parliament. Clearly, the rationale behind this trend is to grant parliament the power to change legislation implementing a treaty whenever national interests are regarded as paramount. Indeed, a later statute can override an earlier treaty. In the US, treaties have the status of federal law and prevail over State law, but can be superseded by a later federal law. (It follows, among other things, that interpretations of treaties made by the US Supreme Court are binding upon State courts.)

There are, however, many States (such as China and a number of English-speaking African countries such as Ghana, Uganda, Nigeria, Tanzania, etc.) that have not made any provision in their constitutions or national legislation for the implementation of treaties. In these countries, treaties are incorporated by means of ad hoc mechanisms. The rank of treaties within the national legal order thus depends on the rank and status of the ad hoc implementing legislation.

In those States where treaties, once incorporated, assume the rank of ordinary legislation, conflicts between treaties and subsequent legislation may frequently arise. To narrow the range of such possible conflicts, courts tend to uphold the principle of interpretation whereby in case of doubt a national statute must be so construed as not to conflict with an international treaty ratified by the State. The Italian Court of Cassation clearly set out this principle in 1954 in the *I. Whittingham & Sons Ltd.* v *Fratelli D'Amico* case. In upholding that the Brussels Convention of 1924 on the unification of certain rules on the bill of lading had to prevail over the Italian maritime code of 1932, the Court stated that:

> [t]he existence of an international undertaking ... and, even more, its implementation by the national legislature cannot but amount to a means of interpretation of subsequent legislation. Consequently, failing a clear and manifest intention of the lawmakers to repeal the law implementing a treaty, that is to say to cast off the international undertaking, one ought to think that the legislature intended to abide by the general and fundamental rule of international law commanding respect for the treaties.

US courts have taken the same approach. Thus, for instance, in *United States* v *Palestine Liberation Organization*, the Southern District Court of New York decided in 1987 that the Anti-Terrorism Act of 1988 did not supersede the Headquarters Agreement made by the US with the UN in 1946, on account of the principle at issue, which the Court set out as follows: 'Only where a treaty is irreconcilable with a later enacted statute and Congress has clearly evinced an intent to supersede a treaty by enacting a statute does the later enacted statute take precedence'.

Some legal scholars have criticized this approach, which the courts of other States have also taken. In their view, to claim that a national statute can derogate from an international treaty only when the law-makers have clearly expressed the intent to make the law prevail over the previous treaty is to propound a hypothesis that is abstract and pointless. In fact, so they argue, parliaments very seldom deviate from treaties with the express intent to do so. When national legislation turns out to be contrary to international rules, this is often merely as a result of lack of co-ordination or even owing to an oversight. It could, however, be objected that this principle of construction, however artificial, ultimately constitutes a sound device forged by courts to make good mistakes or oversights of the legislature, with a view to ensuring consistency of national legislation with international legal standards.

An approach akin to that just outlined was taken in the 1996 South African Constitution, section 233 of which provides that:

> [w]hen interpreting any legislation, every court must prefer any reasonable interpretation of the legislation that is consistent with international law over any alternative interpretation that is inconsistent with international law.

It would seem that this wording is sufficiently flexible to grant substantial leeway to courts when confronted with cases of conflict between national legislation and international treaties.

A number of Italian international lawyers, and a Russian scholar, have propounded an interesting view, designed to make treaties prevail over subsequent contrary domestic legislation, because of the unique nature of the origin of the norm. According to this view, when interpreting and applying norms coming from international treaties that might be inconsistent with national legislation, one ought to proceed on the basis of the notion that the legislation implementing the treaties makes up 'special' law on account of the special origin of the norm. This special character does not lie in the fact that the legislation governs a class of facts or persons more limited than that envisaged by the general rule (the usual notion of speciality). Rather, it lies in the origin and role of the rules implementing the treaty at the national level. These rules differ from ordinary municipal legislation in that they have the particular aim of adjusting the national legal order to an international treaty. They derive their origin and *raison d'être* from the existence of the treaty, and are designed to put it into practice in municipal law. This is the sort of 'speciality' that should make them prevail over subsequent legislation, on the strength of the traditional principle that a later and general rule does not supersede an earlier and special rule. Ultimately the Court of Cassation in Belgium reached the same conclusion in *S.A. Fromagerie Franco-Suisse 'Le Ski'* v *État Belge*. The Court held that treaties must prevail over national legislation because 'the primacy of the treaty results from the very nature of international treaty law'.

One of the most striking features of modern international law is that some intergovernmental organizations are empowered to adopt binding decisions, some laying down rules producing outside effects, others consisting of 'administrative acts', that is, binding decisions concerning the internal life of the organization. To be put into operation, these decisions too need to be implemented at the national level. This in particular holds true for such acts as the economic and diplomatic sanctions adopted by the UN Security Council (e.g. those against South Africa, Southern Rhodesia, Iraq, the Federal Republic of Yugoslavia (Serbia and Montenegro), etc.), as well as for the Statutes of the ICTY and the ICTR, enacted by the Security Council in 1993 and 1994 respectively, by a decision taken under Chapter VII of the UN Charter. Of great importance also is the implementation of regulations, directives, and other acts adopted by the organs of the European Union.

Normally, national legal systems do not contain any special provision on the automatic or ad hoc incorporation of decisions of international organizations. Exceptions can be found in the constitutions of such States as the Netherlands, Greece, and Spain, or in the judicial practice of such States as France. These countries take a modern and internationally oriented attitude, by providing that internationally binding resolutions and decisions of intergovernmental organizations become binding within the internal legal system simply upon their publication in the State's Official Journal. It is submitted that it would be excessive to claim that those decisions or resolutions should become binding *ipso facto*, without even being published in the Official Journal of the relevant State. Since normally there is no international judicial review of binding acts of international organizations, it would seem that States are entitled to exercise some sort of minimal scrutiny of the legality of those acts, that is, their consonance with the organization's rules, before applying them internally.

Whenever this is not the case, or if the international normative acts, being non-self-executing, require implementing legislation, specific legislative enactments prove necessary. There have been many such enactments. A number of States have passed legislation for the specific purpose of adjusting their national legal system to the Statutes of the ICTY and the ICTR, in particular with a view to specifying the national judicial bodies entrusted with the task of ensuring co-operation with the Tribunals. Other States, including the Russian Federation, did not need such legislation to put the Statutes into practice.

The situation is different in relation to the national implementation of acts adopted by organs of the European Union. The Treaty on the Functioning of the European Union provides that regulations are 'directly applicable' in the national legal order of the various Member States (see e.g. Article 288 TFEU). As for directives, the case law of the European Court of Justice (ECJ) has clarified that at least three categories of them are directly applicable in national legal systems. In other instances, the passing of implementing legislation by each Member State is needed. This feature of EU acts, that is, their being directly applicable in the national legal systems of Member States, is warranted (i) by the need for the EU immediately to produce the same legal effects within the legal systems of all these States;

and (ii) by the existence of a Court (the ECJ) entrusted with the task of undertaking judicial review of any EU act allegedly contrary to the treaties. The exclusive and unique role of the ECJ in this regard was recently reaffirmed by the Court itself through a press release after the judgment of the German Constitutional Court which had challenged the activities of so-called 'Quantitative Easing' of the European Central Bank.

11.3.6 HIERARCHICAL RELATIONS BETWEEN INTERNATIONAL AND DOMESTIC LAW

The choice of mechanisms for implementing international rules within national legal systems is the acid test for establishing to what extent States are open to international values. Those States which are sensitive to international demands opt for automatic standing incorporation mechanisms for customary law, treaty rules, and decisions of international organizations. In addition, they grant those international rules and decisions a higher rank than 'ordinary' law.

Very few countries adopt such an overall internationalist outlook. Three in particular stand out: Greece, the Netherlands, and Spain. They all adopt the automatic standing incorporation system. In addition, in Greece, both customary international rules and treaties override national legislation, a clear demonstration of Greece's consistent and courageous internationalist approach. In the Netherlands, international treaties override the Constitution. In Spain provision is made not only for the primacy of international treaties over national legislation, but also for the obligation of national authorities to construe national legislation on human rights in the light of international instruments. However, to safeguard the requirements of democratic governance, this internationalist attitude is counterbalanced in Spain by the firmly required intervention of Parliament: under the interpretation the Council of State (*Consejo de Estado*) set forth in numerous 'opinions', Parliament's authorization or approval is required by Article 94 of the Constitution not only for making treaties, including agreements 'in simplified form' (e.g. through exchange of diplomatic notes), but also for appending or withdrawing reservations, making unilateral declarations (whether creating new obligations or simply interpreting existing obligations), amending multilateral treaties, or denouncing treaties or agreements, as well as in cases of adhesion or accession of States to a multilateral treaty already binding upon Spain; in contrast, parliamentary authorization is normally not required for the provisional application of treaties.

Conversely, most States still take a rather nationalist approach to the implementation of international law. They do not make international values, as sanctioned in international rules, prevail over domestic interests and concerns. By putting international rules on the same footing as ordinary national legislation, they retain the power to disregard international values at any time by passing municipal legislation inconsistent with international law. The most extreme of nationalist attitudes would seem to be that of States such as the UK which, out of respect for parliamentary prerogatives, require, for treaty rules to be binding at the national level, that the treaty be translated into national legislation by Act of Parliament.

Other States, such as France and the Russian Federation, have adopted a partially internationalist approach, in that they make at least a part of international law prevail over national legislation. They tend, however, to take this attitude only with regard to treaties (whereas they take a traditional, statist approach with regard to customary law). This trend is probably accounted for by a widespread distrust of customary rules, a body of law regarded as uncertain in its contents, and at any rate as not so reliable as written law. There may be another possible factor: in the case of treaties, normally parliament is associated with their birth, at least in that it authorizes their ratification or their implementation, and such association gives an imprint of popular legitimation to the rules contained in the treaty.

In sum, most States do not accord primacy to international rules in their national legal systems. Thus, it may be concluded that most members of the world community tend to play down the possible role of international legal standards in their domestic legal setting. It does not follow, however, that they normally and systematically disregard international norms. The contrary is rather the rule. The failure of States to accord to international law pride of place at home only means that they do not intend to tie their hands formally, at the constitutional or legislative level. In other words, subject to the few exceptions already referred to, States ultimately prefer not to enshrine in their constitutions or in their laws a firm and irrevocable commitment to unqualified observance of all international rules.

To limit, at least in part, the markedly statist outlook taken by many States, courts may play a crucial role by stepping in to ensure compliance with international legal standards. Whenever their national legislation does not provide them with the legal means for making international values prevail, they have at least two interpretative principles available: the principle concerning the presumption in favour of international treaties, and the principle of speciality (see **11.4.1**). By judiciously resorting to either of these principles, courts may advance international law in a significant way.

Furthermore, one should consider that in modern international law we are faced with a phenomenon of increasing importance: there are more and more international rules that address themselves directly to individuals, either by imposing obligations (see **Chapter 19**) or by granting rights (see **Chapter 18**). These rules intend to, and do, reach individuals directly, that is, not through the medium of the municipal law of States. They are thus operative as soon as they emerge, regardless of what is provided for in any particular national legal systems, and even contrary to possible national rules. Whereas, in the old international community, international law and national legal systems made up two distinct spheres of law, there has been an increasing tendency, since at least the First World War, for many international rules to operate everywhere in the world immediately, that is, to penetrate and directly affect individuals living under national systems of law. Clearly, for these rules, the passing, if any, of national implementing legislation only serves to strengthen their effectiveness. If they are matched by national rules, their impact on the conduct of individuals becomes even stronger.

11.4 HIERARCHICAL RELATIONS AMONG INTERNATIONAL LEGAL NORMS: EMERGENCE AND DEVELOPMENT OF *JUS COGENS*

11.4.1 GENERAL

Normally, in municipal law there exists a hierarchy both of sources of law and of legal rules produced through such sources. Thus, for instance, in States having a 'rigid' constitution and also a constitutional court monitoring compliance with it, normally there are three main sources of law, each prevailing over the one below: the constitution; laws enacted by parliament; and administrative regulations passed by political and administrative bodies, or by-laws made by subordinate bodies (government departments, local authorities, etc.). The hierarchy is even more extensive in such federal States as the US: there, one must distinguish between the Constitution, federal laws, state laws, and subordinate legislation such as local regulations. The hierarchy of *sources* entails a hierarchy of *rules*: a law may not derogate from or be inconsistent with a constitutional provision; a regulation may not run counter to a law (and *a fortiori* to a constitutional rule). This normative hierarchical structure reflects the will of the people to make some legal commands (those comprised in the Constitution) more important and 'stronger' than others, for they reflect values shared by the overwhelming majority of citizens, while rules set through a law may only reflect the will of the majority.

In contrast, in classic international law there did not exist any hierarchy of rules of international law, at least as between the two primary law-creating processes, that is, custom and treaty (see **Chapter 9**). Both these processes and the sets of rules created through them possessed equal rank and status. The reason for this state of affairs is that States did not intend to place limitations on their sovereign powers that they had not expressly or implicitly accepted. Therefore, even if the custom-creating process was general in nature and brought about rules binding on the whole international community, such rules could not override a contrary treaty entered into by two or more States in derogation from the customary rule. The complete interchangeability of the two sources plainly sanctioned the wish of sovereign States not to tie their hands for good; they were able to dispose of their obligations by mutual agreement as soon as fulfilling them proved contrary to the parties' interests.

As a result of the lack of any hierarchy, the relations between rules generated by the two primary sources were governed by the three general principles which in all legal orders regulate the relations between norms deriving from the *same* source (a later law repeals, or may derogate from, an earlier one; a later law, general in character, does not derogate from an earlier one, which is special in character; a special law prevails over a general law). Thus, two or more States could elect to derogate *inter se* from customary international law; by the same token, a new customary rule could supplant a treaty concluded by two or more States.

An obvious corollary of the full interchangeability of the two sources was that both categories of norms could regulate any subject matter, and in any manner the parties concerned agreed upon.

This general condition has recently changed in some respects. No hierarchy has been created encompassing the two main *sources of law*, which remain on the same footing. Nor has a hierarchical order been established embracing *all* the rules generated by one source (say, custom) and those set through the other source (treaty). Rather, a special class of *general rules* made by custom has been endowed with a *special legal force*: they are peremptory in nature and make up the so-called *jus cogens*, in that they may not be derogated from by treaty (or by ordinary customary process); if they are, the derogating rules may be declared null and void. Thus, these peremptory norms have a rank and status superior to those of all the other rules of the international community.

11.4.2 THE EMERGENCE OF *JUS COGENS*: ESTABLISHMENT AND SCOPE

The upgrading of certain fundamental rules produced by traditional sources of law occurred in the late 1960s, chiefly as a result of the endeavours of socialist and developing countries. These countries claimed that certain norms governing relations between States should be given a higher rank than ordinary rules deriving from treaties and custom. According to the proponents of this view, the norms in question covered self-determination of peoples, and the prohibition of aggression, genocide, slavery, and racial discrimination (in particular, racial segregation or apartheid).

What were the political and ideological motivations behind this move? It seems that the two groups of countries were impelled by slightly different, though somewhat overlapping, motives.

To developing countries, the proclamation of *jus cogens* represented a further means of fighting against colonial (or former colonial) countries. The representative of Sierra Leone at the 1968 Vienna Conference made this point, when he noted that the upholding of *jus cogens* 'provided a golden opportunity to condemn imperialism, slavery, forced labour, and all practices that violated the principle of the equality of all human beings and of the sovereign equality of States' (UN Conference on the Law of Treaties, First Session (1968), *Official Records*, at 300, §9). To socialist countries, on the other hand, peremptory norms represented the hard core of those international principles which, by proclaiming the peaceful coexistence of States, permitted and safeguarded smooth relations between States having different economic and social structures. The upgrading of such principles to *jus cogens* further reinforced them, as it offered them protection against the risk of being nullified by any future treaty. In short, to socialist States *jus cogens* was a political means of crystallizing once and for all the 'rules of the game' concerning peaceful coexistence between East and West.[4]

From the outset, Western countries were on the defensive: some of them (in particular, France (ibid., at 309–10, §§26–34)[5] and, less strongly, Switzerland (ibid., at 323–4, §§25–31)) immediately expressed serious doubts, while others (such as the Scandinavian countries and a number of others, including Greece (ibid., at 295, §§18–19), Cyprus (ibid., at 305–6, §§66–71), Israel (ibid., at 310, §§35–38), Italy (ibid., at 311, §§41–43), Spain (ibid., at 315, §§1–5), and Canada (ibid., at 323, §§21–24)) became aware of the need to bow to the will of the majority, either because of their strong humanitarian or legal tradition, or under the influence of national jurists who had supported the concept of *jus cogens*. In the event, Western countries, with the support of some Latin American and Afro-Asian States, accepted the socialist and developing countries' initiative, subject however to a strict condition: that some mechanism for judicial determination of peremptory norms be set up. In their view, since no general agreement existed on the list of specific rules having peremptory character, in order for them to accept the new notion it was necessary to ensure that an impartial judicial body be called upon to establish, in case of dispute, whether or not an alleged peremptory rule did in fact belong to this corpus of higher-ranking norms. This judicial mechanism was embedded in the International Court of Justice (ICJ).[6] Thus, in Vienna a sort of package deal was made: *jus cogens* was accepted but on condition that any State invoking it be prepared to submit its determination to the ICJ.

The Vienna Convention on the Law of Treaties of 1969 (as well as that of 1986) provides, in Article 53, as follows:

> A treaty is void if, at the time of its conclusion, it conflicts with a peremptory norm of general international law. For the purposes of the present Convention, a peremptory norm of general international law is a norm accepted and recognized by the international community of States as a whole as a norm from which no derogation is permitted and which can be modified only by a subsequent norm of general international law having the same character.

---

[4] This concept was set forth most clearly in the statements made at Vienna by Romania (UN Conference on the Law of Treaties, First Session (1968), *Official Records*, 312–13, §§55–63) and Ukraine (ibid., at 322, §6), which, curiously, were echoed by Mali (ibid., at 327, §§68–70).

[5] See also UN Conference on the Law of Treaties, Second Session (1969), *Official Records, Verbatim Records of the Plenary Meetings*, 93–5, §§7–18.

[6] The introduction of this notion into international law in a sense translated into terms of positive law concepts and constructs that had been propounded in the seventeenth and eighteenth centuries by some lawyers, in particular, the German jurists Samuel Rachel (1628–91), Christian Wolff (1679–1754), and Georg Friedrich de Martens (1756–1821), and the Swiss publicist and diplomat Emer de Vattel (1714–67). They had divided the legal order into *three spheres*: (i) internal law (*jus civile*) pertaining to the internal life of the State; (ii) the law applicable to relations among civilized States, that is the law pertaining to the international society, and primarily composed of treaties (*jus gentium*, also called *jus voluntarium*, on account of its consisting of the merger of the wills of the various States); and (iii) natural law (*jus naturae*), regulating the life of mankind, the *societas humani generis*; this law made up *jus necessarium*, or a necessary body of law, in that it derived from reason and humanity; as such it perforce prevailed over *jus voluntarium* or treaties.

(See also Article 64, whereby '[i]f a new peremptory norm of general international law emerges, any existing treaty which is in conflict with that norm becomes void and terminates'.)

As a great authority, Jimenez de Aréchaga, rightly emphasized, the definition of peremptory rules contained in these provisions is very defective. As he put it:

> [T]his description of *jus cogens* fails to apprehend its real essence, since the definition is based on the legal effects of a rule and not on its intrinsic nature; it is not that certain rules are rules of *jus cogens* because no derogation from them is permitted; rather, no derogation is allowed because they possess the nature of rules of *jus cogens*.[7]

Article 66(a) (and Article 66.2 of the 1986 Convention) provide for resort to the Court in the event of disputes on the actual content of *jus cogens* in specific instances. Pursuant to these provisions if, in the case of dispute on the applicability of *jus cogens*, no solution has been reached through conciliation, within a period of 12 months following the date on which the objection to the applicability of *jus cogens* was raised, 'any one of the parties to a dispute concerning the application or the interpretation of Articles 53 or 64 may, by a written application, submit it to the International Court of Justice for a decision unless the parties by common consent agree to submit the dispute to arbitration'.

Clearly, a peremptory norm can only take shape if the most important and representative States from the various areas of the world consent to it. It is in this sense that R. Ago, the President of the Vienna Diplomatic Conference, authoritatively interpreted the formula of Article 53 of the 1969 Vienna Convention.[8] The president of the Drafting Committee in Vienna, Ambassador Yasseen, had to some extent adumbrated this interpretation (and also elaborated upon its implications) when he had noted that:

> by inserting the words 'as a whole' in Article 50 the Drafting Committee had wished to stress that there was no question of requiring a rule to be accepted and recognized as peremptory by all States. It would be enough if a very large majority did so; that would mean that, if one State in isolation refused to accept the peremptory character of the rule, or if that State was supported by a very small number of States, the acceptance and recognition of the peremptory character of the rule by the international community as a whole would not be affected. (ibid., at 472, §12)

It could be contended that peremptory norms ultimately rest on the consent or acquiescence of the *major members* of the world community. However, it is difficult for a State, whether or not it is a Great Power, to oppose the formation of a peremptory norm: numerous political, diplomatic, or psychological factors dissuade States from assuming a hostile attitude towards emerging values which most other States consider to be fundamental.

For all its innovative impact, the concept of peremptory rules should not be overestimated. Jimenez de Aréchaga, speaking as the delegate of Uruguay, rightly stressed this point at Vienna (ibid., at 303, §48). He noted that at the time of their proclamation the provisions of the Vienna Convention on *jus cogens* aroused greater hopes, in some, and fiercer opposition and fear, in others, than was warranted by a realistic prospect of their application. In fact, instances of flagrant violations of *jus cogens* would be infrequent. One should therefore not make of those rules a mystique 'that would breathe fresh life into international law' or 'an element of the destruction of treaties and of anarchy'.[9] Nonetheless, much headway was made, in that a body of supreme or 'constitutional' principles was created.

---

[7] E. Jimenez de Aréchaga, 'International Law in the Past Third of a Century' (1978-I) 159 *RCADI* 64.
[8] R. Ago, 'Droit des traités à la lumière de la Convention de Vienne' (1971-III) 134 *RCADI* 297.
[9] See UN Conference on the Law of Treaties, First session (1968), *Official Records*, 303, §48.

11.4.3 EXAMPLES OF PEREMPTORY NORMS

So far, no *State practice* proper has developed with the attendant *opinio juris* or *opinio necessitatis* (that is, legal conviction) of the peremptory character of a specific norm. In particular, no dispute has arisen between States as to the *jus cogens* nature of a specific rule. Nor have one or more States insisted on the peremptory nature of a rule in a dispute with other States, accompanied by either acquiescence by other States or contestation by them. Nor has any international Tribunal, let alone the ICJ, settled any dispute revolving around the question of whether or not a specific rule must be regarded as belonging to the corpus of norms under discussion.

Nevertheless, considerable agreement has evolved among States at the level of *opinio juris* (or *opinio necessitatis*), to the effect that certain rules indisputably belong to *jus cogens*.

An important clue to the identification of peremptory norms can be found in the former Draft Article 19 of the Articles on State Responsibility (as adopted on first reading by the International Law Commission (ILC) but not included in the final text of the ILC Articles for reasons other than the enumeration of fundamental norms; see **12.8**). In that provision, proposed by the Special Rapporteur R. Ago and initially accepted by the ILC, mention was made of norms laying down international obligations 'so *essential for the protection of fundamental interests of the international community* that [their] breach [was] recognized as a crime by that *community as a whole*' (emphasis added). By way of illustration, reference was made there to the norms prohibiting aggression, 'the establishment or maintenance by force of colonial domination', slavery, genocide, or apartheid, as well as 'massive pollution of the atmosphere of the seas'.

One could add the norms prohibiting the use or threat of force (see **3.4**). In this respect, it is interesting to note that, as the ILC rightly emphasized (Commentary on Article 40(2) ILC Articles on State Responsibility), the UN Security Council regarded the annexation of Kuwait by Iraq in breach of the ban on the use of force laid down in the UN Charter as null and void (resolution 662 (1990)). Although the Security Council did not use the term *jus cogens*, the implication is evident that it substantially relied upon this notion, for it clearly articulated the idea that the illegality of Iraqi occupation rendered the occupation legally invalid and all other States were bound not to recognize the annexation. One may also mention the customary rules banning racial discrimination[10] or torture[11] as well as the general rules on self-determination (see **3.8**). In addition, at the Vienna Diplomatic Conference on the Law of Treaties, various delegates stated that the fundamental principles of humanitarian law belong to *jus cogens*,[12] a statement echoed in 1993 by the Hungarian Constitutional Court[13] and in 2000 by the ICTY in *Kupreškić et al.*, where the Tribunal referred to 'most norms of international humanitarian law, in particular those prohibiting war crimes [and] crimes against humanity' (at §520).

---

[10] See e.g. The American Law Institute, *Restatement of the Law Third—The Foreign Relations Law of the United Nations* (St Paul, MN: American Law Institute Publishers, 1987), ii, at 167.

[11] See *Furundžija*, Trial Chamber, §§153–157; the House of Lords in *Pinochet* (in particular, Lord Browne Wilkinson, Lord Hope of Craighead, and Lord Millet).

[12] Delegates of the following States took this position: Finland (UN Conference on the Law of Treaties, First Session (1968), *Official Records*, 294–5, §13, on the treatment of war prisoners); Lebanon (ibid., at 297, §297, on the treatment of war prisoners, the wounded, and the civilian population); Poland (ibid., at 302, §35, on 'some of the rules of land warfare'); Italy (ibid., at 311, §41, on the four Geneva Conventions; see also UN Conference on the Law of Treaties, Second Session (1969), *Official Records, Summary Records of the Plenary Meetings*, 104, §38); Switzerland (First Session, op. cit., at 324, §26, referring to the four Geneva Conventions). See also the ICJ's Advisory Opinion in *Legality of the Threat or Use of Nuclear Weapons*, §79.

[13] In *Law on 'Procedures Concerning Certain Crimes Committed During the 1956 Revolution'*, the Hungarian Constitutional Court held that '[t[he rules relative to the punishment of war crimes and crimes against humanity are *jus cogens* norms of international law, because these crimes threaten mankind and international co-existence in their foundations. A State refusing to undertake this obligation may not participate in the international community' (at 2836).

A Belgian *juge d'investigation* in *Pinochet* (at 286), and the Swiss government in an official 'message' to Parliament of 2000,[14] took the same stand, with reference to crimes against humanity.

It is apparent from the examples mentioned above that all the peremptory norms that have so far evolved in the international community impose community obligations and by the same token confer community rights (on these notions see **1.8.2**).

An important effort to flesh out the notion and implications of 'peremptory norms of general international law (*jus cogens*)' has been undertaken by the ILC since 2015, under the guidance of Special Rapporteur Dire Tladi. In 2019, the ILC adopted on first reading a set of 23 draft conclusions with commentaries on the topic, which provides further substance to the issue of identification and consequences of *jus cogens*. These draft conclusions (see 2019 ILC Report A/74/10, chapter V) include as an annex a non-exhaustive list of peremptory norms (see draft conclusion 23) which include the prohibition of aggression, genocide, crimes against humanity, racial discrimination and apartheid, slavery and torture, as well as the basic rules of international humanitarian law (IHL) prohibition of racial discrimination and the right of self-determination. The ILC, relying substantially on the Vienna Convention for the definition and general consequences (draft conclusions 2–4), indicated that the bases for peremptory norms to come into existence can be both customary law as well as treaties (draft conclusion 5). At the same time, it specified that for a norm to be identified as peremptory 'there must be evidence that such a norm is accepted and recognized as one from which no derogation is permitted' (draft conclusion 6). Moreover, the Commission further devoted specific attention to one of the most intriguing aspects of the very coming into existence of the notion: its effects.

11.4.4 LEGAL EFFECTS OF *JUS COGENS*

Traditionally, the issue of the effects of *jus cogens* has been one of the most debated questions. In theory, the only consequence provided by the Vienna Convention is the invalidity of treaties, which has not been resorted to in practice. Whereas scholarly opinions, case law, and state practice have on a number of occasions shown that there is room for further effects.

In Part three of its draft conclusions, the ILC courageously tackles the issue of legal consequences. In so doing, the Commission deals first with treaty law (draft conclusions 10–13) and other customary rules, but also acts of international organizations as well as unilateral acts of States (draft conclusions 14–16). It also links the work of the ILC on the responsibility of States for internationally wrongful acts (in draft conclusions 16–19) with the topic. In this regard it indicated that '[p]eremptory norms of general international law (jus cogens) give rise to obligations owed to the international community as a whole (obligations erga omnes), in which all States have a legal interest' and clarified that '[a]ny State is entitled to invoke the responsibility of another State for a breach of a peremptory norm of general international law (jus cogens), in accordance with the rules on the responsibility of States for internationally wrongful acts' and specified consequences and modalities of the reaction of States to violations of peremptory norms by identifying a duty to co-operate to bring an end to violations and restating the duty of non-recognition (see draft conclusion 19(2)).

As already stated, the typical effect of peremptory norms is that, as States cannot derogate from them through treaties (or customary rules not endowed with the same legal force), any treaty or customary rules contrary to them are null and void *ab initio* (that is, since the moment the rules came into being) (see ILC draft conclusion 10).

---

[14] See the message of the Swiss government (*Conseil fédéral*) to Parliament: *Message relatif au Statut de la Cour pénale internationale, à la loi fédérale sur la coopération avec la Cour pénale internationale ainsi qu'à une révision du droit pénal*, 15 November 2000, 470, §5.2.

However, other less far-reaching consequences than *invalidity* may be envisaged. Thus, for instance, there is justification for contending that a consequence of a peremptory norm may be that a court will simply *disregard* or declare *null and void* a single treaty provision that is contrary to *jus cogens*, if the remaining provisions of the treaty are not tainted with the same legal invalidity. Admittedly, the 1969 Vienna Convention does not explicitly allow for this possibility and can probably be taken to even exclude it (see Article 44(5)). However, one fails to see why a whole treaty should be invalidated if only one of its provisions is contrary to a peremptory norm and the other provisions are not closely intertwined with, or dependent on, the invalid one. If Article 44(5) is literally construed and the possibility in question is excluded for States parties to the Vienna Convention, one could nevertheless admit it under the customary rule on *jus cogens*, whenever the States at issue are not at the same time bound by that Convention. The ILC adheres to the more rigorous reading as far as a treaty is originally contrary to *jus cogens* (draft conclusion 11(1) provides that '[a] treaty which, at the time of its conclusion, conflicts with a peremptory norm of general international law (jus cogens) is void in whole, and no separation of the provisions of the treaty is permitted'), while under certain circumstances it permits separation when dealing with *jus cogens superveniens* (draft conclusion 11(2)). In addition, the ILC confirms that when interpreting the law, treaty provisions possessing dubious scope must be interpreted in a sense consistent with a peremptory norm on the matter, rather than in any other sense (see draft conclusion 10(3)). This equally applies to resolutions adopted by the UN Security Council. Indeed, peremptory norms are also binding on the UN Security Council, as the ICTY Appeals Chamber rightly held, albeit *obiter*, in 1999 in *Tadić (Appeal)* (at §296) (and as Judge Sir Elihu Lauterpacht had already stated in his Separate Opinion in *Genocide (Bosnia and Herzegovina v Yugoslavia (Serbia and Montenegro) (Further Request for the Indication of Provisional Measures)* (at §§100 and 102)). It follows that if the Security Council disregards one of those norms, its resolution ought to be interpreted in such a manner as to be rendered consistent with *jus cogens*, unless the incompatibility is such that the resolution must be held to be invalid (or, if possible, partly invalid).

Peremptory norms can also produce other effects. A first effect is essentially meta-legal. As the ICTY Trial Chamber emphasized in *Furundžija* (with specific reference to the norm prohibiting torture), peremptory norms produce a 'deterrent effect' in that they signal to all States and individuals that their prohibition enshrines absolute values 'from which nobody must deviate' (at §§154–157).

Furthermore, *jus cogens* may have a bearing on *recognition of States*. The Arbitration Commission of the Peace Conference on Yugoslavia rightly stated in its *Opinion No. 10 (Federal Republic of Yugoslavia and Serbia Montenegro)*, that:

> while recognition is not a prerequisite for the foundation of a state and is purely declaratory in its impact, it is nonetheless a discretionary act that other states may perform when they choose and in a manner of their own choosing, subject only to compliance with the imperatives [*normes impératives du droit international général*, in the French authoritative text] of general international law, and particularly those prohibiting the use of force in dealings with other states or guaranteeing the rights of ethnic, religious or linguistic minorities.

It would follow, among other things, that whenever an entity with all the hallmarks of statehood emerges as a result of aggression, or is grounded on systematic denial of the rights of minorities or of human rights, other States are legally bound to withhold recognition. This is confirmed by ILC draft conclusion 19.2 which establishes that '[n]o State shall recognize as lawful a situation created by a serious breach by a State of an obligation arising under a peremptory norm of general international law (jus cogens)' and it adds 'nor render aid or assistance in maintaining that situation'.

Another effect of peremptory norms relates to the *entering of reservations* to multilateral treaties. Some members of the ICJ (Padilla Nervo, Tanaka, and Sørensen) had already noted in 1969, in their Separate or Dissenting Opinions in the *North Sea Continental Shelf* cases (respectively at 97, 182, and 248), that inconsistency with a peremptory norm makes a reservation inadmissible. In 1994 the UN Human Rights Committee took up this issue and stated cogently in its General Comment no. 24 of 1994, that:

> [r]eservations that offend peremptory norms would not be compatible with the object and purpose of the [UN] Covenant [on Civil and Political Rights]. Although treaties that are mere exchanges of obligations between States allow them to reserve *inter se* application of rules of general international law, it is otherwise in human rights treaties, which are for the benefit of persons within their jurisdiction. Accordingly, provisions in the Covenant that represent customary international law (and *a fortiori* when they have the character of peremptory norms) may not be the subject of reservations. (at §8)[15]

ILC draft conclusion 13 (inspired by the ILC Guide to Practice on Reservations to Treaties, Official Records of the General Assembly, Sixty-sixth Session, Supplement No. 10 (A/66/10/Add.1)) indicates that '[a] reservation to a treaty provision that reflects a peremptory norm of general international law (jus cogens) does not affect the binding nature of that norm, which shall continue to apply as such' and naturally that '[a] reservation cannot exclude or modify the legal effect of a treaty in a manner contrary to a peremptory norm of general international law (jus cogens)'. The draft conclusions, however, do not shed light on the positions of the States involved with regard to the treaty, nor do they specifically tackle the issue of human rights treaties. As stated in the Commentary, what matters appears to be 'that, whatever the validity of the reservation in question, a State cannot escape the binding nature of a peremptory norm of general international law (*jus cogens*) by formulating a reservation to a treaty provision reflecting that norm'.

Jus cogens may also have a bearing on the operation of specific treaties, for example *treaties of extradition*. As the *Institut de droit international* implied in a resolution adopted in 1983 (60 Annuaire Part II, 306), the possible violation of a peremptory norm, for instance those against torture or persecution on racial, religious, or ethnic grounds, would authorize a State not to comply with an extradition treaty under which it would otherwise be obliged to extradite an individual. The Swiss Supreme Court has taken a similar and much clearer position in some decisions regarding extradition treaties (e.g. the *Bufano* case) where the Court pronounced on the potential effects of the actual operation of the treaty in the specific case rather than the normative validity by excluding the legality of implementing treaty provisions that could lead to effects contrary to peremptory norms.

Other effects are even more controversial. It had been suggested that peremptory norms may impact on *State immunity from the jurisdiction of foreign States*, in that they may remove such immunity. Judge Wald, a member of a US Court of Appeals, convincingly argued in her Dissenting Opinion in *Princz* v *Federal Republic of Germany* that 'a State is never entitled to immunity from any act that contravenes a *jus cogens* norm, regardless of where or against whom that act was perpetrated' (at 618). Also, as the ICTY Trial Chamber held in *Furundžija* (at §§154–157), peremptory norms may produce legal effects *at the municipal law level*: they delegitimize any legislative or administrative act authorizing the prohibited conduct. Consequently, national measures (including national laws granting amnesty to the authors of the prohibited conduct) *may not be accorded international legal recognition* or at any rate are *not opposable* to other States. In addition, according to the ICTY:

> Proceedings could be initiated by potential victims [of conduct contrary to *jus cogens*] if they had *locus standi* before a competent international or national judicial body with a view to asking it to hold the national measure to be internationally unlawful; or the victim could bring a civil suit for

---

[15] The General Comment is online at http://hei.unige.ch/humanarts/gencomm/hrcomm24.htm.

damage in a foreign court, which would therefore be asked *inter alia* to disregard the legal value of the national authorizing act. (at §155)

A string of decisions in Italy, starting with the *Ferrini v Federal Republic of Germany* case (see **6.3.2**), had shown a similar understanding. However, the ICJ in *Jurisdictional Immunities of the State (Germany v Italy: Greece intervening)* clarified that rules on State immunity and *jus cogens* are bodies of law which operate on different levels; while the former are procedural in nature, the latter relate to the merits of a case. Therefore, according to the Court, immunity provisions always apply with priority (i.e. prior to moving to the merits); by applying these rules prior to any assessment of the merits, it would appear that *jus cogens* rules cannot be used to set aside State immunities.

It is interesting to note that the idea that the *jus cogens* nature of certain rules (and the ensuing hierarchy) may authorize judges (and other interpreters of the law) to logically derive consequences entailing the setting aside of any rule contrary to peremptory norms in specific cases, has been adopted also with regard to other situations. For example, Spanish courts have taken this position with regard to *amnesty laws*, which they have held not applicable as contrary to *jus cogens* (e.g. see *Scilingo*, Legal Ground 8, and *Pinochet*, Legal Ground 8). Argentinean courts (e.g. in *Simon Julio, Del Cerro Juan Antonio*, at 64–104) have taken the same position, as well as the Swiss government, with regard to genocide.[16]

Finally, according to various courts,[17] one of the consequences of the peremptory character bestowed upon the prohibition of certain acts may be the granting to State courts of *universal criminal jurisdiction* over the alleged authors of those acts.

11.4.5 THE LIMITED RELIANCE ON *JUS COGENS* IN INTERNATIONAL DEALINGS

As pointed out earlier, strikingly, although the concept of *jus cogens* has been in existence in the world community for a number of decades, so far it has not been used to invalidate treaty provisions. However, it has been invoked on a number of occasions to make arguments in favour of a hierarchical articulation of international provisions and to promote the pursuance of some of the fundamental goals of international law. The ILC has taken up the topic and will hopefully contribute to the debate, particularly if States react positively to the Commission's suggestion and provide contributions to the further development of the system. On the other hand, the ICJ has carefully avoided pronouncing on the matter or has used rather elusive language.[18] As recently noted by Judge Robinson, in his Separate

---

[16] See *Message relatif à la Convention pour la prévention et la répression du génocide, et révision correspondante du droit pénal*, sent to Parliament on 31 March 1999, 4916.

[17] See the ICTY Trial Chamber in *Furundžija* (§156), a Belgian investigating judge in *Pinochet* (at 288), Judge Wald's Dissenting Opinion in *Princz v Federal Republic of Germany* (at 618), the Italian Court of Cassation in *Ferrini v Federal Republic of Germany* (at §9 with regard to *civil* litigation), as well as at least one judge of the House of Lords, namely Lord Millet, in *Pinochet*.

[18] E.g. in its order of 15 December 1979 in *United States Diplomatic and Consular Staff in Tehran (United States of America v Iran) (Provisional Measures)*, the Court stated that 'while no State is under any obligation to maintain diplomatic or consular relations with another, yet it cannot fail to recognize the imperative obligations inherent therein, now codified in the Vienna Conventions of 1961 and 1963, to which both Iran and the United States are parties' (at §41). In the Advisory Opinion on *Legality of the Threat or Use of Nuclear Weapons*, the Court stated that the fundamental rules of humanitarian law applicable in armed conflict 'are to be observed by all States whether or not they have ratified the conventions that contain them because they constitute intransgressible principles of international customary law' (at §79). However, President Bedjaoui, in his Declaration, said that those rules 'form part of *jus cogens*' (ibid., at 273, para. 21). In 1986, in *Nicaragua (Nicaragua v United States of America)* the Court mentioned that both Nicaragua and the US, respectively in their Memorial and Counter-Memorial, had asserted that the prohibition of the use of force had come to be recognized as *jus cogens*. After mentioning these concordant views, the Court refrained however from setting forth its own view on the matter (at §§190–191).

Opinion in *Legal Consequences of the Separation of the Chagos Archipelago from Mauritius in 1965*, 'the most striking feature of the Court's case law is the apparent reluctance that it reveals on the part of the Court to engage fully with the subject of *jus cogens*, at times only finding its application in an indirect and oblique manner, and at other times, not pronouncing on the application of the norm. Consequently, the keen observer may conclude that, despite finding the application of *jus cogens* several times in its work, the Court's embrace of the concept is somewhat hesitant' (at §82).

All this can be easily explained. As emphasized earlier, peremptory rules primarily pursue a *deterrent effect*. Jimenez de Aréchaga perceptively underlined this unique feature. After noting that a set of values of vital importance has emerged in the international community (peace, respect for human rights, etc.), he pointed out that it was not considered sufficient to attach special consequences to their violation (on aggravated responsibility, see **12.8**). It also was felt

> necessary to lay down in anticipation the preventive sanction of absolute nullity in respect of one of the preparatory acts, namely the conclusion of a treaty by which two or more States contemplate the execution of acts constituting a violation of those basic principles. The function of *jus cogens* is thus to protect States from contractual arrangements concluded in defiance of some general interests and values of the international community as a whole. (159 RCADI (1978-I), at 65)

Furthermore, at present, States still hesitate to raise crucial issues of alleged deviance from the basic values accepted in the world community, the more so because to do so often presupposes a general interest in invoking a peremptory norm. In other words, States still incline to act out of self-interest, within a 'bilateralist' or 'private' paradigm; they are therefore prepared to contest the inconsistency of a treaty with *jus cogens* only to the extent that this serves to promote their own interests. In short, the furtherance of 'public' interests still remains in the background, in the present international community.

On the other hand, one should not underrate the role peremptory norms may play in guiding and channelling the conduct of States. The existence of a core of fundamental values enshrined in peremptory norms may serve, and indeed is serving, to bar States from behaving in a certain manner and at the same time to induce them to fashion their conduct consistently with those values. In other words, *jus cogens* is already working as a host of 'world public order' standards, sometimes dissuading States from performing certain acts, and at other times impelling them to behave in a certain manner. This *preventive* role may—to some extent—account for the lack of invocation of *jus cogens* in disputes between States.

Be that as it may, the fact remains that, undeniably, at least at the level of State-to-State relations, hitherto peremptory norms have largely remained *a potentiality*.

PART IV

IMPLEMENTATION OF INTERNATIONAL LAW

12

INTERNATIONAL STATE RESPONSIBILITY FOR WRONGFUL ACTS

12.1 INTRODUCTION

The international legal system is at such an embryonic stage that the archaic concept of collective responsibility still prevails (see **1.4**). The reason is that international law mainly aims at regulating the behaviour of States, which are thus the primary subjects of this body of law and the main bearers of international obligations. Being corporate structures, States can act only through individuals. As a rule of thumb, therefore, the individual State agent who materially infringes a rule of international law does not bear responsibility at the international level. It is the State on behalf of which he or she has acted that incurs international responsibility, and it is the State that has to take all the required remedial measures. These measures might include the punishment of the individual State agent who has materially carried out the unlawful conduct, as a form of 'satisfaction' (see **12.7.1**). However, in this scenario the responsibility of the individual would be a consequence of the international responsibility of the State and not a form of the international responsibility of the individual as such.

The principles and rules regulating the international responsibility of States for violations of international law have gradually grown over the years. They have also been the subject of the groundbreaking work of codification by the UN's International Law Commission (ILC), which has greatly contributed to the development of this key field of international law. As we shall see, the ILC's codification on State responsibility also addresses the question of the international responsibility of non-State armed actors but is limited to the conduct of insurrectional movements that eventually become the government of a new State (see **12.4.1**). The rise of non-State armed actors during the second half of the twentieth century and the first decades of the twenty-first, their increased involvement in armed conflicts, and their impact on global policy accentuate the need to address comprehensively the question of their international responsibility. The principles and rules on State responsibility could be in part transposable to these actors. Any transposition however should be approached with caution for a variety of reasons, above all the lack of legitimacy of non-State armed groups in international law and the traditional hostile position of States in granting them international legal status.[1]

---

[1] See further J. Kleffner, 'The Collective Accountability of Organized Armed Groups for System Crimes' in A. Nollkaemper and H. van der Wilt (eds), *System Criminality in International Law* (Cambridge: Cambridge University Press, 2009), 238.

Be that as it may, the international principles and rules on State responsibility are generally considered as the frame of reference for the international responsibility of other subjects of international law, in particular international organizations. The ILC's codification on State responsibility has therefore constituted the basis for the codification of the law on the international responsibility of these important players on the international stage (see **7.7**). At the same time, the notion of individual criminal responsibility for some types of serious violation of international law has gradually taken shape, particularly in the aftermath of the Second World War, and has enormously expanded in recent decades. Individuals, be they State officials, members of non-State armed groups, or private persons, can now incur criminal responsibility under international law for international crimes (war crimes, crimes against humanity, genocide, terrorism, etc., see **Chapter 19**).

Considering its pivotal role in the system of international responsibility, what follows will focus exclusively on the law of State responsibility for wrongful acts, emphasizing the main developments that have materialized in this field. Readers can refer to the aforementioned chapters of this volume for more specific discussion on the international responsibility of international organizations and the international criminal responsibility of individuals.

12.2 THE CODIFICATION OF THE LAW OF STATE RESPONSIBILITY

The first attempt at codification of the international rules on State responsibility can be traced back to the period 1924–30.[2] A committee of jurists appointed by the League Council concluded that one of the seven topics ripe for codification was 'Responsibility of States for Damages Done in their Territory to the Person or Property of Foreigners'. However, a Codification Conference held at The Hague in 1930 showed that there was disagreement on the matter, among other things on the issue of responsibility for the treatment of aliens (some States proposing that aliens should be granted the 'national treatment', that is, equated with the nationals of the host State, others—principally Western countries—suggesting that they should instead be treated according to the 'minimum standard' principle, that is, they must be afforded the possibly higher protection deriving from the set of international rules making up the so-called 'minimum standards of civilization').

This attempt shows that the customary rules on State responsibility were at the time normally lumped together with the substantive rules governing State behaviour, chiefly with the customary rules concerning the treatment of foreigners. This was because in essence the customary rules on State responsibility crystallized as a result of disputes concerning the treatment, chiefly by non-industrialized countries (e.g. Latin American countries), of nationals of industrialized States. Hence a tendency evolved to associate rules on State responsibility with breaches of those international rules which imposed on States the obligation to respect the rights of foreign nationals and their property.

In addition, the rules on State responsibility were rudimentary. In particular, it was not clear whether State responsibility could arise only if State officials of the allegedly delinquent State had acted wilfully and maliciously or negligently (*culpable negligence*) or if instead the simple fact that one or more of a State's officials had breached a rule of international law was sufficient, without there being any *intent* or *fault*. As for the consequences of the wrongful act, it was clear only that there was an obligation to make reparation. However, it was not specified whether one form of reparation was to be preferred to another and, if

---

[2] State responsibility is an area of international law that has also been the subject of a number of 'private' codification efforts. See in this regard L. Laithier, 'Private Codification Efforts' in J. Crawford, A. Pellet, S. Olleson, and K. Parlett (eds), *The Law of International Responsibility* (Oxford: Oxford University Press, 2010), 53.

so, subject to what conditions. It was generically provided that reparation could take the form of restitution in kind (re-establishment of the situation as it existed before the wrongful act); compensation (payment of a sum of money); or satisfaction (apology, expression of regret, salute to the flag, etc.). As a rule of thumb, it was held that satisfaction should be the consequence of a breach of international rules protecting the honour or dignity of a State. However, all these classes of reparation were resorted to in State practice as possible instances of reparation, not as legal categories to which recourse should be made under certain circumstances and not under others. The choice of each class was left to the parties concerned. Furthermore, it was left to the injured State to decide whether and at what stage to resort to enforcement measures, as well as what measures to take. Moreover, State responsibility amounted to a *bilateral relation* between the delinquent State and the injured State. It was for them to agree (or, depending on the case, disagree) on the form of reparation; it was for the injured State alone to choose—subject to a few requirements including proportionality—the form of self-help, if it decided to enforce its rights. Only if the parties entered into negotiations and reached agreement could they establish a dispute settlement mechanism.

In 1948, the UN General Assembly selected State responsibility amongst the first topics assigned to the newly established ILC. The process leading, after almost five decades, to the accomplishment of one of the most successful works of codification of the ILC was thus put in motion.

The work of the ILC on the topic formally began in 1956 under Special Rapporteur F. V. García Amador (Cuba). His reports focused mainly on State responsibility for injuries to aliens and their property, but also discussed some general issues. There was, however, disagreement within the ILC as to the way forward and therefore, also because of other commitments, the ILC postponed any detailed discussion of García Amador's reports. In the meantime, the idea that the codification on State responsibility had to be disentangled from the substantive rules on the treatment of aliens gained support. In 1963, the ILC formally approved this approach and decided to deal only with the general rules on State responsibility, applicable in case of violations of rules of international law irrespective of their content. The ILC appointed Roberto Ago (Italy) as Special Rapporteur. The reports prepared by Ago, his predecessor, and the subsequent Special Rapporteurs (W. Riphagen, G. Arangio-Ruiz, and J. Crawford); the debates in the Commission; and the reaction of States, expressed both individually and in discussions in the UN General Assembly, have gradually led to the adoption, in 2001, of the 'Draft Articles on Responsibility of States for Internationally wrongful Acts' (the 'ILC's Articles on State Responsibility' or 'the ILC Articles'). The ILC Articles to a large extent reflect existing law, while in some respects progressively developing that law. These rules are applicable by default, that is, they apply unless excluded in individual treaties or otherwise (Article 55, ILC Articles).

One of the main merits of the ILC Articles is the unfastening of the law on State responsibility from the set of substantive rules on the treatment of foreigners, with which—as already noted—it had been previously bound up. Roberto Ago must chiefly be credited for this major clarification of the matter. The ILC Articles have also clarified and given precision to a number of previously controversial rules: for instance, the question of whether fault is a necessary legal element of an internationally wrongful act, the nature of the damage required for a State to be considered 'injured' by the wrongful act of another State, the circumstances precluding wrongfulness, etc. A further major achievement of the ILC Articles is the acknowledgement that there is a set of rules protecting fundamental values for the international community, the violation of which gives rise, under specific circumstances, to additional legal consequences. Finally, the ILC Articles clarify the relationship between the obligation of the responsible State to provide reparation to the injured State and the right of the latter to resort to countermeasures as a means to ensure cessation of the wrongful act and reparation by the responsible State. The nature, functions, and limits of countermeasures have also been clarified and developed (see **14.2**).

The ILC Articles have not (yet) been adopted in a binding treaty. In 2001, the UN General Assembly 'took note' of the Articles and 'commended' them to the attention of governments 'without prejudice to the question of their future adoption or other appropriate action' (resolution 56/83). By so doing, the General Assembly followed the recommendation of the ILC itself which, after discussing the question of the future status of the Articles, resolved to recommend that the General Assembly take note of them and postpone the decision on their possible adoption in a binding treaty to a later stage. Since then, the matter has remained on the agenda of the UN General Assembly, which in a string of resolutions has reiterated its commendation of the ILC Articles to governments; requested the Secretary-General to prepare and update the compilation of decisions of international courts, tribunals, and other bodies referring to the Articles; and created a Working Group of the Sixth Committee with the task of further examining the question of a convention on responsibility for internationally wrongful acts or other appropriate action. The Sixth Committee has discussed the question of the future status of the Articles at various meetings, but has been unable so far to reach a decision. Although some delegations have pressed for a diplomatic conference to consider the Articles, others have preferred to maintain their status as an ILC text commended to States by the General Assembly. The matter is therefore still pending.[3]

The ILC Articles, though not contained in a binding treaty, are nonetheless generally considered to reflect customary international law and have been widely applied or referred to by international courts and tribunals, including by the International Court of Justice.

12.3 PRELIMINARY NOTIONS

At the outset, a definition of State responsibility may prove useful. This notion designates the legal consequences stemming from the commission by a State of an internationally wrongful act. The international rules on State responsibility must therefore be distinguished from the international liability resulting from activities not prohibited by international law, usually hazardous activities (e.g. industrial, mining, energy production, or transport activities).[4] In the present state of international law, such liability is imposed on economic operators rather than on States (except when these act as economic operators) (see **20.5.4**). For over two decades, the ILC considered the topic of *International Liability for Injurious Consequences Arising from Acts Not Prohibited by International Law*. In 1997 it decided to split it into two parts, namely prevention of transboundary damage from hazardous activities and international liability for loss from transboundary harm arising out of hazardous activities. The work in these two strands was completed in 2001 and 2006 respectively, with the adoption of a set of Draft Articles and a set of Draft Principles[5] which have been commended to the attention of governments by a string of resolutions of the UN General Assembly.[6] Yet, whereas the Draft Articles on Prevention concern the characterization of

---

[3] See F. Paddeu, 'To Convene or Not Convene? The Future Status of the Articles on State Responsibility: Recent Developments' (2018) 21 *Max Planck Yearbook of United Nations Law Online* 83.

[4] See P.-M. Dupuy and J. E. Viñuales, *International Environmental Law*, 2nd edn (Cambridge: Cambridge University Press, 2018), chapter 8.

[5] See the ILC Draft Articles on Prevention of Transboundary Harm from Hazardous Activities (adopted in 1998) and the Draft Principles on the Allocation of Loss in the Case of Transboundary Harm Arising out of Hazardous Activities (adopted in 2006).

[6] See e.g. UN GA resolution 62/68 'Consideration of Prevention of Transboundary Harm from Hazardous Activities and Allocation of Loss in the Case of Such Harm', 6 December 2007.

the prevention principle as a primary norm, the Draft Principles focus on the liability of economic operators rather than States. Thus, the initial attempt at developing a 'strict' or 'objective' liability regime for States was lost in translation.

The international rules on State responsibility are considered to be 'secondary rules', that is, rules establishing (i) on what conditions a breach of a rule of international law may be held to have occurred, (ii) the legal consequences of this breach, and (iii) the processes through which responsibility may be invoked. Secondary rules must be distinguished from rules prescribing the observance of a certain conduct by States, so-called 'primary rules' of international law. The body of primary rules is vast and diverse. Most chapters of this book focus on primary rules in areas from the law of the sea, to investment or trade, to human rights or international humanitarian law, to principles.

Finally, two different forms of State responsibility may be distinguished. The first concerns the 'ordinary' form of responsibility, embracing the legal consequences of violations of international rules laying down 'synallagmatic' obligations protecting reciprocal interests of States (economic and commercial relations, the reciprocal treatment of nationals and of consuls or diplomats, etc.). These rules are by far the most numerous and traditional rules of international law. Even in the case of rules addressing a given number of States (e.g. rules contained in a multilateral treaty or having a customary nature), the breach of any such rule creates a 'bilateral relation' between the responsible and the wronged State. Hence the whole relation remains a 'private' or 'horizontal' matter between the two States. The second form of State responsibility can be described as 'aggravated' State responsibility, since it relates to the legal consequences of violations of rules laying down 'community obligations' (see **1.8.2**). The specific content of State responsibility for violations of any of such obligations is still debated. The ILC Articles have taken in this respect a cautious and minimalistic approach, which arguably does not fully conform with the most progressive international practice in the field (see **12.8.1**).

We shall now examine the ordinary form of State responsibility, and then move to analyse the distinguishing traits of the aggravated form with respect to the former.

12.4 THE INTERNATIONALLY WRONGFUL ACT

The basic precondition for State responsibility to arise is the commission of an internationally wrongful act by a State. Conversely, every internationally wrongful act of a State entails its international responsibility (Article 1, ILC Articles). For an internationally wrongful act to occur, there must be: conduct (an act or an omission) of persons or entities that is attributable to a State (see **12.4.1**), and this conduct must be contrary to an international obligation incumbent upon the relevant State (Article 2, ILC Articles) (see **12.4.2**).

12.4.1 ATTRIBUTION OF CONDUCT TO A STATE

In the ILC Articles, the rules of attribution of conduct of persons or entities to a State are set forth in Articles 4 to 11. These rules enshrine normative criteria under international law whereby the conduct of persons or entities is attributed to a State for the purpose of its international responsibility. Let us examine them in turn.

(1) *Conduct of State organs*: in the first place, the conduct of any State organ is attributed to the State, whatever position the organ holds in the organization of that State, and regardless of its functions (including legislative and judicial authorities) or its character (central government or territorial unit, for example, the component State of a federal State such as

the US). This rule is enshrined in Article 4 of the ILC Articles and can be considered a well-established rule of international law (see e.g. the Advisory Opinion of the International Court of Justice (ICJ) in *Difference Relating to Immunity from Legal Process of a Special Rapporteur of the Commission on Human Rights* (at 87, §62)).[7]

Any conduct performed by a State organ in that capacity shall be considered an act of that State under international law, even in case of acts *ultra vires*, namely acts performed by the State organ exceeding its authority or contravening instructions (Article 7, ILC Articles).[8] Whether an organ acts in its capacity usually requires examining whether it uses the means and powers pertaining to its status. For instance, in *Francisco Mallén (United Mexican States) v United States of America*, a Mexican consul had been violently attacked and beaten twice by an American police officer, who evidently had a profound aversion to the consul. As for the first attack, with respect to which Mexico did not allege the 'direct responsibility' of the US, but a denial of justice, the Mexico–US General Claims Commission found that the evidence indicated 'a malevolent and unlawful act of a private individual who happened to be an official'. On the second attack, the American policeman, 'showing his badge to assert his official capacity', struck Mallén with among other things his revolver, and then took him at gunpoint to the El Paso county jail. The policeman was brought to trial and contended in court that he had arrested Mallén because of his illegally carrying a gun, a contention that according to the Mexico–US General Claims Commission had no merit. The police officer was sentenced by a US court in Texas to pay a small fine, which he never paid. The Commission held that there was no doubt as to 'the liability on the part of American authorities for this second assault on Mallén by an American official' and stressed that he 'could not have taken Mallén to jail if he had not been acting as a police officer' (at 174–5, 177).[9]

---

[7] For cases where the US and other federal States were held responsible for acts of member States, see *Davy* (at 468), brought before a UK–Venezuela Mixed Claims Commission; *Pellat* (where a France–Mexico Claims Commission held in 1929 that 'a federal State is considered responsible for acts of member States causing damage to citizens of other States, even when the Constitution denies to the central government the right to supervise the action of the member States or the right to demand that they conform their conduct to the prescriptions of international law', at 536); and *Galvan* (at 274: the US was held responsible for the action of the authorities of the state of Texas against a Mexican national).

[8] In *Caire* an officer and two soldiers of the forces in control of Mexico had asked Mr Caire, a French national, to give them US$5,000 in gold, under threat of death; as he refused to comply, stating that he did not possess that amount of money, they detained him for some time and then had him shot. Verzjil, the President of the France–Mexico Claims Commission, held Mexico responsible for the act. He stated that States bear international responsibility for all acts committed by their officials or organs which are contrary to international law, regardless of whether the official or organ has acted within the limits of its competency or has exceeded those limits. However, in order to justify the admission of this 'objective responsibility' of the State for acts committed by its officials or organs outside their competence, it is necessary that 'they should have acted, at least apparently, as competent officials or organs, or that, in acting, they should have used powers or measures proper to their official character' (at 530).

[9] Another relevant case is *Youmans*. Some American nationals, following a labour dispute, were threatened by a mob of Mexican nationals. At the request of the mayor of the town, Mexican troops were sent to quell the riot and put an end to the attack on the Americans. However, the troops, on arriving at the scene of the riot, instead of dispersing the mob opened fire on the house where the Americans had withdrawn. As a result, two Americans were killed by the troops and members of the mob. No one appeared to have been punished for the crime, although some prosecutions were begun and some mobsters were sentenced in absentia, but then the sentences were modified. In 1926 the Mexico–US General Claims Commission found Mexico responsible, stating the following: '[W]e do not consider that the participation of the soldiers in the murder [of one of the Americans] can be regarded as acts of soldiers committed in their private capacity when it is clear that at the time of the commission of these acts the men were on duty under the immediate supervision and in the presence of a commanding officer. Soldiers inflicting personal injuries or committing wanton destruction or looting always act in disobedience of some rules laid down by superior authority. There could be no liability whatever for such misdeeds if the view were taken that any acts committed by soldiers in contravention of instructions must always be considered as personal acts' (at 116).

The question arises of identifying which persons and entities are State organs for the purpose of the international rules of attribution. In this respect, one should refer first of all to the municipal law of the State. Thus, if a person or an entity is a State organ under the law of that State (namely, he or she is *de jure* an organ), that person or entity will also be considered a State organ for the rules of attribution. This principle is codified in Article 4(2) of the ILC Articles. There may be however persons or entities who do not qualify as State organs under the relevant domestic law but that can be assimilated to a State organ for the particular function they perform within the structure of the State. These individuals or entities might therefore qualify as de facto State organs according to international law, and by consequence their conduct is attributable to the State. Article 4(2) recognizes this possibility implicitly. It establishes that a State organ 'includes' persons or entities having this status under the municipal law of the State, implicitly recognizing that persons and entities other than *de jure* organs under the municipal law can be considered as State organs under international law.

In the judgment on the merits of the *Genocide (Bosnia and Herzegovina v Yugoslavia (Serbia and Montenegro))* case, the ICJ clearly took this stand when considering whether the military and paramilitary groups in Bosnia-Herzegovina fighting against the central government could be considered as de facto organs of Serbia-Montenegro under Article 4 of the ILC Articles. In reaching a negative conclusion, the ICJ resorted to a high demanding test, the so-called 'complete dependence test' whereby the requirement for persons or entities to be considered as de facto organs of a State is that they depend completely on the State (at §§386–394, esp. at §392).

The ICJ has not clarified the basis upon which it relied in applying this demanding test, which would require evidence that persons or entities are under the complete control of the State and that the State actually exerts control 'in all fields' of activity of the group of people and entities. However, this test had been already applied by the ICJ in the *Nicaragua (Nicaragua v United States of America)* case (although without expressly using the term 'complete dependence'). In that case, the ICJ examined *inter alia* whether the anti-Sandinista armed group in Nicaragua (the *contras*) could be equated for legal purposes with an organ of the United States government and reached a negative conclusion. This is because it was not satisfied on the basis of the evidence that the United States had created the *contras* nor that it provided direct and critical combat support to all their military operations. In addition, the Court found that the US government was supporting the military and paramilitary activities of the *contras* in Nicaragua, but considered this assistance insufficient to demonstrate the complete dependence of the *contras* on the United States. The Court thus rejected the claim of the government of Nicaragua attributing responsibility to the United States for *all* the activities of the *contras*, which Nicaragua regarded as 'essentially the acts of the United States' (at §§104–114).

Similarly, in the *Armed Activities on the Territory of the Congo (Democratic Republic of the Congo v Uganda)* case, the ICJ did not find sufficient evidence to establish that the Movement for the Liberation of Congo (MLN), backed by the government of Uganda through training and military support, was created by the latter or that Uganda could control the manner in which the MLC put this assistance to use. Consequently, the Court concluded that there was no credible evidence to suggest that the conduct of the MLC was that of an organ of Uganda under Article 4 of the ILC Articles (at §160).

(2) *Conduct of persons or entities exercising elements of governmental authority*: there may be cases where a State is responsible at the international level for the conduct of persons or entities which are not organs (*de jure* or de facto) of that State, but which exercise elements of governmental authority for that State. This might happen on the basis of the law of the State. The conduct of these persons or entities is attributed to the State, to the extent that

they act in that capacity (Article 5, ILC Articles) and also if they exceed their authority or contravene instructions (Article 7, ILC Articles). This rule of attribution takes into account the conduct of so-called 'parastatal entities' or former State corporations that, after privatization, retain some public or regulatory functions (e.g. State-owned or private airlines having certain powers in regard to immigration control). The rule clearly requires determining what is meant by 'governmental authority', which in turn may depend on a particular society, its history and traditions, as the ILC noted in its commentary to Article 5.

Another scenario is when an organ of one State is put at the disposal of another State to carry out specific governmental tasks or functions for the latter State. Article 6 of the ILC Articles provides that the conduct of the organ of the former State is attributed to the State at whose disposal it is placed if the organ is acting in 'the exercise of elements of the governmental authority' of this State. Examples in the ILC commentary include a section of the health service of a State placed under the orders of another State to assist in overcoming an epidemic or natural disaster. The rule excludes situations where the organ of a State is sent to another State but retains its own autonomy and status (e.g. cultural missions, diplomatic or consular missions, and foreign relief or aid organizations). It also excludes the case where the organ of one State acts on the joint instructions of its own and another State, since this would trigger attribution to both States.

The rules of attribution also cover the situation where persons or groups are 'in fact exercising elements of the governmental authority in the absence or default of the official authorities and in circumstances such as to call for the exercise of those elements' (Article 9). In this situation, which is exceptional and arises rarely in practice, the conduct of these persons or groups is attributed to the State. The commentary of the ILC mentions situations occurring during revolution, armed conflict, or foreign occupation, where the authorities of the State have been suppressed or are disintegrating or are being inoperative. An example expressly quoted is that of the so-called *levée en masse*, concerning the case of the inhabitants of a territory during a military invasion, who spontaneously take up arms to resist the invading troops without having had time to organize themselves into regular armed forces (see **17.3.1**).

(3) *Conduct of private persons or group of persons*: generally, the conduct of private persons or groups of persons is not considered attributable to a State under international law. As a consequence, States are not responsible for violations of international law committed by private persons or groups, unless they violate their own *due diligence* obligations under international law. In this latter scenario, however, States incur responsibility for their own conduct, which usually consists in the failure by the State organs (or other competent authorities) to take all necessary measures in preventing the wrongful conduct by the private persons or groups or in punishing them. For instance, in the case of injury inflicted by private persons against foreign diplomats, nationals, or installations, the State is not responsible for the acts of those private persons (commission), but might incur responsibility for the acts of its organs if they failed to exercise due diligence in preventing the injury or in punishing wrongdoers (conduct by omission).

The *US Diplomatic and Consular Staff in Tehran* case, decided in 1980 by the ICJ, is illuminating. The Court divided the Iranian militants' attack on the US embassy and consular premises in Tehran into two phases. In the first stage, the attack was carried out by militants who had no 'form of official status as recognized "agents" or organs of the Iranian State' (at §58). Therefore, according to the Court, the militants' conduct in mounting the attack, storming the embassy, and seizing the inmates as hostages could not be 'imputable to the State on that basis'. Nevertheless, Iran was held responsible in that it failed to protect the US premises as required by international law (at §§59–68). The second phase started after completion of the occupation of the US embassy. At this stage, the Iranian government was legally bound to bring to an end the unlawful occupation and pay reparation. Instead, it approved and endorsed the occupation and even issued, on 17 November 1979, a decree stating that the US personnel 'did not enjoy international diplomatic respect'. As a result, in the view of the Court, the 'occupants' 'had now become agents of the Iranian State for whose acts the State itself was internationally responsible' (at §74). The Special Rapporteur J. Crawford pointed out in his First Report on State Responsibility (1998) that that acknowledgement and approval by a State of conduct 'as its own' may have retroactive effect (A/CN.4/490/Add.5, §§283–284). Article 11 of the ILC Articles upholds his suggestion and provides that conduct which is not attributable to a State under any other rule of attribution enshrined in the Articles 'shall nevertheless be considered an act of that State under international law if and to the extent that the State acknowledges and adopts the conduct in question as its own'.

The situation is different when private persons or groups carry out conduct on behalf of a State, without meeting the requirements for being equated to organs of the State. In this hypothesis, the conduct is considered as an act of the State if the person or group of persons is 'in fact acting on the instructions of, or under the direction or control of, that State *in carrying out the conduct*' (Article 8, ILC Articles). This rule of attribution reflects another test adopted by the ICJ in the aforementioned *Nicaragua* case to establish whether, in the civil war in Nicaragua, the breaches of international humanitarian law perpetrated by the *contras* were to be attributed to the US. As clarified earlier, the Court excluded the possibility that the *contras* could be considered as completely dependent on the US, and therefore excluded on that basis that their activities could be considered as the activities of the US. The Court however further examined whether these activities could be attributed to the US because they were carried out under 'the effective control' of that State or under its 'specific instructions', and concluded in the negative. By contrast, the Court considered that the acts of some Latin American operatives (so-called UCLA, or Unilaterally Controlled Latino Assets) had to be attributed to the US either because, in addition to being paid by that government, they had been given specific instructions by US agents or officials and had acted under their supervision, or because 'agents of the US' had 'participated in the planning, direction, support and execution' of such specific operations by the UCLA as attacks on oil and storage facilities, or the blowing up of underwater oil pipelines in Nicaraguan ports (at §§75–86, 93–115).

In *Tadić (Appeal)* the ICTY Appeals Chamber partially departed from the tests propounded by the ICJ in *Nicaragua* and subsequently adopted by the ILC in Article 8 of the Articles. The ICTY had to establish whether some individuals (Bosnian Serbs) fighting what prima facie appeared to be civil war (between Bosnian Serbs and the central authorities in Bosnia and Herzegovina) had in fact acted on behalf of a foreign country (the Federal Republic of Yugoslavia (Serbia and Montenegro)), thus turning the civil conflict into an international armed conflict. The ICTY held that international law provides for three alternative tests to establish whether acts by private individuals can be attributed to a State as de facto State organ. First, whether single individuals or militarily unorganized groups act under specific instructions of a State (or subsequent public approval). Secondly, in the case of armed groups or militarily organized groups, whether they are under the *overall control* of a State (without this State necessarily issuing instructions concerning each specific action). Thirdly, whether individuals actually behave as State officials within the structure of a State (at §§98–145). The first and third tests do not differ in substance from the tests already propounded by the ICJ. By contrast, the second test (the overall control test) constitutes a radical departure from the effective control test applied by the ICJ in *Nicaragua* and allowed the ICTY to conclude, in the case at stake, that the armed conflict in Bosnia and Herzegovina was not actually an international armed conflict.

Judge Shahabuddeen, in his Separate Opinion (at §§17–18), took a critical view of the majority's decision, stressing that the context of the two decisions (by the ICJ in *Nicaragua* and the ICTY in *Tadić*) was different, the former dealing with State responsibility, the latter with individual criminal responsibility. J. Crawford adhered to this view in his Commentary to the ILC Articles on State Responsibility (see §5 of his Comment on Article 8). In the *Genocide (Bosnia and Herzegovina v Yugoslavia (Serbia and Montenegro))* case, the ICJ also noted that the overall control test applied by the ICTY in *Tadić* could be relevant for classifying an armed conflict, but is not applicable in the framework of State responsibility.[10] This is because 'logic does not require the same test to be adopted in resolving the two issues, which are very different in nature' (at §405). It can be noted, with respect, that the basic question at issue was the same in both cases: to establish the conditions under which a private person may be held to be acting on behalf of another State (see the decision in *Tadić (Appeal)*, at §104). The real problem, it is submitted, is whether or not the appraisal of customary international law made by the ICTY is more persuasive than that made by the ICJ.[11]

In practice the effective control test set forth by the ICJ (and accepted by the ILC) makes it very difficult to prove that a State is responsible for acts performed by non-State armed groups backed by that State. Indeed, it becomes necessary to prove that every single action contrary to international law has been the subject of specific instructions by the State or under its effective control. Instead, under the overall control test propounded by the ICTY (and which this Tribunal held to be more in keeping with international customary law than the one suggested by the ICJ), whenever an individual is a member of a military unit or of a militarily organized group, it is sufficient to prove that a State exercises overall control over that unit or group, for such a State to incur international responsibility for unlawful acts performed by members of that unit or group. Thus, the test involves a significant broadening of State responsibility in the context of armed conflict and other violent situations.

(4) *Conduct of insurrectional or other movements*: Article 10 of the ILC Articles regulates two exceptional scenarios, namely that of an insurrectional movement which becomes the new government of a State and that of a movement, insurrectional or otherwise, which establishes a new State on the territory of a pre-existing State or on a territory under its administration. In both cases, Article 10 provides that the conduct of the movement is attributed to the State for the purpose of State responsibility. The assumption is that there is continuity between the movement and the State. Importantly, Article 10 covers exclusively the attribution of conduct of a *successful* insurrectional movement for the purpose of the international responsibility of a State (pre-existing State with a new government or new State) towards another State. The conduct of the movement that is *defeated* is not attributable to the State, and the latter will not therefore bear international responsibility for breaches of international law committed by the insurrectional movement during the uprising vis-à-vis other States.[12] The insurrectional movement might be directly responsible for those breaches, particularly where it has gained control over part of the territory of a

---

[10] Interestingly, the overall control test has been also applied for the classification of armed conflicts by the International Criminal Court (ICC). See e.g. *Lubanga Dyilo*, §541; *Katanga*, §1178; *Bemba Gombo*, §130. The ICC has however refrained from clarifying whether it considers this test to be applicable based on the rules of attribution in the framework of State responsibility or on other relevant rules.

[11] The criticism raised by A. Cassese on the position adopted by the ICJ in the *Genocide* case is further developed in 'The Nicaragua and Tadić Tests Revisited in Light of the ICJ Judgment on Genocide in Bosnia' (2007) 18 *EJIL* 649.

[12] See e.g. the 1920 arbitration between the US and the UK in *Home Frontier and Foreign Missionary Society of the United Brethren in Christ*, where the Tribunal held (at 44): 'It is a well-established principle of international law that no government can be held responsible for the act of rebellious bodies of men committed in violation of its authority, where it is itself guilty of no breach of good faith, or of no negligence in suppressing the insurrection.' See also Commentary Article 10 of the ILC Articles, §2.

12.4.2 INCONSISTENCY OF STATE CONDUCT WITH AN INTERNATIONAL OBLIGATION

The conduct of a State is inconsistent with an international obligation when it is contrary to an obligation stemming for that State from an applicable rule or principle of international law, whatever the nature of the obligation breached (that is, whether it is imposed by a customary rule, a treaty provision, a binding decision of an international organization, etc.) (Article 12, ILC Articles). The wrongful conduct may consist either of an action or of the failure to take a prescribed action.

Plainly, for State responsibility to arise, it is necessary that the obligation was in force when it was breached. This rule is enshrined in Article 13 of the ILC Articles and reflects the so-called principle of *tempus commissi delicti*. With respect to the law of treaties, a parallel rule is contained in Article 28 of the Vienna Convention of the Law of Treaties, providing that unless a different intention appears from the treaty or is otherwise established, treaty provisions 'do not bind a party in relation to any act or fact which took place or any situation which ceased to exist before the date of the entry into force of the treaty with respect to that party'.

Furthermore, one shall distinguish between so-called *instantaneous* violations and *continuing* violations. The former occur when the material act of the State ends as soon as it is committed. In this case, the breach of an international obligation occurs at the moment when the act is performed, even if its effects continue (Article 14(1), ILC Articles), as is the case, for instance, of the killing of a foreign diplomat by a State organ. By contrast, continuing violations occur with respect to an act having a continuing character, for instance the unlawful annexation of foreign territory, in which case the violation extends in time during the entire period during which the continuing act in question continues in breach of the relevant international obligation of the State (Article 14(2), ILC Articles).

The distinction between these two types of violations is crucial, among other things, to determine whether an international court or tribunal has temporal jurisdiction over a particular dispute: if an act began before the jurisdiction of the international court or tribunal was accepted, but continued after the acceptance of jurisdiction by the relevant State, then the court or tribunal has temporal jurisdiction over the dispute. In this regard, one can mention the case law of the Inter-American Court of Human Rights. In a string of cases, the Court has applied the doctrine of continuing violations to assert its temporal jurisdiction over violations of the American Convention which started before the acceptance of the Court's contentious jurisdiction by the respondent State. For instance, in *Blake*, concerning the disappearance and murder of an American journalist by the Guatemalan military, the Court has asserted its temporal jurisdiction over the case even if it found that the deprivation of Mr Blake's liberty and his murder were completed in March 1985, two years before Guatemala's acceptance of the contentious jurisdiction of the Court. The Court however established that, since the death of Mr Blake, Guatemala 'committed subsequent acts [which implied] complicity in, and concealment of, Mr. Blake's arrest and murder' and that these acts continued past the acceptance of the Court's jurisdiction.[13]

---

[13] *Blake v Guatemala (Preliminary Objections)*, §34.

12.4.3 THE RELEVANCE OF FAULT

By 'fault' is meant a psychological attitude of the wrongdoer consisting of either 'intention' (the intent to bring about the event resulting from the conduct; for instance, the intent to expel all the nationals of a foreign country in breach of an international treaty), or 'recklessness' (awareness of the risk of the prohibited consequences occurring; for instance, a State puts in place provisional military installations on the high seas, knowing that it may thus jeopardize the freedom of other States to fish in that area or that those installations may imperil important natural resources).

Normally, international courts do not inquire whether or not persons whose conduct is attributable to a State and who have allegedly performed an international wrong acted intentionally. They only consider the question of fault if the allegedly responsible State objects that it did not act willingly and invokes, for instance, *force majeure*. The ILC Articles have endorsed this approach in that they do not envisage intention or fault as a distinct subjective element of the internationally wrongful act, but only take fault into account when dealing with circumstances precluding wrongfulness (when lack of fault may exclude the arising of State responsibility under the claim of *force majeure* or *distress*: see **12.6.1**), or for establishing the amount of compensation due (Article 39, ILC Articles).

However, fault—in the form of knowledge—amounts to an indispensable subjective element of State responsibility in three scenarios, all of them concerning the responsibility of one State in connection with the internationally wrongful act of another State: (i) aid or assistance (Article 16, ILC Articles); (ii) direction and control (Article 17, ILC Articles); and (iii) coercion (Article 18, ILC Articles). In these three scenarios, the State not directly committing the wrongful act nonetheless incurs international responsibility if it has knowledge of the circumstances of the act and if the act would be, if committed by such State (or by the coerced State, in the absence of coercion), an internationally wrongful act.

12.5 THE QUESTION OF DAMAGE

Under the ILC Articles, the commission by a State of an internationally wrongful act is sufficient to trigger its international responsibility. The ILC excluded the requirement that damage caused to another State was a necessary additional element, arguing that this was a matter pertaining to the content of the primary rule rather than a necessary condition for international responsibility to arise. As an example, the ILC Commentary to the Articles mentions the obligation under a treaty to enact a uniform law: the failure by a State party to comply with this obligation would be sufficient to engage the international responsibility of the State, without the need for another contracting State to point to any damage caused by such failure. However, according to the ILC Articles, damage (material or moral)[14] may be taken into account when appraising the modalities and the *quantum* of the ensuing reparation.

The ILC Articles have thus expressly departed from the view whereby State responsibility may only arise when, in addition to the violation of an international obligation, a State also causes material or moral damage to another State, which it is then obliged to make good. The then Special Rapporteur, Roberto Ago (in the footsteps of Anzilotti)[15] suggested

---

[14] Material damage is any prejudice caused to the economic or patrimonial interests of a State or its nationals; moral damage is any breach of a State's honour or dignity (e.g. burning the flag of a State, or violating with military aircraft the airspace of a foreign country without causing any material damage, or through State agents trying to carry out official functions in a foreign territory without prior permission).

[15] D. Anzilotti, *Teoria generale della responsabilità dello Stato nel diritto internazionale* (Firenze: Lumache, 1902), reprinted in *Scritti di diritto internazionale pubblico* (Padova: Cedam, 1956), ii, 89, and *Corso*, at 425.

the view eventually accepted by the Commission,[16] according to which any breach of an international obligation necessarily causes a *legal injury* to another State, in the form of the violation of the international right corresponding to the obligation breached. If—so the argument goes—the commission of an internationally wrongful act by a State necessarily causes damage or prejudice to a *legal right* of another State, there is no point in insisting that damage, or prejudice, should be regarded as a *distinct* element to engage the international responsibility of the former State.

This view is in some respects sound. However, three nuances are in order. First, it is no coincidence that most illustrations of responsibility arising out of a mere breach of an international obligation without involving any material or moral damage, advanced in the ILC Reports, belong to an area where State responsibility takes on different connotations, namely, the legal regime of what is here called 'aggravated responsibility' (the ILC referred to breaches by a State of the human rights of its own nationals, as well as violations by a contracting State of ILO conventions ((1973-II) *YILC*, at §12) which, as is well known, are conventions laying down obligations *erga omnes*, the violation of which does not bring about material or moral damage to other contracting parties). This suggests that, in practice, whereas material or moral damage is usually part of the wrongful act in the case of 'ordinary responsibility', as we shall see later, it *is not indispensable in the case of 'aggravated responsibility'*.

The second nuance is grounded on the analysis of State practice. In the case of 'ordinary' responsibility, based on a one-to-one legal relation (between the responsible State and the injured State), normally the injured State is entitled to request reparation only because one of its rights has been breached and this breach has caused material or moral damage. It is easy to explain why in international case law damage has not been *explicitly* required as one of the basic elements of international responsibility (except in those cases where courts have insisted that only direct damage, and not so-called indirect damage, gives rise to responsibility):[17] when the States concerned in an alleged breach have brought cases to international courts, courts have not felt the need to satisfy themselves that the State other than the one allegedly breaching the international obligation was a damaged party. This was simply taken for granted. Indeed, international substantive rules aim at protecting specific interests of States in their bilateral relations with any other member of the international community. In practice, States undertake legal démarches with a view to invoking State responsibility vis-à-vis another State only when the action of that State directly affects them in their economic, commercial, diplomatic, or political sphere. State practice shows that, most of the time, if a State is not injured at the material or moral level by the action of another State, it does not invoke international rules on State responsibility against that State (unless the legal regime of 'aggravated responsibility' may be triggered, on the conditions we will set out in what follows, and the State decides to exercise its right to invoke the international responsibility of the offending State).

Thirdly, it is then the vagueness of the concept of legal injury that requires clarification. In most cases of ordinary responsibility, in the absence of material damage, the legal injury at stake will likely reach the level of moral damage. Situations where the legal injury necessary for triggering the rules of State responsibility remains below the level of moral damage would be rare in ordinary State responsibility and, in the overwhelming majority of cases, they will be based on treaty law (e.g. the violation of a procedural rule which amounts to

---

[16] See R. Ago's Third Report on State Responsibility, (1971-II) *YILC*, First Part, §§73–74.

[17] See *Yuille, Shotridge and Co.* (*United Kingdom*/Portugal), 109; *Alabama* (*United States/Great Britain*), 893 and 889; PCIJ, *The S.S. Wimbledon* (*United Kingdom, France, Italy, Japan v Germany*); *Naulilaa* (*Portugal v Germany*); *Eagle Star and British Dominions Insurance Company (Limited) and Excess Insurance Company (Limited)* (*Great Britain* v *United Mexican States*), 141-2.

a legal injury without being moral damage). By contrast, the legal injury does not need to reach the level of direct moral damage to a given State (the injured State) in the context of primary norms which create *erga omnes* obligations and, hence, give rise to international responsibility of an aggravated nature. That would be consistent with the wording of Article 48 of the ILC Articles, which refers to States 'other than the injured State'. Here, the nature of the primary norm (peremptory norms but also norms creating obligations *erga omnes* and *erga omnes partes*) would allow for a pure legal injury to justify the invocation of State responsibility by a State 'other than the injured State'.

In sum, contrary to what the ILC suggested in its Articles, it is warranted to hold that to trigger the legal regime of 'ordinary' State responsibility in general international law the additional element of *material or moral damage* is required.

12.6 CIRCUMSTANCES PRECLUDING WRONGFULNESS

An internationally wrongful act, as already seen, triggers the international responsibility of the State to which the wrongful conduct is attributable. However, an allegedly responsible State could claim the existence of circumstances which would preclude the wrongfulness of the act and thus allow it to escape international responsibility.[18] The existence of any of these circumstances generally shall be proven by the State allegedly responsible for the internationally wrongful act. This means that the general rules on State responsibility establish a system of so-called 'relative objective responsibility', namely a strict but not absolute regime of responsibility (the latter is, for instance, the regime of responsibility arising in case of causation of damage, as is the case of responsibility for ultra-hazardous activities).

12.6.1 THE CODIFICATION OF THE ILC ARTICLES

The ILC Articles codify six circumstances precluding wrongfulness: (1) consent of the State injured (Article 20); (2) self-defence (Article 21); (3) countermeasures (Article 22 and further elaborated upon in the Part on the consequences of a wrongful act); (4) *force majeure* (Article 23); (5) distress (Article 24); and (6) state of necessity (Article 25). The Commentary to the ILC Articles clarifies that these are the circumstances precluding wrongfulness *presently* recognized under international law, thus indirectly recognizing that international rules on new circumstances may develop.

(1) *Consent* by a State with respect to activities carried out by another State that would otherwise breach an international obligation vis-à-vis the consenting State precludes the wrongfulness of those activities. This is an application of the principle *volenti non fit injuria* (to one willing, no harm is done). Examples include consent by the relevant State to station foreign troops on its territory; to authorize a foreign State to fish, or drill for oil, in its

---

[18] See generally discussion of the five circumstances precluding wrongfulness mentioned in the ILC Articles: F. Paddeu, *Justification and Excuse in International Law* (Cambridge: Cambridge University Press, 2018). For an analysis of how exceptions to a rule can be designed in international law see J. E. Viñuales, 'Seven Ways of Escaping a Rule: Of Exceptions and their Avatars in International Law' in F. Paddeu and L. Bartels (eds), *Exceptions in International Law* (Oxford: Oxford University Press, 2020), 65.

territorial waters; or to perform such enforcement tasks as the arrest of suspects, as in the *Savarkar* case (at 252–5), etc.

Consent precludes the wrongfulness of the conduct of another State to the extent that the conduct of the latter remains within the limits of consent. This point was for instance clarified by the ICJ in the *Armed Activities on the Territory of the Congo (Democratic Republic of the Congo v Uganda)*.[19]

Consent must be validly given. The ILC Articles do not clarify the criteria of the validity of State consent for the purpose of precluding the wrongfulness of acts of other States. The Commentary to the ILC Articles simply makes a *renvoi* to the pertinent rules of international law. Arguably, these rules can be drawn, by analogy, from the rules regulating the expression of consent to be bound by a treaty, codified in the 1969 Vienna Convention on the Law of Treaties (see **Chapter 10**). In addition, consent shall be clearly established and cannot be presumed. It must be given prior to the conduct that would be otherwise unlawful, or at least while the conduct is taking place. Consent subsequent to the conduct does not preclude the wrongfulness of that conduct, but implies renunciation by the consenting State to the consequences of the wrongful act, in particular reparation.

Finally, consent shall be given by the competent authorities of the State. This usually requires determining the nature and character of the conduct with respect to which consent is given. In other words, consent by junior officials or non-governmental agencies of the State may exclude the wrongfulness of an act of another State if the officials and agencies operate within the scope of their competence and in accordance with the principles of actual or ostensible authority (see ILC Commentary, at 164).

(2) *Self-defence* and (3) *countermeasures* are discussed elsewhere (see **16.5** and **14.2.3**). Suffice it here to say that both measures constitute means that allow a State which has been injured by an internationally wrongful act by another State to react in response to such act. These measures are thus measures of self-help, although (as we shall see) they exhibit very different features. Importantly, *self-defence* consists in the international use of armed force in response to an armed attack and for the purpose of repelling it. By contrast, countermeasures are allowed in response to any breach of international law and consist in the violation of a rule of international law by the State that has suffered such a breach vis-à-vis the State allegedly responsible. Both self-defence and countermeasures are subject to specific requirements and limitations, failing which they will not preclude the wrongfulness of the measures taken by the injured State.

(4) *Force majeure* is defined in Article 23(1) of the ILC Articles as follows: 'the occurrence of an irresistible force or of an unforeseen event, beyond the control of the State, making it materially impossible in the circumstances to perform the obligation'. Paragraph 2 adds that *force majeure* does not apply if '(a) the situation of *force majeure* is due, either alone or in combination with other factors, to the conduct of the State invoking it; or (b) the State has assumed the risk of that situation occurring'.

---

[19] In examining the scope of the consent by the Democratic Republic of the Congo to have Ugandan troops operating in its territory, the ICJ pointed out that the consent was not open-ended, but was subject to certain restrictions in terms of geographical location and objectives (*Armed Activities on the Territory of the Congo, (Democratic Republic of the Congo v Uganda)*, 198, §52).

Gill is often mentioned as an illustration of *force majeure* but does not seem to be germane to this matter.[20] In the *Serbian Loans* case, the PCIJ did not admit the Serbian claim that the First World War had made it impossible for Serbia to repay loans (at 39–40). In the arbitration concerning the *Rainbow Warrior (New Zealand v France)* case, France claimed that urgent medical reasons had imposed repatriation to France, without the consent of New Zealand, of a French agent, Major Mafart, from a French military facility on the island of Hao. For France those medical reasons amounted to *force majeure*. The Arbitral Tribunal rejected the French claim. Quoting the works of the ILC, it held that *force majeure* 'is generally invoked to justify involuntary, or at least unintentional conduct' and relates to 'an irresistible force or an unforeseen event' against which the State has no remedy and which makes it 'materially impossible' for the State to act in conformity with its obligation. The Tribunal went on to note that the test for applying the doctrine of *force majeure* was one of 'absolute and material impossibility', whereas a 'circumstance rendering performance [of the obligation] more difficult or burdensome' did not constitute such a circumstance precluding wrongfulness (§§76–77).

(5) *Distress* has been defined in Article 24(1) of the ILC Articles as a situation where 'the author of the [otherwise wrongful] act . . . had no other reasonable way, in a situation of distress, of saving the author's life or the lives of other persons entrusted to the author's care'. Paragraph 2 goes on to provide that distress does not apply if '(a) the situation of distress is due, either alone or in combination with other factors, to the conduct of the State invoking it; or (b) the act in question is likely to create a comparable or greater peril'.

According to the ILC,[21] illustrations of distress are the unauthorized entry of an aircraft into foreign territory to save the life of passengers, or the entry of a military ship into a foreign port without authorization due to a storm (this happened in the case of *The Creole*: at 704–5). In 1946, following a diplomatic incident caused by some unauthorized flights of US military aircraft over Yugoslavia, the two countries agreed that only in cases of emergency rendered necessary by the need to save the life of the crew could such flights be admissible in absence of consent.[22]

Distress, unlike *force majeure*, requires that the person whose behaviour is attributable to the State be aware of behaving contrary to international law. This person, in theory, could choose to face the serious danger to life and comply with international rules, rather than try to save his life or those of others by behaving contrary to international law. In fact, this choice is only apparent.

It is worth stressing that the ILC has rightly insisted that distress may operate as a circumstance excluding wrongfulness only when the *life* of one or more persons, not their physical integrity, is at stake. Nevertheless, in at least one case international jurisprudence has taken a different view, admitting that a serious threat to physical integrity may amount

---

[20] Gill, a British national working at a power plant in Mexico, was forced to flee in night attire with his family when revolutionary forces attacked the power plant. During the attack a considerable amount of personal property was taken or destroyed by the revolutionary forces. The Claims Commission held that Mexico was responsible for its failure to suppress or punish the attack. However, the Commission stated that 'there may be a number of cases, in which absence of action is not due to negligence or omission but to the impossibility of taking immediate and decisive measures, in which every Government may temporarily find themselves, when confronted with a situation of a very sudden nature . . . authorities cannot be blamed for omission or negligence, when the action taken by them has not resulted in the *entire* suppression of the insurrections, risings, riots or acts of brigandage, or has not led to the punishment of *all* the individuals responsible. In those cases no responsibility will be admitted' (at 159).

[21] See (1979-II) *YILC*, First Part, 60, §131.

[22] Ibid., at §130. See also the more recent commentary to Article 24 of the ILC Articles (online at http://www.un.org/law/ilc).

to distress as a ground for removing the illegality of State conduct. This is the aforementioned *Rainbow Warrior* case (in the arbitration phase). The Arbitral Tribunal established by France and New Zealand held that France's violation of the obligation to obtain the prior consent of New Zealand to the removal to mainland France of Major Mafart was justified by distress, namely 'the existence of very exceptional circumstances of extreme urgency' involving medical considerations (at §§78–79). However, the Tribunal found that France incurred responsibility in not returning Major Mafart to the island of Hao once the medical reasons had terminated (at §§83–88).

(6) *Necessity* as a ground for excluding wrongfulness involves, like distress, a situation of danger. What is now in danger, however, is not the life of a person acting on behalf of the State and the persons who may have been entrusted to him, but the *State as such or its population* (or part of the population).

Article 25(1) of the ILC Articles defines necessity as the condition where an otherwise unlawful act is performed and such act '(a) is the only means for the State to safeguard an essential interest against a grave and imminent peril; and (b) does not seriously impair an essential interest of the State or States towards which the obligation exists, or of the international community as a whole'. Paragraph 2 adds that, '[i]n any case, necessity may not be invoked by a State as a ground for precluding wrongfulness if: (a) the international obligation in question excludes the possibility of invoking necessity; or (b) the State has contributed to the situation of necessity'. Thus, necessity may not be relied upon when the very legal obligation that a State violates rules out, either expressly or implicitly, the possibility of invoking this ground for excluding wrongfulness: an illustration is the rules of international humanitarian law that, as rightly pointed out by the ILC, apply precisely in exceptional circumstances of danger for the State and its essential interests.

Given its very restrictive requirements, the state of necessity is seldom established. In this regard, one can mention the *Neptune* case, decided in 1797 by a United States–Britain Mixed Commission. In 1795, during the Anglo-French war, an American-owned vessel, 'laden with rice and other foodstuffs' on a voyage from the US to France, was captured by a British ship of war, and the cargo was taken over for the British government, the owners being allowed the invoice price plus a mercantile profit of 10 per cent. The owner claimed before the United States–Great Britain Mixed Commission the difference between what had thus been paid to them and the price the goods would have fetched at Bordeaux, if they had not been seized. Britain claimed among other things that the seizure was justified by necessity, for Britain 'was threatened with a scarcity of those articles directed to be seized'. Judge Pinkney, writing as a member of the majority that issued the award, dismissed the British argument, essentially on two grounds: (i) the 'evil' was only 'seen in perspective', namely was 'imaginary', not 'real and pressing', and in addition (ii) no attempt had been made to find other means of supply 'which were consistent with the rights of others and which were not incompatible with the exigency'. The judge also tackled the issue of compensation. He held that, assuming a necessity existed in Britain for the seizure of the cargo, the British government could have pre-empted the cargo only upon giving the neutral traders as much as they would have earned in the port of original destination.[23]

In the *Case Concerning the Gabčíkovo-Nagymaros Project (Hungary/Slovakia)* before the ICJ, Hungary had contended that in 1989 it had suspended a treaty obligation imposing the joint construction with Czechoslovakia of a dam in the Danube on account of 'a state of ecological necessity'. The other party to the dispute, Slovakia, contested the claim. The Court dismissed the Hungarian submissions. It noted that 'the state of necessity is a ground recognized by

---

[23] See also a summary of the case in (1980-II) *YILC*, First Part, 34, §48.

customary international law for precluding the wrongfulness of an act not in conformity with an international obligation ... Such ground ... can only be accepted on an exceptional basis.' The Court then enumerated most of the conditions set forth in the ILC Articles (at the time not yet adopted by the ILC), adding that they 'reflect customary international law'. After applying some of those conditions to the case at issue, the Court concluded that 'the perils invoked by Hungary, without prejudging their possible gravity, were not sufficiently established in 1989, nor were they "imminent"; and ... Hungary had available to it at that time means of responding to these perceived perils other than the suspension and abandonment of works with which it had been entrusted. What is more, negotiations were under way which might have led to a review of the Project and the extension of some of its time-limits, without there being need to abandon it' (at §§51–52, 56–57, and 58–59).[24]

Finally, one can also mention a string of cases arising out the Argentinean economic and financial crisis of 2001, where Argentina unsuccessfully raised (among other things) state of necessity as a ground for avoiding liability in response to claims brought by US investors in public utilities in that country. In all cases, the tribunals established under the ICSID rules (see **21.4.3**) recognized that Article 25 of the ILC Articles on necessity reflected a rule of customary international law, but a large majority of them found that the relevant requirements were not cumulatively fulfilled.[25]

12.6.2 THE RELEVANCE OF *JUS COGENS*

As the ILC rightly specified in Article 26 of its Articles, circumstances precluding wrongfulness do not operate when they involve the breach of obligations deriving from a peremptory norm. Thus, for instance, consent does not preclude the wrongfulness of any activities contrary to obligations stemming from *jus cogens* (such as consent for foreign armed forces to enter the territory to massacre civilians or a specific ethnic group).

As the ILC put it in its Commentary on Article 26, '[w]here there is an apparent conflict between primary obligations, one of which arises for a State directly under a peremptory norm of general international law, it is evident that such an obligation must prevail'. However, arguably, this limitation does not apply to self-defence: as self-defence consists of the use of force, this ground for excluding the wrongful nature of conduct necessarily implies a breach of the ban on the use or threat of force, a ban that indubitably has the character of *jus cogens*.

12.6.3 THE RELATIONSHIP WITH THE OBLIGATION TO PAY COMPENSATION

If one of the circumstances discussed above can be proved, no responsibility is incurred by the State invoking that circumstance. This State may nevertheless have to pay compensation for any material harm or loss caused by its conduct. Article 27(b) of the ILC Articles provides that 'the invocation of a circumstance precluding wrongfulness ... is without prejudice to ... the question of compensation for any material loss caused by the act in question'.

---

[24] The ICJ Advisory Opinion on *Legal Consequences of the Construction of a Wall in the Occupied Palestinian Territory* is also worth mentioning: the ICJ excluded the possibility that Israel's construction of the wall could be justified on the basis of a state of necessity because it was not convinced that 'the construction of the wall along the route chosen was the only means to safeguard the interests of Israel against the peril which it has invoked as a justification for that construction' (at §51).

[25] See J. E. Viñuales, 'Defence Arguments in Investment Arbitration' in J. E. Viñuales and M. Waibel (eds), *ICSID Reports*, vol. 18 (Cambridge: Cambridge University Press, 2020).

It would seem appropriate, and in keeping with the spirit of international principles on the law of State responsibility, to hold that compensation must not always be paid. First of all, one should exclude the case of self-defence or countermeasures, where the action is only taken to react to the wrongful act of another State. As for self-defence, the right to compensation could accrue to the aggressor only if self-defence resulting in material harm or loss had been disproportionate. One fails to see why, instead, a State acting in self-defence to repel aggression should also be called upon to pay compensation for the material harm it may have caused (e.g. for lawful collateral damage to civilians or civilian objects, or destruction of such lawful military objectives as railways, bridges, or radio communication centres). The same holds true, *mutatis mutandis*, for countermeasures.

It seems that compensation should also be excluded with regard to some other circumstances precluding wrongfulness. For instance, if a State has consented to the commission of a specific activity that otherwise would have been unlawful, one might consider as implicit in the specific consent to the specific activity the waiver of any claim to compensation in the case of damage. This conclusion is grounded on the assumption that the consenting State knew or should have known that material harm or loss was most likely to occur.

12.7 CONSEQUENCES OF THE INTERNATIONALLY WRONGFUL ACT

The commission of an internationally wrongful act gives rise to a new legal relationship between the responsible State and the injured State. The obligations and rights forming this new legal relationship constitute the content of State responsibility under international law. To put it differently, the notion of State responsibility designates the legal consequences of the internationally wrongful act of a State, namely, the obligations of the wrongdoer, on the one hand, and the rights and powers of any State injured or otherwise affected by the wrong, on the other.

12.7.1 OBLIGATIONS OF THE RESPONSIBLE STATE AND FORMS OF REPARATION

The responsible State is under several obligations, owed to the injured State and to it alone, as a result of the commission of an internationally wrongful act (so-called 'secondary obligations'). In particular: (i) it must cease the wrongful act, if it is continuing (obligation of cessation), and 'offer appropriate assurances and guarantees of non-repetition, if circumstances so require' (Article 30, ILC Articles); (ii) it must make full reparation for the injury caused; injury includes 'any damage, whether material or moral, caused by the internationally wrongful act' (Article 31, ILC Articles); (iii) it must accede bona fide to any attempt peacefully to settle the dispute made by the injured State if it refuses to make reparation or to pay compensation to the extent required by the injured State. This obligation is not included in the ILC Articles, but shall be considered as a corollary of the obligation enshrined in Article 2(3), of the UN Charter on the peaceful settlement of disputes (see **3.5** and **Chapter 13**).

As far as the obligation to provide *full reparation* for the injury caused, the various forms of reparation are: (1) restitution in kind; (2) compensation; and (3) satisfaction:

(1) *Restitution in kind* and (2) *compensation* are due when the internationally wrongful act causes material damage, namely damage to the property or other interests of a State or of its nationals that is assessable in financial terms. The primary obligation of the responsible

State is to provide *restitution in kind*, to the extent possible. Pursuant to Article 35 of the ILC Articles, restitution means:

> to re-establish the situation which existed before the wrongful act was committed, provided and to the extent that restitution:
>
> (a) is not materially impossible;
> (b) does not involve a burden out of all proportion to the benefit deriving from restitution instead of compensation.

Only if restitution is not possible[26] or can allow only partial recovery of the material damage suffered, must the responsible State make compensation. Under Article 36 of the ILC Articles:

> 1. The State responsible for an internationally wrongful act is under an obligation to compensate for the damage caused thereby, insofar as such damage is not made good by restitution.
> 2. The compensation shall cover any financially assessable damage including loss of profits insofar as it is established.

Examples of restitution include: making the use of a house available (under a treaty with Britain, the Sultan of the Spanish zone of Morocco had built a house for the private residence of the British consul. Later the house was destroyed by Spanish troops; the arbiter, Huber, held in *Spanish Zone of Morocco Claims (Great Britain v Spain)* (at 722–7) that Spain—the protector State—was to give Britain 'the usufruct for a consular residence', that was to be 'as convenient' as the destroyed house); deciding that, 'as a form of reparation', the respondent State must recognize the rescinding of the obligation or payment previously imposed (*Martini*, at 1002); and ordering that government taxes and import duties unlawfully paid must be returned.[27]

(3) *Satisfaction* is due when the injury caused by an internationally wrongful act cannot be made good by restitution or compensation; it is however not a standard form of reparation, since injury caused by an internationally wrongful act can usually be fully repaired by restitution and/or compensation. Satisfaction is however the remedy available when the wrongful act does not cause any material damage, but nonetheless consists in an affront to another State ('non-material damage'). Satisfaction may be provided by the responsible State by 'an acknowledgement of the breach, an expression of regret, a formal apology or another appropriate modality' but shall not be 'out of proportion to the injury and may not take a form humiliating to the responsible State' (Article 37, ILC Articles).

For instance, on 19 February 1998 five Israeli secret agents tried to plant listening devices in an apartment building in the outskirts of Berne (one of the tenants was suspected of being connected to a Palestinian or Lebanese militant group); the Swiss police detained

---

[26] In *Avena and other Mexican Nationals (Mexico v United States of America)*, the ICJ rejected Mexico's request for *restitutio in integrum*, §§115–125.

[27] See *The Palmarejo and Mexican Gold Fields Ltd* (UK–Mexican Claims Commission), 301–2; *Compagnie générale des asphaltes de France*, 389–98. The Umpire stated the following: 'The umpire is not disregardful of the claim of the honourable Commissioner for Venezuela that, since the duties were not, in fact, again paid, the claimant company has suffered no loss, and hence, in equity, has no rightful demand for their repayment; but it is the opinion of the umpire that an unjustifiable act is not made just because, perchance, there were not evil results which might well have followed. The claimant Government has a right to insist that its sovereignty over its own soil shall be respected and that its subject shall be restored to his original right before consequent results shall be discussed. The umpire having found that the requirement of import duties before clearance was an unlawful exaction and a wrongful assumption of Venezuelan sovereignty on British soil, it is just and right, and therefore justice and equity [sic] that these duties be restored to the claimant company' (at 398).

them, but then released four and held one. The Swiss authorities accused Israel of violating Swiss sovereignty and demanded an apology; on 27 February, Israel formally apologized and the Israeli agent was released.[28] Similarly, on 11 April 2001, the US government apologized to China for a US military aircraft entering China's airspace and landing in Hainan airport without prior authorization.[29] Other instances of satisfaction may be the symbolic payment of a very modest sum. In *The Carthage* and *The Manouba*, France had asked the Arbitral Tribunals to hold that Italy—having breached international law by capturing and temporarily detaining, on the high seas, during the Turco-Italian war in 1912, two French steamers allegedly carrying war contraband—was to pay to France, in addition to compensation for moral and material damage, also one French franc for the offence on the French flag. In both cases the Tribunal held that finding that Italy had breached international law was by itself a 'serious sanction' and only obliged Italy to pay compensation for the moral and material damage. The decision by an arbitral or judicial body that the State had committed an international wrong was also held to constitute fair satisfaction in *Corfu Channel* (at 35) and the arbitration in the *Rainbow Warrior* case (at §123). Another instance of satisfaction may be the punishment by the national authorities of the responsible State of the individuals who have caused the wrong; or formal assurance by the responsible State that it will not repeat the wrong.[30]

Although restitution and compensation should normally be resorted to in the order we have outlined, nothing prevents States from combining them, and if need be also providing satisfaction, to the extent that this is feasible or asked for.

12.7.2 THE NOTION OF INJURED STATE

The injured State has the right to claim compliance by the responsible State with the secondary obligations stemming from the commission of an internationally wrongful act. Having ruled out that damage is a necessary requisite for State responsibility to arise, the ILC has upheld a notion of the injured State that is not based on the infliction of damage. Article 42 of the ILC Articles indeed stipulates:

> A State is entitled as an injured State to invoke the responsibility of another State if the obligation breached is owed to:
>
> (a) that State individually; or
> (b) a group of States including that State, or the international community as a whole, and the breach of the obligation:
>
> (i) specially affects that State; or
> (ii) is of such a character as radically to change the position of all other States to which the obligation is owed with respect to the further performance of the obligation.

Thus, the ILC Articles have identified three distinct categories of 'injured State': (i) when the wrongful act is a breach of rules based on reciprocity, the injured State is the State holder of the right corresponding to the obligation breached (Article 42(a)); (ii) when the wrongful conduct constitutes a breach of community obligations, the 'injured State' is

---

[28] See http://www.fas.org/irp/news/1998/02/980227_mossadf.htm.
[29] See text of the letter of the US ambassador in *International Herald Tribune*, 12 April 2001, 8 ('We are very sorry the entering of China's airspace and the landing did not have verbal clearance'). The Chinese government had insisted that the Chinese authority had heard no distress calls or requests for permission to enter Chinese airspace and so the landing was illegal (see *International Herald Tribune*, 14–15 April 2001, 1 and 41).
[30] In *LaGrand (Germany v United States of America)* the ICJ held an apology did not suffice 'in cases where the individuals concerned' had been subjected to 'prolonged detention or convicted and sentenced to heavy penalties' (at §125).

that on which the wrongful act has a particular bearing, so that it is specially affected by that wrong. The ILC Commentary gives as an illustration the pollution of the high seas in breach of Article 194 of the Law of the Sea Convention, which 'may particularly impact on one or several States whose beaches may be polluted by toxic residues or whose coastal fisheries may be closed' (at §12, Commentary on Article 42). In such cases that State may be considered 'injured', although there is a general interest among all the contracting States in the protection of the marine environment; (iii) the wrongful conduct may breach so-called 'integral obligations'[31] (that is, obligations normally deriving from treaties, and necessarily dependent on a corresponding performance by all the other parties, since it is of the essence of treaties laying down such obligations that the undertaking of each party is given in return for a similar undertaking by the others);[32] if this is the case, all the States to which the obligation is owed must be considered 'injured'.

Article 42 provides that the 'injured State', in one of the three different classes just referred to, is entitled to invoke the responsibility of the delinquent State, in particular: it has the right to ask for the cessation of the wrongful act (if it is continuing) and assurances and guarantees of non-repetition (if circumstances so require), and to obtain full reparation for any injury caused by the wrongful act. However, as we shall see later (see **12.8.1**), the ILC has also identified another category of States which, although not 'injured', under certain circumstances are nevertheless entitled to invoke the fulfilment by the responsible State of these obligations.

The injured State, if it decides to invoke the responsibility of another State for the commission of a wrongful act, must take the following steps.

First, it must 'give notice of its claim to that State' and specify in particular '(a) the conduct that the responsible State should take in order to cease the wrongful act, if it is continuing; (b) what form reparation should take' (Article 43, ILC Articles).

Secondly, if the responsible State does not comply with its request, the injured State must endeavour to settle the dispute by peaceful means and in particular embark upon, or at least propose, negotiations, mediation, conciliation, or arbitration (Article 52(1)(b)

---

[31] For this notion see G. Fitzmaurice, *Second Report on the Law of the Treaties* (1957-II) YILC §126.

[32] Most, if not all, treaties on disarmament or arms control are based on the assumption of similar performance by the other contracting States, with the consequence that, if a State breaches the treaty, the other States may suspend its application or withdraw from the treaty, pursuant to Article 60 of the Vienna Convention on the Law of Treaties. Plainly, these obligations, although laid down in multilateral treaties, are based on reciprocity, and only 'ordinary responsibility' ensues from their violation. Most disarmament treaties include a clause providing for withdrawal. As an example of these clauses Article X(1) of the 1968 Treaty on the Non-Proliferation of Nuclear Weapons may be mentioned: 'Each party shall in exercising its national sovereignty have the right to withdraw from the Treaty if it decides that extraordinary events, related to the subject matter of this Treaty, have jeopardized the supreme interests of its country. It shall give notice of such withdrawal to all other Parties to the Treaty and to the UN Security Council three months in advance. Such notice shall include a statement of the extraordinary events it regards as having jeopardized its supreme interests.' It is submitted that this clause, when inserted in treaties providing for a collective monitoring and sanctioning mechanism in case of breach by one of the contracting parties, should be strictly construed and only made applicable to cases where the non-compliance with the treaty, established by the collective monitoring body, is very serious, and the responsible State does not discontinue it in spite of the findings and possible sanctions of the collective body. This proposition applies to such treaties as the 1967 Tlatelolco Treaty Banning Nuclear Weapons in Latin America; the 1972 Convention on the Prohibition of the Development, Production and Stockpiling of Bacteriological (Biological) and Toxin Weapons and on Their Destruction; and the 1993 Convention on the Prohibition of the Development, Production, Stockpiling and Use of Chemical Weapons and on Their Destruction.

of the ILC Articles only requires that the injured State must 'offer to negotiate' with the responsible State).

Thirdly, only if the responsible State refuses to make reparation or to enter into negotiations, or other dispute settlement procedures, or manifestly does not act bona fide in responding to the offer for negotiations or dispute settlement, is the injured State entitled to resort to countermeasures (according to Article 52(1) of the ILC Articles, countermeasures may be taken after the failure of the parties concerned to negotiate with a view to settling the matter). As stated earlier, the need to go through this process before initiating countermeasures follows from the general obligation to endeavour, in good faith, to settle disputes peacefully.

In 1978 a US–France arbitral tribunal took a contrary view in the *Case concerning the Air Service Agreement of 27 March 1946*. France had contended that countermeasures could be resorted to only in the absence of other legal channels to settle the dispute. The Tribunal dismissed this submission, stating that,

> [u]nder the rules of present-day international law, and unless the contrary results from special obligations arising under particular treaties, notably from mechanisms created within the framework of international organizations, each State establishes for itself its legal situation *vis-à-vis* other States. If a situation arises which, in one State's view, results in the violation of an international obligation by another State, the first State is entitled, within the limits set by the general rules of international law pertaining to the use of armed force, to affirm its rights through 'countermeasures'. (at §81; see also §§84–98)

It is submitted, with respect, that the Tribunal did not take into sufficient account the recent evolution of general international law, and in particular its emphasis on the peaceful settlement of disputes, as can be inferred from the evolution of the obligation of Article 33 of the UN Charter into a general obligation laid down (or codified) in the 1970 Friendly Relations Declaration.

As for the other conditions on which countermeasures are admissible, they will be discussed in **Chapter 14** (see **14.2.3** and **14.2.4**).

12.8 AGGRAVATED STATE RESPONSIBILITY

The idea that violations of rules protecting fundamental values of the international community should give rise to a form of responsibility different and more serious than the ordinary one (applicable by default to any breach of international rules) has emerged as a result of a number of concomitant factors.

The UN Charter provision prohibiting the use of armed force in international relations and the modalities for both centralized and non-centralized responses to its violations and to acts of aggression clarified that there existed rules envisaging reactions to international delinquencies different from and more serious than the usual response. The practice concerning reaction to gross and large-scale violations of human rights has also shown that, in other areas too, responses to breaches are permissible which, although less institutionalized and conspicuous than those against unlawful use of force and aggression, may however take a collective dimension unusual in the consequences of 'ordinary' wrongs. More generally, the emergence in the world community of values (peace, human rights, self-determination of peoples) deemed of universal significance and not derogable by States in their private transactions has led many States to believe that gross infringements of such values must perforce require a reaction different from those normally taken in response to violations of bilateral legal relations, and allow collective[33] or 'public' reaction, as opposed to the bilateral and 'private' responses to ordinary responsibility.[34]

The works of the ILC also gave impetus to the idea that violations of rules of international law protecting fundamental values were subject to specific consequences other than the one concerning 'ordinary' breaches. In 1976, the then Special Rapporteur, R. Ago, prompted the inclusion in the first Draft of the ILC Articles (subsequently adopted on first reading by the ILC in 1996) of a provision (Draft Article 19) concerning the so-called 'international crimes of States'. Crimes of States were proposed as a specific category of internationally wrongful acts (to be distinguished from so-called 'international delicts', namely all other breaches of international law) that—in the view of Ago—should have been subject to a specific regime of State responsibility. However, the ILC—after an extensive debate and triggered reactions, both positive and negative, from States—eventually jettisoned Draft Article 19 and the idea of a separate regime of State responsibility for serious violations of international law. Most States were indeed reluctant to accept the notion that they might be accused of 'crimes'. At the same time, the ILC was unable to pinpoint the specific content of a separate regime of State responsibility for these serious violations of international law. In the end, as we shall see in what follows, the ILC followed a *minimalist approach*.

12.8.1 THE REGULATION IN THE ILC ARTICLES

In the ILC Articles, there are two set of rules that are pertinent in respect of violations of rules protecting community values: (1) the rules applicable in case of serious breaches of peremptory norms of general international law (Articles 40 and 41, ILC Articles); (2) the rules allowing States other than an injured State to invoke the international responsibility of another State in case of violations of *erga omnes* and *erga omnes partes* obligations and to take measures against the latter to induce compliance with its secondary obligations (Articles 48 and 54, ILC Articles).

(1) Concerning the rules applicable in case of *serious breaches of obligations under peremptory norms of general international law*, Article 40(2) of the ILC Articles clarifies that a breach is serious if 'it involves a gross and systematic failure by the responsible State to fulfil the obligation'. It also explains that the term 'gross refers to the intensity of the violation or its effects', while 'systematic' indicates that 'a violation would have to be carried out in an organized and deliberate way'. Therefore, not every violation of a peremptory norm triggers the applicability of the specific set of consequences described in Article 41.

---

[33] E.g. in the field of international humanitarian law, Article 1 common to the four Geneva Conventions of 1949 obliges any contracting party 'to respect and to ensure respect' for the Conventions 'in all circumstances'. This obligation, which reflects a rule of customary international law (ICJ in *Nicaragua (Nicaragua v United States of America)*, §220), arguably empowers and even obligates any State party (and under customary international law, any State or other international entity) to demand of another State party (or any other State or entity) that it comply with its obligations under the Conventions (or with the fundamental principles of humanitarian law codified in the Conventions or arising out of the Conventions). It follows that the provision also entitles each State party to demand the cessation of a serious violation of the Conventions or of the general principles of humanitarian law (as well as, as the case may be, the punishment of the culprits). See further R. Geiß, 'The Obligation to Respect and to Ensure Respect for the Conventions' in A. Clapham, P. Gaeta, and M. Sassòli (eds), *The 1949 Geneva Conventions: A Commentary* (Oxford: Oxford University Press, 2015), 111.

[34] For instance, in the area of human rights (see **Chapter 18**) States have set up special bodies and institutions charged with supervising compliance and, if need be, requesting the responsible States to take remedial action. In other words, in most cases, to avoid politicization of the matter, the responsibility of States infringing human rights has been invoked not by other States but by international agencies pre-established by groups of States.

The ILC Commentary explains that this qualification is necessary 'in order not to trivialize the breach and it is not intended to suggest that any violation of these obligations is not serious or is somehow excusable'.[35]

The consequences stemming from serious violations of peremptory norms identified by the ILC are however limited. They consist essentially in a set of obligations incumbent upon States other than the responsible State, and which are additional to those normally flowing from an ordinary wrongful act. Under Article 41 of the ILC Articles, these additional obligations are: (i) to co-operate 'to bring to an end through lawful means' the wrongful act; (ii) not to recognize 'as lawful a situation created' by the wrongful act nor 'render aid or assistance in maintaining that situation'. The first obligation clearly consists in a positive obligation, which can be implemented within or outside a competent international organization (such as the UN). The other two obligations are instead negative obligations, which arguably reiterate pre-existing primary obligations under international law and apply regardless of the characterization of the breach as a serious violation of a peremptory rule of international law.

In the Advisory Opinion in *Legal Consequences of the Construction of a Wall in the Occupied Palestinian Territory*, the ICJ seems to have confirmed the approach adopted by the ILC in Articles 40 and 41. After finding that Israel had violated various international obligations in building a wall in the Palestinian Occupied Territories, the Court considered the legal consequences arising for Israel as the responsible State and for other States and, where appropriate, for the United Nations. Concerning the legal consequences arising for other States, the Court observed that the obligations violated by Israel in building the wall included certain obligations *erga omnes*, specifically the right of the Palestinian people to self-determination and certain obligations under international humanitarian law (at §155). According to the Court:

> given the *character and the importance of the rights and obligations involved* . . . all States are under an obligation not to recognize the illegal situation resulting from the construction of the wall in the Occupied Palestinian territory, including in and around East Jerusalem. (emphasis added)

In addition, the Court asserted that 'they are also under the obligation not to render aid or assistance in maintaining the situation created by such construction' and, 'while respecting the United Nations Charter and international law, to see to it that any impediment, resulting from the construction of the wall, to the exercise by the Palestinian people of its right to self-determination is brought to an end' (at §159). As for the legal consequences arising for the United Nations, the Court stated that 'the United Nations, and especially the General Assembly and the Security Council, should consider what further action is required to bring to an end the illegal situation resulting from the construction of the wall' (at §160). Admittedly, the Court has not clearly linked these legal consequences to serious violations of peremptory rules, as is the case for the ILC Articles, but to the *erga omnes* character of the obligations breached by Israel. However, it has also referred to the 'character and the importance of the rights and obligations involved', which can be considered as an implicit reference to the *jus cogens* nature of the obligations breached and the seriousness of their violations.

(2) As for the legal consequences of violations of rules setting *erga omnes* and *erga omnes partes* (i.e. within a treaty) *obligations*, the ILC Articles provide that any State other than the 'injured State' (which, as already stated, is the State 'whose individual right has been denied

---

[35] For a critical analysis, see P. Gaeta, 'Grave Breach of a Peremptory Obligation Owed to the International Community: the Character of the Breach' in J. Crawford, A. Pellet, S. Olleson, and K. Parlett (eds), *The Law of International Responsibility* (Oxford: Oxford University Press, 2010), 421.

or impaired by the internationally wrongful acts or which has otherwise been particularly affected by that act') *may invoke the responsibility of the delinquent State* and in particular may claim: (i) 'cessation of the internationally wrongful act and assurances and guarantees of non-repetition' (Article 48(2)(a)); (ii) 'performance of the obligation of reparation', 'in the interest of the injured State' (if there is an injured State, that is a State 'specially affected' by the breach) or of 'the beneficiaries of the obligation breached' (Article 48(2)(b)). In addition, pursuant to Article 54, any State other than the injured State may 'take *lawful measures*' (emphasis added) against the delinquent State 'to ensure cessation of the breach and reparation in the interest of the injured State or of the beneficiaries of the obligations breached'.

The ILC has thus envisaged a reaction to those breaches of community obligations hinging on the action of individual States, more than on a collective and in a way 'public' action. More importantly, the ILC has not clarified what is the scope of the term 'lawful measures', and it has not taken a clear stand on whether the term also includes resort to countermeasures by non-injured States to induce compliance by the delinquent State. According to the ILC, at the time of the adoption of the Articles, there was 'no clearly recognized entitlement of States ... [other than the injured State] to take countermeasures in the collective interest'. Consequently, the ILC considered that it was not appropriate 'to include in the present articles a provision concerning the question whether other States ... [other than the injured State], are permitted to take countermeasures in order to induce a responsible State to comply with its obligations'. The matter was thus left for resolution 'to the further development of international law'.[36]

This legal scheme concerning what is called in this book 'aggravated responsibility' lends itself to a number of criticisms. First, the ILC Articles do not provide for a collective, 'public' response to serious breaches of community obligations, a response upon which the individual response by each State should be made contingent. This is not in conformity with international practice, indicating that so-called sanctions are often resorted to by a large (and increasingly diverse) number of States acting within the framework of competent international organizations (at the universal, regional, or intra-regional level) to react to serious assaults on the international public order.[37]

Secondly, in substance the ILC scheme boils down to granting to all States other than the responsible State, in the case of very serious breaches of obligations flowing from *jus cogens*, the same rights accruing to any injured State toward the responsible State (claim to cessation and reparation, albeit for the benefit of the injured State), *plus* the additional obligations referred to above, but *minus* the right to resort to countermeasures proper. The crucial point of what measures other States could lawfully take to react to the gross breaches and induce compliance with international law has been left in abeyance. Again, the approach taken by the ILC is not in conformity with State practice, which, rather than being 'embryonic', as the ILC contended in adopting Article 54, clearly indicated that States have the right to resort to countermeasures against the responsible State if the 'public'

---

[36] For a critical analysis see, among others, A. Pellet, 'The New Draft Articles of the International Law Commission on the Responsibility of States for Internationally Wrongful Acts: A Requiem for States' Crime?' (2001) 32 *NYIL* 55.

[37] This is also what then Special Rapporteur, J. Crawford, clarified in his *Third Report* by noticing that the general law the law of State responsibility 'can only play an ancillary role in this field'. This is because 'the primary means in present international relations for dealing with emergencies affecting the very existence of States or the security of populations do not lie within the scope of the secondary rules of State responsibility. They are, inter alia, a matter for the competent international organizations, in particular the Security Council and the General Assembly' (at §372).

response by international organizations is not possible or is not adequate. Recent practice on the measures adopted by certain States confirms this view.[38]

Thirdly, a particular point deserves attention. The ILC has attached crucial importance to the notion of 'specially affected State' (that is, the State that may have suffered a particular prejudice) in the identification of an injured State. This State is entitled to react to wrongful acts—through, among other things, countermeasures—when such acts breach community obligations, *whether or not such breach is gross and large-scale*. Two consequences follow: (i) Violations of community obligations (such as a sporadic disregard for a human right, or the delivery of arms by a State to insurgents fighting in another State) are put on a par with very serious breaches of such obligations (such as massacres, large-scale torture, aggression, and so on). In other words, any breach of a community obligation, whatever its gravity, can trigger the same legal reaction. This is not consistent with State practice, which tends to distinguish between the two categories; (ii) What is even more striking, when a community obligation is seriously breached, for the ILC any other State not 'specially affected' would *not* be entitled to resort to countermeasures. This, again, seems to be in conflict with international practice. Thus, for instance, if a State ill-treats, on account of their religious beliefs, all its nationals that are Muslim, any other Muslim country might consider itself as 'specially affected' and would be entitled to adopt countermeasures; such a right would accrue to the State even if the ill-treatment is sporadic and inconspicuous. If, however, a State very seriously and consequently ill-treats such categories of its nationals as women or the handicapped or political opponents, no other State would be 'specially affected', with the consequence that no other State would be authorized to react to such serious breaches of community obligations by taking lawful countermeasures. The ILC approach is all the more surprising because, in some provisions of the ILC Articles, the Commission uses, to designate obligations *erga omnes* protecting some basic values, the expression 'obligations owed [by individual States] to the international community as a whole' (Articles 42(b) and 48(1)(b)), as if such community were personalized as an international subject and consequently held rights vis-à-vis its members.[39]

12.8.2 AGGRAVATED STATE RESPONSIBILITY IN LIGHT OF INTERNATIONAL PRACTICE

Let us now propose an alternative legal scheme on aggravated State responsibility, pointing out what, in our view, and in accordance with international practice, are the distinguishing traits of this form of State responsibility.

(1) *Preconditions for aggravated State responsibility*. The first distinguishing trait for aggravated responsibility is that, unlike ordinary State responsibility, the former is triggered by the breach of a '*community obligation*', that is, an obligation concerning a *fundamental value* (peace, human rights, self-determination of peoples, protection of the environment); *owed to all the other members* of the international community; having as its correlative position a '*community right*', that is, a right belonging to any other State (meaning that this right may

---

[38] See M. Dawidowicz, 'Third-party Countermeasures: A Progressive Development of International Law?' (2016) 29 *QIL, Zoom-in* 3, examining State practice in reaction to: the brutal repression of civil protest in Libya by the regime of Gaddafi in 2011, the massive violations of human rights and international humanitarian law by the Syrian regime since May 2011, and the role of Russia in the Ukrainian crisis. For a thorough examination of the relevant practice, see in particular M. Dawidowicz, *Third-Party Countermeasures in International Law* (Cambridge: Cambridge University Press, 2017).

[39] On this issue see generally S. Villalpando, *L'émergence de la communauté internationale dans la responsabilité des Etats* (Paris: LGDJ, 2005).

be exercised by any other State, whether or not damaged by the breach; and the right is exercised on behalf of the international community and not in the interest of the claimant State) (see **1.8.2**).

Furthermore, the breach of this obligation *must be gross or systematic*; in other words, it may not be a sporadic or isolated or minor contravention of a community obligation (e.g. the infringement of the right of an individual to a fair trial). It must be serious or large-scale (e.g. aggression, genocide, or grave atrocities against one's own nationals or all persons belonging to an ethnic group). One may think, for instance, of the aggression launched by a State against another State, but also of a relatively less grave breach, such as the military assistance by a State to insurgents fighting in another State against the central authorities (as the ICJ held in *Nicaragua (Nicaragua v United States of America)*, at §191, this breach is less serious than that of Article 2(4) of the UN Charter and the corresponding customary rule banning resort to force). In both cases the ensuing responsibility is different from 'ordinary' responsibility, although, as we shall see, not all consequences flowing from serious violations of community obligations apply to minor violations of such obligations.

Let us now consider the question of *damage*. As we saw earlier, and unlike the approach taken in the ILC Articles, material or moral damage should be considered an element of the wrongful act that may trigger the 'ordinary responsibility'. Things are however different in the case of 'aggravated responsibility'. Here a State is responsible towards all other States simply for breaching an international obligation, regardless of whether or not a particular State has been materially or morally damaged. If a State grossly violates human rights of its own nationals, no material or moral damage is caused to any other State; only a *legal injury* is brought about to the right of *every other State*. Or it may happen that by the same wrongful act (e.g. a massacre of a State's nationals together with the nationals of another State, belonging to the same ethnic or religious or racial group), a State may cause material or moral damage to one particular State, and by the same token bring about a legal injury to all States.

Finally, let us consider the *subjective element* required for the commission of a wrongful act. While in cases of ordinary breaches the subjective element is not required, and the claimant State does not need to prove it, the opposite is arguably true for aggravated responsibility. In other words, the seriousness of the breach and the fact that the obligation violated is of fundamental importance for the community as a whole should entail that the violation is carried out with intent by the responsible State, as for instance is the case for *genocide* (which requires the *special intent* to destroy, in whole or in part, a national, ethnic, racial, or religious group as such) or in the case of aggression (arguably, for a State to be responsible for aggression, there should be the *animus aggressionis*, namely the intention to invade and conquer foreign territory, destroy the foreign State apparatus, and so on).

(2) *Content of aggravated State responsibility.* In the case of 'aggravated' responsibility, the offending State has obligations *towards all other States*. The wrongdoer is under all the obligations incumbent upon any author of an international delinquency with regard to 'ordinary responsibility'. However, now these obligations are owed not only to the injured State, if any, but also to all the other members of the international community. In other words, the legal consequences of the wrongful act no longer consist merely of a 'bilateral relation' (between the responsible State and the State victim of the wrongful act), but of a 'community relation' between the wrongdoer and all other States.

Restitution, compensation, or satisfaction in some instances may prove relevant when the wrongful act has caused a material or moral damage to a particular State (e.g. in cases of aggression, or in cases of serious violations of the human rights of nationals of that State). In such cases, the offending State is obliged to make reparation to the State damaged.

In *most* cases of serious and massive breaches of 'community obligations', however, reparation in its various forms may turn out to be inconsequential. Take the example of large-scale or gross violations of human rights perpetrated by a State against its own nationals. Plainly, it is difficult to see how, under normal circumstances, it is possible to demand ordinary forms of reparation from the responsible State. Nevertheless, one may envisage the possibility that the responsible State may pay compensation to the victims, or to the relatives of the victims, of those gross breaches.

All other States have rights, powers, and obligations consequent upon the wrongful act, vis-à-vis the delinquent State. It is more important to establish the legal position of other States (namely, any member State of the international community, whether or not damaged by the wrong, provided it has the legal entitlement or right corresponding to the obligation breached by the responsible State).

The first set of consequences of gross or systematic breaches of community obligations has been rightly set out by the ILC in Article 42 of its ILC Articles, providing that, in case of serious violations of peremptory rules, all States other than the responsible State are under the obligations: (a) not to recognize as lawful the situation created by the breach; (b) not to render aid or assistance to the responsible State in maintaining the situation so created; (c) to co-operate as far as possible to bring the breach to an end.

In addition, all States other than the wrongdoer have *powers, rights, or claims*. First, all States other than the wrongdoer have the right to invoke the aggravated responsibility of the delinquent State, by bringing their claim to the notice of that State. Secondly, they have the right to demand cessation of the wrong, if it is continuing, and to request assurances and guarantees of non-repetition. Thirdly, they are entitled to claim reparation in a form consistent with the nature of the wrong (if a State has been materially or morally damaged—and thus is an injured State—it may claim reparation, as may other States to the benefit of the victim State, or, as in the case of gross violations of human rights, to the benefit of the individuals that have suffered from the wrongful act). These rights and claims have been also identified in the ILC Articles, but in relation to every violation of obligations *erga omnes*, irrespective of its character as gross or systematic violation.

If the responsible State does not take immediate action to discontinue the wrongful act or does not comply with the form of reparation sought by the claiming States, arguably the latter have additional rights and powers. In particular, they have the right to bring the matter to the attention of the competent international bodies (universal, regional, or intraregional), requesting them publicly to discuss the wrong done by the delinquent State with a view to attaining public exposure of that wrongdoing, or to adopting collective sanctions. The need for States to take steps within international organizations or other appropriate collective bodies seems to be warranted and indeed dictated by the inherent nature of this class of responsibility. This responsibility arises out of a gross attack on community or 'public' values. The response to the wrongdoing must therefore be, as much as possible, *public and collective*. It would be incongruous and contradictory to contemplate on the one hand a form of States' aggravated accountability for gross breaches of fundamental values of concern to all members of the world community, and then to envisage, on the other hand, a response left to the 'private' initiative of each individual member of such community.

If those bodies take no action, or their action has not brought about cessation of the wrong or adequate reparation (if only in the form of strict assurances not to repeat the same or similar wrongs in the future), arguably all States are empowered to take *countermeasures* on an individual basis. As mentioned earlier, State practice clearly points in this direction, and arguably already pointed in this direction at the time of the adoption of the ILC Articles. The cautious approach taken by the ILC in Article 54 was thus unwarranted.

When States opt for individual countermeasures, these must be subject to all the conditions and limitations that apply to these measures of self-help (see **14.2.4**). In particular, before taking countermeasures, the claimant States must (a) offer to negotiate with the responsible State as well as propose other means of peacefully settling the dispute such as mediation and conciliation, if appropriate, or arbitral or judicial settlement; (b) duly notify the responsible State of their intention to resort to countermeasures; (c) comply with the limitations as regards the content of countermeasures (such as the prohibition of countermeasures consisting in violations of the ban on the use of armed force). Plainly, if more than one State decides to resort to countermeasures, a problem of co-ordination may arise.[40] Finally, in case of armed aggression, as we shall see later, States are further entitled to resort to collective self-defence (subject to the request or consent of the State which is the victim of aggression; see **16.5**).

A caveat must now be entered. The above measures do not affect or prejudice the possible operation of the *UN security system*. If the UN Security Council considers that a gross violation of community obligations amounts to a threat to the peace, a breach of the peace, or an act of aggression, it may recommend or decide what measures not involving the use of force States are entitled or obliged to take under Article 41 of the UN Charter, or may authorize States to take forcible measures against the wrongdoer. In other words, faced with an internationally wrongful act that it deems covered by Article 39 of the UN Charter, *the Security Council takes over*, and individual States may only take action to the extent allowed by the UN Charter (individual or collective self-defence), or recommended, authorized, or decided upon by the Security Council.

A final point also needs to be made. As has already been stressed, violations of community obligations may well cause material or moral damage to a particular State. Thus, for example, in the aforementioned case of gross violations of human rights by a State, the victims of those violations may include both nationals of that State and citizens of, say, other States. In this case all States members of the international community may invoke the aggravated responsibility of the wrongdoer. In addition, the State whose nationals were victims of the wrongful act may complain that it has been damaged by the international delinquency, and claim reparation accordingly. For this purpose, it is necessary for the State to prove that some of the victims were nationals of that State. In contrast, for other States it is sufficient to prove that gross violations of human rights have been perpetrated, regardless of the victims' nationality.

In sum, international practice clearly shows that States consider that (i) the protection of some fundamental values laid down in legal obligations requires that the legal reaction to possible breaches of such obligations be different from that envisaged for 'ordinary' wrongful acts; (ii) such reaction should first of all be decided or agreed upon within the framework of international bodies, such as the UN Security Council and General Assembly, as well as organs of regional organizations; organizations such as NATO; or international human rights bodies. It has been rightly felt that collective action was preferable to the action of individual States, which may have political, ideological, or economic underpinnings, or may lend itself to distortions, or may acquire political overtones. International practice also shows that (iii) in some instances States tend however to 're-appropriate' the enforcement function with which they had (partially and imperfectly) entrusted international bodies, and to take, on an individual basis, countermeasures for the purpose of seeking compliance

---

[40] Article 54(3) of ILC Draft (2000), subsequently deleted, rightly provided that '[w]here more than one State takes countermeasures, the States concerned shall cooperate in order to ensure that the conditions laid down ... for the taking of countermeasures are fulfilled'.

with community obligations. Admittedly, in a few cases States, by taking such countermeasures, may have so acted because the community concern upon which they were acting coincided with their national policy or international agenda. The fact remains, however, that they have demanded compliance with community obligations; in so doing, they have acted, albeit individually, on behalf of the whole international community.

12.8.3 THE CURRENT ROLE OF AGGRAVATED RESPONSIBILITY

It must be emphasized that at present 'ordinary responsibility' is still firmly embedded in the world community and 'aggravated responsibility' plays a relatively minor role. In their daily international dealings, many States still cling to the idea that they should take action in the world community primarily to protect their own interests. They are bent on avoiding any meddling with matters that are not of direct concern to them. For them, State responsibility still is primarily a private matter, arising within the framework of a bilateral legal relation.

Nevertheless, no one can deny the existence of a consistent practice pointing to the emergence of a legal regime of 'aggravated responsibility'. Moreover, here, as in other areas of international law, it is important for *forward-looking legal means and instrumentalities* to be available. Sooner or later, international subjects will make use of them, thus fully implementing those fundamental values they tend to proclaim and even tout, but then occasionally forget to put into practice.

13

PEACEFUL SETTLEMENT OF INTERNATIONAL DISPUTES

13.1 INTRODUCTION

In every national legal system there are various rules establishing the authority of courts of law to adjudicate disputes arising between members of the community. By virtue of these rules, a person can be brought to trial even if he is unwilling to submit to court. Normally, for the institution of proceedings a suit by another subject is sufficient. In addition, the system for establishing whether in specific instances substantive rules are violated is so elaborate and complex that a basic dichotomy exists between civil and criminal proceedings. In the latter, most offences can be submitted to court by any individual who happens to be cognizant of the offence, by a prosecutor, or by enforcement officers. While this is the rule, there is also the exceptional procedure of arbitration whereby disputes on civil or commercial matters can be settled by a third party chosen by the litigants. The main feature of arbitration is that, if admitted by State legislation and within the limits set out by such legislation, it rests on the agreement of the contending parties: the arbitrator cannot pronounce on the dispute if he has not been granted the power to do so by both sides.

By comparison, the position of the international community appears far more rudimentary. Until the adoption of the UN Charter in 1945, States were authorized to resort to force to impose their terms of settlement, unless they had entered into treaties requiring self-restraint on the matter (the Covenant of the League of Nations of 1919, and the Paris Pact of 1928 were among these treaties; see **2.4.3** and **16.1**). States were authorized to enforce, even militarily, their rights without previously endeavouring to seek a peaceful solution of their differences. Thus, while in municipal systems third-party ascertainment of possible breaches of law normally precedes enforcement, in international law this intermediate stage was not necessary, and in fact was normally skipped. However, one should not think that no means other than war were available to States for settling their disputes. Over the years States had gradually forged some institutions or mechanisms, available to those willing to resolve their disagreements peacefully. Things changed considerably after the Second World War, chiefly as a result of the establishment of the UN and the introduction of a general ban on the use or threat of force (see **3.4**). States revitalized and strengthened the traditional means for settling disputes and, in addition, established innovative and flexible mechanisms for preventing disputes or, more generally, inducing compliance with international law.[1]

---

[1] For authoritative overviews of the main means of international dispute settlement see L. Caflisch, 'Cent ans de règlement pacifique des différends interétatiques' (2001) 288 *RCADI* 245; J. G. Merrills, *International Dispute Settlement*, 6th edn (Cambridge: Cambridge University Press, 2017); Y. Tanaka, *The Peaceful Settlement of International Disputes* (Cambridge: Cambridge University Press, 2018).

13.2 OBLIGATION AND MEANS OF DISPUTE SETTLEMENT

According to a celebrated definition of the International Court of Justice (ICJ), 'a dispute is a disagreement on a point of law or fact, a conflict of legal views or of interests between two persons' (*Mavrommatis Palestine Concessions (Greece v United Kingdom) (Objections to the Jurisdiction)*, at 11),[2] which leads to a claim by one party that is positively opposed by the other party (*South West Africa* cases *(Preliminary Objections)*, at 328).[3] The determination of its existence is a matter 'of substance, not of form', which means that the dispute shall exist objectively and is not dependent upon a self-assertion by the parties (*Interpretation of Peace Treaties with Bulgaria, Hungary and Romania* (first phase), at 74).[4] That means that even if a party believes a dispute to exist, it still bears the burden of establishing the objective existence of a dispute (*Marshall Islands*, at 273, §45 of the judgment in the case against India).[5]

The UN Charter enshrines the legal obligation for Member States to settle disputes by peaceful means (Article 2(3)) and lays down in Chapter VI a set of provisions dealing with disputes that may endanger international peace and security (Article 33(1)) (see **3.5** and **15.3.3**). Article 2(3) of the UN Charter is broad in scope, encompassing the peaceful settlement of all disputes, while Article 33 only imposes the obligation of peaceful settlement with regard to 'disputes, the continuance of which is likely to endanger the maintenance of international peace and security'. However, this loose terminology makes it clear that, since in practice any dispute may be likely to jeopardize peace and security, the obligation of peaceful settlement might concern all disputes. In any event, the obligation of peaceful settlement of disputes has been confirmed and further developed in a number of international

---

[2] Notably, in the *Marshall Islands* cases, for the first time the ICJ declined to exercise jurisdiction based on the absence of a dispute between the parties at the time of the submission of the application. The case was brought by the Marshall Islands (which has suffered enormously from nuclear testing) against a host of nuclear countries (but eventually the Court added on its docket only the cases against India, Pakistan, and the UK), for a violation of Article VI of the Treaty on Non-Proliferation of Nuclear Weapons (NPT) concerning the obligation of the States parties 'to pursue negotiations in good faith on effective measures relating to cessation of the nuclear arms race at an early date and to nuclear disarmament', and of customary international law. The decision of the Court to dismiss the case has been harshly criticized, including because it manifested the 'increasing disconnect between the ICJ and the outside world' that in turn 'may lead to the progressive disempowerment of international law as an emancipatory tool to bring about more justice and fairness in international affairs' (A. Bianchi, 'Choice and (the Awareness of) Its Consequences: The ICJ's "Structural Bias" Strikes Again in the Marshall Islands Case' (2017) 111 *AJIL Unbound* 81–7, at 87.

[3] More recently, the ICJ has clarified that 'a dispute exists when it is demonstrated, on the basis of the evidence, that the respondent was aware, or could not have been unaware, that its views were "positively opposed" by the applicant' (*Marshall Islands* case, §38 of the judgment in the case against India, where the Court also refers to prior case law on the requirement of 'awareness').

[4] Determining the existence of a dispute requires therefore an examination of facts (*Application of the International Convention on the Elimination of All Forms of Racial Discrimination (Georgia v Russian Federation) (Preliminary Objections)*, §30).

[5] As aptly noted by a commentator, in its most recent case law, the ICJ seems to have chosen to rely almost exclusively on diplomatic correspondence. Therefore, '[w]hen objections are raised on grounds of a lack of a dispute, the case often turns on finding the document which clearly sets out the parties' opposing views over the subject-matter of the case submitted to adjudication. This masterpiece evidence, in which a high official of one party clearly disagrees with the views of the other party, is the sesame which would open the gates in The Hague. If the right words have not been spelled out, there is a possibility for the case to be rejected by the ICJ *in limine litis*, on the grounds that the existence of a dispute was not established—in that respect the two States might as well fight on a battlefield!' (A. Miron, '"Establishing the Existence of a Dispute before the International Court of Justice": Between formalism and verbalism', Blogpost: *Questions of International Law*, 31 December 2017, online at http://www.qil-qdi.org/establishing-the-existence-of-a-dispute-before-the-international-court-of-justice-between-formalism-and-verbalism/).

instruments, including UN General Assembly resolution 2625 (XXV) on Principles of International Law concerning Friendly Relations and Co-operation among States[6] and the Manila Declaration on the Peaceful Settlement of International Disputes.[7] These instruments have codified a customary rule that is fully consistent with, and spells out the essence of, the legal system inaugurated by the UN Charter whereby States are obliged to settle *any dispute* by peaceful means. This obligation thus complements the obligation not to resort to the threat or use of armed force in international relations (see **3.4**).

The obligation to settle disputes by peaceful means does not imply, however, that States actually have to settle them. To put it differently, the obligation enshrined in Article 2(3) of the UN Charter and the corresponding customary rule is an obligation of conduct, establishing how States shall settle their disputes, and not an obligation of result. States shall *endeavour* to resolve their disputes peacefully, before taking any enforcement action, although they are not duty-bound to *settle* those disputes at any cost.[8] At the same time, however, the obligation of peaceful settlement necessarily implies that the parties to a dispute shall carry out negotiations in good faith to reach a settlement acceptable to the parties or to agree on a means of peaceful settlement. Nonetheless, they remain free to choose any means of peaceful settlement they prefer and they cannot be compelled to submit their dispute to any kind of pacific settlement without their consent (this is the so-called principle of the free choice of means of settlement).[9] The obligation of peaceful settlement is thus marred by the absence of any provision establishing by what specific modalities disputes shall be solved. No general rules have evolved to the effect that States must submit to the authority of bodies empowered to dictate the terms of settlement; in particular, no adjudicating organ endowed with *general and compulsory* jurisdiction has ever been created.

It is not difficult to grasp the reasons for this utterly unsatisfactory state of affairs. All members of the world community have come to realize that it is too dangerous to allow disagreements to be resolved by violent means: the threat or use of force between two States can easily involve other countries as well, since international subjects are interconnected by a variety of links. Hence, the establishment of the general obligation referred to above. However, a profound chasm exists among States as to the modalities for settlement. On the one hand, many countries claim that conciliation and judicial review are the best procedure for settlement and that they should therefore be compulsory for all States. In contrast, many other nations contend that negotiation is more appropriate; more generally, they argue that States should be left free to choose the best mechanisms in each specific case.

States solve their disputes by resorting to a variety of means. Nonetheless, one can distinguish two classes of means or methods of settling disputes. The first class includes those means which aim at inducing the contesting parties to reach agreement. These are the so-called 'diplomatic' or 'political' means, which may involve a third entity in the dispute, such as inquiry, good offices, mediation, or conciliation. The second class includes the means designed to confer on a third party the power to settle the dispute by a binding decision

---

[6] GA resolution 2625 (XXV), 'Declaration on Principles of International Law concerning Friendly Relations and Co-operation among States in accordance with the Charter of the United Nations', 24 October 1970, Annex.

[7] GA resolution 37/10, 'Manila Declaration on the Peaceful Settlement of Disputes', 15 November 1982.

[8] The non-settlement of disputes, at least for a limited period, may be not as disruptive as one might think: see P. Tzeng, 'The Peaceful Non-Settlement of Disputes: Article 4 of the *CMTAS* in *Timor-Leste v. Australia*' (2017) 18 *Melbourne Journal of International Law* 349, referring to the dispute on the sovereignty over the Antarctic; the dispute over the independence of Taiwan; and the Lake Constance delimitation dispute (at 349).

[9] *Status of Eastern Carelia*, 27; *East Timor (Portugal v Australia)*, §26.

(so-called 'judicial means', namely international arbitration and judicial settlement). The agreement by the parties and the third-party decision contain a legally binding assessment on the opposing claims of the parties that have given rise to the dispute. The agreement by the parties ends the dispute, while this may be not the case with the issuance of a third-party binding decision. One or both of the parties to the dispute may indeed fail to conform to the terms of settlement contained therein and insist on their own claim and position. This is the main reason why one generally distinguishes between diplomatic and judicial means.

States solve their disputes often by resorting to a combination of diplomatic and judicial means of settlement. In addition, in certain fields (e.g. in the protection of the environment: see **20.4.4**), they have felt the need to develop specific procedures to ensure compliance with legal standards alternatives to traditional dispute settlement procedures (so-called non-compliance and supervisory procedures).

13.3 DIPLOMATIC MEANS OF DISPUTE SETTLEMENT

There are several diplomatic means of dispute settlement. These are also referred to as 'political' because the resolution of the dispute does not result from the application of international legal rules, but the term 'political' has connotations that may not fully reflect the operation of certain means, such as inquiry or fact-finding bodies, which are expected to establish the facts objectively, or certain forms of conciliation, which operate in a quasi-judicial manner. The operation of these means may not be adequately captured by the term 'diplomatic' either, but for present purposes, it is useful to retain the terminologies in use. There are several diplomatic means of dispute settlement:

(1) *Negotiations*. The most elementary method of settling international disputes is resort to *negotiation* between the contending parties. Characteristic of this method is the total absence of a third party, be it another State or an international institution. The advantage is that the solution is left entirely to the parties concerned, without any undue pressure from outside. In addition, as the goal of negotiation is to achieve agreement over the conflicting claims, a further and more important element is that there will be no loser and no winner, for both parties should derive some benefit from the diplomatic exchange. However, it has two major shortcomings. First, negotiation seldom leads to an in-depth determination of the facts or, when legal disputes are at issue, to the identification of the rules applicable in the specific case. Secondly, the stronger party is more likely to apply pressure to its counterpart than the other way around. More important still, the stronger State may easily subdue the other litigant by resorting to a host of means available to it on account of its de facto superiority. Thus, negotiation may turn out to be a way in which powerful States bend the will of lesser States, settling the issue to their own advantage.

Negotiation is still the most widespread means of settling disputes peacefully. Some treaties make recourse to it compulsory, in the form of mandatory 'consultations' or 'exchange of views'. A case in point is Article 283(1) of the Montego Bay Convention on the Law of the Sea,[10] providing that:

> [w]hen a dispute arises between States Parties concerning the interpretation or application of this Convention, the parties to the dispute shall proceed expeditiously to an exchange of views regarding its settlement by negotiation or other peaceful means.

---

[10] United Nations Convention on the Law of the Sea, 10 December 1982, 1833 UNTS 397.

This obligation to resort to direct negotiations between the parties to the dispute, however, does not entail that they shall continue ad infinitum when it is clear that they will not arrive at a positive conclusion.[11] More generally, the obligation to resort to direct negotiations must be performed in good faith. In this respect, the ICJ has clarified that the parties must conduct negotiations in a meaningful way, 'which will not be the case when either of them insists upon its own position without contemplating any modification of it'[12] or if, during the negotiations, one party adopts the measure concerned in the negotiations and thereby deprives the latter of any meaningful character.[13] That said, unless a treaty provision specifically requires it,[14] international law does not impose an obligation to reach a certain outcome in the negotiations.[15]

(2) *Inquiry* is a method envisaged in the Hague Convention for the Peaceful Settlement of Disputes 1899 (revised and improved upon in 1907) (the Russian publicist Fyodor Fyodorovich de Martens must be credited with strongly and successfully advocating at the Hague Conferences this means of promoting the settlement of disputes). By inquiry is meant a scheme whereby the contending parties agree to set up an international body, consisting of independent and impartial individuals, for the limited purpose of 'elucidating the *facts* [in dispute] by means of an impartial and conscientious investigation' (Article 9 of the 1907 Convention; emphasis added), the presupposition being that they agree on the applicable law. It is for the contestants to decide whether the findings of the body conducting the inquiry shall, or shall not, be legally binding on them. States can also decide to entrust the inquiry commission with establishing where the responsibility lay. This was for instance the case of inquiry relating to the so-called *Incident in the North Sea (Dogger Bank (Great Britain/Russia))*.[16] Finally, inquiry may also be, and more often is, a stage of a more complex settlement of disputes process: it aims at establishing facts with a view to facilitating the task of a conciliation commission or an arbitral or judicial body (see e.g. Article 50 of the Statute of the ICJ, pursuant to which '[t]he Court may, at any time, entrust any individual, body, bureau, commission, or other organizations that it may select, with the task of carrying out an enquiry or giving an expert opinion').

Whereas, as in the past, inquiry as a 'bilateral' method organized by the disputant States has seldom been used (with a few notable exceptions),[17] inquiry or *fact-finding*, as it is now

---

[11] See in this regard the interpretation on the scope of Article 283(1) of the Montego Bay Convention adopted by an Arbitral Tribunal established based on the procedure envisaged in the same Convention: *Arbitration between Barbados and the Republic of Trinidad and Tobago, Relating to the delimitation of the exclusive economic zone and the continental shelf between them*, §§201–203.

[12] *North Sea Continental Shelf* cases, 47, §85.

[13] *Pulp Mills on the River Uruguay (Argentina v Uruguay)*, §§146–147.

[14] *Legality of the Threat or Use of Nuclear Weapons*, §99 (concerning the obligation to negotiate with a view to achieve total and complete disarmament under Article VI of the Treaty on the Non-Proliferation of Nuclear Weapons).

[15] *Obligation to Negotiate Access to the Pacific Ocean (Bolivia v Chile)*, §87.

[16] During the Russo-Japanese war (1904–05) Russian warships fired on a British trawler fleet that was fishing on the Dogger Bank in the North Sea, believing that they were Japanese torpedo boats. The Commission of Inquiry had to establish facts and allocate responsibility: see the Report of the Commission of Inquiry of 26 February 1905. See also A. Mandelstam, 'La commission internationale d'enquête sur l'incident de la Mer du Nord' (1905) *RGDIP* 161, 350–415. For a retrospective account see J. M. Lemnitzer, 'How to Prevent a War and Alienate Lawyers: The Peculiar Case of the 1905 North Sea Incident Commission' in I. de la Rasilla and J. E. Viñuales (eds), *Experiments in International Adjudication: Historical Accounts* (Cambridge: Cambridge University Press, 2019), 76.

[17] A notable exception is recourse to this method by the US and Chile in 1992, in the *Letelier and Moffit* case: these two persons had been assassinated in Washington, DC in 1976, allegedly by a Chilean intelligence officer acting under instructions of the central Chilean authorities. Chile denied responsibility but was prepared to make an *ex gratia* payment equivalent to the amount it would have paid had its responsibility been established. The Inquiry Commission was thus simply called upon to determine the quantum of the *ex gratia* payment.

more often termed, has increasingly acquired importance as a means of establishing facts employed by international organizations or bodies. For instance, the ILO has frequently resorted to this method (under Article 26 of the Organization's Constitution), as have the UN Security Council (Article 34), the General Assembly, or the UN Secretary-General, as well as the Council of the International Civil Aviation Organization (ICAO). Mention should also be made of the International Fact-Finding Commission, provided for in Article 90 of the First Geneva Additional Protocol of 1977. However, this Commission has not become operative so far. As a result, parties to international conflicts have been loath to request it to act (see **17.8.1**).

Inquiry is increasingly used in the field of the international protection of human rights. For instance, some of the so-called Human Rights Treaty Bodies of the UN (see **18.4.6**) can carry out inquiry procedures *ex officio* to investigate grave and systematic violations of human rights.[18] In addition, the Human Rights Council (see **18.4.6**) has established several international commissions of inquiry to investigate crises and determine whether violations of human rights or international humanitarian law have occurred. These commissions and others established by other UN bodies typically do not have the power to make binding findings and recommendations; nonetheless they play an important normative role by engaging in a broader process of law enforcement (e.g. by guiding prosecutorial strategies and investigations in the field of the repression of international crimes or leading to the establishment of international criminal courts or tribunals).[19]

(3) *Good offices*, *mediation*, and *conciliation* denote three gradations of third-party participation in the settlement of disputes.

In the case of *good offices*, a third State or an international body is asked, or offers, to induce the contending parties to negotiate an amicable settlement. The UN Secretary-General has often offered his good offices to facilitate negotiations between the parties of a dispute independently from a mandate by the Security Council or the General Assembly, based on the so-called 'Peking Formula' established in the mid-1950s by the then-Secretary-General Hammarskjöld. The UN General Assembly had mandated Dag Hammarskjöld to offer his good offices for the release of an American aircrew imprisoned by the People's Republic of China (PRC) since the Korean War. Instead of acting on the basis of the mandate conferred by the General Assembly (where the PRC was not yet represented), Hammarskjöld dissociated himself from the General Assembly's resolution, which he considered too partial to the American position in the dispute, and assumed a neutral stance. In this way, he clearly asserted his office's power to intervene, on the basis of Article 99 of the UN Charter, with or without the prior approval of a political organ. The mission was successful, and the PRC released the aircrew expressly as a gesture of 'friendship with Hammarskjöld'.[20] Since then, the UN Secretary-General's good offices role has developed significantly, intervening on very numerous occasions, whether directly or through the appointment of Special Envoys who act on his behalf.[21]

---

[18] This is the case for the Committee Against Torture (CAT), the Committee for the Elimination of Discrimination Against Women (CEDAW), the Committee on Enforced Disappearance (CED), the Committee on the Rights of Persons with Discapacities (CRPD), the Committee on Economic, Social and Cultural Rights (CESCR), and the Committee on the Rights of the Child (CRC).

[19] See in this regard M. Frulli, 'Fact-Finding or Paving the Road to Criminal Justice?' (2012) 10 *JICJ* 1323.

[20] See UN Doc. A/2888 of 17 December 1954; Report SG A/2954 of 9 September 1955. On the specific circumstances of Hammarksjöld's actions see B. Urquhart, *Hammarskjöld* (New York: Alfred A. Knopf, 1972), 99ff.

[21] See T. Franck, 'The Secretary-General's Role in Conflict Resolution: Past, Present and Pure Conjecture' (1995) 6 *EJIL* 1; A. Day, 'Politics in the Driving Seat: Good Offices, UN Peace Operations, and Modern Conflict' in C. de Coning and M. Peter (eds), *United Nations Peace Operations in a Changing Global Order* (London: Palgrave Macmillan, 2019), 67.

In *mediation*, the third party takes a more active role in the dispute settlement, by participating in the negotiations between the two disputants and informally promoting ways of settling the dispute. As a rule, mediation is more effective when the mediator is a dignitary of a Great Power or a senior civil servant of an international organization. For instance, on 8 January 1979, Chile and Argentina asked Pope John Paul II to mediate the dispute between them over the Beagle Channel; following the Pope's 'proposals, suggestions and advice' of 12 December 1980, they entered into an agreement in 1984.[22] Similarly, in 1979, the US President, Jimmy Carter, mediated between Egypt and Israel and achieved the Camp David Agreement. In 1994–95 the so-called Group of Contact (consisting of a number of States including the US, Britain, and Russia) mediated between the conflicting States in the former Yugoslavia, and promoted the conclusion of the Dayton/Paris agreement of November 1995. In 1999, at the request of the Foreign Ministers of the Group of Seven Industrialized Countries and the Russian Federation, the President of Finland, Mr Ahtisaari, and the Russian former Prime Minister, Mr Chernomyrdin, discharged the task of finding a political settlement of the Kosovo crisis; they eventually proposed a settlement that was accepted both by the Federal Republic of Yugoslavia (Serbia and Montenegro) and by NATO countries, and was later endorsed by the UN Security Council by resolution 1244 (1999).

Conciliation designates an even more active role of the third party, which carefully considers the various factual and legal elements of the dispute and formally proposes the terms of settlement (which, however, are not legally binding on the disputants). Among the treaties establishing the right of States parties to unilaterally resort to conciliation (the so-called 'compulsory conciliation procedure'), one should mention the 1969 Vienna Convention on the Law of Treaties (see **Chapter 10**). Under Article 66(b), any party to a dispute concerning any provision on the invalidity of treaties other than those on *jus cogens* can set in motion the conciliation procedure by submitting a request to this effect to the UN Secretary-General within 12 months of its beginning. The Conciliation Commission, appointed from a list drawn up by the Secretary-General, 'shall hear the parties, examine the claims and objections, and make proposals to the parties with a view to reaching an amicable settlement of the dispute' (Article 5 of the Annex to the Convention). Clearly, the Commission has quasi-judicial powers, for it can look into both the facts and the law. However, its findings and proposals are not binding, for the report of the Commission 'shall have no other character than that of recommendations submitted for the consideration of the parties in order to facilitate an amicable settlement of the dispute' (Article 6 of the Annex).[23]

Some multilateral treaties provide the possibility for the parties to a dispute to resort unilaterally to conciliation. Usually, the establishment of compulsory conciliation is the upshot of two conflicting approaches. On the one hand, there is the position of those countries which argue that the drafting of new international substantive rules can only make sense if some compulsory means of settling disputes is established. On the other hand, there are the views of the vast majority of States. These States, while conceding the paramountcy of the general principle on peaceful settlement of disputes, do not wish to tie their hands by accepting a priori the obligation to have recourse to one or another of the specific methods of settlement; in particular, they strongly oppose any settlement procedure

---

[22] Treaty of Peace and Friendship of 1984 between Chile and Argentina, 29 November 1984, 1399 UNTS 103.

[23] Nonetheless, the authority of the Commission's conclusions and recommendations cannot fail to have a great impact on the parties. It is likely, therefore, that in actual fact the weight of the Commission's report will be no less than that of a legally binding judgment. It should, however, be added that, in practice, the mechanism has never been utilized.

leading to a 'win or lose' conclusion. Faced with this rift, international law-makers have eventually struck a balance by making resort to conciliation compulsory.

One major illustration is the Montego Bay Convention on the Law of the Sea, which provides for resort to conciliation in the framework of an elaborate arrangement for the settlement of disputes. If negotiations fail and no other means of settlement is agreed upon, each contending party has the right to propose resort to conciliation. If the offer is not accepted or the parties do not succeed in agreeing upon the conciliation procedure (under Article 284), then any party to the dispute is entitled to resort to arbitration or adjudication. This procedure has been used only once so far, but very successfully. In the recent case opposing Timor-Leste to Australia regarding the delimitation of their continental shelves in the Timor Sea, Timor-Leste triggered the compulsory conciliation procedure (*Timor Sea Conciliation (Timor-Leste v Australia)*). Despite the highly tense overall context of the dispute, marked by Australia's historical co-operation with Indonesia, the occupying Power until Timor-Leste's independence, as well as by espionage incidents involving the Australian secret service, the Conciliation Commission skilfully led the two parties, together with other relevant stakeholders (including private energy companies), to a peaceful resolution of the dispute and delimitation of the area, in a treaty signed by the two parties and recorded in the decision of the Commission.[24]

In practice, however, resort to conciliation has been limited compared to the number of treaty provisions on compulsory conciliation procedures as a means of settling disputes.

13.4 JUDICIAL MEANS OF DISPUTE SETTLEMENT

The mechanisms of dispute settlement that lead to a legal decision binding on the parties are arbitration and adjudication (also called judicial settlement). As in the case of conciliation, the relevant body (a court or an arbitral tribunal) makes a thorough examination of both the facts at issue and the law governing them. Unlike conciliation, however, the findings concerning both the facts and the law are legally binding on the contending parties, in as much as they are set out in the operative part (*dispositif*). In many respects, arbitration and adjudication involve a qualitative leap. The dispute is no longer settled for the sole purpose of safeguarding peaceful relations and accommodating the interests of the conflicting parties in a mutually acceptable manner. An additional goal is pursued—that of patching up the differences on the basis of international legal standards previously accepted by States and by virtue of a binding decision (usually an arbitral award, in the case of arbitration, or a judgment for adjudication).

The main difference between arbitration and adjudication lies in the degree of institutionalization of the court or tribunal that pronounces upon the dispute. In the case of arbitration, the parties to the dispute or to a series of disputes (i) create the tribunal ad hoc; (ii) appoint (or participate in the appointment of) the arbitrators; and (iii) decide the law and the procedure that the tribunal shall apply. By contrast, in the case of adjudication the court is permanent, composed of judges previously elected by the States parties to the relevant treaty establishing the court, and decides the dispute based on predetermined applicable law and procedure. Nonetheless, international arbitration and adjudication inevitably

---

[24] Maritime Boundary Treaty signed by the Parties on 6 March 2018, Annex 28 to Conciliation Between the Democratic Republic of Timor-Leste and the Commonwealth of Australia, Report and Recommendations of the Compulsory Conciliation Commission Between Timor-Leste and Australia on the Timor Sea (9 May 2018) PCA 2016–10, online at https://pcacases.com/web/sendAttach/2327.

present common features, being both governed by the principle of consent whereby an international court or tribunal cannot exercise its jurisdiction without the consent of the defendant State and exceptionally of all States 'whose legal interests would form the very subject matter of the decision'. This is the so-called *Monetary Gold* principle, set forth by the ICJ in its 1954 judgment in the *Monetary Gold* case.[25] In addition, certain aspects of international arbitration may also appear in judicial settlement (e.g. in the possibility for the parties of the dispute to appoint ad hoc judges before the ICJ).

(1) *Arbitration*. The modern era of arbitration as a means of settling international disputes can be traced back to the 1794 Jay Treaty between Great Britain and the US. Since then it has become a regular feature of international diplomacy, but its heyday was the period between the two world wars when Western States still made up a relatively homogeneous group and were still paramount in the world community. Tradition, domestic legal philosophy, and attachment to the principle of the rule of law all prompted Western States to submit to adjudication. Even more importantly, during that period States were under the influence of the Wilsonian concept of 'open diplomacy', according to which the 'reign of law' and voluntary submission to impartial judgment would save the world community from another conflagration by relaxing dangerous tensions.

Permanent bodies have been set up and a whole corpus of rules of procedure has been developed to facilitate recourse to this means of settlement. The process began in 1899, when the Hague Convention on the Peaceful Settlement of International Disputes set up the Permanent Court of Arbitration (PCA), and in 1907, the subsequent Hague Convention (Article 41) undertook to maintain it.[26] The PCA is still in existence, since both Hague Conventions are still in force. Each State member of the PCA can appoint up to four persons (the so-called national group)[27] who are included in a list of qualified persons who can be selected as arbitrators in procedures carried out under the auspices of the PCA. The administrative infrastructure of the PCA (the Permanent Administrative Council and the International Bureau) acts as a secretariat once an arbitral tribunal is established.[28] The rules of procedure of the arbitration are set out in the 1899/1907 Hague Conventions, but the parties to the dispute may agree to apply other rules if they decide otherwise (and actually, most arbitrations currently administered by the PCA apply different rules). The methods of conferring jurisdiction on the PCA are twofold: first, the conclusion of an agreement submitting a certain dispute to the Court (the so-called *compromis*), and, secondly, the making of a treaty containing a clause whereby each contracting party is empowered to submit to the Court any dispute with another contracting party relating to the interpretation or application of the treaty (the so-called *arbitral clause*). The PCA was originally established to settle interstate disputes, but has evolved also to encompass so-called mixed arbitration, dealing with disputes between a State

---

[25] *Monetary Gold Removed from Rome in 1943 (Italy v France, United Kingdom of Great Britain and Northern Ireland and United States of America) (Preliminary Question)*, 32.

[26] On the contribution to arbitration of the 1899 and 1907 Hague Conferences see S. Rosenne (ed.), *The Hague Peace Conferences of 1899 and 1907 and International Arbitration: Reports and Documents* (The Hague: T.M.C. Asser Press, 2001).

[27] Importantly, each national group nominates candidates for the election of judges to the International Court of Justice (Article 4, Statute of the International Court of Justice).

[28] The essential features of the Court were described in 1907 by Fyodor Fyodorovich de Martens, who had played a central role in setting it up in 1899. He said that '[t]he Court of 1899 is only a shadow which, from time to time, materialises, only to fade away once again'. Martens' statement is quoted in League of Nations, Permanent Court of International Justice, *Advisory Committee of Jurists* (1922), 22 and 695. In a similar vein, the Dutch jurist Asser, at the same 1907 Conference, stated that the PCA was 'only a phantom, an impalpable ghost, or, in plain words, it consisted of a Registry and a list'. Conférence de La Haye, *Actes et Documents* (The Hague, 1907), ii, at 235. See also *Advisory Committee of Jurists* (ibid., at n. 4), 695.

and a foreign private party (e.g. in the field of foreign investment, see **21.4.3**), and other types of arbitration (e.g. disputes between non-State actors).²⁹ It has therefore developed Optional Rules, each concerning the various types of arbitration that can be submitted to it. These Optional Rules are based on the arbitration rules promulgated by the United Nations Commission on International Trade Law (UNCITRAL). The establishment of the Permanent Court of Justice and, subsequently, the International Court of Justice led to a decline of the PCA. However, in recent decades, its role has been revitalized, particularly in the field of mixed arbitration.

The PCA has made its facilities and staff available, *inter alia*, to the Iran–US Claims Tribunal. This arbitral tribunal was established in 1981 under the Algiers Accord concluded following the 1979 hostage crisis and the consequent freezing by the US government of Iranian assets in the US or under US jurisdiction or control, and the taking of trade sanctions against Iran. The Tribunal was granted jurisdiction over: (a) claims of US nationals against Iranian authorities as well as claims of Iranian nationals against the US; (b) claims of each State against the other, arising out of contractual arrangements for the purchase or sale of goods or services; (c) claims of one State against the other concerning the interpretation and performance of the obligations laid down in the General Declaration forming part of the Algiers Accord. The Iran–US Claims Tribunal has ruled on hundreds of disputes, some of which involved crucial aspects of international law (e.g. on expropriation and State responsibility).³⁰

In the field of arbitration for the settlement of investment disputes, the International Centre for Settlement of Investment Disputes (ICSID) stands out.³¹ In 1965 a Convention was concluded under the auspices of the World Bank (see **21.2.3**). The purpose was to establish a mechanism that could take into account and protect the interests of both investors (normally nationals or corporations from industrialized countries) and States where investments were made (normally developing countries). Thus, a legal framework was set up, available to States, individuals, and corporations. No permanent tribunal was established, only an Administrative Council, consisting of all member States, and a Secretariat. In addition, panels of conciliators and arbitrators (experts in the fields of law, industry, or finance) were set up. Parties to investment disputes may thus select conciliators or arbitrators from those panels. So far ICSID has proved very successful, primarily in the field of arbitration, although it has also come under much criticism (see **21.4.3**).

(2) *Adjudication*. This means of settlement is characterized by the establishment of permanent judicial bodies, made up of independent judges, adjudicating international disputes based on a predetermined set of rules of procedure, and rendering decisions that are binding on the parties.³²

The first permanent court with jurisdiction over States ever created is the Central American Court of Justice (the Court of Cartago), established in 1907 by the five Central

---

[29] In 1934, the Bureau of the PCA for the first time accepted the request of a tribunal established under a contract between the Radio Corporation of America and China to use the PCA's facilities, thus considering that its mandate did not encompass only interstate arbitration (see *Radio Corporation of America v The National Government of The Republic of China*).

[30] On the practice of the Iran–US Claims Tribunal see G. Aldrich, *The Jurisprudence of the Iran–United States Claims Tribunal* (Oxford: Clarendon Press, 1996).

[31] See C. Schreuer, L. Malintoppi, A. Reinisch, and A. Sinclair, *The ICSID Convention: A Commentary*, 2nd edn (Cambridge: Cambridge University Press, 2010).

[32] For a comprehensive analysis of the phenomenon of international adjudication see C. P. Romano, K. J. Alter, and Y. Shany (eds), *The Oxford Handbook of International Adjudication* (Oxford: Oxford University Press, 2013).

American Republics (Convention for the Establishment of a Central American Court of Justice).[33] The Court carried out its activities for a decade; it had jurisdiction not only in interstate disputes but also over complaints brought by nationals of the contracting States against these States (but not against their own government). The Court heard only three interstate disputes and received seven complaints by individuals (although the Court admitted only one). The Court dissolved in 1918, in accordance with the expiration date established in the Convention and there was no attempt to revive it due to its limited success.

The Court of Cartago, however, constituted a precedent for the establishment in 1921 of the Permanent Court of International Justice (PCIJ), as a response to the increased impetus to create a permanent international court to facilitate the international settlement of disputes.[34] The PCIJ was not an organ of the League of Nations, but it was open to its members, and the main features of its jurisdiction had been agreed and included in Article 14 of the Covenant of the League. Moreover, its establishment was to give effect to the objectives of the League to prevent recourse to war. The framers of the PCIJ Statute found four great merits in its institution. Since it consisted of a group of sitting judges, 'the contesting parties no longer [had] the choice of the judges'. As it was made up of judges 'permanently associated with each other in the same work, and, except in rare cases, retaining their seats from one case to another', the Court could 'develop a continuous tradition and assure the harmonious and logical development of international law'. While with the PCA the fear is that judges would be inclined to regard cases 'from a political standpoint', in the case of the PCIJ '[l]aw necessarily [became] more authoritative and also, possibly, more severe'. While the PCA could include 'politicians in addition to Jurisconsults', the Court would comprise, 'besides Jurisconsults, great judges'.[35] In short, the Court was not a court of arbitration 'but a Court of justice'.[36]

The PCIJ was a landmark international judicial body, whose main legal features have been maintained in the Statute of its successor, the International Court of Justice (ICJ) (see **15.2**).[37] The Court is the 'principal judicial organ' of the UN (Article 92 of the UN Charter), created and regulated by the UN Charter and the Statute of the Court, which is an integral part of the UN Charter. Like its predecessor, the ICJ can decide any dispute that States decide to submit to it. In other words, the Court has 'general' jurisdiction differently from other permanent judicial bodies whose jurisdiction is limited to disputes concerning specific matters (see later in the chapter). Unlike other permanent judicial courts and tribunals, however, only States are admitted as parties in adversarial proceedings before the ICJ. International organizations may have recourse to the ICJ not to solve disputes but through the possibility of requesting an Advisory Opinion. Under Articles 96 of the UN Charter and 65 of the ICJ Statute, the Court may render an Advisory Opinion at the request of the UN General Assembly or the UN Security Council as well as of other bodies that may be authorized by or in accordance with the UN Charter. In practice, this possibility

---

[33] See F. Baetens, 'First to Rise and First to Fall: The Court of Cartago (1907–1918)' in I. de la Rasilla and J. E. Viñuales (eds), *Experiments in International Adjudication: Historical Accounts* (Cambridge: Cambridge University Press, 2019), 211.

[34] For prospective and retrospective views see H. Wehberg, *Das Problem eines internationalen Staatengerichtshofes* (München and Leipzig: Duncker & Humblot, 1912); O. Spiermann, *International Legal Argument in the Permanent Court of International Justice* (Cambridge: Cambridge University Press, 2005).

[35] See the Final Report of the Committee of Jurists, in *Advisory Committee of Jurists* (n 29), at note 4, 695.

[36] Ibid., at 696.

[37] Within the voluminous literature on the ICJ see H. Lauterpacht, *The Development of International Law by the International Court* (London: Stevens & Sons, 1958); R. Kolb, *The International Court of Justice* (Oxford: Hart, 2013); M. Shaw, *Rosenne's Law and Practice of the International Court (1920–2015)*, 4 vols, 5th edn (The Hague and Leiden: Brill/Nijhoff, 2016); H. Thirlway, *The International Court of Justice* (Oxford: Oxford University Press, 2016).

has often been relied upon to address legal issues arising in interstate disputes, particularly when there is no consent to submit that specific issue to adjudication.[38]

Indeed, as for any international court or tribunal settling international disputes, the jurisdiction of the Court is governed by the principle of consent, meaning that the Court cannot decide a dispute unless States parties to it have accepted the jurisdiction of the Court. States may accept the jurisdiction of the Court in a variety of ways. First, States parties to a dispute can conclude a special agreement after the dispute has arisen[39] (the *compromis*, also used to establish an ad hoc arbitral tribunal[40]). Secondly, States can accept the jurisdiction of the Court by virtue of a treaty[41] or a treaty provision for disputes that may eventually arise in the future.[42] Under these treaties or treaty provisions, the Court can be seized unilaterally by each State party to a dispute that is also a party to the relevant treaty, which however must also have been accepted by the other party to the dispute. This is the so-called compulsory jurisdiction of the ICJ.[43] Thirdly, States can accept the so-called *optional clause* of the jurisdiction of the Court (Article 36(2) of the Court's Statute). By virtue of this clause, every State can declare that it accepts *ipso facto* and without special agreement the compulsory jurisdiction of the Court in relation to any other State accepting the same clause.[44] Finally, the Court has developed in its case law another method of accepting the Court's jurisdiction, based, as much as the other modes, on consent, which in this case is tacit or

---

[38] See most recently GA resolution 71/292 'Request for an advisory opinion of the International Court of Justice on the legal consequences of the separation of the Chagos Archipelago from Mauritius in 1965', 22 June 2017, A/RES/71/292, and the subsequent Advisory Opinion of the Court in *Legal Consequences of the Separation of the Chagos Archipelago from Mauritius in 1965*. The questions asked of the Court in the UN General Assembly's request were: (a) whether the process of decolonization of Mauritius had been lawfully completed when it was granted independence in 1968, following the separation of the Chagos Archipelago from Mauritius and having regard to international law; (b) what were the consequences under international law flowing from the United Kingdom's continued administration of the Chagos Archipelago, including with respect to the inability of Mauritius to implement a programme for the resettlement on the Chagos Archipelago of its nationals, in particular those of Chagossian origin. The questions were closely related to a long-standing dispute between Mauritius and the United Kingdom on the sovereignty over the Archipelago which the United Kingdom did not agree to submit to judicial decision. In the Advisory Opinion, the Court reached the conclusion that Mauritius' decolonization was not lawfully completed in 1968 following the separation from the Chagos Archipelago, and that the United Kingdom is under an obligation to bring to an end its administration of the Chagos Archipelago as rapidly as possible.

[39] Cases submitted to the ICJ by means of a *compromis* include *Corfu Channel (United Kingdom v Albania)*, (although the first phase proceeded through voluntary acceptance by Albania); and *Case Concerning the Gabčíkovo-Nagymaros Project (Hungary/Slovakia)*.

[40] Two prominent examples of arbitral proceedings based on a *compromis* are *Alabama (United States/Great Britain)* and *Trail Smelter Arbitration (United States/Canada)*.

[41] See e.g. the American Treaty on Pacific Settlement (Pact of Bogotá), 30 April 1948, 30 UNTS 55, Article XXXI (relied on *inter alia* in *Certain Activities Carried Out by Nicaragua in the Border Area (Costa Rica v Nicaragua)* and *Construction of a Road in Costa Rica along the San Juan River (Nicaragua v Costa Rica)*, 690–1, §§54–55); European Convention for the Peaceful Settlement of Disputes, 29 April 1957, 320 UNTS 243, Article 1 (relied on in *Jurisdictional Immunities of the State (Germany v Italy: Greece intervening)*, 118–19, §§41–44).

[42] See e.g. Optional Protocol to the Vienna Convention on Diplomatic Relations, concerning the Compulsory Settlement of Disputes, 18 April 1961, 500 UNTS 241, Article 1, and Optional Protocol to the Vienna Convention on Consular Relations concerning the Compulsory Settlement of Disputes, 24 April 1963, 596 UNTS 487, Article 1 (relied on *inter alia* in *United States Diplomatic and Consular Staff in Tehran*, §§45–49; *Jadhav (India v Pakistan)*, §§34–38).

[43] E.g. under the Vienna Convention disputes relating to *jus cogens* may be submitted to the ICJ at the request of one party only, after 12 months have elapsed since the start of the dispute without any settlement being reached (Article 66(a)).

[44] See e.g. *Nicaragua (Nicaragua v United States of America) (Jurisdiction and Admissibility)*. On the operation of this clause see C. Tomuschat, 'Article 36' in A. Zimmermann et al. (eds), *The Statute of the International Court of Justice: A Commentary*, 3rd edn (Oxford: Oxford University Press, 2019), 712, §§70–84.

implied: the so-called *forum prorogatum*. According to this method, once a State institutes proceedings before the Court against another State that has not previously accepted the Court's jurisdiction, the jurisdiction of the Court is established if the respondent State shows that it accepts the Court's jurisdiction by some act (such as appearing before the Court and arguing the case on its merits). This doctrine was first set out by the PCIJ in 1925,[45] then taken up by the ICJ in 1951.[46]

Since the end of the Cold War, States, chiefly developing countries as well as States belonging to the former socialist bloc, have increasingly had recourse to the ICJ, in the correct belief that independent and impartial third-party binding settlement of disputes constitutes a helpful way of bridging international differences. Conversely, many Western States, contrary to the previous trend emphasized earlier, have tended to shun the Court, presumably out of distrust for the judicial settlement of disputes. The docket of this Court has greatly augmented, and its judgments tend to cover a growing range of subjects, including politically sensitive issues such as self-defence, indirect armed aggression, self-determination of peoples, the legality of the threat or use of nuclear weapons, genocide, and so on.

(3) *Proliferation of international courts and tribunals.* Together with the increasing importance of the ICJ, another signal phenomenon of recent decades is the proliferation of permanent judicial bodies.[47] In this connection, one could mention the courts and tribunals set up at the regional level in the area of human rights (the European Court of Human Rights, the Inter-American Court of Human Rights, and the African Court of Human and People's Rights, see **18.4.7**) and in the field of economic integration and free trade (e.g. the Court of Justice of the European Union, the Court of Justice of the European Free Trade Association, the Court of Justice of the Common Market for Eastern and Southern Africa, the Court of Justice of the Economic Community of West African States, the Court of Justice of the Andean Community of Nations, and the Caribbean Court of Justice). In addition, many international organizations have set up administrative tribunals to settle disputes with members of their staff (e.g. the Administrative Tribunal of the International Labour Organization, sitting in Geneva, which also settles disputes between other organizations of the UN family and their staff). One should also mention the International Tribunal for the Law of the Sea (ITLOS), sitting in Hamburg, established under Annex VI of the UN Convention on the Law of the Sea. The ITLOS is one of the four judicial bodies to which contracting States parties to a dispute may turn, when the dispute cannot be solved through negotiations, conciliations, or other means[48] (the ITLOS has exclusive jurisdiction, through its Seabed Disputes Chamber, over disputes relating to activities in the international seabed area; in addition, it has special jurisdiction in matters calling for provisional measures). Finally, one should mention the courts and tribunals established in the field of international criminal law, in particular the International Criminal Court (see **19.3.3**). Unlike the courts and tribunals mentioned so far, they do not adjudicate disputes between States or between States and private parties or between other subjects of international law, but they rule on the criminal responsibility of individuals accused of crimes

---

[45] *Mavrommatis Palestine Concessions (Greece v Great Britain) (Objections to the Jurisdiction)*, 27–8.

[46] *Haya de la Torre (Colombia v Peru)*, 78.

[47] For overviews see P.-M. Dupuy and J. E. Viñuales, 'The Challenge of Proliferation: An Anatomy of the Debate' in C. Romano, K. Alter, and Y. Shany (eds), *The Oxford Handbook of International Adjudication* (Oxford: Oxford University Press, 2014), 135; Y. Shany, 'No Longer a Weak Department of Power? Reflections on the Emergence of a New International Judiciary' (2009) 20 *EJIL* 73, at 75–6; C. Romano, 'The Proliferation of International Judicial Bodies: The Pieces of the Puzzle' (1998–99) 31 *NYU Journal of International Law* 709.

[48] The other three judicial bodies available to the parties are the ICJ, an arbitral tribunal set up in accordance with Annex VII to the Convention, and a special arbitral tribunal constituted in accordance with Annex VIII.

under their respective jurisdictions. States are not called to account before these courts and tribunals (although indirectly their conduct is taken into account when the defendant acted as a State agent, and more particularly if he or she was a prominent figure in the apparatus of the State).

Some commentators have considered the multiplication of international arbitral or judicial bodies as likely to lead to discrepancies and conflicts in the interpretation or application of international law, and hence to a fragmentation of this body of law. Also, it has been suggested that the ICJ, as the principal international judicial organ, should be given the role of the court having the final word on international legal issues. It may be contended that, by itself, the proliferation at issue is not a negative phenomenon, as it may stimulate courts and tribunals to hand down better-reasoned and more convincing judgments. As a consequence, those judgments which stand out both for the compelling nature of their legal reasoning and for the balanced nature of their findings will also enjoy greater authority.

13.5 INTERPLAY BETWEEN DIPLOMATIC AND JUDICIAL MEANS

The growing network of international courts and tribunals coexists with the continued use of diplomatic means of dispute settlement, which remain the preferred choice of States, mainly because they have control over the outcome. This coexistence has sometimes led to complex interactions.[49] The two approaches can be combined into a broader dispute settlement mechanism, as illustrated by the WTO dispute settlement approach.

(1) *The ongoing importance of diplomatic means.* The proliferation of international courts and tribunals and the progressive institutionalization of the legal methods of settlement through treaty provisions providing compulsory resort to arbitration or adjudication constitute a key development of the international legal order. Nonetheless, diplomatic means of settlement continue to play a crucial role in current international practice for a variety of reasons.

First, despite the mushrooming of judicial means, courts and tribunals are still very limited and have limited jurisdiction over disputes, one reason being that the parties to a dispute must have consented to submit it to the relevant court or tribunal. Recourse to diplomatic means of settlement may thus, in some scenarios, be the only option available.

Secondly, courts and tribunals operate in the context of political processes and necessarily interact with political institutions. Prior negotiations between the parties, possibly facilitated by a third party, are often necessary (see **13.2**) to agree to submit the dispute to arbitration or judicial settlement. In other instances, the submission of a dispute to a legal method of settlement is the outcome of processes occurring within an international organization, whether regional or universal (e.g. think of the powers that the UN Security Council exercises under Chapter VI of the Charter: see **15.3.3**).

Thirdly, the existence and availability of judicial means for the settlement of a dispute may facilitate and encourage recourse to diplomatic methods. This is particularly the case when the parties to the dispute, given the importance of the issues at stake, prefer to avoid a winner/loser solution that is often the outcome of arbitration and adjudication, making them unattractive and too risky in specific instances.

---

[49] On this interplay see the contributions in L. Boisson de Chazournes, M. Kohen, and J. E. Viñuales (eds), *Diplomatic and Judicial Means of Dispute Settlement* (The Hague: Brill, 2012).

Finally, and closely related to the last point, disputes may show a strong political dimension that at the same time makes them unsuitable for legal settlement (which, however, does not mean that the dispute cannot be solved by judicial means, to the extent that the dispute concerns a legal issue and not only a political one).

(2) *The dispute settlement of the WTO.* As mentioned previously, States usually resort to a combination of means of dispute settlement. It is therefore no surprise that multilateral treaties on specific matters provide for systems of settlement that combine diplomatic and judicial means (e.g. as the Convention on the Law of the Sea).

An extremely original method for settling disputes has been established within the World Trade Organization (WTO) (on the WTO see **21.4.2**). This system is an inventive admixture of conciliation, negotiation, and adjudication, with an interesting follow-up of enforcement, and traditional arbitration as a final and *extrema ratio* mode of resolution. Clearly, this unique procedure is warranted by the subject matter that involves huge economic interests. In addition, there is often the need to take account of the specific problems besetting certain countries or some sectors, a need that, however, must be reconciled or balanced with the requirement to ensure non-discrimination, that is, equality of treatment and absence of unjustified distortions of world trade.

The Dispute Settlement Understanding (DSU), annexed to the WTO Agreement, regulates the dispute settlement procedure. It hinges on the following points:

(i) Each contracting State must *notify* the Organization and the other parties of its adoption of trade measures affecting the operation of the substantive provisions of an agreement on trade. Notification is followed by *consultation*. The other contracting parties must respond to requests for consultation promptly and conduct these consultations with a view to reaching mutually satisfactory solutions. Should consultations fail to lead to an acceptable settlement, the parties may ask for the use of *good offices* or *conciliation* by the WTO.

(ii) If no settlement is reached, a contracting party may submit a *complaint* to a panel of independent experts. The complaint, it should be emphasized, does not necessarily concern a breach of a WTO provision. What a State may complain of is the *'nullification or impairment' of benefits accruing to it*, brought about by the measures adopted by the party complained of. What matters is not whether a State has violated a specific treaty provision, but rather whether or not it has caused that 'nullification or impairment of benefits' (indeed, a 'nullification or impairment of benefits' may come about even in the absence of a breach of the relevant agreement; conversely, a State can breach the agreement without such breach amounting to a 'nullification or impairment of benefits').

(iii) The complaint may emanate from a single State or more States (multiple complaint). It is submitted to a panel of three (unless the parties agree on a panel of five) experts in international trade law or policy, serving in their individual capacity. Panels are established by the WTO Dispute Settlement Body (DSB), on which representatives of all contracting parties sit. The members of each specific panel are however nominated by the WTO Secretariat; if the parties do not agree to the composition of the panel, membership is determined by the Director-General of the WTO in consultation with the chairman of the DSB and the chairman of the Council or Committee established under the relevant WTO Agreement.

(iv) The panel hears submissions from each complainant as well as the State complained of. Third States may also be heard. In making their findings on the facts and law, panels proceed in two stages. First, they issue an *Interim Report* with their findings and conclusions. The parties may comment on it and request a further meeting of the panel

(Article 9); the 1966 Covenants on Human Rights (Articles 16 and 40 respectively); the 1956 Slavery Convention (Article 8); and the 1984 UN Convention against Torture (Article 19). One should also mention the Universal Periodic Review, established within the Human Rights Council, which allows the latter to examine the reports submitted by all States members of the UN on the implementation of human rights (see **18.4.6**), as well as the procedures established in the field of the protection of the environment (see **20.4.4**).

(2) *Inspection*, far more effective and penetrating than the examination of States' reports, where the inquiring body must confine itself to the data provided by the State concerned. On-the-spot investigations allow international organs (or, as in the case of the treaties on Antarctica and outer space, the other States parties to the treaty) to satisfy themselves as to whether a State respects or disregards the treaty. This class of monitoring is, for example, provided for in the Treaty on the International Agency for Atomic Energy (Article 12(6)), the Antarctic Treaty (Article VII), and the 1967 Treaty on the Peaceful Use of Outer Space (Article XII). Inspection is also provided for in many treaties on protection of the environment (see **20.4.4**).

(3) Supervision by treaty-based monitoring bodies, based on quasi-judicial procedures, for instance in the field of the protection of human rights (see **18.4.6**) or to monitor respect for international labour standards (see the procedures provided for in Articles 22(3), 24(5), and 26(9) of the ILO Constitution).

(4) Adoption of measures designed to forestall the possible commission of international delinquency by a State. So far, this unique form of *'preventive' supervision* has been chiefly established in the area of the peaceful use of atomic energy and protection of the environment (see **20.4.4**). The special nature of the subject matter accounts for the exceptional characteristics of this international scrutiny. For instance, some treaties make the delivery of nuclear material conditional on a preventive control of the facilities of the recipient party by the granting State. Only if those facilities are considered consistent with the general standards set out in the agreements can the material be delivered. In this case, the extreme importance of the matter, that is, the danger that nuclear material might be used for military purposes, warrants resort to a very advanced type of supervision, which States would otherwise find unacceptable.

There are two main reasons explaining the establishment of non-compliance and supervisory procedures. First, in the aftermath of the First World War, States started to resort to international treaties to regulate matters which until then had remained within their domestic jurisdiction. These issues included the protection of minorities; the regulation of labour conditions and the rights of workers; the establishment of international mandates over territories which up to that time had been under the exclusive control of sovereign Powers; the regulation of narcotic drugs; and unique matters such as the relations between the Free City of Danzig (now Gdansk) and Poland, and more generally the protection of the rights of the City laid down in the Treaty of Versailles. The new international legislation presented one remarkable feature: it did not impose reciprocal obligations, that is to say obligations entailing each contracting party being interested in complying with the rules for fear the other contracting State might feel free to disregard them. Rather, the new rules belonged to that unique class of norms which protect the interests of entities other than the subjects assuming the rights and obligations in question—such as individuals, groups, populations subject to the mandate system, associations of workers and employers, and so on. The second reason is that in these new areas it was difficult to establish mechanisms for ensuring that the new international rules were faithfully observed. Resort to adjudication was not feasible on a number of grounds, including the fact that States, although they had accepted such new and bold obligations, were reluctant to submit to judicial bodies. Furthermore, the unique features of the subject matter meant that adjudication was scarcely appropriate. Indeed, the non-reciprocal character of the obligations laid down in those rules meant that infringement of one of them might be passed over in silence, if it was only the other contracting States that had the right to demand compliance. It was, therefore, only logical to bestow the right to exact respect for the rules upon the very entities for whose benefit they had been agreed upon. However, it would have been impossible for States to accept the granting of *locus standi* before international courts to individuals or groups. A compromise was reached. It lay in allowing individuals or groups to petition international bodies that were devoid of any judicial function and power.

To satisfy all the requirements mentioned above, imaginative monitoring systems were contrived. To make them acceptable to States, it was deemed necessary to water down their possible impact on State sovereignty. To this effect, no binding force was attached to the final assessment of supervisory bodies. In addition, side by side with organs consisting of impartial individuals, bodies composed of State representatives were set up (plainly, they are more sensitive to States' exigencies and, therefore, more inclined to attenuate possibly harsh evaluations). It was also decided that the meetings or sessions of the monitoring bodies should normally be held *in camera*, for the manifest purpose of shielding States from public exposure.

Supervisory systems proved a balanced and relatively effective means of impelling States to live up to their international undertakings. It is, therefore, not surprising that certain of them survived the Second World War (e.g. the ILO mechanisms for monitoring the application of international labour conventions, and the systems for scrutinizing conventions on narcotic drugs). In other areas new control machinery was instituted. The *fields in which supervision is at present most widespread* are (a) international labour conventions, (b) treaties and other international standards on human rights, (c) the peaceful use of atomic energy, (d) the environment, (e) the Antarctic and outer space, (f) international economic law, and (g) international and internal armed conflict.

Plainly, the expansion of supervision to so many important areas testifies to its responsiveness to States' needs. In addition, it also proves that all groups of States are ready to submit to supervision, for even those countries which are loath to accept other international means of investigation do not oppose international monitoring. This, of course, is mainly due to its flexibility and to the fact that supervisory bodies do not put States in the dock, but tend to persuade them, even before any possible breach occurs, by dint of cautious diplomatic and moral pressure, to abide by those rules which they may be inclined to disregard.

14

ENFORCEMENT

14.1 DECENTRALIZED ENFORCEMENT IN HISTORICAL PERSPECTIVE

14.1.1 GENERAL

In domestic legal orders enforcement strictly denotes all those measures and procedures, mostly taken by public authorities, calculated to impel compliance, by forcible and other coercive means, with the law. Consequently, there exists a clear-cut distinction between those measures and procedures, that is, *sanctions*, on the one hand, and, on the other hand, forcible acts which, since they do not amount to an authorized institutional reaction to a wrong, are unlawful. By contrast, in the old international community this distinction could not be made. There existed no central authorities responsible for enforcing the law on behalf of the whole community: *self-help* prevailed, that is, only the aggrieved State was authorized to react to what it considered a breach of its rights by another State. What is even more striking, the law applicable before the First World War also allowed resort to force for the protection of one's own interests. Consequently, there was *no substantial difference* between legitimate forcible 'sanctions' and resort to military force for safeguarding or furthering one's own interests. States were only to respect certain modalities: if they decided to engage in war, they were to express their *animus belligerandi* (intent to wage war) in some way, with the consequence that all the rules on war and neutrality became applicable. If, instead, they preferred to resort to coercion short of war, they were to make it clear that they did not mean to render the laws on war and neutrality applicable, but preferred to remain within the province of the laws of peace. Other modalities concerned the proper use of force: in the case of war, various rules on warfare placed restraints on the conduct of hostilities; in the case of forcible measures short of war, a few general principles gradually evolved.

A further distinguishing trait of traditional law was that even when a State resorted to armed force in order to react to wrongful behaviour by another State, no prior exhaustion of peaceful remedies was requested; much less was the State required to wait for a third party to pronounce on whether international law had actually been broken. Thus, while in domestic legal systems enforcement is normally carried out after judicial ascertainment that a breach of law has indeed occurred, in traditional international law States were authorized to judge by themselves, that is to base their possible resort to force on their own unilateral assessment of wrongdoings by other countries.

Both before and after the First World War, State practice and legal literature tried to identify the various forms which the use of force could take. In particular, the distinction between armed intervention (whereby States act to protect their own interests) and armed reprisals (reactions against wrongful acts of another State), a distinction States often relied on, was rather blurred in actual practice, for two reasons. First, States were, in any case, authorized to use armed force to pursue their interests, and so it did not make much difference whether they engaged in military action to react to an instance of unlawful conduct by another State, or to safeguard their own interests. Secondly, all too frequently States invoked legal considerations as a cloak to cover their action in cases where they acted out of mere political interest; conversely, in some instances, when they were the victims of breaches by other States, their reaction was not explicitly based on legal arguments. Yet it may be useful to discuss some of these traditional categories.

14.1.2 FORCIBLE INTERVENTION

Forcible intervention meant compelling another State, by the threat or use of force, to do something (e.g. to change its government, to enter into a treaty, to cede territory, or to carry out certain actions in its territory) in the interest of the intervening State. Forcible intervention took the form of military occupation of the territory of another State; naval demonstrations; naval blockade (that is to say the blocking by men-of-war of a portion of the coast of another State); embargo (in the old sense, that is the seizure of ships belonging to the other State or its nationals), and so on. International practice is replete with cases of armed intervention. In some instances, armed intervention in the territory of other States was officially justified by the intervening State on the grounds of 'self-defence and self-preservation'.

As early as 1817 the US occupied *Amelia Island* (off East Florida, at the mouth of St Mary's river, near the boundary of the State of Georgia), then under Spanish sovereignty, on the grounds that it had become a centre of illicit trafficking harmful to the US and over which the Spanish authorities were unable to exercise control.[1] In 1817, the American troops invaded Western Florida, which was also still under Spanish sovereignty, to repel the Seminole Indians living in Florida.[2]

Another famous incident is that of the *Caroline*. On the occasion of the Canadian rebellion of 1837 against the British authorities (Canada being at the time under British sovereignty), rebels were assisted by American citizens who several times crossed the Niagara (the border between Canada and the US) on the *Caroline* to provide the insurgents with men and ammunitions. A party of British troops headed by Captain McLeod was then sent to attack the ship. They boarded it in the US port of Fort Schlosser, killed a number of men, set the ship on fire, and cast it adrift towards Niagara Falls. The US government protested against this violation of its territorial sovereignty. A characteristic feature of the *Caroline* incident is that Britain saw no need to justify its behaviour by invoking a breach of international law by the US. Rather, it claimed that its violation of US sovereignty had been rendered necessary by the fundamental right of 'self-defence and self-preservation'. However, the ensuing diplomatic correspondence enabled the two States to agree upon a delimitation of the instances in which armed attack on the territory of another State was allowed. According to the definition by the US Secretary of State, Webster, the attacking State must show a 'necessity of self-defence, instant, overwhelming, leaving no choice of means and no moment for deliberation'. This formula, which became famous and was taken up in subsequent years, initiated an international practice which gradually led to the placing of some restrictions on the unfettered freedom of States to use force for the protection of their interests.[3]

---

[1] On the *Amelia Island* case see Moore, *Digest*, ii, 406; *Right to Protect Citizens in Foreign Countries by Landing Forces*, Memorandum of the Solicitor for the Department of State, 5 October 1912, 2nd edn (Washington, DC: Government Printing Office, 1929), 51.
[2] See Moore, *Digest*, ii, at 402–5; *Right to Protect Citizens in Foreign Countries* (n 1), 52–3.
[3] On the *Caroline* case see Moore, *Digest*, ii, at 409–14; Lord McNair, *International Law Opinions* (Cambridge: Cambridge University Press, 1956), ii, at 221–30; R. Jennings, 'The *Caroline* and *McLeod* cases' (1938) 23 *AJIL* 82.

In other instances, States sent armed troops abroad for the purpose of protecting their own nationals. In such cases, the justification normally invoked by the invading State was that the territorial State had failed to take all the precautionary and other measures necessary for safeguarding the life and property of foreigners. It therefore proved imperative to substitute for this omission. Plainly, this sort of justification lent itself to many abuses.

According to the American writer Offutt,[4] between 1813 and 1928 US troops were sent abroad at least 70 times in order to protect US nationals or 'US interests'. Not unexpectedly, most military expeditions were carried out by the US in Latin American countries, but US troops also landed in other countries, such as Japan (1853, 1854, 1863, 1864, 1868); China (1854, 1856, 1859, 1900); Egypt (1858 and 1882); Kisembo (on the west coast of Africa) in 1860; Formosa (now Taiwan) (1867); and Korea (1871, 1888, 1894). During the same period, British forces landed in Honduras in 1873 and in Nicaragua in 1895 and 1910, and German forces in Samoa in 1899.

In other earlier instances, chiefly in the nineteenth century, States used force abroad allegedly for the purpose of protecting the life or assets of individuals (not necessarily their nationals) threatened by civil commotion (so-called *humanitarian intervention*). In fact there were military interventions by European countries in other States (e.g. the Ottoman Empire) designed to further political or diplomatic interests of the intervening Powers.

14.1.3 REPRISALS

Reprisals indicate acts or actions in response to an unlawful act by another State. They consist of violations, by the allegedly wronged State, of international rules vis-à-vis the wrongdoer. In other words, reprisals are unlawful acts that become lawful in that they constitute a reaction to a delinquency by another State. It obviously follows that, if the State against which reprisals are taken had not in fact breached international rules, the State resorting to reprisals can be held responsible for a violation of international law. In traditional international law reprisals were aimed at either impelling the delinquent State to discontinue the wrongdoing, or at punishing it, or both.

They are usually divided into 'peaceful' and 'military'. The former term covers actions that may consist of the failure to apply towards the alleged author of a breach of international law, a treaty or a customary rule (e.g. on the treatment of foreigners), the mass expulsion of nationals of a State with which the State taking reprisals had concluded a treaty prohibiting such expulsion, and so on. The latter category includes any act implying the threat or use of military force against the State responsible for a wrongful act. This category, therefore, included the actions indicated above under the heading of intervention (blockade, embargo, and so on).

The famous *Naulilaa (Portugal v Germany)* case may be mentioned as it illustrates the rules on reprisals at the beginning of the twentieth century. In 1914, while Portugal was still neutral, German forces from the German colony of South West Africa (at present Namibia) crossed the border with Angola, then under Portuguese domination, in order to meet Portuguese authorities and initiate negotiations concerning the importation of food and the setting up of postal relations with Germany through Angola. At the Portuguese post of Naulilaa, on the southern border of Angola, the head of the German team, the governor of a district in South West Africa, and two German officers were killed following a misunderstanding caused primarily by the linguistic incompetence of the German interpreter, who hardly spoke and read Portuguese. By way of military reprisal, German troops were sent to destroy Portuguese

---

[4] M. Offutt, *The Protection of Citizens Abroad by the Armed Forces of the United States* (Baltimore: Johns Hopkins University Press, 1928), 12ff.

posts and kill Portuguese soldiers. The Special Arbitral Tribunal instituted by Germany and Portugal determined in 1928 the following in relation to reprisals: first, they comprise acts which would normally be illegal but are rendered lawful by the fact that they constitute a reaction to an international delinquency; secondly, they must be 'limited by considerations of humanity (*les expériences de l'humanité*) and the rules of good faith applicable in the relations between States'; thirdly, they must not be excessive, although they need not be strictly proportionate to the offence; fourthly, they must be preceded by a request for peaceful settlement (they must 'have remained unredressed after a demand for amends'); fifthly, they must 'seek to impose on the offending State reparation for the offence, the return to legality and the avoidance of new offences'. It is interesting to note that in this case, the Tribunal held that Germany had violated international law because: (i) the Portuguese had not acted contrary to international law, since the killing of the three Germans was not a wilful but a fortuitous, if deplorable, incident; (ii) the Germans had not made a request for peaceful settlement before resorting to force; (iii) the force used by Germany was 'excessive' and 'out of any proportion' to the conduct of the Portuguese authorities (at 1026–9).

Clearly, the requirement whereby armed reprisals are lawful only to the extent that they constitute a reaction to a wrong committed by another State presupposes the emergence of a rule prohibiting forcible intervention, that is, any interference in another State by the threat or use of force (see **3.4**). So long as such intervention was admitted, armed reprisals hardly made up a separate category, for it did not matter very much whether forcible measures short of war were to be labelled 'intervention' or 'reprisals'.

International law did not impose the choice of one form of reprisal rather than another. Until the First World War international law did not exercise any restraints. Afterwards the restrictions on war laid down in the Covenant of the League of Nations and the concomitant limitations on forcible intervention led States to gradually restrict resort to armed reprisals as well.

14.1.4 WAR

As stated earlier, until 1919 States were free to resort to war whenever they considered it fitting. In 1899 a Convention adopted by the Hague Peace Conference (Hague I) prescribed a declaration of war or an ultimatum (namely, a declaration making the beginning of hostilities contingent on the non-observance by the other party of the conditions set forth therein). The 1899 Hague Convention, which was restated in 1907 and arguably turned into customary international law (unless it is held that it in fact codified a pre-existing customary rule), can, however, be violated without this breach implying that war, in the full sense of the word, has not started: if a State initiates warlike action against another State without complying with the Convention, it only makes itself answerable for a breach of international law; nevertheless the so-called state of war (namely the entering into operation of the laws of war and neutrality) comes into force.

14.2 ENFORCEMENT OF INTERNATIONAL RULES IN CONTEMPORARY INTERNATIONAL LAW

14.2.1 GENERAL

After the First World War, between 1919 and 1938, there were three major developments: (i) A customary prohibition of war as a means of protecting one's own interests slowly emerged. (ii) Consequently, a set of rules evolved permitting recourse to armed force under exceptional circumstances (reprisals, self-defence, protection of nationals abroad whose life and assets were in peril because the territorial State was unable or unwilling to protect them); in particular, rules evolved setting out the conditions on which armed reprisals were lawful, and better distinguishing them from retortion (a mere unfriendly act, not per se unlawful, on which see **14.2.2**); these rules crystallized both as a result of the aforementioned *Naulilaa* case and under the impulse of a resolution adopted in 1934 by the *Institut de droit international*.[5] (iii) A gradual process circumscribing the grounds for forcible intervention in the territory of another State led to the formation of a rule prohibiting 'dictatorial intervention', that is, the threat or use of force for the purpose of imposing on the will of another State.

At present, as discussed earlier in this book (see **3.4**), force and the threat of force 'against the territorial integrity or political independence of any State, or in any other manner inconsistent with the Purposes of the United Nations' are prohibited by the ban laid down in Article 2(4) of the UN Charter and a corresponding customary rule. In consequence, non-armed or peaceful reprisals have become the most widespread means of enforcing international rules. Two trends have emerged.

First, on account of the ban on force, *armed* reprisals in time of peace are considered unlawful, except when resorted to against unlawful small-scale use of force (see **16.5.6**); by contrast, in time of war, belligerent reprisals against some limited targets are allowed (see **17.8.2**). To differentiate these prohibited reprisals from those which are permitted, it is now preferred to term the latter 'countermeasures' (an expression used for the first time in 1978 by the US–France Arbitral Tribunal in *Case Concerning the Air Service Agreement*, at 417). There is no point in objecting that, if armed reprisals are ruled out, the weakness and the frequent failures of the UN collective security system, as well as the ineffectiveness of many economic sanctions, would leave a victim State at the mercy of States bent on violating international law. In fact, the collective security system of the UN Charter was not engineered in 1945 to *enforce international law*, but only to *maintain or restore international peace and order* (see **Chapter 15**). Any time a violation of international law does not amount to a threat to the peace or a breach of the peace, that collective security system may not be triggered. By the same token, States remain bound by the prohibition laid down in Article 2(4). Consequently, they may only resort to peaceful countermeasures.

Secondly, there is a growing tendency towards the adoption of 'sanctions' by international organizations, particularly as a *reaction to serious and large-scale breaches of international law* (see **14.4**). Clearly, while countermeasures are actions taken by *individual* States, sanctions are *collective* responses undertaken within an institutional framework (although some States do employ the same name to identify unilateral measures).

14.2.2 RETORTION

Retortion embraces any retaliatory act by which a State responds, by an unfriendly act not amounting to a violation of international law, to either (a) a breach of international law, or (b) an unfriendly act, by another State. Illustrations of retortion include the breaking off of diplomatic relations; non-recognition of acts of a law-breaking State; withholding of economic assistance; discontinuance or reduction of trade and investment; denial of economic or financial benefits; curtailment of migration from the offending State; expulsion (on condition that such expulsion does not infringe treaty or customary rules) of nationals of the State that has done the unfriendly act; imposition of heavy fiscal duties on goods

---

[5] See text in H. Wehberg, *Institut de Droit International: Tableau général des résolutions (1873–1956)* (Basle: Editions juridiques et sociologiques S.A., 1957), 167.

from the offending State; requiring visas for entry into the country or enforcing other strict passport regulations, etc.

Retortion must meet two conditions. First, the noxious act by which a State retaliates against a breach or an unfriendly act should be *proportionate* in gravity to that conduct. Secondly, the act should be *discontinued* as soon as the unfair, unfriendly, or wrong behaviour to which it is intended to react ceases.

Typical instances of retortion can be seen in the measures adopted since 1989 by the US against Burma/Myanmar on account of the gross violations of human rights perpetrated by that country, violations strongly condemned by various UN bodies including the General Assembly. In 1989, the US President suspended Burma's eligibility for the trade preferences normally available to developing countries. In 1993, the US authority suspended munitions export licences to Burma. In 1997, the US Congress prohibited bilateral aid to that State and the President prohibited new investment by US nationals.[6]

14.2.3 COUNTERMEASURES IN GENERAL

In the event of a breach of international law, the injured State (see **12.7.2**) is legally entitled to *disregard* an international obligation owed to the delinquent State.

Countermeasures, whether taken to react to cases of 'ordinary responsibility' or to respond to instances of 'aggravated responsibility' (see **12.7** and **12.8**), must, however, fulfil some basic conditions, and in addition are subject to a set of limitations. The general conditions are as follows:

(1) States are not allowed to resort to them as soon as the wrong occurs; the injured State must first call upon the responsible State to discontinue the wrongful action, in cases of a continuing delinquency, or make reparation, in other cases.

(2) If the cessation of the wrong is not obtained or no reparation is made, the injured State must endeavour to obtain it through *negotiations*. The aim of negotiations is either to settle the dispute or to agree upon another means of settlement. This requirement follows from the general principle (see **3.5** and **Chapter 13**), whereby States are under the general obligation to settle their disputes peacefully. Only when the author of the wrongdoing refuses to engage in negotiations, or wilfully or *mala fide* hampers the working of other means of adjustment available, can the injured State consider in good faith that no other choice is available, and resort to countermeasures.

In the particular case where States have already undertaken to submit their disputes to a compulsory settlement mechanism, countermeasures are not allowed until such time as the settlement mechanism has been activated. This view is not unanimously shared. Whether or not one agrees to it, it seems nevertheless certain that some treaties implicitly or explicitly rule out resort to countermeasures, as a settlement of dispute mechanism is available, and in addition it is backed up by an international organization. This applies, for instance, to disputes relating to the interpretation or application of the European Convention on Human Rights, the American Convention on Human Rights, the European Community Treaty, and WTO Agreements. The principle was clearly stated by the US–France Arbitral Tribunal in *Case Concerning the Air Service Agreement of 27 March 1946*: the Tribunal held that any State can establish for itself whether another State has violated its international rights and, if so, take countermeasures, 'unless the contrary results from special obligations arising under particular treaties, notably from mechanisms created within the framework of international organizations' (at §81).

---

[6] See also, for the relevant references, L. F. Damrosch, 'Enforcing International Law Through Non-Forcible Measures' (1977) 269 *RCADI* 91.

As for the different question of whether a State may resort to countermeasures in a case of *failure* of an institutional settlement of dispute mechanism, see **12.8** (with specific reference to 'aggravated' responsibility arising out of gross violations of community obligations enshrining fundamental values).

14.2.4 LIMITATIONS ON COUNTERMEASURES

There are limitations on the countermeasures that may be taken within the framework of both 'ordinary' and 'aggravated' responsibility. Countermeasures (taken in time of peace) cannot consist of the violation of a host of international rules enshrining basic values protecting the interests of the international community as a whole.

(1) *Obligations concerning the threat or use of force*. Countermeasures may not derogate from the obligations concerning the threat or use of force. The principle, evolved after the gradual turning of Article 2(4) of the UN Charter into a customary rule endowed with the force of a peremptory norm, was clearly laid down in Principle 1.6 of the 1970 UN Declaration on Friendly Relations, whereby 'States have a duty to refrain from acts of reprisal involving the use of force'. This provision may be deemed to reflect or codify customary international law (see also Article 50(1)(a) of ILC Articles on State Responsibility).

The ICJ, when it has pronounced on the matter, which admittedly has only been in passing, has never *explicitly* held armed reprisals to be contrary to law. This holds true both for *Nicaragua (Nicaragua v United States of America)* (at §§176 and 198) and *Legality of the Threat or Use of Nuclear Weapons* (where the Court stated that the reprisals at issue 'are considered to be unlawful' (at §§37–50, in particular 42 and 46)). When faced with cases of armed reprisals, the UN Security Council has often tended to condemn them, not because of their inconsistency with the Charter and general international law, but rather because they were 'disproportionate'.[7] Nevertheless, the principle at issue is firmly rooted in the present international legal system.[8]

(2) *Protection of human rights*. Countermeasures may not disregard international rules for the protection of human rights or, more generally, the dignity and welfare of human beings. This serious limitation follows from the general principle on respect for human rights discussed elsewhere in the book (see **3.6** and **Chapter 18**), which has acquired such importance in the world community that it is no longer possible to sacrifice the interests and exigencies of human beings for the sake of responding to wrongs caused by States. Consequently, if a State breaks an international rule, the aggrieved party is not authorized to violate international rules protecting the rights or interests of nationals of the delinquent State. States cannot make the consequences of international misbehaviour fall upon innocent people.

The limitation under discussion, upheld in Article 50(1)(b) of the ILC Articles on State Responsibility, was partially codified in the 1969 Vienna Convention on the Law of Treaties (even though it is open to debate whether this belongs to the same branch of international law). Article 60(5) of this Convention lays down that a material breach of a bilateral or multilateral treaty cannot be invoked by a party as a ground for terminating the treaty or suspending its operation, in whole or in part, in the case of 'provisions relating to the protection of the human person contained in treaties of a humanitarian character, in particular to provisions prohibiting any form of reprisals against persons protected by such treaties'.

---

[7] For this practice see D. Bowett, 'Reprisals Involving Recourse to Armed Force' (1972) 66 *AJIL* 7, n. 23.

[8] See the practice carefully reported and perceptively commented upon by R. Barsotti, 'Armed Reprisals' in A. Cassese (ed.), *The Current Legal Regulation of the Use of Force* (Dordrecht, Boston, and Lancaster: Martinus Nijhoff Publishers, 1986), 79.

This provision codifies only in part the general limitation upon reprisals, for it rules out disregard of a treaty whenever the treaty itself is broken by another party. By contrast, the general limitation set forth above is intended to protect human beings even if the breach relates to a rule other than that which might be violated by way of reprisal. International rules designed to protect human beings must be observed under any circumstances, whether or not they themselves are the subject of a breach and regardless of whether they are contained in a treaty or are customary in nature.

The general qualification under discussion does not apply solely to treaties or general rules on human rights or to the humanitarian law of armed conflict. It also extends its reach to rules protecting *fundamental interests or needs of human beings*. Thus, for instance, if a State acts contrary to international law (e.g. by mistreating foreign diplomats, or unlawfully hampering innocent passage through its territorial sea), the injured State cannot reciprocate by terminating (or suspending the application of) a treaty which provides for economic aid to the defaulting State for the purpose of alleviating the plight of a segment of its population. This kind of retaliation would ultimately damage the needs and interests of human beings. Similarly, if a State unlawfully expropriates the assets of foreigners, the national State of the expropriated companies cannot react by terminating a commercial treaty intended to benefit poor sections of the population of that State. (In this instance, we are also dealing with the breach of an international rule protecting interests and rights— those relating to property—which the two 1966 UN Covenants consider as not worthy of the same international protection as other interests and needs of the human person. Consequently, we are faced with two conflicting interests, one of which outweighs the other in international consideration. This condition reinforces the obligation not to disregard, by way of countermeasure, the rule protecting fundamental human interests.) In a nutshell, the reciprocity principle does not apply when basic concerns and exigencies of human beings are at stake.

(3) *Obligations imposed by peremptory norms of general international law*. Countermeasures may not disregard obligations imposed by norms of *jus cogens* (see also earlier in the chapter). This prohibition, restated in Article 50(1)(d) of the ILC Articles on State Responsibility, aims at filling any gap left by the ban on countermeasures derogating from norms on the threat or use of force, or human rights and humanitarian law. It is therefore a 'residual' prohibition. It covers such areas as self-determination of peoples and protection of the environment.

It is doubtful whether countermeasures consisting of violations of diplomatic or consular immunities are prohibited. Article 50(2)(b) of the ILC Articles on State Responsibility rules out countermeasures directed to derogate from 'obligations to respect the inviolability of diplomatic or consular agents, premises, archives and documents'. The ICJ judgment in *US Diplomatic and Consular Staff in Tehran* (at §§80–89), as well as State practice, seem to support this proposition, subject to a caveat: practice shows that States feel authorized to derogate from diplomatic or consular immunities by way of *specific* countermeasures against *violations of these immunities* by the counterparty.

(4) *Countermeasures must not breach the rights of third States*. Generally speaking, countermeasures may only target the State allegedly responsible for an international wrongful act. Hence, among other things, it is not permitted to violate, through a countermeasure, an international rule imposing community obligations (that is to say, obligations *erga omnes* giving rise to correlative rights *erga omnes*: see **1.8.2**). For instance, it is not permitted, through a countermeasure, to disregard treaty obligations granting rights to other States. Indeed, the violation of such an obligation would result in the breach of the right of all the States other than the wrongdoing State; it would be inadmissible, for these States have nothing to do with the initial delinquency.

It is in the light of these principles that one should consider the application by the US authorities of the Helms–Burton Act of 12 March 1996 and the D'Amato–Kennedy Act of 5 August 1996. The first Act, intended both to help the people of Cuba 'to restore its freedom' and to protect US nationals against Cuban acts of confiscation and illicit traffic of confiscated assets, allowed among other things unilateral measures against foreigners or foreign companies engaging in commercial activities involving assets 'confiscated' in Cuba in early 1960. The second Act aimed at depriving what the US considered 'rogue' States of financial means for supporting international terrorism; it provided for 'sanctions' against any person or company investing in Iran or Libya US$40m in oil activities. The implementation of these laws entailed that, to 'punish' Cuba, Iran, or Libya, the US authorities were empowered to breach international agreements (bilateral treaties or the WTO rules) vis-à-vis third States whose nationals or companies engaged in forms of 'prohibited' trade with Cuba, Iran, or Libya. Plainly, the two Acts were in breach of international law. This is borne out by the harsh reaction of Latin American countries, Canada, the EU, as well as the OECD and the Secretariat of the WTO.

(5) *Proportionality*. A further limitation upon countermeasures is that they *must not be out of proportion* to the breach by the delinquent State.

The application of the proportionality principle raises two problems: the exact scope of proportionality, and the standards by which proportionality should be gauged.

As the Arbitral Tribunal stated in *Naulilaa*, no strict proportionality was required at the time in the case of armed reprisals (at 1026–8). The same consideration holds true for countermeasures, if only because it is always difficult to ascertain whether they are strictly commensurate with the wrongdoing. What is exacted by international law is that countermeasures be not grossly disproportionate in gravity and magnitude: the importance of the rule disregarded by way of countermeasure, as well as the duration and global effects of its non-application, should roughly correspond to those of the unlawful act to which one retaliates.

The US–France Arbitral Tribunal rightly held in *Case Concerning the Air Service Agreement of 27 March 1946* that 'it is essential, in a dispute between States, to take into account not only the injuries suffered by the companies concerned but also the importance of the questions of principle arising from the alleged breach' (at §83). In addition, in *Case Concerning the Gabčíkovo-Nagymaros Project (Hungary/Slovakia)*, the ICJ held that 'the effects of a countermeasure must be commensurate with the injury suffered, taking account of the rights in question' (at §85).

As for the standard of evaluation to be taken into account, it may be noted that in the aforementioned cases, that is, both in *Naulilaa* and in the judgments delivered by the US–France Arbitral Tribunal and the ICJ, courts have pronounced upon proportionality by balancing the *injury* caused by the wrongdoing State with that brought about by the countermeasure: the latter was proportionate if it did not seriously exceed the injury resulting from the previous international wrongful act. The rationale behind this approach possibly lay in the idea that countermeasures aimed at 'punishing' the delinquent State for its misconduct. However, in current international law the purpose of countermeasures must rather be seen in impelling the offender to discontinue its wrongful conduct or to make reparation for it. If this is so, the proportionality must be appraised by establishing whether the countermeasure is such as to attain this *purpose*. For instance, in the case of violation by a developing State of an obligation owed to a major Power, it may not prove necessary to retaliate by bringing about an injury of the same magnitude as that caused by the breach; to obtain cessation of the wrong or reparation, it may suffice to respond by causing damage of a lesser magnitude, in view of the impact that such a damage may in any case have on the weaker State (on proportionality, see now *Beit Sourik Village Council* v *Government of Israel*, §§40–43).

14.2.5 COUNTERMEASURES AND AGGRAVATED STATE RESPONSIBILITY

As has been pointed out earlier (see **12.8**), in the area of aggravated responsibility, countermeasures, in addition to having to meet the limitations already set out, are subject to a special legal regime.

Here it may suffice to mention that the current international practice of States includes cases where countries, individually or jointly, have decided to react against gross violations of basic international norms by other States by adopting economic measures against the delinquent State. Thus, for example, the US put into effect economic countermeasures (suspension of deliveries of corn, withholding of industrial goods, etc.) against the USSR as a consequence of the Soviet 'invasion' of Afghanistan in 1979. Also, the US decided to call the USSR to account for the Soviet attitude towards Poland in 1981.

The difficulty of making an impartial and balanced assessment of economic and other collective countermeasures taken so far by States outside any prior specific authorization of a representative international body helps to explain why countermeasures produce such widely varying reactions in the world community. Thus, for example, the USSR consistently rejected as unlawful the countermeasures applied by the US in response to the Soviet 'invasion' of Afghanistan. As for Argentina, a few socialist countries (Albania, Bulgaria, Byelorussia, the then German Democratic Republic, the former Czechoslovakia), plus Laos, argued in November 1982 in the General Assembly that the 'collective sanctions' imposed by some European countries against its invasion of the Falklands/Malvinas were unlawful. However, they did not specify to which international norms they ran counter. Poland, the Soviet Union, and Panama had contended in May 1982, in the Security Council, that the sanctions violated the UN Charter.

14.3 CAN NATIONAL COURTS ENFORCE INTERNATIONAL RULES?

The problem has arisen on many occasions of whether national courts of a State can contribute to enforcing international rules by either (a) denying legal domestic recognition to acts performed by foreign States contrary to international law, or even (b) deciding that, in the event of a foreign State taking an internationally unlawful decision or conducting a transaction injuring the interests of the court's nationals, the court could oblige the foreign State to pay compensation to the injured individuals.

The question has cropped up in the matter of nationalization by a foreign State (after the 1917 Soviet nationalizations, those of Iran in 1951, those in Indonesia in 1959, the Cuban nationalization of US-controlled banks, as well as tobacco and sugar plantations in 1959–60, the Chilean nationalization of the copper industry in 1971, and so on).

The question also arose of (a) whether a court could pass judgment over the domestic validity and enforceability of foreign legislation on nationality contrary to international law; or (b) whether a court could pronounce on the internal validity of measures taken by a foreign State as a result and on the strength of internationally unlawful annexation of territory. Finally, the question arose of (c) whether individuals could, before their own national courts, sue for damage a foreign State that had caused them injuries as a result of an allegedly illegal conduct in the course of an international armed conflict.

National courts have taken conflicting approaches. Thus, for instance, Japanese and German courts tend to exclude the power to adjudicate allegedly illegal foreign sovereign acts.[9] In particular, in *Shimoda and others*, the Tokyo District Court upheld the doctrine of sovereign immunity of foreign States (at 1699–1700) (see **6.2**) and therefore dismissed the claim for compensation lodged by the victims or relatives of the atomic bombing of Hiroshima and Nagasaki. However, more recently Japanese district courts have taken a somewhat different approach with regard to acts performed by Japanese troops against foreign civilians. In some cases, they have rejected claims for compensation while establishing the facts (with regard, for instance, to the so-called 'comfort women', or to Chinese or Korean nationals subjected to forced labour, or to the use by Japanese armed forces of biological weapons in China). Instead, in a few cases district courts have not upheld the various doctrines on the basis of which the Supreme Court in Japan normally dismisses foreign private claims against Japan, in particular: (i) the doctrine whereby the Fourth Hague Convention of 1907 does not grant any direct claim to individuals to sue a State for compensation; (ii) the doctrine whereby in Japan the State is immune from any civil responsibility for official acts; (iii) the doctrine based on the applicability of the statute of limitation. See, for instance, the decision of the Yafmaguchi District Court of 1998 in *Korean 'comfort' women v Japan*, the decision of the Tokyo District Court of 2003 in the case of *Forced transportation and labour of Chinese*, and the decision of the Niigata District Court of 2004 on *Forced transportation and labour of Chinese workers*.[10] Other courts, for instance, in France,[11] the Netherlands,[12] Aden,[13] and Italy,[14] consider themselves authorized to establish whether the foreign act is contrary to international law, particularly with regard to foreign nationalization. Greek courts have taken contradictory views. For instance, in 2000 the Greek Supreme Court (*Areios Pagos*) held in *Prefecture of Voiotia v Germany* that Greek courts had jurisdiction over the civil suit brought against Germany by the relatives of the victims of the massacre of civilians perpetrated by German troops at Distomo (near Delphi) in 1944. However, when the plaintiffs sought the execution of the decision by trying to obtain the attachment of certain assets of the German State in Greece, the same court in 2002 disallowed the request, by arguing that such execution was not lawful with regard to foreign property necessary for discharging sovereign functions or for maintaining friendly relations. That same year, a claim (in *Margellos v Germany*) similar to that brought in *Prefecture of Voiotia v Germany* was submitted to the Supreme Special Court (*Anotato Eidiko Dikasterio*) which, under Article 100.1(f) of the Greek Constitution, is responsible for pronouncing on cases involving the interpretation of international rules. This Court held that Germany enjoyed immunity from jurisdiction, regardless of whether or not the acts at issue were contrary to *jus cogens* (at §14).[15] US courts, after admitting judicial review of foreign State acts only under strict conditions (*Banco Nacional de Cuba v Sabbatino*), have eventually broadened the scope of this judicial review (see *Bernstein v N.V. Nederlandsche Amerikaansche*

---

[9] See Tokyo Higher Court, in *Anglo-Iranian Oil Co. v Idemitsu Kosan Kabushiki Kaisha* (*Nissho Maru* case), 312–16; Hamburg Court, *Chilean Nationalization of El Teniente Mine* case, 274. The Court held that the claimants *as individuals* were not entitled to claim damages in international law, nor were they able, as a result of the *doctrine of sovereign immunity*, to pursue a claim under municipal law, in the US.

[10] On the recent Japanese case law see in particular Shin Hae Bong, 'Compensation for Victims of Wartime Atrocities: Recent Developments in Japan's Case law' (2005) 3 *JICJ* 187.

[11] See *Moraly et société 'Maison Moraly'* and *Kassab*.

[12] *Nv. Assurantje Maatschappij de Nederlanden van 1845 v Pt. Escomptobank*, 31–5.

[13] Aden Supreme Court, 9 January 1953, *Rose Mary* case, 317.

[14] Venice Court, *The Miriella (Anglo-Iranian Oil Company Ltd v Supor Company)* case, 23. See also *Ferrini, v Federal Republic of Germany* §§2–12.

[15] On these cases see the important paper by A. Gattini, 'To What Extent are State Immunity and Non-Justiciability Major Hurdles to Individuals' Claims for War Damages?' (2003) 1 *JICJ* 356.

Stoomvaart-Maatschappij, Alfred Dunhill of London Inc. v *Republic of Cuba*, as well as *Forti* v *Suarez-Mason*).[16]

It would seem that there exist in this matter *two conflicting requirements*. On the one hand, there is the need to respect the independence and sovereign equality of foreign States. The rationale is that interstate transactions are to be dealt with at the diplomatic and political level, by organs that may take decisions on the strength of broad political and diplomatic criteria. Judicial decisions simply based on the illegality of a foreign act could easily beget frictions and unsettle international relations. There also exists another, and contrary, requirement: to ensure by all means the supremacy of international law and, in a way, supplement the failings of international mechanisms for enforcing international rules by having recourse to national courts.

A balanced solution may reside in considering national courts as entitled to pronounce on the international legality of those foreign (legislative, administrative, or judicial) acts which, depending on their conformity or inconsistency with international law, may or may not take effect in the *domestic legal system of these courts*. In contrast, it is still doubtful, because of the risk of abuse, whether it is in keeping with the spirit of general international law to authorize national courts to pronounce judicially on claims for compensation brought by individuals allegedly injured by a public executive action of the foreign State that does not take legal effect abroad (these cases may take the form of egregious violations of international law in the responsible State's territory). Nevertheless, any time there is a close link between the gross violation of international law and a foreign State, the courts of this State are warranted to pronounce on the matter.

The *Letelier* case is illustrative of the problems arising in this matter. In 1980, a US district court in *Letelier et al.* v *Republic of Chile* (at 260–6), after finding that, in 1976, agents of Chile had caused the death in Washington of a Chilean (Orlando Letelier) and a US citizen (Ronni Moffit), held that it had subject-matter jurisdiction over a civil action brought by the relatives of the deceased; it found that employees 'of the Republic of Chile, acting within the scope of their employment and at the direction of Chilean officials who were acting within the scope of their office, committed tortious acts ... that were proximate cause of the deaths' of the two (at 266). The court thus granted a default judgment against Chile and awarded the plaintiffs compensatory and punitive damages. However, in 1984, a Court of Appeals rejected an action by the plaintiffs aimed at subjecting the assets of the Chilean airline (owned by the Chilean State) to execution to satisfy the default judgment (*Letelier et al.* v *Republic of Chile*, at 790–801). The court held that the US Foreign Sovereign Immunities Act did not allow execution against the assets of a State-owned airline. Subsequently, following diplomatic negotiations between the two governments, Chile paid compensation, although it claimed that this was made *ex gratia* and without admission of any responsibility (30 ILM (1992), 422 and 31 (1993) at 1). In Italy, in 2004, the Court of Cassation issued an important ruling in *Ferrini* v *Federal Republic of Germany* (§§2.1–2.11). The plaintiff had sued Germany for damages, claiming that in 1944 he had been detained by the German army in Italy and taken to Germany, where he had been subjected to slave labour until 1945. The Court of Cassation held that Italian courts had jurisdiction over the 'civil' consequences of this war crime, chiefly on the grounds that (i) war crimes are prohibited by international peremptory rules, which as such override customary rules on State immunity from the jurisdiction of foreign courts (at §§9–9.1), and (ii) the offence had commenced in Italy (at §10).

Of course, national courts contribute to the enforcement of many international rules on human rights or on the prohibition of international crimes, by instituting *criminal*

---

[16] See T. Buergenthal and S. D. Murphy, *Public International Law*, 3rd edn (St Paul, MN: West Group, 2002), 251.

proceedings against individuals allegedly guilty of violations of those rules (see **19.3.1**) or, as is the case in the US, by authorizing aliens to *sue for compensation*, before US courts, foreign State officials (or persons acting in a private capacity) who have assertedly perpetrated abroad gross breaches of human rights or humanitarian rules (see **18.4.8**).

Finally, national courts can naturally be a forum for the implementation of international trade and economic law (or at least some aspects of it), through their function of enforcement of foreign (non-domestic) arbitral awards. The 1958 New York Convention on the Recognition and Enforcement of Foreign Arbitral Awards (adopted on 10 June 1958 and entered into force in 1959) enables the courts of each contracting State (there are 161 to date) to recognize and enforce arbitral awards made outside domestic jurisdiction. This Convention, or other mechanisms providing for analogous solutions, generally applies to transnational arbitrations (for which it is made applicable), the outcome of which can be enforced in the forum State where recognition and implementation is sought. In this way 'external values', through mutually agreed procedural solutions, can be given access to the domestic legal system and concretely implement the awards, including relevant provisions of international law. In any case, the circulation of arbitral awards is made very much easier and economic actors can find solutions which reconcile both efficiency and legal certainty, and ensure eventual implementation.

From the earlier discussion, and the examples illustrated, one can conclude that domestic judges may operate as agents of the international legal order, including by enforcing international law at national level both as a form of reaction to non-compliance by foreign States, as well as through more ordinary forms of recognition of international and foreign judgments and arbitral awards. Clearly such a key role, which is becoming increasingly relevant in today's international society, presents several dimensions of interaction with the issue of implementation of international rules in domestic legal systems, in which other actors are more heavily involved (i.e. governments and parliaments).

There are nonetheless limits to the potential role of domestic judges. On the one hand, in their enforcement role they will of course have to respect several principles of international law, including, for example, immunities under international law—as it does not seem acceptable that immunities can be set aside altogether as a form of countermeasure. Secondly, when acting as enforcers of international law, domestic judges will most likely face major difficulties in appropriately balancing the values enshrined in the provisions deriving from the international (or foreign) legal order against those protected by their own domestic system. Normally, under municipal law, the latter are deemed to be prevailing in the context of domestic judicial proceedings; hence, it would seem more than appropriate for governments and parliaments to stand ready to support enforcement through correct implementation of international law at normative and administrative level. Yet, when domestic judges act as agents for the enforcement of international law they should operate as much as possible (that is as much as their domestic legal order allows them to) as if they were 'organs' of the international legal system (and thus prefer interpretation more consistent with international law). Finally, it is worth noting, of course, that national courts should be primarily implementing the obligations of their own state within their domestic legal system.

14.4 COLLECTIVE ENFORCEMENT MEASURES (SANCTIONS PROPER)

14.4.1 GENERAL

One of the most notable trends in the present international community is for international bodies, and principally international organizations, to react to breaches of international law by States. This is to be regarded as a healthy development: for all their defects (in particular, the possible slowness of the response to a wrong and the frequent need to resort to complex or even cumbersome procedures), collective responses (that may be termed 'sanctions properly so called') are to be preferred to countermeasures by individual States. Centralized countermeasures (that is, measures that are (i) in breach of international obligations, (ii) intended to respond to an international wrongful act of another State, and (iii) taken jointly by a plurality of States upon decisions or recommendation of an international organization)[17] may be based on a more balanced appraisal of the illegal situation and take into account the general interest of respect for the law combined with the need to safeguard peaceful international relations.

In practice, one can distinguish between collective countermeasures *decided* by international bodies, and those *authorized* or *recommended* by such bodies. In both cases it is States that take the sanctions; in the former case States are legally bound to do so, whereas in the latter case they are not.

The UN Security Council has on many occasions decided on or recommended economic sanctions such as the breaking off of economic relations, embargoes on imports and exports, the blocking of financial operations, as well as other sanctions (such as embargoes on weapons, the suspension of co-operation in the scientific and technical fields, etc.): against South Africa, Southern Rhodesia, Iraq, Somalia, the former Yugoslavia, Libya, Liberia, Angola, Rwanda, Sudan, Sierra Leone, etc.[18] The UN General Assembly has recommended sanctions: for instance, against Spain (in 1951), North Korea and China, South Africa, Israel, etc.[19] In 1982, the 10 EEC countries decided upon economic sanctions against Argentina for her invasion of the Falklands/Malvinas. As noted earlier, in 1995 the European Community and its Member States requested Canada immediately to discontinue a wrongful act (the unlawful arrest of a Spanish fishing vessel, the *Estai*). Canada in fact complied.

Such economic and other measures are often taken in consequence of a breach of international rules imposing community obligations. Sanctions such as these amount to centralized countermeasures when they consist of actions that undo previous legal commitments made by the sanctioning States (e.g. suspension of trade agreements). They are instead 'political sanctions' when they consist of actions that are not per se illegal, but which amount to unfriendly conduct (e.g. the breaking off of diplomatic relations). Attention must however be drawn to the fact that the UN may decide upon or recommend sanctions even in instances of threats to the peace not amounting to violations of international law (see **16.2**).

In the case of Afghanistan, the resolution adopted by the UN General Assembly by a very large majority, on 14 January 1980 (resolution ES–6/2), 'deploring' the 'armed intervention in Afghanistan as being contrary to the fundamental principle of respect for sovereignty, territorial integrity and political independence of States' (the USSR, however, was not named), can be regarded as warranting the economic sanctions taken by individual States or a group of States. In the case of the Falklands/Malvinas, the resolution adopted by the UN Security Council on 3 April 1983, to the effect that Argentina had committed a 'breach of the peace' (UNSC resolution 502 (1983)), can be considered sufficient international authority for imposing economic sanctions on that country. The decision of the EEC Council of Ministers gave added weight to the Security Council pronouncement.

There is a basic requirement that economic and other sanctions should meet: they must aim at inducing the delinquent State to discontinue its misbehaviour; these measures are

---

[17] For the various notions of sanctions, see **14.4**.
[18] See, in particular, B. Conforti, *The Law and Practice of the United Nations* (The Hague, London, and Boston: Kluwer Law International, 2000), 185.
[19] Ibid., at 214–17.

not so much to be seen as a punishment for the deviant conduct. Additionally, they ought not to be used as an instrument for gaining political or diplomatic advantages. In short, they must not be abused.

Let us now ask ourselves what motivates economic and other peaceful sanctions, and whether these sanctions have proved effective. It seems that they may serve two purposes. First, they may act as the catalysing factor uniting a group of States opposed to the alleged misbehaviour of another State: by taking sanctions the collective bodies intend to rally States behind their censorious attitude. Secondly, they may be a symbol of public exposure and condemnation of the States allegedly misbehaving. They are not intended to damage the delinquent State in the economic field—the history of international relations speaks volumes for the ineffectiveness in practice of economic sanctions. They are primarily intended to dramatize and articulate the condemnation of a certain form of behaviour and, by the same token, to 'delegitimize' it, or, to put it differently, to prove to world public opinion that the responsible State was wrong, inasmuch as it had acted contrary to internationally accepted standards. Illustrations of these trends may be found in the sanctions decided upon by the Security Council against Iraq, Libya, and the Federal Republic of Yugoslavia (Serbia and Montenegro).

From this point of view the sanctions may be said to have been relatively effective. On other scores they have not achieved major results.

14.4.2 SANCTIONS AND RESPECT FOR HUMAN RIGHTS

It has become increasingly clear that international sanctions designed to impel ruling elites of States grossly violating international legal standards to discontinue such violations may have serious adverse impacts on the most vulnerable groups in the targeted country. Some of these consequences were illustrated in 1997 by the UN Committee on Economic Social and Cultural Rights (CESCR, the body monitoring compliance with the UN Covenant on Economic, Social and Cultural Rights of 1966), in its important General Comment no. 8: it stated that collective sanctions

> often cause significant disruption in the distribution of food, pharmaceuticals and sanitation supplies, jeopardise the quality of food and the availability of clean drinking water, severely interfere with the functioning of basic health and education systems, and undermine the right to work. (at §3)

It follows that economic sanctions, in particular, may seriously affect and jeopardize the basic human rights of children, the elderly, the sick, women, and other vulnerable members of the civilian population. Aware of these consequences, the Security Council has increasingly included in its resolutions on sanctions humanitarian exemptions with a view to permitting the flow of essential goods and services destined for humanitarian purposes. However, as noted by the CESCR in its aforementioned General Comment (at §5), these exemptions have not produced the intended effects.

What does international law prescribe with regard to these situations? A few general standards may be drawn from the general spirit and tenor of principles and rules on human rights.

First, as rightly pointed out by the CESCR, the *general assumption* from which all States and international organizations must start is that:

> the inhabitants of a given country do not forfeit their basic economic, social and cultural rights by virtue of any determination that their leaders have violated norms relating to international peace and security. (at §16)

Secondly, the general community obligation to refrain from engaging in, or bringing about, gross and large-scale violations of human rights is binding upon both States and international organizations. In particular, they are bound to refrain from causing, to the vulnerable members of the civilian population, suffering that is *manifestly disproportionate* to the aim of stopping the State's misconduct. It follows that international bodies such as the Security Council, when deciding on collective sanctions against a State, must consider whether such sanctions may cause egregious violations of the social, economic, or cultural rights of the vulnerable members of the civilian population. If this consequence looks likely to come about, they must opt for alternative courses of action, or differently shape their sanctions. By the same token, if after sanctions have been imposed it turns out that they cause very serious and disproportionate infringements of the human rights of the population concerned, collective bodies are under the obligation to take all the necessary measures to alleviate the plight of vulnerable groups, including, if need be, discontinuance of sanctions.

Thirdly, the State targeted by the sanctions must take all the measures necessary to *spare as much as possible its civilian population*: that State

> remains under an obligation to ensure the absence of discrimination in relation to the enjoyment of such rights [that is, economic, social, and cultural rights], and to take all possible measures, including negotiations with other States and the international community, to reduce to a minimum the negative impact upon the rights of vulnerable groups within the society. (at §10)

It is for these reasons that, progressively, collective enforcement measures addressed to States as a whole have been supplanted by new measures, called targeted or smart sanctions, which are aimed at specific individuals or groups of individuals with the idea of trying to avoid the negative effects of indiscriminate sanctions for civilian populations (for this new kind of measure adopted by the UN Security Council see **16.2.1**).

PART V
CONTEMPORARY ISSUES IN INTERNATIONAL LAW

15

THE ROLE OF THE UNITED NATIONS

15.1 THE GRAND DESIGN OF THE POST-SECOND WORLD WAR PERIOD

As the US Secretary of State, Cordell Hull, recalled, '[f]rom the moment when Hitler's invasion of Poland revealed the bankruptcy of all existing methods to preserve peace, it became evident... that we must begin almost immediately to plan the creation of a new system'.[1]

The US and the British did most of the planning. Two grand designs soon emerged, one advocated by the Americans, the other by the British. The former, strongly championed by Cordell Hull and President Roosevelt, hinged on a few main points: (i) resort to military force in international relations had to be banned; (ii) the traditional system of unilateral action, of military and political alliances, of spheres of influence and balance of power ought to be removed; all these mechanisms and practices had to be replaced by a universal organization set up by peace-loving nations; (iii) in this organization a major role was to be given to the most powerful allies fighting against the Axis Powers, namely the US, the USSR, as well as Britain and France (which still had huge colonial empires), and China, which was to be associated with them. They were to be allotted the role of world policemen, responsible for enforcing peace; (iv) economic and social co-operation was to be promoted so as to ensure economic progress and better working conditions with a view to forestalling future armed conflict resulting from dramatic economic inequalities; (v) colonial empires were to be dismantled, particularly if they belonged to 'weak nations', on three grounds: (a) for ideological reasons, that is, in order to realize the principle of self-determination of peoples throughout the world; (b) for political reasons, namely to avert future clashes and conflicts resulting from the existence in the world of over one billion 'brown people' resenting the domination of white minorities;[2] (c) for economic reasons: colonial empires distorted equality and free trade on the world market, one of the primary goals of the US neo-liberal approach; indeed, the colonial Powers had access to cheap labour and cheap primary commodities in their colonies. However, the break-up of the colonial system should not be abrupt but gradual: an international trusteeship system was to gradually bring about the demise of that system.

The British scheme, relentlessly propounded by Churchill, accepted the idea of banning force and promoting economic and social co-operation, but also hinged on (i) the notion that world security could be safeguarded by the setting up of regional councils under a

---

[1] C. Hull, *Memoirs* (New York: Macmillan, 1948), ii, at 1625.
[2] The expression 'brown people' was used by President Roosevelt, according to a memo by C. Taussig: see W. R. Louis, *Imperialism at Bay: The United States and the Decolonization of the British Empire, 1941–1945* (New York: Oxford University Press, 1978), 486.

world council; (ii) the maintenance of colonial empires or, alternatively, their gradual change into self-governing entities.

As the US was by far the more powerful country, and had indeed become the most industrialized and militarily powerful State in the world, it easily gained the upper hand. However, it had to compromise with Britain over the question of colonialism, the more so because another future 'policeman', France, although temporarily 'defeated', very much clung to its colonial empire.

The Soviet Union played a relatively minor role in the establishment of the universal organization, the UN, and was primarily vocal on some political issues such as the veto power in the Security Council (SC), the proposed participation in the founding of the Organization of all 16 Soviet republics (eventually accepted by the Western allies only for Byelorussia and the Ukraine), and the upholding of the principle of self-determination.

The fundamental tenets of the future UN Charter were gradually agreed upon. This was done first in the Atlantic Charter, drafted by the US and Britain in 1941, then by the three victorious Powers (the US, Britain, and the Soviet Union) plus China, in a string of summits: at Moscow (October 1943), at Dumbarton Oaks (an estate in Washington DC, from 21 August to 7 October 1944), and at Yalta (4–11 February 1945, without the participation of China). When the diplomatic conference designed to work out and approve the UN Charter was held (San Francisco, 25 April–26 June 1945), it was presented with a text elaborated by the Great Powers. To this text amendments, requiring a two-thirds majority, were technically permitted, although politically they were allowed only on relatively minor points. The 50 States gathered at San Francisco (most States of the world at the time: the four convening Powers, the 42 States, including India, not yet independent that had declared war either on Germany or on Japan, plus Argentina, Denmark, Byelorussia, and Ukraine, the last two not yet recognized as independent States) could not but accept the key provisions of the Charter. Among these were: the provision on the establishment of a central organ, i.e. the Security Council, consisting of a few countries (nine originally, 15 today), dominated by the five permanent members with veto power, and responsible for the maintenance of international peace and security; and the provision on domestic jurisdiction,[3] corresponding to the present Article 2(7), which was closely intertwined with the traditional principle of non-interference in the internal affairs of States (see later in the chapter). However, small and medium-sized countries were able to contribute on some points, chiefly: (i) the laying down, in Article 51 (see **16.5**), of the right to individual and collective self-defence; (ii) the expansion of the competence of the General Assembly (GA) (i.e. the collective body where every member State had one seat and one vote), which was empowered both to discuss any matter within the scope of the Charter and to make recommendations on questions concerning peace and security not being dealt with by the Security Council (see Articles 10 and 12); (iii) the elevation of the Economic and Social Council, ECOSOC (the body charged with promoting co-operation on economic, social, cultural, educational, health, and related matters) to the rank of one of the principal organs of the new Organization; (iv) the adoption of provisions on colonial matters (such as the Declaration regarding non-self-governing territories, contained in Article 73, and those on the trusteeship system); and (v) the insertion of a provision establishing the prevalence of obligations imposed by the UN Charter over conflicting obligations, if any, deriving from other treaties (Article 103). A point of some contention was the principle of non-intervention, which was dear to the hearts of Latin American and other small countries

---

[3] On the various proposals relating to domestic jurisdiction see in particular R. B. Russell, *A History of the United Nations Charter: The Role of the United States 1940–1945* (Washington, DC: The Brookings Institution, 1958), 463–4, 785, 900–10.

(as was pointed out by a distinguished commentator: 'there was a widespread conviction among the middle and lesser States that some formal safeguard against intervention in their internal affairs was needed in an Organization in which the great Powers were to play a dominant role').[4] This principle was intended to be put into what became Article 2(4) (banning the use of force); the motion of Latin American and other countries had enough support to be inserted by a divided vote. However, in the end, the compromise (probably a perverse one) was to put it into Article 2(7) (safeguarding member States' 'domestic jurisdiction' from undue interference by the Organization, without prejudice to enforcement measures decided by the Security Council).

It must be stressed that, from the outset, the new Organization was envisaged as a political body dominated by the Great Powers. They had taken upon themselves the task of safeguarding peace and security on behalf and in the interest of all nations of the world, but did not intend to make major concessions to other nations on matters they regarded as of crucial importance. In this connection, an exchange of views between Stalin, Churchill, and Roosevelt that took place on 4 February 1945, at Yalta, is illuminating. While discussing the issue of voting procedures in the Security Council, Stalin noted that 'he would never agree to having any action of any of the Great Powers submitted to the judgment of the small powers'.[5] The other two leaders substantially agreed.[6]

Furthermore, the new Organization was to be a political entity pursuing political objectives, albeit within a legal framework. In its action it was to be untrammelled by legal technicalities, let alone by judicial restraints: efforts to make disputes on the interpretation of the Charter subject to the mandatory jurisdiction of its principal judicial organ, the ICJ, were rejected at San Francisco (they secured majority support but not the requisite two-thirds majority).[7]

15.2 GOALS AND STRUCTURE OF THE ORGANIZATION

In the view of the founding fathers, the new Organization was to pursue a number of fundamental purposes: (i) to maintain peace and security (Article 1(1)); (ii) to bring about by peaceful means the adjustment or settlement of international disputes or situations which might lead to a breach of the peace (Article 1(1)); (iii) to develop friendly relations among nations based on respect for the principle of equal rights and self-determination of peoples

---

[4] L. Preuss, 'Article 2, Paragraph 7 of the Charter of the United Nations and Matters of Domestic Jurisdiction' (1949-I) 74 *RCADI* 573.

[5] See FRUS, *The Conferences at Malta and Yalta—1945*, 589, which can be read at https://history.state.gov/historicaldocuments/frus1945Malta. On the same occasion A. Y. Vyshinsky ('First Deputy People's Commissar for Foreign Affairs', in other words, Deputy Foreign Minister, of the Soviet Union) 'said to Mr Bohlen [Assistant to the US Secretary of State and interpreter of President Roosevelt at the Yalta Conference] that they would never agree to the right of the small powers to judge the acts of the Great Powers, and in reply to an observation by Mr Bohlen concerning the opinion of the American people he replied that the American people should learn to obey their leaders', ibid., at 590.

[6] See ibid., at 589–91. Churchill quoted the saying 'The eagle should permit the small birds to sing and care not wherefor they sang' (at 590), while Bohlen (see n 5), in reply to an inquiry by Churchill about the US position on the voting procedure in the Security Council, mentioned 'the story of the Southern planter who had given a bottle of whiskey to a Negro as a present. The next day he asked the Negro how he had liked the whiskey, to which the Negro replied that it was perfect. The planter asked what he meant, and the Negro said if it had been any better it would not have been given to him, and if it had been any worse he could not have drunk it' (at 590–1).

[7] See UNCIO, 13, at 633–4, 645–6.

(Article 1(2)); in short, to promote, if not yet the gradual and internationally organized demise of colonial systems, at least the slow awakening of colonial countries to self-government; (iv) to foster economic and social co-operation (Articles 1(3), 55); (v) to promote respect for human rights and fundamental freedoms for all persons (Articles 1(3), 55).

Other purposes of the Organization, clearly considered of minor importance by the founding fathers, were: (vi) to promote disarmament and the regulation of armaments (Article 11(2)); (vii) to further respect for international law (Preamble) and encourage the progressive development of international law and its codification (Article 13(1)(b)).

Plainly, maintenance of peace and security was the crucial goal of the new entity. In 1939–45 the tension between force and law—endemic in the international community, as in any human grouping—had been magnified by the war. It had become clear that unless serious restraints were put on violence, the world would be heading for catastrophe. One should not believe, however, that the leaders were so naïve as to think that in 1945 one could radically break with the approach so forcefully set forth by Bismarck in the nineteenth century, when he reportedly said that 'the questions of our time will not be settled by resolutions and majority votes, but by blood and iron'.[8] Perhaps it was rather thought that, faced with two radically opposed methods for settling friction and disagreement, 'bullets' or 'words' (as Camus put it in 1947),[9] one ought bravely to endeavour to opt as much as possible for the latter, while however being aware that the former would continue to be used.

Let us take a quick glance at the structure of the new Organization and how the various organs were to pursue the goals set by the founding fathers (and mothers).

The Security Council and the General Assembly are the two principal political organs. The General Assembly, consisting of all member States, each having one vote, was granted a very broad competence: it was authorized to discuss and pronounce upon any matter within the province of the Organization (subject to some procedural restraints whenever a question relating to peace and security is being handled by the Security Council: see Article 12). Its decisions 'on important questions' (listed in Article 18(2)) are taken by a two-thirds majority of the members present and voting; others are taken instead by a majority of the members present and voting (Article 18(3)). Its resolutions (recommendations, Declarations, etc.) are not legally binding per se (except for decisions concerning the 'internal life' of the Organization, such as those apportioning UN expenses among the member States (see Article 17(2)); adopting rules of procedure (Article 21); establishing subsidiary organs (Article 22); electing members of the various other bodies, such as the SC, ECOSOC, etc.; appointing the Secretary-General (Article 97); electing members of the ICJ pursuant to Article 8 of the Court Statute, etc.).

The Security Council consists of 15 members,[10] 5 permanent (the so-called Big Five: China, France, the UK, Russia, and the US), and 10 others elected by the GA for a term of two years (every year there is the election of five members), representing the five geographical groups operating in the UN for rotation purposes (the groups of African, Asian, Eastern European, Latin American, and Caribbean States, as well as the Western European and Others group). The SC competence is 'limited' to the maintenance of peace and security. Its decisions, except for those on procedural matters and on the election of members of the ICJ, may only be taken with an affirmative vote (or at least the abstention) of the five permanent members (hence, if one of the Big Five votes against, the resolution will not be adopted); this is the so-called veto power (see Article 27(3)). The decisions are taken by

---

[8] See A. J. P. Taylor, *Rumors of War* (London: Hamish Hamilton, 1952), 44.
[9] A. Camus, *Essais* (Paris: Gallimard, 1984), 352.
[10] Originally the Council was only composed of 11 member States, the five permanent members plus six others elected by the General Assembly. In 1965, an amendment to the Charter brought the total number to 15 in order to reflect the expansion in the membership of the Organization.

a vote of nine members (with the exception of those on the election of judges of the ICJ, which may be taken by a vote of eight members: see Article 10 of the ICJ Statute, merely requiring the absolute majority of members of the Security Council).[11] They may either be recommendatory in nature, or legally binding, pursuant to Article 25; the distinction between them can be made based on the wording of the relevant decisions, but these are not always clear and often some ambiguity and uncertainty is left on purpose.

The Security Council was to be assisted and advised by the Military Staff Committee, consisting of the Chiefs of Staff of the permanent members; this body was to be responsible 'under the SC' for the strategic direction of any armed forces placed at the disposal of the Council. What is even more important, the military contingents that under Articles 43–45 member States were to put at the disposal of the Security Council for enforcement action in case of threats to the peace, breaches of the peace, or aggression, were to act under SC control.

The Security Council and the General Assembly are at the top of the Organization. Their principal instrumentality was to be the *Secretariat*, headed by a *Secretary-General*, appointed by the Assembly upon the recommendation of the Council (Article 97). Three other main organs were to fulfil specialized functions: in the field of economic and social co-operation, the *Economic and Social Council* (ECOSOC); in some colonial matters, the *Trusteeship Council*; and in matters concerning international legal disputes and advisory opinions, the *International Court of Justice* (ICJ).

ECOSOC consists of 54 member States elected by the General Assembly for three years: its main task is to discuss; propose; recommend; promote studies; co-ordinate the action of specialized agencies (such as the International Labour Organization (ILO), the United Nations Educational, Scientific and Cultural Organization (UNESCO), the Food and Agriculture Organization (FAO), the World Health Organization (WHO), etc.); set up subsidiary bodies (such as the Commission on Human Rights, established in 1946 on the strength of Article 68, and operational until 2006 when it was replaced by the Human Rights Council: see **Chapter 18**), etc. in the fields within its competence.

Matters relating to some categories of non-independent countries (territories that were still under mandate, territories detached from 'enemy States as a result of the Second World War', other territories such as colonies voluntarily placed under trusteeship by the States responsible for their administration) were to be brought under the trusteeship system by virtue of special agreements. They were thus put under the control of the Trusteeship Council, consisting of members administering trust territories, permanent members of the Security Council that were not in such a position, and a number of members elected by the General Assembly so as to ensure that membership was equally divided between States that administered trust territories and those which did not (Article 86). The Charter puts the Trusteeship Council under the control of the General Assembly or, when trusteeship agreements relate to 'strategic areas', of the Security Council (Article 83). As all trust territories have become independent, the Trusteeship Council has become substantially inoperative (since 1994, when Palau, an island in Oceania under US administration, reached independence). However, it still meets periodically to elect its President and Vice-President.

The ICJ is the principal judicial organ of the UN, authorized to settle legal disputes between States by binding judgments, or to issue advisory opinions at the request of the principal organs of the UN, that is the Security Council, the General Assembly, or any other organ or specialized agency authorized by the Assembly. The ICJ consists of 15 judges elected by the General Assembly and the Security Council (when they elect judges for the ICJ, permanent members of the Council have no veto power; as already pointed out, it is therefore sufficient for a candidate to obtain 8 out of 15 votes, whether or not the votes in his or her favour include those cast by the permanent members).

---

[11] It is worth recalling that for candidates to be elected as judges of the ICJ, the concurrent positive vote (with absolute majority) of both the General Assembly and the Security Council is required.

15.3 PRINCIPAL ACHIEVEMENTS AND FAILURES OF THE UN

15.3.1 GENERAL

From the outset, agreement among the Great Powers who had drafted the Charter was considered the indispensable underpinning of the Organization (at Yalta, on 6 February 1945, Stalin had noted that 'the main thing was to prevent quarrels in future between the three Great Powers [US, Britain, and the USSR] and the task, therefore, was to secure their unity for the future';[12] President Roosevelt fully shared this view).[13] However, as is well known, agreement did not last and the sudden worsening of relations between the two leading States, the US and the USSR, undermined the establishment of the collective security system. During the Cold War (1946–89), the world split into two groups, each led by a superpower. President Roosevelt's idea of the Security Council as 'a board of directors of the world' responsible for 'enforcing the peace against any potential miscreant'[14] fell apart. Each of the two leading Powers took care of its own bloc to enforce order and stability there, and each respected the other's sphere of influence. Competition and conflict primarily erupted in relation to the Powers' grip on developing countries and control over strategic areas.

Since the collapse of the Soviet Union and the end of the confrontation between the Eastern and Western coalitions, the world has been increasingly dominated by one superpower, the US. Nevertheless, the drastic change in the international scenario has not entailed the implementation of the security system envisaged in the Charter. The prevention of international and internal armed conflict or the prompt re-establishment of peace when these conflicts break out, the fight against terrorism, disarmament, and a satisfactory regulation of international economic relations conducive to political stability in many countries, have remained the principal sore points.

Surprisingly, the UN has achieved much more in those areas that had been left somewhat in the background in 1945, than in those on which the founding fathers and mothers had focused their attention (maintenance of peace and security, and settlement of disputes likely to endanger peace). The lukewarm attitude taken towards colonial countries was overturned and, by the early 1960s, colonialism had been practically swept away. In the area of development, the General Assembly and the ECOSOC, thanks to the key role of many developing countries, made sustained progress. More recently, in 2015, the General Assembly adopted resolution 70/1 whereby the commitment of member States (and of the Organization) to the pursuit of the Sustainable Development Goals (the SDGs) has been affirmed.[15] In the area of human rights immense progress was made, with the adoption of exceedingly important Declarations and Conventions. The progressive development of international law was attained by the adoption of a number of Conventions codifying and developing international law.

15.3.2 MAINTENANCE OF PEACE AND SECURITY

The system inaugurated in 1945 was revolutionary indeed. It postulated that, in future, States ought to endeavour to settle their disputes peacefully and never use force (see Article 2(3) and 2(4) of the UN Charter), subject to the exception of self-defence; and that an

---

[12] See FRUS, *The Conferences at Malta and Yalta—1945*, 666.
[13] Ibid., at 667.
[14] H. Kissinger, *Diplomacy* (New York: Simon and Schuster, 1995), 395.
[15] See UN Doc. A/RES/70/1.

international authority, the UN, would act as a world policing and enforcement agency. Thus, forcible self-help, traditionally a characteristic feature of the international community, was significantly restricted: it was left in the form of self-defence, provided for in Article 51 of the UN Charter, as well as, under Article 106 (a 'transitory' provision on what were then enemy states—Germany, Italy, and Japan in the context of the Second World War—that has now become obsolete), in the form of possible collective action by the five Great Powers to maintain peace, pending the coming into force of the agreements, referred to in Article 43, designed to make available to the Security Council armed forces, assistance, etc. And a centralized body (the Security Council) was vested with broad powers of forcible intervention (see Chapter VII of the Charter): any time it determined under Article 39 that there was a threat to the peace, a breach of the peace, or an act of aggression, it could decide upon measures not involving the use of armed force, under Article 41, or take armed action against the aggressor or the State threatening the peace, under Article 42.

There were two momentous consequences. First, whereas previously the distinction between lawful and unlawful use of force either could not be made or was blurred, it had now become possible to say—at least in theory—whether a specific instance of use of force was lawful. Secondly, whereas previously (until the establishment of the League of Nations) force could be used without any previous assessment by a third party, now an international body, the Security Council, could decide to enforce peace after having determined the existence of a threat to the peace, a breach of the peace, or an act of aggression.

Self-defence was envisaged as an exception to this centralized collective security system. However, the UN Charter also set a number of limitations upon the right of self-defence enshrined in Article 51. This provision, subsequently turned into general international law, only allows the use of force in order to repel an 'armed attack', and subject to the procedural requirements that the Security Council must be immediately informed of the armed action in self-defence (Article 51 thus envisages self-defence as a sort of preliminary or provisional measure by which the victim of an armed attack may safeguard its rights for a limited period of time until such time as the centralized security mechanism begins to function).

The basic deficiencies of the collective security system outlined in the UN Charter were fourfold. First, the idea of a collective monopoly of force by the five permanent members of the Security Council was, of course, based on their continuing agreement; in the case of dissent, the so-called veto power (advocated by the US and strongly endorsed at Dumbarton Oaks by the USSR) gave any of the five the right to cripple the functioning of the collective security system. (The veto power would have had a more sweeping scope and would have been essentially unqualified had the USSR prevailed in its opposition to Roosevelt's view—up to a point shared by Britain—that, when the Security Council was dealing with the *peaceful* settlement of disputes, but not with enforcement matters, a party to a dispute, including any of the Big Five, should not be entitled to cast a vote, because 'American concepts of fair play required that a party to a dispute not vote in judgment on itself'.)[16]

---

[16] In the opinion of the US, permanent members of the Security Council were to place themselves, at least with regard to judicial or quasi-judicial procedures, on an equal footing with other States. For the US position, see FRUS, *The Conferences at Malta and Yalta—1945*, 46–7; see also 56–62, 66–8, 660–2, 682–4, 995–6. See also E. R. Stettinius, Jr, *Roosevelt and the Russians: The Yalta Conference* (Garden City, NY: Doubleday and Co., 1949), 135–50. In this regard, it is interesting to note that despite the prevailing interpretation of the provisions of Article 27(3) of the Charter, in March 2014, when the Council met at the demand of Ukraine to discuss the legality of a referendum regarding the status of Crimea, the Russian Federation—arguably an interested party in the situation—did take part in the vote (with little or no opposition from other Members) and eventually vetoed the resolution which would have expressed condemnation for the prospective referendum. For the British position, see FRUS, at 46, 663–7. As to the Soviet position, see ibid., at 46, 63–4, 68–71. See also R. B. Russell (n 3), at 445–50, 458–9, 497–506.

Secondly, the 'army' which should have been put at the disposal of the UN was not envisaged as an international army proper, exclusively dependent on the Security Council. Rather, it was to be composed of contingents placed at the disposal of the Security Council by the various member States through special agreements governing the number and type of forces and their degree of readiness. The Council would exercise its authority over national forces, which would act under the strategic and military direction of the 'Military Staff Committee'. The Charter did not envisage that the State sending a contingent would continue to exercise command and control over it. However, the possibility of a 'dual allegiance' was not excluded altogether. Such a possible dual allegiance could not but result in a dangerous likelihood of the 'army' being paralysed by national States.

Thirdly, force was only banned in 'international relations' (Article 2(4)); it was consequently allowed in 'internal' affairs (e.g. against rebels in the case of civil strife), and in the relations between colonial Powers and dependent territories. As tensions within the various colonial empires had already become apparent and were to increase, the Charter left a huge host of potentially dangerous strains to be dealt with at the discretion of individual States, should political dissension and demands for change intensify to the point of armed conflict.

Fourthly, to a large extent the UN Charter tended to uphold a concept more of 'negative peace', or absence of war, than 'positive' peace, or the introduction of justice for the purpose of preventing as far as possible political tensions from degenerating into armed conflicts. This is not to say that the UN closed its eyes to political reality and refrained from suggesting political solutions calculated to prevent armed conflicts. Indeed, co-operation in the economic, social, and political fields was promoted, obligations were imposed on colonial Powers, and a role for the UN was also envisaged to further co-operation as regards disarmament. However, this part of the UN Charter proved rudimentary and weak. Particularly unsatisfactory were the provisions concerning colonies and economic relations.

As a result of the Cold War, the attempt at centralizing the use of force ended in failure and a 'UN army' was never established. The old institution of self-help acquired new importance, albeit with a number of qualifications. As a consequence, the following developments have occurred.

(1) The two contending blocs set up separate organizations for 'collective self-defence' (NATO in 1949, which still exists and now comprises several States which once were part of what was at the time the 'Communist bloc', and the Warsaw Pact in 1955—which dissolved in 1991). The world community returned to the traditional system of opposing political and military alliances.

(2) A trend emerged which was to become one of the distinguishing features of the present international community, namely, the tendency of States to make increasing use of the right of individual self-defence, to such an extent that a number of States now feel relatively confident to engage in war under the cloak of 'self-defence', without having to fear any decisive hindrance from the UN. At the same time, States have endeavoured to broaden the concept of self-defence so as to include major forms of use of force short of war not covered by Article 51 of the Charter. Resort to unilateral use of force, under the cover of self-defence, or protection of nationals abroad, or pre-emptive self-defence, has occurred in a number of cases (for details, see **16.5**).

(3) The Security Council's inability to enforce peace led to two major developments: on the one side, enforcement by UN member States at the request, or *upon authorization*, of the Council (see **16.4**); on the other, establishment of *peacekeeping* as a less intrusive replacement of or substitute for peace enforcement proper (see **16.3**).

15.3.3 PROMOTION OF THE PEACEFUL SETTLEMENT OF DISPUTES LIKELY TO ENDANGER PEACE

The Charter enshrines the legal obligation of settling disputes by peaceful means (Articles 2(3), 33(1)). However, the draftsmen were not interested in the peaceful settlement of *any* interstate dispute. They were particularly concerned about disputes that could degenerate and imperil *peace*. They therefore laid down in Chapter VI of the Charter a set of provisions dealing with 'disputes the continuance of which is likely to endanger the maintenance of international peace and security'.

The purpose of intervention by the UN bodies is to prevent the breaking out of armed conflict. The machinery provided for in the UN Charter refers both to legal and to political disagreement, although, as we shall see, in the case of legal disputes a specific mode of settlement is suggested. The lack of distinction between the two classes of disputes is a sound development. All too often, clashes between legal claims are politically motivated, or they have strong political implications, whereas political feuds frequently present legal overtones, or else one of the parties—or even both of them—employs legal arguments to buttress their political demands. If one of the major purposes of the world community is reconciliation of disputants so as to prevent their crossing swords, the better course of action is that taken in 1945, of not making the selection of a certain mode of settlement conditional on the intrinsic character of the dispute.

The basic philosophy underlying the Charter is that every effort should be made to maintain peace and security. An obvious corollary is that whenever disagreements between States threaten to become explosive and to endanger peace, the UN must step in and endeavour to defuse the situation. This, of course, implies that the Organization must always watch out for possible cracks in the fragile edifice of peace. The field of action of the Organization thus becomes very broad, for any disagreement may evidently escalate into a major conflict, except for the very minor and peripheral ones. Ross aptly stressed the great novelty of the Charter system in the following terms:

> The essence of the Charter, the point where it definitely breaks with the rules of traditional international law, is that it establishes the principle that every dispute (the continuance of which is likely to endanger the maintenance of international peace and security) is a public matter, so that whether the parties wish it or not, they must accept the fact that the dispute may be debated in the SC ([or] the GA), if that organ considers such debate to be in the interests of peace. The parties are not obliged to seek the assistance of the Organization, but they are obliged to put up with its intervention.[17]

With regard to disputes likely to endanger peace, the UN Charter provided that (i) each party to the dispute has the obligation to seek a solution 'by negotiation, enquiry, mediation, conciliation, arbitration, judicial settlement, resort to regional agencies or arrangements, or other peaceful means of their choice' (Article 33(1)); (ii) any other State is authorized to bring any dispute or situation likely to endanger peace to the attention of the Security Council or the General Assembly (Article 35; pursuant to paragraph 2, if the State is not a member of the UN, it must accept in advance the obligations of pacific settlement provided in the Charter; hence the Council's decision regarding the mode of peaceful settlement becomes binding on it); (iii) whenever there is a dispute or situation which no State brings to the Security Council, this body is empowered to call upon the parties to settle their dispute by peaceful means (Article 33(2)); (iv) the Security Council can investigate any dispute or situation in order to establish whether its continuance is likely to endanger peace (Article 34); (v) the Security Council can *recommend* 'appropriate procedures or methods of settlement' (Articles 36(1) and 37(2)).

---

[17] A. Ross, *The United Nations: Peace and Progress* (New York: The Bedminster Press, 1966), 190.

Clearly, the UN machinery for dispute settlement was rather weak, not only because the class of disputes or situations susceptible of being considered by the Security Council was relatively limited, but also because the powers of this body were confined to issuing recommendations (except for decisions to initiate investigations under Article 34). Nonetheless, scrutiny of UN practice shows that member States have also brought to the attention of the Security Council disputes that sometimes did not appear likely to endanger the peace, and it has considered itself empowered to issue recommendations.[18]

The fulfilment of this task has not, however, led to any major achievements, on many grounds. The Security Council has not fully used the powers it derives from Chapter VI. Furthermore, sometimes the public airing of the grievances of the parties to a dispute or those concerned in a situation was considered less appropriate for achieving a prompt settlement of the dispute or situation than 'confidential' collective diplomacy. In addition, sometimes it has been felt that the Security Council sided with one of the parties concerned, rather than acting as a neutral promoter of the dispute settlement. On other occasions the contesting parties have felt that the Council was not prepared to push for a prompt and determinative settlement, nor was it willing, in the case of failure, to proceed to apply Chapter VII. This lack of political will has played into the hands of the contesting parties, or of one of them, with the resulting failure of the attempt at solving the case.

It should be noted that, under Article 14, the General Assembly may recommend measures for achieving a 'peaceful adjustment of any situation . . . which it deems likely to impair the general welfare or friendly relations among nations'. This provision, couched in very broad terms, has given rise to an interesting practice.

In addition, the UN Secretary-General may play a role in dispute settlement. The Charter does not expressly give him this function, but many Secretaries-General have been asked, or have offered themselves, to act as mediators. The political and moral authority deriving from this high position within the UN structure has often proved useful at least to bring the parties to a common table by exercising good offices (see **13.3**). In one case the Secretary-General was asked to act as arbitrator: in 1986, France and New Zealand jointly invited Pérez de Cuéllar to arbitrate their dispute over the sinking of the *Rainbow Warrior (Case concerning the differences between New Zealand and France arising from the Rainbow Warrior affair)*. Moreover, at least in theory, the Secretary-General could resort to his power under Article 99 of the Charter to bring to the attention of the Council 'any matter which in his opinion may threaten the maintenance of international peace and security'. Such power could be used to induce States in dispute to find a reasonable settlement, rather than being 'deferred' to the Security Council.[19]

---

[18] The Security Council has exercised its powers under Chapter VI on numerous occasions: in 1947, when it dealt with the dispute between Britain and Albania over the mines laid by Albania in the Corfu Channel (a dispute that was then submitted to the ICJ); in 1948, when it handled the Kashmir dispute between India and Pakistan; and in 1949, when it considered the dispute between Israel and Arab States. Later on it dealt with disputes over the Suez affair, the Congo, Namibia, Southern Rhodesia, up to, more recently, the crises in Nicaragua, Honduras, El Salvador, Guatemala, Cambodia, etc.

[19] It is well known that traditionally such a power has always been used with great caution by the Secretary-General. Nonetheless, the case was made—notably by Secretary-General Kofi Annan—that such a tool could be resorted to more effectively for the purpose of preventing the escalation of crisis situations. For more details see *Repertory of Practice of the UN Security Council*, Supplement no. 10 (2000–2009) vol. 6, available online at http://legal.un.org/docs/?path=../repertory/art99/english/rep_supp10_vol6_art99.pdf&lang=E. More recently, Secretary-General António Guterres sent a letter to the Security Council (S/2017/753) regarding the Rohingya refugee crisis. While not mentioning Article 99 explicitly, the Secretary-General brought the situation to the Council's attention. More generally, even the Council itself has recognized the potential of Article 99 and the essential role of the Secretary-General. In particular, mechanisms of early warning or briefings on particularly sensitive situations could be useful tools to allow the UN to discharge its preventive role. For more details on practice relating to Article 99 see https://www.scprocedure.org/chapter-3-section-10b.

15.3.4 SELF-DETERMINATION OF PEOPLES

Despite the attempt of the USSR to set out in the Charter the goal of promoting independence for the colonial countries, in fact what was agreed upon in San Francisco was the gradual attainment of self-government by dependent peoples (and concomitantly, a moderate overhauling of colonial empires). The reference to self-determination contained in Articles 1.1 and 55 was conceived of in this limited manner. Article 73 (under Chapter XI, entitled 'Declaration regarding non-self-governing territories') concerned the colonial territories that colonial Powers were not prepared to put under the trusteeship system, and with regard to which the relevant colonial Power simply had to report to the Secretary-General on minor matters (pursuant to Article 73(e)). Article 73 consistently envisaged that member States taking responsibility for the administration of territories whose peoples had 'not yet attained a full measure of self-government' should engage in assisting them to develop self-government and build free political institutions. In contrast, the provisions on the international trusteeship system (to be established under UN authority for the administration and supervision of some limited categories of colonial territories) contemplated self-government of colonial peoples, but also independence as might 'be appropriate to the particular circumstances of each territory and its peoples and the freely expressed wishes of the peoples concerned' (Article 76(b)). Complex machinery was set up, hinging on the Trusteeship Council, for national administration, under international supervision, of trust territories.

In short, the Charter kept alive the colonial system, although it divided colonial peoples into *two classes* (non-self-governing territories and trust territories) and envisaged some measure of international scrutiny over the attainment, by the colonial Power, of the objectives of self-government (or, exceptionally, independence) that the colonial Power was now to pursue.

This is the area where the UN has been most successful. It is reported that, at San Francisco, it was widely believed that the UN could achieve general disarmament in a decade, whereas decolonization would take a century. Instead, only a few years after the adoption of the Charter the UN succeeded in beginning to dismantle colonial empires. It rapidly moved from a moderate, substantially neo-colonialist scheme primarily geared to self-government, to a courageous search for and promotion of independence. This bold development was facilitated by various factors: (i) the strong push given by the Soviet Union and eastern European socialist States to the fight against colonialism; (ii) the increasingly lukewarm support of the US for its colonial allies and the revival of the anti-colonialist attitude of that Great Power; (iii) the growing insistence of colonial peoples on their 'right' to gain independence; this awareness was inculcated and spread by many debates in the Organization and the consequent UN resolutions and Declarations, which hence were objectively instrumental in subverting the existing world order; it appears indisputable that those texts greatly incited national liberation movements to fight against colonialism, thereby contributing to the demise of the colonial system; (iv) the growing economic and social costs, for European Powers, of maintaining their colonial systems, coupled with the decreasing importance and economic attractiveness, for them, of the primary goods they formerly exploited in colonial territories; (v) the rise to power in European colonial States of powerful social democratic (Labour) parties adopting anti-colonialist stances.

Thus, in a matter of three decades (between 1947 and 1975), colonial empires were substantially brought down. The last colonies to acquire independence were the Portuguese colonies of Angola and Mozambique, in 1975, and Namibia, formerly a territory held by

South Africa under a League of Nations mandate, in 1990. The status of Western Sahara and some small territories (the Virgin Islands, under the US; New Caledonia, under French control; Tokelau, under New Zealand; plus some territories still under British control, such as the British Virgin Islands, Bermuda, and the Falklands/Malvinas) remains one of the few unresolved problems. (It should however be noted that the population of some of these territories does not want independence, and neither the UN Charter nor the relevant GA resolutions require that they must choose independence.)

One of the merits of the UN was that it promoted the independence of colonial peoples (a) by peaceful means and, generally speaking, (b) by respecting the wishes and aspirations of the peoples concerned (through plebiscites and referendums).

However, the success of the UN in implementing self-determination was limited to colonial peoples (including Southern Rhodesia (now Zimbabwe) in 1980). Outside this category, it promoted (internal) self-determination in South Africa (in 1994) and the external self-determination of Eritrea (in 1996) and of East Timor (in 1999; in 1974 East Timor had been annexed by Indonesia, although the UN continued to consider that it was under Portuguese administration). Because of the basic attitude of most States towards territorial integrity and national sovereignty, the UN has been able or willing to foster internal self-determination in sovereign States only where it was to bring down governments practising an apartheid policy. However, the UN has played an important role in electoral assistance and, more generally, the promotion of democracy.

15.3.5 ECONOMIC AND SOCIAL CO-OPERATION

In the area of economic and social co-operation the Charter simply stated, in Article 13(1)(b), that the GA could initiate studies and make recommendations. However, a specialized body, the Economic and Social Council (ECOSOC) was made responsible for preparing studies, reports, and draft conventions, as well as recommendations (Article 62). Also, Article 55 (at subparagraphs (a) and (b)) dealt with economic and social development, in particular with the creation of conditions necessary for social and economic progress. Here again, as in many other provisions of the UN Charter, a link was established with the maintenance of international peace and security. Conditions of stability and well-being were considered essential for the development and maintenance of peaceful relations among States. The link could also work the other way round: peace and security ensure a proper environment for economic and social development.[20]

However, no general principle was laid down in the Charter on the direction that economic and social co-operation should take in future. Policy decisions were left to the General Assembly and ECOSOC or, more precisely, to the majority of States prevailing within them.

Over the years the General Assembly and ECOSOC have undoubtedly promoted a great deal of co-operation among States in the social area, particularly with regard to human rights (see **Chapter 18**). However, in the field of economic co-operation the *huge hurdles to progress towards closing or at least narrowing the gap between developed and developing countries* have prevented any major breakthrough. The 1974 GA Declaration on the New International Economic Order and the Programme of Action relating thereto,[21] as well as the 1974 Charter on Economic Rights and Duties of States,[22] the 1986 Declaration

---

[20] See GA resolution S-18/3, adopted on 1 May 1990, during the Special Session on International Economic Co-operation.

[21] GA resolution 3201(S-VI), adopted on 1 May 1974; GA resolution 3202 (S-VI), adopted the same day.

[22] GA resolution 3281(XXIX), adopted on 13 December 1974.

to discuss their comments. The panel then adopts a *Final Report*, which is transmitted to the parties and the DSB.

(v) The panel's report is adopted by the DSB unless (a) it decides by consensus not to adopt it, or (b) a party to the dispute appeals against the report.

(vi) If an appeal is made, it is heard by a standing seven-member *Appellate Body* established by the DSB. The Appellate Body has jurisdiction solely on questions of law. That body may of course also pronounce on questions of interpretation of the relevant provisions, but it is bound by the *interpretations* of the WTO Agreement and the various Multilateral Trade Agreements, adopted by the WTO Ministerial Conference and General Council (both consisting of representatives of all member States of the WTO), interpretations taken by a three-quarters majority of States.

(vii) Reports of the Appellate Body are *automatically adopted* by the DSB unless it decides by consensus not to adopt them.

(viii) *Monitoring* of compliance with the panel's or Appellate Body's report is exercised by the DSB. In addition, if the State concerned does not comply with the report, the complainant State may request the DSB to authorize it to take countermeasures, namely, to *suspend* the application, vis-à-vis the State concerned, of concessions or other obligations laid down in the relevant agreement. This suspension may concern either the same trade sector or another sector or even obligations deriving from another WTO agreement.

(ix) If the State against which the suspension is carried out objects to it, the matter must be referred to *arbitration* and the findings of the Arbitral Court are final.

Up until the appointment of members of the Appellate Body was blocked by the US, effectively preventing its operation as of December 2019, the procedure proved exceedingly useful and successful. A great number of cases have been brought before the competent WTO organs or panels.[50] When we consider that at present WTO membership runs to 164 members and that all are bound by this procedure, we may surely contend that it has proved to be one of the best means, by far, of settling international disputes in the world community.

13.6 NON-COMPLIANCE AND SUPERVISORY PROCEDURES

There are certain fields regulated by international law where States have felt the need to develop specific procedures to ensure compliance with legal standards alternative to traditional dispute settlement procedures, in particular adjudication. These alternative procedures are mechanisms designed to *monitor compliance* with international legal standards on a permanent basis, with the ultimate goal of *preventing* or *deterring* as much as possible deviation from those standards. There are four *principal modalities* through which supervision is effected:

(1) *Examination of periodic reports* submitted at predetermined intervals by the States concerned to the supervisory body (usually composed of individual experts). For example, the reports by the member States of the ILO concerning the application of international labour conventions under Article 22 of the ILO Constitution; the reports provided for in various human rights conventions, such as the 1965 Convention on Racial Discrimination

---

[50] At the time of writing, it is reported that since 1995, 593 disputes have been brought to the WTO and over 350 rulings have been issued.

on the Right to Development,[23] and the 1990 Declaration on International Economic Co-operation and the Revitalization of Economic Growth and Development of Developing Countries,[24] have proved to be a relative failure—among other things because the principles laid down there were a far cry from real economic relations (see **21.3**). A shift has occurred over the years: while in the 1970s industrialized countries were called upon to support developing countries in their efforts to further progress, recently the emphasis has been laid on the need for each country to be responsible for designing and implementing its own development policies.

Nevertheless, the UN has promoted economic co-operation in various fields, through some of its specialized agencies (FAO, WHO, the International Fund for Agricultural Development (IFAD)), or through such organs as the UN Conference on Trade and Development (UNCTAD) or the UN Development Programme (UNDP). UNDP has become very important as a means of co-ordinating various UN technical assistance activities. In 1970 the General Assembly established a UNDP country-programme process, which was later strengthened and became the basic framework for co-ordinating assistance activities at the national level.[25] In addition, through one of its specialized agencies, the UN Industrial Development Organization (UNIDO),[26] it has promoted entrepreneurship and self-reliance, as well as cost-effective, ecology-sensitive industry in developing countries. Furthermore, it has promoted industrial co-operation and technology transfer. It also has served as a 'matchmaker' for North–South, South–South, and East–West investment and, more recently, the organization of partnerships with the private sector.

A further attempt to advance and promote the action of the UN and of its member States has been launched through the Millennium Development Goals adopted at the margins of the 2000 Millennium Summit, which helped, for example, to reduce extreme poverty, and the 2015 Sustainable Development Goals (the SDGs), which were affirmed on the occasion of the Summit on the 70th anniversary of the Organization. The process also involved structural changes, as, in 2013, on the basis of the outcome document of the Rio+20 UN Conference on Sustainable Development of 2012, the General Assembly established the High Level Political Forum (an ad hoc meeting at which States should be represented at political level, which replaced the UN Commission on Sustainable Development, and is designed to oversee the implementation of development policies by member States and by the UN system).[27]

Within the general domain of economic and social co-operation, the UN activity that stands out for its importance and novelty is that concerning protection of the environment. As this topic will be discussed in **Chapter 20**, it may suffice here to recall that the UN has not only adopted three important Declarations (in 1972, 1982, and 1992), but also set up the United Nations Environment Programme (UNEP).[28] This body, together with the World Meteorological Organization (WMO), has been instrumental in highlighting the damage caused to the earth's ozone layer. In addition, UNEP has led major efforts to clean up pollution in the Mediterranean Sea as well as on beaches in a number of countries including Syria, Israel, Turkey, and Greece. Together with other specialized agencies such as FAO, the UN has also contributed to curbing global warming, preventing

---

[23] GA resolution 41/128, adopted on 4 December 1986.
[24] See GA resolution 45/199, adopted on 21 December 1990.
[25] See GA resolution 2688(XXV), adopted on 11 December 1970; GA resolution 32/197, Annex, adopted on 20 December 1977.
[26] GA resolution 2152(XXI), adopted on 17 November 1966.
[27] The HLPF was established on the basis of the Rio+20 Conference outcome document (*The Future We Want*) reflected in UN GA resolution 66/288 as implemented by GA resolution 67/290.
[28] GA resolution 2997(XXVII), adopted on 15 December 1972.

overfishing, and limiting deforestation. Moreover, it is within the framework of the UN that the Conferences on Climate Change have been established and led to the adoption in 2015 of the Paris Agreement.[29]

Finally, through the UN International Children's Fund (UNICEF), the UN has attempted to raise the general level of children's health and welfare in many developing countries. The UN has also provided an appropriate forum for negotiating the Convention on the Rights of the Child, the most widely ratified treaty ever, which entered into force in 1990.

In sum the UN, although it has greatly expanded, over the years, its range of action and tackled the most sensitive problems of our time, in the various social and economic fields with which it has dealt, has been unable to go beyond *co-ordination and promotion*. This is only natural, since decision making in these matters still remains in the hands of *sovereign States*, and States are deeply divided by conflicting economic, political, and ideological interests. However, in the economic field the UN must be credited with promoting a shift (a) from government-to-government assistance to assistance by multilateral institutions, and (b) from public investment to private investment as the engine of development (see generally **Chapter 21**).

The efforts of the General Assembly and the ECOSOC in the area of development, coupled with social and environmental challenges—what is today called 'sustainable development'—must be credited as fruitful. The Organization and its member States, through the SDGs, conceived an ingenious path towards trying to achieve a balanced promotion of development and economic co-operation in keeping with the protection of the environment and human rights. Through high-level summits and the adoption of ambitious Declarations setting out not only development objectives, but also the means and ways to reach them, as well as the systems for measuring progress in pursuing such goals, the UN has provided a platform which may be instrumental in achieving sustainable development.

15.3.6 HUMAN RIGHTS

In the area of human rights as well the Charter was extremely cautious and tepid. In Article 55(c) it laid down that the Organization would 'promote' universal respect for human rights. In Article 13(1) it simply provided that the GA should 'initiate studies and make recommendations' for the purpose of 'assisting in the realization of human rights and fundamental freedoms for all without distinction as to race, sex, language, or religion'. Only 'studies and recommendations' were envisaged. However, ECOSOC could also prepare draft conventions and reports (Article 62).

In 1945, the international community still lacked an internationally agreed *list* of human rights to be respected by States and an internationally agreed *definition* of those rights. This is one of the reasons why it was still inconceivable that an international body could limit States' sovereignty by intruding in their internal affairs and making comments or recommendations on governments' internal structure or the relations between the State authorities and individuals. Therefore, it was only natural for States to introduce Article 2(7) into the Charter. This clause, in providing for protection of States' 'domestic jurisdiction', objectively constituted a huge stumbling block to any incisive action by the UN in the field of human rights. It substantially barred the Organization from taking any step other than *general* recommendations (that is, recommendations addressed to all States), *general* studies or reports, and draft conventions. In other words, the Organization could not address matters relating to human rights in a specific country, for these were matters 'which are essentially within the domestic jurisdiction' of that State.

---

[29] See https://unfccc.int/process-and-meetings/the-paris-agreement/the-paris-agreement.

Admittedly, in addition to envisaging tasks for the Organization, the Charter also laid down an obligation for States: through Article 56 all member States pledged themselves 'to take joint and separate action in co-operation with the Organization for the achievement of the purposes set forth in Article 55', including respect for human rights. This 'pledge' was however extremely vague.

In short, the Charter provisions concerning human rights only set forth a general programme of action. Detailed obligations and implementation mechanisms were not provided for. The Charter intended simply to proclaim human rights as a general goal both for States and for the Organization.

Over the years the UN has proved successful in promoting respect for human rights. In a matter of a few years the General Assembly, by adopting in 1948 the Universal Declaration, was able to turn the few loose provisions of the Charter into a *decalogue of fundamental human rights and freedoms* (which, albeit without any legally binding force, possessed great moral authority). The next steps were the two Covenants of 1966 (see **18.4.3**). They translated the provisions of the Declaration into binding legal rules. A string of treaties and Declarations followed (see generally **Chapter 18**). In addition to laying down obligations concerning respect for human rights, the Organization also set up a host of monitoring bodies.[30]

The action of the UN in this area is impressive. Admittedly, many of the treaties concluded under the auspices of the Organization are still not universally binding. Furthermore, most monitoring mechanisms could be more effective and hard hitting. Nevertheless, for all its flaws, the whole array of instruments and mechanisms dealing with human rights at the universal level constitutes a great achievement. This becomes apparent if one considers the action of the UN in this field against the general background of an international community consisting of sovereign States, each eager to protect its own independence and autonomy against outside interference. The UN, by strongly and unflinchingly promoting human rights, has introduced *a new ethos* in the international community. It has gradually brought about a sort of Copernican revolution: while previously the whole international system hinged on State sovereignty, at present individuals make up the lynchpin of that community. To be sure, States still play a crucial role in international dealings. However, they are no longer looked upon as perfect and self-centred entities. They are now viewed as structures primarily geared to the furtherance of interests and concerns of individuals. Only a universal intergovernmental organization of the calibre of the UN could have achieved this momentous result.

15.3.7 DISARMAMENT

In the field of disarmament the Charter reached its lowest point. Article 11(1) simply provided that the General Assembly might 'consider general principles of co-operation ... including the principles governing disarmament and the regulation of armaments'. It added that the Assembly could 'make recommendations with regard to such principles to the Members or to the SC or to both'. Thus a matter indisputably of crucial importance was relegated in the Charter to the back row. Probably the founding fathers and mothers felt that the failure of all the provisions on this matter contained in the Covenant of the League of Nations warranted a cautious approach and no great illusions. By and large the framers of the Charter assumed that disarmament was a project to be negotiated among a relatively

---

[30] One of the major achievements of the Organization was its remarkable contribution to putting an end to racist white supremacy in Southern Rhodesia (Zimbabwe) in 1980, and to bringing about the downfall of apartheid in South Africa in 1994. The UN has also been instrumental in promoting the spread of democracy in the world. By providing electoral advice, assistance, and monitoring of electoral consultations, it has assisted (or, as in the case of Cambodia, enabled) people in a great many countries (including Namibia, El Salvador, Eritrea, Mozambique, Nicaragua, and South Africa) to participate in free and fair elections.

few key States, but subject to principles agreed among the members of the Security Council and the General Assembly.

However, the General Assembly took action to deal with the matter. Its first Committee (responsible for political and security matters) specialized in disarmament and from the outset discussed questions falling within this purview. In addition, in 1983 and 1988 the Assembly held a special session devoted to disarmament. It also set up the Committee on Disarmament, transformed in 1984 into the Conference on Disarmament, which is tasked with preparing draft treaties to be submitted to the Assembly for adoption.[31] There is also a UN Commission on Disarmament (created by the General Assembly in 1952) where States may discuss any issue relating to disarmament and suggest to the Assembly the adoption of recommendations.[32] Furthermore, in 1984 the General Assembly established (resolution 39/148H) UNIDIR, a research institute on disarmament, as a subsidiary organ.

It is notable that a major disarmament treaty, namely the 1968 Treaty on the Non-Proliferation of Nuclear Weapons, was negotiated following a GA resolution (1665(XVI) of 5 December 1961) and within the UN Committee on Disarmament; it was eventually adopted as resolution 2373(XXII) of 12 June 1968. In addition, the Treaty is subject to the verification procedures of an institution closely linked to the UN, the International Atomic Energy Agency (IAEA). Furthermore, many treaties concluded under the auspices of the UN include clauses on disarmament or denuclearization.[33]

Additionally, the 2017 Treaty on the Prohibition of Nuclear Weapons was adopted at the initiative of the General Assembly, which, by resolution 71/258, decided to convene a UN conference open to all member States. Despite the fact that several States did not participate (in particular those possessing nuclear weapons), the Conference took place in New York in 2017, and eventually adopted the Treaty (122 States in favour, one against, and one abstention) on 7 July 2017. At the time of writing, the treaty is not yet in force as it requires the deposit of the instrument of ratification by 50 States (around 30 States have already ratified) (see also **17.6.3**).[34]

Moreover, after several rounds of unsuccessful negotiations, it is in the framework of the General Assembly that a seminal treaty, regulating the international trade in conventional arms, the 'Arms Trade Treaty', was eventually adopted in 2013, entering into force on 24 December 2014.[35]

Nevertheless, other major treaties on disarmament have been negotiated and concluded *outside the UN*, or the Organization has played a relatively minor role in their negotiation.

---

[31] Formally speaking, the Conference is independent of the UN, although it uses UN staff and annually reports to the General Assembly, which can address recommendations to it. The Conference, which consists of 65 member States, meets in Geneva in one or more sessions and discusses a variety of issues relating to disarmament, although with little chance of conducive deliberations since it adopts its decisions by consensus. It is probably for this reason, given the divisions existing over disarmament issues among the member States, that the work of the Conference is seriously hampered. Nonetheless, it remains a forum for States to share opinions and present their views.

[32] The UN Commission reports annually to the First Committee of the General Assembly. After a gap of years since the last document was adopted, it recently approved a set of 'Recommendations on practical confidence-building measures in the field of conventional weapons' as an annex to its 2017 Report UN Doc. A/72/42, 11–14. For more details on the Commission and its activities see online at https://www.un.org/disarmament/institutions/disarmament-commission/.

[33] E.g. the 1959 Treaty on the Antarctic, Articles I and V; the 1967 Treaty on outer space, Article 4; and the 1979 Treaty on the moon and other celestial bodies, Article 3.

[34] For background information on this treaty and the update on the status of ratifications see online at https://www.un.org/disarmament/wmd/nuclear/tpnw/.

[35] The Arms Trade Treaty was adopted by the UN General Assembly on 2 April 2013 with 154 votes in favour, three votes against, and 23 abstentions, after the unsuccessful conclusion of the Conference the previous year. The treaty opened for signature on 3 June 2013 and entered into force on 24 December 2014 following its ratification, acceptance, or approval by 50 states (in accordance with Article 22(1)).

The reason is simple: the major nuclear Powers have felt that they had to reach agreement on crucial military matters on their own and outside a multilateral forum, where they are likely to be subject to political and ideological pressure. Thus, the idea underlying the UN Charter, that States without major armaments would have a voice through the General Assembly, proved unworkable.[36]

Nonetheless, the UN, through the IAEA, has helped minimize the threat of nuclear war by inspecting nuclear reactors in at least 90 countries, to verify that nuclear materials were not diverted for military purposes.

Finally, one should highlight the role that the Security Council has played in the disarmament area, more specifically with regard to weapons of mass destruction, both in general terms under resolution 1540 (2004), whereby a Non-proliferation Committee has been established, as well as concerning specific situations such as those of the Democratic Republic of Korea, Iraq, Iran, or Syria. For example, regarding Syria, the Security Council together with the Organization for the Prohibition of Chemical Weapons (the OPCW) established monitoring missions to oversee the dismantling of the Syrian chemical weapons arsenal, as well as fact-finding missions to shed light on incidents regarding the unlawful use of such weapons.[37] With regard to Iran, the Council endorsed through resolution 2231 (2015) the agreement, known as the Joint Comprehensive Plan of Action (JCPOA) (from which the Trump Administration subsequently withdrew in 2018), between Iran and the P5+1 that was concluded in July 2015 outside the context of the UN by the permanent members of the UN Security Council and the European Union with Iran, regarding the monitoring of the Iranian Nuclear Programme.

15.3.8 CODIFICATION AND PROGRESSIVE DEVELOPMENT OF INTERNATIONAL LAW

Mention of international law was made in the Charter's preamble (where it was stated that one of the goals of the Organization was 'to establish conditions under which justice and respect for the obligations arising from treaties and other sources of international law can be maintained'). Article 1(1) provided that disputes should be 'settled peacefully in conformity with the principles of justice and international law'. Only Article 13(1)(a) envisaged action on the matter: the General Assembly was entrusted with undertaking studies and making recommendations for the purpose of 'encouraging the progressive development of international law and its codification'. Clearly, international law was not considered as one of the pillars for the construction of a new 'world order'. However, the need was felt to promote its updating and elaboration.

This is no doubt an area where the UN has gone beyond any expectation. It has fostered international law in a number of ways, some more traditional, others distinctly novel. First, various UN bodies, in particular the General Assembly, have succeeded in adopting draft

---

[36] The treaties negotiated outside the UN include agreements on nuclear disarmament, agreements on arms control, and treaties on denuclearization. Some have been directly negotiated by the two Great Powers: e.g. the Moscow Treaty of 5 August 1963 on nuclear testing in outer space; the treaty of 10 September 1996 on nuclear tests; the 1971 treaty banning the placing of nuclear weapons on the ocean floor; the 1972 treaty between the USSR and the US on antiballistic missiles modified in 1974 (Salt I), followed by that of June 1979 (Salt II); the Washington treaty of 7 December 1987 on short-range missiles; and the Start agreements I, of 31 July 1991, and II of 3 January 1993. Other treaties have been negotiated within the Conference on Disarmament: e.g. the 1993 convention on chemical weapons, and the 1996 treaty for the complete ban on nuclear tests. A number of treaties have been negotiated within regional frameworks: e.g. the 1967 treaty of Tlatelolco (Mexico) for the denuclearization of Latin America; the 1985 treaty of Rarotonga (Cook Islands) denuclearizing the South Pacific; the 1995 treaty of Bangkok, for the denuclearization of South East Asia; and the 1996 treaty of Pelindaba (South Africa) for the denuclearization of Africa.

[37] See e.g. UN SC resolutions 2118 (2013) and 2235 (2015).

conventions on major issues such as genocide, human rights, protection of women, rights of children, etc. These conventions, patiently worked out within UN bodies, chiefly the General Assembly, have subsequently been ratified by a large number of States.

Secondly, the International Law Commission (ILC), a body consisting of experts in international law and diplomacy, has elaborated some important draft treaties codifying and progressively developing crucial areas of traditional international law (e.g. diplomatic immunities, consular immunities, the law of treaties, the law of the treaties between States and international organizations, State succession). These draft treaties, after receiving the approval of the General Assembly, have been submitted to a Diplomatic Conference. The resulting legal texts have subsequently been ratified by a large number of States; in addition, they have exercised considerable influence even outside the group of contracting parties.

Thirdly, there are areas where the conflict between the political or economic interests of the various groups of States is staggering: for instance, regulation of international economic relations, protection of the environment, and the enunciation of the general principles that should govern international relations. In these areas, where it proved impossible to work out treaties, either directly by the General Assembly or through the ILC, the General Assembly has had recourse to creative legal thinking. It has promoted the elaboration of Declarations or general resolutions. These texts, albeit devoid of any legally binding force, have the advantage of (i) laying down the major areas where most States may have reached some sort of understanding or agreement; (ii) setting forth the major goals as well as the consequent policies that States ought to pursue in those areas; (iii) establishing a sort of blueprint for international and national action; (iv) laying the groundwork for future developments, at least on some of the issues envisaged; (v) gradually generating the possible crystallization of general binding rules or principles on some of the issues.[38]

Fourthly, various other UN bodies have greatly contributed to international law. Of course the principal merits in this area go to the ICJ, which through its judgments and Advisory Opinions has fleshed out many international rules or provided authoritative interpretations or elaborated on their contents and scope. However, also such political organs as the Security Council or the General Assembly have provided in their resolutions, recommendations, or decisions a number of pronouncements on legal issues that significantly clarify or develop some areas of international law.[39]

---

[38] As examples of these Declarations, one may recall the 1948 Universal Declaration on Human Rights (which had an important follow-up in the two 1966 Covenants and the numerous subsequent treaties); the 1960 Declaration on the granting of independence to colonial countries and peoples; the 1962 Declaration on permanent sovereignty over natural resources; the 1963 Declaration on principles governing activities in outer space; the 1970 Declaration on principles governing the seabed and ocean bed beyond national jurisdiction; the 1970 Declaration on Friendly Relations; the 1974 (ill-fated) Declaration on a New International Economic Order; the 1974 Declaration on the Definition of Aggression; the 1972 Stockholm Declaration on the Human Environment; and the 1992 Rio Declaration on Environment and Development.

[39] Suffice it to mention a few examples: (i) in 1970, by laying down in the 1970 Declaration on Friendly Relations that colonial peoples may fight with all necessary means against colonial Powers forcibly depriving them of their freedom and independence, the General Assembly contemplated a right to use force in international relations that was not envisaged in the UN Charter; (ii) in 1990 and 1991 the Security Council adopted resolutions 662 (1990) and 687 (1991) declaring among other things the annexation of Kuwait by Iraq to be null and void; (iii) in 1991 the Security Council, by resolution 687 of 3 April 1991, adopted a decision regarding the delimitation of the frontier between Iraq and Kuwait, subsequently demarcated by the Secretary-General (S/22558); (iv) again in 1991 the Security Council took the unprecedented step of establishing, by resolution 692 of 20 May 1991, the UN Compensation Commission charged with managing a fund for paying compensation for war damage caused by the unlawful Iraqi invasion and occupation of Kuwait; (v) the Security Council, by establishing in 1993 and 1994 the two International Criminal Tribunals (one for the former Yugoslavia, the other for Rwanda), imaginatively interpreted and applied Chapter VII, in particular Article 41 of the UN Charter (on measures not involving the use of force, that may be taken to counter a threat to the peace), as the ICTY stated in *Tadić* (*Interlocutory Appeal*) (at §§32–37).

15.4 THE CURRENT ROLE OF THE UN

It is apparent from the above survey that since it came into existence the UN has often failed in three areas: (a) maintenance of peace and security, (b) disarmament, and (c) bridging the gap between industrialized and developing countries.

However, it would be disingenuous to apportion the blame to the UN itself. True, no one should gloss over the indisputable flaws of the Organization: bureaucratization; frequent mismanagement; overemphasis on discussing *ad infinitum* controversial matters; and passing hundreds of resolutions, as if verbal struggles and the consequent production of more written texts were by themselves to lead to changes in the political, diplomatic, and economic realm. However, for all its deficiencies and in spite of the lack of vision of some of its Secretaries-General, the primary failings of the UN must be traced back to the States behind it, chiefly the Great Powers. One should always bear in mind a few well-known, but true facts.

The Organization was established as a mechanism directed at co-ordinating the efforts of member States towards the gradual achievement of some major collective goals. It was still largely based on the 'Grotian paradigm' (typical of an anarchical society consisting of self-centred actors, each pursuing its short-term interests and scarcely concerned about community values), in that it bowed not only to State sovereignty as an insurmountable and quintessential element of the world community but also to the Great Powers' dominant position. However, by trying to co-ordinate the action of States, it *also* tended to move towards a new vision of the world community, the 'Kantian model' (which hinges on co-operation and the promotion of common, meta-national values). With the passage of time, gradually the UN has come to be increasingly geared to the Kantian model. At present, although the world community and the 'UN community' almost coincide as far as their membership is concerned, their structure and orientation are significantly different (this is why it still seems questionable to speak of the UN Charter as 'the constitution' of the world community). As a result of the substantial chasm between the two models, the Organization must strive hard to rally all or most member States behind some general principles, in order to orient and channel their actions in a way conducive to the promotion of those common values and goals. In addition, the Organization, as such, lacks any real economic, political, or military power of its own. It must perforce rely on the support of member States, chiefly the Great Powers. However, only as long as the Great Powers consider that their general agendas can be reconciled with those of the Organization, are they prepared to lend it their support.

Furthermore, the structure of the Organization is in substance still that established in 1945 at San Francisco (except for some organs, such as the Trusteeship Council, which have lost their *raison d'être* in light of historical changes). The world, however, has changed radically. A more efficient apparatus would be needed, together with a Security Council representing not only the victors of the Second World War but the present constellation of economic and military power in the world. However, the two-thirds majority (including all the permanent members of the Council) required by Article 108 for amending the Charter makes it exceedingly difficult to introduce any major change.

Moreover, only minimal reform of the Charter appears realistic at this stage, and yet there are several significant changes which can be made within the system that can help ensure better delivery.[40] It is premature to say whether the reforms launched by Secretary-General Antonio Guterres within the Secretariat functioning will achieve desired results in

---

[40] See P. Alston, 'The United Nations. No Hope for Reform?' in A. Cassese (ed.), *Realizing Utopia: The Future of International Law* (Oxford: Oxford University Press, 2012), 38.

bringing fewer costs and more efficiency, increasing the conflict prevention capabilities of the Organization, ensuring coherent implementation of human rights policies, increasing the impact of development assistance, and making the delivery of humanitarian aid more timely, but certainly there is consciousness in the Organization, both in the Secretariat and among member States that some aspects need adjustment.

Also, the approach of the US towards the Organization over time does leave much room for improvement. Since the 1990s, US policy, as set out in 'Presidential directive no. 25' of 5 May 1994, makes it clear that the US is prepared to participate in peacekeeping or peace-enforcement operations only to the extent that this participation is warranted by national US interest (and so long as the operations pursue clear objectives, are being sufficiently financed, and are of limited duration). According to the US State Department 'neither the US nor the international community have the mandate, nor the resources, nor the possibility of resolving every conflict . . .'.[41] As rightly noted by Bertrand,[42] this statement is in fact a death sentence for collective security. Despite inevitable oscillation linked to different approaches taken by subsequent Administrations as to the amount and the method of involvement of the US in international affairs, the stance taken towards the Organization has hardly changed. The US military cannot operate under UN command and control—it would be contradictory with US standing as a superpower. The Organization is supported insofar as its agenda coincides with the advancement of American interests and as far as it promotes values in line with US policies (and yet with surprising U-turns in the area of human rights and the rule of law at various points in time). Moreover, the fact that the US bears the largest portion of the budget of the Organization makes it a priority for any American Administration to keep UN funding under control and find ways to reduce the impact on the US budget. In this regard, for example, the reform of the UN advocated by the US is of limited scope: the US essentially insists on better management and budget cuts for the Secretariat; on the need for Germany and Japan to become permanent members of the Security Council (primarily to involve these two States more in financing peacekeeping operations)[43] without, however, any veto power; and closer association of the UN with regional organizations or other organizations such as NATO, the European Union, or the African Union, when it comes to UN missions, including peace enforcement (also with a view to obtaining significant cost sharing).

Finally, no one could deny that in the world community there are a number of political problems that are objectively intractable on account of deep-rooted tensions and conflicting ethnic, political, and ideological claims. Conspicuous illustrations are Kashmir, Cyprus, the Middle East, and the Western Sahara, where the UN has been present for decades, as well as more recent situations and conflicts in which the UN is involved, from Somalia to Libya, from Syria to Yemen. In these situations, not only UN diplomacy but also the diplomatic efforts undertaken by some Great Powers, chiefly the US, have not led to any major breakthrough. It would be ungenerous to lay the blame at the door of the Organization for its failure to settle those situations and instead freezing them through its peacekeeping operations. Sometimes partial management of problems, albeit in a scarcely satisfactory manner, and even delaying an appropriate solution may prove to be a better option than either outright neglect or else handling of those issues by individual States or by groups of States substituting themselves for the UN.

---

[41] Cited by M. Bertrand, 'The UN as an Organization. A Critique of its Functioning' (1995) 6 *EJIL* 352.

[42] Ibid.

[43] During the Obama Administration overtures were also made, albeit for different reasons, to India (probably to counterbalance the increasing power of China in Asia and in the rest of the World), see online at https://www.nytimes.com/2010/11/09/world/asia/09prexy.html.

It should be added, on the other hand, that over the years the UN has proved indispensable and indisputably successful in a great many areas.

Membership of the Organization has by now become a *test of legitimation* for any State. No new State can claim to be a legitimate and fully fledged member of the international community if it has not gained admission to the UN. This is also confirmed by recent practice: for example in 2011, soon after independence, South Sudan obtained admission to the UN as 193rd member State.[44] At the same time, Palestine, after its 2010 admission to UNESCO, sought membership in the UN to find confirmation of its having become a fully fledged State (see **Chapter 4**). A similar role can be played by recognition of credentials by the UN General Assembly. Again in 2011, in September, the new Libyan government—while the conflict was still ongoing—presented credentials to participate in the 66th Session of the General Assembly and, upon approval by the Credentials Committee and the General Assembly, overcame remaining uncertainty as to who should represent Libya at the UN (this was contested by some States and the report of the Credentials Committee approved by vote).[45] These episodes are confirmation that, somehow, the UN is often seen as the embodiment of international legitimacy.

In addition, as everybody knows, the UN constitutes an *indispensable forum* where States may get together and engage in multilateral diplomacy, with a view to achieving political or legal agreement. The lack of such a world forum would render international dealings even more difficult.

Furthermore, what the UN has done in the fields of *decolonization, human rights, protection of the environment, and the development of international law*, besides furthering *a set of new community values* (such as the principles of *jus cogens*) constitutes a great legacy. If the international community is so starkly different from that existing before the Second World War, this is primarily due to the UN.

Another major achievement of the UN has been to gradually get *non-State actors*, chiefly non-governmental organizations, but also some national liberation movements, involved in the international diplomatic process. In Article 71 the UN Charter only referred to non-governmental organizations ('The Economic and Social Council may make suitable arrangements for consultation with non-governmental organizations which are concerned with matters within its competence'). Since 1945, the UN has gradually integrated those organizations into its action and, by so doing, has been one of the factors promoting their creation and activities. This is an exceedingly significant development: it shows that at the interstate level an attempt has been made, with success, to integrate actors other than States into international dealings, to listen to their voices, to pay attention to their demands, and to uphold their concerns as much as possible. At a later date, the same has occurred with regard to national liberation movements, which have been granted observer status in some UN bodies, and thus enabled to voice their claims (see **7.5**).

Finally, one should not underestimate the increasing tendency of the UN to link up with *regional organizations* (the Organization of American States (OAS), the African Union (AU, formerly Organization of African Unity (OAU)), the Arab League, the European Union (EU), the Council of Europe, etc.) and even organizations that, geographically speaking, are not regional (e.g. the North Atlantic Treaty Organization (NATO) and the Organization for Security and Co-operation in Europe (OSCE)), to promote and enhance their role in areas envisaged in Articles 52–54 of the UN Charter, that is, in peaceful

---

[44] See https://news.un.org/en/story/2011/07/381552.
[45] The report of the Credentials Committee was adopted with a favourable vote of 114 member States, 17 against, and 15 abstentions. For the discussions concerning the credentials of the new Libyan government see UN Doc. A/66/PV.2, 16 September 2011, in particular at 7–16.

settlement of disputes and enforcement of peace and security. At present the UN is endeavouring to work in much closer partnership with those organizations. Indeed, in recent times some seminal ideas deeply rooted in Churchill's international vision of the 1940s and early 1950s, in particular the idea of the possible crucial role of regional organizations in the international community, are proving more and more fecund. It is highly probable that the international community will increasingly direct itself towards combined action of the universal Organization with regional bodies. Cross-fertilization, mutual assistance, and a wise *division of labour* may in the end prove instrumental in somewhat narrowing—to the extent that this is feasible—the present fissures of the world community.

As weakened and 'wrinkled' as it might be on its 75th birthday (in 2020), the UN represents the very idea that matters of a supranational nature are to be addressed through international co-operation and co-ordinated efforts, rather than merely at the domestic level through the individual actions of each sovereign State. In this direction, the unanimous adoption by the General Assembly, during the mayhem of the Covid-19 crisis (at a time when the UN headquarters building in New York was closed and delegations were operating remotely), through a newly adopted emergency procedure,[46] of a resolution entitled 'Global solidarity to fight the coronavirus disease 2019 (COVID-19)' represents a significant reaffirmation of the commitment of member States to multilateralism and international co-operation.[47] At the same time, one cannot fail to note that the Security Council (and hence mainly the Great Powers) remained divided and failed to adopt timely measures, for example, the global ceasefire invoked by the Secretary-General and by His Holiness Pope Francis, and supported by over 125 member States.

---

[46] The procedure was adopted through decision 74/544 of the GA, adopted on 27 March 2020; for more details see online at https://www.un.org/pga/74/covid-19/.

[47] See operative paragraph 1 of UN GA resolution 74/270 entitled 'Global solidarity to fight the coronavirus disease 2019 (Covid-19)', adopted on 2 April 2020, online at https://undocs.org/en/A/RES/74/270.

16

COLLECTIVE SECURITY AND THE USE OF ARMED FORCE

16.1 INTRODUCTION

One of the main problems of the modern international community, at least since the 1648 Peace of Westphalia, has been to devise ways to keep the use of armed force under control and determine when and under what conditions States were entitled to resort to war. Under traditional international law, a few fundamental tenets emerged with regard to the use of (armed) force in interstate relations: (i) the unfettered freedom of States to use force; (ii) the consequent lack of a clear-cut distinction between enforcement proper (that is, resort to coercive action to compel observance of law) and use of force for realizing one's own interests; (iii) the licence to use force without previously getting an international authority to establish whether a subjective right of the State resorting to force had in fact been violated; (iv) the absence of any 'solidarity link' between the injured party and any third State, authorizing the latter to intervene to protect the rights of the former; international wrongs remained a 'private' occurrence between the delinquent State and the aggrieved party, except for those instances where there were already links based on treaties of alliance, in which case an ally might be affected by the wrongdoing and feel authorized to intervene; (v) the lack of any international agency capable of at least co-ordinating resort to force by individual States. In short, the 'old' law favoured major Powers: minor States derived no protection from general rules and consequently their own safeguard lay in the conclusion of treaties of alliance with one or more Great Powers.

In the twentieth century, in the immediate aftermath of the First World War, States had already tried to limit resort to war by creating the League of Nations (1919). At that time, however, the Covenant did not manage to prohibit resort to armed force, it merely proceduralized the decision to use force and subjected it to a 'cooling off' period (see **2.4.3**). Moreover, the League of Nations had other weaknesses which made it unsuitable for the task of restraining the willingness of States to go to war. In 1928, with the Kellogg-Briand Pact, an additional step was taken whereby the adhering States were renouncing war as an instrument of international politics.

However, it was only in 1945, after the Second World War, that consensus emerged to the effect that peace should constitute the overriding purpose of all members of the world community. Consequently, States agreed that the maintenance of peace should become a 'public' affair, that is to say, a matter of general concern, and that no country should be allowed to break or even jeopardize peaceful relations. The ensuing legal position is as follows:

(1) The previously untrammelled right to use force has been suppressed; any unilateral use of armed force except in self-defence is totally banned. It should be noted, however, that the new

international law has not abrogated the norms concerning the *modalities* of the use of force. In other words, if a State legally or illegally engages in military action, it is bound to respect certain general principles and rules placing restraints on such action (see **Chapter 17**), the purpose being, of course, to ensure that any breaches of the general prohibitions referred to above do not degenerate into barbarism.

(2) There is an international organization, the UN, which, at least in theory, is endowed with collective responsibility both for safeguarding peace, irrespective of any action taken by the aggrieved party (hence also in the event of its remaining passive in the face of aggression), and, more specifically, for enforcing the law in extreme cases (i.e. when breaches of international rules jeopardize peaceful relations). Serious international breaches have become 'public' events, of concern to the whole international community.

(3) Theoretically, the UN has a monopoly of force, in that it should intervene militarily in all the extreme cases just referred to.

(4) Whenever international rules are disregarded without the breach falling within the category of 'armed attack', States are not authorized to react by force. Self-help, although still allowed, must be confined to *peaceful* reaction to international wrongs.

(5) Even peaceful countermeasures must be preceded by resort to other, peaceful, means of conflict resolution. Judicial adjudication, however, is not made compulsory. It may suffice for some peaceful settlement mechanism to be used. Thus, even contemporary international law has not yet reached the stage typical of domestic legal systems, where ascertainment of legal situations must precede law enforcement.

(6) A marked distinction between peaceful measures of enforcement—which are lawful—and other instances of use or threat of military force—which are unlawful—has emerged. Thus, gradually, international law has come to uphold a distinction which is of fundamental importance and has for centuries been acted upon in municipal legal systems. As in municipal systems, in international law only the supreme collective body, the Security Council, is authorized to depart in exceptional circumstances from this distinction in the interest of the whole community. It can both *enforce the law* and *exercise 'police power'*. Unfortunately, what strongly differentiates the world community from domestic legal systems is both the rudimentary character of the international enforcement machinery and also the fact that this distinction becomes somewhat blurred, in practice, owing to disagreement among States over the exact boundaries of the classes of lawful and unlawful use of force.

In many respects this legal regime is a great innovation as compared with the previous one, but in the most important area, namely, the status of Great Powers, it has left the existing position almost unaffected. While in the past the lack of substantial restraints on the use of force simply confirmed that these Powers were the overlords in the world community, now the law goes as far as consecrating their might, providing, as it does, that while they must not use force contrary to the UN Charter, transgression will not invite sanction under Chapter VII of the Charter owing to the veto power conferred on each of them. In spite of this huge shortcoming in the law, the UN Charter system was designed to afford legal and institutional protection to smaller or middle-sized countries, whenever they were not involved in a fight against one of the major Powers. To this extent the Charter made much headway towards the introduction of some kind of safeguard for peace. In addition, one should not pass over in silence a major factor which helps to forestall the most serious breaches of international law by States: the role of public opinion, especially in democratic countries.[1]

The system envisaged in the UN Charter for the maintenance of international peace and security has never been implemented as designed. In the era of a bipolar world the antagonism of the two blocs prevented the adoption, by the Security Council, of the measures not involving the use of armed force (for the few exceptions, see **16.2.2**), provided for in Article 41 of the UN Charter, nor were the special agreements for the establishment of UN armed forces under Article 43 ever concluded. Hence, the two limbs of the collective security system seemed to remain a dead letter.

Nonetheless, the Security Council and the General Assembly, being unable to take the measures provided for in the Charter, fell back on different measures, labelled 'sanctions',[2] which, although devoid of coercive force, at least served to stigmatize some deviant State conduct (and in more recent times also the conduct of individuals or groups of individuals). Furthermore, the inability to set up UN armed forces led to the establishment of an innovative alternative mechanism: peacekeeping operations.

Only at the end of the Cold War was the Security Council able to take some of the measures short of force under Article 41 and to develop the practice of 'authorizing' the use of armed force by States, acting individually or within the framework of regional organizations, in the face of serious threats to the peace or breaches of the peace. It was a practice which became accepted and was largely considered to be in keeping with the UN Charter system; and it became a substitute for the use of force by the UN.

16.2 MEASURES SHORT OF ARMED FORCE AND THE UN SYSTEM

16.2.1 GENERAL

Article 41 of the UN Charter provides that:

> [t]he Security Council may decide what measures not involving the use of armed force are to be employed to give effect to its decisions, and it may call upon the Members of the United Nations to

---

[1] In this regard, see the remarks of J. L. Brierly, on the enormous importance which international public opinion can and does have for the observance of the 'law of nations'. He noted in 1931 that international public opinion contains an apparent paradox: 'It is intrinsically a weaker force than opinion in the domestic sphere, yet it is in a sense more effective as a sanction of the law. For whereas an individual law-breaker may often hope to escape detection, a State knows that a breach of international law rarely fails to be notorious; and whereas again there are individuals so constituted that they are indifferent to the mere disapproval, unattended by pains and penalties, of others, every State is extraordinarily sensitive to the mere suspicion of illegal action' (J. L. Brierly, 'Sanctions' (1931), in H. Lauterpacht and C. H. M. Waldock (eds), *The Basis of Obligation in International Law* (Oxford: Clarendon, 1958), 203).

[2] A few logical and terminological distinctions about the notion of sanctions are necessary. By speaking of 'sanctions' (or sanctions *lato sensu*) reference is made here to all those measures taken by groups of States or bodies of international organizations for the purpose of reacting to deviant conduct of States or other international subjects. This broad category is thus an umbrella concept that embraces (i) *collective countermeasures* (measures in breach of international law taken by a multiplicity of States, without any authorization of an international organization, in response to a violation of international law by another international subject, which are lawful in that they are intended to react to that breach and force its author to obey international law); (ii) *sanctions properly so called* or sanctions *stricto sensu* ('centralized' countermeasures decided upon or recommended by an organ of an international organization); as well as (iii) *political sanctions*, that is, *measures imposing hardship*, which do not involve a breach of international law and are taken by international organizations in reaction to deviant conduct of a member State (regardless of whether or not such conduct contravenes international norms).

apply such measures. These may include complete or partial interruption of economic relations and of rail, sea, air, postal, telegraphic, radio, and other means of communication, and the severance of diplomatic relations.

Clearly these measures are not a substitute for military action, which would still be possible in the Charter system under Article 42. It is however a fact that the relative failure of the UN collective system, and even of the imaginative substitutes subsequently set up, of necessity led to *magnification* of the role and importance of these 'sanctions'. They have been resorted to, both to respond to serious violations of international law amounting to a threat or a breach of peace, as well as to react to situations which, although not constituting a violation of international law, imperilled peace and security (triggering powers under Chapter VII presupposes a threat or breach of international peace and security under Article 39).

Often resort to these so-called sanctions is inversely proportional to their coerciveness; in other words, the less coercive they are, the more frequently and effectively they are used. The reason is simple: States and international institutions cannot do without 'sanctions'. In the face of paralysis of collective enforcement machinery, the solution lies in relatively mild forms of pressure or exposure not provided for in Article 41. When there is agreement in the Security Council, these measures at least serve to express collective condemnation of misbehaviour by States. However, the effectiveness of the measures taken by the Council under Article 41 depends first and foremost on the level of support they actually enjoy among all member States (as they may only be implemented with the active support of UN member States) and, secondly, on the quality of targeting.

It is worth adding a few words with regard to the targets of the 'repressive' measures decided upon by the Security Council. Although Article 41 does not explicitly clarify this matter, it would seem that these measures, or at least those enumerated in the provision, may be taken by the Council to impel a *State*, 'guilty' of threatening or breaching peace, to discontinue its deviant conduct. However, the spread of international terrorism, and the criticism of sanctions against States primarily affecting an innocent population, have led the Security Council to also decide upon measures against individuals or groups of individuals, for instance, the measures adopted against Al-Qaeda and its members, as well as those against ISIS/Daesh, but also in the context of other situations against those responsible for jeopardizing peace processes or engaging in serious violations of international humanitarian law.

More broadly, targeted or smart sanctions as they are also called (i.e. sanctions targeting individuals, e.g. suspected terrorists, high-level State officials, or groups of individuals, including rebels and other non-State actors as well as their leaders) have become a new tool for the Security Council to overcome the criticism of measures that did not distinguish between those that were actually responsible for the violations of international law and those (often the people) who were among the first victims of their own governments.

When adopting sanctions, the Security Council does not normally cite any specific provision of the Charter, but generically refers to Chapter VII. Yet, under Article 41, which is presumably the legal basis for SC sanctions, there are a variety of available measures: economic, political, technical, as well as institutional (e.g. the establishment of subsidiary organs, such as the Sanctions Committees or the UN Ad Hoc Tribunals for the former Yugoslavia and Rwanda, the 'ICTY' and the 'ICTR': see **19.3**). The characteristic that these measures share is that they do not entail use of armed force against a State.

Since 1966, the Security Council has established some 30 sanction 'regimes' (in 2020, 14 are still operational) from Southern Rhodesia to South Africa, from the former Yugoslavia to Haiti, from Iraq to Yemen, from South Sudan to Mali, as well as specific mechanisms against ISIS/Daesh, Al-Qaeda, and the Taliban.[3] Security Council sanctions have taken a number of different forms, in pursuit of a variety of goals. The Security Council has applied sanctions to support peaceful transitions, fight against terrorism, stigmatize human rights violation, and pursue non-proliferation policies. Measures have ranged from comprehensive economic and trade sanctions to more targeted measures such as arms embargoes, travel bans, and financial or commodity restrictions.

One of the criticisms advanced against targeted measures (i.e. those imposing limitations on physical or legal persons) has been that they do not give sufficient consideration to the due process rights of those involved. In 2005, even the General Assembly called on the Security Council to improve the fairness and due process for the imposition of sanctions measures. As a consequence, for example, in the framework of the Al-Qaeda Committee (established under resolutions 1267(1999) and 1989(2011)), the UN established an Office of the Ombudsperson to which individuals can apply to have their situation examined, and focal points for delisting requests were established. Nonetheless, the progress made has been deemed insufficient by many, including the Court of Justice of the European Union, which has considered unlawful certain targeted measures for violation of due process rights (see e.g. the *Kadi* case). In addition, the improvement made has been sectoral as it did not entail broader consideration of due process rights of the targeted individuals under the other sanctions regimes.

16.2.2 ECONOMIC AND OTHER 'SANCTIONS'

As mentioned earlier in the chapter, sanctions can be characterized according to their nature, for example, in a few cases the Security Council has *decided* that member States should take certain *economic* or *commercial* measures against a State. Cases in point have been Southern Rhodesia (1966–79) and South Africa (1977–94), when the Council explicitly acted under Article 41 of the Charter, imposing an embargo on the import and export of certain goods, in the former case, and an embargo on the import of arms and other military materials, in the latter. After the end of the Cold War, the Council imposed economic sanctions or military embargoes on a number of occasions in different situations ranging from those against Iraq after the invasion of Kuwait in 1990 (resolution 661 of 6 August 1990) to those against the former Yugoslavia in the 1990s (resolution 757 of 30 May 1992, followed by many resolutions against the FRY in 1992–93) to more recent measures concerning Eritrea (2009, lifted in 2018) or the Central African Republic (2013), North Korea (2006), or South Sudan (2018). In most of these more recent situations the Security Council has established a 'sanction committee' (composed of representatives of the 15 States which are members of the Council) acting as a subsidiary organ to work out the details of the sanction regime and handle the concrete determination of the measures adopted.

In other instances, either the Security Council or, when the Council is unable to make a determination, the General Assembly, has *recommended* the adoption of measures such as the *breaking off of diplomatic relations*: for example, against South Africa (since 1962 on account of apartheid and later on also because of its illegal occupation of Namibia) and Portugal (between 1963 and 1975 because of its colonial policy). Some of these decisions or recommendations have gone unheeded, owing to the lack of unanimous and substantial

---

[3] See https://www.un.org/securitycouncil/sanctions/information and the publication *Subsidiary Organs of the United Nations Security Council: 2020 Fact Sheet*, by the Department of Political Affairs (updated on 10 February 2020), online at https://www.un.org/securitycouncil/sites/www.un.org.securitycouncil/files/subsidiary_organs_factsheet.pdf.

support by the whole international community (often the target State was aided by one or more Powers, which inevitably undermined UN condemnations). In other cases, these measures have been successful and have contributed to peaceful settlement. It should be emphasized that often the success of the measures depends on whether they are coupled with a sufficiently robust engagement for a political process, and, in any case, they always require sustained coherence and consistency by member States in their implementation.

16.2.3 NON-RECOGNITION OF ILLEGAL SITUATIONS

On several occasions, faced with the unlawful behaviour of States that it was not in a position to terminate, or against which it proved unable to recommend or enjoin effective sanctions, the UN has fallen back on declaring the non-recognition of the illegal situation. As already mentioned (see 1.7), the doctrine of non-recognition was first enunciated in early 1932 by US Secretary of State Stimson,[4] and, soon afterwards, the Special Assembly of the League of Nations adopted on 11 March 1932 a resolution along the same lines. In 1938, at Lima, the Conference of American States passed a resolution on the non-recognition of acquisition of territory by force.

In the UN era, the Security Council has resorted to this class of sanctions with respect to a number of States: Israel, South Africa, Southern Rhodesia, Cyprus, and, in 1990, Iraq (by resolution 662 of 9 August 1990, the Council stated that the annexation of Kuwait by Iraq was null and void). In cases where the Security Council is not in a position to take such a stance (generally owing to the veto or prospective veto of one of its permanent members), similar pronouncements have been passed by the General Assembly. For example, referring to the situation of Crimea, on 27 March 2014, through resolution 68/262, the General Assembly '[c]alls upon all States, international organizations and specialized agencies not to recognize any alteration of the status of the Autonomous Republic of Crimea and the city of Sevastopol on the basis of the [above-mentioned] referendum and to refrain from any action or dealing that might be interpreted as recognizing any such altered status'. A non-recognition request was also issued by the General Assembly in relation to the US decision to move their embassy in Israel from Tel-Aviv to Jerusalem. After a failed attempt in the Security Council,[5] on 21 December 2017 the General Assembly convened in the resumed tenth emergency session, and adopted a text (very similar to the one vetoed in the Council) as resolution ES-10/19 (by 129 votes in favour, nine against, with 35 abstentions), whereby it '[a]ffirms that any decisions and actions which purport to have altered the character, status or demographic composition of the Holy City of Jerusalem have no legal effect, are null and void and must be rescinded in compliance with relevant resolutions of the Security Council, and in this regard calls upon all States to refrain from the establishment of diplomatic missions in the Holy City of Jerusalem, pursuant to Council resolution 478 (1980)' and '[d]emands that all States comply with Security Council resolutions regarding the Holy City of Jerusalem, and not recognize any actions or measures contrary to those resolutions'.

---

[4] After the Japanese invasion of the Chinese province of Manchuria, H. L. Stimson, the US Secretary of State, declared that his government could not 'admit the legality of any situation de facto nor does it intend to recognize any treaty or agreement entered into between these Governments or agents thereof which may impair the treaty rights of the United States ... and ... it does not intend to recognize any situation, treaty or agreement which may be brought about by means contrary to the covenants and obligations of the Treaty of Paris of August 27, 1928' ((1932) 26 *AJIL* 342).

[5] On 18 December 2017, at the initiative of Egypt, a draft resolution was tabled before the Security Council; the text obtained 14 votes in favour, but failed to be adopted owing to the veto by the US.

What is the import of UN pronouncements on non-recognition? Politically they rest on the idea that all actions contrary to certain basic values commonly accepted by the world community amount to deviations that should not be legitimized. Their aim is to isolate the delinquent State and compel it to change the situation that has been condemned. They constitute a political measure in those cases where the UN has proved unable to bring about a return to legality by resorting to the 'sanctions' provided for in the Charter: since the international organized community cannot nullify power, it must confine itself to emphatically withholding its endorsement.

Legally speaking, these UN pronouncements entail a mutual undertaking on the part of the supporting States. States pledge themselves to avoid any international or internal act capable of turning the de facto situation into an internationally legal one. It follows that domestic courts of all those States must treat acts and transactions carried out with unlawful authority as null and void; on an international level, no act should be performed that might result in legalizing the situation in any way. The ensuing state of affairs is likely to be very complex: although many customary rules of international law have in fact been modified to take account of the universal principles which have emerged and been consolidated (see **Chapter 3**), those States which do not vote in favour of the UN resolutions cannot be forced to take the view that the effective situation is contrary to international law. Invoking the principle of effectiveness (see **1.7**), they can claim that they are entitled to consider that situation lawful and act accordingly. By contrast, the States that support the UN resolutions are authorized to regard the effective situation as unlawful, and to behave accordingly. Here, as in many other instances, one is confronted with a split in the attitude of the world community. Current international law makes allowance for this rift: although it does not render both tendencies legally warranted, it affords no means of making the majority view prevail.

16.2.4 THE ESTABLISHMENT OF INTERNATIONAL CRIMINAL TRIBUNALS

On two occasions the Security Council, acting under Chapter VII, has *set up international criminal tribunals* designed to prosecute and punish the authors of atrocities perpetrated during armed conflict (see **19.3**). It first established the ICTY, in 1993, and one year later the ICTR. They can be classified as measures not involving the use of force provided under Article 41 of the Charter, as the ICTY Appeals Chamber held in the *Tadić (Interlocutory Appeal)* (at §§31–40).

The Council resorted to a similar measure, although with the consent of the territorial State, with regard to the establishment of the Special Tribunal for Lebanon (see **19.3**), which is based on an agreement between the government of Lebanon and the UN that entered into force, under Chapter VII, on the basis of SC resolution 1757 (2007).

16.2.5 ACTION BY THE GENERAL ASSEMBLY IN CASE OF GROSS VIOLATIONS OF INTERNATIONAL LAW

The failure of the UN Security Council to get to grips with the tremendous problems posed by forcible implementation of international law has impelled it to fall back on yet another 'sanction': public exposure of gross violations. This 'sanction' normally consists in the adoption by the General Assembly of resolutions condemning the unlawful conduct of States and in calls for the discontinuation of the deviant behaviour. So far the General Assembly has passed resolutions of this class on several occasions, chiefly when member States have violated human rights or when they have disregarded basic principles of the Organization (as in the case of South Africa and Israel).[6]

Similarly, in other recent cases, the General Assembly has adopted resolutions expressing concern for serious human rights violations and abuses in Syria, in Myanmar (relating to the treatment of the Rohingya), and in Ukraine.

Of course, one should not expect too much from this category of 'sanction', for more often than not the State concerned turns a deaf ear to international organizations. However, the beneficial effects of public condemnation can be appraised in the long term. It appears that States increasingly endeavour to avoid public strictures. In particular, they try to avoid being the target of repeated moral chastisements.

A recent evolution of the power of the General Assembly to intervene in these areas, on account of the inability of the Security Council to take any steps, has been the establishment of mechanisms to support investigations into the crimes committed in Syria and in Myanmar. Through resolution 71/248 (21 December 2016) the General Assembly has contributed to the promotion of accountability for serious human rights violations by creating the International Independent and Impartial Mechanism to support investigations into crimes committed in Syria since 2011. This Mechanism represents an interesting experiment that goes beyond condemnation and entrusts this body with the task of gathering materials and prospective evidence of serious crimes for future prosecution before competent domestic authorities (or international trials should the international community find an agreement to do so). In other words, the UN acts as a repository for evidentiary materials to which domestic prosecutorial entities may be able to resort when bringing to justice those responsible for war crimes, crimes against humanity, and genocide committed in Syria. The Human Rights Council, through resolution 39/2 on 27 September 2018, adopted a similar decision to establish an ongoing independent mechanism to collect, consolidate, preserve, and analyse evidence of the most serious international crimes and violations of international law committed in Myanmar since 2011 and to prepare files in order to facilitate and expedite fair and independent criminal proceedings, in accordance with international law standards, in national, regional, or international courts or tribunals that have, or may in the future have, jurisdiction over these crimes, in accordance with international law. Thereafter, the creation of such a mechanism was welcomed by the General Assembly in its resolution 73/264, adopted on 22 December 2018.

Broadly speaking, all these alternative measures (the implementation of which is very much dependent on their voluntary implementation by States given their non-binding nature) demonstrate the willingness of the majority of States in the General Assembly to be innovative in resorting to the tools provided for by the UN system and try to address gross violations of international law, particularly when the Security Council is unable to act due to the veto or the threat of the veto by one of the five permanent members.

---

[6] The fact that mere resort to exposure is seen as a 'sanction' need not surprise us. Time and again States themselves have admitted the importance that public exposure can have as a means of exercising leverage on States. Thus e.g. in 1975 the Greek representative said in the General Assembly: 'Only intervention by various international and national organizations or protests of foreign Governments which truly respected the principles of freedom and democracy could exert an influence on dictators and guarantee some protection to political prisoners under totalitarian regimes' (see GAOR, XXX Session, 3rd Committee, 2160th Meeting, §14). In the same vein, the UK delegate pointed out that 'if it was accepted that exposure was the most potent weapon available for combating torture, then the responsibility of the UN was very great indeed and there was cause to be grateful for the response to the GA's resolution [on torture, passed in 1975]' (ibid., 2167th Meeting, at §1).

16.3 PEACE OPERATIONS—FROM PEACEKEEPING TO PEACE ENFORCEMENT AND PEACE BUILDING

In some instances, the UN is able to act more incisively and set the stage for putting boots on the ground. Although the 'enforcement' system envisaged in the Charter did not become a reality, as early as 1956—exploiting a temporary convergence between the two superpowers (the US and USSR)—the Secretary-General (Dag Hammarskjöld at that time) and the General Assembly filled the vacuum left by the Council. In the context of the Suez Crisis, the elaboration of a new and imaginative scheme was devised: the creation of 'peacekeeping' forces (generally known, on account of their headgear, as the UN Blue Berets). On that occasion, to circumvent the British and French vetoes the General Assembly entrusted the Secretary-General with the establishment of UNEF (United Nations Emergency Force), a military force mandated to secure the cessation of hostilities and the withdrawal of British, French, and Israeli forces from Egyptian territory, and—after the withdrawal—to serve as a buffer force between the Egyptian and Israeli armies.

UNEF provided the model for what were to become traditional peacekeeping operations, which have the following distinguishing features:

(1) They are composed of military personnel put at the disposal of the UN by member States and deployed in a troubled area with the consent of the territorial State.

(2) They are generally under the exclusive authority of the Security Council (but can occasionally be under the authority of the General Assembly, as happened with the creation of UNEF). The Council therefore bears responsibility for their overall political direction. In addition, their executive direction and command is entrusted to the UN Secretary-General, while command on the ground is given to the Chief of Mission.

(3) They have no power of military coercion, but can resort to arms only in self-defence (see, however, later in the chapter).

(4) They are always requested to act in a neutral and impartial way.

(5) They are financed through regular contributions by the member States. The expenditure for peacekeeping forces relates to the maintenance of international peace and security; therefore, they are obligatorily allotted by the General Assembly under Article 17(2), as confirmed by the ICJ in its Advisory Opinion on *Certain Expenses* (at 151). Given the high costs of peacekeeping operations, the General Assembly has occasionally established Special Funds inviting voluntary contributions from member States to cover expenses.

Since 1956, the UN has established a large number of peacekeeping operations in different areas of the world. Classical peacekeeping operations, created on the basis of the UNEF model, have the main function of separating the contending parties, forestalling armed hostilities between them, and maintaining order in a given area. However, over the years they have come to perform a variety of tasks. Their number and complexity have greatly expanded since the end of the confrontation between Western and Eastern blocs: whereas 15 operations were set up before 1988, more than 50 operations have been established since that date.

Over the years, peacekeeping operations have evolved through peace enforcement, into peace operations *tout court* and there has been an increasing tendency towards attributing more complex tasks to UN missions. Innovation related especially to the abandonment of the principle providing for the use of force only in self-defence, but also to a more general broadening of the mandate which now may range from providing capacity building to support for national institutions in specific areas, to forms of territorial administration where required.

As early as 1961, the United Nations Operation in Congo (ONUC) represented the first remarkable exception: the Security Council authorized ONUC to use force 'if necessary, in the last resort' to prevent 'the occurrence of civil war in the Congo' (resolution 161 (1961)) and later on to arrest and bring to detention foreign military and paramilitary personnel and mercenaries (resolution 169 (1961)). After the end of the Cold War, in the 1990s, the Security Council radically altered the nature of the peacekeeping operation in Somalia (which was thus transformed from UNOSOM I into UNOSOM II), endowing it with enforcement powers under Chapter VII of the Charter (resolution 814 (1993)). Through resolution 836, adopted in June 1993, it also authorized UNPROFOR (the peacekeeping operation deployed in the territory of Bosnia and Herzegovina), 'acting in self-defence, to take the necessary measures, including the use of force, to reply to bombardments against the safe areas by any of the parties'. In all three cases, UN forces were deployed where there was actually no peace to keep—that is, in situations of ongoing conflicts within States—and where a partial or total breakdown of governmental authorities had taken place. This trend of entrusting peacekeeping forces with enforcement functions has however been strongly criticized and did not develop to the point of creating a special category of UN peace-enforcement units, as Secretary-General B. Boutros Ghali had envisaged in his 'Agenda for Peace' in 1992.

The vast majority of UN forces have responded to intrastate conflicts or have intervened in internal disorder or immediate post-conflict situations. Several forces were established as a result of comprehensive peace agreements which, among other provisions, asked the UN to supervise respect for and implementation thereof (UNAVEM I, II, and III in Angola; ONUMOZ in Mozambique; UNAMIR in Rwanda; ONUSAL in El Salvador; and UNTAC in Cambodia). Accordingly, UN forces have included a large civilian component engaged in several other activities, including providing humanitarian assistance, furthering national reconciliation and promoting respect for human rights and fundamental freedoms, organizing and monitoring elections, and occasionally also assisting in rebuilding institutions and national capacities.

In the late 1990s, operations were entrusted with the task of administering a region for a transitional period: for example, the UN Mission in Kosovo (UNMIK), which was created by resolution 1244 (1999) to perform, *inter alia*, basic civilian administrative functions where and for as long as required, organizing and overseeing the development of provisional institutions for democratic and autonomous self-government pending a political settlement, including the holding of elections; supporting, in co-ordination with international humanitarian organizations, humanitarian and disaster relief aid; maintaining civil law and order, including establishing local police forces and meanwhile, through the deployment of international police personnel to serve in Kosovo, protecting and promoting human rights and assuring the safe and unimpeded return of all refugees and displaced persons to their homes in Kosovo.

Similarly, the UN Transitional Authority in East Timor (resolution 1272(1999)), established after the riots following the referendum granting the people independence from Indonesia, was assigned the following tasks: to provide security and maintain law and order throughout the territory of East Timor; to establish an effective administration; to assist in the development of civil and social services; to ensure the co-ordination and delivery of humanitarian assistance, rehabilitation, and development assistance; to support capacity building for self-government; and to assist in the establishment of conditions for sustainable development. The precedent for this kind of operation was set in 1962 when the General

Assembly established—upon the request of Indonesia and the Netherlands—a temporary executive authority (UNTEA) to administer the territory of West New Guinea pending its transfer to Indonesia (where it now forms the province of Irian Jaya).

Complex situations have occasionally affected two other critical features of traditional peacekeeping operations: consent of the territorial State and impartiality. In some cases, peacekeeping operations proceeded on the basis of a partial consent, in that they lacked the consent of one or more of the parties involved. As a consequence, impartiality too was jeopardized. Nonetheless, the UN has always referred, and still does, to these features as the distinguishing features of peacekeeping operations.

The 'peacekeeping' system—like the 'authorizations regime'—is at odds with that envisaged in Chapter VII of the UN Charter. Nevertheless, it has become one of the most important UN tools—often the only available one—and at present is universally recognized as consistent with the Charter.

On balance, peacekeeping operations have proved useful principally for the purpose of making the contending parties stop fighting, thereby avoiding more bloodshed. They have also turned out to be very helpful in assisting in the fulfilment of complex peace processes where the parties were willing to co-operate and build for the future. They are not actually designed to compel the parties to accept a solution imposed by the UN, but serve to help put into practice, on the spot, the solution agreed upon by the contending States. However, in the long run, peacekeeping operations may turn out to be counterproductive, for they freeze the situation without providing a real solution to the basic problems at the root of the conflict.

One of the crucial problems the Organization faces regarding its operations is how to devise appropriate 'exit strategies' from situations in which it had to establish a presence on the ground (and there are several instances in which the UN cannot leave a country for decades, e.g. Cyprus or Democratic Republic of the Congo (DRC)) and the cost of the operations is a matter of concern for the member States, which repeatedly invoke the need for financial cuts.

Conscious of these concerns, the UN has been trying to find ways to reshape its approach to peacekeeping operations. It moved from peacekeeping to peace building, and more recently has placed stronger emphasis on the need for preventive action so as to try to avoid the need to establish peace operations.

In 2005, on the basis of the World Summit Outcome document, a new organ was established, the Peace Building Commission (a subsidiary organ of both the Security Council and the General Assembly), to assist—including with country-specific configurations—the relevant political processes and help provide financial support with external resources. In 2010 a review of peace operations was launched, laying the groundwork for UN peace operations in the new millennium.

Broadly speaking, the approach is that peace operations of a new generation tend to be developed in ways that acknowledge the fact that peacekeeping is often closely linked with, and needs to provide support for, State (re-)building processes, requiring broader mandates for UN missions on the ground, while at the same time integrating political processes within the scope of UN action. All this without jeopardizing the fundamental principles of impartiality and neutrality.

To sum up, it might be useful to recall that, at least since the 1990s, the UN has periodically reflected on its peacekeeping dimension. The vision of UN peacekeeping has been the object of a fundamental tension between two strands of opinion. On the one hand, those who consider it necessary to expand the tasks and roles assigned to peacekeepers, giving them broader mandates, which should include an enforcement dimension. On the other, those that deem it more prudent to stick to a traditional notion of peacekeeping as mere interposition with very limited (or no) enforcement tasks, strict adherence to the mandate, and always requiring the consent of the territorial state and leaving to political negotiations the organization of the post-conflict dimension of territorial administration and reconstruction.

These tensions re-emerge periodically. For example, they surfaced on the occasion of the adoption of some recent SC resolutions regarding UN operations in the DRC and in Mali, where the Council eventually opted for the creation of 'intervention brigades' within those UN peacekeeping missions. These resolutions have assigned the relevant UN forces the task of 'neutralizing armed bands'. In these cases, and for the limited purpose of enforcing the resolutions, the UN forces are acting, in a way, as domestic enforcement authorities. The tension between an interventionist and a more traditionalist vision of peace operations is confirmed, *inter alia*, by the express statement in those resolutions that such a measure (the establishment of the intervention brigade) shall not constitute a precedent and that the (three) basic principles of peacekeeping are reaffirmed (i.e. consent of the parties, impartiality, and non-use of force except in self-defence; to the latter category, in recent times, the expression 'and in defence of the mandate' has been added to justify the enforcement dimension of new peace operations).

16.4 ENFORCEMENT ACTION UPON AUTHORIZATION OF THE SECURITY COUNCIL

Being unable to set up the UN armed forces envisaged in Article 43 of the Charter, especially after the end of the Cold War, the UN Security Council has gradually developed a practice of authorizing the use of force by individual member States or coalitions of States, including regional organizations. This practice has taken three forms: (1) on some occasions the Security Council has authorized States to resort to force after a State had engaged in acts of aggression against another State, which had reacted in individual (and collective) self-defence; in other instances, (2) the Council has authorized States to use force individually or to establish multinational forces, to confront threats to the peace, which included ongoing international or internal armed conflicts, humanitarian crisis, or other varied situations.

(1) On a few occasions, the Security Council has authorized States to use force against another State that had committed a breach of the peace or had engaged in aggression. In 1950, taking advantage of the absence of the Soviet delegate (who did not attend SC meetings in protest over the failure of the UN to allow China to be represented in the UN by the People's Republic of China rather than nationalist China), the Security Council authorized member States, acting under US command, to assist South Korea in repelling by force the aggression of North Korea and allowed them to use the UN flag in the course of military operations (resolutions 82, 83, and 84 (1950)). Similarly, in 1990 the Council authorized member States to use all necessary means—that is, to use force on a large scale—to repel the Iraqi aggression against Kuwait (resolution 678 (1990)). In 2001, after the terrorist attack by Al-Qaeda against the US (Twin Towers, Pentagon, Pennsylvania), under resolution 1368 (2001) on 12 September, the Council condemned the attacks while '[r]ecognizing the inherent right of individual or collective self-defence in accordance with the Charter'.

(2) In other instances, the Security Council has authorized States to use force when faced with a threat to the peace. This has in particular occurred with *humanitarian crises*. Indeed, the Security Council has gradually established a direct link between humanitarian crises and threats to the peace, one of the three possible conditions that could trigger SC action under Chapter VII. The Council has thus considerably enlarged the concept of threat to the peace laid down in Article 39 of the UN Charter, so as to include humanitarian crises

within one State, which once were deemed to fall primarily within domestic jurisdiction. It has subsequently authorized member States to use force to establish a secure environment for humanitarian relief operations. For example, efforts were made to protect safe havens in Bosnia and Herzegovina on the basis of resolutions 836 and 844 (1993) authorizing member States, through the use of air power, to deter attacks against the safe areas. Operation *Restore Hope* in Somalia and Operation *Turquoise* in Rwanda were launched, respectively, on the basis of resolutions 794 and 929 (1992 and 1994). They consisted of large-scale military operations conducted by two 'coalitions of the willing'—led respectively by the US and France—in order to achieve humanitarian objectives such as providing security and support for the distribution of relief supplies or ensuring the protection of displaced persons, refugees, and civilians at risk.

However, this practice of elevating humanitarian crises to threats to the peace is not without its dangers. The Security Council is eager to retain discretionary power in this matter and tends to avoid explaining the nature of the link and the reasons for its action. As a result its practice lacks consistency and turns out to be selective. For instance, African countries have railed against the fact that some humanitarian disasters in Africa, such as that in Sierra Leone, have not motivated the Security Council as strongly as some previous crises, such as that in Somalia.

Through the enlargement of the notion of 'threat to the peace' the Security Council also authorized member States, acting nationally or through regional organizations or arrangements, to use force with a view to restoring democracy or public order. By resolution 940 (1994) the Council, after condemning the behaviour of the illegal de facto regime set up in Haiti, authorized member States to establish an international force and to use all necessary means to facilitate the departure of the military leaders and allow the return of the legitimately elected President, Jean-Bertrand Aristide.

In 1997, following a request by Albania for SC action, the Security Council authorized member States to intervene there (resolution 1101 (1997)). It also authorized intervention in East Timor (resolution 1264 (1999)) to prevent internal disorders from degenerating into combat situations, as well as in Liberia, pursuant to resolutions 1497 (2003) and 1509 (2003).

In 2004, after a new conflict erupted in Haiti, the Council intervened again by authorizing a Multinational Force (mainly consisting of US troops) which subsequently was converted into a UN stabilization force (under resolution 1542 (2004)) and thereafter a mission.

More recently, on 17 March 2011, the Security Council, through resolution 1973 (2011), authorized States 'acting nationally or through regional organizations or arrangements [...] to take *all necessary measures* [...] to protect civilians and civilian populated areas under threat of attack in the Libyan Arab Jamahiriya'. This authorization, which implied the availability to member States of the option to resort to armed force (all necessary means), permitted the NATO operation against the Libyan armed forces acting under the instructions of the government of Colonel Gaddafi. The intervention soon became contested in the international community as it appeared to aim at replacing the existing government rather than being merely protective of the civilian population.[7] Nonetheless, it represented a form of authorization of the use of armed force in the implementation of the so-called 'responsibility to protect' doctrine.[8]

---

[7] UN SC resolution 1973 (2011).

[8] Resolution 60/1, 2005 World Summit Outcome, 24 October 2005, §§138–139, subsequently elaborated in a Report from the UN Secretary-General, Implementing the Responsibility to Protect, 12 January 2009, UN Doc. Ae/63/677. The UN Security Council has relied on this doctrine on several occasions, including Darfur (2006), Libya (2011), Côte d'Ivoire (2011), South Sudan (2011), Yemen (2011), Syria (2012), and the Central African Republic (2013). See N. Michel, 'La responsabilité de protéger—Une vue d'ensemble assortie d'une perspective suisse' (2012) 131 *Revue de droit suisse* 5.

The Security Council also authorized member States to use force for several other different purposes. For instance, it adopted numerous authorizations to enforce economic measures previously decided upon under Article 41. This happened first in 1966, when the Council called upon the UK to halt, 'by the use of force if necessary', ships carrying oil destined for Southern Rhodesia in flagrant breach of the embargo imposed by the Council against that country (resolution 221 (1966); there ensued the incident of the Greek ship *Manuela*).[9] Since then, particularly after the end of the Cold War, the Security Council has often recommended States to undertake a limited use of force to secure compliance with economic sanctions previously adopted. Thus, for instance, by resolution 665 of 25 August 1990, the Security Council invited member States to inspect and verify the cargo and destination of every ship crossing the Gulf in order to ensure that they were not violating embargo measures imposed on Iraq. The Security Council also requested States to halt all inward and outward maritime shipping to ensure strict implementation of economic measures decided upon against the Federal Republic of Yugoslavia (resolutions 787 (1992) and 820 (1993)), Somalia (resolution 794 (1992)), Haiti (resolutions 875 (1993) and 917 (1994)), Liberia (resolution 1083 (1997)), and Sierra Leone (resolution 11 (1997)). Similarly, the Council authorized NATO air strikes against Serb forces in Bosnia and Herzegovina.

Similar authorization measures (albeit with the consent of the coastal States) were adopted for the purpose of ensuring antipiracy activities off the coast of Somalia in resolution 1846 (2008). And the same approach was taken with regard to the authorization of the EU mission in the Southern Mediterranean (EUNAVFOR MED), off the coast of Libya, to prevent violations of the arms embargo, as well as countering all forms of trafficking under resolution 2292 (2016).

Over the years, the 'authorization regime' has evolved along three main lines. First, with regard to the purpose of the use of force authorized by the SC, this body has increasingly defined in a clearer manner the *objectives* States were to pursue when using force. It is necessary only to think, in contrast, of the broad purpose of the use of force set out in resolution 678 (1990) concerning Iraq. The Security Council decided that States had to use all means necessary 'to uphold and implement resolution 660 (1990) and all subsequent resolutions and to restore international peace and security in the area'. This sweeping mandate enabled some States (in particular the US and the UK) to argue that the air raids against Iraq designed to ensure respect for the subsequent SC resolutions were authorized by resolution 678 (1990). Clearer and more specific objectives were set forth in resolution 1511 (2003) and, even more, in resolution 1546 (2004) (see e.g. §§9–14), both on Iraq.

Secondly, the *duration* of the mandate given by the Security Council has been increasingly defined. Initially this duration was not specified (see e.g. resolution 678 (1990) concerning Iraq, resolution 770 (1992) relating to the former Yugoslavia, and resolution 794 (1992) concerning Somalia). At present the Council tends to provide for a time limit in its resolutions authorizing the use of force. Sometimes this limit is a 'functional deadline', as is the case with resolution 940 (1994) concerning Haiti, which provides in §8 that the multinational force will terminate its mission as soon as 'a secure and stable environment has been established and UNMIH [UN Mission in Haiti] has adequate force capability and structure to assume the full range of its functions' (a determination entrusted to the Council itself). In other situations (e.g. the counterpiracy operations in Somalia, or

---

[9] This Greek ship was stopped and searched by a British man-of-war without opposition from the Greek authorities. Another Greek ship, the *Joanna-V*, had been searched on the high seas off the coast of Beira, Mozambique, prior to the SC resolution, triggering strong protests from the Greek government. On these two incidents see, for the relevant references, V. Gowlland-Debbas, *Collective Responses to Illegal Acts in International Law* (Dordrecht, Boston, and London: Nijhoff, 1990), 400 as well as B. Conforti, *The Law and Practice of the United Nations*, 2nd edn (The Hague, London, Boston: Kluwer, 2000), 280.

countertrafficking measures in Libya) the timeframe has been set at 12 months. The practice of providing for a time limit is important, particularly when a permanent member of the Council takes part in the military operations, given that, if the permanent member for its own reasons is not interested in the cessation of the operations, it could veto any SC decision designed to terminate the authorization to use force.

Thirdly, the Security Council has increasingly imposed upon States the duty to report to it, frequently and in a detailed manner, on the conduct of military operations.[10]

Clearly, this evolution of UN practice tends to make such practice more consonant with the UN Charter. The Security Council now increasingly tends to exercise control over and supervision of the way States put into effect its authorization to use force. It is thus gradually recovering that primary authority and responsibility in the area of peace and security that the Charter had bestowed upon it. This evolution is however opposed by those States which, in participating in military operations, prefer to act outside international restraints and supervision.

The practice, which has gone unopposed, whereby the Security Council authorizes States to use force is not envisaged in the UN Charter and indubitably constitutes an innovation, since no provision of the Charter may be held to warrant it, not even by implication. One cannot argue that the practice is implicitly justified by Article 51 on collective self-defence, for the actions undertaken now do not need to meet the requirements of immediacy, necessity, and proportionality (and, in addition, they do not necessarily constitute a response to an armed attack). Nor can one argue that the Security Council, being empowered under the Charter to establish a UN multinational force, is implicitly authorized to delegate such power to member States: indeed, the lynchpin of the Charter provisions is the notion that the use of force is kept in the hands of a central body, whereas the new system hinges on the idea of such force being spread out among States, that is, being 'decentralized', albeit upon authorization of that body.

The question therefore arises of whether the practice, initially contrary to, or at least deviant from, the UN Charter, is now legally sanctioned by international law. Given the lack of any significant opposition and the widespread resort to such practice, it is reasonable to argue that a *customary* rule has evolved in the international community, which is also operative within the UN legal system, in that it broadens the scope of Chapter VII of the Charter.

16.5 SELF-DEFENCE AND ITS MANY FACES

16.5.1 INDIVIDUAL AND COLLECTIVE SELF-DEFENCE

When States are not authorized by the Security Council, they must refrain from the use of armed force, unless they act in self-defence. As pointed out earlier in this book (see **3.4**), under Article 2(4) of the UN Charter (and the corresponding customary rule of

---

[10] Initially this obligation was not stringent. E.g. resolution 678 (1990), on Iraq, simply provided that States were 'to keep the Security Council regularly informed on the progress of actions undertaken' (at §4). In fulfilling this broad obligation some States confined themselves to submitting to the Security Council short and general reports on the military operations that were under way. At present, this obligation is no longer general and loose. In some cases the Security Council also requests the Secretary-General to report on the conduct of operations, so as to have other standards of appraisal available in addition to (or in place of) the information given by States. E.g. resolution 1546 (2004) concerning Iraq provides in §30 that the Secretary-General must 'report to the Council within three months from the date of this resolution on UNAMI [UN Assistance Mission for Iraq] operations in Iraq, and on a quarterly basis thereafter on the progress made towards national elections and fulfillment of all UNAMI's responsibilities'.

international law) 'all Members shall refrain in their international relations from the threat or use of force against the territorial integrity or political independence of any state, or in any other manner inconsistent with the Purposes of the United Nations'. In the Charter scheme, member States can resort to armed force only if ordered or authorized by the Council or if they act in self-defence. This latter inherent right to act in individual or collective self-defence is clearly recognized in Article 51 of the UN Charter.[11] Both rules are generally considered to correspond to customary international law, and the prohibition on using armed force—particularly the ban on aggression—is part of *jus cogens* (see **11.4.3**).

Self-defence is the lawful reaction to an 'armed attack', that is, to massive armed aggression against the territorial integrity and political independence of a State that imperils its life or government ('less grave forms of the use of force' may not be considered as armed attack, as the ICJ held in 1986 in *Nicaragua (Nicaragua v United States of America)* (at §191) and confirmed in 2003 in *Oil Platforms (Islamic Republic of Iran v United States of America)*, at §§51, 64, and 72). In addition, the attack must be of such magnitude that one cannot repel it otherwise. Contrary to what the ICJ states in *Nicaragua* (at §195) and in 2004 in the Advisory Opinion on the *Legal Consequences of the Construction of a Wall in the Occupied Palestinian Territory* (at §139)—a holding highly criticized by Judge Higgins in the Separate Opinion she appended to the latter Court's pronouncement (at §33)—the aggression need not come from a State; it can also emanate from a terrorist organization or even from insurgents (aggressing a State other than the one on whose territory they operate). Including attacks by such groups within this concept may provide an explanation of the overall positive reaction of the international community to the US reaction against Afghanistan following the 9/11 terrorist attack on the Twin Towers in New York and the Pentagon in Washington DC.

Since aggression constitutes a violation of the sovereign rights of the victim, in resorting to self-defence the latter engages in legal enforcement. This implies that self-defence must limit itself to rejecting the armed attack; it must not go beyond this purpose. As the ICJ stated in *Nicaragua*, self-defence only warrants 'measures which are proportional to the armed attack and necessary to respond to it' (at §176; see also *Legality of the Threat or Use of Nuclear Weapons*, at §141, and *Oil Platforms*, at §§51, 73, and 76–77; in this case the Court found that the forcible measures taken by the US against Iran were not 'a proportionate use of force in self-defence', at §77). The requirements of necessity and proportionality must be strictly construed, so as to restrict States' room for manoeuvre: as the ICJ held in *Oil Platforms*, 'the requirement of international law that measures taken avowedly in self-defence must have been necessary for that purpose is strict and objective, leaving no room for any "measures of discretion"' (at §73).

Consequently, (i) the victim of aggression must use an amount of force strictly necessary to repel the attack and proportional to the force used by the aggressor; (ii) it may only attack 'legitimate military targets' (*Oil Platforms*, at §51), in keeping with principles and rules of international humanitarian law; also, the necessary precautions must be taken to minimize incidental damage to civilians; (iii) the State that has been the target of an 'armed attack' must not occupy the aggressor State's territory, unless this is strictly required by the need to hold the aggressor in check and prevent him from continuing the aggression by other means. Furthermore, (iv) self-defence must be terminated as soon as the Security Council

---

[11] Article 51 states that '[nothing] in the present Charter shall impair the inherent right of individual or collective self-defence if an armed attack occurs against a Member of the United Nations, until the Security Council has taken measures necessary to maintain international peace and security. Measures taken by Members in the exercise of this right of self-defence shall be immediately reported to the Security Council and shall not in any way affect the authority and responsibility of the Security Council under the present Charter to take at any time such action as it deems necessary in order to maintain or restore international peace and security.'

steps in and takes over the task of putting an end to the aggression. This, however, does not imply that self-defence must cease if the Security Council simply pronounces on the matter; self-defence may continue until the Council has taken *effective* action rendering armed force by the victim State unnecessary and inappropriate, and hence no longer legally warranted. If the Security Council fails to take action, (v) self-defence must cease as soon as its purpose, that is, repelling the armed attack, has been achieved. In other words, Article 51 and the corresponding norm of general international law do not authorize or condone any military action overstepping mere opposition to, and repelling of, aggression. In particular, they prohibit prolonged military occupation and annexation of territory belonging to the aggressor.

In addition, Article 51 grants any member State of the UN the right to use force in support of another State which has suffered an armed attack. This right has been interpreted to the effect that the intervening State must not itself be a victim of the armed attack by the aggressor (in which case it would act by way of 'individual' self-defence). Both the NATO treaty and the Treaty on the Warsaw Pact (now extinct) pointed in this direction. However, what is required is a prior bond (e.g. a treaty) between the two States acting in self-defence or, if such a bond is lacking, an express request by the victim of the attack. In other words, a State cannot use force against a country which has attacked another State, without the request or the previous consent of the latter. In addition, it is for the victim State to establish that it has been militarily attacked. As the ICJ held in *Nicaragua*:

> [I]t is the State which is the victim of an armed attack which must form and declare the view that it has been so attacked. There is no rule of customary international law permitting another State to exercise the right of collective self-defence on the basis of its own assessment of the situation. Where collective self-defence is invoked, it is to be expected that the State for whose benefit this right is used will have declared itself to be the victim of an armed attack.[12]

So far 'collective' self-defence (that is, intervention by one or more States in favour of the victim) has been invoked on a few occasions.[13] The relative paucity of reliance on this category of use of force—in itself no doubt a felicitous feature of the present world community—is due to the tendency of States to hold aloof as much as possible from international armed conflicts or to side with one of the contending parties merely by sending arms and military equipment.

As we shall see, *other instances of unilateral resort to force* (protection of citizens abroad, armed intervention with the consent of the territorial State, armed reprisals against unlawful small-scale use of force, use of force to stop atrocities) are instead legally doubtful, for it is not clear whether customary international rules have evolved on the matter, derogating from the general ban on the unilateral use of armed force, laid down in the body of law just referred to. Furthermore, it is a matter of dispute whether a similar derogation has evolved with regard to peoples or racial groups fighting for their self-determination to the effect that such groups or peoples are authorized, subject to some stringent conditions, to use military violence to achieve self-determination.

---

[12] *Nicaragua (Nicaragua v United States of America)*, §§195 and 199. See also *Oil Platforms (Islamic Republic of Iran v United States of America)*, §51.

[13] The US relied on this defence in the case of Vietnam (in various official pronouncements, in particular the State Department Memorandum of 4 March 1966, the US invoked Article 51 for its military action in support of South Vietnam) and in Nicaragua, in 1981–84, as did Britain in 1964 when it attacked Yemen to assist the Federation of Southern Arabia, and the Soviet Union in the case of Czechoslovakia (1968) and Afghanistan (1979). Collective self-defence was also referred to in the preamble to the resolution adopted by the Security Council after the Iraqi attack on Kuwait in 1990 and the request for assistance by the Kuwaiti government in exile (resolution 661 of 1990). However, as is well known, in that instance the Security Council authorized States to react to the Iraqi aggression against Kuwait.

As stated earlier, the failure of the UN collective system for enforcing peace resulted, among other things, in an expansion of resort to self-defence; in other words, it led to the invocation by States of Article 51 in cases which hardly amounted to self-defence or even in cases that were clearly not covered by the provision at issue.[14]

States, particularly Great Powers, have tended to abuse this right. In addition to some of the cases mentioned below, under various headings, mention may be made of some instances where the US has invoked Article 51 to justify military actions that, in fact, had strong *punitive* connotations and also pursued a primarily *deterrent* purpose.

On several occasions States have invoked self-defence in an expansive way; one example is the US attack on Libya carried out on 14 April 1986, made in response to the bombing, in West Berlin, on 5 April, of the *La Belle* disco, allegedly carried out by Libyans. Another instance was the launch of a number of missiles, on 26 June 1993, against Baghdad, allegedly in response to a planned terrorist attack on the former US President, Bush, which was due to have occurred two months earlier (on 14 April 1993), on a visit by Bush to Kuwait. The terrorist attack was not carried out but the reaction took place. In the UN Security Council the US delegate justified the American attack as follows: 'From all the evidence available to our intelligence community, we are ... highly confident that the Iraqi Government, at its highest levels, directed its intelligence services to carry out an assassination attempt against President Bush ... [T]his was a direct attack on the US, an attack that required a direct US response ... as we are entitled to do under Article 51 of the UN Charter, which provides for the exercise of self-defence in such cases. Our response has been proportionate and aimed at a target directly linked to the operation against President Bush. It was designed to damage the terrorist infrastructure of the Iraqi regime, reduce its ability to promote terrorism and deter acts of aggression against the US' (UN Doc. S/PV.3245, at 6). And again on 20 August 1998, US submarines fired missiles against a military training camp in Afghanistan and a chemical plant in Sudan as a response to terrorist attacks organized by the group led by Osama bin Laden, including the shelling of the US embassies in Kenya and Tanzania. The justification given by the US President on 21 August 1998 was as follows: 'The US acted in exercise of our inherent right of self-defense consistent with Article 51 of the UN Charter. These strikes were a necessary and proportionate response to the imminent threat of further terrorist attacks against US personnel and facilities. These strikes were intended to prevent and deter additional attacks by a clearly identified terrorist threat. The targets were selected because they served to facilitate directly the efforts of terrorists specifically identified with attacks on US personnel and facilities and posed a continuing threat to US lives' ((1989) 83 *AJIL* 162).

Clearly, after the attacks of 11 September 2001, broad resort to the notion of self-defence in the wake of what became known as the 'war on terror' has become a distinctive trait of the first 20 years of the twenty-first century, posing new threats of erosion to the ban on the use of armed force in international relations and the UN Charter system.

The war in Afghanistan (2001–02), subsequently the invasion of Iraq (2003–04), and more recently the protracted conflict in Syria (since 2010) have created a number of instances in which the provisions of the Charter have again been severely tested and Article 51 has been invoked beyond its literal terms.

---

[14] Instances where Article 51 was invoked include: the USSR intervention in Hungary in 1956; the US intervention in the Dominican Republic in 1965; the US participation in the Vietnam War in 1966; the Israeli attack on Egypt in 1967; resort to force by the US in the Mayaguez incident in 1975; the USSR intervention in Afghanistan in 1979; Israel's use of unilateral force in Uganda in 1976 (Entebbe airport), in Iraq in 1981 (Osiraq nuclear power station), and against Lebanon a number of times since 1978; the numerous attacks by South Africa on neighbouring States (Angola, Zambia) between 1976 and 1979 allegedly to stop terrorism from abroad; the military action of the UK against Argentina after the latter's invasion of the Falklands/Malvinas in 1982; and the US intervention in Grenada in 1983, in Libya in 1986, and in Panama in 1989.

The conflict in Syria, with its multiple phases and faces, has determined developments in State practice that might be hard to disentangle. While some States intervened in the conflict to support the Syrian government in reacting to internal threats from a variety of sources (in ways which are amenable to being characterized as intervention with the consent of the territorial State), others intervened invoking Article 51 against ISIS/Daesh and the fact that attacks (or threats of attacks) attributable to Daesh had occurred in their territories, by essentially confirming that the armed attack (or threat thereof) may also originate from a non-State entity and that armed force can be resorted to against such entity even in the territory of a third State. This is particularly true when such a State is unable to prevent the terrorist entity from attacking the 'intervening' States. For instance, States such as the US, France, the UK, and Germany intervened by making reference to Article 51 of the Charter, linking their intervention to the threat or the actual occurrence of terrorist attacks in their territories and more broadly on the threat ISIS/Daesh posed to peace and security. In so doing they seem to have shown agreement with a broader notion of armed attack under Article 51, triggering the right to engage in self-defence. In these cases not only was the Security Council kept informed, but it also somehow endorsed some aspects of these positions, which included reference to the right of collective self-defence by the EU Member States (under Article 42(7) of the EU Treaty)—see, for example, resolution 2249 (2015) adopted in the immediate aftermath of the terrorist attacks in Paris on 13 November 2015.

16.5.2 IS ANTICIPATORY SELF-DEFENCE ADMISSIBLE?

A connected problem that has cropped up on several occasions and which in modern international relations has become of *crucial importance* (on account of the kind of weapons that exist) is whether Article 51 allows anticipatory self-defence. This makes reference to a pre-emptive strike once a State is certain, or believes, that another State (or entity) is about to attack it militarily. Israel has resorted to anticipatory self-defence on various occasions: for example, in 1967 against Egypt, in 1975 against Palestinian camps in Lebanon, and in 1981 against Iraq (Israeli aircraft bombed Osiraq, an Iraqi nuclear reactor near Baghdad). Similarly, in 1980, in the Security Council, Iraq justified its armed attack on Iran by relying upon its right to strike pre-emptively at other countries preparing for war. In 2003, the US and the UK invoked pre-emptive self-defence to justify their attack on Iraq, including on the basis of alleged possession of weapons of mass destruction by the regime of Saddam Hussein.

The rationale behind the doctrine of 'anticipatory' self-defence, stressed by all those who advocate it, is a strong meta-legal argument: in an era of missiles and nuclear weapons and of highly sophisticated methods of reconnaissance and intelligence, it would be naïve and self-defeating to contend that a State should await attack by another country, in the full knowledge that it is certain to take place and likely to involve the use of very destructive weapons. As McDougall, one of the leading proponents of this view, wrote, to impose on States the attitude of 'sitting ducks' when confronted with an impending military attack 'could only make a mockery, both in its acceptability to States and in its potential application, of the Charter's main purpose of minimizing unauthorized coercion and violence across State lines'.[15] In 1981 the Israeli delegate echoed this doctrine in the Security Council.[16]

---

[15] M. McDougall, 'The Soviet-Cuban Quarantine and Self-defence' (1963) 57 *AJIL* 601.

[16] He declared that the scope of the concept of self-defence had 'broadened with the advance of man's ability to wreak havoc on his enemies. Consequently, the concept took on new and far wider application with the advent of the nuclear era. Anyone who thinks otherwise has simply not faced up to the horrific realities of the world we live in today, and that is particularly true for small States whose vulnerability is vast and whose capacity to survive a nuclear strike is very limited.' See UN Doc. S/PV.2288, at 40; 19 ILM (1981), 989.

This non-legal rationale has been given a legal foundation by claiming that Article 51 did not suppress the pre-existing international rule on anticipatory self-defence, which was, therefore, left unaffected by the Charter. The argument, developed by some eminent American and British jurists,[17] and advanced by Israel in the Security Council in 1981,[18] has been opposed by other distinguished publicists.[19] These publicists have substantially made two points. First, the alleged customary rule did not envisage a right of anticipatory self-defence proper, but a right of self-defence and self-preservation. Secondly, Article 51 wiped out all pre-existing law, and did not leave any room for self-defence except in the form it explicitly authorized.

However, in *Nicaragua* the ICJ authoritatively placed a different interpretation on Article 51, contrary to the second point just mentioned. It held that '[o]n one essential point, this treaty itself [that is, the UN Charter in Article 51] refers to pre-existing customary international law; this reference to customary law is contained in the actual text of Article 51, which mentions the "inherent right" (in the French text the "droit naturel") of individual or collective self-defence... The Court therefore finds that Article 51 of the Charter is only meaningful on the basis that there is a "natural" or "inherent" right of self-defence, and it is hard to see how this can be other than of a customary nature, even if its present content has been confirmed and influenced by the Charter... customary international law continues to exist alongside treaty law. Moreover, the Charter, having itself recognized the existence of this right, does not go on to regulate directly all aspects of this content' (at §176). Nevertheless, the Court did not specify the contents of the customary rules referred to in Article 51, in particular whether they included the old rule providing for a right to anticipatory self-defence. The Court noted that, as the parties to the dispute had not raised 'the issue of the lawfulness of a response to the imminent threat of armed attack', it did not intend to express any view on the matter (at §194). Thus, this important decision of the Court cannot support any interpretation narrowing or broadening Article 51 with regard to the class of self-defence we are discussing.

If one undertakes a perusal of State practice in the light of Article 31 of the Vienna Convention on the Law of Treaties (see **10.6**), it becomes apparent that such practice does

---

[17] C. H. M. Waldock, 'The Regulation of the Use of Force by Individual States in International Law', (1952) 82 *HR* 498; J. Stone, *Aggression and World Order* (London: Stevens, 1958), 44; D. W. Bowett, *Self-Defence in International Law* (Manchester: Manchester University Press, 1958), 187; M. S. McDougall and F. P. Feliciano (eds), *Law and Minimum World Public Order* (New Haven, CT: New Haven Press, 1961), 232; M. A. Kaplan and N. Katzenbach, *The Political Foundations of International Law* (New York: Wiley, 1961), 210ff; S. Schwebel, 'Aggression, Intervention and Self-Defence in Modern International Law' (1972-II) 136 *HR* 479ff; see also S. Schwebel, Dissenting Opinion, ICJ, *Nicaragua*, ICJ Reports 1986, 347; O. Schachter, *International Law in Theory and Practice* (Dordrecht, Boston, and London: Nijhoff, 1991), 151; R. Higgins, *Problems and Process: International Law and How to Use It* (Oxford: Clarendon Press, 1994), 242.

[18] With reference to the attack on Osiraq, the Israeli delegate stated the following: 'In destroying Osiraq, Israel performed an elementary act of self-preservation, both morally and legally. In so doing, Israel was exercising its inherent right of self-defence as understood in general international law and as preserved in Article 51 of the UN Charter. A threat of nuclear obliteration was being developed against Israel by Iraq, one of Israel's most implacable enemies. Israel tried to have that threat halted by diplomatic means. Our efforts bore no fruits. Ultimately we were left with no choice. We were obliged to remove that mortal danger. We did it cleanly and effectively.' See UN Doc. SPV.2280, 2 June 1981, in ILM (1981), 970.

[19] H. Kelsen, *The Law of the United Nations* (London: Stevens, 1950), 797; H. Wehberg, 'L'interdiction du recours à la force. Le principe et les problèmes qui se posent' (1951-I) 78 *HR* 81; P. C. Jessup, *A Modern Law of Nations: An Introduction* (New York: Macmillan, 1952), 165; I. Brownlie, *International Law and the Use of Force by States* (Oxford: Oxford University Press, 1963), 264ff; K. Skubiszewski, 'Use of Force by States. Collective Security. Law of War and Peace' in M. Sørensen (ed.), *Manual of Public International Law* (London: Macmillan, 1968), 767; P. L. Lamberti Zanardi, *La legittima difesa nel diritto internazionale* (Milano: Giuffrè, 1972), 191ff; B. V. A. Röling, 'On the Prohibition of the Use of Force' in A. R. Blackshield (ed.), *Legal Change: Essays in Honour of J. Stone* (New York: Butterworths, 1983), 276ff.

not evince agreement among States regarding the interpretation or the application of Article 51 with regard to anticipatory self-defence. On many occasions States have used anticipatory self-defence, without however formally invoking it, but rather relying on other legal justifications.[20] In contrast, in other instances States formally invoked anticipatory self-defence or at least argued that it was lawful.[21]

Analysis of State and UN practice thus shows that the overwhelming majority of States firmly believe that anticipatory self-defence is not allowed by the UN Charter. However, a number of States take the opposite view, and the emergence of a specific doctrine regarding the use of armed force against terrorist entities has provided further support. Given the importance and the role of these States, one may not conclude that there is universal agreement as to the illegality under the UN Charter of anticipatory self-defence.

This being so, it would seem that one should resort to the *object and scope of Article 51* and, more generally, Chapter VII of the UN Charter or even, to use the words of the ICJ in *Legality of the Use by a State of Nuclear Weapons in Armed Conflict*, 'the logic of the overall system contemplated by the Charter' (at §26). The purpose of these provisions is to safeguard peace as much as possible, and for this purpose to establish a *collective* and *public* mechanism designed to prevent or put a stop to armed violence. The only exception is the *'private'* right of each State to protect itself against aggression pending the stepping in of collective bodies. Peace is regarded as the supreme value, and whatever may imperil or jeopardize such value should be removed or reined in as much as possible. If this is so, pre-emptive strikes should be banned, since they may easily lead to abuse, being based on subjective and arbitrary appraisals by individual States. It may thus be contended that, however *unrealistic* the ban on pre-emptive self-defence deriving from Article 51 may be in the present circumstances of warfare, States prefer to avoid *risks of abuse*. This should not be surprising. In any legal system, it is well known that some classes of action are not susceptible to being properly defined and circumscribed in advance, although they may have perilous consequences. In these instances, legal legitimation of such actions might produce pernicious effects. Many legal systems make provision for cases where actions may prove illegal but are in some respects justified on other grounds. Usually this is achieved, in criminal law, through the notion of 'mitigating circumstances'. Or else judicial or enforcement bodies in fact decide *not to legally* respond to breaches of law (in a way, this has also happened in the UN: the General Assembly, which could be seen as the 'world jury', for better or worse, has sometimes harshly condemned recourse to force—for instance in the cases of Hungary, Grenada, Panama, and Western Sahara—whereas on other occasions it has seemed to ignore or

---

[20] E.g. in 1962 the US instituted a 'naval quarantine' forcibly to intercept on the high seas ships carrying missiles to Cuba; however, it relied on the legal endorsement by a regional organization, the OAS. In 1967, Israel launched a pre-emptive strike against Egypt (the United Arab Republic), Jordan, and Syria, but claimed that it was a reaction to the 'act of war' constituted by Egypt's preventing the passage of Israeli vessels through the Straits of Tiran. In 1988, the US military ship *USS Vincennes* shot down an Iranian civilian aircraft during the Iran–Iraq war; the US authorities justified the downing of that aircraft by claiming that, as Iranian aircraft and patrol boats had previously fired on American helicopters and ships, the Americans had simply reacted to those attacks.

[21] In 1975, Israel did so when it launched a pre-emptive strike against Palestinian camps in Lebanon. In 1980, Iraq claimed that in attacking Iran it had exercised its right of pre-emptive self-defence (but then quickly changed its attitude and argued that it had reacted to a previous attack by Iran). In 1981, Israel again invoked anticipatory self-defence when it destroyed the Iraqi nuclear reactor at Osiraq. South Africa too relied on the same legal ground when it attacked military bases of the ANC in neighbouring countries (Zambia, Lesotho).

even approve such recourse: for instance in the cases of Goa, Tanzania and Uganda, and the Central African Republic).

As for anticipatory self-defence, it is more judicious to consider such action as *legally prohibited*, while admittedly knowing that there may be cases where breaches of the prohibition may be justified on moral and political grounds and the community will eventually condone them or mete out lenient condemnation. This may in particular occur when the relevant State offers to the world community or to the UN convincing evidence of the impending attack, which it felt justified to pre-empt by use of force, and in addition shows that the anticipatory strike and the subsequent military actions have been proportionate to the threat, and limited to removal of such threat.

Although pre-emptive self-defence is not currently authorized by international law, no one can deny that, as international relations presently stand, not only terrorist action but also violence resorted to by States (or by insurgents attacking a State other than the one on whose territory they lie and against which they fight) may compel States to use force before being attacked. With regard to such extreme cases it may not seem injudicious to put forward legislative solutions *de lege ferenda* (that is, aimed at suggesting the adoption of new rules). These new rules should be designed to take account of exceptional exigencies of States, while at the same time making allowance for the need to avoid risks of abuse and dangerous escalations of armed violence. If gradually accepted, such new rules would on the one hand legitimize some justified security needs while, on the other, ensuring that restraints are placed on armed violence.

From the viewpoint of a possible development of law one could perhaps envisage the possibility of making anticipatory self-defence *lawful* subject to the following strict conditions: (i) the State that decides to resort to such self-defence must have available compelling evidence that another State or a terrorist organization abroad is about to unleash an armed attack; this evidence must be all the more determinative when monitoring inspection procedures, or if conciliation mechanisms are operating with regard to the State or organization suspected to be about to launch aggression (this was clearly the case with Iraq in 2003 before the US and UK attack); (ii) the attack is not only imminent and inevitable but also massive, such that it is likely seriously to jeopardize the population or even imperil the life or the survival of the State; (iii) the use of force in anticipatory self-defence must not be out of proportion to the attack it aims at averting; (iv) anticipatory self-defence must only aim at forestalling the attack; it must not pursue other goals such as the occupation of enemy territory or the overturning of a foreign government (occupation of territory may be temporary and strictly required by the aim of removing the threat of aggression; the overturning of a foreign government may also be an inescapable and natural consequence of the armed attack, not one of its aims); (v) the State resorting to such self-defence must immediately report to the UN Security Council; as soon as the armed clash is over, it must produce convincing evidence to the Council showing that, had it not made the attack, it would have been the object of aggression; (vi) the State at issue must accept the Security Council's subsequent political assessment (if it is one of the five permanent members, it must forgo its veto power when voting on the issue); if the majority of the Council considers that the conditions for resort to anticipatory self-defence were not met, the State must be ready to submit to conciliation or arbitration, if resort to such procedure is requested by the majority of the Council; (vii) if the Security Council or a conciliatory or arbitral body concludes that anticipatory self-defence was not warranted, or that the use of force was disproportionate, or that it also pursued unwarranted goals, the State concerned must be ready to pay compensation to the State attacked.

As it is difficult to amend the UN Charter (the amending procedure being cumbersome and time-consuming), States could agree upon the above (or other) conditions through a resolution unanimously approved by the General Assembly, with the concurring vote of the five permanent members (in which case, the resolution would amount to an agreement in simplified form partly amending Article 27(3) of the UN Charter, in derogation from Article 108 of the Charter).

16.5.3 SELF-DEFENCE AGAINST ARMED INFILTRATION AND INDIRECT AGGRESSION

While Article 51 clearly refers to an actual use of force taking place at a definite time (the crossing of frontiers by military troops, the bombing of territory by foreign aircraft, large-scale attack on foreign ships on the high seas, etc.), international practice shows that military aggression increasingly takes the form of gradual infiltration of armed forces and groups of volunteers supported by a foreign government into the territory of another State. In such cases the 'invasion' of the territory of a State does not take place all of a sudden and on a large scale, but over a long period and piecemeal. This sort of aggression can also consist in organizing, assisting, fomenting, financing, inciting, or tolerating subversive or terrorist activities carried out against another State, either to overthrow its government or to interfere in civil strife (so-called indirect armed aggression). The problem arises of whether international law extends self-defence to include reaction to *invasion through infiltration of troops* and to *indirect armed aggression*.

The US invoked the former category of aggression in the case of Vietnam: the American government consistently held that individual self-defence by South Vietnam and collective self-defence by the US were legitimized by the gradual infiltration of North Vietnamese troops and Vietcong into South Vietnam. The attitude of other States towards this view does not provide compelling evidence of the formation of a customary rule on the matter. However, the view agreed upon by States in the Definition of Aggression adopted in 1974 by the UN General Assembly through resolution 3314(XXIX) seems to reflect customary law, as the ICJ authoritatively held in *Nicaragua (merits)* (at §195). According to this view, one may consider as attacks justifying self-defence those armed attacks made by armed bands, groups, irregulars, or mercenaries *sent by or on behalf of a State* or a terrorist organization, and of such a gravity as to amount to an armed attack conducted by regular forces. Anything short of these requirements may not warrant self-defence.

Various States (chiefly the US, Israel, and South Africa) have claimed that 'indirect aggression' warrants self-defence.[22] However, the reaction of the international community has never been one of full and convinced acceptance of the legal justifications propounded by Israel, Southern Rhodesia, and South Africa. Indeed, the debates that took place on various occasions in the Security Council[23] show that most States were opposed to the

---

[22] In particular, Israel, on the occasion of its attacks against Palestinian camps in Lebanon (1970–83) and in Tunisia (in 1985); Southern Rhodesia (when it attacked Zambia (1978–79)); and South Africa, on the occasion of its attacks on SWAPO camps and troops in Angola and its raids into Lesotho, Zambia, and Swaziland (between 1976 and 1985), claimed that the violation of sovereign rights of the attacked State was justified by the fact that the latter tolerated or actively supported terrorist activities of guerrilla groups against the territory and assets of the attacking States.

[23] In 1976, 1978, 1979, 1980, 1982, and 1984. See references in A. Cassese, in J.-P. Cot and A. Pellet (eds), *La Charte des Nations Unies: Commentaire article par article*, 2nd edn (Paris: Economica, 1991), 781.

invocation of Article 51 and regarded the various instances of resort to force as illegal. In addition, the discussions on the principle of non-intervention which took place in the UN Special Committee on Friendly Relations in the years 1966–70 were revealing.[24]

Furthermore, in *Nicaragua* the ICJ distinguished between various classes of threat or use of force. It pointed out that training or providing economic, military, logistical, or other assistance to rebels fighting against the central authorities in another country may be regarded as a threat or use of force or as an intervention in the internal or external affairs of another State. However, it does not amount to armed attack (unless the provision of significant military support to an insurgency is major and demonstrable) (at §195). Hence, it does not entitle the target State to respond by self-defence against the assisting State (at §§195, 228, and 230).

It thus seems doubtful that Article 51 authorizes self-defence against indirect armed aggression, or that a general rule has evolved authorizing States to invoke self-defence to repel such specific category of aggression. It would seem that State practice shows that entitlement to the right of self-defence against a State supporting an insurgency or terrorism depends on (a) the level of such support, (b) the evidence of that support, and (c) the evaluation of that evidence by the ICJ or by another competent UN organ. It also depends, of course, on (d) the proportionality of the response and (e) the legality of the means used to respond.

16.5.4 FORCIBLE PROTECTION OF NATIONALS ABROAD

In various instances, States have used force for the purpose of protecting their nationals whose lives were in danger in foreign territory. In certain cases, force has been used *without the consent* of the territorial State.[25] In other cases, military intervention was effected

---

[24] In 1964, the UK proposed proclaiming the right of any country to seek military assistance from third States, should it become the victim of unlawful intervention in the form of 'subversive activities leading to civil strife in which the dissident elements are receiving external support and encouragement'. In 1966, a group of Western countries (Australia, France, Canada, Italy, the UK, and the US) took up and broadened that proposal, suggesting that the 'right of States in accordance with international law to take appropriate measures to defend themselves individually or collectively against intervention is a fundamental element of the inherent right of self-defence'. However, this proposal was strongly attacked in the Special Committee by a number of socialist and Third World countries, including Czechoslovakia, the United Arab Republic, Ghana, India, Lebanon, Algeria, and Mexico. They argued that the proposal was 'a dangerous departure from the UN Charter and from international law as generally accepted'; in particular, it ignored Article 51 and led to a dangerous broadening of the range of eventualities in which self-defence could be exercised under that provision of the Charter. As a result of that criticism, the resolution's sponsors withdrew it and the final text of the Declaration on Friendly Relations simply refers to the 'relevant provisions of the Charter'. It should also be noted that the UN Special Committee for the Definition of Aggression eventually took the same stand, as is apparent, in particular, from the debates which took place within the Committee.

[25] Belgium intervened in the Congo in 1960; the US in the Dominican Republic in 1965; the US in Cambodian waters in 1975 (to rescue an American cargo boat and its crew captured by Cambodian armed forces); Israel in Uganda in 1976; and the US in Iran in 1980. In addition, as recalled earlier in the chapter, the US bombed Libya in 1986, Baghdad in 1993, and Afghanistan and Sudan in 1999 as a reaction to terrorist attacks on US nationals. In the first two cases, the territorial State was not responsible for the threat to the life of foreign nationals, for such threat resulted from the collapse of the public order system. By contrast, in the third and fourth cases, the local government was answerable, for it did not protect the lives of foreigners, but tolerated or even aided and abetted the activity of private individuals endangering foreign nationals. For more recent practice see N. Ronzitti, *Rescuing Nationals Abroad through Military Coercion and Intervention on Grounds of Humanity* (Dordrecht, Boston, and Lancaster: M. Nijhoff, 1985), 26ff. For older practice see *Right to Protect Citizens in Foreign Countries by Landing Forces*, Memorandum of the Solicitor for the Department of State, 5 October 1912, 2nd edn (Washington, DC: Government Printing Office, 1929), 51ff.

with the consent of the territorial State.²⁶ In addition to these cases one should mention the Larnaca incident of 1978. It is unique and anomalous and therefore cannot be put into the same category as those just mentioned.²⁷

One thing is striking: in most cases of the use of force to protect nationals, the intervening State is a Western Power, and the State on whose territory the military action is carried out is a developing country. This situation is indicative of the present constellation of power in the world community. Of course, there is no denying that in nearly all the cases at issue there was either a real breakdown in the territorial system of public order, or inability on the part of the local government to prevent the perpetration of unlawful acts against foreigners.

The second remarkable thing is that mostly Western States have expressed the view that armed intervention for the protection of nationals is internationally lawful, being authorized either by Article 51 of the UN Charter or by a customary rule unaffected by the Charter (the US went as far as to adopt, in 1948, regulations laying down the right of the US to use force abroad to protect 'the lives and property' of American citizens 'against arbitrary violence': Article 0614, US Navy Regulations).²⁸

---

²⁶ Thus, the US sent its troops to Lebanon in 1958 (although the principal grounds for American intervention, adduced by both the US and Lebanon, were the request of the Lebanese government and the applicability of Article 51 of the UN Charter, the US delegate to the Security Council also emphasized that US troops had been sent to Lebanon in order to protect American lives; he pointed out that US forces 'will afford security to the several thousand Americans who reside in that country'). Belgium did the same, with help from the US, in the Congo in 1964. The Federal Republic of Germany sent a commando unit to Mogadishu with the consent of Somalia in 1977. In 1978, French and Belgian troops intervened in the Shaba area at the request of Zaire. In 1983 the US sent armed forces to Grenada. (They claimed that this was done at the request of the British Governor-General, due to the collapse of local authorities (see (1984) 78 *AJIL* 200, 662); independent reports disclosed that there was actually no imminent threat or danger to the lives of American citizens; the fact that US troops were stationed on the island after evacuating the American nationals confirmed that the ground for landing troops adduced by the US authorities was indeed a mere pretext for unlawful forcible intervention. The UN General Assembly did not uphold the legal grounds adduced by the US and, by resolution 38/7 of 1984, deplored the US intervention.) In 1989 the US sent armed forces to Panama, among other things 'to protect American lives' after 'the legitimate democratically elected government of Panama [had been] consulted and [had] welcomed [the US] action' (see (1990) 84 *AJIL* 545, 547).

²⁷ In February 1978, two terrorists killed the Egyptian Secretary-General of the Afro-Asian Peoples Solidarity Organization during a meeting of the Organization in Nicosia. After seizing hostages, among whom there were a few Egyptian nationals, the terrorists left Cyprus by aircraft but, being refused access by various countries, were obliged to return to Larnaca airport. While negotiations were under way between the Cypriot authorities and the terrorists, an Egyptian aircraft was allowed to land at Larnaca. When the Cypriot authorities realized that it carried a commando unit, they refused to authorize it to intervene. The Egyptians nevertheless opened fire against the terrorists, whereupon the Cyprus national guard in its turn fired on the Egyptians. As a result of the shoot-out several Egyptians and Cypriots were killed or wounded and the Cypriot authorities arrested the terrorists. A dispute between Egypt and Cyprus ensued. The former—while conceding that Cyprus had not authorized the use of force—claimed that it had not violated Cypriot sovereignty and had acted upon the principle of fighting terrorism. Cyprus, however, rejected Egyptian claims and firmly asserted that its sovereignty had been violated. The case clearly does not fit into the class of incidents where States use force to protect their own nationals, first, because Egypt claimed that its sole aim was to combat terrorists, and, secondly, because it contended that it had used force after being authorized by Cyprus to send a military aircraft to Larnaca (it would seem that in the view of Egypt, such authorization entitled it at least to send in armed forces, from which it followed that it did not breach the sovereignty of Cyprus).

²⁸ In 1993, the UK Foreign Minister stated in the House of Commons that '[f]orce may be used in self-defence against threats to one's nationals if: (a) there is good evidence that the target attacked would otherwise continue to be used by the other State in support of terrorist attacks against one's nationals; (b) there is, effectively, no other way to forestall imminent further attacks on one's nationals; (c) the force employed is proportionate to the threat'. See (1993) 64 *BYIL* 732.

By contrast, other countries have consistently opposed the legality of this class of resort to force. Except for the German intervention in Somalia (where the territorial State gave its consent), foreign intervention has often been attacked as contrary to international law.[29]

On balance, it would seem that the objections of many States have not led to the obliteration of the general rule on the matter, evolved after the First World War. However, this rule—which might be subsumed under the general notion of self-defence pursuant to Article 51 of the UN Charter—may only be resorted to *under very strict conditions*, dictated by the UN Charter system for the maintenance of peace and security. Its applicability in present-day conditions is justified by the weakness of UN collective enforcement (clearly, if the UN had SC armed forces at its disposal, to be dispatched immediately to places where human lives are in serious jeopardy, the rule would no longer be needed). The conditions to be fulfilled for the use of armed force to protect nationals abroad to be lawful, are as follows:

(1) The threat or danger to the life of nationals—due either to terrorist attacks or to the collapse of the central authorities, or to the condoning by those authorities of terrorist or similar criminal activities—is serious.

(2) No peaceful means of saving their lives are open either because they have already been exhausted or because it would be utterly unrealistic to resort to them.

(3) Armed force is used for the exclusive purpose of saving or rescuing nationals.

(4) The force employed is proportionate to the danger or threat.

(5) As soon as nationals have been saved, force is discontinued.

(6) The State that has used armed force abroad immediately reports to the Security Council; in particular, it explains in detail the grounds on which it has considered it indispensable to use force and the various steps taken to this effect.[30]

16.5.5 ARMED INTERVENTION WITH THE CONSENT OF THE TERRITORIAL STATE

We should now ask ourselves whether the principle *volenti non fit injuria* (an illegal act is no longer such if the party whose rights have been infringed previously consented thereto), universally enshrined in State law, is also acknowledged as valid by the international community in the area of armed force.

In traditional international law this principle was obviously in full force—each member being on a par with the others, there were no limits to the freedom of States and all rules could be derogated from. Thus, each State was free to allow another to use force in any form

---

[29] Thus e.g. on the occasion of the armed action by the US in Lebanon in 1958, Ethiopia stated in the General Assembly: 'Ethiopia strongly opposes any introduction or maintenance of troops by one country within the territory of another country under the pretext of protection of national interest, protection of lives of citizens or any other excuse. This is a recognized means of exerting pressure by stronger Powers against smaller ones for extorting advantages. Therefore, it must never be permitted' (see GAOR, 3rd Emergency Special Session, 742nd Plenary Meeting, 20 August 1958, §75). On the same occasion Poland argued that the protection of nationals abroad constituted an 'old pretext' (ibid., 740th Plenary Meeting, at §84). And in 1978, on the occasion of the French and Belgian military operation in Zaire, the Soviet official news agency TASS stated that 'humanitarian intervention' was merely 'a fig leaf to cover up an undisguised interference in the internal affairs of Zaire' (see *Keesings' Contemporary Archives* (1978), 29128).

[30] It follows from this enumeration of conditions that the military interventions of Belgium in the Congo in 1960, of the US in the Dominican Republic in 1965, and of Israel in Uganda in 1976 were lawful. In contrast, the US intervention in Grenada in 1983 was unlawful (in particular, under the heading we are discussing—protection of citizens abroad). Similarly, the US bombing of Libya in 1986, of Baghdad in 1993, and of Afghanistan and Sudan in 1998 were contrary to the UN Charter.

on its own territory. Just as a State was able officially to sanction its own mutilation, dismemberment, or even its total extinction, so it could agree to allow another international subject to use force on its own territory.

Did the situation change once the use of force had been explicitly forbidden in the UN Charter and this ban had been enshrined as one of the mainstays of the international community, with only a few very circumscribed exceptions? Since these exceptions did not include consent, can consent become an implicit exception? A close scrutiny of the Charter allows for only one conclusion: by explicit consent a State may authorize the use of force on its territory whenever, being the object of an 'armed attack', it resorts to individual self-defence and in addition authorizes a third State to assist it in 'collective self-defence'. What if the consenting State is not in fact the object of an 'armed attack'? For example, if there is an insurrection within its territory, or if it is faced with serious disorders, and would like to appeal for help to another member of the international community?

A number of States tend to consider traditional law still fully valid and consequently hold that consent legitimizes the use of force because it precludes the violation of Article 2(4) of the Charter.[31] A survey of practice also shows that some States all too readily claim their own military interventions to be lawful on account of consent (or request) by the State concerned. Thus, on more than one occasion, in cases of subversion in the territory of one State, other States have considered it quite legitimate to intervene, after a request to do so, either because the rebels were said to be receiving aid from third States, or because the consenting State was said to be the object of an 'armed attack', as laid down in Article 51.[32]

---

[31] E.g. in 1958, the British Foreign Secretary asserted: 'The structure of the Charter preserves the customary law by which aid may be given to a nation of the kind which I have described [in the face of civil strife fomented from abroad] ... I do not believe that either the spirit or the letter of the Charter takes away the customary, traditional right' (quoted by Brownlie, *International Law* (n 19), 326).

[32] E.g. the Soviet intervention in Hungary in 1956 (when the USSR did not invoke Article 51); that of the US in Lebanon, and of Britain in Jordan, both in 1958 (when both States invoked Article 51, as well as receiving consent); that of the US in the Dominican Republic in 1965 (when the Americans also invoked the Charter of the OAS), and in Grenada in 1983 (when the US also referred to a regional treaty and to the 'right to protect nationals abroad'); not to mention Soviet intervention in Czechoslovakia in 1968 and in Afghanistan in 1979 (when the USSR both invoked Article 51 and allegedly received the consent of the territorial State in question). To justify its armed intervention in Cyprus in 1964 and 1974, Turkey invoked before the UN Security Council the 1960 Treaty of Guarantee between Cyprus, Greece, Turkey, and the UK, Article IV of which provided that in the event of a breach of the Treaty, and in so far as no common or concerted action proved possible, each of the three Guaranteeing Powers reserved 'the right to take action with the sole aim of re-establishing the state of affairs' created by the Treaty. Before the Security Council, Greece and Cyprus rejected this interpretation, insisting that no 'military' action had been explicitly envisaged in the Treaty and in addition there had been no 'specific' consent by Cyprus to foreign military intervention. The *Panama Canal* case should also be mentioned. Article V of the 1977 Panama Canal Treaty, laying down the principle of 'non-intervention in the internal affairs of the Republic of Panama', was unilaterally interpreted by the US as authorizing the use of force by the US in Panama. When the Treaty was submitted to the US Senate for the necessary authorization to ratification, Senator De Concini proposed a clause, accepted by the Senate as a 'condition' to ratification, whereby, '[n]otwithstanding the provisions of Article V or any other provision of the Treaty, if the Canal is closed, or its operations are interfered with, the United States of America and the Republic of Panama shall each independently have the right to take such steps as each deems necessary, in accordance with its constitutional processes, including the use of military force in the Republic of Panama, to reopen the Canal or restore the operations of the Canal, as the case may be' (see the text of the relevant documents online at http://lcweb2.locgov/frd/cs/panama/pa-appnb.html). The Panamanian government accepted the clause, without submitting it to a new plebiscite (the Treaty had already been approved by plebiscite). However, President Torrijcos stated that Panamanians would not accept US intervention for defending or reopening the Canal, unless the US was specifically invited. In addition, Torrijcos appended a declaration to the Panamanian instrument of ratification, stating among other things that Panama's 'political independence, territorial integrity and self-determination [were] guaranteed by the unshakable will of the Panamanian people' (see W. I. Jorden, *Panama Odyssey*

Clearly State practice makes extensive use of the consent exception, even though this practice hardly conforms to present-day international law. It would appear that most cases of so-called armed intervention were unlawful, either because they were based on a misinterpretation of the relevant rules, or because the specific situation adduced to justify intervention differed in reality from the one depicted by the intervening State. Often the rebels were not in fact receiving any 'external' aid, and certainly not in the form of massive 'military assistance'; or else, the individuals requesting or authorizing foreign intervention could not be regarded as the lawful authority of the 'inviting' State. Furthermore, whenever the intervening State (not to mention the 'consenting' State) justified the use of force by the need to ward off, in conformity with Article 51, an 'indirect armed aggression', the justification was based on a questionable interpretation of Article 51. Indeed, as noted earlier, normally this provision does not allow the use of force against that particular form of 'aggression'.

The present legal regulation may be summarized as follows. First, consent must be freely given (that is, it cannot be wrested by any form of force, coercion, or duress: *coacta voluntas non est voluntas*); it must be real as opposed to merely 'apparent'. Secondly, it must be given by the lawful government, that is, by the authority empowered thereto by the constitution. Thirdly, it may not be given as a blanket authorization for the future; it must be given ad hoc. Fourthly, it may not validly legitimize the use of force against 'the territorial integrity or political independence' of the consenting or requesting State, contrary to Article 2(4) of the UN Charter. For instance, a State may not authorize another State to use force on its territory with a view to establishing control over the population of the consenting State, or to appropriating a portion of territory of that State. Fifthly, consent cannot run counter to other principles of *jus cogens*. This would occur, for example, if force were authorized in order to deny or limit the right of peoples to self-determination, or if force involving atrocities were allowed for the purpose of putting down a rebellion or preventing secession.

16.5.6 ARMED REPRISALS AGAINST UNLAWFUL SMALL-SCALE USE OF FORCE

A few States and also some commentators have contended[33] that a particular class of armed reprisals, that is, military action short of war in response to a single and small-scale armed action by another State, is legally authorized either by Article 51 or by a general rule on the

---

(Austin, TX: University of Texas Press, 1984), 585). The Declaration went on to provide that '[t]herefore, the Republic of Panama will reject, in unity and with decisiveness and firmness, any attempt by any country to intervene in its internal or external affairs' (§3 of the Panamanian Declaration). It would seem that the Panamanian response to the US 'condition' was intended to stultify its purpose of authorizing armed intervention. However, the State Department construed the Panamanian statement as not excluding or modifying 'the De Concini Condition or any other provision of the Treaties as ratified by the Senate' (see (1984) 78 *AJIL* 204). Whether or not this view was correct, it seems indisputable that, as some distinguished American commentators have rightly pointed out, the US invasion and occupation of Panama in 1989 was not lawful, either on this ground (consent) or on any of the other three grounds put forward by the US government, namely 'to safeguard lives of American citizens', to 'help restore democracy', and 'to bring General Manuel Noriega to justice' (statement by the US President G. Bush, 3 January 1990, Office of the Press Secretary, the White House). (See V. P. Nanda, 'The Validity of United States Intervention in Panama Under International Law' (1990) 84 *AJIL* 500; L. Henkin, 'The Invasion of Panama Under International Law' (1991) 29 *CJTL* 302–3, 309–10. A contrary view was put forward by A. D. Sofaer, 'The Legality of the United States Action in Panama' (1991) 29 *CJTL* 287. See also D. Wippman, 'Treaty-Based Intervention: Who Can Say No?' (1995) 62 *U Chi L Rev* 680.)

[33] Bowett, *Self-Defence* (n 17), 270; D. Bowett, 'Reprisals Involving Recourse to Armed Force' (1972) 66 *AJIL* 3; Skubiszewski, 'Use of Force' (n 19), 754; Y. Dinstein, *War, Aggression and Self-defence*, 2nd edn (Cambridge: Cambridge University Press, 1994), 215.

matter. (As for serious violations of rules of international law other than Article 2(4) of the UN Charter, we have seen earlier (see **15.3**) that armed reprisals in response to them are prohibited by current international law, for only peaceful countermeasures are allowed, as even those who are in favour of the legality of the class of reprisals we are now discussing would admit.)

Before discussing this *particular* and *narrow* class of armed reprisals, it is fitting briefly to reconsider the legality of the *general category* of armed reprisals in modern international law. Some States have carried out acts that can be regarded as military reprisals.[34] However, that no customary rule has evolved on this matter is evidenced by the fact that only some Western States have insisted on the legitimacy of armed reprisals when they themselves took such reprisals (strikingly, some of them, that is, France, Britain, and the US, went as far as to criticize resort to those reprisals by *other* member States of the UN). That these reprisals are not authorized by Article 51, read in conjunction with Article 2(4), can be inferred from a literal and logical construction of those provisions and is corroborated by the subsequent practice of UN bodies, as indicative of the legal conviction of the States making up those bodies. In particular, mention may be made of various SC resolutions condemning reprisals 'as incompatible with the purposes and principles of the United Nations'[35] (this pronouncement is, among other things, intended to rule out the possibility of founding this category of reprisals on the last part of Article 2(4)), as well as the statement in the 1970 GA Declaration on Friendly Relations (resolution 2625(XXV) adopted by consensus on 24 October 1970) whereby 'States have a duty to refrain from acts of reprisals involving the use of force' and, again, in 1981, in the GA Declaration on the Inadmissibility of Intervention and Interference in the Internal Affairs of States (resolution 36/103, adopted by consensus on 9 December 1981).

However, as has been rightly pointed out,[36] one should distinguish retaliatory armed force, which is normally a *delayed* response to the unlawful but small-scale use of force by another State, from an *immediate* armed reaction to a minor use of force. In the latter case, it is contended, the armed response is warranted, for otherwise the aggrieved State might turn out to be impotent in the face of a serious violation of international law by another State that causes an immediate and unavoidable threat to the life of the victims: in the end individuals belonging to law-abiding States would remain at the mercy of aggressive States. A commentator crafted a useful expression for designating this class of cases: 'on-the-spot-reaction'.[37] He suggested, as an example, the case of the patrol of a State that, moving along an international border, is hit by intense fire from military outposts of the neighbouring country; in this case, it is argued, the patrol can return fire. He also suggested another instance: the destroyer of one particular State on the high seas drops depth charges against the submarine of another State, 'and the submarine responds by firing torpedoes against the destroyer'. It would seem that in these cases the employment of military force by the

---

[34] They are all in the Western area: Britain, Israel, the US, France, and Portugal. E.g. in 1964, when the US undertook bombing raids against North Vietnam in reply to the Gulf of Tonkin incident, the US Secretary of State, McNamara, spoke of 'retaliation'; the 1965 US air strikes against the same country following the North Vietnamese attacks at Pleiku were termed by the White House 'appropriate reprisal action'. In 1968, the Israeli Chief of Staff, General Bar Lev, defined as 'reprisals' both an Israeli attack against Egyptian installations and a raid against Beirut. Israel has resorted to this class of armed reprisals in many instances since the early 1960s. It would seem that also some cases where a State employed armed force under the cover of self-defence in fact fall into the category of armed reprisals: e.g. the US attack on Libya in 1986 (see **16.5.1**), as well as the US attacks on Sudan and Afghanistan in 1998 (see **16.5.1**).

[35] See e.g. SC resolution 111 of 19 January 1956; SC resolution 171 of 9 April 1962; SC resolution 188 (1964), §1; SC resolution 270 (1969).

[36] See e.g. Brownlie, *International Law* (n 19), 305.

[37] Dinstein, *War, Aggression and Self-defence* (n 19), 214.

target State is justified either because (a) the unlawful action involving force, undertaken by the other State, does not constitute an 'armed attack' pursuant to Article 51 of the UN Charter (the ICJ in *Nicaragua* stated that 'a mere frontier incident' does not amount to an armed attack (at §195)), or (b) there was no other means of avoiding an immediate peril to the life of persons belonging to the victim State: the ICJ in *Corfu Channel* admitted that a warship passing through an international waterway was entitled to 'retaliate quickly if fired upon' by the batteries of the coastal State (at 31).

In any event, the armed response is only authorized if it fulfils the conditions of *necessity* and *proportionality* generally required for the category of specific circumstances precluding wrongfulness of otherwise illegal acts,[38] as well as that of *immediacy*, inherent in the characteristic of this type of military response.[39]

16.5.7 HUMANITARIAN INTERVENTION

In the aftermath of the NATO intervention in the Kosovo situation, arguments have been raised to try to ground justifications for the use of armed force to protect civilian populations from massive human rights violations—arguments very close to those invoked to justify humanitarian intervention. Subsequently, these principles were articulated in the doctrine of the 'responsibility to protect', which—however—allows resort to armed force, only through the United Nations.

Ultimately, despite attempts to broaden the legal basis for the use of armed force, it is apparent from the text and the context of the UN Charter that, although respect for human rights constitutes one of the main goals of the Organization, together with peace and self-determination, the Charter privileges peace to such an extent that it prohibits breaches of peace and security needed for ensuring observance of human rights. In other words, the Charter does not authorize individual States to use force against other States with a view to stopping atrocities. Such use may only be resorted to when the Security Council considers that this is exceptionally justified and acts accordingly, by authorizing the use of force. That this is the right interpretation of the Charter is borne out by the holding of the ICJ in *Nicaragua* (at §268). State practice confirms the proposition.[40] It is apparent from

---

[38] In *Nicaragua*, the ICJ mentioned that the parties agreed 'in holding that whether the response to the [armed] attack is lawful depends on observance of the criteria of the necessity and the proportionality of the measures taken in self-defence' (at §194), and seemed implicitly to uphold this view.

[39] Cf. Dinstein, *War, Aggression and Self-defence* (n 19), 215.

[40] India justified its armed intervention in East Pakistan in 1971 as (among other things) an act of self-defence against the Pakistani aggression and also on account of the inhuman conditions of the Bengali population in what later became Bangladesh. However in the Security Council, the US objected to the use of force, and in the General Assembly, opposition came from China, Albania, Jordan, Sweden, and other States (for the appropriate references see Ronzitti, *Rescuing Nationals Abroad* (n 25), 95; S. D. Murphy, *Humanitarian Intervention* (Philadelphia: University of Pennsylvania, 1996), 99). When Vietnam intervened militarily in Cambodia in 1978, relying upon the notion of self-defence, in the ensuing debate in the UN Security Council many States clearly asserted that the UN Charter did not allow foreign intervention for the alleged purpose of safeguarding human rights (for references see Ronzitti, *Rescuing Nationals Abroad* (n 25), 98; Murphy, *Humanitarian Intervention*, 103). When Tanzania attacked Uganda, in 1979, thus toppling the dictator Idi Amin, it to some extent relied on humanitarian grounds, citing the atrocities ordered or committed by the Ugandan dictator. However, although the attack was not discussed in the UN Security Council or in the General Assembly, it would seem that eventually the international community did not endorse or condone the intervention, although it did not pronounce on its illegality (for references see Ronzitti, *Rescuing Nationals Abroad* (n 25), 102; Murphy, *Humanitarian Intervention*, 105). When the French intervened in 1979 against Emperor Bokassa of the Central African Republic, after the atrocities had been condemned by the OAU Judicial Commission, there was no official pronouncement on that intervention. On the occasion of the 1999 NATO armed intervention in Kosovo, which had not been authorized by the Security Council, a number of States claimed that resort to force was

a survey of such practice that an international customary rule, legally entitling individual States to take forcible measures to induce a State engaging in gross and large-scale violations of human rights to terminate such violations, has not crystallized. Indeed, *usus* is extremely limited and *opinio necessitatis*, though widespread, does not fulfil the requisite conditions of generality and non-opposition (though, interestingly, Article 4(h) of the 2000 Constitutive Act of the African Union (a treaty ratified by 53 States) lays down 'the right of the Union to intervene in a Member State pursuant to a decision of the Assembly [which may decide by a two-thirds majority under Article 7(1)] in respect of grave circumstances, namely: war crimes, genocide, and crimes against humanity'). After the General Assembly resolution adopting the 2005 World Summit Outcome document (A/Res/60/1), the new concept of responsibility to protect was established (§§138–139 of the said resolution). Today, this notion has largely superseded the most relevant (and potentially lawful) aspects of what was previously labelled humanitarian intervention.

The system created by the UN Charter entails the existence of a corresponding customary rule whereby armed force cannot be resorted to unless under the strict conditions laid down in the Charter as reflected in the practice (i.e. in self-defence and through collective action authorized by the Security Council). All attempts to justify different forms of resort to armed force, albeit limited or value-oriented (humanitarian intervention, or against rogue non-State actors), too easily translate into abuses and engender a potential for further violations of international law.

---

legally warranted by the urgent need to put a stop to a 'humanitarian catastrophe' or, as other States put it, to the atrocities being perpetrated by the Serbs in Kosovo. (This stand was taken by such States as the US, the UK, France, Canada, Belgium, the Netherlands, Italy, and others.) However, many other States (including Russia, China, Cuba, Belarus, Ukraine, Namibia, and India) strongly objected to that military action, arguing that it was blatantly contrary to the UN Charter, as it had not been authorized by the Security Council (for the indication of the position of various States see A. Cassese, 'A Follow-Up: Forcible Humanitarian Countermeasures and *Opinio Necessitatis*' (1999) 10 *EJIL* 791).

17
LEGAL RESTRAINTS ON VIOLENCE IN ARMED CONFLICT

17.1 INTRODUCTION

It has become fashionable to quote the famous observation made in 1952 by Sir Hersch Lauterpacht that 'if international law is, in some ways, at the vanishing point of law, the law of war is, perhaps even more conspicuously, at the vanishing point of international law'.[1]

There is a lot of truth in this. More than any other corpus of legal rules, international law directly and transparently reflects power relations. War marks the passage from relatively harmonious relations to armed contention. War is the area in which power politics reach their peak and law to a large extent relinquishes its control over international dealings. In the daily wrangle between force and law, the latter, of necessity, loses ground: international legal rules only partially hold Armageddon at bay. First, it does not impose restraints on the most dangerous forms of armed violence. Secondly, all too often existing legal restraints are check-mated by sheer power. This state of affairs is only natural, given the mental disposition of most people and, what is even more important, the division of the world community into self-serving nation States, each of them claiming—as Suarez observed—to be a *communitas perfecta* (a perfect community). Therefore, realistically one can only expect international law to mitigate at least some of the most frightful manifestations of the clash of arms and ensure as far as possible the protection of the victims of war. This is precisely what the international rules on warfare, comprising the so-called international law of armed conflict, or international humanitarian law (IHL) as it is more commonly described, endeavour to do.

Before examining the substantive content of these rules, an important clarification is in order. Since the adoption of the UN Charter, the notion of 'war' has become less relevant in international law. This is because resort to war, and more generally, to the use of armed force as an instrument of foreign policy of States is forbidden under the UN Charter and customary international law (see **3.4** and **Chapter 16**). Since resort to war is prohibited, but nonetheless the use of armed violence between and within States has not disappeared, the term 'armed conflict' is currently used to describe situations of violence that are specifically regulated by international law and trigger the applicability of the relevant rules of IHL. There is no single or unitary legal definition of what constitutes an armed conflict, but it is generally accepted that 'an armed conflict exists whenever there is a resort to armed force between States or protracted armed violence between governmental authorities and

---

[1] H. Lauterpacht, 'The Problem of the Revision of the Law of War' (1952) 29 *BYIL* 360, at 382.

organized armed groups or between such groups within a State'.[2] A distinction is usually drawn, therefore, between international armed conflicts (IACs), consisting in resort to armed force between States, and non-international armed conflicts (NIACs), namely protracted armed violence within a State between the State's forces and armed groups or between such groups. NIACs may also exhibit transnational features, namely when a State opposes a non-State armed group in the territory of another State. As will be clarified later, there is extensive treaty regulation of IACs as compared to NIACs.

Notwithstanding the outlawing of war and the use of 'armed conflict' as the technical term of art to describe situations in which IHL applies, the notion of 'war' retains legal significance.[3] For instance, a formal declaration of war still triggers the applicability of the pertinent rules concerning IACs, even in the absence of actual fighting. In addition, in national legal orders, the existence of a 'state of war' may trigger certain specific rights and obligations (such as in relation to contracts that do not apply in times of war). At the same time, the notion of war 'plays on our emotions and imagination' as references to the 'war on terror' in the aftermath of the terroristic attack of 11 September 2001 have shown.[4]

Finally, it is worth emphasizing that, since time immemorial, wars have involved in their cruelty and devastation the whole population of the contending parties, with civilians suffering no less than combatants. For a number of historical reasons, between 1648 and 1789, wars tended to take the shape of contests between professionals, conducted as a sort of game and without any direct involvement of the civilian population.[5] However, the new ideals of the French Revolution and their implementation in this particular field (soldiers were no longer professionals; every citizen became a patriot and a member of a mass army) begot so-called *total* wars. The devastating armed conflicts in which Napoleon engaged (1792–1815) soon provided an even more forceful negation of Rousseau's maxim that war was not a relationship between man and man but between State and State, where private persons were enemies only incidentally. The Prussian general, von Clausewitz, who had fought against Napoleon, eventually asserted in his treatise *On War* (1832) the need for wars to be life or death struggles involving the whole of the population of the contending States.

Most of the armed conflicts which spread after the Napoleonic period and are still raging today belong to the class described by von Clausewitz as total wars and civilians are unfortunately the primary victims of violations of IHL. In addition, contemporary armed

---

[2] ICTY, *Tadić (Interlocutory Appeal)*, §70. The legal use of the term 'armed conflict' instead of 'war' originates in the 1949 four Geneva Conventions for the protection of the victims of warfare (see **17.2.3**). As the Commentary to Common Article 2(1) of the Geneva Conventions clarifies, 'the substitution . . . was deliberate. A State can always pretend, when it commits a hostile act against another State, that it is not making war, but merely engaging in a police action, or in legitimate self-defence. The expression "armed conflict" makes such arguments less easy.'

[3] A. Clapham, 'The Concept of International Armed Conflict' in A. Clapham, P. Gaeta, and M. Sassóli (eds), *The 1949 Geneva Conventions: A Commentary* (Oxford: Oxford University Press, 2015), 3, at 4.

[4] Ibid. The metaphor of 'war' is also used in the current COVID-19 pandemic, as is often the case in the field of infectious diseases. A humanitarian advocacy officer of the Italian Red Cross has however underlined that using the metaphor of war to address the dramatic challenges of the spreading of COVID-19 can have dangerous consequences on the real front lines of armed conflict: A. Iaria, 'We Are Not at "War" with COVID-19: Concerns from Italy's "Frontline"', Blogpost, *Humanitarian Law & Policy*, 9 April 2020.

[5] This was due to many factors: reaction to the sanguinary and drawn-out wars of the early seventeenth century; the development of costly armies consisting of highly trained professionals, whose death in war would be a great loss for States; the lack of national allegiance in military men and the consequent marked reluctance to fight unto the bitter end in defence of the State; the fact that the military profession was almost everywhere an apanage of the nobility, with the consequent feeling of belonging to the same social class common to the officers of all countries; and the influence of aristocratic principles of chivalry.

conflicts increasingly involve non-State armed groups.[6] The latter have emerged as key actors in contemporary armed conflicts. However, the rules of IHL have developed upon the understanding that wars are clashes between States' armies and therefore belligerents have to distinguish between combatants and civilians to shield the latter as much as possible from armed violence. In other words, the rules of IHL are mainly based on the 'Rousseauesque', not the 'Clausewitzian' conception of war. It is therefore no surprise that the question of the scope of application and enforcement of these rules in armed conflicts involving non-State armed groups has repeatedly arisen. At the same time, it is no surprise that the question of protection of civilians in armed conflict is one amongst the periodic challenges to the implementation and enforcement of IHL and amongst the constant priorities of relevant international institutions, such as the United Nations and the International Committee of the Red Cross (ICRC).

17.2 THE CORE INTERNATIONAL LEGAL FRAMEWORK

17.2.1 THE ORIGIN OF INTERNATIONAL HUMANITARIAN LAW AND EARLY KEY INSTRUMENTS

The crucial moment for the birth of modern IHL is linked to the activities of Henri Dunant (a Swiss banker).[7] His activism and proposals led to the creation of the Committee of Five (the Permanent International Committee for the Relief of Wounded Soldiers, which later became the ICRC), and of the Red Cross Societies (followed by the Red Crescent Societies and later on by the International Federation of Red Cross and Red Crescent Societies). The Committee of Five also prompted the Swiss Confederation to convene a diplomatic conference in Geneva, which finally led to the adoption on 22 August 1864 of the Convention for the Amelioration of the Condition of the Wounded in Armies of the Field. The Convention established for the first time the main principles for the protection of the wounded on the battlefield that were maintained and developed by all the subsequent Geneva Conventions and Protocols on the same subject.

Another key contribution to the birth and development of modern IHL is the so-called Lieber Code, named after its main author, Francis Lieber, a respected professor at Columbia Law School who had immigrated to the United States from Prussia. During the American Civil War, he drafted the text that, with minor modifications, was then promulgated, in May 1863, by the Union President, Abraham Lincoln, as 'General Orders, No. 100: Instructions for the Government of Armies of the United States in the Field'. The Lieber Code contains a rather detailed regulation of a variety of issues that are still relevant today (such as the prohibition of torture, rape, and pillage, just to name a few). Its importance lies in the fact that it influenced the adoption of similar regulations by other States, thus contributing to the development of State practice and the formation of customary rules of international law that were reinstated and further codified in the Hague Conventions (see **17.2.2**).

---

[6] According to the *2018 War Report* prepared by the Geneva Academy of International Humanitarian Law and Human Rights, under the supervision of A. Bellal, at least 51 NIACs in 23 States occurred in 2018, compared with seven active IACs and 11 situations of belligerent occupation.

[7] The story is well known. Dunant wrote a short book called *Un souvenir de Solferino* ('A memory of Solferino'). In this book he described the terrible suffering of the survivors of the battle of Solferino (24 June 1859), one of the bloodiest since Waterloo. In the book Dunant proposed the adoption of an international convention that would create societies in every European State to care for the wounded on the battlefield, irrespective of the army they belonged to. From that moment Dunant became an active promoter of humanitarian ideas.

As for the means of warfare (weapons and arms), one may mention the Declaration of St Petersburg (1868) that was adopted at the initiative of the Russian government. The Declaration was actually an international agreement, the first aimed at prohibiting the use of a certain weapon in war, in this case explosive projectiles weighing less than 400 grams. The Preamble of the Declaration enounced the principle grounding the prohibition, namely the principle according to which the employment of arms 'which uselessly aggravate the sufferings of disabled men, or render their death inevitable' is contrary to 'the laws of humanity' and exceeds 'the only legitimate object which States should endeavour to accomplish during war', namely 'to weaken the military forces of the enemy'. This is the principle of military necessity that is at the heart of further instruments of modern IHL.

Finally, one may also refer to the Project of an International Declaration concerning the Laws and Customs of War (the so-called 'Declaration of Brussels') of 1874 and the Oxford Manual of 1880. The former, based on a Russian draft and adopted at the end of a Conference convened in Brussels at the initiative of the Czar, contained a set of basic rules on a variety of issues (for instance, the treatment of prisoners of war, belligerent occupation, the treatment of civilians, and the conditions under which guerrilla fighters can wage war as lawful combatants). It never became a binding instrument but formed the basis of the codification of laws of war at the Hague Conferences in 1899 and 1907. The Oxford Manual was adopted by the *Institut de droit international*, a prestigious scientific association founded in 1873 to promote the progress of international law, on the basis of a text prepared by Gustav Moynier, one of the founders of the *Institut* itself and (together with Henri Dunant) of the aforementioned Committee of Five (which later became the ICRC). The Oxford Manual was drafted with the intent to codify the laws and custom of war developed until that time and to impact the national legislation of individual States on the matter.

17.2.2 THE HAGUE CONVENTIONS (1899–1907) AND THE MARTENS CLAUSE

By the turn of the new century, the main principles and rules restraining the use of violence in warfare had thus taken shape and the time was ripe to codify and further develop them through binding treaties.

This task was accomplished by a number of Conventions adopted at the two international conferences that took place in The Hague, respectively in 1899 and 1907. Among these Conventions, one which is particularly still relevant today is the Convention IV on the Laws and Customs of War in Land and its Annexed Regulations ('Hague Regulations'). Other Conventions were adopted on the adaptation of the principles of the 1864 Geneva Convention to maritime warfare, on the rights and duties of neutral Powers and persons in case of war on land, and on the opening of hostilities and on various issues related to war at sea. Further, three Declarations were accepted—one prohibiting the use of asphyxiating gases, another prohibiting the use of expanding bullets (dumdums), and another prohibiting the discharge of projectiles or explosives from balloons.

The Preamble of the 1899 Hague Convention II containing the Regulations on the Laws and Customs of War on Land included for the first time the so-called 'Martens Clause', mentioning the 'laws of humanity' and the 'requirements of the public conscience' as sources of the principles of the law of nations affording protection in war to populations and belligerents. The Clause was reinstated in the 1907 Hague Convention IV on the same matter and subsequently reiterated (with some adaptations) in other instruments of international humanitarian law, including the 1949 Geneva Conventions on the protection of the victims of warfare and the Additional Protocols thereto (on the 1949 Geneva Conventions[8] and Additional Protocols,[9] see **17.2.3** and **17.2.4**). This Clause is very loosely worded and has consequently given rise to a multiplicity of often conflicting interpretations. Nonetheless, and arguably precisely because of its evasive yet appealing content, the Martens Clause has been very frequently relied upon in international relations, restated in treaties, cited by national and international courts, and invoked by organizations and individuals. In sum, the Martens Clause has by now become one of the legal myths of international society and has been hailed as a significant turning point in the history of IHL. In spite of its ambiguous wording and undefinable purport, it has responded over the decades to the deeply felt and widespread demand that the requirements of humanity and the pressure of public opinion be duly taken into account when regulating armed conflict. As for its impact on IHL, the Martens Clause may serve as fundamental guidance in the interpretation of IHL treaty rules. In addition, it has an indirect impact on the customary process, making the requirement of *usus* (namely, general practice) less stringent in the formation of customary international humanitarian law, while giving the requirement of *opinio juris* special prominence (see **9.3**).[10]

It is worth noting that, at the time, the applicability of the Hague Conventions on warfare was always uncertain and precarious. Indeed, all these Conventions included the so-called *si omnes* clause (namely, the general participation clause), whereby they applied to a war on condition that all the belligerents were contracting parties. Consequently, it was sufficient for one belligerent not to be bound by a certain convention for the convention to become inapplicable to the relationships between the other belligerents *inter se*. This is because belligerents feared that, if another belligerent was not bound by a particular convention while they were, an imbalance would ensue to their disadvantage. They therefore preferred to opt for a solution favourable to them (but detrimental to civilians and to combatants): the convention would not apply to, hence restrain the freedom of, *any* belligerent. It follows that only customary law—hence the most general but also the loosest body of legal rules—was indisputably applicable in any war.

17.2.3 THE 1949 GENEVA CONVENTIONS AND COMMON ARTICLE 3

The tragic experience of the First World War had already shown the limits of the Hague Conventions, which were mainly devoted to the regulation of warfare and the law of belligerency. After the War, a few treaties were adopted to revise and update pre-existing treaties for the protection of the victims of warfare, namely the Convention for the Amelioration of the Condition of the Wounded in Armies in the Field and the Convention Relative to the Treatment of Prisoners of War (both adopted in Geneva in 1929 and entered into force in 1931). However these Conventions also contained the *si omnes* clause, which—during

---

[8] Article 63 of Convention (I) for the Amelioration of the Condition of the Wounded and Sick in Armed Forces in the Field (GC I), Geneva, 12 August 1949; Article 62 of Convention (II) for the Amelioration of the Condition of Wounded, Sick and Shipwrecked Members of Armed Forces at Sea, Geneva, 12 August 1949 (GC II); Article 142 of Convention (III) relative to the Treatment of Prisoners of War, Geneva, 12 August 1949 (GC III); Article 158 of Convention (IV) relative to the Protection of Civilian Persons in Time of War, Geneva, 12 August 1949 (GC IV).

[9] Article 1(2) of Protocol Additional to the Geneva Conventions of 12 August 1949, and relating to the Protection of Victims of International Armed Conflicts (Protocol I), 8 June 1977; Preamble of Protocol Additional to the Geneva Conventions of 12 August 1949, and relating to the Protection of Victims of Non-International Armed Conflicts (Protocol II), 8 June 1977.

[10] See in more detail A. Cassese, 'The Martens Clause: Half a Loaf or Simply Pie in the Sky?' (2000) 11 *EJIL* 187.

the Second World War—allowed Germany to refuse the application of the Convention on Prisoners of War in relation to the conflict with the Soviet Union (which was not a party to the Convention, and also not a party to Hague Convention IV). This had abominable consequences on the treatment of prisoners of war on both sides.

The horrific sufferings inflicted on civilians during the Second World War, as a consequence of the bombardment of cities or on civilians in occupied territories or detained by the enemy, also demonstrated that there existed a serious gap in the international regulation. The tragic experience of the Second World War thus brought about a shift in the international approach regulating warfare, which since then started to be predominantly focused on affording or enhancing protection to those who do not take part in hostilities (civilians) or have ceased to take part in the hostilities (wounded, sick, shipwrecked, and prisoners of war). At the initiative of the Swiss government, a diplomatic conference was thus convened in Geneva to discuss the drafts prepared by the ICRC for the protection of the victims of war. The diplomatic conference concluded its work on 12 August 1949, with the adoption of four Conventions (GCs), each devoted to the protection of a specific category of persons: *Wounded and Sick in Armed Forces in the Field* (GC I), *Wounded, Sick and Shipwrecked Members of Armed Forces at Sea* (GC II), *Prisoners of War* (GC III), and *Civilian Persons in Time of War* (GC IV). This last Convention significantly elaborated upon the Hague Convention IV Regulations' protections for the most vulnerable category of persons in war, namely civilians and the civilian population, thus strengthening a key objective of the regulation of warfare.

Another key achievement of the 1949 Geneva Conventions was the inclusion of a common provision, namely common Article 3, regulating NIACs. All the previous international legal instruments applied only in international wars, while civil wars were not regulated at the international level, mainly because States considered these conflicts to pertain exclusively to internal matters.[11] However, the civil war in the territory of Upper Silesia in 1921 and the Spanish Civil War in which the ICRC had intervened on a humanitarian level clearly illustrated that internal conflicts are no less serious and no less cruel than those between States. At the Diplomatic Conference in Geneva the ICRC presented its proposal to extend *in toto* the Conventions which were about to be adopted to internal conflicts. This proposal was not accepted because of the opposition of a large number of delegations, but the compromise solution was to dedicate a common article of the Conventions enshrining a short catalogue of humanitarian principles applicable to situations of non-international armed conflicts, with a view to ensuring minimum guarantees of protection to civilians and those who were no longer participating in the hostilities. It was with a hint of criticism that the Soviet delegate Morozov referred to common Article 3 as a 'convention in miniature'.

The 1949 Geneva Conventions have by now achieved almost universal ratification. Most of their provisions, including common Article 3, are widely considered to reflect customary international law. Notably, none of the four Conventions contains the *si omnes* clause: even if one of the Powers in conflict is not bound by the Geneva Conventions, the non-customary provisions of the Geneva Conventions continue to apply between and among the other Powers in conflict who are party to the Geneva Conventions (common Article 2(3) GCs).

---

[11] See in more detail A. Cassese, 'La guerre civile et le droit international' (1986) 90 *Revue générale de droit international public* 553, republished in English, 'Civil War and International Law' in P. Gaeta and S. Zappalà (eds), *Antonio Cassese: The Human Dimension of International Law: Selected Papers* (Oxford: Oxford University Press, 2008), 110.

17.2.4 THE 1977 ADDITIONAL PROTOCOLS

On 8 June 1977, at the fourth session of a Diplomatic Conference convened in Geneva by the Swiss Federal Council (the first session was held in 1974), two Additional Protocols to the GCs were adopted.[12]

The *first Additional Protocol* (AP I)[13] updates and innovates the law applicable to international armed conflicts as defined in common Article 2 of the GCs. Importantly, it also includes within its scope of material application the so-called 'wars of national liberation', namely 'armed conflicts in which peoples are fighting against colonial domination and alien occupation and against racist régimes in the exercise of their right of self-determination' (Article 1(4)). This provision thus recognizes that wars of national liberation shall be equated to international armed conflicts for the application of IHL[14] and arguably it crystallized the emergence of a new customary international law rule.[15]

As for its content, AP I develops the rules contained in the 1949 Geneva Conventions protecting the victims of warfare (e.g. by extending the protection granted under the Geneva Conventions to all medical personnel, units, and means of transport, whether civilian or military). It also updates and codifies the new rules on conduct of hostilities that had developed since the adoption of the Hague Conventions, enhances the protection of civilians from the effect of hostilities, and adapts the rules of IHL to guerrilla warfare. It also establishes the International Humanitarian Fact-Finding Commission (Article 90), a new mechanism to strengthen compliance with the rules of IHL (which however has so far failed to fulfil this expectation: see **17.8.1**).

The *second Additional Protocol* (AP II),[16] develops and supplements common Article 3 to the Geneva Conventions, particularly by extending and giving more precise formulation to the fundamental guarantees of persons who do not participate or no longer participate in hostilities. Excluding 'wars of national liberations' covered by AP I, it applies to all armed conflicts

---

[12] The negotiations of the Protocols, based on drafts of the ICRC, were particularly arduous, also because of the involvement of new countries that had emerged from decolonization and had not participated in the adoption of previous conventions on the laws of war and the protection of victims of war. Indeed, one half of the countries participating in the drafting of the Protocols had not taken part in the drafting of the Geneva Conventions. Moreover, in 1974–77 the Afro-Asian States were able to command a comfortable majority; acting in concert with either the socialist or Latin American States they could achieve a two-thirds majority. The Western European States and the United States, which had until that time left their mark on the international regulation of armed conflict, were no longer the dominating diplomatic figures. This had an impact on the content of some rules and principles enshrined in two Additional Protocols, as will be shown in this chapter.

[13] Protocol Additional to the Geneva Conventions of 12 August 1949, and relating to the Protection of Victims of International Armed Conflicts (Protocol I), 8 June 1977.

[14] The process that led to the inclusion of this provision in AP I began with the adoption by the UN General Assembly of a string of resolutions proclaiming that wars of national liberation were to be treated as international armed conflict proper (see e.g. resolution 2383-XXIII of November 1968 and resolution 3103-XXVIII of 12 December 1973).

[15] These resolutions were instigated and supported by the socialist and developing countries, but opposed by the Western States which maintained that these wars were not dissimilar from civil strife. It comes therefore as no surprise that in 1974, the text of a draft article that later became current Article 1(4) of AP I, was provisionally adopted at the Diplomatic Conference with the negative vote of the Western States and the support of the developing and socialist countries (70 votes to 21 with 13 abstentions). However, the Western opposition diminished throughout the sessions of the Diplomatic Conference, so that Article 1(4) was finally adopted at the plenary session in 1977 with 87 votes in favour, one against (Israel), and 11 abstentions (the UK, the US, Federal Republic of Germany, Canada, Italy, France, Spain, Ireland, Monaco, Japan, and Guatemala). Despite the abstentions, it is apparent from the declarations made by various countries that in actual fact only one State (Israel) totally rejected the principle enshrined in the rule.

[16] Protocol Additional to the Geneva Conventions of 12 August 1949, and relating to the Protection of Victims of Non-International Armed Conflicts (Protocol II), 8 June 1977.

which take place in the territory of a High Contracting Party between its armed forces and dissident armed forces or other organized armed groups which, under responsible command, exercise such control over a part of its territory as to enable them to carry out sustained and concerted military operations and to implement this Protocol. (Article 1(1))

It does not apply to 'situations of internal disturbances and tensions, such as riots, isolated and sporadic acts of violence and other acts of a similar nature' (Article 1(2)). The material scope of application of AP II is thus narrower than the material scope of application of common Article 3, which applies generally to 'armed conflict not of an international character occurring in the territory' of a member State. Thus, the progress made in 1977 turns out to be limited on account of the fact the regulation contained in AP II does not cover all classes of internal armed conflicts, but only those above a certain 'threshold'.

Unfortunately, during the negotiations AP II was mutilated and stripped of some very significant provisions at the eleventh hour which were included in earlier drafts. For instance, unlike AP I, the final text of AP II does not contain specific provisions relating to means or methods of warfare. Nonetheless, AP II does contain provisions that have implications in determining the lawfulness of military attacks. For instance, Article 4 prohibits ordering that there shall be no survivors (the prohibition of giving no quarter), while Article 13 affords general protection to the civilian population and individual civilians 'against the dangers arising from military operations'. To give effect to this general protection, Article 13 further provides that '[t]he civilian population as such, as well as individual civilians, shall not be the object of attack. Acts or threats of violence the primary purpose of which is to spread terror among the civilian population are prohibited'. Article 14 further prohibits '[s]tarvation of civilians as a method of combat'. All the same, the Protocol represents the maximum which States participating in the Geneva Conference, and particularly Third World countries, were prepared to concede. To attain a more satisfactory general treaty regulation of non-international armed conflicts it will be necessary to await the appearance of a more favourable attitude of States.[17]

Currently, a great number of the States parties to the 1949 Geneva Conventions are also parties to both Additional Protocols (with more States parties to AP I than to AP II). Among the absentees are the US, Israel, Iran, Pakistan, and Turkey (not parties to either Protocol). Syria and Iraq have instead not ratified AP II. This means, therefore, that the two Protocols do not apply qua treaty law in the NIACs currently fought in Syria, Iraq, Pakistan, and Turkey (just to mention a few). In addition, States not parties to AP I (notably the US) are not bound to apply it, including when they are involved in an IAC against States that are instead parties to it. However, it can be argued that most of the rules contained in AP I and AP II now mirror the content of corresponding rules of customary international law with the effect that they are also binding on States not parties qua customary international law. However, if one applies the theory of 'persistent objector' to the formation of a specific customary norm (see **9.3.4**), the possibility remains that some rules of AP I or AP II reflecting customary international law are not applicable to persistently objecting States

---

[17] What matters here is to emphasize that although nearly all the provisions of AP II were adopted by consensus, and although the Protocol itself was the subject of consensus approval, a number of Third World countries raised strong and unequivocal objections. These objections were phrased in the language of sovereignty and effective response to rebellion and were situated in the particular context of the recent independence of many of these States and their efforts to consolidate national identities in the face of colonially exacerbated ethnic and religious divisions, secessionist movements, and external intervention. The number and content of the objections was such as to lead the Turkish delegation to state that the consensus was only apparent. For the various statements on Protocol II, see Diplomatic Conference on Humanitarian Law of Armed Conflict (1974–77), *Official Records*, vii, at 199, 201, 203, 250, 251.

(which are also not parties to AP I or AP II). This could be the case of Articles 43–44 of AP I, defining the notion of the armed forces of a party to the conflict and of combatants in an innovative way with respect to previous regulation (see **17.3.1**).

17.2.5 OTHER LEGAL INSTRUMENTS AND CUSTOMARY INTERNATIONAL LAW

The 1949 Geneva Conventions and the two 1977 Additional Protocols currently form the core of the international legal regulation applicable in armed conflicts. They are supplemented by a number of treaties on specific matters, particularly those restricting the choice of weapons (see **17.6.3**) or protecting cultural heritage (the 1954 Hague Convention on Cultural Property and its Protocols), some of which are applicable in both IACs and NIACs. However, not all the provisions contained in each of these treaties have ripened into customary international rules with similar or identical content. As a consequence, there may be cases where the international regulation contained in a specific treaty exclusively governs the conduct of the States parties.

Despite the web of treaties pertaining to IHL, customary international law thus continues to be an important source of law regulating armed conflicts, as also pointed out by the ICJ (Advisory Opinion on *Legality of the Threat or Use of Nuclear Weapons*, at §75). This is particularly true as regards the international legal framework applicable in NIACs, with respect to which treaty regulation is scant when compared to IACs. As a matter of fact, by way of customary international law there has been increasing extension of the principles on conduct of hostilities applicable to international armed conflicts to NIACs.[18]

The rules of customary international law that have emerged to become applicable to NIACs are, for instance: the ban on deliberate bombing of civilians; the prohibition on attacking non-military objectives; the rule concerning the precautions which must be taken when attacking military objects; and the rule forbidding reprisals against enemy civilians. Arguably these rules only apply to NIACs that exhibit features comparable to international wars proper (such as the Spanish Civil War (1936–39)). That is to say, the insurgents or other relevant non-State armed groups must exhibit the following features: an organized administration effectively controlling a portion of the State's territory and organized armed forces capable of abiding by international humanitarian law. Non-international armed conflicts having a lesser degree of intensity, for example, instances of minor rebellions, or uprisings which do not take on the proportions of a civil war proper, would not be covered by these rules.[19]

---

[18] The rationale for this development was spelled out by the ICTY's Appeals Chamber in *Tadić (Interlocutory Appeal)*: '[E]lementary considerations of humanity and common sense make it preposterous that the use by States of weapons prohibited in armed conflicts between themselves be allowed when States try to put down rebellion by their own nationals on their own territory. What is inhumane, and consequently proscribed, in international wars, cannot but be inhumane and inadmissible in civil strife' (§119).

The ICTY's Appeals Chamber also found four reasons for this development: the growing frequency of these conflicts; their becoming increasingly cruel and protracted; the difficulty for third States to remain aloof; and the impetuous propagation of the human rights doctrine in the international community. Therefore, as clarified by the Appeals Chamber (§97ff), since the 1930s, the traditional dichotomy between interstate conflicts and civil strife, the former category governed by numerous international rules, the latter substantially left to the operation of national criminal law, has become blurred. As a consequence, increasingly, the shield of State sovereignty cannot bar the regulation of internal armed conflicts by customary international law rules.

[19] It is however contended that these rules would also be applicable to NIACs that do not take the proportions of civil war proper, e.g. when the non-State armed group does not exercise control over a portion of the State's territory. See M. Sassóli, *International Humanitarian Law: Rules, Controversies, and Solutions to Problems Arising in Warfare* (Cheltenham: Edward Elgar Publishing, 2019), MN 6.34.

Another body of customary rules has evolved out of common Article 3 of the Geneva Conventions, to become applicable qua customary international law to *any armed conflict* (international or non-international). This stand was clearly taken in 1986 by the ICJ in the *Nicaragua (Nicaragua v United States)* case. The Court held that the provisions of common Article 3 'constitute a minimum yardstick' applicable to any armed conflict and 'reflect what the Court in 1949 [in the *Corfu Channel* case] called "elementary considerations of humanity"' (at §218). This Article has a much broader field of application than the aforementioned general rules on civilians, for it applies to any internal armed conflict, whether or not they reach a high level of intensity. Common Article 3, which makes a point of leaving the legal status of insurgents unaffected, is, however, meant to protect only the victims of hostilities, namely 'persons taking no active part' in them, to whom it grants a set of basic humanitarian safeguards.[20]

The ICRC has conducted a study indicating the rules that in its view have acquired customary status both in international and non-international armed conflicts (the 'ICRC Study on Customary IHL'). This study does not constitute an official codification of the rules of customary international law in armed conflict and is not a binding document. However, it constitutes an important reference point to identify relevant practice and *opinio juris* in the field of IHL and is constantly updated by the ICRC. The ICRC Study confirms the trend identified earlier, namely that the bulk of the international rules on conduct of hostilities applicable in international armed conflict contained in relevant treaties have turned into customary rules and are equally applicable (with some exceptions) to non-international armed conflicts.

Since IHL also regulates NIACs and is therefore equally addressed to non-State armed actors, the question arises whether their practice and *opinio juris* are relevant for the formation of customary international law. According to the International Law Commission (ILC), the answer is in the negative.[21]

17.2.6 INTERNATIONAL HUMANITARIAN LAW AND INTERNATIONAL HUMAN RIGHTS LAW

International humanitarian law is a 'specialized' body of law, meaning that it regulates a specific subject matter, as other branches of international law do (environmental law, the law of the sea, international criminal law, international trade law, and so on). International

---

[20] The trend towards the gradual extension of principles and rules governing IACs to cover NIACs was strengthened and bolstered by the gradual jettisoning of the notion whereby war crimes can only be perpetrated in interstate wars. In 1995, the ICTY's Appeals Chamber, in the aforementioned decision in *Tadić (Interlocutory Appeal)*, set forth the view that serious violations of customary or treaty rules governing non-international armed conflicts may also amount, subject to certain conditions, to war crimes (at §§128–134). This view was confirmed by the Statute of the ICTR (Article 4), the case law of both the ICTY and ICTR, Article 8(2) of the 1998 Statute of the ICC dealing with war crimes in non-international armed conflict, and the 1999 UN Secretary-General's 'Bulletin on Observance by United Nations Forces of International Humanitarian Law'(UN Doc. ST/SGB/1999/13, of 6 August 1999).

[21] ILC, 'Draft conclusions on identification of customary international law and commentaries thereto', Report of the International Law Commission, Seventieth Session (30 April–1 June and 2 July–10 August 2018), UN Doc. A/73/10 (2018) 119. See Draft conclusion 4, providing that the requirement of a general practice, as a constituent element of customary international law, refers primarily to the practice of States and, in certain cases, the practice of international organizations, while the practice of other actors may be relevant only to assess the practice of States and international organizations.

According to a distinguished commentator, however, '[i]n order to ensure that customary rules are realistic for all belligerents and to give non-State armed groups a sense of ownership over customary IHL of NIACs, it is important that the practice and statements of armed groups are taken into account when determining customary rules applicable in NIACs'. As the same commentator acknowledges, there are nonetheless 'several conceptual difficulties in considering the practice of non-State armed groups in the norm-creating process' (Sassóli (n 19), at 50).

human rights law also is a specialized branch of international law. At the same time, however, it is a body of law whose development has introduced a new paradigm in the international legal order, that has influenced all other fields of international law in various forms and to various degrees (see generally **Chapter 18**).

The question of whether and to what extent international human rights law has (or should have) an impact on IHL is a difficult one. The reason is that, like international human rights law, IHL is premised on the need to respect basic values of humanity shared by every civilization. IHL however intends to minimize human sufferings in specific contexts, namely in armed conflicts. Unlike international human rights law, the content of the rules of IHL thus reflect a constant balance between the needs for humanitarian protection and military necessity. Since international human rights law continues to apply in armed conflicts, there can be situations where the joint operation of the relevant rules pertaining to each body of law leads to conflicting results. The question of how to solve the conflict thus arises, requiring clarification of the relationship between these two branches of international law.

There is a considerable body of literature on the matter. A distinguished commentator has wittily noticed that those who have engaged in finding the key word best describing the relationship between IHL and international human rights law have almost exhausted the relevant words found in the 'c' portion of the dictionary. As he has explained, the two branches have been characterized as 'concurrent, coexisting, convergent, coterminous, congruent, confluent, corresponding, cumulative, complementary, compatible, cross-fertilizing, contradictory, competitive, or even in conflict', and has added that his contribution to the debate is the following: 'It's contextual and it's complicated.'[22]

The ICJ has expressly addressed this matter, but without clarifying it entirely. In the Advisory Opinion on *Legality of the Threat or Use of Nuclear Weapons*, by referring to the International Covenant on Civil and Political Rights, the Court stated, first of all, that its protection 'does not cease in times of war' and then continued as follows:

> [W]hether a particular loss of life, through the use of a certain weapon in warfare, is to be considered an arbitrary deprivation of life contrary to article 6 of the Covenant [protecting the right to life], can only be decided by reference to the law applicable in armed conflict and not deduced from the terms of the Covenant itself. (at §25)

This passage can be interpreted in two ways. According to one view, the Court has here embraced the so-called theory of *lex specialis*, at least with respect to the relationship between the two branches of international law in the field of the use of lethal force. According to this theory, when there is an armed conflict, international human rights law would constitute the *lex generalis* while IHL should be characterized as the *lex specialis*, being designed to regulate armed conflicts. As a consequence, the latter would prevail over the former, whenever their joint application produces conflicting results. The ICRC accepts this theory with respect to the assessment of the lawfulness of the use of lethal force against military targets in international armed conflicts. The US, more broadly, seems to accept it with regard to conduct of hostilities and the protection of war victims.[23] According to another view, however, in the aforementioned passage the Court simply intended to clarify that the protection of the right to life enshrined in Article 6 of the Covenant 'has to be read and understood in conjunction with the rules of IHL', and not as an 'abandonment of the introductory sentence about the continuity of human rights in wartime' as the *lex specialis* theory would imply.[24]

---

[22] A. Clapham, 'Human Rights in Armed Conflict: Metaphors, Maxims, and the Move to Interoperability' (2018) 12 *HR&ILD* 9, at 10.

[23] Ibid., at 21, note 49, also for the relevant references.

[24] C. Tomuschat, 'Human Rights and International Humanitarian Law' (2010) 21 *EJIL* 15.

In 2004, in its Advisory Opinion on *Legal Consequences of the Construction of a Wall in the Occupied Palestinian Territory*, the Court has addressed the matter again. Being confronted with the obligations of Israel to respect the relevant human rights treaties, over and above those stemming from IHL, the Court stated:

> As regards the relationship between international humanitarian law and human rights law, there are thus three possible situations: some rights may be exclusively matters of international humanitarian law; others may be exclusively matters of human rights law; yet others may be matters of both these branches of international law. In order to answer the questions put to it, the Court will have to take into consideration both these branches of international law, namely human rights law and, as lex specialis, international humanitarian law. (at §106)

The Court has however not provided any guidance on how to determine which rights belong to which of the three aforementioned categories.[25]

The question of the interplay between IHL and international human rights law is particularly debated in relation to: (1) the use of lethal force against members of non-State armed groups, and (2) detention abroad in relation to NIACs. In both scenarios, international human rights is more protective than IHL rules. Let us examine them briefly in turn.

(1) Concerning *the use of lethal force* by the law enforcement authorities of a State, international human rights law permits it only as a means of last resort. In addition, it requires an assessment of the respect of the principle of proportionality in light of the relevant circumstances of the case, and taking into account the right to life of the person killed.[26] In practice, proportionality 'sets a maximum on the force that might be used to achieve a specific legitimate objective'.[27] Thus, according to the European Court of Human Rights, law enforcement authorities cannot use lethal force against an escaping suspect who does not pose a threat to life 'even if a failure to use lethal force may result in the opportunity to arrest the fugitive being lost' (*Nachova v Bulgaria*, §95). On the other hand, IHL does not prohibit the use of lethal force by belligerents against legitimate military targets (combatants, members of non-State armed groups, and civilians directly participating in hostilities: see **17.3**, **17.4**, and **17.5**). In addition, incidental civilian casualties are not unlawful, to the extent that the military attack was carried out in conformity with the relevant requirements, among which there is the principle of proportionality. This principle is however not assessed as being within the framework of human rights law (see **17.4**). IHL is even construed as 'permitting' the use of lethal force against military targets (subject, *inter alia*, to the proportionality rule) or, as it has been put, as providing 'a licence to kill', including in the context of NIACs.

The latter approach provides legal grounds for the so-called policy of targeted killings (see **17.5.2**) by States such as the US or Israel against members of non-State armed groups (including terroristic organizations) engaged in NIACs, even in locations outside areas of

---

[25] In *Armed Activities on the Territory of the Congo* (*Democratic Republic of Congo v Uganda*), §216, the ICJ reproduced the description of the relationship between the two bodies of law set forth in the 2004 Advisory Opinion, but without the final sentence referencing the *lex specialis* principle.

[26] The right to life is enshrined in Article 3 of the Universal Declaration of Human Rights (1948) and in all general human rights conventions, in particular: Article 6 of the International Covenant on Civil and Political Rights (1966); Article 2 of the European Convention for the Protection of Human Rights and Fundamental Freedoms (1950); Article 4 of the American Convention on Human Rights (1969); and Article 4 of the African Charter on Human and Peoples' Rights (1981).

The right to life is not absolute, since certain limitations are allowed. The European Convention contains a list of these limitations, bound together by the principle of proportionality. The other conventions implicitly envisage limitations, since they forbid arbitrary deprivations of the right to life. The term has been interpreted as including, among others, disproportionate measures by the State enforcement authorities.

[27] Human Rights Council, *Report of the Special Rapporteur on Extrajudicial, Summary or Arbitrary Executions, Christof Heyns*, A/HRC/26/36, 1 April 2014, §66.

active hostilities with the relevant armed group. For instance, in 2019 the US government issued an update to a previous Report noting that 'as a matter of international law' air strikes in Libya, Yemen, and Somalia against members of the so-called Islamic State (ISIS/Daesh) had been conducted at the request and with the consent of the relevant governments of the two countries, in the context of the ongoing armed conflict against ISIS/Daesh and also in furtherance of US national self-defence.[28]

The new General Comment on the right to life from the Human Rights Committee[29] states that, while the right to life as protected by Article 6 of the International Covenant on Civil and Political Rights (ICCPR) continues to apply in situations of armed conflict, the 'use of lethal force consistent with international humanitarian law and other applicable international law norms is, in general, not arbitrary', and hence in accordance with the aforementioned Article 6. 'By contrast'—the General Comment continues—'practices inconsistent with international humanitarian law ... would also violate article 6 of the Covenant'. In addition, it seems that for the Human Rights Committee the protection that Article 6 would continue to afford beyond that offered by IHL rules consists in the disclosure by the States parties of 'the criteria for attacking with lethal force individuals or objects whose targeting is expected to result in deprivation of life' and in the obligation '[to] investigate alleged or suspected violations of article 6 in situations of armed conflict in accordance with the relevant international standards' (at §64).

Arguably, the Committee could have gone further. During the drafting process of the General Comment, the Committee had received submissions according to which there are cases where international human rights law takes priority over IHL. This would be when lethal force is used against members of non-State armed groups in situations where IHL is applicable, but nonetheless active hostilities are absent. Under this view, the applicable legal framework should switch in favour of IHL only on the outbreak of active hostilities.[30]

(2) *Detention abroad in relation to NIACs.* International human rights conventions prohibit arbitrary arrest and detention, namely the arrest and deprivation of liberty of a person except as provided for by law, and provided that the law itself and the manner of its execution are not arbitrary.[31] According to the ICRC Study on Customary IHL, customary international law also prohibits arbitrary deprivation of liberty both in IACs and NIACs (Rule 99).

Prolonged detention outside a criminal process of enemy fighters, combatants, and civilians is a constant feature of both IACs and NIACs. Also, to overcome the limited territorial scope of application of national laws on deprivation of liberty (national laws regulating the grounds and procedures for deprivation of liberty usually do not apply extraterritorially), IHL contains rules on this matter.

These rules, however, are more developed with respect to IACs, including because they also establish grounds for detention and internment. The 1949 GCs provide that, during an IAC, each belligerent has the right to detain prisoners of war (PoWs), that is, combatants

---

[28] Report on the Legal and Policy Frameworks Guiding the United States' Use of Military Force and Related National Security Operations. In support of this view, see R. Goodman, 'Drone Strikes Outside "Areas of Active Hostilities"' (A Memo to the Human Rights Community), Blogpost on *Justice Security*, 4 October 2017.

[29] General Comment No. 36 (2018) on Article 6 of the International Covenant on Civil and Political Rights, on the right to life.

[30] See Clapham (n 22), at 21, quoting the comments by Lubell and Murray to the Human Rights Committee during the drafting process of the General Comment.

[31] Article 9 of the Universal Declaration of Human Rights, Article 9(1) of the ICCPR, Article 7 of the American Convention of Human Rights, Article 6 of the African Convention of Human and People's Rights, and Article 14 of the Arab Charter of Human Rights. By contrast, Article 5 of the European Convention for the Protection of Human Rights and Fundamental Freedoms lists exhaustively the permitted grounds for detention, and does not include internment in armed conflicts.

who have fallen into the hands of the enemy (see **17.3**) until the end of hostilities.[32] In addition, they set forth an individualized procedure for the internment or the administrative detention (namely, outside a criminal process) of protected civilians on the basis of imperative security reasons.[33] Failing applicable national legislation, these rules may thus constitute the only relevant legal framework granting States the authority to deprive persons of their liberty for reasons linked to the armed conflict. Respect for these rules by belligerents can therefore be considered compatible with the human rights protection against arbitrary detention. In the *Hassan v UK* case, for instance, the European Court for Human Rights held that the UK had the authority to detain without trial an Iraqi individual suspected of participating in armed hostilities in occupied Iraqi territory based on the relevant rules of the Geneva Conventions. According to the Court,

> It can only be in cases of international armed conflict, where the taking of prisoners and the detention of civilians who pose a threat to security are accepted features of international humanitarian law, that Article 5 [protecting the right to liberty] could be interpreted as permitting the exercise of such broad powers. (at §104)

By contrast, the relevant rules of IHL applicable in NIACs do not provide any express ground for detention or internment for reasons linked to the armed conflict. In particular, they do not grant authority to States to detain members of non-State armed groups (upon capture or surrender) until the end of the hostilities, by analogy with captured combatants in IACs.[34] Arguably, because of this gap, no contradiction may be deemed to exist with international human rights law. In other words, absent a legal basis for internment or administrative detention in IHL, international human rights law is clearly the *only* applicable international legal framework to assess (eventually taking into account IHL) NIAC-related cases of deprivation of liberty of persons without a criminal charge. Consequently, under international human rights law, there must be a national law or alternative legal basis providing States with the authority to detain.

The lack of grounds for detention in the IHL rules governing NIACs may not raise problems when the conflict is confined to the territory of one State, without foreign involvement. This is because members of non-State armed groups engaging in armed violence within the State violate the domestic law of that State and can be equated to criminals or terrorists: national law will thus normally provide the legal ground for detention by the relevant State authorities. States may however be engaged in armed conflicts with non-State armed groups in the territory of another State (these are the so-called transnational NIACs) or may assist another State involved in an NIAC within its territory. The armed conflicts in Iraq, Afghanistan, and Syria are just a few examples of foreign State involvement in NIACs in the territory of another State. As mentioned earlier, however, national legislation regulating the deprivation of liberty does not usually apply overseas. In addition, the territorial State involved in an NIAC may not have domestic legislation on internment (as was the case e.g. in Afghanistan). States fighting abroad against non-State armed groups, however, do regularly hold captured enemy fighters in security detention. The question of whether these States respect the prohibition on arbitrary detention enshrined in human rights treaties when they intern or detain enemy fighters without criminal charge thus arises repeatedly.

---

[32] Article 21 GC III. Interning PoWs is not mandatory. The right to intern PoWs is based on the need both to prevent their further participation in the hostilities and to protect them.

[33] Article 42 GC IV (on internment of civilians on own territory) and Article 78(1) (on internment of civilians in occupied territories).

[34] Common Article 3 of the GCs and Article 6 of AP II establish the judicial guarantees of persons detained based on a criminal charge. Article 5(1) and (2) and Article 6(5) of AP II mention internment, but only for the purpose of regulating the treatment of internees. According to the 2016 ICRC Commentary on GC I, these references confirm that administrative detention 'is a form of deprivation of liberty inherent to non-international armed conflict' (at §720).

The US and Israel argue that IHL implicitly grants them the authority to detain or intern without criminal charge. They mainly rely on the notion of unlawful combatants (see **17.5.1**, also termed 'unprivileged belligerency'). According to this notion, members of armed groups, in contexts where either the individual or the group does not meet the requirements for combatant status, can be attacked everywhere and at any time (including by resorting to so-called targeted killings (see **17.5.2**)). Since lethal force can be used against them, so the argument goes, they can also be detained indefinitely without trial (by analogy with captured lawful combatants). In the US, this legal position was confirmed by the Supreme Court in *Hamdi* v *Rumsfeld*). By contrast, the UK has justified prolonged security detention by its armed forces in Iraq and Afghanistan based on the authority deriving from relevant SC resolutions.[35] The UK Supreme Court has adopted this legal position in *Serdar Mohammed* v *Ministry of Defence* concerning the security detention of Mr Serdar Mohammed in Afghanistan, following his capture by British armed forces.[36] The majority considered it unnecessary to express a concluded view on whether customary international law (in the field of IHL) authorizes the detention of members of armed groups in NIAC. Lord Reed, in his dissent, however concluded that no such authority exists under customary international law.

The simplest solution to the problem would be for States to reach an international agreement on detention and internment in relation to their involvement in NIACs occurring in another State or in transnational NIACs. Unfortunately, States have been reluctant so far to take such a step. The main reason is that they fear that by establishing under international law their authority to detain in NIACs, they would implicitly confer on members of the enemy non-State armed groups rights hampering their authority to use lethal force against them. There is also the risk that this would imply, either legally or politically, recognition of the combatant status of the members of the group (on this notion, see below).[37]

17.3 COMBATANT STATUS

The international regulation of the use of military force in armed conflicts, as will be further clarified later in the chapter (see **17.6.1**), is premised on the fundamental distinction between combatants and civilians.

With respect to IACs, there are rules determining the criteria to be fulfilled for a person to possess 'combatant status' (so that that person is considered a lawful or legitimate belligerent). Combatants do not enjoy protection from military attack under the relevant rules of IHL (meaning that a military attack directed against them is prima facie lawful under IHL, unless it is carried out through prohibited means of warfare or in violation of other relevant rules on conduct of hostilities), and have the right to participate directly in hostilities. If captured they enjoy prisoner-of-war status (unless they have the nationality of

---

[35] As for Iraq, resolutions 1511 (2003) and 1546 (2004) authorize 'all necessary measures to contribute to the maintenance of security and stability in Iraq'. According to the UK, the end of the occupation of Iraq in 2004 did not terminate the authority to undertake prolonged security detentions as 'a necessary measure', as provided for by the SC resolution. As for Afghanistan, the UK has developed a similar argument by relying on resolution 1386 (2001) (extended by subsequent resolutions). Resolution 1386 authorized the International Security Assistance Force (ISAF), whose mandate included assisting the Afghan authorities in maintaining security, to 'take all necessary measures to fulfil its mandate'.

[36] The Court reversed on this matter the Court of Appeal but found however that the UK violated the European Convention of Human Rights on the review process of the detention.

[37] E. Debuf, *Captured In War: Lawful Internment In Armed Conflict* (Oxford/Paris: Hart/Pedone, 2013), 459.

the Detaining Power, or owe a duty of allegiance to such Power).[38] This involves that they: (i) may not be punished for the fact of merely having participated in hostilities (so-called 'combatant immunity'); (ii) are entitled to the treatment (rights and privileges) accorded to prisoners of war; and (iii) may only be tried and punished for any conduct that was criminalized in the law of the Detaining Power or in international law, at the time of commission.

17.3.1 REQUIREMENTS FOR COMBATANT STATUS

The rules establishing the requirements for combatant status have significantly developed since the adoption of the Hague Regulations and are subject to some controversy when it comes to the relevant rules contained in AP I, particularly concerning guerrilla warfare. The matter is further complicated because the 1949 Geneva Conventions do not define expressly who are the persons entitled to combatant status, but those who are qualify for prisoner-of-war status once they have fallen into the power of the enemy and are thus protected under Article 4(A) of GC III. Since combatants are entitled to the status of prisoners of war upon capture, however, the latter provision serves to establish indirectly the requirements for combatant status.

(1) *Categories of combatants under GC III*. In general, all *members of the army* of the State are combatants.[39] This is a rule that corresponds to customary international law. It goes back to the Hague Regulations and is restated in Article 4(A) GC III of 1949. Importantly, since the army of a State may be constituted in full or in part by militia or volunteer corps, the members of such groups are also *ipso facto* combatants (see Article 1 of the 1907 Hague Regulations, further restated in Article 4(A)(2) GC III of 1949, concerning the definition of prisoners of war, and consolidated within the definition of 'armed forces' by Article 43(1) of AP I).

Another class of combatants is constituted by the members of *militias and volunteer corps* not part of the army of a State, provided they fulfil the following conditions, namely: (i) they are commanded by a person responsible for his subordinates; (ii) they have a fixed distinctive sign recognizable at a distance; (iii) they carry arms openly; (iv) they conduct their operations in accordance with the laws and customs of war; and (v) they belong to a party to the conflict. This last requirement, not contained in the Hague Regulations, was added in Article 4(A)(2) GC III of 1949 (see on this issue the *Kassem* case, at 476–8). Plainly, the rationale for adding this requirement was that, in this way, at least the most glaring abuses were prevented (by extending prisoner-of-war status in case of capture to these irregular forces), greater onus was placed on irregular combatants, and belligerents were implicitly made accountable for any misconduct by irregulars.

Combatant status is further recognized to 'the inhabitants of a territory not under occupation who, on the approach of the enemy, spontaneously take up arms to resist the invading troops without having the time to organize themselves' (the so-called *levée en masse*). In addition to the requirement that the territory is *not under occupation*, two conditions must be fulfilled, namely that: (i) they carry arms openly, and (ii) they respect the laws and customs of war.

In addition to the preceding categories of persons entitled to combatant status already under the 1907 Hague Regulations, *partisans* were for the first time recognized as entitled to combatant status after the Second World War. As is well known, during the Second World War partisans and resistance movements played a remarkable role in certain European countries occupied by Germany (Yugoslavia, France, the Netherlands, Poland, and the

---

[38] See in this respect the stand taken by the British Privy Council specified in *Public Prosecutor v Koi et al.* (at 856–8). *Contra* see *In Re Territo* (about American soldiers who were granted PoW status by the US), as well as (among various scholars arguing that nationality is irrelevant to granting PoW status) Ka Ho Tse, 'The Relevancy of Nationality to the Right to Prisoner of War Status' (2009) 8 *Chinese JIL* 395.

[39] Only military medical and religious personnel, even though members of armed forces, are not considered combatants (Article 43(2) of AP I).

Soviet Union) as well as in Italy from 1943 to 1945. They were not formally permitted by existing law to take up arms against the occupier, because they operated in territories under military occupation, and also because they often lacked one or more of the requirements needed for lawful combatants. In particular, they did not normally carry arms openly, nor did they wear a distinctive sign recognizable at a distance. After the war, a general feeling emerged among the Allies that resistance movements had acted for politically sound reasons; some provision should therefore be made in future for granting them legitimacy. To take into account the partisan war waged in many occupied countries of Europe during the Second World War, partisans were therefore recognized (*ex post facto*) as belonging to the category of combatants. Article 4(A)(2) GC III of 1949 indeed recognizes the status of prisoners of war (and therefore indirectly combatant status) for the members of 'organized resistance movements . . . operating in or outside their own territory, *even if this territory is occupied*', provided that these resistance movements fulfilled the aforementioned five conditions for combatant status of militias and volunteer corps not part of the army of a State.

(2) *The legal framework under AP I*. The requirements for combatant status were further developed in AP I, particularly to take into account guerrilla warfare which had spread throughout the colonial countries.

First of all, AP I adopts a broad definition of 'armed forces'. According to Article 43(1), 'the *armed forces*' of belligerents comprise 'all organized armed forces, groups and units' that: (i) are under a command responsible to a Party to the international armed conflict; and (ii) are 'subject to an internal disciplinary system which, *inter alia*, shall enforce compliance with the rules of international law applicable in armed conflict'. Under Article 43(1), the traditional distinction between 'regular armed forces' and 'irregular armed forces' therefore disappears in favour of a unified definition. Under subsequent paragraph 2 of the same Article, all members of the armed forces (as broadly defined by paragraph 1) of a party to a conflict (other than medical personnel and religious personnel) are combatants and 'have the right to participate directly in hostilities'. Thus, the formalistic criteria of wearing a uniform or, more generally, having a fixed distinctive sign recognizable at a distance, are not *sine qua non* requirements for members of the armed forces for being considered combatants under AP I.[40] This way of regulating the conditions for belligerency was precisely intended to take account of some characteristics of guerrilla warfare.

In order to be entitled to prisoner-of-war status upon capture, however, combatants have to fulfil the conditions spelled out in Article 44. According to the first sentence of Article 44(3) 'combatants are obliged to distinguish themselves from the civilian population while they are engaged in an attack or in a military operation preparatory to an attack' (presumably by insignia or any appropriate outward token, or by openly carrying weapons). This stipulation, read in conjunction with the definition of armed forces in Article 43(1), does not substantially alter the requirements set forth in the Hague Regulations and GC III of 1949 for combatant status of members of irregular forces (namely, militias and volunteer corps). Indeed AP I leaves unaffected three of the requirements for combatant status provided for in the previous legal framework (namely, being linked to a party to the conflict, being under a responsible command, and complying with the laws of war), while it reduces the other two criteria (having a distinctive sign recognizable at a distance, and carrying arms openly) to the one set forth in the first sentence of Article 44(3) (the obligation to distinguish themselves from the civilian population while engaged in an attack or in a military operation preparatory to an attack). Thus, the two traditional requirements

---

[40] See Commentary on the Additional Protocols, §1672. See also the UK *Manual of the Law of Armed Conflict* (UK Ministry of Defence) (Oxford: Oxford University Press, 2004), §4.3.

for combatant status of members of irregular forces are relaxed to the general condition of 'distinction from civilians'. In addition, this condition must be fulfilled *during* an armed attack or immediately *prior* to it.

The requirements just mentioned are further relaxed with regard to specific situations such as *wars of national liberation* and *belligerent occupation*. With respect to these situations, the second sentence of Article 44(3), recognizing that 'there are situations in armed conflicts where, owing to the nature of the hostilities an armed combatant cannot so distinguish himself', only requires that such a combatant should carry his/her arms openly '(a) during each military engagement, and (b) during such time as he is visible to the adversary while he is engaged in a military deployment preceding the launching of an attack in which he is to participate'. This second requirement has been widely interpreted to the effect that a combatant is required to carry arms openly as from the moment he/she is visible while moving to the place from where the attack is going to be launched. Thus, guerrillas fighting in wars of national liberation or in occupied territory are favoured by the regulation contained in AP I in two respects: first, the requirements exacted from them are less stringent than those necessary for irregular combatants fighting in 'normal' situations; secondly, they must fulfil these requirements under circumstances ('military engagement', etc.) which are narrower in scope than those for which guerrillas in 'normal' fighting must fulfil their conditions. However, in another important respect Article 44 is more exacting, or stricter, with guerrillas fighting in 'special' situations: if irregular combatants not satisfying the requirements of the second sentence of Article 44(4) are captured in the course of a war of national liberation or in occupied territory, pursuant to Article 44(4) they forfeit their status as lawful combatants and cannot therefore enjoy prisoner-of-war treatment (but shall nevertheless 'be given protections equivalent in all respects to those accorded to prisoners of war by the Third [Geneva] Convention and by this Protocol').[41]

Since AP I has not been universally ratified, and the absentees include some important States (such as the US, but also Iran, Turkey, and Israel), it is open to question whether the aforementioned rules reflect the content of corresponding rules of customary international law.

Finally, one may mention the question of *mercenaries*. In 1960–70, the number of mercenaries became conspicuously large in Africa, where they were used both by African States (for internal security, intelligence, the training of special commandos, etc.) and by foreign Powers as tools for organizing or strengthening movements to destabilize African regimes. Many African States took a strong stand against the latter practice. Accordingly, both in the UN and at the Geneva Conference of 1974–77, African States claimed, with the support of other developing countries and the socialist group of countries, that mercenaries should be treated as unlawful combatants (and hence not entitled to be treated as prisoners of war on capture). Western countries retorted that mercenaries fulfilling the various requirements of international law should be regarded as legitimate combatants, lest an ideological element be introduced into the laws of warfare, contrary to the basic humanitarian principle of equality of treatment.

The growing insistence on this issue by countries in the UN and the Organization of African Unity (now AU) found official recognition in the adoption of Article 47 of AP I

---

[41] The illustration given by G. Aldrich (a distinguished US lawyer who, as head of the US delegation, greatly contributed to the elaboration of Article 44) may be recalled. He mentioned the case of a guerrilla fighting in an occupied territory, who disguises himself as a civilian; if he is stopped and searched by occupying troops and suddenly draws his weapon and opens fire on the soldiers, on capture he will be deprived of prisoner-of-war status provided it can be proved that he was engaged in a military deployment preceding the launching of an attack. Only if he was not so engaged must he be treated as a prisoner of war (G. Aldrich, 'New Life for the Laws of War' (1981) 75 *AJIL* 764, at 773–4).

at the Geneva Conference. The provision states in paragraph 1 that 'a mercenary shall not have the right to be a combatant or a prisoner of war' and then gives, in paragraph 2, a detailed definition of a mercenary.[42]

17.3.2 RECOGNITION OF BELLIGERENCY

Rules governing NIACs do not grant insurgents, rebels, or members of non-State armed groups (as they are often described today) the status of lawful combatants. In the eyes of both the government against which they fight and of other States, these individuals are often considered criminals (even 'terrorists') infringing domestic penal law. Consequently, if captured, they do not enjoy the status of prisoner of war but can be tried and punished for the mere fact of having taken up arms against the central authorities.

Rebels can be 'upgraded' to the status of lawful combatants only if the incumbent government decides to grant them the so-called *recognition of belligerency*. This recognition was only accorded in the past and in extreme situations (see **8.4**). The obsolescence of the recognition of belligerency derives mainly from the desire of the governments involved in civil commotion to wipe out rebellion as soon as possible, as well as from the interest of other States in either remaining aloof or meddling de facto in the conflict without, however, going to the lengths of granting rebels international legitimation. Thus rebels are normally in a greatly inferior position to that of the government forces against whom they fight.

However, it is important to emphasize that while the absence of a formal combatant status in NIACs means that members of non-State armed groups do not enjoy combatant immunity, the functional distinction between those who participate in hostilities and civilians in terms of who can be the subject of attack applies also in NIACs. This raises the question of determining how to identify membership of an armed group for the purpose of targeting decisions, as discussed next.

17.4 MEMBERS OF NON-STATE ARMED GROUPS

The principle of distinction must be respected not only in IACs, but also in NIACs. Article 13 of AP II prohibits attacks against the civilian population and individual civilians (unless they participate in hostilities and only during such direct participation). As a distinguished commentator has forcefully put it, civilians can be defined only by opposition to those who fight.[43] This consequently raises the (difficult) question of determining, for the purposes of targeting decisions, who is a 'fighter' and who is not.

---

[42] 'A mercenary is any person who (a) is specially recruited locally or abroad in order to fight in an armed conflict; (b) does, in fact, take a direct part in the hostilities; (c) is motivated to take part in the hostility essentially by the desire for private gain and, in fact, is promised, by or on behalf of a Party to the conflict, material compensation substantially in excess of that promised or paid to combatants of similar ranks and functions in the armed forces of that Party; (d) is neither a national of a Party to the conflict nor a resident of territory controlled by a Party to the conflict; (e) is not a member of the armed forces of a Party to the conflict; and (f) has not been sent by a State which is not a Party to the conflict on official duty as a member of its armed forces.'

[43] As M. Sassóli lucidly argues, the view according to which in NIACs everyone is a civilian, meaning that no one can be the object of a military attack unless he/she directly participates in hostilities, is untenable, based on the correct interpretation of the relevant rules of IHL, in particular Article 13 of AP II and common Article 3. In addition, he notes that prohibiting the governmental forces from attacking active members of non-State armed groups (fighters) until and only during they participate directly in hostilities 'is militarily unrealistic as it would oblige [the governmental forces] to react to rather than prevent attacks while facilitating hit-and-run operations by the rebel group' (Sassóli (n 19), at 601–2.

Under the prevalent view, and by way of analogy with members of the regular armed forces of a State, the criterion to be applied is membership of an armed group. Under this view, members of non-State armed groups may be attacked at any time following the principle applied to members of State armed forces.[44] IHL treaties, however, do not even refer to the notion of membership of an armed group, which raises a series of issues that still remain controversial.[45] According to the ICRC, 'the decisive criterion for individual membership in an organized armed group is whether a person assumes a continuous function for the group involving his or her direct participation in hostilities'.[46]

Following this view, therefore, individuals who support an organized armed group but who do not assume a continuous combat function shall not be considered as members of the group and enjoy immunity from attack. This would be the case for 'recruiters, trainers, financiers and propagandists', as well as for persons in charge of 'purchasing, smuggling, manufacturing and maintaining of weapons and other equipment outside specific military operations' and collecting 'intelligence other than of a tactical nature'.[47] By contrast, the notion of continuous combat function would allow consideration, as members of a non-State armed group, of individuals who are actually fighting or involved in execution or planning of attacks, or commanding acts amounting to direct participation in hostilities.[48] In addition, an individual who has been recruited, trained, and equipped to assume a continued combat function for the group is considered as a member of the group for targeting purposes, irrespective of whether he or she has actually carried out a hostile act for the duration of the continuous combat function within the group. This function will last until he or she disengages from it.

The approach taken by the ICRC remains controversial. For the US, membership of armed groups depends on being associated formally or integrated functionally with an organization that has been designated as hostile. On this basis, it is claimed that members of an armed group can be attacked at all times, regardless of the activities in which they are engaged at the time of the attack.[49] Under this view, for instance, the killing in Pakistan on 2 May 2011 of Osama bin Laden (the founder of Al-Qaeda) by the US special operation forces was in conformity with IHL, since he was a member of an organized armed group (Al-Qaeda) taking part in the armed conflict in Afghanistan.[50]

Practice on how States concretely determine whether an individual is a member of a non-State armed group is generally unavailable, being classified. However, based on publicly available information, membership of an armed group for targeting purposes (e.g. by drone strikes) seems to be broadly understood.[51]

The issue of identifying who is a member of an armed group in an NIAC has recently arisen in the context of the military air strikes against the training camps of the Islamic State in Syria and Iraq (ISIS/Daesh), carried out by the US-led anti-Islamic State coalition since July and August 2014. More specifically, the question relates to the attacks against the training camps of the so-called 'foreign fighters', namely the individuals trained to carry out

---

[44] ICRC Commentary to AP II, §4789.

[45] See in this regard G. Gaggioli, 'Targeting Individuals Belonging to an Armed Group' (2018) 51 *Vanderbilt J of Trans'l Law* 901, at 910–16.

[46] ICRC, *Interpretive Guidance on the Notion of Direct Participation in Hostilities under International Humanitarian Law* (ICRC DPH Guidance), 33.

[47] Ibid., at 34–5.

[48] Ibid., at 34.

[49] US Department of Defense, *Law of War Manual* (December 2016), §5.7.3.

[50] Apparently, however, bin Laden was wounded but not yet dead when the members of the special operation forces fired several rounds into his chest and killed him. If this was the case, as a commentator has aptly noted, the killing would amount to the war crime of intentionally killing a person *hors de combat* (see K. J. Heller, 'Author of "No Easy Day" Admits to Committing a War Crime', Blogpost on *OpinioJuris*, 29 August 2012).

[51] See again G. Gaggioli, (n 45), at 914.

terrorist attacks in Europe. It is reported, for instance, that France carried out such military attacks around Raqqa in the fall of 2015.[52] May individuals specifically recruited and trained by ISIS/Daesh for carrying out terrorist acts in Europe be considered as members of an armed group engaged in an NIAC in Iraq and Syria? Is carrying out a terrorist attack in Europe a combat function performed for the armed group? Can foreign fighters be killed if they return to their home country, based on the view that they are members of an armed group involved in an NIAC?

These are just some of the thorny questions that arise in contemporary armed conflicts involving terrorist and other non-State armed groups. There is a high risk that States, in reacting to terrorist attacks, operate in grey zones of the existing legal framework, putting in danger the foundational principles of international humanitarian law.

17.5 DIRECT PARTICIPATION IN HOSTILITIES

Both in IACs and in NIACs, civilians are protected from military attacks, unless and for such time as they take a direct part in hostilities (Article 51(3) AP I; Article 13(3) AP II; see also the ICRC Study on Customary IHL, Rule 6).[53] The notion of 'direct participation in hostilities' is therefore crucial to establish when civilians can be targeted, without violating a fundamental principle of IHL (and committing the war crime of attacking civilians (on war crimes see **19.2.1**)).

IHL treaties do not define the term 'direct participation in hostilities'. In its 'Interpretive Guidance on Direct Participation in Hostilities', the ICRC has introduced the criterion of the continuous combat function to determine membership in non-State armed groups (see **17.4**). Military attacks against these members would therefore not be unlawful under IHL. According to the ICRC, the notion of direct participation in hostilities for targeting purposes is relevant only for those individuals who carry out acts of hostilities without being members of any such groups. Under the ICRC Interpretative Guidance, an act amounts to direct participation in hostilities if it meets the following three cumulative requirements: '(1) a threshold regarding the harm likely to result from the act, (2) a relationship of direct causation between the act and the expected harm, and (3) a belligerent nexus between the act and the hostilities conducted between the parties to an armed conflict' (at 56).

The approach adopted by the ICRC remains controversial. According to another view, the term 'direct participation in hostilities' may include any member of an armed group, not only those who fight or assume a combat function.[54] In addition, from a practical point of view, it is undoubtedly difficult (if not impossible) to determine that individuals have a 'continuous combat function' for an organized armed group, unless they commit hostile acts. It has been therefore convincingly suggested that, absent sound intelligence information or clear appearance to the contrary, 'those who do not identify themselves as members of an armed group are civilians who may only be attacked if and for such time as they commit acts of direct participation'.[55]

---

[52] E. Pothelet, 'Are People in Islamic State Training Camps Legitimate Targets?', Blogpost on *Just Security*, 4 March 2016.

[53] Common Article 3 refers to 'active participation in hostilities'. The term is considered equivalent to 'direct participation in hostilities', in light of the French authentic text using 'participation directe' both in common Article 3 and Article 13(3) of AP II.

[54] According to Sassóli, this view 'is incompatible with the terms "direct participation", which hint to an activity and puts "genuine" civilians into danger because it opens the definition of what makes them lose protection subject to creative interpretations' (*International Humanitarian Law* (n 19), at §8.316).

[55] Ibid., at §8.318.

17.5.1 UNLAWFUL COMBATANTS?

What is the status upon capture or surrender of individuals who have taken direct part in hostilities? In IACs, where the status of lawful combatant exists, if it is not clear whether they are entitled to such status, they shall enjoy the protection of the GC III on Prisoners of War 'until such time as their status has been determined by a competent tribunal' (Article 5 GC III). If it is determined that these persons do not enjoy the status of prisoners of war, and hence do not enjoy combatant immunity, they can be charged and tried in accordance to domestic criminal law for the mere fact of having participated in the hostilities (including if they respect all rules of IHL). There are also those who have contended that by taking up arms and being engaged in hostilities these civilians have committed a war crime. This view is based on the assumption that participation in hostilities without the requirements of combatant status is a violation of IHL.[56]

Importantly, in IACs direct participation in hostilities does not deprive civilians of the protection of GC IV. Subject to the nationality requirements of Article 4, the Convention's protection is extended with restrictions by Article 5 to persons 'definitely suspected of or engaged in activities hostile to the security' of the enemy State or the Occupying Power, as well as to an 'individual protected person ... detained as a spy or saboteur' by the Occupying Power.[57] Therefore, those who participate in hostilities in the context of an IAC without fulfilling the requirement for combatant status are also granted key protections afforded to civilians once it has been determined that they are not entitled to the status of prisoners of war. No protection gap exists in the framework of the GCs. A person who is in the hands of the enemy is either a lawful combatant (and therefore entitled to the status of prisoner of war and protected under GC III) or a civilian (and therefore protected under GC IV, plus supplementary protection afforded by AP I and customary international law). This is also the view currently held by the ICRC.

Since the famous US case *ex parte Quirin* (concerning seven German servicemen who in 1942 landed in the US, abandoned their uniforms, and set off to carry out acts of sabotage; at 468–74), there are those who propound the view that 'unlawful combatants' (also termed later by R. R. Baxter 'unprivileged combatants'[58]) would constitute an intermediate category between combatants and civilians.[59] According to this view, unlawful combatants would be entitled neither to the protection afforded to prisoners of war (because they did

---

[56] In the earlier edition of this book, A. Cassese had also taken this view and argued that participation in hostilities without the requirements of combatant status is a war crime (at p. 409) and cited some authorities in support of this statement, namely: L. Oppenheim and H. Lauterpacht, *International Law*, 7th edn (London, New York, Toronto: Longmans, Green and Co., 1952), 567 and 574; M. Greenspan, *The Modern Law of Land Warfare* (Berkeley: University of California Press, 1959), 61, 265; as well as 1958 British *Manual of Military Law*, Article 626(p). This view, however, is not generally shared. See in this respect, also for further reference, L. Olson, 'Status and Treatment of Those Who Do Not Fulfil the Conditions for Status as Prisoners of War' in A. Clapham, P. Gaeta, and M. Sassóli (eds), *The 1949 Geneva Conventions* (n 3), 911, at 913 (note 11) and at 915–17.

[57] Article 5 provides for two key derogations. If the protected person is in the territory of the party to the conflict, the protected person is not 'entitled to claim such rights and privileges ... as would ... be prejudicial to the security' of the State. If the protected person is in occupied territory, that person forfeits his or her rights of communication 'where absolute military security so requires'. Article 5 specifies, however, that the right to 'humane treatment' and of 'fair and regular trial' may not be derogated from, and that restricted rights are to be restored 'at the earliest date consistent with the security of the State or the Occupying Power'.

[58] R. R. Baxter, 'So-called "Unprivileged Belligerency": Spies, Guerrillas and Saboteurs' (1952) 28 *BYIL* 323.

[59] See for relevant references K. Dörmann, 'Unlawful Combatants' in A. Clapham and P. Gaeta (eds), *The Oxford Handbook of International Law in Armed Conflict* (Oxford: Oxford University Press, 2014), 605, esp. at 607, note 8.

not have combatant status upon capture or surrender) nor to that afforded to civilians in the hands of the enemy (because they did take part in hostilities). Under this view, unlawful combatants may be held in administrative detention without trial and without the attendant privileges of prisoners of war.[60]

Recent practice shows that the notion of 'unlawful combatant' has been used to deny any specific protection to captured members of so-called terrorist groups. For instance, during the US war against Afghanistan, on 7 February 2002 President Bush declared that captured Taliban personnel and Al-Qaeda fighters were not entitled to prisoner-of-war status under GC III or to the protection of civilians in the hands of the enemy under GC IV. The US Supreme Court has partially redressed this approach and held that captured enemy fighters are entitled to the *habeas corpus*, if they are US citizens (*Hamdi v Rumsfeld*), or, in the case of non-citizens, if they are detained in places where the US 'exercises plenary and exclusive jurisdiction . . .' even if it does not exercise *de jure* sovereignty (as in Guantánamo Bay, Cuba) (*Rasul v Bush*).

However, as one commentator has correctly noted, the view according to which unlawful combatants would constitute a 'third legal category', breaking the binary distinction of combatants/civilians, is not supported by any detailed legal reasoning.[61]

17.5.2 TARGETED KILLINGS AND THE 'WAR ON TERROR'

The notion of 'unlawful combatants' has been also used by some States (notably Israel and the US, but also others) to justify the so-called practice of 'targeted killings' against persons suspected of belonging to terrorist organizations, killed in surprise attacks (e.g. while they are travelling in a private car or a taxi, or are in their homes). More generally, some States have argued that they are engaged in a 'war on terror' against terrorist groups, and that many current rules of international humanitarian law could hardly apply to such a war, including with respect to suspected terrorists who could be considered as lawful military targets at any time.

This stand was taken in particular by the US administration of President George W. Bush after the terrorist attacks on 11 September 2001, to describe the armed conflict it launched against Al-Qaeda and associated groups. This armed conflict consisted both of a military campaign against Afghanistan (which at the time was ruled by the Taliban government, and allegedly harbouring the Al-Qaeda leaders) and of a series of attacks against or arrests of suspected Al-Qaeda members or other terrorists elsewhere in the world. The argument has been also used by Israel, to launch surprise military attacks against suspected terrorist leaders, more specifically since 2000, in reaction to a series of suicide bombings during the so-called second Intifada.

In this respect, it must be pointed out, first of all, that while it may be argued that a new type of armed conflict (namely to fight 'terrorist groups') is de facto developing as a historical phenomenon, no such category can be said to exist *de jure* under contemporary international law. As mentioned earlier, an 'armed conflict' exists when there is 'resort to armed force between States or protracted armed violence between governmental authorities and organized armed groups or between such groups within a State'. In occupied territories, the armed conflict which takes place between an Occupying Power and rebel or insurgent

---

[60] Y. Dinstein, *The Conduct of Hostilities under the Law of International Armed Conflict* (Cambridge: Cambridge University Press, 2004), 31.

[61] In this vein, see Dörmann (n 59), at 608.

groups—whether or not they are terrorist in character—amounts to an international armed conflict.[62] Therefore, the killings of suspected terrorists in the context of the so-called 'war on terror' must be assessed against the pertinent rules of IHL regulating international and non-international armed conflicts.

Arguably, with regard to *suspected* terrorists who are not presently engaging in armed hostilities on the battlefield, the belligerent is free to arrest them (and of course once detained, they could not claim any prisoner-of-war status). It has to be proved by judicial means, that is, through a fair trial, that they intended to commit a hostile act or had done so (the *Kassem* and *Mohamed Ali* cases provide clear examples of such trials).[63] In other words, suspected terrorists may be arrested in order to ascertain their responsibility, as is the case for other combatants who do not distinguish themselves from the civilian population (namely spies, saboteurs, and irregular fighters). Such civilians may be tried and punished for unlawfully participating in armed hostilities.

When it proves impossible to capture the suspected terrorists who are not presently directly participating in hostilities, belligerents may use lethal force against them only as an *extrema ratio*, when any other method has proved or may reasonably prove pointless. As the Inter-American Court of Human Rights held in a number of cases (*Velásquez Rodríguez*, at §154; *Godínez Cruz v Honduras*, at §162; and *Neira-Alegría et al. v Peru*, at §75), 'regardless of the seriousness of certain actions and the culpability of the perpetrators of certain crimes, the power of the State is not unlimited, nor may the State resort to any means to attain its ends'. It follows that belligerents must always try first of all to detain civilians suspected of having engaged or intending to engage in hostilities and use lethal force only if it proves absolutely impossible to arrest or capture them. This test was spelled out by the European Court of Human Rights in the *McCann and others* case, in the context of a law-enforcement operation.[64] It is submitted that it is also applicable with respect to suspected terrorists or civilians who are not presently directly participating in hostilities, given the applicability of international human rights law also in the context of armed conflicts (see **17.2.6**).

---

[62] There are three reasons for this proposition: (i) internal armed conflicts are those between a central government and a group of insurgents belonging to the same State (or between two or more insurrectional groups belonging to that State); (ii) the object and purpose of international humanitarian law require that in case of doubt the protection deriving from this body of law be as extensive as possible, and it is indisputable that the protection accorded by the rules on international conflicts is much broader than that relating to internal conflicts; (iii) as belligerent occupation is governed by GC IV and customary international law, it would be contradictory to subject occupation to norms relating to international conflict while regulating the conduct of armed hostilities between insurgents and the Occupant on the strength of norms governing internal conflict. It follows that the rules on international armed conflict also apply to the armed clashes between insurgents in occupied territories and the belligerent Occupant.

[63] In *Kassem* the Israeli Military Court held that 'International Law is not designed to protect and grant rights to saboteurs and criminals. The defendants have no right except to stand trial in court and to be tried in accordance with the law and with the facts established by the evidence, in proceedings consonant with the requirements of ethics and International Law' (at 483). Similarly, in 1969 in *Mohamed Ali* the Privy Council upheld the conviction of two members of the Indonesian armed forces for entering Malaysian territory wearing civilian clothes and committing acts of sabotage (at 2–9).

[64] The case concerned the use of lethal force, by British enforcement officials, against terrorists. The European Court stressed that: (i) a very strict and compelling test of 'necessity' must be employed when determining if lethal force is necessary to fight terrorism (at §149); (ii) the State's response to the perceived threat of a terrorist attack must be proportional to the threat in question (at §156); and (iii) it is always necessary to take into account whether there are acceptable alternatives to the use of lethal force (at §§205–214).

17.6 RESTRICTION ON THE USE OF MILITARY FORCE AND THE CHOICE OF WEAPONS

There are two sets of international rules regulating the use of military force in warfare (the so-called rules on the 'methods and means of warfare'): those meeting the needs of all belligerents; and those which instead were intended to favour, directly or indirectly, the stronger States.

The former include rules in the Hague Regulations such as those prohibiting treachery (Article 23(b)); the killing or wounding of enemies who have 'laid down their arms or, no longer having any means of defense, have surrendered at discretion' (Article 23(c)); the declaration that no quarter will be given, in other words that even the defeated enemies willing to surrender will be killed (Article 23(d)); the improper use of flags of truce, of national flags, of the military insignia and uniform of the enemy, or of the distinctive signs of the Geneva Conventions (Article 28)); and, lastly, pillage (Article 23(f)). All these norms were clearly intended to introduce a minimum of fair play into the conduct of hostilities and actually serve the interests of all potential belligerents.

In short, the international regulation is built upon two fundamental principles: (i) the principle of distinction, whereby it is prohibited to attack civilians or civilian objects deliberately or to launch indiscriminate attacks that hit military and civilian objects without distinction; and, (ii) the principle of proportionality, according to which an attack on military objectives shall not be expected to cause incidental loss of civilian life, injury to civilians, or destruction of civilian objects which are out of proportion to the direct and concrete military advantage anticipated. These two principles and the rules fleshing them out are formulated loosely and lend themselves to the most divergent interpretations. Nonetheless, they still provide a standard for at least the most glaring cases of unlawful conduct in warfare. Were they lacking, no restraints on military power would exist and any war would soon turn into carnage even worse than the armed conflicts we have known so far.

17.6.1 THE PRINCIPLE OF DISTINCTION

Under this principle, it is prohibited to attack civilians or civilian objects deliberately. Therefore indiscriminate attacks (that is, attacks which are not or cannot be directed against military objectives) are also banned. This principle is laid down in customary international law and is restated in Articles 51 and 52 of AP I and Article 13 of AP II.

Civilians are those who are not combatants. In addition, as already clarified, they lose protection from military attacks 'for such time as they take direct part in hostilities', raising the issue of determining the exact meaning of 'direct participation in hostilities' (see **17.5**). Civilian objects are 'all objects which are not military objectives'. For a long time, however, the very concept of 'military objective' had not been clearly defined, and could therefore be extended at discretion. A broad definition was agreed upon in 1977 and became Article 52(2) of AP I. It defines as military objectives:

> [t]hose objects which by their nature, location, purpose or use make an effective contribution to military action and whose total or partial destruction, capture or neutralization, in the circumstances ruling at the time, offers a definite military advantage.

This definition can be held to have become part of customary international law, and can therefore be considered as binding even on States that are not party to AP I. The interpretation of the definition, however, and in particular the meaning of 'effective contribution to military action', remains controversial. This is because the definition covers both objects that have a clear military use (such as enemy armed forces, garrisons, military weapons, vehicles, equipment and installations, military aircraft, airports, and munitions factories), but also objects that *may* serve such a purpose (e.g. bridges, roads, railways, factories, power stations, communication towers, electricity and oil refineries, but also e.g. a school building or a hotel used by military troops). The appraisal of whether, 'in the circumstances ruling at the time', the object does offer 'a definite military advantage' falls of course to the belligerent about to launch the attack. Although the belligerent thus enjoys great latitude, such latitude may not be exercised arbitrarily, but is restrained by the terms of the definition, including the requirements that the 'contribution to military action' be 'effective', and the 'military advantage' be 'definite'. It is, for instance, significant that the ICRC in its Commentary to AP I has pointed out that 'it is not legitimate to launch an attack which only offers potential or indeterminate advantages' (at §2024). The Commentary also emphasizes that 'there must be a definite military advantage for *every* military objective that is attacked' (at §2028).

State practice shows however that on many occasions belligerents tend to place an exceedingly liberal interpretation on that definition, specifically with respect to dual-use and war-sustaining economic facilities. For instance, in 1991, in the war against Iraq after its invasion of Kuwait, the allies considered Iraqi power stations as legitimate targets, because they supplied power to a national grid providing power to both civilians and military forces. More recently, the US, the UK, France, and Russia have justified attacks on Iraqi civilian oil infrastructure and assets controlled by the so-called Islamic State (ISIS/Daesh) on the grounds that they provided revenues which sustain ISIS operations. During the NATO air operations against Yugoslavia (Operation Allied Force), NATO forces considered the radio and television station in Belgrade as a legitimate target, including because it contributed to the war effort by disseminating propaganda in favour of the government. This argument was discredited by a Committee of experts established by the Office of the Prosecutor of the ICTY.[65]

Arguably, this practice may be accepted subject to some conditions, dictated by the general logic and purpose of international humanitarian law: (i) in the case of attacks on objectives that are not exclusively used for military purposes, for instance television stations, power stations, railways, bridges, etc., belligerents should take all the necessary precautionary measures to avoid hitting civilians or civilian personnel who may be working in, or regularly using, such installations; such precautions may include a prior warning that the objective may be attacked (effective advance warning, for instance, was not provided for the NATO bombing of the RTS in Belgrade); (ii) such attacks should be limited to neutralizing the military potential of the object (which in practice, however, is difficult to assess); they should not aim at all-out destruction of enemy objects, in view of the need for the enemy belligerent to use those installations for peaceful purposes once war is over.

17.6.2 THE PRINCIPLE OF PROPORTIONALITY

The principle that when attacking military objectives belligerents must make sure that any collateral damage to civilians or civilian objects is not out of proportion to the military advantage anticipated also turns out to be rather imprecise.

It has been argued that 'proportionality' is by definition very questionable, except in extreme cases (e.g. if, in order to destroy a tiny garrison controlling a bridge, the adversary

---

[65] See 'Final Report to the Prosecutor by the Committee Established to Review the NATO Bombing Campaign Against the Federal Republic of Yugoslavia', 14 June 2000, §76, online at http://www.icty.org/en/press/final-report-prosecutor-committee-established-review-nato-bombing-campaign-against-federal.

annihilates a whole village surrounding the place where the garrison is located). However, it would be important to try to define this principle as precisely as possible, with a view to restraining the otherwise unfettered power of belligerents—all the more so if one takes into account the possible criminal consequences of violations of the principle (its breach might entail the criminal liability for war crimes of those who have ordered it or carried it out, as for instance provided in Article 85(3)(b) of AP I).

The rule of proportionality is set out in identical terms in Article 51(5)(b) of AP I (as an example of an indiscriminate attack) and in Articles 57(2)(a)(iii) and 57(2)(b) of AP I (in the context of precautionary measures). These provisions prohibit the launching of attacks 'which may be expected to cause incidental loss of civilian life, injury to civilians, damage to civilian objects, or a combination thereof, which would be *excessive in relation to the concrete and direct military advantage anticipated*' (emphasis added).

Arguably, this provision reflects customary international law, or at least it can be held that it has contributed to the formation of a customary international rule,[66] and is also applicable to NIACs. However, certain States made reservations to this provision. For instance, the UK stated that the military advantage anticipated from an attack should be intended 'to refer to the advantage anticipated from the *attack considered as a whole* and not only from isolated or particular parts of the attack'.[67] Subsequently the framers of the Rome Statute establishing the International Criminal Court (ICC) (see **19.3.3**) adopted a similar notion, although in the framework of a treaty containing provisions on war crimes falling under the Court's jurisdiction (i.e. Article 8(2)(b)(iv)).

This notion is broadly considered to represent the current status of customary international law. However, it is problematic on at least two grounds. First, because it broadens the discretionary power of the attacking belligerent, since it is for him to decide whether the military advantage anticipated from an attack justifies the incidental loss of or injury to civilians. Secondly, such a broad notion becomes almost incapable of verification and criminal application. It is submitted therefore that this broad notion should be subject to a host of measures, as follows: (i) all feasible precautions must be taken in the choice or means and methods of attack 'with a view to avoiding, and in any event minimizing, incidental loss of civilian life, injury to civilians and damage to civilian objects' (Article 57(2)(ii) of AP I); (ii) where it appears that the collateral damage would be disproportionate or excessive, belligerents must refrain from launching the attack (Article 57(2)(iii) of AP I); (iii) belligerents must verify that the objectives are not subject to special protection; such objectives encompass 'objects indispensable to the survival of the civilian population' (Article 54 of AP I) and 'works and installations containing dangerous forces', namely dams, dykes, and nuclear electrical generating stations (Article 56 of AP I).

Arguably, it would be consonant with the humanitarian purpose of international rules on armed conflict to postulate that a belligerent should be prepared to accept *independent verification* in case of dispute after an attack. In particular, a belligerent who, when attacking military objectives, causes purportedly disproportionate collateral damage, should be prepared to submit to independent and impartial inquiry either during hostilities or at their end, or in any case must be willing to offer to any competent international body all the evidence about the overall military advantage anticipated, available to him before launching the attack.

---

[66] The best application of proportionality can be found in the judgment of the Israeli Supreme Court in *Beit Sourik Village Council* v *Government of Israel*, where three sub-tests for applying the principle are set forth (at §§40–43; see also §§44–86).

[67] In A. Roberts and R. Guelff, *Documents on the Law of War*, 3rd edn (Oxford: Oxford University Press, 2000), 511.

17.6.3 RESTRICTIONS ON THE CHOICE OF WEAPONS

The choice of the so-called means of warfare (namely, weapons) is not unlimited. Two fundamental principles must be respected and they were both spelled out in the Hague Regulations. First, it is expressly forbidden to employ arms, projectiles, and material calculated to cause unnecessary suffering. Secondly, indiscriminate weapons (that is weapons which do not distinguish between combatants and civilians) are prohibited. Both principles are, however, too vague to function as a workable standard of behaviour (except in extreme cases). Therefore, the adoption of international rules to set forth specific bans on specific arms or weapons has provided useful clarity.

(1) *Treaties containing specific bans*. At the time of the Hague Conventions, only those agencies of destruction which either were relatively ineffective or might imperil the life of the users themselves were proscribed. Thus, explosive projectiles weighing under 400 grams were prohibited as belonging to the former category, whereas the other banned category covered such weapons as poison or poisonous weapons, asphyxiating or deleterious gases, and automatic submarine contact mines. In 1925 the Geneva Protocol prohibited the use of chemical and bacteriological weapons. In 1972, the ban on bacteriological means of warfare was restated and strengthened by a specific Convention designed to prohibit the manufacture and stockpiling of these agents of destruction. In 1976, a Convention was adopted within the UN on the prohibition of military and any other hostile use of environmental modification techniques. In 1980, the use of three categories of weapons was proscribed by the Convention on Certain Conventional Weapons, to which three Protocols were annexed (a fourth Protocol was adopted in 1995). The first Protocol prohibits any weapon whose primary effect is to injure by *fragments non-detectable* in the human body by X-rays. The second bans the use on land of *mines, booby traps*, and *other devices*, if employed indiscriminately or when directed against civilians (it was amended in 1996 with a view to strengthening restrictions on the use of land mines). The third proscribes *incendiary weapons*, not per se but if such weapons are used to attack civilians or civilian objects, or military objectives 'located within a concentration of civilians'. The fourth Protocol prohibits blinding laser weapons. Strikingly, the First Protocol banning the use of 'any weapon the primary effect of which is to injure by fragments which in the human body escape detection by X-rays', concerns weapons that in fact do not exist. When the first move to ban such weapons was made, it was erroneously believed that US military forces had used them in Vietnam. Although it was later made clear that the weapons had actually not been used or even manufactured and that no State planned to include them in its arsenal, the ban was enacted, probably because major military Powers wished to show their readiness to make concessions and, in any case, the issue was harmless (though the ban can serve the purpose of discouraging States from engaging in the manufacture of the weapon in question). In 1997, States agreed upon the Ottawa Convention on the prohibition of the use, stockpiling, production, and transfer of antipersonnel mines and on their destruction.

The prohibition of specific weapons by specific bans or restrictions has two undoubted advantages. First, since these bans or restrictions refer to weapons by describing their objective features, a high degree of certainty is provided about the kind of weapons outlawed. By the same token, the prohibitions and restrictions are capable of providing normative guidance which is effective, even in the absence of an enforcement authority, as can be seen from the fact that, generally speaking, the various prohibitions of specific weapons have been respected in spite of occasional violations.

This approach presents, however, two major drawbacks. First, even the bans on minor weapons can be easily bypassed by elaborating new and more sophisticated weapons which, while they are no less cruel, do not fall under the existing prohibition owing to new features.

Secondly, so far, international bans have concerned only those weapons which proved to be of minor military effectiveness or which, although militarily effective, might also present a risk to the belligerent using them.

(2) *Nuclear weapons.* In light of the above, it comes as no surprise that no specific treaty banning the use of atomic and nuclear weapons has yet been enacted. A treaty on the Prohibition of Nuclear Weapons has been adopted by the UN General Assembly on 7 July 2017, following the informal effort by a group of States (including Norway, Mexico, and Austria) willing to reframe the debate on nuclear weapons based on the catastrophic and lasting consequences of their use on health, societies, and the environment (the so-called 'humanitarian initiative'). The treaty, however, is not yet in force. It will enter into force 90 days after the fiftieth instrument of ratification, acceptance, approval, or accession has been deposited (Article 15). The prospects for ratification of this treaty by nuclear-weapon States are scant. In addition, no specific customary rule prohibiting the use of nuclear weapons has evolved on the matter (as the ICJ rightly held in *Legality of the Threat or Use of Nuclear Weapons*, at §266).

This does not mean that the use of nuclear weapons, although not directly prohibited by a specific international rule, is lawful under IHL (or under the international rules banning the threat or use of armed force in international relations). On 10 August 1945, the Japanese Imperial government lodged a protest with the US government, through Switzerland, stating that the atomic bomb dropped on Hiroshima (an instance of *first use in a conventional war*) was contrary to international law since it 'produced suffering not inferior to that caused by other weapons specifically prohibited by international law'. In 1962, the Tokyo District Court also concluded that the bombings of Hiroshima and Nagasaki were unlawful for they were contrary both to the principle prohibiting indiscriminate attacks on undefended towns, and to the principle forbidding the use of weapons causing unnecessary suffering (*Shimoda et al.*, at 1688ff).

The stand taken by the Tokyo District Court is convincing. The first use of nuclear weapons in a conventional war would not be warranted by any norm or principle and indeed would exacerbate the conflict by bringing about an escalation in the use of weapons of mass destruction. More generally, it is doubtful whether nuclear weapons can ever be used in such a manner as to meet the requirements deriving from two fundamental principles of international humanitarian law: that on the protection of civilians, with the consequent obligation of always distinguishing between civilian and military objectives, and the principle whereby it is prohibited to cause unnecessary suffering and superfluous injury to combatants. In addition, it is also doubtful whether nuclear weapons could ever be used respecting the principle of neutrality, whereby belligerents must respect the inviolability of neutral Powers.[68]

Some nuclear Powers claim that so-called tactical nuclear weapons may be used in keeping with international humanitarian law and the aforementioned principles.[69] In its Advisory Opinion on *Legality of the Threat or Use of Nuclear Weapons*, the ICJ has reached

---

[68] Under the international rules of neutrality, a State which is not participating in an armed conflict or which does not want to become involved has certain rights and duties. In particular, it has the right not to be adversely affected by the conflict, and the duty of non-participation and impartiality. The rules on neutrality are contained in the Hague Conventions V and XIII and in some provisions of the four Geneva Conventions and Additional Protocol I.

[69] Some authors have suggested possible illustrations of allegedly lawful uses of nuclear weapons: e.g. the nuclear bombing of troops and armour in an isolated desert 'with a low-yield air-burst in conditions of no wind' (M. N. Schmitt, 'The International Court of Justice and the Use of Nuclear Weapons' (1998) 362 *Naval War Coll Rev* 108), or the detonating of a 'clean' nuclear weapon 'against an enemy fleet in the middle of the ocean' (Y. Dinstein (n 60), at 79).

the same conclusion (at §§42, 78–87, 88–89). Surprisingly the Court also held that 'in view of the current state of international law, and of the elements of fact at its disposal, [it could not] conclude definitively whether the threat or use of nuclear weapons would be lawful or unlawful in an extreme circumstance of self-defence, in which the very survival of a State would be at stake' (at §§96–97, and 105E). Two objections can be made against this ambiguous ruling. First, it does not clarify whether, in the instance of self-defence to which it alludes, the aforementioned requirements must be respected. In other words, did the Court intend to say that the law does not specify whether in the case of self-defence 'in which the very survival of the State would be at stake', that State could breach the principles of proportionality, the other two fundamental principles of humanitarian law, and the principle of neutrality? Secondly, did the Court intend self-defence to encompass anticipatory or pre-emptive self-defence?

(3) *Lethal autonomous weapons.* The arms industry is developing technology to produce so-called lethal autonomous weapons systems (LAWS), that is, weapons that can find, track, and fire on targets without human supervision. Numerous studies have already been conducted on a range of legal issues relevant to the development of LAWS. These include studies focusing on whether LAWS can be developed and used in compliance with the IHL rules on targeting and how and to what extent there could be an 'accountability gap' in case of violations of these rules, including those amounting to war crimes. A campaign has been launched to call for a preventive ban on the development of these weapons, without exception, based on the catastrophically destabilizing effects they would cause to society (*Campaign to Stop Killer Robots*). States parties to the Convention on Conventional Weapons have agreed to establish a Group of Governmental Experts, mandated to examine issues related to emerging technologies in the area of LAWS. Up to now, the main relevant legal point of the discussions has focused on the required level of human control for the use of these weapons. Some delegations have agreed on the criterion of so-called 'meaningful human control', while other delegations have proposed the alternative criterion of 'appropriate level of human judgment'.

Undoubtedly, facing the development of new weapons based on algorithms and artificial intelligence, there is a pressing need to adopt the appropriate legal framework, including to fill possible gaps. Though clearly, the crux of the matter is not legal. Increasing automation brings many benefits to society and may even bring benefits in warfare.[70] However, does robotism—the mindless automation of our lives—risk leading us into 'insane societies', as predicted by Erich Fromm in his book, *The Sane Society* (1955)? 'The danger of the past was that men became slaves. The danger of the future is that men may become robots.'

17.7 PROTECTION OF WAR VICTIMS

Unlike the international rules governing the conduct of hostilities, there are extensive and detailed international rules protecting war victims, namely all the persons who do not take part in hostilities (civilians) or, having engaged in combat, are no longer in a position to do so (prisoners of war, the wounded, sick, or shipwrecked). The reason is that humanitarian considerations have counted more in this area than in others, where they have been outweighed by military demands. Plainly, while it is in the interest of all belligerent Powers to afford strong protection to war victims (if only for humanitarian reasons), major military Powers are less concerned with prohibitions or restraints on the conduct of hostilities.

---

[70] See e.g. Sassóli (n 19), according to whom the use of lethal autonomous weapons may have many advantages compared with other lethal weapon platforms (at §10.81).

In the area of protection of victims of warfare, the Hague codifications of 1899 and 1907, as well as the 1864, 1906, and 1929 Geneva Conventions, made much headway. At present, with respect to international armed conflicts, the pertinent rules are to be found both in the four Geneva Conventions of 1949, and in Additional Protocol I.

According to these rules, lawful combatants who fall into the hands of the enemy, either because they surrender or because they are wounded, sick, or shipwrecked, are entitled to the status of prisoner of war. They may be interned in prisoner-of-war camps (which must be located far from the combat zone). They must be held in good health and be treated humanely. They also have a set of rights (e.g. against violence, intimidation, or insult); GC III spells them out in detail. Various international judicial bodies (e.g. the ICJ in the Advisory Opinion on the *Legality of the Threat or Use of Nuclear Weapons* (§79) and the Eritrea–Ethiopia Claims Commission)[71] have held that most of the rules of the Geneva Conventions have turned into customary international law.

Under GC IV and AP I, civilians are satisfactorily protected to the extent that they are in the 'hands of the adversary' (namely on enemy territory) or in occupied territories. Additional Protocol I also enhances the protection of the civilian population in the theatre of hostilities, expanding the rules enshrined in GC IV for the general protection of the civilian population against the effects of warfare. As for civilians in occupied territories, the relevant provisions of GC IV build upon the 1907 Hague Regulations governing belligerent occupation. The latter however proved inadequate to afford protection to the civilian population of occupied countries during the Second World War. The Geneva Convention, however, does not contain a legal definition of occupation, which is instead defined in Article 42 of the Hague Regulations. According to this definition, '[t]erritory is considered occupied when it is actually placed under the authority of the hostile army. The occupation extends only to the territory where such authority has been established and can be exercised.'

The need for the second requirement has sparked a vivid debate, particularly in light of the so-called 'disengagement' of the Israeli armed forces from the Gaza Strip in 2005, calling into question whether this territory is still occupied.[72] This debate shows that the international rules regulating the powers and duties of the Occupying Power, despite their significant development after the Second World War, still face significant challenges of interpretation.

As for NIACs, common Article 3 of the 1949 Geneva Conventions contains some minimum rules that must be respected by the parties to the conflict. This provision, on the face of it, does not have any direct bearing on the actual conduct of hostilities. However, on close scrutiny, one could argue that it contains some indirect regulation.[73] Banning the visiting of violence upon the lives and persons of those who do not take part in hostilities or no longer participate in hostilities can be interpreted to include the following prohibitions. First, these persons must not be attacked; in other words, they must not be seen as a military target and can never be the object of deliberate attacks. Furthermore, the contending parties must not resort to measures intended to intimidate or terrorize the civilian population. In this connection, it is interesting to recall that in a memo of 30 January 1970, the

---

[71] See the following awards of the Eritrea–Ethiopia Claims Commission, and with reference to GC III: *Prisoners of War—Ethiopia's Claim 4* (at §§29–33, 52, 61, 64, 75–76, 78, 124–125, 134, 150), and *Prisoners of War—Eritrea's Claim 17* (at §§39–40, 58, 64, 70, 81, 84–85, 87–88, 116–117).

[72] On this issue, see J. Grignon, 'The Geneva Conventions and the End of Occupation' in A. Clapham, P. Gaeta, and M. Sassóli (eds), *The 1949 Geneva Conventions* (n 3), 1575, at 1591–6.

[73] This view is not shared by the ICRC (see the Commentary to AP I, §4365, and more recently the 2016 Commentary on Geneva Convention I, §389).

Legal Bureau of the Canadian government stated, *inter alia*, that common Article 3 outlaws 'acts of the type occurring at My Lai [in Vietnam]' ((1971) 9 *CYIL* 301). This statement referred to the ban on physical violence against civilians, stemming from common Article 3. Secondly, pursuant to common Article 3, the taking of hostages is prohibited. This practice, it must be emphasized, has frequently been resorted to during civil wars, including the Spanish conflict; the relevant provision is, therefore, of great value. Thirdly, all reprisals involving violence to the lives and persons of non-combatants, or outrages upon their personal dignity, are forbidden. Fourthly, if members of the armed forces of the adversary, or civilians belonging to the opposing party and suspected of supporting it, are arrested and detained, or are put into internment camps, they must be treated humanely. In particular, no discriminatory treatment may be meted out to them, nor may they be submitted to torture, or to cruel, humiliating, or degrading measures. In the event of their being brought to trial, all judicial safeguards provided for in paragraph 1(d) of common Article 3 must be observed. Finally, the wounded and sick, including those belonging to the adversary, must be collected and cared for.

State practice developed after 1949 shows that Article 3 was invoked, reaffirmed, and relied upon on a number of occasions. Even when it was disregarded in practice, no State admitted to having violated it. This should not come as a surprise, for common Article 3 essentially enshrines a handful of humanitarian principles proclaimed by States in other contexts, such as in the various treaties on human rights. The fact remains, however, that the instances of violation of or disregard for the provisions of common Article 3 greatly outnumber the instances of compliance. Nonetheless, all these instances of non-observance have not been such as to erode the rule. (Similarly, domestic criminal laws are not obliterated by their daily violation.)

17.8 PREVENTIVE AND REPRESSIVE MEASURES TO ENSURE COMPLIANCE

There are no effective mechanisms for determining when a belligerent has violated the rules of IHL. As we shall see, there are some specific institutions to which the Geneva Conventions and AP I assign monitoring functions. Yet, these institutions are not functioning as they should, or they have limited authority.

There are also other institutions that monitor compliance with the rules of IHL in armed conflicts, for instance independent and authoritative non-governmental organizations, or commissions of inquiry set up by UN bodies (such as those established by the Human Rights Council or by the Security Council).[74] However, these institutions also face significant challenges, for instance concerning access to the territory where the armed conflict is fought, expertise in IHL and the scope of their mandate, to mention only a few.

In some instances, it has been possible to resort to international courts or tribunals. The European Court of Human Rights and the Inter-American Court of Human Rights have dealt with numerous cases originating from situations of armed conflict. The Eritrea–Ethiopia Claims Commission was set up in 2000 to decide, 'through binding arbitration all claims for loss, damage or injury by one Government against the other' relating to the 1998–2000 armed conflict and resulting from 'violations of international humanitarian law, including the 1949 Geneva Conventions, or other violations of international law' (Article 5 of the

---

[74] On these commissions, see T. Boutruche, 'The Role of United Nations Commissions of Inquiry in the Implementation of IHL: Potential and Challenges' in D. Djukić and N. Pons (eds), *The Companion to International Humanitarian Law* (Leiden; Boston: Brill Nijhoff, 2018), 98. See also P. Alston, 'The Darfur Commission as a Model for Future Responses to Crisis Situations' (2005) 3 *JICJ* 600.

2000 Algiers Agreement). Also, there have been situations which have prompted the establishment of ad hoc international or mixed criminal tribunals, having jurisdiction over war crimes committed in specific armed conflicts (e.g. the ICTY, the ICTR, or the Special Court for Sierra Leone) and there are situations in respect of which the ICC can exercise its jurisdiction over war crimes (see **Chapter 19**). In general terms, however, the 'legal' perspective (including the 'criminal law perspective') is not necessarily the most effective way to ensure compliance with the rules of IHL. Arguably, the need is for flexible bodies, not quasi-judicial ones but rather organs adapted for the minute and daily monitoring of the conduct of the parties to the conflict. These supervisory bodies should obviously be impartial beyond any doubt and be composed of military experts and specialists of international humanitarian law. They should be set up to verify on the ground and from the start of the conflict compliance with the rules of IHL. Their reports should be disclosed only to the parties to the conflict, but automatically published at the end of the conflict. However, they could also be made public during the conflict in case of repeated violations of IHL.

17.8.1 SPECIFIC INSTITUTIONS

(1) The *ICRC* is currently the leading institution that promotes compliance with IHL. The ICRC's delegates carry out visits and inspections to places of detention for prisoners of war or other detainees and, more generally, monitor respect for international humanitarian law by the parties to an armed conflict. The ICRC reports and its findings are strictly confidential and are only forwarded to the party concerned. Sometimes, however, the ICRC issues public statements and appeals of a general nature, where it calls upon the party concerned to abide by the rules and principles of humanitarian law. Although the rule of confidentiality is crucial to the effective functioning of the ICRC as a supervisory body (otherwise, it is claimed, States would not accept its intervention), perhaps in exceptional situations where a belligerent, after repeated confidential reports and appeals, fails to comply with humanitarian law and persists in its flagrant breaches of such law, the ICRC might consider the advisability of 'going public'. A case in point was the widespread US practice of ill-treating or even torturing prisoners of war in Iraq. It is now common knowledge that the ICRC issued various confidential reports without the US authorities taking immediate and drastic measures. Perhaps a public appeal disclosing at least the essence of the confidential findings might have proved effective.[75]

Some of the activities of the ICRC in promoting compliance with IHL rules are envisaged in the 1949 Geneva Conventions and other relevant treaties. However, the role of the ICRC goes beyond the express treaty-based mandate and covers a variety of activities characterized by the discretion and flexibility of this institution. As aptly noted by a commentator, there is today a high expectation by and on States to allow the ICRC to insert itself in situations of armed conflict or other situations of violence that clearly bypasses the limited responsibilities conferred on it by IHL treaties.

(2) After the Franco-Prussian War of 1870–71, and at least until the Second World War, belligerents resorted to the system of *Protecting Powers* for the purpose of safeguarding

---

[75] It should be recalled that this is what the 1987 European Convention for the Prevention of Torture provides for. It is also interesting to recall that, in 2003, the Eritrea–Ethiopia Claims Commission held that the ICRC insistence on confidentiality was questionable. Both States possessed ICRC reports concerning visits to prisoner-of-war camps and other ICRC communications, and both agreed that such documents should be provided to the Claims Commission. Nevertheless, the ICRC refused to disclose any documents except for those which had already been made public. The Claims Commission expressed its 'disappointment' in its awards (*Prisoners of War—Ethiopia Claim 4*, §§45–48; *Prisoners of War—Eritrea's Claim 17*, §§50–53).

their interests in warfare (in particular when diplomatic relations were severed) as well as impelling the adversary to abide by the rules of warfare. This system was codified and improved by the 1949 Geneva Conventions and further developed by Article 5 of AP I.[76]

In a nutshell, the system provides that each of the belligerents shall appoint a third State (a neutral State or a State not party to the armed conflict) as 'Protecting Power', either to safeguard its interests (diplomatic mandate) or to monitor the implementation of the rules of IHL (humanitarian mandate), or both. The humanitarian mandate of the Protecting Power is defined in the relevant rules of the 1949 Geneva Conventions and AP I. For the designated State to accomplish its tasks the consent of both belligerents is necessary. Under the Conventions, the other belligerent must accept the appointment of the Protecting Power but can oppose the appointment on specific grounds (e.g. because the proposed State is not sufficiently neutral or independent). Thus, the system hinges on a 'double-decker three-sided' relationship: the two belligerents and two third parties. Once a triangular agreement is reached, a third party could act as a 'Protecting Power' on behalf of each belligerent and scrutinize the implementation of the rules of IHL. Nothing, of course, rules out the possibility of a third State acting as Protecting Power for both belligerents. As the consent of all the States involved is necessary for the appointment and functioning of Protecting Powers it follows that if one of them withdraws consent the Protecting Power ceases to act.

A significant advance of the 1949 Geneva Conventions lies in the provision of 'Substitutes for the Protecting Powers'. Of the three possibilities envisaged in this regard by the Conventions, the third stands out on account of its mandatory character: under common Article 10/10/10/11, paragraph 3, the Detaining Power (that is, the State detaining the enemy wounded, shipwrecked, prisoners of war, or civilians) is duty-bound to accept 'the offer of the services of a humanitarian organization, such as the International Committee of the Red Cross to assume the humanitarian functions performed by Protecting Powers under the present Convention'.

In practice, since the Second World War, the system of Protecting Powers has fallen into disuse and has proved to be a (relative) failure. It has been resorted to in only five cases: in 1956, in the Suez conflict (only, however, between Egypt on the one hand and France and the UK on the other); in the French–Tunisian conflict over Bizerte in 1961; in the short Goa affair in 1961, when India invaded the Portuguese colony; in the Indo-Pakistani war in 1971, although India soon withheld its consent; and in the 1982 Falklands/Malvinas conflict between Argentina and the UK (Switzerland acted on behalf of the UK whilst Brazil protected the interests of Argentina; however, neither State was formally designated as a Protecting Power). The various causes for the failure of this system include belligerents' fear (when they do not recognize each other) that the appointment of Protecting Powers may be interpreted as implicit recognition, or, instead, the desire not to sever diplomatic relations when they continue to entertain such relations and therefore to consider the appointment of Protecting Powers unnecessary; the marked tendency not to enter into any agreement with the adversary; the shortness of the armed conflict (whereas the appointment of Protecting Powers may be a long process); and the reluctance of third States to become entangled in armed conflict involving many States. One should also note both the

---

[76] The scheme provided for in Article 5 AP I substantially takes up the 1949 system. It spells out that consent of all the parties concerned is of the utmost importance. It is indeed made the lynchpin of the system, and any automatic obligation, even that laid down in common Article 10/10/10/11, paragraph 3 of the 1949 Conventions concerning the ICRC is done away with. Also (in para. 3) it sets up a procedure for facilitating the appointment of Protecting Powers: it eliminates some of the practical or political obstacles to the appointment of Powers, by specifying in paragraphs 5 and 6 that the designation and acceptance of Powers does not affect the legal status of the parties to the conflict or of any territory, and that diplomatic relations can be maintained by the belligerents despite the appointment of Protecting Powers.

propensity of States not to accept the offers of the ICRC to act as a substitute, as well as the reluctance of the ICRC to step in and take on the role of substitute.

(3) Finally, a third specific institution for promoting compliance with the rules of IHL is the *International Humanitarian Fact-Finding Commission*, established by Article 90 of AP I. This is a permanent body, officially constituted in 1992, which is competent to enquire into any grave breach or other serious violation of the Geneva Conventions and AP I, and to facilitate 'through its good offices, the restoration of an attitude of respect' of the Conventions and the Protocol. The Commission can exercise its mandate only if the parties involved express their consent, through modalities resembling the expression of consent to the exercise of jurisdiction of the ICJ. Since its establishment, the Commission has declared that it would be ready to carry out its functions also in situations of non-international armed conflict, provided it had the consent of the parties involved. Unfortunately, the lack of political will and the requirement of consent have prevented the Commission from exercising its functions, at least so far.[77] Frits Kalshoven therefore appropriately described the Commission as the 'Sleeping Beauty of the Forest'.[78]

17.8.2 REACTIONS TO VIOLATIONS

(1) Under the traditional framework of the laws of war, belligerents enjoyed great discretion in resorting to *belligerent reprisals*, consisting in the violation of rules of warfare in response to an alleged prior violation by the other belligerent (on the general notion of reprisals, see **14.1.3**). Instances of belligerent reprisals were the maltreatment of prisoners of war, the unlawful bombardment of 'undefended' localities or of buildings immune from attack, etc. This made belligerent reprisals a barbaric institution, ultimately leading to the killing of innocent people, punished for the misdeeds of their fellow countrymen. In addition, they lent themselves to abuses owing to the absence of any impartial verification of violations by the enemy.

Therefore, progressively, there has been a trend towards banning or restricting recourse to belligerent reprisals. The 1949 Geneva Conventions have banned reprisals against 'protected persons' (prisoners of war, the wounded, sick, or shipwrecked, and civilians who found themselves in the hands of the enemy). Additional Protocol I has extended the ban to a series of civilian persons or civilian objects (Articles 51(6), 53(c), 54(4), 55(2), and 56(4) of AP I). It can be argued that this ban reflects the current status of customary international law, and thus binds all States regardless of whether they are parties to it or have entered reservations.[79]

---

[77] Albeit outside of its treaty mandate, the Commission concluded its first and only inquiry on an accident which occurred in Ukraine in 2017, upon request of the OSCE. A redacted summary of the report is available online at https://www.osce.org/home/338361.

[78] F. Kalshoven, 'The International Humanitarian Fact-Finding Commission: A Sleeping Beauty?' (2002) 4 *Humanitäres Völkerrecht* 213, reprinted in F. Kalshoven, *Reflections on the Law of War: Collected Essays* (Leiden: Brill, 2007), 835.

[79] See the decision of the ICTY in *Kupreškić et al.*, where Trial Chamber II put forward the proposition that 'the demands of humanity and the dictates of public conscience, as manifested in *opinio necessitatis*, have by now brought about the formation of a customary rule also binding upon those few States that at some stage did not intend to exclude the abstract legal possibility of resorting to the reprisals [against civilians not in the hands of the enemy belligerents, i.e. in the combat zone]' (at §533). The Court among other things based its contention on the notion that 'while reprisals could have had a modicum of justification in the past, when they constituted practically the only means of compelling the enemy to abandon unlawful acts of warfare and to comply in future with international law, at present they can no longer be justified in this manner. A means of inducing compliance with international law is at present more widely available and, more importantly, is beginning to prove fairly efficacious: the prosecution and punishment of war crimes and crimes against humanity by national or international courts' (at §530).

Belligerent reprisals that are still not prohibited are subject to a number of conditions: (i) resort to them must be preceded by a warning to the adversary (the purpose of such warning obviously being to enable the enemy to terminate the breach forthwith); (ii) they must be proportionate to the violation against which they react; (iii) the decision to visit reprisals on the adversary must be made at the highest level, not by the combatants in the field (the rationale for such condition being that the overall effects and implications of taking reprisals must be weighed before resorting to such a perilous means of enforcement of the law); (iv) reprisals must be terminated as soon as the adversary's breach comes to an end (otherwise they lose their rationale and turn into an unlawful use of military force).

(2) Another traditional means of ensuring compliance with the rules of IHL is the punishment of enemy combatants or civilians guilty of *war crimes*, that is, serious violations of the laws of warfare. As will be pointed out later in this book (see **19.2.1**) war crimes may be prosecuted and repressed both by national courts (that is, those of the national or territorial State, or of a third State, whenever the requisite conditions are met), and at the international level (by the ICTY, the ICTR, the ICC, the Special Court for Sierra Leone, or other international criminal court or tribunal as long as it has jurisdiction). For a specific class of war crimes (the so-called 'grave breaches'), the Geneva Conventions and AP I enshrine mandatory prosecution or extradition by domestic jurisdictions under the so-called *aut dedere aut iudicare* principle.

17.8.3 COMPENSATION FOR DAMAGE

It is well known that under international law a State that commits a wrongful act is liable to make reparation, and that reparation may take various forms, including monetary compensation (see **12.7**). As for violations of rules of IHL, the obligation to provide for compensation is detailed in Article 3 of the 1907 Hague Convention IV, which provides that belligerent parties which violate the Annexed Regulation are liable to pay compensation. This obligation is reaffirmed in Article 91 of AP I.

As the ICRC Commentary on AP I aptly observes, the purpose of both Article 3 of Hague IV and of Article 91 of AP I 'is specifically to prevent the vanquished from being compelled in an armistice agreement or peace treaty *to renounce all compensation* due for breaches committed by persons in the service of the victor'.[80] According to the ICRC Commentary, this implies that:

> on the conclusion of a peace treaty, the Parties can in principle deal with the problems relating to war damage in general and those relating to the responsibility of starting the war ... On the other hand, they are not free ... to deny compensation to which the victims of violations of the rules of the Convention and Protocol are entitled.

In light of the above, one may therefore clearly distinguish between the so-called 'war indemnities' or 'war reparations', requested by the victor once the war is over and usually covering the damage caused by starting the war (while the defeated had no means of doing likewise), and compensation for violations of the rules of warfare, which are due by all parties to the conflict in case of violations of the rules of warfare. The post-conflict settlements concluded to deal with war-related claims thus have no bearing on the interpretation of the relevant provisions of Hague Convention and AP I. This practice does not relate to the application of the obligation to provide for compensation enshrined in those provisions. These post-war settlements did not cover any injury or loss inflicted by the victorious states

---

[80] ICRC Commentary to Additional Protocol I, §3651 (emphasis added).

as a result of violations of rules of warfare, and are therefore in clear contrast with the wording, scope, and purpose of the aforementioned provisions on compensation.

Claims for compensation are normally dealt with in interstate relations, and compensation can be paid directly by the responsible State to the claimant State (e.g. this happened in the case of the unlawful bombing of the Chinese embassy in Belgrade by US air forces in 1999, during the NATO bombing campaign against Yugoslavia (Operation Allied Force)).[81] Claims for compensation for breaches of IHL have also been brought by individuals suing the alleged responsible State either before the courts of such State or the courts of other competent States.

These claims have often been dismissed on a variety of grounds, such as that foreign States enjoy sovereign immunity for acts of war,[82] or because individuals do not have any claim to compensation under international law for violations of IHL,[83] or by invoking the political question doctrine or the act of state doctrine, also called the doctrine of non-accountability of the State for its official acts.[84] The cases where courts have upheld jurisdiction and where such cases were decided on the merits are relatively few.[85]

Arguably, denying individuals the right to seek compensation before domestic courts for violations of rules of IHL by the application of doctrines such as that of sovereign immunity, non-justiciability, or similar doctrine is at odds with the current evolution of international law and its progressive 'individualization'. Belligerents owe specific duties in relation to individuals in the event of armed conflicts and there is no reason why individuals should not also enjoy the right to reparation in cases of violations of the relevant rules of IHL. Their claims should therefore be heard at the domestic level, especially when recourse to national courts is the only means available to seek reparation for the injuries which they have suffered.

17.9 AN OVERALL ASSESSMENT

Over the years, humankind has witnessed steady progress in the sophistication, the devastating effects, and the cruelty of weapons and methods of combat. International *legal control* of warfare has kept pace with the developments in organized armed violence only to a

---

[81] On 8 May 1999, US aircraft bombed the Chinese embassy in Belgrade, causing the death of three 'journalists' and injuring 20 Embassy staff members. On 17 June 1999, a US senior official (Ambassador Thomas Pickering, Under Secretary of State) stated in Beijing that 'the attack was a mistake', resulting from 'a series of errors and omissions'. The bombing was 'accidental' and 'completely unintended'. The US official offered 'sincere apologies' to China's leaders and 'sympathy to the families of those who died and to the injured' (see the text of the statement of Mr Pickering online at http://www.state.gov/documents/organization/ 6524.doc). On 30 July 1999, the two States made an agreement on compensation to the victims and their families (http://www.state.gov/documents/organization/6526.doc). On 16 December 1999 the US and China then entered into an agreement providing for compensation to China (see online at http://www.state.gov/documents/organization/ 6521–6522.doc). Interestingly, the agreements did not specify that the US was responsible for violating China's rights, nor that the payment was *ex gratia*.

[82] See e.g. the numerous cases brought before Japanese courts for violations of the laws of warfare in the Second World War, such as, *Filipino 'comfort' women* v *Japan*, and *Sjoerd Albert Lapre and others* v *Japan*; one may also mention *Margellos*, brought before the Greek Supreme Special Court provided for under Article 100.1(b) of the Greek Constitution, as well as some American cases: *Princz* v *Federal Republic of Germany*, and *Fishel* v *BASF Group and others*; *Kalogeropoulou and others* v *Greece and Germany*, a case taken to the European Court of Human Rights should also be mentioned.

[83] See e.g. the *Chinese Women* case.

[84] See e.g. *Shimoda* v *Japan*, and *Presidenza del Consiglio dei Ministri* v *Marković and others*.

[85] See e.g. *Korean 'Comfort' Women* v *Japan*, *Prefecture of Voiotia* v *Germany*, as well as *Ferrini* v *Federal Republic of Germany*.

limited extent. States and, in particular, major military Powers have not accepted sweeping restraints, with the consequence that this body of law is beset with deficiencies, loopholes, and ambiguity.

However, legal rules, no matter how weak and defective, do restrict the behaviour of States and non-State armed groups and do introduce a modicum of humanity into utterly inhuman conduct. The absence of normative standards would be even more regrettable: it would leave belligerents free of any restraint. Furthermore, it is precisely the nature of the laws of warfare (see **17.1**) which makes it clear that here, more than in any other area, legal standards possess significant juridical value: they also serve as a moral and political yardstick by which public opinion and non-governmental groups and associations can appraise if, and to what extent, belligerents misbehave.

18
THE PROTECTION OF HUMAN RIGHTS

18.1 INTRODUCTION

Since 1945, the doctrine of human rights has been troubling and upsetting some, inflaming and thrilling others, whether individuals, groups, or non-governmental organizations, or members of cabinet, diplomats, or other State officials. At the State level, since the Second World War this doctrine has become, for some countries, one of the significant postulates of their foreign policy, of great use when blaming or denouncing other countries, or guiding their actions within international organizations. To other States this doctrine has turned out to be an incubus instead: it serves as a yardstick by which their behaviour is gauged and may be censured in international fora.

The arrival of human rights on the international scene is, indeed, a remarkable event because it is a *subversive* theory destined to foster tension and conflict among States. Essentially it is meant to tear aside the veil that in the past protected sovereignty and gave each State the appearance of a fully armoured titanic structure, perceived by other States only 'as a whole', the inner mechanisms of which could not be tampered with. Today, the human rights doctrine forces States to give account of how they treat their own nationals, administer justice, run prisons, and so on. Potentially, therefore, it can subvert their domestic order and, consequently, the traditional configuration of the international community as well.

On the whole, one can say that within the international community this doctrine has acquired the value and significance which, within the context of domestic systems, was accorded to Locke's theory of a social contract, Montesquieu's concept of the separation of powers, and Rousseau's theory of the sovereignty of the people. Just as these political ideas eroded absolute and despotic monarchy, democratizing the foundations on which kingdoms rested, so the doctrine of human rights has lent, and still lends, in the world community, tremendous impetus to respect for the dignity of all human beings, and also to the democratization of States.

Why then did States support and even advocate this 'theory' at an international level, knowing full well that it diverged radically from the political philosophy of State sovereignty and the basic principle on which the 'Grotian model' rested? What political and ideological motives induced certain members of the international community to propound ideas likely to undermine and disrupt their own authority?

18.2 CLASSICAL INTERNATIONAL LAW

Traditionally, individuals were under the exclusive jurisdiction of the State of which they were nationals and where they lived. No other State could interfere with the authority of that State, which in a way had a sort of right of life and death over those individuals. Beyond national boundaries individuals could only be taken into consideration qua *citizens* of a foreign State. If they suffered damage abroad, their interests were safeguarded only to the extent to which their national State decided to exercise diplomatic protection (by approaching through diplomatic channels the State that had allegedly wronged one's nationals in their person or property, with a view to obtaining compensation for the damage caused and possibly punishment of the wrongdoers), or judicial protection (by bringing a claim on behalf of one's nationals before an international arbitral tribunal or court). Individuals were mere 'appendices' of the State to which they belonged, simple pawns in its hands, to be used, protected, or sacrificed according to what State interests dictated.

Gradually, however, a few exceptions took shape. Treaties prohibiting the slave trade were concluded in the nineteenth century. Others banning both the slave trade and slavery as such were made during the twentieth century. Conventions were concluded after the First World War, under the auspices of the International Labour Organization (ILO), to protect the rights of workers. In the same period various treaties safeguarding religious, ethnic, and linguistic minorities were agreed upon. All these conventions and treaties, although founded to a great extent on humanitarian considerations, were also motivated by the self-interest of the contracting States.[1] Even so, it remains true that one of the motivations behind these three classes of treaties was the concept that certain groups or categories of individuals ought to be protected by international law for their own sake.

After the Second World War, international protection of human beings as such increased at a staggering pace. Individuals were no longer to be taken care of, on the international level, qua members of a group, a minority, or other category. They began to be protected qua single human beings. Furthermore, the international standards on the matter were no longer motivated, even in part, by economic interests, although they were often dictated by political considerations.

Why did things change so drastically? The main reason was the shared conviction, among all the victorious Powers, that the Nazi aggression and the atrocities perpetrated during the war had been the fruits of a vicious philosophy based on utter disregard for the dignity of human beings. One means of preventing a return to these horrors was the proclamation at all levels of certain basic standards of respect for human rights. This view was propounded with the greatest force by the Western Powers (in particular the US), for the simple reason that their whole political philosophy and, indeed, for some of them, the fundamental legal texts of their national systems, was based on a 'bill of rights'. Therefore, it came naturally to them to project their domestic concepts and creeds onto the international community.

The victors adopted a two-pronged strategy. They pursued, on the one hand, the development of international criminal law to meet the immediate need of bringing to justice and punishing German and Japanese war criminals who had committed inhuman acts. On the other hand, they set out to elaborate a set of general principles on human rights designed to

---

[1] The pressure to put a stop to the trade in black slaves came in part from those European countries which no longer had colonial interests in the Americas and were consequently keen to end the flow of cheap manpower to other countries. In the case of ILO Conventions, guaranteeing uniformity of treatment to workers in all the major areas of the world prevented certain countries from taking unfair advantage in the international market of low labour costs at home. The treaties on minorities (with Czechoslovakia, Greece, Poland, Rumania, and Yugoslavia) as well as the peace treaties including clauses on minorities (those with Austria, Bulgaria, Turkey, and Hungary) were to some extent politically motivated: those European countries which had ethnic, linguistic, or religious affinities with groups living in other countries were eager for these groups to be respected and immune from undue hindrance and interference. What is even more important—as President Wilson pointed out at the Peace Conference on 31 May 1919, in an attempt to rebuff the opposition of States where minorities existed—the international protection of minorities aimed at safeguarding peace, besides attenuating the often harsh consequences of the territorial partitions effected in Europe by the Great Powers (see FRUS, *The Paris Conference 1919*, iii (Washington, DC: Government Printing Office, 1943), 406).

serve as guidelines for the UN and its member States, the intention being that they would be gradually implemented and elaborated upon through traditional normative means, that is to say, treaties.

These two approaches, although distinct, supplement each other. Both stemmed from the desire to punish those guilty of atrocities and, by the same token, prevent the recurrence of similar acts in future by setting standards to be observed even in peacetime.

18.3 THE TURNING POINT: THE UN CHARTER

As pointed out earlier, the lead was taken in 1945 by Western countries and chiefly by the US. President Roosevelt, in his message to Congress of 6 January 1941, had already listed the 'four freedoms', which he saw as important goals of future US foreign policy:

> In the future days, which we seek to make secure, we look forward to a world founded upon four essential human freedoms. The first is freedom of speech and expression—everywhere in the world. The second is freedom of every person to worship God in his own way—everywhere in the world. The third is freedom from want—which, translated into world terms, means economic understandings which will secure to every nation a healthy, peaceful life for its inhabitants—everywhere in the world. The fourth is freedom from fear—which translated into world terms, means a world wide reduction of armaments to such a point and in such a thorough fashion that no nation will be in a position to commit an act of aggression against any neighbour—anywhere in the world.[2]

The elevated concepts enunciated by Roosevelt were taken up in the Atlantic Charter of 14 August 1941 and subsequently amplified by the US delegation to the Dumbarton Oaks Conference in 1944. In the 'US Tentative Proposals for a General International Organization' of 18 July 1944, it was suggested that the General Assembly of the UN should be responsible for

> initiating studies and making recommendations for ... the promotion of the observance of basic human rights in accordance with the principles or undertakings agreed upon by the States members of the International Organization.[3]

It is apparent from this proposal that, once one moved from the proclamation of lofty principles at the political level to the adoption of treaty provisions, even the very State which had championed the inclusion of human rights among the matters under UN jurisdiction eventually proceeded with the utmost caution. Indeed, it took pains to spell out that the Organization should have limited powers only. In particular, the standards on human rights by which member States should be guided were to be first accepted by them through the traditional process of treaty making. The American restraint was clearly motivated by domestic reasons: there were constitutional problems, which the acceptance of international obligations on human rights might raise, but also, and more importantly, in the US in 1945 various racist laws were in force—and continued in force until the 1960s. These laws might easily expose the US government to international censure if internationally binding obligations on human rights were enacted through the UN Charter.

At the Dumbarton Oaks Conference (August–October 1944), the initial opposition of the UK and the USSR led the US to water down its proposals even further. In fact, the provision on human rights produced by the four Powers (the US, the USSR, the UK, and China)

---

[2] See US Congress, *Hearings Documents*, 77th Congress, 1st Session.
[3] See the text of the 'Tentative Proposals' as an appendix to R. B. Russell, *A History of the United Nations Charter: The Role of the United States 1940–1945* (Washington, DC: The Brookings Institution, 1958), 995, at 997.

was quite weak. However, when the San Francisco Conference (April–June 1945) began, the four sponsoring Powers were confronted with a spate of bold amendments, mostly emanating from Latin American countries. This, as well as the conversion of the USSR to the cause of human rights (it put forward specific proposals on the matter, particularly on non-discrimination and self-determination of peoples), led the four Powers to consider it advisable to strengthen their proposals.

In the course of the San Francisco Conference three alignments emerged. On the one hand, there was a group of vocal Latin American countries (chiefly Brazil, Colombia, Chile, Cuba, the Dominican Republic, Ecuador, Mexico, Panama, and Uruguay) plus a few Western States (Australia, New Zealand, and Norway) joined by such nations as India. These countries put forward amendments substantially calculated to lay down an obligation to respect human rights. The second group of States included major Western Powers which, though favourable to the promotion of human rights, opposed the attempts to expand the sphere of action of the UN and to lay down definite obligations to respect human rights. The US took a lead on this score, by objecting strongly to the broadening of Article 56 (on member States' joint and separate action for the promotion of economic and social co-operation) and also by insisting on the need to provide a safeguarding clause protecting State sovereignty from undue interference from the Organization (the proviso that later became Article 2(7) on domestic jurisdiction). A third group, consisting of socialist countries (Byelorussia, Czechoslovakia, and Ukraine) led by the USSR, although substantially upholding the restrictive attitude of the second group just mentioned, distinguished itself by stressing the importance of the right of peoples to self-determination (a right which major Western countries, together with such colonial Powers as Belgium, strongly opposed).

In addition, the USSR put forward proposals clearly showing that differences existed even in areas where there seemingly was agreement between East and West. Thus, for instance, when the four Great Powers met in San Francisco and discussed the proposal that the UN should promote 'respect for human rights', the USSR suggested that this should be followed by the words: 'in particular, the right to work, and the right to education'. The US and the UK opposed this proposal, on the grounds that if it was specified which rights were to be protected, then others should be added—in particular freedom of information and freedom of religion. Similarly, when at San Francisco the report of 'Technical Committee 3' (charged with discussing matters relating to economic and social co-operation) came to be discussed within Commission II of the Conference, the Soviet delegate drew attention to the part played by the USSR in improving on the Dumbarton Oaks proposals and specifically mentioned the principle of respect for human rights. He only spoke of economic, social, and cultural rights, however.[4]

The upshot of the lengthy discussions at San Francisco was that the first group of States did not obtain any substantial gains, while the other two groups reached a compromise which, to some extent, accommodated their mutual demands. The compromise took shape in the following provisions: (i) there was *no specific obligation* to take separate action for the promotion, let alone the protection, of human rights (see Article 56); (ii) the right of self-determination of peoples was proclaimed (Articles 1 and 55), but only as a guiding principle for the Organization and in the *emasculated version of self-government*; (iii) the powers of the General Assembly in the field of human rights, already very weak (they boiled down to *making recommendations* and *conducting studies*), were further limited by the proviso of Article 2(7) (on domestic jurisdiction); (iv) the Charter provisions on human rights were inspired by the conviction that respect for human rights should only be furthered as *a means of safeguarding peace*.

---

[4] For the relevant statements on human rights made at San Francisco see in particular UNCIO, vol. 3, 296ff, vol. 8, 56, 80–1, 85, 90–1. In particular, for the Soviet statement referred to in the text, see vol. 8, 56–7.

18.4 TRENDS IN THE EVOLUTION OF INTERNATIONAL ACTION ON HUMAN RIGHTS

18.4.1 GENERAL

Faced with this normative framework, member States of the UN were to decide how to make use of the loose formulas of the Charter. Generally speaking, two possible courses of action were open to them.

First, they could confine themselves to using the General Assembly as a 'regular diplomatic conference' and accordingly draft conventions or stimulate States to pursue certain objectives by addressing general recommendations to them, in keeping with a liberal construction of Article 2(7) of the UN Charter. Arguably, to have achieved this would by no means have been a poor performance: the mere fact of detailing and spelling out in international instruments the human rights and fundamental freedoms, for the promotion of which States should strive, would have constituted a major accomplishment. Alternatively, a less moderate course of action was available. By placing a strict interpretation on Article 2(7), the Organization could go beyond the mere elaboration of international standards, and call States to account, at least in cases of massive infringements of human rights. To this effect, the UN could turn the General Assembly into the 'conscience of the world', by endowing it with the role of watchdog, to forestall or castigate egregious deviations from basic standards on human rights. In the following pages we shall see that the UN (and regional organizations) gradually took the second path.

The majority in the UN and consequently the prevailing political philosophy underpinning UN action changed in the course of time. One can pinpoint four different phases. The first stage, which dated from the adoption of the UN Charter to the late 1950s, was characterized by Western dominance. At the regional level this approach led to the adoption, within the Council of Europe, of the 1950 European Convention on Human Rights, a landmark in the evolution of the international protection of human rights. The second stage, which started with the strengthening in the UN of the socialist group in 1955 and its taking the lead among developing countries, had as its main feature the need for the West to come to terms with the other two groups, with the consequent striking of a number of important compromises such as the two Covenants on human rights of 1966. The third stage, which began around 1974 and ended around 1990, was marked by the prevalence of developing countries. It launched a new doctrine of human rights, which eventually gained the upper hand in many respects and aimed to supplant or at least tone down, as much as possible, the views previously upheld by the General Assembly. The main feature of the present stage, which opened with the end of the Cold War, is the disappearance of three markedly differentiated groupings of States and the emergence of broad consensus on the need to consider respect for human rights a *sine qua non* for full international legitimation, that is, in order to participate in international intercourse. In the following sections, the main milestones and mechanisms of this overall development are introduced.

18.4.2 THE UNIVERSAL DECLARATION (1948)

The first step was the attempt by the UN General Assembly to draw up an international document on human rights acceptable to all members of the international community: to States as dissimilar ideologically and politically as the US and the USSR; to nations with such different economic and political structures as the Western countries on the one hand and Ethiopia, Saudi Arabia, and Afghanistan on the other; to countries upholding differing religious philosophies, ranging from Christian (the nations of the West and Latin America) to Muslim (such as Saudi Arabia, Afghanistan, Turkey, Pakistan, etc.), Hindu (such as India), and Buddhist (such as China).

It was therefore necessary to find the lowest common denominator, as regards the conception both of the relationship between State and individual, and of basic human rights. The attempt to forge a single, collective stand, a general 'philosophy' of human dignity, was successful, although agreement was only reached after lengthy discussions. The ensuing political document, the Universal Declaration of Human Rights of 10 December 1948, has two basic characteristics, one to do with its formal structure and the other with its content.

In formal terms, it is not legally binding, but it possesses moral and political force. In other words, it is simply a *recommendation* to States. Regarding its content, on the whole, the view of human rights expressed in it is a Western one. More space and importance are allotted to civil and political rights than to economic, social, and cultural rights, and no mention at all is made of the rights of peoples. The position taken with regard to colonized peoples, who had been partially or completely denied their right to freedom, was purely formal. Nor did the Declaration say anything specific about economic inequalities between States (although today many commentators cite with increasing frequency Article 28 whereby '[e]veryone is entitled to a social and international order in which the rights and freedoms set forth in the Declaration can be fully realized'). In addition, one could note that the Declaration did not consider the fact that some States, being underdeveloped, faced special problems when trying to guarantee certain basic rights, such as those to work, to education, to suitable housing, etc.

How did the West succeed in imposing its 'philosophy'? The socialist countries, though putting up a strong resistance to the fact that so little importance was being attributed to economic, social, and cultural rights, were in a minority. All they could do was abstain. Moreover, they had not yet fully worked out a clear strategy of their own. As for the Third World, it was at this stage largely made up of Latin American countries with a Western outlook; the remaining countries simply did not have the strength or authority to stand up to the Western Powers, which incidentally numbered among their delegates influential figures such as Eleanor Roosevelt and René Cassin.

In spite of its limitations, the Declaration was, nevertheless, of great importance in stimulating and directing the international promotion of human rights. It formulated *a unitary and universally valid concept of what values all States should cherish within their own domestic orders*. One particular category of States, the socialist countries, did not support it enthusiastically. Yet neither the socialist nor the developing nations regarded the Declaration as something from which they felt estranged—rather, they looked upon it as a document containing a valid core in need of completion. Consequently, their subsequent efforts were directed not at eroding, let alone jettisoning, the Declaration, but rather at filling its gaps.

On the whole the Declaration remains a lodestar, which has guided the community of States as they gradually emerged from the dark age when the possession of armies, guns, and warships was the sole factor for judging the conduct of States, and there were no generally accepted principles for distinguishing good from evil in the world community.

18.4.3 HUMAN RIGHTS TREATIES

Even before the Universal Declaration was adopted, States had basically agreed on the need to translate its general principles into legally binding instruments.

A twofold strategy gradually unfolded. First, it was felt necessary to spell out the general standards of the Declaration in legally binding instruments of *general purport*, that is, covering the whole range of human rights. This was to be done both at the universal and at the regional level, where the relative political, ideological, and economic homogeneity of States rendered the task less difficult. Secondly, treaties were to be worked out in *specific* areas, notably those considered by the majority of States to be of greater significance and more in need of urgent international legislation (such as genocide, racial discrimination, etc.).

Thus, at the universal level the International Covenant on Civil and Political Rights (ICCPR) (with an Optional Protocol) and that on Economic, Social and Cultural Rights (ICESCR) were adopted in 1966. At the regional level the European Convention on Human Rights was adopted in 1950, the American Convention on Human Rights in 1969, and the African Charter on Human and Peoples' Rights in 1981; in 1994, the Council of the Arab League (with a membership of 22 States) passed the Arab Charter on Human Rights.[5] In parallel, a panoply of other treaties protecting specific rights were adopted at both universal and regional level.

The International Covenants cover the whole range of fundamental rights. However, characteristically the right of property does not figure in either of them. Arguably, this was not due to the fact that the right was no longer considered a value worthy of international protection on a universal level, but rather to the inability of East and West to agree on the issue of compensation in case of expropriation. Be that as it may, this omission was in line with the trend to erode and revise international customary law which in the past had protected the private property of foreigners, requiring 'prompt, adequate, and effective' compensation in the case of expropriation or nationalization (see **21.4.3**).

In addition, for the first time in an international legal document we find that formal or legal equality makes little sense if deep practical inequalities exist. This being the case, it appears right to give legal sanction to certain types of distinction when they come into being as a consequence of practical inequalities. Thus, Article 2(3) of the Covenant on Economic, Social and Cultural Rights lays down that developing countries 'may determine' to what extent they 'would guarantee' the economic rights specified in the Covenant 'to non-nationals'. In other words, they are authorized to discriminate between nationals and foreigners, so long as (a) this is justified by the country's economic circumstances and does not amount to discrimination against citizens of a particular State, and (b) the refusal to award the same status to foreigners and nationals does not lead to serious violations of other human rights. Other treaties that contain provisions envisaging 'affirmative action' for groups discriminated against include the 1965 Convention on racial discrimination (see e.g. Article 1(4)) and the 1979 Convention on discrimination against women (see e.g. Article 4).

At the same time, a host of specific treaties was hammered out, particularly at the universal level. Suffice it to mention, among the most important, the Conventions against genocide (1948), against racial discrimination (1965), on discrimination against women (1979), against torture (1984), on the rights of the child (1989), and on migrant workers (1990), and the 2000 Optional Protocols on the Involvement of Children in Armed Conflict, and on the Sale of Children, Child Prostitution and Child Pornography; as well as the 2002 Optional Protocol to the Torture Convention, the Convention on enforced disappearances (2006), and the Convention on the rights of persons with disabilities (2007).

18.4.4 THE TENDENCY TO OVERRULE THE OBJECTION OF DOMESTIC JURISDICTION

Over the years, the UN tended to reject the objection of State sovereignty put forward by a number of States, and discussed various questions concerning human rights. In general,

---

[5] Although this instrument is not yet in force; see also the Draft Arab Charter on Human Rights, adopted on 5–14 January 2004 by the Arab Standing Committee for Human Rights, online at http://www.pogar.org/themes/reforms/documents/dacharter.pdf.

however, these questions concerned large-scale, flagrant violations of human rights, rather than isolated cases. The UN justified its 'intervention' on the grounds that these violations constituted a threat to peace and to friendly relations between States. The line taken was warranted in the same terms as those used while drafting the UN Charter: respect for human rights as a means of securing peace, thereby dispelling misgivings that the Organization would suffer from a paralysing fear of trespassing on State sovereignty. This 'intervention' could take various forms: public discussion in a UN body, adoption of a resolution on the matter, the making of appeals, requesting the State concerned to stop the violations forthwith, or even recommending to member States that peaceful 'sanctions' should be taken against the delinquent State.

However, as a result of the growing network of international treaties and the establishment of the monitoring procedures to which we shall shortly refer, the conviction gradually took hold among UN members that 'intervention' in the affairs of individual States was fully justified, so long as *serious and large-scale violations* had been allegedly committed, regardless of whether they amounted to a threat to peace or to friendly relations between States.

To grasp the importance of this new trend and the sea change that has occurred, over the last few decades, in the relations between universal interstate organizations and individuals living within member States and whose human rights are allegedly breached, one need only remember how the Council of the League of Nations reacted to the complaint of a German national of Jewish origin in 1933 (the *Bernheim* case), and, more generally, to large-scale and harsh discrimination against Jews in Germany.[6]

---

[6] In 1933 Franz Bernheim complained to the Council of the League of Nations about the breaches by Germany of the German-Polish Treaty of 1922, protecting minorities in Upper Silesia (at the time belonging to Germany); in particular, he insisted on the fact that the anti-Jewish laws promulgated in Germany in 1933, and by virtue of which he (like all Jewish employees) had been sacked by a German firm, were contrary to the Treaty (see League of Nations, *Official Journal*, Year XIV, July 1933, 833–935 and October 1933, *Special Supplement* no. 114, 1–3 and 22). The German delegate asked that the complaint be dismissed because Bernheim had no link with Upper Silesia (League of Nations, *Official Journal*, Year XIV, July 1933, 839). The Polish delegate noted that admittedly from a formal point of view the Council could only deal with the fate of Jewish minorities in Upper Silesia. Nevertheless, '[a]ll members of the Council had ... at least a moral right to make a pressing appeal to the German Government to ensure equal treatment for the Jews in Germany' (ibid., at 841). He wrapped up his eloquent speech by stating that '[a] minimum of rights must be guaranteed to every human being, whatever his race, religion, or mother tongue' (ibid.). A Committee of Jurists was appointed. It found Germany in the wrong but decided to take note of an assertion made previously by the German delegate: if some blame had to be assigned to Germany, confined obviously to Upper Silesia, it could only derive from 'errors due to misconstructions of internal [German] law by subordinate authorities; these errors would be corrected' (at 842). On the strength of this affirmation the Council adopted a report inviting Germany to bring the violations to an end. It would seem that Germany made no follow-up to the Council's exhortation. But the question of discrimination against Jews did not rest there. A few months later the question of whether in every modern civil State all citizens ought to enjoy equal treatment came up before a Committee of the League's Assembly. Germany insisted that this was an internal matter, while France took the contrary position, contending among other things that if a treaty protected minorities in one part only of a country, minorities were nonetheless to be protected in other parts of the territory of the country as well, for the treaty provisions must not be interpreted as excluding some categories of citizens from the benefits they granted (a clear reference to the *Bernheim* case) (League of Nations, *Official Journal*, 1933, *Special Supplement* no. 120 (Minutes of the Sixth Committee—Political questions), 28). The German delegate retorted that 'the Jewish problem in Germany [was] a special problem *sui generis* and [could] not possibly be treated ... simply like an ordinary minority question' (ibid., at 42). Although amended by the Greek delegate, N. Politis, the French proposal was rejected by Germany. Consequently, pursuant to Article 5 of the Covenant that required unanimity, the French-Greek proposal did not carry. Only three days after the rejection of that proposal, on 14 October 1933, Hitler announced Germany's withdrawal from the League, because other States were not prepared to grant it 'true equality of rights', and thereby put Germany in an 'undignified' position. Respect for human dignity thus came up against its first stumbling block in Germany's firm stance that national sovereignty could not tolerate any international interference by an international body in internal affairs.

18.4.5 EXPANSION OF THE TERRITORIAL SCOPE OF HUMAN RIGHTS OBLIGATIONS

When States undertake obligations in the area of human rights, they tend to consider that such obligations apply to individuals subject to their jurisdiction in their own territory. In other words, they construe these obligations as having a strictly territorial scope. This, for instance, was the interpretation they inclined to place on Article 2 of the Covenant on Civil and Political Rights, whereby '[e]ach state Party . . . undertakes to respect and to ensure to all individuals within its territory and subject to its jurisdiction the rights recognized in the present Covenant'.

However, international bodies responsible for scrutinizing compliance with human rights standards have increasingly interpreted those obligations as also having an *extraterritorial scope*. Thus, for instance, in 1995 the UN Human Rights Committee, in commenting on the report submitted by the US, noted that it could not share the view of the US government that the ICCPR lacked extraterritorial reach under all circumstances:

> Such a view [it went on to point out] is contrary to the consistent interpretation of the Committee on this subject that, in special circumstances, persons may fall under the subject matter jurisdiction of a State party even when outside that State territory.[7]

More specifically, in *Delia Saldías de Lopez (on behalf of her husband Sergio Ruben Lopez Burgos) v Uruguay* the Committee had already ruled that Uruguay had violated the Covenant when its security forces had abducted and tortured in Argentina a Uruguayan citizen living there. It had noted that:

> The reference in Article 1 of the Optional Protocol to 'individuals subject to its jurisdiction' does not affect the above conclusion [that the Covenant also covered conduct of Uruguayans acting on foreign soil] because the reference in that Article is not to the place where the violations occurred, but rather to the relationship between the individuals and the State in relation to a violation of any of the rights set forth in the Covenant, wherever they occurred. Article 2(1) of the Covenant places an obligation upon a State party to respect and to ensure rights 'to all individuals within its territory and subject to its jurisdiction', but it does not imply that the State party concerned cannot be held accountable for violations of rights under the Covenant which its agents commit upon the territory of another State, whether with the acquiescence of the Government of that State or in opposition to it . . . In line with this, it would be unconscionable to so interpret the responsibility under Article 2 of the Covenant as to permit a State party to perpetrate violations of the Covenant on the territory of another State, which violations it could not perpetrate on its own territory. (at §§12.2–12.3)[8]

In an important case *(Loizidou v Turkey (Preliminary Objections))*, the European Court of Human Rights carried this doctrine even further. The question had arisen of whether the denial by Turkish armed forces stationed in Northern Cyprus, of the Cypriot applicant's access to her property in Northern Cyprus, was imputable to Turkey and consequently fell under Turkey's jurisdiction pursuant to Article 1 of the European Convention on Human Rights. The Court gave an affirmative answer, ruling that what mattered was that Turkey had effective or overall control over the armed forces stationed in an area outside its national territory (at §57). The Inter-American Commission of Human Rights spelled out this doctrine more forcefully in *Coard et al. v US*. The question at issue was whether the US could be held responsible for violating the 1948 American Declaration on the Rights

---

[7] UN Doc. CCPR/C/79/Add 50 (1995), 19.
[8] See also *Lilian Celiberti de Casariego v Uruguay*, §5 and *Montero v Uruguay*, §§10.1–10.3.

and Duties of Man for allegedly holding incommunicado and mistreating 17 Grenadian nationals in Grenada in October 1983, when US and Caribbean armed forces invaded the island, deposing the 'revolutionary government'. In its report of 29 September 1999 the Commission replied in the affirmative.[9]

This case law (restated and confirmed by the ICJ in *Legal Consequences of the Construction of a Wall*, at §§108–111), is consistent with the object and purpose of human rights obligations: they aim at protecting individuals against arbitrariness, abuse, and violence, regardless of the location where the State conduct occurs.

It follows from the above that States are to respect human rights obligations not only in their own territory but also abroad, when they exercise there some kind of authority or power, whether the individuals subject to this authority or power have the State's nationality or are foreigners. In addition, the meaning of 'exercise of authority' should be interpreted as encompassing not only the display of sovereign powers (law-making, law enforcement, administrative powers, etc.), but also any exercise of power, however limited in time (e.g. the use of belligerent force in an armed conflict).

Indeed, recent pronouncements have confirmed the notion that human rights obligations extend beyond the territory of the State. The Human Rights Committee, for example, discussing the right to life, clearly reaffirmed that each

> State part[y has] an obligation to respect and to ensure the rights [of] all persons who are within its territory and [of] all persons subject to its jurisdiction, that is, all persons over whose enjoyment of the right to life it exercises power or effective control. This includes persons located outside any territory effectively controlled by the State, whose right to life is nonetheless impacted by its military or other activities in a direct and reasonably foreseeable manner. States also have obligations under international law not to aid or assist activities undertaken by other States and non-State actors that violate the right to life. Furthermore, States parties must respect and protect the lives of individuals located in places, which are under their effective control, such as occupied territories, and in territories over which they have assumed an international obligation to apply the Covenant.[10]

Moreover, a similar approach has been invoked for economic, social, and cultural rights, with the idea that an extraterritorial scope for obligations under the ICESCR would entail a greater (and much needed) co-operation by States parties in achieving the goals promoted by the treaty.[11]

---

[9] It noted that, '[g]iven that individual rights inhere simply by virtue of a person's humanity, each American State is obliged to uphold the protected rights of any person subject to its jurisdiction. While this most commonly refers to persons within a State's territory, it may, under given circumstances, refer to conduct with an extraterritorial locus where the person concerned is present in the territory of one State, but subject to the control of another State—usually through the acts of the latter's agents abroad. In principle, the inquiry turns not on the presumed victim's nationality or presence within a particular geographic area, but on whether, under the specific circumstances, the State observed the rights of a person subject to its authority and control' (at §37).

[10] See UN Doc. CCPR/C/GC/36, HRC General Comment No. 36 dated 3 September 2019 (adopted at the 8 October–2 November 2018 session) online at https://tbinternet.ohchr.org/_layouts/15/treatybodyexternal/Download.aspx?symbolno=CCPR%2fC%2fGC%2f36&Lang=en.

[11] See UN Doc. E/C.12/GC/24, 10 August 2017, General Comment No. 24 (2017) on State obligations under the International Covenant on Economic, Social and Cultural Rights in the context of business activities, online at https://tbinternet.ohchr.org/_layouts/15/treatybodyexternal/Download.aspx?symbolno=E%2fC.12%2fGC%2f24&Lang=en.

18.4.6 UNIVERSAL SUPERVISORY MECHANISMS

Clearly, in general, the best means of ensuring respect for a right is to back it up with legal guarantees to be administered by a court of law. We have, however, already mentioned that in the international community the judicial settlement of disputes is often rendered all but impossible by the lukewarm attitude of many States. In the case of human rights, opposition to international adjudication is even stronger. The need to strike a compromise between State sovereignty and the requirement that States comply with international standards on human rights led to the establishment of a number of monitoring mechanisms—which are weaker than international adjudication but nevertheless important.

The principal mechanisms created in this period at the *universal* level were of two kinds: those established by international treaties and those set up by UN resolutions. Among the former, one should mention—at the world level—the procedures created by the 1965 Convention on racial discrimination (monitored by the Committee on the Elimination of Racial Discrimination); the Covenant on Civil and Political Rights of 1966, with its Optional Protocol (the monitoring body is the Human Rights Committee); the mechanism established in 1985 on the strength of the 1966 UN Covenant on Economic, Social and Cultural Rights, further enriched by the 2008 Optional Protocol which entered into force in 2013 and which has also enabled the Committee on Economic, Social and Cultural Rights to hear individual complaints; the 1979 Convention on the elimination of discrimination against women (establishing a Committee with the same name, whose powers were strengthened by the 1999 Optional Protocol); the 1984 Convention on torture (on the strength of which the Committee against Torture was established); the supervisory mechanism established by the 1989 Convention on the protection of the child (Committee on the Rights of the Child); and the Committee established by the 1990 Convention on the Rights of Migrant Workers and Their Families, as well as the 2006 Convention on Enforced Disappearances and the 2007 Convention on the Rights of Persons with Disabilities (which provide for the establishment of independent monitoring Committees).[12]

Normally, the Conventions just mentioned establish three supervisory procedures: (i) A procedure based on the examination of *periodic reports* submitted by States. (This is, of course, the weakest and it is no coincidence that it is the scrutiny applicable to all contracting States.) (ii) The procedure for the examination of *interstate complaints*, which a contracting State can set in motion against another party. (It can work only with regard to those States which, in addition to ratifying the Convention, have also accepted a special clause providing for the procedure. So far it has not yielded any major result, for of course States refrain from engaging in reciprocal accusations.) (iii) The procedure operating at the *request of individuals* or groups of individuals, who may file with the supervisory body a 'communication' setting out the violations allegedly perpetrated by a State. (Like the previous procedure, it is provided for in an 'optional clause', but it has proved effective, within the limitations inherent in any supervisory mechanism: see **13.6**.)

In addition, more recent treaties provide for the possibility of establishing independent inquiries (e.g. the 2007 Optional Protocol to the Convention on the Rights of Persons with Disabilities and the 2008 Optional Protocol to the ICESCR). Inquiries represent a new instrument in the toolbox of monitoring bodies, which can become useful in establishing facts in a more accurate manner and preserving them for future reference.

At UN level there have been two major areas of institutional development concerning human rights monitoring mechanisms. First, the establishment of an ad hoc body,

---

[12] For the full list see the dedicated website of the UN Office of the High Commissioner for Human Rights, at https://www.ohchr.org/EN/HRBodies/Pages/Overview.aspx.

consisting of elected member States, which organizes thematic as well as country-specific monitoring procedures of various kinds. This body was initially the Commission on Human Rights (established by the ECOSOC in 1946 and operational until 2006), replaced since 2006 by the Human Rights Council (composed of 47 States elected by the General Assembly).[13] The HR Council—which builds on the experience of the Commission—is 'responsible for promoting universal respect for the protection of all human rights and fundamental freedoms for all, without distinction of any kind and in a fair and equal manner'.[14] The Council, which has its seat in Geneva, operates through a variety of mechanisms. The system provides for three main kinds of mechanism: (i) the 'Universal Periodic Review', which is an assessment of the human rights situations in all member States (every year a group of States submits its reports to the Council and is 'examined'); (ii) the system of 'complaint procedures' which allows individuals and organizations to bring human rights violations to the attention of the Council; and (iii) the activities through the UN Special Procedures (most of which were already established by the old Commission on Human Rights), which are today overseen and co-ordinated by the Council. These special procedures assume various forms, which could be the appointment of Special Rapporteurs (normally on thematic issues), or special representatives, independent experts, or working groups. The essence is that these organs assist in the effort of monitoring and examining on thematic issues or the situation regarding human rights in specific countries.

The other important development has been the creation in 1993 of the UN Office of the High Commissioner for Human Rights,[15] which laid the foundations for a stable and focused UN Secretariat structure specifically in charge of human rights issues throughout the system. The primary function of the High Commissioner is to play 'an active role ... in preventing the continuation of human rights violations throughout the world'. In order to do so, the Office provides technical assistance to member States to help them fulfil their obligations, and advises other UN organs with a view to mainstreaming human rights. Moreover, the High Commissioner as the leading UN figure in this area is assigned the task of addressing major human rights violations in a timely and objective manner. The role of the High Commissioner can be instrumental in drawing attention to gross violations, calling upon States to abide by international standards. Moreover, the Office—which today comprises 1,300 people and has its headquarters in Geneva—also has field presence in several countries and is involved in UN peace operations and missions across the globe.

In order fairly to appraise the effectiveness of the aforementioned mechanisms, it must be appreciated that (a) they operate in an area where States, although they may have assumed international obligations, are not prepared to submit to international judicial scrutiny; and (b) this area covers matters which are politically extremely sensitive, and which may have international implications at the diplomatic, economic, or commercial level. Consequently, international bodies must tread gingerly, lest States withhold co-operation, thus leaving them unable to act, except for the adoption of condemnatory resolutions. Hence, the various international bodies concerned avoid taking an accusatory approach, that is, they prefer not to engage in the attribution of responsibility to individual governments. Rather, they tend to opt for public exposure and pressure. (However, things are gradually changing in this respect; thus, for instance, the Working Group on Arbitrary Detention issues opinions which do in effect attribute 'responsibility' and various other rapporteurs increasingly tend to write their reports in a similar way.) More generally, they are inclined to take a *'conciliatory'* rather than a *'confrontational'* approach. Seen against

---

[13] The Council was created by the United Nations General Assembly on 15 March 2006 by resolution 60/251.
[14] UN GA resolution 60/251, op. para. 2.
[15] UN GA resolution 48/141.

this backdrop, the mechanisms under discussion may be considered to be reasonably effective in (a) focusing on countries or problems that deserve to be carefully scrutinized; (b) drawing the attention of States, international organizations, NGOs, and public opinion at large to some pivotal issues concerning human rights; (c) exerting pressure upon States with a view to inducing them gradually to improve their human rights record; (d) contributing to the creation of an international ethos requiring respect for at least some core human rights; and (e) serving as a catalyst for the gradual elaboration of new international conventions or the adoption of general resolutions.

However, one should not ignore some major failings of these mechanisms: (i) They tend to be so conditioned, in their unfolding, by political and diplomatic considerations, that often their final result is rather weak, being couched in terms that are too general or too diplomatic. (ii) The reports of the various working groups or individuals often fail to trickle down from the body of specialists or specialist organizations to public opinion at large. Consequently, a wealth of monitoring, information, and expertise is eventually little used outside some restricted circles within the UN.

18.4.7 REGIONAL SUPERVISORY MECHANISMS

Regional supervisory mechanisms are more advanced. They are normally judicial bodies, such as the European Court of Human Rights (ECHR), the Inter-American Commission (IACommHR) and the Inter-American Court of Human Rights (IACHR), and the African Commission and Court on Human and Peoples' Rights.

Among the various judicial bodies just mentioned, the ECHR is by far the most advanced. Under the 11th Protocol of 1994, as well as the subsequent Protocols 14, 15, and 16, the system has been considerably modified compared to the previous system provided for under the 1950 European Convention on Human Rights.[16] Actually, the Court's success has entailed a huge workload (it reached about 70,000 cases in the early 2000s and was at 56,000 pending cases at the beginning of 2019[17]), which has prompted the member States of the Council of Europe to adopt major changes. Today the Court consists of one judge per member State, elected for a single non-renewable term of nine years. Naturally, as an expression of the principle of independence, judges do not represent their country

---

[16] Protocol no. 14 (13 May 2004), by which major changes are made to the European Convention on Human Rights. The principal ones are as follows: (i) the Court's articulation in judicial formations has been increased: under Article 6 the Court 'shall sit in a single-judge formation, in committees of three, in chambers of seven judges and in a Grand Chamber of seventeen judges'; under Article 7 a single judge, assisted by non-judicial rapporteurs, will decide upon so-called 'clearly inadmissible cases' submitted by individuals (currently this is done by committees of three); committees of three judges also have the same power, but in addition, under a simplified summary procedure, can pronounce on the merits of so-called 'repetitive cases', that is, cases concerning questions already 'the subject of well-established Court's case law' (Article 8); (ii) the standards of admissibility of cases have been changed, so as to add to already existing criteria (exhaustion of local remedies, six-month time limit, incompatibility with the Convention, manifestly ill-founded nature of the application, etc.) the criterion of whether or not an individual applicant 'has suffered a significant disadvantage' (Article 12); however, even where no significant disadvantage has been suffered, the Court will nevertheless go fully into the case and pronounce on the merits if (a) respect for human rights requires such examination, or (b) even if the applicant makes minor complaints, the case has however not been duly considered by a domestic court. Changes have also been made to the term of office of judges (from the present six-year renewable term to a single, nine-year term; see Article 2) and to the supervision of the execution of the Court's judgments by the Committee of Ministers (Article 16); in addition, provision has been made for the possible accession of the European Union to the European Convention on Human Rights (Article 17). Pursuant to Article 19 the Protocol shall only enter into force after ratification by all 45 States parties to the European Convention on Human Rights, and this may take some time.

[17] https://www.echr.coe.int/Documents/Stats_pending_2019_BIL.pdf.

of nationality but sit in a personal capacity and are bound neither to seek nor to receive instructions from any source. To face the increasing workload, the Court operates in several judicial formations: a single judge, a panel of three judges, chambers of seven judges, and the Grand Chamber comprising 17 judges.

Each of the States parties to the Convention may refer to the Court any alleged violation of the Convention and its Protocols by another contracting State. In addition, any person, non-governmental organization, or groups of individuals subject to the jurisdiction of any of the contracting States may address a petition to the Court claiming to be the victim of a violation of the Convention or the Protocols. The petitioner fully participates in the proceedings before the Court, on the same footing as the respondent State.

Another important feature of the Court's system today is the procedure for 'pilot judgment', which has been established through practice and subsequently codified in rule 61 of the rules of procedure of the Court. This is an innovative tool which allows the Court, in cases relating to one country which are identical as to the subject matter, to pronounce not only on the specific violation of the Convention in the individual case, but more broadly regarding the structural problems that might affect the actual enjoyment in that country of determined rights provided for under the ECHR.[18]

Moreover, on the basis of Protocol 16 (enacted in 2013, entered into force in 2018) a new system allowing the Court to issue Advisory Opinions has been created. According to the Optional Protocol, the '[h]ighest courts and tribunals of a High Contracting Party [...] may request the Court to give advisory opinions on questions of principle relating to the interpretation or application of the rights and freedoms defined in the Convention or the protocols thereto'. The first Advisory Opinion was rendered on 10 April 2019 on issues regarding the effects of gestational surrogacy on the relationship between the child and the mother.[19]

Despite indisputable organizational problems, the huge backlog, and the slowness in bringing about changes in the legal systems of the various member States, no one can deny that the Court is playing a pivotal role in Europe. It is promoting and seeking to ensure full respect for human rights in countries as diverse as the UK and the Russian Federation, France and Slovakia, Germany and the former Yugoslav Republic of Macedonia. The Court is gradually effecting a harmonization, in the vast area of human rights, of the various legal systems. It is thus contributing to the creation of an extensive region in Europe where arbitrary or discriminatory action by governments is being strongly curtailed.

In the Americas, too, supervisory bodies have been successful (despite both Canada and the US not having accepted the relevant monitoring mechanisms); the Commission and Court are playing an important role. The IACommHR, the headquarters of which are in Washington DC, is an autonomous organ of the Organization of American States (OAS) consisting of seven members elected by the General Assembly of the OAS. It applies the

---

[18] Rule 61—'Pilot-judgment procedure: 1. The Court may initiate a pilot-judgment procedure and adopt a pilot judgment where the facts of an application reveal in the Contracting Party concerned the existence of a structural or systemic problem or other similar dysfunction which has given rise or may give rise to similar applications.' See Rules of Court (3 June 2019) online at https://www.echr.coe.int/Documents/Rules_Court_ENG.pdf.

[19] See ECHR, Grand Chamber, *Advisory Opinion requested by the French Court of Cassation (Request no. P16-2018–001)* concerning the recognition in domestic law of a legal parent–child relationship between a child born through a gestational surrogacy arrangement abroad and the intended mother. A second request for Advisory Opinion was introduced by the Constitutional Court of Armenia in September 2019, related to a provision in Armenia's Criminal Code which penalizes the overthrowing of the Constitutional order. The discussion concerns the proceedings against the former President. See ECHR Press Release 343 (2019), dated 11 October 2019, online at https://hudoc.echr.coe.int/eng-press#{%22itemid%22:[%22003-6534292-8633878%22]}.

1969 American Convention on Human Rights, ratified by 25 States out of the 34 member States of the OAS (contracting parties include Latin American and Central American countries, plus Mexico; as mentioned, neither the US nor Canada is a party to it). The Commission may receive individual petitions alleging human rights violations perpetrated by a member State of the OAS. (For those that are not parties to the Convention, the Commission applies the American Declaration of Rights and Duties of Man adopted in Bogotá in 1948.) If the petition is not held inadmissible, the Commission may carry out investigations, including on-site visits, and hold hearings. It then offers to assist the parties in negotiating a friendly settlement, if they so desire. It may prepare a confidential report, containing possible recommendations to the respondent State. After a certain delay, and if the State has not taken any action on the report, the Commission may decide either to take the case to the Court, or to prepare a second report (giving, among other things, a period of time to the State to resolve the case). After the lapse of that period, the Commission may make its report public.

The Court is composed of seven judges (elected by the States parties to the American Convention on Human Rights) and has its seat in San José (Costa Rica). Only the Inter-American Commission and the States parties to the American Convention may bring cases before the Court. Proceedings may only be initiated against States that are both parties to the Convention and have recognized the Court's jurisdiction. The Court is also endowed with an advisory jurisdiction: it may issue an Advisory Opinion at the request of a member State or of an organ of the OAS. The Court may also issue, at the request of any member State of the OAS, an Opinion on the compatibility of one of its national laws with Inter-American international instruments on human rights. This is a mechanism whereby the Court has issued important pronouncements on thorny legal issues; for example, in 2014 at the request of four States (Argentina, Brazil, Paraguay, and Uruguay) the Court issued an important Advisory Opinion declaring the illegality of the detention of migrant children solely on account of their migration status (*Advisory Opinion OC-21/14*) and, more recently, on 15 November 2017, at the request of Colombia, the Court issued a landmark Opinion on the protection of environment and human rights (*Advisory Opinion OC-23/17*).

In spite of numerous difficulties of all kinds, the Commission and Court have done a remarkable job so far. They have issued important decisions as well as, in the case of the Court, Advisory Opinions. Given the survival (or resurgence) of some authoritarian States on the American continent, the contribution of the two bodies to progress, the rule of law, and respect for human rights should be highlighted.

Finally, the picture is completed by the African Commission and the African Court on Human and Peoples' Rights. The Court was established in 2006 on the basis of the specific 1998 Protocol to the African Charter on Human and Peoples' Rights. Today, about 30 States[20] have ratified the Protocol granting the Court jurisdiction over intrastate disputes concerning the interpretation and application of the African Charter as well as competence to hear cases filed by the African Commission, and to issue Advisory Opinions on human rights obligations of States parties. As of 2019, only nine have made an 'Article 34(6) declaration' recognizing the competence of the Court to receive complaints from

---

[20] Algeria, Benin, Burkina Faso, Burundi, Cameroon, Chad, Comoros, Congo, Côte d'Ivoire, Gabon, The Gambia, Ghana, Kenya, Lesotho, Libya, Malawi, Mali, Mauritania, Mauritius, Mozambique, Niger, Nigeria, Rwanda, Sahrawi Arab Democratic Republic, Senegal, South Africa, Tanzania, Togo, Tunisia, and Uganda.

NGOs and individuals (Benin, Burkina Faso, Côte d'Ivoire, Gambia, Ghana, Mali, Malawi, Tanzania, and Tunisia). The Court is composed of 11 judges elected for a six-year term, renewable only once.

18.4.8 HUMAN RIGHTS, HUMANITARIAN LAW, AND LITIGATION BEFORE DOMESTIC COURTS

In some countries national courts take over, in a way, the functions of governments (which, all too often, seem unmoved by grave violations) and substitute themselves for international enforcement agencies that either do not exist or have proved extremely ineffectual.

Thus, since no international body had passed judgment on whether or not the atomic bombing of Hiroshima and Nagasaki was lawful, and in addition the Japanese government had eventually changed its mind on the matter (in 1945 it had protested, claiming that the bombing was contrary to the laws of warfare), in 1963 a group of survivors sued the Japanese government before the Tokyo District Court. They claimed compensation, arguing that by the peace treaty of 1952 the government had unlawfully waived its rights and claims and those of its nationals towards the US government, including the claims to compensation for the illegal atomic bombing. The court pronounced the bombing illegal, although in the final analysis it held against the complainants (this is the famous *Shimoda* case). In other cases domestic courts pass criminal judgment on individuals whom the territorial State failed to prosecute. The most important in this respect is the famous *Eichmann* case. In its judgment of 29 May 1962, the Supreme Court of Israel dismissed all the submissions of the appellant Eichmann who claimed that Israeli courts lacked jurisdiction over his alleged crimes because there was no territorial or personal link between those crimes and Israel.[21]

This judgment was in a way taken up by a US court in the *Yunis* case. Yunis, a resident and citizen of Lebanon accused of participating in the hijacking of a Jordanian airliner which resulted in the passengers (including several Americans) being held hostage, was brought to trial in the US after being arrested by US authorities on the high seas. Yunis challenged the US courts' jurisdiction, arguing that there was no nexus between the hijacking and the US territory (the aircraft never flew over US airspace and had no contact with US territory). In its judgment of 12 February 1988, the US District Court of the District of Columbia dismissed the defendant's motion and affirmed the jurisdiction of US courts. It held:

> Not only is the United States acting on behalf of the world community to punish alleged offenders of crimes that threatened the very foundations of world order, but the United States has its own interest in protecting its nationals. (at 903)

The country where national courts have taken the most vigorous action against crimes involving serious violations of human rights committed abroad is the US, where individuals and courts have taken down from the shelves and skilfully dusted off an old statute passed in 1789. This is the Alien Torts Claim Act, under which '[t]he [US] district courts shall have original

---

[21] In its final remarks the Court held as follows: 'Not only do all the crimes attributed to the appellant bear an international character, but their harmful and murderous effects were so embracing and widespread as to shake the international community to its very foundations. The State of Israel therefore was entitled, pursuant to the principle of universal jurisdiction and in the capacity of a guardian of international law and an agent for its enforcement, to try the appellant. That being the case, no importance attaches to the fact that the State of Israel did not exist when the offences were committed' (at 304).

jurisdiction of any civil action by an alien for a tort only, committed in violation of the law of nations or a treaty of the United States'. The US courts have applied this statute to gross violations of human rights perpetrated abroad by State officials (or individuals acting in a private capacity) against foreigners, thus obliging the culprits to pay compensation for those violations.[22]

No one can deny the great significance of these US court decisions. In all these cases, US courts filled the gap existing both at the international level (no international collective body took action, nor did other States intervene against the State to which the offending State officials belonged), and at the domestic level (no authority of the territorial State stepped in). Those courts therefore acted on behalf of the international community at large, to vindicate rights pertaining to human dignity. In so doing they proclaimed in judicial decisions some fundamental human values.

However, one should not be unmindful of the limits of this approach. First, these are *civil cases*, where the alleged perpetrator of serious crimes is only enjoined to pay compensation; no conviction is issued at the criminal level. Secondly, as these are cases involving civil litigation only, the person sued may be, and normally is, absent (it is sufficient for him to be served a suit when in the US). Thus, no in-depth examination of evidence takes place. Thirdly, this judicial trend has only occurred in one country. There is the danger for courts of that country of setting themselves up as universal judges of atrocities committed abroad, a sort of humanitarian imperialism that may turn out to be highly controversial. By itself, this trend might not arouse misgivings, if it did not go hand in hand with the tendency of the US Executive to take upon itself the task of policing the world.

18.5 HUMAN RIGHTS AND CUSTOMARY INTERNATIONAL LAW

A significant feature of international legislation, case law, and monitoring activity of the relevant UN organs is that they have had a huge bearing on the traditional configuration of the international community. The human rights doctrine has substantially shaken up that configuration, bringing about significant changes in many areas of international law.

First of all, *certain important customary norms have gradually evolved*, foremost among them being the norm forbidding grave, repeated, and systematic violations of human rights (see **3.9**). Consistent practice and *opinio juris* or *opinio necessitatis* show that other rules now belong to the corpus of customary law: those banning slavery, genocide, and racial discrimination; the norm prohibiting forcible denial of the right of peoples to self-determination; and the rule banning torture. It should be noted that these rules not only bind all States belonging to the international community, whether they have ratified conventions on the subject or not; they also impose community obligations, as the ICJ stressed in the celebrated dictum in the *Barcelona Traction (Belgium v Spain)* case (at §33). Moreover, they have also acquired the status of *jus cogens* (see **11.4.3**).

---

[22] Since 1980, US courts have thus pronounced on torture in Paraguay (*Filartiga v Peña-Irala*); torture and racial discrimination for economic gain in Argentina (*Siderman de Blake v Republic of Argentina*); torture, arbitrary arrest, and forced disappearance in Argentina (*Forti v Suarez-Mason*); arbitrary killing and summary executions in East Timor (*Todd v Panjaitan* and *Doe v Lumintang*); torture, summary execution, and forced disappearances in the Philippines (*Marcos*); atrocities in Bosnia and Herzegovina (*Karadžić*); torture and arbitrary detention in Haiti (*Paul v Avril*); torture in Guatemala (*Gramajo*); torture in Ethiopia (*Hirute Abebe-Jira and others v Kelbessa Negewo*); terrorist bombing in Lockerbie, Scotland (*Abdelbaset Ali Mohmed Al-Megrahi and Al Amin Khalifa Fhimah*); and torture in El Salvador (*Ford et al. v García et al.*). In 2004, in *Sosa v Alvarez-Machain*, the US Supreme Court upheld, subject to some qualifications, the legal significance of the US Statute used to react to gross violations of human rights abroad, normally the Alien Torts Claims Court.

In addition, since these customary rules impose community obligations (see **1.8.2**), there now exists a *legal entitlement* for any State or international organization competent in the area of human rights to request States where gross and large-scale violations of human rights are allegedly occurring to discontinue such violations. If they are not ended, States are authorized to take, in addition to diplomatic or economic steps amounting to retortion proper (see **14.2.2**), peaceful countermeasures (suspension or termination of treaties, withholding of economic assistance provided for in bilateral or multilateral treaties, etc.).

Individual countermeasures may be taken after the various means available within collective bodies have been exhausted, or have proved ineffective, or they may be taken with the authorization of an intergovernmental organization (see **14.2.3**). In contrast, it would seem that, so far, no customary rule has yet evolved to legitimize *forcible* countermeasures against massive and egregious infringements of human rights amounting to crimes against humanity (see **14.2.4**).

In practice, States tend to employ retortion more frequently than countermeasures proper. One may recall, for example, the action taken since 1989 by the US against Burma/Myanmar. Mention may also be made of the decision of the Italian Senate in 1999, upheld by the Italian government,[23] to make economic assistance by Italy to Guatemala contingent upon Guatemala's implementation of the recommendations contained in the Final Report of 25 February 1999 of the Commission for Historical Clarification established through the Accord of Oslo of 23 June 1994 between the Government of Guatemala and the Guatemalan National Revolutionary Unity.[24] It would appear that, in view of the Guatemalan failure to comply with the Report's recommendations, the Italian decision was carried through, although Guatemala considered that it amounted to unlawful interference in its domestic affairs.[25]

Arguably, in addition to the rules already referred to, which have no doubt evolved in the world community, another customary rule is gradually crystallizing as a result of a host of UN GA resolutions and international treaties, as well as the increasing case law of the ICTY on rape and sexual assault; this is the rule banning gender discrimination. Probably another general norm is currently in the process of coming into being: the rule that grants a *right to democratic governance* to all persons under the jurisdiction of a State.[26] However, for the time being, the right to democracy has not yet taken root either as a human right belonging to all the individuals living in a State, or as a legal entitlement accruing to any

---

[23] See *Senato della Repubblica*, XIII Legislatura, 634th Seduta pubblica, *Resoconto sommario e stenografico*, 17 June 1999, 16–27, and 36–9, online at http://www.senato.it/service/PDF/PDFServer/BGT/5335.pdf.

[24] See *Guatemala—Memory of Silence, Report of the Commission for Historical Clarification—Conclusions and Recommendations* (1999).

[25] See C. Tomuschat, 'Vergangenheitsbewältigung durch Aufklärung: Die Arbeit der Wahrheitskommission in Guatemala' in U. Fastenrath (ed.), *Internationaler Schutz der Menschenrechte* (Dresden and Munich: Dresden University Press, 2000), 173, n. 53.

[26] This general norm was first propounded as a result of the 'codification' of existing practice, in the principle of internal self-determination laid down in the 1970 UN Declaration on Friendly Relations; at that stage it was however confined to granting the right to equal access to government to racial groups denied such access. A number of subsequent factors gradually expanded that notion: the increasing ratification by States of the UN Covenants (which confer the right to internal self-determination on the whole people of each contracting State); the signing by 53 States (in Europe, and the US and Canada) of the 1975 Helsinki Declaration (which explicitly grants the right of self-determination to all peoples) and its follow-up Declarations adopted by the Conference on Security and Co-operation in Europe (CSCE, as it then was) and explicitly laying down a right to democracy or to democratic institutions as a goal to be pursued by all States; the attitude taken in 1991–92 by the European Community on the occasion of the break-up of the Soviet Union and Yugoslavia and, in particular, the great emphasis laid by the 12 EC States (as they then were) on respect for democracy and the rights of minorities; the spread of democratic governance to many Latin American countries, coupled with the formal upholding of the

State, to claim respect for democracy by other States. At present, the notion of democracy is being used in international fora, on different scores. Thus, for instance, respect for democracy may constitute one of the criteria States adopt for according or withholding recognition of new States (see **4.3**). Similarly, that notion may be used in the UN in accrediting the representatives of the government of a State: as has happened in many instances (Haiti in 1992, Liberia in 1991–96, Afghanistan in 1996–98, Sierra Leone in 1997, and Cambodia in 1997–98), the UN Credentials Committee has accredited, and entitled to participate in the UN GA as representatives of their respective States, the delegates of the government it considered democratic, even though that government was not yielding control over the population and the territory of the State.[27]

18.6 THE IMPACT OF HUMAN RIGHTS ON CLASSICAL INTERNATIONAL LAW

The human rights doctrine has positively *influenced various fields of classical international law*. It has helped to introduce a new paradigm in the international community, as the ICTY Appeals Chamber stated in 1995 in its seminal decision in *Tadić (Interlocutory Appeal)* (at §97).

Suffice it to mention here the impact on recognition of new States or governments (see **4.3**), international legal personality (see **8.2**), customary law (see **9.3**), the structure of international obligations (see **1.8**), reservations to treaties (see **10.5**), termination of treaties (see **10.9**), *jus cogens* (see **11.4**), international monitoring of compliance with law (see **13.6**), enforcement, including countermeasures (see **14.2**), the administration of international criminal justice (see **Chapter 19**), the laws of warfare or, to use a modern expression, the humanitarian law of armed conflict (see **Chapter 17**).

---

principles of democracy by both these States and other developing countries in other continents; the adoption of resolutions on democracy by the UN General Assembly (e.g. resolutions 50/172, and 50/185, both of 1996), by the UN Human Rights Commission (e.g. resolutions 1999/57 of 28 April 1999, 2000/47 of 25 April 2000, 2000/167 of 4 October 2000), and by the General Assembly of the OAS (e.g. resolution 1080 (XXI-O/91) of 5 June 1991). Mention should also be made of mechanisms and institutions set up within the UN, the OSCE, or the OAS on the monitoring of elections, to ensure a democratic process. All these factors are clear indications of an important trend: States are increasingly accepting the idea that the right to democratic governance (also termed, less stringently, internal self-determination) should have a broad purport and consequently apply to the people of each sovereign State. The fact that pronouncements of States to the contrary are isolated seems to bear out the contention that customary law is in the process of emerging. What is meant by democracy? Many non-Western States have opposed the Western model (see e.g. the statements made in 1999 by various States in the UN Human Rights Commission: India (*Summary Records*, 57th Meeting, E/CN.4/1999/SR 57, §7), Pakistan (ibid., at §11), Cuba (ibid., at §21), Russia (ibid., at §29), Indonesia (ibid., at §40), and China (ibid., at §§41–42), see online at https://documents-dds-ny.un.org/doc/UNDOC/GEN/G99/131/87/pdf/G9913187.pdf?OpenElement. See also the statements made by some States in the same organ, in 2000: Pakistan (*Summary Records*, 62nd meeting, E/CN.4/2000/SR.62, §§11 and 43–45), Cuba (ibid., at §§40–42 and 56), Sudan (ibid., at §47), China (ibid., at §§52–53), and Swaziland (ibid., at §54)), see online at https://documents-dds-ny.un.org/doc/UNDOC/GEN/G00/134/67/pdf/G0013467.pdf?OpenElement. This opposition leads one to believe that only some features of that model are now widely accepted: *representative* governance based on *regular, free, and fair elections*, and accountable to the electorate; *respect for human rights*; *rule of law*. It would seem that instead the notion of a multiparty political system is not yet agreeable to many States and therefore has not become part of the emerging international notion of democracy. All official UN documents are available online at https://documents.un.org/prod/ods.nsf/home.xsp.

[27] For the necessary references, see also M. Griffin, 'Accrediting Democracies: Does the Credentials Committee of the United Nations Promote Democracy Through its Accreditation Process, and Should It?' (2000) 32 *NYUJ Int'l Law & Pol* 725, in particular 745ff.

In all these areas the human rights doctrine has operated as a potent leaven, contributing to shifting the world community from a reciprocity-based bundle of legal relations, geared to the 'private' pursuit of self-interest, and ultimately blind to collective needs, to a community hinging on a core of fundamental values, strengthened by the emergence of community obligations and community rights and the gradual shaping of public interests.

18.7 THE PRESENT ROLE OF HUMAN RIGHTS

The steady insistence on the need to respect human rights, by international law-making and monitoring bodies, and the impact these bodies have gradually had on States' behaviour, has produced a significant ripple effect. The whole international ethos has gradually, if almost imperceptibly, changed, so much so that some international supervisory bodies now consider it warranted to depart from notions they themselves traditionally upheld. They currently consider it appropriate to place on those notions a much broader interpretation.

This trend has especially manifested itself in Europe and has in particular become apparent in the case law of the European Court of Human Rights. Indicative of this trend is the judgment delivered in 1999 by the European Court in *Selmouni v France*. There, the Court, sitting as a Grand Chamber, unanimously held that the serious ill-treatment of persons detained in police custody, that it had regarded in previous cases (e.g. in 1992 in *Tomasi v France*, at §§115–116) as manifestations of inhuman or degrading treatment contrary to Article 3 of the European Convention, was now to be termed torture, that is, a much more serious breach of Article 3. The Court stated the following: '[H]aving regard to the fact that the [European Convention on Human Rights, of 1950] is a "living instrument which must be interpreted in the light of present-day conditions" . . . the Court considers that certain acts which were classified in the past as "inhuman and degrading treatment" as opposed to "torture" could be classified differently in future. *It takes the view that the increasingly high standard being required in the area of the protection of human rights and fundamental liberties correspondingly and inevitably requires greater firmness in assessing breaches of the fundamental values of democratic societies*' (§101, emphasis added).

Along the same lines, the Court has modified, or even reversed, its jurisprudence in a number of other cases, all directed at enhancing, more than in the past, the protection of human rights.[28] Another example of the constant evolution of the approach taken by the Court to human rights is the case law of the Court concerning the controversial issue of compatibility of whole-life imprisonment sentences with Article 3 of the Convention. The Court has progressively reduced the margins for States actually to carry out the enforcement of such penalties with no availability of alternatives to detention for the convicted person.[29] Eventually, the approach taken by its most recent case law is that States must always ensure that punishment is directed at rehabilitation (at least potentially) and thus

---

[28] See e.g. *Borgers v Belgium*, where it would seem that the Court reversed its previous judgment in *Delcourt v Belgium*. See also *Labita v Italy*, where the Court expanded the scope of Article 3 by holding that 'the lack of a thorough and effective investigation into the credible allegation made by the applicant that he had been ill-treated by wardens when detained' in a specific Italian prison, amounted to a violation of Article 3 (§§130–136). See further *M.C. v Bulgaria*, where the Court held Bulgaria in breach of Articles 3 and 8 of the European Convention, for it had failed to discharge its 'positive obligations' under these provisions to ensure that the alleged rape of a girl by two young men be duly prosecuted, in accordance with the requirements 'to establish and apply effectively a criminal-law system punishing all forms of rape and sexual abuse' (at §§185–187).

[29] For a concise illustration of the main features of the evolution, in recent years, of the case law of the Court on life imprisonment and its compatibility with Article 3 of the European Convention see online at https://www.echr.coe.int/Documents/FS_Life_sentences_ENG.pdf.

individual convicts cannot *a priori* be excluded from the possibility of benefiting from alternative measures implying early release, outside work, or other forms of treatment, without an individualized assessment of their personal circumstances during the enforcement phase (*Marcello Viola v Italy (No. 2)*). These pronouncements have been criticized by some as misinterpreting the dangers of 'organized crime', as well as the 'human rights concerns' of the actual and potential victims of criminal organizations (including protected witnesses). Nonetheless, this jurisprudence can be seen as evidence of the role human rights doctrines are supposed to play in society, and of the influence they are meant to exercise on State authorities. The underlying message being that under no circumstances can States combat crime by bending human rights norms.

In addition, the human rights doctrine has had the great merit of projecting domestic bills of rights onto the international stage, thereby pushing for the worldwide recognition of certain basic values hitherto upheld only within the national setting of a few countries. It also must be credited with prompting the UN to promote a deep sense of social justice and indignation against 'structural violence', in particular those historical situations (such as colonial or neo-colonial domination and apartheid, as well as poverty, malnutrition, and starvation in many poor countries) which have deprived whole groups or peoples of basic rights and freedoms. In other words, the UN has succeeded in moving from a static concept of human rights (conceived as a means of realizing international peace) to a dynamic doctrine which extends to promoting conflict and the disruption of the status quo for the sake of introducing social justice and respect for human dignity (this, as Röling correctly emphasized,[30] is what happened in the case of apartheid and the former Rhodesia, where the UN willingly promoted rebellion against structural violence in the form of 'white rule').

It can be said that by now all, or nearly all, States agree on the following essential points. First, the dignity of human beings is a basic value that every State should try to protect, regardless of considerations of nationality, race, colour, gender, etc. Secondly, it is also necessary to aim at the achievement of fundamental rights of groups and peoples. Thirdly, racial discrimination is universally considered one of the most repulsive and unbearable conditions. Fourthly, even though some States may find it hard (either for economic reasons, or on organizational grounds) to achieve full respect for human rights, no State must engage in grave, repeated, and large-scale violations of these rights. Fifthly, when these large-scale violations are perpetrated, the international community is justified in 'intervening' by peaceful means.

Impressive headway has been made as far as norm setting is concerned, both at the universal and at the regional level. In contrast, from the vantage point of international scrutiny of observance of human rights, the balance sheet is less optimistic, at least at the universal level. Although a few important monitoring procedures have been instituted within the UN system or on the strength of some Conventions, so far they have not yielded conspicuous results. However, in assessing these procedures one ought to bear in mind that they are neither legally binding nor coercive (see **18.4.6**). In consequence they can only be effective by exerting moral, psychological, and political pressure and by making use of public opinion (in the country concerned and in the whole international community). It follows that their effects can only be appreciated in the long run.

A general appraisal of the spread of the human rights doctrine and its incarnation in international rules and institutions should not, however, ignore one important fact: at the regional level, originally in Europe but today also in America and Africa, advanced judicial

---

[30] B. V. A. Röling, 'Peace-Research and Peace-Keeping' in A. Cassese (ed.), *United Nations Peace-Keeping: Legal Essays* (Alphen: Sijthoff and Noordhoff, 1978), 250.

mechanisms have been set up that remedy in a substantially satisfactory manner violations of human rights perpetrated by member States.

Two additional areas are worth mentioning, as they have attracted the attention of both scholars and practitioners, as well as of some UN bodies. On the one hand, the application of human rights obligations to private actors (e.g. multinationals or non-State actors' armed groups). On the other, the impact of new technologies and the advent of the digital era on the enjoyment of human rights (ranging from the protection of data to the threat posed to civil liberties by increased surveillance mechanisms, as well as the rise in the use of autonomous weapons). While developments in these areas do not necessarily entail a paradigm shift, there is little doubt that, increasingly, the challenge for human rights doctrines is to look beyond State sovereignty and encompass in their actions scrutiny over a wide range of other actors (ranging from multinational corporations to international organizations, from rebel groups to criminal organizations).

Finally, a point which still entails substantial division in the world community is the question of whether resort to armed force might be justifiable/permissible to react to massive human rights violations occurring within domestic borders. The notion of 'responsibility to protect'[31] was developed to this effect, deriving from reflections on theories of 'humanitarian intervention' (which had been largely abused in the past). The idea, which developed between the end of the old and the first part of the new millennium (perhaps crystallizing in the aftermath of the NATO air campaign Operation Allied Force against Yugoslavia, in relation to the Kosovo conflict), was solemnly proclaimed in 2005, at the World Summit, and as such reflected in paragraphs 138 and 139 of the outcome document.[32] Nonetheless, despite the reaffirmation of State sovereignty through the recognition of the primary responsibility of governments towards their civilian populations[33] and the decision appropriately to channel the armed reaction of the international community through the UN Charter (and in particular Chapter VII and the Security Council),[34] the notion has become rather controversial. For example, various States have challenged the application of such a doctrine in the Libyan situation in 2011, arguing that the notion had been abused by NATO more with a view to overturning the Gaddafi government than to

---

[31] For reference materials and more information see online at http://www.globalr2p.org/about_r2p.
[32] UN Doc. A/RES/60/1, of 16 September 2005.
[33] Paragraph 138 states: 'Each individual State has the responsibility to protect its populations from genocide, war crimes, ethnic cleansing and crimes against humanity. This responsibility entails the prevention of such crimes, including their incitement, through appropriate and necessary means. We accept that responsibility and will act in accordance with it. The international community should, as appropriate, encourage and help States to exercise this responsibility and support the United Nations in establishing an early warning capability.'
[34] Paragraph 139 indicates that '[t]he international community, through the United Nations, also has the responsibility to use appropriate diplomatic humanitarian and other peaceful means, in accordance with Chapters VI and VIII of the Charter, to help to protect populations from genocide, war crimes, ethnic cleansing and crimes against humanity. In this context, we are prepared to take collective action, in a timely and decisive manner, through the Security Council, in accordance with the Charter, including Chapter VII, on a case-by-case basis and in cooperation with relevant regional organizations as appropriate, should peaceful means be inadequate and national authorities are manifestly failing to protect their populations from genocide, war crimes, ethnic cleansing and crimes against humanity. We stress the need for the General Assembly to continue consideration of the responsibility to protect populations from genocide, war crimes, ethnic cleansing and crimes against humanity and its implications, bearing in mind the principles of the Charter and international law. We also intend to commit ourselves, as necessary and appropriate, to helping States build capacity to protect their populations from genocide, war crimes, ethnic cleansing and crimes against humanity and to assisting those which are under stress before crises and conflicts break out.'

protect all Libyans.[35] In the years following the intervention in Libya, the divide widened between those who often have a rather traditional view of domestic jurisdiction, cautioning against resorting to armed force to react to human rights violations (even with SC authorization), and those considering that when confronted with large-scale violations the international community must react, including, if need be, with the use of armed force. At the moment, the divide remains and emerges periodically on the occasion of the debates in the General Assembly on the Reports of the Secretary-General on the responsibility to protect,[36] as well as in the activities of the Security Council (where the P5 are divided, with China and Russia on one side, and France, the UK, and the US on the other). Nonetheless, despite controversies on aspects regarding the use of armed force, there is no doubt that mechanisms for preventing massive human rights abuses, as well as the activities of the UN and international civil society in this area, have been significantly strengthened by the advent of this doctrine.

---

[35] See e.g. the position of Brazil which—despite being a supporter of human rights—in the aftermath of Libya proposed a new notion, 'responsibility while protecting': see the statement of the President of Brazil Dilma Rousseff at the opening of the 66th session of the General Assembly, verbatim records A/66/PV.11, dated 21 September 2011.

[36] See e.g. the statement by the Russian delegation at 2011 UN General Assembly Informal Interactive Dialogue on the Responsibility to Protect, online at http://www.globalr2p.org/media/files/russia2.pdf.

19

THE REPRESSION OF INTERNATIONAL CRIMES

19.1 INTERNATIONAL CRIMES

In the old conception of the international community, individuals were not normally direct addressees of international rules. It followed that at the international level they could not be held personally responsible for any breach of those rules. If they misbehaved, contrary to international law, either in a private or in an official capacity (e.g. if they ill-treated foreigners, attacked foreign diplomats, murdered a foreign Head of State, or unlawfully expelled foreigners), they could be prosecuted and punished by the competent authorities of a foreign State, within the *national system* of that State, on the following conditions: (i) the international rules against which the individuals had acted had been implemented in the domestic order of the forum State, thereby becoming part and parcel of that State's criminal legislation; (ii) national courts possessed jurisdiction (that is, they did not lack jurisdiction because the individual in question enjoyed immunity from prosecution on the strength of international law); (iii) there was a link between the offence and the forum State (the offence had been perpetrated on the territory, or by a national of the relevant State).

A few exceptions existed. One of them was piracy, a practice that was widespread in the seventeenth and eighteenth centuries, and has recently regained some importance.[1] All States of the world were empowered to search for and prosecute pirates, since piracy is committed on the high seas, and usually regardless of the nationality of the perpetrator and of whether the proceeding State had been directly damaged by piracy. Also, the fact that the pirates happened to have the status of State officials when they had engaged in piratical acts while pursuing private ends did not impede their prosecution and punishment by other States (unless of course they could show that they had acted on behalf of a State, in which case State responsibility arose). The pirates were regarded as enemies of humanity (*hostes humani generis*) in that they hampered the freedom of the high seas and jeopardized private property.

---

[1] Under Article 101 of the 1982 Convention on the Law of the Sea, which can be deemed to reflect and codify customary international law, piracy consists of any of the following acts: '(a) any illegal acts of violence, detention or any act of depredation, committed for private ends by the crew or passengers of a private ship or private aircraft and directed: (i) on the high seas, against another ship or aircraft, or against persons or property on board such ship or aircraft; (ii) against a ship, aircraft, persons or property in a place outside the jurisdiction of any State; (b) any act of voluntary participation in the operation of a ship or of an aircraft with knowledge of facts making it a pirate ship or aircraft; (c) any act of inciting or of intentionally facilitating an act described in subparagraph (a) or (b)'. See generally A. P. Rubin, *The Law of Piracy*, 2nd edn (The Hague: Brill, 1998). On the resurgence of piracy off the coast of Somalia affecting oil tanker transit routes see J. Ashley Roach, 'Countering Piracy off Somalia: International Law and International Institutions' (2010) 104 *American Journal of International Law* 397.

Things gradually changed, and new classes of acts emerged that were considered punishable as international crimes under international law, namely, offences entailing the personal criminal liability of the individuals concerned (as opposed to the responsibility of the State) directly under international law and thus irrespective of the existence of a parallel national criminal rule. The prosecution and repression of these crimes occur both at the domestic level, often based on criminal legislation enacted to implement international treaties on the matter (see **19.3.1**), or directly at the international level. The establishment of international criminal courts and tribunals (such as the ad hoc Tribunals for the former Yugoslavia (ICTY) and Rwanda (ICTR), the International Criminal Court (ICC), and a host of so-called 'hybrid' or 'mixed' courts and tribunals) has built upon the legacy of the Nuremberg and Tokyo trials to enhance the opportunities for the repression of international crimes (see **19.3.3**).

Before considering some of the major categories of such international crimes, it should be specified that international crimes can be held to include the following. First, violations of either international *customary rules* which are intended to protect values considered important by the whole international community and consequently bind all States and individuals, or of *treaty rules* that spell out, clarify, develop, or elaborate upon such customary rules, and are applicable in the case at issue. Secondly, since there exists a universal interest in repressing these crimes, under international law their alleged authors *may* be prosecuted and punished *by any State*, regardless of any territorial or nationality link with the perpetrator or his victim when the crime was committed, provided, however, that the suspect or the accused is on the territory of the forum State when jurisdiction is exercised (this is the so-called 'universality principle': see **19.3.1**). Thirdly, if the perpetrator has acted in an official capacity, the State on whose behalf he has performed the prohibited act is *barred* from claiming that he enjoys immunity from the civil or criminal jurisdiction of foreign States accruing under customary law to State officials acting in the exercise of their functions (see **19.3.1**).

Under this definition, international crimes include war crimes, crimes against humanity, genocide, torture (as distinct from one of the categories of war crimes or crimes against humanity), aggression, and terrorism. By contrast, it does not include apartheid, the illicit traffic in narcotic drugs and psychotropic substances, the unlawful arms trade, the smuggling of nuclear and other potentially deadly materials, and money laundering. The latter crimes are not directly criminalized by relevant rules of customary international law, although their criminalization has to be implemented by States through their national criminal legislation in accordance with the relevant treaties or resolutions of international organizations dealing with such crimes.[2]

19.2 CATEGORIES OF INTERNATIONAL CRIMES

19.2.1 WAR CRIMES

In a broad sense, war crimes encompass all wartime atrocities. As a term of art, however, war crimes are violations of rules of international humanitarian law (see **Chapter 17**) giving rise to the criminal responsibility of individuals directly under international law, and without prejudice to the international responsibility of States and other relevant international actors (e.g. non-State armed groups). Not every violation of international humanitarian law gives rise to a war crime. According to the Appeals Chamber of the ICTY, the violation

---

[2] As for apartheid, it would seem that under customary international law it is prohibited as a State delinquency; as a crime of individuals it falls within the broad category of crimes against humanity, as may also be inferred from Article 7(1) of the Statute of the ICC.

must be *serious*, namely: 'it must constitute a breach of a rule protecting important values, and the breach must involve grave consequences for the victim' (*Tadić (Interlocutory Appeal)*, at §94).[3]

Traditionally war crimes encompassed only breaches of international rules regulating war proper, that is, international armed conflicts and not civil wars. Since the aforementioned ICTY decision in *Tadić* (at §§95–137), it is now widely accepted that serious violations of rules of customary international law regulating non-international armed conflicts must also be regarded as amounting to war crimes proper.[4] As evidence of this new trend, suffice it to mention Article 8 of the Rome Statute of the ICC, which includes as war crimes serious violations of both the law regulating international armed conflicts (IACs) and rules covering non-international armed conflicts (NIACs).

There is no authoritative exclusive list or official codification of serious violations of rules of international humanitarian law amounting to war crimes. The 1949 Geneva Conventions (GCs) (see **17.2.3**) and Additional Protocol I (AP I) (see **17.2.4**) list the violations of the GCs and the Protocol that States parties have to criminalize in their respective domestic legal orders. These violations are termed *grave breaches* of the GCs and AP I respectively and are considered to constitute war crimes under customary international law. In addition, States parties have the obligation to bring before their own courts (including under the universality principle) persons allegedly responsible for such grave breaches or to surrender them to another State that has a prima facie case in accordance with their national legislation.[5]

To identify additional serious violations of rules of international humanitarian law amounting to war crimes, one has to rely on the usual means of establishing the existence of rules of customary international law. This requires identifying whether States consider the violation of a rule of international humanitarian law as serious, and entailing individual criminal responsibility under international law. The most relevant means of identifying the existence of customary international rules on war crimes are military manuals, national and international case law, national criminal legislation, and the rules on war crimes contained in the statutes of international criminal courts and tribunals.

Article 8 of the Rome Statute of the ICC ('Rome Statute'), supplemented by the Elements of Crimes relevant to this provision, defines war crimes under the jurisdiction of the ICC. The list of war crimes contained therein is an exclusive list, which distinguishes between war crimes committed in IACs and NIACs. The list of war crimes in IACs further distinguishes between grave breaches of the Geneva Conventions and AP I (Article 8(2)(a)) and 'serious

---

[3] The Tribunal went on to give an example of a non-serious violation: 'the fact of a combatant simply appropriating a loaf of bread in an occupied village' would not amount to such a breach, 'although it may be regarded as falling foul of the basic principle laid down in Article 46(1) of the [1907] Hague Regulations [on Land Warfare] (and the corresponding rule of customary international law) whereby "private property must be respected" by any army occupying an enemy territory'.

[4] The ICTY Appeals Chamber stated the following: 'A State-sovereignty-oriented approach has been gradually supplanted by a human-being-oriented approach. Gradually the maxim of Roman law *hominum causa omne jus constitutum est* (all law is created for the benefit of human beings) has gained a firm foothold in the international community as well. It follows that in the area of armed conflict the distinction between interstate wars and civil wars is losing its value as far as human beings are concerned. Why protect civilians from belligerent violence, or ban rape, torture or the wanton destruction of hospitals, churches, museums or private property, as well as proscribe weapons causing unnecessary suffering when two sovereign States are engaged in war, and yet refrain from enacting the same bans or providing the same protection when armed violence has erupted "only" within the territory of a sovereign State. If international law, while of course duly safeguarding the legitimate interests of states, must gradually turn to the protection of human beings, it is only natural that the aforementioned dichotomy [belligerency–insurgency] should gradually lose its weight' (ibid., at §97).

[5] On the system of repression of grave breaches, see among others: P. Gaeta, 'Grave Breaches of the Geneva Conventions' in A. Clapham, P. Gaeta, and M. Sassóli (eds), *The 1949 Geneva Conventions: A Commentary* (Oxford: Oxford University Press, 2015), 615.

violations of the laws and customs applicable in international armed conflict, within the established framework of international law' (Article 8(2)(b)). War crimes belonging to this latter category mainly include violations of the rules on conduct of hostilities, but also violations of other rules not specifically envisaged as grave breaches by the relevant provisions of the GCs and AP I. Similarly, war crimes in NIACs consist of serious violations of common Article 3 of the GCs (Article 8(2)(c)) and 'other serious violations of the laws and customs applicable in armed conflicts not of an international character, within the established framework of international law' (Article 8(2)(e)). The latter considers as war crimes violations of rules of international humanitarian law in NIACs other than common Article 3.

It is worth mentioning that Article 8(1) of the Rome Statute provides that the Court 'shall have jurisdiction in respect of war crimes in particular when committed as part of a plan or policy or as part of a large-scale commission of such crimes'. This provision does not spell out a legal ingredient of war crimes, but suggests a jurisdictional threshold for the ICC (as the term 'in particular' makes clear). In addition, the list of war crimes contained in Article 8(1) does not codify customary international law but is intended to establish the scope of jurisdiction of the ICC.

(1) *Legal elements*. Identifying the main legal elements of war crimes, that is, the prohibited physical act (*actus reus*) and the required mental element (*mens rea*), requires an examination of the content of the rule of international humanitarian law allegedly breached. Reliance on rules of international humanitarian law for the identification of criminal acts can raise difficult issues, since these rules are not criminal rules addressing individuals and therefore lack the required precision.

As for the *actus reus*, the relevant rule of international humanitarian law may not be clear with respect to whether the corresponding war crime will necessarily entail harmful consequences (thus constituting a so-called 'crime of result') or whether it consists of the violation of the prescribed conduct, regardless of harmful consequences (so-called 'crime of conduct'). For instance, Article 51(2) of AP I and Article 13(2) of AP II prohibit 'acts or threats of violence the primary purpose of which is to spread terror among the civilian population'. These provisions, however, fail to specify whether a war crime is committed when the breach causes harmful effects on the civilian population, or only by carrying out the wrongful conduct. The Appeals Judgment of the ICTY in *Galić* has adopted the former approach, having clarified that the war crime of terror requires that acts of violence directed against the civilian population or individual civilians cause death or serious injury to body or health within the civilian population (§104).

Rules of international humanitarian law may sometimes clarify the relevant mental element for corresponding war crimes.[6] When this is not the case, and the relevant rule does not provide for a mental element, arguably what is required is the *intent* or, depending upon the circumstances, *knowledge* or *recklessness* prescribed in most legal systems of the world

---

[6] Thus e.g. Article 130 of GC III (on prisoners of war) enumerates among the 'grave breaches' of the Convention the 'willful killing [of prisoners of war], torture or inhuman treatment, including biological experiments' as well as 'willfully causing great suffering or serious injury to body or health' of a prisoner of war, or 'willfully depriving a prisoner of war of the rights of fair and regular trial prescribed in [the] Convention'. The word 'willful' clearly presupposes a criminal intent, namely the intention to bring about the consequences of the act prohibited by the international rule. (E.g. in the case of 'willful killing' proof must be produced of the intention to cause the death of the victim; in the case of 'willfully causing great suffering' it must be proved that the perpetrator had the intention to cause great suffering, etc.) The same holds true for other similar provisions, such as Article 147 of GC IV (on civilians) as well as provisions of other treaties, such as Article 15 of the 1999 Second Hague Protocol for the Protection of Cultural Property in the Event of Armed Conflict; this provision, in enumerating the serious violations of the Protocol entailing individual criminal liability, makes such liability contingent upon the fact that the author of the 'offence' has perpetrated it 'intentionally'.

for the underlying offence (murder, rape, torture, destruction of private property, firing on undefended localities, pillage, etc.). Generally speaking, it appears reasonable to contend that, for war crimes, culpable negligence (*culpa gravis*) may be sufficient; that is, the author of the crime, although aware of the risk involved in his conduct, is nevertheless convinced that the prohibited consequence will not occur (whereas in the case of recklessness or *dolus eventualis* the author knowingly takes the risk). Indeed, the consequent broadening of the range of acts amenable to international prosecution is in keeping with the general object and purpose of international humanitarian law. In the Rome Statute, however, the general rule on mental element (that is, the one applicable 'unless otherwise provided') is enshrined in Article 30, requiring intent with respect to the conduct and consequence, and knowledge with respect to the circumstances and consequences of the crime.

(2) *The requirement of nexus*. Domestic crimes can be committed during an armed conflict and may consist in criminal conduct also prohibited under international humanitarian law (e.g. the killing of an innocent civilian by a soldier). In these circumstances, the need arises to clarify whether the criminal conduct under domestic law also amounts to a war crime, giving rise to individual criminal responsibility under international law. This function is served by the so-called 'nexus requirement', according to which the criminal conduct will be closely linked with the armed conflict to constitute a war crime. How to determine the existence of such nexus? According to the Appeals Chamber of the ICTY (*Kunarac*, at §§58–59), the requirement of nexus means that:

> the existence of an armed conflict must, at a minimum, have played a substantial part in the perpetrator's ability to commit [the crime], his decision to commit it, the manner in which it was committed or the purpose for which it was committed.

The Appeals Chamber has listed a few factors that one can use to establish the required nexus, namely:

> the fact that the perpetrator is a combatant; the fact that the victim is a non-combatant; the fact that the victim is a member of the opposing party; the fact that the act may be said to serve the ultimate goal of a military campaign; and the fact that the crime is committed as part of or in the context of the perpetrator's official duties.

Clearly, the broader the nexus requirement, the less it serves its purpose of distinguishing between war crimes and other international crimes or relevant domestic offences committed in the course of an armed conflict.

19.2.2 CRIMES AGAINST HUMANITY

During the Second World War, the Allies became aware that some of the most heinous acts of barbarity perpetrated by the Germans were not prohibited by traditional international law. The laws of warfare only proscribed violations involving the adversary or the enemy populations, whereas the Germans had also performed inhuman acts for political or racial reasons against their own citizens (Jews, trade union members, social democrats, communists, gypsies, and members of the church) as well as other persons not protected by the laws of warfare.[7] In addition, in 1945 such acts as mere persecution on political or racial grounds were not prohibited, even if perpetrated against civilians of occupied territories.

---

[7] E.g. citizens of the Allies (such as French Jews under the Vichy regime (1940–44)); nationals of States not formally under German occupation and, therefore, not protected by the international rules safeguarding the civilian population of occupied territories: this applied to Austria, annexed by Germany in 1938, and Czechoslovakia (following the Munich Treaty in 1938, the Sudeten territory was annexed by Germany, and the rest of the country became the so-called Protectorate of Bohemia and Moravia, in 1939). The Germans also harassed and murdered stateless Jews and gypsies.

In 1945, at the strong insistence of the US, the Allies decided that a better course of action than simply to execute all the major war criminals (as initially suggested by Winston Churchill and other members of the British Cabinet),[8] would be to bring them to trial (it appears that Stalin also opposed summary execution).[9] The London Agreement of 8 August 1945 embodying the Charter of the International Military Tribunal sitting at Nuremberg ('Nuremberg Tribunal') included a provision under which the Tribunal was to try and punish persons guilty, among other things, of 'crimes against humanity'. These were defined as:

> murder, extermination, enslavement, deportation, and other inhumane acts committed against any civilian population, before or during the war, or persecutions on political, racial, or religious grounds in execution of or connexion with any crimes within the jurisdiction of the Tribunal [that is, either 'crimes against peace' or 'war crimes'], whether or not in violation of the domestic law of the country where perpetrated.

One major shortcoming of this definition is that it closely links crimes against humanity with the other two categories of offences, namely war crimes and crimes against peace. As Schwelb rightly remarked, this association meant that only those criminal activities were punished which 'directly affected the interests of other States', either because these activities were connected with a war of aggression or a conspiracy to wage such a war, or because they were bound up with war crimes, that is, crimes against enemy combatants or enemy civilians.[10] Plainly, in 1945 the Allies did not feel that they should legislate in such a way as to prohibit inhuman acts with a merely 'domestic' scope (that is, devoid of consequences or implications for third States), and thus required that crimes against humanity be linked with an armed conflict.

Despite this limitation, the creation of the new category marked a great advance. First, it indicated that the international community was widening the category of acts considered of 'meta-national' concern. This category came to include all acts running contrary to those basic values that are, or should be, considered inherent in any human being (in the notion, humanity did not mean 'mankind' or 'the human race' but the 'quality' or concept of human being). Secondly, inasmuch as crimes against humanity were made punishable even if perpetrated in accordance with domestic laws, the 1945 Charter showed that in some special circumstances there were limits to the 'omnipotence of the State' (to quote the British Chief Prosecutor, Sir Hartley Shawcross) and that 'the individual human being, the ultimate unit of all law, is not disentitled to the protection of mankind when the State tramples upon his rights in a manner which outrages the conscience of mankind'.[11]

---

[8] See the statements made on 2 February 1945, at the Malta Conference, by the British Foreign Secretary, Anthony Eden (in FRUS, *The Conferences at Malta and at Yalta, 1945*, at 507) and on 9 February 1945 at Yalta, by Prime Minister Churchill (ibid., at 849). See also the Memorandum of 4 September 1944 on 'Major War Criminals', by the Lord Chancellor, Sir John Simon, reproduced in B. F. Smith, *The American Road to Nuremberg: The Documentary Record, 1944–1945* (Stanford, CA: Hoover Institution Press and Stanford University, 1982), 31 and notes at 227. Another member of the Cabinet, Clement Attlee, had proposed including industrialists and military leaders, plus von Papen and Seyss Inquart, in the shoot-on-sight list (see Smith, at 227).

Later Churchill changed his mind (see his top secret telegram to Roosevelt of 22 October 1944, in FRUS, at 400).

[9] The Soviet position is reported by the British Foreign Secretary, Eden, in FRUS (n 8), at 507 ('Mr. Eden said that when this [question] was discussed in October [1943, at the Moscow meeting of Foreign Ministers] Marshal Stalin had disagreed with our view favouring some summary executions and had said that some form of judicial procedure was necessary').

[10] E. Schwelb, 'Crimes against Humanity' (1946) 23 *BYIL* 193, at 206–7. The words cited in the text are at 207.

[11] Sir Hartley Shawcross, in *Speeches of the Chief Prosecutors at the Close of the Case Against the Individual Defendants* (London: HM Stationery Office, Cmd. 6964, 1946), 63.

In the wake of the major war trials momentous changes in international law took place. On 11 December 1946, the UN General Assembly unanimously adopted resolution 95-1 'affirming' the principles of the Charter of the Nuremberg Tribunal and its judgment. In recent times, a conspicuous number of international instruments, including the Statutes of the ICTY, the ICTR, and the ICC, then have embodied the prohibition of crimes against humanity, certain of which improved and extended the definition contained in the London Agreement. In August 2019, the International Law Commission (ILC) presented the final text of Draft Articles and commentary for a Convention on the Prevention and Punishment of Crimes against Humanity.[12] The definition of crimes against humanity enshrined in the Draft Articles reproduces the definition contained in the Rome Statute, with only minor changes (in particular, it removes the definition of gender contained in Article 7(3) of the Rome Statute and restricts the definition of persecution contained in Article 7(1)(h) of the Rome Statute).

(1) *Legal elements*. The definition of crimes against humanity embodied in the relevant statutes of international criminal courts and tribunals established so far encompasses actions that share a set of common features. First, these crimes are particularly odious offences in that they constitute a serious attack on human dignity or a grave humiliation or degradation of one or more human beings. The list includes the following acts: (i) acts that domestic legal systems usually criminalize (e.g. murder, extermination, and rape); (ii) persecution on enumerated discriminatory grounds; and (iii) other inhumane acts. Secondly, these acts shall be not isolated or sporadic events, but shall be part of a context of violence (the so-called contextual element of crimes against humanity, discussed later). Isolated acts may constitute grave infringements of human rights or, depending on the circumstances, war crimes, but fall short of meriting the stigma attaching to crimes against humanity. An individual, however, may be guilty of crimes against humanity even if he or she is responsible for one or two of the acts mentioned above or engages in one such offence against only a few individuals, provided those offences are part of a consistent pattern of misbehaviour and that he or she acted with the required mental element.

The determination of the *mental element* of crimes against humanity has proved particularly difficult and controversial. This is because the mental element is not simply limited to the criminal intent required for the underlying offence (murder, extermination, deportation, rape, torture, persecution, etc.). The viciousness of these crimes goes far beyond the underlying offence, however wicked or despicable it may be. This additional element—which also may help to distinguish crimes against humanity from war crimes—consists of *awareness* of the broader context into which this crime fits, that is, knowledge that the offences are part of a systematic policy or of widespread and large-scale abuses. In addition, when these crimes take the form of persecution, another mental element is required: a persecutory or discriminatory animus, namely to subject a person or group to discrimination, ill-treatment, or harassment, to bring about great suffering or injury to that person or group on religious, political, or other such grounds. This added element for persecution amounts to an aggravated criminal intent (special intent or *dolus specialis*).

(2) *The contextual element*. As already mentioned, the definition of crimes against humanity in the London Charter linked these crimes to the other two categories of crimes within the jurisdiction of the Nuremberg Tribunal (namely war crimes and crimes against peace). In other words, in 1945, the definition of crimes against humanity required a link with an armed conflict. The definition of crimes against humanity enshrined in the ICTY Statute

---

[12] Report on the work of the seventy-first session (2019), A/74/10, Chapter IV.

has kept the need for this link, although the Appeals Chamber of the Tribunal asserted that this requirement was a jurisdictional limitation and did not reflect the definition of crimes against humanity under customary international law (*Tadić (Interlocutory Appeal)*, at §141). On the other hand, the definition of crimes against humanity in the Statute of the ICTR did not require the link with an armed conflict, but the existence of a 'widespread or systematic attack against any civilian population on national, political, ethnic, racial or religious grounds'. This has paved the way for the adoption of the definition of crimes against humanity in the Rome Statute, that similarly does not require the link with an armed conflict, but a widespread or systematic attack against a civilian population (without any reference to discriminatory grounds mentioned in the ICTR Statute). It seems therefore that, at present, the definition of crimes against humanity under customary international law no longer attaches any importance to the link with an armed conflict.

The question however arises of the meaning of the term 'widespread or systematic attack'. In the case law of international criminal courts and tribunals, 'systematic' refers to the 'organized nature of the acts of violence and the improbability of their random occurrence' (*Kunarac* (Appeals Chamber), at §98), while 'widespread' relates to the large-scale nature of the acts or their magnitude (*Tadić* (Trial Chamber), at §648). The term 'attack' is defined in Article 7(2) of the Rome Statute as a course of conduct involving the multiple commission of prohibited acts against any civilian population, 'pursuant to or in furtherance of a *State* or *organizational* policy to commit such attack' (emphasis added). Based on this definition, the ICC has asserted that also non-State entities can carry out an attack against a civilian population and that they are not limited to entities showing features similar to a State. According to the ICC, 'the formal nature of a group and the level of its organization should not be the defining criterion', but that 'a distinction should be drawn on whether a group has the capability to perform acts which infringe on basic human values' (*Kenya Decision*, at §§90–93). This criterion however is somewhat circular: it identifies the organization behind the attack for the purpose of crimes against humanity by referring to the capability of the organization to do so.

19.2.3 GENOCIDE

Genocide, that is, activities directed at the destruction of groups as such, was not included as a crime under the jurisdiction of the Nuremberg and Tokyo Tribunals. The word genocide had just been coined by Polish jurist Raphael Lemkin in his work *Axis Rule in Occupied Europe* (1941), to describe the destruction of essential foundations of the life of Jews in Eastern Europe (*genos* is the Greek word to describe social groups with common descent and *caedere* is a Latin word for 'to kill'). In dealing with the extermination of Jews and other ethnic or religious groups, the Nuremberg Tribunal therefore mostly referred to the crime of persecution as a crime against humanity.[13]

Genocide acquired autonomous significance as a specific crime in 1948, when the UN General Assembly adopted the Convention for the Prevention and Repression of the Crime of Genocide. The Convention has numerous merits. Among other things, it sets out a careful definition of the crime. This definition has been reproduced verbatim in the Statutes of the ICTY, the ICTR, and the ICC and is considered to reflect the definition of the crime under customary international law. In addition, the Convention makes punishable other acts connected with genocide (conspiracy, complicity, etc.) and it prohibits genocide whether it is perpetrated in time of war or peace. Finally, the Convention considers

---

[13] However, genocide was discussed in a few other cases: in particular *Hoess*, decided by a Polish court in 1948 (at 1520) and *Greifelt et al.*, decided in 1948 by a United States Military Tribunal sitting at Nuremberg (at 17).

genocide both as a crime involving the criminal responsibility of the individual and an international delinquency entailing the responsibility of the State.[14] However, one should not be unmindful of the flaws of the Convention. The most blatant one is that the definition of genocide does not include the extermination of a group on political grounds, nor cultural genocide (that is, the destruction of the language and culture of a group). In addition, the enforcement mechanism envisaged in the Convention is mostly ineffective.[15]

By contrast, much headway has been made both at the level of prosecution and punishment of genocide by international criminal tribunals, and at the normative level. Genocide having been provided for in the Statutes of both the ICTY and the ICTR as well as the ICC, the first two courts have had the opportunity to try quite a few persons accused of this crime, and have delivered important judgments on the matter.[16] At the normative level, some major advances should be emphasized. The major substantive provisions of the Convention have gradually turned into customary international law, as was held by the ICJ in its Advisory Opinion on *Reservations to the Convention on the Prevention and Punishment of Genocide* (at 23). In addition, at the level of State responsibility it is now widely recognized that customary rules on genocide impose community obligations, that is, towards all other member States of the international community, and at the same time confer on any State the right to require that acts of genocide be discontinued (community rights). Finally, those rules now form part of *jus cogens* or peremptory norms, that is, they may not be derogated from by international agreement (nor *a fortiori* by national legislation).

(1) *Legal elements.* Article II of the Genocide Convention clearly defines the acts that may amount to genocide:

> (a) killing members of the group; (b) causing serious bodily or mental harm to members of the group; (c) deliberately inflicting on the group conditions of life calculated to bring about its physical destruction in whole or in part; (d) imposing measures intended to prevent birth within the group; (e) forcibly transferring children of the group to another group.

The list is closed and it focuses on acts that may lead to the 'biological' destruction of groups. In particular, the list does not include the conduct currently termed 'ethnic cleansing', that is, the forcible expulsion of civilians belonging to a particular group from an area, a village, or a town.[17]

Each of the aforementioned acts amounts to genocide if carried out 'with intent to destroy, in whole or in part, a national, ethnical, racial or religious group, as such'. This element describes an aggravated criminal intention (special intent or *dolus specialis*), required

---

[14] This stand was taken by the ICJ in the *Genocide (Bosnia and Herzegovina v Yugoslavia (Serbia and Montenegro))* case, §§161–167. For a critical assessment, see P. Gaeta, 'On What Conditions Can a State Be Held Responsible for Genocide?' (2007) 18 *EJIL* 631.

[15] In Article IV, the Convention contemplates trials before the courts of the State on the territory of which genocide has occurred, or before a future 'international penal tribunal'; Article VIII provides that any contracting party 'may call upon the competent organs of the United Nations to take such action' under the Charter 'as they consider appropriate' for the prevention or suppression of genocide, whereas Article IX confers on the ICJ jurisdiction over disputes between States concerning the interpretation, application, or fulfilment of the Convention.

[16] The ICTR particularly in *Akayesou*; *Kayishema and Ruzindana*; *Musema*; *Rutaganda*; and the ICTY in *Jelisić*; *Krstić* (Trial Chamber); *Krstić* (Appeals Chamber); and *Stakić*.

[17] In the course of the drafting of the Genocide Convention, Syria proposed an amendment designed to add as an act of genocide: 'Imposing measures intended to oblige members of a group to abandon their homes in order to escape the threat of subsequent ill-treatment' (see UN Doc. A/C6/234). However, the draftsmen rejected this proposal.

in addition to the criminal intent accompanying the prohibited acts. In other words, it must be proved that the perpetrator, in addition to willing, for instance, the death of the victims (killing a member of a group), also intended to destroy in whole or in part the group to which they belonged. Murder was thus a *means* of achieving the *goal* of partial or total destruction of the group. Importantly, however, genocide is committed even if the intention to destroy the group is not achieved: the destruction of the group is relevant only as an objective of the perpetrator, regardless of its accomplishment.

The perpetrator aims at the destruction of only 'national, ethnical, racial or religious' groups. Political, economic, social, gender, and other groups are excluded from the protection against genocide under the definition of the Convention. Some national legislations have expanded the list of the protected groups. Article 211-1 of the French Criminal Code, for instance, adds to the definition of genocide the intention to destroy any group based on any arbitrary criteria (*'un groupe déterminé à partir de tout autre critère arbitraire'*). International criminal courts and tribunals have identified these groups mostly by combining an objective and a subjective approach, namely by referring to objective criteria (e.g. the colour of the skin or some other criterion) and by the social perception of the distinctiveness of the group.[18]

Finally, the special intent may consist in the partial destruction of the group. According to international case law, this means that the perpetrator aims at destroying a substantial portion of the group, which in turn can be established by taking into account the size of the targeted part of the group or its prominence within the group (see e.g. *Kristić* (Appeals Chamber) at §12).

(2) *The question of the genocidal context.* The definition of the crime of genocide in the 1948 Convention and the corresponding provisions included in the statutes of international criminal courts and tribunals do not provide for a contextual element. Genocide can therefore be committed even absent a widespread or systematic practice of violence against members of a protected group. The ICTY and ICTR have endorsed this interpretation, and have clarified that the existence of a genocidal plan or policy is not a legal ingredient of the crime, although it may become an important factor to prove the specific intent of the perpetrator.[19]

The situation at the ICC is different, since the Elements of Crime (that complement the Rome Statute) expressly provide that the prohibited genocidal conduct 'took place in the context of a manifest pattern of similar conduct directed against that group *or* was conduct that could itself effect such destruction'. The first part of the Elements of Crime for genocide clearly requires the existence of a contextual element. The second part, however, makes the existence of the contextual element irrelevant when the conduct 'could itself effect the destruction of the group', thus allowing for the so-called *lone genocidaire* scenario (e.g. an individual possessing a weapon of mass destruction and using it against members of a protected group). In the *Decision on Confirmation of Charges against Omar Hassan Ahmad Al Bashir*, the Pre-Trial Chamber of the ICC stated that there is no 'irreconcilable contradiction between the definition of the crime of genocide provided for in article 6 of the Statute and the contextual element provided for in the Elements of Crimes with regard to the crime of genocide'. This is because the crime of genocide requires 'for its completion an actual threat to the targeted group, or a part thereof' (at §133). Therefore, the Pre-Trial Chamber concluded that the contextual element in the Elements of Crime is consistent with the definition of genocide contained in the Rome Statute

---

[18] For an analysis of the case law of the ICTY and ICTR, see A. Szpak, 'National, Ethnic, Racial, and Religious Groups Protected against Genocide in the Jurisprudence of the Ad Hoc International Criminal Tribunals' (2012) 23 *EJIL* 179.

[19] For a critical view see, among others, A. K. A. Greenwalt, 'Rethinking Genocidal Intent: the Case for a Knowledge-Based Interpretation' (1999) 99 *Colum L Rev* 22.

19.2.4 THE CRIME OF AGGRESSION

Aggression was first regarded as an international crime in the London Agreement of 8 August 1945 establishing the Nuremberg Tribunal. Article 6(a) of the Charter of the Tribunal, annexed to the Agreement, provided as follows:

> The following acts, or any of them, are crimes coming within the jurisdiction of the Tribunal for which there shall be individual responsibility: (a) CRIMES AGAINST PEACE: namely planning, preparation, initiation or waging of a war of aggression, or a war in violation of international treaties, agreements or assurances, or participation in a Common Plan or Conspiracy for the accomplishment of any of the foregoing.

Thus, wars of aggression were only one of the sub-categories of the broad category of 'crimes against peace'. The Nuremberg Tribunal dwelt at some length on this category to prove that it had already been established before 1945 and consequently the punishment of such crimes did not fall foul of the principle of legality in criminal matters (*nullum crimen sine lege* principle). The Tribunal went so far as to define aggression as the 'supreme international crime' (at 186). Some defendants were found guilty on this count and sentenced either to death or to long terms of imprisonment. Subsequently the Tokyo Tribunal found some defendants guilty of aggression. The definition of crimes against peace and its application by the Nuremberg Tribunal was formally subsequently endorsed by the UN General Assembly, with the adoption of the aforementioned resolution 95-I affirming the 'principles of international law recognized by the Charter of the Nuremberg Tribunal and the judgment of the Tribunal'. However, there was no follow-up to this specific matter in later years.

The problem with aggression was that the major Powers preferred to avoid defining this breach of the ban on force laid down in Article 2(4) of the UN Charter, so as to retain as much leeway as possible in the application of that provision both by each of them individually and by the Security Council collectively. The definition of aggression remained in abeyance, with regard to aggression both as a State delinquency entailing the international responsibility of the State and as an international crime involving criminal liability. Later, the UN General Assembly adopted resolution 3314 (XXIX) of 14 December 1974 on the Definition of Aggression ('1974 Definition'). However, the 1974 Definition was deliberately incomplete, for Article 4 provided that the list of acts amounting to aggression was not exhaustive and left to the Security Council a broad area of discretion, by stating that it was free to characterize other acts as aggression under the Charter. Furthermore, the 1974 Definition did not specify that aggression may entail both State responsibility and individual criminal liability: in Article 5(2) it simply provided that war of aggression is a crime against international law, adding that it 'gives rise to international responsibility'. In addition, the definition propounded in the Draft Code of Crimes against Peace and Security of Mankind, adopted by the UN International Law Commission in 1996, is rather poor and disappointing.[20]

Originally, the Rome Statute provided the jurisdiction of the Court over the crime of aggression, but envisaged a subsequent amendment of the Statute on definition of the crime and the relevant conditions for the exercise of jurisdiction (Article 5*bis* of the Statute). This amendment was adopted at the Kampala Review Conference in 2010 and, after being ratified by the requested minimum number of States parties, has led to the activation of the jurisdiction of the Court over the crime of aggression as from 17 July 2018 (resolution

---

[20] Article 16 of the Draft Code provides that '[a]n individual, who, as leader or organizer, actively participates in or orders the planning, preparation, initiation or waging of aggression committed by a state, shall be responsible for a crime of aggression' (UN Doc. A/51/332).

ICC-ASP/16/Res.5 of the Assembly of States Parties). The Kampala amendment on aggression has added a few provisions to the Statute: (i) Article 8*bis*, on the definition of the crime of aggression, which will be discussed in what follows; (ii) Articles 15*bis* and *ter*, on the conditions for the exercise of the jurisdiction of the Court over this crime; and (iii) Article 25(3)*bis*, to align the different modes of responsibility set forth in the Statute with the definition of aggression as a crime that can be committed by some individuals only.

Not surprisingly, since the Nuremberg and Tokyo trials there have been no national or international trials for alleged crimes of aggression,[21] although undisputedly in quite a number of instances States have engaged in acts of aggression, and in a few cases the Security Council has determined that a State had committed such acts.[22] At the national level, the principal problem is that most States lack any legislation granting their courts jurisdiction over the crime of aggression. The tide is now turning. States parties to the Rome Statute that have ratified the Kampala amendment are passing national legislation criminalizing aggression within their legal orders, although with some deviations with respect to the definition enshrined in Article 8*bis*.[23] At the international level, the Security Council did not entrust the ICTY and ICTR with jurisdiction over the crime of aggression or other crime of a similar nature.[24] It is to be hoped that the ICC will make good use of the unprecedented judicial role the Assembly of States Parties assigned to it in activating its jurisdiction over the crime of aggression.

(1) *Legal elements*. Aggression is an area where States deliberately want to retain a broad margin of discretion. Nevertheless, at least some more *traditional* forms of aggression are prohibited by customary international law, which therefore can be held to provide the objective elements of the crime. These instances of aggression, constituting the core of the notion at issue, are taken directly from the 1974 Definition,[25] and confirmed, at least in part, by the ICJ in *Nicaragua (Nicaragua v United States)* (at §195). The definition of the crime of aggression can therefore be built upon planning, organizing, preparing, or participating in the first use of armed force by State officials against the territorial integrity of another State

---

[21] The Iraqi Special Tribunal for Crimes Against Humanity, established as part of the national judiciary of Iraq by the Interim Governing Council (following the invasion of Iraq by coalition forces in 2003), did however have jurisdiction over the following crime: 'The abuse of position and the pursuit of policies that were about to lead to the threat of war or the use of the armed forces of Iraq against an Arab country, in accordance with Article 1 of Law Number 7 of 1958' (Article 14(third) of the Statute). It does not seem, however, that there have been trials based on this charge.

[22] The Security Council has defined as 'acts of aggression' some actions or raids by South Africa and Israel. See e.g. resolution 573 of 4 October 1985 (on Israeli attacks on PLO targets) and resolution 577 of 6 December 1985 (on South Africa's attacks on Angola).

[23] A. Hartig, 'Post Kampala: The Early Implementers of the Crime of Aggression' (2019) 17 *JICJ* 485.

[24] This failure has been strongly criticized by some commentators, e.g. D. Zolo, 'Who is Afraid of Punishing Aggressors? On the Double-Track Approach to International Criminal Justice' (2007) 5 *JICJ* 799.

[25] This category comprises the following instances: (1) The invasion or the attack by the armed forces of a State on the territory of another State, or any military occupation, however temporary, resulting from such invasion or attack, or any annexation by the use of force of the territory or part of the territory of another State. (2) Bombardment, or use of any weapon, by the armed forces of a State, against the territory of another State. (3) Blockade of the ports or coasts of a State by the armed forces of another State. (4) Attack by the armed forces of a State on the land, sea, or air forces, or marine and air fleets of another State. (5) The use of armed forces of one State which are within the territory of another State with the agreement of the receiving State, in contravention of the conditions provided for in the agreement, or any extension of their presence in such territory beyond the termination of the agreement. (6) The action of a State in allowing its territory, which it has placed at the disposal of another State, to be used by that other State for perpetrating an act of aggression against a third State. (7) The sending by or on behalf of a State of armed bands, groups, irregulars, or mercenaries, which carry out acts of armed force against another State of such gravity as to amount to the acts listed above, or the State's substantial involvement therein.

in contravention of the UN Charter, provided the acts of aggression concerned, or their consequences, are large-scale and serious.

Article 8*bis* of the Rome Statute reflects this approach. First, it lists the acts enumerated in the 1974 Definition (Article 8*bis*(2)) as acts of aggression constituting the material element of the crime of aggression. Secondly, it establishes a threshold for the criminalization of acts of aggression: under the Statute, crime of aggression means:

> the planning, preparation, initiation or execution ... of an act of aggression which, by its character, gravity and scale, constitutes a manifest violation of the Charter of the United Nations (at Article 8*bis*(1)).

There is therefore no correspondence between an act of aggression and the crime of aggression, since only the acts of aggression listed in Article 8*bis* that manifestly and given their 'character, gravity and scale' violate the UN Charter can give rise to individual criminal responsibility for the crime of aggression. This mismatch has raised some concerns since, for the first time, the international prohibition on aggression is disconnected from its criminalization.[26] On the other hand, the criminalization only of the most blatant and serious violations of the ban on the use of armed force ensures that the Court is not involved in current legal controversies on the breadth of this ban (e.g. on the legality of humanitarian intervention, see **16.5.7**, or on anticipatory self-defence, see **16.5.2**).

As for the mental element, this crime too requires criminal intent (*dolus*). It must be shown that the perpetrator intended to participate in aggression and was aware of the scope, significance, and consequences of his action. This is the case also for aggression under the Rome Statute, given the application of the standard rule on the mental element (Article 30). Arguably, however, the crime of aggression should also require a special intent, that is, the intention to achieve territorial gains or other advantages.[27] In any case, this special intent is not provided in the definition of aggression in the Rome Statute.

(2) *Other conditions.* Article 8*bis* of the Rome Statute requires the planning, preparation, initiation, or execution of the criminal act of aggression 'by a person in a position effectively to exercise control over or to direct the political or military action of a State'. This requirement entails that aggression under the Rome Statute is a so-called *leadership* crime that is committed only by political or military leaders or other senior State officials. Thus, for instance, the pilots carrying out air raids in foreign territory in execution of an aggressive plan by the political and military authorities of the State cannot be responsible for the crime of aggression. In addition, this requirement clearly establishes that the person shall exercise control over or shall direct the political or military action *of a State*. Leaders of non-State armed groups cannot therefore be responsible for the crime of aggression under the Rome Statute (unless one demonstrates that they control or direct the military action of a State).

Finally, it is worth noticing that Article 8*bis*(2) generally defines as 'act of aggression' the use of armed force *by a State* against the sovereignty, territorial integrity, or political independence of another State. The individual criminal responsibility for the crime of aggression is thus dependent upon the commission of an act of aggression *by a State*. Again, this excludes the possibility that the illegal use of force by non-State armed groups operating from one State against the sovereignty, territorial integrity, and political independence of another State gives rise to individual criminal responsibility for aggression of their leaders.

---

[26] See the pertinent remarks by M. O'Connell, 'What is Aggression? Comparing the Jus ad Bellum and the ICC Statute' (2012) 10 *JICJ* 189.

[27] See A. Cassese and P. Gaeta, *Cassese's International Criminal Law*, 3rd edn (Oxford: Oxford University Press, 2013), 142.

In other words, Article 8*bis* provides a State-centred definition of the crime of aggression, raising doubt in light of the contemporary forms of warfare increasingly involving non-State armed actors.

19.2.5 TORTURE

Torture may amount to a crime against humanity when it is committed as part of a widespread or systematic attack against any civilian population. Torture may also amount to a war crime when it is committed, during an armed conflict and in connection with it, against persons not taking part or no longer taking part in the hostilities. Finally, torture may constitute a crime per se (in other words, a discrete international crime) under the 1984 UN Convention against Torture and Other Cruel, Inhuman or Degrading Treatment or Punishment ('UN Torture Convention'). As explained in what follows, the definition of torture under the Torture Convention, however, does not coincide with the definition of torture as a crime against humanity and torture as a war crime,

(1) *Legal elements.* According to Article 1(1) of the UN Torture Convention:

> torture means any act by which severe pain or suffering, whether physical or mental, is intentionally inflicted on a person for such purposes as obtaining from him or a third person information or a confession, punishing him for an act he or a third person has committed or is suspected of having committed, or intimidating or coercing him or a third person, or for any reason based on discrimination of any kind, when such pain or suffering is inflicted by or at the instigation of or with the consent or acquiescence of a public official or other person acting in an official capacity. It does not include pain or suffering arising only from, inherent in or incidental to lawful sanctions.

According to this definition, the conduct prohibited is the infliction of 'severe pain or suffering, whether physical or mental', on a person, excluding pain or suffering arising 'only from' or 'inherent in or incidental to lawful sanctions'. The same prohibited conduct is enshrined in the definition of torture as a crime against humanity and as a war crime.[28]

In addition, under the definition of the UN Torture Convention, the prohibited conduct: (i) shall be carried out for one of the purposes specifically listed, and (ii) shall be inflicted by a public official or other person acting in an official capacity, or with their involvement (in the form of instigation, consent, or acquiescence). In the Elements of Crime of the ICC, the crime against humanity of torture does not require either of these two elements, but instead establishes that the victims must be in the custody or under the control of the perpetrator. By contrast, for the war crime of torture (both in international and non-international armed conflict) they retain the need for the prohibited conduct to be carried out for one of the enumerated purposes (reproducing almost literally those listed in the Torture Convention). The main difference between the definition of torture as a discrete crime and torture as a crime against humanity and a war crime thus lies in the fact that the former requires that the prohibited conduct is inflicted by or with the involvement of a public official or other person acting in an official capacity. Arguably, this requirement is needed because torture, as a discrete crime, is punishable even when it constitutes a single or sporadic episode and in the absence of an armed conflict. There is consequently the necessity to distinguish between the infliction of serious pain and suffering amounting to a common or 'ordinary' crime (e.g. on a woman by her husband, or on a boy by a group of

---

[28] See the Elements of Crime of the ICC: Article 7(1)(f), for the crime against humanity of torture, Article 8(2)(a)(ii) for the war crime of torture in international armed conflict, and Article 8(2)(c)(i) for the war crime of torture in non-international armed conflict.

hooligans) and the infliction of serious pain and suffering as an international crime covered by international rules on human rights.[29]

As for the mental element, the infliction of serious pain and suffering must be intentional in all cases (namely, for torture as a discrete crime, a crime against humanity, and a war crime). As already mentioned, for torture as a discrete crime and torture as a war crime under the ICC Elements of Crimes (but not for torture as a crime against humanity), it must be carried out for one of the enumerated purposes. Finally, for torture as a crime against humanity and a war crime there needs to be the general mental element of these two categories of crimes.

(2) *Torture by non-state actors*. For torture as a discrete crime, the question arises of whether and to what extent the prohibition applies to activities carried out by persons who do not qualify as public officials or persons acting in an official capacity. As noted earlier, the main difference between torture as discrete crime and torture as a crime against humanity or a war crime lies in the involvement of a public official or person acting in an official capacity. This is a requirement only for torture as a discrete crime.

In this regard, it is important to clarify that the UN Torture Convention does not consider torture to be a crime *only if* committed by a 'public official or other person acting in an official capacity'. The Convention includes such a possibility (the public official or the person acting in an official capacity is the perpetrator) but also covers activities carried out by a private person subject to the involvement of a public official or other person acting in an official capacity in one of the forms mentioned in Article 1(1) (instigation, consent, and acquiescence). In other words, private individuals may commit the crime of torture, subject to the involvement of a public official or person acting in an official capacity.

Do members of a non-State armed group qualify as 'public officials' or 'persons acting in an official capacity'? The UK Supreme Court has discussed the question recently in *R v Reeves Taylor*. The defendant (the former wife of the ex President of Liberia, Charles Taylor) was a member of an armed group, the National Patriotic Front of Liberia, seeking to take control of Liberia (which occurred in 1997, when Charles Taylor became President of Liberia). The defendant was arrested in the UK in 2007, and charged with various counts of torture under section 134 of the Criminal Justice Act 1988 (implementing the UN Torture Convention in the UK), with respect to events that occurred in 1990, during the early stages of the Liberian civil war. The question raised and discussed before the UK Supreme Court concerned the correct interpretation of the term 'person acting in an official capacity'. In particular, the Court had to clarify whether the term included 'someone who acts otherwise than in a private and individual capacity for or on behalf of an organisation or body which exercises or purports to exercise the functions of government over the civilian population in the territory which it controls and in which the relevant conduct occurs'. The Court answered in the affirmative (Lord Reed dissenting), finding that the term is sufficiently wide 'to include conduct by a person acting in an official capacity on behalf of an

---

[29] The ban on torture perpetrated under these circumstances has evolved over a long time, during which significant contributions at the norm-setting level were made by: (a) an important Declaration passed by the UN General Assembly (resolution 3452(XXX) adopted on 9 December 1975); (b) the increasing importance of the 1984 UN Convention on Torture; (c) general treaties on human rights and the judicial practice of the bodies responsible for their enforcement; (d) national case law (in particular cases such as *Pinochet* (UK); and (e) the judgments of the ICTY in *Furundžija* (Trial Chamber) and the European Court of Human Rights in *Aksoy* and *Selmouni*. Suffice it to mention that in *Filartiga* v *Peña-Irala* a US court held that 'the torturer has become, like the pirate or the slave trader before him, *hostis humani generis*, an enemy of all mankind' (at 980). And in 1998, in *Furundžija* the ICTY, after mentioning the human rights treaties and the resolutions of international organizations banning torture, stated that 'the existence of this corpus of general and treaty rules proscribing torture shows that the international community, aware of the importance of outlawing this heinous phenomenon, has decided to suppress any manifestation of torture by operating both at the interstate level and at the level of individuals. No legal loopholes have been left' (at §146).

entity exercising governmental control over a civilian population in a territory over which it exercises de facto control'. The Court considered this interpretation in conformity with the object and scope of the UN Torture Convention, which is 'to establish a regime for the international regulation of "official" torture as opposed to private acts of individuals' (at §76). The Court, however, underlined that the exercise of governmental functions by the organization or body controlling the territory is a core requirement. For the Court, this requirement involves a case-by-case assessment of whether the entity in question has a sufficient degree of organization and actual control over an area and whether it exercises the type of functions which a government or governmental organization would exercise (at §79).

19.2.6 TERRORISM

For decades, States have debated in the UN the question of punishing terrorism. However, as it will be clarified in what follows, they have been unable to adopt a foundational or comprehensive treaty for the repression and punishment of the crime.[30] In consequence, the majority of UN members have preferred to take a different approach, namely to draw up conventions prohibiting sets of well-specified acts (so-called 'sectoral conventions').

Since 1963, 16 international conventions of universal scope (and supplementary Protocols) have been adopted under the auspices of the UN and its specialized agencies. These conventions criminalize specific acts, such as acts of aircraft hijacking, aviation sabotage, and violence at airports; acts against the safety of fixed platforms located on the continental shelf; acts against internationally protected persons; acts of unlawful taking and possession of nuclear material; acts of hostage-taking; acts of terrorist bombings; and financing terrorist acts and terrorist organizations.[31] The most recent sectoral convention is the 2005 International Convention for the Suppression of Acts of Nuclear Terrorism, covering a broad range of acts and possible targets, including nuclear power plants and nuclear reactors. Some of these conventions have been widely ratified (e.g. as is the case of the 1999 International Convention for the Suppression of the Financing of Terrorism). By following a sectoral approach in the international criminalization of acts of terrorism, States have thus circumvented the thorny question of hammering out a comprehensive definition of the crime of terrorism.

(1) *The definition of the crime of terrorism.* In 2000, India informally circulated a draft treaty text for a comprehensive convention to the Ad Hoc *Committee on International Terrorism* (report C.6/55/L.2, Annex II) and since then UN member States have been negotiating the text of the Draft Comprehensive Convention on International Terrorism. This Convention would complement existing sectoral conventions and would strengthen the normative and moral stance of States against all forms of terrorism.

The text of the Draft Convention is almost ready. However, States have not reached final agreement on a definition of the crime of terrorism, essentially because they cannot agree on its exceptions, particularly with regard to the use of violence during armed conflict. Some States are adamant that the definition of the crime of terrorism excludes the acts of the so-called freedom fighters (namely armed groups engaged in wars of self-determination), even when they consist in attacks against civilians. Other States however disagree because they do not wish to include this exception. The Draft Convention cannot therefore be finalized and adopted while disagreement persists on this core issue.

---

[30] An early attempt to agree upon a universal definition of terrorism as an international crime is the 1937 Convention for the Prevention and Punishment of Terrorism, which never came into force.

[31] See the list of the Conventions and Protocols prepared by the UN SC Counter-terrorism Committee, online at https://www.un.org/sc/ctc/resources/international-legal-instruments/.

Arguably, however, a general definition of terrorism as a crime when it is committed in *peacetime* may be discerned based on national legislations, judicial decisions, regional and international treaties, and UN resolutions.[32] The Appeals Chamber of the UN Special Tribunal for Lebanon (STL) has also taken this view in its *Interlocutory Decision on the Applicable Law* (at §§83–113).[33] In a similar vein, the UK Court of Appeal (Criminal Division) in *R v Mohammed Gul* has asserted that there exists a generally agreed definition of the crime of terrorism in time of peace, by explicitly referring to the STL Interlocutory Decision (at §35).[34] By contrast, a broader norm, that would outlaw terrorist acts during times of armed conflict, has not yet emerged but may be considered as being about to emerge (STL, *Interlocutory Decision*, at §107).

(2) *Legal elements*. Following the STL *Interlocutory Decision*, in peacetime, the crime of terrorism would consist of the following three key elements: (i) the perpetration of a criminal act (such as murder, kidnapping, hostage-taking, arson, etc.), or threatening such an act; (ii) the intent to spread fear among the population (which would generally entail the creation of public danger) or directly or indirectly coerce a national or international authority to take some action, or to refrain from taking it; (iii) a transnational element of the criminal act (at §85). This last element rules out purely domestic offences, making the definition of terrorism applicable only to acts of international terrorism.

As for the emerging norm on terrorism in times of armed conflict, the STL *Interlocutory Decision* has placed great emphasis on the definition of the crime of financing terrorism enshrined in the 1999 International Convention for the Suppression of the Financing of Terrorism, providing that the crime is committed *among other things* if the person collects or provides funds to commit

> [a]ny other act intended to cause death or serious bodily injury to a civilian, or to any other person not taking an active part in the hostilities in a situation of armed conflict, when the purpose of such act, by its nature or context, is to intimidate a population, or to compel a government or an international organization to do or to abstain from doing any act. (Article 2(1)(b))

According to the STL *Interlocutory Decision*, the emerging norm on the crime of terrorism in armed conflict similarly would require that the perpetration of the criminal act should target civilians who do not take an active part in armed hostilities (these acts, in addition, could also be classified as war crimes). By contrast, acts directed against military targets may not be classified as terrorism (at §108). However, absent a general definition of terrorism in armed conflict, national laws have adopted a very broad definition of terrorism which also applies to military attacks by members of non-State armed groups against State military objectives.[35]

---

[32] This view has been propounded by A. Cassese in various scholarly works, particularly in the second edition of this book (*International Law* (Oxford: Oxford University Press, 2005), 449–50); in *International Criminal Law* (Oxford: Oxford University Press, 2003), 120; and in 'The Multifaceted Criminal Notion of Terrorism in International Law' (2006) 4 *JICJ* 933.

[33] Antonio Cassese was the President of the Appeals Chamber and his scholarly works on the matter might have had a significant influence on the content of the decision. The majority of States and scholars still do not recognize a customary crime of terrorism. For a critical analysis of the decision of the Tribunal, see B. Saul, 'Legislating from a Radical Hague: The United Nations Special Tribunal for Lebanon Invents an International Crime of Transnational Terrorism' (2011) 24 *LJIL* 677.

[34] The view seems to have been further confirmed (or at least not rejected) by the UK Supreme Court in the same case (*R v Gul (Appellant)*, §45).

[35] See e.g. the UK definition of the crime of terrorism, discussed by the UK Supreme Court in *R v Gul (Appellant)*, §45.

19.3 PROSECUTION AND PUNISHMENT OF INTERNATIONAL CRIMES

The penal repression of international crimes can be better assessed in its merits and shortcomings if considered in the light of the fundamental distinction drawn by Röling, between 'individual' and 'system' criminality.[36] The former encompasses crimes committed by individuals acting on their own initiative and for 'selfish' reasons (rape, looting, murder, etc.). The latter refers to crimes perpetrated on a large scale, chiefly in furtherance of the policy of a State or non-State armed group or other entity, or at least with the encouragement or toleration of the government authorities or the leaders of the group or entity in question. Normally 'individual criminality' is repressed by the culprit's national authorities (army commanders do not like this sort of misbehaviour, because it is bad for the morale of the troops and makes for a hostile enemy population). By contrast, 'system criminality' is normally repressed only by international tribunals or by the national courts of the adversary. There are, of course, exceptions, such as the *Calley* case, 'a typical example of system criminality',[37] urged upon the US authorities by American and foreign public opinion. By and large, repression of 'individual criminality' is a more frequent occurrence than that of 'system criminality', for the simple reason that the latter involves an appraisal and condemnation of a whole system of government, of misbehaviour involving the highest authorities of a country.

19.3.1 PROSECUTION AND PUNISHMENT BY STATE COURTS

(1) *Grounds of criminal jurisdiction*. States bring to trial before their courts alleged perpetrators of international crimes on the strength of one of two principles traditionally enshrined in national laws and also adopted for the repression of domestic offences: *territoriality* (the offence has been perpetrated on the State territory), or *active nationality* (the perpetrator is a national of the prosecuting State). Normally, the territoriality principle is preferred, both for ideological reasons (need to affirm the territorial sovereignty) and because the territory where the alleged crime has been committed is the place where it is easier to collect evidence (it is therefore considered the *forum conveniens*, or the appropriate place of trial, as the Supreme Court of Israel rightly stated in *Eichmann*, at 302–3). In addition, they also resort to the principle of *passive nationality* (the victim is a national of the prosecuting State). Notably, this occurs also in common law countries that usually contest the possibility of resorting to this ground of jurisdiction for the repression of purely domestic offences.

In more recent years, the so-called principle of *universality* has also been upheld, whereby any State is empowered to bring to trial persons accused of international crimes regardless of the place of commission of the crime, or the nationality of the author or of the victim. This principle has been advanced in two different versions.

According to the most widespread version, only the State where the accused is in custody can prosecute him or her (so-called *forum deprehensionis*, or jurisdiction of the place where the accused is apprehended). This class of jurisdiction is accepted, at the level of customary

---

[36] B. V. A. Röling, 'The Significance of the Laws of War' in A. Cassese (ed.), *Current Problems of International Law* (Milan: Giuffrè, 1975), 137. The distinction was propounded with respect to war crimes, but can be extended to other categories of international crimes as well.

[37] Ibid., at 139.

international law, with regard to piracy. At the level of treaty law it has been upheld with regard to grave breaches of the 1949 Geneva Conventions and the First Additional Protocol of 1977, and torture (under Article 7 of the 1984 UN Torture Convention), as well as terrorism (see the various UN-sponsored treaties on this matter).[38] The presence of the suspect on the territory of the State is requested in most criminal legislations, either as a basis to establish jurisdiction or as a requirement for its exercise.[39]

Under a different version of the universality principle, a State may prosecute persons accused of international crimes regardless of their nationality, the place of commission of the crime, the nationality of the victim, and even whether or not the accused is in custody in the forum State. This principle was upheld in national legislations such as Spain (in particular, with regard to genocide, war crimes, crimes against humanity, and terrorism; see Article 23 of the Law on Judicial Powers of 1985), as well as Belgium (see the Laws of 1993 and 1999). In these two countries, this broad variant of the principle of universal jurisdiction has led to a few cases and complaints against current or former senior State officials of foreign States. For instance, General Augusto Pinochet was arrested in London further to a Spanish warrant issued based on universal criminal jurisdiction (for crimes committed in Chile while he was in power). In Belgium, victims of serious human rights violations filed judicial complaints against prominent leaders, such as the then Israeli Prime Minister Ariel Sharon (for his role in the Sabra and Shatila massacre), the former Chinese President Jiang Zemin (for international crimes allegedly committed against Falungong practitioners), and former US President George W. Bush and the then Secretary of Defense Dick Cheney (for war crimes allegedly committed in the 1991 Gulf War). The issuance and international circulation by Belgium of an arrest warrant against the then acting Minister for Foreign Affairs of the Democratic Republic of Congo (DRC) also triggered a dispute between the two countries before the International Court of Justice, on the legality of the exercise of universal jurisdiction and the respect of the international immunities of the RDC. The Court eventually did not pronounce on the claim on universal jurisdiction principle, but even a cursory look at the individual Opinions of the judges appended to the judgment reveals how divisive the matter was. In Spain and Belgium, the broad variant of the principle of universal jurisdiction has been subsequently restricted by amendments to the relevant national provisions.[40] The question of whether States can assert 'absolute' universal jurisdiction now seems less topical than it was in the aftermath of the *Pinochet* case, having lost significance in practice.

(2) *International immunities*. As discussed earlier in the book (see **Chapter 6**), a State can claim immunity from foreign jurisdiction of its officials who have acted on its behalf and for acts or transactions carried out in an official capacity (so-called *functional immunities*). In addition, States are entitled to immunity from civil and criminal jurisdiction of some classes of State officials, chiefly Heads of State and Government, Ministers of Foreign Affairs, and diplomats (these are the so-called *personal* or *diplomatic immunities*). The question arises of whether both classes of immunities apply with respect to the prosecution and repression of international crimes before foreign national jurisdictions.

With respect to *personal* or *diplomatic immunities*, the ICJ has clarified that no customary rule has evolved derogating from the customary obligation of States to respect these

---

[38] These treaties, however, do not confine themselves to granting the power to prosecute and try the accused. They also oblige States to do so, or alternatively to extradite the defendant to a State concerned (the principle of *aut prosequi et judicare, aut dedere*).

[39] See P. Gaeta, 'Principle 21: Measures for Strengthening the Effectiveness of International Legal Principles Concerning Universal and International Jurisdiction' in F. Haldemann and T. Unger (eds), *The United Nations Principles to Combat Impunity: A Commentary* (Oxford: Oxford University Press, 2018), 226, at 238.

[40] Ibid.

immunities, as far as international crimes are concerned. According to the Court, incumbent Heads of State and other persons protected by these immunities may not be arrested in a foreign country and brought to trial for alleged international crimes, as long as they are in office and unless their State waives the immunity (*Arrest Warrant of 11 April 2000 (Democratic Republic of Congo v Belgium)*, at §§58–61). As for *functional immunities*, arguably since the Second World War the principle has been established according to which these immunities are not applicable in relation to international crimes. The statutes of the Nuremberg and Tokyo Military Tribunals contained respectively a rule on the irrelevance of having acted in an official capacity for the purpose of criminal responsibility. The same rule has been included in the statutes of modern international criminal courts and tribunals such as the ICTY, the ICTR, and the ICC. National proceedings have also been brought against persons accused of international crimes for their activities carried out in an official capacity, on behalf of their own State (see e.g. the trial of Eichmann in Israel). Finally, States have adopted treaties establishing the mandatory exercise of their criminal jurisdiction over persons responsible for specific classes of international crime (e.g. genocide, grave breaches of the Geneva Conventions and Additional Protocol I, torture). The object and scope of these treaties would be frustrated, should State parties respect the international rules on functional immunities.[41]

However, in recent times (probably, following the *Pinochet* case in the UK and other attempts to bring to justice former senior State officials based on the principle of universality), the irrelevance of functional immunities for international crimes has been put into question in academic and diplomatic circles. The matter has been also the object of a vivid debate within the International Law Commission, in the context of its work on the immunities of State officials from foreign jurisdiction. In 2017, the Commission adopted Draft Article 7 and an associated draft annex, providing that functional immunities shall not apply before foreign criminal jurisdictions in respect of genocide, crimes against humanity, war crimes, apartheid, torture, and enforced disappearance. This draft provision has however not been adopted without difference of opinion and criticism in the Commission, so the question cannot be considered at this stage to have been finally solved.[42]

19.3.2 THE DEMAND FOR INTERNATIONAL CRIMINAL JUSTICE

(1) *The origins.* The demand for international criminal justice blew up, as it were, in the 1990s. However, this was not new. As early as 1919, after the First World War, the victors had provided in the peace treaty with Germany, signed at Versailles, for the punishment of the major parties responsible for war crimes and went so far as to lay down in Article 227 the responsibility of the German Emperor (Wilhelm II) for 'the supreme offence against international morality and the sanctity of treaties'. However, the Emperor was not prosecuted, because the Dutch government refused to extradite him.

The attempt was repeated in similar historical circumstances, namely after the Second World War. Again, this was 'victors' justice'. Two 'international' tribunals were set up, one to try the major German 'war criminals' (the Nuremberg Tribunal), the other to try the major Japanese leaders and politicians accused of very serious breaches of international law (the Tokyo Tribunal). The Allies instituted other tribunals in Germany: these were courts composed of judges from some of the allied countries (primarily US nationals) sitting in judgment over minor alleged war criminals. Furthermore, German courts were authorized, and

---

[41] See also for the necessary references, A. Cassese, 'When May Senior State Officials Be Tried for International Crimes? Some Comments on the Congo v. Belgium Case' (2002) 13 *EJIL* 853.

[42] ILC, Report on the Work of Its Sixty-Ninth Session, UN Doc. A/72/10. The text of Draft Article 7 is at 176.

indeed requested, under Law no. 10 passed by the Control Council established by the four major Powers (the US, Britain, France, and the Soviet Union) to try persons accused of war crimes, crimes against humanity, or crimes against peace.

The major drawback of the Nuremberg and Tokyo Tribunals was that in practice they were composed of judges appointed by each of the four Powers; the prosecutors too were appointed by each of those Powers and acted under the instructions of each appointing State. Thus, it must be pointed out that the two Tribunals were not international courts proper, but judicial bodies acting as organs common to the appointing States. The Nuremberg Tribunal admitted this legal reality when it stated that:

> [t]he making of the Charter [of the IMT] was the exercise of the sovereign legislative power by the countries to which the German Reich unconditionally surrendered; and the undoubted right of these countries to legislate for the occupied territories has been recognised by the civilised world ... The Signatory Powers created this Tribunal, defined the law it was to administer, and made regulations for the proper conduct of the Trial. In doing so, *they have done together what any one of them might have done singly*; for it is not to be doubted that any nation has the right thus to set up special courts to administer law. (at 218; emphasis added)

In spite of all their deficiencies, it was salutary that, by setting up these two 'international' Tribunals, for the first time States broke the monopoly of national jurisdiction over international crimes, a monopoly that until then had been the rule.

(2) *The turning point in the early 1990s.* A major breakthrough occurred in the early 1990s, paving the way for the establishment by the UN Security Council of the two ad hoc Tribunals for the former Yugoslavia and Rwanda and, subsequently, for the creation of the ICC and a host of mixed/hybrid criminal tribunals. Various factors led to a new ethos in the world community and a strong call for international criminal justice. Two, in particular, should be underscored.

First, the *end of the Cold War* proved to be of crucial importance. It had significant effects. For one thing, the animosity that had dominated international relations for almost half a century dissipated. In its wake, a new spirit of relative optimism emerged, stimulated by the following factors: (i) a clear reduction in the distrust and mutual suspicion that had frustrated friendly relations and co-operation between the Western and the Eastern blocs; (ii) the successor States to the USSR (the Russian Federation and the other members of the Confederation of Independent States) came to accept a growing number of principles and rules of international law; (iii) as a result there emerged unprecedented agreement in the UN Security Council and increasing convergence in the views of the five permanent members, with the consequence that the institution was able to fulfil its functions more effectively.

Another effect of the end of the Cold War was no less important. Despite the problems of that bleak period, during the Cold War era the two power blocs had managed to guarantee a degree of international order in that each of the superpowers had acted as a sort of policeman and guarantor in its respective sphere of influence. The collapse of this model of international relations ushered in a wave of negative consequences. It entailed a fragmentation of the international community and intense disorder which, coupled with rising nationalism and fundamentalism, resulted in a spiralling of mostly internal armed conflicts, with much bloodshed and cruelty. The ensuing implosion of previously multi-ethnic societies led to gross violations of international humanitarian law on a scale comparable to those committed during the Second World War.

The second crucial factor was the *increasing importance of the human rights doctrine*. Its emphasis on the need to respect human dignity and consequently to punish all those who seriously attack such dignity gave rise to the quest for, or at least gave a robust impulse to, international criminal justice.

19.3.3 THE ESTABLISHMENT OF INTERNATIONAL CRIMINAL COURTS AND TRIBUNALS

(1) *The two ad hoc Tribunals for the Former Yugoslavia and Rwanda.* In the early 1990s, the conflicts which erupted in, amongst other places, the former Yugoslavia and Rwanda and the atrocities they engendered served to rekindle the sense of outrage felt at the closing stages of the Second World War. By way of response, the UN Security Council, pursuant to its power to decide on measures necessary to maintain or restore international peace and security under Chapter VII of the UN Charter, set up two ad hoc Tribunals: in 1993, by resolution 827 (1993), the International Criminal Tribunal for the former Yugoslavia (ICTY), and in 1994, by resolution 955 (1994), the International Criminal Tribunal for Rwanda (ICTR).

The ICTY closed down on 21 December 2007. Established in The Hague, in the Netherlands, the ICTY was empowered to exercise jurisdiction over grave breaches of the Geneva Conventions, violations of the laws and customs of war, genocide, and crimes against humanity allegedly perpetrated in the former Yugoslavia since 1 January 1991. The Tribunal indicted over 160 persons, including Heads of State, Prime Ministers, army chiefs of staff, Interior Ministers, and many other high- and mid-level political, military, and police leaders from various parties to the Yugoslav conflicts. The indictments addressed crimes committed between 1991 and 2001 against members of various ethnic groups in Croatia, Bosnia and Herzegovina, Serbia, Kosovo, and the Former Yugoslav Republic of Macedonia. The Tribunal heard significant cases, such as the case against Ratko Mladić (commander of the main staff of the Bosnian-Serbian army) for his role in the genocide in Srebrenica and the extermination and persecution in the municipalities of Bosnia Herzegovina. Through its seminal and rich case law, the ICTY has made an enormous contribution to the very creation of modern international criminal law and the current system of international criminal justice.

The ICTR closed down on 31 December 2015. Established in Arusha, Tanzania, it was called upon to adjudicate on genocide, crimes against humanity, violations of Article 3 common to the Geneva Conventions and of the Second Additional Protocol, allegedly perpetrated in Rwanda (or in 'the territory of neighbouring States' by Rwandan citizens) between 1 January and 31 December 1994. The ICTR indicted over 90 people and heard cases against prominent figures, including the former Prime Minister of Rwanda, Jean Kambanda. By sentencing him to life imprisonment in 1998, the ICTR was the first international tribunal to issue a judgment against a Head of Government since the Nuremberg and Tokyo Tribunals. Like the ICTY, the ICTR played a pioneering role in the establishment of the current system of international criminal justice and contributed to the clarification and development of international criminal law by producing a substantial body of jurisprudence on a variety of issues. In particular, the ICTR defined rape in international criminal law and recognized it as a means of perpetrating genocide. It was also the first international tribunal to hold members of the media responsible for incitement to commit genocide through broadcasting.

The ICTY and ICTR have attracted criticism, particularly with respect to the selection of cases. For instance, facing allegations of war crimes by members of the NATO forces in the bombing campaign against the then Federal Republic of Yugoslavia, the Prosecutor of the ICTY eventually decided not to start investigations. The Prosecutor took this decision based on the report issued by an ad hoc Review Committee, although the report was not binding and arguably was inconclusive in excluding the commission of war crimes by members of NATO forces.[43] As for the ICTR, it failed to prosecute war crimes and crimes against humanity committed in 1994 by members of the Rwandan Patriotic Front (RPF), the rebel group at the time fighting against the central government that ended the genocide and that subsequently became the Rwanda's ruling party.[44]

In 2010, the Security Council established the Mechanism for the International Criminal Tribunals (MICT) as a successor court of its own to the ICTY and ICTR (SC resolution 1996 of 22 December 2010). The MICT continues 'the jurisdiction, rights and obligations and essential functions of the ICTY and the ICTR' and comprises two branches: one for the ICTR (based in Arusha and active since 1 July 2012), the other for the ICTY (based in The Hague and active since 1 July 2013). The MICT will continue to operate until the Security Council decides otherwise. During the initial years of its existence, the MICT operated in parallel with the ICTR and the ICTY.

(2) *The International Criminal Court.* The ICC was created in 1998 by a Diplomatic Conference held in Rome. The Court has jurisdiction over only 'the most serious crimes of concern to the international community as a whole' (Rome Statute, Preamble, §4), which according to Article 5(1) of the Rome Statute are: genocide, crimes against humanity, war crimes, and the crime of aggression. Generally speaking, this reflects the jurisdictional reach of the ad hoc Tribunals, being a combination of Articles 2–5 of the ICTY Statute and Articles 2–4 of the ICTR Statute, to which the crime of aggression had been added. The key aspects of the 'jurisdictional architecture' of the Rome Statute are the following.

First, the jurisdiction of the ICC can be activated in three ways (Article 13 of the Rome Statute): (i) when a situation where one or more crimes under the jurisdiction appear to have been committed has been referred to the Prosecutor by a State party to the Statute, (ii) when a situation where one or more crimes under the jurisdiction appear to have been committed has been referred to the Prosecutor by the Security Council acting under Chapter VII of the UN Charter, or (iii) where the Prosecutor him/herself initiates an investigation over a case. This latter route to the seizing of the Court was particularly controversial and a number of safeguards—or barriers—were therefore erected to guard against the possibility of an autonomous Prosecutor exercising excessive zeal. In particular, under Article 15 the role of the Prosecutor is to examine 'information' and he must seek the authorization of a pre-trial Chamber of the Court itself if there is to be a thorough 'investigation' of the case. By contrast, there is no need for the Prosecutor to seek authorization if a situation was referred by a State party or by the Security Council. Moreover, Article 16 permits the Security Council, by means of a resolution adopted under Chapter VII of the UN Charter, to block the 'commencement or continuance of investigations for a period of up to 12

---

[43] See in particular P. Benvenuti, 'The ICTY Prosecutor and the Review of the NATO Bombing Campaign against the Federal Republic of Yugoslavia' (2001) 12 *EJIL* 503. As the then Prosecutor of the ICTY, Carla Del Ponte, has subsequently clarified in her memoirs, the decision not to open an investigation was dictated essentially by her conviction that otherwise the States members of NATO would have stopped co-operating with her office in all other procedures. According to her view, this would have prevented her office from exercising its functions and fulfilling the mandate to prosecute the crimes committed by local forces since 1991: C. Del Ponte and C. Sudetic, *Madame Prosecutor: Confrontations with Humanity's Worst Criminals and the Culture of Impunity* (New York: Other Press, 2009), 60.

[44] See T. Cruveillier, *Le tribunal des vaincus: un Nuremberg pour le Rwanda?* (Paris: Calmann-Levy, 2006).

months'.⁴⁵ This possibility is open to the Security Council whatever the mechanism that triggered the jurisdiction of the Court. These safeguards notwithstanding, the US maintained its objections to the referral of situations by States parties and *proprio motu* powers of the Prosecutor, arguing that this rendered members of the US armed forces participating in peacekeeping operations around the world open to prosecution by the ICC and that, in consequence, it might be faced with cases motivated by political hostility.⁴⁶

Secondly, the Court can only exercise its jurisdiction if one of the two preconditions is fulfilled (Article 12 of the Rome Statute): (a) 'the State on the territory of which the conduct in question occurred or, if the crime was committed on board a vessel or aircraft, the State of registration of that vessel or aircraft' is a party to the Rome Statute or has accepted ad hoc the jurisdiction of the Court under Article 12(3), or (b) the 'person accused of the crime is a national' of a State party to the Statute or of a State that has accepted ad hoc the jurisdiction of the Court. Of course, this means that the Court can exercise jurisdiction over individuals who are nationals of States that have not ratified the Statute if the act in question was performed in the territory of a State that has ratified the Statute or the crime was committed on board a vessel or aircraft of such State (this is because of the disjunctive formula used in Article 12 of the Rome Statute).

Importantly, there is no need for either of the two preconditions to exist when the Security Council triggers the jurisdiction of the Court. This has occurred twice. On the first occasion, the Security Council referred to the ICC the situation in the Darfur region of Sudan and required Sudan and all other parties to the conflict in Darfur to co-operate fully (SC resolution 1593, adopted on 31 March 2005). The second time, the Security Council referred to the ICC the situation in Libya since 15 February 2011 (which can be considered as the starting date of the civil war which led to the fall of Gaddafi's rule) (SC resolution 1970, adopted on 26 February 2011).

In a decision concerning the crimes committed against the Rohingya in Myanmar (a State not party to the Rome Statute), the Court has clarified that the precondition of territoriality under Article 12(2)(a) is also fulfilled when only one element of the crime took place on the territory of a State party to the Statute (*Rohingya Decision*). It has thus asserted its power to exercise jurisdiction over the crime against humanity of deportation, allegedly committed against members of the Rohingya who have crossed the border of Bangladesh, which is a State party to the Rome Statute. This is because, according to the Court, the crime against humanity of deportation necessarily includes the element of crossing the frontier of another State. Until now, the Court has not yet asserted its power to exercise jurisdiction solely because of the fulfilment of nationality requirement of the accused. On 13 May 2014, upon receipt of new information, the Prosecutor reopened a preliminary examination on alleged crimes committed by nationals of the UK (a State party) in the territory of Iraq (a non-State party), in the context of the Iraq conflict and occupation from 2003 to 2008, including murder, torture, and other forms of ill-treatment. Formal investigations have however not yet commenced.

The third critical feature of the functioning of the ICC is that its jurisdiction is *complementary* to that of national criminal justice systems (Preamble, §10, and Article 1 of the

---

[45] See SC resolution 1422 (12 July 2002) and resolution 1487 (12 June 2003) which remove *en bloc* from the jurisdiction of the Court cases that may arise 'involving current or former officials or personnel from a contributing state not a party to the Rome Statute over acts or omissions relating to a United Nations established or authorized operation' for a 12-month period. The Security Council expressed the intention to renew this request annually 'for as long as necessary' (but it was not renewed in 2004).

[46] Statement by the Hon. Bill Richardson, US Ambassador to the UN (17 June 1998). The US has now entered into a series of bilateral treaties with States under the terms of which it is agreed that no US servicemen serving in UN-authorized operations in a State party to the Statute will be transferred to the jurisdiction of the Court.

Rome Statute). It does not replace national courts; indeed, national jurisdictions enjoy priority over the ICC. According to Article 17 of the Statute, a case is therefore to be declared inadmissible if it is being investigated or prosecuted (or has been investigated) by national authorities, unless the State in question is unable or unwilling genuinely to carry out the investigation or prosecution. This flows naturally from principles of State sovereignty and means that the ICC jurisdiction should have something of a residual flavour. This is the reason why some commentators have criticized the way the Court has interpreted and applied Article 17 to date. In particular, the Court has adopted very stringent requirements to establish whether a national jurisdiction is actually investigating and prosecuting the same case pending before the ICC. The approach taken by the Court is considered incompatible with the jurisdictional architecture established by the Rome Statute, which would require the ICC to declare a case inadmissible whenever the national authorities are making a genuine effort to bring a suspect to justice.[47]

(3) *Hybrid criminal courts or tribunals.* After deciding to create the ICTR, which took considerable time and effort, the Security Council arguably reached a point of 'tribunal fatigue'. Indeed, the logistics of setting up the ad hoc Tribunals for the former Yugoslavia and Rwanda had strained the capacity and resources of the United Nations and the time of the Security Council, which frequently found itself seized with issues and problems concerning the Tribunals and their administration. Thus, the desire to establish such tribunals waned and, furthermore, the Council did not consider other international conflicts to be of a scale sufficient to justify their establishment.

Nevertheless, with the passing of time, the Security Council came to consider situations that required some sort of international involvement in the delivery of criminal justice. The solution has not been to create an ad hoc tribunal along the lines of the ICTY or ICTR, but to establish courts or tribunals exhibiting features of both national and international jurisdiction. One can distinguish two different phases in this regard.[48] The first, addressing accountability dilemmas, has led to the establishment of courts such as the Special Court for Sierra Leone, the Special Panels for East Timor and Kosovo, the Extraordinary Chambers for Cambodia, the War Crimes Chamber in Bosnia Herzegovina, and the Special Tribunal for Lebanon. The second phase is characterized by the involvement also of international actors other than the UN (notably, the African Union and the European Union). In contrast to the previous phase, the second one seems to take more account of certain advantages that this model of justice would possess with respect to international criminal courts in addressing issues of accountability.[49]

The common feature of the aforementioned courts or tribunals is that they are judicial bodies with a mixed composition, consisting of both international judges and judges having the nationality of the State where trials are to be held. This is why they are termed 'hybrid', 'mixed', or 'internationalized'. Some of them are part of the judiciary of the relevant State, and therefore are national courts (although exhibiting specific features). This is, for instance, the position of Cambodian Extraordinary Chambers. Alternatively, other courts or tribunals are truly international in nature, meaning that they are not part of the national judiciary and are bodies belonging to the international legal order (e.g. this was the case for the Special Court for Sierra Leone and is the case for the Special Tribunal for Lebanon).

---

[47] See in this respect K. Heller, 'Radical Complementarity' (2016) 14 *JICJ* 637.

[48] See C. Stahn, *A Critical Introduction to International Criminal Law* (Cambridge: Cambridge University Press, 2019), 197, speaking of 'two waves'.

[49] For an excellent overview of the features and activities of these different mixed courts and tribunals, see ibid., at 199–209.

The establishment of hybrid courts and tribunals to address issues of accountability may prove advantageous in numerous ways. For example, it might help taking into account nationalistic concerns about handing over the administration of justice—an essential prerogative of sovereign power—to international bodies. In addition, hybrid courts and tribunals allow for the involvement of local prosecutors and judges who are familiar with the mentality, language, and habits of those with whom they are coming into contact. They might also allow for more expeditious prosecution whilst not compromising international standards. Moreover, holding trials in the territory where the crimes have been committed ensures maximum visibility, which can have a cathartic effect as regards victims or their relatives, and through the public stigmatization of culprits and the issuance of just retribution, thereby contributing to the process of gradual reconciliation. At an even more general level, the experience of participating in hybrid justice might produce a significant spill-over effect, in that it might assist in promoting the democratic legal training of the local prosecuting and judicial authorities.

19.3.4 MERITS AND DISADVANTAGES OF INTERNATIONAL CRIMINAL TRIALS

(1) *Main merits.* International criminal courts and tribunals enjoy a number of advantages over domestic courts, particularly those sitting in the territory of the State where atrocities have been committed.

First, it is a fact that national jurisdictions are not inclined to institute proceedings for crimes that lack any territorial or national link with the State. National judicial authorities are still State-oriented and loath to try foreigners who have committed crimes abroad against other foreigners. For them, the short-term objectives of national concerns seem still to prevail. This is also due in part to the failure of national parliaments to pass the necessary legislation granting courts universal jurisdiction over international crimes. As for crimes committed by nationals in the State territory, courts may be reluctant to bring the suspects to trial whenever they happen to be senior State officials or persons strongly supported by such officials.

Secondly, the crimes at issue being serious breaches of international law, international courts are the most appropriate bodies to pronounce on them. They are in a better position to know and apply the relevant law, that is, international rules.

Thirdly, international judges may be more impartial and unbiased, or at any rate more even-handed, than the national judges who have been caught up in the milieu in which the crime under trial has been perpetrated. The punishment of alleged authors of large-scale crimes by international tribunals normally meets with less resistance than national punishment, as it hurts national feelings much less.

Fourthly, international courts can investigate crimes with ramifications in many countries more easily than national judges. Often the witnesses reside in different countries, other evidence needs to be collected thanks to the co-operation of several States, and, in addition, special expertise is needed to handle the often complex and difficult legal issues raised in the various national legislations involved.

Fifthly, trials by international courts may ensure some sort of uniformity in the application of international law, whereas proceedings conducted before national courts may lead to a great disparity both in the application of that law and the penalties meted out to those found guilty.

Finally, the holding of international trials—enjoying greater visibility than national criminal proceedings—signals the will of the international community to break with the past, by punishing those who have deviated from acceptable standards of human behaviour. In delivering punishment, the international community's purpose is not so much retribution as stigmatization of the deviant behaviour, in the hope that this will have some deterrent effect.

(2) *Main disadvantages.* International criminal courts and tribunals however have at least two main disadvantages over domestic criminal prosecutions.

First, they pronounce on crimes committed on the territory of a State of which they are *not* the judicial organ. Normally they do not sit in the country where crimes falling under their jurisdiction have been perpetrated. They are located in a distant country, or at any rate in a country not necessarily close to the scene of the crimes. In short, they are not the *forum delicti commissi.*[50]

Secondly, international criminal courts and tribunals exercise jurisdiction directly over individuals living in a sovereign State and subject to the jurisdiction of that State. In addition, in most cases, when perpetrating the alleged crime these individuals have acted qua State officials, or at least at the instigation or with the support or the endorsement or acquiescence of State authorities. In principle, international criminal courts and tribunals are therefore intended to cast aside the shield of sovereignty. However—and this is another salient trait—in fact they cannot reach those individuals without going through national authorities. These courts do have the power to issue warrants for the seizure of evidence or the searching of premises, and to issue subpoenas or arrest warrants. However, they cannot enforce the acts resulting from the exercise of those powers, for lack of enforcement agents working under their authority and empowered freely to enter the territory of sovereign States and exercise enforcement functions there, notably vis-à-vis individuals acting as State officials. This is the major stumbling block of these courts and tribunals. They lack an autonomous *police judiciaire* overriding national authorities. They are like giants without arms and legs, who therefore need artificial limbs to walk and work. These artificial limbs are the State authorities. If the co-operation of States is not forthcoming, these courts and tribunals are paralysed and can hardly fulfil their mandate.

---

[50] This is also the *forum conveniens.* As the Supreme Court of Israel stated in *Eichmann,* 'normally the great majority of the witnesses and the greater part of the evidence are concentrated in … the State [where the crimes were committed] and [this] is therefore the most convenient place (*forum conveniens*) for the conduct of the trial' (at 302).

20
THE PROTECTION OF THE ENVIRONMENT

20.1 INTRODUCTION

The UN Charter makes no reference to environmental protection. In the aftermath of the Second World War, the natural wealth of countries and non-self-governing territories was only understood through the prism of the exploitation of 'natural resources'. This prism became even more important in the context of the decolonization process, with the efforts of developing and newly independent countries to gain economic independence and promote socio-economic development.

Yet, throughout the 1960s and early 1970s, a series of events and developments both at the domestic and the international levels started to draw attention to a range of issues, such as air pollution (e.g. 'acid rain'), pollution of the seas (e.g. oil spills), nuclear energy and waste, endangered species, degradation of certain spaces, large-scale industrial activities, over-exploitation of fisheries, among others, which required a concerted response rather than a purely domestic one. At the domestic level, a series of influential publications unveiled the side effects of activities which, until then, had been one-sidedly perceived as positive.[1] For example, Rachel Carson's famous book *Silent Spring* unveiled the adverse effects on birds resulting from the use of DDT as a pesticide.[2] Also during this period, the link between inequality, race, and environmental degradation became increasingly visible, particularly in the comparison of where most waste was being generated (wealthy areas populated by white people) and where it was disposed of (poor areas populated by black people).[3] At the international level, oil spills such as the one resulting from the grounding of the Liberian tanker *Torrey Canyon* in 1967[4] gave a sense of urgency to claims about marine and air pollution, through the more complex (less visible) phenomenon of 'acid rain' experienced in Scandinavian countries and in Canada.[5] The conservation of nature and wildlife in newly independent countries emerging from the decolonization process

---

[1] See e.g. K. E. Boulding, 'The Economics of the Coming Spaceship Earth' in H. Jarrett (ed.), *Environmental Quality in a Growing Economy* (Baltimore: Johns Hopkins University Press, 1966), 3; M. Nicholson, *The Environmental Revolution: A Guide for the New Masters of the World* (London: Hodder & Stoughton, 1969); B. Commoner, *The Closing Circle: Nature, Man, and Technology* (New York: Alfred Knopf, 1971); D. H. Meadows, D. L. Meadows, J. Randers, and W. W. Behrens III, *The Limits to Growth* (New York: Universe Books, 1972).

[2] R. Carson, *Silent Spring* (Boston: Houghton Mifflin, 1962).

[3] R. D. Bullard, *Dumping in Dixie: Race, Class, and Environmental Quality* (Boulder, CO: Westview Press, 1990).

[4] On 18 March 1967, the *Torrey Canyon*, a ship registered under the flag of Liberia, ran aground off the British coast spilling over 117,000 tons of crude oil into the English Channel and causing extensive damage to the English and French coasts.

[5] See G. E. Likens et al., 'Acid Rain' (1979) 241 *Scientific American* 43.

also led to calls—not without a paternalistic tone—for the creation of protected areas to safeguard the nature of newly independent countries.[6]

The emergence of 'environmental protection' as an area of co-operation at the international level therefore has a diverse range of sources, some largely preceding the post-1945 architecture and others more directly prompted by the challenges, mostly pollution, faced by industrialized countries. This chapter begins with a brief survey of three important precedents of international environmental law and then examines tour à tour the process leading to the formulation of the main principles in this area, their extension and specification through soft-law instruments, multilateral environmental agreements (MEAs), implementation techniques, and international institutions, and, finally, the role of State responsibility and civil liability for environmental harm (see **20.5**).[7]

20.2 PRECEDENTS

Well before the emergence of environmental protection as an area of international co-operation in the late 1960s and early 1970s, three important cases laid the ground for subsequent developments relating to transboundary relations and the protection of the global commons.

(1) Somewhat unintuitively, the oldest precedent is possibly also the most progressive in the argumentation developed by one of the parties, albeit not accepted by the tribunal. Indeed, in the *Bering Fur Seals arbitration* (1893) between the United States and United Kingdom, the idea of the preservation of a resource, even if located outside of a State's jurisdiction, was articulated in detail by counsel of the US. The context of the case is given by the wide disagreements among a group of States (the US, the UK, France, Germany, Japan, Russia, Sweden, and Norway) interested in fur seals in the Bering Sea on how to tackle the indiscriminate destruction and extermination resulting from over-exploitation. It is, therefore, about what today would be called a 'tragedy of the commons' by reference to G. Hardin's classic piece[8] and, even more remarkably, it offers the concept of public trust as the appropriate legal frame.

The US and the UK submitted to arbitration various issues relating to jurisdictional rights and the preservation of fur seals. In particular, one of the issues raised before the arbitral tribunal was the question whether the US had 'any right ... of protection or property in the fur seals frequenting the islands of the United States in the Bering Sea when such seals are found outside the ordinary three-mile limit'.[9] On this issue, counsel for the

---

[6] See S. Macekura, *Of Limits and Growth: The Rise of International Sustainable Development in the Twentieth Century* (Cambridge: Cambridge University Press, 2015), 54.

[7] The account relies on P.-M. Dupuy and J. E. Viñuales, *International Environmental Law*, 2nd edn (Cambridge: Cambridge University Press, 2018) (Dupuy and Viñuales). Other reference textbooks include P. Sands, J. Peel, A. Fabra, and R. MacKenzie, *Principles of International Environmental Law*, 4th edn (Cambridge: Cambridge University Press, 2018); P. Birnie, A. Boyle, and C. Redgwell, *International Law and the Environment*, 3rd edn (Oxford: Oxford University Press, 2009).

[8] See G. Hardin, 'The Tragedy of the Commons' (1968) 162 *Science* 1243.

[9] J. B. Moore, *History and Digest of the International Arbitrations to which the United States has been a Party* (Washington, DC: Government Printing Office, 1898), vol. I, at 801. It should be noted that as early as 1887 the US Secretary of State, Bayard, had sent a note to France, Germany, Britain, Japan, Russia, Sweden, and Norway, urging international co-operation, and stating among other things that '[i]t is well known that the unregulated and indiscriminate killing of seals in many parts of the world has driven them from place to place, and, by breaking up their habitual resorts, has greatly reduced their number' (ibid., at 776). The note went on to stress 'the common interest of all nations in preventing the indiscriminate destruction and consequent extermination of an animal which contributes so importantly to the commercial wealth and general use of mankind' (ibid.).

US expressed an unusual and novel view. Referring to 'the established principles of the common and the civil law … the practice of nations … the laws of natural history, and … the common interests of mankind',[10] he asserted that the US had a right of property over the fur seals outside its territorial sea; this right, however, did not make the US 'absolute owners', for it was 'coupled with a trust for the benefit of mankind'; 'the human race [was] entitled to participate in the enjoyment'.[11] The US also claimed to be the only State possessing the power of preserving fur seals: '[t]he United States, possessing, as they alone possess, the power of preserving and cherishing this valuable interest, are in a most just sense the trustee thereof for the benefit of mankind and should be permitted to discharge their trust without hindrance'.[12] In explaining the concepts of property and trust, it argued that:

> [e]very nation, so far as it possesses more than enough of the fruits of the earth to satisfy its own needs, is a *trustee* of the surplus for the benefit of those in other parts of the world who need them and are willing to give in exchange for them the products of their own labour, and this trust is *obligatory*.[13]

Subsequently, the argument foreshadowed a concept that in the second half of the twentieth century would become controversial, namely the common heritage of mankind as applied to natural resources:

> The coffee of Central America and Arabia is not the exclusive property of those two nations; the tea of China, the rubber of South America, are not the exclusive property of those nations where it is grown; they are, so far as not needed by the nations which enjoy the possession, the common property of mankind; and if nations which have the custody of them withdraw them, they are failing in their trust, and other nations have a right to interfere and secure their share.[14]

The British submissions were that the US claim was 'entirely without precedent'[15] and 'shorn of all support of international law and of justification from the usage of nations'.[16] It ran counter to the basic principles on the high seas and the right of all nations of the world to navigate and fish there. The tribunal upheld the British view, holding that the US had no 'right of protection or property in the fur-seals'.[17] It thus implicitly dismissed, among other things, the concept of 'trust for the benefit of mankind'. However, it also adopted regulations for the protection and preservation of fur seals. These regulations restricted fur seal capture in many respects: under Article 1, the US and the UK were to 'forbid their citizens and subjects … to kill, capture or pursue at any time and in any manner whatever' fur seals 'within a zone of sixty miles around the Pribilov Islands, inclusive of the territorial waters'; Article 2 extended this prohibition to certain areas of the high seas for the period May–July; pursuant to Articles 3 and 4, only 'sailing vessels' with a 'special licence' were permitted to carry on fur seal capture operations; under Article 6 the use of 'nets, fire arms and explosives' in such operations was however prohibited.[18]

---

[10] Moore, *History and Digest*, 811. See also at 827–9.
[11] Ibid., at 834–5.
[12] Ibid., at 814.
[13] Ibid., at 834.
[14] Ibid., at 853.
[15] Ibid., at 819.
[16] Ibid., at 845. See, at 870–1 and 875–7, the sharp and rather sarcastic British comments on the US views on the right to 'property and protection'.
[17] Ibid., at 939 (original text of the award in French) and 849 (English translation).
[18] Ibid., at 949–51. See, at 922–9, a report on the negotiations on the regulations.

(2) Although less prescient, the *Trail Smelter (United States of America/Canada)* case was much more influential. A Canadian smelter of zinc and lead ores, located in Trail, in British Columbia (Canada) was alleged to cause damage to trees, crops, and land in the American State of Washington due to the emission of sulphur dioxide fumes from the plant. These fumes, proceeding down the Columbia river valley and otherwise, entered US territory. The arbitral tribunal appointed by the US and Canada by means of a *compromis* was called upon to decide whether Canada was responsible for the damage and, if so, what indemnity it should pay to the US.

It is important to note that the tribunal was asked to apply 'the law and practice followed in dealing with cognate questions in the United States of America as well as international law' (Article IV of the 1935 arbitration agreement). In its second decision (handed down on 11 March 1941), the tribunal stated that, generally speaking, every State has a duty at all times to protect other States against injurious acts by individuals within its jurisdiction (at 1963); more specifically:

> [U]nder the principles of international law, as well as the law of the United States, no State has the right to use or permit the use of its territory in such a manner as to cause injury by fumes in or to the territory of another or the properties or persons therein, when the case is of serious consequence and the injury is established by clear and convincing evidence. (at 1965)

Consequently, the tribunal held Canada responsible for the conduct of the Trail Smelter and enjoined it to pay compensation to the US. In addition, interestingly, the tribunal also provided for future monitoring of the effects of the factory's activities on the environment, to prevent possible future damage to the US environment.

For the first time, an international tribunal propounded the principle that a State may not use, or allow its nationals to use, its own territory in such a manner as to cause injury to a neighbouring country, and this in a specifically environmental context.

(3) Later, the idea gradually emerged that natural resources may be relevant not only to the individual States that can exploit them but also to all members of the international community and could be used in the interest of mankind. Thus, for instance, in the *Lac Lanoux (Spain/France)* case (1957) the arbitral tribunal, while taking a traditional view of international law regulating relations between neighbouring States, alluded to the possibility of natural resources such as the water of a lake being exploited 'in the common interests of everybody'.

France had notified the Spanish government that it intended to authorize the construction of a barrage utilizing the water of Lake Lanoux. This lake lies in French territory at a very high altitude. Its waters flow through a tributary, the River Carol, an international waterway passing through France and Spain. The purpose of the barrage was to channel the lake's water through a hydroelectric power plant; the lake's water would have stopped flowing, so as to be used for the plant. To compensate for the cessation of the water flow, France would build a subterranean canal returning the same amount of water to the Carol river, at a point prior to its use by farmers in Spain. Spain objected that this scheme was contrary to treaty and customary law.

The tribunal held, however, that France's actions did not infringe Spain's rights: France would neither pollute the waters to be returned to Spain, nor return less water than the quantity it intended to divert. It concluded that, 'assuming there was (*en admettant qu'il existe*) a principle which prohibits the upstream State from altering the waters of a river in such a fashion as seriously to prejudice the downstream State', in any event such principle did not apply in the case at issue because the French scheme did not alter the waters of the River Carol (at 308). The tribunal went so far as to hold that there was no general international rule 'forbidding one State, acting to safeguard its legitimate interests, to put itself in a situation which would in fact permit it, in violation of its international pledges, seriously to injure a neighbouring State' (at 305). However, the tribunal also stated that 'the growing ascendancy of man over the forces and secrets of nature has put into his hands instruments which he can use to violate his pledges just as much as for the common good of all (*pour le bien commun de tous*)' (at 305).

20.3 THE PRINCIPLES OF INTERNATIONAL ENVIRONMENTAL LAW: 1972–2020

The birth of modern international environmental law can be situated at the Stockholm Conference on the Human Environment held in June 1972.[19] This conference was convened on the initiative of Sweden.[20] By letter of 20 May 1968, Ambassador Sverker Astrom, then Sweden's Permanent Representative to the UN, requested the UN Secretary-General to inscribe in the agenda of the Economic and Social Council of the UN (ECOSOC) an item entitled '[t]he question of convening an international conference on the problems of human environment'.[21] In the enclosed memorandum, 'problems of human environment' were 'understood to mean, on the one hand, the changes in the natural surroundings of man brought about, without adequate control, by the use of modern technological advances in industry and agriculture, and on the other hand, the impact of this process on man himself'. The memorandum made reference to the ongoing work of certain UN specialized agencies, such as the work on water and air pollution by the World Health Organization (WHO), that on the depletion of soil and fisheries by the Food and Agriculture Organization (FAO), that on conservation by the United Nations Educational, Scientific and Cultural Organization (UNESCO), and, of course, the work on environmental pollution within ECOSOC. However, the memorandum noted that these prior activities:

> ha[d] not yet been given the prominence in the deliberations of the competent organs of the United Nations, in particular the General Assembly and the Economic and Social Council, which is necessary if they are to have maximum impact on the practical actions of Governments and intergovernmental and non-governmental organizations ... There [was], therefore, an indisputable need to create a basis for comprehensive consideration within the United Nations of the problems of human environment.[22]

Three years later, after a rather convoluted process which faced resistance from developing countries and was eventually boycotted by the Soviet bloc, the Stockholm Conference was held, resulting in the introduction of the protection of the environment as a field of co-operation within the UN remit. This step was consolidated by the establishment of the UN Environment Programme,[23] following a recommendation from the Stockholm

---

[19] 'Report of the United Nations Conference on the Human Environment, Stockholm 5–16 June 1972' UN Doc. A/CONF.48/14/Rev1 (1973). On this major milestone see A. Kiss and D. Sicault, 'La Conférence des Nations Unies sur l'environnement (Stockholm, 5–16 June 1972)' (1972) 18 *Annuaire français de droit international* 603; W. Rowland, *The Plot to Save the World: The Life and Times of the Stockholm Conference on the Human Environment* (Toronto: Clarke, Irwin & Company, 1973); M. Strong, 'One Year after Stockholm: An Ecological Approach to Management' (1973) 51 *Foreign Affairs* 690 (the Canadian Maurice Strong was the Secretary-General of the Stockholm Conference and went on to become the first Executive Director of the newly established United Nations Environment Programme). On this evolution see generally J. E. Viñuales, 'The Rise and Fall of Sustainable Development' (2013) 22 *RECIEL* 3.

[20] 'Problems of the Human Environment', 3 December 1968, UN Doc. 2398 (XXIII).

[21] Letter dated 20 May 1968 from the Permanent Representative of Sweden addressed to the Secretary-General of the United Nations, E/4466/Add.1, 22 May 1968 (Swedish Letter).

[22] Ibid., Memorandum, §5.

[23] 'Institutional and Financial Arrangements for International Environmental Cooperation', 15 December 1972, UN Doc. A/RES/2997/XXVII.

Conference,[24] with its headquarters in Nairobi, as a gesture to assuage the concerns of developing countries. No less important was the adoption, at Stockholm, of a Declaration on the Human Environment,[25] which formulated the principle which would progressively establish itself as the cornerstone of international environmental law. Indeed, Principle 21 of the Stockholm Declaration stated:

> States have, in accordance with the Charter of the United Nations and the principles of international law, the sovereign right to exploit their own resources pursuant to their own environmental policies, and the responsibility to ensure that activities within their jurisdiction or control do not cause damage to the environment of other States or of areas beyond the limits of national jurisdiction.

This principle has been examined earlier in this book (see **3.10**). As noted in that section, the principle was subsequently restated in Principle 2 of the Rio Declaration on Environment and Development,[26] which constitutes, so far, the main statement of the principles of international environmental law.[27] The latter was adopted during the second major milestone in the history of global environmental governance, namely the UN Conference on Environment and Development held at Rio de Janeiro from 3 to 14 June 1992.[28] The Rio Conference took place in an entirely different context, marked by the end of the Cold War and an atmosphere of increasing assertiveness by developing countries. Some observers saw the balance struck at Rio with a critical eye due to the great space accorded to development considerations.[29] This shift was symbolically introduced in the formulation of Principle 2, which refers to a State's 'own environmental *and developmental* policies'. However, with the benefit of hindsight, the Rio Declaration must be seen as a major and still unsurpassed statement of the main principles of international environmental law. It is therefore important to examine its contents in some more detail before turning to the evolution of global environmental governance between 1992 and 2015, the date of the subsequent major milestone, and the ongoing efforts to adopt a Global Pact for the Environment.

The Rio Declaration includes a preamble and 27 principles but only a sub-set of them specifically concern environmental law. Among the latter, the most important ones are the triad of principles which have been recognized by the ICJ and other international courts and tribunals as principles of customary international law,[30] namely the prevention principle (Principle 2), which is an advanced form of the older 'no harm' rule and the duty of 'due diligence', the requirement to conduct an environmental impact assessment or 'EIA' (Principle 17), and the duty to co-operate in a transboundary context, particularly through notification and consultation (Principles 18 and 19). Other important principles include the precautionary approach (Principle 15), the polluter-pays principle (Principle 16), intergenerational

---

[24] 'Action Plan for the Human Environment', 16 June 1972, UN Doc. A/CONF 48/14, 10–62.

[25] 'Declaration of the United Nations Conference on the Human Environment', Stockholm, 16 June 1972, UN Doc. A/CONF 48/14/Rev.1, 2ff (Stockholm Declaration). On this declaration see L. B. Sohn, 'The Stockholm Declaration on the Human Environment' (1973) 14 *Harv Int'l LJ* 423.

[26] 'Rio Declaration on Environment and Development', 13 June 1992, UN Doc. A/CONF.151/26. Rev.1 (Rio Declaration).

[27] On this declaration see J. E. Viñuales (ed.), *The Rio Declaration on Environment and Development: A Commentary* (Oxford: Oxford University Press, 2015), Preliminary study.

[28] On the Rio Conference see A. Kiss and S. Doumbé-Bille, 'La Conférence des Nations Unies sur l'environnement et le développement (Rio de Janeiro, 3–14 juin 1992)' (1992) 38 *Annuaire francais de droit international* 823; P. H. Sand, 'International Environmental Law After Rio' (1993) 4 *EJIL* 377.

[29] See e.g. M. Pallamaerts, 'International Environmental Law from Stockholm to Rio: Back to the Future' (1992) 1 *RECIEL* 254.

[30] See P.-M. Dupuy, G. Le Moli, and J. E. Viñuales, 'Customary International Law and the Environment' in L. Rajamani and J. Peel (eds), *The Oxford Handbook of International Environmental Law* (Oxford: Oxford University Press, 2020), chapter 23.

equity (Principle 3), the principle of common but differentiated responsibilities or 'CBDR' (Principle 7), integration (Principle 4), and the principle of public participation (Principle 10). The wording of Principle 1 of the Rio Declaration is more ambiguous—particularly when compared to that of the Stockholm Declaration (Principle 1)—on the recognition of a right to an environment of a certain quality. This right, which has been recognized at the regional level,[31] has not yet received a clear statement in a binding instrument with global scope.[32] The following paragraphs provide a brief examination of these principles, starting with those that flesh out the broad idea that it is better to prevent than to repair (prevention, EIA, co-operation, and precaution) and then moving to those which are mostly concerned with distributive justice matters (polluter-pays, intergenerational equity, CBDR, public participation, and sustainable development):

(1) *Prevention of environmental harm*: as discussed in **3.10**, the principle stated in Principle 21 of the Stockholm Declaration and Principle 2 of the Rio Declaration both recognizes the sovereign right of States to exploit their 'natural resources' and subjects the exercise of such right to the duty to prevent significant harm to the environment.[33]

The latter is a duty of *due diligence* and not an obligation of result.[34] That means that the occurrence of the requisite harm or the creation of risk thereof are not sufficient, in and of themselves, to breach the principle. Although neither the Stockholm nor the Rio formulation qualify the level of harm (they use the term 'damage'), it is widely accepted that only *significant* harm is to be prevented as, otherwise, the sovereign right to exploit natural resources would be excessively restricted.[35] Risk of significant harm is also to be prevented and its occurrence (e.g. a neighbouring nuclear facility operating under low safety standards) may be sufficient to breach the prevention principle.[36] In addition, whereas the duty of prevention in its embryonic 'no harm' form sought to protect the interest of other States, hence its 'transboundary' spatial dimension, the prevention principle seeks to protect the *environment* per se, irrespective of its location.[37]

---

[31] See the African Commission on Human and Peoples' Rights in the *Ogoni case*, §52 (referring to Article 24 of the African Charter: the right to a generally satisfactory environment); the ECOWAS Court of Justice in *SERAP* v *Federal Republic of Nigeria*, §§91–121 (referring to Article 24 of the African Charter); the ACHR in the *Advisory Opinion OC-23/17 (Colombia Request): Environment and Human Rights*, §§56–57 (incorporating Article 11 of the San Salvador Protocol, which enshrines the right to a healthy environment, into the American Convention, through the operation of Article 26 of the latter).

[32] Report of the Special Rapporteur on the Issue of Human Rights Obligations Relating to the Enjoyment of a Safe, Clean, Healthy and Sustainable Environment', UN Doc. A/73/188 (19 July 2018), para. 37; Statement by David R. Boyd, Special Rapporteur on Human Rights and the Environment at the 73rd Session of the General Assembly (25 October 2018).

[33] See generally Xue Hanqin, *Transboundary Damage in International Law* (Cambridge: Cambridge University Press, 2003); L.-A. Duvic Paoli and J. E. Viñuales, 'Principle 2: Prevention' in J. E. Viñuales (ed.), *The Rio Declaration on Environment and Development: A Commentary* (Oxford: Oxford University Press, 2015), 107; L.-A. Duvic Paoli, *The Prevention Principles in International Environmental Law* (Cambridge: Cambridge University Press, 2018).

[34] *Pulp Mills on the River Uruguay (Argentina* v *Uruguay)*, §197; the ITLOS Advisory Opinion on *Responsibilities and obligations of States sponsoring persons and entities with respect to activities in the Area*, §§111–116.

[35] *Trail Smelter (United States of America/Canada)*, at 1980; Draft Articles on the Prevention of Transboundary Harm from Hazardous Activities, 12 December 2001, GA resolution 56/82, UN Doc. A/RES/56/82 (ILC Articles on Prevention of Transboundary Harm), Article 2(a); *Pulp Mills on the River Uruguay (Argentina* v *Uruguay)*, §101.

[36] ILC Articles on Prevention of Transboundary Harm, Article 3.

[37] *Dispute Concerning Delimitation of the Maritime Boundary between Ghana and Côte d'Ivoire in the Atlantic Ocean (Ghana/Côte d'Ivoire) (Provisional Measures)*, §§68–73; *Request for an Advisory Opinion Submitted by the Sub-Regional Fisheries Commission (SRFC)*, §§111, 120; *South China Sea Arbitration*, §927.

Finally, the prevention principle is given expression by other more specific duties, such as the requirement to conduct an EIA and the duty to co-operate, discussed next. Yet, these other duties are but some of the expressions of the prevention principle and do not exhaust its content. In other words, the prevention principle is not a mere 'label' used to refer to a set of some more specific duties; it is a stand-alone 'norm' which requires the exercise of due diligence to avoid significant harm to the environment or risk thereof and the normative pull of which continues to operate irrespective of the application of other norms (e.g. EIA or co-operation) to a given situation. This is the understanding that has been recognized by the ICJ and other international courts and tribunals as a reflection of customary international law.[38]

(2) *Environmental impact assessment*: this requirement is an extrapolation from a domestic law practice which, starting with the 1969 National Environmental Policy Act in the US, became generalized to most countries.[39] Its authoritative formulation appears in Principle 17 of the Rio Declaration:

> Environmental impact assessment, as a national instrument, shall be undertaken for proposed activities that are likely to have a significant adverse impact on the environment and are subject to a decision of a competent national authority.

The ICJ first recognized its customary law character in the *Pulp Mills on the River Uruguay (Argentina v Uruguay)* (at §204) case and later confirmed it in *Certain Activities carried out by Nicaragua in the Border Area (Costa Rica/Nicaragua)* (at §104).

The operation of this norm in customary international law raises three main difficulties. The first concerns the content to be given to the norm. According to the ICJ, international law relies, for the definition of the specific contents of the EIA, on domestic law.[40] It is important not to misunderstand this point. This is certainly not a licence for States to unilaterally define utterly inadequate contents so as to promote unbridled economic development. Whatever the contents set by domestic law, the State remains subject to the general duty of due diligence arising from the prevention principle. The second difficulty relates to the spatial operation of this requirement. In *Pulp Mills on the River Uruguay (Argentina v Uruguay)*, the ICJ referred only to a 'transboundary' context.[41] The following year, the Seabed Chamber of the International Tribunal for the Law of the Sea (ITLOS) recognized the operation of the norm beyond national jurisdiction.[42] The application of the duty to activities which may cause significant harm to the environment per se, irrespective of its location, is consistent with the prevention principle. Thirdly, the trigger of the duty to conduct an EIA also calls for some comment. The English, French, and Spanish texts of Principle 17 refer to 'proposed activities' ('*activités envisagées*'; '*actividad propuesta*'), which would suggest that Strategic Environmental Assessments (SEAs) of policies (instead of those of activities) are not covered by the customary norm. But even within proposed activities, there is an ambiguity regarding the level of impact which subjects an activity to a prior EIA. The English text of Principle 17 refers to a 'significant adverse impact', which would suggest that the threshold is similar to that envisaged by the prevention principle, whereas the French text speaks of '*effets nocifs importants*', which is different from the threshold used for prevention. In *Certain Activities carried out by Nicaragua in the Border*

---

[38] *Certain Activities carried out by Nicaragua in the Border Area (Costa Rica/Nicaragua)*, §104.
[39] National Environmental Policy Act, 42 USC, chapter 55. See N. A. Robinson, 'International Trends in Environmental Impact Assessment' (1992) 19 *BC Envtl Aff L Rev* 591.
[40] *Certain Activities carried out by Nicaragua in the Border Area (Costa Rica/Nicaragua)*, §104.
[41] *Pulp Mills on the River Uruguay (Argentina v Uruguay)*, §§204–205.
[42] *Responsibilities and obligations of States sponsoring persons and entities with respect to activities in the Area*, §§145, 148.

Area (Costa Rica/Nicaragua), the ICJ maintained this difference of language in the English and French versions of its judgment (at §104).[43] Whether the trigger of the EIA requirement is similar or not to the threshold of harm of the prevention principle, the latter principle remains applicable and, therefore, lack of diligence that creates a risk of significant harm would constitute a breach of prevention.

In addition to these three difficulties, the *Certain Activities carried out by Nicaragua in the Border Area (Costa Rica/Nicaragua)* case introduced some ambiguity in the sequence between the EIA obligation and the duty to notify and consult. According to the Court, the latter duty only arises after an EIA has been effectively conducted and it has shown that there is indeed a risk (at §104). Given the fact that the State of origin is thus given the unilateral power to define the content of the EIA, decide whether an EIA is necessary or not, and actually conduct (or review the conduct of) the EIA before a requirement to make potentially affected States aware of the situation emerges, the understanding of the Court should be subject to caution. But, again, the conduct of the State of origin remains generally subject to the due diligence duty arising from prevention at all levels, which may require—independently from the customary norm governing the EIA—notification and consultation much earlier and, in all events, remains controlling as regards the content and conduct of the EIA.

(3) *Co-operation*: the duty to co-operate in good faith is not confined to environmental matters[44] (see **3.6**), but it is in this area that it has particularly developed since the 1980s, following the Chernobyl catastrophe. In the field of environmental co-operation, two main aspects must be clarified.

The first is the nature and content of the norm itself. Despite some initial divergence, particularly throughout the 1960s when the Friendly Relations Declaration was being negotiated, co-operation is more than a mere 'purpose' (as it appears in Article 1(3) of the UN Charter); it is a principle (as it appears in the Friendly Relations Declaration) and, more specifically, it is a widely recognized norm of customary international law creating a duty to co-operate in good faith.[45] In the context of the Rio Declaration, two varieties of co-operation appear, namely co-operation in a transboundary context (Principles 19 and 18) and co-operation in a spirit of global partnership (Principles 7 and 27). So far, its customary grounding is only settled with respect to the former version, although the latter is gaining ground due to the daunting challenges faced by humanity. There are, in addition, many multilateral environmental agreements which flesh out the duty to co-operate in a spirit of global partnership, typically by creating institutions that meet regularly to manage a common problem, such as climate change, biodiversity loss, desertification, chemical and waste management, and many other issues. In its customary international law version, the duty to co-operate lies midway between two extremes, namely refusal of any interaction and a specific result. Indeed, the duty to co-operate is an obligation of means and it does not require a specific result.[46] Specifically, the existence of a duty to co-operate does not mean that a State which may be affected by an activity conducted in another State has a veto over

---

[43] English version: 'significant adverse impact in a transboundary context'; French version: '*risque de dommage transfrontière important*'.

[44] See e.g. *North Sea Continental Shelf*, §85; *Legality of the Threat or Use of Nuclear Weapons*, §§98–103; *Obligation to Negotiate Access to the Pacific Ocean (Bolivia v Chile)*, §87.

[45] *Pulp Mills on the River Uruguay (Argentina v Uruguay)*, §§77, 102, 144–146; *Certain Activities carried out by Nicaragua in the Border Area (Costa Rica/Nicaragua)*, §§104, 106; ITLOS, *Request for an Advisory Opinion Submitted by the Sub-Regional Fisheries Commission (SRFC)*, §§139–140; *Dispute Concerning Delimitation of the Maritime Boundary between Ghana and Côte d'Ivoire in the Atlantic Ocean (Ghana/Côte d'Ivoire) (Provisional Measures)*, §73; *South China Sea Arbitration*, 946, 984–5.

[46] *North Sea Continental Shelf* cases, §85; *Land and Maritime Boundary between Cameroon and Nigeria (Cameroon v Nigeria: Equatorial Guinea intervening)*, §244; *Case Concerning the Gabčíkovo-Nagymaros Project (Hungary/Slovakia)*, §141.

such activity or that its consent is required to pursue it.[47] Yet, co-operation is not a mere pro forma condition. Thus, a State is specifically required to notify and consult with States potentially affected by an activity or accident occurring in the former State,[48] and while a process of negotiation is ongoing, States are required not to take any action that would defeat the outcome of the co-operation process.[49]

The second clarification concerns the relationship between co-operation and other principles, particularly the prevention principle and the requirement to conduct an EIA. As noted in connection with the latter, in *Certain Activities (Costa Rica/Nicaragua)* the ICJ suggested the existence of a rigid sequence between the conduct and findings of the EIA and the obligation to notify and consult. This view is inconsistent with both the requirements of the prevention principle (because the exercise of due diligence may require, in the circumstances, that potentially affected States be notified and consulted earlier and even as part of the EIA), and with the duty to co-operate itself, which is not limited to notification and consultation and may indeed require different forms of co-operation from an early stage in the planning of the activity. Much like prevention, which entails more than just co-operation and the EIA requirement, co-operation entails more than the mere notification and consultation of potentially affected parties. The latter are two expressions of co-operation, among several others, which may require the involvement of international bodies; the exchange of information, technical, and financial co-operation; and prior informed consent.

(4) *Precaution*: Principle 15 of the Rio Declaration gives expression to a norm which has attracted both great attention and criticism. The wording retained for Principle 15 is as follows:

> In order to protect the environment, the precautionary approach shall be widely applied by States according to their capabilities. Where there are threats of serious or irreversible damage, lack of full scientific certainty shall not be used as a reason for postponing cost-effective measures to prevent environmental degradation.

The use of the term 'approach' (rather than of 'principle', as suggested by European countries and, indeed, EU law) and the many ambiguities in the formulation and understanding of the norm have hindered its recognition as a part of customary international law. At present, no international court or tribunal has unambiguously recognized such customary grounding,[50] although some have come close to doing so.[51] The ICJ has limited itself to the laconic observation that precaution 'may' be relevant for interpretation purposes.[52] For present purposes, five main aspects of precaution call for further comment.

First, the domain of precaution must be clearly distinguished from that of prevention. Whereas prevention concerns 'risk', namely a reliable probability (large or small) of an adverse outcome, precaution concerns 'uncertainty', namely those cases in which the science has not yet charted a certain issue and, more specifically, where it cannot be determined whether one of the outcomes of the relevant activity is adverse.[53]

---

[47] *Lac Lanoux (Spain/France)*, §§13, 22.
[48] *Corfu Channel (United Kingdom v Albania)*, 22; *Certain Activities carried out by Nicaragua in the Border Area (Costa Rica/Nicaragua)*, §§104, 108, 168.
[49] *Pulp Mills on the River Uruguay (Argentina v Uruguay)*, §144.
[50] The WTO dispute settlement organs have cast doubt about the customary grounding of precaution. See *European Communities—Hormones Measures Concerning Meat and Meat Products*, §§123–125; *European Communities—Measures Affecting the Approval and Marketing of Biotech Products*, §7.88.
[51] See the European Court of Human Rights in *Tatar v Romania*, §120; and ITLOS, *Responsibilities and obligations of States sponsoring persons and entities with respect to activities in the Area*, §135.
[52] *Pulp Mills on the River Uruguay (Argentina v Uruguay)*, §164.
[53] See A. A. Cançado Trindade, 'Principle 15: Precaution' in J. E. Viñuales, *The Rio Declaration on Environment and Development: A Commentary* (Oxford: Oxford University Press, 2015), 403; A. Trouwborst, *Evolution and Status of the Precautionary Principle in International Law* (The Hague: Kluwer, 2002). See further, in the EU context, *Pfizer Animal Health SA v Council*, §§126–127 (subsequently, this case blurs the terminology but not the concepts).

Secondly, precaution concerns uncertainty about the science, not about a causal link which is ascertainable in the current state of science but has not been ascertained. In other words, precaution does not release the regulating State from its duty of due diligence in ascertaining the scientific basis for regulatory action. This point is often misunderstood. Precaution comes into play only when, after exercising all the diligence that can be expected from the relevant authorities, it has not been possible to determine whether an activity would lead to an adverse outcome or not, and this because the matter is unsettled or uncharted in the current state of the science.[54] A relation between an activity and an adverse outcome that is clearly ascertainable in the current state of science is not a matter of precaution but one of prevention, and the regulating State is therefore required to exercise due diligence in determining the scientific basis for its regulatory intervention.

Thirdly, the uncertain outcome must be potentially 'serious or irreversible damage' and not merely 'significant harm'. The threshold is therefore higher because the State is intervening without a sufficient scientific basis. Thus, precaution is not about regulating any activity that may remotely have some impact, but about not postponing regulation of activities which, despite the inconclusive state of the science, could potentially lead to an aggravated threshold of damage.

Fourthly, the lack of a sufficient basis also explains why the measures adopted to tackle the potential 'serious or irreversible damage' must be 'cost-effective' or, in other words, 'proportional' and not more restrictive than necessary. Such has been the interpretation given to the operation of the precautionary principle in what may be seen as a sophisticated and far-reaching system recognizing it, namely European Union law.[55]

Finally, there is significant ambiguity regarding the purport of the norm. The wording of Principle 15 envisages a situation in which a State refrains from taking action to regulate an activity for the reason—or the pretext—that the science is not yet clear. In the early 1990s, this formulation reflected the fears relating to regulatory competition, that is, the race to lower environmental regulation in order to attract investment or promote national industry. The change in the perception of environmental regulation since the 1990s has been substantial. Today, the fears arise from over- rather than under-ambitious precautionary regulation. Yet, the question of the specific purport of the norm remains. The formulation of Principle 15 can accommodate two different conceptions of precaution, one in which a State is 'required' to act even in the absence of full scientific certainty and the other in which a State is 'entitled' to act in such circumstances. In the first case, precaution would be a 'primary norm' of conduct whereas in the second it would be a 'defence' justifying action.[56] Instead, the term 'approach' used in Principle 15, which was introduced at the request of the United States during the negotiation of the Rio Declaration, would suggest the second understanding, but the context of the statement (the need to avoid pretexts for inaction) supports the first. The term 'approach' has also been used to refer to precaution as an interpretive device. In *Pulp Mills on the River Uruguay (Argentina v Uruguay)*, the ICJ noted that 'while a precautionary approach may be relevant in the interpretation and application of the provisions of the Statute, it does not follow that it operates as a reversal of the burden of proof'.[57] The purport of the norm remains unsettled in general international law and, so far, it has only been pinned down when there is a treaty basis fleshing out the content and operation of precaution, as is the case in the EU context.

---

[54] *Gowan Comércio Internacional e Serviços Lda v Ministero della Salute*, §§75–76; *Queisser v Germany*, §§56–57.

[55] *Queisser v Germany*, §§59–60.

[56] In the EU context, the precautionary principle has operated to require action in *Pfizer Animal Health SA v Council*, §§139–140; *Gowan Comércio Internacional e Serviços Lda v Ministero della Salute*, §§75–76; *Blaise and others*, §43.

[57] *Pulp Mills on the River Uruguay (Argentina v Uruguay)*, §164.

(5) *Polluter-pays principle*: this principle is peculiar in that it is designed to operate at the domestic level and not at the interstate level. Thus, there is no clear authority to conclude that the polluter-pays principle has a basis in general international law. According to Principle 16 of the Rio Declaration:

> National authorities should endeavour to promote the internalization of environmental costs and the use of economic instruments, taking into account the approach that the polluter should, in principle, bear the cost of pollution, with due regard to the public interest and without distorting international trade and investment.

In this formulation, the principle has four main aspects that all concern how its logic is implemented in domestic law.

First, the principle calls for States to adopt measures that 'internalize' the cost of pollution. The language reflects an economic logic which, although widely accepted for decades, today rings hollow, namely that of negative 'externalities'. According to this conception, negative externalities are the cost of a transaction between two market actors which are borne by third parties and not reflected in the price. Internalization is therefore seen as a way of correcting this side effect by making the actors engaged in the transaction bear the cost they impose on society. Of course, this may or may not lead to actual prevention of the cost. Whether internalization does so will depend on how much of the cost is internalized as well as on a range of other factors, including, most fundamentally, the accuracy of the economic prediction according to which a certain increase in the cost borne is capable of driving behaviour. Thus, the polluter-pays principle is not about prevention but about allowing the transaction to continue while allocating the cost.

The second aspect concerns the selection of the cost-bearer. By definition, it has to be one of the entities involved in the transaction rather than a third party (or the environment as such, which is only taken into account in this representation of reality indirectly, through the cost borne by society). But the possibility of placing it on the producer of the good or service is limited by the latter's ability to 'transfer' the cost to consumers. Such transfer remains an acceptable form of internalization to the extent that the consumer is a party to the transaction and hence also a 'polluter'. However, the transfer generates the same type of inequitable results as an indirect tax, which raises the price of a good/service by the same amount for everyone, despite the very different purchasing power and needs of the people acquiring the good/service. In recent years, attempts by governments to internalize the cost of fossil fuels by removing transport and gasoline subsidies had led to civil unrest in countries such as Argentina or France. Despite the strong need, from an environmental perspective, to remove distortive subsidies to fossil fuels, the inequitable effects of such measures have made them politically difficult.

The latter point highlights the importance of the third aspect, namely the methods of internalization. Principle 16 refers to 'economic instruments', also known as 'market mechanisms'. These include essentially taxes, trading schemes, and corrective subsidies. The key commonality of such economic instruments is that (i) they consider any form of harm as acceptable, (ii) as long as the cost is internalized, (iii) with the expectation that market forces will correct the negative externality. Implicit in the use of market mechanisms is the idea that the underlying transaction can be continued. For example, emissions of greenhouse gases or even of toxic air pollutants would thus be allowed to continue, that is, the harm they cause is 'acceptable', as long as the cost is internalized. An alternative to such an approach, which remains the rule in domestic and international law, is the adoption of regulatory measures that define a certain level of harm as unacceptable and require polluters to avoid it (e.g. by using different technologies, such as an engine design). Such measures have sometimes been portrayed as 'inefficient'. Yet, market mechanisms are mired with limitations[58] and misuses,[59] and they only offer a 'theoretical' promise of effectiveness, alas so far unfulfilled in practice.

Perhaps the crux of the polluter-pays principle, its true goal, is conveyed by the fourth aspect, namely the emphasis placed on not 'distorting international trade and investment'. This principle is specifically designed not to interfere with the underlying economic transaction, on the assumption that trade and investment are desirable in all circumstances. That may have been the ideological substrate in the early 1990s, with the end of the Cold War, but the last three decades, including the world economic crisis of 2008 and, even more so, the daunting existential threat faced by humanity as a result of climate change and other forms of environmental degradation, have emphasized the need to revisit our priorities. International trade and investment certainly remain useful, within limits. Such limits cannot rely solely on the polluter-pays principle, with its large deference to the underlying transaction, and need a wider and deeper set of requirements, including some—such as the prevention principle—that prohibit certain transactions because they may cause significant harm to the environment.

(6) *Intergenerational equity*: the scale of our interference with the global environment calls for a balance to be struck between the needs of present and future generations. Principle 3 of the Rio Declaration states, in this regard, that '[t]he right to development must be fulfilled so as to equitably meet developmental and environmental needs of present and future generations'. This statement embodies the need for balance, but it does not provide any clear guidance on how to strike it.[60] The wording recognizes the 'right to development', which had been a major symbolic achievement of developing countries during the 1980s (see **21.3.3**). But it also refers to the needs of future generations, an addition which was introduced at the request of developed countries in order to tame unbridled development.

Over time, the latter addition has become the defining component of Principle 3. At the World Summit held in Rio de Janeiro in June 2012, dubbed 'Rio + 20' by reference to the two decades elapsed since the 1992 Rio Conference, the idea of institutionalizing intergenerational equity gained traction. In a report from the office of the UN Secretary-General, different institutional options to give voice to future generations were explored, including the establishment of commissioners acting as representatives of future generations.[61] In the case law, intergenerational equity has featured in various ways, including as part of the assessment of the legality of nuclear weapons,[62] or in the review of domestic procedures granting permits for the development of natural resources,[63] or, again, as a basis to extend *locus standi* to future generations.[64]

---

[58] According to a World Bank study, 51 per cent of the emissions of greenhouse gases subject to a pricing system (taxes or trading systems) are priced below US$10 per tonne of carbon dioxide equivalent. See World Bank, *State and Trends of Carbon Trading 2019* (Washington, DC: World Bank, 2019), 10.

[59] See M. W. Wara, 'Measuring the Clean Development Mechanism's Performance and Potential' (2008) 55 *UCLA Law Rev* 1759.

[60] For an influential statement of the principle of intergenerational equity see E. Brown Weiss, *In Fairness to Future Generations: International Law, Common Patrimony, and Intergenerational Equity* (Dobbs Ferry: Transnational Publishers, 1989).

[61] See UN Secretary-General, *Intergenerational Solidarity and the Needs of Future Generations: Report of the Secretary-General*, 15 August 2013, UN Doc. A/68/322.

[62] *Legality of the Threat or Use of Nuclear Weapons*, §36.

[63] See the Supreme Court of India in *State of Himachal Pradesh and others v Ganesh Wood Products and others*.

[64] See the Supreme Court of the Philippines in *Minors Oposa v Secretary of the Department of Environment and Natural Resources* (DENR), 185. See however the Human Rights Committee in *E.H.P. v Canada*, §8(a) (where future generations are referred to as a mere 'expression of concern').

(7) *Common but differentiated responsibilities*: in addition to equity *inter* generations, much attention was paid at the Rio Conference to equity *intra* generations, that is, equity within the present generations.[65] Principles 6 and 7 of the Rio Declaration give expression to such concerns alongside many other references to the special situation and the interests of developing countries in several other principles. Of particular note, Principle 7 states the principle of common but differentiated responsibilities (CBDR):

> States shall cooperate in a spirit of global partnership to conserve, protect and restore the health and integrity of the Earth's ecosystem. In view of the different contributions to global environmental degradation, States have common but differentiated responsibilities. The developed countries acknowledge the responsibility that they bear in the international pursuit of sustainable development in view of the pressures their societies place on the global environment and of the technologies and financial resources they command.

This provision is drafted in a manner which can accommodate widely different interpretations, including one which would see an equitable implementation of the prevention principle and another that would make CBDR the nemesis of prevention, as it would only call for prevention action by developed countries. Despite this wide scope, the different interpretations of the principle of CBDR share a common core, namely (i) its focus on global environmental problems, such as ozone depletion,[66] climate change,[67] and biodiversity;[68] (ii) its allocative nature among States (rather than at some other level); and (iii) with the burden distributed on the basis of three criteria: historical contribution to the problem, financial means, and technological means. The reference to the 'pressures their [developed countries'] societies place on the global environment' would suggest that any country which places similar pressures would also have to acknowledge its 'responsibility'. However, the implications of the principle of CBDR remain widely contested and deeply controversial, particularly in the area of climate change. The diplomatic approach to containing such potential for controversy has been, much as for sustainable development, to preserve the ambiguities.

(8) *Public participation*: Principle 10 of the Rio Declaration introduced requirements regarding access to environmental information, participation in environmental decision making, and access to justice in environmental matters. The wording specifically avoided the use of the term 'right':

> Environmental issues are best handled with the participation of all concerned citizens, at the relevant level. At the national level, each individual shall have appropriate access to information concerning the environment that is held by public authorities, including information on hazardous materials and activities in their communities, and the opportunity to participate in decision-making processes. States shall facilitate and encourage public awareness and participation by making information widely available. Effective access to judicial and administrative proceedings, including redress and remedy, shall be provided.

---

[65] See P. Cullet, 'Principle 7: Common but Differentiated Responsibilities' in J. E. Viñuales (ed.), *The Rio Declaration on Environment and Development: A Commentary* (Oxford: Oxford University Press, 2015), 229; L. Rajamani, *Differential Treatment in International Environmental Law* (Oxford: Oxford University Press, 2006).

[66] Vienna Convention for the Protection of the Ozone Layer, 22 March 1985, 1513 UNTS 293, Article 2(2); Montreal Protocol on Substances that Deplete the Ozone Layer, 16 September 1987, 1522 UNTS 29 (Montreal Protocol), Article 5(1).

[67] United Nations Framework Convention on Climate Change, 9 May 1992, 31 ILM 849 (UNFCCC), Article 3(1); Kyoto Protocol to the United Nations Framework Convention on Climate Change, 11 December 1997, 2303 UNTS 148 (Kyoto Protocol), Article 3 compared to Article 10; Adoption of the Paris Agreement, Decision 1/CP.21, 12 December 2015, FCCC/CP/2015/L.9, Annex, Article 2(2).

[68] Convention on Biological Diversity, 5 June 1992, 1760 UNTS 79 [CBD], Article 20(4).

Despite this formulation, 'rights' language has prevailed both in treaty-making, particularly with the adoption of the 1998 Aarhus Convention on Access to Information, Public Participation in Decision-making and Access to Justice in Environmental Matters,[69] the 2010 UNEP 'Bali Guidelines',[70] and the 2018 Escazú Agreement,[71] and in the case law, with the European Court of Human Rights notably referring to such environmental participatory rights in several decisions, including in cases against a State, such as Turkey, which is not a party to the Aarhus Convention (*Taskın and others* v *Turkey*, §§99–100).

The three components described by the principle of public participation in environmental matters have been discussed and refined in the decisions of the Compliance Committee of the Aarhus Convention.[72] Some observations in this regard may be useful. First, 'environmental information' is widely defined, including processes but also raw data[73] and a range of activities and measures.[74] Secondly, public participation requirements apply to processes concerning proposed activities, but also plans, programmes, policies, and even laws and regulations, although different requirements are attached to different types of acts.[75] Such requirements fall short of 'consent' and, therefore, they do not subject the act to the consent of the public. Yet, public participation cannot be satisfied by merely pro forma consultations. Thirdly, the right of access to justice in environmental matters entitles members of the public 'to challenge acts and omissions by private persons and public authorities which contravene provisions of its national law relating to the environment' (Article 9(3) of the Aarhus Convention).[76] One of the main challenges in implementing this right has been the cost of litigation. The Aarhus Compliance Committee has considered that, in order for such access to be effectively granted, the legal recourse must not be 'prohibitively expensive'.[77]

(9) *Sustainable development*: the concept of sustainable development can be analysed at two main levels. At the policy level, it has featured widely in international policy statements, declarations, action plans, and reports since the outcome report of the World Commission on Environment and Development,[78] to the 1992 Rio Conference,[79] the 2002 Johannesburg Summit on Sustainable Development,[80] the 2012 Rio + 20 Conference,[81] and until the 2030 Agenda for Sustainable Development adopted in 2015, which sets 17

---

[69] Aarhus Convention on Access to Information, Public Participation in Decision-making and Access to Justice in Environmental Matters, 25 June 1998, 2161 UNTS 447 (Aarhus Convention).

[70] UNEP Guidelines for the Development of National Legislation on Access to Information, Public Participation and Access to Justice in Environmental Matters, adopted by the UNEP Governing Council in decision SS.XI/5, 26 February 2010 (Bali Guidelines).

[71] Regional Agreement on Access to Information, Public Participation and Justice in Environmental Matters in Latin America and the Caribbean, 4 March 2018.

[72] See generally A. Andrusevich and S. Kern (eds), *Case Law of the Aarhus Convention Compliance Committee (2004–2014)*, 3rd edn (Lviv: RACSE, 2016).

[73] See *United Kingdom* ACCC/C/2010/53, ECE/MP.PP/C.1/2013/3 (11 January 2013), §§73–74.

[74] This covers related contracts, *Moldova* ACCC/C/2008/30, ECE/MP.PP/C.1/2009/6/Add.3 (8 February 2011), §29, including financing contracts *European Community* ACCC/C/2007/21, ECE/MP.PP/C.1/2009/2/Add.1 (11 December 2009), §30.

[75] *United Kingdom* ACCC/C/2010/53, ECE/MP.PP/C.1/2013/3 (11 January 2013), §82.

[76] On the operation of this obligation see *Denmark* ACCC/C/2006/18, ECE/MP.PP/2008/5/Add.4 (29 April 2008), §28; *European Union* ACCC/C/2008/32 (Part I), ECE/MP.PP/C.1/2011/4/Add.1 (May 2011), §77 (no requirement to enact an *actio popularis*).

[77] See *United Kingdom* ACCC/C/2008/27, ECE/MP.PP/C.1/2010/6/Add.2 (November 2010), §44.

[78] Report of the World Commission on Environment and Development, 'Our Common Future', 10 March 1987.

[79] Mainly through the Report of the United Nations Conference on Environment and Development, A/CONF.151/26/Rev.1 (Vol. 1), Resolution 1, Annex 2: Agenda 21 (Agenda 21).

[80] Report of the World Summit on Sustainable Development at Johannesburg (South Africa), 26 August–4 September 2002, UN Doc. A/CONF.199/20 (Implementation Plan).

[81] The Future We Want, 11 September 2012, UN Doc. A/Res/66/288.

Sustainable Development Goals (SDGs).[82] At this level, the very ambiguity of the concept has been the main condition for its success in building momentum for the adoption of several important treaties over the 1990s.[83]

By contrast, at a legal level, the ambiguity of the concept has prevented it from playing, as such, a significant role in international environmental law. The controversy surrounding sustainable development at a legal level has concerned not only its content and operation but also its very nature as either a 'principle' or a 'concept'.[84] From a legal standpoint, two main questions must be clarified.[85] The first question is whether sustainable development is a 'norm' (irrespective of whether it is formulated as a principle or as a normative concept). If the answer is affirmative, then the second question concerns the content and operation of such norm. Both questions require an inductive or empirical inquiry: the answer depends on how sustainable development features in legal instruments and practice.

Regarding the first question, there is a wealth of evidence for the proposition that sustainable development is not a mere concept (such as 'degrowth', 'eco-development', or the 'green economy') but a 'norm'. Aside from its inclusion in policy instruments, which would not be sufficient to disentangle the legal and policy levels, sustainable development features in a wide range of treaties[86] and judicial decisions.[87] Such references lead to the conclusion that sustainable development is indeed a norm and, more specifically, a norm of international law.

---

[82] See resolution 70/1, Transforming our World: The 2030 Agenda for Sustainable Development, 21 October 2015, UN Doc. A/RES/70/1 (2030 Agenda for Sustainable Development).

[83] See Viñuales, 'The Rise and Fall of Sustainable Development' (n 19).

[84] See V. Lowe, 'Sustainable Development and Unsustainable Arguments' in A. Boyle and D. Freestone (eds), *International Law and Sustainable Development: Past Achievements and Future Challenges* (Oxford: Oxford University Press, 1999), 19; N. Schrijver, 'The Evolution of Sustainable Development in International Law' (2007) 328 *RCADI* 217; V. Barral, 'Sustainable Development in International Law: Nature and Operation of an Evolutive Legal Norm' (2012) 23 *EJIL* 377.

[85] This discussion follows J. E. Viñuales, 'Sustainable Development' in L. Rajamani and J. Peel (eds), *The Oxford Handbook of International Environmental Law* (Oxford: Oxford University Press, 2020), chapter 17.

[86] See e.g. UNFCCC, Article 3(4); Kyoto Protocol, Articles 2(1), 10 (chapeau), 12(2); Paris Agreement, Preamble, Articles 2(1), 4(1), 6(1), (2), (4), (8), (9), 7(1), 8(1), 10(5); Nagoya Protocol on Access to Genetic Resources and the Fair and Equitable Sharing of the Benefits arising from their Utilization to the Convention on Biological Diversity, 29 October 2010, CBD Decision X/1 (2010) Annex I (Nagoya Protocol), Preamble; United Nations Convention to Combat Desertification in those Countries Experiencing Serious Drought and/or Desertification, Particularly in Africa, 17 June 1994, UN Doc. A/AC.241/15/Rev. 7 (1994) (UNCCD), Preamble, Articles 1(b), 5(b), 9(1), 18(1), Annex I, Article 6, Annex II, Article 3(1), Annex III, Article 2(c), Annex V, Article 2(i); Agreement for the Implementation of the Provisions of the United Nations Conventions on the Law of the Sea of 10 December 1982 relating to the Conservation and Management of Straddling Fish Stocks and Highly Migratory Fish Stocks, 4 August 1995, 2167 UNTS 3 (Straddling Fish Stocks Agreement), Article 24(1); United Nations Convention on the Law of the Non-Navigational Uses of International Watercourses, 21 May 1997, 36 ILM 700 (New York Convention), Article 24(2)(a); Rotterdam Convention on the Prior Informed Consent Procedure for Certain Hazardous Chemicals and Pesticides in International Trade, 10 September 1998, 2244 UNTS 337 (Rotterdam Convention), Preamble; Protocol on Water and Health to the 1992 Convention on the Protection and Use of Transboundary Watercourses and International Lakes, 17 June 1999, 2331 UNTS 202 (Protocol on Water and Health), Preamble, Articles 1, 4(4)(c); Stockholm Convention on Persistent Organic Pollutants, 22 May 2001, 40 ILM 532 (Stockholm Convention), Article 7(3).

[87] See *Case Concerning Gabčíkovo-Nagymaros Project (Hungary/Slovakia)*, §140; WTO Appellate Body Report on *U.S.—Import Prohibition of Certain Shrimp and Shrimp Products*, §§131, 153; *Ogoni* case, §52; *Hatton v UK*, Joint Dissenting Opinion of Judges Costa, Ress, Turmen, Zupancic, and Steiner, §1; *Arbitration regarding the Iron Rhine ('Ijzeren Rijn') Railway between The Kingdom of Belgium and The Kingdom of the Netherlands*, §§57–59; *Pulp Mills on the River Uruguay (Argentina v Uruguay)*, §§75–77, 177; *Indus Water Kishenganga Arbitration (Islamic Republic of Pakistan v Republic of India)*, §§448–452; *China—Measures Related to the Exportation of Various Raw Materials*, §306; *China—Measures Related to the Exportation of Rare Earths, Tungsten, and Molybdenum*, §7.263; *Advisory Opinion OC-23/17 (Colombia Request): Environment and Human Rights*, §§52–55.

The second question is more difficult to answer. As a general matter, however, it can be said that development which is 'sustainable' from a legal standpoint means both (i) development which, as a procedural requirement, takes into consideration environmental protection (Principle 4 of the Rio Declaration); and (ii) which is consistent with the obligations arising for a given State from the multilateral environmental agreements to which it is a party and, at the very least, from the customary international environmental law principles applicable to all countries (prevention, the requirement to conduct an EIA, and the duty to co-operate). This is the understanding that emerges from a close analysis of the first recognition of the norm (indeed the 'concept') of sustainable development by the ICJ in the *Case Concerning the Gabčíkovo-Nagymaros Project (Hungary/Slovakia)*. According to the Court:

> Throughout the ages, mankind has, for economic and other reasons, constantly interfered with nature. In the past, this was often done without consideration of the effects upon the environment. Owing to new scientific insights and to a growing awareness of the risks for mankind for present and future generations of pursuit of such interventions at an unconsidered and unabated pace, *new norms and standards have been developed, set forth in a great number of instruments during the last two decades. Such new norms have to be taken into consideration, and such new standards given proper weight, not only when States contemplate new activities but also when continuing with activities begun in the past*. This need to reconcile economic development with protection of the environment is aptly expressed in the *concept of sustainable development*.[88]

Thus understood, the legal concept of sustainable development has performed what could be called an 'architectural' or programmatic function in the development of treaties[89] and an interpretive function (shedding light on the scope and content of the primary norm of conduct applicable in a given case) in the case law of international courts and tribunals.[90]

In the period from 1972 to 2020, the principles of international environmental law emerged, consolidated, and developed significantly. Yet, despite some attempts in the past, there is still no framework treaty providing a binding formulation of such principles, which could be relied on by both domestic and international courts to infuse environmental considerations in the wider body of international and domestic law. Following the adoption of the Paris Agreement in December 2015, an initiative was launched to add this missing piece to the global environmental architecture in the form of a Global Pact for the Environment.[91] This initiative was endorsed by the UN General Assembly in 2018 and examined in more detail by a working group during the first half of 2019.[92] The opposition of a handful of nations, including the United States and Russia, has blocked the process so far, but the process remains open, with a conference to be convened in 2022 in commemoration of the 1972 Stockholm Conference on the Human Environment.

---

[88] *Case Concerning the Gabčíkovo-Nagymaros Project (Hungary/Slovakia)*, §140 (emphasis added).

[89] See Viñuales, 'The Rise and Fall of Sustainable Development' (n 19).

[90] See e.g. *China—Measures Related to the Exportation of Various Raw Materials*, §306; *China—Measures Related to the Exportation of Rare Earths, Tungsten, and Molybdenum*, §7.263; *Hatton v UK*, Joint Dissenting Opinion of Judges Costa, Ress, Turmen, Zupancic, and Steiner; *Arbitration regarding the Iron Rhine ('Ijzeren Rijn') Railway between The Kingdom of Belgium and The Kingdom of the Netherlands*, §§57–59, 222; *Indus Water Kishenganga Arbitration (Islamic Republic of Pakistan v Republic of India)*, §§450–452; *Advisory Opinion OC-23/17 (Colombia Request): Environment and Human Rights*, §55.

[91] See online at https://globalpactenvironment.org/en/.

[92] See Y. Aguila and J. E. Viñuales, 'A Global Pact for the Environment: Conceptual Foundations' (2019) 28 RECIEL 3.

20.4 CONTEMPORARY REGULATION OF ENVIRONMENTAL CHALLENGES

20.4.1 OVERVIEW

The principles and concepts discussed in the previous section have been implemented by means of a wide range of instruments, including 'soft law' instruments and multilateral environmental agreements (MEAs), mechanisms, and institutions. The term 'implementation' in this context must be understood broadly as encompassing both instruments which specify more general principles, but which also call for implementation, and implementation techniques *stricto sensu* such as processes, implementing bodies, and international institutions entrusted with these matters. These aspects of international environmental law present some peculiar features and reflect a significant degree of legal experimentation.

The next sections present these specific features focusing on (i) the substantial role played by soft law instruments, such as non-binding resolutions, declarations, action plans, guidelines, and the like; (ii) the characteristic design features displayed by MEAs, particularly the framework convention/protocol approach and other similar techniques; (iii) the supervisory, preventive, and non-adversarial mechanisms developed to 'regulate' compliance with the main standards set by a treaty system, which play a more important role in practice than judicial procedures; and (iv) a number of international institutions that have been established with the general task of promoting environmental protection.

As will become clear, States have shown considerable imagination and engaged in innovative legal engineering. They have crafted principles, rules, and monitoring mechanisms designed to strike a balance between two conflicting requirements: the dramatic urgency to put a stop to the deterioration of the environment in addition to forestalling new damage, on the one hand; and the necessity realistically to take into account the economic and social costs involved in this process both for developed States and even more for developing countries, on the other.

It will also become clear that, because of the need to weigh up and reconcile as much as possible these two conflicting requirements, at the legal level progress has been less substantial than one would have expected or desired. True, the environment is no longer conceived of in a State-sovereignty-oriented perspective, as an asset that may belong to each State and in whose protection only the State concerned may be legally and practically interested. The environment has come to be regarded as a common good in the safeguarding of which all should be interested, regardless of where the environment is, or may be, harmed.

20.4.2 THE ROLE OF 'SOFT LAW' INSTRUMENTS

Soft law instruments, whether in the form of non-binding declarations, codification efforts, guidelines, action plans, or even fully fledged 'Strategic Approaches',[93] have played a major role in the emergence, development, and consolidation of international environmental law.

As noted earlier in this chapter, the 1972 Stockholm Declaration on the Human Environment defined the remit of environmental protection as a global concern to be tackled through international co-operation under the aegis of the United Nations. The 1992 Rio Declaration on Environment and Development provided a consolidated and mature formulation of most principles of international environmental law, and it has been relied on ever since as their canonical formulation. The codification efforts of the UN International

---

[93] See e.g. UNEP, *Strategic Approach to International Chemicals Management. SAICM Texts and Resolutions of the International Conference on Chemicals Management*, 2007, online at www.unece.org.

Law Commission in connection with the scope of the prevention principle (the 2001 ILC Articles on Prevention of Transboundary Harm) or the principles governing the non-navigational uses of international watercourses, to name but two examples, have been very influential.

A host of non-binding yet authoritative guidelines have also been adopted in areas as diverse as land-based pollution of the marine environment,[94] public participation in environmental matters,[95] nuclear safety,[96] the protection of traditional knowledge,[97] the control of certain pesticides,[98] and many others. Such guidelines have sometimes been used as a first step to familiarize States with a co-operation approach, which has thereafter been formalized in treaty language. A case in point is the move from two sets of guidelines on the transboundary movements of certain pesticides to the adoption, in 1998, of the Rotterdam Convention on Prior Informed Consent.[99] Another illustration is offered by the 2002 Guidelines on Access and Benefit Sharing adopted by the Conference of the Parties of the Convention on Biological Diversity,[100] which later led to the adoption of the 2010 Nagoya Protocol on Access and Benefit Sharing. However, such transitions from soft to hard law are far from automatic, as demonstrated by the great difficulties in developing a treaty instrument on land-based pollution at the global level, despite the adoption of guidelines in this area or, still, by the current travails of the initiative towards a Global Pact for the Environment, despite the formulation of most principles in the Rio Declaration.

Since the inception of modern international environmental law in the 1972 Stockholm Conference, plans of action on environmental matters have enjoyed a prominent place. The Plan of Action adopted at Stockholm led, among other things, to the establishment of UNEP.[101] The 'Agenda 21' adopted at the 1992 Rio Conference was widely influential in shaping an integrated environment-development agenda on many areas. Similarly, the Plan of Implementation adopted at the 2002 Johannesburg World Summit for Sustainable Development mainstreamed the idea of relying on 'Public-Private Partnerships' (PPPs) for sustainable development. Perhaps most important, for a contemporary account of international environmental law, is the 2030 Agenda for Sustainable Development adopted by the UN General Assembly in 2015.[102] This important plan of action includes, as noted earlier in this chapter, 17 Sustainable Development Goals (SDGs), further specified through 169 targets and to be measured by reference to 230 indicators. Out of the 17 SDGs, 16 are of substantive nature covering the following matters: SDG 1 (no poverty); SDG 2 (zero hunger); SDG 3 (good health and well-being); SDG 4 (quality education); SDG 5 (gender equality); SDG 6 (clean water and sanitation); SDG 7 (affordable and clean energy); SDG 8 (decent work and economic growth); SDG 9 (industry, innovation, and

---

[94] See e.g. 'Global Programme of Action for the Protection of the Marine Environment from Land-Based Activities', UN Doc. UNEP (OCA)/LBA/IG.2/7.

[95] See e.g. Bali Guidelines.

[96] See the many international standards adopted by the International Atomic Energy Agency on the basis of Article III.A.6 of the Statute of the International Atomic Energy Agency, 26 October 1956, as amended on 28 December 1989, online at https://www.iaea.org.

[97] See e.g. 'Mo'otz Kuxtal Voluntary Guidelines', 17 December 2016, CBD/COP/DEC/XIII/18.

[98] See e.g. 'International Code of Conduct on the Distribution and Use of Pesticides' (1985) and the 'London Guidelines for the Exchange of Information on Chemicals in International Trade' (1987).

[99] See A. M. Mekouar, 'Pesticides and Chemicals—The Requirement of Prior Informed Consent' in D. Shelton (ed.), *Commitment and Compliance* (Oxford: Oxford University Press, 2000), 146.

[100] See 'Bonn Guidelines on Access to Genetic Resources and Fair and Equitable Sharing of the Benefits Arising out of their Utilization', 7–19 April 2002, COP 6 Decision CBD/COP/DEC/VI/24.

[101] 'Action Plan for the Human Environment', 16 June 1972, UN Doc. A/CONF 48/14, 10–62.

[102] See 2030 Agenda for Sustainable Development.

infrastructure); SDG 10 (reduced inequalities); SDG 11 (sustainable cities and communities); SDG 12 (responsible consumption and production); SDG 13 (climate action); SDG 14 (life below water); SDG 15 (life on land); and SDG 16 (peace, justice, and strong institutions). The remaining SDG 17 concerns the means of implementation of substantive SDGs. Two noteworthy features of the SDGs concern the bottom-up and inclusive process which was followed for their development as well as the fact that the SDGs are addressed to all States, not just developing countries. Thus, the term 'development' in this action plan means overall prosperity.

These are not the only forms of 'soft law' that have played a major role in international environmental law. Another normative phenomenon, which is midway between soft and hard law, are the numerous decisions adopted by a range of Conferences of the Parties (COPs) established by MEAs. Due to the—in most cases—non-binding character of these decisions and resolutions, this *'droit dérivé'* cannot be assimilated to treaty law. Yet, it plays a key role in the specification and development of environmental treaty regimes, as discussed next.

20.4.3 MULTILATERAL ENVIRONMENTAL AGREEMENTS (MEAs)

A very large number of treaties have been concluded in this area, both bilateral and multilateral, regional and universal in scope. The choice of treaties as the preferred law-making process is only natural: in an area where enormous economic interests are at stake, and where scientific and technological advances are constantly affecting the understanding of a problem, States prefer to proceed with the utmost prudence and are prepared to be legally bound only by those rules which they themselves have contributed to formulating. In contrast, they are not willing to be bound by general rules emerging in the international community as a product of the majority of States. In short, in this delicate area States prefer to adopt a consensual attitude.

For presentation purposes, the numerous MEAs adopted in this area can be organized from three main perspectives. The first concerns the nature of the problem addressed by the MEA. A broad distinction can thus be made between 'first generation' environmental problems, that is, more direct, visible, and tangible ones (e.g. marine pollution, air pollution, or the depletion of certain species), and 'second generation' environmental problems, which are much more complex to detect and understand (e.g. ozone depletion, climate change, biodiversity loss, or desertification). The second perspective concerns the broad areas of the environment concerned, that is, the hydrosphere, the atmosphere, the biosphere, and dangerous substances/activities. The third perspective is more granular and focuses on the type of treaty-making and design techniques used to tackle important issues such as trade-offs with economic development, scientific/technological change, and the need to include a wide range of States in very different situations. These three perspectives will be examined in turn.

(1) *First and second generation environmental issues*: the distinction between first and second generation environmental issues is of a historical rather than a conceptual nature. First generation issues, such as different forms of marine pollution (e.g. dumping, vessel-source pollution, land-based pollution); transboundary air pollution (e.g. acid rain); pollution from waste (including nuclear waste); and the need to protect certain areas facing massive degradation (e.g. wetlands of international importance or sites of outstanding universal value) or species facing extinction (e.g. whales, endangered species, migratory birds), arose since the very inception of modern international environmental law. Throughout the 1970s, a range of MEAs were concluded at the global level to tackle such issues,

including the 1971 Ramsar Convention on Wetlands,[103] the 1972 World Heritage Convention,[104] the 1973 Convention on the International Trade of Endangered Species (CITES),[105] the 1979 Convention on Migratory Species,[106] the 1972 London Convention on Dumping,[107] the 1973/78 MARPOL Convention dealing with vessel-source pollution,[108] and the 1979 UNECE Convention on Long-Range Transboundary Air Pollution (LRTAP).[109] Also during the 1970s, an ambitious framework for the protection of the marine environment was negotiated under the aegis of the Third Conference on the Law of the Sea, which led to the adoption of Part XII of the UN Convention on the Law of the Sea.[110]

Scientific development and, no less importantly, improvements in the science–policy interface allowing the international community to become more aware of global environmental change, led to the realization that a range of more complex, less visible, yet globally crucial problems were being caused by human action, including the progressive depletion of stratospheric ozone (due to emissions of certain ozone-depleting substances such as chlorofluorocarbons); climate change (driven by the increasing concentrations of greenhouse gases in the troposphere as a result of human emissions of carbon dioxide, methane, and nitrous oxide, among others); biodiversity loss (driven by several phenomena, including habitat degradation, excessive harvesting, and a range of indirect threats, e.g. acidification of the oceans); or desertification of certain areas (driven also by several factors, such as climate change and land-use practices). As these global problems became better understood, States started to adopt global conventions defining a framework to tackle the problem, followed by more specific instruments developing State obligations. Major examples include: the 1985 Vienna Convention on the Protection of the Ozone Layer, followed by the landmark 1987 Montreal Protocol on Substances that Deplete the Ozone Layer; the 1992 UN Framework Convention on Climate Change (UNFCCC), followed by the 1997 Kyoto Protocol; and, more recently, the 2015 Paris Agreement; the 1992 Convention on Biological Diversity (CBD), followed by protocols on genetically modified organisms[111] and on access to genetic resources and benefit sharing; and the 1994 UN Convention to Combat Desertification (UNCCD).

These are just some prominent examples of MEAs adopted around the time of the 1972 Stockholm Conference and the 1992 Rio Conference, which played the role of powerful catalysts for environmental action at the global level.

(2) *The environment as a mosaic of objects and problems*: another vantage point for the same reality organizes these numerous MEAs on the basis of the broad areas of the

---

[103] Convention on Wetlands of International Importance especially as Waterfowl Habitat, 2 February 1971, 996 UNTS 245 (Ramsar Convention).

[104] Convention Concerning the Protection of the World Cultural and Natural Heritage, 16 November 1972, 1037 UNTS 151 (WHC).

[105] Convention on International Trade in Endangered Species of Wild Fauna and Flora, 3 March 1973, 993 UNTS 243 (CITES).

[106] Convention on the Conservation of Migratory Species of Wild Animals, 23 June 1979, 1651 UNTS 333 (CMS).

[107] Convention on the Prevention of Marine Pollution by Dumping of Wastes and Other Matter, 29 December 1972 (London Convention), subsequently modified by the Protocol of 7 November 1996 to the Convention of 1972 on the Prevention of Marine Pollution by Dumping of Wastes and Other Matter, 7 November 1996, 1046 UNTS 120 (London Protocol).

[108] International Convention for the Prevention of Pollution from Ships, 2 November 1973, amended by the Protocol of 17 February 1978, 1340 UNTS 184 (MARPOL 73/78).

[109] Convention on Long-Range Transboundary Air Pollution, adopted in Geneva on 13 November 1979, 1302 UNTS 217 (LRTAP Convention).

[110] United Nations Convention on the Law of the Sea, 10 December 1982, 1833 UNTS 396 (UNCLOS).

[111] Cartagena Protocol on Biosafety to the Convention on Biological Diversity, 29 January 2000, 2226 UNTS 208 (Biosafety Protocol).

environment with which they are mostly concerned. Despite the famous dictum of the ICJ in its Advisory Opinion on the *Legality of the Threat or Use of Nuclear Weapons* that 'the environment is not an abstraction but represents the living space, the quality of life and the very health of human beings, including generations unborn' (at §29), from a legal standpoint international environmental law approaches the environment as a series of discrete, often overlapping, objects and problems, which can be broadly organized according to whether they concern the hydrosphere, the atmosphere, the biosphere, or dangerous substances/activities.

Within the *hydrosphere*, the main MEAs concern the protection of the marine environment at the global[112] and regional levels,[113] and that of international watercourses.[114] With respect to the *atmosphere*, three main objects stand out, namely, transboundary air pollution,[115] ozone depletion,[116] and climate change.[117] The *biosphere* (including wildlife and nature conservation) is addressed through a dense network of MEAs concerning the protection of species,[118] spaces (whether understood as 'sites', 'habitat', 'ecosystems', 'areas' etc.),[119] and biodiversity (the diversity both of and within species, and that of ecosystems).[120] The regulation of *dangerous substances and activities* seeks to cover the life-cycle of pollutants, from their production/use, to their transboundary movements, to their disposal. Some level of integration has been achieved in this regard, whether through the co-ordination of pre-existing treaties, for example the BRS system (Basel, Rotterdam, and Stockholm Conventions),[121] or within a single MEA devoted to particular pollution, for example the Minamata Convention on Mercury.[122]

---

[112] See *inter alia* the 1982 UNCLOS, the 1972 London Convention (and 1996 London Protocol), and MARPOL 73/78.

[113] Following a recommendation from the 1972 Stockholm Conference on the Human Environment, UNEP set up a Regional Seas Programme (RSP), which provides an umbrella for 13 action plans for the main marine regions of the world, nine of which benefit from framework conventions supplemented by protocols (the Mediterranean, the Black Sea, West Africa, East Africa, the Pacific South-East, the Pacific South-West, the Red Sea and Gulf of Aden, the Kuwaiti regional action plan, and the Caribbean). There are also governance regimes for regional seas not included in the RSP, namely the Arctic, Antarctica, Baltic region, Caspian Sea, and the North-East Atlantic. All but the Arctic benefit from dedicated treaty regimes.

[114] See *inter alia* the 1997 New York Convention, the Convention on the Protection and Use of Transboundary Watercourses and International Lakes, 18 March 1992, 1936 UNTS 269 (Helsinki Convention), and the substantial number of watercourse specific agreements. On the latter, see UNEP/Oregon State University/FAO, *Atlas of International Freshwater Agreements* (Nairobi: UNEP, 2002), 3.

[115] See mainly the 1979 LRTAP Convention and its eight Protocols.

[116] See the 1985 Vienna Convention and the 1987 Montreal Protocol.

[117] See the 1992 UNFCCC, the 1997 Kyoto Protocol, and the 2015 Paris Agreement.

[118] See, among many others, the International Convention for the Regulation of Whaling, 2 December 1946, 161 UNTS 361 (Whaling Convention), the 1973 CITES, and the 1979 CMS.

[119] See e.g. the Ramsar Convention, the WHC, and the Protocol to the Antarctic Treaty on Environmental Protection, 4 October 1991, 30 ILM 1455 (Madrid Protocol).

[120] See mainly the 1992 CBD, the 2000 Biosafety Protocol, and the 2010 Nagoya Protocol.

[121] See Basel Convention on the Control of Transboundary Movements of Hazardous Wastes and their Disposal, 22 March 1989, 1673 UNTS 57 (Basel Convention), Rotterdam Convention, and Stockholm Convention. These three treaties have undergone a 'synergy process'. See Decision SC-4/34, 'Enhancing Cooperation and Coordination among the Basel, Rotterdam and Stockholm Conventions', 8 May 2009, UNEP/POPS/COP.4/38; Decision RC-4/11, 'Enhancing Cooperation and Coordination among the Basel, Rotterdam and Stockholm Conventions', 31 October 2008, UNEP/FAO/RC/COP.4/24; Decision BC-IX/10, 'Cooperation and Coordination between the Basel, Rotterdam and Stockholm Conventions', 27 June 2008, UNEP/CHW.9/39. On the progress made in this process so far see *Report on the overall review of the synergies arrangements. Note by the Secretariat*, 24 November 2016, UNEP/CHW.13/INF/43, UNEP/FAO/RC/COP.8/INF/29, UNEP/POPS/COP.8/INF/43, Annex.

[122] Minamata Convention on Mercury, 10 October 2013. On this treaty see H. H. Eriksen and F. Perrez, 'The Minamata Convention: A Comprehensive Response to a Global Problem' (2014) 23 *RECIEL* 195.

Although the understanding of MEAs as a mosaic, rather than as a recognizable 'regime', may be conceptually unsatisfying, it is a much closer depiction of reality than artificial labels such as 'environmental law' or the 'environmental regime'. Moreover, the complexity of this mosaic, with its internal synergies, conflicts, and rivalries, but also gaps, has been a major driver for the initiative to adopt a Global Pact for the Environment.

(3) *MEA design*: in order to understand the operation of MEAs and, specifically, the techniques developed to manage the challenges arising from political economy considerations, scientific/technological change, and universalization/differentiation, it is useful to examine three main types of techniques or approaches by reference to some illustrations.

One important technique that was used early on is the adoption of a *framework instrument*, defining the problem, setting broad principles, and establishing institutional co-operation, followed by the adoption of *more specific instruments*, typically termed 'Protocols', laying down rules and obligations to achieve the broad objective set in the framework instrument. An early illustration of this approach is offered by the 1979 LRTAP Convention, which was subsequently specified through no less than eight Protocols, seven of which focused on specific pollutants (e.g. sulphur dioxide, nitrous oxide, volatile organic compounds, heavy metals, and persistent organic pollutants) and problems (acidification, eutrophication, etc.).[123] Another illustration is the 1985 Vienna Convention on the Protection of the Ozone Layer which merely identified the problem, set the broad principles, and established institutions which, subsequently, enabled the adoption of the 1987 Montreal Protocol. The latter sets quantified obligations for both developed and developing countries regarding the production/consumption of certain specified substances, which have been expanded over time—through amendments to the Protocol—from chlorofluorocarbons and halons at the beginning, to hydrofluorocarbons, with the 2016 Kigali Amendment.[124] Of note, the latter are not, technically, substances that deplete the ozone layer but powerful greenhouse gases. They have been regulated through the Montreal Protocol both due to their close relationship with other regulated substances and, above all, because of the more ambitious top-down structure of the Protocol, which makes it better suited than the Paris Agreement for such a purpose. Yet another illustration of this approach is the UNFCCC, which defined in broad terms the goal of limiting concentrations of greenhouse gases in the troposphere to a level which avoids dangerous human interference with the climatic system; formulated several guiding principles (most notably precaution, intergenerational equity, and CBDR in a specific version); and established a sophisticated institutional structure to negotiate further obligations. The latter came in the form of the 1997 Kyoto Protocol, which required States listed in Annex I to the UNFCCC (mirrored in Annex B of the Kyoto Protocol) to meet quantified emission reduction commitments structured around a baseline year (in most cases 1990) and a commitment period (2008–12). States listed in Annex B were required to reduce or control their emissions of the greenhouse gases identified in the Kyoto Protocol (Annex A) in the commitment period as compared to the baseline year. The Paris Agreement, although it also implements the UNFCCC, has a hybrid form which makes it unsuitable as an example of the framework convention/protocol approach.

---

[123] Protocol to the 1979 Convention on Long-Range Transboundary Air Pollution on the Reduction of Acidification, Eutrophication and Ground-Level Ozone, 30 November 1999, Document of the Economic and Social Council EB.AIR/1999/1 (Gothenburg Protocol).

[124] Decision XXVIII/1, 'Further amendment of the Montreal Protocol', 14 October 2016, Doc. UNEP/OzL.Pro.28/CRP/10; Decision XXVIII/2, 'Decision related to the amendment phasing down hydrofluorocarbons', 14 October 2016, Doc. UNEP/OzL.Pro.28/CRP/10 (together the 'Kigali Amendment').

Another important technique used in MEAs to keep pace with constant changes in the scientific understanding of environmental problems is what one might call the *list technique*, namely a threefold structure of certain treaties which includes a list (of either protected objects, e.g. species or spaces, or prohibited/restricted substances); certain obligations applicable to the items listed; and a system to update the list.[125] This technique is at the heart of several MEAs dealing with matters as diverse as endangered species of flora and fauna,[126] world heritage sites,[127] transboundary movements of chemicals and pesticides,[128] or persistent organic pollutants,[129] among other things. This approach can become extremely complex depending on the specific features of the list (which may be more than one), the associated obligations (which may also be different from one list to the other), and the updating system (which may include several flexibilities, such as the possibility of objecting—opting out—or of preserving certain activities or uses of a listed substance). A good illustration is offered by the 2001 Stockholm Convention on Persistent Organic Pollutants, which prohibits the production/use of the substances listed in Annex A (Elimination) and imposes restrictions on those listed in Annexes B (Restriction) and C (Unintentional production). The system for the updating of the lists is very structured and institutionalized, with powers of initiative, review, and adoption allocated among several bodies. Moreover, the obligations associated with the listing admit several flexibilities to accommodate different national (and industrial) situations. Over time, the number of substances listed in Annex A has slowly increased from an initial list of 12, known as the 'dirty dozen', to 24 as of the last revision.

The latter point raises the question of *differentiation*. Differentiation techniques are aimed at facilitating the participation of the widest possible number of countries while, at the same time, accommodating their special circumstances without defeating the purpose of the MEA. The many flexibilities offered by the Stockholm Convention offer one approach to differentiation. Another approach is illustrated by the Montreal Protocol, which subjects all member States (developed and developing countries) to essentially similar obligations, with developing countries (called countries operating under Article 5) enjoying more time to meet their obligations[130] as well as assistance (financial and technological) to support compliance.[131] A third, quite extreme, approach to differentiation is epitomized by the 2015 Paris Agreement which, effectively, has enshrined a system of 'self-determined' differentiation, in that each member State can choose its level of ambition (what it intends to do) with respect to mitigation of greenhouse gases.[132] Under Article 4(2), '[e]ach Party shall prepare, communicate and maintain nationally determined contributions that it intends to maintain'. Parties are free to select the policies and what they intend to achieve, as made evident in the very terminology used to describe the exercise: 'nationally determined contributions' (NDCs). Unlike the Kyoto Protocol, however, this obligation applies to all parties. The only requirement is that, at least every five years, each party must communicate a new NDC (Article 4(9)) 'which will represent a progression beyond the Party's then current nationally determined contribution and reflect its highest possible ambition' (Article 4(3)). In practice, the NDCs communicated to the Secretariat have been widely diverse in form and substance, raising concerns regarding the overall viability of the approach.

---

[125] See Dupuy and Viñuales (n 7), at 213 (this concept is introduced by reference to CITES).
[126] CITES.
[127] WHC.
[128] Rotterdam Convention.
[129] Stockholm Convention.
[130] Montreal Protocol, Article 5.
[131] Montreal Protocol, Articles 10 and 10A.
[132] Paris Agreement, Article 4(2).

This can be contrasted with more rigid approaches which rely on categories (e.g. 'developed countries' vs 'developing countries' or Annex I—of the UNFCCC—vs non-Annex I countries or, again, countries operating under Article 5—of the Montreal Protocol—and the others). At the same time, the extreme freedom that comes with self-determined differentiation may jeopardize the overall objective of an MEA, which is not merely to bring all countries on board, but to do so in order to effectively tackle a common environmental problem. In the specific context of the Paris Agreement, self-determined differentiation was widely seen as the price to pay to bring developing countries, which include some of the world's main emitters of greenhouse gases, such as China and India, under some form of mitigation discipline.

20.4.4 MECHANISMS TO PROMOTE AND MANAGE COMPLIANCE

States have rightly felt that there was little point in trying to ensure compliance with international rules on environmental protection by resorting to traditional judicial mechanisms and, in cases of persistent non-compliance, to rules on State responsibility. Environmental disputes can seldom be settled by black-and-white decisions, that is by simply deciding whether a State has or has not abided by an international rule. First, most of the time international rules governing this matter are formulated as standards, allowing for a significant margin of interpretation and flexibility. Secondly, once the breach of a rule has occurred it may be too late for judicial or quasi-judicial bodies to step in, for the damage to the environment may be of such magnitude that the payment of compensation proves inadequate to the loss or destruction of precious natural assets. Thirdly, the delinquent State may be unable to pay compensation, because of its dire financial conditions, its under-development, or for other reasons. Fourthly, the damage may have been caused by private persons, without any State responsibility (e.g. on account of lack of due diligence) being involved. Fifthly, it may happen that the damage has been caused not to one or more specific States but to the whole international community, and for diplomatic, political, or other reasons no State is prepared to institute judicial or other proceedings against the law-breaking State. In short, it has been rightly considered that this is an area where what is needed is prevention, carried out by collective bodies acting on behalf of the international community or at least a group of States. It has been felt that the primary task of these bodies should be to monitor the conduct of States and, in case of non-compliance, assist the deviant State in remedying the damage. Sanctions should be envisaged only as a last resort and in case of repeated non-compliance.

The above remarks are not intended to imply that legal disputes may not arise between two or more States and that they may not be settled by recourse to arbitral or judicial proceedings. Indeed, MEAs do not rule out such recourse; they even explicitly provide for it. This, for instance, holds true for the Vienna Convention on the Protection of the Ozone Layer (Article 11) and the UNFCCC (Article 14).[133] The fact however remains that in reality States tend to shun judicial proceedings and rely primarily on supervisory procedures. The latter, unlike arbitral and judicial procedures, are not intended to characterize certain conduct as a breach and derive the attendant legal consequences (responsibility) but to monitor and facilitate 'compliance' and, when necessary, manage 'non-compliance' with the applicable international standards on protection of the environment. They therefore

---

[133] See generally O. Lecucq and S. Maljean-Dubois (eds), *Le rôle du juge dans le développement du droit de l'environnement* (Bruxelles: Bruylant, 2008); T. Stephens, *International Courts and Environmental Protection* (Cambridge: Cambridge University Press, 2009); A. Boyle and J. Harrison, 'Judicial Settlement of International Environmental Disputes: Current Problems' (2013) 4 *JIDS* 245.

act on behalf either of the collectivity of States behind a particular treaty, or of the whole of humanity (in the case of bodies established within universal organizations such as the UN). Monitoring mechanisms have the task of both verifying whether States are complying with international standards and promoting respect for such standards. Clearly, the role these mechanisms play is well attuned to the realities of the present international community.

A survey of the numerous MEAs[134] shows that the most widespread supervisory systems may be grouped into four main classes: (1) States' self-reporting procedures, (2) inspection, (3) so-called non-compliance procedures, and (4) preventive global monitoring.

(1) *Self-reporting*: MEAs routinely provide for the obligation of States to prepare periodic reports on their implementation. These reports are normally transmitted to the Secretariat established by the treaty, or to the Secretariat of the organization in charge of the particular treaty (this, for instance, is provided for in Article VIII of CITES). In other cases, the reports are submitted, through the Secretariat, to the COP (e.g. this is provided for in Article 12 of the UNFCCC; a similar provision can be found in Article 26 of the CBD). In most cases State reports are examined by the Secretariat or by a subsidiary body (a technical body or a 'Compliance Committee'), which submits to the COP draft recommendations, to be discussed and, as the case may be, adopted by it.

(2) *Inspection procedures*: monitoring through on-site or other forms of independent inquiries is far more incisive, and therefore rarer. Inspections are made either by a joint organization or body or by individual contracting States. This supervisory method is envisaged, for instance, in the 1959 Antarctic Treaty, under which each State party may carry out inspections and report to the 'Consultative Parties', which then discuss the reports in their meetings (the 1991 Madrid Protocol on Environmental Protection strengthens this monitoring). The 1973/78 MARPOL entrusts with monitoring tasks both the flag State and the State where ships dock. The 1992 Niue Treaty on Cooperation in Fisheries Surveillance and Law Enforcement in the South Pacific Region[135] provides for inspection on the sea (carried out on the strength of the Pacific Patrol Boat Programme, by boats of the contracting States) and by the air (carried out by aircraft of Australia and New Zealand). Other treaties confer the power of inspection on collective bodies. For example, the Schedule adopted in 1971 to the Whaling Convention established a scheme of international observers, appointed by the International Whaling Commission, but nominated and paid by governments. CITES provides that the Secretariat, after receiving States' reports, may authorize an inquiry, the result of which is submitted to the COP, which in turn may make recommendations to the relevant State (Article 13). A more effective supervisory system is that provided for in the World Heritage Convention, under which an intergovernmental Committee ensures 'systematic' monitoring of the state of conservation of world heritage sites, as well as 'reactive' monitoring when these sites are threatened by natural disasters or human activities.

(3) *Non-compliance procedures*: a third and more advanced supervisory system, the so-called 'non-compliance' procedures, was first established in 1990 under the aegis of the Montreal Protocol.[136] It has subsequently been taken up in many other MEAs, including some which preceded the Montreal Protocol but which were updated through the

---

[134] See generally J. E. Viñuales, 'Managing Abidance by Standards for the Protection of the Environment' in A. Cassese (ed.), *Realizing Utopia* (Oxford: Oxford University Press, 2012).

[135] Niue Treaty on Cooperation in Fisheries Surveillance and Law Enforcement in the South Pacific Region, 9 July 1992, 1974 UNTS 45.

[136] 'Non-compliance Procedure', Decision IV/5, 25 November 1992, UNEP/OzL.Pro4/15, Annex IV (Report of the Parties) as subsequently amended.

establishment of such procedures, such as the London Dumping Convention, CITES, and the LRTAP Convention.[137]

This monitoring system is much stronger than the others and shares some features with the judicial settlements of disputes. In particular, (i) the proceedings may, in some cases, unfold in an adversarial manner (the State complained of may appear before the monitoring body to put forward its arguments and submissions); (ii) in the most advanced examples, the procedure may be triggered not only by a State party to the MEA or the Secretariat (this latter option is rare for political reasons) but also by the public;[138] and (iii) the outcome of the procedure may be the adoption of a recommendation which, in some cases, may 'declare' the situation of non-compliance and even have the effect of suspending the advantages derived from the relevant MEA (e.g. assistance or participation in market mechanisms).

Taking the procedure of the Montreal Protocol as an illustration, it is possible to describe the process as follows.[139] If, after examining States' periodic reports, the Secretariat considers that a State is not complying with the treaty, it may make a report to the Meeting of States Parties (MOP) as well as the Implementation Committee (a permanent body consisting of representatives of 10 contracting States, and normally meeting twice a year). Similarly, the Secretariat may forward to the Committee the objections and misgivings (called 'reservations') expressed by a State party, and supported by 'corroborating information', concerning another contracting State's implementation of its obligations. In addition, a State party may report to the Committee, through the Secretariat, that, 'despite having made its best, bona fide efforts, it is unable to comply fully with its obligations'. The Committee discusses the Secretariat's report, or the complaining State's 'reservations', or the submission of a State about its own inability to fulfil the Protocol's obligations. It may invite to its discussion the State complained of or self-reporting. It then makes a report to the MOP. This gathering shall 'decide upon and call for steps to bring about full compliance with the Protocol'. The measures that the MOP may adopt, listed in Annex V, include: (a) 'appropriate assistance, including assistance for the collection and reporting of data, technical assistance, technology transfer and financial assistance, information transfer and training'; (b) the issuing of cautions; (c) the 'suspension, in accordance with the applicable rules of international law concerning the suspension of the operation of a treaty, of specific rights and privileges under the Protocol, whether or not subject to time limits, including those concerned with industrial rationalization, production, consumption, trade, transfer of technology, financial mechanism and institutional arrangements'. The latter amount, essentially, to the suspension of the benefits of the treaty, which may generate pressure on the non-compliant government both directly and indirectly, that is, through pressure from the domestic industries affected by the suspension.

In practice, the procedure has been mostly used at the initiative of the Secretariat or by 'submission' (self-reported non-compliance) and, aside from deficient reporting of data relating to the consumption of ozone-depleting substances, cases of non-compliance with

---

[137] On these procedures, see generally M. Koskenniemi, 'Breach of Treaty or Non-Compliance? Reflections on the Enforcement of the Montreal Protocol' (1992) 3 *YIEL* 123; T. Treves et al. (eds), *Non-Compliance Procedures and Mechanisms and the Effectiveness of International Environmental Agreements* (The Hague: TMC Asser Press, 2009); S. Urbinati, *Les mécanismes de contrôle et de suivi des conventions internationales de protection de l'environnement* (Milano: Giuffrè, 2009).

[138] See 'Review of Compliance', Decision I/7, 2 April 2004, ECE/MP.PP/2/Add.8, Annex, §18; 'Review of Compliance', Decision I/2, 3 July 2007, ECE/MP.WH/2/Add.3, EUR/06/5069385/1/Add.3, §16.

[139] See F. Romanin Jacur, 'The Non-Compliance Procedure of the 1987 Montreal Protocol to the 1985 Vienna Convention on Substances that Deplete the Ozone Layer' in T. Treves et al. (eds), *Non-Compliance Procedures and Mechanisms and the Effectiveness of International Environmental Agreements* (The Hague: TMC Asser Press, 2009), 11.

the substantive (phase-out) obligations of the Protocol have also been common in respect of transitional countries and developing countries. In some cases, such as a procedure concerning the Russian Federation conducted in the mid-1990s, the MOP has adopted trade bans of ozone-depleting substances to induce a return to compliance. In many other cases, particularly those concerning developing countries, a facilitative and non-adversarial approach has been followed resulting in assistance for improving compliance.

(4) *Neutral data collection and monitoring*: a fourth system is different from those so far discussed in that it is not primarily designed to verify whether States infringe international rules for the protection of the environment. Rather, it aims at collecting data and information on the environment so as better to prevent possible damage to the environment and, above all, guide international and domestic action. An early example of this category is the Global Environment Monitoring System (GEMS) established within the framework of the Earth-Watch Programme designed by UNEP. It is directed 'to assemble and assess information on the human and natural environment in order to anticipate environmental degradation and alert the international community to ways in which human activities may be interfering with the functioning of the biosphere and with human well-being'.[140] Another encompassing effort has taken the form of the Global Environment Outlooks (GEOs) prepared by UNEP since the 1990s, to monitor progress with the Agenda 21 adopted at the 1992 Rio Conference. So far, six GEOs have been published, most recently GEO-6 of 2019.[141] These are just two examples of what can be seen as a general effort to consolidate a global science–policy interface.

The most sophisticated model for such an interface developed so far is the Intergovernmental Panel on Climate Change (IPCC), an international institution created in 1988 at the initiative of the International Union for the Conservation of Nature (IUCN), the International Council for Science (ICSU), and UNEP.[142] It brings together State representatives and scientists in a highly structured effort to assess, every five to seven years, the current state of knowledge with respect to climate change, focusing on the physical science basis of climate change, its impact, and its mitigation. The IPCC does not conduct research; its vast network of scientists, who work pro bono, reviews research already conducted over the reference period and comes to a unified view of what is known, on balance, about climate change. This takes the form of an Assessment Report (AR). So far, five ARs have been published, respectively in 1990 (AR1), 1995/96 (AR2), 2001 (AR3), 2007 (AR4), and 2013/14 (AR5).[143] The development of global climate policy has been profoundly influenced by these ARs, with the adoption of the UNFCCC after AR1, that of the Kyoto Protocol following AR2, and the entire negotiation process (organized by a negotiating mandate known as the 'Durban Platform for Enhanced Action'[144]) leading to the 2015 Paris Agreement being structured so as to wait for the publication the previous year of AR5. The IPCC also prepares 'Special Reports' on particular issues, most recently on the impact of limiting greenhouse gas concentrations to 1.5 degrees Celsius above pre-industrial times (i.e. to a global average temperature of 15.5 degrees Celsius, rather than 16) (2018), on climate change and land (2019), and on climate change, oceans and the cryosphere (2019).

---

[140] See generally M. D. Gwynne, 'The Global Environment Monitoring System (GEMS) of UNEP' (1982) 9 *Environ Conserv* 35.

[141] See generally the website of the GEO: https://www.unenvironment.org/global-environment-outlook.

[142] On the IPCC as an institution see R. Encinas de Munagorri (ed.), *Expertise et gouvernance du changement climatique* (Paris: LGDJ, 2009).

[143] Online at https://www.ipcc.ch/reports/.

[144] 'Establishment of an Ad Hoc Working Group on the Durban Platform for Enhanced Action', Decision 1/CP.17 (11 December 2011), Doc. FCCC/CP/2011/9/Add.1.

The success of the model, despite some controversies about the reliability of its procedures, has led to its replication. In 2012, an Intergovernmental Science-Policy Platform on Biodiversity and Ecosystem Services (IPBES) was established following the model of the IPCC. The IPBES has issued several assessment reports (akin to the IPCC's Special Reports) focusing on certain issues (e.g. pollinators and food production, land degradation, and biodiversity and ecosystem services in different areas).[145] In 2019, it published its first Global Assessment Report, which highlighted the dire and extremely urgent situation of global biodiversity loss.[146] A similar approach to the science–policy interface, that is the establishment of a 'Scientific Panel on Water', has been recommended by a 2018 report from a High-Level Panel on Water,[147] although so far this recommendation has not been given any concrete form.

20.4.5 INTERNATIONAL INSTITUTIONS IN CHARGE OF ENVIRONMENTAL PROTECTION

As soon as it emerged that the protection of the environment was bound to become one of the crucial issues of the whole international community, international bodies were set up and entrusted with broad powers of promoting protection of natural resources and the human environment.

Among the institutions with a universal scope, mention should be made of a body which has already been referred to in this chapter, namely, the United Nations Environment Programme (UNEP). UNEP is technically a subsidiary body of the UN established in 1972 by UN GA resolution 2997.[148] UNEP consists of: (a) a Governing Council, which initially had 58 members elected by the General Assembly meeting annually and reporting to it but was later (following the Rio + 20 Summit) expanded to all members of the UN General Assembly, which now sits every two years as the UN Environment Assembly (UNEA);[149] and (b) a Secretariat, which has its headquarters in Nairobi, a decision taken in the early 1970s to assuage the concerns expressed by developing countries with respect to global environmental governance. UNEP promotes international environmental co-operation, co-ordinates programmes and projects on the environment, and stimulates action by States and international organizations in this area.

In 1992, the UN General Assembly established by resolution 47/191 the UN Commission on Sustainable Development (CSD), consisting of 53 States elected by ECOSOC and a Secretariat based in New York. The main function of the CSD was to monitor the implementation of Agenda 21, but its work was discontinued by a decision taken at the Rio + 20 Summit and replaced with a High-Level Political Forum on Sustainable Development, which is to monitor the implementation of the 2015 SDGs.

These two institutions are only two illustrations of a wide and diverse landscape of international organizations, non-governmental organizations, and mixed entities which

---

[145] See L.-A. Duvic-Paoli, 'The Intergovernmental Science-Policy Platform for Biodiversity and Ecosystem Services or the Framing of Scientific Knowledge within the Law of Sustainable Development' (2017) 19 *Int CL Rev* 231.

[146] Online at https://www.ipbes.net/global-assessment-report-biodiversity-ecosystem-services.

[147] HLPW, *Making Every Drop Count: An Agenda for Water Action* (14 March 2018), 9 and 31 (Recommendation 10).

[148] 'Institutional and Financial Arrangements for International Environmental Cooperation', 15 December 1972, UN Doc. A/RES/2997/XXVII.

[149] The Future We Want, §88. See online at http://web.unep.org/environmentassembly/.

are active in global environmental governance. These include not only the IUCN, IPCC, and IPBES—already mentioned—and several UN Specialized Agencies, for example, the Food and Agriculture Organization (FAO), the UN Education, Scientific and Cultural Organization (UNESCO), the International Maritime Organization (IMO), or the World Meteorological Organization (WMO), but also a wide range of institutions created by MEAs; others set up with different purposes but active in environmental matters (e.g. the Organisation for Economic Co-operation and Development (OECD) and of course the European Union); and a myriad NGOs, large (e.g. Greenpeace, the World Resources Institute, and the World Wildlife Fund) and small.

The most striking feature of this daunting landscape is the conspicuous absence of a World Environment Organization, despite several attempts over the years, lastly in the run-up to the Rio + 20 Summit, to create such an organization.[150] The reluctance of States to do so may be the result of different factors. There is a certain international organization 'fatigue' in States due to the sheer number of entities which deal with different aspects of global governance, together with a reluctance to engage additional costs to support international bureaucracies. But that is not all. There are also reservations regarding environmental matters specifically, most notably fears that such an organization may interfere with economic development or simply add 'red tape' to business as usual. In addition, the specific functions that such an organization would perform remain unsettled. But, given the extremely urgent and dangerous challenges posed by global environmental change and a progressive shift in the perception of such challenges, which now rank at the very top of the global—and in some countries also domestic—political agenda, one can expect that the need for such an organization will be better understood in the future.

20.5 RESPONSIBILITY AND LIABILITY FOR ENVIRONMENTAL HARM

20.5.1 OVERVIEW

Under general rules on 'ordinary' State responsibility (see **Chapter 12**) States incur international responsibility when their conduct breaches a norm of international law owed to another State or to the international community. The question which arises, however, is whether the injuring State bears responsibility on account of fault (i.e. if it failed to exercise due diligence) or instead regardless of any negligence, that is simply because of its risk-creating conduct or the occurrence of damage. A further problem is whether States are responsible for activities that are not prohibited by international law, and nevertheless cause harm or damage to other States.

In some rare cases, these difficult questions have been settled by treaty. For instance, the 1972 Convention on International Liability for Damage Caused by Space Objects[151] provides for various forms of responsibility: absolute liability (Article II)[152] and liability based on

---

[150] See B. Desai, *International Environmental Governance: Towards UNEPO* (The Hague: Brill, 2014).

[151] Convention on International Liability for Damage Caused by Space Objects, 29 March 1972, 961 UNTS 187 (Convention on Liability for Space Objects).

[152] Convention on Liability for Space Objects, Article II stipulates that '[a] launching State shall be absolutely liable to pay compensation for damage caused by its space object on the surface of the earth or to aircraft in flight'.

fault (Article III). In addition, it contemplates causes of exoneration from absolute liability (Article VI).[153] However, in virtually all other cases, there is no clear legal basis ascribing consequences for the conduct of activities which are lawful and which are diligently conducted, even when harm occurs. Historically, States have been extremely reluctant to accept 'strict' or no-fault liability for their activities, including dangerous and ultrahazardous activities. This introduces a stark contrast between domestic law and international law. In domestic law, strict liability (other expressions referring to different forms of no-fault liability include 'absolute liability', 'responsibility *sine delicto*', 'objective responsibility', etc.) is very frequent, whether on producers placing products on the market or operators of certain dangerous activities or even drivers of cars and builders of certain works. By contrast, in international law, except for those rare cases where this is established by treaty (e.g. liability for space objects), States themselves are not liable for the injurious consequences of lawful activities.

This is of course problematic from the perspective of environmental protection, given that the broad category of lawful activities includes most of the drivers of global environmental degradation, from climate change, to land-based marine pollution (e.g. plastics or agricultural run-off), to biodiversity loss. In response to this major challenge, three main approaches have been followed over time: (i) the payment of compensation *ex gratia*, that is, without recognizing any obligation, or on the basis of a specific clause; (ii) the development of standards of environmental protection, including for the prevention of risk, which turn a large part of what were previously seen as lawful activities into lawful but negligently (unlawfully) conducted activities resulting in State responsibility for internationally wrongful acts; and (iii) the development of 'civil liability' regimes, that is, strict liability for economic operators and not for States (unless States or State entities are themselves the relevant economic operator).

Of these three approaches, the first one is by far the weakest and least developed, which highlights the continued reluctance of States to bring international law closer to the approach of domestic law in this area. That reluctance can be observed even in the third approach, which remains confined mainly to oil pollution damage and nuclear accidents. It is therefore the second approach which has greatly developed, hence the importance of principles of international environmental law and, above all, of the prevention principle both for prevention and for responsibility. The three approaches will be briefly presented in the order mentioned.

20.5.2 COMPENSATION *EX GRATIA* OR STRICT LIABILITY OF STATES

Two illustrations of this approach can be provided, although the State paying compensation did not recognize the existence of an obligation in either one. In 1954, a US nuclear test off the Marshall Islands in the South Pacific caused injury to many members of the crew of the Japanese fishing boat *Fukuryu Maru*, which was exposed to nuclear fallout. It should be noted that before the conduct of the tests, the Japanese ambassador to the United States had requested assurances from the US that compensation would be paid in the event of damage or economic loss to Japanese fishermen resulting from the nuclear test.[154] After the tests the

---

[153] Under Article VI.1 the launching State can be exonerated from absolute liability if it establishes 'that the damage has resulted either wholly or partially from gross negligence or from an act or omission done with intent to cause damage on the part of the claimant State or of natural or juridical persons it represents'. Paragraph 2 provides that '[n]o exoneration whatever shall be granted in cases where the damage has resulted from activities conducted by a launching State which are not in conformity with international law including, in particular, the Charter of the United Nations and the Treaty on Principles Governing the Activities of States in the Exploration and Use of Outer Space, including the Moon and Other Celestial Bodies'.

[154] See the Japanese note of 25 January 1956 in Whiteman, 4, at 575.

US government agreed to pay US$2 million, without however formally admitting liability.[155] The same occurred as a result of the disintegration over Canadian territory of the Soviet satellite *Cosmos 954*, in 1978. The Canadian authorities, after searching and finding the partly radioactive debris scattered on Canadian territory, requested compensation for the cost incurred in locating and recovering the debris. In 1981, the Soviet Union agreed to pay compensation (CA$3 million), without recognizing any liability it might have incurred.[156]

An additional illustration, from contemporary international law, is provided by a relatively recent action area within the climate change treaty regime, namely, 'loss & damage'. Behind this obscure expression lies a tension between, on the one hand, the claims of low-lying small island nations and other developing countries for reparation of the harm already caused to them as a result of climate change and, on the other hand, the staunch refusal of developed countries to admit any ground for liability and see any contribution as *ex gratia* 'aid' or 'assistance'. The current state of this tension is consecrated in two provisions of the Paris Agreement (Articles 8 and 9) and a paragraph in the Decision of adoption of this instrument. Article 8 anchors 'loss & damage' within the treaty, but Article 9 carefully omits any financing obligation of developed countries relating to Article 8. Moreover, paragraph 51 of the Decision of adoption provides that the COP 'agrees that Article 8 of the Agreement does not involve or provide a basis for any liability or compensation'.

20.5.3 STATE RESPONSIBILITY FOR ENVIRONMENTAL HARM OR RISK

Recognizing the importance of environmental harm resulting from lawful activities, in 1978, albeit based on an earlier mandate, the UN International Law Commission undertook an effort towards the codification/progressive development of the issue. The question of strict liability of States for the consequences of lawful activities (technically designated by the expression 'international liability for injurious consequences arising out of acts not prohibited by international law') was mired in ambiguity for almost two decades and, in 1997, the ILC decided to distinguish two tracks in this work. The first track focused on prevention, that is, a primary norm of conduct, whereas the second was devoted to international liability.

The work on prevention led to the adoption, in 2001, of a set of Draft Articles on Prevention which clarify the level of diligence that must be observed by States in connection with activities that present a risk of significant transboundary environmental harm. Of note, the ILC Articles on Prevention of Transboundary Harm (unlike Principles 21 of the Stockholm Declaration and 2 of the Rio Declaration) clarify the level of harm required for a breach of the prevention principle, that is, 'significant' harm, although they leave its determination for the adjudicator in each case.[157] In addition, and importantly, the ILC Articles on Prevention of Transboundary Harm contemplate the possibility that 'risk' of significant environmental harm may constitute a breach of the prevention principle, even in the absence of harm.[158] Lawful activities that present a risk of significant harm, such as ultrahazardous activities, are thereby brought under the umbrella of a primary norm, the prevention principle, which circumscribes the level of diligence in a demanding manner, as discussed earlier in this chapter and in **3.10**. The key instrument to enable the possibility of 'breach', hence of negligence and not of no-fault liability, despite the absence

---

[155] See 1956 Settlement of Japanese Claims for Personal and Property Damages Resulting from Nuclear Tests in the Marshall Islands, in *Treaties and Other International Acts Series (United States)*, 3160.
[156] See 18 ILM (1979), at 899.
[157] ILC Articles on Prevention of Transboundary Harm, Commentary Article 2, at §4.
[158] ILC Articles on Prevention of Transboundary Harm, Article 3, Commentary Article 2, §§1–2.

of any 'damage', is the conformity of the activity with international standards setting best practices and a range of other procedural obligations, such as the conduct of an EIA and the duty to co-operate. Thus, this work addressed the initial question of the liability for consequences arising from lawful activities by raising the level of diligence for the conduct of the activity to be considered lawful. Whether damage is required or not depends on the primary norm at stake. For ultrahazardous activities, negligence in generating risk (by not applying sufficiently demanding standards) would be enough for 'breach' of the prevention principle, even in the absence of actual damage. The consequences of 'breach' are, as for other breaches of primary norms, governed by the customary law of State responsibility for internationally wrongful acts. The other track of the codification was indeed confined to some broad guidelines on 'civil liability' of operators (see **20.4.4**).

Some commentators have noted that the operation of the rules of State responsibility for internationally wrongful acts in an environmental harm context may have to face a host of legal problems as well as serious practical hurdles:

(1) It may be difficult to prove the existence of a causal link between the culpable activity and the harm, particularly in the case of climate change (which arises from the emissions from many sources in many States) or when it is asserted that the damage has arisen as a result of activities performed years before (the issue of 'historical responsibilities').

(2) Moreover, harmful effects may arise as a result of many concomitant factors (e.g. the emissions of greenhouse gases from different sources/countries over time interact with a range of other human factors, deforestation and land-use change, biodiversity loss as a result of species or ecosystem tipping points, and the role of the oceans both as a sink and as vector of temperature regulation, possibly triggering other tipping points) which influence processes that also affect the dynamics of the climatic system.

(3) Furthermore, it may prove difficult to identify the responsible author of environmental harm, particularly in the case of emissions of greenhouse gases.

(4) In most cases, harmful effects are caused by individuals or multinational corporations. Thus, States, in addition to being responsible for the conduct of persons who are State officials or who act on behalf of the State, may also be responsible for their lack of due diligence in regulating private activities of persons or entities.

The State's duty of prevention, including the requirement not to allow its territory or the spaces under its jurisdiction to be used in a manner that violates international obligations owed to other States or to the international community, has been long recognized. Due diligence was seen as a requirement already at the time of the *Alabama (United States/Great Britain)* arbitration and applied in the specific context of transboundary environmental harm in the *Trail Smelter (United States of America/Canada)* case. The same duty is part of the prevention principle, and it was recognized by the ICJ already in *Corfu Channel (United Kingdom v Albania)*.[159]

---

[159] The Court held that 'as State practice shows ... a State on whose territory or in whose waters an act contrary to international law has occurred, may be called upon to give an explanation ... A State cannot evade such a request by limiting itself to a reply that it is ignorant of the circumstances of the act and of its authors. The State may, up to a certain point, be bound to supply particulars of the use made by it of the means of information and inquiry at its disposal' (*Corfu Channel (United Kingdom v Albania)*, at 18). However, the Court went on to say that the mere fact of a State's control over a territory does not entail that the State knew or ought to have known of the commission of unlawful acts. 'This fact [the Court concluded] by itself and apart from other circumstances, neither involves *prima facie* responsibility nor shifts the burden of proof' (ibid.).

(5) The assessment of damages may be extremely difficult and complicated in view of the numerous factors that should be taken into account. This is suggested by the decision delivered in 1984 in the *Amoco Cadiz* case by the US District Court for the Northern District of Illinois, which envisaged numerous categories of damage, such as clean-up operations by public employees, the cost of using public buildings for those operations, coastline and harbour restoration, ecological harm, etc.[160] Similarly, the UN Compensation Commission set up after the 1990–91 Gulf War to assess the extent (but not the principle) of Iraq's liability for losses during the war, including claims for environmental harm (so-called 'F4' claims), faced daunting challenges regarding the determination of the amount and form of reparation.[161] More recently, the ICJ has recognized that the services provided by ecosystems may be taken into account as part of the assessment required by general international law.[162]

20.5.4 CIVIL LIABILITY OF ECONOMIC OPERATORS

The third approach, which was adopted early on in connection with oil pollution damage and nuclear accidents, consists of channelling liability, indeed 'strict liability', to the economic operator who has effective power over the relevant activity. The treaties embodying this approach set harmonized standards that must be followed by States parties to ensure that (i) victims are treated on an equal footing with respect to reparation, (ii) there are sufficient funds for repairing what can be very significant harm, and (iii) the economic operator is placed in a situation where its activity can be continued (i.e. its economic exposure is not too high) but where there is a strong incentive to actively prevent any potential harm. These goals are pursued through a combination of techniques, including strict liability with compensation ceilings, mandatory insurance, and additional layers of compensation by beneficiaries of the activity or the State. These are also the techniques that are suggested in the 2006 ILC Draft Principles on the Allocation of Loss in case of Transboundary Harm from Hazardous Activities,[163] which can be seen as an attempt to generalize resort to standardized civil liability systems.

For present purposes, it is useful to present the main components arising from the two main systems which are in force: oil pollution and nuclear accidents. The first relies on a system developed after the 1967 *Torrey Canyon* incident, later revised in 1992[164] and supplemented in 2003.[165] The second is based on two distinct treaty regimes, one concluded

---

[160] See also the subsequent decision of 1992 *In the matter of Oil Spill by the Amoco Cadiz off the Coast of France on March 16, 1978*. On the various problems referred to in the text, see, in particular, A. Kiss and D. Shelton, *International Environmental Law* (New York and London: Transnational Publishers Inc. and Graham and Trotman Ltd, 1991), 350ff.

[161] Of the US$85 billion claimed for environmental damage and resource depletion under F4 claims, the UNCC awarded compensation of US$5.3 billion only. On the valuation methods used see O. Das, *Environmental Protection, Security and Armed Conflict: A Sustainable Development Perspective* (Cheltenham: Edward Elgar, 2013), 200–5.

[162] *Certain Activities (Costa Rica/Nicaragua) (Compensation)*, §52.

[163] Draft Principles on the Allocation of Loss in case of Transboundary Harm from Hazardous Activities, GA resolution 61/36, UN Doc. A/RES/61/36 (ILC Principles on the Allocation of Loss in case of Transboundary Harm).

[164] See the Protocol amending the International Convention on Civil Liability for Oil Pollution Damage, 27 November 1992, online at www.ecolex.org (CLC/92), and the Protocol to Amend the International Convention on the Establishment of an International Fund for Compensation for Oil Pollution Damage, 27 November 1992, also at www.ecolex.org (FUND/92).

[165] Protocol to the International Convention on the Establishment of an International Fund for Compensation for Oil Pollution, 16 May 2003, online at www.ecolex.org (FUND/2003).

among OECD States[166] and the other in the context of the International Atomic Energy Agency,[167] and linked by a joint protocol.[168] Both systems share four broad components:[169]

(1) *No-fault liability of the economic operator for the damage*: channelling liability to the operator requires the identification of the *liable entity* and the *nature and extent of its liability* (including any possible exoneration causes). The liable entity selected is typically the one with effective power over the activity and/or the beneficiary. In the regime concerning liability for nuclear accidents, the 'operator'[170] meets both conditions, while the regime relating to liability for oil pollution damage places liability on the ship owner,[171] which has effective control over the activity, and brings the beneficiary (the oil industry) in as part of the additional layers of compensation. When damage is caused by more than one entity, the two regimes establish a system of joint liability[172] whereby each entity is liable for the entire amount of compensation but can then bring a claim against other liable entities. Regarding the nature and extent of liability, the two regimes establish a no-fault 'strict' liability system applicable to the liable entity. For the latter, the system has the disadvantage of triggering liability on the basis of damage only (with some limited grounds for exemption, e.g. armed conflict, force majeure, etc.[173]) but also the advantage of defining liability caps,[174] which must be set at a level that strikes a compromise between making pursuance of the activity possible while incentivizing a high level of diligence. When there is serious fault on the part of the operator, these caps are lifted, and the operator is therefore exposed to a far higher level of liability.[175]

(2) *The obligation of economic operators to take out insurance*: this obligation[176] is imposed on the liable entity to exclude the risk of insolvency, ensure the adequate compensation of the victims, and spread its costs through insurance techniques. The insurance policy normally covers the amount up to the cap applicable to the liable entity and the details will be set in the contract subject to domestic law. The insurer can invoke the exoneration causes available to the liable entity.[177]

---

[166] Convention on Third Party Liability in the Field of Nuclear Energy, 29 July 1960, 956 UNTS 251 (Paris Convention), supplemented by the Convention Supplementary to the Paris Convention of 29 July 1960 on Third Party Liability in the Field of Nuclear Energy, 31 January 1963, 1041 UNTS 358, and subsequently amended several times.

[167] Convention on Civil Liability for Nuclear Damage, 21 May 1963, 1063 UNTS 265 (Vienna Convention), amended by the Protocol to amend the Vienna Convention on Civil Liability for Nuclear Damage, 12 September 1997, 2241 UNTS 302, which leaves in place the two systems (initial system and amended system), supplemented by the Convention on Supplementary Compensation for Nuclear Damage, 12 September 1997, IAEA INFCIRC/567, not in force.

[168] Joint Protocol Relating to the Application of the Vienna Convention and the Paris Convention, 27 September 1988, 1672 UNTS 293.

[169] See Dupuy and Viñuales (n 7), 319–20, and Survey of Liability Regimes relevant to the Topic of International Liability for Injurious Consequences arising out of Acts not prohibited by International Law (International Liability in case of Loss from Transboundary Harm arising out of Hazardous Activities), 24 June 2004, UN Doc. A/CN.4/543 (Survey of Liability Regimes).

[170] Paris Convention, Articles 1(a)(vi) and 3; Vienna Convention, Articles I(a)(c) and IV(1).

[171] CLC/92, Articles I(3), III(1) and (4).

[172] CLC/92, Article IV; Vienna Convention, Article II(3)(a); Paris Convention, Article 5(b).

[173] CLC/92, Article III(2)–(3); Vienna Convention, Article IV(2)–(3); Paris Convention, Article 9.

[174] On the relevant amounts see ILC Principles on the Allocation of Loss in case of Transboundary Harm, Article 4, Commentary, §23 and notes.

[175] See CLC/92, Article V(2); ILC Principles on the Allocation of Loss in case of Transboundary Harm, Article 4, Commentary, §24.

[176] See CLC/92, Article VII(1); Vienna Convention, Article VII; Paris Convention, Article 10.

[177] CLC/92, Article VII(8); ILC Principles on the Allocation of Loss in case of Transboundary Harm, Article 4, Commentary, §34.

(3) Establishment of additional layers of compensation in case the first layer (borne by the economic operator or its insurer) is insufficient: given the magnitude of the harm that may result from oil spills and nuclear accidents, civil liability regimes establish additional layers of compensation on top of the cap placed on the liability of the economic operator or its insurer. The resources for these additional layers are contributed by the beneficiaries of the activity (the oil industries of member States in the oil pollution damage regime) or by States themselves (in the nuclear accident regime). They serve to cover the damages in case of insolvency of the liable entity (or its insurer) and/or when damages exceed the applicable cap and/or when the duty to compensate cannot be imposed on the economic operator.[178] Because such funds serve as a fall-back redress mechanism, they normally cannot invoke the bases of exoneration available to the economic operator.[179]

(4) Non-discrimination of victims with respect to redress mechanisms: the very objective of these civil liability regimes is to harmonize the situation of victims. The systems set certain parameters that must be complied with by all member States,[180] which, in addition, are required not to discriminate between national and foreign victims with respect to access to redress.[181]

These broad components are also present in other civil liability regimes, which have been developed in connection with the movements of hazardous waste[182] and genetically modified organisms,[183] as well as for industrial accidents.[184] These systems have struggled to achieve a sufficient number of ratifications to enter into force. The same applies to the failed attempt to enact, under the aegis of the Council of Europe, a general environmental liability treaty, that is, the Lugano Convention, which may never enter into force.[185] The limited support given on the international plane to environmental liability regimes suggests that, since its modern inception in the 1972 Stockholm Conference on the Human Environment, international environmental law has been built around the ideas of prevention (rather than reparation) of environmental harm and a balanced allocation of the benefits/burdens among present and future stakeholders.[186]

---

[178] FUND/92, Article 4.
[179] FUND/92, Article 4(2).
[180] See CLC/92, Article X(2).
[181] Paris Convention, Article 14(a); Vienna Convention, Article XIII.
[182] Convention Relating to Third Party Liability in the Field of Maritime Carriage of Nuclear Material, 17 December 1971, 944 UNTS 255; International Convention on Liability and Compensation for Damage in Connection with the Carriage of Hazardous and Noxious Substances, 3 May 1996 (amended by the Protocol of 30 April 2010), online at www.ecolex.org (not in force); Basel Protocol on Liability and Compensation for Damage resulting from Transboundary Movements of Hazardous Wastes and their disposal, 10 December 1999, also at www.ecolex.org (not in force).
[183] Nagoya–Kuala Lumpur Supplementary Protocol on Liability and Redress to the Cartagena Protocol on Biosafety, 15 October 2010, UNEP/CBD/BS/COP-MOP/5/17 (not in force).
[184] Protocol on Civil Liability and Compensation for Damage Caused by the Transboundary Effects of Industrial Accidents on Transboundary Waters, 21 May 2003, Doc. ECE/MP.WAT/11-ECE/CP.TEIA/9 (not in force).
[185] Convention on Civil Liability for Damage Resulting from Activities Dangerous to the Environment, 21 June 1993, online at www.ecolex.org (not in force).
[186] On this distinction see Viñuales, 'Managing Abidance' (n 134).

21

INTERNATIONAL LAW AND THE GLOBAL ECONOMY

21.1 INTRODUCTION

The Second World War left Europe in a shambles. The economies of both Western European countries and the Soviet Union had been disrupted by the fighting or converted to the war effort. Japan too was on its knees. The United States was the only Power whose territory had been spared from invasion or bombardment and whose economy had been boosted by the war. After the war, it became by far the most powerful State militarily; it was in its interest, both politically and economically, to support the post-war reconstruction through a policy designed to stabilize trade and currency exchanges while allowing—although subject to limitations—capital movements.[1] The US economic expansion on European territory and in the Far East was salutary, at least in the short run, to the countries disrupted by war. The flow of American capital into their markets was much needed. Hence, they warmly welcomed the restructuring of international economic relations propounded by the United States. To implement the new scheme it was, however, necessary to dismantle all the barriers that over the years had been erected in the world community by States increasingly bent on protectionism (this of course included colonialist countries, which drew much benefit from the exploitation of primary commodities produced in colonial territories). Thus, the United States launched a free trade and free market philosophy, which rested upon a global architecture consisting of three important international institutions, the International Bank for Reconstruction and Development (the IBRD or World Bank), the International Monetary Fund (IMF), and the General Agreement on Tariffs and Trade (GATT),[2] which was expected to prepare the ground for an International Trade Organization. This triad was aimed at supporting the reconstruction effort and limiting the possibility of succumbing to the competitive currency devaluations and protectionist trade policies that most saw as a major cause of the war.

The World Bank was given the task of mobilizing and collecting money from a range of sources with a view to lending it to those States most in need of foreign investment for their reconstruction and development efforts. The IMF was designed to ensure international monetary stability. It aimed to ensure that single States did not alter international trade conditions by monetary contrivances (such as unilateral devaluations of their currencies)

---

[1] See M. Daunton, 'The Inconsistent Quartet: Free Trade versus Competing Goals' in A. Narlikar, M. Daunton, and R. M. Stern (eds), *The Oxford Handbook of the World Trade Organization* (Oxford: Oxford University Press, 2012), 40.

[2] On the evolution of the legal principles underlying the global economy since 1945 see J. Kurtz, J. E. Viñuales, and M. Waibel, 'Principles Governing the Global Economy' in J. E. Viñuales (ed.), *The UN Friendly Relations Declaration at 50: An Assessment of the Fundamental Principles of International Law* (Cambridge: Cambridge University Press, 2020), chapter 14.

designed to protect the national economy at the expense of foreign countries. In addition, it was designed to help finance temporary balance-of-payment deficits of member States, caused by fluctuations in the price of products on the international market, or by domestic problems. Such financing was clearly to serve as a device for preventing States from finding themselves constrained to resort to protectionism. The GATT was intended to progressively reduce traditional tariff restrictions on free trade and to prohibit discrimination, which greatly hampered free competition on the world market.

In the two decades which followed their establishment, these institutions and their underpinning philosophy came under harsh criticism from developing and newly independent countries. Their great success in the struggle for political independence, embodied in their numerical majority in the UN General Assembly, led a large number of States which, with some variation, were called non-aligned States, 'Third World' States, the Group of 77, or 'developing countries', to claim both economic emancipation and the redefinition of the international economic order created after the Second World War. They advocated three principles conflicting with the prevailing free market philosophy: 'permanent sovereignty over their natural resources', 'differential treatment', and 'positive discrimination', which found expression in what became known as the 'New International Economic Order'. As a result of such pressure from developing countries, but also Cold War politics as well as increasingly apparent design flaws, the international economic architecture underwent substantial changes in the 1960s and 1970s. Such changes involved (i) a partial modification of international economic and financial institutions so as to make them more responsive to the needs of developing countries; (ii) the promotion of multilateral co-operation geared towards the development of those countries; (iii) the rise of the 'Permanent Sovereignty' movement, particularly as regards the energy resources located in developing countries.

With the end of the Cold War, the early 1990s saw once again an expansion of the free market philosophy, embedded in what was by then known as the 'Washington consensus'. Although the World Economic Crisis of 2008 left this consensus in tatters, the major pillars of contemporary international economic law remain those laid down in the early 1990s, most notably the World Trade Organization established in 1994, a financial system geared towards the prevention of financial crises and contagion, and a surge of claims against States on the basis of bilateral investment treaties. At present, there are increasingly strong signs of yet another swing of the pendulum towards sovereignty and limitation of economic liberalization. This backlash has not yet translated into a settled transformation of international legal structures.

21.2 THE POST-1945 GLOBAL ECONOMIC ARCHITECTURE

21.2.1 TWO FOUNDATIONAL CONFERENCES: BRETTON WOODS AND HAVANA

The organization of the post-war economic architecture began during the war and, indeed, very early on, when the likely outcome of the war was still unknown. The trade and monetary policies of the 1930s were widely seen as a major cause of the war. The tariff increase of approximately 20 per cent introduced in the United States, through the infamous 1930 Smoot-Hawley Tariff Act, to protect its industry from foreign products triggered a chain reaction of retaliatory policies from other States.[3] In May and, above

---

[3] See D. A. Irwin, *Peddling Protectionism: Smoot-Hawley and the Great Depression* (Princeton, NJ: Princeton University Press, 2011), 144.

all, in September 1930, Canada, then the largest trading partner of the United States, retaliated with a substantial increase in the tariffs applied to American products.[4] In November 1931, the United Kingdom adopted the Abnormal Importation Act, massively increasing tariffs on manufactured goods from outside the Empire. This was soon followed, in 1932, by the Import Duties Act, increasing tariffs on non-Empire fruit and vegetables, and by the Ottawa Conference, which consolidated the imperial preference.[5] Preferential intra-bloc trade was also embraced by Imperial Japan and Germany during the 1930s.[6] Writing in 1941, former League of Nations economist J. B. Condliffe observed by reference to trade in the inter-war years: 'it is now so obvious as to hardly need statement that bilateral trade took on aggressive and destructive aspects as international rivalries were sharpened in the era of what is now known as pre-belligerancy'.[7] US President F. D. Roosevelt and UK Prime Minister Winston Churchill were well aware of this. When, on 14 August 1941, they met 'somewhere in the sea', their joint declaration, known as the 'Atlantic Charter', contained two principles devoted to economic cooperation. Under the fourth principle, the US and the UK undertook to 'endeavor […] to further the enjoyment by all States, great or small, victor or vanquished, of access, on equal terms to the trade and to the raw materials of the world', while the fifth principle stated their 'desire to bring about the fullest collaboration between all nations in the economic field with the object of securing, for all, improved labour standards, economic advancement and social security'.[8]

As early as 1943, preparations began for the establishment of a post-war international economic architecture which would both stabilize exchange rates (to avoid competitive currency devaluations) and organize a multilateral (rather than intra-bloc or bilateral) trading system. The two main proposals, often known as the Keynes Plan,[9] named after prominent Cambridge economist J. M. Keynes, and the White Plan,[10] named after United States Assistant Treasury Secretary Harry Dexter White, concerned mostly what became known as the Bretton Woods institutions, namely, the IMF and the World Bank. United States Treasury Secretary Hans Morgenthau believed in the priority of currency disorders as the catalyst of the war. In his opening address to the United Nations Monetary and Financial Conference, held in July 1944 in Bretton Woods, New Hampshire, he emphasized such priority in unambiguous terms:

> All of us have seen the great economic tragedy of our time. We saw the worldwide depression of the 1930s. We saw currency disorders develop and spread from land to land, destroying the basis for international trade and international investment and even international faith. In their wake, we saw unemployment and wretchedness—idle tools, wasted wealth. We saw their victims fall prey, in

---

[4] See J. McDonald, A. P. O'Brien, and C. M. Callahan, 'Trade Wars: Canada's Reaction to the Smoot-Hawley Tariff' (1997) 57 *J Econ Hist* 802.

[5] See A. de Bromhead, A. Fernihough, M. Lampe, and K. H. O'Rourke, 'When Britain Turned Inward: The Impact of Interwar British Protection' (2019) 109 *Am Ec Rev* 325.

[6] See K. A. Chase, *Trading Blocs: States, Firms and Regions in the World Economy* (Ann Arbor: University of Michigan Press, 2005), chapter 3.

[7] J. B. Condliffe, *The Reconstruction of World Trade: A Survey of International Economic Relations* (London: George Allen and Unwin, 1941), 287.

[8] Joint Declaration of President F. D. Roosevelt and Prime Minister W. Churchill, 14 August 1941, known as the 'Atlantic Charter'. On this declaration see M. Bennouna, 'Atlantic Charter (1941)', *Max Planck Encyclopedia of Public International Law*, November 2007.

[9] Proposals for an International Clearing Union, Cmd. 6437 (London, 7 April 1943).

[10] Preliminary Draft Outline of a Proposal for an International Stabilization Fund of the United and Associated Nations (Washington, 10 July 1943).

places, to demagogues and dictators. We saw bewilderment and bitterness become the breeders of fascism, and, finally, of war.[11]

The outcome of the Bretton Woods Conference was the result of a joint US–UK proposal, which was much closer to White's plan than to Keynes'. The architecture arising from the Bretton Woods Conference consisted of two main components, which are examined in more detail in the next sections. First, the Conference established a system of fixed but adjustable exchange rates among convertible currencies. Adjustments to the fixed exchange rate remained possible but they were managed through the IMF. The idea behind this was to allow for cases in which, in the absence of an adjustment, the economy of a Member would suffer significantly and thereby lay the political ground for the demagogic movements observed in the inter-war period. Thus, the objective was to stabilize exchange rates to avoid competitive devaluations, while allowing a managed adjustment when there was a genuine disequilibrium. Secondly, investment in support of reconstruction and development were to be channelled through the IBRD, better known as the World Bank. The volatility of foreign capitals in the inter-war period had been seen as a contributing factor leading to the war. To provide greater certainty in the financial flows to nations and, given the fact that private investment could not be expected in sufficient amounts in the immediate aftermath of the war, the World Bank would be entrusted with stimulating private investment by offering guarantees (thus reducing risk) and with financing worthy projects for which private capital would not be forthcoming. Of note, the Bretton Woods system explicitly allowed, indeed encouraged, countries to establish capital controls to regulate 'hot money', that is, short-term speculative capital flowing in and out. Such capital movements were a destabilizing factor for exchange rates, reconstruction, and development efforts.

Although trade was also a key component of the United States post-war economic order, the negotiation of this aspect followed a separate process. On 6 December 1945, the United States and the United Kingdom issued a proposal for an 'International Conference on Trade and Employment'.[12] Discussions between the two countries had begun earlier. US Secretary of State, Cordell Hull, was a firm believer in trade integration as a vehicle of peace, and British economist James Meade had suggested the creation of a multilateral trading system, a 'Commercial Union', already in 1942.[13] Following the joint US–UK proposal, a series of preparatory meetings were held, most notably in Geneva in 1947, leading to the United Nations Conference on Trade and Employment, held in Havana from November 1947 to March 1948. In Geneva, the GATT was adopted as an interim arrangement[14] for what was expected to become the International Trade Organization (ITO). The ITO's Charter, the 'Havana Charter', was effectively adopted at the Havana Conference.[15] Yet, it came under

---

[11] United Nations Monetary and Financial Conference, Proceedings and Documents (US Department of State, International Organizations and Conferences Series, Washington DC, 1948), I, at 81, reproduced in M. Daunton, 'Britain and Globalisation since 1850: III Creating the World of Bretton Woods, 1939–1958' (2008) 18 *Transactions of the Royal Historical Society* 1, at 2–3.

[12] Proposals for Consideration by an International Conference on Trade and Employment as Transmitted by the Secretary of State of the United States of America to His Majesty's Ambassador at Washington, 6 December 1945, Cmd. 6709. On the process leading to this proposal and the origins of the Havana Charter see R. Toye, 'Developing Multilateralism: The Havana Charter and the Fight for the International Trade Organization' (2003) 25 *IHR* 282.

[13] See S. Howson (ed.), *The Collected Papers of James Meade, III: International Economics* (London: Unwin Hyman, 1988), 27–35, referred to in Toye (n 12), at 286.

[14] General Agreement on Tariffs and Trade, 30 October 1947, TIAS No. 1700, 55 UNTS 194.

[15] Final Act and Related Documents of the United Nations Conference on Trade and Employment, Havana, Cuba, 21 November 1947 to 24 March 1948, UN Doc. ICITO/1/4 (1948).

much criticism within the US which never ratified it. Under these circumstances, the trade pillar envisioned during the war remained confined to the GATT until the early 1990s.

The following sections examine the three pillars of the post-1945 international economic architecture, that is, the two Bretton Woods institutions (the IMF and the World Bank) and the GATT. This examination is intended to provide the necessary background to understand the struggle for a 'New International Economic Order' in the 1960s and 1970s and the contemporary international law of the global economy.

21.2.2 THE INTERNATIONAL MONETARY FUND (IMF)

The IMF was established to ensure monetary and financial stability in international relations. It also aimed at promoting the development of international trade, by ensuring the stability of foreign exchange. In addition, it was intended to prevent crises in the balance of payments.

Through the Agreement establishing the Fund,[16] the previously unrestricted sovereignty of States in monetary matters was seriously limited. The Agreement required Members to set a fixed exchange rate, the 'par value', by reference to a reserve currency, the USD, itself convertible into gold at a fixed rate of US$35 per ounce. The objective of this system was to stabilize exchange rates to avoid the currency disorders, such as competitive devaluations, of the inter-war years, while at the same time allowing Members to manage their exchange rates, within a 1 per cent band of their set exchange rate, and potentially adjust, through a managed process with IMF intervention, in case of 'fundamental disequilibrium' of their balance of payments. In an attempt to strike a balance between the negative effects of currency disorders and those of maintaining a fixed exchange rate despite a genuine imbalance (which would make exports artificially expensive), the IMF Articles of Agreement introduced a system of fixed but adjustable exchange rates.

In case of liquidity shortages, that is, lack of sufficient foreign reserves to intervene in the foreign exchange markets to maintain the par value, each Member could draw from the IMF a certain amount of foreign reserves against payment of an equivalent amount in the Member's currency. However, there were limitations on this drawing right. A Member could only draw up to 25 per cent in excess of its national quota per year and the IMF's holdings of the Member's currency could not exceed 200 per cent of that Member's quota. In case of more fundamental disequilibria, a Member could propose to the Fund an adjustment of its exchange rate, the par value, which required the Fund's approval when the adjustment exceeded 10 per cent of the par value. In addition, Member States also undertook to refrain from introducing restrictions on payments or transfers for current international transactions as defined by the Fund's Articles of Agreement, multiple currency practices, or discriminatory arrangements, unless authorized by the Articles of Agreement or by the Fund. Of note, Article VI, section 3 of the Articles of Agreement specifically authorized Members to introduce controls on short-term movements of speculative capital. This was seen, at the time, as a way of preserving the ability of Members to resort to monetary policy (increasing and decreasing interest rates) to pursue domestic purposes without facing massive and sudden capital flights (in search of higher interest rates abroad).

This system faced challenges very early on and, by the late 1960s, it became untenable. One major reason was famously singled out by Yale economist Robert Triffin. The 'Triffin dilemma' pointed to the fact that, under the Bretton Woods system, the world needed more USD to support growth, which could only be achieved by printing more USD and

---

[16] Articles of Agreement of the International Monetary Fund: adopted at the United Nations Monetary and Financial Conference, Bretton Woods, New Hampshire, 22 July 1944.

thereby undermining confidence in it.[17] Other important issues included the fact that, over time, the Yen and the Deutsche Mark became artificially cheap, thus granting Japan and Germany a comparative advantage that some compared to the competitive devaluations of the inter-war years. Finally, on 15 August 1971, the United States suspended the convertibility of the USD into gold. After a failed attempt at reinstating a system of fixed exchange rates, including a devaluation of the USD and a re-evaluation of the Deutsche Mark and the Japanese Yen, in the Smithsonian Agreement of December 1971, the Bretton Woods system collapsed for good. Exchange rates were thus left to each country to decide in what some economists called a 'non-system'.[18] An amendment of the IMF Articles of Agreement in 1976, effective in 1978, endorsed this non-system, allowing Members to freely choose their own exchange rate systems (new Article IV(2)(b)) but maintaining the prohibition of exchange rate manipulation (Article IV(1)(iii)).[19]

The role of the Fund also shifted towards a focus on surveillance, technical assistance, and conditional lending, a matter that in time came under great criticism from developing countries. As noted by a prominent American scholar writing in the mid-1980s:

> [t]oday, the original concept of the international oversight of domestic policies exists only in relation to the developing countries, which must seek IMF approval for their adjustment programmes as the price of access to the Fund resources and Fund-approved restructuring of their external debt.[20]

Conditionality became a major source of friction in North–South relations, with developing countries claiming that it amounted to economic coercion from rich States, which controlled voting in the IMF, and developed countries viewing it as a form of co-operation and technical assistance freely sought by recipients.

21.2.3 THE INTERNATIONAL BANK FOR RECONSTRUCTION AND DEVELOPMENT (WORLD BANK)

The World Bank is an intergovernmental organization, created in 1944 at the Bretton Woods Conference.[21] It later became a UN specialized agency. It is corporate in form, all its capital stock being owned by its member States; the amount of their shares is established on the basis of the quotas set for participating in the IMF. The central organ is the Board of Governors, consisting of a Governor and an alternate appointed by each member State. Its decisions are taken by a 'weighted voting' system.

The Bank's primary statutory goals, namely 'the restoration of economies destroyed or disrupted by war' and 'the re-conversion of productive facilities to peacetime needs', were primarily attained through activities carried out directly by the United States. It must be recalled that, after the Second World War, the economies of most countries were devastated and there were very limited capital surpluses that most countries or their investors could lend to other countries. Moreover, the US had a very important trade surplus as most other countries imported American products purchased with their scarce holdings

---

[17] R. Triffin, *Gold and the Dollar Crisis: The Future of Convertibility* (Princeton, NJ: Princeton University Press, 1960).

[18] J. Williamson, 'The Benefits and Costs of an International Monetary Nonsystem' in E. M. Bernstein et al. (eds), *Reflections on Jamaica* (New Jersey: International Finance Section, 1976), 54.

[19] See R. M. Lastra, *International Financial and Monetary Law*, 2nd edn (Oxford: Oxford University Press, 2015), 423.

[20] See R. N. Gardner, 'Sterling-Dollar Diplomacy in Current Perspective' (1985–86) 62(1) *Int Aff* 21, at 27–8.

[21] International Bank for Reconstruction and Development, Articles of Agreement, adopted at the United Nations Monetary and Financial Conference, Bretton Woods, New Hampshire, 22 July 1944.

of USD. The shortage of liquidity, that is, of USD or other convertible currencies to fuel the economies, led the US to take several important steps to reconstruct post-war economies. One was the European Recovery Programme, better known as the 'Marshall Plan', the management of which was entrusted to the Basel-based Bank of International Settlements, established following the First World War. This initiative came in addition to the initially designed Bretton Woods institutions and largely in order to facilitate performance of the latter's functions.

Within the Bretton Woods institutions, the World Bank was designed to perform a stimulus function. Given the scarcity of capital lending, the Bank was to facilitate such lending either through direct loans under certain conditions or through loan guarantees, which made such loan transactions less risky (for other public or private lenders) and costly (for the borrower). Lending activities were primarily targeted to member States, to 'political subdivisions thereof', or to business enterprises in the territory of members. If the borrower was not a government, the loan had to be guaranteed by the government in whose territory the project financed by the loan was located. Loans, made only for technically and economically valid projects, were long term and incurred current interest rates.

Over time, in order to cater for more specific needs, some activities of the Bank were allocated to other bodies and agencies of what became the 'World Bank Group'. The International Finance Corporation (IFC) was set up in 1956 to engage directly with the private sector through loans and loan guarantees. The International Development Agency (IDA) was established in 1960 with the aim of providing differential financial assistance in the form of low or no-interest loans and grants to developing and less developed countries. Two other institutions of the World Bank Group came later, namely the International Centre for Settlement of Investment Disputes (ICSID), established in 1966 following the adoption of the 1965 ICSID Convention,[22] and the Multilateral Investment Guarantee Agency (MIGA), set up in 1988 to provide insurance to foreign investors against political risk.[23] These two institutions connect the Bretton Woods and, more generally, the post-1945 global economic architecture to an area of particular importance today, which at the time remained largely unregulated or only through the old techniques of diplomatic protection, namely, international investment law. This will be discussed in **21.4.3**.

21.2.4 THE GENERAL AGREEMENT ON TARIFFS AND TRADE (GATT)

The combination of international currency stability and the institutionalized mobilization of private capital to promote the free flow of investment to countries short of money did not suffice for the realization of the grand design launched by the United States in the post-war period—a design which constituted a bold projection onto the world community of a pattern of economic order typical of capitalist countries. As noted earlier in this chapter, the free enterprise, free market, and free competition postulates would have become empty words if protectionism in trade had survived. Hence, after the establishment of the IMF and the World Bank, the need soon arose to complete the foundations of the new economic order by tackling trade barriers.

---

[22] Convention on the Settlement of Investment Disputes between States and Nationals of Other States, 18 March 1965, 575 UNTS 159 (ICSID Convention).

[23] Maurizio Ragazzi, 'World Bank Group', *Max Planck Encyclopaedia of International Law*, October 2017, §1.

In 1947 a new scheme was set up in the form of the General Agreement on Tariffs and Trade.[24] The GATT was seen, at the time, as a stepping stone in the run-up to the UN International Conference on Trade and Employment, held in Havana from November 1947 to March 1948, which was expected to lead to the creation of an International Trade Organization. The constitutive instrument of the latter, the Havana Charter, never entered into force and the interim GATT moved to centre stage. Unlike the Articles instituting the Bank and the IMF, the GATT did not create an international organization; however, over the years an organizational structure did evolve, operating between the 'sessions' of the contracting parties, held twice a year in Geneva. Unlike the Bank and the IMF, the GATT is based on the equal voting power of each party or, in other words, not on the weighted-voting system.

The GATT is still a key pillar of the rules-based international trade system established in the 1990s.[25] The core of the GATT is the set of obligations it imposes on the contracting States, a very complex and technical network of stipulations. They are briefly described in this section in preparation for the discussion of contemporary international trade law in **21.4.2**.

The first obligation is the requirement that each member grant all other parties *most-favoured-nation treatment* (Article I) in connection with duties and charges imposed on imports or exports, that is, treat other GATT members in the same manner as the country to which it grants the most favourable conditions. Why was this clause deemed necessary for the purpose of achieving free trade? Clearly, if a great number of States loyally apply this clause, it follows that discriminations between them tend gradually to fall away and a regime of equality in their trade relationship is established. The MFN clause, as this requirement is known, has a long history in commercial dealings, which largely predates modern international law.[26] Its use became more frequent with the push for liberalization led by UK treaty practice in the second half of the nineteenth century, of which the 1860 Cobden-Chevalier Treaty became emblematic.[27] By the end of the Second World War, trade liberalization was widely seen as an instrument for peace. The then US Secretary of State, Cordell Hull, has sometimes been described as a reincarnation of Richard Cobden,[28] who had expounded the view that international trade provides a powerful safeguard against war. It is therefore unsurprising that Article I of the GATT opens the text with a statement of the MFN requirement.

Another obligation prescribes that imported goods be treated *no less favourably than domestic goods under internal taxation or regulation measures* (Article III). Thus, while the MFN clause is designed to provide non-discriminatory treatment for imports from

---

[24] General Agreement on Tariffs and Trade, 30 October 1947, 64 UNTS 187. Following the adoption of the Marrakesh Agreement establishing the World Trade Organization, 15 April 1994, 1867 UNTS 154 (WTO Agreement), the pre-1994 instrument came to be known as GATT 1947. It is technically defunct but its text was entirely incorporated (with some adjustments) into the GATT 1994, which also contains some 'Understandings' on Articles of the GATT 1947, essentially interpretive additions.

[25] On the history of the GATT system from a legal perspective see generally J. Jackson, *World Trade and the Law of GATT* (Indianapolis: Bobbs-Merrill, 1969); R. Hudec, *Enforcing International Trade Law: The Evolution of the Modern GATT Legal System* (Salem, MA: Butterworth, 1993); D. Irwin, P. Mavroidis, and A. Sykes, *The Genesis of the GATT* (Cambridge: Cambridge University Press, 2008).

[26] See B. Nolde, 'La clause de la nation la plus favorisée et les tarifs préférentiels' (1932) 39 *RCADI* 1, at 25.

[27] Treaty of Commerce between the United Kingdom and France, 23 January 1860, named after Richard Cobden and Michel Chevalier, who negotiated. It famously contained a MFN clause and led to an expansion of similar instruments, although its effects on trade liberalization have been challenged. See O. Accominotti and M. Flandreau, 'Bilateral Treaties and the Most-Favored-Nation Clause. The Myth of Trade Liberalization in the 19th Century' (2008) 60 *World Politics* 147.

[28] Daunton (n 11), at 3.

different foreign countries, this obligation puts foreign goods on the same footing as those produced domestically. The obligation, it is plain, strikes at the very heart of the protectionist tendency of most States. The idea underlying the 'national treatment' clause, as this requirement is known, is to ensure that tariff reductions, which are another essential component of the GATT system, are not undermined by the imposition of discriminatory internal measures on foreign goods after they have cleared through customs. Taken together, the MFN and the national treatment clauses embody the requirement of non-discrimination in international trade transactions.

These two obligations are closely related to, and supported by, the general obligation gradually to reduce customs duties by way of *bilateral or multilateral negotiations* ('*rounds*') (Article XXVIII*bis*). It must be kept in mind that, originally, the GATT was envisioned as an agreement to support the implementation of the tariff concessions agreed by countries during the negotiations of the ITO.[29] The first rounds dealt mainly with tariff reductions and were conducted bilaterally, whereas later negotiations, conducted on a multilateral basis, included other areas (anti-dumping and non-tariff measures). The trajectory over time has been described as a thickening of the legal constraints accepted by States as well as a progressive reduction of tariffs, most notably at the negotiation rounds known as the Kennedy Round (1964–67) and the Tokyo Round (1973–79).[30] As discussed later in this chapter (see **21.4.2**), the Uruguay Round (1986–94) led to an overhaul of the entire system embodied by the establishment of the WTO.

While these are the principal obligations laid down in the GATT, they are attended by further obligations calculated to strengthen the principle of non-discrimination and equality of treatment in other specific areas, where States tend to depart from free trade postulates. Thus the Agreement prohibits quantitative restrictions on both imports and exports (such restrictions are often introduced to protect national products from foreign competition) (Article XI) and dumping, that is, the practice by which 'products of one country are introduced into the commerce of another country at less than the normal value of the products', if 'it causes or threatens material injury to an established industry in the territory of a contracting party or materially retards the establishment of a domestic industry' (Article VI). In addition, the Agreement restricts the freedom of States to grant subsidies, particularly export subsidies (Article XVI).

When imposing all these obligations, the framers of the GATT were, of course, aware that special situations existed of which they ought to take account. This is why they provided for a set of exceptions, some of which were laid down in the original Agreement, whereas others were added in later years when the practical operation of the GATT rendered them necessary. The exceptions can be grouped under three different headings. The first group of exceptions is aimed at *general situations*. Thus, Article XXV stipulates that the contracting parties, acting jointly, may by a specific vote waive an obligation laid down in the Agreement. Article XIX provides for the use of temporary restraints on imports if the latter are causing serious injury to domestic industry. Furthermore, Articles XII to XIV permit the use of quotas on imports in case of balance of payments crises. Finally, Articles XX and XXI provide for exceptions for the purpose of implementing national health and safety regulations as well as those pertaining to national security. A second group of exceptions aims at allowing the furtherance of *economic integration* between members of special regional groupings (Article XXIV). These exceptions in particular concern such groupings

---

[29] See W. Brown, *The United States and the Restoration of World Trade* (Washington, DC: The Brookings Institution, 1950), 131.
[30] On the significance of the Tokyo Round see G. R. Winham, *International Trade and the Tokyo Round Negotiation* (Princeton, NJ: Princeton University Press, 1986).

as customs unions (e.g. the then European Economic Communities) and free trade areas (e.g. EFTA). A third group of exceptions, as will be seen, relates to the *differential treatment of developing countries*.[31] As discussed next, the latter became a particular focus in the revindications of developing and newly independent countries starting in the 1960s.

21.3 DECOLONIZATION, DEVELOPMENT, AND THE STRUGGLE FOR A NIEO

21.3.1 THE NORTH-SOUTH DIVIDE

The global economic architecture described in the previous section was largely designed by the victorious Powers and, above all, by the United States. However, in the 15 years following the end of the Second World War, the composition of the international community of States changed radically, not only as a result of the East-West divisions but, more fundamentally, due to the accession to independence of numerous non-self-governing territories which joined the ranks of what started to be referred to as developing countries. In the 1960s, this new constituency of the international community achieved a majority of the voting Powers in the UN General Assembly and sought to redefine, at least in part, the rules of the global economic architecture that had been set without their full or effective participation. Thus, in a period of essentially two decades, from the mid-1950s to the mid-1970s, the international community awoke to the plight of these countries and redefined the rules to take into account their needs and special situation.

Although, in hindsight, one may gather the impression that the international law of development belongs to a bygone era, the efforts of developing countries led to several significant achievements which are still part of contemporary international law. Overall, four main factors account for this breakthrough: (i) the gradual dismantling of colonial empires unveiled the real conditions of colonial territories and made it clear that political independence was not sufficient; (ii) the increasing impact of socialist ideologies on international relations convinced political leaders that they could no longer turn a blind eye to cruel social realities; (iii) some emerging leaders of developing countries, fully aware of the real conditions of their nations, started vociferously to demand assistance as a way of compensation for the past exploitation by colonial States; (iv) the UN offered emergent States a crucial forum where they could put forward their demands and try to reach some sort of compromise with the industrialized States. These four factors must be kept in mind to understand the origins of the North-South divide, the struggle for a New International Economic Order or NIEO, and the vehicles through which this struggle found expression at a normative and institutional level.

21.3.2 THE ECONOMIC STRUCTURE OF UNDER-DEVELOPMENT

It is impossible to accurately set down, in just a few paragraphs, the principal economic features that characterized the economies of developing countries in the decades following the Second World War, if only because these nations differ widely. They include huge and populous countries such as China, India, Nigeria, Indonesia, and Brazil and much smaller

---

[31] See the Decision of the GATT Parties 'Generalized System of Preferences', Decision of 25 June 1971 (L/3545), which granted a waiver and which was subsequently replaced at the end of the Tokyo Round by the so-called 'Enabling Clause', 'Differential and more favourable treatment, reciprocity and fuller participation of developing countries', Decision of 28 November 1979 (L/4903).

countries such as Grenada, Eswatini, and Nauru. Nevertheless, a few generalizations are possible, with the usual caveat that they over-simplify reality.

The broad characteristics of a situation of under-development may be summed up as follows:

(1) The dominant economic activity focuses on agriculture or the production of raw materials.

(2) Often a 'dual' or 'hybrid' economy exists.[32] This term refers to the coexistence of two different patterns of economic activity, namely: (a) a foreign-dominated dynamic and modern sector, export oriented, based on the capitalistic model, and benefiting from cheap local labour; and (b) the general sector of the economy, essentially based on pre-capitalistic structures and geared to subsistence agriculture. Sometimes the economy even consists of three sectors: the traditional area where subsistence (agricultural) economy predominates; the sector geared to foreign trade (production and export of raw materials, which has sometimes been termed a *monoculture economy*); and a sector of light industry producing articles of general consumption such as textiles and processed foodstuffs, earmarked for the domestic market.

(3) Both agriculture and manufacturing are often conducted on a family basis, that is, primarily in family-size, cottage-type units, rather than in industrial productive units.

(4) The agricultural and industrial equipment is rudimentary, or at any rate not very sophisticated; as a consequence, labour productivity is relatively low and the output comparatively poor.

(5) So-called concealed unemployment prevails, that is, a situation whereby if the number of workers employed is reduced, there is no fall in production, even without changing the capital stock and the production techniques.

(6) There is a low level of capital stock. The accumulation of capital necessary for the acquisition of better industrial equipment and more generally for productive investment, in particular with a view to terminating the monoculture economy and thus undertaking differentiated economic activities, often does not come about. There are two principal reasons for this failure. First, the low labour productivity does not give rise to that excess of production over consumption which allows private saving. In other words, agricultural and industrial output primarily serve to ensure the subsistence of workers. Secondly, that part of the national product not earmarked for labour force subsistence often goes to a small wealthy elite, normally made up of landowners, a few industrial entrepreneurs, and political leaders. This causes what economists call 'the vicious circle of poverty':[33] the labour output is too small to permit the accumulation of capital necessary to improve and modernize the agricultural and industrial equipment, so as to increase labour and investment productivity.

(7) What economists call 'conglomerative factors' worsen the economy of these countries. The industrialization of an area presupposes a number of infrastructures (lines of communication, electric power, supplies of piped water, training of local manpower, public administration, etc.). In turn, these infrastructures make further investment profitable. Lack of, or scant, industrialization and ancillary facilities in developing countries make it more

---

[32] For this notion see C. Furtado, *Development and Underdevelopment* (Berkeley: University of California Press, 1964), 127, in particular at 129.

[33] For this, and other economic notions used in this chapter, see C. Napoleoni, *Economic Thought of the Twentieth Century*, trans. and ed. A. Cigno (London: Martin Robertson and Co., 1972), 145ff.

advantageous for capital-exporting countries to invest in industrialized areas of the world. Indeed, even cheap manpower in developing nations does not outweigh the profitability of investment in areas where a whole range of infrastructures already exists. In addition, conglomerative factors also operate with regard to the demands of industrial workers. If a factory is set up in a backward area, the workers' earnings cannot be spent only on purchasing the factory's output; a market must be created, which itself can further stimulate economic activity. The optimum solution would lie in setting up, instead of one big factory, a number of small industrial units capable of producing a wide range of products to be sold to the workers. However, below a minimum size, modern factories are not profitable. Consequently the installation of a new factory in a developing country may be attended by the lack of an adequate domestic market, so that all the beneficial effects of industrialization fail to materialize.

(8) A further complicating factor for the economy of these countries is the steady increase in population.

In addition to the aforementioned features characterizing economic under-development, developing countries faced other challenges, in some cases of their own making. First of all, many of these countries faced important governance, institutional, and rule-of-law challenges, largely resulting from an authoritarian government structure. It was not unusual for political leaders to be inclined to act more in the interest of the ethnic group or the elite to which they belonged than in the interest of the whole population, and in particular that of the innumerable people who suffered from poverty, malnutrition, and lack of education and health care. Frequently corruption was rife, both among civil servants and at a higher level, politicians. In many countries, internecine conflicts or tensions between ethnic, tribal, or religious groups were and remained rampant, and they resulted in armed clashes and much bloodshed. On top of that, some States tended to choose inadequate economic policies that often led to imbalances in the public budget, high inflation, and increases in the foreign debt. All this created conditions unfavourable to foreign investments and private initiative.

Plainly, whenever developing countries are beset with these problems, foreign assistance may only prove fruitful if accompanied by better or more democratic governance at home.

21.3.3 THE STRUGGLE FOR A NEW INTERNATIONAL ECONOMIC ORDER (NIEO)

Initially (between 1946 and the late 1950s) disadvantaged countries insisted on their need to obtain financial and technical assistance from industrialized nations, so as rapidly to get off the ground. Then they gradually realized that this sort of assistance was totally inadequate to cope with the far-reaching problems besetting them. The prices of the agricultural primary commodities (tobacco, oilseed, animal and vegetable oils, etc.), as well as other agricultural goods (sugar, coffee, tea, etc.) they produced, were steadily declining on the world market, while at the same time there was a steady increase in the price of manufactured or semi-manufactured goods, that is, goods which poor countries had to import both to meet their growth requirements and also to create the infrastructure necessary for promoting foreign investment. In consequence, a decline in the exports of developing countries and an increase in their imports took place; as a result, their balance of payments deficit worsened at staggering speed. From the early 1960s to the early 1970s they therefore increasingly insisted on 'trade, not aid', that is, trade conditions more favourable to them.

Over this same period, the accession of a great number of formerly dependent African and Asian countries to political independence rendered developing countries more pugnacious and vocal. In addition, following the 1973 Arab–Israeli war, the Arab members of the Organization of Petroleum Exporting Countries (OPEC), which had been created in 1960 with the purpose of exercising and expanding powers over energy resources, imposed an embargo on the United States and other industrialized countries which supported Israel in the war. Between October 1973 and March 1974, when the embargo came to an end, the price of a barrel of oil had been multiplied by four.[34] The worried reaction of the West emboldened the Arab States, which understood that their power over certain strategic natural resources, particularly oil, was a powerful lever. Their numerical majority and their newly found powers arising from resource sovereignty *inter alia* led developing countries to (a) reconsider the whole international economic system, and (b) put forward audacious and far-reaching demands concerning the reshaping of international economic relations, so as to adopt measures that, instead of being palliatives, could change structural relations.

To attain their political objectives, the numerical superiority of developing countries in the UN General Assembly allowed them to adopt several important resolutions. One prominent example is resolution 1803 (XVII) of 1962 on 'Permanent Sovereignty over Natural Resources',[35] which within 15 years was deemed by an arbitral tribunal to have reached customary status.[36] In a similar vein, in 1967, Maltese Ambassador Arvid Pardo launched the idea in the General Assembly that the seabed and subsoil underneath the high seas should be considered the 'common heritage of mankind'.[37] This initiative led to the adoption, in 1970, of resolution 2749 (XXV) consecrating this idea,[38] which was subsequently taken up in treaty form in Article 136 of the United Nations Convention on the Law of the Sea.[39] Other resolutions went further, although their very ambition prevented them from achieving a similar degree of recognition. Thus, in 1974, the UN General Assembly adopted a 'Declaration on the Establishment of a New International Economic Order of 1974'[40] and a programme of action in the form of a 'Charter of Economic Rights and Duties of States'.[41] Yet, these two instruments were too controversial to be acceptable to the eyes of industrialized States. The NIEO was intended to be a global challenge to existing international economic relations. Its main tenets were the following:

(1) Developing countries must be entitled to regulate and control the activities of multinational corporations operating within their territory.

(2) They must be free to nationalize or expropriate foreign property on conditions favourable to them; this tenet went further than the more nuanced formulation retained for resolution 1803 (XVII) on the same issue.

(3) They must be free to set up associations of primary commodities producers similar to OPEC; all other States must recognize this right and refrain from taking economic, military, or political measures calculated to restrict it.

---

[34] See G. J. Ikenberry, 'The Irony of State Strength: Comparative Responses to the Oil Shocks in the 1970s' (1986) 40 *Int'l Org* 105.

[35] GA resolution 1803 (14 December 1962) UN Doc. A/RES/1803(XVII).

[36] See *Texaco Overseas Petroleum Company and California Asiatic Oil Company v The Government of the Libyan Arab Republic*, §87.

[37] See A. Pardo, *The Common Heritage: Selected Papers on Oceans and World Order 1967–74* (Malta: Malta University Press, 1975), 31, 64, 85.

[38] GA resolution 2749 (XXV), 'Declaration of Principles governing the Sea-Bed and the Ocean Floor, and the Subsoil Thereof, beyond the Limits of Nations Jurisdiction', 17 December 1970.

[39] United Nations Convention on the Law of the Sea, Montego Bay, 10 December 1982, 1833 UNTS 33.

[40] GA resolution 3201 (1 May 1974) UN Doc. A/RES/3201.

[41] GA resolution 3281 (12 December 1974) UN Doc. A/RES/3281.

(4) International trade should be based on the need to ensure stable, equitable, and remunerative prices for raw materials and generalized non-reciprocal and non-discriminatory tariff preferences.

(5) Industrialized countries must transfer technology to developing countries and provide economic and technical assistance without any strings attached.

By and large, the principles laid down in the General Assembly resolutions embodying the NIEO amounted to a set of standards with great political and rhetorical value, but little purchase on reality. With the passage of time, it became increasingly clear that they could not be translated into reality unless some conditions, including a favourable attitude on the part of industrialized countries, were met. Nevertheless, although the NIEO never really got off the ground as a normative scheme, some of its mechanisms proved viable. Two examples are the Restrictive Business Practice Code, or RBP Code, adopted in 1980 by the General Assembly as a non-legal, non-binding code of conduct,[42] and the Common Fund for Commodities, which came into force in 1989 to assist commodity-producing emergent countries.[43]

Moreover, during the 1980s, the recognition of a 'right to development' gained ground. The principle whereby all human beings have a right to development had first been suggested by Senegal in the General Assembly as early as 1966. It was later enshrined in various General Assembly resolutions, culminating in the 1986 'Declaration on the Right to Development'.[44] It has the following main components:

(1) The right to development is an inalienable right whereby 'every human being and all peoples are entitled to participate in, and contribute to, and enjoy economic, social, cultural and political development' (Article 1 of the Declaration).

(2) 'The human person is the central subject of development and should be the active participant and beneficiary of the right to development' (Article 2(1)).

(3) States have 'the right and the duty to formulate appropriate national development policies' (Article 2(3)) and the 'duty to take steps, individually and collectively, to formulate international development policies with a view to facilitating the full realization of the right to development' (Article 4(1)).

Plainly, these provisions, and others included in the Declaration, set out loosely worded political goals, rather than legal guidelines. In addition, they did not specify to what extent the right at issue should be conceived of as a right of individuals towards their States, or of peoples, and whether the holder of the corresponding obligations should be States vis-à-vis individuals or States towards one another. On the whole, this and other similar texts were misguided. Their motivation was twofold. Proclaiming the 'right to development' meant reformulating the whole problem of development in terms of a 'fundamental right'. This served to bring the demand for a restructuring of the world economic order into focus and indeed to dramatize this demand. Secondly, the new concept served to bring the whole momentum of the human rights doctrine—with its panoply of ideas, patterns, and machinery—to bear on all the problems of international economic relations. Nevertheless, developing countries won a pyrrhic victory, for the verbal proclamation and the verbal insistence on the new 'right' did not lead to any major tangible result. Perhaps the chief merit of the whole action

---

[42] See J. Davidow, 'The UNCTAD Restrictive Business Practices Code' (1979) 13 *The International Lawyer* 587.

[43] Agreement Establishing the Common Fund for Commodities, 27 June 1980, 1538 UNTS 3. Known as the CFC, as of October 2019, the Fund had 101 member States and nine Institutional Members.

[44] GA resolution 41/128 (4 December 1986), UN Doc. A/RES/41/128.

for this new 'right' was to bring to the fore two important underlying ideas: development does not merely amount to economic growth, but also involves a human dimension; and it directly concerns not only governments but the whole population—consequently its realization should not be to the sole advantage of ruling elites.

Despite the fact that this normative strategy led, on the level of principles, to essentially symbolic results, throughout the three decades it lasted, several important steps were taken at the more concrete institutional level to promote co-operation for development. As discussed next, these steps concerned all areas of the global economic architecture.

21.3.4 MULTILATERAL CO-OPERATION FOR DEVELOPMENT

The notion of development co-operation commonly covers all the activities undertaken by the more industrialized States to promote the economic progress of the more disadvantaged countries. When States carry out these activities within the framework of an international organization, development co-operation takes on the nature of multilateral co-operation, in contrast to the co-operation that every State, in pursuing its foreign policy goals, may undertake at the bilateral level.

In addition to these two modalities of co-operation, recently forms of so-called multi-bilateral co-operation have taken shape. They are mixed in nature: they are performed by an international organization, but subject to the priorities and conditions established by the industrialized State willing to finance the specific co-operation activities. This class of co-operation has the advantage of reconciling the interests of all the parties concerned. The granting States, as in bilateral co-operation, are in charge of the policy decisions, management, and financing; international organizations, as in the case of multilateral co-operation, are entrusted with implementation; the beneficiary States, in their turn, may count on a relatively steady flow of assistance, which however is filtered through the international organization.

At the universal level, the UN and its specialized agencies constitute the necessary reference point for development co-operation of a technical nature. Through the transfer of technology and know-how, co-operation primarily aims at furthering the most efficacious use, by the beneficiary States, of their own economic resources. In contrast, development co-operation of a financial nature is organized, at the universal level, by the organizations falling within the ambit of the World Bank, notably the International Development Agency (IDA). This class of co-operation aims at mobilizing capital so as to increase the financial resources of poor countries. Unlike technical co-operation, it is channelled through loans to developing and less developed countries on conditions more advantageous to them than those prevailing on financial markets.

The concept of *North–South co-operation* has been accompanied by the gradual emergence of the concept of the need for development co-operation between countries belonging to the same class of less industrialized States: so-called *South–South co-operation*. The final Act of the Bandung Conference of 1955 (attended by 29 Afro-Asian countries) for the first time officially recognized this form of co-operation. Significant developments followed in the first seven conferences of non-aligned countries as well as, within the UN framework, in UNCTAD (UN Conference on Trade and Development), discussed later in this chapter. South–South co-operation pursues the goal of establishing an economic circuit alternative to the existing one; to this end, it emphasizes the importance of the collective autonomy of developing countries. The ensuing economic relations established by the countries under discussion, defined as Technical Co-operation between Developing Countries (TCDC), have had many ups and downs. Nevertheless, in the 1980s and 1990s, trade exchanges between developing countries increased.

The following paragraphs review several important channels of co-operation for development, both within the framework of the United Nations or its specialized agencies and in other institutional contexts, such as the Bretton Woods institutions:

(1) In an *initial stage*, namely between 1946 and the early 1960s, the lack of both clear vision and an operational scheme, on the part of most developing countries, and the resistance of developed countries, resulted in the establishment, within the UN, of forms of technical co-operation largely inadequate for coping with the far-reaching problems of developing countries. The UN at first dealt with the issue by establishing the Technical Assistance Programme (TAP).[45] This Programme, financed through the system provided for in Article 17.2 of the UN Charter (that is, through compulsory apportionment by the General Assembly), mainly envisaged the sending of missions of experts and technicians to developing countries, the granting of scholarships, and the establishment of training and research centres. Later the General Assembly established the Expanded Programme of Technical Assistance (EPTA).[46] This Programme was financed by a Special Fund, contributed to voluntarily by member States. The assistance provided mainly consisted of furnishing expert advice, the individual training of local personnel, the provision and dissemination of technical information, and the supply of equipment for demonstration purposes.

(2) The *establishment of the United Nations Development Programme (UNDP)* in 1965 was a turning point. In the late 1950s and early 1960s, the prices of the primary commodities produced by developing countries were steadily declining on the world market while the prices of manufactured or semi-manufactured goods developing countries had to import were steadily increasing. It thus became imperative to reconsider the whole international economic system. It is within this new context that the General Assembly, by resolution 2029-XX of 22 November 1965, established the UNDP. This Programme, which replaced both EPTA and the Special Fund, was set up in order to co-ordinate and streamline the assistance previously granted by various UN specialized agencies. It is at present the UN's largest source of development assistance and the main body responsible for co-ordinating assistance.

UNDP's resources consist of voluntary contributions, which States announce in a special conference ('pledging conference') annually convened by the UN Secretary-General. There also exist the so-called contributions for the financing of activities provided for in the programmes; they are paid by the countries benefiting from the activities carried out by the UNDP on their territory. UNDP is a subsidiary organ of ECOSOC. It is headed by an Administrator, responsible to an Executive Board consisting of 36 States representing all major regions and both donors and 'programme countries'. The Board reports, through ECOSOC, to the General Assembly. It sets policy guidelines and discusses and approves the volume of assistance allocated to each country, as well as all country programmes. With a view to realizing a decentralization of the Programme, side by side with this central structure there exists a local structure, consisting of Country Offices, resident representatives, the resident co-ordinator, and regional bureaux.

(3) Another major step was the establishment of the *United Nations Conference on Trade and Development (UNCTAD)*. UNCTAD's principal purposes are 'to maximize the trade, investments and developing opportunities of developing countries'. It was established in 1964 by the UN General Assembly, after a Conference held under the auspices of the UN

---

[45] GA resolution 200(III) (4 December 1948).
[46] GA resolution 304(IV) (16 November 1946).

had adopted a set of resolutions laying down the principles on which the institution was to work in future. Legally speaking, UNCTAD is a subsidiary body of the General Assembly. However, it has an autonomous and conspicuously complex structure, consisting of: (a) a Conference, composed of all the member States and meeting every four years; (b) a permanent executive body, the Trade and Development Board, open to most (157) of all the current 195 members; it meets twice a year (for 'regular sessions') and up to three times a year for 'executive sessions' dealing with urgent policy issues as well as management and institutional matters; and (c) a Secretariat, headed by a Secretary-General, who is appointed by the UN Secretary-General and needs to be confirmed by the General Assembly.

UNCTAD has an operational budget (covering the organizational expenditures) drawn from the UN regular budget, and a budget covering its technical co-operation activities, that is instead financed from extra-budgetary resources provided by donors (the major industrialized States including France, Germany, Italy, Japan, the Netherlands, Sweden, Switzerland, the UK, and the US), beneficiary countries (developing countries are increasingly financing UNCTAD's technical co-operation activities in their own territory), as well as organizations (UNDP, the World Bank, the Inter-American Development Bank, the EU Commission, etc.).

It is within UNCTAD that a new philosophy and an attendant new strategy of development were worked out and approved, at the instigation of developing nations. They basically hinged on (i) the need to pursue an international division of labour; (ii) the elimination by developed countries of existing trade barriers hampering the access of primary products from developing countries; (iii) the stabilization of the price of primary commodities; (iv) non-reciprocity in commercial agreements, which means that differential treatment must be granted to developing countries whereas the latter are not required to reciprocate.

(4) Another important institution was established in 1966: the *UN Industrial Development Organization (UNIDO)*. It was set up by General Assembly resolution (2152(XXI)). It has the status of a specialized agency. UNIDO neither provides nor lends money to developing countries. It carries out studies and surveys geared to the problems of industrialization of poor countries. It also serves as a global forum for the exchange of information, analysis, and advice on industrial policies and institutions, between industrially developed and developing countries, business associations, and individual companies. Furthermore, it serves as a provider of services to governments, institutions, and enterprises in recipient (that is, developing) countries. These services range from simple advice and counsel to providing engineers to implement global agreements on reducing greenhouse gases and industrial pollution, or transferring appropriate technology from one country to another, or helping solve sensitive problems of waste management. Normally, in agreement with the client country, UNIDO makes available its own experts or may draw upon specialists from other agencies or from States or private corporations. Similarly, UNIDO may find investors for projects and industries, or providers of equipment, technology, or techniques.

UNIDO is composed of 170 States, mostly developing countries, plus a number of industrialized States (the US and Canada are conspicuously absent). It is made up of a General Conference, which meets every two years and, among other things, elects representatives to the 53 seats on the Industrial Development Board and to the 27 seats on the Programme and Budget Committee, besides appointing the Director-General. UNIDO's financial resources come from a '*regular budget*'. This budget, covering expenditures to be met from assessed contributions, provides for administration, research, and other regular expenses of the Organization. In contrast, and acceding to a request made at the outset by industrialized countries, technical co-operation is funded, through the '*operational budget*', from other sources (voluntary contributions from donor countries and institutions, allocations by the UNDP, etc.).

(5) The *GATT* also came to take progressively into account the specific problems and needs of developing countries. These countries, due to their economic structure and insertion in the global market, ran the risk of specializing in agriculture and in the production of primary goods, and this could put in jeopardy the entire process of their industrial development. For developing countries, the temporary protection of some of their industries and the setting up of customs barriers to their imports therefore proved justified. Furthermore, it turned out to be necessary for industrialized States to grant differential treatment to exports from these countries. The MFN clause referred to earlier did not meet the demands of emergent countries. It was designed to put on the same footing States having similar economic structures, whereas it was ill-suited for developing countries. In addition, until the 1986–94 Uruguay Round, the clause did not cover areas crucial to developing countries, namely agriculture, textiles, and clothing, areas in which industrialized States permitted levies, quotas, and subsidies so as to protect themselves from the products of developing countries.

The need for a differential treatment of developing countries was first acknowledged through the revision, brought about at the Review Session of 1954–55, of Article XVIII of the GATT. The amendment essentially recognized the structural nature of developing countries' balance of payments problems and attenuated the requirement of prior approval in regard to measures deviating from the GATT's obligations for the promotion of a particular industry.

Subsequently, in 1965, more significant changes were introduced. A Protocol amending the GATT was adopted and a special section, Part IV, called 'Trade and Development', was added to it. Part IV of the GATT codifies in the multilateral trading system the concept of *non-reciprocity* in trade negotiations between developed and developing countries. Thus, developing countries were allowed: (i) with a view to promoting the establishment of particular industries, to modify or withdraw tariff concessions previously made for manufactured products of industrialized countries; (ii) to impose quantitative restrictions on the importation of foreign goods in order to safeguard their financial position and ensure an adequate level of monetary reserves. Industrialized countries, in turn, undertook, first, to accord high priority to the reduction or elimination of barriers to products of particular export interest for developing countries; secondly, to refrain from introducing, or increasing the incidence of, customs duties or non-tariff import barriers on those products; and, thirdly, to refrain from imposing new fiscal measures which could hamper significantly the growth of consumption of primary products from developing countries.

Part IV of the GATT was further elaborated in 1979, in the decision known as the *Enabling Clause*.[47] This Clause consolidated both the concept of 'differential and more favourable treatment' for developing countries and the principle of non-reciprocity in trade negotiations. Under the Clause, members of the GATT, which are parties to a trade agreement, were authorized 'to accord differential and more favourable treatment to developing countries, without according such treatment to other contracting parties'. However, this Clause has the drawback that it does not legally oblige industrialized States to grant the treatment it provides for to developing countries. It merely authorizes them to grant that treatment.[48]

---

[47] As noted earlier in this chapter, initially, the GATT Parties adopted the 'Generalized System of Preferences', Decision of 25 June 1971 (L/3545), which granted an MFN waiver to developing countries. This Decision was subsequently replaced, at the end of the Tokyo Round, by the so-called 'Enabling Clause', 'Differential and more favourable treatment, reciprocity and fuller participation of developing countries', Decision of 28 November 1979 (L/4903).

[48] See A. A. Yusuf, 'Differential and More Favourable Treatment: The GATT Enabling Clause' (1980) 14 *JWTL* 488.

The World Trade Organization (WTO), which will be discussed later in this chapter, takes part in technical co-operation by (i) assisting recipient countries in understanding and implementing agreed international rules on trade, (ii) achieving their full participation in the multilateral trading system, and (iii) directing technical assistance towards human resource development and institutional capacity building.[49] The WTO pursues these goals by carrying out an array of activities, some in the country or the region concerned, others at the WTO headquarters in Geneva: seminars (e.g. on anti-dumping, customs valuation, subsidies, and countervailing measures, or on broader topics such as the functioning of the WTO and multilateral trade negotiations); workshops; technical missions (designed to assist countries in drafting and preparing legislation and regulations, etc.); briefing sessions for Geneva-based delegations or visiting officials; or technical co-operation in electronic form. Funding for technical co-operation comes from three sources: (i) the WTO's regular budget; (ii) voluntary contributions from WTO members (a number of WTO members have decided, as an interim solution, to finance the activities at issue through the establishment of a Global Trust Fund (GTF) for WTO Technical Co-operation; one of its aims is to minimize the administrative costs and procedures following from a multiplicity of trust funds on a national basis); and (iii) cost sharing, either by the host country or by other countries. Technical co-operation activities are overseen by a Committee on Trade and Development (CTD).

(6) Regarding the *role of the World Bank*, one of its statutory goals is 'the encouragement of the development of productive facilities and resources in less developed countries'. Since its early years the Bank has pursued this goal. As noted earlier in this chapter, within the World Bank Group, financial co-operation with developing countries is effected mainly by the International Development Association (IDA).

The IDA was established in 1960 on the initiative of the United States. It is an affiliate of the World Bank, and it avails itself of its structure. Its financial resources consist of capital subscribed by the member States and by supplementary contributions from several members. The IDA supplements the World Bank's functions and pursues the primary task of financing the development of poor countries by granting development loans on terms more liberal than those granted by the Bank. These are long-term loans (normally for a 30-year period), on particularly favourable conditions (there is normally a 10-year initial grace period, no interest charge, and a service charge of three-quarters of one per cent per annum), in order to finance various projects. Besides the length of the term of loans and the lack of any interest charge, another feature of IDA's operations was designed to uphold some developing countries' requests: greater participation of such countries in the decision-making process. However, the fact remains that the majority is firmly kept in the hands of industrialized States. In the 1960s, loans were directed to the financing of investment projects in infrastructures. Since the 1980s, most loans are aimed at supporting macro-economic and institutional reforms, particularly in the field of education and health.

(7) Last but not least, *the IMF also gradually opened to the specific needs of developing countries*. This opening took place both through the growing participation of these countries in the IMF decision-making process, and through the growing influence of developing countries on the drafting of provisions regulating the IMF and the use of its resources. Moreover, in order to meet the specific needs of developing countries, the Fund set up mechanisms designed to increase the lending of financial resources to those countries. This was done through the increase in the maximum limit on authorized drawing, and through

---

[49] For a contemporary account of the role of the WTO in development see S. E. Rolland, *Development at the WTO* (Oxford: Oxford University Press, 2013).

the establishment of special resources designed to take into account the wide range of causes of disequilibria in the balance of payments. Initially loans were made in the form of stand-by arrangements, in order promptly to intervene in the event of balance of payments crises; they were granted for short periods and were to be repaid within a brief time span. Subsequently the Compensatory Financing Facility (CFF) was established in 1963 (which was expanded in the following years). It was designed to provide additional resources to States exporting primary products and encountering problems due to temporary shortfalls in receipts for exports.

The awareness that many crises originated in structural disequilibria in the balance of payments led in 1974 to the establishment of the Extended Fund Facility (EFF), which grants assistance, for a longer period of time and in larger amounts than normal, to States suffering from serious deficits in their balance of payments owing to structural maladjustments in production, trade, or prices. In 1987, the Enhanced Structural Adjustment Facility (ESAF) was established. It had the same purposes as EFF but was designed to assist low-income countries with loans at an interest rate of 0.5 per cent. The establishment of this programme shows that, since the mid-1980s, assistance to poor countries had become part and parcel of the Fund's objectives. Such assistance culminated in 1996 in the setting up of the programme for alleviating the debt of 'heavily indebted poor countries' (HIPC) that the Fund co-ordinates together with the Bank. Towards the end of the 1990s, the reduction of poverty appeared to be a specific objective of policies favouring developing countries, with the transformation of the ESAF into the Poverty Reduction and Growth Facility (PRGF) and the strengthening of the HIPC programme.

These changes in the IMF's policies to some extent constituted a response to the numerous criticisms that had targeted the Fund. It had been attacked on account of the relative ineffectiveness of its adjustment programmes, as well as the high number and wide-ranging scope of the conditions imposed upon States. Although the IMF's conditionality is limited to the economic area, the Fund came under much criticism for its excessive interference in internal economic affairs, which—it was claimed—effectively removed important decisions from the national democratic process. A change in its assistance strategy to low-income countries occurred when the Fund began to concede that the success of the adjustment programmes crucially depended on whether local governments shared the programmes' objectives as well as the programmes' 'ownership'. To gain the co-operation and commitment of the local authorities in those countries, in 1999 the Fund and the Bank produced a 'Poverty Reduction Strategy Paper'. According to this document, it is for the local authorities to set out the development programme, and to set priority objectives as well as the strategy for achieving them.

21.4 INTERNATIONAL LAW AND THE GLOBAL ECONOMY TODAY

21.4.1 THE POST-1990 GLOBAL ECONOMIC ARCHITECTURE

The three decades since the end of the Cold War have been eventful in many ways, including for the redesign of the global economic architecture. Three main developments stand out in the areas covered by this chapter, namely the redesign of the world trading system, the surge in international investment treaties, and the financial instability generated by debt crises, particularly in 2007.

It is useful to begin with the latter because, despite its massive importance economically and financially, it has left a less lasting impact on international economic law than the other two. The 2007 economic crisis originated in a sub-prime mortgage crisis in the United States, which was further disseminated across the entire world through certain credit instruments (securitized structured instruments and credit swaps) held in large quantities by banks and other financial institutions, which suddenly lost their value leading to a global financial crisis.[50] This was not the only major debt crisis of the period. Some others include the Argentine crisis of 2002, which led to the largest default of payment in recent history, and the sovereign debt crisis faced by some EU Member States (most notably Greece) starting in 2010, as a result of many factors relating in part to European monetary integration and in part to fiscal imbalances. These crises led to the strengthening of standard-setting in the areas of prudential financial regulation and the limitation of systemic risks, in particular through the creation of the Financial Stability Board (FSB) in 2009[51] and, at the EU level, the European Stability Mechanism (ESM). Together with an enhanced role and budget for the IMF,[52] the objective of these changes is both to ensure tighter regulation of financial transactions and entities, and to provide rapid financial assistance to defuse imbalances before they spark a crisis.

Despite their importance, these developments are mainly oriented towards the co-ordinated (standardized) domestic or EU-level regulation of financial transactions and entities, and they are therefore less significant from the perspective of international law. By contrast, the establishment in 1994 of the World Trade Organization and the surge of international investment treaties and arbitration have left a lasting mark on post-1990 international economic law.

21.4.2 THE WORLD TRADE ORGANIZATION (WTO)

The Uruguay Round's Final Act of 1994 strengthened the GATT's institutional machinery through the establishment of the World Trade Organization. This organization is a single *institutional framework* encompassing the GATT plus all the agreements and legal instruments negotiated in the Uruguay Round (the GATT, now called the GATT 1994, and other agreements relating to trade in goods; the General Agreement on Trade in Services (GATS); the Agreements on Trade-Related Aspects of Intellectual Property (TRIPs) and on Trade-Related Investment Measures (TRIMs); the Understanding on Dispute Settlement (DSU); and so on).[53]

---

[50] Mario Giovanoli, 'The Reform of the International Financial Architecture After the Global Crisis' (2009) 42 *NYUJ Int'l Law & Pol* 81, 86.

[51] G-20, 'The Global Plan for Recovery and Reform' (2 April 2009), online at http://www.g20.utoronto.ca/2009/2009communique0402.pdf.

[52] G-20, 'Declaration on Delivering Resources Through the International Financial Institutions' (2 April 2009), online at http://www.g20.utoronto.ca/2009/2009delivery.pdf.

[53] The Final Act of the Uruguay Round, adopted on 15 April 1994, includes the WTO Agreement and Annexes I to IV. Annex I is divided into A (Goods), B (Services), and C (Intellectual Property Rights). Annex IA includes: GATT 1994, GATT 1947, six 'Understandings', the Marrakesh Protocol to the GATT 1994, the Agreement on Agriculture, the Agreement on the Application of Sanitary and Phytosanitary Measures (SPS Agreement), the Agreement on Textiles and Clothing, the Agreement on Technical Barriers to Trade (TBT Agreement), the Agreement on Trade-Related Investment Measures (TRIMs), the Agreement on Implementation of Article VI of the General Agreement on Tariffs and Trade 1994 (Anti-Dumping Agreement), the Agreement on Preshipment Inspection, the Agreement on Rules of Origin, the Agreement on Import Licensing Procedures, the Agreement on Subsidies and Countervailing Measures (SCM Agreement), and the Agreement on Safeguards. Annex IB appends the General Agreement on Trade in Services (GATS). Annex IC appends the Agreement on Trade-Related Aspects of Intellectual Property Rights (TRIPs Agreement). Annex II appends the Understanding on rules and procedures governing the settlement of disputes [DSU]. Annex III includes the Trade Policy Review Mechanism. Finally, Annex IV includes several 'Plurilateral Agreements' binding only the Members that have adhered to them (rather than all WTO Members).

The WTO is not a successor organization to the GATT. However, contracting parties to GATT 1947 that accept all the undertakings deriving from the Uruguay Round automatically become original Members of the WTO. Other States may accede to the Organization, on condition that they accept the undertakings deriving from the Uruguay Round (some exceptions are however envisaged, concerning the so-called 'pluri-lateral agreements'). As of 2020, the WTO had 164 Members (some two-thirds are developing countries), accounting for over 90 per cent of world trade. Currently, 23 other States are negotiating accession to the membership.

The structure of the WTO is largely based on the practice which had progressively developed under the GATT, but it goes beyond it. It consists of a Ministerial Conference (meeting at least every two years); a General Council (composed of the representatives of the Member States—it meets in the intervals between each session of the Conference and also meets as the Trade Policy Review Body or the Dispute Settlement Body); the Goods Council, Services Council, and Intellectual Property Council, reporting to the General Council; and a Director-General heading the staff and appointed by the Ministerial Conference. The first and second Ministerial Conferences (Singapore, 1996; Geneva, 1998) strengthened the WTO structure by establishing working groups relating to specific sectors within the general field of action of the Organization. As in the GATT, decisions are normally taken by consensus; majority voting is envisaged, but not used in practice.

The WTO, more than the GATT,[54] must be seen as a wide-ranging network of agreements covering different types of transactions (trade, services, IPRs) and sectors (including agriculture, government procurement, civil aircraft, and a range of services). For the purpose of an introduction to its operation, four main components can be singled out, namely: (1) rules on market access (progressively reduced tariff barriers; prohibited forms of non-tariff barriers, i.e. quantitative barriers; regulated forms of non-tariff barriers, i.e. regulations); (2) trade disciplines applicable to the conduct of trade policy (above all non-discrimination, i.e. MFN and national treatment clauses, and rules on unfair trading, i.e. dumping and subsidies); (3) certain exceptional regimes defined by the reference to certain parties (economic integration areas and general system of preferences), measures (e.g. government procurement exemption), or purposes (overriding societal goals); and (4) a centralized dispute settlement mechanism. Each of these components will be briefly discussed in the next paragraphs:[55]

(1) The rules on *market access*, particularly those regarding the progressive negotiation of tariff reductions, were the initial bargain of the post-1945 trade system, and they remain at the heart of the contemporary system. Under the WTO agreements, tariffs are acceptable, although they are reduced over time, whereas non-tariff barriers to trade are either banned (Article XI on quantitative barriers) or tightly regulated (essentially through the TBT Agreement and the SPS Agreement).

---

[54] On what has been called the 'transformation' of the world trading system see E.-U. Petersmann, 'The Transformation of the World Trading System through the 1994 Agreement Establishing the World Trade Organization' (1995) 6 *EJIL* 161; J. Pauwelyn, 'The Transformation of World Trade' (2002) 104 *Michigan Law Review* 1. For a wider perspective on the WTO and its history see Narlikar, Daunton, and Stern (n 1).

[55] For detailed treatment of the rules governing international trade see *inter alia* M. J. Trebilcock, R. Howse, and A. Eliason, *The Regulation of International Trade*, 4th edn (London: Routledge, 2013); P. C. Mavroidis, *The Regulation of International Trade* (Cambridge, MA: MIT Press, 2016); P. Van den Bossche and W. Zdouc, *The Law and Policy of the World Trade Organization: Text, Cases and Materials* (Cambridge: Cambridge University Press, 2017). See also P. Delimatsis, *International Trade in Services and Domestic Regulations* (Oxford: Oxford University Press, 2007); C. Correa, *Trade Related Aspects of Intellectual Property Rights: A Commentary on the TRIPS Agreement* (Oxford: Oxford University Press, 2007).

Tariffs can be defined as financial duties imposed on foreign goods as a result of their importation, typically as a percentage of their value (*ad valorem*). The tariff applicable to a certain good is defined by reference to three main instruments, namely, the category under which the good falls (categories are defined through a Harmonized Commodity Description and Coding System); the Member's Schedule of Concessions (which typically sets the maximum level or 'tariff binding' for a certain category of goods); and its tariff list (the actual level of the tariff, which is typically lower than the tariff binding). Two additional technical questions that may have a significant impact on the determination of the applicable tariff or its actual cost concern the determination of the origin of the product (as products subject to differential trade regimes or within a free trade area will be subject to a lower tariff or none at all, and those from certain destinations may be subject to anti-dumping duties, countervailing duties, or safeguards) and the valuation of the goods at customs (as most tariffs are *ad valorem*). The WTO system therefore contains detailed rules of origin[56] and customs valuation.[57] It is lawful for a Member to increase its tariffs on a category of goods within the ceiling set by the tariff binding, as long as this is not done in a discriminatory manner. However, Article XXVIII*bis* of the GATT foresees the organization of negotiation 'rounds' towards the reduction of tariffs ('tariff concession' or 'tariff bindings') for certain categories of products. So far, eight such rounds have been completed, the latest one (the Uruguay Round) having led to the establishment of the WTO. A round launched in November 2001 at the Doha Ministerial Conference is still ongoing, and it has so far achieved limited results, most notably an Agreement on Trade Facilitation governing a certain type of non-tariff barriers and a 'Nairobi Package' relating to agriculture and commodities in least-developed countries.

As tariff bounds are increasingly reduced, *non-tariff barriers* to trade become more and more important. Such non-tariff barriers may include a wide range of measures, such as quotas (quantities of products imported/exported); licensing procedures; customs formalities; and technical regulations regarding the characteristics, safety, production process, packaging, labelling, sanitary and phytosanitary requirements, etc. Given the substantial restrictive and distortive potential of these measures, the WTO system is an attempt to strike a balance between legitimate regulatory action and undesirable protectionism. Non-tariff barriers are subject to two main approaches. On the one hand, the system bans quantitative restrictions to both imports and exports (Article XI(1) of the GATT), understood as restrictions on the quantity of an imported or exported good.[58] On the other hand, some WTO agreements (on TBT, SPS, Import Licensing Procedures and Trade Facilitation[59]) introduce specific disciplines to keep under check other non-tariff barriers, particularly by seeking to harmonize the requirements imposed by such domestic regulations. Under the TBT and SPS Agreements, regulated measures are subject to a number of disciplines (e.g. non-discrimination, proportionality, transparency), compliance with which is presumed if the measure abides by (is 'based on' or 'conforms to') international standards, namely those

---

[56] The rules of origin are set in domestic law, but the Agreement on Rules of Origin sets detailed disciplines for their harmonization, although such disciplines are less demanding for the harmonization of the rules applicable to differential trade with developing countries.

[57] GATT 1994, Article VII, and Agreement on the Implementation of Article VII of the GATT 1994 (Customs Valuation Agreement).

[58] WTO Appellate Body, *Turkey—Restrictions on Imports of Textile and Clothing Products*, §9.63.

[59] On this rather new agreement reached within the framework of the Doha Round see A. Eliason, 'The Trade Facilitation Agreement: A New Hope for the World Trade Organization' (2015) 14 *World TR* 643.

adopted by widely recognized standardization bodies with a membership open to all WTO Members on a non-discriminatory basis.[60]

(2) To ensure the effective functioning of the market access system, the WTO regime provides, as did the GATT, for a variety of trade disciplines aimed at levelling the playing field or, in other words, at ensuring *non-discrimination* and preventing *unfair competition*. Although both considerations are closely connected, it may be useful to discuss them separately for presentation purposes.

The two main *non-discrimination standards*, the MFN clause (Article I of the GATT) and the national treatment clause (Article III of the GATT), have already been introduced.[61] The Uruguay Round extended them to trade in services (Articles II and XVII of the GATS) as well as to other more specific measures.[62] Generally speaking, the test that must be met for a breach of these two disciplines has three main components: (i) the type of measure must fall within the scope of the relevant provision; (ii) the measure must have certain effects amounting to a different treatment of two products (or services) originating in different countries (national and foreign, for the national treatment clause); and (iii) these products (or services) must present some degree of similarity or likeness, which would command their equal treatment. These three components take different forms in the context of each specific provision.

MFN treatment in Article I(1) applies to a very broad set of measures, including but not limited to customs duties, affecting both imports and exports, whether at the border or internally (the provision refers to Article III(2) and (4)).[63] The measure must confer 'any advantage' to the products of one Member State over those of another. The two products concerned must be 'like products', a requirement that, despite its apparent simplicity, is complex to pin down conceptually because it does not have the same meaning in different provisions. As noted by the WTO Appellate Body, '[t]he accordion of "likeness" stretches and squeezes in different places as different provisions of the WTO Agreement are applied'.[64] The question of likeness has been less debated in the context of Article I(1) than in relation to national treatment, perhaps because of the possibility for States to differentiate among foreign products through the use of different tariff bindings.[65] Yet, the reference in Article I(1) to the measures covered by the national treatment clause (Article III(2) and (4)) raises the issue of likeness for the two clauses. In *EC—Asbestos*, the WTO Appellate Body identified the following criteria to determine whether two products are alike:

> (i) the physical properties of products; (ii) the extent to which the products are capable of serving the same or similar end-uses; (iii) the extent to which consumers perceive and treat the products

---

[60] See the WTO Appellate Body, *United States—Measures Concerning the Importation, Marketing and Sale of Tuna and Tuna Products*, §§349–380 (examining the TBT Agreement).

[61] For a detailed account of their operation see W. J. Davey, *Non-discrimination in the World Trade Organization: The Rules and the Exceptions* (The Hague: Hague Academy, 2012) (pocketbook version of Davey's course at the Hague Academy of International Law).

[62] For a detailed discussion see Davey (n 61), at 94–119.

[63] Like Article III itself, which expressly excludes from its remit certain measures such as public procurement (Art. III(8)), the reference to Article III(2) and (4) made in Article I(1) also excludes from its scope such measures. See WTO Panel Report in *European Communities—Measures Affecting Trade in Commercial Vessels*, §7.85.

[64] WTO Appellate Body, *Japan—Taxes on Alcoholic Beverages*, 21.

[65] WTO Panel Report, *Canada/Japan—Tariff on Imports of Spruce, Pine, Fire (SPF) Dimension Lumber*, §§5.9–5.16.

as alternative means of performing particular functions in order to satisfy a particular want or demand; and (iv) the international classification of the products for tariff purposes.[66]

Article I(1) further requires any advantage granted to a product to be also granted 'immediately and unconditionally' to all 'like products' of Member States. This means, essentially, that the extension of the advantage must be effected without delay and that no conditions having 'a detrimental impact on the competitive opportunities for like imported products' are attached.[67] As will be discussed later, the MFN clause has several exceptions, including preferential treatment within free trade areas and of the products benefiting from the general system of preferences.

The *national treatment* clause in Article III is more complex. This clause is, indeed, halfway between non-discrimination and fair competition. It targets above all internal measures which, if left unchecked, could defeat the entire purpose of granting tariff concessions. Article III concerns internal taxes and internal regulations. Internal taxes are subject to two distinct, albeit broadly equivalent, disciplines. Article III(2) first sentence requires 'internal taxes' directly or indirectly applied on a product (a terminology intended to exclude customs duties[68] and income taxes), imposed on imported products, not to be 'in excess of' the taxes imposed on 'like' domestic products. The characterization of likeness used in Article III has been discussed earlier. It must be noted that the third requirement ('in excess of') has been interpreted strictly in the case law and it is deemed breached even by a slight difference in taxation.[69] Article III(2) second sentence imposes a distinct obligation, as emphasized by the interpretive note to Article III(2).[70] This discipline applies to internal taxes, but instead of likeness, it only requires the affected products to be 'directly competitive or substitutable products' (pisco is certainly not like whisky and yet it has been found to meet the test[71]), and it also admits some small variations in taxation as long as the taxation level is 'similar'. In addition, Article III(2) second sentence is only breached if the dissimilar taxation is imposed 'so as to afford protection to domestic production'. This is ascertained by reference to 'the design, the architecture, and the revealing structure of a measure' and '[t]he very magnitude of the dissimilar taxation in a particular case may be evidence of such protective application'.[72] In addition to internal taxes, Article III(4) covers internal 'laws, regulations and requirements' 'affecting'[73] the 'internal sale, offering for sale, purchase, transportation, distribution or use' of 'like' foreign and domestic products. Treatment accorded to foreign products must be 'no less favourable', which is understood as treatment which does not change the conditions of competition in an adverse manner.[74]

The WTO rules aimed at *preventing unfair competition* go beyond the requirements of national treatment. They include detailed rules on certain practices that distort fair trade. One such practice is called dumping, that is, the selling of products in foreign markets at a price below the 'normal value' of the product, typically to gain market share and defeat

---

[66] WTO Appellate Body, *European Communities—Measures Affecting Asbestos and Products Containing Asbestos*, §101.

[67] WTO Appellate Body, *European Communities—Measures Prohibiting the Importation and Marketing of Seal Products*, §5.88.

[68] See WTO Appellate Body, *China—Measures Affecting Imports of Automobile Parts*, §§161–163.

[69] See *Japan—Taxes on Alcoholic Beverages*, at 23; the WTO Panel Report in *Argentina—Measures Affecting the Export of Bovine Hides and Import of Finished Leather*, §§11.187–11.191.

[70] See *Japan—Taxes on Alcoholic Beverages*, 24.

[71] WTO Panel Report, *Chile—Taxes on Alcoholic Beverages*, §§7.80–7.88 (this finding was not appealed).

[72] *Japan—Taxes on Alcoholic Beverages*, 29.

[73] See e.g. WTO Appellate Body, *United States—Tax Treatment of 'Foreign Sales Corporations'—Recourse to Article 21(5) of the DSU by the European Communities*, §§207–213.

[74] See WTO Appellate Body, *Korea—Measures Affecting Imports of Fresh, Chilled and Frozen Beef*, §142.

competition. WTO rules regulate what State Members are authorized to do in response to dumping by foreign producers, which amounts essentially to imposing measures on those products (anti-dumping duties) to erase the unfair advantage sought through dumping.[75] Similarly, when foreign goods benefit from subsidies, that may also distort competition if the subsidies are contingent on the exporting of the good, they are contingent on the substitution of foreign goods for local ones (import substitution subsidies), or if they are specific enough and have a distortive effect in practice. Because subsidies are given by governments, WTO rules regulate both the granting of the subsidy (export-contingent and import-substitution subsidies are prohibited and specific/distortive subsidies are actionable)[76] and the measures that may be adopted to counter the unfair advantage they provide (countervailing duties).[77] Anti-dumping duties and countervailing duties imposed are generally referred to as 'trade remedies'. These are adopted by Member States to neutralize an unfair advantage, but their legality remains subject to the disciplines of the WTO agreements, and it may be challenged through the Dispute Settlement Body.

(3) Trade liberalization, non-discrimination, and the levelling of the competitive playing field may, under some circumstances, collide with other societal values which deserve overriding protection or, more generally, that Member States wished to exclude from the application of the WTO system or from certain specific disciplines. Three *main types of exceptions* can be identified for present purposes: (i) differential trade with developing countries, (ii) free trade areas, and (iii) some 'measures' and situations that are excluded from the remit of the rules or subject to exceptional treatment.

The origins of *differential trade with developing countries* were briefly introduced in **21.3.4**. The Enabling Clause adopted in 1979 permits the granting of 'differential and more favourable treatment to developing countries, without according such treatment to other contracting parties', and such treatment does not require reciprocity, that is, the developing countries benefiting from such treatment are not required to offer the same advantages to developed countries offering differential and more favourable treatment. The WTO system expanded the differential treatment given to developing countries to a range of clauses in many of its agreements.[78] One issue that arose in practice is the possibility to offer more favourable treatment to certain developing countries than to others on the basis of certain behaviour-inducing tariff reductions. In particular, under the so-called 'Drug Arrangements', the EU offered tariff reductions to 12 countries for taking measures against drug production and trafficking. Pakistan was included in the beneficiary list, but India was not. The latter country challenged the conformity of the Drug Arrangements with the Enabling Clause and the WTO Appellate Body sided with India.[79]

The second major exception concerns *free trade agreements* establishing some degree of economic integration among two or more WTO Members. Such agreements may be referred to by different names, such as 'Regional Trade Agreements'

---

[75] See Article VI, GATT 1994, and the Anti-Dumping Agreement. See WTO Appellate Body, *United States—Final Anti-Dumping Measures on Stainless Steel from Mexico*, §§83–94.

[76] See Article XVII, GATT 1994, and Articles 3 to 9 of the Agreement on Subsidies and Countervailing Duties. A representative case relating to subsidies is WTO Appellate Body, *European Communities and Certain Member States—Measures Affecting Trade in Large Civil Aircraft*.

[77] See Article VI, GATT 1994, and Articles 10 to 23 of the Agreement on Subsidies and Countervailing Duties.

[78] See e.g. Article XVIII:A, GATT 1994; Article 15, Anti-Dumping Agreement; Article 27, SCM Agreement; Article 66(1), TRIPs Agreement.

[79] WTO Appellate Body, *European Communities—Conditions for the Granting of Tariff Preferences to Developing Countries*.

(RTAs),[80] 'Free Trade Agreements' (FTAs), 'Preferential Trade Agreements' (PTAs), or by some other label that refers to the nature of the integration achieved, such as a 'customs union' (tariff reduction or elimination and common external tariff) or 'free trade area' (tariff reduction or elimination but without a common external tariff) or 'mega-regionals' (a label that emphasizes the comprehensive nature of the goods and services covered by the agreement).[81] For WTO purposes, the main difference is between these agreements, which may be called for ease of reference FTAs, and the agreements establishing differential trade with developing countries, which are subject to more lenient conditions and do not require reciprocity of treatment among the members of the area thus created. FTAs have grown exponentially since the 1990s. The conditions established by such agreements necessarily entail a measure of discrimination with respect to countries not included in the agreement. Yet, Article XXIV of the GATT 1994 allows for the conclusion of such agreements, subject to certain requirements (Article XXIV(5) and (8) and Understanding on Article XXIV), because they are seen as a stepping stone in the wider process of trade liberalization (Article XXIV(4)). Such agreements must be notified to the WTO and their consistency can be challenged before the WTO Dispute Settlement Body. However, this has never been done, most likely because virtually all WTO Members are also Members of one or more FTAs.[82] Of note, the Understanding on Article XXIV contains a paragraph (12) that has been interpreted as bringing within the jurisdiction of the WTO's Dispute Settlement Body disputes arising from the potential violation of an FTA.[83]

The third type of exception concerns a range of provisions in the GATT 1994, as well as in other WTO agreements, which either reserve the power of Members to adopt certain measures (e.g. Article III(8)(a) on government procurement measures[84] or Article XXI on national security measures[85]) or excuse their adoption under certain situations (e.g. Article XI(2)(a), which allows temporary export restrictions of 'essential products' in critical shortages;[86] Article XIX—together with the Agreement on Safeguards—relating to 'safeguard' measures to temporarily protect the domestic industry in case of emergency

---

[80] Some major examples include, in addition to the European Union (which as part of its integration process includes trade integration), also the North-American Free Trade Agreement (NAFTA), the Southern Common Market (MERCOSUR), the Southern African Development Community (SADC), the Common Market of the Caribbean (CARICOM), and the ASEAN Free Trade Area (AFTA).

[81] On this phenomenon see S. Griller, W. Obwexer, and E. Vranes (eds), *Mega-Regional Trade Agreements: CETA, TTIP, and TiSA* (Oxford: Oxford University Press, 2017).

[82] Some guidance on the meaning of the requirements of Article XXIV of the GATT 1994 can be derived, however, from the WTO Appellate Body in *Turkey—Restrictions on Imports of Textile and Clothing Products*. The claim brought by India concerned certain quantitative restrictions on textiles imposed by Turkey. Turkey sought to justify these measures by reference to Article XXIV (relevant due to Turkey's FTA with the then EC) but this argument was rejected by both the Panel and the Appellate Body (which corrected the Panel's reasoning on this point).

[83] See WTO Appellate Body, *India—Quantitative Restrictions on Imports of Agricultural, Textile and Industrial Products*, §§80–109.

[84] For an interpretation relating to the important issue of support for renewable energy see WTO Appellate Body, *Canada—Certain Measures Affecting the Renewable Energy Generation Sector*, §§5.109–5.220.

[85] The first judicial examination of this provision appears in the WTO Panel Report in *Russia—Measures Concerning Traffic in Transit*, §§7.53–7.149 (finding that Russia can avail itself of Article XXI(b)(iii) of the GATT 1994).

[86] This provision is relevant for the restrictions imposed by many States on the export of personal protective equipment (PPE), in very short supply during the COVID-19 pandemic. This is particularly the case of large suppliers of PPE, with a high number of infected people and overstretched public health services. In the UK, a major problem was the lack of appropriate PPE for medical and health-related staff, who were on the front line of the pandemic and who, if infected, may in turn infect people seeking assistance.

arising from a massive increase of imports;[87] or Articles XII and XVIII(B)—together with the Understanding on the Balance of Payments Provisions—on measures adopted to tackle, through quantitative restrictions or value-based restrictions, a balance of payment emergency[88]). The most emblematic provision regarding exceptions is Article XX of the GATT, which contains different types of general exceptions. Article XX has two main components. First, it has a list of exceptional measures or situations which are excused (letters (a) to (j)). These include measures 'necessary'[89] to protect 'public morals'[90] or 'human, animal or plant life or health'[91] or 'necessary to secure' compliance with laws or regulations[92] or, again, measures 'relating to the conservation of exhaustible natural resources'[93] or 'essential to the acquisition or distribution of products in general or local short supply'.[94] Each of the letters of Article XX has its own specific requirements, which have been clarified in the jurisprudence of the WTO dispute settlement organs. Several letters (a, b, d, and g) have been widely relied upon to excuse environmental measures, although in most cases unsuccessfully. This outcome is partly the result of the operation of the second component of Article XX, namely the 'chapeau', which requires that 'measures are not applied in a manner which would constitute a means of arbitrary or unjustifiable discrimination between countries where the same conditions prevail, or a disguised restriction on international trade'. Importantly, the WTO dispute settlement organs have developed a jurisprudence regarding the operation of these components, according to which the general exception clause only intervenes as an excuse, that is, after a breach of a primary norm (e.g. Articles I, III, or XI) has been found, and the order of analysis starts at the level of the letters and moves to the examination of conditions stated in the chapeau only if the requirements of one or more letters are met.[95] Overcoming the requirements of the chapeau has proved to be a formidable challenge in practice.[96]

(4) The most salient difference between the WTO system and the situation prevailing before it is the establishment of a sophisticated dispute settlement mechanism organized by the Understanding on rules and procedures governing the settlement of disputes (DSU), appended as Annex 2 of the WTO Agreement (see **13.5**). The possibility of bringing complaints existed in the original GATT and, over the long period leading to the Uruguay Round, it slowly evolved from a diplomatic negotiation system, to a more structured one managed by a 'Working Party' (including the parties to the dispute as well as a small number of other countries, some of which were 'neutrals'), and later to 'panels' (first of neutrals and then, progressively, of experts).

The Uruguay Round strengthened and further institutionalized the panel system. Acceptance of the compulsory jurisdiction of the dispute settlement organs became a

---

[87] For an application see WTO Appellate Body, *United States—Definitive Safeguard Measures on Imports of Circular Welded Carbon Quality Line Pipe from Korea*.

[88] For guidance see WTO Panel Report, *Chile—Price Band System and Safeguard Measures Relating to Certain Agricultural Products*, §7.68; WTO Appellate Body, *India—Quantitative Restrictions on Imports of Agricultural, Textile and Industrial Products*, §§5.134–5.135 and §§5.155–5.156; WTO Appellate Body, *Korea—Measures Affecting Imports of Fresh, Chilled and Frozen Beef*, §§728–731 and §§732–745.

[89] See WTO Appellate Body, *Brazil—Measures Affecting Imports of Retreaded Tyres*, §150.

[90] WTO Appellate Body, *European Communities—Measures Prohibiting the Importation and Marketing of Seal Products*, §5.199.

[91] WTO Panel Report, *Brazil—Retreaded Tyres*, §§7.40–7.216.

[92] WTO Appellate Body, *India—Certain Measures Relating to Solar Cells and Solar Modules*, §§5.92–5.93.

[93] WTO Appellate Body, *United States—Import Prohibition of Certain Shrimp and Shrimp Products*, §§129–132.

[94] WTO Appellate Body, *India—Certain Measures Relating to Solar Cells and Solar Modules*, §§5.51–5.52.

[95] WTO Appellate Body, *United States—Standards for Reformulated and Conventional Gasoline*, 22.

[96] For an overview on the WTO jurisprudence on the chapeau see WTO Appellate Body, *European Communities—Measures Prohibiting the Importation and Marketing of Seal Products*, §§5.296–5.306.

pre-condition of accession to the WTO. A two-tiered system was created, consisting of 'panels', established at the request of a party after a process of consultations has not permitted to solve a given dispute, and of an Appellate Body, which can hear appeals against reports of the panels. The reports of panels or of the Appellate Body are then submitted for adoption by the Dispute Settlement Body, that is, the General Council sitting as the DSB, which can only reject their adoption by consensus. Thus, it is very difficult for a report not to be adopted. Once adopted, reports become binding on all WTO Members.

Implementation of the reports is a managed process whereby the Member found in breach of a trade discipline must remove or adjust its non-conforming measures within a reasonable period of time (which may be set through an arbitration under Article 21(3)(c) DSU). Failure to do so opens the way for a further stage of negotiations on compensation, understood not as a payment but as an offset (e.g. offering other trade advantages), although this is rare. If this does not work either, the complainant States can be authorized by the DSB to adopt countermeasures ('suspending concessions or other obligations under the covered agreements', in accordance with Article 22(2) DSU). Because the level of suspension thus authorized must be 'equivalent' to the impairment suffered in the first place, there is a further system of checks and balances in the form of arbitration proceedings to assess whether the retaliation is excessive (Article 22(6) DSU). The system thus provides a detailed—albeit not comprehensive—set of 'secondary norms' of State responsibility, which operate as a *lex specialis* to the general international law rules on this matter. This is not to say that the WTO system evolves in 'clinical isolation' from general international law,[97] as the *lex specialis* principles cannot be simplistically interpreted as creating a bubble within the fabric of international law.

21.4.3 THE RISE OF INTERNATIONAL INVESTMENT LAW AND ARBITRATION

In addition to the reorganization of the world trade system, the early 1990s saw the beginning of another major legal development, namely, the rise of international investment agreements (IIAs), mostly in the form of bilateral investment treaties (BITs) or investment chapters in FTAs. Many more IIAs were concluded from the 1990s onwards than in previous decades, a phenomenon which led to a network of some 3,000 IIAs as of 2020. Equally important is the fact that foreign investors became more and more familiar with the possibilities offered by these treaties, which led to a surge of investment claims against host States before international arbitration tribunals, on the basis of the arbitration clauses contained in most IIAs. The estimated number of known disputes today exceeds 980 and there are likely many more which are not public.[98]

In parallel to this major development, the old technique used to protect the rights of aliens operating in foreign States, namely, the exercise of diplomatic protection, tended to be less and less used, although some cases continued to be brought before the ICJ. There are some points of connection between the two, such as the inclusion of interstate dispute settlement clauses in some IIAs, which have been rarely used, or the recognition of the possibility for non-disputing parties (i.e. States which are parties to an IIA but not involved in a given dispute) to file briefs with the relevant arbitration tribunal in order to share their views on the proper interpretation of the applicable IIA.[99] But the very idea underpinning

---

[97] WTO Appellate Body, *United States—Standards for Reformulated and Conventional Gasoline*, 17.

[98] See UNCTAD's Investment Policy Hub, online at https://investmentpolicy.unctad.org/investment-dispute-settlement.

[99] See e.g. NAFTA, Article 1128.

the system of foreign investment designed by means of IIAs was to bypass the system of diplomatic protection so as to avoid the political tensions in which this type of action has been mired in the past.[100]

In the following paragraphs, after a brief introduction on the rights of 'aliens' under international law, these two trends are discussed. Although diplomatic protection has been largely replaced with the system of investment protection, the latter has come under severe criticism from very different circles including both developed and developing countries. At stake is the fact that three arbitrators, which are unaccountable private persons directly or indirectly selected by the parties to a dispute, are given the power to decide matters that concern the public interest, such as human rights, public health, or environmental protection.[101] Moreover, the body of decisions emerging from this system is volatile, with examples of contradictory decisions adopted by separate tribunals on virtually the same facts and law.[102] The lack of accountability and legal certainty arising from the investment case law has led, more recently, to a major 'backlash' against investment arbitration as such,[103] with reform proposals from the EU aimed at establishing a standing investment court rather than a system of dispute-specific arbitration tribunals.

The overall historical backdrop of the discussion is provided by the protection of the rights of aliens operating abroad, particularly in the nineteenth and early twentieth centuries. From the nineteenth century, customary rules and treaty provisions on the treatment to be accorded to foreigners placed some limitations upon State sovereignty. Although foreigners are under the territorial supremacy of the host State and are bound to comply with its laws and regulations, they also benefit from a host of rights laid down in international rules that confer international rights on their national State. The relevant international rules were intended to protect the life, person, and property of foreigners. However, their content was rather loose and, for a long time, two different approaches were advocated: one, propounded by capital-importing countries since the times of the independence of Spanish colonies in Latin America,[104] argued that it was sufficient for foreigners to be treated as the nationals of the host State, no less but no more. The other approach, chiefly supported by capital-exporting countries, was instead that foreigners must enjoy a minimum standard of civilization, regardless of how the citizens of the host country are treated by their own authorities.[105] Eventually, the latter approach prevailed with the increasing recognition of

---

[100] Article 27(1) of the ICSID Convention states that '[n]o Contracting State shall give diplomatic protection, or bring an international claim, in respect of a dispute which one of its nationals and another Contracting State shall have consented to submit or shall have submitted to arbitration under this Convention, unless such other Contracting State shall have failed to abide by and comply with the award rendered in such dispute'.

[101] See G. van Harten, *Investment Treaty Arbitration and Public Law* (Oxford: Oxford University Press, 2007).

[102] See e.g. *CME Czech Republic B.V. v The Czech Republic*, where the tribunal found a breach of all the provisions invoked by the investor and awarded damages; *Ronald S. Lauder v The Czech Republic*, where the tribunal found a breach of one provision, rejected all other claims, and awarded no compensation. See generally P. Mayer, 'Conflicting Decisions in International Commercial Arbitration' (2013) 4 *JIDS* 407.

[103] See M. Waibel, A. Kaushal, Kyo-Hwa Chung, and C. Balchin (eds), *The Backlash Against Investment Arbitration: Perceptions and Reality* (The Hague: Kluwer, 2010).

[104] See J. E. Viñuales and M. J. Langer, 'Foreign Investment in Latin-America: Between Love and Hatred' in C. Auroi and A. Helg (eds), *Latin America. Dreams and Legacy 1810–2010* (London: Imperial College Press, 2011), 319.

[105] Two apposite early illustrations settled by the Mexico–US General Claims Commission are *Harry Roberts (United States) v United Mexican States* and *L.F.H. Neer and Pauline Neer (United States) v United Mexican States* (1926) 4 RIAA 60. In the first, the United States claimed that its citizen, H. Roberts, had been arbitrarily and illegally arrested, held in detention for an excessive length of time, and, while in prison, subjected to cruel and inhumane treatment. The Commission dismissed the claim of illegal arrest. As for the excessive period of imprisonment, the Commission stated that 'clearly there is no definite standard prescribed by international law by which such limits (i.e. the limits within which an alien charged with crime may be held in custody pending the investigation of the charge against him) may be fixed. Doubtless an examination of local laws fixing a maxi-

an international minimum standard of treatment (IMST).[106] Under the IMST, which is still in operation today, foreigners enjoyed some basic standards of treatment, such as (i) the protection against discrimination; (ii) the right to respect for their life and property; (iii) their right not to be collectively expelled from the territory or on national, racial, religious, or ethnic grounds; and, more generally, (iv) the right to judicial remedies to vindicate their rights in the host country, particularly the protection of property. The territorial State authorities' refusal to afford such remedies, or their resort to abusive or harassing procedures, or serious prosecutorial misconduct, may amount to a denial of justice (*déni de justice*) or miscarriage of justice, a serious breach of international rules on the protection of foreigners.[107] The concrete protection of these rights, however, was clearly dependent on the willingness of the State of nationality of the foreigner to step in and espouse the claims of its nationals in the form of diplomatic protection.

The right of States to exercise diplomatic protection, that is, to claim compliance with international rules to the benefit of their nationals, was recognized early on. In *Mavrommatis Palestine Concessions* (1924), the PCIJ famously noted that:

> [i]t is an elementary principle of international law that a State is entitled to protect its subjects, when injured by acts contrary to international law committed by another State, from whom they have been unable to obtain satisfaction through the ordinary channels. By taking up the case of one of its subjects and by resorting to diplomatic action or international judicial proceedings on his behalf, a State is in reality asserting its own rights—its right to ensure, in the person of its subjects, respect for the rules of international law. (at 12)

The act of espousing the claim is discretionary and a State is free to do so or not depending on a range of legal and diplomatic considerations. Under international law, individuals do not have a right to demand from their State of nationality the exercise of diplomatic protection, although, over time, this tended to be recognized as a natural expectation.[108] In addition, the admissibility of the claim brought against the State of nationality is conditioned on

---

mum length of time within which a person charged with crime may be held without being brought to trial may be useful in determining whether detention has been unreasonable in a given case' (at 79). The Commission then examined the relevant Mexican legislation and found that this legislation had been contravened in the case at issue. It therefore concluded that Mexico was responsible for a breach of international law in this respect. As for the allegation of ill treatment, the Commission dismissed the Mexican claim that Roberts had been 'accorded the same treatment as that given to all other persons'. It pointed out that 'facts with respect to equality of treatment of aliens and nationals may be important in determining the merits of a complaint of mistreatment of an alien. But such equality is not the ultimate test of the propriety of the acts of authorities in the light of international law. That test is, broadly speaking, whether aliens are treated in accordance with ordinary standards of civilization' (at 80). The Commission concluded that Harris had been held in prison in a cruel and inhumane manner; therefore an indemnity was warranted. In the *Neer* case, the Commission held that the bad treatment of aliens, to constitute a violation of international law, 'should amount to an outrage, to bad faith, to willful neglect of duty, or to an insufficiency of governmental action so far short of international standards that every reasonable and impartial man would readily recognize its insufficiency' (at 61–2). This is a difficult threshold to meet, and it is still referred to by respondent States in today's investment jurisprudence.

[106] See M. Paparinskis, *The International Minimum Standard and Fair and Equitable Treatment* (Oxford: Oxford University Press, 2013).

[107] See J. Paulsson, *Denial of Justice in International Law* (Cambridge: Cambridge University Press, 2005).

[108] E.g. in 2002, a UK Court of Appeal, in *Abbasi v Secretary of State for Foreign and Commonwealth Affairs and others*, held that under British law a British national has a 'normal expectation that, if subjected abroad to a violation of a fundamental right, the British Government will not simply wash their hands of the matter and abandon him to his fate' (at §98). 'However, whether to make any representations [to a foreign State] in a particular case, and if so in what form, is left entirely to the discretion of the Secretary of State ... The Secretary of State must be free to give full weight to foreign policy considerations, which are not justiciable. However, that does not mean the whole process is immune to judicial scrutiny. The citizen's legitimate expectation is that his request will be "considered", and that in that consideration all relevant factors will be thrown into the balance' (at §99).

the exhaustion of domestic remedies of the host State by the individual concerned.[109] The rationale behind the customary rule on the prior exhaustion of domestic remedies is that there is no point in bringing a claim on the international plane if there is a chance that it can be settled at the domestic level, by municipal courts that may be better placed to appraise the facts and apply national law. As a result of the important development of human rights doctrines in the international community, the rules on treatment of foreigners have to a large extent been absorbed by rules on human rights. As a consequence, many international rules now tend to protect, more than individuals qua foreigners, individuals as such. It follows that there now exist general rules of international law that impose limitations on States even with regard to their own nationals and any other individuals subject to their jurisdiction (i.e. their *de jure* or de facto authority) (see **Chapter 18**). That may explain why, in recent times, despite the adoption by the International Law Commission in 2006 of a set of draft articles on the topic, resort to diplomatic protection has become rare, although the docket of the ICJ has seen some cases which are either technically examples of diplomatic protection[110] or analogous to it.[111] But the main reason why the importance of diplomatic protection has receded is the surge in both IIAs and investment claims brought by foreign investors under them.

Traditional international rules governing foreign investment required that any time a country, to which foreign capital had been exported or where companies had been established, nationalized or otherwise expropriated their property, it had to pay compensation. These rules were contested by the Soviet Union following the Soviet nationalizations in 1918 and 1925 and by Mexico in the wake of the nationalizations involved in the Mexican Agrarian Reform of 1927 and the nationalization of foreign oil property in 1938. Eventually the Soviet Union had to bow to the economic and political pressure of other States and grudgingly complied with the prevailing international standards. As for Mexico, it admitted that 'adequate compensation' was to be paid but insisted that (i) international law only required that foreigners be treated no less favourably than were nationals, and (ii) the time and manner of payment must be determined under the laws of the expropriating State.[112] The United States reacted indignantly and the Secretary of State, Cordell Hull, in a famous note of 22 August 1938, formulated the US doctrine of compensation, as follows: 'No government is entitled to expropriate [foreign] private property, for whatever purpose, without provision for *prompt, adequate and effective payment* therefor.'[113] Mexico eventually yielded to the economic pressure of the US and this celebrated formula was subsequently considered by Western countries to encapsulate the basic requirements for lawful expropriations.

The problem emerged again after the Second World War, when capital-importing territories increasingly became politically independent and tried to get off the ground economically as well. They felt impelled to expropriate foreign property because their natural resources were to a large extent in foreign hands. One of the ways of achieving rapid economic development lay in appropriating foreign assets without this constituting an excessive financial burden for the expropriating State.[114] Developing States increasingly challenged the 'prompt, adequate and effective' formula and contended that (a) only

---

[109] *Interhandel (Switzerland v United States) (Preliminary Objections)*, 26–9.

[110] See *Ahmadou Sadio Diallo (Republic of Guinea v Democratic Republic of the Congo)*.

[111] See the so-called 'death row' cases brought by Germany, Mexico, and Paraguay against the US: *Vienna Convention on Consular Relations (Paraguay v United States of America) (Provisional Measures)*; *LaGrand (Germany v United States of America)*; *Avena and Other Mexican Nationals (Mexico v United States of America)*.

[112] In Hackworth, *Digest of International Law*, vol. 3 (1942), 655–61.

[113] Text in (1938) 32 *AJIL Suppl.*, 192 (emphasis added).

[114] In addition to those carried out by eastern European socialist countries in 1946–48, expropriations were made by Iran in 1951, Egypt in 1956, Cuba in 1959, Sri Lanka in 1963, Indonesia in 1965, Tanzania in 1966, Bolivia in 1969, Algeria in 1971, Somalia in 1970–72, Chile in 1972, and Libya in 1978.

'adequate' or 'appropriate' compensation was due, and in addition (b) the modalities of its determination were to be left to the nationalizing State. Their demands were upheld first in General Assembly resolution 1803 (XVII) and then reflected in Article 2(2)(c) of the Charter of Economic Rights and Duties of States. However, most Western States voted against that provision or abstained, making clear that in their view it ran counter to existing law. Although the Hull formula has been widely relied on by investment tribunals, it must be noted that some important contrasting stances can be found in international jurisprudence. In 1994, the Iran–US Claims Tribunal, in *Shahin Shaine Ebrahimi and others v The Government of the Islamic Republic of Iran*, did not take a position favourable to it.[115] In a well-argued and elaborate decision, the Tribunal held that the Hull formula does not represent 'the prevailing standard of compensation'. Rather, in its view customary international law favours an 'appropriate compensation' standard (at §88). The Tribunal also specified the purport of this standard:

> The gradual emergence of this [customary international] rule [on 'appropriate compensation'] aims at ensuring that the amount of compensation is determined in a flexible manner, that is, taking into account the specific circumstances of each case. The prevalence of the 'appropriate' compensation standard does not imply, however, that the compensation *quantum* should be always 'less than full' or always 'partial'. (at §88)

The relevance of this stance must not be underestimated or, indeed, overestimated. A substantial practice has developed in the application of IIAs by hundreds of investment arbitration tribunals that, although often contradictory, suggests that the Hull formula enjoys wide acceptance. Yet, even more important than the specific standard relating to compensation for expropriation, is the overall system of investment promotion and protection that has developed under the aegis of IIAs. To describe the basic tenets of this system, it is useful to focus on the three main components underpinning it,[116] namely, (1) the protected transactions, (2) the applicable standards, and (3) the prevailing dispute settlement mechanism.

(1) *The protected transaction* envisaged by the efforts to promote and protect foreign investment was initially 'foreign direct investment' (FDI) in infrastructure and in the exploitation of natural resources. FDI differs from 'portfolio investment' in that it establishes a 'lasting interest' in the venture rather than a short-term capital investment.[117] As noted earlier in this chapter, the control of short-term speculative capital movements was an important consideration in the aftermath of the Second World War. In the 1960s and 1970s, the objective of granting protection to foreign investment was both to promote FDI capable of contributing to the development of the host State[118] and to protect such ventures from the political risks arising from long-term exposure of substantial investments to often unstable regimes.

However, the major scale-up in both IIAs and investment arbitration observed since the 1990s has challenged this initial understanding. IIA have tended to include increasingly broad definitions of the covered 'investments', routinely encompassing 'shares, stocks or

---

[115] The Award was rendered by Chamber Three, presided over by Judge G. Arangio-Ruiz. See also the Separate Opinion of Judge Allison, §§4–37 (on the standard in question).

[116] This account follows J. E. Viñuales, 'Foreign Direct Investment: International Investment Law and Natural Resources Governance' in E. Morgera (ed.), *Research Handbook on International Law and Natural Resources* (Cheltenham: Edward Elgar, 2016), 26.

[117] See *OECD Benchmark Definition of Foreign Direct Investment* (2008), para. 11, online at http://www.oecd.org/daf/inv/investmentstatisticsandanalysis/40193734.pdf.

[118] See the preamble of the ICSID Convention, §1 (considering: 'the need for international co-operation for economic development, and the role of private international investment therein').

other forms of equity' but also 'bonds [...] other debt instruments, and loans' and even assets such as 'intellectual property rights'.[119] No less importantly, arbitration tribunals constituted to hear investment disputes under IIAs have interpreted the term investment in a very broad manner, which includes not only portfolio investment and commercial loans[120] but also, quite unintuitively, sovereign bonds.[121] Also, the need for the investment to contribute to development has been played down.[122] Given the importance of the interpretation of the term 'investment' for the assertion of jurisdiction by investment arbitration tribunals, it is possible to conclude that the surge in the number of investment arbitrations is partly—but of course not only—explained by such an expansive interpretation of this term. At present, the controversy raised by this phenomenon has led some major emerging economies, such as India, to redefine the term investment so as to require an element of permanence and of contribution to the prosperity of the host State.[123] In addition, as discussed under point (3) below, the unruly nature of the investment arbitration jurisprudence has also sparked efforts to redefine the mechanisms for dispute settlement provided for in IIAs.

(2) *The applicable substantive standards* have significantly evolved over time, becoming far more diverse, encompassing, and specific. Whereas, historically, the focus was on measures of the executive resulting in an uncompensated expropriation or on measures of the judiciary resulting in a denial of justice, the standards of investment protection most commonly included in contemporary IIAs cover much more ground and in greater detail. In addition to the international minimum standard of treatment and the prohibition of denial of justice, IIAs routinely provide *inter alia* for the requirement of 'fair and equitable treatment', 'full protection and security', the protection against unlawful expropriation, non-discrimination standards (MFN and national treatment), and the so-called 'umbrella clause', that is, the undertaking to respect obligations entered into by the host State in contracts with foreign investors.

The latter emerged from the ambiguities in the law applicable to so-called 'State contracts', namely major contracts between a foreign investor and a host State relating most often to infrastructure development or natural resources. The complexities raised by the selection of 'international law' as the law applicable to a contractual relationship involving one private party led certain capital-exporting countries, such as the UK, to include umbrella clauses (or respect for undertakings clauses) in their model IIAs.[124] The effect sought by such clauses was to 'elevate' a contractual commitment to the level of international law, transforming breaches of contract into breaches of treaty. Yet, when decades later such clauses were first interpreted and applied, their effects led to much controversy.[125] The main area of controversy concerns the specific terms of a contract which may be thus 'elevated' to the level of a treaty.[126]

---

[119] See e.g. US Model BIT (2012), Article 1.

[120] See e.g. *Ceskoslovenska Obchodni Banka, A.S. v The Slovak Republic*, §§76–89.

[121] See *Abaclat and others v Argentine Republic*, §§373–380 (with Abi-Saab dissenting). By contrast, in *Poštová banka, a.s. and Istrokapital s.e. v Hellenic Republic*, §§308, 331, 371, the tribunal declined jurisdiction.

[122] See *Malaysian Historical Salvors v Malaysia*, §§62–63, 69, 71–72.

[123] See e.g. the Model text for the Indian Bilateral Investment Treaty, 2015, Articles 1(6) and 1(2)1. The text is online at https://mygov.in.

[124] On the origins of the umbrella clause see H. Abs and H. Shawcross, 'The Proposed Convention to Protect Private Foreign Investment: A Round Table' (1960) 1 *JPL* [now *Emory Law Journal*] 115.

[125] See e.g. J. Antony, 'Umbrella Clauses Since *SGS v Pakistan* and *SGS v Philippines*—A Developing Consensus' (2013) 29 *Arb Int'l* 607.

[126] See *SGS Société Générale de Surveillance S.A. v Islamic Republic of Pakistan (Jurisdiction)*, §§146–173; *SGS Société Générale de Surveillance S.A. v Republic of the Philippines (Objections to Jurisdiction)*, §§97, 113–163.

Another important standard, which can be seen as a revised and possibly more demanding version of the international minimum standard of treatment, is the 'fair and equitable treatment' (FET) standard. FET clauses laconically state that States 'shall accord fair and equitable treatment' to the investors of the other contracting party. That leaves a wide margin of interpretation to arbitration tribunals, which, over time, have generated an important body of jurisprudence on the specific meaning of the FET standard.[127] One important implication of the FET clause as it has been interpreted by investment tribunals is the protection of 'reasonable' or 'legitimate' expectations, namely the expectations generated by the conduct of the host State on the basis of which the investor made its investment. The concept and its application are fraught with ambiguities and, in practice, are driven by the specific circumstances of the dispute, the ability of counsel to present the case, and the assessment conducted by the arbitration tribunal. Perhaps as a result of such ambiguities, the ICJ has felt compelled to clarify the state of general international law as regards the protection of these expectations:

> [R]eferences to legitimate expectations may be found in arbitral awards concerning disputes between a foreign investor and the host State that apply treaty clauses providing for fair and equitable treatment. It does not follow from such references that there exists in general international law a principle that would give rise to an obligation on the basis of what could be considered a legitimate expectation.[128]

This is an indication that the content of IIAs, although broadly formulated, may not be taken as a reflection of general international law on this point.

Other important standards included in IIAs concern the protection against discrimination in a form analogous to that in international trade, namely, through the MFN and national treatment clauses.[129] Non-discrimination is also protected in other standards, such as FET, which may cover discriminatory action affecting two investors of the same nationality, or the protection against expropriation, which requires non-discrimination for expropriation to be lawful. As discussed in point (3) below, MFN clauses have been relied upon in an unexpected manner, namely, to import more favourable arbitration clauses from other IIAs.

All in all, the standards of investment protection resemble the broad protections offered by certain human rights, such as the right of equal treatment, economic freedoms, and the right to property. Both share a common history in the historical rights accorded to aliens. However, investment protection standards must be interpreted as 'disciplines' imposed on State action to the benefit of investors of certain nationalities, as a result of reciprocal advantages conferred by the State of nationality. Despite the similarity of content of these disciplines with some human rights, the foundations of the latter are fundamentally different, as they are entirely independent of any nationality requirement and they are inherent to human dignity. For this reason, human rights are 'rights' whereas investment protection standards are 'disciplines'. Such a difference can be traced back to the distinction made by the ICJ in the *Barcelona Traction (Belgium v Spain)* case between reciprocal concessions and obligations *erga omnes* (at §33), which has been recalled in the case law of the Inter-American Court of Human Rights:

---

[127] See generally I. Tudor, *The Fair and Equitable Treatment Standard in the International Law of Foreign Investment* (Oxford: Oxford University Press, 2008); R. Kläger, *'Fair and Equitable Treatment' in International Investment Law* (Cambridge: Cambridge University Press, 2011).

[128] *Obligation to Negotiate Access to the Pacific Ocean (Bolivia v Chile)*, §162.

[129] On the similarities and differences in the operation of non-discrimination standards in these two contexts see J. Kurtz, *The WTO and International Investment Law. Converging Systems* (Cambridge: Cambridge University Press, 2016).

[T]he Court considers that the enforcement of bilateral commercial treaties negates vindication of non-compliance with state obligations under the American Convention; on the contrary, their enforcement should always be compatible with the American Convention, which is a multilateral treaty on human rights that stands in a class of its own and that generates rights for individual human beings and does not depend entirely on reciprocity among States.[130]

(3) Perhaps the most striking development in this area since the 1990s is the surge in investment arbitration proceedings brought by foreign investors against host States on the basis of IIAs. This possibility, first recognized in a 1990 award rendered in *Asian Agricultural Products Ltd v Republic of Sri Lanka*, paved the way for foreign investors to bring 'treaty claims' directly on the basis of an arbitration clause appearing in an IIA, in the absence of any privity of contract between the host State and the foreign investor.[131] In some cases where the arbitration clause in the treaty was restrictive, foreign investors have relied, often successfully, on the operation of the MFN clause to 'import' more favourable arbitration clauses (e.g. not requiring preliminary steps akin to the exhaustion or use of domestic remedies) from other treaties.[132] In addition, the jurisprudence arising from the surge in investment disputes is often inconsistent or even contradictory, a feature which has created significant legal uncertainty.

Investment arbitration tribunals normally consist of three members, two appointed by the parties to the dispute and the third, the chairperson, selected by the two party-appointed arbitrators or, in the absence of agreement, by an appointing institution. The proceedings conducted by these tribunals can be governed by the ICSID Convention and its Arbitration Rules or by other systems and rules, most notably the UNCITRAL Arbitration Rules.[133] The difference between ICSID and non-ICSID arbitration is significant in a number of ways. As a general matter, ICSID arbitrations are largely detached from domestic jurisdictions for a range of matters, particularly set-aside, recognition, and enforcement. In the case of non-ICSID arbitrations, the latter are in most cases governed by the 1958 New York Convention on the Recognition and Enforcement of Foreign Arbitral Awards,[134] a feature which has blurred the boundaries between public and private international law.

In recent years, the wide powers conferred by IIAs on such 'private' or 'ephemeral' tribunals, as they have been designated by commentators, on matters of public concern, as well as the fact that several developed countries, such as Australia, Canada, Germany, or Spain, have faced massive investment claims, has generated a 'backlash' against investment arbitration proceedings, including a process under the aegis of the UN Commission on International Trade Law (UNCITRAL) to study the reform of the investor-State dispute settlement system.[135]

---

[130] *Case of Sawhoyamaxa Indigenous Community v Paraguay*, §140.

[131] See J. Paulsson, 'Arbitration Without Privity' (1995) 10 *ICSID Review—Foreign Investment Law Journal* 232.

[132] The first decision to address this issue is *Maffezini v Kingdom of Spain (Jurisdiction)*, §64.

[133] GA resolution 31/98 (15 December 1976), UN Doc. A/RES/31/98 (1976), revised in 2010.

[134] New York Convention on the Recognition and Enforcement of Foreign Arbitral Awards, 10 June 1958, 330 UNTS 3.

[135] See S. Puig and G. Shaffer, 'Imperfect Alternatives: Institutional Choice and the Reform of Investment Law' (2018) 112 *AJIL* 361.

INDEX

accession 208
adjudication 285–8
  arbitration, and 283–4
  ICJ 286–7
  PCIJ 286
  permanent courts, creation of 285–6
African Commission 418
African Court on Human and Peoples' Rights
  Advisory Opinions 418
  judges 419
  jurisdiction 418
aggravated responsibility *see under* international State responsibility for wrongful acts
aggression
  crime of *see* crime of aggression
  definition of 58
  indirect aggression *see under* self-defence
Ago, R. 247, 256–7
agreements *see under* treaties
airspace, law of 118–20
  air services agreements 118–19
  civil aircraft enjoying 'freedoms of the air' 118 118
  height of airspace 118
  measures taken by States to contain spread of COVID-19 119–20
  State enjoying sovereignty over airspace above territory and territorial sea 118
aliens *see under* international investment law and arbitration
Annan, Kofi, 322
annexation 59, 69, 97, 236, 255, 303.340, 351,
Anzilotti, D. 143, 159, 188, 194, 196, 198, 212, 219, 256
apartheid 48, 233–7, 324, 339, 424, 428
arbitration 284–5
  adjudication, and 283–4
  investment law, and *see* international investment law and arbitration

permanent bodies 284–5
WTO dispute settlement, and 291, 518
Area *see under* law of the sea
armed conflict
  international rules imposing obligations on individuals for 159–60
  legal restraints on violence *see* legal restraints on violence in armed conflict
armed force, use of *see* collective security and use of armed force
arms trade treaty 177, 328
attribution of conduct *see under* international State responsibility for wrongful acts

bays *see under* law of the sea
belligerency, recognition of 384
belligerent occupation 369
  civilians, and 396
  combatant status 383
belligerent reprisals 400–1
  barbaric nature of 400
  belligerent's discretion in resorting to 400
  conditions applicable to belligerent reprisals 401
  trend towards banning or restricting recourse to 400
Bretton Woods
  Conference 491–3
  IMF *see* international Monetary Fund (IMF)
  Keynes Plan and White Plan 492–3
  World Bank *see* World Bank
Briand-Kellogg Pact (1928) 11, 35
  banning/restricting use of force 57
Bull, H. 19

Calvo, C 30
Calvo doctrine 30
Cassin, René 409
Chagos Archipelago 40, 68–70, 99, 241, 287
children's health and welfare 326

civilians
  belligerent occupation 383
  belligerent reprisals against, banning of 400
  detention of 378–9
  direct participation in hostilities 386, 389
  internment 379
  military attacks, and *see* direct participation in hostilities
  principle of distinction, and 384, 390
  protecting 371
    victims of war, as 395, 396
  sanctions, and 309
  shielding from armed violence 368, 371
  see also legal restraints on violence in armed conflict
  use of armed force to protect from human rights violations 364–5
codification
  codification treaties 200
  circumstances precluding wrongfulness, codification of 258–62
  customary rules, codification of 41
  development of international law, and 200–1
  direct negotiation among States 200
  effects of codification treaties
    crystallizing effect 201
    declaratory effect 200–1
    generating effect 201
  ILC, and *see* International Law Commission (ILC)
  law of the sea, codification of 103–4
  State responsibility, codification of law of 200, 246–8
  codification of circumstances precluding wrongfulness 258–62
  States, and codification, preference for 191

codification(*Continued*)
   treaties, natural preference for 191, 200
   UN codification and progressive development of international law 329–30
coercion
   economic coercion against developing States 58
   extreme forms of economic coercion
      breach of non-intervention principle, as 60
      threat to peace, as 60
   ground of invalidity of treaty, as 214, 215
   specific forms of intervention, as 56
Cold War 491
   period after end of 41–2
   period from UN Charter to end of 36–41
   start of 39
collateral damage 391–2
collective responsibility
   examples of 6–8
   legal feature of international community, as 6–8
   meaning of 6
collective security and use of armed force 335–65
   enforcement action on authorization of the Security Council 346–9
   authorizations to enforce economic measures 348
   authorizing use of force against another State using aggression 346
   authorizing use of force when faced with threat to peace 346–7
   defining objectives of States when using force 348
   duration of Security Council mandate increasingly defined 348–9
   enlargement of notion of 'threat to the peace' 347
   ensuring antipiracy activities 348
   'responsibility to protect' doctrine, use of armed force to implement 347
   States required to report to Security Council on military operations 349
jus cogens, norms as 236
legal position 58–60, 335–7

anticipatory or pre-emptive self-defence not permitted 58–9
distinguishing grave from less grave uses of force 58
extreme forms of economic coercion as threat to peace 60
no use of force to acquire another State's territory 59–60
no use of force to repel indirect armed aggression 59
no threat or use of force against States or national liberation movements 58
peaceful means of conflict resolution 336
peaceful measures of enforcement 336
right to use force, suppression of 335–6
sanctions, use of 337
Security Council authorizing States to use force, development of 349
States not authorized to react by force except to armed attack 336
UN's collective responsibility for safeguarding peace 336
UN's monopoly of force 336
measures short of armed force and the UN system 337–42
   economic and other sanctions 339–40
   see also sanctions
   establishment of international criminal tribunals 341
   general 337–9
   General Assembly action for gross violations of international law 341–2
   non-recognition of illegal situations 340–1
   UN Charter 337–8
peacekeeping, peace enforcement and peace building 343–6
   capacity building civilian administrative functions, performing 344–5

enforcement function 344, 346
exit strategies, devising 345
features of traditional peacekeeping operations 343
growth in peacekeeping operations 343–4
moving from peacekeeping to peacebuilding 345
Peace Building Commission 345
UNEF 343
prohibition of the threat or use of force 38, 57–60
   general observations 57–8
   legal scope of principle 58–60
   non-intervention principle, and 53
   UN Charter, enshrined in 57–8
self-defence *see* self-defence
combatants
   combatant status 380–4
   direct participation in hostilities 387–8
   protection of lawful combatants as victims of war 396
   recognition of belligerency 384
   requirements for combatant status 381–4
      categories of combatants under GC III 381–2
      legal framework under AP I 382–4
   unlawful combatants 379–80, 387–8
      direct participation in hostilities 387–8
      terrorists 388
common but differentiated responsibilities 460, 467
   meaning of principle 467
   widely different interpretations 467
common heritage of mankind international seabed *see under* law of the sea
outer space 120–1
community rights and obligations 14–16
   Art 1 Geneva Conventions, and *see under* Geneva Conventions (1949)
   common good of the whole world 15

community rights, nature
  of 15
community obligations
  significance of 16
  unique features of 15
  emergence of new values
    worthy of special
    protection 14
  traditional means of redress,
    use of 15
compensation
  environment, protection
    of 484–5
  civil liability of economic
    operators 487–9
  international investment
    law 521–2
  State responsibility 262–3, 265
  violence in armed
    conflict 401–2
  belligerent parties liable to
    pay compensation 401
  claims often dismissed 402
  individuals bringing
    claims 402
  violations of rules of
    warfare, for 401
  war reparation 401
  WTO, dispute settlement
    of 518
Concert of Europe 27, 38
conciliation 282–3
consent
  arbitration and
    adjudication 284
  armed intervention with
    consent of territorial
    State 360–2
  circumstances precluding
    wrongfulness 259
  ICJ jurisdiction 287–8
  jus cogens, consent not
    precluding wrongfulness
    under 262
  peremptory norms resting
    on consent of major
    States 235
  treaties
    binding on States on
      consent 208
    expression of consent
      to 208–9
    termination by
      consent 216
consular agents, immunities
  of *see* immunities of foreign
  State officials
contiguous zone 108
continental shelf *see under* law
  of the sea

co-operation
  development
    co-operation 504
  duty to co-operate *see* duty to
    co-operate
  economic and social
    co-operation 324–6
  Environmental impact
    assessment (EIAs),
    and 463
  human rights law 324
  multilateral co-operation for
    development *see under*
    global economy and
    international law
  principles of international
    environmental law 462–3
  technical co-operation, WTO
    providing 508
corporations *see sui generis*
  entities, corporations and
  NGOs
Council of Europe 142, 163,
  333, 408
countermeasures 299–308
  aggravated responsibility,
    and 299, 303
  States' individual
    countermeasures
    273–4, 274–5
  circumstances precluding
    wrongfulness 259
  community rights, exercised
    through 15
  conditions for 299
  economic countermeasures 7
  human rights violations,
    for 421
  in general 299–300
  limitations on
    countermeasures 300–3
  countermeasures must not
    breach rights of third
    States 301–2
  obligations concerning
    threat or use of
    force 300
  obligations imposed by
    peremptory norms of
    general international
    law 301
  proportionality 302–3
  protection of human
    rights 300–1
countervailing duties 515
courts *see* international courts
  and tribunals; national legal
  systems
COVID-19 15, 63, 119–120,
  334, 367, 516

crime *see* international crimes,
  repression of; international
  criminal tribunals
crimes against humanity
  8, 431–4
  contextual element 433–4
  definitions 432, 433–4
  ILC Draft Articles 433
  international instruments,
    in 433
  legal elements 433
    aggravated criminal
      intent 433
    mental element 433
  Nuremberg Tribunal 432, 433
crime of aggression 437–40
  definition 437–8, 439
  international crime, as 437
  legal elements 438–9
    other conditions 439
  Nuremburg Tribunal 437
custom/customary international
  law 184–92
  armed conflicts 374–5
  civil wars 374
  codification of customary
    rules 41
  Common Article 3, and 375
  continental shelf 186
  customary rules, existence
    of 187–8
  courts establishing
    existence of customary
    rule 187–8
  rule evolving from clash of
    interests 188
  definition of 184
  domestic implementation of
    customary international
    law 225–6
  duty to co-operate in a
    transboundary context 459
  elements of 184–7
  general practice 184–5, 186
  opinio juris 184, 185–6
  opinio necessitatis 184, 185
  time element in formation
    of customary
    rules 186–7
  environmental impact
    assessments, duty to
    conduct 459, 461–2
  erga omnes obligations 13
  formation and
    identification 184–92
  human rights, and 420–2
    countermeasures 421
    customary rules imposing
      community obligations,
      effect of 421

custom/customary international
    law (*Continued*)
    democratic governance,
        right to 421–2
    gender discrimination,
        banning 421
    important customary
        norms, evolution of 420
    retortion 421
    States' response
        to continuing
        violations 421
    individuals, and *see under*
        individuals
    interactions among sources of
        law 202–3
    limitations imposed upon
        State sovereignty 91
    local customary rules 190–1
        customary rules binding
            on States of geographical
            area/region 190
        elements and requirements
            of regional customary
            rule 190–1
    no hierarchy between treaties
        and customs as sources of
        law 202
    non-international armed
        conflicts 171–2, 374
    outer space 120–1, 186
    pacta sunt servanda principle
        as part of customary law 65
    persistent objector
        doctrine 188–9
        nature of doctrine 188
        support for doctrine 189
    present role of custom 191–2
        demotion of custom 191
        preference for codification
            and multilateral
            treaties 191
        world community divided
            economically and
            politically 192
    prevention of significant
        environmental harm,
        principle of 73, 459
    riparian State's right to free
        navigation 14
    self-defence 58–9
        anticipatory or pre-emptive
        self-defence 59
    succession of States 87
cyberspace 56

Declaration of Brussels
    (1874) 369
Declaration of St Petersburg
    (1868) 369

Declaration on the Right to
    Development 503–4
see also developing States
democracy
    democratic governance, right
        to 421
    respect for democracy as
        criteria for recognition of
        States 422
    right to 421–2
    UN role in promotion of 324
desuetude 217
developing States
    command over UN General
        assembly 39, 40
    developing countries
        becoming more
        vocal 501–2
    numerical superiority of
        developing States 502
    economic coercion against 58
    characteristics of under-
        development 499–501
    agriculture and
        manufacturing
        conducted on family
        basis 500
    agriculture as dominant
        economic activity 500
    concealed
        unemployment 500
    conglomerative
        factors 500–1
    'dual' or 'hybrid' economy
        existing 500
    low level of capital
        stock 500
    population increases 501
    primitive agricultural
        and industrial
        equipment 500
    development
        co-operation 504
    expansion and updating of
        Charter principles 46
    forcible protection of
        nationals abroad in
        developing States 359
    GATT, differential treatment
        under 499, 507, 515
    greater access to world
        markets, seeking 42
    Global South, as 43
    Group of 77, as 41, 42
    IMF, and 508–9
    jus cogens as means of fighting
        colonial countries 233–4
    law of the sea, and 93
    multilateral co-operation for
        development 504–9

channels of co-operation
    for development 505–9
loans to developing
    States 504
nature of 504
North–South
    co-operation 504
South-South
    co-operation 504
technical assistance 505
NIEO: main tenets regarding
    developing States
    free to nationalize or
        expropriate foreign
        property 502
    free to set up associations
        of primary commodities
        producers 502
    international trade based
        on stable, equitable
        prices 503
    regulating multinational
        corporations 502
    transfer of technology to
        developing States 503
no longer ideologically
    oriented 42
permanent sovereignty over
    natural resources 40, 502
racial equality 40
right to development 503–4
    human person as
        beneficiary of 503
    right to development as
        inalienable right 503
    State's right and duty to
        facilitate full realization
        of 503
self-determination 40
development *see* global economy
    and international law
diplomatic protection 153, 159,
    199, 405, 496, 518–21
diplomats and diplomacy
    binary rules in their specific
        operation, splitting into 13
    community rights, exercised
        through 15
    immunities *see* immunities of
        foreign State officials
    international investment law,
        and 518–19, 520
    settlement of disputes *see
        under* peaceful settlement
        of international disputes
    see also Vienna Convention
        on Diplomatic Relations
        (1961)
direct participation in
    hostilities 386–9

civilians 386, 387
criterion of continuous
  combat function 386
targeted killings and 'war on
  terror' 388–9
unlawful combatants
  379–80
  civilians 387, 388
disarmament 327–9
  actions taken by General
    Assembly 328
  Charter provisions 327
  role of Security Council 329
dispute settlement
  diplomatic means of *see
    under* peaceful settlement
    of international disputes
  international investment law
    and arbitration 525
  judicial means of *see under*
    peaceful settlement of
    international disputes
  PCIJ 36
  peaceful settlement *see*
    peaceful settlement of
    international disputes
  WTO *see under* World Trade
    Organization (WTO)
distinction, principle of 384,
  390–1
  civilians, prohibition against
    attacking 384, 390
Drago doctrine 31
Drago, Luis Maria 30–1
dualism *see under* international
  legal norms, implementation
  and hierarchy of
due diligence, duty of 459
  environmental protection
    due diligence, need to
      display 74–5
    prevention of
      environmental
      harm 460, 461
  pandemics, due diligence duty
    to prevent spread of 15
dumping 498, 514–15
Dunant, Henri 368
duty to co-operate 46, 62–4
  dimensions of
    co-operation 62–4
    broad domain of duty to
      co-operate 53
    co-operation as a duty of
      States 62–3
    duty to co-operate in
      transboundary/global
      context 63
  purposes of duty
    related but distinct

from domains of
  o-operation 64
environmental matters,
  and 462–3
duty to co-operate in good
  faith 462
nature of duty 462–3
relationship between
  co-operation and other
  principles 463
risk of significant harm,
  and 485–6
general observations and
  nature of duty 62

Economic and Social Council
  (ECOSOC) 316, 317, 318
economic and social
  co-operation 324–6
environment, protection of 458
United Nations
  Development
  Programme
  (UNDP) 505
human rights 163, 326
  Commission on Human
    Rights 415
  role 314
sustainable development 326
economic crisis, 2007 510
economic operators' liability *see
  under* environmental harm,
  responsibility and liability for
economic pressure and
  coercion 55–6
  conditionality, IMF and 495
  developing States, against 58
  extreme forms of economic
    coercion as breach of non-
    intervention principle 60
  extreme forms of economic
    coercion as threat to
    peace 60
effectiveness, principle of
  creation of States, and 81
  interpretation of
    treaties 212–13
  nature of 12
  overriding role in
    international law 12
  recognition, and 83
employment disputes *see under*
  immunities of States
enforcement 294–309
  collective enforcement
    measures (sanctions
    proper) *see* sanctions
  decentralized enforcement
    in historical
    perspective 294–7

forcible
  intervention 295–6
general 294–5
reprisals 296–7
war 297
enforcement of international
  rules in international
  law 297–303
  countermeasures *see*
    countermeasures
  general 297–8
  retortion 298–9
national courts enforcing
  international rules
  9, 303–6
  conflicting approaches
    adopted by States 304–5
  conflicting
    requirements 305
  criminal proceedings
    against
    individuals 305–6
  forum for implementation
    of international trade
    and economic law,
    as 306
  limits to potential role of
    domestic judges 306
environment, protection
  of 454–89
  common but differentiated
    responsibilities *see*
    common but differentiated
    responsibilities
  compensation *ex gratia* or
    strict liability of States *see
    under* environmental harm,
    responsibility and liability
    for
  compliance, mechanisms
    to promote and
    manage 478–82
    inspection procedures 479
    neutral data collection and
      monitoring 481–2
    non-compliance
      procedures 479–81
    self-reporting 479
  contemporary regulation
    of environmental
    challenges 471–82
    MEAs *see* multilateral
      environmental
      agreements (MEAs)
    mechanisms to
      promote and manage
      compliance 478–82
    overview 471
    role of 'soft law'
      instruments 471–2

environment, protection of (*Continued*)
  economic operators, civil liability of *see under* environmental harm, responsibility and liability for
  environmental impact assessments *see* environmental impact assessments (EIAs)
  intergenerational equity *see* intergenerational equity
  international institutions in charge of environmental protection 482–3
    NGOs 483
    UN Commission on Sustainable Development (CSD) 482
    UN Specialized Agencies 483
    UNEP *see* United Nations Environment Program (UNEP)
  polluter-pays principle *see* polluter-pays principle
  pollution and environmental problems 454–5
  precaution, principle of *see* precautionary principle
  precedents 455–8
    Fur Seal Arbitration 455–7
    Lac Lanoux (Spain/France) 457–8
    Trail Smelter (United States of America/Canada) 457
  prevention of environmental harm, principle of 73–5, 460–1
    duty of due diligence 460, 461
    EIAs, and 461
    general observations 73–4
    legal scope of principle 74–5
  principles of environmental protection 74–5
    due diligence, need to display 74–5
    duty to co-operate in good faith 75
    limiting harm to State's own environment 75
    nature of 'significant' harm 75
    need not to cause significant harm to other States or areas 74–5
    polluter-pays principle 75
    principle of permanent sovereignty over natural resources 74
    requirement to conduct environmental impact assessment 75
  principles of international environmental law: 1972–2020 458–70
    common but differentiated responsibilities 467
    co-operation 462–3
    environmental impact assessment 460–1
    intergenerational equity 466
    polluter-pays principle 465–6
    precaution 463–4
    prevention of environmental harm 460–1
    public participation 467–8
    Rio Declaration and principles 459–60, 471
    Stockholm Conference as birth of modern environmental law 458
    Stockholm Declaration 459, 471
    sustainable development 468–70
  UN Environment Programme, establishment of 458–9
  public participation *see* public participation, principle of
  responsibility and liability *see* environmental harm, responsibility and liability for
  'soft law' instruments 471–3
    Draft Articles on Prevention of Transboundary Harm 471–2
    non-binding, authoritative guidelines 472
    plans of action on environmental matters 472
    Rio Declaration and principles 471
    Stockholm Declaration 471
    Sustainable Development Goals 472–3
  sustainable development *see* sustainable development
  treaties and instruments relating to environmental protection, growth of 73
  UN role 325–6
environmental harm, prevention of *see under* environment, protection of
environmental harm, responsibility and liability for 483–9
  civil liability of economic operators 487–9
    establishment of additional layers of compensation 489
    ILC Draft Principles on the Allocation of Loss 487
    no-fault liability of economic operator for damage, 487, 488
    non-discrimination of victims with respect to redress mechanisms 489
    nuclear accidents 487–8
    obligation of economic operators to take out insurance 488
    oil pollution 487
  compensation *ex gratia* or strict liability of States 484–5
    climate change treaty regime 484
    no recognition of existence of obligation 483–4
  overview 483–4
    absolute liability, treaties providing for 483–4
    'ordinary' State responsibility 483
    States reluctant to accept no-fault liability 484
  State responsibility for environmental harm or risk 485–7
    assessment of damages, difficulties of 487
    causal link, proving 486
    harm from concomitant factors 486
    greenhouse gases 486
    ILC's Draft Articles on Prevention clarifying diligence level 485–6
    risk of significant harm 485–6

States' duty to prevent
    harm 486
States' responsibility
    for individuals and
    corporations 486
ultrahazardous
    activities 486
whether damage
    required 486
environmental impact
    assessments (EIAs) 461–2
co-operation, and 463
difficulties in operation
    of 461–2
requirement to conduct 74,
    75, 459, 463
risk of significant harm,
    and 485–6
environmental information *see
    under* public participation,
    principle of
equidistance, principle of
    delimitation of maritime
    areas 113
equity, and 198
not a rule of customary
    law 186–7
equity 197–8
international law, in 197–8
material component in general
    principles of law 198
role in the interpretation
    of relevant applicable
    rules 198
erga omnes obligations 13
aggravated State
    responsibility 269–70
community obligations, as 15
pandemics, due diligence duty
    to prevent spread of 15
European Court of Human
    Rights (ECtHR)
Advisory Opinions 417
decisions enhancing
    protection of human
    rights 423–4
torture 423
whole life prison
    sentences 423–4
individuals' petitions 417
judges 416–17
pilot judgments 417
pivotal role of 417
State referrals 417
workload 416, 417
European Union 42, 86, 94, 142,
    146, 230, 329, 332–3, 451
evolution of international action
    on human rights, trends
    in 408–20

expansion of territorial scope
    of human rights obligations
obligations interpreted as
    having extraterritorial
    scope 412, 413
States' obligations arising
    where exercise of
    authority 413
general 408
human rights, humanitarian
    law and litigation in
    domestic courts 419–20
national courts substituting
    for international
    enforcement
    agencies 419
US courts hearing cases
    of gross violations of
    human rights 419–20
human rights treaties
    409–10
legally binding
    instruments of general
    purport 409–10
treaties in specific areas,
    development of 410
regional supervisory
    mechanisms 416–19
African
    Commission 418–19
African Court on
    Human and Peoples'
    Rights 418–19
ECtHR 416–17
IACommHR 416
IACourtHR 416
tendency to overrule
    objection of domestic
    jurisdiction 410–11
interventions regarded
    as justified for
    serious/large-scale
    violations 411
UN rejecting
    objection of State
    sovereignty 410–11
UDHR *see* Universal
    Declaration of Human
    Rights (1948)
universal supervisory
    mechanisms 414–16
effectiveness of
    mechanisms 415–16
examination of inter-State
    complaints 414
examination of periodic
    reports from States 414
Human Rights
    Council 415
independent inquiries 414

individuals filing a
    'communication' with
    supervisory body 414
mechanisms established
    by international
    treaties 414
mechanisms set up by UN
    resolutions 414
UN ad hoc body
    organizing monitoring
    procedures 414–15
UN Office of the High
    Commissioner for
    Human Rights 415
exclusive economic zone *see
    under* law of the sea
execution, immunity from *see
    under* immunity of States
expanding bullets, prohibition
    of 29
extradition treaties 238

fact-finding *see* inquiry
First World War 6, 32–4
force majeure 259–60
forcible intervention 295–6
forcible protection of
    nationals abroad 358–60
free trade agreements
    (FTAs) 515–16
growth in 516
types of 515–16

General Agreement on Tariffs
    and Trade (GATT) 490, 491,
    496–9, 507
bilateral or multilateral
    negotiations ('rounds') 498
contracting parties to GATT
    1947, WTO and 511
creation of 497
developing States, and 499, 507
Enabling Clause 507, 517
exceptions
    differential treatment
        of developing
        countries 499, 507, 515
    general situations/
        exceptions 498, 517–18
    FTAs/maintenance
        of economic
        integration 498–9,
        515–16
GATT 1994 510
general obligation to reduce
    customs duties 498
non-discrimination/
    preventing unfair
    competition 513
countervailing duties 515

General Agreement on
Tariffs and Trade (GATT)
(*Continued*)
  dumping 498, 514–15
  exceptions 515–17
  most favoured nation
    clause 497, 513–14
  national treatment
    clause 497–8, 514
  non-discrimination
    standards 513
  rules preventing unfair
    competition 514–15
  subsidies 515
  trade remedies 515
non-reciprocity in trade
  negotiations 507
quantitative restrictions,
  prohibition of 498
restrictions on freedom
  of States to grant
  subsidies 498, 515
voting 497
general principles of law
  recognized in domestic
  systems 192–5
attempt to codify resort to
  principles 1921 193–4
equity as material
  component 198
general 192–3
  norm-setting processes,
    as 193
  subsidiary sources, as
    193, 202
past and present role of
  principles 194–5
  compatible with essential
    features of world
    community 195
General Assembly, UN *see*
  United Nations General
  Assembly
Geneva Conventions
  (1949) 370–1
belligerent reprisals 400–1
combatant status,
  requirements for 381–4
  categories of combatants
    under the third Geneva
    Convention 381–2
  legal framework under
    the first Additional
    Protocol 382–4
Common Article 1
  community rights and
    obligations, and 16–19
  operation with regard to
    other primary rules 17
  provisions of 16–17

Common Article 3 371, 375
  protection of victims of
    war 396–7
enshrining principle of
  community protection of
  universal values 17
exercise of legal entitlement
  not specified 17
first Additional Protocol
  (AP1) 372, 373–4, 382–4
  International Humanitarian
    Fact-Finding
    Commission 400
  Protecting Powers
    system 399
national courts endowed with
  universal jurisdiction over
  grave breaches 18
prisoners of war 381, 400
Protecting Powers system 399
second Additional Protocol
  (AP2) 372–4
State practice since 1950 18
war crimes as grave
  breaches 429
  mandatory prosecution/
    extradition for 401
genocide 8, 434–6
definition 434–5
genocidal context, question
  of 436
Genocide Convention 434–5
legal elements 435–6
  special intent 435–6
safeguards against,
  introduction of 14
Gentili, Alberico 22
global economy and
  international law 490–525
decolonization, development
  and struggle for a new
  international economic
  order 499–509
  economic structure
    of under-
    development 499–501
  multilateral co-operation
    for development 504–9
  north-south divide 499
  struggle for a new
    international economic
    order 501–4
international law and global
  economy today 509–25
  international investment
    law *see* international
    investment law and
    arbitration
  post-1990 global economic
    architecture 509–10

WTO *see* World Trade
  Organization (WTO)
multilateral co-operation for
  development 504–9
  advantages of 504
  development co-operation,
    notion of 504
  Expanded Programme
    of Technical
    Assistance 504
  GATT 507
  IMF 508
  loans to developing
    States 504
  nature of 504
  North–South
    co-operation 504
  South-South
    co-operation 504
  Technical Assistance
    Programme 505
  UNCTAD 505–6
  UNDP 505
  UNIDO 506
  World Bank 508
post-1945 global economic
  architecture 491–9
  Bretton Woods and Havana
    Conferences 491–4
  General Agreement on
    Tariffs and Trade
    (GATT) 496–9
  International Bank for
    Reconstruction and
    Development 495–6
  International Monetary
    Fund 494–5
under-development,
  economic structure *see*
  under developing States
Global North and Global
  South 43
good faith, principle of 64–6
general observations 64–5
  principle inseparable
    from existence of
    international law 64–5
  ubiquitous nature of
    principle 64
specific expressions of good
  faith 65–6
  basis for recognition of
    binding character of
    States' unilateral acts 65
  clean hands doctrine, good
    faith and 65
  estoppel, good faith
    and 66
good faith principle
  important for

INDEX

interpretation of
treaties 66
negotiations and duty to
co-operate must be
conducted in good
faith 66
pacta sunt servanda as
foundational norm 65
rights not to be exercised in
abusive manner 66
States mandated *bona fide*
to try to resolve disputes
peacefully 60
UN, and 45, 46
good offices 281
greenhouse gases 486
Grotius, Hugo 22, 103, 134
Guterres, Antònio 322, 331

Hague Conference 369
Declaration prohibiting
expanding bullets 29, 30
Hague Conference, Second
31–2, 369
Hague Conventions
(1899–1907) 369–70
Hammarskjöld, Dag 281, 343
Havana Conference 493–4, 497
GATT, adoption of 493
Havana Charter, adoption
of 493–4
Head of State or
Government 207–8, 427, 448
high seas *see under* law of the sea
historical evolution of
the international
community 20–44
Cold War end to
present 41–2
emerging
'multipolarity' 43–4
unipolarity 42–3
emergence of international
community before Peace of
Westphalia 20–3
First World War to Second
World War 32–4
League of Nations 34–5
legal output 35–6
Soviet Union splitting
international
community 32–4
turning point of First
World War and its
consequences 32
Peace of Westphalia to end of
First World War 23–32
Great Powers' dominance,
efforts to restrain
30–2

international community,
balance of power 26–8
international community,
composition of 23–6
main features of
international law 28–30
UN Charter to end of Cold
War 36–41
international community,
changes in composition
of 39–40
legal change 40–1
Second World War, main
consequences of 37–8
United Nations,
establishment of 38–9
Holy See 173
human rights *see* international
human rights law/human rights
Human Rights Council 415
humanitarian
intervention 364–5
forcible intervention,
humanitarian reasons
for 56–7
resort to armed force only
through UN 364–5
humanitarian law *see*
international humanitarian law
immunities of foreign State
officials 130–9
diplomatic and consular agents,
immunities of 133–5
agent with nationality
of receiving State
or 'permanent
residence' 134
consular agents 135
family members 134–5
immunities relating to
property 133–4
personal immunities 134
termination of diplomat's
functions 135
types of immunities 133
functional immunities 131–3
acts of officials imputed to
State 132
acts performed in
exercise of official's
functions 131
international crimes,
officials criminally liable
for 132–3
international crimes,
temporary immunity of
senior officials 132
personal liability for
the individual,
circumstances of 132

high rank State officials,
immunities of 135–9
arrest and surrender to an
international court 138
cessation of mission, effect
of 137
civil claims against
officials 139
international crimes,
temporary immunity
from prosecution 137–8
nature of
immunities 135–6
officials not enjoying
personal immunities,
prosecution of 138–9
waiver of immunity by
States 137, 138
types of immunities 130–1
functional and personal
immunities 130–1
waiver of immunity by
States 131

immunities of international
organizations and their
agents 147–52
agents' immunity as
international civil
servants 150–3
'experts on mission',
immunity for 152
Special treatment for
broader categories of
personnel 152
UN officials 151–2
immunity from State courts'
jurisdiction 148–50
determining scope of
actual immunity 149
ensuring organizations'
accountability and
independence 149–50
general trend
towards restricting
immunities 149
immunity essentially
functional 149
right to claim immunity
from jurisdiction/
execution of national
courts 148
importance of
immunities 147
immunities of States 122–30
employment disputes 124–6
criteria establishing
immunity in
international
instruments 125–6

immunities of States (*Continued*)
   distinction between
      ancillary and directly
      related activities 125
   private nature of
      employment contracts,
      emphasis on 125
   States not interfering in
      internal organization of
      foreign States 124
   execution, immunity
      from 129–30
      bank accounts 130
      courts protective of State
        sovereignty 129–30
      property or assets of
        foreign States destined
        for private function 130
      running in parallel
        to immunity from
        jurisdiction 129
   human rights
      interventions regarded as
        justified for serious/large-
        scale violations 411
      UN rejecting
        objection of State
        sovereignty 410–11
   jus cogens, and 238–9
   jurisdictional
      immunity 122–4
      absolute immunity 123, 124
      acts by foreign State
        in private capacity/
        restrictive immunity
        doctrine 123–4
      defining acts performed by
        foreign State in private
        capacity 124
      immunity of foreign
        States from jurisdiction
        of forum State,
        rationale 122–3
   jurisdictional immunity,
      jus cogens and 126–9
      proper role of domestic
        courts 129
      protection of sovereign
        immunities where
        violations of *jus*
        cogens 126–7
      State practice continuing to
        evolve 127–8
      traditional vision of State
        sovereignty 129
   sovereignty and
      immunities 122
   State immunities from
      jurisdiction and
      execution 122–30
employment
   disputes 124–6
   execution, immunity
      from 129–30
   jurisdictional
      immunity 122–4
   jurisdictional immunity,
      jus cogens and 126–9
   violations of IHL, dismissing
      claims for 402
impact assessments,
   environmental *see*
      environmental impact
      assessments (EIAs)
implied powers, doctrine of
   ICJ, and 199, 213
   international
      organizations 145–7
   constitutive instruments,
      interpretation of 146
   expansive interpretation
      of international
      organizations'
      competences 147
   international organizations
      acting on basis of
      conferred powers 145–6
   interpretation of treaties,
      and 146, 213
   origins of doctrine 213
   theory of implied
      powers 146–7
individuals: rights and
   duties 158–65
   customary rules imposing
      obligations on
      individuals 159–60
   armed conflict, obligations
      on individuals
      for 159–60
   expansion of international
      legal personality 156–8
   attributing international
      status to individuals,
      ideological aspect
      of 156
   human rights norms and
      individual criminal
      responsibility, effect
      of 157
   general remarks 158–9
   general position of
      international law
      with regard to
      individuals 158
   States losing exclusive
      monopoly over
      individuals 159
   holders of corresponding
      rights 160–1
   enforcement by
      individuals 160
   growing direct impact
      of international
      legal system on
      individuals 161
   individual responsibility,
      evolution of 8
   national systems
      contractual freedoms and
      constraints in 10
   individuals as principal
      legal subjects in States 3
   international rules
      addressed directly to
      individuals 232
   officials, immunities of *see*
      immunities of foreign State
      officials
   treaty provisions
      conferring rights on
      individuals 161–5
   individuals' lopsided
      position in international
      community 164
   individuals possessing
      limited *locus standi* and
      legal capacity 164–5
   limitations on
      international right to
      petition international
      bodies 162–4
   right to lodge complaint
      with an international
      body 162
indiscriminate weapons 393
infiltration, armed *see under*
   self-defence
inquiry
   bilateral method, as 280
   fact-finding by international
      organizations 280–1
   human rights breaches,
      into 281
   meaning 280
Institut de droit international
   29, 41
insurgents 167–72
   conduct of hostilities and the
      protection of victims of
      warfare 171–2
   Declaration on Friendly
      Relations governing 47
   duties of third States 170
   foreign representatives,
      treatment of 171
   foreigners, treatment
      of 170–1
   international legal subject,
      as 156

lawful countermeasures,
taking 171
nature of 79
limited international
capacity, having 172
State-like subjects, as 172
no right of sovereignty proper
over territory under
effective control 172
non-international armed
conflict, and 171–2
non-intervention principle,
States refraining from
assisting under 53
recognition of
belligerency 168–9
recognition of
insurgency 168
reluctance of States
to recognise
insurgents 169–70
reluctance to give civil
upheaval the status of
international armed
conflict 167–8
requirements for eligibility
to become international
subject 168
States suppressing on own
territory 57
subjects of international
community, as 79
treaty-making by
insurgents 170
Inter-American Commission
(IACommHR) 416
individual petitions 418
membership 417–18
Inter-American Court of Human
Rights (IACourtHR) 416
Advisory Opinions 418
judges 418
jurisdiction 418
intergenerational equity 460, 466
balance needs of present and
future generations 466
basis to extend *locus standi* to
future generations 466
Intergovernmental Panel on
Climate Change (IPCC)
482, 483
creation of 481
role and function 481
internal waters *see under* law of
the sea
international arbitration *see*
international investment law
and arbitration
international armed conflicts
(IACs)

combatant status 380–1
see also combatants
direct participation in
hostilities 386–8
unlawful
combatants 387–8
IHL, and *see* legal restraints
on violence in armed
conflict
meaning of 367
war crimes 429–30
International Bank for
Reconstruction and
Development *see* World Bank
International Centre for
Settlement of Investment
Disputes (ICSID) 285, 525
International Civil Aviation
Organization (ICAO) 119
guidelines on 'Aviation and
COVID-19' 120
International Committee of the
Red Cross (ICRC) 174–5
compliance with IHL, role in
promoting 398
functions and purposes 175
Geneva Conventions, and
17, 175
history of 174–5
international personality,
possessing 174, 175
observer status in General
Assembly 175
origins 368
publishing appeals to
belligerents 18
structure 175
treaty-making 175
international community
balance of power 26–8
coexistence of old and new
patterns of law in 19
composition of 23–6
changes in
composition 39–40
diversification of poles of
power 42
Great Powers' dominance,
efforts to restrain 30–2
history of *see* historical
evolution of the
international community
horizontal structure 12
international relations *see*
international relations,
fundamental principles
governing
legal features of *see* legal
features of international
community

multipolarity, emerging 43–4
peace as principal goal 37, 57
Soviet Union, and *see under*
Soviet Union
States, and *see* States
three postulates of
freedom, equality and
effectiveness 45
unipolarity 42–3
International Court of Justice
(ICJ) 181–2
Advisory Opinions 286–7,
317, 330
classes of threat or use of
force, distinguishing
between 358
custom 184–5
equity 197–8
general principles of law
recognized by civilized
nations 192
implied power doctrine
199, 213
importance of decisions 199
injured State, notion of 265–6
judicial decisions
and teaching of
the most qualified
publicists 199–200
jurisdiction 286
forum prorogatum 287–8
governed by principle of
consent 287–8
local custom 190–1
membership 317
normative role 199, 330
resolutions of the UN General
Assembly, effects of 201
State immunity and *jus
cogens* 239
unilateral acts 195–6
international crimes,
prosecution and punishment
of 444–53
demand for international
criminal justice 446–8
increasing importance
of human rights
doctrine 447–8
origins 446–7
turning point in the early
1990s 447–8
'individual' and 'system'
criminality 444
international criminal
courts and tribunals,
establishment of 448–52
ad hoc Tribunals for the
Former Yugoslavia and
Rwanda 448–9

international crimes, prosecution
and punishment of
(*Continued*)
    hybrid criminal courts or
        tribunals 451–2
    ICC 449–51
    Mechanism for the
        International Criminal
        Tribunals 449
    prosecution and punishment
        by State courts 444–6
    grounds of criminal
        jurisdiction 444
    international
        immunities 445–6
    principle of
        universality 444–5
international crimes, repression
    of 427–53
    categories of international
        crime 428–43
    crime of aggression *see*
        crime of aggression
    crimes against
        humanity *see* crimes
        against humanity
    genocide *see* genocide
    terrorism *see* terrorism
    torture *see* torture
    war crimes *see* war crimes
    demand for international
        criminal justice 446–8
    immunity, and
        international crimes,
            officials criminally liable
            for 132–3, 137
        international crimes,
            temporary immunity of
            senior officials
            132, 137
international crimes, nature
    of 427–8
    definition of international
        crimes 428
    historically 427
    offences entailing personal
        criminal liability of
        individuals 428
    merits and disadvantages
        of international criminal
        trials 452–3
    prosecution and
        punishment *see*
        international crimes,
        prosecution and
        punishment of
International Criminal Court
    (ICC) 195, 401
    creation 449
    crime of aggression 449

crimes against humanity 433,
    434
genocide 434–5
jurisdiction 449
    activating, ways of 449–50
    jurisdiction
        complementary to
        national criminal justice
        systems 450–1
    pre-conditions
        to exercising
        jurisdiction 450
    war crimes under jurisdiction
        of 429–30
international criminal courts
    and tribunals
    ad hoc Tribunals for the
        Former Yugoslavia and
        Rwanda 448–9
    collective security measure,
        as 341
    establishment of 448–52
    hybrid criminal courts or
        tribunals 451–2
        accountability issues,
            addressing 452
        judicial bodies with a
            mixed composition 451
        potential advantages 452
    ICC *see* International
        Criminal Court (ICC)
    Mechanism for the
        International Criminal
        Tribunals 449
    merits and disadvantages
        of international criminal
        trials 452–3
        main disadvantages
            over domestic
            prosecutions 453
        main merits 452–3
    war crimes, prosecuting 401
international criminal justice *see*
    international crimes,
    prosecution and punishment
    of
International Criminal Tribunal
    for Rwanda 401, 447, 448–9
    capacity and resources of UN
        strained by 451
    closure of 448
    crimes against
        humanity 433–4
    criticisms of 448–9
    genocide 434–5
International Criminal Tribunal
    for the Former Yugoslavia
    (ICTY) 18, 401, 447, 448–9
    capacity and resources of UN
        strained by 451

closure of 448
crimes against
    humanity 433–4
criticisms of 448–9
genocide 434–5
influencing classical
    international law 422
rape and sexual assault case
    law 421
International Development
    Agency (IDA) 496, 504
    establishment of 508
    financing developing
        States 508
international disputes, peaceful
    settlement of *see* peaceful
    settlement of international
    disputes
International Finance
    Corporation (IFC) 496
international human rights law/
    human rights
    armed force to protect
        civilians from human rights
        violations, use of 364–5
    classical international
        law 404–6
        international protection
            of human beings
            increasing 405
        promoting respect for
            human rights 405–6
        prosecuting German
            and Japanese war
            criminals 405
    classical international law,
        impact of human rights
        on 422–3
        core of fundamental values,
            developing 423
    co-operation among
        States 324
    countermeasures for
        protection of human
        rights 300–1
    customary international law
        and human rights 420–2
        countermeasures 421
        customary rules imposing
            community obligations,
            effect of 421
        democracy, right to 421–2
        gender discrimination,
            banning 421
        important customary
            norms, evolution of 420
        retortion 421
        States' response
            to continuing
            violations 421

demand for international
    criminal justice,
    and 447–8
human rights treaties,
    succession of States and 88
increasing importance
    of human rights
    doctrine 447–8
inquiry into human rights
    breaches 281
international humanitarian
    law, and 375–80
    detention abroad
        in relation to
        NIACs 378–80
    lethal force, use of 377–8
    specialized body of law,
        as 376
    whether international
        human rights law impact
        on IHL 376–7
non-intervention principle,
    and 76
present role of human
    rights 423–6
    ECtHR decisions
        enhancing protection of
        human rights 423–4
    dynamic doctrine, human
        rights as 424
    human rights bodies,
        impact on States
        behaviour of 423
    judicial mechanisms
        established at regional
        level 424–5
    monitoring procedures,
        limited results from 424
    private actors, application
        of human rights
        obligations to 425
    responsibility to protect
        doctrine, controversial
        nature of 425–6
    UN promoting deep sense
        of social justice 424
    worldwide recognition of
        certain basic values 424
respect for human rights,
    principle of 71–3
    foundations of
        obligation 72
    general observations 71–2
    legal scope of
        principle 72–3
respect for human rights,
    sanctions and 308–9
    avoiding suffering
        that is manifestly
        disproportionate 309

humanitarian
    exemptions 308
general standards to
    be observed by
    States 308–9
sanctions adversely
    impacting most
    vulnerable groups 308
sparing as much as possible
    civilian population 309
targeted or smart
    sanctions 309
supervisory mechanisms,
    regional 416–19
supervisory mechanisms,
    universal 414–16
treaties on human rights
    reservations 212
trends in evolution of *see*
    evolution of international
    action on human rights,
    trends in
UN, and 45, 326–7
    promoting respect for
        human rights 327
    UN Charter 327, 406–7
International Humanitarian
    Fact-Finding
    Commission 400
international humanitarian
    law (IHL)
    armed conflicts, and *see* legal
        restraints on violence in
        armed conflict
    human rights, and *see under*
        international human rights
        law/human rights
    jus cogens, as 236
    specialized' body of law,
        as 375
international institutions *see*
    international organizations
    and institutions
international investment law and
    arbitration 518–25
    aliens
        exhaustion of domestic
            remedies of host State
            by 520–1
        historical protection of
            rights of aliens operating
            abroad 519–20
        international minimum
            standard of
            treatment 520–1
        right of State to
            exercise diplomatic
            protection 520
    applicable substantive
        standards 523–5

expropriation 285, 410,
    521–523
fair and equitable treatment
    standard 524
human rights protections,
    resembling 524
protection against
    discrimination 524
umbrella clause 523
backlash against investment
    arbitration 519
criticism of investment
    protection system 519
diplomatic protection system,
    by-passing 518–19
growth in international
    investment
    agreements 518
Hull formula/
    compensation 521–2
system of investment
    promotion and protection
    under international
    investment agreements
    (IIAs) 522–5
    applicable substantive
        standards 523–5
    prevailing dispute
        settlement
        mechanism 525
    protected
        transactions 522–3
    traditional international
        rules on foreign
        investment 521–2
International Labour
    Organization (ILO) 14, 405
    establishment of 142
    trade union associations filing
        complaints with 36–7,
        162, 163
international law
    armed conflict, violence
        in *see* legal restraints on
        violence in armed conflict
    armed force, use of *see*
        collective security and use
        of armed force
    classical international
        law 404–6
    impact of human rights
        on 422–3
    laissez-faire approach
        of 45
    development and
        identification of 199–202
        codification *see*
            codification
        jurisprudence and
            doctrine 199–200

international law (*Continued*)
  soft law 201–2
  dispute settlement *see*
    peaceful settlement of
    international disputes
  domestic law, and *see*
    international law in
    domestic systems,
    implementing
  enforcement *see* enforcement
  environment, and *see*
    environment, protection of
  global economy, and *see*
    global economy and
    international law
  history of *see* historical
    evolution of the
    international community
  international crimes *see*
    international crimes,
    repression of
  international legal
    subjects *see* international
    legal subjects
  international relations *see*
    international relations,
    fundamental principles
    governing
  international rights
    and obligations *see*
    international rights and
    obligations
  investment law *see*
    international investment
    law and arbitration
  law-making *see* law-making
    processes
  legal features of international
    community *see* legal
    features of international
    community
  main features
    historically 28–30
    international norms and
      principles framed by
      Great Powers 28–9
    rules and principles as
      product of Western
      civilization 28
  norms *see* international legal
    norms, implementation
    and hierarchy of
  States, and *see* States
  treaties *see* treaties, law of
International Law Commission
  (ILC)
  aggravated responsibility,
    regulation of 268–71
  Articles on State
    Responsibility 245, 258–62
    achievements 247–8
    attribution of conduct to a
      State 249–55
    codification of
      circumstances precluding
      wrongfulness 258–62
    compensation 262–3
    customary international
      law, reflecting 248
    damage 256–8
    inconsistency of
      State conduct with
      an international
      obligation 255
    relevance of fault 256
    status of Articles 248
  circumstances precluding
    wrongfulness,
    codifying 258–62
  codification, and 200, 246–8
  Draft Principles on Allocation
    of Loss in case of
    Transboundary Harm 487
  Draft Articles on Prevention
    and Punishment of Crimes
    against Humanity 433
  Draft Articles on Prevention
    of Transboundary
    Harm 471–2, 485–6
  Draft Articles on
    Responsibility
    of International
    Organizations 154–5
  Guide to Practice on
    Reservations to
    Treaties 211–12, 238
  Guiding Principles
    applicable to unilateral
    declarations 196
  international
    organizations 202
  law of the sea, codifying 103
  peremptory norms 237
  role of 41, 330
  study on the Fragmentation of
    International Law 202
  UN establishment of ILC 41
international law of armed
  conflict *see* legal restraints on
  violence in armed conflict
international legal norms,
  implementation and hierarchy
  of 218–41
  domestic implementation of
    customary international law
    automatic standing
      incorporation 225–6
    customary law overriding
      inconsistent 'ordinary'
      national legislation 226
    later national law
      prevailing 226
    non-self-executing
      customary rules 226
  domestic implementation of
    treaty law 226–31
    incorporation of decisions
      of international
      organizations 230–1
    legal standing of treaties
      within domestic legal
      orders 228
    legislation implementing
      treaties as 'special'
      law 229–30
    mechanisms of
      incorporation 226–7
    national statute construed
      not to conflict with
      international treaty 229
    rigid constitutions 228
    treaties containing
      non-self-executing
      provisions 227–8
    treaties incorporated by ad
      hoc mechanisms 229
    treaties possessing same
      rank as laws enacted by
      parliament 228
  dualism, monism, and
    reality 218–21
    dualistic doctrine, nature
      of 219–20
    monistic theory 220–1
  hierarchical relations between
    international and domestic
    law 231–2
    courts' role in ensuring
      compliance with
      international legal
      standards 232
    few countries adopting
      overall internationalist
      outlook 231, 232
    international rules
      addressed directly to
      individuals 232
    partially internationalist
      approach 231
  international law in
    domestic systems,
    implementing 221–32
    automatic standing
      incorporation of
      international rules
      223, 225
    domestic implementation
      of customary
      international law
      225–6

domestic implementation
of treaty law 226–31
duty to enact legislation to
implement treaties 222
general 221–3
hierarchical relations
between international
and domestic law 231–2
legislative ad hoc
incorporation
of international
rules 223–4
rank of international
rules within domestic
systems 224–5
States may not use
internal law to justify
not performing
treaties 221–2
trends in domestic
systems 223–4
jus cogens, emergence and
development of 232–41
establishment and scope
of 233–5
examples of peremptory
norms 236–7
general 232–3
limited reliance on *jus
cogens* in international
dealings 240–1
rank of international
rules within domestic
systems 224–5
international rules having
higher rank than
national legislation 224
international rules on
same footing as national
legislation 224
rigid constitutions
224–5
statist or nationalist
approach 225
international legal
personality 156–8
international legal subjects
expansion of international
legal personality 156–8
international status
for individuals and
national liberation
movements 156
large variety of entities
acquiring some status
under international
law 156–7
individuals *see* individuals:
rights and duties
insurgents *see* insurgents

international
organizations *see*
international organizations
and institutions
nature of 3–4
people and national liberation
movements 165–7
States *see* States
*sui generis entitles see
sui generis* entities,
corporations and NGOs
International Maritime
Organization (IMO) 483
International Monetary Fund
(IMF) 142, 490–1, 492,
494–5, 497, 510
developing States 508–9
conditionality, objections
to 495
Enhanced Structural
Adjustment Fund
Facility 509
Extended Fund
Facility 509
growing participation
in IMF
decision-making 508
lending financial resources
to 508–9
enhanced role following
economic crisis of
2007 510
purpose and function
490–1, 494
role of IMF shifting 495
restricting sovereignty
of States in monetary
matters 494
system of fixed but adjustable
exchange rates 493, 494–5
collapse of Bretton Woods
system 495
international organizations and
institutions 140–55
binding decisions of 197
enacted in conformity with
constituent treaty
197, 202
secondary source of law,
as 202
criminal courts and
tribunals *see* international
criminal courts and
tribunals
Declaration on Friendly
Relations governing 47
development of 40, 140–2
agencies increasingly
endowed with
autonomous powers 140

creation of new
organizations no longer
viewed positively 143
criticisms of 141–2
need for strong network
of international
instrumentalities 141
enforcement of rights 154
environmental protection,
and *see under*
environment, protection of
immunities *see* immunities of
international organizations
and their agents
proliferation of international
courts and tribunals 288–9
recognition of legal
personality 143–5
activities requiring
recognition of
autonomous
personality 143–4
effective position of entity
in the international
community 144
intention of founders 144
organizations not satisfying
the tests, position of 145
tests for determining
whether organization
is international
subject 144–5
responsibility of international
organizations 154–5
ILC Draft Articles
on Responsibility
of International
Organizations 154–5
violations of international
law, responsibility for 154
right to bring a claim 153–4
right to enter into
international
agreements 153
right to protection for
agents 153
scope and limits: implied
powers and principle of
speciality 145–7
constitutive instruments,
interpretation of 146
expansive interpretation
of international
organizations'
competences 147
international organizations
acting on basis of
conferred powers 145–6
theory of implied
powers 146–7

international organizations and
  institutions (*Continued*)
  States' membership of 89
  types of 142–3
    first international
      organizations 142
    structure of 143
    variety in size, objectives
      and membership 142–3
  see also individual
    organizations and
    institutions
international relations,
  fundamental principles
  governing 45–76
  characterization of 45–9
  duty to co-operate *see* duty to
    co-operate
  Friendly Relations
    Declaration
    conflicting views of
      States 47
    constitutional principles
      of international
      community, as 47
    expansion and updating of
      principles in 41, 46
    nature of principles 46
    overriding legal standards,
      as 47
  good faith *see* good faith,
    principle of
  human rights, respect
    for 71–3
  interactions among
    fundamental
    principles 75–6
  non-intervention, principle
    of *see* non-intervention,
    principle of
  peaceful settlement of
    international disputes *see*
    peaceful settlement of
    international
    disputes
  prevention of significant
    environmental harm *see
    under* environment,
    protection of
  prohibition of threat or use
    of force *see* collFective
    security and use of armed
    force
  self-determination of
    peoples *see* self-
    determination of peoples
  States as primary subjects
    of *see* States as primary
    subjects of international
    law

States, sovereign equality
  of *see* sovereign equality
  of States
  three postulates of
    freedom, equality and
    effectiveness 45
  UN role in development of
    international law 329–30
international rights and
  obligations
  exception in general rule on
    piracy 13–14
  reciprocity as basis of 12–14
  respect for law made
    dependent on power 13
international seabed and common
  heritage of mankind *see under*
  law of the sea
International Sea-Bed
  Authority 117
international State responsibility
  for wrongful acts 245–75
  aggravated State
    responsibility 267–75
  countermeasures,
    and 273–4, 274–5, 303
  current role of 275
  gross violations of
    fundamental rules,
    accountability for 8,
    267–8
aggravated State responsibility
  in light of international
  practice 271–5
  content of aggravated State
    responsibility 272–3
  countermeasures on State
    individual basis 273–4,
    274–5
  damage 272
  gross or systematic
    breaches 272
  pre-conditions for
    aggravated State
    responsibility 271–2
  reparation 272–3
  rights and obligations of all
    other States 273
  subjective element 272
  UN security system,
    and 274
aggravated State
  responsibility, regulation in
  ILC Articles of 268–71
  criticisms of 270–1
  notion of 'specially affected
    State' 271
  rules for *erga omnes* and
    erga omnes partes
    obligations 269–70

rules for serious breaches
  of obligations
  under peremptory
  norms 268–9
attribution of conduct to a
  State 249–55
  conduct of insurrectional
    or other
    movements 254–5
  conduct of persons
    exercising elements
    of governmental
    authority 251–2
  conduct of private
    persons 252–4
  conduct of State
    organs 249–51
circumstances precluding
  wrongfulness 257–63
  codification of ILC
    Articles 258–62
  relationship with
    obligation to pay
    compensation 262–3
  relevance of *jus cogens* 262
codification of
  circumstances precluding
    wrongfulness 258–62
  consent of the State
    injured 258–9
  countermeasures 259
  distress 260–1
  force majeure 259–60
  necessity 261–2
  self-defence 259
codification of law of State
  responsibility 245, 246–8
  historically 246–7
  work of ILC 247–8
consequences of
  internationally wrongful
  act 263–7
  notion of injured
    State 265–7
  obligations of
    responsible State and
    reparation 263–5
damage, question of
  aggravated
    responsibility 257
  moral damage 257–8
  'ordinary' State
    responsibility 257–8
  requirement for
    damage 256–8
injured State, notion of
  265–7
  categories of 'injured
    State' 265–6
  rights of injured State 267

steps to be taken by injured
State 267–8
internationally wrongful
act 249–56
attribution of conduct to a
State 249–55
inconsistency of
State conduct
with international
obligation 255–6
instantaneous
and continuing
violations 256
relevance of fault 256
preliminary notions 248–9
aggravated State
responsibility 249
definition of State
responsibility 248
international
liability and State
responsibility 248–9
'ordinary' form of
responsibility 248
rules on State responsibility
as secondary rules 249
reparation, forms of 263–5
compensation 262–3, 265
restitution in kind
263–4, 265
satisfaction 264–5
intervention
non-intervention see non-
intervention, principle of
specific forms of 55–7
investment law see international
investment law and
arbitration

Jimenez de Arechaga, E.
235, 241
judicial decisions and
teaching of most qualified
publicists 199–200
judicial means of dispute
settlement see under peaceful
settlement of international
disputes
jurisdiction of States 95–7
adjudicative jurisdiction
based on principles of
territoriality 96
nature of 96
principle of universality,
and 96
competences of States are
exercised through assertion
of jurisdiction 94
enforcement
jurisdiction 96–7

normally confined to
acts committed on the
territory 96
taking enforcement
measures abroad 96–7
extraterritorial
jurisdiction 94–5
jurisdictional
immunity 122–4
absolute immunity 123,
124
acts by foreign State
in private capacity/
restrictive immunity
doctrine 123–4
immunity from execution,
and 129–30
immunity of foreign
States from jurisdiction
of forum State,
rationale 122–3
jurisdictional immunity, *jus
cogens* and 126–9
proper role of domestic
courts 129
protection of sovereign
immunities where
violations of *jus
cogens* 126–7
State practice continuing to
evolve 127–8
traditional vision of State
sovereignty 129
prescriptive jurisdiction
allocating responsibility,
for purposes of 96
exercising universal
jurisdiction over serious
international crimes 95
main forms in
contemporary
international law 95–6
market power laws 95
nature of 95
territorial jurisdiction 94
jus cogens 126–9
circumstances precluding
wrongfulness 262
consent not precluding
wrongfulness 262
derogation not
permitted 47–8
emergence and development
of 232–41
establishment and scope
of 233–5
developing Sates 233–4
peremptory norms resting
on consent of major
States 235

socialist States 234
Western States 234
examples of peremptory
norms 236–7
customary rules banning
racial discrimination or
torture 236
fundamental principles of
humanitarian law 236
general rules on
self-determination 236
norms essential to
protect fundamental
interests 236
norms prohibiting the use
or threat of force 236
general 232–3
jurisdictional immunity,
and see under jurisdiction
of States
legal effects of 237–40
deterrent effect of
peremptory norms
238, 241
entering reservations
to multilateral
treaties 238–9
invalidity of single treaty
provisions 238
invalidity of treaties 237
recognition of States,
and 238
State immunity from
jurisdiction of foreign
States 238–9
treaties of extradition 238
limited reliance on *jus
cogens* in international
dealings 240–1
peremptory norms guiding
States' conduct 241
States acting out of
self-interest 241
peremptory norms as 47
protecting fundamental
values of the international
community 183
protection of sovereign
immunities where violations
of *jus cogens* 126–7
States' freedom of action,
impact on 11
treaties, and
conflict with *jus cogens* as
ground of invalidity 215
disputes on content of *jus
cogens* 235
termination and
suspension of
treaties 217

jus cogens (*Continued*)
    treaties subject to *jus cogens* 183

Kelsen, Hans, 59, 159, 184, 220–1, 350
Kosovo 42, 69, 76, 85–6, 282, 364–5
land territory of States 97–103
    absolute nexus between territory and sovereignty 97
    acquisition of territory 98–9
        conquest no longer admissible 98
        contemporary law of territory 98–9
        current modes of acquisition of territory 'derivative' in nature 98
        principal modes of acquiring territory 98, 99
    definition of 97–8
    delimitation of boundaries: *uti possidetis* doctrine 102–3
        relevance of principle beyond context of decolonization 103
    titles, *effectivités* and their interactions 98–102
        acquiescence, title by 100
        different titles conferring different powers over spaces 99–100
        effective occupation by a State with requisite *animus domini* 100
        interactions between title and *effectivités* 101
        nature of titles conferring territorial sovereignty 100
        title arising from coming into existence of a State 100
        title arising from treaty lawfully concluded 100
        title conferred by political adjudication or attribution 100

Lauterpacht, Sir Hersch 204, 366
law of the sea 103–18
    bays 107–8
        coasts of bays belonging to more than one State 107–8
        definition 107
    codification of 103–4

Conferences on the Law of the Sea 103–4
    UNCLOS as 'a constitution of the oceans' 104
contiguous zone 108
continental shelf 110–11
    coastal State's 'sovereign rights limited to certain specific activities 111
    customary rule, as 186
    nature of 110
    outer limit of 110, 111
    Truman Proclamation 110
delimitation of maritime areas 112–13
    equidistance method 113
    guidance for 112–13
    importance of 112
development dictated by State sovereignty and nationalism 93
exclusive economic zone 108–10
    coastal State's broad prescriptive jurisdiction 109
    coastal State's extensive powers of enforcement 109–10
    coastal State's 'sovereign rights' in some specific matters 108
    duty to have 'due regard' for rights of flag States 110
    nature of 108
high seas 114–16
    arrest and seizure of ships 114–15
    bunkering, regulation of 115–16
    res communis omnium, as 114
    States exercising jurisdiction over foreign ships 114
internal waters 106–7
    exceptions to unfettered right of coastal State 106
    foreign ships, offences and 107
    subject to full and exclusive sovereignty of State 106–7
international seabed and common heritage of mankind 116–18
    exploration of the Area 117–18
    International Sea-Bed Authority, establishment of 117

main elements of common heritage of mankind 116–17
    nature of international seabed 116
territorial sea 104–6
    archipelagic baselines, drawing 105
    baselines, definition of 105
    coastal State's full sovereignty, subject to right of innocent passage 106
    definition 104
    innocent passage, meaning of 106
    straight baselines, general criteria for drawing 105
    width of territorial sea 103–5
    traditional international law, in 92
law-making processes 181–203
    binding decisions of international organizations 197
        enacted in conformity with constituent treaty 197, 202
        secondary source of law, as 202
    custom
        elements of custom 184–7
        existence of customary rules 187–8
        general 184
        local customary rules 190–1
        persistent objector 188–9
        present role of custom 191–2
        process whereby rules binding on all States are created 184
    development of international law 199–202
        codification *see* codification
        jurisprudence and doctrine 199–200
        soft law 201–2
    equity as formal source 197–8
    general principles of law 192–5
        attempt to codify resort to principles in 1921 193–4
        general 192–3
        past and present role of principles 194–5

subsidiary source of
international law,
as 193, 202
interactions among
sources 202–3
sources through which
international rules
created 181–2
States continuing to be main
makers of international
rules 181
treaties as law-making
processes 182–3
all treaties subject to the
same rules governing
formation 183
jus cogens, treaties subject
to 183
most frequent means of
creating international
rules, as 182
treaties applicable to
contracting parties
only 182–3
treaties establishing rules of
general purport 183
unilateral acts of States 195–6
ILC Guiding Principles
applicable to unilateral
declarations 196
promise as unilateral
declaration 196
protest 195–6
recognition 196
renunciation 196
source of international law,
as 195, 202
League of Nations 34–5, 38, 103
Covenant of League of
Nations 22, 276
banning/restricting use of
force 57
PCIJ 286
placing restraints on States'
resort to war 11, 34
creation of 34, 142
flaws in League system 34–5
minorities, protection of 36
Slavery Convention 36
lethal autonomous weapons 395
lethal force 377–8, 380
terrorists, use against 389
legal features of international
community 3–19
central authority, lack of 4–6
power fragmented
and dispersed
in international
community 5
collective responsibility 6–8

decentralization of legal
'functions' 4–6
effectiveness, overriding role
of 12
horizontal structure of
international community 5
international rules translated
into national legislation,
need for 8–9
nature of international legal
subjects 3–4
'fictitious person' in
international law 4
States as principal legal
actors internationally 3
old and new patterns,
coexistence of 19
States' freedom of action,
range of 9–11
traditional and new
trends 12–19
community rights and
obligations 14–16
community rights and
obligations, merits and
flaws of 16–19
reciprocity as basis of
international rights and
obligations 12–14
legal restraints on violence in
armed conflict 11, 366–403
choice of weapons,
restrictions on 393–5
choice of means of warfare
not unlimited 393
indiscriminate weapons
prohibited 393
lethal autonomous
weapons 395
nuclear weapons 394–5
treaties containing specific
bans 393–4
weapons calculated to
cause unnecessary
suffering prohibited 393
combatant status *see*
combatant status
core international legal
framework 368–80
Additional Protocols
(1977) 372–4
Geneva Conventions
(1949) and Common
Article 3 370–1
Hague Conventions
(1899–1907) and
Martens Clause 185–6,
369–70
international humanitarian
law and international

human rights
law 375–80
origin of international
humanitarian law/early
key instruments 368–9
other legal instruments and
customary international
law 374–5
direct participation in
hostilities *see* direct
participation in hostilities
IACs *see* international armed
conflicts (IACs)
NIACs *see* non-international
armed conflicts (NIACs)
non-State armed groups,
members of *see* non-State
armed groups
preventive and repressive
measures to ensure
compliance 397–402
belligerent reprisals 400–1
compensation for
damage 401–2
ICRC's role in promoting
compliance with
IHL 398
International
Humanitarian
Fact-Finding
Commission 400 400
no effective mechanisms to
determine violation of
IHL 397
Protecting Powers
system 398–400
punishment of enemy
combatants or civilians
for war crimes 401
reactions to
violations 400–1
resort to international
courts or
tribunals 397–8
specific
institutions 398–400
restrictions on use of military
force and choice of
weapons 390–5
principle of
distinction 390–1
principle of
proportionality 391–2
restrictions on choice of
weapons 393–5
war victims, protection
of 395–7
civilians 395, 396
Common Article 3 396–7
lawful combatants 396

legal restraints on violence in
  armed conflict (*Continued*)
  NIACs 396–7
Lieber Code 368

Manchuria 12
maritime areas, delimitation
  of *see under* law of the sea
Martens Clause 185–6, 369–70
Mechanism for the International
  Criminal Tribunals
  (MICT) 449
mediation 282
mercenaries
  combatant status 383–4
  prisoners of war, as 383–4
  self-defence, and 357
  sent by or on behalf of a
    State 357
Millennium Development
  Goals 325
monism *see under* international
  legal norms, implementation
  and hierarchy of
most favoured nation
  clause 497, 513–14
multilateral environmental
  agreements (MEAs) 472–8
  environment as mosaic
    of objects and
    problems 474–6
  atmosphere 475
  biosphere 475
  dangerous substances and
    activities 475
  hydrosphere 475
  first and second generation
    environmental
    issues 473–4
  first generation
    issues 473–4
  global conventions
    followed by specific
    instruments 474
  MEA design 476–8
  differentiation
    techniques 477–8
  framework
    instruments 476
  list technique 477
  Protocols 476
  States preferring to adopt
    consensual attitude 473
multipolarity 43–4

national legal systems
  domestic implementation of
    customary international law
  automatic standing
    incorporation 225–6

customary law overriding
  inconsistent 'ordinary'
  national legislation 226
later national law
  prevailing 226
non-self-executing
  customary rules 226
domestic implementation of
  treaty law 226–31
incorporation of decisions
  of international
  organizations 230–1
legal standing of treaties
  within domestic legal
  orders 228
legislation implementing
  treaties as 'special'
  law 229–30
mechanisms of
  incorporation 226–7
national statute construed
  not to conflict with
  international treaty 229
rigid constitutions 228
treaties containing
  non-self-executing
  provisions 227–8
treaties incorporated by ad
  hoc mechanisms 229
treaties possessing same
  rank as laws enacted by
  parliament 228
dualism, monism, and
  reality 218–21
few countries adopting
  overall internationalist
  outlook 231, 232
international law in
  domestic systems,
  implementing 221–32
  automatic standing
    incorporation of
    international rules
    223, 225
  domestic implementation
    of customary
    international law
    225–6
  domestic implementation
    of treaty law 226–31
  duty to enact legislation to
    implement treaties 222
  general 221–3
  hierarchical relations
    between international
    and domestic law 231–2
  legislative ad hoc
    incorporation
    of international
    rules 223–4

rank of international
  rules within domestic
  systems 224–5
States may not use
  internal law to justify
  not performing
  treaties 221–2
trends in domestic
  systems 223–4
international rules, national
  courts enforcing *see under*
  enforcement
Geneva Conventions, courts
  jurisdiction over grave
  breaches of 18
highly developed nature
  of 4–5
human rights
  human rights,
    humanitarian law and
    litigation in domestic
    courts 419–20
  national courts substituting
    for international
    enforcement
    agencies 419
  tendency to overrule
    objection of domestic
    jurisdiction 410–11
  US courts hearing cases
    of gross violations of
    human rights 419–20
immunity from State courts'
  jurisdiction 148–50
individual responsibility,
  notion of 6
international crimes,
  prosecution and
  punishment by State
  courts 444–6
  grounds of criminal
    jurisdiction 444
  international
    immunities 445–6
  main disadvantages of
    international courts over
    domestic 453
  principle of
    universality 444–5
international rules, national
  courts enforcing *see under*
  enforcement
key elements of 5
need for international rules to
  be translated into national
  legislation 8–9
war crimes, prosecuting 401
  principle of universality,
    and 429
see also States

national liberation movements
  first Additional Protocol, and 372
    combatant status 383
  assistance to 53
  attributing international status to 156
  Declaration on Friendly Relations governing 47
  peoples and national liberation movements 165–7
    disposal of claimed territory by organized peoples 167
    international legitimation based on principle of self-determination 165
    movements as international subjects acquiring control over territory 166
    liberation movements on the wane 165
    representative organization, need for 166
    rights and duties of organized peoples 166
  self-determination of peoples, and see self-determination of peoples
  use of force against 57–8
national treatment clause 497–8, 514
nationals
  aliens operating abroad, as see under international investment law and arbitration
  forcible protection of nationals abroad see under self-defence
  right to respect for life and property of 52
NATO 42, 56, 142, 274, 282, 320, 332–3, 347–8, 351, 364, 391, 402, 425, 448–9
natural resources
  permanent sovereignty over 40, 502
  principle of 74
  substances originating in celestial bodies as natural resources 121
necessity
  armed response fulfilling condition of 364
  circumstances precluding wrongfulness 261–2

New International Economic Order (NIEO) 491, 501–3
  developing States, main tenets regarding
    free to nationalize or expropriate foreign property 502
    free to set up associations of primary commodities producers 502
    international trade based on stable, equitable prices 503
    regulating multinational corporations 502
    transfer of technology to developing States 503
  General Assembly's adoption of plan of action for 41
  General Assembly's Declaration 503
non-governmental organizations (NGOs) 176–7
  characteristics of 173
  environmental protection, and 483
  established as legal subjects with personality 176
  fundamentally subject to authority of States 177
  general 173
  increasingly allowed to participate in international settings 176–7
non-international armed conflicts (NIACs)
  belligerency, recognition of 384
  civil wars 374
    Common Article 3, and 371
    customary international law applying to 374
    internal matter, as 371
    new entities resulting from 83
    non-intervention principle, and 53
    revolutionary change following, effects of 86–7
    taking hostages 397
    war crimes, and 429
  civilians, avoiding collateral damage to 392
  combatant status 384
  detention abroad in relation to 378–80
  direct participation in hostilities 386–9

unlawful combatants 387–8
IHL, and see legal restraints on violence in armed conflict
indiscriminate attacks, principle of proportionality and 392
lethal force in, use of 377, 380
meaning of 367
protection of victims of war 396–7
scant treaty regulation of 374
transnational NIACs 379
war crimes 429–30
non-intervention, principle of 47, 52–7
  general observations 52–3
    prohibiting interference in organization of a foreign State 52–3
    prohibition on use of force, and 53
    refraining from assisting insurgents 53
    refraining from supporting activities prejudicial to foreign countries 53
  specific forms of intervention 55–7
    coercion, existence of 56
    cyberspace, interference through 56
    economic pressure 55–6
    human rights breaches 76
    humanitarian reasons for forcible intervention 56–7
  UN Charter 47, 54
  UN General Assembly, development by 48, 54–5
    core components of non-intervention principle 55
    Friendly Relations Declaration, principle re-Stated in 54
    new authority to non-intervention principle 54
non-recognition, doctrine of 340–1
non-State armed groups
  combatant status 384
  IHL, and see under legal restraints on violence in armed conflict
  members of 384–6
    continuous combat function, whether requirement for 385

non-State armed groups (*Continued*)
  criterion for individual membership 385
  terrorism 385–6
NIACs, in *see* non-international armed conflicts (NIACs)
non-State actors, torture by 441
norms/normative interactions *see* international legal norms, implementation and hierarchy of
nuclear accidents 487–8
nuclear weapons 394–5

occupation 12, 26, 31, 58–9, 68–70, 76, 81, 98–00, 120, 165, 169, 236, 252–3, 295, 339, 351, 268–9, 372, 381–3, 396, 450
officials, foreign *see* immunities of foreign State officials
outer space, law of
  basic principles of legal regime 120
  customary rule on 120–1, 186
  definition of outer space 120
  res communis omnium, as 120
  substances originating in celestial bodies as natural resources 121

pacta sunt servanda principle 65, 209
Palestine 86, 333
peaceful settlement of international disputes 45, 46, 60–2, 276–93
  diplomatic means of settlement 279–83
    conciliation 282–3
    good offices 281
    inquiry/fact-finding 280–1
    judicial means of settlement, and 289–91
    mediation 282
    negotiations 279–80
    ongoing importance of 289–90
  general observations/nature of principle 60
  judicial means of dispute settlement 283–9
    adjudication 285–8
    arbitration 284–5
    arbitration and adjudication, comparison between 283–4
    diplomatic means of settlement, and 289–91
  proliferation of international courts and tribunals 288–9
  legal scope of principle 61–2
  'free choice of means' to achieve settlement 60
  States bound to continue to try to settle peacefully 60
  States mandated *bona fide* to try to resolve disputes peacefully 60
  States refraining from action that may aggravate situation 61–2
  non-compliance and supervisory procedures 291–3
    effectiveness 293
    examination of periodic reports 291–2
    inspection 292
    preventive supervision 292
    reasons for the establishment of procedures 292–3
    supervision by treaty-based monitoring bodies 292
  obligation and means of dispute settlement 277–9
    means or methods of settling disputes 278–9
    no general and compulsory jurisdiction 278
    UN Charter obligations 277–8
  UN promoting peaceful settlement of disputes likely to endanger peace 321–2
    General Assembly recommending measures 322
    Secretary-General, role of 322
    States' obligation to seek solution 321
  WTO, dispute settlement of 290–1
  see also World Trade Organization (WTO)
peacekeeping, peace enforcement and peace building 320, 343–6, 337
  basic principles of peacekeeping 346
  capacity building 344
  civilian administrative functions, performing 344–5
  domestic enforcement authorities, UN forces acting as 346
  enforcement function 344, 346
  exit strategies, devising 345
  features of traditional peacekeeping operations 343
  growth in peacekeeping operations 343–4
  moving from peacekeeping to peacebuilding 345
  Peace Building Commission 345
  UNEF 343
Perez de Cuellar, Javier 322
Permanent Court of Arbitration (PCA) 284–5
Permanent Court of International Arbitration (PCIJ) 36, 286
persistent objector doctrine 188–9
piracy
  direct obligations on individuals, and 159
  enemies of humanity, as 427
  general rule on 13–14
  pirates criminally liable under international law 8, 427
  Security Council authorizing antipiracy activities 348
Politis, N. 37
polluter-pays principle 75, 459–60, 465–6
  emphasis on not 'distorting international trade and investment' 466
  methods of internalization 465–6
  operating at domestic level 465
  selection of the cost-bearer 465
  States adopting measures internalizing cost of pollution 465
pollution
  environmental problems, and 454–5
  land-based marine pollution 484
  oil pollution 487
  polluter-pays *see* polluter-pays principle
precautionary approach 459, 463–4
  measures for potential serious damage must be 'cost-effective' 464

nature of principle 463
prevention, distinguishing
   from 463
significant ambiguity
   regarding purport of
   norm 464
uncertain outcome must
   be potentially 'serious or
   irreversible damage' 464
uncertainty about the science
   concerning 464
prevention of significant
   environmental harm, State's
   duty of 73, 459, 486
duty of due diligence 460, 461
EIAs, and 461
general observations 73–4
legal scope of principle 74–5
precautionary approach,
   and 463
prisoners of war 370–1
belligerent reprisals against,
   banning of 400
detention of 378–9
Geneva Conventions,
   and 381
mercenaries 383–4
protection and treatment
   of 396
qualifying for status of 381
suspected terrorists 389
prohibition of the threat or use
   of force *see* collective security
   and use of armed force
promise as unilateral
   declaration 196
proportionality, principle of
amount of force necessary to
   repel attack 350
avoiding suffering
   that is manifestly
   disproportionate 309
armed response fulfilling
   condition of 364
civilians, avoiding collateral
   damage to 391–2
countermeasures 302–3
criminal consequences of
   violations of 392
customary international
   law 392
lethal force, use of 377–8, 380
Protecting Powers
   system 398–400
fallen into disuse 399–400
Geneva Conventions
   codifying 399
'Substitutes for the Protecting
   Powers' 399
three-sided arrangement 399

protest as unilateral act of
   States 195–6
public participation, principle
   of 460, 467–8
Aarhus Convention 468
access to environmental
   information 467
environmental information
   widely defined 468
public participation
   requirements, application
   of 468
right of access to justice
   467, 468
publicists, teachings of most
   qualified 199–200

racial equality 40
rebels *see* insurgents
reciprocity
international rights and
   obligations, as basis
   of 12–14
non-reciprocity in trade
   negotiations 507
recognition of States
concept and effects of
   recognition of States 82–4
   act of recognition having
      no legal effect on
      personality of entity 83
   change in factual
      conditions States require
      for recognition 84
   legal consequences where
      recognition precipitately
      granted 83–4
   threefold significance of
      recognition 83
contested Statehood 84–6
   application of general
      international rules 85
   emergence of new
      States attracting
      controversy 84–6
   withholding of
      recognition 85
role of recognition 82–6
unilateral act of State, as 196
regionalization
growing trend towards 42
human rights, regional
   supervisory mechanisms
   for 416–19
renunciation 196
reparation
compensation for violations
   of IHL 401–2
environmental harm, State
   compensation for 484–5

State responsibility 263–5
   compensation 262–3, 265
   restitution in kind
      263–4, 265
   satisfaction 264–5
reprisals 296–300
   armed reprisals 363–4
      see also self-defence
   belligerent reprisals *see*
      belligerent reprisals
   peaceful reprisals *see*
      countermeasures
Responsibility to Protect
   doctrine 56
   human rights violations,
      and 425–6
   resort to armed force only
      through UN 364–5
   use of armed force to
      implement 347
restitution in kind
   263–4, 265
retortion 298–9
   conditions for 299
   human rights violations, for 421
right to development *see under*
   developing States
Rio Declaration and
   principles 459–60, 471, 485
rivers, navigable 14
Rohingya 342, 450
Rome Statute
see also ICC 171, 228, 392,
   429–40, 451
Roosevelt, Eleanor 71, 409
Roosevelt, President Franklin
   Delano 313, 315, 318–9,
   406, 492
Roosevelt, President
   Theodore 31

sanctions 306–9
   collective security,
      and 339–40
   effectiveness 338
   expressing collective
      condemnation 338
   sanctions regimes 338–9
   targeted or smart
      sanctions 338, 339
   economic sanctions 307–8,
      337, 339–40
   diplomatic relations, breaking
      off 339–40
   general 306–8
      countermeasures decided
         by international bodies
         or authorized 307
      UN economic
         sanctions 307–8, 337

sanctions (*Continued*)
  non-recognition of illegal situations 340–1
  respect for human rights, and 308–9
    avoiding suffering that is manifestly disproportionate 309
    humanitarian exemptions 308
    general standards to be observed by States 308–9
    sanctions adversely impacting most vulnerable groups 308
    sparing as much as possible civilian population 309
    targeted or smart sanctions 309
satisfaction 264–5
seas *see* law of the sea
secession 68–9, 76, 83, 87–9, 99–100, 168
Second World War 37–8
Security Council, UN *see* United Nations Security Council
self-defence 349–65
  anticipatory or pre-emptive self-defence, admissibility of 59, 353–7
    exceptional exigencies of States, recognition of 356
    issue of crucial importance, as 353
    making anticipatory self-defence lawful subject to strict conditions 356–7
    no customary basis for 59
    no universal agreement as to illegality under the UN Charter 354–6
    rationale behind doctrine 353–4
  armed infiltration and indirect aggression, self-defence against 357–8
    ICJ distinguishing between various classes of threat or use of force 358
    military aggression increasingly taking form of gradual infiltration 357
    States' views on legality of 357–8
  armed intervention with consent of territorial State 360–2

present legal regulation of consent exception 362
State practice making extensive use of consent exception 362
volenti non fit injuria principle, application of 360–1
armed reprisals against unlawful small-scale use of force 363–4
  conditions of necessity and proportionality, armed response fulfilling 364
  legality of general category of armed reprisals 363
  retaliatory armed force and immediate armed reaction, distinguishing 363–4
  whether military action short of war lawful 362–3
circumstances precluding wrongfulness 259
collective self-defence 320
forcible protection of nationals abroad 358–60
  most use of force carried out in developing States 359
  rule may be resorted to under very strict conditions 360
  States' views on legality of 359–60
  use of force to protect nationals in danger abroad 358–9
humanitarian intervention 364–5
  resort to armed force only through UN 364–5
  use of armed force to protect civilians from human rights violations 364
increasing use of right of individual self-defence 320
individual and collective self-defence 349–53
  amount of force necessary to repel attack and proportionate, use of 350
  attacks only on 'legitimate military targets' 350
  collective self-defence, nature of 351
  expansion of resort to self-defence 352

occupation of aggressor State's territory 350
other instances of unilateral resort to force, lawfulness of 351
self-defence as lawful reaction to 'armed attack' 350
termination of self-defence, circumstances of 350–1
when Member States can resort to armed force 350
UN, and 319, 320
self-determination of peoples 57, 66–71
  categories entitled to self-determination 58
  developing States, and 40
  evolution of principle in world community 66–7
  formation of international entities based on free will of populations 67
  legal scope of principle 67–9
    anti-colonialist standard, as 67
    ban on foreign military occupation, as 67
    external and internal self-determination 67, 68
    national liberation movements, use of force by 70
    requirement that all racial groups be given full access to government, as 67
  limits of the principle 71
    acceptance of principle selective and limited 71
    political stability and the territorial integrity, importance to States of 71
  military violence to achieve self-determination, use of 351
  national liberation movements *see* national liberation movements
  rights and obligations 69–70
    acquisition, transfer, and loss of title over territory 70
    international humanitarian law, self-determination and 70
    legal right to external or internal self-determination 69

States duty bound to allow
free exercise of right to
self-determination 69
States legally authorized to
support peoples entitled
to self-determination 70
transfer of territories
requiring consultation
of the population 70
rules of self-determination
as *jus cogens* 236
use of force, self-
determination and 70
sovereign equality, and 76
UN role in 40, 45, 46, 323–4
promotion of
democracy 324
success of UN role 323
ships
arrest and seizure of 114–15
States exercising jurisdiction
over foreign ships 114
internal waters, foreign ships
in 107
slavery 36, 48, 233–7, 292,
405, 420
slave trade 29
Slavery Convention 36, 292
Treaties prohibiting 405
soft law
customary international law,
and 202
development of international
law, and 201–2
environmental protection,
role in *see under*
environment, protection of
features of 201–2
legally binding undertaking,
and 201
meaning of 201
sovereign equality of States 45,
46, 49–52
fundamental principle of
international law, as 45,
46, 90
general observations 49
legal equality 52
self-determination, and 75
sovereignty *see* sovereignty
treaties derogating from
47–8
UN Charter 49
Sovereign Order of Malta 174
sovereignty 8–9, 50–2, 90–1
competence and
jurisdiction 94–7
competences of a State 94
conceptual
distinctions 94–5

exercise of jurisdiction *see*
jurisdiction of States
evolving concept of 90–1
current problems requiring
State co-operation 91
limitations of power of
sovereign States 91
return to more traditional
version of international
legal order 90
sovereignty not
unfettered 90
immunities, and *see*
immunities of foreign State
officials; immunities of
States
jurisdictional immunity,
and *see under* jurisdiction
of States
key trait of Statehood,
as 81–2, 90
legal equality, meaning of 52
natural resources, permanent
sovereignty over 40, 502
no exercise of sovereign
powers over another
equally sovereign State 122
power to freely use and
dispose of territory under
State's jurisdiction 50
power to wield authority over
individuals in territory 50
respect of sovereignty,
principle of 13
right to exclude others from
territory 50–1
right to immunity for State
representatives 51–2
right to immunity from
jurisdiction of foreign
courts 51
right to respect for life and
property of State's nationals
and officials 52
sovereign equality of
States *see* sovereign
equality of States
'sovereign rights', and 94
Soviet Union 38
collapse of 41, 42
isolation of 36
presence of Soviet Union
splitting international
community 32–4
principles advocated by
Soviet Union 33
repudiating unacceptable
treaties 34
speciality, principle of 145–7
Spiers, E.M 29–30

State activities, spatial
dimensions of 92–121
airspace, law of 118–20
land territory *see* land
territory of States
law of the sea *see* law of the
sea
outer space, law of 120–1
sovereignty, competence and
jurisdiction 94–7
conceptual
distinctions 94–5
exercise of jurisdiction *see*
jurisdiction of States
traditional international law,
in 92–3
State responsibility *see*
international State
responsibility for wrongful
acts
States
armed force, use of *see*
collective security and use
of armed force
countermeasures *see*
countermeasures
creation and extinction of *see*
under States as primary
subjects of international
law
duty to co-operate *see* duty to
co-operate
environmental protection,
and *see* environment,
protection of
international investment
law, *see* and arbitration
international investment
law and arbitration
international relations *see*
international relations,
fundamental principles
governing
jurisdiction *see* jurisdiction
of States
nationals abroad, forcible
protection of *see under*
self-defence
spatial dimensions of
activities *see* State
activities, spatial
dimensions of
freedom of action, range
of 9–11
freedom in economic
field 10–11
increasing qualifications on
freedom 11
jus cogens prohibiting
activities 11

States (*Continued*)
    legal restrictions on right to use force 11
    treaties, impact of 11
    untrammelled freedom in classical international law 10
    general principles of law recognized in domestic systems 192–5
    Great Powers' dominance, efforts to restrain 30–2
    immunities *see* immunities of States; immunities of foreign State officials
    individuals as principal legal subjects 3
    international law, in *see* States as primary subjects of international law
    jurisdiction of *see* jurisdiction of States
    land territory *see* land territory of States
    national legal systems *see* national legal systems
    national liberation movements *see* national liberation movements
    non-intervention in affairs of other States *see* non-intervention, principle of
    officials *see* immunities of foreign State officials
    peaceful settlement of disputes *see* peaceful settlement of international disputes
    principal actors internationally, as 3
    right to development, and 503
    riparian State's right to free navigation 14
    self-defence *see* self-defence
    sovereign equality of *see* sovereign equality of States
    State responsibility *see* international State responsibility for wrongful acts
    succession of States *see* succession of States
    threat or use of force by States *see* collective security and use of armed force
    unilateral acts of *see* unilateral acts of States
States as primary subjects of international law 79–91
    continuing pre-eminence of States 79–80
    handful of States enjoying pre-eminent position 79
    States as backbone of the international community 79, 80
    subjects other than States possessing limited legal capacity 80
    continuity, succession and extinction of States 86–9
    changes in government and territory 86–7
    extinction of States 87
    merger of States 87, 88
    revolutionary change 85–6
    State succession *see* succession of States
    creation of States in international law 80–2
    effectiveness and independence, principles of 81
    failed or collapsed States 82
    illegality affecting genesis, effect of 82
    independence, requirement of 81–2
    key structural elements, presence of 80–1
    territory as essential element of Statehood 81
    recognition *see* recognition of States
    sovereignty, evolving concept of *see under* sovereignty
Stimson doctrine
    see also non-recognition 12–4, 340
Stimson, Henry 12
Stockholm Declaration 459, 471, 485
Stockholm Conference as birth of modern environmental law 458
Strayer, J.R. 21
strict liability of States 484–5
Suarez, Francisco 22
subsidies 498, 515
succession of States 87–9
    customary rules addressing succession of States 87
    membership of international organizations, succession to 89
    public debts, succession to 89
    State property, succession to 89
    treaties, succession to 88
    'clean slate' principle 88
    continuity, principle of 88
    human rights treaties 88
    localized treaties 88
    non-localized treaties 88
sui generis entities, corporations and NGOs 173–7
    characteristics of 173
    general 173
    Holy See 173
    International Committee of the Red Cross 174–5
    multinational corporations, regulating 502
    non-governmental organizations 176–7
    Sovereign Order of Malta 174
    States' responsibility for corporations 486
    transnational corporations 175–6
sustainable development 468–70
    ambiguity of concept 469
    featuring widely in international policy statements 468–9
    legal concept of 470
    nature of 74
    norm, as 469
    requirements for 470
Sustainable Development Goals 325, 472–3
    CSD, and 482

Taiwan 85, 278, 296, 340
targeted killings
    IHL, and 377–8
    terrorists 377–8, 379–80, 385–6, 388–9
    'war on terror', and 388–9
targeted sanctions *see under* sanctions
technology transfer to developing States 503
territorial sea *see under* law of the sea
terrorism
    armed force against terrorist entities, use of 355
    devastating importance of 42–3
    international crime, as 442–3
    definition of crime of terrorism 442–3
    legal elements 443
    lethal force against terrorists, use of 389
    NIACs, and 384
    non-State armed groups, and 385

INDEX

553

sectoral conventions on 442
status of 388
suspected terrorists, arrest
  of 389
targeted killings 377–8,
  379–80, 385–6, 388–9
targeted sanctions 338–9
universal jurisdiction over 95
unlawful combatants,
  terrorists as 388
'war on terror' 367, 388–9
  States resorting to notion of
    self-defence 352–3
  targeted killings 388–9
threat or use of force see
  collective security and use of
  armed force
torture 440–2
  crime against humanity,
    as 440
  crime per se, as 440
  definition 440
  legal elements 440–1
    mental element 441
  non-State actors, torture
    by 441–2
  rules banning torture as *jus
    cogens* 236
  Torture Convention 440–1
  war crime, as 440
transnational
  corporations 175–6
  foreign investment disputes,
    role in 176
  powerful actors in international
    relations, as 175
treaties, conclusion of 207–9
  entry into force 208–9
  expression of consent
    accession 208
    exchange of instruments
      forming treaty 208
    executive agreements 208
    means to express
      consent 208
    ratification 208
    signature 208
    treaties concluded in
      solemn form 209
  standard procedure 207
    adoption of text 206
    authentication of text 206
    negotiations by persons
      possessing full
      powers 207
    treaties negotiated
      in international
      conference 207
  treaties binding on States on
    consent 208

treaties, law of 204–17
  amendment of treaties 214
  conclusion of treaties see
    treaties, conclusion of
  contracting parties,
    between 182–3
  domestic implementation of
    treaty law 226–31
  effects and scope of
    application of treaty
      law 209–10
    subsequent treaties 209–10
    third States, position
      of 209
    treaty binding on each
      party in respect of entire
      territory 209
  establishing rules of general
    purport 183
  formation, all treaties
    subject to the same rules
    governing 183
  grounds of invalidity 214–16
    absolute and relative
      grounds of
      invalidity 215–16
    coercion 214–15
    corruption of State
      officials 215
    error 215
    fraud 215
    grounds of invalidity
      historically 214–15
    invalidity under VCLT 215
    jus cogens, treaties contrary
      to 215, 234–5
    nullity invoked by State
      not party to the
      treaty 215–16
    violation of fundamental
      provision of internal
      law 215
  interpretation 212–13
    authoritative texts 213
    effectiveness, principle
      of 212–13
    good faith 212
    implied powers doctrine,
      application of 213
    no binding rules on
      interpretation
      historically 212
    purpose of contracting
      parties 212
    recourse to preparatory
      work 213
    VCLT's literal, systematic,
      and teleological
      interpretation
      212–13

jus cogens, treaties subject
  to 183
law-making processes,
  as 182–3
  interactions among sources
    of law 202–3
  no hierarchy between
    treaties and customs as
    sources of law 202
  treaties as most frequent
    means of creating
    international rules 182
modification of treaties 214
reservations 210–12
  effects of
    reservations 210–11
  human rights treaties 212
  ILC 'Guide to Practice
    on Reservations to
    Treaties' 212, 239
  impairing integrity of
    multilateral treaties 211
  jus cogens, and 237–8
  objections to
    reservations 210
  universality of treaties
    doctrine 210
States' freedom of action,
  limiting 11
succession of treaties see
  under succession of States
termination and suspension
  consent, by 216
  denunciation or
    withdrawal 217
  desuetude 217
  extinction of one of the
    parties 217
  fundamental changes of
    circumstances 217
  jus cogens, conflict
    with 217
  material breach by another
    party 216–17
  supervening impossibility
    of performance 217
types of treaties
  bilateral and multilateral
    treaties 206
  closed treaties 206
  normative and contractual
    treaties 206
  open treaties 206
  political commitments
    compared to
    treaties 205–6
  States full freedom as
    regards modalities and
    form of treaties 205
  universal treaties 206, 210

treaties, law of (*Continued*)
  weapons, treaties containing specific bans on 393–4
  see also Vienna Convention on the Law of Treaties 1969 (VCLT)
Triepel, H. 9

UNCITRAL Arbitration Rules 525
under-development *see under* developing States
unilateral acts of States 195–6
  binding character of 65
  good faith, and 65
  interactions among sources of law 202–3
  law-making process, as
    ILC Guiding Principles applicable to unilateral declarations 196
  promise as unilateral declaration 196
  protest 195–6
  recognition 196
  renunciation 196
  source of international law, as 195, 202
unipolarity 42–3
United Nations (UN) 313–34
  achievements and failures *see* United Nations, principal achievements and failures of
  Charter of *see* United Nations Charter
  codification of customary rules 41
  current role 331–4
    areas of achievements 333
    areas of failure 331
    Covid 19 334
    flaws in Organization 331
    forum for multilateral diplomacy 333
    intractable nature of political problems 332
    membership of UN as test of legitimation for States 333
    reforms 331–2
    regional organizations, links with 333–4
    United States, relationship with 332
  decline as UN as agency for maintenance of peace and stability 42
  development, and *see* global economy and international law

ECOSOC 317
enhancement of powers 40
establishment of 38–9
goals 315–16
grand design of post-Second World War period 313–15
international development, powers expanded to 40
international relations, principles governing 40–1
NIEO *see* New International Economic Order (NIEO)
permanent sovereignty over natural resources 40, 502
power to pass binding resolutions 196
racial equality 40
self-determination 40, 45
social justice, promoting 424
structure 316–17
UN General Assembly *see* United Nations General Assembly
UN Security Council *see* United Nations Security Council
United Nations Charter
  Ch VII 196
  disarmament 327
  duty to co-operate *see* duty to co-operate
  expansion and updating of principles 46
  fundamental purposes and principles, laying down 45–6
  human rights 45, 406–7
  ICJ *see* International Court of Justice (ICJ)
  military force, restraints on Members using 11, 15
  non-intervention principle 47, 54
  peace as principal goal 37
  peaceful settlement of disputes *see* peaceful settlement of international disputes
  prohibition of threat or use of force *see* collective security and use of armed force
  signing 37
United Nations Commission on International Trade Law (UNCITRAL) 285, 525
United Nations Commission on Sustainable Development (CSD) 482

United Nations Conference on Trade and Development (UNCTAD) 505–6
  purposes 505
  structure 506
United Nations Development Programme (UNDP) 505
United Nations Education, Scientific and Cultural Organization (UNESCO) 86, 317
  cultural relations 142
  environment 483, 458
United Nations Emergency Force (UNEF) 343
United Nations Environment Programme (UNEP) 472
  establishment of 458–9
  structure and organisation 482
United Nations General Assembly
  action for gross violations of international law 341–2
  Declaration on Friendly Relations *see under* international relations, fundamental principles governing
  developing States' command over 39, 40, 502
  disarmament 328
  Expanded Programme of Technical Assistance 504
  membership 316
  NIEO 41, 503
  non-intervention principle, development of 48, 54–5
    core components of non-intervention principle 55
    Friendly Relations Declaration, principle re-Stated in 54
    new authority to non-intervention principle 54
  Technical Assistance Programme 504
  UNCTAD 505–6
United Nations Industrial Development Organization (UNIDO) 506
United Nations International Children's Fund (UNICEF) 326
United Nations Office of the High Commissioner for Human Rights 415

INDEX

United Nations, principal
  achievements and failures
    of 317–21
  codification and progressive
    development of
      international law 329–30
    fostering international
      law 329–30
    ILC, role of 330
  disarmament 327–9
    actions taken by General
      Assembly 328
    Charter provisions 327
    role of Security
      Council 329
  economic and social
    co-operation 324–6
    children's health and
      welfare 326
    co-operation among
      States in social area and
      human rights 324
    environment, protection
      of 325–6
    lack of success in economic
      co-operation 324–5
    Millennium Development
      Goals 325
    Sustainable Development
      Goals 325
  general 318
  human rights 326–7
    promoting respect for 327
    UN Charter 327, 406–7
  maintenance of peace and
    security 318–20
    deficiencies of the
      collective security
      system 319–20
    enforcement by member
      States 320
    lawful and unlawful use of
      force 319
    peacekeeping 320
    self-defence 319, 320
  promotion of peaceful
    settlement of disputes likely
    to endanger peace 321–2
  self-determination of
    peoples 323–4
United Nations Security Council
  acting under Ch VII of
    Charter 196
  authorizing enforcement
    action see collective
    security and use of armed
    force
  collective security 39, 40
  disarmament 329
  divisions in 334

membership 316–17
MICT 449
permanent members, powers
  of 39, 316–17
power to pass binding
  resolutions 196
power to take sanctions 38,
  196
public condemnation, effect
  of 342
resolutions condemning
  unlawful conduct 341–2
structure
veto power 316–17, 342
Universal Declaration of Human
  Rights (1948) 72, 217, 408–9
  forging general 'philosophy' of
    human dignity 409
  General Assembly
    adopting 327, 409
  importance of 409
  not legally binding 409
  Western view of human
    rights, expressing 409
universality, principle of
  adjudicative jurisdiction
    based on 96
  forum deprehensionis 444–5
  States exercising universal
    jurisdiction over serious
    international crimes 95
  national courts having
    universal jurisdiction
    over grave breaches 18
  versions of principle
    broad variant of 445
    State where accused in
      custody, prosecution
      by 444–5
  war crimes, prosecution in
    national courts for 429
unlawful combatants *see under*
  combatants
use of force *see* collective security
  and use of armed force
uti possidetis doctrine 102–3
  relevance of principle
    beyond context of
    decolonization 103

Vattel, Emeric de 52
victims of war, protection
  of 395–7
  civilians 395, 396
  Common Article 3 396–7
  lawful combatants 396
  NIACs 396–7
Vienna Convention on
  Diplomatic Relations
  (1961) 133

immunity of diplomatic
  agents 13, 134, 135
protection of foreign
  diplomats 9
Vienna Convention on the Law
  of Treaties 1969 (VCLT)
  amendment of treaties 214
  application and scope 205
  codifying/developing
    customary rules of law of
    treaties 204–5
  conclusion of treaties *see*
    treaties, conclusion of
  grounds of invalidity 215,
    234–5
  absolute and relative
    grounds of
    invalidity 215–16
  interpretation of treaties *see
    under* treaties, law of
  modification of treaties 214
  pacta sunt servanda
    principle 65, 209
  reservations 210–11
  suspension of treaties 216–17
  termination of
    treaties 216–17
  treaty, meaning of 206
Vitoria, Francisco de 15, 22
violence in armed conflict *see*
  legal restraints on violence in
  armed conflict

war
  aggression as international
    crime, war of 38
  armed conflict, violence
    in *see* legal restraints on
    violence in armed conflict
  armed force, use of *see*
    collective security and use
    of armed force; self-defence
  civil wars *see* non-
    international armed
    conflicts (NIACs)
  Cold war *see* Cold War
  crimes *see* war crimes
  enforcement, as 297
  First World War 32–4
  formal declaration of war,
    consequences of 367
  historically 367–8
  legal significance of notion of
    'war' 367
  national liberation, wars of 372
    see also national liberation
    movements
  Second World War 37–8
  state of war, effect of 367
  war victims *see* victims of war

war crimes 428–31
  civil wars 429
  courts with jurisdiction 401
  ensuring compliance with
    IHL by punishing for 401
  establishing existence of rules
    of customary international
    law 429
  expansion of categories of 8
  grave breaches 429
    mandatory prosecution/
      extradition for 401
    universality principle 429
  IACs and NIACS 429–30
  ICC jurisdiction 429–30
  legal elements
    actus reus 430
    mens rea 430–1
  meaning of 401
  nexus, requirement of 431
  personal individual
    responsibility for 8
  prosecuting German
    and Japanese war
    criminals 405
  torture, as 440
  violations of rules of
    international humanitarian
    law, as 428–9
'war on terror' *see under*
  terrorism
Washington consensus 55, 491
weapons
  expanding bullets, prohibition
    of 29
  indiscriminate weapons 393
  lethal autonomous
    weapons 395
  nuclear weapons 394–5
  restrictions on choice of 29,
    393–5
  treaties containing specific
    bans 393–4
  weapons calculated to cause

  unnecessary suffering
    prohibited 393
Wight, M. 19
workers' rights 14
World Bank 490, 495–6, 504
  Bretton Woods 493–4
  developing States, and 508
  goals 495–6, 508
    stimulus function 496
  IDA 508
  reconstruction and
    development through 493
  structure 495
  World Bank Group 496, 508
World Health Organization
  (WHO) 317
  controlling spread of
    disease 63
  Covid 19 119–20
World Trade Organization
  (WTO) 508, 510–18
  Dispute Settlement Body
    (DSB) 290, 291
    monitoring role 291
    reports submitted to 518
  dispute settlement of
    WTO 290–1, 517–18
    appeals/Appellate
      Body 291, 518
    compensation 518
    countermeasures 518
    Dispute Settlement
      Understanding 290,
      510, 617
    implementation of
      reports 518
    Interim and Final
      Reports 290–1
    nature of 290
    panel system,
      strengthening of 517
    procedure 290–1
    retaliation 518
  establishment of 510

  exceptions in WTO
    system 515–17
    differential trade with
      developing States 499,
      507, 515
    FTAs/maintenance
      of economic
      integration 498–9,
      515–16
    Members' reserved
      power to adopt certain
      measures 516–17
    types of general exceptions
      in Art XX 517
  market access rules 511–13
  membership 291, 511
  non-discrimination/
    preventing unfair
    competition 513
    countervailing duties 515
    dumping 498, 514–15
    exceptions 515–17
    most favoured nation
      clause 497, 513–14
    national treatment
      clause 497–8, 514
    non-discrimination
      standards 513
    rules preventing unfair
      competition 514–15
    subsidies 515
    trade remedies 515
  non-tariff barriers 512–13
  structure 511
  tariffs 512
  technical co-operation,
    providing 508
  wide-ranging network of
    agreements, as 511
wrongful acts *see* international
  State responsibility for
  wrongful acts